MW00561832

DOCUMENTARY HISTORY OF THE FIRST FEDERAL CONGRESS OF THE UNITED STATES OF AMERICA

4 March 1789–3 March 1791

SPONSORED BY
THE NATIONAL HISTORICAL PUBLICATIONS AND RECORDS COMMISSION
AND
THE GEORGE WASHINGTON UNIVERSITY

This book has been brought to publication with the generous assistance of the National Historical Publications and Records Commission.

NHPRC

DOCUMENTING DEMOCRACY

National Historical Publications and Records Commission

This volume has been supported by a grant from the National Endowment for the Humanities, an independent federal agency.

NATIONAL
ENDOWMENT
FOR THE
HUMANITIES

PROJECT STAFF

CHARLENE BANGS BICKFORD, *Co-Editor*
KENNETH R. BOWLING, *Co-Editor*
HELEN E. VEIT, *Associate Editor*
WILLIAM CHARLES DIGIACOMANTONIO, *Associate Editor*

VOLUME XIX

CORRESPONDENCE

SECOND SESSION: 15 MARCH – JUNE 1790

CHARLENE BANGS BICKFORD

KENNETH R. BOWLING

HELEN E. VEIT

WILLIAM CHARLES DIGIACOMANTONIO

Editors

The Johns Hopkins University Press, Baltimore

This book has been brought to publication with the generous assistance of the Boone Endowment of the Johns Hopkins University Press.

Printed in the United States of America on acid-free paper
2 4 6 8 9 7 5 3 1

The Johns Hopkins University Press
2715 North Charles Street
Baltimore, Maryland 21218-4363
www.press.jhu.edu

ISBN-13: 978-0-8018-9446-6 (hardcover: alk. paper)
ISBN-10: 0-8018-9446-8 (hardcover: alk. paper)

Library of Congress Control Number: 2009933941

A catalog record for this book is available from the British Library.

To

our always helpful and ever generous colleagues at the
Letters of Delegates to the Congress, 1774–1789
Documentary History of the Ratification of the U.S. Constitution
Documentary History of the Supreme Court of the U.S., 1789–1800
and
The Papers of:
John Adams
Benjamin Franklin
Nathanael Greene
John Jay
Thomas Jefferson
James Madison
Robert Morris
George Washington
for their invaluable assistance over the decades

CONTENTS

ILLUSTRATIONS

Correspondence: Second Session

15–31 March 1790

Monday, 15 March 1790

Rain (Johnson)

Francis Cook to George Thatcher

I take the freedom to inform you that whereas in conformity to the Coasting Law we have to demand a years Tonnage Money for all Vessels employed in the Coasting Trade, when they take a License to Trade (and before it is due as they term it) I meet with no small difficulty with the Masters of Vessels employed in Coasting—The greater part of the Vessels of Burthen belonging to this District are Employed partly in the Coasting Trade, and partly on foreign Voyages and they complain of it as a very great hardship that they have to Pay a years Tonnage as Coasters, when they are Employ'd half of the time upon foreign Voyages, and have to pay Tonnage upon each Entry at their return home—Under our Rate regulations there was a deduction made from the Yearly light money[1] for the time they were Employ'd Already and they think hard that Provision is not now [*lined out*] made for them in the like Circumstances—I have wrote to the Secretary [*Hamilton*] upon subject, and if you sir, think it an Object worth your Attention, please to consult with him what answer is proper for me to give them, Or if you think proper to lay it before Congress I submit it to your Wisdom—In the division of the Districts the Town of Thomastown [*Maine*] being Annexed to the District of Penobscot and as Part of that Town lyeth upon St. Georges River, (altho it has another Harbour below and disconnected with said River,) Mr. [*John*] Lee the Collector for Penobscot *Insisting* that his District takes in the whole of said River, we cannot agree upon a divisional Line—the Inhabitants upon said River Complaining that it will put them to Insuperable Difficulties to have to go to Penobscot to do their Business, the distance being twenty or thirty Miles further than to Wiscassett, and impassable in the winter Season, on account of Snows—The Emoluments which will accrue to either of us from having it annexed to our Districts are hardly worth contending for—But the dissatisfaction of the Inhabitants is such that I cannot comply with his Requisition. I am loth to trouble you with small affairs when matters of so much more Importance call for your Attention, but as the Law points it out as the duty of the Officers to agree upon a *Divisional* line, I think it my Duty to Assign the Reason why I have not.

ALS, Thatcher Papers, MeHi. Written from Wiscasset, Maine.

[1] A special tonnage duty applied to the maintenance of the state's lighthouses.

Thomas Dwight to Theodore Sedgwick

I have just received, Dear Sir. your favor of the 10th inst. the decision of the House on the question of *assuming*, is an event which I have hoped for most earnestly. but not without some fear and trembling—I see no one within the circle of my acquaintance in this quarter, who does not express very great satisfaction in it—I have not indeed enquired of Mr. [*David?*] Smead, Wm. Lyman or Mr. [*Noah*] Goodman. these brave men ride in Mr. A~~dams~~ our Lt. Govr. [*Samuel Adams*] troop, and I suppose are above approving any thing done by Congress under the new Constitution, so that had you resolved that the State debts, should never be assumed by the Continent on any terms whatever they would I presume, declare that you were studying to harrass and oppress the people. Will the Senate concur in this measure of assumption? We have been informed that it is very uncertain what fate the proposition will meet with in that branch. I shall still have some impatience about me, until this business has the fiat of the president.

***

ALS, Sedgwick Papers, MHi. Written from Springfield, Massachusetts. This concludes a letter begun on 14 March, volume 18. The omitted text relates to the appointment and weakness of state revenue collectors.

Edmund Pendleton to John Page

I am much indebted for yr. obliging Favr. of the 27th. past, and the two Packets of papers which accompanied it, and were the more acceptable, as they found me confined to the House by a deep snow and a frost nearly as severe as any we had through the winter, wch. has made sad havock with our Fruit. The papers are a Super-abundant gratificatn. without the Congressional Register, wch. would be generally read even in Our papers before it came to hand. I have also to thank you for yr. kind Attention to Dr. [*David*] Morrow's Application.

I feel at this distance the great weight & importance of the burthen at present on the Shoulders of our Fœdral Representatives, & more especially the discussion of that abstrace, difficult & all-important subject providing for the great Mass & variety of our Public debt. In my recluse state to attempt to develope the various ~~plan~~ parts of the Secretary's Plan, & advise upon them to the collected Wisdom of America, would be as Arrogant, as unnecessary; Thus much I can venture to say, that on its first perusal, I was struck with Sentiments different from his on two great Points, that of discrimination amongst Creditors, & the Assumption of the State debts, Upon both which the arguments I have read since, have confirm'd & not shaken my Opinion. I will just mention as to the first my thoughts on the Subject of Public Faith, wch. no doubt should be sacred—It was pledged & offer'd at full value, was it so accepted? It was by the Creditors, either by Compulsion or voluntarily; If the former no wonder the Faith was low with them, & they carried their Certificates to the first market, but still the loss by the sale of what was then forced on them, was a debt upon Pub. Justice. The Voluntier acceptor proved that he did not want Faith in Government, & his parting with them must be imputed to Necessity—but in either case did the purchaser accept the Pub. Faith at Full value? no, he rated it at a 1/5, 1/6th. 1/8th. or 1/10th. in performing our engagement then, wch. is most just, to give to each Class, the proportion which his expectations reached at the time of contracting, or to disappoint both, giving one much more & the other things depending on Opinions in Social Regulations I suppose my self wrong & a Majority right; I confess indeed my Feelings were wounded by one Observation in the Course of the debate, that a bounty of 250 Dollars (perhaps not worth so many pence) was abundant reward to an All-meritorious Veteran Soldier, whilst the Observer was advocating a measure for putting as many thousand pounds into the Pocket of a Speculator, who to say no more has no Public Merit.

As to Public Credit, If the Secretary thinks his new Paper will have more, by establishing a Principle which allows to Speculators the Full reward of their pious labours, I differ widely from him. As to the Assumption of the State debts, besides my doubts that Virga. would loose & other States gain by the measure, I disapprove of it upon general principles, as tending to accumulate the Fœdral debt & increase its difficulties, and as being a stride towards a consolidated Government, which you know was here made a great Objection to the Constitution, & obviated by shewing from the Delegated Powers, that the Fœdral head were to Act in General concerns, whilst all local matters were to remain wth. the States.

I fear the Secretary's reason for it "that taxation may not be divided, but absorbed by the Genl. Governmt." will Act very differently from a Palliative on the Occasion. The modifications may relieve Virga. but not remove the other general Objections. I beg pardon for taking up so much of yr. precious time.

ALS, The Gilder Lehrman Collection, on Deposit at the New York Historical Society, New York. [GLC 99.142] Written from Virginia. Page apparently gave this letter to Madison, who docketed it and kept it among his papers (*PJM* 17:546).

David Stuart to George Washington

***

Coll. Grayson died on Saturday last—As his death has been expected for some time, I am informed the Executive have been endeavouring to fix on someone to fill up his place—Mr. [*Patrick*] Henry has been applied to, it is said, but will not serve. It is said, he is about to remove off to a territory, he has purchased in partnership from the State of Georgia.

A spirit of jealousy which may become dangerous to the Union, towards the Eastern States, seems to be growing fast among us—It is represented, that the Northern phalanx is so firmly united, as to bear down all opposition, while Virginia is unsupported, even by those whose interests are similar with hers—It is the language of all, I have seen on their return from [*lined out*] New York—Coll. [*Henry*] Lee tells me, that many who were warm Supporters of the government, are changing their sentiments, from a conviction of the impracticability of Union with States, whose interests are so dissimilar from those of Virginia—I fear the Coll. is one of the number—The late applications to Congress, respecting the slaves, will certainly tend to promote this spirit—It gives particular umbrage, that the Quakers should be so busy in this business—That they will raise up a storm against themselves, appears to me very certain—Mr. Maddison's sentiments are variously spoke of—so much so; that it is impossible to ascertain whether they are approved of by a majority or not—The Commercial and most noisy part, is certainly against them—It appears to me, to be such a deviation from the plain and beaten track, as must make every Creditor of the Public tremble—His plan of discrimination, is founded too much on principles of equity, to please even those who have advocated allways a discrimination—If the Public was to gain, what the original holders lost in their sales, I believe it would have pleased this description of Citizens better.

ALS, Washington Papers, DLC. Written from "Abingdon," in present-day Arlington County, Virginia. For the full text, see *PGW* 5:235–36.

Jonathan Trumbull to David Trumbull

I was indeed surprized this last Mail by your very great exertions—and am much obligd to you therefor.

I wrote you last Week respecting your securities—they are still in nearly the same State of Value as then—As I shall probably receive none of my Compensations untill the Sessions is closed—which may not be till sometime in the Summer—I fear it will not be in my power to give you the Aid you wish, in season for your engagements—I shall do the best I can with your Securities if they are sold—If you write me soon, I may receive your Orders, before I make a Visit to Lebanon [*Connecticut*].

***

Congress is constantly employed on the Treasury Reports but where there are so many *Wise* men [*co*]llected—there must be many [*blotted out and torn*] to reconcile there different Opinions is the Work of time—We get on however slowly—& I hope shall come to an Issue which will be effectual to establish public Credit.

Wadsworth is gone to Hartford [*Connecticut*]. two Days ago—on his return if circumstances will permit I hope to pay a visit to my friends.

ALS, Trumbull Papers, CtHi. Place to which addressed not indicated. The omitted text describes Trumbull's efforts to assist an unemployed "Brother Chester," then at New York City.

Other Documents

Abigail Adams to Mary Cranch. ALS, Abigail Adams Letters, MWA. Addressed to Braintree, Massachusetts. For the full text, see *Abigail Adams*, pp. 40–42. In a letter dated 5 October 1789, Joseph Cranch asked his uncle, Mary's husband Richard Cranch, to recommend him to John Adams for an appointment in the federal armory at Springfield, Massachusetts (Christopher Cranch Papers, MHi).

Will mention (Joseph) Cranch's request to Knox; "Mr. Adams deliverd the Letter and talked with the Gen'll about him at the same time"; she will inquire further of Knox if he can do anything for Cranch.

Thomas Hartley to George Washington. ALS, Washington Papers, DLC.

Encloses list of last four mares and will wait upon him as instructed. (This letter concludes a correspondence begun on 1 August 1789 arranging the purchase of mares for Mount Vernon; see *DHFFC* 16:1217.)

Thomas Hartley to Jasper Yeates. ALS, Yeates Papers, PHi. Addressed to Lancaster, Pennsylvania; franked; postmarked.

Encloses newspaper with COWH resolutions on funding (agreed to on 13 March and reported to the House on 29 March); is writing from the floor of the House, where "no material Business has been done this morning";

presumes they will take up the report on public credit "in the Course of a few Minutes"; promises to write "as often as possible."

Woodbury Langdon to John Langdon. ALS, Langdon Papers, NhPoA. Written from Portsmouth, New Hampshire. (For more on the petitions mentioned, on court location and trade policy, see *DHFFC* 8:185–86, 353–54.)
Encloses "the Memorials you desired," subscribed by all but two or three of Portsmouth's principal merchants who are "interested the other way"; hopes they will be attended to as soon as possible; "you will doubtless lay in with a number of the principal Members of both Houses to assist you in the above business."

Edmund Pendleton to James Madison. Noted on a list probably made by Peter Force (*PJM* 13:108). The letter is actually addressed to Page, who gave it to Madison. The docket is in Madison's hand (*PJM* 17:546).

William Pike to Benjamin Goodhue. ALS, Letters to Goodhue, NNS. Written from Newburyport, Massachusetts.
Office seeking: excise collector for Newburyport; has been promised the post of state excise inspector, "so that I may be considered as in the line"; Nicholas Pike and Michael Hodge have "promised to mention" him "on this Subject."

Edmund Randolph to James Madison. AL, Madison Papers, DLC. Written from Williamsburg, Virginia. For the full text, see *PJM* 12:105–6.
Family is sick; if the critical state of his wife's pregnancy improves, he may return by the stipulated date; asks that "the outlines" of his situation be told to the President, as it is an inappropriate subject for a letter to him; requests an immediate response.

Corbin Washington to Hannah Bushrod Washington. ALS, Lee-Ludwell Papers, ViHi. Written from "Chantilly," Westmoreland County, Virginia. This is the postscript to a letter of 10 March.
Came to Chantilly on 7 March to take leave of (father-in-law) R. H. Lee who was setting off for Congress, "but an uninterrupted series of bad weather, & other accidents" prevented Lee from proceeding.

Manasseh Cutler, Diary. Cutler Papers, IEN.
"Drank tea at Mr. Gerry's."

George Washington, Diary. ViHi. For the full text, see *DGW* 6:46. The address from the Catholics, dated 15 March, is printed in *PGW* 5:300–301; the one from the Georgia legislature, dated 22 December 1789, which referred to escaped slaves and relations with the Creeks, is in *PGW* 4:458–59.

Fitzsimons and the Carrolls, accompanied by many residents of New York City, presented an Address from the Roman Catholics of the United States; all three members had signed the Address; Few provided a copy of the Address from the Georgia legislature and asked when it would be convenient to present it formally; finding "it out of the usual style—State politics being blended" in it, Washington informed Few "that as soon as I could make it convenient to receive it He should have Notice thereof."

Tuesday, 16 March 1790

Snow (Johnson)

John Pemberton to James Pemberton

On evening of First day Richard Hallett delivered thy two letters of 11th. Inst.; I had before acknowledged the Receipt of thy favor of the 10th, the sympathy & attention of Friends is Acceptable, it can scarce be expected that this letter will reach thee before the Conclusion of the meeting for Sufferings—We are newly returned from the house which sat sometime after three o'Clock. It was near One o'Clock before the subject of the Adress was entered upon. Smith from S.C. made a short but very pointed. & envious speech representing that the Adresses of the Quakers, were highly improper & was for turning the Adresses & the report wholly aside representing that an evil Spirit Actuated us. Jackson made a speech of about 50 minutes spoke very quick & very vehement. had a long list of Notes. Spoke first on the Impolicy of the subject of the Adress. aluding to none but that from Pensyla.; he produced a book wrote by one Miller[1] to shew the despotic Disposition of the Negroes in Africa particularly Congo that when they went to meals made their wives stand behind to wait upon them, & only had to eat what the Husband left. & skipped to other Nations from the North to the south of Africa, even to the Hottentots, describing the misery they were in In Africa what a kindness it was to them to be brought from their Country. then read part of a News Paper, printed in Virginia describing the state of the Colony sent to Africa from London.[2] mentioned many hundreds being sent thither, that there were few remained, if I remr. right 20 blacks & 6 whites according to what he read. & would insinuate this as the Act of Friends. he expatiated greatly on the large extent of the Country how necessary it was to promote the settlement of the Back Country especially back of Georgia

& south Carolina, that much of it was Rice ground, and brought a great revenue. & that if the Negroes were taken from them Population would be retarded & discouraged, what did the Quakers mean. did they propose that the Whites & Blacks should Intermarry there would soon be a motley breed. if the Good People wanted this, let them go to Africa & take Daughters there for their sons. & Give their sons for Daughters. & after a deal of Rambling attacked Warner Mifflin by Name, representing it was for some great Crime Comitted by him & for fear of being Destroyed by Thunder & Lightning & being Centered in Hell that he set his Negroes free to expiate for his Sins.[3] but he did not believe God required Such sacrifice, he had Warner's Name over several times & desired the Quakers to read ~~a~~ Chapters he referred to in Romans Colossians Timothy &c. J. Vining arose & said he did not mean to follow the Gentleman that spoke, thro' his Vanity, as he did not apprehend it related to the particular matter before the house, it being the Contents of the Comittees report yet remarked upon some parts, & spoke very favorably of W. M[*ifflin*]. said he had known him of a long time that he lived in the state he represented & not in New Jersey as had been mentioned that he had a most Amiable private Character. & that he did not speak as expecting his Vote as had been Insinuated for that W. M. might next Year be in Carolina for what he knew. On the subject of the Memorials—spoke also favorably of Friends & that he believed they were Actuated by An Angelic Spirit & not an evil Spirit & thot. that the members shd. keep to the matter before them. he stood about half An hour. then Tucker moved An Alteration in the first Paragraph of the Report which if Adopted would have set aside if I did hear right the Whole if it. a long debate ensued respecting the propreity of the proposal, & its Consistency with the Order of the House, this took up Considerable time. Bland. Jackson & Smith S.C. often urging. Boudinot Page. Fitzsimons & some others laboured; plainly seeing that those from Carolina & Georgia endeavored to put the subject by & prolong time as it was late. It was moved when to take up the matter. from the southward it was moved 2d. day, that was overuled, then 7th. day proposed that was set by. then to morrow was moved & a great majority approved tho' many of the New England Men Sliped away & some had Voted agst. its being revived this day who heretofore have professed highly respecting freedom & being United with us. The funding System is so much their darling that they want to obtain the favor of those from Carolina & Georgia. The [*New*] York Members except one[4] & Ours with Page, Madison &c. are Steady I find the Conduct of the Georgia & Carolina Members has disgusted some other members who seing their Aim is Delay appear determined to pursue the business. the Issue must be left. I little Admire thou did not get the Copy of the Comittees report before thou see it in a Newspaper on 5th. day I am pretty clear I enclosed it to my Wife [*Hannah Zane Pemberton*] with the Congressional Register as it

was cut out of a News Paper it might be droped by her unnoticed My love to Friends at the meeting for Suffs.; if this gets timely. Job Scott went this day for Longisland Isaac Everet for N. Jersey David Sands is just Come in very wet from Longisland There was a large favored meeting Yesterday Afternoon appointed by Isaac Everet. Myself & Comp[*anio*]ns. are as composed & resigned as we could expect to be under our long Detention, but it is very evident that the subject needs to be followed up & Friends need not fear our promoting, or even the house, any Compromise, it would be Acceptable to be released but I do not find my mind easy to leave my Compns. in their Situation a weight [*of*] Concern attends each of us but more particularly dear Warner & John Parrish. Warner sent a long letter yesterday to smith. S.C.[5] & this morning wrote something of which divers Copies were made out & distributed among the members to bring the Weight over their minds.[6] he is supported both Inwardly & outwardly. I admire most at dear S[*amuel*]. Emlens steady attention & patience he was about 4 hours this day in the house of Representatives. P. S. I wrote thee yesterday. & proposed that thy remarks respectg. Georgia. B. Franklin &c. shall be rendered useful to some. Thy letter of the 14th. Just reced. I wrote ℔ thy neighbour Davis the 10th. & ℔ Post if I remr. right. I wish the whole Speech[7] had come it wd. have been useful; its too late in the evening to get what thou sent.
My love to Ab[*igail*]. Parrish. & A[*nn Emlen*]. Mifflin her letters to her husband [*torn*] [*Warner*] revived him when he has been ready to faint [*torn*].

ALS, Pennsylvania Abolition Society Papers, PHi. Addressed to Second Street, Philadelphia; postmarked; received 18 March at 4 P.M. For the select committee report referred to throughout, see *DHFFC* 8:335–37.

[1] John Millar (1735–1801), professor of law at the University of Glasgow, wrote *Observation on the Distinction of Ranks in Society* (London, 1771). Jackson is known to have quoted from chap. I, sec. I ("The effects of poverty & barbarism, with respect to the condition of women"), chap. IV, sec. II ("The natural progress of government in a rude Kingdom"), chap. VI, sec. III ("Causes of the freedom acquired by the labouring people in the modern nations of Europe"), and chap. VI, sec. I ("The condition of Servants in the primitive ages of the world").

[2] In 1787 the Sierra Leone Company of London established a colony of approximately five hundred British and Anglo-Africans at Granville Town (in present-day Sierra Leone). Two years later, the settlement was destroyed by native Africans. British Quakers were involved as investors but not leaders of the experimental relocation. A second, larger wave of Anglo-African refugees—primarily "Black Loyalists" by way of Canada—established the nation's present-day capital city of Freetown in 1792.

[3] Mifflin verified the truth of this story six years later in his autobiographical "Defence Against Aspersions" (Hilda Justice, ed., *Life and Ancestry of Warner Mifflin* [Philadelphia, 1905], pp. 77–101). How Jackson came to know about it is a mystery, unless Mifflin himself divulged it to him in a conversation or unpreserved letter at the time.

[4] Silvester was the only northerner to vote against commitment of the petition of the Philadelphia yearly meeting.

[5] See 10 March, volume 18.

[6] See Mifflin to the Representatives, under this date, above.

[7] Antislavery speech of William Pinckney before the Maryland House of Delegates in November 1789.

Warner Mifflin to Members of Congress.

QUERY, whether it is not the duty of every friend to humanity, delegated in congress with the power of legislation, to exert the utmost strength thereof, as speedily and efficaciously as circumstances will admit, to prevent any further progress in the African slave trade? Would I could impart to the members of your body, my feelings on that head, which are, supposing I had a father, mother, brother, sister—or, what would be as severely pinching, suppose my beloved wife was there, and likely to be torn from all, which men call dear, and put on board a vessel owned by a citizen of America, and to be fitted out of one of the ports of the united states, the beginning of next month, or by a foreigner coming into one of the aforesaid ports, to procure a cargo, for such a voyage, among which cargo were hogsheads of iron handcuffs made by an American in this land of freedom. Oh! how would a sight of this, fill my very soul with horror.

Thus I view this ugly monster, and cannot help participating somewhat of their bitter cup, in a feeling sympathy with and for those poor unhappy sufferers. And I believe it is the safe way for the members, to determine by endeavouring to make the case of the Africans their own, and if they have not power to prevent ten thousand of the innocent inhabitants of Africa being brought away by robbery and murder, yea, such as is to be exceeded by no savage barbarity; and which on an inquisition for blood (which I believe will be made by that incomprehensible power, who, being omnipotent, knows all the actions of men) all parties concerned, will have their reward therefor, even those whose power and duty it was to prevent, and who neglected the same.

I calculate on the number of Africans torn in this manner, supposing, one-half to be brought to the southern states, and the other by vessels belonging to, or fitted out of American ports, are carried to foreign markets, which clearly congress have power to prevent without touching the constitution, or giving any just occasion of uneasiness.

I am as tenacious of supporting the union, as any of the southern delegates, which, I hope, will be manifested; but it is a common proverb, that the delay of justice, is the denial thereof: and perhaps this very business, being delayed only one month, may occasion thousand of persons to be centered in slavery, worse than death. I should rather my children had a period put to their existence, than to be so dealt by. This is the clear sentiment of a well-wisher to the true interests and welfare of America.

[Philadelphia] *American Museum* 8(Aug. 1790):64–65. Mifflin had this open letter sent by the doorkeeper into the House chamber and distributed to the members in their seats (Mifflin to Benjamin Rush, 19 June, Rush Papers, PPL at PHi).

Letter from Schenectady, New York

From fresh accounts, we learn, that the English are constantly employed in adding to the strength of the forts and posts on our north western frontier; keep a very watchful eye over all visitants, and seem extremely jealous least any of the United States people should be observant of their proceedings. One would conclude from all this, that their nation still has some designs on this country—Several of the old American refugees are said to be resident in those posts, who are mostly very poor, and depend wholly upon the royal rations.

NYDA, 24 March; reprinted at Windsor, Vermont, and Charleston, South Carolina.

Other Documents

George Cabot to Benjamin Goodhue. ALS, Letters to Goodhue, NNS. Written from Beverly, Massachusetts. For the full text and background on the petition referred to, see *DHFFC* 8:366–68.

Cover letter describing the enclosed petition of the proprietors of the Beverly Cotton Manufactory for tariff protection.

Theodore Hopkins to Jeremiah Wadsworth. ALS, Wadsworth Papers, CtHi. Written from London.

Directs what legal proceedings in America are necessary to settle with Silas Deane's creditors in London; will continue Wadsworth's subscription to the *Parliamentary Register* and encloses what has been published of the session up to that point; thanks for "your observations on the state of trade in America."

James Madison to Edward Carrington. No copy known; acknowledged in Carrington to Madison, 27 March.

John Page to St. George Tucker. ALS, Tucker-Coleman Papers, ViW. Addressed to Williamsburg, Virginia; franked; postmarked.

Encloses (unlocated) additions to "my Dodsley," with an explanation of his encryptions; "I can only add & that indeed is enough now that I hope to be married on Saturdy. the 27th. Instt."; of the enclosed (apparently ribald) verses, Page notes, "we are very careful of your Belles of Wmsbg. [*Virginia*] particular Friends only will be entrusted with a Copy."

Timothy Pickering to William Samuel Johnson. ALS, Johnson Papers, CtHi. Written from Philadelphia.

Relates developments in Pennsylvania legislature regarding Connecticut titles in the Wyoming Valley; requests return of Pickering's letter (of 3 March, unlocated), to produce as evidence of agreement with Johnson's legal opinion on the matter.

George Washington, Diary. ViHi. Jones (d. 1826) was a prominent merchant-planter of Charleston, which he represented in the State's House (1782–85, 1878–90) and at the state convention, where he voted to ratify the Constitution (*South Carolina House* 3:387).

At the levee, Smith (S.C.) presented a copy of an Address from the Intendent (Thomas Jones) and Wardens of Charleston, South Carolina, and was told "I would receive it in form" on Thursday at 11 A.M.. (For the Address, see *PGW* 5:189–90.)

From New York. [Boston] *Massachusetts Centinel*, 24 March; reprinted at Portland, Maine.

"Since I wrote you nothing has transpired but what you find in the papers. The Secretary's Report [*on public credit*] will be run through with rapidity. The great questions being now pretty generally decided on."

Letter from London, via Boston. *NYDA*, 29 April (the date on which members of Congress would have seen it); reprinted at Baltimore and probably elsewhere.

"By a late order no article whatever can be admitted into the ports of Great Britain from America, in any vessel whatever, British or foreign except the same is of the actual production of the United States. Forty bales of cotton, from Maryland, in a British ship, are now under seizure: whatever is sent hereafter, of this description, must first be to some admissable port in the continent, from whence it may be carried to Great Britain."

Wednesday, 17 March 1790

Fine Rain (Johnson)

Fisher Ames to [*William Eustis*]

You, who are a Representative as well as myself, can judge of the respect with which I recd. your favour by the post of last Saturday—You call it a

Mr Madison is at the head of it. You will
see by the papers what mutilation the Sec's
proposals suffered in Comee. of the whole
The subject has not been resumed in the
house - I think that a majority will be
found for the assumption and the substan
-tials of the Report - but it is so small that
our progress will be slow painful and
perilous - We are now engaged in an
unfortunate debate about negro slavery on
the petition of the Quakers. Congress have not
much power to meddle - The debate is in
more senses than one unreasonable - and
it has been conducted with a spirit of
acrimony against the Quakers, and as
much in their vindication, which has
discomposed and disgraced the house. I am
ashamed that this subject should be pressd

Fisher Ames to William Eustis, 17 March 1790, ALS, p. 3. In this letter Ames, a leading Federalist and supporter of assumption of the Revolutionary War debts of the states, expresses his opinion that it is unfortunate that the subject of slavery has been introduced and describes the debate that has "disgraced the house." (Courtesy of the Massachusetts Historical Society.)

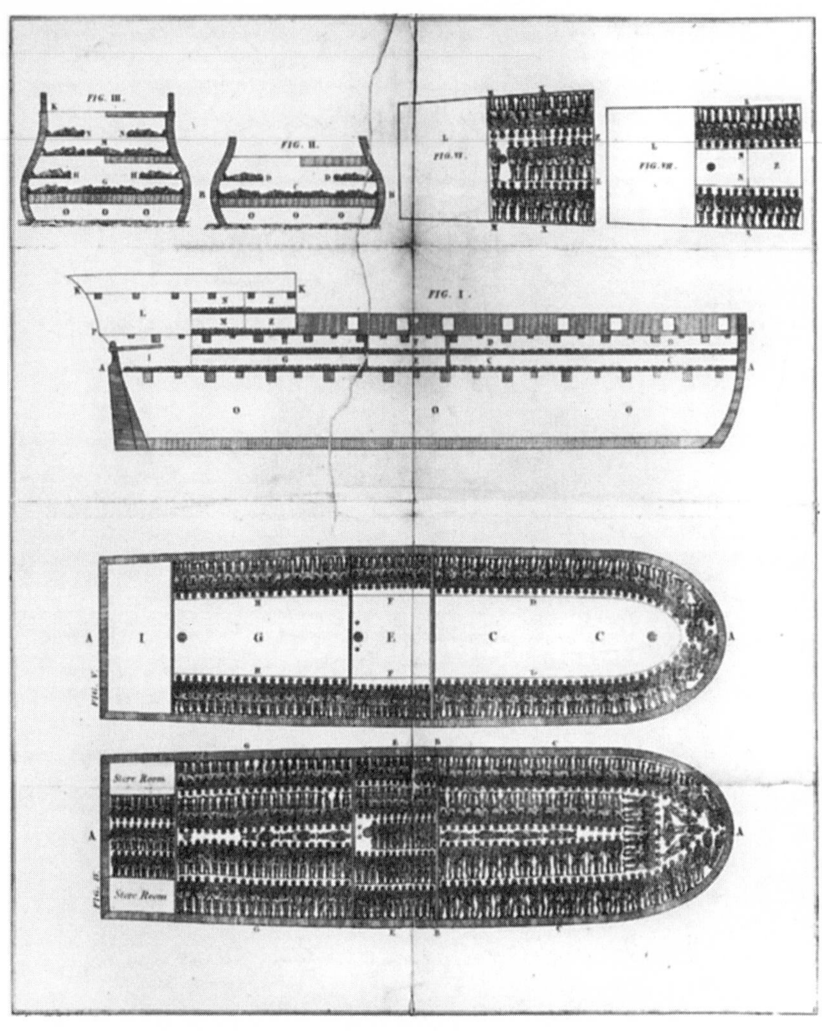

Diagram of a slave ship (1808). This diagram reveals the typically extremely crowded conditions aboard ships in the slave trade. The Quakers and the Pennsylvania Society for the Abolition of Slavery were petitioning Congress to improve conditions by regulating the trade. Illustration from *The History of the African Slave Trade by the British Parliament,* by Thomas Clarkson. (Courtesy of the New-York Historical Society.)

letter of instructions—and I desire you to take notice how cordially I receive them. A representative is a kind of wife to the public—and ought to be submissive as well as faithful. I am afraid that the phrase *wife of the public* will produce some unlucky association of ideas—I trust that, however, to your purity.

I am pleasing myself with the hope of seeing our worthy friend, [*Christopher*] Gore, next week. Before this will reach you he will be on his way. My curiosity has been raised to know what degree of support the Amendmts. [*to the U.S. Constitution*] reported to the [*Massachusetts*] Senate are likely to receive in either house. They have been commented upon here, and are considered as stronger evidence of general uneasiness in the state than I have any reason to believe exist. When shall we find that love of the constitution which is found in other countries in favour of other systems as inferior to our own as can well be imagined! The funding system if well established would give security to the Govt. But I begin to entertain fears that this will be mangled, perhaps delay'd till next session—The opposition is formidable, because Mr. Madison is at the head of it. You will see by the papers what mutilation the Sec.'s proposals suffered in Com[*mitt*]ee. of the whole[1] The subject has not been resumed in the house—I think that a majority will be found for the assumption and the substantials of the Report—but it is so small that our progress will be slow painful and perilous—we are now engaged in an unfortunate debate about Negro Slavery on the petition of the Quakers. Congress have not much power to meddle—The debate is in more senses than one unreasonable—and it has been conducted with a spirit of acrimony against the Quakers, and as much in their vindication, which has discomposed and disgraced the house. I am ashamed that this subject should be prefer'd before the Report of the Secretary. I am no advocate for Slavery in any form—But as Congress may not emancipate, and the happiness of Slaves has not been found to be secured by it, I wish the whole matter could have been kept out of sight till some rational means could be divised to make the benevolent zeal of those who declaim agt. the doctrine more useful than it has hitherto been—we spent great part of yesterday, & I am in fear of wasting a day or two more with this business.

As soon as anything shall be proposed or done in regard to the *Invalids* I will acquaint you, and shall be ready to use my little influence in favour of a good establishment for the poor fellows.

ALS, Eustis Papers, MHi. Place to which addressed not indicated. The recipient's identity is based on the location of the letter as well as the fact that Eustis was a state representative and Gore was a close friend of both men.

[1] Eight resolutions were agreed to by the COWH on 13 March and presented to the House on 29 March. They are printed under that date in *DHFFC* 5:856–59.

Stephen Goodhue to Benjamin Goodhue

*** we here of great things to the Southward and of its raining porrage and no dishes[1] but when we are there with our dishes they remain empty by the Collection of the impost our trade in Common years I think will be equil to any of them *** the tempers of the people much the Same as when I wrote last *** I here nothing of public Securities bying bought or Sold lately I believe the loan Office Certificates are ~~much more Chieff~~ principally in the hands of the great and but few holders ~~than~~ Government Securities are [*Sent out?*] amongst the people but as the old Saying is the fat Sow wants to be greaced in the Arse[2] we have our doubts here as to Congress Assuming the State debts, great men are apt to have great influence it matters not weither they have a title or not if they have but the purse and Intrest Some times will out weigh Patriotism I think. ***

FC:lbk, Goodhue Family Papers, MSaE. Sent from Salem, Massachusetts.

[1] Based on a Scotch-Irish saying, indicating the failure to take advantage of an excellent opportunity.

[2] A version of a Scottish folk saying meaning, the rich get richer.

John Pemberton to James Pemberton

I wrote thee last evening, & just as I was about to fold my letter in order to send to the post office, Thy favor of the 14th. was Delivered me. The business we are here upon was resumed this day some small time before 12. o.Clock. It being the Custom of the House to read Petitions and Reports first, so that our Affair did not Immediately come on, Hartley made a very proper speech. & alluding to the Abuse bestowed on us yesterday representd friends very favorably & laboured that the subject matter should be attended to. Burke arose & stood more than half an hour. I could not hear much what he said but I understand it was principally abuse. & in his Close represented us as satan siting like a Cormorant. his speech often excited Laughter that the Chairman of the Comittee was obliged to Call to Order. & there was great Confusion in the house. which was sometime before it was settled several members Arising at once & speaking. Smith S.C. arose & ran on a Considerable time. & some apprehending he was beside the proper business was Interrupted but this fired Jackson that he was obliged by the Chairman to sit down. & Smith Continued his speech abt. $1\frac{3}{4}$ hours having parts of sevl. news Papers with matter wrote while the subject of Abolition was before the last parliament. then to maintain slavery, Went to Grece, Turkey the Highlands of

JOHN PEMBERTON.

HENRY DRINKER.

JAMES PEMBERTON.

JOHN PARRISH.

John Pemberton, Henry Drinker, James Pemberton, and John Parrish, by Unknown, n.d. John Pemberton's "traveling ministry" led him to New York, where he, along with Drinker and Parrish, was part of a delegation of eleven Quakers to present the Philadelphia Yearly Meeting's petition against the slave trade. Pemberton and Parrish were among the four "deputies" who remained there throughout the lengthy House debate on the subject. Quakers frowned on the vanity of portrait paintings. (Amelia Mott Gummere, *The Quaker: A Story in Costume* [Philadelphia, 1901], p. 72.)

Beloved Brother — New York 3mo; 17. 1790

I wrote thee last evening, & just as I was about to
fold my letter in order to send to the post Office, thy favor
of the 14th; was Delivered me. The business said and hered
upon was resumed this day some small time before 12 o'Clock
it being the custom of the House to read Petitions and
Reports first so that our affair did not Immediately come
on, Hartley made a very proper speech & alluding to the
abuse bestowed on us yesterday, represented Friends very
favorably & laboured that the subject matter should be
attended to. Burke arose & stood more than half an hour
I could not hear much what he said but I understand it
was principally abuse & in his close represented us as
Satan sitting like a Cormorant. his speech oftentimes excited
Laughter that the Chairman of the Committee was obliged to
call to Order & there was great Confusion in the house
which was sometime before it was settled several members
Arising at once & speaking. Smith S.C. arose & run on
a considerable time, & some apprehending he was beside the
proper business was interrupted but this fired Jackson
that he was obliged by the Chairman to sit down &
Smith Continued his speech ab.t 1 3/4 hours having parts
of Scot: News Papers with matter wrote while the subjects
of Abolition was before the last parliament there
to maintain slavery, went to Greece, Turkey the
Highlands of Scotland & various parts to justify it
& at last. hit on the Conduct of the Shaking Quakers.

John Pemberton to James Pemberton, 17 March, ALS, p. 1. Pemberton served as the unofficial scribe and chronicler of the Quaker anti-slavery petition campaign. His letters to his older brother, James, secretary of the Pennsylvania Abolition Society, provide rare details of House procedures and debates—such as the particularly acrimonious debate of this date. (Courtesy of the Historical Society of Pennsylvania.)

Scotland & Various parts to Justify it & at last brot. in the Conduct of the Shaking Quakers.[1] then took up our Adress & went thro' Divers parts of it Representing how Inconsistent our Conduct was with our Principles & the Antient Testimony we published in 1776.[2] part of which he read to shew we Declaimed having any hand in setting up & pulling down Governments. & representing we had nothing to do with Politics he was heard with more patience than he Deserved, for he wearied himself & his hearers Generally except his frd. Jackson—It being after 3. o.Clock the Comittee broke up & the Chairman reported progress—& the speaker resumed the Chair when a debate ensued when the subject shd. be taken up Bland wanted it Adjourned sine Die.[3] however it was at Length determined By a large majority (notwithstanding Divers of the New England Men fled away) to morrow. No time was Allowed for the frds. of Humanity except Hartley. & some remarks made by A. White Pointing to the Immediate parts of the Report respectg. the Discouragment of the Trade—It was abt. 40 minutes after 3. o.Clock when the house broke up James Mot & Silias Hubs from the Country were here & divers frds. of this City also attended. This business does not appear likely to be speedily ended—It is the Contrivance of the So. C. & Georgia men to Weary us—It is Galling to these, we Continue here. My hearing being Defective I can hear but little said by some of the Speakers. I believe I mentioned Yesterday that Smith said we were Actuated By an Evil Spirit I understand since I wrote it was that we hovered (alluding to our being in the Gallery) like evil Spirits. Honest Warner [*Mifflin*] sent or Prepared to send Jackson some texts of Scripture this morning as he Recommended to us Yesterday divers texts.

I hope thou Visits my dr. Wife [*Hannah Zane Pemberton*] often & labours to Cheer her. I still seem bound with my Brethren. the subject is of Great moment & it does not appear safe to leave it.

[*P. S.*] Let S[*arah*]. Emlen know her husband is Well.

P. S. My love to my frd. J[*ohn*]. Wilson & inform him that his letter of 16th Inst. is just read. I have before mentd. that the Papers by R[*ichar*]d. Hallet came to hand but I have not as yet had time to shew them to A. White. ***

ALS, Pennsylvania Abolition Society Papers, PHi. Addressed to Second Street, Philadelphia; postmarked; received 19 March. The omitted text concerns a private business transaction. On the endorsement sheet, James Pemberton listed twelve prominent Quakers from the Philadelphia-Trenton area, perhaps in preparation for the relief delegation hinted at in John's letters home.

[1] A small millenarian sect in England. In 1774 its most prominent convert, "Mother Ann" Lee, took both the name and a small group of adherents to America, where the religious community became known more simply as the Shakers. The group was sometimes called by its earlier name although it attracted many more Baptists than Quakers. Smith's choice of the

term in this instance deliberately associated the Quakers with the unfavorable reputation enjoyed by their more eccentric cousins.

[2] The Philadelphia Yearly Meeting of Quakers published its pacifist "Ancient Testimony" in December 1776, as Sir William Howe's forces first approached Philadelphia.

[3] "Without a day"; without assigning a date for further proceeding.

George Thatcher to Sarah Thatcher

The old saying, that winter will not rot in the sky, has, in some degree, been verified since the month of march come in—For since that time, we have had much cold & severe weather; & on wednesday night last week there fell more snow than all that had fallen thro the winter before—and some of it still remains on the Ground—But this morning the air is perfectly mild & spring-like.

Sunday morning, about the break of day, we were alarmed by the fire Bells—I jumped out of bed, & looked out of the winder, & saw the light of the fire, but it being at a considerable distance—I returned to bed & went to sleep—I have since been to the place of the fire—it broke out in a Malt-house, but it had got to such a prodigious head that the Building was nearly consumed before it could be extinguished, tho every exertion was made for that purpose[1]—The next morning, about half after three, we were again called up by the ring of fire—I looked out of my window & saw the light very bright; it appeared to be not more than two or three houses from the one I was in—I immediately dressed, & with some Gentlemen sallied out to see the fire—when I arrived at the place, which was about a dozen Rods from my Lodgings,[2] & in a range therewith—the fire was busting forth thro several places in the roof. & thro the eves of the house—One engine had got to work, & several others in a few moments arrived there—I took a place, among the bucket-men, not more than two or three Rods from the fire—and with an uninterupted prospect of the whole transaction: having never before been present on such an occasion, I was desirous to see how they conducted—A very fortunate circumstance was, the air was perfectly calm—not a breath of wind was to be percieved—And in about half an hour the fire was quite overcome, & extinguished—But had there been a common breaze of wind the house on fire, with several other adjoining, being all made of wood, must have been demolished—For the Garrett, where the fire first enkindled, was a solid body of fire when discovered—And I must not omit one circumstance, on which account I have wrote this Letter, that is—*The day before, the owner of the house put some* ~~ashes~~ *ashes in the Garret before the fire in the ashes was extinct*—Pray be cautious then how you put away ashes in any part of the house, or elsewhere, before you are certain there is no fire among them—I have known fire to lay concealed in ashes two or three days.

I something expect a Letter from Biddeford this evening; but shall not be much disappointed if I recieve none—for, in that case, I shall conclude that our dear children are still recovering—and that you, my dear, are well.

ALS, Thatcher Family Papers, MHi. Place to which addressed not indicated.

[1] The fire occurred in the kiln and malt house of the Watson and Willet Brewery on Catherine Street (*NYDG*, 15 March).
[2] A rod is a unit of measuring distance equivalent to five and a half yards or sixteen and a half feet; Thatcher resided at 47 Broad Street in April.

Benjamin Rush, Journal

Visited Mr. Jefferson on his way to New York—It was the first time I saw him since his return from France. He was plain in his dress. & ~~a republic~~ unchanged in his manners. He still professed himself attatched to republican forms of Government, & deplored the change of opinion upon this subject in John Adams of whom he spoke with respect & affection as a great & upright Man.

He said Mr. Madison "was the greatest man in the world." That Dr. Witherspoon[1] his master had said of him "that he never knew him do or say an improper thing" when at School. ***

Ms., Rush Papers, PPL at PHi.

[1] John Witherspoon (1723–94) was a Scottish born Presbyterian minister who emigrated to America to serve as president of the College of New Jersey (Princeton), 1768–92. He signed the Declaration of Independence as a member of the Continental Congress, 1776–82. James Madison attracted his personal interest and support while a student there, 1769–71.

A Pennsylvanian

THE report of the Secretary of the Treasury having had a most extensive circulation, it is not to be wondered at that it has attracted the observation of a multitude of people: If it had been published for consideration previous to the meeting of a grand Assembly, it would have furnished an opportunity to the public to have expressed some of their sentiments, and might have proved a satisfaction to a great community; but this not being the case, it is really a matter of amusement, to consider the different effects of this celebrated performance on the minds of different men. I think that the liberty of the press, so much boasted of in this country, is a most valuable privilege, and that it is right for men of abilities to express their sentiments, when they are careful to avoid all personal reflections, and have no other design than to promote the right understanding of any matter for the public benefit. As I believe such is my case with respect to views, I hope there can be no harm in mentioning some of the opinions of others, as I find them published in the various news-papers.

The member of Congress for the state of Pennsylvania, early gave it as his opinion, that it was necessary the House should be *cool and deliberate* in their enquiries, and in the collection of every possible information; for government was bound to do justice, but not to do more than justice.[1]

Another member expressed himself in this manner, "he must renounce every sentiment which he had hitherto cherished, before his complaisance could admit that America ought to erect the monuments of her gratitude, not to those who saved her liberties, but to those who had enriched themselves, in her funds."[2]

Much argument and sound reasoning have arisen from these opinions (published at large in the different papers) and in this display of eloquence, the doctrine that the same principle would apply, as well to a fall of 60 or 70 per cent. as to a fall of 600 or 700 per cent. has been fully refuted: A member observed that a distinction was essential between an extreme case and a case short of it, and explained himself in this very intelligible manner: "Suppose that the distress of the alienating creditors had been ten times as great as it was, that instead of two, three, or four shillings in the pound, they had received a farthing only, and that the certificates lay in the hands of the purchasers."[3] I shall here remark, that such a comparison shews the nature of an extreme case (as the saying is) with a witness, and I shall just ask this question, what should we think of a man who required the value of 20 shillings in payment for such a purchase?

Another member observed, that "it had been asserted, that public opinion should have little influence on the conduct of legislators: But notwithstanding the plausible reasonings he had heard on that head, he was satisfied a regard was due, and must be had to the opinions of the people and to their feelings. Government, he said, was formed for their benefit, and he could not belive the legislature ought to be indifferent as to their sentiments."[4]

These and such like subjects have been learnedly discussed by several in a great Assembly, and if I am of their opinion in many respects, I do not know that there is any impropriety, in expressing such agreement with those distinguished gentlemen.

As to the effects of the report on another class of men, they are so visible, and have been propagated in so extraordinary and extensive a manner, that I think it would be quite supernumerary to say much on that head. The idea of the pleasure of rolling in carriages, perhaps on the other side of the ocean, will be the delightful object of foreign speculators, while the residents in the United States may be laboring to pay a perpetual tax for their emolument.

As to my own countrymen, I should be sorry they should imagine that

I am so contracted in my notions, as to have any objection to their riding in the finest coaches, even with twenty horses in their train, from the most northern to the most southern states, provided they should do it by means of wealth obtained in an honorable manner, and without any infringement of the rights of their fellow men.

But when we see the following extract of a letter, published in a newspaper, it must require the philosophy of a Stoic, not to feel, at this enlightened period, on an occasion of such illiberality of sentiment.

Extract of a letter from New-York, dated Feb. 4, 1790

"Monday next will be an important day—the friends of discrimination, it is generally believed, will be ashamed to show their faces; their doctrine, since the report of the Secretary was published, has become very unpopular."

Is it not a great pity however, that the writer of this letter would hardly let the report be published before he made this observation; perhaps the importance of the day was so much in his head that he forgot every other circumstance. To proceed with the effects of this renowned report, I shall mention an instance of another kind. A writer of Connecticut proposes a plan for paying off the domestic debt of America at once, and that by direct taxes. In the course of this plan, after mentioning a number of particulars, he says, "I wish and pray to heaven, that there may be one nation on earth free from a national debt, and from tontines, state lotteries, and stock jobbing, the mysteries and snares of the ignorant, &c. and wishes that these states may have it in their power to appropriate some part of their revenues to works of public utility, to make roads, open canals, found useful institutions in favor of arts, sciences, commerce, agriculture and manufactures." He concludes his plan with saying, "It is my Hobby Horse that the whole national debt should be paid at once by a direct tax, without any burthen to the people, and if I do not see through my own plan, I am just like other projectors who attempt what they do not understand."[5] Another writer (who calls himself Necker) in the Gazette of the United States,[6] printed at New-York, is remarkably serious on this occasion, and really deserves great credit for the evident marks of his sensibility, and strong attachment to the public welfare. He says, "this is an awful crisis. The decision of Congress on the public debt renders it eminently so. To retain the confidence of the wise, the well informed, and the honest of the whole world, Americans and Foreigners, is the task assigned them. To their native stock of wisdom and virtue, let them carefully and anxiously strive to add all the information they can obtain. A well informed conscience is the best of human guides," &c. Thus this gentleman goes on with a number of free sentiments to elucidate the propriety of his opinions respecting reason and justice on this occasion, and concludes his performance with this remarkable paragraph.

"If an examination were carefully made into the operation of this unexceptionable touch-stone of substantial justice, upon the various debts of the union, and of the states, a great and rightful reduction of their immense amount will be the consequence. Let it not be said that it will produce too much delay, for justice is the object. Let not an ill-judged œconomy of time occasion a profusion of public money. Let not the husbandman be twice condemned to pay, by the sweat of his brow, the debts occasioned by the late distressful war."

I shall just mention one more writer who has appeared in print, and calls himself A Farmer;[7] he has expressed his sentiments in a very free manner, and has furnished an eminent proof of the liberty of the press in the city of Philadelphia.

Thus having attempted, in a brief manner, to point out the different effects of the same thing on the minds of different men, I shall go a little further with what I suppose to be another instance of it in the following adventures, being a copy of a manuscript which was never that I know of offered to any Printer for publication, but was actually found in the entry of a merchant's house, in one of the great cities on this continent, more than five weeks since—Whoever the writer is, he certainly appears to have been in a very pleasant humour, and withal so exceedingly modest, that I have not been able to discover the word Report in the whole history, though I have read it over several times.

If I could think that the foregoing remarks would be as pleasing to others, as that chance performance has been to me, I shall just say, it would be a real satisfaction, and that the public should be perfectly welcome to the whole communication.

P. S. As I have seen some verses about coaches in this day's paper, I have thought it might possibly be suspected, that I was the writer of that or some other publication on the subject of the report; but in order to obviate such suspicion, I now declare that I have never yet had a hand in any thing whatever which I have seen published on this subject, in any of the public papers.

PG, 24 March. The piece is headed, "For the Pennsylvania Gazette."

[1] For Scott's speeches of 9 February, which are paraphrased here, see *DHFFC* 12:214–15, 225.

[2] The precise quotation has not been located but its content and tone suggest Jackson; see especially his speeches of 28 January in *DHFFC* 12:107, 113–14.

[3] For this quote from Madison's speech of 18 February, see *DHFFC* 12:424–25.

[4] For this quote from Seney's speech of 19 February, see *DHFFC* 12:449.

[5] A Private Citizen, [Hartford] *Connecticut Courant*, 25 February.

[6] 24 February.

[7] *PG*, 27 January, 3, 10, 17 February.

Letter from Harrisburg, Pennsylvania

Friday passed through here, on his way to New-York, Captain Alexander Thompson, from Muskingum, who informs us, that the Indians have committed depredations on the Ohio river—that they took several boats going to Kentucke, and killed the people—that the Shawanese and Cheorkees had been particularly mischievous at the Three-Dolands, above Lime-Stone—that the Spanish governor had invited the Indians to remove to his territory; and informed them, that the American people were surveying their lands, and would take it from them, and kill them, as they did their Moravian brethren[1]—that five runners from the Wiandots, with their half-king, and White-Eyes of the Delawares,[2] arrived at the Muskingum, two days before his departure, informing of the Savages being near that place, with design to attack it, as they were determined to leave their mark behind them, before they went off.

PP, 5 April; reprinted at Windsor and Bennington, Vermont; Keene, New Hampshire; Boston, Northampton, and Pittsfield, Massachusetts; Providence, Rhode Island; Hartford and New London, Connecticut; New York City (*NYDA* and *NYDG*, both 8 April) and Poughkeepsie, New York; Burlington, New Jersey; Philadelphia; Wilmington, Delaware; Annapolis, Maryland; and Charleston, South Carolina.

---

[1] A reference to Pennsylvania militia units' retaliatory raid against the Moravian community of Gnadenhütten, Ohio, on 9 March 1782, in which ninety-six Christianized Delaware Indians were massacred.

[2] George Morgan White Eyes (ca. 1772–1798) became a ward of the Continental and Confederation government after the death in 1779 of his father and the government's ally, Delaware Indian chief White Eyes. The younger White Eyes returned to live among the Delawares in Ohio shortly after the FFC made its last appropriation for his support. See *DHFFC* 8:137–38.

Other Documents

William Few to Governor Edward Telfair. Letter continued on 18 March. No copy known; mentioned as received on 24 April, Georgia Executive Council Journal, G-Ar.

Benjamin Goodhue to Stephen Goodhue. ALS, Goodhue Family Papers, MSaE. Addressed to Salem, Massachusetts; franked; postmarked.

Private commercial business; will ship to Lisbon corn purchased from Connecticut and the Hudson River valley as soon as ice permits; they have had no business of consequence in the House that week; no more done on funding since his last letter.

John Hurd to John Adams. ALS, Adams Family Manuscript Trust, MHi. Written from Boston; answered 5 April. Hurd enclosed a copy in his letter to Langdon, 17 April, below.

Office seeking: "any opening" offering a decent support for his family in Massachusetts, New Hampshire, "or either of the New States"; is well known to several members, particularly Langdon and Livermore.

Nicholas Low to William Bingham. ALS, Montgomery Collection, NNC. Addressed to Philadelphia; postmarked.

Not clear that assumption of the states' war debts will take place that session, but when it does, understands that every species of state debt may be subscribed to the new loan.

Jacob Milligan to Pierce Butler. ALS, Butler Papers, PHi. Written from Charleston, South Carolina; postmarked.

Office seeking: seeks any federal office that Butler thinks would suit him for the support of his family.

Theodore Sedgwick to Pamela Sedgwick. No copy known; acknowledged in Pamela to Theodore Sedgwick, March 1790 Undated.

Theodore Sedgwick to [*Ephraim*] Williams. ALS, Sedgwick Papers, MHi. Place to which addressed not indicated. The recipient was identified from his handwriting on the docket.

"We have been these two days past delayed by the quaker petition—a very foolish thing and very indiscreetly managed."

Jonathan Trumbull to Horatio Gates. No copy known; acknowledged in Gates to Trumbull, 23 April.

Francis Adrian van der Kemp to John Adams. ALS, Adams Family Manuscript Trust, MHi. Written from Kingston, New York.

Hopes that the "interference" he solicited from the President, on Adams's advice (regarding van der Kemp's loan to the Dutch province of Utrecht), "wil be promoted by you in the Same manner"; discusses Adams's theories of republican government and suggests that Vermont and Kentucky, if "acknowledged as independent States, in alliance with us," might be persuaded to adopt those theories and see what "might accrue to the State"; ponders the expediency of dismembering the union in fifty years, into two or three governments.

Otho H. Williams to Philip Thomas. ALS, Williams Papers, MdHi. Written from Baltimore; place to which addressed not indicated.

Smith (Md.) "was liberal in his communications to me, and wanted to collect the sentiments of his constituents" on Hamilton's funding plan; has written on the subject, "suspecting that my letters might be made use of, as a sort of corroborating testimony of the public opinion"; encloses *NYDG*, 8 March, "which contains the first part of my letters," and the manuscript of the remainder.

Richard Henry Lee, Journal. Brock Collection, CSmH.

Left "Chantilly," (Westmoreland County, Virginia), for New York; before leaving, received money from George Mason, Jr., to pay for a subscription to *GUS*.

George Washington, Diary. ViHi.

Gave Few notice that Washington would receive the Address from the Georgia legislature at 10:30 Thursday.

NYDG, 17 March. Wister Butler Papers, PHi. Annotated by Butler to indicate the article for which he retained the issue.

Welcome address from the citizens of Albemarle County, Virginia, to Thomas Jefferson and his reply (12 February).

From Richmond. *NYDG*, 10 April.

George Mason was appointed to Grayson's Senate seat by the Virginia executive.

Letter from a Well Informed London Commercial House. *NYDG*, 29 April (the date on which members of Congress would have seen it); reprinted at Baltimore and Charleston, South Carolina.

British customs officials have interpreted the proclamation regulating commercial intercourse between the United States and Great Britain to exclude (even in British ships) all articles not of the growth or produce of the United States; followed by a commentary signed "A Merchant" calling for a commercial treaty with Great Britain.

THURSDAY, 18 MARCH 1790

Warm (Johnson)

Thomas Fitzsimons to Samuel Meredith

I have during the Course of my Treasurearship[1]—I have drawn for

Dolls.	3000
	2000
	1000
	166.30
	669.38
	38
	300
	7173.68

Seven thousand one hundred Seventy three 68 Cents—And have delivered a draft on Otho Williams. 1000 dollars—to Mr. Anderson[2] three books of Indents. for which his bal. is in the Chest the Key [*to?*] the Chest left with Mrs. Daubeny[3] to be delivered to Col. Cadwalader.

The Check for 300 dollars was drawn to Supply some my Colleagues & Inclosed as My Note the [*illegible*] Which I will settle with You.

ALS, Dreer Collection, PHi. On the address sheet, Fitzsimons also wrote: "A fourth book of Indents to Mr. Anderson" and "March. 19. a Check to Genl. [*John*] Lamb for 8000."

[1] Meredith returned from a trip to Philadelphia on 21 March (to Margaret Meredith, 22 March; calendared below). Apparently, during his absence, Fitzsimons informally took on some of the duties of his friend the treasurer before himself departing for Philadelphia for a two week leave granted him this day.

[2] Samuel Anderson was Meredith's clerk in New York.

[3] Mary Dobiney was landlady to Meredith's brother-in-law Cadwalader at 15 Wall Street.

Daniel Hiester to John Nicholson

I take just time to beg the favor of You to furnish me if you can do it without much trouble with the amount of the tax on Carriages, on Writs, &c. &c. annually in Pennsylva. to form some extimate of what may be expected to be raised by Mr. Hamiltons Report of the 4th.[1]

We shall hardly do much at the funding business this week we have since Tuesday been taken up with the Report of the Petition of the Committee of the Yearly meeting[2] &c.—the debates were very warm for two day this day the[*y*] have been more moderate—I have sent Dr. [*James*] Hutchinson some papers containing the debates next week shall write You more fully.

ALS, Gratz Collection, PHi. Addressed to Philadelphia; franked; postmarked; received 20 March; answered.

[1] For the report, see *DHFFC* 5:852–55.
[2] The Philadelphia Yearly Meeting of Friends was one of the three Quaker-sponsored antislavery petitions being debated at this time.

William Irvine to [*John Nicholson*]

I wrote you yesterday by Mr. Evans, who did not set out til this afternoon, another member of Penna. got leave of absence to day—Mr. F-t-s [*Fitzsimons*]—there must be something extraordinary hatching—perhaps to prevail on the Assembly to Resolve as South Carolina has[1]—"that if the U. States will assume the State debts they will relinquish all claim to any balance"—or probably the assembly have no men in it fit to examine into the State of the Accounts—(which by the by I fear is too true) til the gentleman above alluded to directs them—but then on his present system of burning the books after the Assumption of State debts, what need is there to be at any trouble with them—however no inconsistency is too great, when a diabolical end is to be answered—But perhaps they have found out that the assumption is not so agreeable in Pennsylvania, and that they mean to be out of the way, when the question is taken in the house—to let it be lost, as I think it will with or without them—especially if people of your State oppose it—I know the advocates of that measure despair of carrying it when the Bill comes forward, if people continue to speak and write against it.

What would you think of this Barter—Viz. ~~Pensya.~~ a Vote for the Assumption on condition that the Eastern & Southern members give them the seat of Govt. at, either Trenton or Germantown—this is conjecture, but from symptoms it is not without some rational ground—They say little about the new [*Pennsylvania*] State Constitution, but they do not like it, and will not loose sight of an oppertunity to injure it, but this as they are its Fathers must be secret & cautious.

It is thought Scott is rather on a stool of repentance since a member of Assembly of his County [*Thomas Ryerson*] was here who, it is said brought word that the Secretarys Report [*on public credit*] was not popular in the State at large—but this will not be the last of it with him—I did not think of writing til evening late, that some of these things have occurred—and the mail will close in two minutes—I scarce know what I have written being in such haste & but no matter as it is confidential.

ALS, Miscellaneous Collection, WHi. Place to which written not indicated; received 20 March; answered. Enclosed two newspapers. The identity of the recipient is based on the endorsement in Nicholson's hand.

[1] On 19 January South Carolina instructed its congressional delegation to vote for assumption.

William Samuel Johnson and Oliver Ellsworth to Governor Samuel Huntington

We receiv'd yr. Excelly. favr. of the 6th. of Feby. & are sorry we cannot yet acquaint you with the final determinats. of Congress relative to the Funding of the public Debt. That Interesting subject yet continues before the House of Representatives. The Commee. of the whole have Indeed adopted the general Principles & provisions of the Secret[*ary'*]s. Report including the Assumption of the State Debts & have Reported the same to the House but the business is yet very far from a Conclusion. Their [*lined out*] Disputes upon the subject have been extremely long & laboured, but as the substance of them ~~are~~ is published in the Papers ~~it is unnecessary for us to Attempt~~ yr. Excelly. is no doubt fully acquainted with them. The Senate in the mean time have been attending to the several matters which could properly come before them & particularly such as the House at Intervals had dispatch'd. That which has been the principal subject of Argumt. in Senate ~~was~~ is the Naturalizatn. Bill which is not yet finished. There is no forming any Idea as yet when the session of Congs. will terminate. But it appears to be the general wish that it may be as soon as possible—Their appears not the best probabty. from the enquerys. & observats. we have made to expect that the Presidt. of the U.S. will Issue any Proclamatn. for a Fast this Spring, indeed it is the Opinion of many Gentn., in which we concur that except on most ~~Natl~~ National Occasions the appt. of both Fasts & Thanksgivings should be left to the ~~particular~~ States. In the Course of the Debate on the Questn. of the Assumption of the State Debts The House of Reps. thot. proper to call upon the Secrty. of the Treasy. to state to them the Funds he has in Contemplation for Securing the paymt. of Interest on those Debts this Rept. upon that ~~subject~~ occasion we enclose you.[1]

FC:dft, hand of Johnson, Johnson Papers, CtHi.

[1] See *DHFFC* 5:852–55.

Samuel Johnston to James Iredell

I am very much obliged to you for your Letter of the third which has this moment come to hand, and am very glad to know that you have got your

Commission and pray that you may live & keep your health long to enjoy it, I am told that the Southern Circuit is assigned to you and Mr. Rutledge for this time it is expected that the Judges will take it in Rotation, it is not necessary that you should write to the Senate, it will be sufficient that you write to the President, Majr. Butler & Colo. Hawkins A Vessell will sail on Sunday by which I will send you the News Papers which you will be pleased to distribute in my name to such of our Friends as you may think proper, I will likewise send some Sassaparilla for your Brother [*Thomas*] I am very happy to hear that he is better and that the rest of your Family are well.

ALS, Iredell Papers, NcD. Addressed to Edenton, North Carolina; franked.

John Page to St. George Tucker

I have sent you your Brothers [*Thomas Tudor Tucker*] *Quis, que* [*who?*], & promised, his *Quid*, which you shall soon have, as it first stood, & as amended. I now send you his *Quando* [*when?*]—with my Reply—as that will shew you how Matters stand with me.

P. S. as I could not lay yr. Brothers Verses before me I could not recollect them so as to answer them in their order or more pointedly.

Jefferson is just arrived.

[*Enclosure*]

Quando? by T. T. T. M. D.

Far scatter'd be every Cloud,
  Serene let the Sunshine appear;
All Nature, look Joyful & proud,
  That the Hour of Transport is near.
Be still'd the rude Storm of the main,
  With their warblings let Birds please the Ear;
Be sportive, ye Flocks on the Plain,
  For the Hour of Transport is near.
Gay Flowers, enliven the Field,
  That the Landscape may smile to the Eye;
Your Perfumes more abundantly yield,
  For the Hour of Transport is nigh.
Assemble, ye Nymphs, with your Loves,
  With Dances beat Time on the Ground;
Let your Voices be heard thro' the Groves,
  Let the Hills with your Musick redound.
With Hymen, ye Cupids attend,

To accomplish the Work ye've begun;
Nor cease with your Smiles to befriend
Whilst *Page* & his Peggy are *one.*

Answered March the 17th. 1790 in the House of Representatives whilst Mr. Smith [*S.C.*] was Justifying Slavery & abusing the Quakers by J. P—e.

Though Clouds should the Heaven o'erspread,
And the Sun be quite hid from my Eye;
Yet chearful I'll hold up my Head,
For the Day of my Transport is nigh—
Though Storms should deep plow up the Main,
And Thunders should shake the whole Land;
Quite free should I be from all Pain;
For the Day of my Transport's at hand—
Though the Flocks from their Folds should all flee,
And Wolves should be prowling around;
Yet I'll smile with a Heart full of Glee;
For the Day of my Transport [*lined out*] I've found
For Peggy's as Sunshine to me;
She brightens my Prospect each day;
By her I now clearly can see
On Earth, & to Heaven, my Way—
When Peggy's soft Voice I shall hear,
No Storms of the Mind can arise,
But sooth'd & serene I'll appear,
Though Whirlwinds should darken the Skies—
But, should Heaven be pleased to smile,
On the Day which makes Peggy my own;
May [*lined out*] Swains, & Nymphs their Cares then beguile,
Their Bosoms with Joy overflown!
May the Sun shine serene in the Sky,
All Nature partake of my Joy;
May none on that Day heave a Sigh;
With their Bliss may they have no Alloy!
To reply to your Question my Friend,
When the Hour of my Transport will be,
Ten Days I must bid you attend,
Before you can hear it from me.

ALS, Tucker-Coleman Papers, ViW. Place to which addressed not indicated. Thomas Tudor Tucker's poem and Page's response relate to Page's upcoming marriage to Margaret "Peggy" Lowther, which took place on 27 March.

John Pemberton to James Pemberton

The Enemies of Righteousness made a terrible rattle again this day, Our Cause came on pretty early, but it was 1½ hour before the Speaker could get to leave the Chair, though often attempted it. the southern men often starting up. & strove much to set aside wholly the report of the Comittee. & to treat, with Contempt the Memorials. Jackson saying if they had been treated as they ought they would have been thrown under the Table & Kicked out of Doors. &c. used Opprobrious expressions as well as did Smith & Burke. & they were often up. & yet some others had time to say something E. Boudinot in Particular, Gerry, Vining &c. near 1 o.Clock the Comittee sat & held until ¼ past 3 o.Clock. The Debates yesterday, & the day before, & more than an hour, near two, this day, did not Carry them further than the first paragraph. & this after many proposals during the several debates was very little altered. the word *prior* instead of *until* was the principal for on this & other matters when yea's and nay's were Called went in our favor. & the house was Charged with being Influenced by us. & some have given frequent intimations they could Dispense with our Attendance. the second & third propositions of the Comittee were to be struck out & Madison proposed some lines which were adopted instead of them, the objections were repeatedly made by Smith (S.C.) & urged the words humanity & Good Policy ~~words~~ made use of, shd. be struck out but when voted was Carried, to stand. The house has agreed to resume the subject to morrow. divers members seeing the drift of the southern men is to prolong. & weary out are determined to preserve the subject. I wrote thee last evening & my wife [*Hannah Zane Pemberton*] this morning to her ⅌ a private Conveyance, Inclosed three letters which came ⅌ the Packet for Dear Mary & Jane, & a news paper Containing Jackson's speech on 3d. day [*16 March*] & the Extract thou sent me in thy last which I hope will be delivered in season. Fitzsimons asked liberty of Absence for two weeks which was granted tho' objected to by J. Vining &c. I think he shd. have Continued while this momentous subject is under debate. G. Clymer went away sometime past. Wadsworth is also absent who was friendly to the Cause. The Gallerys have been exceedingly crouded. these three days past. A very Venomous piece came out this day in the News paper signed a Citizen of the Union, it looks like the production of Smith (S.C.) as he said he had a rod prepared for Warner.[1] It may create an expence of 3d, yet think to Inclose it.

***

[*P. S.*] W[*arner*]. M[*ifflin*]. thinks Baldwin had a principal hand in this scurrilous Publication. he has been silent upon the memorials from the two first days they were read, until this day when he was very loud Clamorous & Abusive.

ALS, Pennsylvania Abolition Society Papers, PHi. Addressed to Second Street, Philadelphia; postmarked. For the select committee report referred to throughout, see *DHFFC* 8:335–37. The omitted text reports news from British Quakers, including progress by abolitionist lobbyists in Great Britain and France.

[1] Probably A Citizen of the Union to Mr. Greenleaf, below. Smith's wording may have been an allusion to the story then circulating that credited Mifflin's abolitionism to his conversion experience during a thunderstorm; see John to James Pemberton, 16 March, n. 3, above.

William Smith (Md.) to Otho H. Williams

When I wrote you last, I was much indisposed with a head Ache & Sore throat. which continued till *Tuesday.* I am now pretty well recovered but feel *still*, a little weakened, although I could Scarcely be called Sick. I have nothing to communicate, therefore would not [*have*] troubled you at this time, but that you might conclude from my Silence I was Unable to write.

Nothing has been done further in the funding business, since I wrote you, & there seems to arise more doubts on that head at present than heretofore. Some Warm gentlemen have declared, if they cannot have the Assumption business to their Satisfaction they will be opposed to all funding Systems. And I am of opinion *That* Measure is yet doubtfull. The house has been employed, *foolishly*, all this week on the quaker's memorial And probably, will be so, to the end of it. Certificates have fallen here to 7/ If they will bring 8/6 certain with you & *Cash*, it might be worth while to Speculate in that trade.

ALS, Williams Papers, MdHi. Addressed to Baltimore.

William Smith (S.C.) to Tench Coxe

I reproach myself for having so long neglected noticing some of your obliging Letters. When I sent you the Secretary's Report [*on public credit*], I wrote you a few Lines which in my hurry I omitted including in the cover & found some days after. Since that time I have from the multiplicity of public business & private avocations been unwillingly delayed from writing to you, acknowledging your politeness in sending me several valuable communications, for which I now offer you my thanks. I read your little Book[1] with much satisfaction; your sentiments on the subject of American Commerce & Impost were particularly acceptable, because they gave validity to similar opinions which I have always entertained.

I am sorry you[*r state constitutional*] Convention have not compleated your

Constitution, for I find they have left several defects in it; they appear to have wanted sufficient firmness & were too much biassed by popular prejudices.

I wish I had it in my power to return your civilities by sending you some agreable or useful Papers, but none have lately appeared. Congress have been much engaged for some days past in a very unpleasant business, which the improper interference of the Quakers & the impudence of some Members who have countenanced them have led us into. We have not yet got rid of it.

Much time has already been engaged in the Funding Business, but yet there remains Much to be done. great opposition has been & will still be made to the assumption of the State Debts, but I do not see how the Government can get along without it & I am persuaded that it will be impossible to have any funding System of which the State debts shall not make a part. To sacrifice the State Creditors would be such a violent act of injustice as would convulse the Union & defeat the national revenue. I hope the good sense of a majority of Congress will lead them to harmonize the several parts of the Continent & give stability to the government.

Mrs. [*Charlotte Izard*] Smith desires to add her respects to mine & to present them to Mrs. [*Rebecca Coxe*] Coxe. Mrs. S. & her son [*Thomas Loughton Smith*] are well.

We have been much disappointed at not seeing the Allens,[2] which we hear was unfortunately occasioned by an accident to Miss Peggy. I hope you will accompany them should they come here.

ALS, Coxe Papers, PHi. Addressed to Philadelphia; franked; postmarked 19 March.

---

[1] Probably Evans 21774, *Observations on the Agriculture, Manufactures, and Commerce of the United States* (New York, 1789). Although Jacob E. Cooke argues (*Coxe*, p. 150n) that Coxe was not the author, the long pamphlet, or "little book" as Smith called it, has chapters on both commerce and the impost and is prefaced by the comment that what followed were the author's "sentiments."

[2] Coxe's favorite sister Sarah (ca. 1751–1825) married the prominent Philadelphia lawyer Andrew Allen, Sr. (1740–1825) in 1768. Andrew, Sr., then a member of the Continental Congress, swore allegiance to the British Crown in 1776 and two years later emigrated to London. His wife and their children—Andrew, Jr., and Margaret ("Peggy")—followed in 1783, although the latter continued to visit their uncle Tench Coxe in Philadelphia often (*Drinker*, p. 2108; *Coxe*, pp. 11, 60n, 237–38). Smith no doubt became acquainted with the family while residing in London (1770–83).

William Vans to Benjamin Goodhue

***

As it appears probable that the Union will assume the State Debts, & consequently will take the Excise into their hands, I should be happy, if you thought me equal to the place, that you would hand my name to the Presidt. when nominations may be called for—I am sensible you have many friends that may claim yr. attention before me, but as I have the suffrages of this State & am now in post, & shall collect what is or may be due on the Old Act to the 1st May next, for these reasons I flatter myself youl not oppose me, if you dont think propper to apply in my behalf. The Excise for some time past has not been very productive, owing to the many loop holes made by Draw backs[1] which have swallowed up near 3/4 of the Revenue—I hope & trust the Wisdom of Congress will guard their Acts for Excise better than our Courts have done, especially in the Old Act which expires on the 1st. May next.

Small Excise without draw backs (in any case whatever) will be more productive than a large duty with drawbacks, as the latter would encourage evasion—there is one Article Mr. Hamilton has not mentioned that I think would be very productive viz. Leather of all kinds, even at a Cent ℔ pound it would produce a very large Revenue anually, & it might be easily collected from Tanners & Curriers who are but few in Number in each County—Mr. Hamilton I observe estimates Excise on Wine & Spirits sold by retail at only 200,000 Dollars, I am apt to think it will produce four times that sum throughout the Union, the county of Essex only has produced in years past I beleive about £6000. Curr[*enc*]y. the cheif of which has airisson from Wine & Spirits, but I must conclude with an appology for giving you even the trouble of reading this Epistle & Remain D. sir in haste.

ALS, Letters to Goodhue, NNS. Written from Salem, Massachusetts. The omitted text reports Vans's appointment as a state excise collector in Essex County.

[1] Refunds of a portion of a duty based on the fact that the dutied item was exported.

Henry Wynkoop to Reading Beatty

We have not received a single Line from Bucks [*County, Pennsylvania*] this Week, which induces me to suspect that those Communications must have miscarried.

Tuesday & wednesday were unfortunate Days relative to the Debates of Congress, owing to a Subject being introduced relating to the abolition of slavery, this is one in which the States of South-Carolina & Georgia are extremely interested & determin'd to give every Opposition to the Measure the Debate on their part was conducted with an unusual degree of warmth & not without severe Invective against the Quakers, who seated in the Gallery, bore the Basteing as they term'd it, with all the Composure of true Philosophers, I am happy to inform You that the Boisterous Commotions of the two past Days have subsided on this, and as after a Storm fair Weather ensues, the House this day in Committee of the whole have with great Calmness & moderation proceeded in discussing the Report of the special Committee on the Memorials of the Quakers & the Society of Philadelphia on the Emancipation of Slaves,[1] and after all, considering the small degree of Authority in the National Government, it is nowise probable any thing will be done that can afford the least ground of Alarm to those Southern States.

Were it in my power to cast a Veil over the Debates of the two past days, I should undoubtedly do it, but as they were public & will appear to the World, however small the Credit to be derived from them, I send You the Dayley Advertiser by way of Example.

Mama [*Sarah Newkirk Wynkoop*] has Work enough upon her hands I dont know wether she will not have to do like some other People, make an elopement to avoid paying their Debts. Drinking Tea with Mrs. Kuensey[2] this evening who is Sister to the Speaker & General [*Peter*] Mughlenberg, I met with a Man from Montgomery County [*Pennsylvania*], with whom I sent my home Communications, to be left at Ledoms.

We are told that the day before yesterday a Snow fell above the high Lands near two feet thick.

ALS, Wynkoop Papers, PDoBHi. Place to which addressed not indicated.

[1] For the petitions and the select committee report on them, see *DHFFC* 8:322–26, 335–37.

[2] Margaretha "Peggy" Henrietta Kunze (1751–1831).

A Citizen of the Union to Mr. Greenleaf

THE Quakers are bustling with a degree of ardor & activity in the cause of freedom—There is a phlegmatic insensibility, and apathy, usually in the character of this sect, that they are rarely moved into brisk action in private or political concerns, but by the powerful *stimulus* of avarice, interest, passion, or fanaticism—This enthusiasm in the cause of freedom and humanity is not consistent with their political principles or conduct, during the American revolution. Here was a glorious opportunity for the display of their love of liberty. Did these lovers of freedom support the revolution with their monied or personal services? Were they always ready to feed the hungry army with the produce of their farms, or with the *morsels that fell from their plentiful tables.* Did the charity or patriotism of this sect, ever induce them to send voluntary contributions of cloathing, to cover the nakedness of their military neighbours? Did they *chearfully* assist the war-worn and disabled soldier with their *pampered horses* to transport his *little* baggage? Did the uniform humanity and christianity of this sect, open their doors to the wounded soldier, and did they, like the good *Samaritan*, pour "*oil into their wounds*?"[1] Did these lovers of Mammon support the value of the paper currency by their example or conversation? Or did they not very early endeavour to destroy the confidence of the people? And did not their Jesuitical and Jewish artifices accelerate the depreciation?

I have heard it often reported that a great man [*George Washington?*], when Pennsylvania was the theatre of war, declared that the Quakers and Tories would ruin America. If this is a fact, they do not merit from the national representatives a *forgiveness of their injuries*, much less any peculiar marks of respect, because they have influence in elections in *West Jersey* and *Pennsylvania*.

When Gen. [*Sir William*] How inflicted every kind of cruelty on the American prisoners,[2] did [*t*]his humane and Christian sect petition him for the mitigation of their sufferings when their *favorite army* was burning whole towns, and their *loyal allies*, the savages, were murdering man, woman and child? Did they offer up prayers publicly in their temples to the throne of grace, to soften the hardness of *Pharaoh's* heart?[3] Did they petition their favorite government [*Great Britain*] to mitigate the ferocity of war? And to accommodate the hostilities to the practice of civilized nations? Has this wealthy and charitable sect ever contributed any sum for the release of American slaves in Algiers?[4] These superior Christians, who boast that *they are not like other men*, and whose boasted professions of superior piety do not comport with the humility of the gospel, ought to form a fund of humanity for the purpose of releasing American christians, from the chains of slavery, and from the rancour of Mahometanism. This costly effort of humanity is not to be expected. They mean to practise humanity with their *characteristic œconomy*. Their present efforts, they mean shall be at the unequal expence of the southern citizens of the union. If they had property of this kind, and made sacrifices to the objects of humanity and philanthrophy, their sincerity, disinterestedness, and virtue would appear in a more favorable light: "*Render unto Cæsar the things that are Cæsars*:"[5] But these indefatigable readers of the gospel, and these meek servants of Christ, mean to reduce the opulent families of the south, because of the *yearning of their bowels*.[6] Humanity dictates a pious robbery; their justice and their liberality holds out no equivalent or compensation for so partial a sacrifice. No sect except the Jesuits ever pursued the good of their society with more indeviate aim. *That charity begins at home*[7] is the favorite proverb and principle of this sect—Their private and public liberality never extends beyond the families of *friends* and the limits of the society.

These people have pursued the object of emancipation, with such a blind zeal, that their humanity will probably terminate in the misfortune of the slaves, and their *gentle mercies* will become cruelties.[8] If an immediate emancipation could take place, thousands would die of hunger, and with the fainting voice of death, they would curse the cruel mercy of the Quakers. A sensible humanity should pause, look into futurity, and reflect, that those whose estates depended on this mode of cultivation, would be reduced to poverty and distress. Policy should consider the dereliction of the southern states, and the loss of the articles of southern commerce as a serious event. The charity of this opulent sect should make previous provision, for the naked and famished negroes, and for the children of the ruined planters, whose heroism and military efforts deserve national delicacy and indulgence. All the debts owed by the individuals of these states, ought to be paid by a sect, which unites opulence and humanity. Their present efforts may loosen the fidelity of the slave to his master; the bloody standard of rebellion may be raised, reciprocal massacre and carnage may ensue; Conspiracies may take place in the bosom of every family, and whole sleeping families, in the midnight hour, may be destroyed by the poignard of the treacherous slave. These horrors, this blood, this guilt, their own consciences, and the sorrowful voice of the fatherless and the widow, may ascribe to their injudicious and meddlesome interference. The fierce ghost of the gibeted and tortured slave, who was contented with slavery, who whistled and sung in the field of his master, and the gentle and plaintive ghost of widows and children may disturb the nocturnal tranquility of these friends to peace, who profess *charity* and *good will to all*—If they should be removed from all personal injury from the hand of spirits, and their pusillanimity should find security from this circumstance, they ought to reflect that they cannot escape the vengeance of an all seeing God, who knoweth the secret workings of the heart and tryeth the reins of man.[9]

If generosity and discernment was mixed in the character of these pious petitioners, they would not alarm the southern proprietors with their illiberal, violent, and abusive petitions. They would perceive, that the labor of slaves was necessary to their soil, climate, produce, and to the habits of their education. The lands may be cultivated in all those parts of the union, where meek and simple Quakerism resides, by the labor of their children, and by hired servants. The habitual frugality of these Christians, who are so eminently endowed with *saving grace*, makes the service of slaves unnecessary. These slaves to system, impose the burden of domestic duty on the tender shoulders of their wives, and the labors of the field are encountered by the tender and unformed limbs of their children. The houses of these lovers of freedom present a gloomy system of despotism. The wife of his bosom, and the issue of his loins are mere machines and automatons. The principle of passive obedience and non-resistence, actuates their public and private conduct, and is their chief pivot of action. These friends to liberty are slaves to their tenets, and submit to more cruel and scurvy freaks of the spirit, than any slave suffers from the caprice of his master.

They prostitute holy writ for the purposes of robbery. If the puritanical persecution of their now eastern advocates had drove them to the southward, and they had purchased slaves under the sanction of government and the laws, and had cultivated swamps at an immense expense, and had borrowed money for the purpose, and were now fixed in all the comforts of ease and opulence, would they not (if any fanatics or obscure sect attempted to deprive them of their hard earned poverty) call them impertinent meddlers? And would they not, with great propriety, say to them, "*Do unto others as you would that others should do unto you.*"[10]

The southern people are attached to all the polite ceremonies of life, and having liberal and enlarged ideas of religion, cannot conceive, that it consists in *clownish rudeness.*

Suppose that they should insist, that the Quakers should be covered in the presence of magistrates, and the representatives of the people; the meek spirit of these Christians would, no doubt, be provoked to murmur and complain. These people are now attempting political and agricultural alterations, that will destroy the political balance of the union, and cut up all private independence by the root, and they hear the alarms of the southern people with the insensible muscles of statues. It is a tenet with the southern people that slaves are indispensably necessary to the cultivation of their country. The Quakers are principled against oaths, and the common courtesies of life, and government indulges them; both principles deserve toleration, and they ought never to disturb a government, which allows them such signal privileges. The affirmation gives them dangerous advantages in society, and these Jesuits may always turn the scale of justice, in all legal litigation by their bold affirmations. If the southern government should invade this dangerous privilege, the spirit of bigotry would take the alarm, and their petitions would groan with vituperative eloquence. They ought then to reflect, and re invite to their meetings, the spirit of peace, and to extinquish their *Council fires* of persecution.

These people were generally averse to the revolution, and, in various instances, state governments were obliged to use all the severity, vigilance, and authority of government to restrain their inimical and mischievous intrigues. These events are strongly impressed on their memories, and I sincerely believe, that their vaunted humanity originates in pious resentment, vindictive malice, and Jesuitical artifice. With the *fair seeming* pretexts of piety, humanity, and the popular love of freedom, they mean to wound the Constitution, and scatter us again into a *rope of sand.*[11] When a society, who professed the wisdom of the serpent, and the abhorent simplicity of the dove, whose passions and principles are directed to the aggrandizement of their own sect—when this society is organized into a strong, efficient, and united system of government, and is influenced and moved by the blind, but powerful stimulus of fanaticism—when this society, emerges from political ostracism, disgrace, and lethargy, and commences its political career, by bold and daring strokes at the Constitution, it ought to spread a political alarm—*Blow ye the Trumpet in Zion.*[12] The political interference of religious sects is not much relished in America. This state, whose constitution is much admired, absolutely interdicts all ecclesiastical interference in political concerns,[13] and the temper of no state approves a political meddling in their clergy. This circumstance ought to excite jealousy, as every Quaker is an occasional *priest.*

These people have instituted seminaries, and here they will qualify their emissaries and instruments. From these seminaries, the Jesuits extended their influence, and every court in Europe had some of their pupils. There are such strong and marked symptoms of persecution in our meek and charitable friends, that if they cannot obtain a legislative emancipation, they will endeavor, by their missionaries, to stir up the slave to rebellion and conspiracy.

If they only wish to satisfy their conscience, they ought to rest satisfied with their present efforts, and ought to acquiesce in *passive obedience* to the wisdom of the convention. If religion and conscience really actuate them, they ought to abstain from all traffick, in West India or southern produce. These articles are important in the system of American commerce, and it would be a folly to expect, that a people, notoriously devided between *God and Mammon*, would make such an exemplary sacrifice. These conscientious Christians should negotiate like the patriarchs of old, with the flocks of their field, and the produce of their farms, and should not covet, with such avidity, silver and gold, the fruits of the most cruel slavery. I am told the Quakers view the idolatry of the Jews to the *golden calf*[14] with great indulgence.

Slavery is no novelty; it has existed in all ages, and may be found in the greatest part of the present world. The Jews were slaves to the Egyptians,[15] and I sincerely believe, some sect, like the Quakers, instigated them to run away, and rob their masters. The wives of Solomon were slaves,[16] and here wisdom countenances the practice, and the Quakers have imitated the royal example. The universality of slavery proves, that slavery is connected with the natural order of society; freemen and slaves; the weak and the strong; the foolish and the wise; the deformed and the beautiful; the rich and the poor are the natural links of the social chain. Slavery exists in Africa, and if friend M-ff-n [*Warner Mifflin*] was on the slave coast, they would hang him for his doctrines.

The Quakers receive some happy compliments from those people, who study popularity. They have influence in elections, because they are united, as merchants, as lawyers, and as ambitious men; it is their interest to cultuate their good will, and to white-wash them with flattery.

The eastern people now combine with the Quakers; and the coalition, though a little *outres* in the cause of persecution, will be a formidable union, when the object is to destroy the southern states. It is certainly the policy of the eastern states to diminish the population of the southern states. This will give them a decided balance of power and votes in Congress, when we consider the rule of representation prescribed in the Constitution. The black freemen would emigrate this way to marry Quaker's daughters, and to drink cyder with *eastern representatives.*

In all confederations, either some one state, or some secondary combination of states, will prevail. If the eastern states meant to diminish the weight of the southern part of the union in the scale of politics, and to give law to the continent, the emancipation, by purchase, would be a great stroke of policy. If the votes of a faction should ever give away the property of the southern branch of the great family, they will make animated efforts of resistence. The little state of South-Carolina triumphed over the chosen troops of Britain, and if any part of the union should sacrifice them to the treacherous humanity of Quakers, they will defend their property, and die in the last ditch.

NYJ, 18 March; edited by Thomas Greenleaf; reprinted at Augusta, Georgia. In his letter of this date to his brother James, above, John Pemberton suspects Smith (S.C.) to be the author of this piece, which similarities to Smith's polemical style and the reference to South Carolinian patriotism seem to corroborate. However, the piece's numerous biblical allusions as well as its sole reprinting in Baldwin's home district support Warner Mifflin's suspicion that Baldwin, a former Congregationalist minister, was the author.

---

[1] Luke 10:33–34.

[2] British treatment of American prisoners of war was one of the darker legacies of the Revolution. Particularly notorious were the prison ships moored around New York City, beginning under the command of General Sir William Howe (1729–1814), commander in chief of British forces, 1775–78.

[3] Exodus 7:3.

[4] The reference is to the dozens of American seamen captured by the Muslim "Barbary Pirates," including the fourteen then held hostage at Algiers; for more on this issue, see *DHFFC* 2:425–49, 8:1–2.

[5] This quote from Jesus appears in each of the Synoptic Gospels (e.g., Matthew 22:21).

[6] Bowels were frequently referred to, in the Bible and other literary sources of the time, as the seat of pity and compassion (e.g., Genesis 43:30).

[7] Proverb based on 1 Timothy 5:4.

[8] Proverbs 12:10.

[9] Paraphrase of Jeremiah 20:12.

[10] Paraphrase of Matthew 7:12.

[11] A commonly used metaphor for the United States under the Articles of Confederation.

[12] Joel 2:15.

[13] Article 38 of the New York constitution of 1777 declared that as "we are required by the

benevolent principles of national liberty, not only to expel tyranny, but also to guard against that spiritual oppression and intolerance wherewith the bigotry and ambition of weak and wicked priests and princes have scourged mankind," we declare "that the free exercise and enjoyment of religious profession and worship, without discrimination or preference, shall forever hereafter be allowed," while Article 39 prohibited clergy from holding public office (civil or military) within the state.

[14] Exodus 32:4.

[15] Exodus passim.

[16] 1 Kings 11:1–3.

A Janisary, ex officio, to Mr. Greenleaf

It was not without strong emotions of indignation that I cast my eye on a piece signed Machiavel in your Journal of the 4th inst. evidently intended to turn into ridicule the character of a man [*Hamilton*] to whom this country stands indebted for many of the blessings it now enjoys. It is a happy circumstance, however, that every sensible citizen of these states are well acquainted with the person and abilities of the worthy gentleman at whom Machiavel has levelled his envenomed darts. His character is also as much esteemed in Europe and the other quarters of the Globe as it is at home. His very *name* has raised the American stocks at 50 per cent. on the exchange of London. His credit in Holland will effect any loan, and his friends, who are above 19/20ths of the whole inhabitants of America, are so much attached to him that they have justly compared him to the great Sully, without whose aid Henry the IVth could not have closed his career of glory.[1] Even the ladies, who, in this country, vie with the accomplished fair politicians of France, have expressed their approbation of their favourite P-b-s,[2] by every mark of regard. Nay, I have heard some ladies declare, that he was worthy to be "Cut out in little pieces and stuck up on the firmament, to make the face of Heaven look brighter."[3] This warmth of style must be forgiven the fair sex. But, setting all extravagance aside, Mr. Printer, I believe his very enemies, if he has any, yea, the malicious Machiavel must admit, that his splendid abilities have raised him above the common race of men; and his supporters, many of them, are persons of the highest reputation, notwithstanding all that can be said of his connections with speculators, his sophistry, and all such kind of abuse: I would, therefore, advise your correspondent, Machiavel, to desist from his vain attempt to turn such a character into ridicule, least he gets himself into a dilemma, from which nothing less than a broken head will relieve him.

NYJ, 18 March; edited by Thomas Greenleaf. Janissaries were a class of Turkish soldier-slaves who accepted absolute obedience to the sultan. Despite the fact that this piece is an attack on Machiavel, which the editors believe to have been authored by Maclay, it is likely that Maclay wrote this satirical piece as well.

[1] Maximilien de Béthune, duc de Sully (1560–1641), superintendent of finance under Henry IV of France.

[2] Publius, the pseudonym employed by Hamilton, Madison, and Jay for the series of eighty-five pro-ratification essays first published serially at New York between October 1787 and May 1788, and later that year in book form. Although the precise attribution of sixteen of the essays is still disputed, Hamilton was the first of the three authors whose identity was speculated upon publicly as early as December 1787 (*DHROC* 13:488–89).

[3] A rough paraphrase of Shakespeare's *Romeo and Juliet*, Act III, scene 2.

Ximenes to the Printers

By publishing the following, you will publish the sentiments of every friend to Connecticut.

In examining the Constitution of the United States, I found it written, that "No person should be a senator who shall not have attained to the age of 30 years, and been nine years a citizen of the United States, and who shall not, when elected, be an *inhabitant* of that state for which he shall be chosen." Had this clause of the Constitution been considered and applied to a senator from this state,[1] I never would have taken up my pen on this subject, even though he has been confirmed in his seat. Nor would I have written on the subject, had his lot fallen among those who are to vacate their seats the second year; but for us to have a senator from the state of New-York, for six years, may materially affect our interest as a state. In a word, the state of New-York has three senators in congress, and the state of Connecticut but one. I venerate the man, but if he remain in congress, let it be as a senator for New-York, and not for Connecticut.

At the time of his election he was an *inhabitant* of New-York, if I can understand the meaning of the word. His family was in that state, his fixed employment was in that state, and he considered it as the place of his residence. Indeed he was in this state on the day of his election; but his presence on that day, and a few preceding days will not constitute inhabitancy.

To assert that he had the other necessary qualifications, will not excuse the want of this. If he has not all the qualifications, he cannot by the Constitution be considered as legally elected, with any more propriety than if he had none of them, nor is he any more a lawful member of congress than an inhabitant of the Indies. Why was he chosen? I answer, the members of our legislature were probably ignorant of the place of his residence. The circumstance of his late removal from this state, and of his being a member of our council, must have contributed to the error. That error, however, will not enforce on us an obligation of being represented in the senate from the state of New-York.

If it is a privilege to have two senators from each state, it is equally a privilege to have those who are inhabitants of the state. We cannot suppose that our interest will be so fairly represented by members from any other state, as by those from our own: particularly by those from the state of New-York, whose interest in a commercial view is altogether repugnant to ours. But if the gentleman is concerned for the interests of this state, he will certainly grant that we ought to be represented from among ourselves; and if he is not concerned that we should be fairly represented, he is not the man for us.

[New Haven] *Connecticut Journal*, March 18. The letter is dated from Connecticut. The pseudonym is from the famous Spanish cardinal of the late middle ages, Francisco Ximenes (Jimenez) de Cisneros (1436–1517). While it may seem a miscalculated public relations ploy in Puritan Connecticut to identify with a Catholic Inquisitor General noted for his massacre of Moors in northern Africa, the author apparently aimed at capitalizing on Ximenes' reputation as a successful reformer of Spain's corrupt clergy and religious orders.

[1] Connecticut Senator William Samuel Johnson served as president of New York's Columbia College, 1787–1800, and resided there full time throughout the first two sessions of the FFC. He resigned his Senate seat effective at the close of the third session.

Letter from Derby, Connecticut

The proposed duty on salt is contemplated with great disgust, the exportation of provisions is become a very important article of commerce; I yearly pack up 500 barrels; the salt amounts to a considerable sum—an enhanced duty will make my beef and pork meet the market at more than a shilling additional price—now, though the business is profitable, yet this duty will entirely break it up; our cattle upon a thousand hills will be a useless burthen on the earth; our pastures will be untenanted, our calves must be all killed—and in short all the graziers, butchers, packers, coopers and shippers of provisions will be ruined by this enhanced duty on salt—There are other articles which might be noticed—shall only mention *snuff*; my wife takes a great deal, much to my comfort you may be sure—she says if it is made dearer by a new duty, *noses*[1] may as well go out of fashion.

GUS, 27 March; reprinted at Salem and Boston, Massachusetts; Lansingburgh, New York; Philadelphia; Baltimore; and Fredericksburg and Richmond, Virginia.

[1] Probably a double entendre for "penis," as in Laurence Sterne's novel, *Tristram Shandy*.

[*William Maclay*,] Intelligence Extraordinary

WE hear, that two chosen Janissaries[1] have been dispatched by the Grand Vizir,[2] about 100 miles south of this capital, to take off the heads of certain malcontents, who have dared to whisper dissatisfaction at the present measures of government.[3] Should success attend this undertaking, there is no doubt but the first honors of the state, will reward the enterprise, though in the opinion of the impartial, it justly merits a bow-string. In the mean while, the deliberations of the Divan[4] are suspended, or diverted, to some petty regulations about the slaves, for the double purpose of attending to the secret expedition and waiting the return of their celebrated partizans, whose voices in council are equally necessary with their customs abroad.

IG, 27 March; reprinted at Litchfield, Connecticut. Addressed from the imaginary "Hamiltonople," a place name employing the Greek suffix for "city." Maclay wrote this piece on 21 March (*DHFFC* 9:224).

---

[1] Thomas Fitzsimons and George Clymer.

[2] The secretary of the treasury. The grand vizir was the chief minister of the sultan of Turkey.

[3] The report on the public credit.

[4] Congress. The divan was the privy council of Turkey.

Other Documents

Christian Philippe Carl Brenneysen to George Washington. LS, Miscellaneous Letters, Miscellaneous Correspondence, State Department Records, Record Group 59, DNA. For the full text, see *PGW* 5:247.

Mentions Peter Muhlenberg as a reference while soliciting Washington for money to return to Prussia.

Phineas Miller to Jeremiah Wadsworth. ALS, Wadsworth Papers, CtHi. Written from "Mulberry Grove," Chatham County, Georgia; carried by Capt. Joseph Burnham; postmarked New York, 3 April.

Asks to forward enclosed letter to Decius Wadsworth.

Samuel Penhallow, Jr. to John Langdon. ALS, Langdon Papers, NhPoA. Written from Portsmouth, New Hampshire; postmarked 19 March.

Office seeking: secretary to the "Resident or Ambassador" to Great Britain or any post at home or abroad; asks advisability of going to New York to pursue it; if the "delicacy of the Business" prevents Langdon from nominating him, recommends King, with whom he is "well acquainted," or Strong, with whom he is "sufficiently acquainted."

Edmund Randolph to James Madison. ALS, Madison Papers, DLC. Written from Williamsburg, Virginia. For the full text, see *PJM* 12:108–9.

Has expressed "your decided negative" in reply to Governor Beverley Randolph's inquiry about Madison's wishes in the case of the Senate vacancy caused by Grayson's imminent death; generally rumored in James City, Virginia, that Madison had become a Methodist; "it will be no easy matter to impress upon some of your friends, that you have fastened Yourself to any sect"; Virginia's federal district court is thought to lack jurisdiction or have "equivocal cognizance" in case of two recent indictments for perjury.

Hezekiah Rogers to George Thatcher. ALS, Chamberlain Collection, MB. Written from New Haven, Connecticut; franked; postmarked.

Encloses "Edwards reply" (Jonathan Edwards, Jr.'s *Salvation of All Men Strictly Examined* [New Haven, Conn., 1790]) to (Charles) "Chaunceys System"; asks in return "the honor of a Letter and the pleasure of hearing a little news if any there be as no article is more scarce in the country."

George Washington, Diary. ViHi. The address from the Charleston city government, dated 18 February, congratulated Washington on his presidency (Washington Papers, 38:108, DLC).

Few and the three Georgia Representatives presented the Address of their state's legislature; Smith (S.C.) presented the Address from the Intendent and Wardens of the City of Charleston, South Carolina; Otis, Beckley, Livermore, A. Foster, Partridge, Thatcher, Sherman, Fitzsimons, Hartley, Seney, R. B. Lee, Burke, Tucker, Baldwin, Jackson, and Mathews dined at the President's.

NYDG, 29 March.

Abigail Otis, the sixteen year old daughter of the Secretary of the Senate, died at Boston, after "a tedious illness." (A poem in her honor appeared in the [Boston] *Herald of Freedom*, 23 March.)

Friday, 19 March 1790

Cold (Johnson)

John Quincy Adams to John Adams

***

The public mind here seems chiefly agitated by the late discussions, relation to *discrimination* and to the *assumption* of the debts. The decision upon the former of these subjects, meets with the approbation of almost all the persons with whom I have had opportunities of conversing; but I am very apprehensive, that unless the consent of the States in their respective legislatures is requested by Congress to the assumption, that measure will be extremely unpopular, even in this Commonwealth, burthened as it is with one of the heaviest debts in the union. And if that consent should be required, I am informed by those, who are more connected with political affairs, that even our general Court, will never grant it, though in their late Session they have not made provision for the payment of a quarter part of the interest upon their debt. New Hampshire whose debt is comparatively trifling will be still more opposed to this measure. This opposition is not confined to the party who were termed antifederalists. Some of the most strenuous advocates for the cons[*t*]itution, are alarmed, at the prospects of a consolidation of the States and of the dissolution of the particular governments. And they dread to see an article so weighty and important as the State debts taken from one scale, and added to the other.

***

ALS, Adams Family Manuscript Trust, MHi. Written from Newburyport, Massachusetts. The omitted text discusses Massachusetts politics and J. Q. Adams's future residence and professional prospects.

John Carnes to Benjamin Goodhue

***

One thing I will mention as privacy, which I just thought of, and that is, that some Person has thrown out to the Governour [*John Hancock*] many things to the prejudice of My Friend, George Thacher Esqr., upon the head of Libertinism in Sentiment; & Conduct in not paying a proper regard to the public worship of God upon the Sabbath. He has lately said much to me about it, and I have endeavoured to make him believe that he had been misinformed. Do advise him to set an Example to Others, let his Sentiments be what they will. The Governour is high about it.

Be so kind as to let Mr. Otis know, that I have reported upon his Account, & the Account of the other Commissioners;[1] & excuse my not Writing to him as I have not time to write by this Stage. As I did not mention it to his Son [*Harrison Gray Otis*], I suppose he knows not of it, and may think I have neglected him. Tell him all is well.

The remainder of the room I must fill up, with expressing my Obligations to You, & Thanks, for your kind Favours by the Stage, and your Exertions in the matter of my Son, & my late Brothers Children.[2]

And it wou'd be unfriendly not to let You know, that your Conduct at Congress as a Representative, not only gives satisfaction to your own County, but to the public at large; *and my Friend, we are proud of You.*

Please Sir to give my respectful Compliments to the Gentlemen of our Acquaintance.
P. S. Tell Mr. Dalton that I hope what was done relative to our Fisheries,[3] is to his Mind; & to the wish of Others.

[*Nathaniel*] Gorham & [*Oliver*] Phelps's matter is like to be settled, but not to my mind. *Some men are artful.*

ALS, Letters to Goodhue, NNS. Written from Lynn, Massachusetts; postmarked Boston, 21 March. The omitted text relates to Massachusetts state politics.

[1] As a state representative, Carnes was actively involved in settling Otis's public accounts. Otis had served on the Massachusetts Board of War during 1775 and 1776.

[2] For the petition of Joseph Henderson and John Carnes, Jr., executors for Edward Carnes, see *DHFFC* 7:43–47.

[3] For the Representation of the Massachusetts legislature sent to Dalton and Strong on 13 March, see *DHFFC* 8:144–45. The Senators were not satisfied with the document and returned it to the governor for clarification on 23 March. It was presented to the House on 14 April.

Benjamin Lincoln to Theodore Sedgwick

The Light houses &c. are not to be at the expence of the Union after Augt. 15 Next unless before that time the State or States respectively in which they are shall vest in the United States all such Light houses &c. together with the Land & tenements thereunto belonging and together with the *jurisdiction of the same.* What is meant by the jurisdiction of the same? Our people are afraid of these words I wish to know the understanding of Congress in this business.

I wish to be informed, whether, in your opinion, there will be any material alterations in the mode of collecting the impost during the present session of Congress—And if any what that will be There ought to be a farther allowance to the collector 1/2 ℔ Cent is not an equal compensation for receiving & paying out the monies—Indeed half ℔ Cent is only paid on part of the sum collected and paid out The allowance of 1/2 ℔ Cent is on such sums only as are paid into the *treasury* of the *United States,* By this resolution all expences, bounties, draw backs &c. are received paid and accounted for without a fee—I think that one ℔ Cent should be allowed on all monies received and paid out—People here in general are much pleased with the Majority of Congress.

We hear that Colo. Grout is ~~gains~~ against the measure of Congress embracing the debts of the several States I hope he will be convinced of his errour before it is too late as it regards himself as well as his constituents I never knew him tread on ground so unpopular before—Why should he wish to burden the landed interest by a provision for the interest of our State debt—He will not say, I presume, that the lands will not be burdened if Congress will leave the State creditors in the hands of the several States that they can continue the same line of Conduct which has marked their doings for a number of years past He will not I presume think that a spung will satisfy the people, He cannot flatter himself with enjoying the pleasure of holding his whole property while his neighbour equally meritorious and equally entitled to the protection of his country must lose the whole of his—I say those cannot be his ideas—Therefore when he reflects that the debt must be paid that it must be honestly paid he will see that it is best for the ~~continent~~ Union to do it as all systems of finance in exercise among the same people should originate in the same source & be under the same controul other wise there will be those militations which in the end will prove ruinous to the General as well as ~~the~~ particular interest.

ALS, Sedgwick Papers, MHi. Written from Boston.

Pamela Sedgwick to Theodore Sedgwick

I have omited writeing by the Last Post because I had some faint hope that I should before this folded in my Arms the friend of my heart—I receivd yours my dearest by Mr. Kingsley—notwithstanding you mention so frequently your expectations of Being at home in your Last letters I cannot say I am greatly disapointd For so very Slow are the motions of great Bodies That I dare not allow my self to depend on your Being at home at the Time you wished as I knew your Leving N. York would depend on the Progress of the Business before Congress—Mr. Sedgwick will be home and I expect pappa this eveing has filld evry mouth for several days Past—indeed my Love I cannot say That I really wisht you to make us a Visit at this uncomfortable season I had rather wait a few days Longger for that Pleasure than have you obliged To suffer the Inconveniences ~~of~~ and fatigues of a Journey In the Stage from N. York at this disagreeable [*lined out*] weather and Worse Roads—Last Eveing my dear I receivd a letter from your Brother [*John*] in which he tells me that your dear Mother [*Ann*] receivd on the 10 Instant a severe Shock of the Palsy which much impaired her Reason and left one side wholly Useless—but that theay have hopes that she may Recover.

The Little Boys have been very unwell This week past with hard Coulds and Coughs and [*lined out*] Little Catherine also who is still unwell—Elisa Poon Give begs Pappa will excues her not writeing a fortnight since she intended to have wrote but met with the Misfortune of being Turnd over in a Sleigh by which means she was considerably hurt uppon her head and her face very much Scratcht and Bruised—last week pappa will Certainly come—and now She is very unwell with a paind swollen face oing to Takeing Could after haveing Some Teeth drawd and one Set in again—Frances is gone out—I know not what excues she make except hurry of Business.

*** may the most Gatious God Preserve your Preatious life and health my dearest Love and again return you in Safety to the Arms of your Pamela Sedgwick.

[*P. S.*] Will you be pleasd to let Agrippa [*Hull*] Get me Some Garden Seeds and forward them in Season.

Poor Little Robert seems this some days Past to be much Lamer—I can perceive no material alteration in the Looks of his ancle.

ALS, Sedgwick Papers, MHi. Written from Stockbridge, Massachusetts. The omitted text reports on local court business.

Letter from Philadelphia

The situation of Doctor Franklin is such, that some politicians finding he cannot be of much further service to them, presume to abuse him, who heretofore were as extravagant in extolling; but if they had the opportunity of conversing with him, would discover his faculties of mind to be vigorous beyond all expectation, and his judgements on the natural rights of men unfettered by the shackles of slave holding, and therefore was induced to sign the memorial on the principles of justice and conviction.[1] I am not disappointed to find that his name has galled some of those, who if he was present would be able to instruct, and shew what might be done without violation of the articles of the constitution.

It must be a very bad cause which requires scurrility to support it. The abusive invectives against the friends of humanity[2] are unworthy of attention, and must with all judicious persons turn to their own shame. If they could prevail with themselves dispassionately to read some of the Essays which have been published on the subject of *slavery* and the *slave trade* their sentiments must change; so that I attribute their warmth of opposition to prejudice and ignorance.

NYDA, 19 March; reprinted at Providence and Newport, Rhode Island; and Philadelphia.

[1] During the House debates of 8 March, Jackson speculated that only the onset of senility could explain Benjamin Franklin's signing the Pennsylvania Abolition Society's petition despite constitutional protections of slavery. John Pemberton's letter of that date to his brother James, above, is the only known source for this detail; no New York City newspaper coverage of the day's debate repeated the comment.

[2] Quakers.

Letter from Louisville, Kentucky

We arrived safe at this place the beginning of February, from Pittsburg, and a dreadful passage we had of it: The waters of the river, which had risen rapidly since January, now poured down in a perfect torrent; and we were almost in as much danger of foundering at their rapids, as we should have been in the middle of the Atlantic in a severe gale. We were frequently too, in the most immenent danger of our lives, from the limbs of trees hanging just above the water, and through which we were often hurried at the rate of seven miles an hour, by the impetuosity of the stream. If any of our canoes had been entangled amongst these branches (which in many places hang very thick over the river) they must inevitably have been overturned, and buried their freight in the bottom of the Ohio. Fortunately no such accident happened to us. Louisville is a tolerable village every thing very dear, excepting beef—common rum, from 1 to two and one-half dollars per gallon, and other imports in proportion.

Another paragraph of the same letter says, from Fort Lawrence to the mouth of Siota river on a westerly course to the Illinois, is generally a rich, level country, abounding with living springs, and navigable waters, and situated under a pure and moderate climate. Imagination wanders with surprise over those vast tracts northwest of the Illinois, where exist the most extraordinary remains of the labours of great and powerful nations. The fortifications from all appearance are of very great antiquity, and seem to have been constructed with as much art and regularity as those of Europe. Some of them are incredibly large, and must, at some period or another, have contained vast numbers of people. The pyramids of earth are also very numerous, although large trees are grown upon most of them. Whoever the ancient inhabitants of America might have been, they in all probability were a ferocious, warlike people, acquainted with the use of iron and the art of war. Probably a hundred ages hence, Europe may present the same spectacle. At certain periods there seem to be revolutions in nature, which entirely obliterates the memory of the past.

NYDG, 10 May (the date on which members of Congress would have seen it); reprinted at Boston and Pittsfield, Massachusetts; Philadelphia; and Charleston, South Carolina.

From Our Correspondent

Slave Trade

The report of the select committee on the memorials of the Quakers and others, respecting the SLAVE TRADE, occupied the attention of the House the principal part of these days [*17–19 March*]. The respectability of the memorialists, and the importance of the cause in which they had stepped forward, made the adoption of the report interesting to one part of the House: While motives of interest and policy induced others to endeavour to put a negative on it. The debate was warm and able—many of the southern members reprobated, in the strongest terms, any interference of the government in the business; and the character and conduct of the Quakers during the war, were highly and severely censured by Messrs. BURKE and BROWN: While their probity, piety, humanity, and attachment to good government, were the theme of the applause of other members. Nothing finally was decided on, excepting a negative of the 4th proposition, respecting a duty of 10 dollars on slaves imported—and an adoption of the 5th proposition, as modified by Mr. MADISON, viz. "Congress have authority to restrain the citizens of the United States, who are concerned in the African trade, from supplying foreigners with slaves; and to provide for their humane treatment, while on their passages to the United States."

Reports from the heads of the several departments on petitions, &c. were read.

Two Bills, with amendments, came down from the Senate, viz. An *Act* to provide for the remission or mitigation of fines, &c. in certain cases: And, an *Act* to establish a uniform rule of Naturalization.

[Boston] *Massachusetts Centinel*, 31 March. Although this account appeared under a 17–19 March dateline, the amendments it describes, to the committee report on the slave trade, occurred on 19 March.

OTHER DOCUMENTS

Alexander Hamilton to Benjamin Huntington. ALS, Bright Collection, NRom. Written from the "Treasury Department." For the full text, see *PAH* 26:524–25. The verso contains Huntington's draft reply of the same date, below.

Asks whether the treasury could issue an order on the Bank of Boston, rather than cash, to pay the $1,000 advance on William Ellery's salary (as continental loan officer, which Huntington was authorized to receive under Ellery's power of attorney).

Alexander Hamilton to Robert Morris. ANS, privately owned in 1970; *PAH* 26:526. The editors of *PAH* concluded that the note relates to Morris's bid to purchase shares in the Bank of North America offered by Hamilton's brother-in-law and client, John B. Church. Negotiations concerning the sale started in November 1789 and concluded in early April 1790, but no specific transaction is known to coincide with this note.

"I find that I cannot answer as soon as I expected. The absence of a Gentleman, who has taken a ride out of town, will probably postpone my decision till afternoon. The moment I am ready, you shall hear from me."

Samuel Henshaw to Theodore Sedgwick. ALS, Sedgwick Papers, MHi. Written from Northampton, Massachusetts; franked; postmarked New Haven, Connecticut, 25 March.

Office seeking: asks whether it is necessary to write to the President again (concerning an excise appointment) or to write to "Goodhue, Gerry, Ames or any body"; he relies on Sedgwick; "Strong will give you information"; suggests Sedgwick write to Benjamin Lincoln about anything further that might be done to help.

Benjamin Huntington to Alexander Hamilton. FC:dft, Bright Collection, NRom. For the full text, see *PAH* 26:525. This draft was composed on the verso of Hamilton's letter of this date to which this is the reply, above.

Acting as William Ellery's attorney for receiving and remitting money, quotes from Ellery's letter to him of 8 March (see volume 18) relating an immediate request for $300 of the salary due; authorizes the Treasury to retain the balance pending Ellery's further directions; Huntington prefers this measure to the risk of holding the money himself.

Manasseh Cutler, Diary. Cutler Papers, IEN.

"Spent the Eve[*nin*]g. with Members of Congress."

Saturday, 20 March 1790

Rain (Johnson)

John Adams to Jabez Bowen

If your state would as you hint in your letter of the 9th all turn tories and go back to Britain openly; I should not be obliged to rack my invention to point out the advantages which would result to the United States. For as this would oblige us to chastise the treachery, insolence and ingratitude of your people, it would be an exemplary vengeance to all others whose hearts are no better than theirs: and consequently would sufficiently strengthen the national government. A remonstrance or Address from Congress would employ them better than the Quaker petition: but there are other things which await their decission, of much more in import than either. As I know it to be impossible that Congress should interpose by an address; so I hope they will no more interpose by their lenity: but treat Rhode Island in all points as a foreign state. If your people are desirous of trying their strength and their wit with us, I am for joining the issue I shall feel for you and some others. But I say "Come out from among them."[1]

FC:lbk, Adams Family Manuscript Trust, MHi. Sent to Providence, Rhode Island.

[1] 2 Corinthians 6:17.

John Adams to Henry Marchant

Your favours of 19. Decr. 18. Jan. and 7. March are all before me. I am much obliged to you for the accurate and useful Information, in all of them. It is a mortifying Thing to be obliged to take so much Pains with a Man to prevent him from Setting Fire to his own House, when he knows that he must burn the whole Town with it.

I can give you no other Advice my Friend than to persevere, with the Same Zeal Candour Honour, Probity and public Virtue, which you have hitherto discovered and leave the Event to Time. Congress I hope will now take a firm Part and make Rhode Island Cheese Butter Lime and every Thing else *foreign*. To be trifled with again would be too much.

***

Your Exertions and your Influence, my good Friend have hitherto done a great deal to procure mercy to your fellow Citizens. That Esteem and Respect in which you are held, and a few others will Still induce many to wish that the day of Grace may be prolonged. I cannot say it will not: but I must say I believe it will not; and that I think it ought not.

There are three Sorts of Men, who are like three discordant materials in a Chimical Composition; The old Whiggs; the old Tories; and the Youngsters. The old Whigs are hated by the old Toris and envied by the Youngsters. Hatred and Envy have therefore allied themselves together. and the old Whigs have many of them given great Advantages against themselves to this confederacy by an obstinate Attachment to very ignorant notions and pernicious Principles of government: which will end in their ruin. But not perhaps till they have excited a civil War and involved their Country in Calamities, more dreadful than those We have escaped. Rhode Island is pursuing a Conduct more directly tending to this End than any other State. The Character of a Legislator, has in all Ages been held above that of an Hero. Lycurgus[1] and Solon are ranked higher than Alexander[2] or Cæsar. The most profound and Sublime Genius, the most extensive Information and the vastest Views h[*ave*] been always considered as indispensible. a consu[*m*] mate Master of science and Literature, a long Experience in affairs of Government, travel through all the known World were among the ancients thought little enough for a Founder of ~~Nations~~ Laws. But in America Dr. [*Thomas*] Young, Common sense [*Thomas*] Pain, Samuel Adams and R. H. Lee have been our Founders of Empires. I esteem them all. But God knows there is no Legislator among them. and if this poor People will not learn to discover Some better Plan of Government than those Gentlemen even with the assistance of Dr. [*Richard*] Price, Mr. Turgot[3] & Dr. [*Benjamin*] Franklin are capable of, they will attone with their blood in a civil War for their Negligence, Rashness and Willful Ignorance.

ALS, Autograph Collection, MH. Place to which addressed not indicated. The omitted text discusses the Rhode Island Antifederalists and their contacts in other states.

---

[1] Lycurgus was the legendary founder of the constitution of the ancient Greek city state of Sparta, sometime between 800–600 B.C.

[2] Alexander the Great (356–323 B.C.) was king of the northern Greek state of Macedon but better known for his military conquest of the Persian Empire.

[3] Anne Robert Jacques Turgot (1727–81) was an economist whose tenure as France's comptroller of finance (1774–76) instituted radical but short lived reforms inspired by the Enlightenment.

George Clymer to William Rawle

Amongst the arguments urged to a Committee of your house, of which you was the chairman, by an agent of the Pennsylvania claimants to induce a report for the repeal of the wioming bill; one was, as I am informed, that the members the most active in obtaining the law,[1] were specially interested in it—for in surrendering one part of the country in which they had little or no property, they thought more effectually to secure the undisturbed possession of another in which they had a great deal. My name being mentioned among these, I have waited in town several days after the particular business which brought me from New York was finished, in the hope of being able to refute this miserable calumny, but am obliged to leave it without that satisfaction, from the absence of Mr. Wallace [*Samuel Wallis*], who in a general draught of the County of Luzerne, has markt every survey in which I have any interest, but which there can, as I [*am*] told by Mr. [*John*] Adlum, be no access to in his absence. I must therefore be content with observing to the members of the Committee that I am not a land jobber, that all the property of mine which could have been affected by any decision respecting the wioming controversy, was not very considerable, that of this property I had always supposed a large portion would fall within the limits of the ceded territory—but be that as it may, it is clearly in my recollection that once when the wioming subject was before the house Mr. Charles Steuart, surveyor, one of the petitioners for the repeal and through whose hands the lands in question chiefly came, endeavoured to convince me, that by the part I was taking, nearly the whole of my property would be Lost. The notes I then made as he ran over the surveys, were mislaid, or, not foreseeing their future use as evidence, perhaps destroyed.

I have been accused too of misrepresentation—having declared it seems to a committee of which I was the chairman that the Pennsylvania claimants would generally acquiesce in the proceedings of the assembly—I have but a faint recollection of such declaration, but am willing however to confess and justify—for this disposition was certainly once discoverable in them—I do not pretend it is so now—it is possible that with the times many ~~of them~~ may have changed opinions or sides—one gentleman now a leading advocate for the repeal was to my knowledge not content only with the law, but condemned the opposition to it as unreasonable and vexatious.

Such observations here as go to my own vindication, against ungenerous representations, made in the presence of the Committee you will ~~will~~ suffer me to claim as a right—the following asks for you indulgence—it is, that whatever may be the issue of any attempt to abolish the law, the integrity of the law itself, or the honour of those who made it, can never justly be impeached, unless ~~it~~ [*lined out*] ~~be~~ what is impossible, it should be reconsidered under all the original impressions which induced it.

ALS, Chamberlain Collection, MB. Place to which written not indicated. The endorsement sheet of a copy in the hand of Timothy Pickering (Pickering Papers, MHi) notes that it was read in the Pennsylvania Assembly on 25 March.

[1] The Pennsylvania act that would be passed on 1 April repealing the Wyoming Act of 1787.

James Madison to Benjamin Rush

I recd. your favor of the 10th. instant some days ago. Altho' I feel the force of many of your remarks, I can not embrace the idea to which they lead. It would not be consistent with the view I have taken of the subject; nor indeed promise any chance of success agst. the present politics of the House.

The Petitions on the subject of slavery have employed more than a week, and are still before a Committee of the whole. The Gentlemen from S. Carolina & Georgia are intemperate beyond all example and even all decorum. They are not content with palliating slavery as a deep-rooted abuse, but plead for the lawfulness of the african trade itself—nor with protesting agst. the object of the Memorials, but lavish the most virulent language on the authors of them. If this folly did not reproach the public councils, it ought to excite no regret in the patrons of Humanity & freedom. Nothing could hasten more the progress of those reflections & sentiments which are secretly undermining the institution which this mistaken zeal is laboring to secure agst. the most distant approach of danger.

A British Packet arrived a day or two ago, but I do not find that she throws much light on the affairs of Europe. Those of France do not go backward, but they go forward so slowly as to beget apprehensions for the event.

ALS, Madison Papers, DLC. Place to which addressed not indicated. For background on the antislavery petitions, see *DHFFC* 8:314–38.

John Pemberton to James Pemberton

I have no letter from thee later than 14th Inst.—yesterday the subject of our [*antislavery*] Adress was resumed about 1 o'Clock & Continued in Debate until after 3 o'Clock, much scurrility & abuse from Jackson. Burke & Smith who were not willing any should say much but themselves, & their party. Smith laboured to represent that the memorial was Answered by what passed the preceeding days, & therefore was not needful to be taken up again, representing in as strong terms as possible, what alarms would take place in the southern states. & Burke threatned if any of the Quakers came into So. Carolina to sow their sedition they might expect to be treated as some of their forefathers were by the men in New England.[1] & represented he would promote a Law for their being hanged, Yet this man the day before at Table at the Presidents acknowledged, & said it was a truth that the Quakers in Carolina who had no slaves lived abundant better & got rich faster than they who kept Slaves. & lived as clean as a Nail. I understood the President Smiled at the Conversation, which Passed between Burke & Thatcher a New England Delegate—however the Billingsgate Language[2] has given much Disgust to many members. & divers of the New England men are much Galled. they brot. in Mellasses & Cyder. striking at them. it was veryly a shame that such language & abuse was suffered in the house of Representatives of the United States of America. however when matters come to be voted. the southern men are Cant. The principal matter is yet to be Concluded upon. they suffer other matters to be proceeded upon for near 2 hours after meeting. that Sufft. time is not allowed on our business, Considering the Opposition from the south. I proposed to send herewith some of the News Paper which Contain some of the speeches, those in our favor not printed, & the others tho', still black enough, and much moderated by Omissions &c.

"The 4th. Proposition respecting a Duty of 10 Dollars on slaves imported being read it was moved that it be struck out which motion after much

Debate was adopted. several modifications of the 5th. Proposition were offered, but the following in Substance offered by Madison was agreed to. Vizt. Congress have Authority to restrain the Citizens of the United States who are Concerned in the African trade from supplying foreigners with slaves & to provide for their humane treatment while on their passages to the United States." This was much opposed by Smith in particular, who said that it might come to that to allow only one two or three slaves in a ship & so Annihilate the Trade effectually, some of their hearts seem hard, & as Jackson said, would dispute every Inch of Ground.

In One of the News Papers of this date[3] ~~says~~—
"a Correspondent observes it has been said, if Congress should interfere in the Regulation of the slave trade in one Instance they may in another, & under the pretence of introducing humane regulations they may interdict the business altogether. This is undoubtedly a fact, for it is impossible to interpose the offices of humanity to any effect, in respect to this business without encreasing the expence of importation in such manner, as to amount to a prohibition The truth is, if you were obliged to build barns on board of Ships for the Transportation of Horses. they could not be sent out of the Country; if you say that negroes shall be brought into the Country in any other way than as Brutes, you must Interdict the trade; to Import them as Human Beings, is entirely out of the Question."

ALS, Pennsylvania Abolition Society Papers, PHi. Addressed to Philadelphia; answer dated 25 March, mailed the following day. The conclusion of this letter was written on 21 March and is printed under that date, below.

---

[1] Laws suppressing Quakerism quickly followed the arrival of its first missionaries in Massachusetts in 1656. Friends' "preaching" became a capital offense in 1658 and four were hanged before the persecution ceased in 1661 under pressure from Charles II.

[2] Coarsely abusive language.

[3] *GUS*.

David Sewall to George Thatcher

Yours of the 7. & 9th. Instant, have come to hand since my last, By Which I percieve The Important Resolution for an assumption of the State's Debts has passed in the Committee. But I am Sorry to find, so large a Number against the Measure. Because I have supposed it to be a *very Important* Step in which small minds with local prejudices. Would be opposed [*blotted out*]. However I hope since it is carried, There will be a greater Number in support of the measure, When the Resolution comes to be put into Force and efficacy—My Ideas upon this Subject I have I think Shortly Stated in a Letter to you or Mr. Sedgwick, and I shall not now repeat them—They do not, Originate, I humbly concieve, from, from any particular advantage or Benefit that will result to my Self Personally, my Individual Friends or Connections; or to the State of Which I am a Cytizen. But from a Comprehensive View of the Subject when applied to the U.S. at large, The Justness and Equity of the measure and its Tendency in Strengthning the Union, by taking away the cause of What would otherwise Be a Continual Theem of bickerg. and What would be always in the Way of Congress in their extensive Plans of Finance— *** I am Sir with Respectfull Compliments to your Brethen of the Massachusetts Delegation, and to Whom I Wish all that Wisdom Patience and perseverance in discharging the duties devolved upon them, in the great Business of the Nation, that their Importance require.

ALS, Washburn Papers, MHi. Written from York, Maine; postmarked Portsmouth, New Hampshire, 23 March. The omitted text relates to the status of Massachusetts court judge Nathaniel Wells.

Henry Sewall to George Thatcher

I wrote you the 27. of January last, but have as yet found no acknowledgement of its receipt; nor indeed any thing from New York (except what appears in the Newspapers at an old date) since the opening of the present session of Congress. I am at a loss to conceive what is become of my acquaintance in New York, who solicited a correspondence when I left it, and to whom I have repeatedly written—particularly our friend Mr. [*Samuel*] Loudon.

It is true, we have seen *by the bye*, (and without being immediately indebted to Mr. Thatcher) the reports of the Secretary of the Treasury, and the Secretary at War. The former, so far as it is understood, is generally approved; but the latter I believe, is neither approved, nor fully understood. Two weighty objections lay against it; viz. the heavy expence of the annual camps—and their natural tendency to corrupt that class of our youth who will be in the very season of life to imbibe a train of vices very pernicious to society. But, perhaps, from this plan the outlines of a system for regulating the militia, might be framed, and improved in such manner as to become acceptable and highly beneficial to the community.

We are anxious to see the enumeration Act—but especially the Act for establishing the fees in the Judicial department. ***

I have taken the liberty to forward the enclosed under your cover, to secure its passage—hope it will claim your attention.

ALS, Chamberlain Collection, MB. Written from Hallowell, Maine. The omitted text relates to federal district court business, the upcoming state elections, and the recent severe weather and resulting shortage of feed.

Jonathan Trumbull to David Trumbull

By Capt. [*Jonathan*] Culver[1] I have an opportunity of sending you the promised Report of the Secretary of the Treasury—with some other papers which may be matters of curiosity to you.

The Report on finance is still under consideration—our progress not being much advanced since writing you last—some other matters intervening to gain attention—particularly the Petitions of a number of Quakers—& the Society for the Manumission of Slaves—requesting the interference of Congress—these have given Alarm to the States of So. Carolina & Georgia who opp[*ose the*] consideration of the Matter on the Ground t[*hat*] Congress have no right to interfere in any Manner prior to the Year 1808[2]—if ever—& are exerting themselves on the occasion as tho their very Existence [*wa*]s depe[*ndin*]g on the Fate of this subject—altho nothing has been done or proposed by Congress that can affect their real Interests—but the subject seems to them to be a Noli me tangere.[3]

I hope some time next Month to have the pleasure to see you & my other Friends in Lebanon [*Connecticut*].

ALS, Trumbull Papers, CtHi. Place to which addressed not indicated. The recipient was identified from the reference to Lebanon, where David lived, and the closing, "Affec[*tionate*]. Br[*othe*]r."

[1] Jonathan Culver (ca. 1745–1807) of Norwich, Connecticut.
[2] Article I, section 9, paragraph 1.
[3] Do not touch me; John 20:17.

William Webb to George Thatcher

Your letter of the 21st Ulto. is now before me, I am happy to find thereby that yr. Hon. agrees in Opinion with the people on this River [*Kennebec*] in regard to this Port being made a Port of Delivery for foreigners and that you have hopes of accomplishing so necessary an object—am fully sensible that yr. Hon. will not be wanting on yr. part in anything that may serve to forward the obtaining the Desired amendment of the Law [*Collection Act HR-11*]—as well as all other matter that may serve to promote the happiness of the district of maine, so far as may be consistant with the Wellfare of the UNITED STATES at large.

In regard Sir, to a Post Office in this Town, I wrote yr. Hon. the 22d. Ulto. on that subject, wherein I mentioned the necessaty of a Post Office at Bath, & Sir, I am fully of Opinion that the Public wou'd be benefited thereby—It wou'd certainly be of service to me, as now my Letters from the Treasury Department are carried on to Wiscasset in the male & some times I do not receive them in 3 or 4 days, from there, and it has been the case by reason of bad weather they have been at Wiscasset a week—some times they contain Laws of Congress which I shou'd want as early as possible for my Government, In my letter before mentioned I recommended Dummer Sewall Esqr. as Post Master who I talked with on the subject & have no doubt but he wou'd accept it, and it is most certainly my opinion I know of no person in this Town better qualified in every respect for that purpose.

***

ALS, Thatcher Papers, MeHi. Written from Bath, Maine; franked. The omitted text recommends R. (Richard?) Kimbal be continued as post rider from Portland to Wiscassett, Maine. Webb believed that Kimbal had already asked Thatcher "to determine and agree for his compensation" if reappointed.

Hugh Williamson to Governor Alexander Martin

Your favour of 27th ult. came to Hand on the 18th inst. There would be much Propriety in the federal Court sitting at the Place where the State Legislature sets or at the Seat of Govt. if Govt. had any Seat, which I hope it will have before long in N.C. In the mean while I have Doubts whether Fayette Ville would ~~be the most~~ be a proper Seat for a Federal Court because as I am informed there is not any Prison in the Place and the U.S. do not wish to be at the Expence of building Prisons, on the Contrary they have counted upon being allowed the Use of those that are the Property of the several States, for the Use of which they make an Allowance. Perhaps it may be proper to give the Judges Authority or Instructions to hold Courts at Fayette Ville as soon as a good & sufficient Prison shall have been erected. However as maritime affairs must chiefly engage the attention of that Court it must doubtless generally sit at some of the Sea Port Towns.

I wrote you 10 days ago requesting that you would be so good as endeavour to obtain from the Comptroller [*Francis Child*] and forward [*lined out*] ~~Amt. of~~ the Amount of Certificates that have been sunk or called in by our State since the Peace by Taxes, the Sales of confiscated Property, of vacant Lands or otherwise. The Object of many of the States is to assume the Payment of all the State Securities, by which they mean, of all those in Circulation and Nothing is to be allowed for the Mass that has been sunk. It is true they talk of giving us a Credit upon a general Settlement but if it is the Interest of a Majority to make the Assumption they also may so manage it as to prevent any Settlement by eternal delays. I have 2 Capital Objections to the Assumption viz. 1st It will occasion national Taxes much too large to be conveniently paid, for there is no variety of Taxes that can equally fit both Ends of the Union. 2nd It will deprive N.C. at least for many Years of getting any Advantage from her Exertions in sinking Part of the national debt though she must endure Taxes for sinking the very Paper Money which is the medium by which Part of the Certificate Debt has been sunk. Thus we should pay a double Tax. Observe that I am speaking the Opinion of an individual. My Collegues may happen to be of a different Mind. When the Subject is resumed in Congress you will hear the particulars on this Subject.

I wrote you that Notwithstanding my appointment in Congress I shall be able to give Col. [*Abishai*] Thomas every Assistance he may need in the settlement of our Accounts during the Session of Congress. not proposing in the mean Time to charge the State any Thing for such Service. Perhaps the Settlement of Accounts may be put into a new Train before the Adjournment. By the next Session of our Legislature we shall doubtless be able to inform them what or whether any other Provision is to be made or other Document brot. forward in Support of our Claims.

ALS, Governors' Papers, Nc-Ar. Addressed to Danbury, North Carolina; marked "Private"; franked.

Q to Drawcansir

If you can dip your tongue in gall,
And with Stentorian lungs can brawl;
If you in person are but small,
And straight can fire a *pistol* ball;
Or, if a *privilege* you boast,
A shield to screen you from a host—
You may securely then abuse
Quakers, Christians, Turks, and Jews:
Their hands, and eke their tongues are ty'd,
And may *most bravely* be bely'd.

NYDG, 20 March. A Drawcansir is a bullying braggart given to drink, named for a character in *The Rehearsal* (1671) by George Villiers, second Duke of Buckingham (1628–87). The satirist takes aim at a noted duelist who also played not only a prominent but a loud and vitriolic role in the antislavery debates, making the most likely candidate Jackson, a noted duelist whose thunderous speeches caused the Senate to close its windows at least once (Ames to Thomas Dwight, 25 July, volume 20).

[*William Maclay?*] Oculus Mundi to the Independent Gazetteer

I AM one among the many who have exercised their thoughts upon the great political question, whether there shall be *discrimination*, or *no discrimi-*

nation, between the numerous original holders, and the voracious handful of buzzards, who are glutted with the rotten carcase of our public credit. I have turned the question upward and downward, backward and forward, and have viewed it in every light which my fancy could suggest. I have contrasted the merits and services of those who procured for us (I dare not yet say an *happy*) independence, with the new class of beings who have sprung up in the country to claim for themselves the earnings of our best blood, and the property of our best citizens. I have recurred to those repeated pledges, and solemn appeals to Heaven, of the former Congress, to compensate the personal and pecuniary services then rendered, by the patriotic citizens: But I also remembered how those promises had been fulfilled—PAPER WITHOUT FUNDS! I adverted to a thousand other facts, which it would pain as much my feelings to ennumerate, as yours to read. My reflections produced this inference: "If Congress," said I to myself, "are lovers of equity (and equity is the essence of justice) they will consider well the merits and sufferings of the soldier, the patriotic citizen, the widow, and the orphan—They will think of the means by which they became creditors of their country, and how numerous they are—how respectable they once were. They will weigh *their* pretensions against the claims of those men who have gotten possession of their property, and who are well known by the odious epithet of *Speculators*. Congress will blush," said I, "to find any of their brave officers degraded to the rank of the latter class, and revelling on the hard earnings of their poor followers.

If the public faith be pledged to two, and must for expedience sake be violated with one, the breach ought surely to be made where the least degree of injustice will follow, and, especially, where *cruelty* and *ingratitude* will not lie." My mind was absorbed in the contemplation of my subject, my feelings were tremblingly alive to the honor, the justice, the humanity of my country, and I suddenly fell back in my chair.

In a moment I found myself in a vast croud of all sorts of citizens, who were retiring from the galleries of a great hall, in which the representatives of the union had met, and who were then in the act of adjourning to the neighbouring fields, conformable to a resolution which had just been taken.

They were preceded by a gigantic female, with an aspect indiscribable, who bore in her right hand a huge pair of scales, and in her left the pointless sword of mercy. I inquired, of almost every person who had been in the gallery, the name of this extraordinary personage, but, strange! no one could, or would tell me, till, addressing myself to a tattered figure in the same groupe, whose air and countenance strongly indicated that he had seen better days—"The name of that personage," said he, "is JUSTICE."

Being now assembled on a spacious common, proclamation was made, that all original holders of, and all speculators in public securities, should instantly repair to the spot, and arrange themselves in two separate classes. At the same time a trumpet was blown, which seemed to rend the Heavens with its sound, and to reach the most distant parts of the earth. Instantly some hundred thousands of the first description appeared on the left, while a few hundreds only of a motly appearance (some of whom I had seen in arms against the country) arranged themselves on the right. I also perceived with astonishment, that many of the persons who had occupied seats in the hall joined the latter. Justice next commanded the speculators into one scale, and the original creditors into the other. The spirits of the departed heroes had heard the sound of the trumpet, and joined these—but—ghosts weigh nothing. Millions of spectators silently waited the event — — — — — She drew up the scales, when lo! about 4000 persons made 400,000 kick the beam.[1] The latter immediately, and with one voice exclaimed, "Foul play! foul play!" Here Justice knit her brows, and demanded the reason of such a charge. "It is this, may it please your Highness" replied the tattered figure before-mentioned (who happened to be in the scale whence the cry issued) "the pockets of the Speculators are filled with gold, while ours, on the contrary, are perfectly light and empty." At this the countenance of the Goddess brightened up: With a mixture of indignation and pleasantry she now commanded the Speculators to deposit all their gold in a heap on the ground, declaring that, for the trick attempted to be put on her, it should belong to that class only which should outweigh the other. The money was discharged, and the scales immediately changed position. The prize was now adjudged to the original creditors, who accordingly shared it among themselves, amidst the applauding chorus of the millions of spectators! I threw up my hat, shouting, "Long live"—and awoke with—JUSTICE! on my lips.

IG, 20 March. The editors are printing this piece because the viewpoints of the author and the place in which it was published, as well as its style, suggest that Maclay may be the author. "Oculus Mundi" means "eye of the world" in Latin. The concluding dream's stylistic resemblance to the Book of Revelation suggests that the name may be intended as an allusion to that source's symbol for the watchfulness of God's throne, which is guarded by four beasts (later identified with the four evangelists) "full of eyes before and behind" (Revelations 4:6–7).

[1] When one scale pan flies upward because it weighs less or is of less consequence.

A Real Soldier to Mr. Russell

YOU are requested to insert the following sentiments of a Soldier—they are not dressed in the language of an experienced writer; it is simple, and contains the situation of him who wrote it, as well as the principal part of those who served in the army.

No one can feel the weight of the arguments for and against the discrimination, so long debated in Congress, as those who are interested. Every one knows the situation of the army at the time it was disbanded—they were without money—they were without friends—and but one to five hundred had parents or connections they could return to that would support them, while they could put themselves in some kind of employment. What, then, must be the alternative? They must dispose of their ideal pay, or they must go hungry. What was the encouragement when they offered their paper for sale? That government would never be able to pay it, and that it was not worth more than 2/. for 20/. This was the language of all the purchasers. Law is on one side of the question, Humanity and Justice on the other—Now which had ought to influence? The answer is easy, and the candid may judge. It is grievous, that the very persons who were the instruments in raising the United States from a state of slavery, to that of independence and respectability, should be the first to be enslaved; and slaves to those, who, in the whole course of the war, lived in ease and affluence; who knew not an hour's suffering of a soldier; who could retire to his bed without anxiety, or dread of alarm—To those we have to pay 20/. taxes, for that which cost only 2/. It is notorious, that we see the poor, emancipated soldier, hungry and naked, in many instances, (not from any misconduct of their own, but mere misfortune) now wandering from one extreme part of the Continent to the other—friendless and helpless; like the Jews, though not merited like them, scattered to assemble no more, until that trumpet sounds that assembles all nations.[1] Poor, unfortunate men! Thy situation in life is deplorable—and thou art the only sufferers, by that which ought to have been to thy advantage—and thy being had ought to have been that of envy, rather than ridicule. But, thank God! there lives a MADISON to propose justice; a JACKSON to advocate; and a WASHINGTON to approve—They are thy friends, and thy prospects may be more bright in future.

[Boston] *Massachusetts Centinel*, 20 March, edited by Benjamin Russell; reprinted at Exeter, New Hampshire.

[1] The summoning of the dispersed tribes of Israel at the Apocalypse is a frequent motif in the Bible; e.g., Isaiah 27:13.

OTHER DOCUMENTS

John Adams to Joseph Mandrillon. FC:lbk, Adams Family Manuscript Trust, MHi.

Wonders that more patriots of the United Provinces, especially those who have been banished, don't settle in the United States.

John Adams to Charles Storer. FC:lbk, Adams Family Manuscript Trust, MHi. Sent to Troy, New York.

Advises about the poor prospects for office seeking; "the executive authority is so wholly out of my sphere, and it is so delicate a thing for me to meddle in, that I avoid it as much as possible"; nevertheless, will recommend him to the President "for any thing you may think of."

Elias Boudinot to Joseph Shotwell. No copy known; acknowledged in Shotwell to Boudinot, 12 April.

Stephen Goodhue to Benjamin Goodhue. FC:lbk, Goodhue Family Papers, MSaE.

"Fanny" (Frances Ritchie Goodhue) and the children are all well.

Benjamin Goodhue to Nicholas Pike. No copy known, acknowledged in Pike to Goodhue, 6 April.

Patrick Henry to John Dawson. Copy, Patrick Henry Papers, DLC. Written from Prince Edward County, Virginia. The endorsement notes the letter is "private."

Laments the death of Grayson, an "agreeable acquaintance" and "an upright & able servant" to the public, who possessed "genius, learning, & a general knowledge of men & things," more particularly, of anecdotes about American history of the previous twenty years; declines offer to fill Grayson's vacant Senate seat; "my mind revolts at the idea of accepting."

Benjamin Huntington to Governor Samuel Huntington. No copy known; acknowledged in Samuel to Benjamin Huntington, 24 April.

Richard Henry Lee to Justices of the Fauquier County Court. ALS, privately owned in 1983. Written from Dumfries, Virginia (en route to New York).

Regarding the donation of land for a new courthouse.

Rebecca Leppington to Abigail Adams. ALS, Adams Family Manuscript Trust, MHi. Written from Boston.

Office seeking: some appointment for "the Gentleman with whom I have lived for Several years"; requesting that his enclosed letter of application be forwarded to the Vice President; "you doubtless will be at a loss to account for *my* addressing *you* on this subject I am full in the beleif that many Ladies have been as instrumental in promoting both Publick & private good as the Gentlemen."

James Lovell to John Adams. ALS, Adams Family Manuscript Trust, MHi. Written from Boston; answered 5 April. Encloses a list of measures and dates showing how the Continental Congress "was obliged to turn & twist under the Difficulties of a depreciating Currency." For background on James Warren's claim for a depreciation allowance, see *DHFFC* 7:1–4.

"Your old Friend" James Warren failed to procure from Lovell a testimonial in support of his claim (for a depreciation allowance); Warren will be visiting Adams soon and may address him too upon the subject; thinks Gerry's "Regard for the Genl. [*Warren*] and perhaps his *individual* Intention" may provide him a favorable testimonial; Andrew Craigie is handling unsettled business for him related to renewal of destroyed certificates and vouchers; hopes that the secretary of the treasury has "discretionary power" to renew destroyed certificates and that Adams will assist Craigie if asked.

William Maclay to Robert Morris. Maclay Diary, DLC. For the full text, see *DHFFC* 9:223–24.

A description of Northumberland County, Pennsylvania.

James Madison to John Dawson. No copy known; acknowledged in Dawson to Madison, 13 April.

Abijah Poole to George Thatcher. ALS, Thatcher Papers, MeHi. Written from Portland, Maine; franked.

Encloses power of attorney to obtain commutation and veterans' land bounties for Poole, William Stanwood, Samuel Thomas, John Lemont, and Richard Mayberry; prefers the land be in Lincoln or Cumberland County, Maine; "we will amply satisfy you for your attention to the business."

Sunday, 21 March 1790

Abraham Baldwin to Ruth Barlow

I received your good letter of friday, and am glad to find you mend in your morals. If by laughing, or scolding, or talking politicks I can keep your widowship in good humour with yourself and your friends, I shall answer my purposes, and you may set it down all a joke. But if you are serious in telling me to talk politicks with you, beware of the trouble you are bringing upon yourself, I shall talk you blind if not deaf, for I know how your poor eyes used to find fault with my scrawls, and I grow worse in that as well as in every thing else. about speaking—in the first place we have so many magpies, it is difficult for a bird of but common note, to get any chance to chatter: in the second place. I was chairman all the time[1] and had no right to speak but to keep them in order: and the subject did not deserve any speak neither, for however you may like the man and his words,[2] the proposition was but whimsical. There has been as much cause for every state heretofore in settling their accounts, to have pursued that method, and it was vastly more practicable for them, they are like a family compared with us, they knew almost all the individuals, and their accounts were in small and manageable shape, yet not one of them ever attempted such a plan, which is a sufficient proof that it was a wild goose scheme.

If there is any vessel going to Europe you will see it mentioned in the papers, I have not noticed any, when the spirit moves write your letter and send it along; I am told love does not grow cold by lieing, particularly if it is in good hands.

Every body here says how d'ye, and I always say the same to them for you.

AL, American Manuscripts, CSmH. Addressed to Greenfield, Connecticut. The salutation reads "Dear Sis."

[1] Baldwin served as chairman of the COWH from 9 January through 22 February.

[2] Madison and his proposal for discriminating between original and secondary public securities holders.

William Bradford, Jr. to Elias Boudinot

I had the pleasure of receiving your letter last night; but I have not yet seen Mr. Fitzsimons to whom you refer me for the state of matters in N. York. I have no doubt but there must be some essential reasons for adopting the state debts—but the measure has created alarm & despondency among the public creditors here, and indeed among all others who wish to see the credit of the United States properly supported. I have met with several original holders of certificates who seem determined to embrace the next gust of hope to sell out. They consider *that* assumption as a millstone about the neck of the whole system which must finally sink [*lined out*] it. The value of certificates is sinking, & tho' people are unwilling to sell at their present rate, yet scarce any purchasers can be found at it. I believe the price is about 7/. It has been above 9/. For my own part, I parted with all the money I could spare in the beginning of last week when they were at 7/6—but the more people reflect Upon the amount of the debt the more the efforts of their despondency are visible. The reputation of the Secretary [*Hamilton*] is deeply at stake: & unless he can devise means of reviving the public confidence by stating those resources which he has in reserve, ~~the~~ I am apprehensive that his plan will defeat itself. Some persons are of opinion that the measure has been insidiously urged by those who wished for a discrimination in order to ~~produce~~ gain that point by a side wind. I am sorry any interruption has taken place—& still more that it has been occasioned by any disputes, that have a tendency to create ill blood & lessen the harmony that has generally prevailed in your body.

***

ALS, Wallace Papers, PHi. Written from Philadelphia. The omitted text relates to proceedings of the Pennsylvania legislature and supreme court, the health of Boudinot's daughter, Susan Bradford (who intends "to write a few lines, if her head ach should leave her"), the price of public securities, and Boudinot's receiving a payment on Bradford's behalf.

Tench Coxe to James Madison

***

An artist of this city[1] communicated to me some time ago information that he had discovered a method of obtaining an invariable standard of Measures recoverable at all times and in all places. As the President in pursuance of one of the Articles of the Constitution had recommended to Congress the establishment of Uniformity of weights & Measures, and the Subject was refered by your house to the Secy. of State I presumed it might be proper to communicate this Matter to Mr. Jay, having understood that he would have the charge of the department of State 'till Mr. Jeffersons arrival. Mr. Jay was good enough to write me that he only continued his Attention to foreign Affairs, but that he should hand my letter over to the Secy. of State on his Arrival. When Mr. Jefferson was in town I should have done myself the honor to procure an introduction to him, & to have waited upon him with the artist to communicate the Invention to him, but I was confined with a wounded ankle that has made me a prisoner for some days. Having lost that opty. and not having the pleasure of knowing Mr. Jefferson I take the liberty, Sir, to enclose the communication to you. Doctor [*Benjamin*] Franklin, Mr. [*David*] Rittenhouse, Mr. [*Robert*] Patterson the Secy. of the Phil[*osphical*]. Society & I are all the persons the artist has entrusted, and we have each given him a written declaration of the time of Exhibition. His confidence in me has induced him to permit me to chuse a friend thro whom I might lay it before the Secy. of State, with a request that at present the knowlege of the thing may lie with him & yourself—and that it might not without his Consent be made known to any other person, except the President to whom of course he respectfully wishes it may be freely made known, if the Secretary thinks it proper to lay it before him. Tho the apparatus is extremely simple the Object has been industriously pursued for many years by the Philosophers &

Mechanicians of Europe as Mr. Jefferson & you must well know. The Society of Arts &ca. in London have offered 100 Guineas for the discovery, which the inventor is determined not to apply for, but to devote it to the Service of his native Country. The simplicity of the Apparatus however will spread it in a year over the civilized part of the World.

I have the satisfaction to inform you that the Artist, who undertook to make the machine for spinning flax, hemp & wool by water has completed the model & that it is now in my hands ready for an application for a patent, which he will make as soon as the Law shall pass.[2] The drawings and description are prepared. He has added another invention of wch. he has deposited the drawing with me to make cordage of 1½ In. diameter, and he has furnished me with a drawing of a two-part water engine to grind optical glasses or lenses, and to polish them when ground. This engine is capable of grinding & polishing above 1000 glasses in a day & requires but one man and a small constant stream. He also has furnished me with the great movements of [*Sir Richard*] Arkwrights *cotton* spinning Mill, and some of the lesser ones, but this material is more perfectly manufactured by the Milne's improvement on Arkwrights Machinery now established in France.[3] Mr. [*William*] Bingham informs me that Mr. Jefferson wrote him that this Mill might be got in France for 12,000 livres, or 2000 silver Crowns of that Kingdom. To procure and record the drawings & descriptions of Machinery and Apparatus in the useful Arts and Philosophical Science appears to me a very great Object. It is manifest that without depending *inconveniently* upon manual labor we may, by Mechanism and a knowlege of the nature of sensible Objects and their effects upon each other, save great sums of Money, raise our character as an intelligent Nation, and encrease the comforts of human life and the most pure & dignifying Enjoyments of the mind of man. No man has a higher confidence than I, in the talents of my Countrymen & their ability to attain these things by their native ~~talents~~ strength of mind, but I would nevertheless draw upon that great fund of skill & knowlege, particularly of the useful Arts, wch. Europe possesses. For this reason I saw with regret the truth of your apprehension, that the benefit of a patent could not be constitutionally extended to imported objects—nor indeed, if it were within the verge of the powers of Congress, do I think any clause to that effect could be safely modified. Private acts would be wise and safe, if they could be thought constitutional, but I think they cannot without an Amendment, by striking out all of the clause that follows the word "*by*" in the 8th. parag. of the 8th. Sec. of the first Article[4]—or something to that purpose. An Idea however has struck me upon the Subject which I have several times mentioned, and now trouble you with. It is that Congress should lay off a million of Acres of the nearest, least broken & most valuable land in their western Territory as a fund to reward the introduction of Machinery inventions, arts, and other things of that nature from foreign Countries, and Inventions and discoveries first communicated to us by Natives or foreigners the benefits of which, tho of no considerable importance to them, should be useful to the United States. From two years attention to this Subject and a constant observation ~~of~~ on foreigners I am satisfied it would have a very beneficial effect, & that our knowlege of Manufacturing Machinery would quickly equal our capital to carry them on, even supposing public Securities to become so stable in value as to grow into a circulating Medium. I cannot however pass from this Subject without observing that such a plan must prove advantageous to me from the several objects I possess some of wch. are not inventions, but importations. These I trust you will believe I could relinquish, if it would obviate the least impediment in the way of the plan. I will just add that the public benefit from such a measure would arise, in my Opinion, from the assurance it would hold out to the world of the Regard of Congress for the Advancement of the useful Arts and manufactures—and the Idea of a solid, tho not a pecuniary reward to those who enrich our domestic Stock of profitable and liberal Knowlege.

Some time after you passed thro Philadelphia I requested the favor of Colonel Hamilton to shew you two or three of the papers I had sent him, particularly that on the present state of the Navigation of Pennsylvania with a comparison of the same with that of the principal Nations of Europe—and that on the Succedanea for foreign liquors.[5] If they are yet in your hands & you think them worthy of his perusal I would wish them shewn to Mr. Jefferson, from whose Administration the people of this state have very high expectations.

***

ALS, Madison Papers, DLC. Written from Philadelphia. For the full text, see *PJM* 13:111–15. The omitted text relates to ratification of the Constitution in Rhode Island, and mentions the enclosure of a medal of Washington and a copy of the proposed Pennsylvania state constitution for consulting in the reform of Virginia's own constitution, as "our second Revolution" could not be considered complete until the state governments were reformed.

---

[1] Robert Leslie, a Philadelphia watchmaker who was employed by Coxe in various business ventures. Leslie's suggested substitution of a "uniform cylindrical rod" for an oscillating pendulum was subsequently incorporated—with due credit—in Jefferson's final draft of his seminal Report on Weights and Measures (*Coxe*, p. 218; *DHFFC* 8:485).

[2] The "artist," George Parkinson, received the patent for his water-driven spinning machine on 17 March 1791 (*Coxe*, p. 190).

[3] The Milne family's introduction of Arkwright's machinery into Catalonia spurred that region's successful textile industry in the late eighteenth century (J. K. J. Thompson, "Explaining the 'Take-Off' of the Catalan Cotton Industry," *Economic History Review*, vol. 58, 4[Nov. 2005]:701–35).

[4] The Constitution's provision limiting the promotion of the arts and sciences to patent and copyright protection.

[5] "Spanish Wool" was the third piece that Coxe intended Hamilton to share with Madison; see Coxe to Madison, 6 April, below.

Manasseh Cutler to Oliver Everett

I sincerely thank you for your kind favor of the 6th instant, received by the last mail. I fear that I have been troublesome in requesting the particular information respecting G.'s [*Nathaniel Gorham*] purchase. When I wrote you, our business was in a train that rendered it probable such information might be useful, but it has since taken a different turn. Our object is to obtain a reduction of the price we were to give for the land. We have not yet applied to Congress, but we have reason to believe we shall succeed to our utmost wishes.

Our time has been employed in securing the interest of the members, by stating to them, at their private lodgings, the principles and facts on which we shall found our petition, while we have been waiting for Congress to fix the price for future sales. If we obtain our lands at twenty cents, of which I at present have little doubt, we shall make a saving to the [*Ohio*] Company of more than $500,000, and in the same proportion increase the value of the shares.

Mr. M—n [*Madison*] has disgusted many of his friends by taking a part different from their expectations in almost every question on the Secretary's report. His enemies charge him with duplicity, some with dishonesty. It is said that he at first appeared to be pleased with the system; that he repeatedly intimated to H—l—n [*Hamilton*] his approbation, and suggested that he should support it. However this might be, he has not appeared to me to favor the leading principles of this system in the House, nor has he directly opposed them. But it must be acknowledged that he is possessed of excellent abilities. He distinguishes himself much in his speeches by the accurate arrangement of his ideas, and in the happy choice of words to express them. I must confess there are few in Congress whose air and address is more pleasing to me, tho' he appears less animated than many others. His speeches are sentimental, and when he descends to sophistical reasoning, which he has lately often done, he manages it with great art. To me he appears to be possessed of much art, exceedingly local in his views of national objects, and disposed to sacrifice every thing to what he conceives to be for the interest or would be gratifying to his constituents. His talent at artful management has been amply displayed in the opposition that has been made to the assumption. For it has been made against the clearest and most forcible reasoning, as well as every principle of justice, honor, and sound policy. There has been no occasion that has brought forth the whole ability of Congress so clearly as in discussing this question, and it is so very clear that the fairest reasoners and the best politicians have been on the affirmative side of it. Mr. M—n may plume himself on the numbers that have been with him, but I am sure he can not be pleased with his company.

You have seen by the papers that the Committee of the whole House on the Secretary's report have made their report to the House, but the assumption will undoubtedly meet with another severe combat. It was expected that the report would have been taken up by the House last week, but the *cons* are endeavoring to keep it off until the arrival of the N. Carolina members, who, it is supposed will all be against it; the *pros* have been afraid to bring it forward until the return of several members on their side the question, who are now absent,[1] but are expected in the course of the present week. There is yet some ground to fear whether the assumption passes this session, though most of the friends of this measure are pretty sanguine that it will be adopted. They view it as the Key-Stone to the present Government, and will never give up the object while they are members of the House.

It has not been in contemplation to fix the interest of the national debt lower than four per cent. I believe all who are not for four are for six per cent. It indeed seems to be a prevailing wish of the House to fund the debt in such a mode as will approach as near to six per cent as the present state of the country will admit. But at whatever rate interest is fixed, at least, if it is above three per cent, foreigners will speculate in our funds; and if this is an evil, which I am upon the whole inclined to doubt, the higher the interest, the greater will be the evil. Probability of the transfer of a great part of our domestic debt to foreigners has been much talked of in Congress, but the result seems to have been, by a pretty general agreement, that Congress have it not in their power to guard against foreign speculation, and that they ought to pay no regard to this matter in their establishment of a funding system.

It is mortifying to see so many, as there appears to be, in our national legislature who pay little regard to national honor or credit, but I am persuaded there is a respectable majority who pay a proper attention to these great objects. Some acts may possibly pass derogatory to a national character which ought to be immediately established. Yet I think the honor and credit of this country will be pretty well supported during the existence of the present Congress.

It was my intention to have mentioned several other matters when I sat down to write, but I have been much interrupted by a room full of company, and the hour is now arrived (8 o'clock) at which the mail closes.

Cutler 1:461–63. Place to which addressed not indicated.

[1] Clymer, Fitzsimons, and Wadsworth were three prominent supporters of assumption who were absent from Congress at this time.

Thomas Hartley to Jasper Yeates

The last week has past without a Letter from you—but my Friendship as you say is above Etiquette—and therefore tell you that we have made but little Progress in the Finance Business since my last.

Upon the Slave Trade and Manumission have we been engaged.

The Poor Quakers have been pummeled wonderfully and after one Month I revolted in Favor of the persecuted and was obliged to make use of some warm Expressions or rather sensure upon the Gentlemen of the South. They have not pushed me too hard and it is possible that by to Morrow or next Day we shall get through that Business.

The Secretarys Report will come on on Wednesday or sooner—It is not improbable that the Assumption of the State Debts will be lost in the Discussion of the Report to the House—I should not so much regret the Misfortune—provided the Rejection did not tend to a total Disruption of the Business this Session.

I inclose you a News Paper.

ALS, Emmet Collection, NN. Place to which addressed not indicated.

Samuel Henshaw to Theodore Sedgwick

I rejoice with you on the prospect of an assumption of the State debts, & felicitate my Country thereon—and thank you for the part you have taken to effect it—I have read, & read again, with great pleasure & satisfaction, your observations on the Subject, as printed by [*John*] Fenno—Go on my Freind, & do honor to yourself by rendering Service to your Country—Keep yourself cool & collected, & you will certainly force conviction by eloquence & argument—And while your weather cock politicians are whiffled about by the foul breath of popularity, *my* Freind will have his eye steadily fixed on great national Objects—and *your* Freinds will also, at the same time, have their eyes fixed on *your* Interest, & that of our common Country!

But as I cannot in my retired and humble situation, give you any political information, worthy your attention, you will suffer me to advert a little to my own concerns. I observe, That the Secy., in his Statement of funds to pay the Interest of the State debts, mentions an excise on wine & Spirits *by retail.* Is it in his Idea to have the excise paid by the licenced Retailer? and so to have Collectors of excise in the inland Counties? Should this be the case, and could I obtain an appointment where I am, (that would be worth accepting) I should rather have it here, than to move my family again—Sure I am, that I must get into some other business than farming, or I shall soon be beggared! But as you are in the focus of influence & information, I shall conduct in the affair, agreeably to your directions, and shall ever be ambitious to render myself worthy of your Friendship & Patronage!

Have you heard & do you beleive, that Noah Goodman is appointed Collector of Excise for this County—A poor Devil! too illiterate to write a page, or to state the most simple A/C [*accounts*]. But I suppose S[*amuel*]. Lyman will write to Mr. Ellsworth & some others, in his favour—if a federal Excise should be collected from the Retailers.

I hope your Excise System will be in operation before our General Court [*legislature*] meet in May, that they may repeal our excise act before ~~it has~~ any duties are collected from it.

I cannot help mentioning again, that I could wish most heartily to have an appointment ~~when~~ in this County, even if it should not be so lucrative, rather than to move to Boston. For it is my firm belief that I shall enjoy much better Health in the Country than in the Town—And if "Licenses to Practisers of the Law—law proceedings &c. &c." should obtain, I am apprehensive that the Collectors business in this County will be worth something pretty.

Out of the abundance of the Heart the mouth speaketh,[1] and the pen writeth—but I will not trouble you any more—pardon this—and know that I am your fast, faithful Friend.

ALS, Sedgwick Papers, MHi. Written from Northampton, Massachusetts. A postscript dated 25 March is printed below.

[1] Matthew 12:34.

Samuel Johnston to James Iredell

I had the pleasure of receiving your Letter by Captn. [*Abishai*] Thomas yesterday, I think nothing of your Blunder in writing to the President[1] compared to one of my own when I wrote to you on Thursday evening last. I franked the Letter before I put it under cover with the News papers, and verily believe I omitted to frank the outside cover, the mistake occurred to me after I went to bed but could not recover my letter to correct it. You are entitled to pay from the date of your Commission, your Salary is payable quarterly and I beleive there is no doubt but you may draw with a certainty that your Bill will be paid when due, the Bill making appropriations for the Services of the present year [*Appropriations Act HR-47*] is now before the Senate and will pass in the course of this week, I have understood that ~~you~~ the Southern Circuit is assigned to you & Mr. [*John*] Rutledge. I dont know what kind of Gowns the Judges wear but suppose that your Bar Gown may answer your purpose till you can be better informed which will not probably be till you come to this place, I shall be very happy to take charge of my Sister [*Hannah Johnston Iredell*] and the dear Children and keep them as my own till you were to receive them. I think it may be a prudent as well as Economical plan to settle them somewhere in this Neighbourhood, this matter may be concerted hereafter.

I have heard that Mr. Jefferson is come to Town, but have not yet been to pay my respects to him.

P. S. It is now uncertain whether Jackson's Vessell will Sail to Edenton or not I therefore send this by Post and will watch the first opportunity to send the Sassaparella.

ALS, Charles E. Johnson Collection, Nc-Ar. Addressed to Edenton, North Carolina; franked; postmarked 21 March.

---

[1] Possibly Iredell's letter accepting the appointment as Supreme Court justice, 3 March (*DHSCUS* 1:67).

James Madison to Edmund Randolph

Your favor of the 10th. came to hand yesterday. I feel much anxiety for the situation in which you found Mrs. [*Elizabeth*] Randolph; but it is somewhat alleviated by the hopes which you seem to indulge.

The Language of Richmond on the proposed discrimination does not surprize me. It is the natural language of the towns, and decides nothing. Censure I will know would flow from those sources. Should it also flow from other sources, I shall not be the less convinced of the right of the measure or the less satisfied with myself for having proposed it. ~~making the~~ [*lined out*] The conduct of the gentlemen in Amherst & Culpeper [*William Cabell, Sr. and French Strother*], proves only that their personal animosity is unabated. Here it is a charge agst. me, that I sacrificed the federal to antifederal sentiments. I am at a loss to divine the use that C—b—ll & S—t—r can make of the circumstance.

The debates occasioned by the Quakers have not yet expired. The stile of them has been as shamefully indecent as the matter was evidently misjudged. The true policy of the Southn. members was to have let the affair proceed with as little noise as possible, and to have ~~taken~~ made use of the measure to obtain along with an assertion of the powers of Cong[*res*]s. a recognition of the restraints imposed by the Constitution.

The State debts have been suspended by the preceding business more than a week. They lose ground daily, & the assumption will I think ultimately be defeated. Besides short of objections agst. the propriety of the measure in its present form, its practicability becomes less & less evident. The case of the paper money in Georgia S.C. N.C. &c. to R. Isld. is a most serious difficulty. It is a part of the debts of those States, and comes in part within the principle of the assumption.

A packet arrived a few days ago but throws little light on the affairs of Europe. Those of France do not recede but their advance does not keep pace with the wishes of liberty.

[*P. S.*] Mr. Jefferson is not yet here. the bad roads have retarded him. We expect him to day or tomorrow—I am this instant told he is come.

ALS, Madison Papers, DLC. Place to which addressed not indicated.

Robert Morris to Walter Stone

I have received & read with pleasure your favour of the 25th of Feby., when you intend to embark for London give me timely Notice and I will chearfully furnish you with some introductory letters, our Friend Govr. Morris will still be in Europe I expect when you get there and may possibly be usefull to you—I have insisted on a full investigation of my official Conduct as Superintendant of Finance and have now got appointed a Committee of Five respectable Members of the House of Representatives for the purpose,[1] you & I know that the Result must be favourable to me. My Necessities oblige me to draw upon your House for $600 which is about the Balance due to me exclusive of interest and I depend that you will honor the bill and if you can pay it in Baltimore it will be an additional Accomodation.

ALS, Stone Papers, DLC. Addressed to Port Tobacco, Maryland; franked; postmarked.

[1] For background on the FFC investigation into Morris's accounts, including their referral to a House select committee (Madison, Sherman, Sedgwick, Laurance, and Smith [*S.C.*]) on 19 March, see *DHFFC* 8:663–75.

John Pemberton to James Pemberton

***

I have received a mournful letter from my Dear Hannah [*Zane Pemberton*], she wants my Company & assistance I trust I am yet where I ought to be. & to be at home without this Evidence will be of little Comfort to herself or me. I wish to be at home, if I felt myself set at liberty, if some frds. Arrive I would hope I may feel more so; for to leave the subject [*antislavery petitions*] in its present situation, could cause Opposers to triumph, & say we had droped the matter, it should be attended to while a Bill is under Consideration, if it is so ordered, but I expect after the Comittee of the House make their report (tho' it is the whole house) that it will be again Disputed. Our appearance in the Gallery tho' our numbers are few has an effect & sertify's that we Consider the subject of Importance tho' it does vex some violent men. Our Character as a Religious society has been much vilified. Burke, "he animadverted with great freedom on the past & present Conduct of the Quakers—he denied that they were the friends of freedom—he said that during the late Warr they were for bringing this Country under a foreign Yoke, they Descended to the Character of Spies—they supplied the Enemy with Provisions, they were guides & Conductors to her Armies, & whenever the American Army came into their Neighbourhood they found themselves in an Enemies Country."[1]

***

[*P. S.*] I forwarded some days ago some letters for our dr. Friends—which I hope got to hand. I not observing M. R. & J. W. at Bottom of One of the letters, hastily broke the seal but did not read a single line immediately seeing my Error & so Closed it again.

S[*amuel*]. Emlen well & desires love. My other Comp[*anio*]ns. also well.

P. S. ***

The News Papers Contain mostly but One side of the Debates.

ALS, Pennsylvania Abolition Society Papers, PHi. Addressed to Philadelphia; answer, dated 25 March, mailed the following day. The omitted text relates to family news and to the antislavery petitioners' efforts to publicize the progress of race relations in France. The beginning of this letter was written on 20 March and is excerpted under that date, above.

[1] From the debate of 17 March as reported in *GUS*, 20 March.

William Smith (Md.) to Otho H. Williams

***

We have nothing new here; The whole of last week has been Spent in foolish debates on the Quakers memorials, owing in a great measure to the Jealousy of the Southeren Members, who were apprehensive, that Congress had in contemplation to interfere in the importation & Manumission of Slaves, a Jealousy without the Smallest foundation.

We have not advanced a Single Step in the funding business since I wrote you last If anything, *perhaps we have advanced backwards*, for I apprehend, the warmest friends for assumption of the State debts, begin to be more doubtfull of Success than they were sometime ago, at least I think it is far from being reduced to a certainty, We will have four No. Carolina members in all this week, & if they Vote agst. the Assumption *as is expected*, the house will be nearly devided. I believe a majority in the Senate are in favor of the measure, should the bill pass our house—Finals @ 7/ One reason assignd for this low price is the *Assumption*, because it would Swell the Federal debt so much, as to make it doubtfull their ability to pay the interest. But I believe a better reason, *is* that many Speculators bought @ 10/ & 11/ on a credit of Six, Eight, & Ten Weeks, the time being elapsed, they are obliged to Sell to raise the money to comply with their engagements. in addition to this the great fall in Exchs. prevents, drawing Bills.

Yesterday arrived in this harbour a Ship from Amsterdam, which it is said has brought Specie. in confirmation of that opinion, the *Crew* fifteen or, Seventeen, in Number, the Mate at their head rose on the Capt. fourteen days before their arrival with a design to Murder him, & carry of[*f*] the Ship. he however, fortunately recd. information of the Plott a few minutes before the time fixed for carrying it into execution, & by a firm resolute conduct [*and*] the assistance of four others overpowered the revolters. & they are now Safe lodged in the goal of this City.

Perhaps this circumstance may have given rise to the report of the Ship having Cash on board, for I know nothing but the report of the morning.

ALS, Williams Papers, MdHi. Addressed to Baltimore. The omitted text reports the likelihood of war in Europe, based on enclosed newspapers.

George Thatcher to Hezekiah Rogers

Last evening I was duly favoured with yours of the 18th. inst. together with Docr. [*Jonathan*] Edwards book—I am particularly obliged to you for the attention you have been so kind to pay to my request relative to the forwarding this book.

The first leisure I can get will be dedicated to the perusal of it—If I mistake not you heard me express an opinion of the subject, last fall, before I had seen or read even one word of the performance This I think is some where, in the good book condemned, every book ought to be read, as well as a culprit heard, before an opinion is made up—But you will, at the same time, recollect it was the subject of the dispute between the two learned Doctors,[1] rather than the manner of execution, that I censured.

I must confess, from the view I have taken of the controversy, I cannot see the mighty consequence it is to mankind whether they believe, with Docr. Chauncy, that the punishment of the wicked will be intolerable for ages of ages—or with Docr. Edwards, that it will be strictly and metaphysically eternal—The man who has a realising faith of the doctrine, as taught by the former, will always find himself sufficiently disposed to eschew such actions as lead to the punishment in his sense—and those who believe in the doctrine, as taught by the latter cannot wish for any thing more—It appears to me the consequences of either doctrine, when believed, will be the same—and neither, to an unbeliever, will have any effect—But I will read the book.

I wish I could write you some news, since this would be more agreeable than any speculations on the Systems of the learned Doctors—but really we have nothing here either interesting or amusing—excepting—For ten days past the house of representatives, in Congress, have suspended all business, merely to attend to the Ravings of the South Carolina & Georgia Delegates, in attempting to prove the Lawfullness and good policy of Slavery—From their declamation, to which it is hardly thought worth while to reply, a stranger would be led to imagine, that Slavery is the only sacred thing in the United States—whilst Religion, Law & Liberty are only of consequence as they are made subservient to the establishment of the most odious Slavery & despotism—Their abuse & scurrilous invectives against the Quakers, which you will read in the papers, are universally condemned, tho by themselves deemed *solid arguments.*

But least I should be wearisom, I will close my Letter, which is already too long.

FC, Thatcher Family Papers, MHi. Sent to New Haven, Connecticut.

---

[1] Jonathan Edwards and Charles Chauncey; see Hezekiah Rogers to Thatcher, 18 March, above.

George Thatcher to Sarah Thatcher

The sun is almost down, and till within a few moments I had concluded not to write you by this post—Indeed this morning the weather was so pleasant & inviting I thought to spend the day in rambling, & to omit, for once, writing to any body—accordingly the forepart of the day I spent in reading, & immediately after dinner, I set out &, rambled four or five miles in the Country—The grass is just begining to sprout, & every thing puting on a more agreeable hue than I have seen since I have been here.

As I walked by the ponds & swamps they seem'd alive by the peeping of frogs—I think you will not have this mark of spring, at Biddeford [*Maine*], for some time yet—I suppose it is good sleighing with you—The difference in the coming on of spring between that place & this is as much as three weeks.

Tell our friend [*Jeremiah*] Hill I have several of his Letters by me unanswered—but tis just now a pretty dry time, either for news or business—Congress grow slower & slower.

Yours of the 10th. inst. I recieved last evening inclosed with friend

[*Thomas B.*] Waites—I had begun to fear lest he would not make you a visit before sleighing was gone—and if he had not, I should have been almost affronted.

I was exceeding glad to hear our old friend Miss __ [*Rebecca?*] Childs was also at our house—I have often thought we did not take so much notice of her as we ought to—especially, as we were quite intimate together about ten years ago at Barnstable [*Massachusetts*]—And now I think of it, 'twas ten years, some time last week, since I set out from Barnstable to go into the eastern Country—I very well recollect the evening I spent, before I went on board, at Dr. [*Samuel*] Savages—What changes have taken place in our situation & circumstances since that time! these we could then only guess at—but I am sure my most aspiring wishes never once reached to what has since become substantial realities. What will be our situation ten years hence? Shall we be alive? shall we be still blessed with our dear children? should they be alive, will they be presages of [*lined out*] still greater comforts, or forebodings of sorrow to us & misery to themselves? These are questions happily concealed from our knowledge ~~at present~~—hereafter, somebody or other will be able to read their true answers, by looking back upon the now future ten years, as we do upon the ten past years—It is enough for us as we always know our present duties to endeavour to discharge them with faithfullness; and lay aside all anxiety for what is to come.

A Letter from Mr. [*Silas*] Lee dated the 7th. inst. informs me they were well & happy—Another from Judge [*David*] Sewall tells me he spent an evening at his house—And that every thing was agreeable—He sais he told Mr. Lee "that his amusements and enjoyments should be guided and directed with a degree of *Temperance*."[1]

It is growing dark, the Bells are tooling for evening Lectures, and I am almost melancholly—but must bid you adieu, for this time, after telling you to kiss the children ten thousand times for their papa—and assuring you how anxious I am to see them & their mamma.

ALS, Thatcher Family Papers, MHi. Place to which addressed not indicated.

[1] A pun on Lee's wife's name, Temperance ("Tempe").

Jonathan Trumbull to Jeremiah Wadsworth

I received yours last Evening the whole of the past Week has been wasted with the Quakers & the Negroes—The So. Carolina & Georgia Members have taken up the Matter with as much warmth & zeal as though the very existence of their States depended on the decision on the Comtee. Report—we shall [*n*]ot finish it 'till tuesday next—in the mean time all discussion of the Secty.s Report is at a stand—& will remain so till yours—Clymers & Fitzsimmons return—(expected in all this Week).

A *Dutchman* is just arrived from Amsterdam—he has been with our little Frind—what his Business I dont know—has Letters from all the great Houses on the other Side the Water.[1]

Mrs. [*Elizabeth Schuyler*] *Hamilton* requests you to bring the Keys of the Book Chests at her House.

ALS, Wadsworth Papers, CtHi. Addressed to Hartford, Connecticut; franked; postmarked.

[1] Probably delivered on the ship mentioned in Smith to Williams of this date, above. Their "little Frind" was likely Hamilton, while the "Dutchman"—probably the same "Dutch gentleman" described in Manasseh Cutler's 7 April letter to Daniel Story, below—was Theophile Cazenove (*DGW* 6:49; Craigie to Haskell, 24 May, below).

William Wetmore to Benjamin Goodhue

This is just to acknowledge the rect. of your friendly letter, and to congratulate you on the progress you have made in the adoption of Mr. Fitzsimmons's propositions [*on funding*]; I trust by this time you have waded thro the depth of the water, and when the *bill* shall be introduced, that you will have few obstacles to impede you; I speak now of a bill taking up those propositions, for as to the bill to establish the excise I think you will have strong & strenuous opposers—I put this question the other day to a merchant in this town—Do you think that the Distillers &c. &c., will submit to the Secretary's strict interior scrutiny? No, said he, if any are to escape; but if Govt. determine to execute their laws, and equal measures, however strict, are observed with all, there will be no difficulty—the good sense of this people was never more conspicuous than at present—the count as to the Assumption of the state debts has been precisely as I expected—notwithstanding the attempts of a few among us, to decry the measure, before the Assumption took place, I have not heard a single objection to it since—the people in fact are for it, and those who intended to make a stalking horse of it, must & do give up the idea—And I am more & more convinced that the Members of Congress may, as they ought to, give the tone to the public sentiment & not take it from any class or collection of men whom some might tho others wd. not call the *people*. I am full in your opinion that you have a conspicuous as well as an important charge, and that no unworthy motives can influence you, but perhaps too much is expected from you—more than human force can effect—yet while you have the confidence of the people as you undoubtedly have I do not despair of seeing this country, rising more rapidly to public wealth, greatness and fame, than ever did any nation since the days of Antient Greece or Rome—I wish one high Officer [*John Adams*] had more of the respect of the people this way than I fear he has, but, he excepted, the general Opinion with us is that the Great Officers of Govt. have the fame Of their country, more in view than individual wealth or honor—but enough on this subject—We have voted the [*state*] Excise but the people say without scruple, we will not pay it, because it will operate in such a manner as to burden honest men and be a gain to rogues—let Congress take it for they will reverse the proposition & make it the gain of honest men & a burden to rogues.

I saw your Essex man & made him blush at his hasty & foolish zeal. we have nothing now—no electioneering—no squibs—no crackers—no tedious political harrangues—all is peace & quiet—the *doings* of Congress, are as impatiently waited for ~~every four~~ every post night, as ever news was from the army during the war on the eve of a battle.

ALS, Letters to Goodhue, NNS. Written from Boston.

From New York

The attention of Congress, I mean the House, has for these three days been given to the subject of the Slave Trade—and the report of the select committee thereon has been closely altercated. The subject is important, and on its decision hangs many interesting events. The southern members view their States as ruined and undone, if any interference takes place. The other members view an interference as an act of benevolence, humanity and national policy. How it will be decided I know not. Both sides, I expect, will concede—and something will be done to alleviate the condition of the wretched Africans: But it will be impossible to do any thing essential, and preserve the Union.

[Boston] *Massachusetts Centinel*, 31 March; reprinted at Portland, Maine; and Exeter and Portsmouth, New Hampshire.

Other Documents

Abigail Adams to Mary Cranch. ALS, Abigail Adams Letters, MWA. Addressed to Braintree, Massachusetts. For the full text, see *Abigail Adams*, pp. 42–43.

John Adams has spoken to Knox and received a promise that he will do something for (Joseph) Cranch within two weeks; wages for servants in

New York City are very high, "especially for such misirables as one is obliged to put up with"; has suffered from a "Nervious Headache" for the past week.

Benjamin Goodhue to Stephen Goodhue. ALS, Goodhue Family Papers, MSaE. Addressed to Salem, Massachusetts; franked; postmarked.

Is sending off five thousand bushels of corn to Lisbon; is thinking of purchasing a load of salt as well; "we have not been doing anything of consequence in Congress this week past."

Jeremiah Hill to George Thatcher. ALS, Chamberlain Collection, MB. Place from which written not indicated; postmarked Portsmouth, New Hampshire, 23 March.

Proceedings of state legislature; wants to know "how political Matters go on," as "I have not heard from my Friend Thatcher this three posts"; asks what Congress is doing about the Coasting Act and about altering the revenue system; forbears asking "an hundred more questions," for fear of becoming "wearisome."

Henry Jackson to Henry Knox. ALS, Knox Papers, Gilder Lehrman Collection, NHi. Written from Boston.

Abigail Otis, daughter of Samuel A. Otis, was buried yesterday.

George Joy to Jeremiah Wadsworth. ALS, Wadsworth Papers, CtHi. Addressed to Hartford, Connecticut.

Brother Benjamin requests letters of introduction to Madeira Islands; reports "serious rumours" that the states' war debts will not be assumed: that North Carolina will oppose it and that two Pennsylvania members "have gone over to the opposition"; the last rumor comes second hand (through James Sebor from Huntington); wishes Wadsworth were in New York to give Joy his opinion "on this interesting subject."

Silas Lee to George Thatcher. ALS, Chamberlain Collection, MB. Written from Wiscasset, Maine.

Still thinks that a post road from Wiscasset to Penobscot would not bear the expense of a rider, but has since learned that a number of post offices, especially to the southward, scarcely pay any of the expense either, "yet Congress have thought it necessary to establish those routs"; it must certainly go through Waldoboro, which would have a "happy tendency ~~Scar~~ to Scatter a number of friend Waits papers [*Thomas B. Wait's Cumberland Gazette*] among the people east, who will thereby gain much information, which otherwise they will be deprived of"; asks to forward an enclosed letter, related to Lee's legal practice, and to provide any assistance the matter may require.

George R. Minot to George Thatcher. ALS, Chamberlain Collection, MB. Written from Boston; postmarked.

Encloses gold for purchasing "the Irish Edition" of *New Abridgment of the Laws* by Matthew Bacon (fl. 1730); if shipping exceeds six shillings, asks Thatcher to send them to Boston in his own trunk of books and to reply with "a few lines in answer to this."

Theodore Sedgwick to [*Ephraim*] Williams. ALS, Sedgwick Papers, MHi. Place to which addressed not indicated. The first name of the recipient is based on the fact that Sedgwick corresponded with only one Mr. Williams at this time.

When he last wrote, he thought he would have already returned from Congress by this date; fears he will not return for another two weeks; instructions for "my men" maintaining his property; "pray tell [*Loring*] Andrews I do not receive his papers," (the [Stockbridge, Massachusetts] *Western Star*).

Thomas Welsh to John Adams. No copy known; acknowledged in Adams to Welsh, April 1790 Undated.

William Samuel Johnson, Diary. Johnson Papers, CtHi.

"St. Pauls."

MONDAY, 22 MARCH 1790

Warm (Johnson)

George Beckwith: *Conversation with Alexander Hamilton*

[*Beckwith*] 7. I am directed by Lord Dorchester to thank you for those expressions of civility which you were pleased to use with respect to him, when I had the pleasure of seeing you in Autumn,[1] and for the confidence you reposed in His Lordship, in the communications made by me upon that occasion, they have been transmitted home, and although the delays incident to the Season of the year have not hitherto enabled His Lordship to hear from Great Britain in reply he has judged it necessary to defer no longer expressing his approbation of the principle, you then laid down "*that it is expedient that a solid friendship should be established between the two countries.*"

I am desired to explain this to you, and to remain a short time here, in case any information from home, subsequent to my leaving Quebec, may enable His Lordship to throw further light on this subject.

[*Hamilton*] I am happy to find Lord Dorchester's sentiments are in favor of that general principle, which I hold to be so evidently compatible with the welfare both of Great Britain and of this Country. . . .[2] My communications with you, you will of course always consider to be informal; but on this particular point I think I speak the sentiments of the majority of those, who are to conduct the affairs of this country; as to my own part my ideas naturally extend to objects, which I hold to be favorable for the general interests of the States, in which view I contemplate a connexion with you, and further than they may have that tendency, I certainly should not go, but with us different gentlemen may view this matter in different lights; the President of the United States I am inclined to think considers this subject in a favorable one. Mr. Jefferson, the Secretary of State, who lately returned from Paris on his private affairs, the condition of France not requiring his presence, and who did not know of his appointment until his arrival in America, is of opinion, that the struggle for freedom in that country will be successful, and when completed, that it will be productive of great commercial benefits to the States, from the influence of the Marquis de la Fayette, who is greatly attached to this country, as well as from that general bias, which those, who guide that party, have always shewn towards us.

From these considerations I am the more strongly disposed to view the present time as particularly favorable for the consideration of a commercial Treaty.

As to Spain no doubt the navigation of the Missisippi does attract the attention of discerning men with us, and it is looked forward to as the probable source of coldness, possibly of difference with that court at a future period, but it does not appear to me, that it could come under immediate consideration. With regard to your Court having a Minister here, I am clear that would be a measure, which would give general satisfaction, the particular rank might depend on the pretensions of the gentleman in question for that station; high appointments in our situation would not be thought eligible; I am not versed in diplomatic distinctions, but am led to think that a Minister Plenipotentiary is of a scale adequate for the purposes of both countries, concluding that a parity of rank would be proper for each.

[*Beckwith*] I am authorized further to say, that it is for your consideration whether in the present stage of this business you may judge it expedient to make any further communications to Lord Dorchester.

[*Hamilton*] I cannot at this moment determine, whether it may be proper to communicate further with Lord Dorchester on this subject, or to carry it forward through a regular official channel.

Mr. Jefferson arrived last night, and these matters are in his department. Pray how long do you intend to remain here?

[*Beckwith*] Until about the middle of April.

[*Hamilton*] It is probable that before that time I shall have it in my power to give you some information on this point.

We observed a paragraph from a London paper, that mentions Lord Hawkesbury and Mr. Grenville being engaged in the framing the outline of a commercial Treaty with us,[3] pray in what official station is His Lordship?

[*Beckwith*] His Lordship has presided at a Committee of the Privy Council for commercial affairs.

***

Ms., Colonial Office, 42/67, pp. 237–41, PRO. The ellipses are in the source. The dating of this conversation is based on the reference to Jefferson's arrival at the seat of government the day before. This conversation is part of a compilation of transcribed conversations sent to Lord Dorchester at Quebec, who sent them to Lord Grenville in London on 27 May 1790. Beckwith identified his interviewees by a numbered code, the key to which was provided in a separate document. Hamilton was "No. 7." Other important interviewees late in the FFC included Schuyler, Johnson, Jay, R. H. Lee, Paterson, Ames, Scott, and Sherman. For an exhaustive treatment of Beckwith's role during the FFC, see Julian P. Boyd, *Number 7: Alexander Hamilton's Secret Attempts to Control American Foreign Policy* (Princeton, N.J., 1964).

[1] See *DHFFC* 17:1727–28.
[2] The clerk who copied the document here omitted "expressions of personal civility."
[3] *GUS*, 20 March.

Benjamin Goodhue to Michael Hodge

Your kind favr. of 12th. I have receiv'd. We have been the week past engaged in the subject of the Quaker memorials touching slavery, and have not yet got through the contentious bussines, the Constitution has effectualy restricted Congress from materialy interferring, yet the members from the two Southern States have kindled into a flame upon the bringing forward a few simple propositions, in such a manner as has not been very honorary to the legislature of the Union. its uncertain when we may renew the subject of the Secry.s report [*on public credit*], but probably in the course of the present week.

Several Ships have lately arrived here for Grain for Europe and many more are expected.

Flour 64/ Wheat 10/6 Corn 4/8.

[*P. S.*] Mr. Fitzsimons tells me he has seen Mr. [*Nathaniel*] Tracey and has done the bussines he wish'd you to attend to.

ALS, Ebenezer Stone Papers, MSaE. Place to which addressed not indicated. For background on the Quaker antislavery petitions, see *DHFFC* 8:314–38.

Theodore Sedgwick to Pamela Sedgwick

Since I wrote yesterday, my dear Lo[*ve*] Mr. [*Richard*] Bailey a very eminent surgeon [*ha*]s called on me. He is by no means discouraged by Doctr. [*Oliver*] Partridge's state of sweet little Roberts case. He says it is a very full, ingenious & inteligible representation. He will more deliberately contemplate the subject, but at present he wishes Doctr. Partridge to consider whether it is not of importance to keep the limb altogether at rest. He says that he is induced to believe that this is essential and ind[*isp*]ensible, and that it may be done by being constantly kept in a sling. and to provide him with a pretty & convenient cruch. but at all events he thinks there should be an imediate attention to keeping his leg perfectly quiet. Mr. Bailey says as soon as his mind is determined he will suggest to Doctr. Partridge his opinion of the p[*rop*]er course to be persued.

ALS, Sedgwick Papers, MHi. Place to which addressed not indicated. The conclusion of this letter was written on 23 March and is printed under that date, below.

Hugh Williamson to George Washington

Mr. John Skinner of North Carolina who is at present in New York has been mentioned by severals of his fellow Citizens as a Gentleman who would discharge the Duties of Marshal with great Reputation.

Mr. Skinner having had the Misfortune to lose his Wife a short Time before the Sitting of our Convention had resolved to attempt the Relief of his Mind by Traveling; for this Reason Governor [*Samuel*] Johnston gave him a Certificate that is inclosed.[1]

The Family and Connections of Mr. Skinner have long been influential and much respected in the State. One of his Unkles Genl. Skinner[2] was Treasurer for many Years and has lately been Officer of Loans. Mr. John Skinner has been a Member of our Legislature, ever since he was eligible, either in the Commons or Senate, except when he has been of the Governors Council. He has ever been distinguished in political Life by a manly firmness as well as by a sound Understanding whence he is generally respected in the State.

The Office of Marshal would probably be the more acceptable to Mr. Skinner from the Idea that it is considered as being honourable rather than profitable. He is very independent in his Circumstances.

Ms., hand of Williamson, Washington Papers, DLC.

[1] Governor Samuel Johnston's certificate, dated 4 December 1789, stated that Skinner "is a Gentleman of respectable Connections & Property within the said State, and hath acquitted himself honorably in the discharge of the Publick Service, as an honest Man, in his private concerns" (Washington Papers, DLC).

[2] William Skinner was, like his nephew, a wealthy planter and a prominent Federalist of Edenton, North Carolina. A brigadier general in the state militia and a state legislator, he voted for the Constitution at the state's first ratifying convention in 1788 and held the office of federal commissioner of loans for North Carolina from 1790 until his death in 1798 (*PGW* 5:269).

Hugh Williamson, Timothy Bloodworth, John Baptista Ashe, and John Steele to George Washington

Being informed that John Skinner Esqr. of North Carolina has expressed a Wish that he may be favoured with the Appointment of Marshal for that District, We beg Leave to represent that Mr. Skinner not only sustains a fair Character but holds a very respectable Rank in the State; From his Integrity, Firmness and good Understanding we believe that he is well qualifyed for an honourable Discharge of the Office and that his appointment would give general Satisfaction to his fellow Citizens.

ALS, hand of Williamson, Washington Papers, DLC. The dating of this recommendation is based on the timing of Williamson's individual recommendation of this date for Skinner, above.

Letter from Philadelphia

A celebrated reformation-monger (I am told) is again coming forward in a few weeks with a new set of arguments, tending to prevent the Greek and Latin languages being taught in future, as parts of a liberal education—This, and negro emancipation seem to be the *mania* of the present hour. But only attend to the consequences resulting from such reformations: If the negroes are liberated, many families that now live in respectable affluence must be reduced to the most abject poverty—and no less certainly if the Greek and Latin languages are banished from our schools, many worthy professors must starve—As to myself, in particular, I candidly confess Latin is my whole dependence, I teach it for a living, understand little or nothing beside, and the instant *that* is out of fashion, I shall be like a man without nerves, a mere perambulating automaton, a useless member of the United States, or lastly, as the vulgar say, the same as a cat in a strange garret.[1] I am told the Quakers are at the bottom of this matter, and it is possible will in time bring it before Congress—may confusion be their lot, is the earnest prayer of him who sendeth you this short epistle.

NYDA, 25 March.

[1] A metaphor describing confusion or unease from being in unfamiliar surroundings.

OTHER DOCUMENTS

Tench Coxe to Thomas Hartley. FC:lbk, Coxe Papers, PHi. Written at 11 P.M.

Private financial transaction; recent news from France and from conversations with Pierre François Barbé-Marbois.

John Hazelwood to George Washington. ALS, Washington Papers, DLC. Written from Philadelphia; franked; postmarked. For the full text, see *PGW* 5:267–68.

Office seeking: superintendent of buoys, beacons, and piers in the Delaware River and Bay, or some other office; lists Morris and Fitzsimons as references.

William Samuel Johnson to Timothy Pickering. ALS, Pickering Papers, MHi. Addressed to Philadelphia; postmarked 23 March; received 25 March.

Is surprised and concerned that the Pennsylvania legislature is about to repeal the 1782 act confirming land titles granted by Connecticut in the Wyoming Valley; has consulted with "Several Gentn. of eminence, who all agree that it is both unjust & impolitik"; returns, as enclosure, Pickering's letter of 3 March.

Samuel Meredith to Margaret Meredith. ALS, Read Papers, PPL at PHi. Addressed to "Green Hill," Philadelphia; envelope endorsed, "Wednesday Evening Recd. and forwarded by Madam . . . T. F."

Arrived at New York the day before and dined with Cadwalader, who is well.

John H. Mitchell to Thomas Tudor Tucker. Copy, Record of the Reports of the Secretary of State, State Department Records, Record Group 59, DNA. Written from Charleston, South Carolina. For the full text, see *DHFFC* 8:504–7.

Transmits specimens of copper coins and Matthew Boulton's proposal to Congress to furnish the United States with a copper coinage.

James Sullivan to Elbridge Gerry. No copy known; mentioned in docket of Sullivan to gerry, 7 March.

A Freeman. [Hartford] *Connecticut Courant*, 22 April.

In a long piece on funding the public debt, regulating the militia, and compensating federal officials, the author mentioned in passing that, "I judge our representatives did not meet with such a cordial reception from their constituents, when they were last at home, as they should have wished."

NYDA, 6 April.

New York Senate concurs in resolution of state Assembly that under the state and federal constitutions it is "incompatible" for a member of Congress or any other federal office holder to serve as a state legislator during his term in office and that his seat ought to be vacated upon accepting a federal office or appointment; concurrence on resolution vacating Schuyler, Hathorn, and Laurance's seats in the state Senate.

Tuesday, 23 March 1790

Rain (Johnson)

Fisher Ames to George R. Minot

You will wonder at the slumber which the report of the Secretary [*of the treasury*] has enjoyed for more than a week; and still more at the business which has waked in its stead, the Quaker memorial. The absence of Messrs. Fitzsimmons, Clymer, and Wadsworth, who vote with us for the assumption of the State debts, has produced a wish to have the report postponed till their return. Clymer is expected today, and Wadsworth at the end of the week. This is some excuse for the delay—but it is not for the violence, personality, low wit, violation of order, and rambling from the point, which have lowered the House extremely in the debate on the Quaker memorial. You will read in the papers sufficient to confirm this representation; but it is scarcely possible to secure, by any description, the full measure of contempt that we have deserved. The Quakers have been abused, the eastern States inveighed against, the chairman [*Benson*] rudely charged with partiality. Language low, indecent, and profane has been used; wit equally stale and wretched has been attempted; in short, we have sunk below the General Court in the disorderly moment of a bawling nomination of a committee, or even of country (rather Boston) town-meeting. The southern gentry have been guided by their hot tempers, and stubborn prejudices and pride in regard to southern importance and negro slavery; but I suspect the wish to appear in the eyes of their own people, champions for their black property, is influential—an election this year makes it the more probable; and they have shown an uncommon want of prudence as well as moderation; they have teased and bullied the House out of their good temper, and driven them to vote in earnest on a subject which at first they did not care much about.

It remains to say something about the resolutions,[1] which have been so many days in debate. They declare the Constitution in regard to the slave-trade, &c. I disapprove the declaring Constitution. It is risky; it is liable to error, by false reasoning, and to carelessness which will not reason at all. It is pledging Congress to dogmas which may be hereafter denied—it is useless, because it leads to no art. Upon the whole, I am ashamed that we have spent so many days in a kind of forensic dispute—a matter of moonshine. It is a question that makes the two southern States mad and furious.

You will judge, my dear friend, how much of this is fit to be read to the club.[2]

A motion was made just now by Mr. Madison, and decided by the yeas and nays, to enter the report of the committee of the whole House on the journals, because it was understood that the subject would not be pressed further. But there did not seem to be much reason for it; for the whole discussion has been justified on two grounds; it was intended to form a result of the opinions on the points which were entertained, and to quiet the alarms, which have agitated the southern States, on account of the emancipation of the slaves. The opinion of the committee of the whole is sufficient for the first point, and public enough for the second purpose; and the insertion of dogmas relating to the constitution on the journals is in my opinion highly exceptionable and imprudent.

Ames 1:75–76. Place to which addressed not indicated. The conclusion of this letter was written on 24 March and is printed under that date, below.

---

[1] On the slave trade, see *DHFFC* 8:335–36.

[2] Boston's Wednesday Evening Club, of which both Minot and Ames were members. Other members included Thomas Dawes, Jr., Samuel Dexter, John Eliot, and Samuel Emery; see *DHFFC* 17:1788, 1792, 1793.

Benjamin Huntington to George Washington

I hope it will not be troublesome or too Officious in me that I mention Dudley Woodbridge Esqr.[1] who is and for about six Months passd. has been a Resident with his Family at Marietta in the Western Territory, as a proper Person to supply the the Vacancy of a Judge in that Department Occasioned by the Death of the late Judge [*Samuel H.*] Parsons—I have been personally acquainted with Mr. Woodbridge for more than twenty Years and know his Character is good—He is the Son of Dr. Dudley Woodbridge[2] a Reputable and wealthy Gentleman in Connecticut his Wife is of one of the best Families in the State & a Niece of Governor [*Matthew*] Griswold.

Honorable Connections are indeed no Qualifications for an Office when not Accompanied with Personal or Professional Accomplishments—Mr. Woodbridge had a liberal Education, After which he Studied Law under the Tuition of Governor [*Samuel*] Huntington he was admitted and Practised as a Lawyer in the highest Courts in the State about five or six Years with Honor and Reputation untill the War at which Time he went into Trade—He took a Decided part with his Country in the Dispute with Great Britain and was a very Useful Man in the Politics and Provisions of his Country—He is about forty Years of age and I make no doubt of his being an Important man in the Western Territory.

This Application is of my own Motion without Solicitation from him or his Connections and hope he will stand first in the List of Candidates for that office and be thought worthy of an appointment.

ALS, Washington Papers, DLC.

---

[1] Woodbridge (1747–1823), a Norwich lawyer, married Lucy Backus Woodbridge in 1774 and soon thereafter became a dry goods merchant. In the fall of 1789, he moved both his family and the business to Marietta, Ohio (Kim M. Gruenwald, *River of Enterprise* [Bloomington, Ind., 2002]).

[2] Woodbridge (1705–90) was a physician at Stonington, Connecticut.

John Pemberton to James Pemberton

I wrote my beloved wife [*Hannah Zane Pemberton*] yesterday & expect she will Communicate the Contents of at least part of it to thee. Thomas Ross proposing to set off for Philadelphia this afternoon embrace the oppertunity to Inclose thee the Papers of Yesterday & this morning. from the latter thou will find advocates arise for us & our Conduct which the vile Aspersions against us produced. It is indeed Astonishing that men endowed with natural Gifts should so pervert them. to justify Slavery among much other Stuff. Jackson said that the poor Irish were fed worse than their slaves, that they did not feed them Potts. [*potatoes*] & sour milk. As the Report of the Comittee [*on antislavery petitions*] was ordered to be laid on the Table, we cannot determine whether it will be taken up or not. If it is, & a Comittee is appointed to prepare a Bill, we probably shall be detained, if some frds. do not come to our Assistance or relief it will not do after so much toil &

patience to let the matter drop. Many of the members are much displeased at the Conduct of the southern members—yet it is very evident that the slave holders in this place join in spirits with these violent men. & I expect for fear of Offending so few friends of this place Unite with us—& give their attendance. Warner [*Mifflin*] is out to Invite some members to dine with us at L[*aurence*]. Embrees this day. he wants to Catch the men from the southward. I expect there may be some warm debates this day. We have been applied to for names of some disowned for Joining the British.[1] I may possibly write this evening & therefore propose to close this.

ALS, Pennsylvania Abolition Society Papers, PHi. Place to which addressed not indicated; received 25 March; answered by post 26 March.

[1] It is not clear whether "joining the British" referred to sympathizing with the British (perhaps by taking an oath of allegiance) or to bearing arms with the British forces, for which Quaker Meetings could "disown" or revoke the membership of Friends as contrary to their longstanding peace testimony. The petitioners' defenders could have been requesting the information as proof of Quaker patriotism during the war, or detractors could have been requesting the information disingenuously, aware that no Quakers are known to have been disowned merely for sympathizing with the British. From the immediate context of the letter, it seems that Pemberton was referring to the latter.

Theodore Sedgwick to Pamela Sedgwick

After writing the above I rode out of town, which I have done for two or three days and called on Mrs. [*Theodosia*] Burr. she is much more composed than when I first saw her and indeed yesterday she appeared quite chearful: Last evening for the first time since I came into town I spent convivially at a gentleman's house, and talked and laughed much, today I feel better for it. I have as its constantly the case in the spring felt for some days a little of those vertiginous sensations, but I think not in so great a degree as the last year—I have indeed been more attentive to my health, than I ever was in my life. Will my dearest life, permit me to ask her to consider this as an example. Knowing how [*blotted out*] little you, my love, can be induced to attend to yourself you will permit me to repeat my solicitude to you on this subject.

It is possible that I shall be at home [*by*] the time this arrives, it is also poss[*ible*] I may be delayed for a fortnight. The truth is we have not only to support our measures, but we have also our party to keep in order. Without the delegation of Pensylvania it is impossible to succeed. Mr. Fitzsimons and Mr. Clymer the only Men in it are but unexpectedly called home, and how soon they will return is uncertain. Wadsworth too has thought it more for his interests to speculate then to attend his duty in congress, and is gone home. These things my dear, are secrets, but they afford another proff of the R__y [*rascallity?*] of man.

Doctr. [*Richard*] Bailey is from home you must wait therefore till the next post or untill my arrival for his further determination.

I have waited till 9 oClock hoping that the northern post would arrive, but this not being the case, I fear I must wait till morning before I enjoy the pleasure of hearing from home—farewell may the almighty bless the dearest object of the tenderest affec[*tions*].

ALS, Sedgwick Papers, MHi. Place to which addressed not indicated. The beginning of this letter was written on 22 March and is printed under that date, above.

Caleb Strong and Tristram Dalton to Governor John Hancock

We have received your Excellencys Letter of the 13th. of March with the Papers accompanying it and shall be happy to promote the Object of the Representation from the Legislature of Massachusetts to Congress.

One Paragraph in the Memorial represents that before the late War about seven thousand Seamen and two thousand four hundred Tons of Shipping were annually employed in the Whale Fishery—We think there must have been a Mistake in the Calculation of the Number of Tons of Shipping or in copying the Memorial, and as the Business now before Congress would in our Opinion prevent an immediate Attention to this Subject, we have inclosed the Memorial and pray your Excellency to direct the Secretary [*John Avery, Jr.*], if a Mistake in copying has been made, to correct ~~and return~~ it and return the Memorial.

ALS, hand of Strong, Smith Collection, NjMoHP. Place to which addressed not indicated. For background on the fisheries petition forwarded by the Massachusetts legislature, see *DHFFC* 8:141–52.

E— to the Daily Advertiser

I have been much puzzled to account for the invectives and abuse thrown out against the Quakers, and the Pennsylvania society for the abolition of slavery, by some members of Congress during the late debate, on the subject of humanity. If this abuse was the reward due to pleading the cause of human nature, the blood spilt, and treasure expended in bringing about the late revolution, has been to little purpose.

When the subject of domestic slavery was first agitated in Congress, I expected that the representatives of the freest people in the universe, would treat it with that dignity which it certainly merits: but the contrary has been the case, invective has supplied the place of argument, and bare assertion that of evidence. In the course of stentorian rhapsody, and quibbling arguments, drawn from the practices of barbarous nations, in the early ages of the world, to prove the original right to hold the human species in slavery, that venerable American patriot, and philosopher, FRANKLIN, with the whole body of Quakers, have received such abuse, as would make even a Wederbourn[1] blush! But as content, is the reward of conscious *virtue*, the shafts of envy, and malevolence, though directed personally to a [*Warner*] *Mifflin*, will have no other effect, but to produce a sigh of pity, for misapplied abilities, or a sound judgment vitiated by interest.

Gentlemen may argue that they cannot commit themselves, that the opinions they give to day, shall not bind them to-morrow: this may be both true and justifiable; but it certainly leads us to conclude, that they either act without information, or want decision: but a laboured oration, adorned with quotations from Scripture, delivered in our national assembly, will not only stamp the political character of the orator on the public mind, in characters too plain ever to be effaced; but serve to convey to posterity, some of the American ideas of liberty. An oration, delivered at this enlightened period, in favour of domestic slavery, must be sufficient to crimson the face of a Botany-Bay[2] politician!

Some gentlemen, in the course of the debates on the negro business, have affected much ignorance of the Quakers; to suppose that this ignorance was not affected would be supposing that they had never read Montesquieu, who has ranked Sir William Penn, (one of the founders of that sect,) with the most illustrious Philosophers, and law-givers of antiquity.[3] Pennsylvania was first planted by that sage—that code of laws, and government, which for sound judgment, and liberality, has scarcely ever been equalled, was the work of that man. To that government, (which with a benevolence almost unknown to other societies, equalized all christian denominations,) Pennsylvania owes its present opulence. And it is to the superior industry, and œconomy of the Quakers of that state, that the state of South Carolina, (notwithstanding all her slaves,) must in part, be indebted for the payment of her public debt.

The Quakers have been accused of being friendly to arbitrary power; this charge is without foundation. It is true, many of them were opposed to the late revolution; but it certainly does not follow from thence that they were friendly to *tyranny*. The fact was, they knew that in times of national convulsions, reason frequently gives way to passion, and religious scruples become either sacrificed, or serve as the ground work of a persecution. From the time of George Fox, to the present day, the Quakers have uniformly born testimony against tyranny.[4] No sect of Christians in Great Britain, made more free with Oliver Cromwell than the Quakers, and when other sects of christians, were flattering and deluding Charles the second, Mr. Barclay, the celebrated author of the Apology, came forward, and in an open, and manly manner, told *his King some plain truths.*[5]

I now call upon the accusers of this sect, to point out one single instance, in which the Quakers have shewn the slightest disposition towards religious persecution, or ever flattered a tyrant; which Doctor [*Joseph*] Priestly[6] justly observes, can not be said of any other christian society, equally numerous in the world.

NYDA, 23 March; reprinted at Providence, Rhode Island.

---

[1] Alexander Wedderburn (1733–1805) was serving as Great Britain's solicitor general when his reputation for invective, sarcasm, and treacherous political maneuvering were showcased during his denunciation of Benjamin Franklin before the Privy Council in January 1774.

[2] Botany Bay, the name popularly given to New South Wales, Australia, became synonymous with lawlessness after Great Britain established a penal colony there in 1788.

[3] The Quaker proprietor of Pennsylvania, William Penn (1644–1718), devised that colony's first form of government in 1682, granting widespread suffrage and religious toleration. As lawgivers, "for the prejudices they have vanquished, and the passions they have subdued," Penn is compared to Lycurgus, the traditional founder of ancient Sparta's constitution, in Montesquieu's *Spirit of the Laws*, part I, book 4, chapter 6, "On some Greek institutions."

[4] George Fox (1624–91) founded Quakerism in England around 1650. The rapport he established during a series of frank meetings between 1653 and 1658 with Oliver Cromwell (1599–1658), Lord Protector of Great Britain during the Commonwealth period (1649–60), is credited with alleviating, although not arresting, the persecution of Quakers.

[5] Robert Barclay prefaced his famous *Apology* with a letter to Charles II, whose reign was marked by open sympathy to Catholics and other persecuted sects. The "epistle" warned that Charles was responsible to God for avoiding lust and vanity.

[6] Joseph Priestly (1733–1804), English scientist and reformer, was the author of *History of the Corruptions of Christianity* (Birmingham, 1782).

[*Benjamin Franklin,*] Historicus to the Editor of the Federal Gazette

READING last night in your excellent paper the speech of Mr. Jackson in Congress,[1] against meddling with the affair of slavery, or attempting to mend the condition of slaves, it put me in mind of a similar one made about one hundred years since, by Sidi Mehemet Ibrahim, a member of the Divan of Algiers, which may be seen in *Martin's* account of his consulship, anno 1687. It was against granting the petition of the Sect called *Erika* or Purists, who prayed for the abolition of piracy and slavery, as being unjust. Mr. Jackson does not quote it; perhaps he has not seen it. If therefore some of its reasonings are to be found in his eloquent speech, it may only show that Men's interests and intellects operate and are operated on with surprising similarity in all countries and climates, whenever they are under similar circumstances. The African's speech, as translated, is as follows:

"*Allah Bismillah, &c. God is great, and Mahomet is his Prophet.*

Have these *Erika* considered the consequences of granting their petition? If we cease our cruises against the christians, how shall we be furnished with the commodities their countries produce, and which are so necessary for us? If we forbear to make slaves of their people, who, in this hot climate, are to cultivate our lands? Who are to perform the common labours of our city, and in our families? Must we not then be our own slaves? And is there not more compassion and more favour due to us Mussulmen, than to these christian dogs? We have now above 50,000 slaves in and near Algiers—This number, if not kept up by fresh supplies, will soon diminish, and be gradually annihilated. If then we cease taking and plundering the Infidel ships, and making slaves of the seamen and passengers, our lands will become of no value for want of cultivation; the rents of houses in the city will sink one half? and the revenues of government arising from its share of prizes must be totally destroyed. And for what? to gratify the whim of a whimsical sect! who would have us not only forbear making more slaves, but even to manumit those we have. But who is to indemnify their masters for the loss? Will the state do it? Is our treasury sufficient? Will the *Erika* do it? Can they do it? Or would they, to do what they think justice to the slaves, do a greater injustice to the owners? And if we set our slaves free, what is to be done with them? Few of them will return to their countries, they know too well the greater hardships they must there be subject to: they will not embrace our holy religion: they will not adopt our manners: our people will not pollute themselves by intermarying with them: must we maintain them as beggars in our streets; or suffer our properties to be the prey of their pillage; for men accustomed to slavery, will not work for a livelihood when not compelled. And what is there so pitiable in their present condition? Were they not slaves in their own countries? Are not Spain, Portugal, France and the Italian states, governed by despots, who hold all their subjects in slavery, without exception? Even England treats its sailors as slaves, for they are, whenever the government pleases, seized and confined in ships of war, condemned not only to work but to fight for small wages or a mere subsistance, not better than our slaves are allowed by us. Is their condition then made worse by their falling into our hands? No, they have only exchanged one slavery for another: and I may say a better: for here they are brought into a land where the sun of Islamism gives forth its light, and shines in full splendor, and they have an opportunity of making themselves acquainted with the true doctrine, and thereby saving their immortal souls. Those who remain at home have not that happiness. Sending the slaves home then, would be sending them out of light into darkness. I repeat the question, what is to be done with them? I have heard it suggested, that they may be planted in the wilderness, where there is plenty of land for them to subsist on, and where they may flourish as a free state; but they are, I doubt, too little disposed to labour without compulsion, as well as too ignorant to establish a good government, and the wild Arabs would soon molest and destroy or again enslave them. While serving us, we take care to provide them with every thing; and they are treated with humanity. The labourers in their own countries, are, as I am well informed, worse fed, lodged and cloathed. The condition of most of them is therefore already mended, and requires no farther improvement. Here their lives are in safety. They are not liable to be impressed for soldiers, and forced to cut one another's christian throats, as in the wars of their own countries. If some of the religious mad bigots who now teaze us with their silly petitions, have in a fit of blind zeal freed their slaves, it was not generosity, it was not humanity that moved them to the action; it was from the conscious burthen of a load of sins, and hope from the supposed merits of so good a work to be excused from damnation. How grossly are they mistaken in imagining slavery to be disallowed by the Alcoran! Are not the two precepts, to quote no more, *Masters treat your slaves with kindness: Slaves serve your masters with cheerfulness and fidelity*, clear proofs to the contrary? Nor can the plundering of infidels be in that sacred book forbidden, since it is well known from it, that God has given the world and all that it contains to his faithful Mussulmen, who are to enjoy it of right as fast as they can conquer it. Let us then hear no more of this detestable proposition, the manumission of christian slaves, the adoption of which would, by depreciating our lands and houses, and thereby depriving so many good citizens of their properties, create universal discontent, and provoke insurrections, to the endangering of government, and producing general confusion. I have therefore no doubt, but this wise Council will prefer the comfort and happiness of a whole nation of true believers, to the whim of a few *Erika*, and dismiss their petition."

The result was, as *Martin* tells us, that the Divan came to this resolution, "The doctrine that plundering and enslaving the Christians is unjust, is at best *problematical*; but that it is the interest of this state to continue the practice, is clear; therefore let the petition be rejected."

And it was rejected accordingly.

And since like motives are apt to produce in the minds of men like opinions and resolutions, may we not, Mr. Brown, venture to predict, from this account, that the petitions to the parliament of England for abolishing the slave trade, to say nothing of other legislatures, and the debates upon them, will have a similar conclusion.

FG, 25 March, edited by Andrew Brown; reprinted at Boston; Newport and Providence, Rhode Island; New York City (*NYDA*, 30 March); and Baltimore. A draft in an unknown hand with corrections in Franklin's hand is in the Franklin Papers, DLC. Among his contemporaries Franklin's authorship was acknowledged almost immediately; see, for example, Benjamin Rush's commonplace book entry for the day after Franklin's death, three weeks after Historicus was published (George W. Corner, ed., *The Autobiography of Benjamin Rush* [Princeton, N.J., 1948], p. 183).

[1] *FG*, 22 March, covered the House debates of 16 March, reprinting Jackson's lengthy pro-slavery speech from *NYDA*, 18 March (*DHFFC* 12:725–34).

OTHER DOCUMENTS

Josiah Burr to Jeremiah Wadsworth. ALS, Wadsworth Papers, CtHi. Written from New Haven, Connecticut; addressed to Hartford, Connecticut.

Oliver Phelps wants to meet with Burr and others who have purchased shares in the Genessee Tract "as we have," in order to make a full settlement; Burr wishes to consult with Wadsworth previous to that meeting; asks to be informed when he will be in New Haven next.

Pierce Butler and Ralph Izard to Thomas Jefferson. Ms., hand of Jefferson, signed by Butler and Izard, Jefferson Papers, DLC. The full text of the receipt is quoted in Jefferson to Boonen Graves and William Crafts; see *PTJ* 16:324.

Receipt for one hundred fifty bonds from the Amsterdam bankers, the Van Staphorsts, delivered by Jefferson, for the state of South Carolina on the order of the governor.

Joshua Fisher to Benjamin Goodhue. ALS, Letters to Goodhue, NNS. Written from Beverly, Massachusetts. For the full text, see *DHFFC* 8:368–71.

Provides background of the Beverly Cotton Manufactory, in support of import protection.

Chauncey Goodrich to Oliver Wolcott, Jr. ALS, Wolcott Papers, CtHi. Written from Hartford, Connecticut.

Reports the probable success of a strong effort to elect (Representative?) Trumbull to the state legislature; Wadsworth had provided a very satisfactory account of Hamilton's high esteem for Wolcott.

Benjamin Huntington to William Ellery. FC, summary, Huntington Papers, R-Ar. This is composed on the last sheet of Ellery to Huntington, 8 March, volume 18.

Has applied to Hamilton for the treasury's advance on Ellery's salary (as continental loan officer), but Hamilton proposed only an order on the Bank of Boston for $1,000; Huntington has received $300 in cash, which he sends by Capt. Brown, and requests Ellery's consent to the issuance of a bank order for the remainder.

Philip Mazzei to James Madison. ALS, in Italian, Madison Papers, DLC. Written from Paris. For the full text, see *PJM* 13:115–16. Arnold Henry Dohrman (1749–1813) was a Dutch merchant and banker based in Lisbon who was appointed by Congress in 1780 as its agent there, with primary concern for American prisoners of war kept there. In 1785 Madison tried unsuccessfully to collect money Dohrman owed to Mazzei (*PJM* 2:34n; Margherita Marchione, ed., *Philip Mazzei: My Life and Wanderings* [Morristown, N.J., 1980], pp. 235, 287).

Introduces the bearer, Count Paolo Andreani, a Milanese nobleman, for whom Mazzei intends to write only this one letter of recommendation, as letters to anyone in addition to Madison would be superfluous; asks Madison to renew his efforts to help collect Dohrman's debt.

Edmund Randolph to James Madison. AL, Madison Papers, DLC. Written from Williamsburg, Virginia. The recipient's identity is based on internal evidence. Reference is to Randolph's motion in the Virginia House of Delegates on 8 December 1789, for a revision of the state constitution. For the full text, see *PJM* 13:116.

Encloses printed copy of Randolph's motion, as well as a duplicate to be forwarded to Jefferson, if Madison approves.

William Smith (Md.) to Otho H. Williams. ALS, Williams Papers, MdHi. Addressed to Baltimore.

Has nothing to communicate; encloses morning's papers with European news; "the Quaker business Still occupy the time of the house, to their disgrace, & where it will end, I know not, while I am now writing, that business is debated with much warmth, as if it had not been under consideration before this morning."

George Washington to Friedrich von Poellnitz. FC:lbk, Washington Papers, DLC. For the full text of the FC:dft, see *PGW* 5:273-74. Baron von Poellnitz (1734–1801), a German noble who married into British aristocracy before settling in New York City in 1784, conducted agricultural experiments on his twenty-three acre estate in the vicinity of present-day Greenwich Village, which was a frequent destination for congressmen in their leisure time (*DHFFC* 9:46, 51n).

Acknowledges Poellnitz's letter suggesting a federally supported experimental farm; thinks he can do no more than the recommendation in his last message to Congress (on 8 January); thinks it improbable that Congress will have time to address the issue in the current session, while the residence and funding questions are still unresolved.

WEDNESDAY, 24 MARCH 1790

Fine (Johnson)

Fisher Ames to George R. Minot

Another member from North Carolina is arrived—Mr. Ashe. We suppose that he will be against the assumption—though we are ignorant of his opinion. The majority, till the return of the absent of our side, will be small. All our State, and all New England (except Livermore, who is not violent and perhaps may concur with us) will vote for the assumption. While the States discover more and more jealousy of the national government, it seems to be proper to secure it against the many dangers which threaten it, and the multitude of such as are now unforeseen and will arise when the present state of harmony shall be changed. Neglecting to do good will be doing evil. In any country, a public debt absolutely afloat, will produce agitation. How necessary then for us to act firmly and justly!

Ames 1:77. This concludes a letter begun on 23 March and printed under that date, above.

Stephen Higginson to John Adams

***

It is cheering to me, to find you so well pleased with the disposition & measures of Government. it confirms me in my belief, that the Secretarys Report [*on public credit*] will be adopted in its leading essential principles; & that Our national Affairs will, by it, assume a new, & more promising appearance. you are certainly right in your Idea, that the opposition thereto has not the support of the people. Their Voice, in this State, is very obviously in favour of the proposed System—so much so, that Those who have laboured to create an opposition to it, are led to desist from any farther attempt, lest they should injure their own interest. no great effect has been visible here from the report of Mr. Dane & others, on the Subject of Amendments.[1] it was not taken up in the Senate; but is now at rest in their files, to the no small mortification of the framers. the rate of interest proposed in the report [*on public credit*]—the exploding all intention of discriminating between the different classes of the Creditors—& the assumption of the State Debts, & the adjustment of their Accounts with the Union, do all meet the public approbation. not a man, that I hear of, ventures openly to condemn either of those principles. the public mind seems to be unusually tranquil, & pleased with the appearance, & intentions of the general Government. nothing will turn up, I hope, to disturb this placidity. ***

I am surprised to find so little apprehension, as to the new duties proposed upon Spirits &c. among the Importers. the high rates, with the novelty & the energy of the mode of collection, might naturally have excited a general alarm. But there seems to be a general disposition, to acquiesce in whatever may be necessary to the support of Government; & a belief, that no measures will be taken, bearing hard on the trade, without necessity. This surely is a favorable appearance. there are two points, which may possibly occasion a clamour, if care is not taken. Should the duties be drawn from the Importers, before They shall have received Them from the consumer, or retailer, by the sale of the Goods, uneasiness may arise. the monied capital of Our Traders is so small, that a compulsary advance of the duty to the Government, would embarrass their business, & create a very unfavorable impression. I have suggested to the Secretary [*of the treasury*] this danger. the other is, obstruction to business, for want of a constant attention of the executive Officers. the checks proposed by the Secretary appear to be necessary to a due collection of the duties. they will at times inevitably retard business, in the supply to Country Traders; but detention, which can not be avoided without hazarding the object, must be submitted to. an extension of the delay from the inattention of the Officers, may be very injurious, & will be considered as a hardship; But this will depend very much on the appointments, and a strict requisition that they attend their duty. after some attention to the Subject, I am of opinion that the System proposed may be here executed without any difficulty, every accomodation being given to the trade, which the case will admit of.

***

The Commerce & the fisheries of this State do yet labour, & can not flourish as they ought, till We get entirely rid of the habits of dissipation & expence contracted during the War. their influence upon those two branches are yet severely felt, by those, who are engaged in them; but time & necessity will bring us to use that industry and oeconomy, which is necessary to our thriving in any branch of Business. Those who built Vessels soon after the peace, whether for the fishery, or foreign Trade, have suffered more by the reduction in their value, than their earnings will pay; And in the old Towns, the unusual profits from the fishery, the four first years after the Peace, were consumed in expences, which They were formerly Strangers to. But those, who live upon Cape Cod, and along the south Shore,[2] who retained their old habits of industry & frugality, applied their gains to increase their Business. These have very much extended their fishery, & will continue to thrive, while the others are declining, & will not recover, but by a change of mariners, & a reduction of their expences.

The great increase of the British & french fisheries, has tended much to check the growth of Ours. the aggregate quantity of their fisheries and Ours, the two last years, has been more than a full supply for all the markets; & the prices have naturally been lower, than either They, or We can well afford to sell at. But their loss has been very great compared with Ours. They have sunk a large part of their capital, while We, with proper oeconomy, should have sunk only a part of Our usual profits. even the last year, the cod fishery on the south Shore was a living business; but in the old Towns, They took less fish, expended much more, & had little or nothing left to support their families. There is a strong probability, that this business will, from the causes mentioned, be in a good degree transferred from the north to the south Shore. This may be, in a national View of no great importance; but the Towns of M[*arble*]. Head and Gloucester &c. may be much distressed, before they recover those habits, which alone can make them to be flourishing & happy. We have so many advantages in this business over the Europeans who pursue it, that I have no fears of our eventually losing it. the fisheries of france and britain are so depressed, by their late losses, that They will not this year be pursued to the same extent. This may give new courage, & more profit to us in future; & the sufferings now complained of, may tend in their effects, to give us a more decided advantage in the business, then We before enjoyed.

The complaints, as to the want of encouragement to extend Our navigation, arise principally from the same ill habits. was this business pursued with the same industry & frugality by us, which the Europeans practice, no new advantages need be given, by Government, to enable us to be the Carriers of Our produce to market. the carrying business ought not, upon principles of policy, to be more than equal to a decent support to those, who pursue it. all beyond this, must tend to check cultivation, or to load Our exports too much for the foreign markets. I am very doubtful, whether any new advantages given to those branches, by bounties &c., would tend eventually to increase them; because, till Our expences of living & carrying on business shall be reduced to the lowest practicable point, we can not derive the greatest possible advantage from them; & that reduction will not take place, but from necessity.

These Sentiments are not popular among mercantile men; but they are, in my mind, well founded, & will in the end be promotive of the true interest of the Country.

I have ventured to give you these hasty Ideas, for your consideration, supposing that questions relative to those Subjects may be soon brought before you.

P. S. you will excuse my not copying this letter, for want of time.

ALS, Adams Family Manuscript Trust, MHi. Written from Boston. For the full text, see *AHA*, pp. 776–80. The omitted text thanks Adams for his pledge of support for a revenue appointment and reports on antifederalism in the state and the decline of local commerce, accompanied by corruption in the administration of inspection laws.

[1] The Massachusetts legislature's joint committee report on additional amendments to the Constitution, reported earlier that month by Senator Nathan Dane; see Stephen Higginson to John Adams, n. 1, 1 March, volume 18.

[2] Massachusetts' coastline between Boston and Cape Cod. Its principal port was Plymouth.

Samuel Johnston to James Iredell

I am told that there will certainly sail a Vessell from this for Edenton to morrow if the wind serves, by which I send you a pound of Sassaparilla which has been waiting some time for an Opportunity also a bundle of News papers which you will be pleased to distribute as you think proper after having done with them yourself.

On thursday evening last I had an attack of something like the influenza, as it is called. it came on with a chillness ~~and~~ which was succeeded by pretty severe pains in the head & different parts of the body with a slight fever which continued about twenty four Hours, it went off gradually without any return of the Ague and I am now quite well. I believe it proceeded from some cold I had taken and should not have thought it worth mentioning but for fear my Friends might have heard of it and been alarmed.

Colo. Ashe and his Lady [*Eliza Montfort Ashe*] got here last night, he has taken his Seat, she is indisposed with the Ague & fever.

I refer you to the papers for all the publick News we have. ***

ALS, Charles E. Johnson Collection, Nc-Ar. Addressed to Edenton, North Carolina. The omitted text includes commodity prices in Europe and news of friends.

Andrew Moore to [*James Breckinridge?*]

I receiv'd your Letter of a Previous date to that Forwarded by Mr. Service—In Which You Mention the Museums [*(Philadelphia) American Museum*] I promisst to Send you I would have sent them—But the Conveyance is uncertain—I intended sending some of my Clothes—And some books I have purchasd by Water to Richmond—I will send them by the first opportunity that offers—I will inclose the Museums I promis't—The Business before us Increases—The Session Will be protracted to a length I did not expect. However I hope to be home Some time in May—We have had under Consideration (for near a Fortnight passt.) a Memorial from the Quakers on the Subject of Negroe Slavery We have determind That Congress have no Power to Interfere—But suppose They may lay a Duty of 10 Dollars on

Each Negroe Imported—That They have Power to prevent foreigners from fitting out Vessels in any of the American Ports for the african trade—And to provide for the Humane Treatment of Slaves on their passage from africa The Business has been discusst with a great deal of Warmth—In Which the Quarkers Sufferd every Censure & Opprobrium thrown on them With the utmost Tranquility—Tomorrow We shall take up the report of the Committee of the Whole—In the House—I expect the Assumption of the State debts will undergo a Second discussion And I think Will probably be rejected Two of the Members from N. Carolina Have arrivd and taken their Seats[1] the others are soon expected—They Will be oppos'd to the Assumption—I have in former Letters stated to you fully the progress of this Business I begin to be Very anxious for home and the more so as I have receivd but two packets of Letters since I arrivd here.

ALS, Rockbridge Historical Society Collection, ViLxW. Place to which addressed not indicated. The existence of a letter from Moore to Breckenridge in the same collection implies that Breckinridge probably was the recipient.

[1] Ashe and Williamson.

John Wendell to Elbridge Gerry

Since my last I am not favoured with Yours I presume the Close Attention paid by the Members of Congress to public Affairs engrosses so much of their Time that they obtain little Relaxation—I have carefully attended to the Arguments respecting a Discrimination and though Mr. Maddison argues like a Man of yr. Judgment—yet I think his Amendment must fall—for the Thing is impractable in its Nature Though I think Speculators cannot expect to fare so well as Original Holders, but the Subject has been so ably, learnedly, and fully discussed, that it is exhausted.

You have procured Many Friends from the decided Manner with wh. you have treated the Proposition, And though I am not a Convert myself to the Justice yet I am to the almost Impossibility of knowing where to stop—If the Domestick Debts of all the States are consolidated in the U.S. States The principle will be as it were lost unless we can make them pass into a Currency for a Medium, or that there could be a public Bank of Gold and Silver where the Holders might convert them to Cash—for Suppose the Holders shd. want the Hard Cash, they must sell them for a Discount; if an Interest of 3 ℔ Cent was allowed in punctual Payment, it is more than the Original Holders ever realized, and therefore it is better for them, and the Purchasers will think themselves amply paid for Speculating, however I shall Submit to the Determination of those Gentlemen, whose Study it is and whose Judgments must bind us in the End—Corn is very Scarce & dear here and tho' some Vessells are gone to the Southward, yet we fear it will come so high that the poor will be unable to purchase it, and therefore an Uneasiness may take Place; the foreign Demand should be attended to that should it be supplied—We shall all feel the Heavy Effects; Vessells arrive here frequently from Nova Scotia and bring in Salt, and other Articles wch. they undersell, and then take in Corn Thus they can come here but we are not suffered to go there, which creates great Uneasiness and our People can scarcely refrain from stopping them by force, however if the Continent can sustain the Exportation (and leave sufficient for Consumption) of Grain for Europe, it will encrease the Revenue by the Act of Tonnage, The Secretary's Plans are not in General liked, If a State Lottery wholly to consist of public Securities, and sold for such only, was to be set ~~off~~ up and the deductions to be applied to the Sinking Fund, it would help us along, a large Addition to Bohea Tea if at least 20 Cents ℔ C. wd. be agreable to the People, Salt must not be encreased.

A Prohibition to all Vessells from any of the Brittish Islands or Colonies wd. be but just upon the Principle of Retaliation and therefore I hope to see it put in Execution—I think our Prospect of raising 3,000,000 of Dollars will be certain, but as you very justly observe we are to be less Generous in the public Expenditures, Salaries and Pensions.

My best Regards to yr. Lady [*Ann Thompson Gerry*] & family and praying a Line When Leisure permit.

[*P. S.*] Give me to ask yr. Care of the Enclosed.

ALS, privately owned in 1995. Dating based on postmark from Boston.

For the Pennsylvania Gazette

On the REJECTION *of Mr.* MADISON'S MOTION, *for dividing the Interest of the Certificates between the* Speculators *and the* Soldiers *of the late American Army.*

PAY the poor soldier! He's a sot,
Cries our grave ruler, B—ud—not [*Boudinot*].
No pity, *now*, from us he claims,
In artful accents, echoes Am—s [*Ames*]:
In *war*, to heroes let's be just,
In *peace*, we'll write their toils in dust;
A Soldier's pay are rags and fame,
A wooden leg—a deathless name.
To Specs [*speculators*], both *in* and *out* of Cong,
The four and six per cents belong.

PG, 24 March; reprinted at Concord, Exeter, and Portsmouth, New Hampshire; Windsor, Vermont; Boston; Newport, Rhode Island; Litchfield, Connecticut; New York City (*NYJ*, 1 April), Albany and Poughkeepsie, New York; and Philadelphia and York, Pennsylvania. Benjamin Rush acknowledged his authorship of this piece in a letter written to Adams many years later, on 10 January 1811 (*Rush* 2:1076–77). In the same letter he described a specific episode of speculators' attempted bribery of congressmen, as disclosed to him firsthand while attending Peter Muhlenberg on his deathbed in the fall of 1807: "During my visits to him he told me that while the issue of the funding system was in suspense, a gentleman came to him and offered him two hundred thousand dollars at 10/ in the pound upon a credit of one year without interest for his single note, without an endorser. Mr. M. instantly rejected the offer. The certificates in the course of that year rose to and sold for 25/ in the pound."

Letter from Boston

It is curious enough to attend to the ideas of some people in this place relative to a *certain* mode of government. Ambition is already at work amongst us, and crowns and sceptres have their partizans, even amongst some of the descendents of old king-killing Oliverians.[1] It is said by some, who ought to know better that mankind are too wicked to live peaceably together for any length of time unless kept under a severe restraint by the glare of royalty and the terrors of monarchical majesty. It may be observed, that wherever mankind are kept in the greatest ignorance, there the power of despotism has been most rigidly enforced, toleration prohibited, and the subject taught to look upon himself as born to be a slave; that the first object of his labour is to make others great and that his true glory consists in being able to contribute, even at the price of life itself to support the splendor and gratify the ambition of his prince. To impress these notions more deeply upon the minds of men a *secondary power* has ever been encouraged by despots, whose interest it was to envelop the truth in darkness, and who by inculcating false principles and creeds, have rendered men the dupes of regal policy. Where religion has rationality for its foundation, there will be no superstition, and when superstition lets go its hold of the mind of man, political liberty will of itself ensue. A republican government seems most natural to man; has ever been attended with the greatest share of liberty to the subject, and where it has proved otherwise we may constantly trace its corruption to the schemes and intrusions of surrounding monarchies. We in America find ourselves already as happy as we have any right to expect under the republican mode of domination—Long may we continue so, and as Plato wrote over his academy,[2] "Let no one enter here who has not studied geometry;" so let us write in letters of gold over the doors of our federal halls, our assembly houses, and every place of national or state debate—*Let no one dare to enter here who is not a determined enemy to monarchical governments.*

NYDA, 3 April.

[1] A reference to the handful of regicides who voted with Oliver Cromwell for the execution of Charles I in 1648 and after the Restoration of 1660 found sanctuary in the New England colonies, where support for Cromwell's Commonwealth was enduring and widespread (Mark L. Sargent, "Thomas Hutchinson, Ezra Stiles, and the Legend of the Regicides," *WMQ* 49, no. 3[July 1992]:431–48).

[2] The school established by the philosopher Plato (ca. 427–347 B.C.) on the outskirts of Athens, possibly as early as 385 B.C. It served as a center for learning, particularly in science and philosophy, until its dissolution in 529 A.D

Other Documents

Nathaniel Barrell to George Thatcher. ALS, Chamberlain Collection, MB. Written from York, Maine. Henry St. John, viscount Bolingbroke (1678–1757) was a British Tory statesman, political philosopher, and essayist.

Thinks Thatcher, upon serious consideration, will agree that righteousness is the foundation of nations, "even tho you have read both *Voltaire and Bollingbrook*"; Thatcher will find this lesson verified in the history of ancient Greece and Rome to which he confines himself, passing over the Jews; thinks the Jews were equal in righteousness to England, which "tho' laudable," falls short "in the horrid practices you point at to discharge her promises"; hopes Thatcher agrees that it is wise "to set out right—and now in our Infant State of Politics to discover to the World *we Aim to be Just*" and "*that Honesty is the best policy*"; is happy to see so many honest men in Congress and thinks "we could not have got better on the continent—your last resolve has every appearance that Justice predominates in your councils."

Silvanus Bourn to Thomas Jefferson. ALS, Washington Papers, DLC. Misdated 25 March. For a partial text, see *PTJ* 16:264.

Office seeking: diplomatic or consular appointment; mentions Adams as reference.

James Bowdoin to John Adams. ALS, Adams Family Manuscript Trust, MHi. Written from Boston.

Office seeking: recommends the bearer, Nathaniel Appleton, for whatever federal office may replace the commissioner of loans for Massachusetts; his qualifications will be considered the best recommendation "by those, who now so worthily direct the helm."

Benjamin Goodhue to Stephen Goodhue. ALS, Goodhue Family Papers, MSaE. Addressed to Salem, Massachusetts.

Is preparing to ship 4500 bushels of corn and fifty to sixty hogsheads of molasses abroad; if the day had not been rainy, the brig would have been ready to sail on the following day or two; "it is generally supposed we may have a recess in June some think in May. We have not yet taken up the funding business again."

Jeremiah Hill to George Thatcher. ALS, Chamberlain Collection, MB. Written from Biddeford, Maine; postmarked Portsmouth, New Hampshire, 26 March.

"I have been mustering up Apologies for you for not writing me these four last posts, but my Invention is shipwrecked. You see my condition."

John Langdon to James Hackett. No copy known; acknowledged in Hackett to Langdon, 3 April (Langdon Papers, NhPoA).

James Madison to Robert Morris. AN, Bortman File, Boston University. For the full text, see *DHFFC* 8:672–73; for background on Morris's petition, see *DHFFC* 8:663–75.

Requests Morris's attendance to confer with a House committee on his petition, meeting the next day at 9:30 A.M. in the Register's office.

William Short to Richard O'Bryen. FC, Short Papers, DLC. Written from Paris. The editors believe that the letter referred to may have been the petition, or have enclosed the petition, of the Algerine captives, presented in the House on 14 May; for background, see *DHFFC* 8:1–4.

Will forward to Congress the letter O'Bryen wrote to Short, to call its attention to the Algerine captives' situation.

George Thatcher to Sarah Thatcher. ALS, Thatcher Family Papers, MHi. Place to which addressed not indicated.

Sent her a handkerchief some time earlier and now sends another along with two newspapers containing an "affecting story"; "I never saw an adventure told in so few words that affected me so much in my Life."

William Samuel Johnson, Diary. Johnson Papers, CtHi.

"Visits."

Noah Webster, Diary. Webster Papers, NN.

Wadsworth left Hartford, Connecticut, for New York.

GUS, 24 March.

Election of Ashe, Bloodworth, Steele, and Williamson as four of North Carolina's five Representatives has been announced.

THURSDAY, 25 MARCH 1790

Warm (Johnson)

Elias Boudinot to William Bradford, Jr.

I have been so engaged lately and have written so much, that I have dreaded to see a Pen & Ink before me—However I now catch a Moment to acknowledge the Rect. of your two Favours of the 21st. & 22d Instt. The assumption of the State debts, I find greatly divide our politicians, but really a Man must be in the House in order to judge of the propriety of the Measure, and even then, he must be acquainted with many secret Movements—I favour the Principle from a thorough Conviction that there can be no funding System without it, and that there are Resources (without great difficulty) sufficient to answer the Purpose—If we could obtain the Funding of the general Debt without it, I would willingly wait one or two years to gain some Experience as to the propriety of the Measure—but being of opinion that even funding our Debt alone, would raise a host of Parties in the different States, of Continental & State Creditors, and that Confusion would pervade our whole System, I confess that I wish to see the whole accomplished—This however is not yet certain—the North Carolina Members divide the House nearly in equal proportions, and they are expected every day.

Certificates are certainly falling but not from this Reason, but from the low state of Bills of Exchange here, the low Price of Silver in England, and the Scarcity of Money in these States.

I have got some Jersey paper Money, and when I can obtain Payment of the Note with you, I will endeavour to turn them into Silver & lay it out in Certificates, as the best thing I can do with it. My hard money is gone, and what I get here will not more than pay my Expences.

We have done with the Negroe Business,[1] which has been carried, by the Southern Gentn., to a most unreasonable length, without other reason, than their private, local Views, in which I believe from their not being unanimous, they will at last be disappointed.

The dignity & honor of the House were greatly lessened by the torrent of Abuse most indiscriminately poured out on the Quakers—They bore it all as usual and reflected it all on the Authors.

I am sorry any unnecessary disputes are arising in the last Moments of your present Legislature—it would have been very desirable to have seen them expire in peace in their *old Age*[2]—I pity [*John*] Nicholson, who can gain but little by it, as I allways considered him as a very extraordinary Officer. It is not to be doubted but he will come off with Reputation.[3]

I should be glad to know the present price of bank Stock.

***

We are in great hopes to compleat our resolutions on the Secy.'s report [*on public credit*] the next week, when I hope to give you the Result—If we once get over this, we shall immediately
***

ALS, Wallace Papers, PHi. Half of the last page of the letter has been cut away. Place to which addressed not indicated. The omitted text includes orders for Bradford's management of Boudinot's "Farm," to which he hopes to make improvements while staying with the Bradfords part of the summer, and a postscript to daughter Susan regarding payment of enclosed money to a Mr. Franklin.

[1] A reference to the Quaker antislavery petitions; for background, see *DHFFC* 8:314–38.
[2] The Pennsylvania Assembly was about to be replaced by a two chamber legislature under the new state constitution.
[3] See Fitzsimons to Tench Coxe, 5 March, volume 18.

Samuel Henshaw to Theodore Sedgwick

Should an inland excise take place, I suppose Mr. Strong will try hard to obtain an appointment for Capt. [*Abraham*] Hunt—No body can object to the Man—Unless it should be thought, that a Person between Sixty & Seventy is rather too far advanced for the most active Scenes of life. Besides He has neither child nor chick to provide for, and has an Estate (as He says himself) that is amply sufficient to answer all his wishes. Should you, my Friend, beleive, that there will be a Collector in this County, would it not be advisable, to remind the President that your Friend lives in the center of the County of Hampshire & would prefer an appointment there rather than in any other place?

ALS, Sedgwick Papers, MHi. Written from Northampton, Massachusetts; signed "God bless you and so good Night." This is a postscript to a letter dated 21 March, above.

Walter Jones to James Madison

Your Letter of the 28. feby. gave me the disagreeable Information of your infirm Health; which I can now, rather earnestly wish than very confidently hope is perfectly restored. your Sedentary Duty is not less adverse to Health, than the pressure of your mind from the magnitude of the objects that engage it, to Say nothing of their Complexion. The latter appears not quite satisfactory to the few of us here who think on public affairs; but whether we think justly or not is another Question. I freely confess, for myself, no small abatement of ardour in the expectations I had formed of the New

Government, because I apprehend that a certain description of men in power have vicious views of Government; that they, with strong auxiliary Numbers have views equally vicious in finance; and that both are in Combination with a predominating Interest in a certain quarter of the union, which is in opposition to the great agricultural Interest of the States at large.

If the Equity of a Composition of some Sort is, as it seems to me, past Controversy, I am sure no degree of pains should have been spared to make it practicable—indeed I am of opinion that the Government Should have gone much farther in this matter; and should have taken its measures with the public Creditors, rather according to what *it can*, than what it ought to pay. when an individual risques his Stock in Trade, and by Casualty becomes Bankrupt, if he fairly distributes his remaining Effects among his creditors, his reputation suffers not, tho they receive a Shilling only in the pound—Government, like an individual is limited in its Resources. it cannot take more than a certain proportion of the property of its Citizens, without rendering them miserable, and thereby defeating the End of its Institution, if therefore these States, in So meritorious an adventure, as was the late Revolution, were obliged to incur expences for the Safety of the Community, which cannot be fully discharged, without marring the Benefits of Success, I am unable to See any reason for such romantic punctilio, as to institute a System of ruinous Taxation, and a monied Interest that seems utterly incongruous to the present Condition of Society amongst us. There seems to be [*lined out*] less [*lined out*] colour for this partial Delicacy towards the present holders of public Securities, as our Governments have been so regardless of the sufferings of innumerable good Citizens from the depreciation of the paper money, in which the public faith was so firmly pledged, as in any other species of its paper debt—I am at a loss to find any difference in the two Cases, except, that the paper money evaporated in the hands of the people at large, who do not urge their claims & Losses Specifically and in Concert, whereas the public Securities are condensed in the hands of a comparatively small number of Speculators & Jobbers, whose united clamours are loudly propagated & reverberated around the seat of government and thro the principal Towns on the Continent.

In great Britain the Interest of money is low; the commerce wealth & resources of the country astonishingly great—the infinite Quantity & variety of art & Labour that are hourly & momentarily at market invigorates Circulation, and, probably makes a Guinea perform more uses in a week, than it does here in six months—yet the ruinous tendency of her national Debt & its consequences, has ever been maintained by the most impartial & enlightened writers & Speakers on the Subject. In these states every thing is proportionably unfavourable to the sustaining national Debt—Interest is indeed fettered by Law, but the natural State of it is most exorbitant—the great Bulk of our productions being annual Crops, our markets become So, and Consequently the Circulation of money is languid—and besides the usual circumstances that are held to incapacitate every Community of farmers & Landholders from bearing high Taxes, the emigrating Turn of our Inhabitants seems to be a peculiar & very weighty one, and from the vast tracts that invite this spirit, is likely to be of long continuance. It is constantly diverting from the old states, the sources of populousness and therefore of Arts Commerce & internal Wealth. The Emigrants are necessarly poor, from the Expensiveness of Emigration, and each emigrant commonly leaves a needy man behind him, who has strained every resource to purchase his possessions—So that with the ballance of Trade against us on the east, the Drain of Emigration on the west, the immense Load of private & public Debt due (and as the Secy. of the Ty. will have it) to be due to foreigners, together with the Shock which between 20 & 30,000,000 £ of property has received by premature & impracticable Steps towards the Emancipation of Slaves, I know not how the landed Interest of the States will answer the additional demands of the System-mongers & fund Jobbers who have become such fashionable Subjects of news paper panegyric—Indeed, Sir, unless I am deluded in the extreme, there are men & measures blended in the Composition of the Government of the union, that should put us much on our guard—I earnestly hope that every attempt to undermine the respectability of the State Governments may be defeated; for if experience should evince that the component parts of the union are too heterogeneous to be kept together, but by the artificial force & *Influence* of Government, those of the States would be potent Instruments in effecting such a modification and reunion of parts, as would cure the mischiefs that arise, when—

Corpore in uno
frigida pugnabant calidis, humentia siccis.[1]

I begin to check myself, by reflecting that I am not only sacrificing your Patience, but perhaps about to incur your Suspicion of some disappointment or Acrimony of temper: but I may be safely beleived, in affirming, that however Visionary my Opinions may be, they are the offspring of a mind deeply interested in, and sincerely devoted to the real public Interest. I may add too that I am Selfish enough to be loth to forego the Gratification, of pouring them forth without Reserve, to men, in whose Talents, Integrity & Candor I have a cordial Confidence. I have often considered, as a misfortune to these States, that we assumed the reins of Government, with so small a fund of practical Knowledge in the art. we instinctively felt the force of the first Aphorism of Hippocrates, Vita brevis, Ars longa, Occasio præceps, experientia fallax, Judicium difficile;[2] and naturally enough resorted to Speculative Opinions of our own, to the Doctrines of Books, or to the Institutions of European Nations—all of them abundant Sources of Error, when unsustained and undigested by Practice & Experience—Hence the frequent fluctuation & unfitness of our legislative Acts—hence, I suspect, the astonishing Acquiescence of most men, in the Introduction of national funds, National Bank, Tontines, and, very probably, ere long of *State Lotteries*, which, I doubt not, Some harbinger will introduce and extol in the Hartford Gazette,[3] as teeming with Benefits & Blessings to the Planters & farmers even of Virginia & Georgia.

I have ever considered the condition of Society in these States to be sui generis[4]—As the characteristic feature of the Scythians[5] is termed pastoral, may we not call ours Agricultural? and from the vast extent of Territory, this characteristic promises to be of long Duration—The general uniformity & Simplicity of our Interests, makes Government, Comparatively, an easy art; and the Equality of our Rights and Rank is naturally allied to a republican form; if therefore some maritime parts of the union are calculated for the more complicated Conditions of Society (and to a great degree it is impossible they should be) they merit due attention but should never be held in Competition, with the great republican, agricultural Interest of the Continent at large. I should, therefore, ever oppose the Introduction of those artificial modes of administration & Influence in the executive departments of Government, which are engendered in the inveterate Corruption and Complex Interests & relations, internal & external, of the old European Governments.

Ere this reaches you I suppose our friend, Mr. Page will be married; I shall not interrupt the little Leisure he has with a Letter on politics. I have referred him to this, which, if you think it worth while, shew to Mr. R. B. Lee, to whom I convey in it my friendly respects.

ALS, Madison Papers, DLC. Place from which written not indicated.

---

[1] "Within one body cold things strove with hot, and moist with dry," from the *Metamorphoses* of the Latin poet Ovid (43 B.C.–A.D. 17).

[2] "Life is short, art is long, occasion brief, experience fallacious, judgment difficult," an aphorism of the Greek physician Hippocrates (ca. 400 B.C.).

[3] Undoubtedly a reference to the widely reprinted Observer essays on American commerce, manufacturing, and finance that first appeared in the Hartford, Connecticut *American Mercury*; see the location note to Observer No. I, 12 October 1789, volume 18.

[4] Peculiar to itself.

[5] A broad characterization for the nomadic tribes of central Asian origin, who inhabited various parts of western Asia and eastern Europe from 1000 B.C.–A.D. 200.

George Thatcher to Silas Lee

Since the States have adopted a general Government, & thereby each having surrendered some rights & powers heretofore exercised by them &

hereafter to be exercised by the former, it has become both usefull & curious to know how these powers & Rights have been used by the States—It will be usefull as we may thereby know what was agreeable to the states respectively; it being presumeable that the Laws of the States were formed according to the general sense of the people thereof—And this is what every one ought to know since he may in those instances become a Legislator for every State in the Union—This information will be a matter of pleasing curiosity to every inquisitive mind, as he will thereby see with what diversity the same power has been exercised in different States, with the same general object in view.

The power of establishing an uniform rule of naturalization is one of those powers which heretofore resided in the Legislatures of the States & now, by them, vested in the Congress of the United States—I shall therefore in this & perhaps, some future Letters, inform you how this power was used by some of the States.

And shall begin with South Carolina—In 1704 Their General Assembly passed an act, entitled "An Act to make Aliens free"—The particulars of this act I cannot learn—but am told it was a very confused rule, and rendered it difficult to ascertain who was intitled to the priviledges of Citizens under it. To remedy this uncertainty, when that State formed their Constitution [*1778*], at the Revolution, the subject was taken up; but the alteration, in the standing Laws, made by the Constitution—rather rendered the subject more perplexing than more simple—as is frequently the case when ancient Laws & usages are changed.

The Legislature being sensible of this increasing perplexity found it necessary to interfere—Accordingly on the 26th. of may 1784. passed an Act. intitled "An Act to confer the rights of Citizenship on Aliens"—which enacted that all free white persons, alien enemies, fugitives from justice, & persons banished from either of the U. States excepted, who then were, or should become residents in that State for one year, & take & subscribe an oath or affirmation of allegiance before one of the Judges of the Court of Common pleas, should be deemed Citizens & entitled to all the rights, priviledges & immunities to that character belonging. Provided that no person is allowed to vote at the election of members of the Legislature, or of the City Corporation untill he had been admitted two years—nor be eligible to the offices of Governor, Lieutt. Governor, or intendant of the City, nor to a Seat in the Privy Council, or in either branch of the Legislature, untill he should have been admitted by special act of the Legislature, to that p[*r*]iviledge, & be qualified agreeable to the Constitution.

This Act repealed the Law of 1704—but it was soon thought to give too easy admission of Aliens to some rights & priviledges—therefore on the 22 day of March 1786—This Law was repealed & another enacted—with the same mode of admission to Aliens, with the same exception of persons—and the following provision—that no such person shall be entitled to vote at the election of members of the Legislature, or of the city council, nor qualified to serve on Juries, (except on coroners inquests, Juries de meditate Lingure,[1] or special Juries in the Court of C[*ommon*]. Pleas) nor be eligible to the offices of Governor, Lieut. Governor, Privy Council, Delegates in Congress, Intendant of the City, or a member of the City Council, nor to a Seat in the Legislature, untill he shall have been naturalized, by a special act of the General Assembly—And no person tho a Citizen having or holding any place or pens[*i*]on from a foreign State or potentate is eligible to their Legislature, or capable of holding any executive or Judicial Office in the State.

Thus stands the Laws of that State—I shall make no observations thereon—but conclude this Letter, by observing—that in the State of New-Jersey, there has never been an Law upon this Subject prescribing an uniform Law—but aliens, from time to time, have applied to the Legislature & obtained an act of naturalization in ther particular case—almost the only qualification was that of a good moral character.

FC, Thatcher Family Papers, MHi.

[1] Juries "de medietate linguæ," or half of one tongue and half of another, were juries permitted under common law to hear either civil or criminal cases in which one of the parties was a non-English speaking alien; half the jurors were English speakers and half speakers of the alien party's language.

Gustavus B. Wallace to James Madison

There are a great number of Small ballances due to the Soldiers and officers of this and the North Carolina line which has been drawn by the paymaster Genl. and Still remains in his hands to the amount as I am inform'd of thirty thousand dollars. there is now in this State a man from newyork by the name of [*James*] Renolds purchaseing these ballances at the rate of 3/ in the pound he was in this town, show'd me his list of Names, from the paymaster books, and the ballances due to each man. he has purchase'd a great many: at the request of some gent. in this place I give you this information that if possible this trade may be put a Stop to and the Soldiers get the whole of their money which may be done with ease by publishing the list of names belonging to each State in the State new[*s*] paper's and the Sums due them.

ALS, Madison Papers, DLC. Written from Fredericksburg, Virginia.

Paine Wingate to Timothy Pickering

I received your's by Mr. Clymer late yesterday, and have not had opportunity of seeing Dr. Johnson since or conversing with any gentleman of the law on your case. Unless I should write by the post this day it is not likely you could receive my letter before your return home. We have nothing new here more than you will see in the enclosed papers. Very little business has yet been compleated in Congress. We go on slow and I fear this session will be protracted beyond my expectation when I left home. We have at last passed a naturalization bill and a bill for appropriation of money for support of government for the present year. A long dispute has employed the house of Representatives upon the slave trade; but it is like to produce nothing more than some resolves on their journal. The state of the national debt remains as it has been for ten days past & I can tell no better than you can what will be the issue. Nathl. Tracy Esq. has come on to Congress petitioning for relief either by a general bankrupt law or a particular one in his favour, setting forth his merits;[1] but at present I think there is no prospect of his obtaining either. Two causes have been tryed at Salem for breaches of the impost law & the jury decided in both instances in favour of the defendants which is supposed to indicate a temper not much in favour of the revenue. By the last accounts from Salem our friends were well. I hear Mr. Francis Cabot has proposed courtship to Betsey Clarke & probably it will be with success. I have not heard from my family lately. I feel anxious for them, especially for Polly who I expect will lye in with her second child in April.[2] I hope you will find your family well on your return & shall be glad to hear from you whenever there is opportunity. I wish your health & prosperity, and particularly a fortunate extrication from the perplexing business in which you are now engaged.[3]

ALS, Pickering Papers, MHi. Place to which addressed not indicated.

[1] For the background and text of Nathaniel Tracy's petition, see *DHFFC* 8:86–89.

[2] Wingate's daughter "Polly" (Mary Wingate Wiggins) gave birth to her second child, Caroline, on 20 April.

[3] The Wyoming affair.

Henry Wynkoop to Reading Beatty

Have received Yours [*of*] the 21st. with those acompanying; the Quaker busyness has given me more uneasiness than any thing which has hapened since my Attendance here, in defiance of all Order, Gentlemen digress'd from the points in question & ran in pursuit ~~of Object~~ of Objects utterly foreign to the Propositions before the Committee, the House has however got rid of this disagreable Busyness & are now again proceeding with their usual good humour in the management of our national Concerns.

Have ordered our light Wagon to meet us at Mortons on Saturday the 3d. April, when should the Roads improve we may be at your House to diner.

The Pollitick & News of this place You have in the papers.

Mama joins in Love to You & Your's.

ALS, Wynkoop Papers, PDoBHi. Place to which addressed not indicated.

For the Independent Chronicle

ONE of your country correspondents, a few days since, saw Mr. *Madison*'s motion for discrimination, & Mr. *Sedgwick*'s excellent speech in opposition to it, and this day, has been charmed with Mr. *Ames*'s, against a discrimination, and for keeping the public faith inviolate; which brought to his mind what he lately read in a commentary on Proverbs, chap. 6. 1, 2, printed one hundred and thirty years since, upon these words, "*My son, if thou be surety for thy friend—if thou hast stricken thy hands with a stranger, thou art taken with the words of thy mouth.*" The author says, "For a bargain binds a man by the law of nature, and of nations: The *Romans* had great care always to perform their word; insomuch, that the first Temple built in *Rome*, was dedicated to the Goddess *Fidelity*. The *Athenians* were so careful this way, that *Atticus testis* is used for one that *keeps touch*; and *Attica fides* is *sure hold*, as contrary, *Punica fides*, there is no hold to be taken of *Carthaginian promises*.[1] Of a certain Pope and his nephew, it is said, that the one never spoke as he thought, the other never performed what he spake—this was small to their commendation."

Righteousness, we are sure, exalteth a nation, and as sure, the violation of public faith, will not only sink the nation into contempt, but destruction.

[Boston] *Independent Chronicle*, 25 March.

[1] That is, treachery.

Newspaper Article

Thursday Divine Service was performed in Trinity Church, which was attended by the President of the United States, the Bishops and Clergy of all denominations, several Members of Congress, and other public officers, together with an immence concourse of citizens.

After the ceremony of consecration, a sermon was preached by the Rev.

Mr. Beach,[1] suited to the occasion, from the following verses of the 28th chapter of Genesis:

"And Jacob awaked out of his sleep, and he said, Surely the Lord is in this place, and I knew it not.

And he was afraid, and said, How dreadful is this place! This is none other but the house of God, and this is the gate of Heaven."

NYWM, 27 March.

[1] Abraham Beach (1740–1828), a 1757 graduate of Yale, was ordained in the Anglican Church in 1767 and served as assistant minister of Trinity Church from 1784 to 1813. The rebuilding of Trinity Church had been begun in 1788, twelve years after the original 1696 structure was destroyed by fire (*New York*, pp. 136–37, 139–40).

Other Documents

Sally Barrell to George Thatcher. ALS, Chamberlain Collection, MB. Written from York, Maine. A postscript in husband Nathaniel's hand indicates Sally insisted on his enclosing it in his letter to Thatcher, 24 March (excerpted above), which he complied with, "being under petty coat Government."

Apologizes for her "misanthrope" husband's last letter, especially what may incur the resentment of the powerful class of soldiers, and requests "you will have so much more prudence than your correspondant, as to suppress whatever he may have said on subjects that would give umbrage"; "I promise my-self much pleasure from your late purchase, as I know your taste is delicate, & refined, and that your friends have always access to your liberary"; heard Sarah Thatcher was well and "continued her Charming Vivacity."

Henry Sherburne Langdon to John Langdon. ALS, Langdon Papers, NhPoA. Written from Portsmouth, New Hampshire.

Town politics and state elections; probably no governor elected; party spirit at the local level "is more prevalent than ever," to Portsmouth's injury.

Robert Morris to Tench Coxe. ALS, Coxe Papers, PHi. Addressed to Philadelphia; franked; postmarked.

Acknowledges receipt of letter of 22 March, and has delivered enclosure to Otis; is ignorant of John Nicholson's official conduct, but always believed him "an Indefatigueable Officer" with the public interest at heart; "We have spent much time here and as yet to very little purpose. but as the business of the Slave Trade is done with; I am in hopes that the Secretary's Report [*on public credit*] will occupy the whole ~~the~~ attention of the Federal Legislature untill the objects Contemplated thereby shall be accomplished."

Richard Peters to Thomas Fitzsimons. Listing, *Henkels Catalog* 1083(1913): item 411. This is probably the letter from Peters to Fitzsimons listed in *The Collector*, January 1947, as dated March 1790 and discussing a meeting at Philadelphia's City Tavern.

William Short to Thomas Jefferson. ALS, Jefferson Papers, DLC. Written from Paris. For the full text, see *PTJ* 16:271–74.

If Madison is to be Jefferson's successor as ambassador to France, "it would be vanity in me" to compete with him "otherwise I would observe that Mr. Madison's talents in the place where he is at present are certainly more necessary—& more difficult to be replaced than any where else."

William Samuel Johnson, Diary. Johnson Papers, CtHi.

"Trinity Ch[*urc*]h. Consecratd. Din'd with Bisho]p. Provost &c."

George Washington, Diary. ViHi.

Chief Justice Jay and wife, Justice Wilson, Hamilton and wife, Knox and wife, Jefferson, Senators Carroll, Henry, and Schuyler and his wife, Representatives Page and Madison, and Catharine Greene dined at the President's.

NYDA, 26 March.

New Trinity Church was consecrated with many members of Congress in attendance.

NYDA, 27 March.

The New York House of Assembly declared King's seat in it vacant.

Friday, 26 March 1790

Rain (Johnson)

Joseph Jones to James Madison

I have avoided opening my usual correspondence with you from a conviction in my own mind that any communications I could make would be uninteresting to you and occasion a waste of your time that might be otherwise more usefully employed in prosecuting your labours in the public service, more especially as I take it for granted Mr. [*John*] Fenno gives us a pretty authentic detail of the proceedings in Congress. I was happy to find from his paper [*GUS*] you had again taken your seat in Congress and was able to take part in the business after geting over the severe attack you experienced on the Journey. We have seen the fate of your proposition for a discrimination, and I suppose you have been informed of its general reception abroad, I mean in the States in the union. I have been told that in the Towns pretty generally it was disapproved but not so generally in the Country. *Here* it was not liked. On that, as on most other matters of a public nature, mens opinions if they think & speak at all, are too generally regulated by interest, the justice and national policy of the measure is seldom properly considered. When I read the proposition my heart approved it, as I felt the force of its equitable principles; at the same time I doubted its practicability, and national policy. It is difficult to resist the impulse of equity in favor of the original holder, who has suffered by the assignment through no fault of his, when opposed to the present holder for an inconsiderable value given compared to what he is to receive. The proposition having taken a middle course and disclaiming all gain to the public by Anothers loss, bid fair to gain friends, but it wod. require the powers of a second Paul,[1] aided as he was, to convince men und[*er*] the strong prepossession of self interest, or the interest of their near connections and friends that the proposal was just or equitable or that any propositions that do not come up to the paymt. of the principal with 6 ₽ Ct. interest are just—hence it is that ~~the present~~ many of the present holders by purchase [*lined out*] clamour agt. the Secretarys plan—altho' I insinuate that interest may have had influence in the decision, I doubt not some, as I confess I should have been, were embarrassed how to decide, from an apprehension that the measure, if carryed, might injure the national Character. There can be no doubt I Presume but the debt will be funded, I mean that funds will be provided for the payment of the interest annually. I am not a competent Judge, but perhaps that is as much as should be done for the present, as I am to learn that public faith and national Character can require more—and if more cannot be demanded, the establishmt. of a strong sinking fund will be found to be of great public benefit. Mr. Jefferson I expect is with you before now, pray tender him my respects. Grayson is at length gone—who will supply his place I know not, the appointment was to have been made *on Thursday* yesterday *last.* [*Patrick*] Henry and [*George*] Mason were written to. Har—n [*Benjamin Harrison, Sr.*] and Jno. W—k—r [*John Walker*] had offered I hear. Had I been some years younger I shod. have been happy in once more being your associate in Congress. Has [*John*] Dawson made you a remittance.

ALS, Madison Papers, DLC. Written from Fredericksburg, Virginia. Jones misdated this letter 25 March; the correct date is supplied from the fact that Jones indicated he was writing on a Friday.

[1] The apostle Paul, author of at least eight of the fourteen so called Pauline Epistles in the New Testament.

William Smith (S.C.) to Gabriel Manigault

. . .

I am not surprised at your anxiety on the question respecting the assumption of the State debts; we are no less agitated about it and are apprehensive of the issue, tho we think it must finally take place; the opposition to it is considerable and the arrival of the North Carolina Members an inauspicious event, as they are expected to be against it. Two of them have taken their seats—one [*Williamson*] is very warmly opposed to it and the other [*Ashe*] doubtful—two others are daily expected. The Committee of the whole have agreed to it by a majority of five but should all the North Carolina members vote against us, the result will perhaps be fatal.

Some memorials from the Quakers and the Penylva. Society for the abolition of Slavery[1] which were presented to our House have thrown us into a flame which is now fortunately extinguished after a considerable loss of time—two unmeaning resolutions have been passed to gratify the memorialists, (Who are much displeased with them by the bye) and we obtained an explicit declaration that Congress have no power to interfere with the emancipation of slaves. The Quakers are gone home much discontented and the House has been censured by the public for taking up the business.

AHR 14(1908–9):778. Place to which addressed not indicated. The ellipses are in the source.

[1] For background on the antislavery petitions and the resulting resolutions, see *DHFFC* 3:314–38.

George Thatcher to Silas Lee

In mine of yesterday I begun with South Carolina, & ended with New-Jersey—I will now begin with Maryland, but where I shall end is uncertain; & depends, as to the Length of this Letter, on the length of the arguments upon the present question [*in the House*] which is the acceptance or non acceptance of the Cession of a tract of Land by N. Carolina to the United States.

Maryland in november 1771 passed a Law enacting, that all foreign protestants, who had been naturalized in that Province, pursuant to a Statute made in the 13th. year of George the 2d. "entitled, An Act for naturalizing such foreign protestants, & others therein mentioned & all others that should thereafterward be naturalized in pursuance of said Act, be deemed & adjudged natural born subjects to all intents & purposes."

In August 1779, they enacted that every person from any nation, State or Kingdom, who should, before the Governor & Council, or before the General Court, or any one of the Judges thereof—or before any County Court, repeat & subscribe a Declaration of his belief in the Christian Religion, & take, repeat and subscribe an oath, or affirmation, that he would thereafter become a subject of the State of Maryland—and bare true faith & allegiance thereto, should thereafter be deemed, & adjudged to be a natural born subject of said State, and be intitled to all the rights, priviledges and immunities of a natural born subject—But he shall not be appointed to any civil office; or eligible as Governor, member of Council, or General Assembly, or Delegate in Congress untill he shall have resided seven years in the State, & have acquired the property & estate required by the Constitution thereof— And to encourage foreigners to settle in Maryland, the same Act declares that no tax shall be imposed on such persons as come there & take the oaths before-mentioned, with an intent to become a Citizen thereof, or on his property, for the term of two years after his arrival into the State.

The State of Delaware has never passed any Laws upon this Subject; neither have any persons been naturalized by special acts of their Legislature, tho many have applied for that purpose—I am informed by a Gentleman from that State that, estates have descended to persons who are foreigners, and legal questions thereon now are, & for a considerable time have been, pending before their Judicial Courts.

The Cession of North-Carolina has been agreed to in the Committee of the whole—the Committee has rose, reported to the House, ~~& accepted~~ and their Report accepted in the House—A motion is this instant made to adjourn to monday.

FC, Thatcher Family Papers, MHi.

Letter from Albany, New York

I am happy to observe that the Legislature has granted eight thousand pounds for building a Government-House. I fear the sum will be insufficient to do justice to the situation on which it is to be placed, which, for my own part, I conceive to be equal to any in America.

I trust the Architect [*Peter C. L'Enfant*], who planned the Federal Building, will have an opportunity of displaying his genious on the present occasion; and, from the taste he has displayed in the alterations and additions to the City-Hall, I have no doubt that he will erect an edifice which will do honour to the city of New-York.

NYDG, 2 April. The Government House, intended to serve as a residence for the President, was to be built at the foot of Broadway on the site of the soon-to-be-demolished Fort George.

Other Documents

James Avery to George Thatcher. ALS, Thatcher Papers, MeHi. Written from Machias, Maine; enclosed in a letter to John Avery, Jr., which was addressed to Boston.

Office seeking: collector for proposed excise; cites service as longtime state revenue collector.

Pierce Butler to Comte Antoine René Charles Mathurin de La Forest. ALS, French Consular Correspondence, BI 910, Ministère des Affaires Étrangères, Archives de France, Paris. Addressed to the "Consul General of France." For the full text, see *Butler Letters*, p. 20.

Recommends George Hooper of Wilmington, North Carolina, who proposes to supply naval stores to the French navy.

Daniel George to George Thatcher. ALS, Chamberlain Collection, MB. Written from Portland, Maine; franked; postmarked. Titcomb (1761–1848) established the *Gazette of Maine* at Portland in October 1790.

Office seeking: excise collector; troubles Thatcher with only the reason that "it might *save me from starving to death*"; nothing novel to report "in these hyperborian regions"; people are "in general satisfied with the proceedings of *The seven-times illustrious Congress*"; "our friend" Thomas B. Wait does not enjoy the good wishes of Portland's merchants, many of whom have encouraged Benjamin Titcomb to set up a rival newspaper.

Daniel Hiester, Account Book. PRHi.

Paid eleven pence for a hack ride to Speaker Muhlenberg, who entertained the delegation.

William Samuel Johnson, Diary. Johnson Papers, CtHi.

"Visits."

SATURDAY, 27 MARCH 1790

Warm (Johnson)

Edward Carrington to James Madison

Upon coming to Town last ev'ning I had the pleasure to receive your several favors of the 10th. 14. & 16 Inst. and am made happy by the freindly manner in which you received my remarks upon your proposition [*on discrimination*]—they were dictated indeed by my own sincerity, and a confidence, not only in the purity of the motive which founded the proposition, but also in your wishes on every occasion to obtain the undisguised sentiments of your Freinds upon such subjects as you do them the favor to present to their consideration. You have added very much to the former obligation by the fulness in which you have now written on the subject. however this proposition might have opposed the interests or opinions of others, it certainly can have furnished no possible ground of illiberality as to the author of it, for having never been an original Creditor, he could not have placed himself in any possible situation to be affected by it otherwise than to his injury, nor was it calculated even to lighten his burthens as a citizen in contributing to the redemption of the debt. I honestly believe the sense of the Country is against the measure, and am equally convinced it has not lessened the author in the public estimation. I agree with you that it is a melancholy truth that the public rewards are transferred in most instances with respect to the public debt, from those who earned them, to those who have paid but little for them, and were I to act from my feelings alone, I should most cordially embrace your proposition, for let the original Cr. have parted with his certificate from ignorance, distrust of the public ability or willingness to pay him, necessity, or licentiousness, I lament his misfortune; nor is this commiseration checked in the smallest degree from any respect I bear towards the speculators in their claims. I know that the Transfers proceeded from all the causes I have mentioned, & I know that the purchases have in many instances be[*en*] made under ~~a~~ dishonorable conduct, and have no doubt that when this has been the case and any species of fraud whatever has resulted from ~~that~~ it, the same releif might be obtained between the individuals in a Court of equity as ~~is equ~~ applies in other instances of deception. I cannot however view the transactions as they stand between the public and the original Creditors as fraudulent. in the Course of the War large demands arose upon the public for services & supplies rendered—upon the conclusion of the War the public was confessedly unable to pay those demands—the creditors demanded then a liquidation of their Claims; ~~and~~ that evidences of the Debt bearing an Interest should be issued to them, and that the faith of Government should be pledged for payment, ~~and although the debt~~ [*lined out*] ~~received certain~~ Government complied with this demand. it was all that could, as Matters then stood be done, it was therefore all that ought to have been required. the certificates soon became a property at Market and have there been bought & sold, of course they are now found in other hands than the original crs. now it appears to me, that at all events, the public can alledge no fraud against those purchasers who met with the certificates and openly gave for ~~it~~ them what the possessors demanded; if this is true, how can it pretend upon any ground of Law or equity to pay to another any part of a claim which the present possessor has thus openly & fairly acquired a right to receive totally. viewing the matter in this light, I am necessarily led to this conclusion: that the original creditors who have transfered their certificates can upon no ground of equity be intitled to any part of them as they now stand in the hands of open & fair purchasers—they can therefore seek no resettlement but out of the public purse: & for the reasons I have already given I think they can have no claim upon that. I have generally observed that the acquiescence of sufferrers is no bad criterion by which to judge whether there is serious ground of dissatisfaction; in the present case permit me to refer you to the sentiments of that class of public creditors, whose losses in these transfers, have excited in the breasts of their generous Countrymen the greatest commisseration, I mean the officers & soldiers. You will, I beleive, find them pretty generally opposed to your proposition—so far as I have seen them they consider their case as hard, but are reconciled to it, as resulting from a State of things beyond the controul of Govt.

I must still be of opinion the the repayments would nearly go in the same manner as the original ones did; ignorance, distrust, and necessity would, of the former causes, still exist with most of the creditors, and these would produce the same effects as they did before; nor do I conceive that the case would be mended by rendering the certificates untransferable for a time, indeed to me it appears that such a circumstance would make it much worse. negotiations would take place, and if the certificates could not be actually transfered, they would ~~still~~ be pledged or in some way or other ~~be~~ subjected to the absolute use of the Speculator for a little ready money, & ~~they~~ the consideration will always be lessened according to the difficulties or hazards of the negotiation. the more easily and freely paper can be dealt for, the higher will be the price of it. indeed if I am to judge from experience I am constrained to say the crs. would complain of it as a greivance that the certificates were not transferable; the first Issues of certificates to the Virga. line for depretiation were, for the reasons you give, not transferable; the Officers and Soldiers clamoured until ~~the assembly~~ they were made transferable, whereupon they immediately sold them for 2 or 3/ in the pound.

Since I wrote you last I have with more attention than I had then done, read the Secretary's plan. I like it so far as it proposes Subscriptions to take a part in new funded Certs. & another small part in Western Lands with a reduction of Interest upon the part funded, but it appears to me that there ought to accompany it, a pledge of the public faith, that the full Interest of the unredeemed Debt shall be hereafter provided for, should the present provision prove insufficient after paying the Interest of the subscribed debt. I do not think that the debt as it stands is above the abilities of the Country, but yet it is thought so, and any modification that will give a better assurance of its being ultimately paid, must be for the mutual advantage of the public & the Creditors, hence I reconcile the giving a preference to those who shall unite with Government in such a modification—I am glad to find that the proposed tontine is struck out of the plan. it was exceptionable if it was only for its being unintelligible to 9/10ths. of the community. one more observation upon this plan, I am apprehensive it will fall far short of producing the estimated Sums. I am indeed pretty well satisfied that there will, upon no principle, be an adequate provision for the public Credit during this session.

As to the assumption of the State debts I think that upon common principles it would be a wise measure; but as Matters *actually* stand amongst the States it is truly iniquitous unless each State were considered as a Creditor for so much of its debts as ~~they~~ it has already redeemed; some States have discharged considerable parts of their debts whilst others have paid not a farthing of theirs. an assumption by the Genl. Government of none but the outstanding debts of the States, would in becoming a common burthen, operate greivous oppressions upon those who have already burthened their people with Taxes to reduce the amount of their debts. in this case Virga. would be a great sufferrer, having paid off 8 or 900,000 £ of her debt. I see by the debates that you and most of yr. Colleagues ~~having~~ have not been inattentive to this circumstance, and that you have struggled hard upon the occasion. the condition you annexed to the measure is all you could get, but I fear it will be of no effectual avail, for the provision for the assumption will be going into effect, while it is to be apprehended that the one for the adjustment of accounts will make little or no progress. I know not whether it might not be preferable to let the whole measure of providing for the public credit, fall for another session rather than annex to it this business of assuming the State debts. it is not a little strange to me that there should be such haste to add to the proper debt of the United States, those of the States, when it is pretty evident that provision cannot, or will not, be made for what is already on their shoulders.

The Act for the enumeration is come to hand, the latitude given for an increase of compensation to assistants in certain situations will I hope enable me to have it well executed. I am well apprised of the importance of the business and shall take great pains to have it well done[1]—there appears however to be one material defect in the Law—the people are not required to render their numbers upon oath—was this mearly an omission, or was intended that the truth of the returns should rest alone upon the penalties? it appears to me so material a defect that I submit it to your consideration whether it ought not still to be conceded.

I am much obliged by your goodness in paying Capt. Bunyans Bill and shall take the first opportunity of remitting you the amount.

ALS, Madison Papers, DLC. Written from Richmond, Virginia.

[1] As the U.S. marshal for Virginia, Carrington had the responsibility for the census in that state.

Thomas Dwight to Theodore Sedgwick

We have reason to fear that the want of exertion, in the good people of this Commonwealth, in regard to our State elections will be followed by no very advantageous consequences; for on these appointments will ultimately depend the propriety or impropriety of appointments to the Genl. Govt.—the causes of this inertness are easily discoverable—wearied with the political blunders of our State Legislature, men of property and abilities place too unreserved a confidence in the Legislature of the Union—in addition to this, you need not be informed Sir, that in some parts of the State we have been subjected to very unusual perplexities in our federal elections, so that with all the efforts of art cunning & perseverance, we have been barely able to carry an honest purpose and get into place such men as would do justice to our country—After such exertions inspired by objects so important, it is difficult to rouse the same spirit for purposes which in a comparative appear to be of very trifling moment, but on which however may depend the respectability, if not the existence of our Federal Government. The influence of good men among us is small, I have some feeble hopes that ~~all~~ the motions of the people will not be very long directed by that evil spirit which has triumph'd already too long.

Your friends here in this [*Berkshire*] County would be very happy to see you, but as much as we love you, we hope you will not attend our April Court unless you shall know the business of assumption to be in a state of perfect safety—the same reasons we hope will have weight with Mr. Strong—Within a fortnight from this time I expect the honor of waiting on you at

N. York, where I intend spending at least one week and that principally in attending to the debates of your House.

I ~~have been~~ am informed that you have been lately in a very ill state of health, hope you have recovered—the weather has been intolerable—the air pregnant with distemper—and I believe not quite so pure with you as in the Country. Our farmers begin to acknowledge the increase of money, among us in some small degree, but whether they will be willing to attribute it to right causes, is matter of doubt. the establishment of a Federal Govt. and the progress made towards the support of public credit undoubtedly have their effect.

*** you will easily perceive that *I* write to you not so much for the *matter* I have to communicate as to shew that I have you in respectful remembrance.

ALS, Sedgwick Papers, MHi. Written from Springfield, Massachusetts.

William Maclay to Benjamin Rush

For near a Week has your letter of the 17th lay by me unanswered. under the Expectation that every day would produce something new in the House of Representatives. The Secretary's People have been afraid to risk any Question of importance [*on funding*]. as some People are gone home, upon whose Votes they depend. I therefore will send You a few lines, tho' without News. Two New Members took their Seats lately from North Carolina. who were said to be opposed to the Assumption of the State debts. One of them is Doctor Williamson who is well known to You. and with whom I could wish You to correspond.[1] Yesterday it was whispered that means had been Used to attach them to the Secretary's System. The small news of this day is, That [*William*] Duer is to resign the Office of Assistant to the Secretary of the Treasury, and that his place is to be given to a noted Gladiator.[2] Gladiators and Janissaries you must know, are cant Phrases, to denote those Persons, who devote themselves to support The Secretary's Measures. You see my dear Friend how a Scarcity of Matters of importance, has forced me into the small Talk, the scandal, of Politicks.

The Presses of this place are all Under, influence of some kind or other. It is true, pieces are put into some of them. that bear hard on the Secretary. but they are generally either pointed personally at him, and of course beneath the attention of the political world, or directed to procure 6 ℔ Cent. on the whole amount of the public debt. The first are generally attributed to Governor [*George*] Clinton. the last spring from the Speculators, & are not considered, as disagreeable to him. The daily Advertiser of yesterday and this day contains a Peice,[3] of a different complexion, from any of the foregoing. I have therefore cut it out & inclosed it to You, agreeable to the request contained in Your last.

Genl. [*Peter*] Muhlenberg sends you his compliments, and information, That he waits only untill some Occurrence worthy of being communicated offers itself. The directions to the Painter have been rejected.[4] as he assures me. The Pennsylvania presses are the only free Ones. You will say the sentiment is a selfish one. but there really is, in my Opinion, more genuine Republicanism in That State, than in all the rest of the Union. Much as the Quakers are abused, and badly as many of them behaved, during the Revolution Yet much of it is owing to them. They really are the sincere friends of equal liberty, and he that departs from this Principle, ought not to call himself a Republican.

ALS, Rush Papers, DLC. Addressed to Third Street, Philadelphia; franked; postmarked 28 March.

[1] Ashe was the other.

[2] Tench Coxe replaced Duer early in April. For more on Duer's resignation, see House Investigation of William Duer, March 1790 Undated, below.

[3] Plain Argument, *NYDA*, 26–27 March, parodies the arguments raised in favor of a public debt. It originally appeared in [Richmond] *Virginia Independent Chronicle*, 10 March.

[4] See P. Muhlenberg to Rush, 22 February, volume 18.

William Maclay to Benjamin Rush

Since writing the letter which incloses this, I opened Yours of the 25th. for which You have my thanks. I feel the finger of Friendship in it. Those who blame me for writing to J[*ohn*]. Nicholson, are either ill informed or do not act with candor.[1] This Man furnished Mr. Morris and myself, with information touching the public Accounts, about a Year ago. and if I remember right, we thought it but Gentlemanly to acknowledge the Recept of his letter. as to myself I have made it an invariable rule; to answer every decent letter, I have received, be the writer who he would. Nicholson wrote me Sundry letters recommending Baily Beard &ca.[2] I not only answered these, but called on him repeatedly; for information respecting the finances of the State. the ~~Subject~~ Detail of our State debt, it was of high importance to know he has given me some information, on this Subject. & I expect more from him. To blame me in this point of View. is in fact blaming me for endeavouring to obtain knowledge, absolutely necessary, to my serving the State well. The information which I wanted, could be had no where, but in his office. so much did I feel the want of information, in many points. that nothing, but my precarious State of health, prevented my taking a Journey to Philadelphia on Purpose to obtain it. I considered J. Nicholson, as an Officer of the State, whom I had a right to call on, nay to command, in every thing respecting the Duties of his Office, and when the interests of the State were concerned. Under impressions of this kind, I inclosed him the Secretary's Report [*on public credit*], and demanded his Opinion of it. all this I considered as Officially done. my business lay with the Comptroller General of the State. I have received sundry letters from him, containing remarks on the report, some of them, in my Opinion pertinent. I have discovered nothing Antifederal in them. for to differ from the Secretary, on the Subject of finance, is no feature of that crime, either in Your Opinion or mine. In short my Friend, I cast criminality far from me, in this Matter. I was ignorant of some points. Whatever Ignorance may be in devotion, I am sure, she is but a bad parent, in politicks.

If I knew who the worst Man in Pennsylvania was, and that he could, and would give me, useful information, I would write to him for it. These things being known, will satisfy You and all my friends. if there are those, who wish for hooks to hang faults on. we must pass them by, taking care to give, no just cause of offense.

ALS, Rush Papers, DLC. Enclosed in an earlier letter to Rush, immediately above.

[1] For background suggesting the political liability of associating with Nicholson, who was under investigation by the state at this time, see Fitzsimons to Coxe, 5 March, n. 1, volume 18.

[2] Francis Bailey petitioned the FFC for patent protection in January 1790 (*DHFFC* 8:73–84); "Beard" is probably John Bayard, who received a number of testimonials from prominent Philadelphians in the first session supporting his application for the collectorship of that port.

Jonathan Trumbull to Horatio Gates

***

Your Letter to my Brother was more fortunate than you perhaps expected—being with me in this City. he recieved it immediately—& I have the early pleasure of conveying to you his reply.[1]

Congress is proceeding slowly on with the great Business before them—if we do but verify at last the old Adage of—*slow & sure*—I shall be content. The Report of the Secrety. of the Treasury on Finance receives much opposition—its foundation so laid perhaps in too extended & perfect a plan for some minds—I have a hope however that it will succeed in most of its parts—Opposite sentiments in Goverment seem necessary—& as you observe may be usefull in its establishment.

You doubtless see the news papers, with all the Debates—it will therefore be useless for me to trouble you with particulars.

ALS, Emmet Collection, NN. Place to which addressed not indicated. The omitted text congratulates Gates on his recent marriage to Mary Vallance.

[1] Gates had written to welcome John Trumbull back to the United States. In his reply of this date, Trumbull outlined his plan of historical portraits and his intention to paint one of Gates (Emmet Collection, NN).

St. George Tucker to John Page

I last Evening, my dear Page, recieved your favor of the 16th. announcing to me that this day was fixed for the Consummation of that Happiness, which after a melancholy interruption of three years, is at length I hope restored to you. At this moment my dear friend my sympathizing imagination transports me to the room where you are sitting with your Bride, & perhaps asking yourself if the dazzling Scene of Bliss now presented to you is not all a delusion. If a Delusion it Should indeed be, may it last at least as long you live. After realizing the Sorrows which we have both experienced,[1] to have the cup of bitterness removed from our Lips, must excite emotions of Joy, & Gratitude which none but those who have been unhappy can feel, or even concieve. That you feel them all, my friend, I am fully persuaded. Methinks you must feel like a shipwreck'd Passenger; who having been plunged into the abyss of despair, finds himself at the moment of perishing, thrown upon his native shore, & surrounded by his dearest Connexions.

***

But this is dwelling too long on an unentertaining Subject. [*Bishop James*] Madison, [*Robert*] Andrews, & one or two other friends dined with me to day, & drank to the health & happiness of yourself & my fair friend, for such, I hope she will permit me henceforth to esteem her. They have just left me, & I could not pass the Evening without greeting you with my warmest Congratulations. Fleur was over here to day from Rosewell. the family he tells me were all well. I communicated to him the intelligence of your intended Marriage; & with that cordiality which the poor fellow seems to possess a great share of, he ejaculated, "I hope he will be happy."

***

You will also find some Lines of a different complexion & St[*ile*]—May the good that I anticipated for you while writing them be fully realized to yourself & your Bride.

Adieu, my friend—May all your days—& all your Nights be as happy as this. Maria & my Children offer you their Congratulations on your present Happiness. Present me to the late Miss [*Margaret*] Lowther, & tell her, that I hope to find in Mrs. Page all that I once lov'd & admired under that name.

ALS, Tucker-Coleman Papers, Colonial Williamsburg, Virginia. Written from Williamsburg, Virginia, at 8 P.M. Signed "Farewell! & Be happy!" The omitted text concerns Tucker's psychological state and travel plans, and Page's "Dodsley" (see Page to Tucker, 26 February, volume 18) for which Tucker encloses a few lines "by way of Tail-piece, or conclusion to the Collection," and states that the printer of Dodsley has "murder'd some things most cruelly."

[1] Page's first wife Frances Burwell died in 1787, leaving him with twelve children. Tucker's wife, the widow Frances Bland Randolph, died in 1788, leaving him with five children.

George Washington to Robert Morris

The President and Mrs. W___ Compliments and thanks to Mr. Morris for his politeness. They have nothing to charge Mr. Morris with but their affectionate regards for Mrs. Morris and the family; and to wish him a pleasanter journey than the state of the Roads promise, and a safe return to this City when his business in Philadelphia shall be accomplished.

AN, Sol Feinstone Collection, David Library of the American Revolution (on deposit at PPAmP).

Oliver Wolcott, Jr. to Oliver Wolcott, Sr.

***

Congress are proceeding slowly but I hope surely in their deliberations a memorial from the Quakers respecting the condition of the Africans has unfortunately occasioned some considerable animation of debate.

That business has now subsided without any thing being accomplished.

What system will be adopted with respect to the public debt cannot be calculated at this time. nothing has been done except to pass a few votes recognizing the obligation of the public, the opposition to what has been yet done, proves that great obstacles are yet to be surmounted.

Such have been the ill consequences of depreciation, that all the arguments in favour of every opinion are plausible and equivocal.

I can consider, a funding system as important in no other respect than as an engine of government—the only question is what that engine shall be—the influence of a clergy, nobility, and armies, are and ought to be out of the question, in this country—but unless some active principle of the human mind, can be interested in support of the government no civil establishments can be formed which will not appear like useless and expensive pageants, and by their u[*n*]popularity weaken the government which they are intended to support—perhaps the great desideratum, is to contrive business to be executed, which shall appear to be important, if it be not so in reality, and at the same time have this business of a kind which shall not depress the spirit, or check the industry of the country—Duties on most of the articles imported ought to be imposed from political considerations, even though the money were to be buried—if the money is paid in such a manner as to interest the people in the government, and at the same time not corrupt their integrity, the circulation of a revenue answers a good purpose—All taxes answer some good purposes—the propriety of imposing them can be estimated only by the circumstances which attend them.

For these reasons I think the States debts ought to be assumed, as without the assumption the political purposes which I have enumerated cannot be attained—this will indeed increase the debt of the United States to a degree which ~~is~~ will be very inconvenient—the Taxes necessary to pay the interest will be burdensome, and they will appear to be just only to those who believe that the good attained, is more important than the evil which is suffered.

The rate of interest in my opinion ought to be as low, as will answer the public expectation & content the public Creditors. on this point the ablest men have expressed different sentiments—the Gentleman from the Northern States suppose the rates proposed too high—the Southern Gentlemen think them too low—the opinions of those who are most accustomed to perform their promises, are perhaps of most weight.

One great evil will at events attend a funding system. the debt will be alienated to foreigners as long as the exchange is against this Country.

This will take place in the same degree let the rate of Interest be fixed as it may, provided the funds are considered as sure—foreigners buy for the sake of the annuity and from a confidence in the resources of the Country—the only question which they ask is what is the value of an Annuity for a given sum payable in America? we cannot check their Speculations except by lessening their confidence in our punctuality.

Though I write in this manner, I am here no politician, I feel no Interest and take no part in any debates—the business in which I am engaged, engrosses my attention, and though it is tedious at present, I shall soon reduce it within limits—I have reason to believe that I have hitherto given satisfaction—the expenses of living here will be greater than I had imagined, I mean however to save something and indulge the fond, but perhaps vain hope of living in the Country.

***

ALS, Wolcott Papers, CtHi. Addressed to Litchfield, Connecticut; carried by Mr. Brach. For the full text, see *Wolcott* 1:43–44.

[*William Maclay*] to the Printer

I am a poor distressed woman,[1] who for the thirteen or fourteen years since I kept house, have had as great a variety of fortune as ever beset any female. Glorious gleams of sunshine indeed have I had, and happiness ever seemed in my reach; yet by the mismanagement of servants, in brakeing cups and saucers, spoiling provisions, &c. I think I am likely to be ruined. A few days ago I expected to put an end to all my troubles, by sending for a worthy gentleman,[2] who had often taken me out of the gutter, when I considered myself as irretrievably fallen. Hearing he was at hand, I requested my neighbour[3] (as good a man I thought as could be) to brush the furniture, and sweep the house, where I used to lodge my best friends.[4] Now could you think it, Sir? Off he runs, and buys such an heap of pots and pans, and dishes and ladles as run me to ten or twelve pounds of expense. Good Lord! and all this after my being so much in debt already. I determined not to pay him. But what of that? *Sawny*[5] the servant, who had the keeping of the trifle of cash I was possessed of, the moment my back was turned, gave him the money. Was there ever such a trick? People tell me the Grand Jury[6] should indict him; but la Sir, the Jury know all about it, and I am afraid will take no notice of him, but lye by, till it suits them too, to get a slap at me.

Mr. Printer, I think I am not deficient in the qualities of my head; my heart I know to be possessed of the principles of rectitude. Is it not dreadful that my concerns should be knocked about at this rate, every body doing what they please with me? After describing my situation, you cannot expect me to tell my name, but pray publish my case, which is a plain one. Perhaps some humane person may direct me how to get out of my difficulties.

IG, 27 March; reprinted at Boston. The manuscript is in Miscellaneous Manuscripts, DLC. Maclay enclosed it in a letter to John Nicholson on 14 February.

---

[1] The United States of America.

[2] George Washington.

[3] Samuel Osgood.

[4] Osgood's house at 3 Cherry Street had been the residence of the presidents of the Confederation Congress.

[5] Alexander Hamilton. Sawny is a play on words. While it is a nickname for Alexander, its colloquial meaning is "fool."

[6] Congress.

[*William Maclay,*] A Pennsylvanian to the Printer

As the assumption of the state debts, by the general government, is now a common subject of conversation, permit me, through the channel of your paper, to offer to the public, some observations on the debt of Pennsylvania, which has been incurred in the general defence, and which, as far as I have been able to learn, is comprised under the following heads.

		Dollars.
1st.	Certificates of depreciation granted to the army, hospital, &c. about	1,403,793
2d.	Certificates for supplies for the army, by act of June, 1780, about	34,583
3d.	Certificates for horses for the army, in the year 1780, about	90,336
4th.	Certificates for the residue of the state debt, funded on interest, about	478,351
		2,007,063

One third of the depreciation debt in the hands of original holders, was paid off in the money of 1781. The interest of the other two thirds was funded on the state excise. The depreciation lands, and confiscated estates, were appropriated, as a sinking fund for the whole.

The certificates mentioned under the second and third heads, were receivable in taxes at the time of issuing, and have generally been paid off, or continue to be paid, at the Treasury in bills of 1781.

The interest on those, under the fourth head, is paid at the Treasury, out of the arrears of taxes, imposts, &c.

All the foregoing certificates are receivable in the Land-Office of the state, and it is reasonable to suppose that nearly one half of them are already taken up by the sale of lands, city lots, confiscated estates, payments of arrears of purchase money, &c.

The whole mass of state debts proposed, to be assumed by Congress, is stated by the Secretary at twenty five millions of dollars: but throw off one million, for that part of the state debt of Pennsylvania which is already paid, and suppose the whole to stand at twenty-four millions; one million of which belongs to Pennsylvania. Now by the effect of the federal impost, it appears that the port of Philadelphia, pays one fourth of the present revenue of the union. Six millions then of the newly assumed debt (on the principle of impost) must be provided by that port. Had Pennsylvania been among the debtor states, there would not perhaps be cause of complaint, but she has ever been considered as a creditor to a great amount.

It may be said all this can be adjusted by a final settlement. There is but a distant prospect of such settlement; and many say it never will, nor can take place. But the settlement, can equally take place after each state has paid her own debt; and there is no doubt but the balances of both debt and credit, would be lessened by postponing it to that period, or by, what amounts to the same thing, giving each state credit in the general account for the amount of her own state debt. The effect of the assumption proposed is virtually (so far as respects Pennsylvania) the assuming to pay six millions of dollars, in order to get rid of the payment of one.

The payment of the state debt of Pennsylvania, in its present form, by receiving the certificates in the Land-Office, may be considered as an accommodation to the landed interest, and will not be attended with new taxes. By the proposed assumption, the debt will not only be increased in proportion of six to one; but the payment must be in cash, raised by new federal taxes. The payments also, to the Land-Office of the state, must in future be in money, instead of certificates.

IG, 27 March. Maclay enclosed this piece for publication in his letter to John Nicholson of 8 February, volume 18.

A Citizen of Pennsylvania to Messrs. Dunlap & Claypoole

In your daily publications of the 23d and 25th current I have read the debates in Congress, on the report of the committee, to whom were referred the petition of the Society for the abolition of Slavery in Pennsylvania, and the memorial of the people called Quakers; some of which debates are founded on such principles of illiberality, that I must beg your indulgence in the insertion of my remarks in your *Daily Advertiser.*

It is contended by a member (Mr. Jackson) that the negroes are a species of beings in their own country that are subject to such servile treatment from their despotic princes that the transporting them from thence is actual humanity, and that a principle of despotism is inherent in their nature; from whom I deviate, and will draw my remarks from occurrences of their habits and dispositions, on the first intercourse of Europeans amongst them; at which time, criminals and offenders were punished in Africa nearly in the same manner as those among other nations, in the same stage of society: but since the introduction of human commerce, all crimes have been punished with slavery. Every artifice is used by the Prince to induce the subject to become a criminal: acts formerly esteemed trivial, are now deemed crimes, for the sake of inflicting the punishment. Formerly they lived in all the harmony common to society in the first state of nature; now, I admit, they subsist in great measure (particularly those despots on what is called the slave coast) by rapine and plunder. Let every rational person appeal to his own breast for the cause, which will be readily pointed out to him, when he reflects that the despots or sovereigns of this people are induced to sacrifice their subjects freedom, from temptations and pecuniary views, which, even amongst those sovereigns that make liberal professions to humanity and benevolence, seldom fails of proving very captivating: if so, I ask, how much more captivating will temptations prove amongst those who remain in a state of savage society? Hence it will appear, that those engaged in this inhuman traffic are far more blameable than the despots of Africa that furnish the supplies. I will pass from this subject to that part of his speech, wherein he justifies the practice of slavery, as allowable under the Christian dispensation, and immediate sanction of the Apostles. I must beg leave to quote his remarks:

"Onesymus," saith he, "notwithstanding his conversion to Christianity, is understood by the Apostle Paul to continue still the slave of Philemon; and it is not to be supposed, that the master, who was also a Christian, was under the obligation to relinquish any part of his authority, far less to give liberty to his servant. For this I refer them to St. Paul's Epistle to Philemon. Do these good Quakers want more texts as proofs? Let them look into the 13th chap. Romans, ver. 14; Ephesians, chap. 6th, ver. 5th; Colossians, chap. 13th, ver. 22d; 1st Timothy, chap. 6th, ver. 6 & 7; Titus, chap. 2 ver. 9 & 10; 1st Peter, chap. 2. ver. 13; 1st Corinthians, chap. 7. ver. 21 & 22."

The first object that claims my attention is to prove how far Onesymus was the slave of Philemon, after his master's conversion to Christianity, who is admitted, by most commentators, to have obtained his freedom. Onesymus was a name common to all slaves in Rome; the signification, in the original, is profitable: the Apostle may be supposed to allude to it, when he tells Philemon, concerning this servant of his, "In time past he was to thee unprofitable, but now profitable to thee and me." Phil. verse II. And indeed so he proved; for not long after his return to his master, he was sent back again to Rome, that he might be of service to St. Paul in prison. We find the epistles which St. Paul wrote in his confinement, were by his hand conveyed to their respective churches. After the Apostle's release from prison, he was assistant to him in the propagation of the gospel, and (according to the apostolic constitution) was by him made Bishop of Berea, in Macedonia, where he suffered martyrdom. It must strike every person very obviously, consistent with the servile and degrading character of a Roman slave, that Onesymus could not at the same time be the slave of Philemon and Bishop of Berea, but must long first have obtained his right of citizenship, so far as an exemption from Philemon. I will now consider, how far the apostolic injunctions will favor a justification of slavery. Let every soul be subject to the higher power (*a*); servants, be obedient to them that are your masters (*b*) Let as many servants as are under the yoke count their masters worthy of all honour; and they that have believing masters, let them not despise them (*d*) Exhort servants to be obedient to their masters, not purloining, but shewing all good fidelity (*e*) Submit yourselves to every ordinance (*f*) Art thou called, being a servant; for he that is called in the Lord, being a servant, is the Lord's freeman (*g*) There is not the most distant confirmation in the foregoing apostolic texts, that justifies any thing more than passive obedience in voluntary servitude; far from admitting the right of the stronger part of the community wresting the weaker part of their rights, and disfranchising them of the privileges delegated by nature, of being born equally free. There are abundant proofs pointedly in opposition to every such species of oppression; instance the injunctions of our Lord, "Do unto all men as ye would they should do unto you." And with what weight must this sentence of our Lord fall—"Not every one that saith unto me, Lord, Lord, shall enter into the kingdom of Heaven, but he that doth the will of my father which is in Heaven." (Matt. chap. 7. ver. 21.) Think seriously, how far our eternal welfare depends on acting consistent with strict justice, and doing unto others as we would they should do unto us. We learn from history, that slavery, wherever encouraged, has sooner or later been productive of very dangerous consequences. Those that are dubious of its truth I refer to the histories of Athens, Lacedemon [*Sparta*], Rome and Spain.

My next consideration is, how far the invective assertions of several of the southern gentlemen in the House of Representatives are founded in justice, against the society of Quakers. They are charged with the unpardonable accusation of wishing to propagate sedition; to destroy the constitution of these states with hypocrisy; and making religion a pretext for their various schemes and wishes; with being avowed enemies to the late cause of America; and a people of a tyrannical and persecuting disposition. It seems as though the southern gentlemen considered the Quakers as the only people engaged on behalf of the negroes; but I will assure them to the reverse. The freedom of this people has engrossed the serious attention (I may with propriety say) of the majority of the free citizens of the northern states; and one or more religious sects are about making rules, besides the Quakers, for the dismemberment of such in communion with them, as remain in the practice of holding slaves: so that the Quakers are not the only people that are volunteering, as termed, in this business. In respect of their being a people fond of discord and sedition, I will assert, that there has not one instance of this nature ever occurred, since they were formed into a religious society. Trace this sect from the middle of last century, up to the present day, analyze their actions collectively as a religious body, and you will find them so far from discord and sedition, that in every instance that had a tendency that way, they have always held such conduct in the utmost detestation. In respect of their setting up and pulling down governments, is a tenet worked into

(a) Romans xiii. 1. *(b) Ephesians vi.* 5. *(c) Colossians xiii* 22 *(d)* 1 *Timothy vi.* 1, 2. *(e) Titus ii.* 9. 10. *(f)* 1 *Peter ii.* 13. *(g)* 1 *Corinthians vii.* 21, 22.

their religious principles, and is considered contrary to that peaceable spirit, which characteristicks the leading principles of their religion; but in all instances are willing to hold themselves in due subordination to that form of government that is set over them. There may have been instances of some of their members, in the late contest, taking an active part on the behalf of the enemies of this county: yet I presume there are few instances wherein their body did not shew a just disapprobation, by the dismemberment of such. How far the Quakers have been guilty of hypocrisy, and making religion a pretext, I will submit to the tribunal of their actions, and will content myself with making an appeal to those acquainted with their conduct, how far they merit such invectives. In respect of tyranny and persecution, there is no religious society of people less clear of than the Quakers. Even Mr. Voltaire, the analyzer of the actions of mankind, places the highest encomiums on them, and the administration of their celebrated Penn. We find, that during a series of administration in Pennsylvania, they exercised no despotic or arbitrary sway on the persons or property of those not in communion with them, but strictly and literally adhered to the constitution granted by their venerable Penn, which provided, that all persons inhabiting in the province, who confessed and acknowledged one Almighty God, the Creator, Upholder and Ruler of the world, and profess themselves to live quietly under the civil government, should not be molested or prejudiced in their persons or estates, because of their conscientious persuasion or practice, nor be compelled to frequent or maintain any religious worship or ministry contrary to their mind: and that all persons who professed to believe in Jesus Christ, the Saviour of the world, should be capable to serve this government (notwithstanding their profession and practices in point of religion) in any capacity, both legislatively and executively.

I now call upon those asserters, who contend the Quakers are friends to persecution; I even appeal to the consciences of the honorable gentlemen (in Congress) themselves, who have calumniated the characters of the Quakers, that their assertions have been founded without truth; and should they persist, I demand their coming forward to prove the invectives they have been so liberal in bestowing on the Quakers.

I must confess, as a citizen and subject of this rising empire, I view with an eye of pity the altercations that have taken place in the House of Representatives, on the subject which ought, consistent with the rights of nature, and that claims so much humanity, to have met with decent discussion; such document will hand to posterity very unfavourable opinions of the boasted liberty we make such professions of.

PP, 30 March, edited by John Dunlap and David C. Claypoole.

Letter from New York

We have a report, that Gen. [*Arthur*] ST. CLAIR, Governour of the Western Territory, and Major [*Winthrop*] SARGEANT, Secretary thereof, are taken prisoners by the Indians. I am now going out to inquire respecting this report. P. S. I cannot learn any thing authentick respecting it.*

The business that has occasioned the shutting of the galleries so frequently, turns out to be, An Act for *augmenting the Troops*, upon the establishment in the WESTERN TERRITORY,[1] from 8[00] to 1600 men. The Bill has passed the *House*, by a small majority. It will, probably, pass the *Senate*, though not without opposition.

It is expected the business of ASSUMPTION will be taken up to-morrow.

As to the OLD CONTINENTAL, I do not think that the report of the Committee, published in the papers, will be adopted[2]—I question, whether any thing will be done with it *this session*.

I have told you there would be no embargo—I am more convinced of it. The price of grain still falls.

**We add the following note—the information contained in which, we received from a gentleman who lately left the Western Territory. In December last, Governour* ST. CLAIR, *with Major* SARGEANT, *and about* 80 *men, sailed from Fort-Harmer, to the Wabash river—a distance of about* 500 *miles, on a visit to the several posts and settlements in the Territory. It was expected he would be absent about eight months. As the* Wabash *Indians are not in treaty with the United States—and are a mischievous, warlike nation—the capture of the above gentlemen would not be a matter of great surprize. We mention the above circumstances, not as* confirming *the truth of the report mentioned by our New-York Correspondent—but as partly* corroborative *thereof.*

[Boston] *Massachusetts Centinel*, 7 April; reprinted at Portland, Maine; Portsmouth, New Hampshire; and Northampton, Massachusetts.

---

[1] Military Establishment Act [HR-50a].

[2] The House committee report on the petition of Richard Wells and Josiah Hart, presented on 23 March and widely printed. For background and text of the petition and report, see *DHFFC* 8:259, 264–68.

Letter from a Master of a Vessel at Falmouth, England, to his Owners at Patuxent, Virginia

I have the pleasure to inform you of my safe arrival here, after a passage of 31 days. I have not received much damage, though, I am sorry to inform you that very few, of a number of arrivals from our Continent, have experienced the same good fortune.

I had much trouble to quell the disturbance of my men, whose anxiety to land gave me the utmost uneasiness; for in that case by a late act of Parliament, my ship was liable to be seized. I have waited here 14 days expecting daily orders, relative to the port where I may be permitted to discharge. Some regulations ought to be made about our sailors; they become, in every voyage, more troublesome than in the former, as if they were in league with the minister of England, to harrass the trade of their own country.

NYDG, 24 May; reprinted at Baltimore.

Other Documents

John Adams to Francis van der Kamp. ALS, Letters of John Adams, PHi; FC:lbk, Adams Family Manuscript Trust, MHi. Sent to Kingston, New York. For the full text, see *DHFFE* 4:288–89.

Dire predictions about revolutionary France's new form of government; compares the American experience to "that of all ages and nations"; sees dangers in "fermentation" during elections for governors; repeats his version of 1788 Presidential election politics; the election of Senators to the FFC was "a Party Business in most of the States," to be remedied only by a second constitutional convention giving Senators longer terms or "if necessary" making them hereditary; Representatives are elected for a short enough period and from a small enough district as to not "enflame the Passions of a whole nation" as elections for Senators or President do, and so present no danger.

Pierce Butler to Edward Butler. FC, Butler Letterbook, ScU. For the full text, see *Butler Letters*, pp. 20–21.

Chastizes Edward for a personal business transaction; has lately been "familiarised with ingratitude" on the part of the recipient and requests that all "my concerns in your hands" be sealed up and sent to him at New York.

John Chenward, Barnabus Deane, and John Caldwell to Jeremiah Wadsworth. ALS, hand of Chenward, Washington Papers, DLC. Written from Hartford, Connecticut.

Office seeking: recommends Hezekiah Merrill as excise collector at Hartford, if one is to be appointed according to Hamilton's proposal; asks the favor of mentioning Merrill's name to the President.

William Constable to Robert Morris. FC:lbk, Constable-Pierrepont Collection, NN.

Asks Morris to deliver the enclosed letter to John Hall either at Samuel Ogden's or at the Delaware Water Works, and to confer with Hall on estimates for improvement of a mill; also requests that Morris procure him a share in the Ohio Company on whatever terms he can.

Ebenezer Hazard to Jeremy Belknap. ALS, Belknap Papers, MHi. Place to which addressed not indicated.

"Did you ever see such a Piece of work as Congress have made of the Quakers Petition about Slaves: they were thrown into a great Ferment by it, & some very indecent Expressions fell from some of the Members: many who are anxious for the honor & dignity of the national Government were extremely hurt by such deviations from the rules of Propriety."

Ebenezer Hazard to Jedidiah Morse. ALS, Miscellaneous Collection, NHi. Addressed to Charlestown, Massachusetts.

The Patents Act [HR-41] and the Copyright Act [HR-43] are both before Congress and not completed; will circulate the "interleaved Copy" of Morse's *American Geography*, to see if he "can get the members of Congress to attend to it, but I suspect they will plead that they cannot as Col. L[*angdon*]. does"; in one of the published speeches on the Quaker antislavery petitions, Smith (S.C.) "charges you with Inconsistency"; Morse and Jeremy Belknap would laugh at "an humourous Piece signed *Crito*" (*NYJ*, 4 March) satirizing Lucy Knox's "lying in, which was pompously announced to the Public."

Joseph McLellan and John Fox to George Thatcher. ALS, Chamberlain Collection, MB. Written from Portland, Maine; franked; postmarked.

Replies to request in Thatcher to Daniel Davis, 24 February, for information relative to the construction, costs, and estimated price (£400) for finishing the Portland Head lighthouse and keeper's house, together with the cost of the land.

John Tucker, Sr. to Paine Wingate. ALS, Wingate Papers, MH. Written from Newbury, Massachusetts.

Thanks for notice in Wingate's last (3 February) that John Tucker, Jr., had been appointed clerk of the Supreme Court; supposes that whether he accepts will depend on the salary; probably to be determined by Congress, "in which case I cannot doubt your using your Influence in his favor, so far as prudence & Equity will permit"; "Letters from you are allways refreshing as tokens of a Friendship I highly value."

Benjamin Vaughan to Thomas Jefferson. ALS, Jefferson Papers, DLC. Written from London. For the full text, see *PTJ* 16:274–75.

Has sent Izard and other prominent Americans samples of "dry rice" from Mr. Anderson of the Botanical Garden at St. Vincent.

Advertisement. *NYP*, 27 March–15 May (all issues).

For rent, the house on Broad Way, opposite the President's, "in which General SCHUYLER now lives," with a garden, coach house, and stable in the rear.

NYP, 30 March.

Page and Margaret Lowther were married in the evening by Rev. Benjamin Moore.

Letter to New York. *GUS*, 14 April; reprinted at New London and Norwich, Connecticut; Poughkeepsie, New York; Burlington, New Jersey; Fredericksburg and Winchester, Virginia; and Edenton, North Carolina. The ellipses are in the source. This extract may have come from a letter that Joseph Ward wrote to John Fenno; see Fenno to Ward, 11 April, volume 19.

". . . but there are many wise men among them [*Congress?*], who are good state pilots; it is however hard labor for them to get the ship along against such an *undertow*, and the *surf* running at the same time: We may give them a *hint* when we conceive they are out of the way, or move too *slowly* in the right way."

SUNDAY, 28 MARCH 1790

William Ellery to Benjamin Huntington

I have received your letters of the 3d. and 8th. of March on the same sheet, and in answer to the first refer you to my letter giving a general account of the proceedings of the Convention,[1] which you had not recd. when you wrote last, only observing that the Anti's wanted time not to give information to their Constituents; for they have studiously endeavoured to conceal it from and to deceive them; but to secure to themselves the administration at the next election, and to put off the adoption of the Constitution as long as it should suit their interest. They have fixed upon their prox[2] for General Officers, and have admitted into it not more than one Fed, and two Mongrels; and those they would have excluded had they not imagined that an admission of them might silence the first, and stimulate the last in their favour. They have dropped Govr. [*John*] Collins, and placed Arthur Fenner of Providence, a violent Anti, at the head of their Prox. They first intended that the Deputy Governor [*Daniel*] Owens should have been the man; but expecting an opposition from the Feds, they chose Fenner on account of his superior influence. Samuel Potter of Southkingston is to be their Depy. Govr. I question whether the Feds will oppose their prox. If they should there is no prospect of their succeeding, and it may be the best policy to exert themselves in procuring a majority in the house of Deputies; and this may possibly be obtained if the Antis should not be alarmed by an opposition to their prox. The Feds will do all they can to increase their weight and influence in the Assembly; but, they are still overpowered by numbers, and are obliged to fight undermost. If they could receive any assistance from Congress before the election, which will be on the third Wednesday in April, it would have a good effect.

The State Debts I am informed your House have voted to assume; but I am yet to learn whether the Senate have concurred or not. In my last letter I advised you that the Secretary of the Treasury had acquainted me that he was ready to advance 1000 Dollars on account of my salary on my accounts being settled at the Treasury, and I took the liberty to inclose in that letter a power of Attorney authorizing you to receive the money for me, and at the same time depose [*?*] you to send 300 dolls. of it by the first packet.

If you should have received the money before this letter gets to hand, please to send four hundred Dolls. by Capt. [*Edward*] Peterson. I have heard that Mr. [*John*] Cochran the Loan Offr. for N. york has applied to Congress for an allowance to Clerks during the time he issued Indents.[3] I should be glad to know whether this be true and, if so, what became of his application. I mean to [*lined out*] apply when it shall be thought most seasonable.

When do you expect Congress will rise? and do you think that Congress will do any thing respecting this State at this Session? Will the goods, wares, ~~and~~ productions and manufactures of this State excepting cheese and rum be Subject to pay ~~the~~ any duty after the first of April without a positive act for that purpose? There is no act of Congress laying a duty upon lime, flaxseed, or barley that I can recollect, and if those articles are allowed to pass into the other States duty free the Antis will not be impelled by a sense of interest to adopt the Constitution, unless Congress should require an immediate payment of a sum of money from the State with an assurance that if not collected an equivalent will be distrained. Whatever Congress mean to do should be done before the Convention meets, and it would be best that it should be done before the third wednesday in April, which is the day of our election.

The Secretary of the Treasury directed his letter to me as *late* Commissioner of the Loan-Office, and I find by one of his reports that he considers the office as ceasing to exist on the 1st. day of Jany. last. Have Congress passed any Act vacating the Loan-offices at that period, or was he invested with a power to vacate them when he should think it necessary. On the 10th of Jany. I wrote to him informd. him that I accidentally heard that the Loan officer for the State of Massachusetts had received directions from him to cease issuing at the end of the year, and that in consequence of this information I stopped issuing at that period; that my accounts to the last day of Sepr. were ready for transmission, and waited only for his direction, and that I should prepare those for the quarter endg. the 31st. of Decr. immediately. On the fourteenth day of Feby. I recd. from him a letter the copy of which is inclosed; and on the 8th of this month I sent him my accounts with a letter advising him that I had authorized you to receive on my account the sum he had promised me to advance on the settlement of my accounts to the last year, and desiring him to inform me what he would have done with the Indents and blank Loan-Office Certificates remaining in my hands, to which I have received no answer; and the letter a copy of which is enclosed is the only letter I have ever received from him. Nor if Congress should conceive that I ceased to exist as a Loan Officer at the time I receivd the Secretary's letter, which was on the 14th. of February ought I not in reason and justice to be allowed a compensation for the time I have been since employed in the office, for office hire, firewood &c. to a certain period. My office hire commenced on the 2nd. day of May and the quarter of course doth not end until the 2nd. day of next May. Indeed I cannot conceive how I can be considered as ceasing to be Loan-Officer until by an Act of Congress the office shall be vacated; or if the Secretary of the Treasury is empowered to vacat the Loan-Offices until he shall have more formally announced the vacation than by inserting the word *late* in the direction of a letter.

I should be glad to have your opinion on this subject.

I made a mistake in my account current for the quarter ending the 31st. Decr. last, which I have pointed out to the Secretary in a letter which will go by this post.

The ~~thre~~ Four hundred dolls. I have desired you to send by Capt. Peterson, are meant to be exclusive of the three hundred dolls. which in my last letter I desired you to send by the first packet.

If you should not have shipped them by the Aurora Capt. Cahoon, or by Capt. Brown, who are daily expected, please to send six hundred dolls. by Peterson.

As I received no letter from you by the post last friday I expect to receive one by Cahoon or Brown.

[*P. S.*] I intended to have sent this letter by Capt. Peterson but he sailed unexpectedly last saturday early in the morning.

[*P. P. S.*] Peterson is driven back by the fog and I now send this epistle by him.

ALS, Benjamin Huntington Correspondence, 1772–1790, R-Ar. Written from Newport, Rhode Island.

[1] Rhode Island's ratification convention convened in South Kingston on 1 March but adjourned five days later after proposing amendments to the Constitution and voting to reconvene on 24 May.

[2] The prox, as practiced in Rhode Island, was a slate of candidates that had been drafted by a party caucus and ratified by a public nominating meeting.

[3] For Cochran's petition, see *DHFFC* 8:91–93.

William Maclay to John Nicholson

Your's of the 22d has been in my hands for some days, and has placed me in a State of anxiety to know when these Violent Measures will end. I trust your difficulties have terminated before this time. and that there is an account of it, on the way for me, tho' not Yet arrived.[1]

It seems I have incurred displeasure in Philada. by corresponding with You. or in other Words by endeavouring to gain that information, (which could be had only from You) ~~which~~ without which, I could but ill perform the Duty, which I owe to the State. I care not however for these things, I will court a continuance of your, or any other Correspondence which I find Useful to me, as a Servant of the Public. I have however some Reason to suspect, that some either of Your or my letters have been intercepted. A Villain has it in his power to do this. Your hand is very remarkable. and my letters to you are franked with my name, if you think there is the least necessity; I will send Your letters Under cover to any Person, you may please to direct And your letters to me, can be directed in a different hand. some time ago, there was something like a pause in our Correspondence. You mentioned in one of your letters, that a certain Peice would be in such a news Paper, and that You would send me one of them. I never heard further of neither Peice nor News paper. perhaps You changed your mind about the Peice, and if so, all is well. But if You forwarded any such letter I never received it. You promised me an Account of the existing State debt. or what amounts to the same thing, the amount of it which had been sunk. I have not heard from You on this Subject. But this I can account for, from Your late embarrassments.

This goes to you Under cover, to my Brother [*Samuel*], who will deliver it to You, and if there appears any the least necessity for our altering the mode of our exchanging Letters. I expect your next will inform me of it.

ALS, Gratz Collection, PHi. Addressed to "Comptroller Genl. of the State of Pennsylvania"; franked; received 31 March.

[1] The Pennsylvania executive council's investigation of Nicholson's public accounts as state comptroller general .

James Madison to Tench Coxe

I have been some days in debt for your favor of the 21st. instant. Accept my thanks for the Medal [*of the President*] and copy of your new Constitution inclosed in it.

I have delivered to Mr. Jefferson the remarks on a standard of measures, and communicated to him the several other interesting matters which you mention. The former will be disclosed to no one else, but remain in his hands for the purpose intended.

Your idea of appropriating a district of territory to the encouragement of imported inventions is new and worthy of consideration. I can not but apprehend however that the clause in the constitution which forbids patents for that purpose will lie equally in the way of your expedient. Congress seem to be tied down to the single mode of encouraging inventions by granting the exclusive benefit of them for a limited time, and therefore to have no more power to give a further encouragement out of a fund of land than a fund of money. This fetter on the National Legislature tho' an unfortunate one, was a deliberate one. The Latitude of authority now wished for was strongly urged and expressly rejected.[1]

Col. Hamilton has been so closely occupied that he has never thought of communicating the papers to which you refer.[2] Whenever the pleasure of perusing them shall be afforded me, I shall not fail to extend it to Mr. Jefferson.

I regret that it is not in my power to supply the explanations you wish with regard to Rho. Island. I have fallen in with no one who seems to possess an accurate and authentic knowledge of the springs which direct the misconduct of that state. My conjectures would resolve it into the contrivances of a few leaders who are interested in keeping the disaffected party together, and the fear that the federal Constitution might present obstacles to some ~~of~~ [*lined out*] unfinished inequities. As the crisis which has arrived in relation to that infatuated people seems to have suggested to you the idea of discussing the subject, it would have given me particular pleasure, if I had been able to contribute any lights that might be of use to you.

The proceedings of Congs. on the Report of Col. Hamilton have been long interrupted by the Memorials relating to slavery. Whether the time of presenting these was proper, will admit of doubt, but there can be none, that the mode of opposing them was improper. Those who attend to the propositions discussed, and agreed to in a Com[*mitte*]e. of the whole, will be astonished at the arguments which charge the H. of Reps. with a design to ~~prohib~~ usurp the power of prohibiting the importation of slaves, and of manumitting those already in the Country.

ALS, Madison Papers, DLC. Place to which addressed not indicated.

[1] Madison's notes on the Federal Convention record that on 18 August 1787 he moved to refer to the committee of detail a list of additional congressional powers that included the power "to encourage by premiums & provisions, the advancement of useful knowledge and discoveries" (Farrand 2:325). There it apparently met the sound rejection that Madison (who was not on the committee) refers to, since the more limited power that became the language of Article I, section 8 was reported out.

[2] See Coxe to Madison, 21 March, above.

George Read to Gertrude Read

Our son John's Letter of the 22d. instant which I received the 26th. gave me a very favourable account of your and the family's health, I cannot say so much in favour of my own since I wrote to you last, however I have been much better for two or three days past; Repeated additions to a Cold I contracted on my Journey hither has been my complaint which produced some Swelling & pain in my face and jaws that proved troublesome for a time. The Weather here hath been very disagreeable for more than Ten days past, the Air remarkably moist & damp—this morning had a favourable appearance but the Wind is changed and all overcast, there are many invalids among the Congressional Men, tho none dangerously ill. A Mr. Page of Virginia of the House of Representatives was married the last Evening to a Miss [*Margaret*] Lowther of a family that Came hither some time during the War from No. Carolina and also a Mr. White of this City to a Miss Marston a granda[*ughte*]r. of Mr. Tom. Lawrence. Report says some others of the Southern delegates here are in a probable way of forming matrimonial Connections particularly in Commodore Nicholson's family.[1]

*** I believe this Session will be a tedious one from the Complection of the business—some of the Eastern people will be very desirous of going home in May and those for Southward very unwilling for any adjournmt. until all is finished for the Year.

Mr. Bassett says he will be at N. Castle the 15th. of next Month and to Return in Eight or ten days after.

I wish you to give every attention to your health the Season requires it.

ALS, Read Family Papers, DLC. Addressed to New Castle, Delaware. The salutation reads "My dear Getty." On the reverse of the last page of the letter are recorded (not in Read's hand) some household expenses paid by "Mrs. Read" between March and July 1790, and a note on the address page in the same hand directs that "This is to be carefully preserved" because of these financial accounts. The omitted text relates to the travel of friends and family, including Read's brother James's intention to visit New York, possibly with Read's son John.

[1] Two of the four daughters of "Commodore" James Nicholson were married to members at the time of the FFC: Few had married Catherine in 1788, and Seney (one of Read's

housemates at 15 Wall Street) would marry Frances on 1 May 1790. A third daughter, Hannah (1766–1849), married Pennsylvania Senator Albert Gallatin in 1793.

William Smith (Md.) to Otho H. Williams

In answer to yours of the 18th & 19th Instant, I have only to observe, That the revision of the Impost law, has not yet been brot. before Congress, nor do I expect it will be taken up, before the funding System is adopted, or dismissed, That business has been Suspended for Some time past, owing to the Quaker memorials, for the abolition of Slavery, & other business of little importance. Indeed there has appeared a backwardness on both sides of the house, to bring forward *again*, that report on accot. of the State debts; *neither* side being certain of their ground. If the No. Carolina members, vote as is expected, on the Negative Side of the question, that proposition, respecting the assumption of the State debts, will probably be Struck out. & that may Shake the whole System, however I believe there is a very great majority of the members disposed to Support Public credit.

I Perfectly agree with you, that a direct Tax, *on real property*, is the most equitable, & Just of any that can be devised, & almost the only one that can reach many of the wealthiest Citizens in this country, I mean a very Small tax, not more than a quit rent, Say half a dolar or 5/ ℔ hundred acres, this might be easily collected & would raise a very large revenue, but there are objections to that measure at present; in my opinion not solid ones. I will take care to give you information when the impost law is taken up in Congress.

***

You will probably have seen the report of a Special committee, on a memorial of Sundry persons, Citizens of Pennsilvania, & holders of old Continental paper praying, That as they had been by law compelled to receive that money in payment for Just debts, that Congress woud make good to Such holders the Value in Specie. The report however of the committee is. "That on their paying into the Treasury of the U.S. such Bills, they Should receive a Certificate therefor, at one for one hundred, with interest, after it Shall be so paid into the treasury."[1] This report I find is not altogether satisfactory to the House. some are of opinion it ought to be called in at 500, others at 40. & many at 75 for one, the latter Sum, I think as likely as any other to be the value when that business is taken up. When I left Baltimore that Species of paper, Sold at 500 for one, if there is Still any of it to be purchased, it would *perhaps* be a better Speculation than *Finals.* I Suppose you know that continental Loan office certificates, of every State (except So. Carolina & Georgia) are Liquidated here, by the Congress Scale, *none lower than forty for one*, & Specie registered certificates given in exche. & the interest, *in indents*, paid up to the 1st. of Jany. 1788. Those Indents will be consolidated with the Principal, when the funding System takes place. If there are any of those for Sale with you, I presume they [*lined out*] may be purchased, by the State Scales, at least as low, or lower, than finals & no interest counted, which is generally ten or twelve years, besides in the years 80 & 81 the Scale is much higher, Say 60 to 100 & upwards for one.

ALS, Williams Papers, MdHi. Place to which addressed not indicated. The omitted text relates to the surveying of some of Smith's land investments outside Baltimore.

[1] For background and text of the petition of Richard Wells and Josiah Hart and the committee report on the petition, see *DHFFC* 8:259, 264–68.

George Thatcher to Sarah Thatcher

In answer to yours of the 15th. inst. relative to the conduct that ought to have been observed with Phillips, in a particular case, I say, generally, your conduct should have corresponded exactly & punctually with what you had said to him—Had I been in your situation, & once told him, he should have no cake if he was not a good boy—I should keep my word, and, taking no notice of him, distribute a piece to every other person in the house, with a charge to them to say nothing to him, *but that he could have no cake because he had not been a good boy*—Much would depend on every ones minding their work, and taking no notice of his pouting, or threatning—in order for the Lesson to have its proper effect—When a child sais, or does many things, which we wish him not to repeat, the best way to hinder him, & prevent such things becoming habitual, is to appear altogether inattentive—If they have no manner of effect upon us, he will soon see it, & not be likely to use them again as means to obtain his wishes—~~And~~ And they will make a less durable impression on his mind then they would were we to rebuke & correct him for them—I am inclined to think that correction in most, if not in all instances, fixes, in the mind of the person corrected, not only a more lively idea of the thing we would correct, but facilitates the return of the idea & thing in his mind—And the moment a child discovers that his ill behaviour, his pouting & refractoriness give us pain, & that we wish him to behave otherwise, he has got possession of an engine he will not fail to use, on all occasions, to bring us to a compliance to his terms.

I believe general observation confirms this truth; That when children pronounce words they dont know the meaning of, & which it is not proper for them to repeat, the only way to break them of it is to take no manner of notice of what they say; but as soon as it can be done without alarming them, or creating their suspicion, to ask them some question, present to them some pleasing object that shall engage their attention, or tell them to do something or other—And then special care must be taken that such words, or any of a similar sound are not pronounced in their hearing.

I have no doubt but the same principle will hold good with regard to the first actions of children.

By your letter I was led to imagine you had inclosed me a small piece of the muzlin of your gown for a pattern—also a measure of your shoes—but I believe you forgot it, for none were inclosed—You shall have both, my dear, if you will send me a pattern, & a measure—I am happy to hear you are attentive to these little things, as you call them—how can you think you shall never want to ware them? banish such an idea, my dear, & don't query about the matter.

I have concluded to get feathers for a bed &c. in this City—and engaged a man to purchase them for me; they will not cost more than two shillings a pound—I shall get sixty weight, & forward them to Boston the first opportunity.

The money I have in Boston I shall desire our friend [*Thomas*] Dakin to receive & forward to you some time in April.

I am distressed at the thoughts of your having the Itch—pray cure yourself if you can—but dont run any risque.

ALS, Thatcher Family Papers, MHi. Place to which addressed not indicated.

George Washington to David Stuart

Your letter of the 15th enclosing the Act of Assembly authorising an agreement with Mr. [*Robert*] Alexander came to my hand in the moment my last to you was dispatched.[1]

I am sorry such jealousies as you relate should be gaining ground, & poisoning the minds of the Southern people. But, admit the fact which is alledged as the cause of them, and give it full scope, does it amount to more than what was known to every Man of information before, at, and since the adoption of the Constitution? Was it not always believed that there are some points which peculiarly interest the Eastern States? And did any one who reads human nature, & more especially the character of the Eastern people, conceive that they would not pursue them steadily by a combination of their force? Are there not other points which equally concern the Southern States?

If these States are less tenacious of their interest, or, if whilst the Eastern move in a solid phalanx to effect their purposes, the Southern are always divided, which of the two is most to be blamed? That there ~~is~~ are diversity of interests in the Union none has denied. That this is the fact also in every State is equally certain—and that it extend, even to Counties, can be as readily proved. Instance the Southern & Northern parts of Virginia—the upper & lower parts of So. Carolina &ca. have not the interests of these always been at varience? Witness the County of Fairfax, has not the interests of the people thereof ~~can be as readily proved as~~ varied, or the Inhabitants been taught to believe so? These are well known truths, and yet it did not follow that seperation was to result from the disagreement.

To constitute a dispute there must be two parties. To understand it well both the parties & all the circumstances must be fully understood. And to accomodate differences good temper & mutual forbearance is requisite. Common danger brought the States into Confederacy, and on their Union our safety & importance depend. A spirit of accomodation was the basis of the present Constitution; can it be expected then that the Southern or the Eastern part of the Empire will succeed in all their Measures? Most certainly not. but I will readily grant that more points will be carried by the latter than the former, and for the reason which has been mentioned—namely—that in all great national questions they move in unison, whilst the others are divided; but I ask again which is most blameworthy, those who see & will steadily pursue their interests, or those who cannot see, or seeing, will not act wisely? And I will ask another question (of the highest magnitude in my mind) and that is, if the Eastern & Northern States are dangerous *in Union*, will they be less so *in seperation*? If self interest is their governing principle, will it forsake them, or be less restrained by such an event? I hardly think it would. Then, independent of other considerations what would Virginia (and such other States as might be inclined to join her) gain by a seperation? Would they not, most unquestionably, be the weaker party?

Men who go from hence without *feeling* themselves of so much consequence as they wished to be considered—disappointed expectants and malignant designing characters that miss no opportunity to aim a blow at the constitution, paint highly on one side without bringing into view the Arguments which are offered on the other. It is to be lamented that the Editors of the several Gazettes of the Union do not more generally & more connectedly publish the debates in Congress on all great National questions that affect different interests instead of stuffing their papers with scurrility & malignant declamation, which few would read if they were apprised of the contents. That they might do that with very little trouble is certain. The principles upon which the difference in opinion arose as well as the decision, would, in that case come fully before the public, & afford the best data for its Judgment.

Mr. Madison, on the question of discrimination, was actuated, I am persuaded by the purest motives; & most heartfelt conviction; but the Subject was delicate, & perhaps had better not have been stirred. The assumption of the State debts by the United States is another subject that has given birth to long and laboured debates without having yet taken a final form. The Memorial of the Quakers (& a very Mal-apropos one it was) has at last been put to sleep, from which it is not probable it will awake before the year 1808.

ALS, Gratz Collection, PHi. Place to which addressed not indicated. For the full text, see *PGW* 5:286–88.

---

[1]The agreement with Robert Alexander (d. 1793) related to the estate of John Parke Custis (1754–81) and his 950-acre "Abingdon" (in present-day National Airport, Arlington County, Virginia) that Custis had purchased from Alexander.

Other Documents

Nathaniel Barrett to John Langdon. ALS, Langdon Papers, NhPoA. Written from Boston.

Requests that Ebenezer Hazard be informed Barrett is too unwell to write; "what is the reason M. Jefferson does not pay you a Visit? I think his Department must want him."

Benjamin Goodhue to Stephen Goodhue. ALS, Goodhue Family Papers, MSaE. Addressed to Salem, Massachusetts.

"Several wet days" have prevented his sending their ship off to Europe with 5200 bushels of corn; reports "nothing new in the political line"; expects they will renew the funding and assumption debates the following day and that assumption will pass "tho' every obstacle will be thrown in the way"; "I expect to draw in a few days for my wages if so, I shall be able probably to send you some money."

Jeremiah Hill to George Thatcher. ALS, Chamberlain Collection, MB. Written from Biddeford, Maine. Hill addressed the cover, "The Honorable Thatcher, Esq. N. B. you see what I have done" (a reference to Thatcher's aversion to being addressed by any title). Closing salutation in French.

"IIII Posts since I received your Last Letter, Quid tum [*what next*]?"

William Irvine to John Nicholson. ALS, Fogg Collection, MeHi. Addressed to Philadelphia; franked; postmarked; received 30 March.

"M-r-s [*Morris*] is gone to arrange matters, to be Governor [*of Pennsylvania*] the members of assembly, ought & must I suppose be dealt with to ensure this before they rise &ca."

Henry Knox to William Eustis. FC:dft, Knox Papers, Gilder Lehrman Collection, NHi.

Is informed "Our [*Massachusetts*] delegates" soon intend to reopen the rolls of eligible invalid pensioners; from his observation of members, thinks new invalid pensions will be difficult to obtain.

Theodore Sedgwick to David Sewall. No copy known; mentioned in Sewall to Thatcher, 8 April.

Caleb Strong to David Sewall. No copy known; mentioned in Sewall to Thatcher, 8 April.

George Thatcher to Joseph Barnard. No copy known; acknowledged in Barnard to Thatcher, 9 April.

George Thatcher to Daniel Cony. No copy known; acknowledged in Cony to Thatcher, 24 April.

George Thatcher to Jeremiah Hill. No copy known; acknowledged in Hill to Thatcher, 8 April.

George Thatcher to Silas Lee. No copy known; acknowledged in Lee to Thatcher, 18 May (Chamberlain Collection, MB).

George Thatcher to David Sewall. No copy known; acknowledged in Sewall to Thatcher, 8 April.

Thomas Tudor Tucker to an Unknown Recipient. Listing of ALS, *Henkels Catalog* 906 pt. II(1904):item 2498.

William Samuel Johnson, Diary. Johnson Papers, CtHi.

"St. Pauls."

MONDAY, 29 MARCH 1790

Cold (Johnson)

Thomas Hartley to Jasper Yeates

I recived your Favor of the 19th. inst. and am glad to hear that your Party was so pleasing and agreeable on the 17th.

We are this Morning upon the Report of the Committee of the whole on the Secretary of the Treasury's Report.

The first Second & third Resolutions are adopted by the House.

And the Assumption of the State Debts is again under Consideration—How it will end I cannot say—Our Delegation is somewhat alarmed on Account of the Alternative of taking one third in Lands—first on account of the uncertainty of the value—& the next that it would tend to a Depopulation of our State. the poorer Part of our People would be tempted to leave the State.

We are on difficult Ground—I wish we may be able to obtain some System of funding.

I inclose you a News Paper.

***

ALS, Yeates Papers, PHi. Addressed to Lancaster, Pennsylvania; franked; postmarked. The omitted postscript relates to private financial transactions, including a possible loan from Yeates.

St. George Tucker to John Page

You will recieve by this days post a long Letter from me, in answer to your favor of the 16th. The weather is so bad this morning that I can not set out on my Journey as I intended, & having accidentally met with a piece in Davis's paper, which I wrote some time ago, I now enclose it for your perusal,[1] & if you think as well of it as I do, you may send it to the [*American*] Museum, in order that it may be more diffusively circulated throughout the States. If you send it to the Museum a short preface may be necessary, stating, "that an Advertisement had appeared in the Virginia Gazette printed by A. Davis, proposing the establishment of a Society for the Abolition of Slavery in Virginia, & inviting all persons, *except the holders of slaves*, to become Members." which gave rise to the enclosed hasty production.[2]

I have since reflected on the Scheme which I have there suggested, & can not help thinking that if any plan for extirpating an Evil so abhorrent to the principles of our Government, as well as to the rights of humanity it must be something of this kind. I have not seen the Quakers petition to Congress, or the debates on it. But I am induced to think, if the Finances of the united States would admit, that a few thousand Dollars per annum might be appropriated to the purpose of promoting such a Society in the several States with advantage—Perhaps too Congress would not exceed the Limits of propriety, should ~~it~~ they take the Liberty of recommending to the States to take up the subject, & to pass such Laws as may be consistent with the Circumstances of the several States, if by way of giving a sanction for so doing, they should proceed, & offer to assign to the persons manumitted either a portion of the western territory, or to give to the Individuals as much Land as they could occupy there.

One advantage appears to me to arise from this plan. it will not liberate persons born in Slavery, & contracting the Ideas & habits of that Condition, but will give birth to free-men. Suppose the Æra of female Emancipation to commence on the first day of the next Century—that of universal freedom to the after born will commence at a period not later than the year 1820. or 1825. Calculating the period of a Slaves Life at fifty years, the progress of Liberty among the blacks would be nearly as follows.

In the year 1800—all would be Slaves—express the number by an Unit.
In 1810—the Slaves would be reduced ~~to~~ [*lined out*] .8 of the blacks among us.
In 1820—their number would be—.6—or under.
In 1830. they may be estimated as low as—.28.
In 1840. not more than—.12, would remain.
In 1850. there would be so few left as not to be regarded.

I have not attempted any thing like accuracy in this Scale—It is probably not rapid enough in ~~the two first~~ any of periods, for as one half of those born in the first & second would be free while all that die may be considered as Slaves born, they would probably be much faster reduced in Numbers.

Though I have written to you on this subject, as to one who thinks with me that Slavery is a curse upon our Country, yet I should inform you that you have perhaps been injured in the Eyes & opinions of your Constituents by a report that you *advocated the Abolition of Slavery by Congress.* Mr. [*Edmund*] Randolph has done you the Justice to explain your Conduct where it has been mentioned in his presence, but perhaps it might be proper for you in some of your Letters to take notice of the report.

[*Enclosure*]

MR. DAVIS,

I CANNOT easily express to you the pleasure that I received from the proposition in one of your late papers, for establishing a society for the gradual abolition of slavery in this country. I view it as a happy presage of the accomplishment of one of the warmest wishes of my heart; for though I am one of those unfortunate men, who, without any act of their own, possess slaves, yet if the policy of our legislature and the present circumstances of our country would admit of a general emancipation, there is no measure in which I should more heartily concur. Yet I was somewhat disappointed in my expectations of that perfect liberality of sentiment which might have been expected to accompany such a proposal, when I found it was intended to exclude from such a laudable association all those who are in a similar predicament with myself. Were that infamous traffic which peopled this country with slaves still continued, there might perhaps be some reason to conclude that whoever was concerned in it, could not be seriously a friend to the rights of mankind. But when we recur to the mistaken policy of our forefathers, for the origin and existence of slavery in Virginia, and remember that even at this day a moiety, or perhaps a majority of its inhabitants are in a state of bondage—That of the other moiety, a large proportion have fulfilled from generation to generation by the labor of their slaves and the produce of their lands only—That those arts which support the multitude in older countries are but little known among us—That it requires time to introduce them to as to afford a mean of support to those, who, though now idle, might be thus beneficially employed—That the spirit of emigration to the western country threatens destruction to the agriculture of the extensive region on this side the Allegheny which we inhabit—That this unhappy species of property often constitutes the whole of that which has obtained a credit to its possessor, or which can be had recourse to, to satisfy his just debts: That even if a general emancipation could be agreed on, it would be difficult to fix the terms on which it might be prudent to adopt it—That this difficulty and these reasons may deter many who would with pleasure, and without any pecuniary consideration, sign the act of their manumission, from pursuing the dictates of their hearts I have but little doubt; and therefore inclined to think that the respectable persons who have it in contemplation to institute the society will find that they have proceeded upon too narrow a foundation. So far from wishing to confine so noble an undertaking to any description of men, or of circumstances, I could wish that every member of the community could be interested in promoting its success. The possession of fifty or an hundred slaves, or any smaller number may not be able [*to*] emancipate them *all* without neglecting the first obligations of social life; the maintenance and education of his family—yet he may chearfully contribute a part of their value for the desirable purpose of promoting such an institution. Again, a person may possess a worthless slave whose liberation from bondage may become a pest to society, yet he may be willing to contribute his value to release more deserving objects from that unhappy fate: I mention these cases only to show that the possessors of slaves ought not to be considered from that circumstance alone as adversary to the abolition of slavery: This must be a work of time—it will require extensive funds and consequently numerous and liberal contributors. It has not for its object a few individuals, but I might say a nation. Posterity ought to be interested in its prosecution and success, and the more extensive it is made, the more extensive will be those sentiments which must support and carry it into effect.

With all respect then to the original proposers of the scheme, to which I most cordially wish success, permit me to suggest to them the propriety of making their society a national, and not merely a partial object.

To this end,

First—It seems proper to establish an annual fund, sufficient to procure the liberation of such persons as may be considered as proper objects of the charity.

Second—Let all persons wanting to subscribe a certain *annual* sum be admitted as members.

Third—Let the contributions of all others be received.

Fourth—Let the legislature be petitioned to pass an act incorporating the society, and appointing trustees, &c. And for such *pecuniary* aid, as the circumstances of the country and its finances will admit.

These objects being attained, it might perhaps be proper for the society to consider how the purposes of it can most effectually be promoted.

Every young female capable of bearing children, when emancipated, may be considered as the means of liberty to five persons in the first generation—to fifteen in the second, and to fifty in the third.

Consequently if the object be the gradual extirpation of slavery, persons of that description should be first sought after.

Many of these are sold yearly under execution for one half the price that the owner would demand.

If proper persons were employed to attend sheriffs sales, it would answer the double purposes of immediate charity to the miserable sufferers, thus exposed like cattle for sale, and of promoting the great ends of the society.

Though the relief of particular individuals should be a secondary object to such a society, yet ought it not to be lost sight of—nor yet be too extensively indulged. The males are more capable of induring hardships: They would cost more to redeem them—and the benefit of the charity would cease with them: for these reasons it seems that they should be postponed to the females who are likely to be mothers.

What provision is proper to be made for those who are thus relieved, must be a subject for legislative consideration.

I have thrown these few hints upon paper with a view to induce the worthy persons who propose to found this humane society, to consider how far it may be proper to depart from the plan they have set out with by extending their views, and the pleasure of contributing to such an institution to all who are willing to become members of their society, upon the terms beforementioned.

Should they persevere in excluding the present holders of slaves from aiding in such a work, I shall lament that their sentiments are not as charitable to a part of their fellow-citizens, as their conduct in every other respect will be worthy of imitation—And shall hope to see a similar institution take place upon a more enlarged plan.

In either case, no man will be more happy to contribute to the accomplishment of such a charitable and christian like work than myself: for I am

A Real Friend to the Abolition of Slavery.

P. S. May we not hope that upon a plan somewhat of the nature of that within mentioned, slavery, in the course of half the next century may be totally abolished in this country. Suppose the legislature after affording every present aid that circumstances will admit, to the establishment of a society for the purposes above-mentioned, should pass an act, declaring, "That all *females* and the *descendents* of such *females* as shall be born in Virginia after the last day of the present century shall be free;" in fifty years time there would scarcely remain a slave among us; nature herself by slow degrees contributing to the change. The advantage of such a measure would be, that no one would be deprived of the labour of a person whom he had ever counted upon as his property. As a compensation to the person in whose family such as may be entitled to freedom should be born, they may be held to service until the age of one and twenty years, or perhaps longer, as may be consistent with sound policy and humanity.

☞*As the subject of this paper may be considered as interesting to the rights of humanity, the writer wishes that the printers in this state would give it a place in all their papers.*

ALS, Pennsylvania Abolition Society Papers, PHi. Written from Williamsburg, Virginia; franked; postmarked 2 April. The letter's location and docketing on the address page by James Pemberton indicate that it was given to the Pennsylvania Abolition Society, presumably by Scott, to whom Page had referred the letter along with Tucker's request for its republication in the *American Museum* (Page to Tucker, 7 June, below). If, as Page said, he had hoped thereby to disassociate himself from any public exertion on Tucker's behalf, the effort was in vain. While Tucker's plan cannot be found in the *American Museum*, his cover letter—boldly identifying Page as the recipient—was printed in its entirety in Philadelphia's *Independent Gazetteer*, 6 November. The letter appeared with other pieces in a column dedicated to reprinting abolitionist extracts. Tucker's enclosure was ultimately printed in the [Richmond] *Virginia Independent Chronicle*, 17 March, from which it is reprinted here.

[1] Augustine Davis published the [Richmond] *Virginia Independent Chronicle* from 1786 to July 1790. Tucker's "scheme" (printed as an enclosure to this document) was later elaborated in his famous *Dissertation on Slavery: With a Proposal for the Gradual Abolition of It in the State of Virginia* (Philadelphia, 1796).

[2] The advertisement to which Tucker was responding appeared in the *Virginia Independent Chronicle* on 24 February.

An Old Freeman to Messrs. Printers

I Observe a correspondent of yours who appears in the Connecticut Courant of March 22, that seems to be a well meaning man, and judges pretty well so far as he is well informed; but I think he is ill informed, or at least uninformed, as to the reception our Representatives met with when they last returned. I thought it was very agreeable; perhaps it might be otherwise in his circle where they were uninformed. I think I had it from good authority that our Assembly gave our Representatives under the old Constitution the same which they now have, and if it is too much, charge the blame where it is due. I believe it would be a new thing under the sun, at least in this State, for the public servants to give themselves less than the assembly gave them. As to the salaries bestowed on the judges, I believe the people in New-England in general think them too high—He should observe that the Western and Southern people are not so near upon a level as we are in New-England, and thence ariseth those high appointments. He should recollect if he ever knew it, that when we first began to oppose the Britons by arms, the Western and Southern people complained of the wages of our rank and file, and said rather than comply, they would fight it out without us; but when they considered that our young men of family were much superior to their grogsters, who would be likely to desert when the grog failed, and which really happened, they contented themselves with raising the officers wages.

As to his regretting that Congress should assume the state debts, I think he is as ill-informed about that matter as any other. I shall not set him right by public information. Let him enquire, and he will find that it is best for all the states, and this in particular, that Congress should assume all the state debts, without he is one of them that would have the state cheat their creditors, and drive them to complain to Congress, which they certainly will do if the state goes on as they have done, about which I shall forbear to mention particulars at the present.

[Hartford] *Connecticut Courant*, 29 March; reprinted at New York City (*GUS*, 7 April).

Letter from Paris

We have numerous applications from different parts of your states to emigrate to America. A printed circular letter has been received from New-York, highly recommending the salubrity of the air and pleasantness of the situation of that part of America. Our main objection is, that your winters are too severe, and which, from the best information, deprive the farmer, and even many of the citizens of the towns of every farthing they can make in the summer. As to Pennsylvania, we have every reason to believe it to be the garden spot of America, and yet even that state has its disadvantages. The capital [*Philadelphia*], we are told, is extremely sickly during the summer and the greater part of the autumn; strangers, as well as the natives, being in these seasons commonly afflicted with putrid fevers, cholera morbus, bilious cholics, sore throats, intermittents, &c.; besides this, we are told that nearly two thirds of the Philadelphia children die every fall—this discourages our women—As to those Frenchmen who return from your settlements, they, in general, speak well of the country but disapprove of your manners, being, I suspect, too simple for those educated in the habits of frivolity and grimace. I can assure you nevertheless, you will have great numbers of emigrants from France, provided those that first go are not *cheated* by cunning land jobbers and unprincipled speculators, which we have *some reason* to apprehend will be the case.

NYDG, 8 June (the date on which members of Congress would have seen it); reprinted at Baltimore.

Other Documents

William Blount to John Gray Blount. AL, John Gray Blount Papers, Nc-Ar. Written from Greeneville, North Carolina; place to which addressed not indicated; carried by "Sam."

Asks him to write Williamson to ensure that the Montfort and McColloch certificates (a variety of the North Carolina state securities) are included in the Funding Bill.

Silvanus Bourn to John Adams. ALS, Adams Family Manuscript Trust, MHi. Place from which written not indicated.

Office seeking: requests "a renewal of your influence with the President & Mr. Jefferson" for "a Secretaryship or other secondary place in the Diplomatic Line—or a Consulate."

William Constable to Robert Morris. FC:lbk, Constable-Pierrepont Collection, NN.

"Perhaps you may have an opp[*ortuni*]ty. of making some Agreement with [*Tench?*] Cox about the right of purchase of the Miami tract of Land."

Benjamin Goodhue to Michael Hodge. ALS, Ebenezer Stone Papers, MSaE. Place to which addressed not indicated.

"I can inform you of nothing interesting that has occur'd since my last—I suppose We shall to day take up again the Secrys. report, and I have the most flattering hopes that we shall retain a majority for the Assumption, tho' I've no doubt every attempt will be made to defeat it in every stage and the modification of those measures which may be calculated for carrying it into effect."

Benjamin Hawkins to Tobias Lear. ALS, Washington Papers, DLC. Written in the Senate Chamber.

"John McCullough is the present collector at the port of Swansborough [*North Carolina*] the Senators know not his character. William Benson is of fair character and would execute the office of Surveyor at Windsor. We have no information respecting a proper person as surveyor at Currituck."

William Samuel Johnson, Diary. Johnson Papers, CtHi.
"Visits."

Henry Knox, Draft of an amendment, presumably to the Military Establishment Act [HR-50a]. AN, Knox Papers, Gilder Lehrman Collection, NHi.
"And be it further enacted. That whenever the said troops shall be formed into seperate detachments in such a manner as that the surgeons, and the surgeons mates, before mentioned shall be deemed inadequate to the charge of the sick of the said seperate detachments, the President of the U.S. shall be and he hereby is empowered to appoint so many assistant surgeons mates, and for such periods as He shall judge the service may require."

Tuesday, 30 March 1790

Fine (Johnson)

Benjamin Chadbourne to George Thatcher

Your repeated favours have laid me under such obligations, that, should I neglect paying you some acknowledgment I should think myself guilty of that ingratitude which I never wish to be charged with, therefore shall notice some of my thoughts upon the times; however undigested they may be, coming from an old friend, who is almost arrived to the age of Seventy two, I doubt not will be acceptable—and your candour towards me will be, that I mean well, which is all that I can expect.

Reading the debates of Congress seems to reanimate me, and calls my attention more on thinking upon public proceedings than ever I design'd at this time of life. The debates in regard of discrimination have been very entertaining. Mr. Madison's motion[1] seemed to be grounded in Justice and Equity, and [*was thro out?*] supported with great abilities—Every thing, was said in favour of it that could be thought of, altho' from my first hearing of it, I doubted the practicability of it's being carried into execution, yet it was pleasing to me to have it brought forward and so well supported by reason and argument and I think does great honour to your house of Representatives, in digesting so important a motion with that deliberation and candour as that was treated with on both sides—It must give satisfaction (I think) to every considerate person in the Union, as the disputants did not seem to aim at victory but light and truth, and in my opinion the motion was fully confected—In your last you mentioned the very important question before Congress in assuming the states debts, and that some states and individuals was opposed to it—Without knowing your Sentiments upon the subject, and perhaps the matter will be decided before this will reach you yet with the greatest defference I wonder at such opposition from States and individuals; it appears to me their Ideas are too local—If the Debt has arisen in carrying on the war, that the State that was most out of the way in making disbursements for supporting the army, is Sir necessary expence in defending against the common enemy can they now say they are not willing to pay their proportion of the whole expense according to their abilities, after their accompts. are justly liquidated would be departing from the principe we at first sat out upon: but I hope better things—I want to see our government so united & consolidated that if a citizen of Newhamshire should travel to South-Carolina, that he may consider himself as a citizen of that, and every other State he may pass through in as full an extent as if he were in Portsmouth—I cannot think of any method of bringing about so desirable an event than Congress assuming all the States debts accrued by the war—that there may be the same fixed currency in every state, a Simularity of Laws, that a man may depend upon the coin, or currency that may be issued by congress, that when he is acquainted with the coin, Laws and regulations of the particular State he may reside in, he may know how to regulate himself in any other State in the Union—Keeping up a distinction between States will always have a tendency to crea[*te*] discord, but when we come to reallize that we were all [*seal*] in one day, and all of one family, and what ever public measure that is taken to promote the prosperity of one, shod. be equally felt by the whole, so far as circumstances will admit and cannot but think, whenever it takes place, it will have a tendency to strengthen our Union, enlarge our Ideas, promote harmony, and the benefits resulting from our constitution will be more sensibly felt.

I will propose one query, and conclude this Letter that is, admitting the original proprietors of the whole domestic debt were now in possession of their securities as they were when first sold, whether Congress would be under obligations in justice to pay them according to the face of their securities?

ALS, Chamberlain Collection, MB. Written from Berwick, Maine; postmarked Portsmouth, New Hampshire.

[1] The motion to discriminate among public creditors when funding the federal debt.

William Coombs, Moses Brown, and David Coats to [*Benjamin Goodhue*]

As there are some Vessels, soon bound to Sea, from hence which, the Owners are apprehensive, the Collector will not clear out without receiving foreign Tonnage, the Payment of which will create great uneasiness, if the Secretary, could consistenly instruct the Collector by Letter to forbear to insist upon this demand 'till some explanatory Act or Resolve may be passed, it will not only ease the Mind of the Collector but give great Satisfaction, to such here as have been the best Friends to the Federal Government, and are most disposed to support it.

LS, incomplete, Letters to Goodhue, NNS. Place from which written not indicated. The recipient's identity is based on the letter's present location and its endorsement in Goodhue's hand.

Lott Hall to George Thatcher

I send this by Mr. [*Lewis R.*] Morris formerly of New york, who now lives about 12 miles above me in this State. I am now confined to my home by a fall I recd. yesterday, & feel very unsuitable for almost every undertaking of any consequence, more especially writing to a Congress-man, but recollecting that we once did so with the greatest freedom, & having so good an oppertunity thought I would not omit it. I view with all due humility those sketches of your conduct, you are pleasd. to let the world see, thro' the medium of Thomas's Spy.[1] and think nothing seem's to embarres your High Mightinesses, more then the business of financering.

Wish you would let me know what probability there is of our coming into the union—And what you think are the easiest terms on which New york will ever admit us ~~in~~to the priviledges of Independence &c. &c.

I have the honour to be with the greatest esteem & respect your most obedt. humble servt.

[*P. S.*] N. B. I belive I have concluded my letter, as they always do letters to great folks, & if I have not, it is because I dont know how too. I live so far up in the woods hear that I dont see but few such things so hope you'll excuses it.

ALS, Chamberlain Collection, MB. Written from Westminster, Vermont.

[1] Isaiah Thomas's [Worcester] *Massachusetts Spy*.

Daniel Hiester to James Hutchinson

I have recd. several Publications covered under your hand writing for which I am much Obliged to You.

All the resolutions lately Passed in the Committee of the whole, excepting the two first, have been recommitted, and are now again under debate in Committee. There is now great reason to believe the Assumption of the State debts will be rejected, if so, it will be by but a small Majority. If any thing in the Progress of this business happens worth your Notice I will inform you of it—The Advocates for general funding threaten if the State debts fail they will do nothing, that however will not lay with them.

The N. Yorkers are going on with their Government House[1] Confident that the Seat of the Gen. Government is theirs for a long time—It is a good deal spoke of to Adjourn in May & to sit again in October or November—I got Historicus republished here as You will See[2]—it is esteemed a well chosen ground taken What is the opinion, who shall be our New Governor.

ALS, Miscellaneous Manuscripts, PPAmP. Addressed to Philadelphia; franked; postmarked.

---

[1] The Government House was, like the remodeling of Federal Hall, a major public improvement project undertaken by state authorities to entice the federal government to prolong its stay in New York City. On 16 March 1790 the state legislature voted to demolish Fort George at the southwestern end of Broadway, between the Bowling Green and the Hudson River, and construct a building for the state government but "to be applied to the temporary use and accommodation of the President of the United States." On 24 March commissioners advertised the public competition for a design to include a room for the formal reception of the legislature, state and private drawing and dining rooms, and a library. Federal Hall's architect Peter Charles L'Enfant was assumed to be the most favored contender, but, insulted by the compensation New York City offered him for his work at Federal Hall—ten acres of central Manhattan Island farmland—he refused to enter the competition. It closed by 26 April, when the commissioners selected the plan for a large Georgian-style mansion, attributed to master carpenter James Robinson. On 21 May the cornerstone was laid at a ceremony attended by Governor George Clinton, Chancellor Robert R. Livingston, and "a great concourse of respectable citizens." After reaching expenses of £9,500, the commissioners declared the Government House officially completed on 1 March 1791, seven months after the seat of government left New York City under the terms of the Residence Act [S-12]. Clinton moved into the building by year's end, followed by Governor Jay in 1795. Ironically, its use did ultimately revert to the federal government: after a brief career as a tavern in 1799, it served as the federal customs house until its demolition in 1815, three years after the demolition of Federal Hall, which became the site of the new customs house (*Iconography* 1:418, 442, 443; 5:1264, 1265, 1267, 1278; 6:48; Kenneth R. Bowling, *Peter Charles L'Enfant* [Washington, D.C., 2002], pp. 19–20).

[2] Historicus, Benjamin Franklin's antislavery parody, 23 March, above, first appeared in Philadelphia on 25 March and was widely reprinted thereafter, beginning with *NYDA*, 30 March.

William Maclay to Benjamin Rush

Courage my dear Friend we gain upon our Adversaries. the State Debts are recommitted, and the Prospect is fair. for the rejection of their Assumption. The Presses are wrenched open, or at least some of them, and light follows the Operation.[1]

I inclose You another Peice for republication, and refer You to that for news.

How is it that our Friends are so sparing of their correspondence. except a line or Two from Yourself. I have not had a word from Philada. for ten days past.

Haste prevents my adding more.

ALS, Rush Papers, DLC. Addressed to Third Street, Philadelphia; franked; postmarked.

[1] Maclay meant that some New York City newspapers were printing articles in opposition to Hamilton's funding plan.

James Madison to Edmund Randolph

Your favr. of the 15. which requests an immediate acknowledgment, by some irregularity did not come to hand till I had recd. that of the 18. nor till it was too late to comply with the request by the last mail. I have been so unlucky also as to miss seeing the President twice that I have waited on him in order to intimate the circumstances which you wish him to know. I shall continue to repeat my efforts until I shall have an opportunity of executing your commands.

The House have recommitted the Resolutions on the Report of the Treasy. Those relating to the assumption of State debts were recommitted by a majority of 2 votes. The others from an extreme repugnance in many to a separation of the two subjects. N. Carolina has 2 votes on the floor which turned the scale. The final decision is precarious. The immediate decision will repeat the former one in favor of the assumption, unless the composition of the House or the Com[*mitt*]ee. s[*houl*]d. be varied tomorrow. Of six absent members, a majority will be opposed to the measure.

ALS, Madison Papers, DLC. Place to which addressed not indicated.

Louis Guillaume Otto to Comte de Montmorin

While Congress with its long debates on the Report of the Secretary of the Treasury tries the public's patience, the principles put forth by this Secretary are openly attacked by some anonymous writers whose sarcasms seemed directed rather against his personal character than against the public officer. Even in the House of Representatives a member [*Burke*] has just given him the lie[1] in the most outrageous terms which might have some disagreeable consequences if they had not established the maxim here that no member of the legislature is responsible outside for what he said in the course of the debates. *** every time it is a question of a new tariff, the American financiers never fail to put at the head a *tonnage duty on foreigners,* an infallible means of gaining *the votes* of the politicians of New England who have been, are and perhaps always will be masters of the principal operations of the government. ***

The interplay of passions and of particular interests means that generally speaking the Federalists in Congress are the zealous defenders of these expedients while the Antifederalists reject them with disdain. This peculiarity, which is the first cause of the almost interminable debates of this assembly about finances and which furnishes the key to all that has been done here for some time, deserves to be explained. The Federalists know very well that time alone can consolidate the new system of government which they have introduced. They know the full scope of the powers which the Constitution gives it, but they avoid exercising them too early in order not to frighten a people generally prejudiced against every kind of direct taxation; but the needs of Congress being considerable, they eagerly sanction the expedients which are proposed to them in order to gain time, waiting to come to the direct taxes when the people will be accustomed to the yoke. The Antifederalists, for their part, affect a sort of unlimited veneration for the Constitution. They wish to set to work all the activities of the government, to use all their powers, to give to Congress some energy, some importance, finally to make the people feel all the weight of the hand which governs them. It follows that the Antifederalists are in Congress the most ardent defenders of the Constitution, completely convinced that when the people feel the check which has been given to them, they will begin to be uneasy and to demolish an edifice which is not yet solidly enough established so as not to be shaken by the least wind. It is remarkable, My Lord, that although these secret motives now divide almost all the members of Congress and the debates are sometimes very animated, they never betray each other by mutually reproaching themselves for their bad faith. But it results from this diversity of interests and views that for three months the House of Representatives has been able to decide, as to finances, only the following points: one, that it is proper to accumulate funds in order to pay the foreign debt, the domestic debt, and the arrears of interest due on these two items; two, that with the consent of the domestic creditors, it is necessary to modify the debt by a new loan while proposing the following alternatives—to fund two thirds at six per cent interest and to pay one third in western lands at twenty cents an acre or to fund two thirds at once and at the end of ten years the remainder at the same rate; three, that from this year they will see to accumulating the funds necessary for these payments but that the sums raised will serve first for the payment of the interest due to the subcribers to the new loan and that the surplus will be paid to the other creditors at the rate of four per cent while reserving to them, however, the right to receive the complete six per cent when the finances of Congress will permit it.

***

O'Dwyer, pp. 426–29. Otto's letters included in *DHFFC* were usually written over the course of days, and even weeks, following the day they were begun. The omitted text describes additional ways and means that might be proposed ("expedient") and the terms of the Appropriations Act [HR-47].

[1] That is, called him a liar; when done publicly, it was intended to provoke a challenge to a duel.

John Trumbull to John Adams

You may easily conceive how much I was pleased, & flattered by your very friendly & confidential letter of the 6th instant.[1]

At the beginning of the war, he who could advance principles the most agreable to popular pride, & the most destructive to all energetic government, was the best Whig & the greatest Patriot. Many of these, who rose into high rank at that time, were not superior as Politicians to the Levellers & King Jesus-men in the times of Cromwell.[2] As we have improved in the science of Government, they have lost their popularity. You have named several of them in your letter, not one of whom has escaped the lash of our political Satirists, & lost his influence with the intelligent part of the community by adherence to his original principles of Democracy.

I agree that the strongest *Envy* against You lies in the Breasts of the two Men You mentioned [*Samuel Adams and John Hancock*], who could not bear your elevation above them—Each of them probably flattered his own vanity with an expectation of the Rank of V.P.—Hancock particularly, after his grand manoeuvre of limning forth,

"With all his imperfections on his heels,"[3]

to propose nonsensical amendments to the Convention of Massachusetts,[4] supposed himself almost sure of the appointment—not knowing that the whole affair was planned & conducted as a political measure by men of more discernment than himself. These two Gentlemen have undoubtedly exerted all their influence to render You unpopular, & to some of their dependants, I am told You are indebted for an attack in metre, intended for a Satire,[5] published some time since at the Southward—But their influence is so diminished, that they have been wholly unsuccessful in the New England States, beyond the circle of their immediate connections.

The real opposition is more to your principles than your Person—& this prevails most in the Southern States. The People in the Southern States are half an age behind us in the knowlege of Policy & the true principles of Government—Aristocratical in their habits & feelings, they are absurdly advocates for a pure Democracy—They must certainly in time become more enlightened, and I hope, especially that the *Antient* Dominion [*Virginia*] may improve as She grows *older.*

The clamour about your Birth, as it has no foundation, has never made any impression in New England—but You are a Witness how frequently it has been echoed in the Southern Papers.

I believe You may thank New England for the penurious grant of your Salary—But I have no reason to believe that any personal insult was intended. High Salaries are always a subject of popular clamour in New England—The Votes of our Senators & Delegates [*Representatives*] on that question were calculated on motives of Self interest, to preserve their own popularity. And after all, the uneasiness on account of the *high Salaries* & wages granted at the last session was very general among us, & the clamour exceedingly loud, till it was quashed at once by the President's Tour thro' New England,[6] & absorbed in the bombastic enthusiasm of our public addresses.

I doubt with You, whether any Man but Washington could at present support the Constitution—But were he dead, I am sure none who has been thought of as your Rival, could support it while You were living & neglected. Jefferson is little known at the Northward, & it would be impossible to persuade our Great Men in New England that he is greater or wiser than themselves. We have an high opinion of Maddison's abilities, tho' it has lately been lessened by his advocating an impossible scheme of discrim[*in*]ation among the public Creditors—To suppose he did not perceive this impossibility would detract from our esteem of his talents—If he did perceive it, we can only ascribe his conduct to the desire of increasing his popularity in his own State, or to motives of envy against the Secretary [*Hamilton*]—But we have never thought of him for V.P.—Mr. Jay is the only Man, who possesses in any considerable degree the general confidence of the Northern States, or is talked of among us as qualified for that Office—But no Party could be formed against *You* in his favour among us.

There is no uneasiness to the danger or even to the unpopularity of the Government from your continuance in Office, but there would arise the greatest confusion from your resignation, which for that reason, I am sure You cannot seriously think of.

ALS, Adams Family Manuscript Trust, MHi. Written from Hartford, Connecticut. The concluding portion of this letter was written on 17 April and is excerpted under that date, below.

[1] Actually Adams's letter of 9 March.

[2] The King Jesus Men, better known as Fifth Monarchy Men, and the Levellers, were radical Puritan groups active in England during Oliver Cromwell's Protectorate in the 1650s. Their religious fanaticism (particularly of the first group) induced them to agitate for a total social upheaval in anticipation of Jesus' imminent thousand-year reign—the fifth and last world empire, following that of the Romans.

[3] "With all my imperfections on my head," Shakespeare's *Hamlet*, Act I, scene 5.

[4] The Massachusetts ratifying convention had been sitting for almost three weeks when a "caucus" of Federalists that included two future members of the FFC (Dalton and King) privately persuaded the popular Governor John Hancock to publicly throw his support behind an unconditional ratification of the proposed federal Constitution, with nine recommendatory amendments (at least one of which was said to have been authored by King). Hancock's proposal of 31 January 1788, immediately supported by Samuel Adams, has been credited with turning the tide in favor of ratification, which took place on 6 February (*DHROC* 6:1119–20; for Hancock's proposed amendments, see the same volume, pp. 1381–82).

[5] A reference to "The Dangerous Vice ——. A Fragment" (Boston, 1789; Evans 21736), generally attributed to Edward Church. Church had mentioned Adams as a character reference in two unsuccessful bids for a revenue appointment in his adopted state of Georgia in May and July 1789. "A Republican" claimed to have discovered the "small manuscript Poem" during a recent trip "to the Southward," and furnished lengthy extracts to Boston's *Massachusetts Centinel*, where they appeared on 22 August 1789. No imprint or newspaper printing originating in the South has been located.

[6] Washington began a highly popular public relations tour of Connecticut, Massachusetts, and New Hampshire on 15 October 1789 and returned to New York City on 13 November.

Letter from London

In the important business of the slave trade, the National Assembly of France have given their decision, declaring that they do not mean to interfere with any species of commerce carried on by the West-India islands, and desiring their colonists to assemble together, and settle their own affairs, as seems most expedient to themselves.[1]

All the sea-ports of France, from Dunkirk to Marseilles, are all full of rejoicings, on account of the decree which the National Assembly made the eighth of this month, concerning the slave trade. Couriers were immediately sent off to carry them the news as the decree passed. At the 'change, and in every public place, the merchants met and felicitated themselves on the event, as much as if the greatest victory had been gained over a foreign enemy. All the vessels in the several ports hoisted their flags in sign of joy.

NYP, 12 June (the date on which members of Congress would have seen it); reprinted at Philadelphia.

[1]On 8 March France's revolutionary National Assembly tried to prevent the spread of egalitarian ideals and safeguard slavery and the slave trade by adopting resolutions of its colonial committee that exempted France's colonies from the country's new constitution and Declaration of the Rights of Man.

OTHER DOCUMENTS

Samuel Meredith to Henry Hill. ALS, John Jay Smith Manuscript Collection, PPL at PHi. Addressed to Philadelphia.

Reports "fears & hopes in the different Members about the Assumption"; "ultimate fate of the proposition doubtful, many are for procrastination others are for bringing it to an immediate decision & are proposing for that purpose amongst themselves that they will not suffer any other business to be taken up until that is concluded"; the length of the session depends on a speedy decision.

Richard Henry Lee, Journal. Brock Collection, CSmH. This journal includes Lee's expenses en route.

Left Alexandria, Virginia, for New York.

WEDNESDAY, 31 MARCH 1790

Cool (Johnson)

Pierce Butler to Alexander Gillon

A singular event took place in the house of Representatives about two hours ago. In order to give you an adequate idea of it I must go back to last summer. On the anniversary of the Cincinatti Col. Hamilton delivered an oration;[1] in the course of which he drew a comparison between the Militia & standing [*Continental*] army; the first he called the mimickry of soldiery. Bourke often mentioned it as more than indellicate; but in the course of a long speech, which he made this day on the assumption, he took occasion to praise the gallantry of the So. Carolina Militia "notwithstanding said he, the affront given them by a Gentleman now high in office last summer in a place and at a time when it cou'd not be resented; he took an unfair advantage: and I now embrace this opportunity to say in the presence of this house that it was a lye: & that Col. Hamilton told a gross lye"[2] The Senate having adjourned early I happened to be in the house. I was surprised & hurt. How must it end? they are both Men of spirit. I wish that neither of them had expressed themselves as they did. Hamilton has a large family depending much on his life I believe.

I thought I should have heard from you by [*Capt. William*] Elliot. I had not a line nor even a newspaper from any one in Carolina by him. I stood alone the only Member of Congress from there without information of the state of things.

Suppose You send forward to your correspondent here the indigo you bought He can remit you I believe for it.

It is possible the State debts will be assumed; it is very probable they will.

A Gentleman here has begged of me to get him all the laws Our State have passed from time to time on our state debt. Do me the favor to get them & send them to me. You never sent me the other papers I wrote to you for, are You grown lazy?

The assumption of the State debts produces some warmth in the house of representatives. The distresses of Carolina & the low price of property there are the only things that induce me to be in favor of the measure. If I vote for it, it must be from these considerations for there are with me many strong objections against it. It will next to annihilate the state Governments; of course, to make use of very common language, the weakest go to the wall. Yet the temporary relief to Carolina from the adoption will be great. I profess I feel a difficulty—possibly I shall yield my judgement of the future consequences that I think will arise from the assumption, to the present distress and necessity of Carolina. Nothing ever appeared dearer to me than that posterity will be sorry for the assumption that is in Carolina. Yet You Gentlemen of the Legislature have unanimously instructed us to vote for it. On your heads be the sin. Long speeches unattended to are made by some to go home to their constituents. I'll answer for it those who make them do not expect to make one convert in their favor; but these speeches with the printer's glossery read well at a distance.

Have you done any thing for me with Bize or Colcock[3] I am persuaded I need not entreat you to attend to these two objects for me. You well know that they are very interesting to me.

How do the trees & plants turn out? I hope well.

FC, Butler Letterbook, ScU.

---

[1] For background on the affair of honor touched off by Burke's belated response in a House speech of this date to a speech by Hamilton at a Fourth of July observance sponsored the year before by the Society of the Cincinnati, see *DHFFC* 8:476–80.

[2] *DHFFC* 12:915–16.

[3] Hercules Daniel Bize was a principal creditor to Butler, who had stood as guarantor for Daniel Bourdeaux's defaulted loan from Bize (*Butler*, pp. 50–51, 509). Job Colcock was one of Butler's debtors.

Tench Coxe to James Madison

I recd. your favor of the 28th. instant by yesterdays post.

I find the idea of a landed fund for the encouragement of manufactures is an old one in my mind. On looking over the little address to the fr[*ien*]ds. of Manufactures in 1787[1] I observe I have hinted it there. You will excuse me therefore, if I wish not to part with it sooner than can be avoided. An infringement of the constitution is a matter never to be intentionally done—at this time an imputation of it ought not to be hazarded. I am not however clear that this case comes at all into view under the Constitution. The United States possess rights that constitution does not contemplate. They are the lords of the fee in all those lands that do not lie within the bounds of any separate state, and which are within the territorial limits settled at the treaty of Paris.[2] They could sell those lands and apply the money to such uses as they saw fit before the late reform of our Government. They also held them independently of any Idea of the severalty of the states. They held them as the representatives of the Sovereignty of this country by right of conquest. I think it necessary to shew by what clause in the constitution their rights of property in the lands in Question have been diminished, or the application of the Monies, for which they might sell them, limited. I consider them as a property intirely different from the funds to be drawn from the people of this country by the powers of the Constitution, which was intended as supplementary and not as the ~~entire~~ sole law of the land. I apprehend that a recurrence to the preceeding course of events, the preceding State of things, the law of Nations and the common law will be found necessary & admissable in many federal affairs. I have hastily retouched this subject, not to draw you into a discussion of it with me, which will waste your time without any resultting benefit, but to suggest the idea of a distinction between the rights of the Sovereign power of the Union in the Case of the western territory & the great mass of political rights they possess.

I had applied my Sunday morning to what I consider as a pious work, some notice of the affairs of R. Isld., before your favor reached me. I had not intended it as argumentative, because I hoped for matter from you. I am sorry to find that it is nothing more than that general depravity, ~~of~~ with which it is too plain that those people are justly chargable. I enclose you the paper above alluded to in the form & manner of which I have endeavoured to address ~~to~~ the seeds of honest & serious feeling which I believe remain in the hearts of the most corrupted people.[3] There is one point on which I have not, from delicacy, laid quite the stress I now think I ought to have done. I mean the personal character of the President which I find every where impressive. It has been so much the custom to seize every opty. to plaister with the praises this excellent gentleman, that I wished to be very brief whenever I found it proper to mention him. It is probable I may use some other notes wch. I have made this unhappy case of R. Island. I own I have great fears of their Obstinacy—and think their reformation an object of the first magnitude to the United states, and interesting in a high degree to every lover of Mankind.

We [*have*] an arrival here of 20,000 dollars in Specie from Amsterdam—the beginning of the tide of coin which a few years of peace must pour into this country. We have unpleasant advices of the middle of Feby. from Spain. The Markets there are very unequal to the prodigious shipments that have been made to the ports of that Kingdom. The arrivals of foreign Ships however continues to be such in our ports, that the farmers are not so likely to suffer, as the merchants, who have already shipt.

I will mention to you *confidentially* that great pains have been heretofore taken to restrain Applications to the general Government on the subject of slave trade. A very strong paper was drawn & put into my hands to procure the signature of Dr. Franklin to be presented to the federal convention—I enclosed to the Dr. with my opinion that it would be a very improper season & place to hazard the Application considering it as an overzealous act of honest men[4]—A s[*e*]cond attempt was made at the meeting of the Government in 1789, wch. was with great difficulty restrained. This third attempt was less opposed because it was believed that the public Debt would have been adjusted before it could be presented. The language of the Society's application is however very free from reflexions—The address of the friends is impolitic and unhandsome. Yet I think the subject has been much tortured, and the errors of the Quakers in point of decorum have been in some degree apologized for by the manner of discussing their Memorial. I lament the interruption of the important business of Congress—and the exposure of some sentiments of our American legislators that have escaped upon this occasion. These remarks I make confidentially to you confiding as I always shall do in your charitable allowance for the errors of my mind.

It appears to me advisable to have the Rhode Island paper reprinted in one of the New York Gazettes, that is least friendly to the constitution.[5] If it is not done within a few days I submit to you whether this step may not be of use.

ALS, Madison Papers, DLC. Written from Philadelphia. Enclosed "Notes upon Spanish Wool" in an unknown hand.

---

[1] *An Address to an Assembly of the Friends of American Manufactures* (Philadelphia, 1787; Evans 20305).

[2] Under the terms of the Treaty of Paris (1783), ending the Revolutionary War, the territorial limits of the United States ran from the unmarked northern state line of Massachusetts (present-day Maine) along the current boundary to the Lake of the Woods, and southward along the Mississippi to the thirty-first parallel. By the end of the FFC, undisputed and

exclusive federal jurisdiction extended to all the territory lying outside the thirteen original states, Kentucky, Vermont, and the part of Georgia that would become Alabama and Mississippi.

[3] Coxe, writing as An American, addressed the people of Rhode Island in the voice of the ghost of its native son, Gen. Nathanael Greene (*FG*, 30 March).

[4] On 2 June 1787, the Pennsylvania Abolition Society adopted a petition imploring the Federal Convention "to make the suppression of the African trade in the United States a part of their important deliberations" (Pennsylvania Abolition Society Papers, PHi). The petition was never presented on the floor of the Convention.

[5] An American (see n. 3, above) was reprinted in *NYP*, 3 April.

Benjamin Goodhue to Michael Hodge

Congress are upon the Assumption, and have got the subject again, very unexpectedly into the Committee of the whole house, this is progressing in a retrograde direction, it was done under pretence of giving the N. Carolina members, two of whom [*Ashe and Williamson*] are here, an opportunity of offering their sentiments on this question—the subject labours and what will eventualy be produced from this important bussines. I cannot satisfy my own mind, sometimes I am pretty sanguine of success at others I have my doubts. Our numbers are so nearly divided as to afford frequent opportunities of manuvering and perplexing a question which its opponents are so zealous in defeating. I most sincerly wish as I regard the peace of the Union and the interest of our State Creditors, that the measure may succeed.

ALS, Ebenezer Stone Papers, MSaE. Place to which addressed not indicated.

Louis Guillaume Otto to Comte de Montmorin

Since the president moved into the comte de Moustier's mansion, he lives with much more pomp than before and fulfills perfectly the expectations of the public. In order to make him resemble the King of England in every way they celebrate his birthday in every state and the Society of the Cincinnati especially have resolved to celebrate every year. Those [Cincinnati] of South Carolina have even presented him with a congratulatory address expressed in the most flattering terms. Always careful not to give offense, the president has replied in the most gracious manner but without once using the term *Cincinnati* which alarms the extreme democrats because it suggests an order of nobility. In Philadelphia they have struck a medal of the president for subscription and the legislature of New York has voted $20,000 to build him a residence; by his prudence and moderation the president continues to merit all the marks of affection and despite his great care not to display any prejudice for any foreign nation he has permitted himself finally to say for the first time *in public* a kind word for France. In responding to an address presented to him by Catholics he added "I hope that you my fellow citizens never forget the part that you have had in the establishment of our government, *nor the important assistance of a great nation that professes the Catholic religion.*" Although the president's sentiments with regards to France may be well known, Sir, I have always attributed his reserve to the impression that must have been made on him by the rumor raised among the English during the war that he had been secretly paid by the French. The president is ordinarily very gracious and modest in those sorts of responses, but he knows to take a firmer and more elevated tone when his dignity is compromised. Georgia having presented him with an address that included some indirect reproaches that he had not supplied more effective aid against the Indians, he replied curtly "that he used the powers the Constitution gave him in the manner that seemed to him the most suitable."

Mr. Jefferson who has finally arrived here and answers perfectly to the opinion that we have formed of him, has already given public proof of his modesty and his good disposition towards France. The citizens of Alexandria [Virginia] having presented him with an address of thanks for the support that he obtained from our government for the commerce of the United States, he told them "truth and candor oblige me to declare that you owe that support *solely* to the friendly disposition of a nation that on every occasion showed itself ready to adopt the means capable of strengthening the ties of a reciprocal interest and friendship." In no case does Mr. Jefferson deny these sentiments; for resources, riches, learning, friendship, and good disposition towards Americans, he places France above all nations and he tires neither of praising it nor of exposing the true and presumptuous instances of the haughtiness and vainglory of England and its hatred for Americans. In accepting the office of secretary of state Mr. Jefferson has submitted to the desire of the president and the public, which follows the preference he has for France. He has started out here with the simplicity of a true republican, his modesty and affability have won for him the hearts of those who for the first time have seen and confirmed the attachment of their old friends. Finally, of all the Americans who have been to France, Mr. Jefferson is, after Dr. [Benjamin] Franklin, the only one who sincerely feels gratitude for the welcome reception he met with. These arrangements are rather more satisfactory, Sir, since the most influential men put extreme confidence in Mr. Jefferson and think that if the United States has the ill fortune to lose the president, the secretary of state will have a better chance than any other to succeed him. There is no more question of Mr. Adams, who has lost all his credit the better one has understood him; there are even some people who doubt he can ever be reelected vice president. Too monarchical in his sentiments, he has even had the imprudence to extol the British Constitution on every occasion with no regard for the principles of the country in which he lives, principles which at the commencement of the revolution he himself had in some ways inspired. Mr. Jefferson is like all the men in the South, republican in spirit and in heart, with the gratitude, to which he is very susceptible, that one does not ordinarily find in a free country. We have so much reason to rejoice at seeing at the head of foreign affairs a man as fair and obliging as Mr. Jefferson and I believe that in every case we can count on his friendship.

Copy, in French, Henry Adams Transcripts, DLC. Received 2 July. Otto's letters included in *DHFFC* were usually written over the course of days, and even weeks, following the day they were begun.

Richard Peters to James Madison

I know your Time is so much occupied that unless on some very *important Occasion* it ought not to be interrupted. I send you a Pamphlet given to me by a Member of our House [*the Pennsylvania Assembly*] Mr. Herman Husbands.[1] As he reprobates the System of Finance it will not be the less pleasing to you on that Account. Having drawn the Principles of the federal Government from higher Sources than we ever thought of he must be a prodigious Genius. I never saw before the Reason of the Jews being federalists 'till I percieved their Fondness for Brokerage was drown'd in their Attachments to their Friends of the old Testament. We must have Husbands in the [*federal*] House of Representatives as he is of the same Side tho' from deeper Motives with some who are already there & who seem to want a Lift.

If Husbands's *Balderdash* does not amuse you it affords me an Opportunity of assuring you of the sincere Esteem with which I am affectionately yours.

[*P. S.*] Please to present my affectionate Compliments to Mr. Jefferson of whose Arrival in our City I was not apprized 'till he had departed for N. York. He has a Head for deep Speculations, perhaps our great political Investigator may afford him some Amusement.

ALS, Madison Papers, DLC. Written from Philadelphia.

---

[1] Herman Husband (1724–95) was a Quaker farmer who became the principal spokesman and publicist for North Carolina's Regulator movement, which sought greater power for politically disenfranchised back country farmers beginning in the mid 1760s. After the movement was militarily suppressed in 1771, Husband settled outside Pittsburgh, Pennsylvania,

where he continued to agitate for political and economic rights in tracts that frequently cited Old Testament prophecy as inspiration. Peters refers to Husband's *Dialogue between an Assembly-Man and a Convention-Man* (Philadelphia. 1790), E-45861. See Woody Holton, "'Divide et Impera': *Federalist 10* in a Wider Sphere," *WMQ* 62, 2(April 2005):175–212.

Bennet Ballew to John Sevier

WITH infinite pleasure I heard of you being appointed commander in chief [*of the militia*] of the district where you reside, which will give great satisfaction and be very pleasing to all well wishers of the western country.

I know that friendship and true generosity reigns in your soul, that pride and ambition is far from your character, which will do honour to the dignified station the legislature have been pleased to place you in.

Matters of great moment call for our most serious attention and deliberation: I called a general council of several nations together, they received the agreeable news and papers from the honourable Commissioners[1] with great alacrity. With indefatigable pains I laboured to introduce every pacific measure, and cultivate a friendly intercourse between the citizens of the United States and those nations; and for the advantage of both parties in future, I have formed a sort of constitution, similar to that of the federal union, which I expect to have ready for the press by the last of July, as we have appointed to meet at the mouth of the Tennesee river, on the Ohio, (Representatives sent by the different nations are Cherokees 12, Chickasaws 8, and the Choctaws 20,) the 30th day of June next; there to enter into a full union, adopt such laws and regulations as may tend to civilization. Notwithstanding the emissaries from Europe and Louisiana, all the principal men are on my side, except a few that have been disappointed in getting commissions with us, who listen to the foreigners; it will make me extemely happy if I can compromise this affair and bring about the glorious work of civilization.

I received a letter lately from Colonel [*Alexander*] McGillivray, informing me he would prevent his Indians from committing hostilities until further orders; I cannot help saying it is with reluctance I carry on my plan, because it makes our nation an object, which they think is a matter worth their notice. I have also had three messages from different foreign powers since I wrote last, they give me some uneasiness, but hope to get relief soon. Pray do all you possibly can with the [*North Carolina*] Assembly, for peace with the Cherokees we must have; I am sorry to say the white people are daily making depredations on their settlements. (The Cherokees, Chickasaws, and Choctaws, are so well pleased with the thoughts of being like the white people in Congress, that they have sent messages to all the neighbouring tribes to attend the grand council at the mouth of the Tennesee. They have already made some laws regulating the trade of their country, dividing their lands, &c. and one which I much approve, viz. no person is allowed to carry more than three gallons of spirits into the nation at one time otherwise it will be confiscated; as was the case of Alexander Dromgold who thought his influence could carry him through, but soon found himself mistaken.) I heartily wish you all success and happiness.

[Philadelphia] *Pennsylvania Mercury*, 6 April. Addressed to Cross Creek (present-day Fayetteville), North Carolina. The dating is based on a similar letter that Ballew wrote from Richmond, Virginia, to a "Gentleman" in New York City on 31 March (*NYDG*, 13 April; *NYDA*, 14 April), reporting on the union formed by the Cherokees, Chickasaws, and Choctaws. Ballew is writing as a diplomatic agent of this "United Nations" of Indians. The letter is addressed to Sevier as a North Carolina state senator and brigadier general of the state militia; his victory in the congressional election for his district on 8–9 March was not announced until 1 April (*DHFFE* 4:361, 363). This letter, or a paraphrase of it, was published at Windsor, Vermont; Portsmouth, New Hampshire; Newburyport, Boston, and Pittsfield, Massachusetts; Albany, Poughkeepsie, and New York City (*NYDA*, 8 April; *NYDG*, 13 April; *NYP*, 15 April), New York; Elizabethtown, New Jersey; Philadelphia; Annapolis, Maryland; Richmond and Winchester, Virginia; and Charleston, South Carolina.

[1] Benjamin Lincoln, Cyrus Griffin, and David Humphreys, the American commissioners sent to the southern Indians in the fall of 1789.

Letter from Charleston, South Carolina, to New Jersey

The petition of the people called Quakers, presented to Congress, on the subject of slavery, has made as great an uproar in these southern States, amongst the slave-holders, as St. Paul's preaching did among the silversmiths at Ephesus; and like them they cry out with one accord, This our craft is in danger, and ye know by it we have our wealth.[1] I believe that it would be more safe for a man to proclaim through this city, that there was no God, than that slave-holding was inconsistent with his holy law; for from the Clergy down to the Peasant, I have heard them defend this inhuman diabolical practice with indignation against every friend to their freedom—yet it is hard to find an advocate for the cause of God, though his laws are daily violated and trodden under foot, unless it is their occupation and interest so to be—And notwithstanding there are many high professors of the Christian name, yet, like the rich man in the parable, they spare of their own flocks and herds, and instead thereof sacrifice the liberty (if not the lives) of their fellow-creatures, and for no just reason under heaven (only might overcomes right) unless it is because their skin is of a darker hue—But what is still more strange, there is a greater noise, and more acclamations to be heard in these southern States on liberty, than in all the middle and northern ones beside. If the fabrick is founded on inhumanity, tyranny, oppression, vice and immorality, in fact they have a larger share than all the rest; but if on equity, justice, humanity, and that golden rule of doing unto others as we would they should do unto us, they have no part nor lot in the matter; nor is there (on those principles, except amongst a few emigrants) the least type or shadow of it left; for I have been both an eye and ear witness in this, and a neighbouring State* in particular, where husbands have been separated from their wives, wives from their husbands, parents from their children, and children from their parents, without the least prospect of ever meeting again in this vale of tears, while their mutual embraces, tears, and lamentations, were enough to pierce the hardest heart (if not adamantine to all good) yet no more feelings of humanity were seen on the occasion, than is common with you round a sty at the tying and separating a parcel of swine: and as the lucre of gain is the main spring that actuates almost all here, it is a matter of no importance to the seller, who the purchaser is, or what he is called, whether a Christian, Jew, or Turk, (often but very little to the poor slave) for like an Algerine, or Turk, he exposes them by publick sale to the highest bidder, (the same as brutes are with you) while the silent tears that often flow down their cheeks, serve only for a bit of diversion, instead of exciting a pity or blush to humanity—so effectually is common humanity banished out of these southern States, as well as that golden rule of doing as we would be done by.

*Georgia.

[Philadelphia] *Pennsylvania Mercury*, 24 July 1790; reprinted at Northampton and Stockbridge, Massachusetts; Newport, Rhode Island; Middletown, Connecticut; New York City (*NYDA*, 31 July [the date on which members of Congress would have seen it]); Burlington, New Jersey; Philadelphia; and Wilmington, Delaware. The piece may have originally appeared in a non-extant issue of the [New Brunswick, New Jersey] *Brunswick Gazette*. For background on the Quaker antislavery petitions, see *DHFFC* 8:314–38.

---

[1] In the first century A.D., the silversmiths of Ephesus (in present-day Turkey) were famous for crafting costly shrines to the local goddess Diana. The threat to their livelihood posed by Paul's successful missionary work led to a short lived uprising against Christian proselytizing (Acts 19:23–41).

Other Documents

John Adams to William Cranch. ALS, privately owned in 1957. Place to which addressed not indicated. The unlocated enclosure, "Character of an Honest Lawyer," was printed in [Boston] *Independent Chronicle*, 20 April (extraordinary). It is an excerpt of a longer piece of the same name that was printed in London in 1676 and authored by Henry Care (1646–88), a British legal essayist and pro-Catholic polemicist.

Encloses "the Character of an honest Lawyer, which I pray you to have printed in every Newspaper in Boston."

Benjamin Goodhue to Stephen Goodhue. ALS, Goodhue Family Papers, MSaE. Addressed to Salem, Massachusetts; franked; postmarked.

The brig sailed the day before for Lisbon with 3300 bushels of corn, half on Goodhue's private account; "the assumption labours, and I do not know what will be its issue"; expects to send some money home with the next post.

Jeremiah Hill to George Thatcher. ALS, Chamberlain Collection, MB. Written from Biddeford, Maine. The score refers to the number of posts since Hill had heard from Thatcher.

"IIII Don't you see my tally Stick."

Richard Price to John Adams. ALS, Adams Family Manuscript Trust, MHi. Written from Hackney, in London.

Introduces the bearer, Count Paolo Andreani.

George Thatcher to Jeremiah Hill. No copy known; acknowledged in Hill to Thatcher, 17 April.

George Thatcher to Sarah Thatcher. ALS, Thatcher Family Papers, MHi. Place to which addressed not indicated.

Discusses bedding for their family and "the man, or boy, who lives with us"; asks whether to buy "bed-tick," and will forward goose feathers via Boston at the first opportunity; encloses celery seed and directions for planting; "it is the very best kind of Sallad; especially in the winter"; suggests she consult with Matthew Cobb or Dr. (Benjamin) Porter for more advice; "gardning, as well as every species of agriculture, is a part of Science I never had much relish for, & I find these things are less and less alluring every day I live."

Benjamin Thompson to Thomas Jefferson. ALS, Washington Papers, DLC. For a partial text, see *PTJ* 16:282–83.

Office seeking: consul at a French port, and, in the meantime, an appointment in the "Office of Foreign Affairs"; mentions New Jersey delegation, Madison, and Vining as references.

William Samuel Johnson, Diary. Johnson Papers, CtHi.

"Visits."

GUS, 31 March.

The [Virginia] *Norfolk and Portsmouth Chronicle* "informs that the Hon. *John Sevier* is chosen a Representative of the United States for the State of North-Carolina."

[Richmond] *Virginia Independent Chronicle*, 31 March.

George Mason appointed Senator in place of Grayson.

[Portland, Maine] *Cumberland Gazette*, 12 April. This is probably a summary of a letter written by Thatcher to the newspaper's editor, Thomas B. Wait.

"By letter from Newyork of March 31 it appears that Congress had not then determined on the Assumption of the State Debts; and whether they finally would, or would not be assumed, was still uncertain."

March 1790 Undated

William Ellery to John Adams

Engaged as you are in public business, and this State not having shown a disposition to join the Union I did not wonder, although I could not but regret, that my letter should remain so long unanswered.

I wish that our affairs now afforded a prospect of a speedy accession.

Before you receive this letter you will have heard of the proceedings of our Convention. They met, framed a bill of rights, collected a long string of amendments to the Constitution, ordered them to be laid before the people at the annual meeting for proxing for Genl. Officers and chusing representatives, and adjourned to the fourth monday in May. Unless something is done by Congress which will make the Antis feel they will in my opinion adjourn again and again. The Feds will continue to exert themselves; but the Antis appear to be steeled against the most powerful addresses to their reason, their passions and their interest. It is the opinion of many that they are supported and hardend in their opposition from the quarters you mentioned; but it cannot yet be reduced to a certainty. The report of the Committee of your State, appointed to consider what further Amendments are necessary to be added to the Constitution of the United States,[1] will give an handle to our Antis to put off our accession. If it is the wish of your State that this State should speedily become a member of the federal government it appears to me that their conduct is altogether impolitic.

Some of our Antis have had the courage to say, that if the State stood out but six months longer, there would be such insurrections in the other States as would overturn the New Government; and that their opposition would be the salvation not only of our own but of the thirteen States.

Others talk as if they really thought Congress would still extend their lenity and indulgence to the trade of this State. When the Federal members of the Convention, in order to obtain an adjournment to the last monday in March, represented in strong, pathetic terms, the distresses in which the Sea-port towns would be involved at the expiration of the Act reviving the suspension of the navigation Act,[2] an Anti replied that they were in no danger, that upon an Application of the merchants further indulgence would be granted; for Congress would do any thing to favour their friends.

The operation of the navigation act will have no influence upon the Antis until the fall, and then they will probably rather pay an advanced freight, and receive less profit upon what they may have to export to the other States, than accede to the Union.

Something must be done.

An Address to the Genl. Assembly at their Session on the first wednesday in May next, setting forth the advantages which will result to the United States and this State from her accession, and the necessity which Congress will be under to use rigorous measures if she should still persist in her opposition might answer the purpose.

A requisition of our quota of the public debt with a declaration that, unless it was collected at the time assigned, an equivalent would be distrained would have a good effect.

If Congress have a right to consider us as a part of the United States, and to extend their Genl. Government to us, and would make a declaration that they have such authority, and would exercise it if the State did not adopt the Constitution, I have no doubt but that it would be adopted at the next Session of the Convention.

Wisdom as Father [*Roger*] Sherman used to say, in difficult cases, is profitable to direct, and the great Council of the United States are [*posse*]ssed of a large share of it.

Uncertain as it is when this State will adopt the New Government, yet it must sooner or later become a member of the Union, and federal Officers be appointed for it.

I am greatly obliged to you for the assurances you have given me of your readiness to promote my views.

When I first wrote to you my view was, through your influence and that of other friends, to obtain the Office of a district Judge, I have since thought that the Office of Collector of the Impost for this district would be more beneficial and suit me better. I was sometime Naval Officer of this State, while we were under the British Government, and was a Commissioner of the Admiralty under Congress; so that the business of the customs would not be altogether new to me if I should be so happy as to be appointed a

Collector of this district. The present custom house offrs. of this district are a worthless sett of Antis. Who are the candidates for the federal collectorship I do not know; but if early and long public services, and losses in the cause of liberty and my country can give any pretensions to an office I shall not be behind the foremost candidate, and if an addition to these, I should be favoured with your recommendation to the President & Senators I should not doubt of success.

ALS, Adams Family Manuscript Trust, MHi. Written from Newport, Rhode Island.

[1] The Massachusetts legislature's joint committee report recommending additional structural amendments to the Constitution; see Stephen Higginson to John Adams, 1 March, n. 1, above.

[2] The North Carolina Act [HR-36] extended until 1 April 1790 "and no longer" the provision of the Collection Act [HR-23] exempting Rhode Island ships from the tonnage and impost due on foreign shipping.

Miers Fisher to Brissot de Warville

***

The Politics of this Country are in a State of Fluctuation as well as those of France—the mode of funding our National Debt has been a long subject of Dispute in Congress & we do not yet certainly know the Event; I had prepared a small Sketch for the Purpose which I communicated to some of the Members at New York, it was well liked by some of them & the preliminary Proposition was moved by A. White Esqr. of Virginia & lost whereby the whole was stoppd[1]—I hope Congress will be wisely directed in this Business but I dont yet see an End to it.

***

ALS, incomplete, Scioto and Ohio Land Company Papers, NN. Addressed to Paris. Fisher's letter to Warville dated 5 July in the same collection indicates that this letter went by way of the "March packet."

[1] Through his connections with the Pennsylvania delegation, Fisher had an influence on such issues considered by the FFC as lighthouses, revenue collection, the Bailey Bill, and the antislavery petitions. In this case, the advice, perhaps in the form of resolutions, was not received favorably. On 8 February Fitzsimons proposed resolutions that became the basis for the House debate on public credit for the next several weeks. On 22 February White unsuccessfully moved that the second resolution, "That permanent funds ought to be appropriated," be amended to read, "That funds ought to be provided." Alternatively, Fisher may have been referring to White's motion on 25 February, adding a proviso to Madison's motion the day before for liquidating and crediting each state's expenditures. Madison's motion passed but White's proviso was disagreed to (*DHFFC* 5:840n).

Thomas Jefferson to James Madison

I forgot to take your final opinion last night as to the mode of conveying *official communications from the states through the channel of the President to the two federal houses.* whether it will be best to do it

1. by message from the presidt. through mr. Lear?
2. by do. through Th. J. appearing personally?
3 by do. through do. by way of letter?

be so good as to say what you think. I must be troublesome to you till I know better the ground on which I am placed. indeed this consultation is by the desire of the president.
R.S.V.P.

AN, Madison Papers, DLC. Addressed to Madison, "of the Virginia delegation in Congress." This note was written in the days immediately before Jefferson conveyed Madison's thoughts to Washington; see 1 April, below. It could have been written as early as 23 March, the day after the first conference between the President and the secretary of state on several issues. Before Jefferson's arrival, communications from governors requesting legislative action were delivered to both houses of Congress by Tobias Lear. This practice was continued throughout the FFC. For more on this issue of executive-legislative protocol, see *PGW* 5:302–3.

Pamela Sedgwick to Theodore Sedgwick

I have Just receivd my dearest Mr. Sedgwick your favour of the 17 Instant I cannot say my love that I am Greatly Dossopointed that you did not arive at the time propoesd. I can so Poorly bear to have my Inclinations croossed that I seldom allow my self to depend on any event which I Consider as uncertain—I really Valleu your Convenience and Comfort so much more than any Pleasure I can enjoy separate from your Happiness that I did not ardently wish you to encounter the fatigues I sopoesd nesecary to bring you home at this season Lest theay might prove dettrimental To your health—I fondly hope by the time the roads are Tollerable your duty to your Country will not detain you Many days from your famely—we all impatiently wish for the Ariveal of that hour that shall welcome the Tenderest of Husbands and the Kindest of Parents to the Arms of a Lonely and Cheerless Family—I consider It as a very unfortunate circumstance that I can never get your letters by the first post after their written.

*** will you Be pleasd my dear to Tell Agrippa [*Hall*] that I will send his money by the first safe opportunity.

The Children are all Better of their Colds—Little Roberts Leg fails him fast. evry day almost wee can perceive it grows Less—will you my Love be

so good as to continew to write me and Let me Know when we may again Look For you home—may Wisdom from above direct all your Councels and Prosper them for the happiness of this Nation—Harry stands by me and desires me to give his duty to pappa and thank you for his Letter and Tell you he has had a very bad Cough—these are his own words—Lenox Court Rise last Eveing—I am my dearest best beloved friend ever yours.
[*P. S.*] Pray let Agrippa get me some Garden seeds—Shall I make a memorandam of what Supplies are Nesessary for the family and send It to you or shall I send by Mr. [*Thomas*] Dwight to N. York—Pray have you heard that the Goverment are Indebted to you one thousand pound for the Jennesee Land you Purchasd of them—A Blessed house we have had to make Bargains advantagous to their Constituents—I am affraid you will not be able to read half my Letter Theay are always wrote in hast ~~a poor excues~~.

ALS, Sedgwick Papers, MHi. Place from which written not indicated. The omitted text discusses Mrs. Theodosia Burr, and the management of Sedgwick's rental properties.

Thomas Lee Shippen to [*Earl of Shelburne*]

*** The Secretary of the Treasury has proposed to Congress a system of Revenue which will be in a great measure adopted. Provisions will be made pursuant to it, for the faithful discharge of all our public engagements and the punctual payment of the interest of our debt. The Secretary at War has brought forward a plan for the organization of our militia, by which if it be adopted we shall have a considerable effective force amply suff[*icien*]t. for all the purposes of defensive war without the ~~vies~~ vices or the dangers of a standing army. Mr. Jefferson who is appointed Sec. of State has been so short a time arrived from Europe that he has not been able yet to digest his diplomatic system. Congress have tyed up his hands for the present year with respect to foreign appointments by voting the trifling sum of £15,000 sufft. for all ~~foreig~~ such expenditures. Some attempts have been made to put a stop to the farther importation of slaves and to effect a gradual abolition of slavery—but they have not been successful. Indeed, slavery seems so engrafted into the policy of the Southern States; their circumstances are so peculiar, that it is rather problematical whether it wd. be a desireable event. The newspapers inform us that our good friends Mr. [*Lord*] Grenville & Lord Hawkesbury are employed in forming a treaty of commerce with the U.S.[1] I am so anxious solicitous for the event that I care not by whose means it is brot. about. Provided we receive the benefit no matter thro' whose hand it comes—I think, I always have thought and your Lordship contributed not a little to confirm & strengthen my opinion that we were designed by

Nature, and that every thing concurs in the same plan, the U.S. & G.B. to be forever in the closest union of interests tho' our governmts. are distinct and that every thing should be done on both sides to banish animosities and to effect a close & firm alliance. The best & most durable basis for such a connection is already laid undoubtedly in the sameness of interest which exists between us.

FC:dft, Shippen Family Papers, DLC. The editors are printing this letter because Shippen, who was living in New York City, was the nephew of R. H. Lee, and because in this letter he communicated information that was likely to reach the British government. The recipient is identified by reference to a prior letter written in 1789 in the Shippen Papers. The dating is based on the content, although it could have been written in early April.

[1] *GUS*, 20 March.

[*Peter Silvester*] to an Unknown Recipient

We complain, as it were instinctively, of the tediousness of our public deliberations in almost every state in the union. But the slowest of them move with the rapidity of a comet, in comparison with those of the federal head. It would be a good rule if the speeches of gentlemen, like the sales of an auction, were to be struck off by an inch of candle. Upon the subject of discrimination the ideas would turn on few points; yet, what will you think of a speech of two hours, when, perhaps, the session of the day is but three? If you read what is published, you will find that these speeches are but the same copies of each other as to substance, though the manner may be widely different; In fact, we seem to be enchanted to a spot. We talk a great deal; but we advance not forward. Hamilton's plan has been before Congress three weeks, and we are not even in the title page—At this rate the Lord only knows when we shall get through it. Some of our orators remind me of the Dutchman, who, in celebrating the literary accomplishments of his father, said he was certainly the greatest writer of the age, for he had published seven folios already. The rate of interest appears to me the only question, and here we shall find a strange contrariety of sentiment among the members: but when the final settlement of our final certificates will take place, is not even within the reach of conjecture.

Extract of a Letter from New York, [Lansingburgh, New York] *Federal Herald*, 22 March. Internal evidence shows that the letter was written early in the month. The editors identified Silvester as the likely author because the letter appears to have been written by a member of Congress and Silvester represented the district that included Lansingburgh.

Letter from Philadelphia

The situation of Dr. Franklin is such, that some politicians, finding he cannot be of much further service to them, presume to abuse him, who heretofore were as extravagant in extolling; but if they had the opportunity of conversing with him, would discover his faculties of mind to be vigorous beyond all expectation, and his judgments on the natural rights of men unfettered by the shackles of slave-holding, and therefore was induced to sign the memorial on the principles of justice and conviction.[1] I am not disappointed to find, that his name has galled some of those, who, if he was present, would be able to instruct and shew what might be done without violation of the articles of the constitution.

It must be a very bad cause which requires scurrility to support it. The abusive invectives against the friends of humanity are unworthy of attention, and must, with all judicious persons, turn to their own shame. If they could prevail with themselves dispassionately to read some of the essays which have been published on the subject of *slavery* and the *slave trade*, their sentiments must change: so that I attribute their warmth of opposition to prejudice and ignorance.

FG, 26 March, From a late New-York Paper.

---

[1] As its president, Franklin signed the Pennsylvania Abolition Society's petition presented to Congress in February. Reference to his lucidity is a defense against Jackson's speculation on the floor of the House that only senility could have induced Franklin to do this; see John to James Pemberton, 8 March, volume 18. For background, see *DHFFC* 8:314–38.

Interesting

A letter from New York to a gentleman in Boston, received on Sunday by a private conveyance, announces, that the question on the Assumption of the State Debts had been taken in the House of Representatives, and passed in the negative, by a small majority. This determination, it is said, was had immediately on the N. Carolina members taking their seats (who unitedly voted against it) and without much discussion on the subject. The friends of the measure expected it would shortly be called up again, and hoped that on a fuller discussion it would be adopted.

ONE Massachusetts member, it is said, opposes the Assumption of the State Debts—upon what principle we are not able to say, as we have never yet seen his arguments on the subject among the debates of the House.[1]

[Massachusetts] *Salem Gazette*, 6 April. The vote referred to was the 29 March vote to recommit the question of assumption to the COWH; it passed 29 to 27.

[1] While neither Grout nor Leonard was recorded to have spoken during the second session, Carnes to Goodhue, 7 March above, indicates that Grout was the member.

Letter from Scotland

The friends of America, amongst whom I reckon myself, in this country, can already perceive a change in our trading people, since the proclamation was issued for allowing the importation of American grain.[1] The Baltic, from whence Britain has been accustomed to receive a supply of grain, is no longer able to afford us relief in case of scarcity, all the grain in that quarter being demanded for the supply of their own armies. The consequence is, that the prospect of being supplied by America, when no other country can afford us assistance, has altered people's minds much in your favour, which I hope will continue to increase until the two countries become firm friends and allies.

NYDG, 8 June 1790 (the date on which members of Congress would have seen it).

[1] Facing poor harvests throughout Europe, Great Britain's order in council of 4 December 1789 lifted the prohibition on the importation of American wheat that had been imposed in June 1788 because of fears of infestation by the "Hessian Fly," a weevil thought to have been introduced in America by German mercenary troops during the Revolutionary War (Charles R. Ritcheson, *Aftermath of Revolution: British Policy toward the United States, 1783–1795* [New York, 1971], pp. 200–202).

Other Documents

Matthew McConnell to Andrew Craigie. ALS, Craigie Papers, MWA. Written from Philadelphia. For background and documents relating to the petition of Richard Wells and Josiah Hart petition presented by Scott on 1 March, see *DHFFC* 8:264–68.

Seems to be no danger of assumption being postponed, but supposes Scott "will endeavour to embarrass the House with that evil designed petition about the old paper money"; asks "your oppinion about the senate, & say if any thing new."

Robert Oliver to [*William Sizer*]. *NYP*, 24 July 1790 (the date on which members of Congress would have seen it). Written from Marietta, Ohio. Printed first in [Northampton, Massachusetts] *Hampshire Gazette*, 25 May.

Reports of serious problems with the Indians are unfounded; "they appear to be very friendly, and to bear a great regard for the Yankies, as they call us"; description of Marietta and the surrounding area.

Theodore Sedgwick to Benjamin Lincoln. No copy known; acknowledged in Lincoln to Sedgwick, 6 April (where a torn page prevents knowing which date in March is referred to).

Observations on Dr. Williamson's Letter. *Massachusetts Magazine; or, Monthly Museum*, March 1790. Signed "L." For Williamson's letter of 14 September 1789, see *DHFFC* 17:1549.

Refutes Williamson's letter attacking the teaching of Greek and Latin.

Eligibility of Members of Congress to Hold State Office

On 22 March, the New York legislature adopted a joint resolution stating that holding elected state office was incompatible with serving in Congress. The state Senate immediately declared the seats of state senators Hathorn, Laurance, and Schuyler vacant. Three days later the House declared state representative King's seat vacant. The action was widely reported in the American press.[1]

In addition to the valid concern that a person who took oaths to support both the federal and state government faced conflicts of interest, the New York resolution had been in part politically motivated. Senator Schuyler was the leader of those New Yorkers who opposed Gov. George Clinton and his powerful political faction, and the Senator reacted quickly and strongly by publishing two lengthy anonymous pieces criticizing the New York legislature. Signed "Tammany," after the legendary Lenni Lenape, or Delaware, sachem Tamanend (ca. 1628–98), they appeared in *NYDG* on 31 March and 2 April. In the same newspaper on the latter date, Z wrote an address to the citizens of New York supporting Tammany. A Citizen responded to Tammany with a lengthy refutation in *NYDG* on 7 April, causing Schuyler, once again as Tammany, to defend his argument in the same newspaper on 13 April. The newspaper debate ceased after A Citizen, writing in *NYJ* on 26 April, identified Schuyler as Tammany.

While no member of the Massachusetts congressional delegation sat in the state legislature, Leonard and Partridge both held local public offices in the state. Soon after the first congressional election in 1788, the legislature informed Gov. John Hancock that under the state constitution Leonard could not sit as a probate judge concurrently with serving in Congress. Leonard gave up the office; he did however retain his seat on a local court of common pleas. On the other hand, the state executive council ruled that Partridge could continue to serve as a county sheriff while he sat in Congress. Bills to prevent members of Congress from holding state office failed in the Massachusetts legislature in 1790 and 1791, although apparently their defeat was tenuous. In January 1791, when David Sewall fought to be allowed to serve simultaneously as federal district judge and state representative but was rejected almost unanimously by the state House, "Many good Federalists" were sorry that he had "made a question of the business."[2]

A similar bill failed in Connecticut in June 1790 after extensive public debate, following which Huntington nevertheless resigned his seat on the state legislative council. In January 1790, the Delaware legislature also defeated a similar bill revealingly entitled "An Act for the Preservation of the Independence of the Delaware State." A proposed bill in Maryland met the same fate in late 1790,[3] but another was successful in 1792, forcing Charles Carroll to give up his seat in the United States Senate so that he could continue as a state senator. In 1790 North Carolina forbade members of its congressional delegation from serving in the legislature.

Article I of the constitutions of South Carolina and Pennsylvania, adopted in 1790, prevented members of Congress from serving in the state legislature; this meant that Clymer and Fitzsimons were no longer able to sit in the Pennsylvania legislature as they did in 1790.

---

[1] See, for example, [New Haven] *Connecticut Journal*, 31 March; [Hartford] *Connecticut Courant*, 7 April; and *FG*, 30 March, stimulating pre-existing concern about this form of dual office holding in other states.

[2] Henry Jackson to Henry Knox, 30 January 1791, Knox Papers, Gilder Lehrman Collection, NHi.

[3] William Vans Murray to Charlotte Huggins Murray, 27 November 1790, Murray Papers, DLC.

[*Philip Schuyler,*] Tammany to the Independent Electors of the City of New York, 31 March

A FELLOW CITIZEN wishes to call your attention to a measure in which he thinks you deeply concerned. Occupied with the important deliberations of Congress, your attention has been withdrawn from the no less important transactions of your own legislature. Questions of the greatest moment are there agitated, without interesting your feelings; your dearest rights are invaded, without exciting alarm or regret. To what cause can we attribute this lethargic effect? Fashionable as it has been to disregard the operations of state policy, this cannot account for your looking with indifference on a late alarming declaration of your Legislature, and the degrading expulsion of those whom you had chosen to represent you. Another reason may be given: averse to a multiplicity of offices in one hand, you regarded only the evil, and did not question the power to cure it. But when you examine the question on constitutional principles, and view the pernicious tendency of its decision, you will then, I am persuaded, think differently on the subject: you will then see, in the declaratory vote, a violent attack on the constitution; and, in the consequent expulsion, an infringement of your rights, daring in itself, insulting in its manner, and unsupported by even the semblance of argument.

That a Legislature can exercise no other powers than those expressly delegated to them by the people, is an axiom in politics. If then, it can be shewn that no such power as that exercised in the case to which I allude has been given by the constitution of this state, all arguments of inconvenience are at an end: constitutional evils cannot be removed by legislative acts; and, however inconvenient a representation in the national, as well as state legislatures, by the same person may be, it is an inconvenience of which you are the only judges, and which you alone can remove. The constitution of this state requires no qualification but a freehold, in a senator; and any male inhabitant, who possesses the confidence of the people, may become a member of the assembly. Every additional qualification, then, required by the Legislature, infringes the rights of the people, because it contracts the circle in which they must find their representative. If the Legislature have a right to declare, that no man holding an office under the United States shall represent you, they have the same right to prescribe the wealth or the rank of your member; and as the right to enlarge is the same as that to restrict, they may open the door that is shut by the constitution, and fill the assembly with bishops and parsons.

Where, then, shall we find an argument in favour of this measure, at best so rash and imprudent? Not in the constitution; *that* lays no restriction: not in the measures of former legislatures: their every act most strongly disavows it; their members always served as delegates to Congress: not even in the conduct of its warmest advocates. If the two offices are incompatible, they are authors of the evil; they sent the Senators to Congress; they suffer them to keep their seats for two whole sessions; they sit with them; they vote with them; they make them partakers of their council; and the very men who do this expel them. Is this legislative wisdom, or the inconsistency of folly? Compared to such conduct, the changes of a weather cock are stability, the chances of the die are certainty itself. If as the vote declares, it is incompatible with the constitution that they should keep their seats, how will the advocates of this measure justify their conduction permitting men, who had no right, to legislate for their constituents.

Reflect on this, my fellow citizens; it merits your attention; examine the arguments I have used, and you will find that your rights are betrayed by ambition, or surrended by folly.

I shall, to-morrow, pursue the subject, nor will I quit it until you are convinced how greatly you are wronged. Although unknown, I feel a secret pride in thus addressing you when abler pens are idle, and triumph in being the first public opponent of a measure so subversive of your rights.

NYDG, 31 March.

[*Philip Schuyler,*] Tammany to the Independent Electors of the City of New York, 2 April

Vir bonus est quis? Qui *consultra patrum* qui legos *jurisque* servat.[1]

An ardent desire to promote your interests, a sincere attachment to your constitution, and a firm persuasion that an attempt is made to abridge the one and violate the other, all prompt me to continue this address, to place the abuse before your eyes, to point out its pernicious tendency, and, if possible, to excite such a marked resentment of the measure as will induce *your* representatives, at least, to take care how *they* violate their charge. The two houses have, by a solemn act, declared that it is inconsistent with the constitution of this state, and that of the United States, that any person in the state legislature should at the same time be a member of, or hold any office under the United States. When you look for those prohibitory clauses, they will be found to exist only in the vote of the legislature; neither in the one constitution, nor the other, is a word that, to any but a mind biassed by interest or blinded by ignorance, will carry the idea; and I am credibly informed that, when the business was agitated in the assembly, no arguments but those of inconvenience were urged in its defence. Is, then, the voice of legislation become the organ of falshood? And not content with depriving you of your rights, with creating a jealousy of the national government, must they also dishonor themselves? If not a respect for the constitution, at least a regard to their own reputations should have deterred them.

I have heard a justification attempted that scarcely deserves a reply: but I am determined to answer every thing that comes, though "questionable," in the shape of argument. It is said, then, that each house is the judge of its own members, and that this power includes the right of expulsion. That each house has the right of judging whether its members are properly chosen, and the power of punishing an infraction of its rules by expulsion, is undoubtedly the fact, and so far the principle is just; but when applied to the present case it is not only ill-founded, but absurd in the extreme. Let us suppose (*for the sake of argument only*) that a majority of the present house of assembly understood both Latin and Greek, and that a member should be elected who was unacquainted with either: might not these men of learning, with equal propriety, declare that they are judges of *qualifications* of their members, and that a man without Latin or Greek, who had never read Tully and admired the beauties of Demosthenes,[2] was *unqualified* to have a seat in that house? and might they not, with equal justice, expel him? Indeed there is one pretty *good reason* why the case I stated will not happen, this session at least; and, however absurd it may seem, it flows directly from this assumed power of judging.

It is not the absurdity only of the proceeding that calls your attention: had it been only ridiculous, former events would have inured us to its effects: but there is danger in it. So open a violation of your rights can never be innocent; nothing can justify, and extreme danger scarcely excuse it. In this instance its consequence may not be felt; but what secures the future? The precedent once formed, pretexts will not be wanting: *expulsion from the Senate may create an object for ambition*; weak men may become the instruments of the designing, one infraction will lead to and justify another, until the majesty of the constitution, violated by its guardians and deserted by its friends, shall fall beneath the attacks of those who ought most firmly to defend it. Your efforts, then, will be too late, and the miseries of an unsettled government will punish your present neglect.

Exert yourselves, then, my fellow-citizens, while you have the power; and, at the ensuing election, withdraw your confidence from those who tamely surrendered or basely betrayed the rights of their constituents. Shall I be told that, if they have infringed the constitution, yet they are *good and undesigning* men, that it was innocently meant, that it was inadvertently agreed to? Away with reasonings like these. Where the priviledges of the people are concerned, carelessness is treason, ignorance the worst of crimes: and, in politics, the only *good man* is the one described in my motto, who obeys the laws and preserve the rights of his country.

The wickedness that originates pernicious measures, the folly that adopts, or weakness that yields to them, and the indolence that boasts an unavailing desire to serve you, are equally dangerous to you.

NYDG, 2 April.

[1] He is the good man who observes the decrees of his rulers, and the laws and rights of his fellow citizens (Horace).

[2] Tully, Marcus Tullius Cicero (106–43 B.C.), ancient Rome's most famous orator, and Demosthenes (384–322 B.C.), his Athenian counterpart.

Z to the Citizens of New York, 2 April

Is it not an extraordinary circumstance, my friends, that, in an age and country enlight[*en*]ed as our's, a measure should be adopted by government, highly injurious to the most sacred of your rights, without the least remonstrance on your part?

The late concurrent resolution of the Senate and the Assembly of this State—tending to sow the seeds of jealousy and mistrust between the general and state governments, breathing the spirit of antifederalism and disunion, subversive of that liberty secured to you by your social compact, insulting to your understandings, and robbing you of your privileges—has made its appearance in the public prints, and scarce any one has dared to complain. There was a time when such a daring invasion of your rights would have called up your resentments. How, then, shall we account for your present apathy? Is it that, engrossed by the government lately framed for the union, you think the priviledges secured to you by your state constitution beneath your attention? Remember that the security of the one is essential to the existence of the other; that the state constitutions are the pillars on which the grand federal edifice is rested: any injury, therefore, which any one of those experience, weakens the whole fabric.

These are not imaginary assertions: they are solemn truths, and deserve your attention. Let us examine the resolution.

The incompatibility it speaks of, is declared to exist in the constitution of this state and of the United States—a falshood which all who read may detect. What are the disqualifications created by the former?

As they relate to the seat in the legislature of the state, they are restricted to the clergy alone; as they respect a seat in Congress, they are confined to certain judicial and executive officers, and even to some of these with certain exceptions. Under the latter, they are not extended beyond the circumstances of age, citizenship and residence. The legislature of the state is the creature of its constitution. Can it then alter that which gave it existence? If it can, whence is the power derived, and what are its limits? If it can create new disqualifications, without even the form of law, if it can alter the constitution at pleasure, what security have we that it may not resolve itself into a permanent body? After violating that clause of our constitution which declares no member of the state shall be disfranchised, or deprived of his rights or priviledges, but by the law of the land or the judgement of his peers, what may we not apprehend? On constitutional grounds, then, the measure cannot be justified; nor can arguments drawn from inconvenience give it the least support. Of these, the people, and not the legislature, are the proper judges. What, then, can be advanced in its vindication? Some flimsy politicians have endeavoured to shelter themselves under the right which each house has to judge of its own members: but is this an authority to create disabilities? or is it only a power to decide agreeable to some known law of the land, or parliamentary rule? The thing speaks for itself. Judges are in no case, where liberty dwells, at once the makers, the expounders, and the executers of the law.

Nor is the absurdity of the measure less glaring than its unconstitutionality. Who placed two of the gentlemen,[1] who were the first victims of the resolution, in the double capacity contemplated by it? Its very framers. If the incompatibility ever existed, it must equally have existed at the first meeting of the present assembly in July last, as now, and should have been an argument against their election. Such an idea, then, I believe, entered the head of no man; and that it has been but lately conceived, is evident from the House of Assembly having elevated one of the gentlemen [*Schuyler*], since their second meeting, to a seat in the Council of Appointment. View the thing as you will, it must be found replete with absurdity, subversive of your rights, and injurious to the success of that infant government you have just given being to. The legislature itself caused the thing it reprobates: it prohibits, without any legal sanction, your being represented by the man of your choice; and excites a spirit of hostility against a government, as yet too feeble for your happiness. Rouse, then, and shew you disapprove of the measure.

NYDG, 2 April.

[1] King and Schuyler, who had been appointed United States Senators in July 1789 by the same session of the state legislature that declared them ineligible for their state office.

A Citizen to the Citizens of New York, 7 April

Latet anguis in herba—A snake lurks in the grass[1]

As the late resolve of the Legislature, vacating the seats of such members as were in Congress or held offices under the United States, has received the approbation of the wise and moderate of all parties, is sanctioned by the general voice of America, and recognized by the principles of the constitution and the maxims of an enlightened policy—the friends of the gentlemen affected by it ought to court its oblivion and patiently submit to the decision of their country: but disappointed ambition, always connected with the vindictive passions, has prompted an attack, as destitute of argument as of decency, upon the representatives of the people, in which they are caricatured as the organs of falsehood, the victims of folly, and the betrayers of liberty.

The publication to which I allude may be seen in the DAILY GAZETTE, under the signature of TAMMANY. If this writer had confined himself to fair and modest reasoning, and to an impartial representation of facts, he, would have merited honor and praise; because, however deficient he may be in understanding, or however mistaken in opinion, he would have shewn a praise worthy disposition to call the attention of the people to a subject important to their happiness: but when a scribbler, with no other gift of persuasion than elegant language, attempts to impose upon the public, falsehood for truth, invective for argument, and malevolence for patriotism, and destroy the well-placed confidence of the constituent in the representative body, he is guilty of high treason against society; and it is the duty of every good citizen, to enter into an examination of the subject, to expose the false reasoning of the writer, and to vindicate the conduct of the representative. Let us then, my fellow citizens, consider the subject with all the apathy and composure which an honest indignation against a demagogue of sedition will permit.

The fair and candid mode of prosecuting the inquiry, is not by considering the vote of the Senate and Assembly as a legislative act creating a disability not previously existing, but as a judicial exercise of a power vested in them by the constitution: that is, not to contemplate them as legislators *enacting a law* founded on ideas of expediency, but as judges declaring their opinion of *a law.* The only question, then, will be respecting the existence of the law, and the sole standards of decision, the constitutions of the United States and of this State. Happily for the public, the inquiry is easy: it is neither involved in clouds and darkness, nor does it reach above the level of a plain understanding. The jargon of lawyers may darken, but cannot illumine it; the honest and sensible citizen can form a just opinion upon the subject, without being swayed by the interested voice of the man of *magpye* eloquence,[2] or the intrusive advice of a person who can tamely submit to the dignified station of a tool, and sacrifice every sentiment of independence and gratitude at the shrine of putative greatness.

It is an axiom in politics, which defies contradiction, that every legislature has a right to compel the service and attendance of its members. This position is warranted by our state constitution, where it gives the Assembly the same powers that were lodged in the Colonial Assembly; and it is expressly recognized by the constitution of United States.[3] If this right is with-held, the existence of the Legislature would depend upon the will and caprice of a minority, who, by withdrawing their attendance, might obstruct all the wheels of government. The establishment of a legislature necessarily involves the power of self-preservation, otherwise a *political monster* would be created; the representatives would be cloathed with the authority of governing the whole community, and at the same time deprived of the right of governing a part of the community; or, in other words, of the power of self-government. Order and subordination might reign in the constituent body, while the legislature would be a troubled theatre of anarchy and confusion. If the principle be admitted, how easy, how conclusive the application: if the same person be a member of Congress and the State Legislature, neither can compel his attendance without interfering with the rights of the other; and hence arises the incompatibility declared in the resolution. Could the Legislature send their serjeant at Arms to the Congress room, and drag their members to the Exchange,[4] without violating the rights of the federal government? The federal constitution requires the attendance of the Congress, and the state constitution the presence of its legislature; now if the same man is in both bodies, both cannot at the same time exercise their constitutional powers over him; and consequently, unless the writer of Tammany can prove what [*that*] he has something like the omnipotent power of ubiquity, or that the same man can be in two different places at the same time, the conclusion that there is a constitutional incompatibility in the two offices, is irresistible. The common objection, that the members of the legislature might serve in Congress under the confederation, is lighter in the scale of argument than dust in the balance. The same inference, drawn from different premises, savours more of weakness than sound argument. The old Congress was not a legislative, but a diplomatic assembly, and the state could recall its members and command their attendance at pleasure; nor had that honorable body any power to compel the presence of its members.

But, says this writer, the only qualification, required by the constitution in a Senator, is a freehold, and every male inhabitant may become a member of the Assembly: any other disability is consequently an abridgement of the people's rights. I would ask this *zealot for liberty*, whether the constitution, in express terms, prohibits the Governor or a Senator from being members of the Assembly? Whether it excludes women, infants, or aliens, from a place in the legislature? And whether it would be an invasion of liberty, or an infraction of the constitution, to vacate the seats of such persons, if elected? The framers of the government evidently entrusted this matter to the wisdom and discretion of the Legislature: and it ought to be governed by the spirit of the constitution, and only exercised in cases of the last importance. Reason cannot be easily reconciled to Tammany's construction of the powers of the Legislature, and particularly of the right to be judges of its own members; for if it only has, as he says, an authority to judge whether its members are properly chosen, and to punish infractions of its rules by expulsion, *convicts* and *negro slaves* may become legislators, and villainy in the representative out of the house may, in this respect, escape with impunity; while a violation of a parliamentary rule will expose to expulsion. The bold assertion of the author of Tammany, that the vote is an abridgement of the rights of the people, is almost too despicably weak to be worthy of a reply. If, as I have shewn, the power of compelling the attendance of the members was given to the legislature by the constitution, the right of electing the same man into the Congress and the State Legislature was surrendered, when the constitution of the general government was ratified; and how a non-entity can be abridged or destroyed, I shall leave to be decided by the voice of common sense.

Every constitutional exercise of power, that prohibits or prescribes certain modes of action, is with equal propriety an abridgement of the rights of the people. But is it not supremely farcical to hear such piteous whining, jesuitical complaints, about an invasion of liberty, merely because a few men are prohibited from holding two incompatible offices at the same time? For this *high-handed offence* a false alarm must be sounded; the public must startle from its lethargic composure, and hear, with the vindictive bitterness of rage, a dismal tale about its much injured servants; in whose behalf, the writer of Tammany addresses the people in the following melancholy notes:

"Your rights are violated because their ambitious views are defeated; your privileges of choosing are taken away because their chance of being chosen is destroyed. Rouse, then, and make their wrongs your own by adoption; sacrifice the men that dared to act contrary to their desires, though it may be coincident with your interests; become the mean instruments of their revenge, and the despicable vassals of their ambition. They have been cruelly treated; they can no longer *smile* in the Assembly, nor *bully* nor *bluster* in the Senate. One prop of their political importance has fallen away, and, unless you apply your necks and you shoulders to the other, their greatness will vanish into smoke."

Instead of violating your rights, instead of ruining your interests, my dear fellow citizens, this vote ought to be recorded in letters of gold: it is a *magna charta*[5] which secures your liberties against the enterprizes of ambition and the strokes of power: it promotes a circulation of offices, redoubles your checks against tyranny, and erects a barrier against Cesars [*and*] Cromwells. If this patriotic conduct in your Legislature does not command your praise and your admiration, you are either blinded by ignorance or cursed with ingratitude. You ought to consider that man as the meanest wretch in society, who would make your honest well meaning passions the ladder of his greatness, and pervert the holy spirit of liberty into a vehicle of personal resentment and aggrandizement, at the expence of your honor, gratitude, and happiness.

The writer again says, "they (the legislature) are authors of the evil; they sent the Senators to Congress; they suffer them to keep their seats for two whole sessions." A refutation of these abusive reflections, requires only a brief statement of facts. The legislature met at Albany for the express purpose of chusing federal Senators; their meeting continued only about two weeks, at the close of which Mr. Schuyler of the Senate, and Mr. King of the Assembly, were elected Senators of the new government. It was understood at Albany, by all parties, that those gentlemen were no longer to hold their seats in the State Legislature, and a general expectation of their non-attendance at a future period, together with the shortness of the meeting, prevented a definitive decision of the legislature on the question. There was, however, at least an implied understanding on the part of the persons deputed to Congress, at the time of their election, to relinquish their seats in the State Legislature. How this tacit agreement was fulfilled is well known to the public; and I should be sincerely sorry if the conscience of any man should prove a sting to his feelings upon that account. At an early period of the present meeting of the legislature, a motion was brought forward by an honorable member (whom the candid public will readily acquit of party spirit) substantially similar to the one agreed to, but the question upon it was procrastinated by means unnecessary to relate. But what does this reasoning of Tammany amount to, allowing it to be true? It proves not that the Legislature were wrong in vacating the seats; it is only an evidence of cool and mature deliberation, and at most shews that they were tardy in doing what ought to have been done before.

Hospitality is an exalted, though commonly a savage virtue. To receive a forlorn stranger with open arms, and to give him the best room in your house is benevolent in the extreme; but if the guest, like the viper in the fable, should rise up against his benefactor, would not every generous feeling of the heart revolt at such conduct? I trust, for the honor of human nature, that nothing in the remotest degree analogous to this, has occurred in the present case. Delicacy, however, cannot forgive the man who, with more than Capadocian[6] impudence, openly advocates his monopoly of honors, and in the face of day votes in his own cause. Prudence, in such case, must fly before ambition, and decency yield to presumption.

There is a certain class of men in every community who rise into popularity and consequence by the storms of party, and sink into their primeval insignificance in the calms of society. It is the interest and the policy of such characters to keep alive the heats of faction, and to blow up the dying coals of animosity. The public ought seriously to consider whether this aspiring writer has not this object in view, by his inflammatory writings.

NYDG, 7 April; reprinted in *NYDA*, 8 April, at the request of several members of the state legislature, according to Another Citizen.

[1] From Book III of the *Eclogue* by Virgil (170–19 B.C.).

[2] The magpie is traditionally regarded as an uncanny bird; hence, a cunning or devilish eloquence.

[3] Article I, section 5, paragraph 1.

[4] The New York state legislature met at The Exchange, located at the foot of Broad Street.

[5] A reference to the Great Charter, signed by King John under duress in 1215, which first acknowledged the rights of English subjects and the principle of the monarch's subservience to law. In Revolutionary America, it was frequently cited as the aggregate and bulwark of civil liberties.

[6] The Cappadocians were an ancient people who resided in the area of present-day east central Turkey.

[*Philip Schuyler,*] Tammany to the Independent Electors of the City of New York, 13 April

WHETHER the man who addresses be a "Zealot for Liberty," or a "Scribbler without the gift of persuasion," is a point of little importance: but it is one of the greatest moment, that you should be well informed on the subject of his address; that you should examine, with an attention bordering on jealousy, the conduct of your representatives, and know with certainty whether the measure they have adopted is an invasion of your rights or the "great charter" of your liberties; whether it should be written in "letters of gold," or blotted with infamy from the book of your laws. In this view of the subject, I am happy to find that my observations have been deemed worthy an answer from the *elegant writer and delicate satyrist* who addresses you under the signature of A CITIZEN. It gives me pleasure, because I am convinced that my principles are well founded, and that every discussion will but evince their propriety and shew the folly, inconsistency, and pernicious consequences of this violent procedure.

As the letter I speak of has been sanctioned by a republication, at the request of several members of the legislature, we must suppose the arguments it contains to be those on which the vote of expulsion was framed. If, then, these arguments can be clearly refuted; if it can be shewn that they are too weak to convince even credulity itself; that they evade, but do not answer the objections I formerly urged: if this can be done (and this, by the blessing of god, I will do) it then must follow, "as the night the day,"[1] that your rights, my fellow-citizens, your dearest, most important rights, have been either basely betrayed or weakly surrendered. The punishment for such conduct is in your own hands; but while I understand the constitution of my country and see it violated, while I feel the conscious dignity of a free citizen, something very different from the abuse, with which I am loaded, must prevent my sounding the alarm.

The question now submitted to the public is easily decided; any man who reads may determine it; and I agree with the citizen, that professional knowledge is not required in its solution. The power exercised by the legislature must be found in the constitution of this state, of the United States, or it is an usurped power. In this position I think we all agree: but the citizen tells you, that it is found in the constitution, and where? Why, concealed, until this time hid from every eye, in that clause that gives a right of compelling the attendance of its members to the legislature. The exercise of this right, in two bodies, upon the same members at the same time, you are told, is impossible without the gift of ubiquity. All this is most undoubted truth; and what is the result? Why, that the people of this state, when they adopted the constitution of the United States, expressly surrendered to Congress all right to compel the attendance of those whom they should elect to represent them in that body. But will it thence follow, that you are to be restricted in your choice in order to give the legislature the exercise of a power you had before deprived them of? Or how can this clause be made [*to rat*]ify a right of expelling every man who [*holds*] an office under Congress?

The whole of this defence, or rather an apology for an indefensible measure, is founded [*on*] a principle that you are told is an axiom in politics, "that every legislature has a right to compel the service and attendance of its members": a position than which nothing is more easily refuted. Every constitutional power is derived from the people; they may either give the right of compulsion to the legislature, or they may modify or withhold it; and many examples may be produced of governments without this power: Congress, under the confederation, is an instance of this kind. It is no answer to tell me that Congress was but a diplomatic body for certain purposes it was a legislative assembly, and in all cases the attendance of its members was necessary for the operations of government. Here, then, is an instance in which the people have refused, and I have shewn that in another they have restricted this pretended inherent right.

The foundation, then, being destroyed, the fabric of metaphysical arguments it supported must dissolve, and will, before the light of reason, vanish into air.

I am asked, with an air of triumphant exultation, "Whether the constitution expressly prohibits the governor, or a senator, from being members of Assembly? whether it excludes women, infants and aliens, from a seat in the legislature?" To the first of these questions I have a very short answer: the constitution draws a distinct line between the executive and legislative branches of government, which, while that constitution is preserved, can never be confounded; and most expressly prohibits any interference between the senate and assembly, by declaring them separate and distinct bodies of men: and even if it did not, as they are all constituent parts of the same government, no such absurd question can possibly arise. As to the case of women, infants and aliens, I would recommend to the Citizen, before he undertakes his next panegyric on the legislature, an attentive perusal of the constitution, and a tolerable acquaintance with the laws it has adopted: he will there find that *female sway* is to be apprehended no where but in the domestic department—that we are in no danger of foreign legislation—and that the wise framers of our constitution have in vain attempted to guard against the influence of *Childish measures*, by the exclusion of infants from office.

NYDG, 13 April.

---

[1] Shakespeare's *Hamlet*, Act I, scene 3.

A Citizen to Great Chief, 26 April

FROM your signature the sons of America were led to believe, that you were a lawful child, but upon investigation your illegitimacy is discovered, by your pompous interference in the cause of that liberty which you say the Legislature has deprived its citizens of, by vacating your seat, and the seats of your colleagues. You claim the honor of being the *trumpetor and centinel* of our rights, whenever the enemy approaches the sacred altar of (what is dearer than life) the *magna charta* of our liberties; but, sir, when the patriotic *citizen* addressed you, in plain language of truth and facts, your second attempt was like the severing of the limbs from the body: Thus you closed your expiring epistle, "The public was so well convinced of the tyrannising act of these Representatives, that further arguments were unnecessary." Pardon me, great sir, for assuring you, that the united voice of the state bears testimony against you and your junto—the *union* recoils at the idea of *voting in your own cause*. Your senatorialship will soon vanish in *fumo*,[1] and your adopted brother will feel the resentment of free Americans.[2]

NYJ, 26 April.

---

[1] Into smoke.

[2] A reference to King, who had moved to New York City at the end of 1788, having failed to be elected a Senator or Representative to the FFC from Massachusetts.

THE HOUSE INVESTIGATION OF WILLIAM DUER

An uncertain chronology, unjournalized House procedures, and a paucity of documents mark one of the most important precedents set by the FFC: the congressional investigation of an executive branch officer, Assistant Secretary of the Treasury William Duer.

Under the Articles of Confederation, all executive functions were performed by officers responsible to Congress, whose investigative power over any facet of governance—a legacy of Parliament's role as "the grand inquest of the nation"[1]—was never challenged. How this power may have been altered by separating the executive and legislative branches of government under the Constitution of 1787 was a question first discussed when Morris petitioned his colleagues in February 1790 for "some method of vindicating" his account keeping as superintendent of finance under the Confederation. Gerry opposed the appointment of a House committee to "enquire" into Morris's accounts, preferring a presidential commission "as placing the business in a more parliamentary and constitutional direction." However, a vocal majority of the House did not share Gerry's preference.[2]

Although no recorded speeches noted the distinction, Morris was not a current member of the executive branch when the House committee conducted its investigation into his accounts as superintendent. For that precedent, historians have routinely cited the investigatory House committee authorized during the Second Congress in March 1792, "to inquire into the causes of the failure of the late expedition under Major General St. Clair" against the Miami Indians of the Northwest Territory the previous November.[3] Even former FFC members who later also voted for or against the St. Clair committee seem themselves uncertain as to what exactly was at stake in the 1792 decision. Representative Smith (S.C.) admonished the House that a motion to investigate Arthur St. Clair's defeat "was the first instance of a proposition on the part of this House to inquire into the conduct of officers who are immediately under the control of the Executive." But either by their recorded speeches or votes, several of Smith's former colleagues who were also in the Second Congress expressed no such scruples against authorizing an investigation, be it by the President (in the opinion of Boudinot and Seney), or Congress (Fitzsimons, Hartley, Madison, Vining, and Williamson), or either branch (Giles and Steele). In no case did any of these former members of the FFC cite the investigation of William Duer in March 1790 as a precedent. But neither do any of them (apart from Smith) appear to deny the existence of an earlier precedent. Perhaps all references to it were deliberately muted because it was an unofficial proceeding.[4]

The sole evidence for that proceeding is a third hand account of a single reference made by Fitzsimons probably more than two years after the fact, during Maryland Federalist William Campbell's campaign for Representative John F. Mercer's seat in the third federal Congress.[5] In a "conversation" between the two candidates in June 1792, Mercer accused the secretary of the treasury of an "immediate Interest" in the securities speculation carried on by the assistant secretary, William Duer. Mercer told Campbell that his belief in Duer's malfeasance was induced by "strong Circumstances," likely meaning the reputation of his informant, Fitzsimons. Campbell repeated the substance of the conversation at a public meeting in Annapolis. Far from retracting any of his statements about Duer's treatment of securities holders, Mercer, who was present at the meeting, added that "a brokers Office was kept next door to the secretarys office for the purpose of buying up their Claims." The charge of misconduct against Duer does not necessarily prove or even imply Hamilton's complicity. Either for that reason, or indeed (as Mercer had hinted privately to Campbell) because it was thought that a sitting congressman's statement of the facts ought to remain discreetly beyond question, there is no evidence that Hamilton ever sought to refute that particular charge against his subordinate.[6]

Like the "secret" (unjournalized) committee that helped to avert a Burke-Hamilton duel in the first week of April 1790, the committee that investigated Duer appears to have been informal and unofficial and may have been composed of members of both houses. Unlike the Burke-Hamilton committee, however, there is no contemporary first hand report of it by a congressman.[7] Except for Fitzsimons' attendance and apparent chairmanship, nothing is known of the committee's membership or proceedings.

Chronology presents another challenge to verifying and assessing Fitzsimons' recollection (as recorded by Campbell, who heard it from Mercer). There is no consensus among the principal agents as to when Duer actually resigned, or at whose instigation. Duer's biographer states that his departure from the Treasury "came suddenly and unexpectedly." Yet letters from a close business associate reveal Duer's plans to resign, "at his own instance," as early as 13 March. On 27 March, Maclay noted Duer's anticipated resignation among the "small News of this day." From London later that summer, John Brown Cutting wondered whether the resignation was owing to Joel Barlow's success in Paris selling land for the Scioto Company in which Duer was so heavily involved. Hamilton's only letter to Duer on the subject, enigmatically referring to "the necessity of your situation" that "compels you to relinquish [*your*] station," has been dated around 4 April, based on evidence that Timothy Pickering in Philadelphia heard about the job opening on the evening of 5 April. On the other hand, given Hamilton's preoccupation with the possibility of a duel with Burke in those same first few days of April, it is possible that his letter acknowledging his friend and assistant's departure did not closely follow the event, and that Duer may have left as early as sometime in March but no later than 4 April. In a 1797 affidavit, Hamilton's successor, Oliver Wolcott, Jr., provides further corroboration that Duer resigned—forced or not—sometime in March 1790.[8]

When Duer left office is relevant to the dating of the congressional committee's investigation into his misconduct because it provides the only more or less solid piece of data in a chain of cause and effect. Another critical link in the chain is the fact that Fitzsimons took an official leave of absence from the House from 18 March to 1 April. Fitzsimons' possible return before his leave expired would allow for his committee's having taken some action in the last days of March, which also accords with Maclay's declaration on the 27th. Alternatively, the committee may have concluded its business before Fitzsimons left New York around the 18th, and its implications for Duer were somehow kept secret (from Maclay at least). This is the most likely scenario in the event that Fitzsimons did not return until 1 April since, between that date and Duer's departure, even if as late as 4 April, there would not have been enough time to conduct a fair investigation and subsequently to compel Duer's dismissal or resignation within a few days—as described by Fitzsimons in the document that follows.

[1] P. D. G. Thomas, *The House of Commons in the Eighteenth Century* (Oxford, 1971), p. 14.

[2] *DHFFC* 8:663–69, 12:801–3.

[3] *Annals* 2:493. The definitive administrative history of the Federalist era also gives pride of place to the St. Clair committee (Leonard D. White, *The Federalists* [Chicago, 1959], pp. 80–81). For a more recent elaboration of the orthodox interpretation, see James T. Currie, "The First Congressional Investigation: St. Clair's Military Disaster of 1791," *Parameters: U.S. Army War College Quarterly* 20(1990):95–102. Much of the blame for St. Clair's defeat focused on the mismanagement of the army's chief contractor, who coincidentally was William Duer (Stanley Elkins and Eric McKitrick, *The Age of Federalism: The Early American Republic, 1788–1800* [New York, 1993], p. 272).

[4] *Annals* (Second Congress), pp. 491–94.

[5] William Campbell (1756–ca. 1825), of Anne Arundel County, Maryland, a former captain in the Continental Army and founding member of the Society of the Cincinnati, was a planter with extensive real estate holdings throughout the state, most prominently in Frederick County. John Francis Mercer (1759–1821), a lawyer from Anne Arundel County, Maryland, served in Congress from 1791 until his resignation in 1794. The Virginia native graduated from the College of William and Mary in 1775 and studied law under Jefferson in between tours of duty in the Continental Army, from which he resigned as lieutenant colonel. He served in the Virginia legislature and in Congress, 1783–84. In 1785 he moved to Maryland, which he represented at the Federal Convention but left in protest before signing the document and later voted against ratification at the state convention. He served in the Maryland House of Delegates (1788, 1791–92, 1800–1801, 1803–6) and as governor, 1801–3 (*DHFFE* 2:239).

[6] *PAH* 13:222–23n. For background on Mercer's election year attack on Hamilton, see *PAH* 12:481–92. Contemporaries and historians alike almost always begin their list of Duer's questionable activities by referring to his "insider trading"—either leaking news that Hamilton would propose the assumption of the states' debts or sharing the Treasury's lists of (primarily southern) veterans with outstanding certificates or warrants for arrears of pay; see, for example, *PTJ* 18:649–58 and *DHFFC* 9:184–85. However, neither of these charges figures in Fitzsimons' explanation for Duer's departure from office.

[7] For more on the committee on the Burke-Hamilton affair of honor, see *DHFFC* 8:476–80.

[8] Robert F. Jones, "William Duer and the Business of Government in the Era of the American Revolution," *WMQ* 23(July 1975):410; William Constable to James Seagrove, 13 March, volume 18, and 4 June, below; Maclay to Rush, 27 March, above; Cutting to William Short, 14 June, below; *PAH* 6:346, 355; *DHFFC* 8:476–80; *PTJ* 18:653.

Certificate of William Campbell, ca. 14–23 November 1792

*** Mr. Thomas Fizsimmons had inform'd him [*John F. Mercer*], that during the second session of Congress, [*William*] Duer, assistant to the secretary, carried his Speculations to such extent as to prevent any Claimant scarcely getting an account passed against the United States, or at leest to cause such delay and difficulty in their Business as to oblige almost every one to sell his Claim for whatever could be obtained for it, and that he,

Duer, had always his Emissaries ready to become the purchasers. That this Conduct excited an Enquiry by Congress and that he Fitzsimmons as one of the Committee for that purpose, after an Investigation, waited on the Secretary [*Hamilton*] and informed him, he must dismiss Duer, or they would be obliged to report unfavorably, and that accordingly, Duer was in a few days dismissed. ***

LS, Hamilton Papers, DLC. For the full text of Campbell's "certificate," and the cover letter dated 23 November 1792 by David Ross, who solicited it and forwarded it to Hamilton, see *PAH* 13:218–28.

April 1790

Thursday, 1 April 1790

Cool (Johnson)

Aedanus Burke to Alexander Hamilton

I was prevented, by business, from answering your letter as early, this day as I wished. I shall now make a few remarks on the subject of it.

The attack which I conceived you made on the southern Militia,[1] was, in my opinion, a most unprovoked and cruel one. Whether the candour of your friends conveyed to you any intimation of it I know not: but the occasion will, I hope, excuse me if I assure you that Gentlemen from every quarter of the Union who were present deemed it a charge of a very extraordinary nature. As to myself, I have nothing to do respecting the feelings of others: I ever govern myself by my own. The insult, which I conceived was thrown at me, the too keen misery I felt from it: the recollection I had of it until yesterday: together with the concurrent testimony of a number of public, and private men who understood you as I did must be, with me, vouchers of equal authenticity with the extract you quote from your performance, which you will recollect you did not read in the delivery of it to the public—That you proclaimed aloud in the face of, I may say, thousands that the Militia were the mere Mimicry of Soldiery: That you spoke these words when you ran into the affairs of the War to the southward, and recounted the exploits of General Greene in that quarter, is not doubted and you will find it on enquiry in this City.

You may have forgot it, but some of your Friends and all your acquaintances have not forgot it. You told us besides, that there was not, to the southward even the Embers (this was the word, I think,) of Spirit to oppose the Enemy until Genl. Greene arrived there, when it is notorious that the Southern Militia under General [*Thomas*] Sumpter and other officers, in various desperate conflicts: the Militia of Kings Mountain, and other places, before ever Genl. Greene came to S. Carolina had turned the tide of fortune against the veteran troops of Britain; and Yet in sight, and hearing of some of us, who were the representatives of a brave Gallant people, was I told publickly that these Men were the mere mimicry of Soldiery.

The torture which the insult inflicted on me I had no other redress for, but to bear it; to call on you in that day would have been down right madness in me—You, on the high full tide of popularity, in your own City: I a stranger, of what little was known of me, unpopular, on the score of the cry of the day, against any one suspected of not approving the new Government: Had I called you to account, and hurt a hair of your head, I knew too well the Spectre of Antifederalism would have been conjured up to hunt me down; nor have I any sort of doubt, but that, from the party heats of that period, which thank Providence are now subsided I should have been dragged thro' the kennel, thrown into east river. And if yesterday I retorted on you rather harshly your own recollection will whisper to you, and your friends will tell you, if I mistake not, that you brought it on yourself. If I did it where you could not reply then are you exactly as I stood the day I alluded to; a situation, from which you may form some faint Idea, what bitterness you gave me to experience. Thus I have very candidly, in this disagreeable business explained my feelings and motives. The conduct arising from them was such as, I trust, will stand the enquiry of all whose approbation I am fond of: Men of Sensibility and honor.[2]

Copy, hand of Otho H. Williams, Williams Papers, MdHi. According to Williams's annotation on this copy, it was made from "Copies of Correspondence" enclosed in an unlocated letter from Burke to "Mr. T. S." in Baltimore, dated 16 April. This letter is a response to Hamilton's letter to Burke of this date, below. For the background on the duel that almost ensued between Burke and Hamilton, see *DHFFC* 8:476–79n.

---

[1] Hamilton's offending remarks were made during his eulogy for Gen. Nathanael Greene before members of the Society of the Cincinnati and others gathered at St. Paul's Church in New York City on 4 July 1789.

[2] This copy of the letter contains a postscript by Burke: "this answer was written the same day with Coll. H______'s letter—In the order of the correspondence it was Coll. H______'s next move—He waited, however, from the first until the fourth, when he sends his friend Mr. Rufus King to offer propositions of accomodation honorable to both of us, thro' Mr. Gerry, my friend, this offer was accordingly accepted by me."

Edward Carrington to James Madison

I will thank you to inform me whether it is likely that any thing will be done this session of Congress for establishing the emoluments of the Marshals office. this becomes an interesting question to those who must from duty be in Situations to incur expense, or hazard a neglect of duty by remaining where it will not be expensive. there was a temporary provision made at the last session by a reference to the allowances of the States[1]—this may probably do for the admiralty business, because the labour of conducting it under the State Government was nearly the same as occurs under that of the United States, and the fees were adapted to it. but as to the Civil business the case will be intirely different. for instance the Sherif of a County serves a Writ for 3/9. this for the State business is sufficient, because his service is confined within a Small district & he has many things to execute, besides that the collection of the Revenue is always in his hands: when Writs and other process are to issue under the Federal Govt. they will be but few and will require the service of the Marshal in various directions and at great distances. a sufficient quantity of business will not be found in any reasonable space to be formed into a district for the employment of a local deputy, the consequence must be that the Marshal will have to provide for the execution of every process by a hand who must in many instances ride a Number of days to serve a single process & the compensation will not even feed his Horse. I just mention this as the present State of the case, without presuming to say what establishment ought to be made. As soon as the Circuit Court has sat at Charlottesville,[2] established rules, & furnished a Seal, several writs will issue, which have already been applied for. they will run into several distant parts of the State, and I am satisfied, cannot be executed for many times the compensation the present Laws authorise. a moments reflection upon this circumstance must convince every Gentleman that something must shortly be done to support the office if it is to be continued. I am well satisfied from the view that I can now take of the business that no fees that it will be reasonable to charge upon the Suitors will be sufficient to sustain the office—Many other things must be made incidental to it, or Salleries must be given. I suppose some calculation has been made of considerable profits from the admiralty business—there has not however been a single Seizure in Virginia—I am led to trouble you on this subject from the situation of the affair, and seeing that ~~it~~ the session is somewhat advanced, and nothing yet said about it. I trust that your own view of the subject, and your acquaintance with me will exempt me in your mind from any charge of a disposition to be dissatisfied.

ALS, Madison Papers, DLC. Written from Richmond, Virginia.

[1] Courts Act [S-4]. During its third session the FFC dealt with the issue of the salaries of marshals in the Judicial Officers Act [HR-133].

[2] Each of the three circuit courts established under the Judiciary Act of 1789 was to convene twice yearly in each of the districts of which they were respectively composed. The middle circuit convened in the Virginia district alternately in Williamsburg and Charlottesville; it was first scheduled to meet at the latter on 22 May 1790.

Alexander Hamilton to Aedanus Burke

I have been informed that in the House of Representatives, yesterday, you made use of some very harsh expressions in relation to me.

As I cannot but ascribe so unprovoked an Attack to misapprehension or misrepresentation, I have concluded to send you an extract from the Eulogium pronounced by me on General Greene, of the part to which alone your animadversions could relate. It is in these words. "From the heights of Monmouth I might lead you to the *plains of Springfield* [*New Jersey*], there to behold the veteran [*Baron Wilhelm von*] Knyphausen at the head of a veteran Army baffled and almost beaten by a General without an Army aided, or rather embarrassed by small fugitive bodies of Volunteer Militia—the Mimicry of Soldiership."

From this you will perceive that the Epithets, to which you have taken exception, are neither applicable to the Militia *of S. Carolina* in particular or to Militia in general, but merely to small *fugitive* bodies of *Volunteer* Militia.

Having thus, Sir, stated the matter in its true light, it remains for you to judge what conduct in consequence of the explanation will be proper on your part.

FC:dft, Hamilton Papers, DLC. For background on the Burke-Hamilton affair of honor that almost resulted in a duel between them, see *DHFFC* 8:476.

Thomas Jefferson to George Washington

Th. Jefferson has the honor to inform the President that Mr. Madison has just delivered to him the result of his reflections on the question *How shall communications from the several States to Congress through the channel of the President be made?*

He thinks that in no case would it be proper to go by way *of letter from the Secretary of State*: that they should be delivered to the houses either by the Secretary of State in person, or by Mr. Lear, he supposes a useful division of the office might be made between these two, by employing the one, where a matter of fact alone is to be communicated or a paper delivered &ca. in the ordinary course of things, and where nothing is required by the President, and using the agency of the other where the President chuses to recommend any measure to the Legislature, and to attract their attention to it.

The President will be pleased to order in this what he thinks best. T. Jefferson supposes that whatever may be done for the present, the final management of business should be considered as open to alteration hereafter. The government is as yet so young, that cases enough have not occurred to enable a division of them into classes, and the distribution of these classes to the persons whose agency would be the properest.[1]

He sends some letters for the President's perusal praying him to alter freely any thing in them which he thinks may need it.

Copy, Miscellaneous Letters, Miscellaneous Correspondence, State Department Records, Record Group 59, DNA.

[1] For more on this issue of executive-legislative protocol, see Thomas Jefferson to James Madison, March 1790 Undated, above.

Henry Knox, Minutes for a Committee of the Senate

3dly. To prevent the intrigues, and depredations of the cunning and lawless whites ~~on the frontiers~~ and to carry into effect the decisions of Congress from time to time relative to the frontiers.

The design in 1787 by sullovan[1]—The orders given on that subject—The information of Congress to Mr. Gardoqui relative to those orders.

Unathorized expeditions to take Indian Country—Rogers[2] & others.

The late Sales of Georgia[3]—The method of touching that business—A Proclamation—what unless aided by troops would be a dead letter.

4thly. To prevent the usurpations of the public lands—To facilitate the Survey & selling the same for the purpose of reducing the public debt—The use of the troops to prevent usurpations to be proved by their conduct in 1784. 1785. 1786. & particularly in 1787. The expedition to post Vincennes.[4]

The Country N[*or*]th. of the Ohio

The Cession of N. Carolina

The probable Cession of Georgia

5thly To cultivate the friendly dispositions of The chickasaws & Choctaws, and to expand the trade to them, agreably to the treaty of Hopewell.[5]

The numbers illustrations and importance of those tribes and their situation to assist In the coercion of the Creeks if necessary—and ~~perhaps~~ possibly their neighbours—The hatred of the chickasaws & choctaws, both to the spaniards—the recent manifestation of that disposition as it relates of the Chickasaws to the Creeks by the application of Pixmingo for Powder[6]—the state of that business—To [*have?*] the further measures by order of the President of the U.S.

A result to the whole
Opinion of the propriety of the augmentation and if necessary
The opinion of the President same subject—both being against the reduction.
Memo. the Posts recommended by the Commissioners
1 St. Marys
1 Beards bluff
1 junction of the Oconee & oakmulgie [*Ocmulgee*]
1 Rock landing
1 Middle trading path[7]
1 ditto Upper ditto.[8]

AN, Knox Papers, The Gilder Lehrman Collection, on Deposit at the New York Historical Society, New York. [GLC 2437.04572] Knox drew up these notes in preparation for an appearance before the Senate committee on the Military Establishment Bill [HR-50a]. His first and second points have not been located.

---

[1] In early 1787, the military adventurer and Continental Army deserter John Sullivan was offering to fight for either side in hostilities he was fomenting between Spain and its neighbors in the southeastern United States. In August of that year, Spain's minister at New York, Don Diego de Gardoqui, transmitted to the Confederation Congress a letter implicating Sullivan in a planned attack on American settlers; two months later, Congress shared evidence of Sullivan's intended attack against the Spanish at New Orleans and passed a resolution formally condemning him. Over the course of the ensuing months Congress conducted investigations into Sullivan's schemes and received additional reports, excerpts of which were then ordered to be communicated to Gardoqui in September 1788 (*DHFFC* 13:1700; *Emerging Nation* 3:571–73, 611–12, 618, 653–55; Edmund C. Burnett, ed., *Letters of Members of the Continental Congress* [8 vols., Washington, D.C., 1936], 8:643n).

[2] Probably George Rogers Clark.

[3] Georgia's December 1789 land sales to the three Yazoo Companies; see George Walton to John Adams, 20 January, n. 3, volume 18.

[4] Following his unsuccessful expedition against Native American villages along the Wabash River in the summer of 1786, Revolutionary War hero and Virginia militia general George Rogers Clark led a group of settlers in a raid on Vincennes (in the Illinois Country, present-day Indiana) and illegally seized goods belonging to Spanish merchants there in retaliation for Spain's closing the Mississippi to American shipping. In April 1787 Congress authorized Knox to recover Vincennes from Clark's "usurpations of the public lands" (*LDC* 24:96, 265).

[5] The Treaty of Hopewell (South Carolina) was actually a series of nearly identical treaties negotiated with various Southern Indian Nations by United States commissioners, who included future FFC member Hawkins. Those treaties with the Choctaw and Chickasaw were signed on 3 January and 10 January 1786, respectively, and included articles reserving to Congress the sole right of regulating their trade with citizens of the United States and are printed in *DHFFC* 2:174–80.

[6] Piomingo, also known as Mountain Leader, was identified in the Hopewell Treaty as the "head warrior and first minister of the Chickasaw Nation" (in present-day northern Mississippi and southwestern Tennessee). During the post-Revolutionary War period, he resisted a Pan-Indian alliance and led the pro-American faction opposed to both the Spanish (to the Chickasaws' west) and Spain's ally, the Creeks (to the Chickasaws' east). In return Piomingo expected material assistance in the face of deteriorating relations with the Chickasaws'

neighbors, which reached a nadir in early summer 1789 when a war party of Creeks killed his brother and nephew. In October of that year he set out for New York with a small party to ask Washington for arms, but the mission proceeded no further than Richmond where the Virginia legislature provided them with two thousand pounds of ammunition and forty gallons of rum for the return journey via the Ohio River (Colin G. Calloway, *The American Revolution in Indian Country* [Cambridge, 1995], pp. 233–38; *PGW* 4:480–81; James R. Atkinson, *Splendid Land, Splendid People: The Chickasaw Indians to Removal* [Tuscaloosa, Ala., 2004], pp. 134–35).

[7] The middle or main branch of the Creek trading path (also called the Oakfuskee Path for the principal Creek village to which it led, at the present-day site of the West Point Dam on the Chattahoochee River) followed a route westward out of Augusta, Georgia, roughly along present-day state highway 16. Knox probably meant specifically the well known meeting ground near the point at which the route crossed the juncture of the Oconee River and Shoulderbone Creek, where Georgia commissioners signed an important treaty with the Creeks in 1786 and where the United States subsequently erected Fort Twiggs in 1793. The seventh and last military post recommended by the commissioners (Benjamin Lincoln, Cyrus Griffin, and David Humphreys) is listed as the "upper trading Path" in their report to Knox dated 20 November 1789 (*DHFFC* 2:237). The upper branch of the trading path ran out of Augusta approximately along present-day interstate highway 20, and crossed near the (now submerged) juncture of the Oconee and Apalachee rivers where the United States erected Fort Phillips, also in 1793. Rock Landing was the third and southernmost point at which a branch of the trading path intersected the Oconee River—then the westernmost frontier of Anglo-American settlement, although that boundary was not formally established until the Treaty of New York in August 1790. For more on the Creek trading paths, see John H. Goff, "The Path to Oakfuskee: Upper Trading Route in Georgia to the Creek Indians," *Georgia Historical Quarterly* 39(March 1955):1–36.

[8] Knox probably meant "Upper ditto ditto."

William Page to Nicholas Gilman

Will you be so good as to excuse my addressing you as a legislatore of the United States, on matters which come before you to determine—Vanity will not allow me to suppose that that I can say any thing new, or thro' any light on a subject that has been discussed before your honble. body. It is to gain information therefore that I attempt to say any thing.

The funding of the debt of the United States by Congress and their making provision for the payment of the interest and principle as fast as the abilities of the Union will admit of, I think no one in reason can object to it—And were the Resources of the United States sufficient to raise a revenue (without burdening the subjects with direct taxes) to pay the interest & principle of the individual States' debts, I suppose that should Congress fund them also it would not operate against the Seperate States, provided they could be Credited for what they have paid their own Creditors, otherwise I think it must fall very unequal on some of the States for suppose New Hampshire to have paid three fourths of their State debt Since the close of the war, & Massachusetts not to have paid any of their State Debt, allowing each State to have been at equal expenses in support of the war & the debts are now to be funded doth not New Hampshire ought to be Credited for the three fourths paid—but I confess in order for one to jud[*g*]e of the propriety of Congress funding the debts and particularly the State Debts I think in the first place he ought to Know the Amt. of the United State Debt—the amt. of the Debts of the individual States—The amt. & proportion of the expences of the Several States Accrued & damages sustained in the war—the amt. of the Civil list & the expences of Military Arrangements Necessary to be made—& the abilities of the States to provide for the whole agreably to a proper arrangements to be made for the manner, times & mode of payment your situation & abilities furnishes you with all the knowledge necessary to judge on matters of such great Importance, and if you can spare the time to send me your Sentiments on the subject I shall esteem it a particular favour & prehaps may be of some Service in preventing some uneasyness that seems to begin to arise on a supposition of Congress's funding the debts and particularly the State debts I hand you this by Col. [*Lewis R.*] Morris who will return to this place in a few days any thing you please to send me he will take the trouble to convey Col. Morris is waiting.

ALS, Gilman Papers, DLC. Written from Charlestown, New Hampshire.

George Thatcher to Alexander Coffin and Marshall Jenkins

The inclosed Letter came to my care last evening from Mr. Shearjashub Bourne of Barnstable, in the County of Barnstable & Commonwealth of Massachusetts—the contents of it must be my apology for troubling you with this—Mr. Bourne wrote me, that he had recieved information, that his son, some time ago, sailed, in a Hermorphradite Brig, [*William*] Folgier Master, from Cape Francois [*Haiti*], bound to Hudson [*New York*]—and which he supposed must arrive about this time.

He informs me his son passes by different names—sometimes by John Lewis, sometimes by John Bourne, & at other times by John Brown, or John Lewis Brown—and is very artfull in not discovering himself—his real name is John Doane Bourne—Mr. Bourne is exceedingly anxious to get certain intelligence of his son, & induce him, if possible, to return home to his father, prother [*brother*] & friends—If he will return home he may be advantageously put into any Business he wishes for.

I have a number of Letters to Mr. Bourns son; & shall forward them to him as soon as I can hear where he is—Also money if he wants, & pleases to call, or draw on me for the same—Should you be able to find this young man, but not prevail on him to return home, or draw on me for money; I take the

Liberty, in behalf of Mr. Bourn his Father, to request you to advance him such sums of money as he may stand in need of to fix him with cloaths &c. &c., for which money thus advanced your Bill on me, at this City, or Mr. Bourne at Barnstable, shall be paid on sight.

Be so kind, Sir, as to let me know as soon as you recieve this, whether the forementioned Brig as arrived, & the probability of your making the discovery wished for.

FC, Thatcher Family Papers, MHi.

Modestus to Mr. Printer

THE Honorable Mr. Jackson, member of the Federal House of Representatives for the state of Georgia, has made considerable use of MILLAR'S OBSERVATIONS ON THE DISTINCTION OF RANKS IN SOCIETY, which is an ingenious and sensible performance.[1] In addition to what the honorable gentleman has quoted, the following extract seems to deserve attention.

After mentioning the benefits that would probably result from the masters of slaves in the then British colonies (A.D. 1771) now the United States, giving them small wages as an encouragement to industry, and after expressing his astonishment, that a practice of that kind had not been adopted there, he proceeds in these remarkable words. "At the same time it affords a CURIOUS SPECTACLE to observe, that the same people, who talk in so high a strain of political liberty, and who consider the privilege of imposing their own taxes, as one of the unalienable rights of mankind, would make no scruple of reducing a great proportion of the inhabitants into circumstances by which they are not only deprived of property, but almost of every right whatsoever. Fortune perhaps never produced a situation more calculated to ridicule a grave and even a liberal hypothesis, or to shew how little the conduct of men is at bottom directed by any philosophical principles."

I am a real admirer of many parts of Mr. Jackson's character. He appears to have naturally a great deal of generous warmth and manliness in his way of thinking, and therefore I am satisfied he has not seen the passage above quoted, or he would not have omitted to mention it. He will find it however in the 241 and 242 pages of the first London quarto edition of Millar's work.

FG, 1 April.

[1] John Millar (1735–1801), a law professor at the University of Glasgow, published *Observations* at London in 1771.

Of the Extent and Value of the North Carolina Cession

The following account of the North-Carolina *Cession, is said to have been communicated to Congress by a Member from that state* [*Williamson*], *while the bill respecting the ceded territory, was on its passage.*

FROM the Stone Mountain by the line that divides North-Carolina from Virginia, to the clear Fork of Cumberland river, the

	Miles
Distance is	112
From the clear fork to the first [*border*] crossing of Cumberland river, above the mouth of Obey river, is	105
Thence to the second crossing of Cumberland river,	130
Thence to the Tenesee river,	9 1/4
Thence to the Mississippi river,	60
The whole distance[1]	416 1/4

The general course of the Stone Mountain, or the Iron Mountain, by which the ceded territory is divided from North Carolina, is south 59 or 60 degrees west. The course of the river Missisippi from lat. 36 degrees, 30 minutes, the northern boundary of North-Carolina, to lat. 35, which is the southern boundary, is generally south, 25 degrees west. It may however be stated at south, 20 degrees west.

The width of the state is 1 degree, 30 minutes, or 104 miles. This gives 24,570,240 acres nearly. The amount of land entered in the office of John Armstrong,[2] since it was opened in 1783, of which some part is to the eastward of the Iron Mountain, is, 4,464,195 1/4 acres. Of the lands granted to officers and privates of the North Carolina line, a correct return is not come to hand, but the highest estimation is 3,000,000 acres. Pre-emptions, guards, and commissioners rights are estimated at 500,000 acres. The amount granted would then be 7,964,195 acres. There remains for the United States above 16,606,045 acres.

Of this there may be mountainous or barren land 5,000,000 acres, which is a great allowance, in so fine and fertile a country. There will remain fit for cultivation and sale at least 11,606,045 acres.

This land, or so much of the same as is, or shall be ceded by the Indians, may be immediately sold at half a dollar the acre, in national securities. It is worth that sum in specie.

NYDA, 1 April; reprinted at Newburyport and Boston, Massachusetts; New York City (*GUS*, 3 April; *NYP*, 20 April; *NYJ*, 25 May); Philadelphia; Baltimore; Edenton, North Carolina; and Charleston, South Carolina. Williamson composed this description as he began work on what became a map of Tennessee.

[1] These geographic references are to the border between Kentucky and Tennessee. Stone (or Iron) Mountain marks the point at which North Carolina, Tennessee, and Virginia meet.

[2] Armstrong was appointed in 1783 as entry taker for land transactions in what became Tennessee. Sales and grants to North Carolina's Continental Army soldiers ceased in 1784 when that state decided to cede its western lands to the United States.

[*William Maclay?*] Assmodeus to Mr. Greenleaf

Some time since, observing a piece signed *Machiavel*, in your Journal, containing instructions for a financier, or first Lord of the Treasury, my curiosity was excited to see the remainder of that correspondent's lesson; but after waiting three whole weeks, without seeing any further communications, and being anxious for the prosperity of my best friends, where ever dispersed, I have thought it prudent to send my advice, in addition to that of my pupil, Machiavel, for the benefit of all young ambitious politicians.[1]

As Machiavel has already mentioned the necessary qualifications, I shall not touch upon that subject at present, but come directly to the point. My plan has been tried and found infallable by several of the first ministers in Europe, instance, Bute, North, and Callonne.[2]

The Plan

First. Let the financier, and all the writers he can procure to write for him, write a great quantity of writing in the news-papers, and amongst these writers let there be a few wretched bunglers taken from some illiterate country acadamy, who have no ideas of their own, and will be ready to swallow any hypothesis which the financier may set up; then let these writers flourish away, first in paragraphs, and afterwards in longer essays, and let the constant theme be *public faith, public credit*, and *national honor*. After having written a great deal upon these subjects, until the ignorant and unwary are captivated with the *principles*, then tell the people, that Mr. Leeward[3] is the only man who can put those principles into practice, and save a ruined state. The minds of men will thus be apt to connect the idea of *public credit, national honor*, and *Mr. Leeward* together, and when this is once effected, he may begin his state tricks as soon as he pleases; that is, after he has secured a good name. As the old adage goes, you know, Mr. Printer, one man may steal a horse where another dare not look over the fence. This is the first act of the drama.

The second will be, to borrow money from any country that will lend it, and to collect all the revenues of his own, besides, into one spot, from whence he will issue *paper notes*, which will be called *money*, and his supporters must swear, that paper is the very essence of joes, half joes, dollars, beef, mutton, bread, and drink. N. B. This may be effected by means of an anonymous partnership of speculators, a number of whom must have seats in a certain great house.[4] By this scheme all the country will be their own, and they may first mortgage it, and in two years after foreclose the mortgage so as that it never can be opened again while this world lasts. The great influx of money from the loans that will be had, and the foreign purchasers, &c. &c. will give an appearance of great wealth to our cities, but it will be too soon yet to drive coaches over the plain citizens, or to crush them to dust in a moment, that business will come on in the third act.

Having collected all the specie into his own hands, and circulated about 100 millions of *Kites*[5] over the face of the earth, it will probably be found, when too late, that agriculture will be as much neglected as it is in Spain, and that population is decreasing. The heavy drain of interest will carry away most of the specie in about six years after the two years of speculation are at an end. But should the people complain, let them again be told, that agriculture, commerce, and manufactures depend upon their bowing to the yoke; by way of demonstration, shew them the grass growing on the wharves, and corn on the house tops—hills overspread with lofty pines, and vallies as rich as a state of nature can make them.

Perhaps some crusty whigs or obstinate patriots may then threaten a revolt and exclaim against the man (for so it was in Britain with lord North) who brought all these new fashioned things about. But if they should threaten to memorial or petition government for his removal, all he has to do is to procure an ambassador's commission and give the people *the bag to hold.* When he gets across the ocean he need not regard their scurvy murmurings. His own and all his friend's fortunes will then be made, and if ever he returns to his country again, it will only be to insult it and ride over the distresses of the poor and wretched inhabitants, who had tamely submitted to be robbed of their liberties, their property, and their spirit.

If the people should make opposition to the taxation scheme, for instance, a tax upon flaxseed, flour, tobacco, &c. or on butter and pork, I would recommend to Mr. Leeward to have a report spread abroad, of an horrible Indian war, and an invasion from Algiers; perhaps some unbelieving persons may say, "That there is no more danger of an invasion either by sea or land, than there is of the Aleghany mountains marching to the siege of Belgrade." But let not such grumblers be minded; make the war inevitable in the mouths of sycophants, and then I will warrant the certainty of the people submitting to any tax, yea, even a tax upon pump-water.

During the time of the rumour about a war, the 100 millions of new government paper money will fall every where at least 50 per cent. or perhaps 75 per cent. This will be a good time for Mr. Leeward's friends (I suppose it may happen about the year 1794) to launch out in the purchasing and speculation line, for they will have all the specie of the continent amongst them. But if they have only about ten millions, that will go near to purchase up the 100 millions, which, as soon as they have compleated, let a peace be struck with the Indians, &c. (who had no hostile intentions all the while) then securities will rise again to 20/. in the pound, with which the holders, in 1794, may purchase all the land in the United States, and become the sole lords of the soil.

I must not omit, however, mentioning, that the anonymous company must inveigle a few unsuspecting honest men to be of their party, in order to give things a good complexion, of these men they must make *cats-paws*,[6] and Mr. Leeward must promise to use his interest to get the shameless ——, who heads the northern Phalanx, a post of two or three thousand dollars per annum (there will soon be about 200 new offices created, such as inspector general of excise, militia, &c. &c.) must ask them to dinner and to ride in his chariot, he must shew that he has rendered the use of the *binominal theorem* familiar amongst all the clerks in his department, so that it will never be doubted but that he is the wisest, greatest, bravest, and most CANDID of mankind.

NYJ, 1 April, edited by Thomas Greenleaf. Although there is no documentary evidence of Maclay's authorship, the satirical nature of the piece, the reference to Maclay's Machiavel, the allusions chosen, and the fact that Maclay sent it to Rush on 2 April strongly suggest his authorship. Asmodeus is the demon in the Book of Tobias in the Catholic Bible.

---

[1] For Machiavel, see 4 March, volume 18; on 25 March *NYJ* reported that Machiavel could not be included because public proceedings had occupied so much space.

[2] John Stuart Bute (1713–92) was George III's influential tutor and secretary of state who spearheaded the king's policies of monarchical supremacy over Parliament. John Wilkes implied that he was a paramour of George's mother. The tenure of Frederick North (1732–92) as prime minister under George III from 1770 to 1782 was marked by his failure to suppress colonial rebellion in North America. Charles Alexandre de Calonne (1732–1802) was the rival of Jacques Necker and failed French comptroller general of finance from 1783 to 1787, the year he fled to England.

[3] Alexander Hamilton, who was born in Nevis, one of the Leeward Islands.

[4] Congress.

[5] Fictitious bills of credit.

[6] To become the tool of another.

Letter to New York

The slow progress in public business, excites very general concern. The Anties laugh: The friends to the National Government mourn. Why does not — rise up and say "Every man has made up his mind, therefore let us talk *less* and vote *more*." It appears to me that Congress are like some physicians, who have long attended a patient, that they have most perfectly *assured* will *soon* be well; but the cure not being performed, the sufferer and his friends are much more sensible of the lapse of time and the consequent loss, than the honest doctors are. Whether this simile properly expresses the idea or not, the plain truth is, that by a delay of the capital concern of the nation, PUBLIC CREDIT, the universal expectation has been disappointed, and the public confidence considerably abated—while *local* state politicians are furnished with pretexts for keeping up the cry of "state sovereignty."

GUS, 14 April; reprinted at Portsmouth, New Hampshire; New London and Norwich, Connecticut; Poughkeepsie, New York; Burlington, New Jersey; Fredericksburg, Richmond, and Winchester, Virginia; and Edenton, North Carolina. This extract may have been taken from a letter Joseph Ward wrote to John Fenno; see Fenno to Ward, 11 April, below.

Other Documents

Charles Carroll to Joshua Johnson. FC:lbk, Arents Tobacco Collection, NN.
Orders from London the French language edition of *Posthumous Works of Frederick II King of Prussia* (Berlin, 1788); expects it to arrive at Annapolis, Maryland, in October.

Mary Smith Cranch to Abigail Smith Adams. ALS, Adams Family Manuscript Trust, MHi. Written from Weymouth, Massachusetts.
Joseph Cranch (her nephew) is indebted to the Adamses for intervening with Knox on his behalf, for a military appointment.

William Irvine to John Nicholson. ALS, Nicholson Papers, PHarH. Place to which written not indicated; received 3 April. Encloses a manuscript essay, dated 1 April and signed "Juniata Man," which is printed under Pennsylvania in the Second Federal Election section in Correspondence: Third Session.
"the assumption of the state debts goes heavily on tomorrow it is thought it will be divided in Committee of the whole but how is uncertain—the Penn[*sylvania*]ns. it is said begin to wobble."

William Samuel Johnson, Diary. Johnson Papers, CtHi.
"Dind. [*Dined at*] Maj. Butlers."

George Washington, Diary. ViHi.
Senator King and Representatives Leonard, Sedgwick, Grout, Van Rensselaer, Hathorn, Clymer, Hiester, Stone, Williamson, Ashe, and Huger dined at the President's.

Friday, 2 April 1790

Rain (Johnson)

John Adams to John Trumbull

***

If the debate and decision on the presidents power of removal has occasioned rancour, would you advise me to give up and destroy the ballance between the executive and Legislative, to avoid that rancour? Give up this equilibrium and you will have a Senate of Venice without an inquisition;[1] and you know that this goodly devise of an inquisition is the only thing which restrains that Senate from being a worse tyranny than they are. Retirement would allow me all the activity I want; which is exercise on my farm, and ardour among my books and papers, where in my opinion I should do as much good to this Country, and more to others than in any office whatever. But if I should return to the Bar; as many Presidents of Congress & Governors of States have done, I could do more service to my sons, who have a great demand upon me, than I could possibly do in public. So that I assure you after very mature deliberation I am quite reconciled and resigned to retire from public life. I beleive I am no more inclined than you are, by principle or by taste or by habit, to an imitation of the pageantry of foreign Courts. You will agree with me that for the President to live in a mean house, to ride in a mean carriage &c. would degrade him in the eyes of all foreigners—and even of our own people. The first man in the nation must not be worse accommodated and make a meaner appearance than ordinary gentlemen of fortune do in our separate States and Capital towns—This would be evidence not only of a sordid character in the Nation but of a false, affected and hypocritical policy. There is therefore a medium to be observed I do however know that magnificence imposes on this people as much as on any other. It has been one great cause of the influence and popularity of Washington [*John*] Hancock and others. The Number who worship splendor are greater than that of those who despise it. [*David*] Humphreys whom I love as you do, may do well to lay aside his French embroidery—I never wore any in Europe; but I must now from necessity wear over again my French cloaths; for my salary will not admit (thanks to New England representatives[2]) of my purchasing new ones, more cheap and plain.

*** The success that has in all this period attended the public in every thing in which I have been engaged, astonishes and overwhelmes me whenever I look back upon it. My mind and heart are full and my eyes flow, not with vanity or pride; but with wonder and with gratitude. Thus far you will say I sett up my pretensions very high But the reverse of the picture mortifies all my vanity and what is more gives me very serious aprehensions of great calamities to the public. Through the whole thirty years I have seen and felt that the public have been served against their wills. I have seen affection and gratitude and enthusiasm for others but never for me. A reluctance to receive and acknowledge my services has ever been apparent.

A constant pleasure has been taken in throwing little slights, and Sly mortifications, and sometimes cruel insults in my way. But this is not the worst. I have seen such characters as Willm. Molineux, Dr. Young Common Sense Paine,[3] and fifty others, run away with the passions and confidence of the people, obtain more influence than I had, and propagate principles and systems destructive to the people and the public good, in spight of all the arguments I could use and all the interest I could make with them, or the people. If there was an end of these things, I should be happy: but there is more of this spirit than ever; and I see my friends and the friends of the public duped in so gross a manner, that I dispair. A lying manœvre brought me into my present seat in a manner that invites every puppy to give himself airs. By writing to the southern states that New England would not vote generally for Washington, and by writing to New England that Virginia and South Carolina would not vote for him, they raised an apprehension that I should be President; to prevent which so many votes were thrown away that I had not a majority; and what hurt me more than all the rest, even Connecticutt was the dupe of this intrigue.[4] The consequence of this is, a general popular opinion that I stand on so weak ground, that I may be insulted in Gazette or pamphlet at pleasure. When my salary came on all possibility was taken away from me either of entertaining foreigners or my own Countrymen, in a manner that is necessary to obtain that general acquaintance and information that is to be desired in my station and that would be indispensible if a certain melancholy contingency should happen—This was New England policy, to give the President one fifth more than he ought to have had and the Vice President one fifth less. This is but one instance among many. When I had been a slave in Europe for many years, and had made them a peace, instead of sending me the commission of an Ambassador, as common decency would have dictated, they sent me a vote, Moved by Massachusetts delegates, cutting off one fifth of my salary.[5] I have seen the utmost delicacy used towards others, but my feelings have never been regarded. There has been more little malignity to me, than to Jonathan Sewal, Silas Dean or Benedict Arnold.[6] Whether this is owing to too much openness, or warmth, or too decided systems I know not. This language of complaint Sir, does not proceed from a mortified heart, but from serious apprehensions for the public. If any aid is expected from me in my present station, towards introducing a right way of thinking among the people, and first principles of a well ordered government, why am I not supported? If the deprecated event should happen, as it may (for this people deserve it for what I know) I must be President or resign. If the friends of the Country will name me a man, in whom the people will unite better than in me, I will resign without hesitation, and should take a greater pride in that resignation, than in serving in the office of President even to general satisfaction: for I know it would be better for me and for my family. In private life I am very sure I should enjoy a green old age contented and healthy, and leave my family prosperous and happy. If that office should ever fall upon me for my sins, I see nothing but vexation disease and death for myself, and nothing but poverty pride and an humiliating fall for my children. I feel the want of a confidential communication with my friends. Serious events await this people if they cannot agree upon a successor to the Chair. The question must be considered; the people are uneasy and will be untill some one is held up to them as likely to succeed without all doubt. Let it be determined and an end put to questions about it—or at all events I will put an end to them, as far as they regard me, by a resignation. I know of no man of your judgment and information, more independent and unconnected than yourself, and therefore I write to you with this freedom and confidence. If I could have foreseen what has happened, I would have refused my present situation. But I was deceived by positive assertions which prove to be without foundation I was assured from many quarters that altho I had not a majority of votes, it was the desire of the Continent that I should be V.P.; this is now suffered to be called in question. I was also assured that a provision should be made for me, that would enable me to support my rank and maintain the reputation I had with foreign nations, as well as the consideration which was due to me and my office from the people of America. These promises have not been fulfilled. The artifice of some and the simplicity of others, has disappointed me; if it affected me and mine only I should be patient: but it injures the public and threatens still greater mischiefs. I must therefore, at all events some how or other get out of this embarrassment. I do not however intend to let you slumber very long. Whether in public or private life I live and die a zealous friend to my country. There are many things which want attention; many things wrong which cannot be set right but by correspondence or consultation among men of knowledge. Our morals, our Commerce, our governments all want reformation. And if you will promise me not to hitch me into some of your satyrical verses, I will descend to some particulars.

P. S. How extensive may be your meaning where you doubt whether any imitation of the pageantry of foreign Courts would strengthen government, may be uncertain: But would you banish Representation and Appearance altogether? How can we agree? South Carolina and Virginia have been used to more representation than Pennsylvania—all the other states are in habits of more of it than New England—Massachusetts and New Hampshire had more than Connecticutt. The Governors of all the states have felt the necessity of preserving since the Revolution nearly the same appearance, which was exhibited before the war. The Common people of the southern States would laugh at a Governor as simple as the chief magistrate of Connecticutt. Some reasonable medium therefore seems necessary for the President. We must consider that he has intercourse not only with the people of all the States but with foreigners. I am a sincere inquirer after truth, and if I am sure of anything from experience I am sure of this; That appearances have great weight on the imaginations of a large majority of the people. Elegant figures graceful attitudes and motions, easy manners, a polite address, a handsome countenance have charms in them among all people that I have seen; and fascinate multitudes on whom reason, eloquence, and virtue would be lost. Many of our own people are bewitched by them, more than any other. In the third volume of Jean Jacques Rousseu's Emile[7] page 230 you will find some thoughts upon this subject, which merit attention—least you should not have the book at hand I will transcribe some of it. If Rousseau was not Republican enough; if he was not a sufficiently zealous advocate for simplicity, frugality, moderation &c. I know not where to find one who is.

***

FC:lbk, Adams Family Manuscript Trust, MHi. The omitted text includes Adams's reflections on the Treaty of Paris of 1783, prompted by his reading of the recently published memoirs of Frederick the Great, and an outline of Adams's public service up to 1790.

---

[1] Adams refers not to the Inquisition established in the late fifteenth century by the Catholic Church to root out heresy but Venice's Inquisitori di Stato, a political body also known as "The Three," established in 1539 to tighten state security. It was responsible only to "The Ten" (Venice's executive council) and served as a much feared check on the Great Council (John Julius Norwich, *History of Venice* [New York, 1985], pp. 500, 597).

[2] No recorded debate or vote substantiates Adams's faulting the New England representatives for the size of his salary under the Compensation Act, unless his comment is meant to indict their failure to affect its increase. Many New England congressmen sympathized with their constituents' often stated complaints about the size of federal salaries generally, but the only known instances of this in Adams's case were Sherman's speech against acceding to a Senate amendment that would have raised the Vice President's salary from five to six thousand dollars and Goodhue's and Livermore's service on the resulting conference committee that also rejected the Senate amendment (*DHFFC* 11:1479).

[3] The merchant William Molineux (1716–74) and Dr. Thomas Young were early leaders of Boston's Sons of Liberty, a radical, extra-legal organization that spearheaded opposition to British colonial measures in the years preceding the Revolutionary War. Adams groups them with Thomas Paine as grass roots spokesmen for the revolutionary movement.

[4] Adams blamed Hamilton for so effectively ensuring the elimination of any threat to Washington's election that Adams won only thirty-four of the sixty-nine votes available for any other candidate. Of the New England states, only Connecticut's electors did not give the same number of their votes to Adams as to Washington. After casting the maximum number of votes they could for Washington, Virginia's electors divided their remaining ten votes among Adams and three other candidates; South Carolina electors cast no votes for Adams (*DHFFE* 4:288; *DHFFC* 1:8).

[5] On 7 May 1784, Congress agreed to a motion by Gerry restricting the salary of a foreign minister from $1,111 to $9,000. Adams overlooked or may not have known that Gerry's motion reversed a motion carried the day before that would have limited the salary to $8,000 (*JCC* 26:349, 353–54).

[6] Jonathan Sewall (1728–96) served as the last royal attorney general of Massachusetts from 1767 until he fled to New Brunswick, Canada, in 1775. Although they were longtime friends, Adams included Sewall, Massachusetts' most prominent Loyalist, alongside the arch-traitor Benedict Arnold and Silas Deane, whose malfeasance as a wartime diplomat to France was the subject of widespread criticism, especially among the Lee-Adams coalition in the Continental Congress.

[7] *Émile*, a novel otherwise known as *Émilius and Sophia* (1762), was Jean-Jacques Rousseau's proposal for a new system of education. Adams's postscript transcribes in French a lengthy passage from Book IV (Allan Bloom, ed., *Émile, or On Education* [New York, 1979], pp. 321–23).

William Maclay to Benjamin Rush

I have not heard from you for some time past. I however continue to fulfill your request in sending you Peices from the News Papers, respecting the Secretary's System. but this like many other Machines when once fairly set in Motion, will go of itself Peices are now recived and published against the Secretary's report with freedom. nay with asperity and perhaps in some instances full much of it. The whole Week has been spent on the Assumption of the State Debts, and no Question is yet taken. But we fear them not. we do not expect to loose this question but if we ever should, Perseverando,[1] shall be our Motto. A Dinner which I cannot avoid, calls me away. let me hear from you.

ALS, Rush Papers, DLC. Addressed to Third Street, Philadelphia; franked; postmarked 3 April. One of the pieces enclosed was probably Assmodeus, *NYJ*, 1 April, printed above; a copy cut from the newspaper is in the Rush Papers, DLC.

[1] It must be persisted in.

Edmund Pendleton to James Madison

I should have sooner acknowledged yr. obliging favr. of March 4th., but was taken wth. a Cold about the time of it's receipt, which, as usual, brought on a fever & short breathing, from which I am but now relieved. I thank you for your Attention to Dr. [*David*] Murrow's application.

The Secretary's Plan of finance is really too deep for my comprehension, I cannot however accord with his position that Public debt is a blessing; it may be a convenient engine to Government, considered as having a distinct

Interest from that of the Citizens, but can never be so, where they are united, as ought to be our case. Upon his principles, I wonder he did not assume all private debts, since it would have increased the Public *Capital*, &, as he reasons, the wealth of America, & would have gained him many Partizans. I did Not know how Virga. might be Affected by this project, but from it's first Appearance, I had feelings repulsive of the measure on general considerations, of the fœdral debt being thus unnecessarily increased, & difficulties in it's adjustment multiplied, and that it was an Officious intermedling wth. the State Governments which will be considered as a stride towards consolidation, and this increased, rather than diminished by his wish to absorb all the Powers of taxation in the fœdral head, as one of the reasons for the Assumption.

My Sentiments on the other great subject you have long known, & I need not repeat them. yr. Opponents appear to me, instead of considering the subject in a great & general view & applying general principles of Justice to a case new & extraordinary, to have become bar advocates for a favourite measure, calling for precedents, and reiterating maxims establishing the general faith of contracts, without distinguishing their ground, and stating the cases [*lined out*] in [*lined out*] which they may be departed from, consistent wth. good faith; As if there were no such things as Vices in Contracts, wch. render them Nul in law, Equity & Honour; and that if a sharper can once get a bond signed, or transfer'd, it becomes like a law of the Medes & Persians unalterable, tho' obtained thro' the weakness, ignorance of the Subject, or necessity of the other, & an Advantage gained wch. no honest man would insist on: whereas it is one of the great purposes of Society & Government to protect it's members from such Oppressions. The Statutes of Usury for instance have this foundation, and Courts of Equity are occupied Perhaps half their Sessions, in giving relief in such instances as laws can't reach & provide against. But "The new Government is declared by the Constitution to be bound for the debts of the old," true & surely they ought to be, but how does this apply? The question is what is the debt, & to whom it is due? when those are ascertain'd, the obligation to pay is indisputable.

I am almost tempted to say of these Advocates As Warburton[1] does of his, that "so far from a good Argument, to the disgrace of their Profession, they can scarce make a tolerable quibble." however, we must submit to a Majority & wish for the best.

The Progress of Illumination & liberty in Europe, is pleasing to my feelings as a Man, but peculiarly grateful to me as an American, since I think we may, without Arrogance, Assert that the foundation was laid in this revolution, and the sensible publications on that Occasion. May it proceed wth. as little bloodshed as may be, 'til all mankind are happy. We have not a word of News.

ALS, The Gilder Lehrman Collection, on Deposit at the New York Historical Society, New York. [GLC 99.143] Written from Virginia.

[1] William Warburton (1698–1779), English bishop and author.

William Smith (S.C.) to Edward Rutledge

State he represents censured & misrepresented—our conduct has been termed folly & extravagance, & he hears it without being at the trouble of a reply—Sumpter too is equally callous—yesterday he heard a Virginia Member say that in a particular engagemt. during the war the Militia consisted only of Virgins. & No. Caras. & that no South Car. were present;[1] Sumpter & Burke sat near me & ~~said~~ told me it was not true. they knew the contrary; I urged Sumpter to rise & contradict it but he would not. Burke has been warmly with us but his mode of speaking & his roughness only excite Laughter [*torn*]: he has by his viol[*ent*] [*one line torn and illegible*] State) in a very disagreable matter. Hamilton, the Secr. of the [*torn*], in his celebrated oration the 4th. July last in speaking of some little fugitive parties of undisciplined militia which Supported Gen. [*Nathanael*] Greene in some battle (I think it was Monmouth but am not sure)[2] with a view to heighthen the character of his Hero who was the subject of his Panegyric, said "only supported by little fugitive parties of undisc[*ipline*]d. militia, *the mere mimickry of Soldiery*"; some persons who had not attended to the whole connection of the Sentence ~~repr~~ were extremely disgusted with Hamilton for calling the Militia the mimicky. of Soldy., but the thing was forgotten. Day before yesterday Burke was making a Panegyric on the Southern Militia & got so warmed by his subject that he expressed himself something to this effect: "and yet a gentleman now high in office in a public assembly called *this* militia, these brave men the mere mimicky. of Soldy.—Sir in behalf of those brave men I give the lie to Col. Hamilton, yes, in the face of this Assembly & in the presence of this gallery" (turning round to a crowded Gallery in which were several Ladies & among them the widows Young & Hyrne) "I say I give the lie to Col. Hamilton" (here he was called to order) Mr. Laur[*anc*]e. a genuine [*friend?*] of Hamilton's then explained very politely that Burke [*was?*] under [*a mistaken impression as?*] the observation alluded not to the South. Milita. Burke insisted on it [*that*] it did for that Hamilton was then recounting the exploits of Greene to the Southward; he was told he was mistaken that he was relating an engagemt. to the northwd. but he would not recant: he then proceeded to account for his not having taken notice of it Sooner; that observation, said he, was like a Dagger in my breast, but it was impossible for me to notice it at the time; I was called an antifederalist, the people of this city were all federalists, Mr. Hamilton was the Hero of the day & the favorite of the people & had I hurt a hair of his head, I am sure I should have been dragged thru the Kennels[3] of New York & pitched headlong into the East River: But now I have an opportunity in as public a manner of retorting *the lie* which he gave to the character of the Militias.[4] Hamilton was immediately made acquainted with this insult & he determined to proceed with deliberation; he said he should at all times disregard any observations applied to his public station as Secrety. of the Treasy. but that *this* was not to be passed over—he then wrote to Burke & inclosed him an exact copy of that part of his oration which contained the offensive sentence & required that Burke would in return communicate exactly [*what*] he [*said*] in the [*torn*] [*intending?*] to shew Burke he had been wrong. I have not heard the result.

Burke was in the house yesterday, but took no part in the business & was fidgetting backwards & forwards the whole morning. I am told he is amazingly intimate with Govr. [*George*] Clinton & that he is supposed to be courting his daughter,[5] for he is there every day; Clinton hates Hamilton mortally & has probably set on Burke.

ALS, incomplete, Smith Papers, ScHi. Place to which addressed not indicated. The opening pages are missing. The editors have dated the letter based on its reference to Burke's 31 March speech as the "Day before yesterday." The letter was continued on 3 April, below.

[1] Moore made this erroneous observation during the COWH debate of 1 April in reference to the Battle of King's Mountain, North Carolina, on 7 October 1780 (*DHFFC* 13:942).

[2] For documents and background on Hamilton's July Fourth oration and the implications for an affair of honor alluded to by Smith (S.C.), see *DHFFC* 8:476–80. The battle Hamilton mentioned was not Monmouth but Hessian General Wilhelm von Knyphausen's unsuccessful raid on Springfield, New Jersey, on 23 June 1780.

[3] Gutters.

[4] For the speech paraphrased here by Smith, see *DHFFC* 12:915–16.

[5] Either Catharine (1770–1811) or Cornelia (1774–1810), whom Abigail Adams Smith described as "a zealous politician, and a high anti-Federalist" (John P. Kaminski, *George Clinton: Yeoman Politician of the New Republic* [Madison, Wis., 1993], p. 137).

John Wendell to Elbridge Gerry

*** I had an Oppertunity of seeing yr. remarkable Speech[1] in Congress a few days past wch. is so full of fair Reasoning, that altho as I wrote you before that I was converted to an Impractability of a Discrimination between the Original Holders and Purchasers of public Securities, yet I thought Justice demanded it, from the very Nature of the Negotiation which appeared evident to Me that when the final Settlements were given to the Soldiery, tho they were only Evidences of the ballances due to them yet as at the Hour of Settlement it was known known they were but of little Value and Government might have had them at the same rate that Speculators purchased, it must be considered as a public Fraud at the very Time, and for the public Faith which was then punical Vox et pretoria Nihil,[2] to be considered now as rigid as the Virtue of an Old Maid in favr. of Speculators I cannot get over it, but yet I find myself overcome upon the principle that there is a Necessity for any nation to recover its Credit let it be lost by any Ways or Means, but my Friend how will Government get over the Old Emission [*Continental*] Money Look into the Records see the solemn Pledges made for its Redemption, the Solemn Calls upon the People even from the Pulpits by Congress to supports its Credit in Decr. 1778[3] and that Forregners & Childn. then unborn wd. appear for its Redemption and at the very Time it was passing at 20 for 1 with [*illegible*] in March 1779 [*1780*] Congress scaled it at 40 for 1 by which I sunk £1000 Sterling that Hour—how can Congress get over this—I know of no way to do it but an Acknowledgment of a National bankruptcy, but to be so rigid now looks farcical, and yet I pray God it may succeed & that we may get Revenues sufficient for the Purposes of so great a Redemption as the public Debt but the profuse and too generous Grants of the public Monies in Salaries alarms the People and the Event Time must bring to Light—it is a Matter of no great Importance in my Mind how the Debt is funded, although we may have a Revenue to pay the Interest in Specie yet the distant Period for its Redemption will depreciate the principal until it comes nearer to its Redemption and I believe they never will fetch more than 10/ in the Pound unless some Security may be had more than the public Faith, should a War happen with any European Powers, the public Notes wd. fall greatly unless we could get them into Circulation for a Medium thro out the Continent, which I wish could be effected I presume 4 P. Cent will be the funded Interest. Is it not practicable for Congress to appropriate 5,000,000 Dollars of the Securities upon Loan for the Special Purpose of a Currency and establish a Spe[*c*]ie Bank upon Loan out of the Revenue and to let all the public Payments be received in such Notes and thereby the Speice be preserved in the Bank, as a sinking Fund for the Redemption of them in four Years, Let an Annual Lottery be made towards a Sinking Fund for the same Purpose—5,000,000 of Dollars wd. create a currency All the Invalid Pensioners might be paid in these Notes I wish your fertile Invention could strike out some Mode for the Benefit of sink[*ing*] Millions which lye dormant in private [*seal*] being an inactive Fund of Property—You cannot secure the public Esteem (which is now rising into perfect Honour not to say Adoration) than by striking out or promoting some currency which wch. may relieve your fellow Citizens from their Debts without the Assistance of silver or Gold which are Extraneous Articles—to measure our Properties by such articles as are dependant upon foriegners seems very injurious to the People at large, you may not be sensible of the Want of ~~sensible~~ Silver or Gold at New York but I have an Estate worth 20,000 & yet cant command a Dollar without sacrificing Property—I lately sold as good a Note as General Washingtons, of £37.20/ for £30 Cash and such Sacrifices I must make to command Cash, This is in Confidence and if you wish to immortalize yr. Memory, think of some Expedient to relieve yr. fellow Men—I am so attached to you by Friendship and Affection that I have been enthusiastic in yr. favr., and though I might have been a Member of Congress (which I have refused) yet I almost repent it fo[*r the*] Sake of our being still nearer connected, I have heard many ill valued Reproaches of yr. Integrity but [*torn*] stood a warm Advocate for you, and very lately ever since yr. Speech One Gentleman acknowledged his Mistake & from hence forth wd. appeal you and whenever you wish yr. private Sentiments may see daylight I have the Command of the Presses in this State—I have wished often to insert Extracts of yr. Letters to Me as a Friend but I have avoided the Incurrence of yr. disallowance—With that Esteem am most sincerely yrs. without adulation or Sychophancy.

ALS, Gerry Papers, MHi. Written from Portsmouth, New Hampshire; postmarked Boston, 4 April; answered 16 May. The omitted text thanks Gerry for his help in a business transaction that involved a Capt. Phillips, who had resided in 1789 at the same boarding house as Goodhue, Wingate, and Thatcher.

[1] For Gerry's speech of 19 February, see *DHFFC* 12:451–59.

[2] A faithless voice and nothing more.

[3] Wendell may have been referring to Congress's Circular Letter of 13 September 1779; it is printed in *DHFFC* 5:830–39.

Alexander White to Horatio Gates

This is intended to introduce to your Notice, Mr. Jacob Heermans a young Gentleman of this State who is about to travel for his health, having the Sweet Springs[1] principally in View. he is recommended to me as a man of character and real worth, that circumstance may in part apologize for the liberty I have taken but I will add another which has for its object, the showing our Country to advantage, I know the effect which the attention of Gentlemen of character to a Stranger, has on the mind, how much more favourably every object is [*lined out*] viewed, and as the Banks of the Patowmack, & the [*Shenandoah*] Valley South of it have been the Theme of so much Disputation I wish him [*lined out*] to return with favourable impressions—I recommended to him to go by Shepherdstown [*West Virginia*]—and intimated that if he wished to see the Works at Harpers [*Ferry, West Virginia*] it was probable some Gentlemen in that Town or Neighbourhood might accompany him—I expect the Public Papers will detail all our News before

Mr. Heermans arrives—Mrs. [*Elizabeth Wood*] White and the young Family join in most respectful Complts.

ALS, Gates Papers, NN. Place to which addressed not indicated.

[1] One of the lesser known but most efficacious medicinal springs in the Allegheny Range, according to Jefferson's *Notes on the State of Virginia*, it was located in Botetourt County, Virginia (now Monroe County, West Virginia), and was one of the sources of the James River.

Letter from Georgetown [*Maryland*]

I can with pleasure inform you that within three weeks past, we have had arrivals of at least 30 boats at the mouth of Watt's Branch, 14 miles from this, loaded with flour, wheat and tobacco, many of them from the head waters of Potowmac. I have seen several of the boatmen, and they are much pleased with the navigation. The Potowmac company's hands are now at work on the rock at the great falls. I hope they will get through that work this present year, then the boats may pass to the little fall, four miles from hence; at the lower part of which as many pair of mill-stones might run, as would manufacture 500 barrels of flour per day, where ships could go up to the spot.

GUS, 14 April, from a non-extant issue of the [Alexandria] *Virginia Gazette*; reprinted at Bennington, Vermont; Salem, Massachusetts; Providence, Rhode Island; Norwich and New London, Connecticut; and Edenton, North Carolina.

Other Documents

Comte De La Forest to James Madison. ALS, Lafayette Manuscripts, Lilly Library, Indiana University, Bloomington.

Introduction for Dr. John Francis Vacher, who served in the Revolutionary War; Vacher has business for which he desires Madison's support.

Daniel Hooper to George Thatcher. ALS, Thatcher Papers, MeHi. Written from Biddeford, Maine; postmarked Portsmouth, New Hampshire, date unreadable.

No news except that flour and corn are very scarce; asks Thatcher for the loan that he had encouraged Hooper to expect.

Peter Silvester to David Van Schaack. ALS, Van Schaack Collection, NNC. Addressed to Kinderhook, New York.

Is glad at the prospects of a good crop, which will revive trade, "the one thing needfull"; "the Opinion of most of the Judicious" is that New York State legislators' holding seats in Congress is not incompatible with the state or federal constitutions, "however otherwise inconvenient or improper it might be," and that no legislative act ought to interfere; "the manner & time in which it is done is also a reflection that has given disquiet"; reports on state legislature's proceedings; will continue to support Van Schaack's recommendations for state offices for various persons; he always franks his letters "when I think of it," but the postmaster "should not charge for such letters as he knows comes from me"; for news, refers to newspapers.

William Samuel Johnson, Diary. Johnson Papers, CtHi.

"Good Fridy. No Senate. St. Pauls."

Letter from Pittsburgh. *NYDA*, 5 May; reprinted at Portsmouth, New Hampshire; Salem and Worcester, Massachusetts; Philadelphia; and Charleston, South Carolina.

"Nothing less than 1800 or 2000 continental troops, stationed in a line of posts, will keep" the Indian nations bordering on the frontier "in a tolerable degree of awe"; that country is too thinly settled to support a militia.

Saturday, 3 April 1790

Cool (Johnson)

Henry Lee to James Madison

I am induced to address you on a subject which violates the rule I had lately prescribed to myself with respect to our public affairs.

A youth the son of Mr. Thomas L. Lee[1] to whom I beleive you was intimately known met me this morning on the road.

Bred to the mercantile line in one of the most respectable houses in our country & cut off from his expectations there, by the death of his principal Mr. Ritchie who was killed the other day in a duel,[2] he is anxious to obtain a place in some of the departments of the genl. govt.—He is very humble in his wishes & is most solicitous to procure a birth under a character from whose example he will derive instruction & on whose patronage he can rely. He mentioned Mr. Jefferson & said that his deceased father & Mr. J. he understood had been very friendly from an early acquaintance—I promised to write to Mr. J. on the subject which I have accordingly done & will thank you if you will remind him of the matter, provided you can do it consistently with your mode of conduct. If the government should continue to exist, which by the bye is more & more eventful, the introduction of the southern youth as clerks in the high departments of the nation seems to me to be a sure tho slow means of Aiding the southern influence. They become as it were from their official education owners of the ministerial functions if their conduct & talents correspond with their prospective stations.

I wish our southern gentlemen would in due time attend to this material truth—if they do not a monopoly will take place from the northern hives in this, as in every thing else in their power.

On the score of propriety & repose I had determined to suppress my anxious attention to the prosperity of the national Govt., for I really know not what conduct I may feel myself bound to observe in consequence of the mad policy which seems to direct the doings of Congress.

Therefore for the sake of propriety I wish to be done with govt.—on the score of tranquility & peace I am also desirous to be quiet, for every day adds new testimony of the growing ill will of the people here to the govt.—To risk repose when good can result from it & the object in view is clearly right, I hold to be the indispensable duty of every good citizen, nor will I ever disobey the sacred injunction, but to do it in reverse circumstances is pursuing the commands of temerity & folly. [*Patrick*] Henry already is considered as a prophet, his predictions are daily verifying—His declaration with respect to the division of interest which would exist under the constitution & predominate in all the doings of the govt. already has been undeniably proved.[3]

But we are committed & we cannot be releived I fear only by disunion To disunite is dreadful to my mind, but dreadful as it is, I consider it a lesser evil than union on the present conditions.

I had rather myself submit to all the hazards of war & risk the ~~poverty~~ loss of every thing dear to me in life, than to live under the rule of a fixed insolent northern majority—At present this is the case, nor do I see any prospect of alteration or alleviation.

Change of the seat of govt. to the territorial center, direct taxation & the abolition of gambling systems of finance might & would effect a material change—But these suggestions are vain & idle—No policy will be adopted by Congress which does not more or less tend to depress the south & exalt the north—I have heard it asserted that your vice president should say the southern people were formed by nature to subserve the convenience & interests of the north—or in plain words to be slaves to the north—Very soon will his assertion be thoroughly exemplified—How do you feel, what do you think, is your love for the constitution so ardent, as to induce you to adhere to it tho it should produce ruin to your native country [*Virginia*]—I hope not, I believe not—However I will be done, for it is disagreable to utter unpleasant opinions.

ALS, Madison Papers, DLC. Written from "Berry Hill," Stafford County, Virginia, the former estate of Thomas Ludwell Lee (1730–78).

[1] Thomas Ludwell Lee, Jr. (ca. 1752–1807).
[2] Robert Ritchie died in a duel with fellow Fredericksburg, Virginia, merchant William Glassell sometime between 27 and 31 March 1790 (*PJM* 13:137n).
[3] See, for example, Henry's speech of 12 June 1788 in the Virginia Ratification Convention (*DHROC* 10:1221–22).

Theodore Sedgwick to Pamela Sedgwick

Your very kind and obliging Letter, dearest and best beloved of my soul, without date I received by the last post—Poor dear little Robert [*Sedgwick*] how very anxious I am about his fate, yet the gentlemen here seem to think his leg may yet be cured. It is surprising that I cannot yet get from them their ultimate advice with regard to the manner in which it shall be treated, should I be unable to do it before this letter goes to the [*lined out*] post office, I shall dispair of ever doing it.

The event of the assumption during the present session grows every day more and more uncertain. Every act which cunning could devise and every falsehood which want of principle could propagate have been practised on this occasion. Should the assumption be defeated, I shall consider myself justifyed to my constituents and to my country to defeat if in my power any funding system at all, because if justice should not be the basis of the administration of this government I beleive it cannot prosper.

Should I be at home in a few days which I fondly hope may be the case, I shall make the necessary arrangements with regard to yoke farm, if not I beleive it will be best not to let it, because without that farm we shall not have sufficient pasture.

***

Whatever supplies you want you will please to direct me to procure.

ALS, Sedgwick Papers, MHi. Place to which addressed not indicated. The remainder of this letter was written the next morning and is printed under 4 April, below. The text omitted from this portion of the letter relates to management of the Sedgwick's rental property.

William Smith (S.C.) to Edward Rutledge

Yesterday being Christmas day [*Good Friday*] we did no business. I dined at Colo. Hamilton's with a large Company—nothing was said about Burke, & I am not able to learn the result of his misconduct, which is highly reprobated by every body I have met with. I saw him with Major Butler yesterday morning in close conversation. Something is going forward, but it [*is enshrouded*] with mystery. I passed the Evening with Mr. Izard, who is excessively agitated indeed about *the Assumption which stands on a very precarious footing*, owing to the North Cara. members & Sumpter, who speaks publickly (tho not in the House) ~~his mind~~ against it: the negro business[1] & Burke's conduct have encreased his distress of mind. Sumpter voted against us on both the late questions, the one for recommitting the proposition of Assumption, which was intended to get rid of it, the other for recommitting the remaining propositions, which was the only chance we had of keeping the question [*be*]fore the H[*ouse*]: Should his vote lose us the Assumption, he will deserve the [*torn*] [*of every*] citizen [*torn*] He is really more a Delegate from Virga. than our State. Some of our people are not very anxious for the ~~question~~ Assumption & are continually going away & absenting themselves when the question is about to be put, which obliges us to manœuvre & put it off to the next day & keeps us perpetually in hot water. We were in hopes of bringing in the No. Cara. members by a compromise, but we soon discovered that it would be offensive to some of our Eastern gentlemen & that we should risk losing more at one end than we gained at the other. I beleive much opposition to this measure springs from a dislike to Massachusets on the part of her rival Virginia; Georgia is envious of So. Cara.

ALS, incomplete, Smith Papers, ScHi. Place to which addressed not indicated. The closing page or pages are missing. The first part of the letter is dated 2 April and is printed above.

[1] The Quaker antislavery petitions.

Paine Wingate to Samuel Lane

I received your letter of March 17th by the last post. It gave me much satisfaction to hear from you, as it has a tendency to preserve the remembrance of that friendship & intimacy, which has subsisted between us, very agreeably to me, and I hope not wholly unprofitably to either of us, for several years. This acquaintance in the course of nature cannot continue a great many years; for we are both advanced considerably toward the close of life, and the late numerous instances of death, mentioned in your letter, must very sensibly admonish us of that approaching event. I had not heard of any of those deaths you mention, and do particularly sympathise with you on account of the death of Mr. Clarke whom I much respected as a worthy and sincerely good man. I am naturally led to reflect what a breach those deaths have made in our church whose numbers before were very small. From a growing indifference to the profession of religion, and an attendance on the special ordinances of it, it seems as though in a few years we should scarce have in many places the remains of a christian church. I wish some of the hindrances & discouragements to a standing in the Ch[*urc*]h. could be removed, and that sober [*lined out*] exemplary persons, who have a competent knowledge of religion, and who in a judgement of charity we ought to think are sincerely religious, though not without imperfections, which we all have, might be admitted to christian fellowship, if they desire it, without complying with some terms heretofore required. What I particularly refer to is the *relation* of their experiences & conversion. Good persons may be over backward in publishing to the world, what looks like boasting of experiences that are known only to God & their own souls. There is a natural diffidence in persons especially in those who are young to come before a whole congregation, consisting of their parents, of their companions, and of the irreligious as well as the religious and there laying open what they conceive to be the secret opperation of god upon their hearts. I believe that many good persons may from mere bashfulness be discouraged from it. And is it proper that we should lay those discouragements in their way? What can we derive from making this a term of communion Can we know their hearts that they are sincere? May they not even be decieved themselves by the power of Enthusiasm & much more others who can look only to the outward appearance. And cannot we judge better by their lives than their words? Does Jesus Christ the head of the Chh. direct that such a relation should be a necessary term of discipleship? I think not. I believe that in the Apostles days, if a man owned that he believed in Jesus & was desireous to become his disciple, he was readily admitted to the priveleges of a christian. And whence have we a right to make the gate of the Christian chh. narrower? Why should we attempt to be wiser & stricter than the lawgiver of his chh.? I wish that we may not be found hurting the cause of religion instead of promoting of it, at a time when it seems almost ready to leave us. What with Deism, on one hand, prevailing among the fashionable world, and Enthusiasm prevailing among the weak & ignorant, I think we are in danger of loosing the substantial form of godliness. I wish that we may not by any unscriptural & useless terms of communion be the means of promoting those evils. I do not doubt that the practice in our Churches was introduced by our Ancestors with a pious intention, & I am sensible that it is hard to overcome the prejudices of long usuages but it is never amiss to endeavour to get righter and with a spirit of moderation & forbearance to reform past errors & promote as far as in lies, the increase & prosperity of Christs chh., & the mutual edification of each other—You will excuse my taking up so long a letter upon this subject, as it forcibly struck my mind on reflecting on the state of our chh. when I read your account of those deaths in it. You ask whether business goes on in Congress agreeably to my mind? I cannot say that it does. We have been a long time engaged on the subject of the national debt & have not yet come to any decisions that can be depended upon. The minds of Congress are much divided, but something must be done though it is yet uncertain what that will be. It gives me much uneasiness to find so many ways for our money to be applyed beside paying our creditors! We are told that the resources of our country are abundant without direct taxes or oppressing any description of men. I ardently wish it may prove so, but cannot rely on it, from what appears to me. I have not room in this letter to give you a more particular account of our doings but you will see by the news papers generally what is doing & I hope to have the pleasure in two months more to communicate to you face to face & that the result of this session will be eventually for the peace & welfare of the country [*lined out*] whose good I sincerely wish.

ALS, Wingate Papers, MH. Place to which addressed not indicated.

Newspaper Article

We are informed that there will soon be published, an history of this, and the preceding session of Congress; and that the object of this history will be to point out the most interesting questions that have been debated, and to make such remarks on the proceedings at large as will shew the general complexion of public business. This history will be rendered singularly entertaining, by furnishing a biographical account of the most distinguished characters in Congress; and by investigating the views and principles which appear to have governed the debates.

GUS, 3 April; reprinted at Portland, Maine; Portsmouth, New Hampshire; Stockbridge, Massachusetts; Providence, Rhode Island; Danbury, New Haven, and Norwich, Connecticut; Philadelphia and York, Pennsylvania; Fredericksburg, Richmond, and Winchester, Virginia; Edenton, North Carolina; and Charleston, South Carolina.

For the Independent Gazetteer

MR. PRINTER,

Be pleased to publish the following in your paper for the good of the public.

IN the debates of Congress, I observe that Mr. Gerry says, that public faith or credit principally depends on the integrity, &c. of Congress, and that their conduct will be critically tried by the people by the standard of morality.[1] This I grant to be true; but let us first fix what morality itself is; for men in all ages have formed different ideas of virtue and vice—the reason of which is, that almost if not every virtue, in all nature, by excess, becomes a vice: Then it follows, that as lawful drinking does by excess become a vice, so when we apply it [*to*] government, though it is found just and necessary to support all men in their bargains and dealings with each other; yet excess herein, like that of beastly drunkenness, has been found the worst of all vices, and the foundation or cause of all the violence, oppression, and slavery of mankind, from *Noah's* days[2] to the present state of all Asia and Europe; which, when we compare to the present taste of freedom that we enjoy, and the glorious prospect of our still growing and future happiness, we ought surely to endeavor to guard against the vice, and its effects, as the curse of all curses, and worse than savage ignorance. And more especially, as we have before our eyes the present troubles and ze[*al*] of the people in Europe, to throw off the effects of th[*is*] excess—their Egyptian task-masters.[3] Therefore, to begin to draw a medium line through, as Pope says,

— — — to know is very nice,

Where ends the virtue, and where begins the vice.[4] Yet we must endeavor to draw the line as near as we can, otherwise all our boasted liberty will be at an end. Now all these ages past, with all their outward learning, have been ignorant of the first principles whereby to draw this line, except a chance Lycurgus, and some travelling Jew, or perhaps the exiled Japthah,[5] very few that were spiritually learned, such as the authors of the scriptures, and founders of the Jewish government, (which scriptures in fact, is our original statute book). For all our present principles of liberty are the effects and fruits of the seeds and principles sown in our said original statute book; and happily we are yet sworn to believe and (consequently) to maintain them. The fixing this medium-line is the most important to the happiness of society, in every part thereof; for those tyrants are themselves deceived from enjoying any real happiness—They are but miserable themselves, if not the most miserable, like the devils in hell. By envying the happiness of others, they are deprived of it themselves.

The first framers of our constitutions, as Israel of old, (who were as hinds let loose[6]) had a feeling sense of these Egyptian task-masters, and endeavored to guard against them by not creating any title of nobility. But we must go farther than the mere name and title; for if we create the property, and support the speculator in holding it to excess, the odious name, with that of landjobber, will serve for all the purposes of the titles of nobility. Nature itself is drawing this line, in thus fixing those odious names of forestallers, engrossers, and extortioners, speculators, landjobbers, &c.

The aim and design of uniting into society was the common happiness of every individual. There cannot be any other social tie than that of the common interest; therefore, nothing can be consistent with the order of society or government, unless it be consistent with the common utility of its members. This is the first principle of morality, and the only criterion whereby the people will try virtue from vice.

Again, Mr. Gerry acknowledges, that in March, 1780, Congress *scaled* their old debt to sink it, and violated their public faith, rather than be enslaved.[7] How was this matter? Their giving up the cause, would not have paid the original creditors; but Congress was absolutely unable to pay off the old score; and rather than our posterity should be enslaved, the same creditors who had compounded with them to take one for forty, now credited them anew. The freedom of our posterity was surely the grand and glorious object which they had in view, otherwise they might as well have submitted to the tax on tea first; for there was not a whig in that day but saw very clearly that the expense of a war would hurt the present age much more than what Britain could possibly impose on them by taxes. All men could see this—and it was always the argument of the unprincipled, ignorant, and short-sighted, selfish tory, against the war. But though these creditors had thus compounded to take one for forty, and began again anew, yet the Congress was still unable to pay, and the debt sunk to a thousand for one, which Congress did not think fit or worth while to *scale* the old debt any more. Here Mr. Gerry argues, that though Congress, in the time of a distressing war, violated their faith—but why not become insolvent? I reprobate that term of *violating public faith*; they were unable to pay; and the principled original creditors did again virtually compound to take 2/6 in the pound. There was no contract, neither verbally nor virtually, between the original creditor and the speculator. Two shillings and 6*d* in the pound was the current value of the certificates; and it was virtually a contract between the creditor and the insolvent nation—and I say an honorable insolvancy—more honorable than that of a private insolvent debtor, even if it was through an accident of fire; therefore, no violation of public faith. Thus nature was doing her work by the true line of justice and principles or morality: and had Congress had the foresight to have added a little art to nature, and *scaled* the debt on this contract of nature (who always does her work aright) all had been well. Indeed such original creditors as kept their certificates in their own hands it may be more right to consider; as thereby they did not appear to agree to compound. But if we follow the known rules in cases of private insolvents, which is every day practised, they have no right to complain. At the time that peace was restored, speculation began. Before that time, as I said, nature was doing her work by the true line of justice and morality; and all who took certificates at the current value, passed them away again as soon as they could; and what they lost by the depreciation while in their hands, they counted as their proportion of taxes to carry on the war. If some few did begin to speculate before, from early intelligence or foresight, how the war would end: As all forestalling and speculation is of the nature of theft and robbery, if we do not punish it by law, at least let us not give it the greatest countenance and encouragement, by funding the debt for them on our posterity. We might, from the same wrong principles of justice, fix a perpetual tax on the children and posterity of every insolvent debtor. On this same argument of Mr. Gerry, viz thus admitting that the Assembly passed an act of insolvency in favor of this insolvent debtor, because he was then in distressing circumstances, having a large family of small children, &c. can this alter the eternal rules of justice, says Mr. Gerry, that now his family of children are grown up to manhood, and their great numbers (which while small distressed him) do now enable the family to pay off the debt, by paying a yearly tax, fixed on each child, and childrens' child, to the end of time, to the heirs of the (say) honest creditor? Yet the argument will not hold.

[Boston] *Independent Gazetteer*, 3 April. The second half of this article is dated 10 April and is printed under that date, below.

---

[1] Gerry's speech of 19 February against discriminating among securities holders (*DHFFC* 12:456).

[2] Ham saw his father Noah naked and drunk in his tent, for which Ham's descendants were cursed (Genesis 9:21–26).

[3] A reference to Exodus 1:11 on the Egyptian treatment of the Hebrews after the death of Joseph.

[4] A paraphrase of "the difference is too nice/where ends the virtue or begins the vice," from Epistle II of Alexander Pope's "Essay on Man" (1732–34).

[5] Jephthah, ruler of the Gileads (Judges 11:1–12:7).

[6] A recurring allusion in the Old Testament, for example, Genesis 49:21 and Psalm 22.

[7] Gerry's speech of 19 February; see *DHFFC* 12:458. In March 1780 Congress revalued the continental currency at forty dollars to one specie dollar; see *DHFFC* 12:238n.

Other Documents

Abigail Adams to Mary Cranch. ALS, Abigail Adams Letters, MWA. Addressed to Braintree, Massachusetts. For the full text, see *Abigail Adams*, pp. 43–45.

"Richmond Hill" "begins to reassume all its Beauty"; "For situation and prospect I know no equal"; has been gardening for more than a week; expects only a short congressional recess; given the importance and duration of Congress's business, "they talk now of only adjourning through the Hot Months"; Knox has promised John Adams he will do something for (Joseph) Cranch; as he "is always very civil polite and social with me, I will drop a word to him if opportunity offers" when she dines at the Knoxes' the following Tuesday (6 April); Jefferson "adds much to the social circle."

William Constable to Gouverneur Morris. FC:lbk, Constable-Pierrepont Collection, NN.

Believes that if no provision is made for the assumption of the states' war debts, no provision will be made for the Continental debt; Robert Morris is expected back from Philadelphia in the course of the week.

Moses Copeland to George Thatcher. ALS, incomplete, Thatcher Papers, MeHi. Place from which written not indicated.

A post road to the Penobscot River will accommodate eight towns without the trouble of going through the woods; will provide distances of alternative routes in a short time; will be happy to provide particulars of his part of the state.

Alexander Johnson to John Adams. LS, Adams Family Manuscript Trust, MHi. Written from Portland Street, London.

Asks Adams's patronage for a remedy that he exhorts magistrates worldwide to adopt, for resuscitating life in victims of accident or violence; institutions were established at Boston and Philadelphia about 1785, to implement the procedure, but he has heard nothing of their success.

John Langdon to Joseph Whipple. ALS, Sturgis Family Papers, MH. Addressed to Portsmouth, New Hampshire; franked; postmarked 4 April.

Asks Whipple to pay Mrs. Elizabeth Langdon one or two hundred dollars, for which Langdon will procure a warrant; "I have not a Single thing to inform you of, worth mention[*in*]g."

Benjamin Lincoln to John Adams. ALS, Adams Family Manuscript Trust, MHi. Written from Boston; answered 19 May.

(William) Frobisher seeks "compensation" from the federal government for improvements to the mode for making pot ash; "he informs me that you are possessed of the art & advised him to apply"; asks Adams to point out to Frobisher the proper mode.

Roger Sherman to Simeon Baldwin. ALS, Sherman Collection, CtY. Addressed to New Haven, Connecticut; franked; postmarked. For background and documents relating to Collins's and Ocain's petitions, see *DHFFC* 7:84–85.

In consequence of a letter on the subject from Jonathan Edwards, Jr., has spoken with C. Carroll about Russ's application to the trustees (probably of Annapolis's St. John's College, of which C. Carroll was a major benefactor) to be hired as a writing master; has been very busy this day, but intends to speak to C. Carroll on the subject again early the next week; has discussed with Justice William Cushing the business of the federal circuit court to be held at New Haven; thought it best that Pitman Collins's petition "should be determined before the other [*Jeremiah Ocain's*] is referred"; encloses issues of *GUS* and directions for binding a complete set.

Frederick William Steuben to Benjamin Walker. One page ALS, in French, *The Collector* 62(1949):item 130. For background on Steuben's petition for compensation, see *DHFFC* 7:203–46.

Hamilton's report on Steuben's petition will be submitted on Monday (5 April), and his friends have assured him of a prompt decision.

Jeremiah Wadsworth to Josiah Burr. No copy known; acknowledged in Burr to Wadsworth, 12 April.

Jeremiah Wadsworth to Catherine Wadsworth. ALS, Wadsworth Papers, CtHi. Place to which addressed not indicated.

Has written instructions for household management to Daniel (Wadsworth); is well except for a cold "which I caught lately I know not how. but it is not bad it makes my Eyes Water & tickles my nose very much."

Samuel Ward to Jeremiah Wadsworth. ALS, Updike Collection, Providence Public Library, Rhode Island. Written from London; addressed to Hartford, Connecticut; postmarked Boston, 27 May.

Met in Amsterdam with Gouverneur Morris, who commented on the improbability of Catharine Greene's securing a Dutch loan with land because of "what seemed to be a general opinion amongst the Dutch monied men—that Landed security in any part of America was very low in value"; "this I think was your opinion when I had the pleasure to see you in New York."

Hopley Yeaton to John Langdon. ALS, Langdon Papers, NhPoA. Written from Portsmouth, New Hampshire.

Thanks Langdon for delivering a letter; is sorry Langdon talks of retiring from Congress: it always wants men like Langdon who "Know what is Right or Rong."

SUNDAY, 4 APRIL 1790

Warm (Johnson)

John Adams to Benjamin Rush

The Tories as you observe in your friendly Letter of 24 Feb. are more attached to each other; they are also, we must candidly confess, more of real Politicians. They make to themselves more merit with the People, for the smallest services, than the Whigs are able to do for the greatest. The Arts, the Trumpetts, the Puffs, are their old Instruments and they know how to employ them. The History of our Revolution will be one continued Lye from one End to the other. The Essence of the whole will be *that Dr.* [*Benjamin*] *Franklins electrical Rod, Smote the Earth and out sprung General Washington. That Franklin electrified him with his Rod—and thence forward these two conducted all the Policy Negotiations Legislatures and War.* These underscored [*italicized*] Lines contain the whole Fable Plot and Catastrophy. if this Letter should be preserved, and read an hundred years hence the Reader will say "the Envy of this J. A. could not bear to think of the Truth! He ventured to scribble to Rush, as envious as himself, Blasphemy that he dared not speak, when he lived. But Barkers at the Sun and Moon are always Silly Curs." But this my Friend, to be serious, is the Fate of all Ages and Nations; and there is no Resource in human nature for a cure. Brederode[1] did more in the Dutch Revolution than William 1st. Prince of orange. Yet Brederode is forgotten and William the Saviour, Deliverer and Founder. limited Monarchy is founded in Nature. No Nation can adore more than one Man at a time. it is an happy Circumstance that the object of our Devotion is so well deserving of it. that he has Virtue so exquisite and Wisdom so consummate. There is no Citizen of America will say, that there is in the World so fit a Man for the head of the Nation. From my Soul I think ~~so~~ there is not. and the Question should not be who has done or suffered most, or who has been the most essential and Indispensible Cause of the Revolution, but who is best qualified to govern Us? Nations are not to sacrifice their Future Happiness to Ideas of Historical Justice. They must consult their own Weaknesses, Prejudices, Passions, Senses and Imaginations as well as their Reason. "La Raison n'a jamais fait grande chose," as the K. of Prussia says in his Histoire de mon temps.[2]

The more Extracts you send me from your Journals, the more will you oblige me—I beg especially a Copy of my Character. I know very well it must be a partial Panegyrick. I will send you my Criticisms upon it. You know I have no affectation of Modesty. My Comfort is that such vain folly as Cicero, Neckar, Sir William Temple and I are never dangerous.

If I said in 1777 that "We should never be qualified for Republican Government till we were ambitious to be poor" I meant to express an Impossibility. I meant then and now say that No Nation under Heaven ever was, now is, or ever will be qualified for a *Republican Government*, unless you mean by these Words, *equal Laws* resulting from a Ballance of three Powers—the Monarchical Aristocratical & Democratical. I meant more and I now repeat more explicitly, that Americans are peculiarly unfit for any ~~but the Mon~~ Republic but the Aristo-Democratical-Monarchy; because they are more *Avaricious* than any other Nation that ever existed the Carthaginians and Dutch not excepted. The Alieni appetens sui profusus[3] reigns in this nation as a Body more than any other I have ever seen.

When I went to Europe in 1778 I was full of patriotic Projects like yours of collecting Improvements in Arts Agriculture, Manufacture Commerce Litterature and science. But I soon found my Error. I found that my offices demanded every moment of my time and the Assistance of two or three Clerks and that all this was not enough. I was obliged to make it a Rule never to go out of my *road* for any Curiosity of any kind. J. J. Rousseau understood it very well when he said that Ambassadors "doivent tout leur tems à cet Objet Unique, ils sont trop honnêtes gens pour voler leur Argent."[4] Emile, Tom. 4. p. 361. If he meant this as a Sarcasm he was in the Wrong. I never knew one who attempted or affected Philosophy, that was good for any Thing in the Diplomatique Line—and I know that every Hour that I might have employed that Way would have been a Robbery upon the Duties of my Public Character.

Your Family pictures are charming; and the tender Piety you express for your Mother, is felt by me in all its force, as I have a Mother living in her Eighty Second Year, to whom I owe more than I can ever pay. This Mother and a Father who died 30 years ago,[5] two of the best People I ever knew, formed the Character which you have drawn. alas! that it is no better! I said before that Vanity is not dangerous. a Man who has bad designs is seldom or never vain. it is such modest Rascals as Cæsar, who play tricks with Mankind. read his Commentaries—what consummate caution to conceal his Vanity! contemptu famæ, fama augebatur.[6] This Tyrants and Villains always know.

Adieu Mon Ami,

[*P. S.*] Pray can you recollect a Feast at Point no Point in the Fall of 1775 and the Company that returned with you and me in a Boat and our Conversation.[7] I want a List of the Names of that Party who returned in the same Boat with us to Philadelphia.

Photostat of ALS, Rush Papers, DLC. Place to which addressed not indicated. Adams wrote an alternative beginning to this letter in a draft dated 28 February, in which he lamented the Tories' influence on how the events of the Revolution "are all forgotten, and no more talked of than if they had happened in the heart of Africa before the flood" (FC:dft, Adams Family Manuscript Trust, MHi).

[1] Hendrik van Brederode (1531–68), a Dutch nobleman active in the early phases (1564–68) of the revolt of the Netherlands against Spanish rule.

[2] "Reason never accomplished anything great," from *L'Histoire de mon temps*, written in 1746 and included in the posthumous sixteen volume *Oeuvres* (Berlin, 1788) of Prussia's Frederick II the Great. Portions had previously been translated into English.

[3] "Covetous of the possessions of others and extravagant with his own," said by the historian Sallust (ca. 86–35 B.C.) of Catiline, one of the most notorious conspirators against the Roman Republic.

[4] Ambassadors ought to devote their time to that single object; they are too honest to steal their money.

[5] "Deacon" John Adams (1691–1761), a typical New England yeoman from Braintree,

Massachusetts, married Susannah Boylston (1709–97) in October 1734; their first son John was born almost exactly one year later. Adams's mother remarried, to John Hall, in 1766.

[6] With contempt of fame, fame grows.

[7] The excursion in row galleys up the Delaware River above Philadelphia by a company of Second Continental Congress delegates, Pennsylvania assemblymen, and Philadelphia notables is described in Adams's diary entry for 28 September 1775, in *LDC* 2:76–77. Returning with Adams and Rush in the galley *Bull Dog* were Owen Biddle, Nathaniel Falconer, Michael Hillegas, David Rittenhouse, John Ross, John Zubly, and the captain, Charles Alexander.

Pierce Butler to Weeden Butler

I cannot let the Packet Sail without my thanks for Your kind letter of the 5th. of January. It is always highly gratifying to Us to hear from You; but still more so when We are informed that all are well with You—We share largely in the satisfaction arising from Mrs. [*Mary Middleton*] Butlers reestablishd health—May She and everything that can Contribute to Your happiness, be long Spared to You—My Dear Wife has been greatly indisposed all the Winter—She is still Confined—Her Spirits are miserably low—She has given up the idea of going to England this Year; indeed She has not strength to attempt the Voyage—I have enough to Encounter in Her indisposition. My anxiety formerly was for my Boy—Now my Dear Girls occupy my anxious mind—My Son has a certain friend and sure Guide in You—Who is to direct and Guide my Girls if they shou'd be deprived of a tender Mother! I must drop the Subject.

I have had a letter from my friend Doctor [*Peter*] Spence from Bath—tho' He Complains, yet He writes in good Spirits—I write to Him and my Boy by this Conveyance.

The mind of all Europe seems alive—The People are agitated with sensations to which they were long Strangers—*Am not I a Man also!*[1] The feelings and opinions of the French will extend—It is probable that the Crowndheads of Europe may have their hands full for many Years—We, the last days Work of Creation, appear now to be beforehand with the European States; while they are Agitated and busied in forming Governments, We are giving Stability to One already formed—While they are breathing the breath of Life into the Nostrils We are giving Strength and Vigour to what is already quickend—The important business of Finance is the Subject of Our present deliberations; truly important it is. difficulties present themselves—If I cou'd see my Son rise in the House of Representatives and, when they are most at a stand, point out the clear and certain road to greatness and Independence, by [*lined out*] present Arrangements—Greatness by an honest and honorable Compliance with their Engagements—Independence by a Wise provision for future events—I woud say with good Old Simeon—Lord now leteth thou thy Servant depart in peace, for mine Eyes

have seen thy goodness[2]—I have greatly at heart His being a finishd Orator and able States Man. You will say, perhaps, that I am not moderate in my expectation, that such a Character is the lott of few—that is very true; but that is no reason why We shoud not Contend for the Goal—If we reach it not, it is Our misfortune—If We gain it We shall be amply paid for Our trouble.
[*P.S.*] Inclosed You have a Bill for £70—at thirty days Sight which when pay'd You pass to my Boys Credit.

ALS, Butler Papers, Uk. Addressed to "Cheyne Walk, Chelsea, near London"; postmarked 7 April; answered 1 June. On the first page, Pierce noted to Weeden Butler that "Tommy's" letter "of this Date was No. 6" and that this letter was answered on 1 June. On the last page is the bill of exchange that Butler mentions, written in an unknown hand, indicating that it was negotiated through William Constable & Co.

---

[1] "Am I Not A Man and a Brother?" was the inscription on the seal of Great Britain's Committee for the Abolition of the Slave Trade, founded in 1787. It helped mobilize public opinion when it was manufactured into Wedgewood medallions that circulated in the thousands throughout the Atlantic world (Simon Schama, *Rough Crossings: Britain, the Slaves and the American Revolution* [New York, 2006], pp. 208–9, 260).

[2] Uttered by Simeon upon Jesus' presentation for circumcision at the Temple, which fulfilled the Holy Ghost's promise that the aged priest would not die before seeing the Messiah (Luke 2:21–34).

Thomas Hartley to Jasper Yeates

I receved your Favor of the 28th. ult. and am glad you succeeded in your Business to Chester.

It would have been as well had the People called Quakers postponed their Application concerning the Manumission of Slaves and the like—but as it was taken up—we were obliged to pay some attention.

The Southern Gentlemen acted with very unbecoming warmth in several Instances—and indeed some of your Friends were very near personal Quarrels with them.

We are still on the Assumption or non assumption of the State Debts—The House as I said is nearly equally divided—The Determination of that Question is very important—The System must take much of its Complexion from this Decision.

Our State ~~was~~ Delegation was pretty unanimous some Days ago—but from Causes which we may speak of at a future Day we are broken to Pieces.

It may be popular for the Moment to vote against the Assumption—but I am convinced the People will think differently at [*lined out*] another Time.

I believe the Farmer would be rather best satisfied to be without a Land Tax of some shillings in the Pound.

I inform myself as well as I can and I am determined to vote according to my Judgment without regard to future Consequences so far as they may affect Myself.

You and a few Friends shall know my Reasons when I see you—The Newspapers may give them in Part—and I am convinced that were our whole Delegation unanimous in Sentiment with me—we could when we agreed to the Assumption—make such Terms as would tend to protect the Manufactures & Interests of our State—we could turn the Scale or alter Tide.

If we carry the Assumption we shall have Mr. Madison and all his Friends to oppose us in every Stage of the Business—If the Question should go in the Negative I fear poor Pennsylvania will again be let down betwen two Stools—I shall {*lined out*} strive to act for the best—if the non assumption Plan carrys—I shall consider it my Duty to support the first Proposition for the Debts of the union only—However in no Stage will I if possible commit myself.

There is a Quarrel on Hand between Judge Burke and Colonel Hamilton—The latter Gentleman in an oraytion delivered on the 4th of July—had said in order to enhance the Character of his Hero General Green that the Militia he met with were the mere mimickry of Sodiers—This gave some offence and on Thursday last Mr. Burke Head over Heels—brought in the Assertion—Said it was False—and called to the Gallery to the House & the world that Colonel Hamilton was a Liar—What will be the Consequence I do not know—Mr. Hamiltons Situation is critical—He is a man of Spirit.[1]

You shall hear again to Morrow.

P. S. If you knew the number of Letters I am obliged to write this Morning you would excuse the Incorrectness of the foregoing.

ALS, Yeates Papers, PHi. Addressed to Lancaster, Pennsylvania; answered 12 April. In a second ALS of the same date, in the same manuscript collection and also answered on 12 April, Hartley drew on Yeates to pay back money advanced on the President's behalf for the purchase of mares for Mount Vernon.

[1] For the Burke-Hamilton affair, see *DHFFC* 8:476–80.

James Madison to Edmund Pendleton

You will see by the papers herewith covered that the proposed assumption of the State debts continues to employ the deliberations of the House of Reps. The question seems now to be near its decision, and unfortunately, tho' so momentous a one, is likely to turn on a very small majority, possibly on a single vote. The measure is not only liable to many objections of a general cast, but in its present form is particularly unfriendly to the interests of Virginia. In this light it is viewed by all her representatives except Col. Bland.

The American Revolution with its foreign and future consequences is a subject of such magnitude that every circumstance connected with it, more especially every one leading to it, is already and will be more and more a matter of investigation. In this view I consider the proceedings in Virginia during the crisis of the Stamp-Act as worthy of particular remembrance, and a communication of them as a sort of debt due from her cotemporary citizens to their successors. As I know of no memory on which my curiosity could draw for more correct or more judicious information, you must forgive this resort to yours. Were I to consult nothing but my curiosity, my enquiries would not be very limited. But as I could not indulge that motive fully, without abusing the right I have assumed, my request goes no farther than that you will, as leisure & recollection may permit, *briefly* note on paper—by whom & how the subject commenced in the Assembly, where the resolutions proposed by Mr. Henry *really* originated, what was the sum of the arguments for and against them, and who were the principal speakers on each side; with any little anecdotes throwing light on the transaction, on the characters concerned in it, or on the temper of the Colony at the time.

ALS, Madison Papers, DLC. Place to which addressed not indicated. A copy of this letter, which from the emendations is clearly a working draft, is in the Wirt Papers, MdHi. Madison later annotated the ALS with the remark that Pendleton's response regarding Patrick Henry's role in the Revolution had been sent to William Wirt to assist in his 1817 biography of Henry and was never returned.

Robert Morris to Gouverneur Morris

I came here last Monday to attend a Lawsuit[1] *** there is another ***, after which I shall return to New York. *** Mr. [*William*] Constable will no doubt write you what is going forward in Congress particularly in regard to the Domestic Debt and the Funding System, [*William*] Duer has quitted his Station in the Treasury Department, The Restrictions under which He held it Cramped his genius for Speculation and I believe He found it absolutely necessary to retire. My Accounts with the Secret Committee were very nearly gone through when I left New York[2] and I regretted the necessity of coming away before they were finished, but I was obliged to leave them, ten days after my return will finish them and enable me to give the Lie to all the abuse which has been lavished on me on that Score. I also got a Committee appointed in the House of Representatives for the examination of my official Transactions as Superintendant of Finance,[3] it is a very respectable Committee Consisting of Mr. Madison, Mr. Sedgewick Mr. Sherman, Mr. Lawrence of New York and Mr. Smith of South Carolina, they are now at work, and I have no doubt but they will do justice to my Character, I wish they may so manage their Report as to enable me to acknowledge your Services[4] & render that Justice which is so eminently due to your Talents and exertions.

*** from Mr. Constable it seems probable that something of the same sort is to happen with one of our Friends there,[5] of which He will probably write you the particulars.

These are Tilting times & they lead me to think I should engage for a party, altho my object, is so fast sinking into Contempt that I believe it may be Wisest to Content myself with the Victory I shall now soon gain over the whole Faction.

Mr. Jefferson arrived in N. York before I came away, We visited and I was in his Company at one or two dinners but he had not then entered upon his Official Duties, by the time I get back it is probable that something in the Diplomatic line may be in agitation.

ALS, Gouverneur Morris Papers, NNC. Written from Philadelphia; place to which addressed not indicated.

[1] Morris returned to Philadelphia on 29 March to hear verdicts delivered on the two lawsuits concluding his longtime litigation with John Holker, which stemmed from Morris's conduct as Holker's agent to the French marine department from 1778 to 1780. The first verdict cleared Morris of a claim for £4700; the second, which Morris expected to be decided on similar principles, is not known. Morris returned to New York by 16 April (*PRM* 9:407, 597–609; *DHFFC* 9:246).

[2] The board of treasury's investigation into Morris's unadjusted secret and commercial committee accounts (for purchasing supplies in Europe prior to 1778) was entrusted to Commissioner Benjamin Walker until his duties were superceded under the new government by the treasury department's auditor and comptroller. Morris and his partners owed $93,312.63 under the settlement of accounts finally concluded in 1795 (*PRM* 9:635n).

[3] For background, texts, and the legislative history of Morris's petition to the FFC for an investigation into his accounts as superintendent of finance (1781–84), see *DHFFC* 8:663–75.

[4] On the basis of an alliance with Morris while serving in the Continental Congress (1778–79) and his authorship of a highly regarded series of articles on public finance published in early 1780, Gouverneur Morris was recruited as deputy in the office of finance and served throughout Morris's term as superintendent of finance (*PRM* 1:96).

[5] A reference to the practice of dueling, of which Morris had just noted several recent instances in the omitted text immediately preceding. The "Friend" he alludes to is Hamilton.

Theodore Sedgwick to Pamela Sedgwick

I have again called on Doctor [*Richard*] Bailey. He says great attention has been paid to little Roberts case, that however he cannot without seeing him be particular. Of two things he seems to have no doubt, first that the bone is not effected, was this the case he says the child would constantly be in pain. and that there would be no intermission in its constantly growing worse. In the next place he is very confident that constant rest is indispensibly necessary. He says he is persuaded that one days use of his leg would do it as much injury as it could derive benefit from many days application of the most proper remedies. Every conversation I have with him he urges the indispensible necessity of an imediate and constant attention to this object. He seems also very well convinced that a constant drain from the part affected should be made and that for this purpose a succession of blisters is the most proper application—If this course should be found ineffectual he seems to advise to his being brought here.

Tomorrow it seems agreed on all hands to take the question, we conceive that we have a majority and they are at least equally confident. Our great difficulty is with the delegation of Pensylvania. They have no hesitation in declaring that they believe the assumption to be indispensible to the welfare of the country, but they seem to consider the measure as unpopular in that state, and have not the firmness of spirit to give a decided preference to the welfare of the people over their own popularity.

Dearest and best beloved of my soul, may you possess that happiness which should be the effect of your many exemplary virtues.

ALS, Sedgwick Papers, MHi. Place to which addressed not indicated. This portion of text, written "Sunday morning," concludes a letter begun on 3 April and printed under that date, above.

Theodore Sedgwick to Henry Van Schaack

I can only excuse my long intermission of writing by the busy scenes with which I have been connected and the suspence in which the event has hung. Tomorrow the great question which has so long been agitated will probably be decided. Both parties flatter themselves with success. There is a real doubt arising from the pendularian disposition of the delegation of Pensylvania. They do not hesitate with regard either to the polocy or justice of the measure, but beleive it to be unpopular in that state: you have doubtless been at a loss to determine from what motives the delegation of N. Carolina is actuated on this occasion. You will cease to wonder when I inform you of a few facts. That state has issued a large sum in paper money, this money by specific taxes laid annually they call into the treasury. It is again issued by the purchase of their securities at 4/. in the pound. By this operation they intend for every 2/6, paid by the citizens to create to themselves a credit of 20/—When you reflect on these circumstances and apply them to a people, with whom honesty has ceased to be a motive, you will perceive the that the conduct of those men is not so grossly absurd as otherwise it might appear.

Let me know how men of inteligence veiw the subject of the assumption. Pray what is the prospect with regard to the election in your district? There is not a more honest and virtuous man on earth than your present representative.[1]

ALS, Sedgwick Papers, MHi. Place to which addressed not indicated.

[1] Woodbridge Little (1741–1813), a lawyer and longtime selectman of Pittsfield, Massachusetts, represented that town in the state House of Representatives from 1788 to 1790.

William Smith (Md.) to Otho H. Williams

I have not heard from Baltimore, for Near Two weeks past, your Absense from home may be a good reason why I have not heard from you. but that appology will not hold good for Polly [*Mary Smith Williams*], nor my other friends who have been all silent.

The question is not yet taken on the Assumpn. of the State debts, the friends to that measure seem afraid to let it come forward, & have by various means, hithertoo prevented a decision. I believe they begin to despair of Success. and many of them have declared in the House, if that is rejected, they will not concur in any funding System; however I have little doubt, a majority of the house will be decided in favor of Supporting public credit. we proceed so slowly in business that it is truly distressing to be detained here so long & do so little good.

In the debates two or three days ago, on the Assumption of the State debts, A mr. Burke from So. Carolina, took occasion to Shew the great Services rendered by the Militia of that State, *in fighting the battles of the United States*, as an argument Why their debts ought to be paid out of the genl. funds. in the course of his argument he took an oppertunity to resent, *what had long rankled in his mind*, some expressions made use of by Colo. Hamilton, in his Eulogium on Genl. [*Nathanael*] Greene, the last summer, by which it was thought he spoke disrespectfully of the Militia.[1] Burke after recapitulating those Services, & remarking on the expressions, *which gave offence.* Said he gladly took that oppertunity of giving that gentleman the *lie*, & doing Justice to the Merits of the So. Carolinians, here, he was called to order, Stop'd & Set down, After [*lined out*] sometime he again rose, & told the Speaker, he was perfectly cool, *never more so in his life*, but Supposing Colo. Hamilton in the Gallery (which was filled with ladies) he faced round to that quarter, & called out aloud, that he threw the lie in Colo. Hamiltons face. here he was again Stoped & was not permitted to proceed. The friends of Hamilton, are very Uneasy abt. this business, some apprehend Serious consequences must ensue. it is Said Mr. Hamilton has wrote him a letter on the Subject, the contents not known, but Supposed making Such demands, as Burke will not comply with. I have been told by some of Burkes intimate friends, that he is obstinate, & will not consent to make any concessions. *He ought most certainly to make an appology to the house*, perhaps that would Satisfy all parties. I apprehend if no appology is made there will be a fight on the occasion.

Finals from 7/ to 7/6, I con[*c*]lude. The doubts that may have arisen, in the minds of the public on the funding business, has opperated on the price of Securities.

ALS, Williams Papers, MdHi. Addressed to Baltimore.

---

[1] Burke's remarks on the floor of the House on 31 March are printed in *DHFFC* 12:915–16. See also *DHFFC* 8:476–80.

George Thatcher to Francis Cook

Your favour of the 15th March came to hand last evening, for which I thank you; and so long as I have the honor of representing the District of Maine, I hope you will continue to acquaint me, from time to time, of whatever you may think to be injurious to the people, or require the attention of Congress for their good.

The difficulty, you state, of collecting the Tonage duty on vessels, that are part of the year employed in coasting, & part of the year sent on foreign voyages, has been taken notice of by several of my correspondents—and I have heard it complained of by others—I am inclined to think a remidy will be attempted in Congress; but am not certain of success, as some think Coasting vessells ought not to go foreign voyages—I believe they wish to seperate, as much as they can, coasting vessells from those employed in foreign Trade—I am sensible this will hurt our part of the Country; because most of the merchants & Traders, who are engaged in foreign Commerce often find it very advantageous to send their vessells a coasting some part of the year.

Some time ago I recieved a Letter from Mr. [*Moses*] Copeland, wherein he represents it as the wish of the people in Thomaston, & on St. Georges River to be annexed to the District of Wiscassett—they complain much of the inconvenience of being obliged to resort to Penobscott to enter & clear their Vessells.

He informed me the people there were about petitioning Congress on the subject—I have wrote him an answer; and shall use my endeavour, when the amendments to the Revenue Laws come before Congress, to get Thomaston

& all St. Georges River annexed to your District—I shall consult with the Secretary of the Treasury on the subject of your Letter.

FC, Thatcher Family Papers, MHi. Sent to Wiscasset, Maine.

George Thatcher to Sarah Thatcher

Yours of the 20th. & 24th. March are before me—The former came to hand on wednesday, & the latter on last evening—The first contained the pattern & measure you mentioned in some former Letter—The latter has an apology for what, you fear, I shall deem a piece of extravagance—Before this time I hope the other handkerchief has come to hand; which, tho a mere trifle, will be a small argument, that I do not look upon the requests you made as extravagant. Whatever you have, or shall write for, it will be my greatest pleasure to procure for you.

I am extreemly grieved on account of the distressing humour that has seized you—for if it is the Itch, I fear it cannot, with safety, be cured—And should it be otherwise, it may be very troublesom—But should it turn out to be the Itch, I think you had better content yourself with backing it by the spirits of Turpentine, than attempt, by sulpher or Dock-root, to cure it—I have had an itching humour all winter, and made pretty free use of Spirits of Turpentine—Sometimes I have thought it to be the proper itch; but by its being periodical, from the full, or three or four days after the full of the moon, to the change I am encouraged to think it is only a bad humour in the blood; or what is usually called the relicks of the Itch—And the spirits of Turpentine generally asswages its itching and burning.

The Miss Lorings [*Sarah Smith Loring and her sister Eunice*] send their Love to you; and, will, with pleasure, execute your commands—Last evening, I recieved a Letter from Tempe [*Temperance Hodge Lee*], dated the 21st. march—She was well & very happy—she expresses the strongest wishes to see her good Uncle & aunt at her little house—She sais she longs to kiss our dear children—whom I likewise long to embrace—You tell me they frequently talk about their papa—this gives me pleasure—I would not have them forget me, tho absent—I was charmed at hearing they now & then drink to me at Table—I hope you let them always set at the Table with you—and behave in the same manner, as tho there was a large company with you at dinner—by this early begining they may be taught, in a good degree, to avoid that bashfullness in company which many suffer under when arrived to years of manhood, & scarcely ever throw off.

Dont let them get a habit of silence when they are spoke to, especially by a stranger—Make them say something, or other—when they are asked, how old they are, or how they do? insist on their answering—no matter what at first—habit will soon form proper replys—teach them, on such occasions to speak their words full, & distinct.

I suppose Eben[1] will want his pay as soon as it becomes due—I am now enquiring after some Bank Bills—to send you, which you can exchange with friend [*Jeremiah*] Hill for the Cash—And it is probable I shall get some in a few days—However, if they should not arrive at the day he wants his money, assure him he shall not loose any thing by a few days delay—And if you want money before I can remit you some, some of our friends will supply you till it arrives.

ALS, Thatcher Family Papers, MHi. Place to which addressed not indicated.

[1] According to the 1790 census, Thatcher's household in Biddeford, Maine, included two free white males over age sixteen. Eben may have been a live-in house servant or hired hand.

George Thatcher to William Webb

Your favours of the 22d February & 20th March are before me—I agree with you that a post-Office, at Bath [*Maine*], is needed, and that Dummer Sewall Esqr. will make a good and faithfull Post-Master, provided he should be disposed to accept—I shall in a few days, write him upon that subject. The emoluments of his office will not be much—but then the duties will not be troublesom or require much time.

Mr. [*Richard?*] Kimball, whom you mention as a proper person to carry the mail, wrote to me, and conversed with me upon that subject, when I was at Portland. There have been some objections to him, on account of his inattention, but I believe they are removed—and he may undoubtedly continue the business. Hitherto he has carried the mail for too small a sum—he ought to have two hundred dollars a year.

I have frequently travled in most parts of the District of Maine, & know pretty well what the roads are, and how difficult it frequently [*is*] to ride from Portland to Wiscassett.

Upon the new establishment, I am of opinion the mail will be carried once a week to & from Wiscassett—for once a fortnight is too seldom to serve the purposes of Trade & commerce, as well as to accommodate the offices of the Revenue—Furthermore, I look upon it [*as*] a general advantage to the people at large, as it gives them an opportunity if they choose, to get the public papers—I was in hopes to have it in my power to inform you, by this time, that Bath was a port of Delivery for Vessells owned by foreigners—but I cannot. The Secretary has not yet reported the amendments to the Revenue Laws—He has been, & still is collecting information from all parts of the

United States, upon that subject—I have been with him several times, & shewn him some Letters from Gentlemen at Kennebeck; particularly one from Mr. [*James?*] Davidson—this is long & very circumstantial, and at the request of Mr. Hamilton I left it with him—it states, with great accuracy & justness the injuries to that part of the Country by the present regulation—and the advantages that may be expected to accrue by opening that port to foreigners; and I think I have convinced the Secretary of the necessity of the measure—and I have no doubt, but before this Session ends of accomplishing the desired object—I can assure you & the Gentlemen on Kennebeck, that nothing on my part shall be wanting to oblige them in this & every other measure touching the District.

FC, Thatcher Family Papers, MHi.

Jeremiah Wadsworth to Tench Coxe

The bearer Mr. Aspinwall[1] is the Father of the Silk Manufacture—he long since began to Plant Mullberry Trees in Connecticut from the leaves of which are now fed so many Worms as to produce sewing Silk more than enough for the use of the State—Permit me Sir to recommend him to your Notice—as an honest Man and every way quallified to introduce the cultivation of Silk.

ALS, Coxe Papers, PHi. Place to which addressed not indicated.

[1] According to Wadsworth's clerk, Peleg Sanford, Prince Aspenwell of Mansfield, Connecticut, had devoted himself almost exclusively to the silkworm industry since he helped to establish it in the early 1770s. The state of Connecticut subsidized it by a bounty from 1784 to 1794. Wadsworth had endorsed his state's textile industry by conspicuously modeling woolen broadcloth suits at Washington's 1789 inauguration and other occasions, and regularly wore hair ribbons made of Connecticut silk (Joseph S. Davis, *Essays in the Earlier History of American Corporations* [1917; reprint, 2 vols., New York, 1965], 2:269; *PAH* 9:355–57).

Letter to New York

The members ought to bear in mind that their constituents in general think their pay is high, and was established without *much loss of time.* I confess myself mortified with the indecision of that assembly, which ought to strike the world with its wisdom, energy and dispatch—Men of sentiment are astonished and extremely disappointed.

GUS, 14 April; reprinted at Portsmouth, New Hampshire; New London and Norwich, Connecticut; Poughkeepsie, New York; Burlington, New Jersey; Fredericksburg, Virginia; and Edenton, North Carolina. This excerpt may have been taken from a letter Joseph Ward wrote to John Fenno; Fenno acknowledged a letter (of unknown date) that relates to this subject in his letter to Ward, 11 April, below.

From New York

The question on *Assumption* was expected yesterday—but an adjournment being called for, it was prevented. It is whispered that *Pennsylvania* will vote with *Virginia, Maryland, &c.* against *Assumption* which will create a majority on that side—but, I can not but suppose the debts will be assumed the present session—If NO ASSUMPTION, then NO FUNDING, is the cry! But I expect that, by compromise, both will be adopted.

The Bill for accepting the cession of Territory, by N. Carolina, and that for preventing the exportation of goods not duly inspected, received THE PRESIDENT's assent yesterday.

There is a strong talk of rising in May—to have another session late in the fall—but I think, except they quicken their motions, they must set forever, if any business is to be completed; but *slow and sure* is a good motto—It is a new business, and omissions are not so bad as errors.

We have several vessels from Europe—a packet in 54 days from St. Maloes [*St. Malo, France*]—All quiet in France, so far as I can hear.

[Boston] *Massachusetts Centinel*, 14 April; reprinted at Portland, Maine; Exeter and Portsmouth, New Hampshire; Northampton, Massachusetts; and Providence, Rhode Island.

Letter from Kentucky to Washington, Virginia

As to the Indians, they have been troublesome all winter, since October last, sixty persons have been killed within the limits of this district [*Kentucky*], besides a number destroyed on the Ohio: among whom is our old acquaintance, Mr. John May, late of Botetourt [*County, West Virginia*], whose exit deserves notice, because he was actuated by motives of humanity: The affair is thus related by a captive that has lately from Fort-Pitt, ashore, at the same place where they had captured Mr. May's; but, luckily, they were discovered in time, and our people sheered off. The enemy, being prepared, suddenly manned the boat taken from Mr. May, with about thirty warriors, and gave chase. The crews of two of the boats, fearing they might be overtaken, quitted them, and went on board the best sailer, where they threw overboard all the horses, and some heavy articles, and plied all their oars to effect their escape. The Indians, also, exerted themselves in the pursuit, keeping on a steady course for about 20 miles, notwithstanding 24 well armed white men were on board the American boat, with one of our Colonels of militia, and the sides of the boat high, and bullet proof. Thus, for want of a little resolution and skill, a favorable opportunity was lost, to destroy a number of the vile enemies to the humane race. The Indians, on their return, took possession of the two boats that were abandoned, and found in them 17 horses, about 5000 dollar's worth of merchandise, and considerable property, belonging to the emigrants.

The prisoner, who since made his escape, informs, that this, with other mischief, has been perpetrated by a banditti of Cherokees and Shawanese not openly acknowledged by the chiefs of either nation; but really connived at, and sometimes encouraged.

Thus, Sir, we find that Indian treaties do not secure our country from the depredations of the savages; and the Governor of the Western Territory has told us, we must abide by those treaties, and by no means attempt retaliation, until we receive his previous consent. A disagreeable dilemma, truly! Our last hope now is, that the President of the United States will, ere long, adopt such measures as will prove the efficiency of the federal government, to protect the citizens of the United States, however remotely situated from the seat of government.

NYMP, 17 May (the date on which members of Congress would have seen it); reprinted at Windsor, Vermont; Exeter, New Hampshire; Boston, Newburyport, Northampton, and Worcester, Massachusetts; Hartford, Connecticut; Philadelphia; Wilmington, Delaware; Baltimore; and Edenton, North Carolina.

Other Documents

John Adams to Thomas Crafts. FC:lbk, Adams Family Manuscript Trust, MHi. Sent to Boston.

Office seeking: military appointment for Martin Brimmer Sohier; has spoken to Knox on his behalf.

William Bradford to Elias Boudinot. ALS, Wallace Papers, PHi. Written from Philadelphia. The court controversy mentioned probably refers to the conclusion of Morris's longtime litigation with John Holker, in which Fitzsimons (and Clymer) had been involved as arbitrators (*PRM* 9:605–7).

Fitzsimons, the bearer, will inform Boudinot of the state's politics; "I have been concerned for Mr. Fitzsimons & also for Mr. Morris, & they have both been successful in the controversy *before the Court*"; Susan (Boudinot Bradford) will set out for New York about 27 April; hopes Fitzsimons's return to Congress "will give you a little more animation on the subject" of the secretary's report; as he is the author of the resolutions (of 8 February), "he will be bound to exert himself to bring them to a conclusion."

Daniel Carroll to an Unknown Recipient. ALS, Gilder Lehrman Collection, NHi. Place to which addressed not indicated.

Encloses bill of lading for articles to be forwarded to Georgetown, Maryland; "I am sorry to inform you that we have as yet come to no final conclusion respecting Finance—the subject of the State Debts has been the cause—On this the House is so equally divided, that whatever may be agreed on in that manner, may be attended with disagreable consequences—I hope some alterations & accomodations may take place, so as to bring this subject to a conclusion which will be generally agreable."

Bossinger Foster, Jr. to Andrew Craigie. ALS, Craigie Papers, MWA. Written from Boston on Sunday evening.

A gentleman named Macaulay arrived in three days from New York with information that a reconsideration of the COWH vote on assumption was to take place "in consequence of the arrival of the Carolina delegates," that a majority of the Senate were opposed to the measure, "and that the Common apprehension was that it could not be effected."

Benjamin Goodhue to Stephen Goodhue. ALS, Goodhue Family Papers, MSaE. Place to which addressed not indicated.

Long letter regarding mercantile ventures; "I have nothing to tell you but that I much fear the assumption will not obtain."

Henry Jackson to Henry Knox. ALS, Knox Papers, Gilder Lehrman Collection, NHi. Written from Boston.

Regarding the plan for a militia, "an establishment for a few *Cadets* to a Regiment, will be the means of introducing a *Class* of gentle young men in to the army."

James Madison to Henry Lee. No copy known; acknowledged in Lee to Madison, 22 April.

Robert Morris to Alexander Hamilton. ALS, Hamilton Papers, DLC. Written from Philadelphia. For the full text, see *PAH* 6:348–49.

Concerns negotiations for Morris's purchase of one hundred shares of John B. Church's stock in the Bank of North America; believes that Fitzsimons (a bank director), who departs for New York the next morning, is authorized to consult further on the Bank's behalf.

William Short to Alexander Hamilton. FC, Short Papers, DLC. Written from Paris. For the full text, see *PAH* 6:349–52.

Supposes it useless to repeat that it would be advantageous for Congress to appoint a representative in Europe with control over finances with the

Dutch; such a commission would have a good effect, particularly if Congress begins to reimburse a part of the continental debt's principal; has heard of plans by the Scioto Company to accept for payment of land sales French government securities transferable for an equal amount of the U.S. continental debt owned by France; such attempts show the necessity of Congress's making known in Europe its intentions regarding funding.

George Thatcher to David Sewall. No copy known; acknowledged in Sewall to Thatcher, 22 April.

William Samuel Johnson, Diary. Johnson Papers, CtHi.
"St. Pauls."

MONDAY, 5 APRIL 1790

Warm (Johnson)

John Quincy Adams to John Adams

I have more than once mentioned to you, the state of retirement from political conversation in which I live, and the restraints which I am endeavouring to lay upon a disposition inclining perhaps with too much ardor, to feel interested in public occurrences. But it sometimes happens that I am accidentally witness to conversations upon these subjects; from which I collect some trifling information, that I imagine might at least not be unentertaining to you, In general I have supposed that your other correspondents in this quarter would anticipate me and that I should only employ your time in reading ~~accounts~~ a relation of occurrences, which would not even have with you the merit of novelty But from some late Letters I have been led (though perhaps erroneously) to imagine your correspondents here have not been so punctual in their communications, as they have been formerly, and I have supposed I might mention some circumstances which though generally known here might not be public; at New-York. It appears to me that the hostile character of our general and particular governments each against the other is increasing with accelerated rapidity; The Spirit which at the time when the constitution was adopted, it was contended would always subsist, of balancing one of these governments by the other has I think almost totally disappeared already; and ~~I think~~ the seeds of two contending factions appear to be plentifully sown. The names of federalist and antifederalist, are no longer expressive of the Sentiments which they were so lately supposed to contain; and I expect soon to hear a couple of new names, which will designate the respective friends of the National and particular Systems. The People are very evidently dividing into these two parties. What the event will be, I hardly allow myself to conjecture,

"but my soul akes,
To know when two authorities are up,
Neither supreme, how soon confusion
May enter 'twixt the gap of both, and take
The one by the other."[1]

In point of measures, the Government of the United States has undoubtedly greatly the *advantage*. But while they are strengthening their hands by assuming the debts, and by making provisions for the support of the public credit, the partizans of our State government are continually upon the rack of exertion, to contrive every paltry expedient to maintain their importance and to check the operations of the Government, which they behold with terror: As they can only clamour upon subjects of importance; their active efforts are used, in appointing a premature fast, or in opposing the cession of a light house. In the last Session of our general Court the light houses in this Commonwealth were not ceded to Congress: And the keeper [*Richard Devens*] of that at the entrance of Boston Harbour has been forbidden upon his peril to receive any directions or pay from the federal officers. But the imbecillity of our Government renders all these exertions—the more ridiculous: for while they endeavour to prevent the assumption of their debt, they cannot even provide for the payment of the interest upon it. And they have never yet paid for two light houses at the entrance of this harbour, although they are so solicitous to retain them.

The History of the additional amendments to the Constitution proposed by a joint committee of our two houses,[2] affords ~~adititional~~ further evidence of the petty arts which are used by the enemies to the national union to turn the tide of popular opinion against the national Government. Mr. [*Benjamin*] Austin who as I have been informed had the principal agency in that affair, never expected, that any amendments would be seriously proposed to Congress by our Legislature; and there is an internal evidence in the report of the Committee, that it was intended for a declamation to the people rather than for amendments to the Constitution. They are not even pretended to be amendments, but after the long common-place rhapsody, upon the dangerous tendency of the government, when we come to the *articles*, we find them pretended to be nothing but *principles* for amendments. The Committee consisted of seven members; of whom only four were present when this report was agreed upon. Mr. [*Nathan*] Dane who drew it up was one of the absent, and it is said, afterwards declared that he should have objected to the two last articles,[3] (perhaps the most important of the whole number) though he drafted them himself. The two other absent members utterly disclaimed the report; and the chairman, who did not vote, was equally opposed to it. Three members only agreed upon the point; and when they produced the paper in the Senate, they obtained a vote to have a certain number of copies printed. It was then dismissed without being suffered to undergo the test of an examination, and Mr. Austin I am told, made no scruple to acknowledge that he had answered his purpose.

Yet, even when opportunities are presented, where the importance of our own Government might be really increased, some other little selfish interested principle steps in, and produces measure, calculated to bring it into contempt. The appointment of N[*athan*]. Cushing upon the bench of our Supreme Court, has certainly not tended to increase the confidence of the people in that Important branch of the government. the appointment was very unpopular; and what perhaps in a political view rendered the measure the more injudicious, is that it is not his integrity but his abilities that are called in question. But personal animosity against the characters who would have added dignity to that Station, the apprehension of giving offence to the late chief Justice [*William Cushing*]; who it is said recommended his cousin too strongly, and the pleasure of removing a troublesome councillor, concurring together were too powerful even for *antifederal* principles, and produced ~~it is said~~ we are told a nomination, which could be accounted for upon no other motives. The only liberal and generous measure by which they have pursued their System has been the raising the Salaries of our Judges and I fear they would not have succeeded even in that, had not the personal interest of certain influential men, of very different principles been engaged, and assisted to promote it. It is melancholy to observe how much even in this free Country the course of public events depends upon the private interests and Passions of individuals.

But the popularity of the general Government is, and for some time to come must continue to be disadvantageously affected, by those very exertions to support the public credit, which must eventually strengthen it so effectually. It must suffer however chiefly in the Sea-ports and among the merchants who find their interests affected by the operation of the revenue Laws. In this town and Still more in Salem there have lately been considerable clamours raised by men who have been the firmest friends to the constitution; and there is now I presume before Congress a petition from the merchants in this town,[4] praying relief from an evil, which has excited great complaints, but which will probably be remedied without difficulty.

Those people among us who are perpetually upon the search, for causes of complaint against the government, are cavilling at the dilatory manner with which the Congress proceed in their business. The decision upon the subject of discrimination, has ~~been~~ met with general approbation in the circles of company where I have heard it mentioned; and from the complexion of our news-papers, I have concluded that the public opinion of which so much was said in the debates, is here much in favour of the measure. I do not think indeed that the public opinion can always be collected from news-papers; but they are never silent upon unpopular topics of so great importance—Mr. Madison's reputation has suffered from his conduct in that affair; and Judge [*Francis*] Dana is the only man I have known whose character gives weight to his opinions, that has adopted those of Mr. Madison.

The report of the Secretary of the Treasury [*on public credit*], has in general met with great approbation. I have heard it almost universally spoken of with great applause. Yet I am almost ashamed to acknowledge, that I know not how justly it is admired, as I have never read it. This neglect has rather been owing to ~~my~~ accident than to inclination, for little as I attend to the public prints I should certainly have noticed a publication of so important a nature had I been in the way of seeing the Gazette of the United States which contains it. I am equally ignorant of the System for the establishment of the militia, which is as much disliked as the treasurer's report is esteemed, the most favourable judgment that I have heard passed upon it was, that however excellent it might be, it would never be submitted to by the people.

I know not, but that I shall incur your censure for ~~thus~~ departing even in this instance from the line which I have prescribed to myself, and losing the lawyer in the politician; and still more for the freedom with which I have express'd myself upon public men and measures: if I should on this occasion meet with your disapprobation, I shall without difficulty observe a more prudent silence upon these subjects in future. The opinions which I have heard express'd are no evidence of the general opinion even throughout the Commonwealth, but in some instances they have been the opinions of men whose influence is great and extensive. But if the information contained in this Letter should compensate in your mind for its tediousness, I shall from time to time continue to give you a similar supply.

ALS, Adams Family Manuscript Trust, MHi. Written from Newburyport, Massachusetts.

[1] Shakespeare's *Coriolanus*, act 3, scene 1.

[2] See Stephen Higginson to John Adams, 1 March, n. 1, volume 18.

[3] The eleventh (of twelve) articles proposed as amendments to the Constitution by a joint committee of the Massachusetts legislature called for federal Senators and Representatives to be paid by the state they represented. The last proposed amendment would have given state legislatures the power to recall their respective federal Senators and limited them to four year terms due to expire simultaneously.

[4] For more on this petition from the merchants and traders of Newburyport, Massachusetts, presented in the House on 9 April, see *DHFFC* 8:418–20.

Pierce Butler to George Hooper

***

If You could have succeeded in purchasing your publick securities you would have made much money by it. I think the State debts that were incurred on acct. of the general cause will be assumed this day—pray how do you distinguish between the certificates that were fraudulently issued and the just ones? Your Militia Certificates I doubt will not be taken into acct.; how are they distinguished from the others. I ask these Questions not for myself but for general information, and to satisfy others. Your Gentry here appear not to have informed themselves fully on these points—Be so good to explain them to me.

Pray were Williamson's speculations in your state money or the final Continental Settlements—I mean your state securities.

I observe what you say respecting the double duties you have payed. It is hard on so good a Federalist—I wish I could get it restored. You must send forward two memorials to the two houses of Congress stating your case fully;[1] there is no other mode by which you can obtain redress.

I think you are wrong in not sending your son [*Archibald Maclaine Hooper*]. the school on Long Island[2] is very cheap, and well spoken of. It is the worst saved money You can save. Besides You would give your Son a better stamina.

*** I shall really take it friendly if you can let me have the Nine hundred pounds I advanced. My crop has fallen sonsiderably short which more than deranges me. I am really distressed on the score of money. You will greatly oblige me therefore by letting me have even a part of it, if it is not convenient to You to pay the whole just now. I rely on Your aid.

[*P. S.*] My best regards to Mr. [*Archibald*] McClain. I hope he received a letter I wrote him lately.

FC, Butler Letterbook, ScU. For the full text, see *Butler Letters*, pp. 24–26. The omitted text describes Butler's formal application on Hooper's behalf to the French consul general, René Charles de La Forest, for a naval stores contract with the French ministry of marine; Butler's intervention in a legal transaction between Hooper and the Dutch banking firm of Lodewijk Hovy and Son; and arrangements for a business partnership between Butler and Hooper.

---

[1] Hooper was one of the signatories of the petition from the merchants of Wilmington, North Carolina, presented to the Senate on 24 May and to the House two days later, seeking relief for having paid state as well as federal duties prior to that state's ratification; see *DHFFC* 8:398–400.

[2] There were two "flourishing" academies on Long Island at this time: Erasmus Hall in Flatbush, Brooklyn, and Clinton Academy in East Hampton (Jedidiah Morse, *The American Geography* [Elizabethtown, N.J., 1789], p. 267).

William Ellery to Benjamin Huntington

***

Before this letter reaches you, you will probably have seen a proposal from a Committee of the town of Providence and some private gentlemen of this town, directed to Arthur Fenner who is at the head of the Antifedl. prox, for a coalition. The design of the Feds in this maneuvre was to introduce, if they could, some fedl. members into the upper house, and thereby increase their strength in the Legislature. If the Feds. had previously concluded to have opposed the Antifedl. prox, the proposal of a coalition might have had an influence upon some moderate men; but without that it could not possibly, in my opinion, answer any good purpose, and so I told the Providence Committee. However they were fierce for the measure, and to gratify them some of our gentlemen joined with them. For my part I esteem honesty to be the best policy, and I have no notion of coalescing with the unfruitful works of darkness. I think I told you in my last that it was not probable that any opposition would be made to this prox; but that the Feds would exert themselves to gain a majority in the Lower House. An opposition would be unsuccessful, and therefore I still suppose will not be made. There is I think a prospect of an addition of strength in the Lower-House. If we should by a superiority in that house be able to ballance their superiority in the Upper House, we may at the election, appoint some federal State officers who would be of great use at a future election of Genl. Officers, and if the Constitution should be adopted we may possibly stand a chance to get one Senator. you mention that common report says the adjournment of the Convention was agreed to in hopes that Congress would in the present Session do something which might be considered by the Antis as alarming, and so to frighten the people still more against adopting the Constitution. This is entirely new to me, and appears to be calculated to prevent Congress from taking any rigorous measures. If Congress do nothing, I am confident the Convention will adjourn again and again. In a former letter I assigned what I take to be the true reasons for their agreeing to adjourn. The only reason in my mind against their adjourning again (they are afraid to reject the Constitution) is this: The longer they delay the adoption of it, the less may be their ability to chuse such Senators as they please, when it shall be adopted; and the two men who wish for that appointment are I beleive anxious to be possessed of that honour and profit. One of them is the famous Jonathan Hazard, and the other is Theodore Foster, a brother in law to Mr. Fenner but a clever fellow and a Fed at heart.

It is regretted that so much time has been spent in a business about which nothing effectual can be done until the year 1808.[1] The Quakers are very persevering in whatever they undertake, and they act in concert. When

Congress are besieged by religious bodies of men, they may expect to be not a little perplexed. At the first session of Congress, under the old Confederation, the Baptists made an application requesting the interference of Congress respecting their persecution in Massachusetts, and they endeavoured to procure aid from the Quakers in Philadelphia; but by the happy management of the Adams's [*John and Samuel*], then delegates from Massachusetts, the Quakers were detached from them, and the danger was averted.

The Vice-Presidt. can tell you the story,[2] I was not then in Congress, and it is worth hearing—The Quakers have several times applied to Congress on the subject of Slavery, and it always occasioned some heat in the Southern members. While they consider the Quakers as enthusiasts, and that it is for their interest to countenance slavery, any attempts to abolish it before 1808, will without doubt disturb them; and it seems to me that any applications for that purpose before that period ought not to be encouraged.

Since I wrote the aforegoing, the Gentlemen of Providence who formed the Committee before mentioned, have advertized the people ~~at large~~ at large meet at Greenwich to morrow to form a prox.[3] If the Antis will not unite in a prox which will admit into it a number of Feds, ~~it is~~ the Feds will either print a prox with a ~~new~~ federal Head; or only insert into their new prox a few federal Assistants leaving to it an Antifedl. head. When they meet if the Antis will not join with them they will do what they think will be most beneficial. I do not expect that the Antis will meet with them; or that any advantage will result from issuing a prox in any form; but some of our principal Feds had proceeded so far, that I beleive it is necessary to go farther.

The goods, wares, productions and manufactures of this State I am told are still admitted into the United States duty free, and they must be so admitted unless Congress passes an Act prohibiting their importation, or laying a duty upon them, and unless one or the other is done the country party, who are the Antis, will feel no inconvenience from not adopting the Constitution—the Feds alone will be the sufferers, and further the former, not suffering any disadvantage from the Impost Act as it now stands, will triumph in their opposition to the Constitution. If a discrimination cannot be made in favour of the Feds, the Antis certainly ought not to be indulged.

ALS, Benjamin Huntington Correspondence, 1772–1790, R-Ar. Written from Newport, Rhode Island; received 10 April. The omitted text relates to financial transactions.

---

[1] Ellery refers to the House's consideration of the Quakers' antislavery petitions in February and March and the prohibition against abolishing the slave trade that appears in Article I, section 9 of the Constitution. See *DHFFC* 8:314–38.

[2] The episode Ellery refers to was an informal four hour meeting convened at 6 P.M. on 14 October 1774 at Philadelphia's Carpenters Hall, attended by several Baptist elders visiting from New England, the Massachusetts delegation to the First Continental Congress,

other congressmen, Philadelphia's mayor, and three of the city's most influential Quakers, including James Pemberton. The latter's role in spearheading the Quaker antislavery petitions to the FFC no doubt affected the disparaging manner in which those petitions were received in the Senate by Adams, who had never forgotten the embarrassment and indignation he experienced at his first introduction to Quaker methods of political agitation sixteen years earlier. If Huntington ever acted on Ellery's suggestion, Adams might have consulted his diary entry to assist in recounting the story, although he treated it more amply in his autobiography begun twenty-five years later, with little variation in tone (*Adams* 2:152–54, 3:311–13). The fullest account was recorded by the Massachusetts Baptist leader Isaac Backus, who was also present (William G. McLoughlin, ed., *Diary of Isaac Backus* [3 vols., Providence, R.I., 1979], 2:916–18).

[3] In a process unique to Rhode Island, nominees to office were chosen in a public meeting from a preliminary slate compiled by a caucus of party leaders.

Benjamin Goodhue to [*Michael Hodge*]

We should have come to the question on the Assumption on Saturday in a Committee of the whole if some of the friends of the measure had not been absent and we were afraid to risque it, if it succeeds it will be but by a majority of one or two—should it not obtain I should not be surprised if the whole funding bussines was postponed till next session, as the assumption forms so essential a part of those advantages which may be expected from the sistem which must establish public credit—I am deeply impressed with those evils which I think must inevitably await a rejection of the proposition, and most ardently wish it may succeed, but I must confess my fears seem to out weigh my expectations—I forbear to express my sentiments ~~which~~ of the motives which may produce this dreaded event; those who are the authors of it must answer for the consequences~~—should it not obtain I sh~~.

ALS, Ebenezer Stone Papers, MSaE. Place to which addressed not indicated. Closes with "I am with great esteem for the Gentlemen of N[*ewbury*]port." The recipient was identified by his handwriting on the docket.

Richard Bland Lee to [*Charles Lee*]

I am just favored with your very acceptable letter of the 29th ult.

As to Mr. Madison's plan [*for discrimination*] you do not seem fully to have understood it. It would not have diminished the amount of the debt, and therefore would not have rendered the burthen less. The public would not have gained a farthing by the operation, but he intended that justice should be done to every class of citizens, to the full extent of the abilities of the country. He conceived the original holders, as well as the present possessors of the debt of the United States, entitled to some consideration;

and as it was evidently impossible to discharge the obligations which the public were under to both, dictates of justice required that there should be a composition of their claims, and every possible justice done. I conceive the equity of this doctrine incontrovertible; and I saw no objection to his plan but the difficulty of the execution—and the danger of the precedent. Such a precedent might be used as a pretext to justify a measure dissimilar in all its leading points at a future day. I felt myself, as you have done, very much irritated at the indelicate treatment which he received. Some seemed to express, by their conduct, a joy, that they had it in their power to depress his importance (as they thought), which rendered it still more necessary for the friends of virtue, and of the Southern interests, to maintain and support him. The debates on this question will better explain to you his conduct.

As to the memorials of the Quakers and others relative to the slave trade, their introduction, from the manner in which the subject was treated, became importunate. The gentlemen from South Carolina and Georgia, by anticipating what was never intended, have been instrumental in sounding disagreeable alarms. If they had said nothing, the House of Representatives without a doubt, would have declared with one voice that Congress had no power to interfere in any manner so as to affect or alter the internal regulations of the States relative to them.

The authors of the petitions were influenced by an honest, though indiscreet zeal on the occasion. They expressly declared that their object was not to injure the property of the Southern States, but to discontinue the slave trade, which they deemed cruel and dishonorable.

By the unfounded apprehensions of the gentlemen from Carolina and Georgia, all the alarms which have been spread were caused. I consider the declaration which we made in a committee of the whole,[1] however, as soon as we were permitted to come to a decision, will not only quiet our fears, but put our slave property on a surer foundation than it before stood; and an interpretation of the powers of Congress given at the time, when the meaning of the parties to the Constitution must be fully understood, may prevent at a future day any improper coercive authority on this subject. I can not, therefore, but flatter myself that the conclusion of this subject will be generally satisfactory to the State of Virginia and that the petitions you mention to be in contemplation to our next Assembly will be found wholly unnecessary on this subject.

As to the assumption of the State debt, this question is still in suspense, and the final determination very uncertain. The Eastern States would carry their point at all hazards—rather than fail they would be contented with a majority of one vote. Three members from the State of North Carolina are now on the floor,[2] which renders the success of their plans still more uncertain. From the present appearance, I can not help thinking that the assumption will not proceed; if it should, it must wear a different countenance than it has at present, and the most effectual provision be made for a speedy and fair settlement of all accounts. I have no doubt negotiations have been commenced, and are yet existing, between the Eastern States and Pennsylvania relative to the permanent seat of government; the Pennsylvanians endeavoring to make the settlement of the seat of government the price of the assumption. But in this business the State of New York is as necessary to carry the point as Pennsylvania and it is not probable that she will be induced to yield up the advantage which she now has over her commercial rival. I have, therefore, no fears that this negotiation will be productive of an establishment in Pennsylvania. As to Potomac, I consider our prospects as very remote. *If the Government lasts so long,* it may erect its capital on its banks at the expiration of twenty years.

I confess that I feel myself often chagrined *by the taunts against the ancient Dominion, but disunion* AT THIS TIME *would be the worst of calamities.* The Southern States are too weak at present to stand by themselves, and a General Government will certainly be advantageous to us, as it produces no other effect than protection from hostilities and uniform commercial regulations. And when we shall attain our natural degree of population *I flatter myself that we shall have the power to do ourselves justice, with dissolving the bond which binds us together.* It is better to put up with these little inconveniences than to run the hazard of greater calamities. Adieu.

Cincinnati Daily Commercial, 6 November 1862. This document, which falls outside the editors' normal search parameters, was brought to our attention by Douglas Clanin. Printed under the headline, "A Curious Revelation of the War. The Doctrine of Secession in 1790," the letter is preceded by a brief paragraph that attributes it erroneously to the "grandfather of the present Commander-in-Chief of the rebel army," refers to its discovery "in the dwelling house of General [*Jeb*] Stuart, in Virginia," and describes it as "one of the most curious epistolary productions brought to light by the war, and furnishes a clear insight into the origin of the rebellion." The recipient's identification is based on R. B. Lee's use of the closing salutation "Adieu" exclusively in his letters to his brothers, of which those to Charles Lee were widely dispersed in the nineteenth century.

[1] For this as well as other documents and background of the Quaker antislavery petitions, see *DHFFC* 8:314–38.

[2] Ashe, Bloodworth, and Williamson.

Other Documents

John Adams to John Hurd. FC:lbk, Adams Family Manuscript Trust, MHi. Sent to Boston.

Office seeking; would be happy to serve him, "But the office I hold is totally detached from the executive authority, and confined to the legislative; which renders it very improper for me to intermeddle in appointments," except when the President "or some of his ministers of State" ask his opinion "of matters of fact."

John Adams to James Lovell. FC:lbk, Adams Family Manuscript Trust, MHi. Sent to Boston. For background on James Warren's claim for a depreciation allowance, see *DHFFC* 7:1–4.

James Warren has arrived but has mentioned nothing to Adams about his petition; will assist Andrew Craigie with "all the aid in my power" regarding Lovell's renewal of destroyed certificates, "but I do not at present see how I can assist him"; the majority in that day's vote on assumption "will not be large"; inquires about public opinion on the new government and the state of trade and shipbuilding in Boston.

John Adams to Thomas Welsh. FC:lbk, Adams Family Manuscript Trust, MHi. Acknowledges receipt of Hurd's letter of application forwarded by Welsh and replied to this day, above.

Office seeking: John Hurd for any post in New Hampshire or Vermont; "he cannot have better advocates than his friends," Langdon and Livermore.

William Samuel Johnson, Diary. Johnson Papers, CtHi.

"Visits."

NYDA, 6 April.

The New York Council of Appointment asked the legislature to decide whether Schuyler's seat on the Council was vacant.

Letter from Washington County, Kentucky. *NYP*, 6 May (the date on which members of Congress would have seen it); reprinted at Boston.

The Indians captured two boys on 26 March and Mrs. Wiley, captured in Montgomery County [*West Virginia*] last September, has returned.

TUESDAY, 6 APRIL 1790

Rain (Johnson)

George Cabot to Benjamin Goodhue

The last post brought me your obliging letter of the 28th ulto., since which some private hands have conveyed to us the disagreeable intelligence of your overthrow in the house in trial for the non assumption of the State Debts [*lined out*]—I never considered the National Govt. as being more than half established by the *nominal* acceptance of the Form—to take from our Newspapers the metaphor they have used, it was an Arch—but to me the keystone was wanting—the actual exercise of [*lined out*] certain powers to the exclusion of the states wou'd be finishing the work—'till this takes place I cannot think the Country completely safe from the danger of disunion & consequently anarchy & wretchedness.

I am no holder of public securities of any kind[1] & never wou'd be interested in any of our funds on any terms but I consider the assumption of all our State Debts as so essential, that as an Individual I wou'd rather pay a 4 fold interest thro' the National Govt. than a 1/2 per cent thro' the medium of the State—because the former *may* give us protection, the latter *cannot*—[*lined out*] I confess to you however that I am still indulging myself in the pleasing idea that you will succeed in this point in the present session—& if you do, I shall think that the Govt. has done every thing its most sanguine Friends & every honest Patriot coud have wished—if you fail, there certainly is reason to apprehend a long & hard contest with the State Govts. for *power*.

Since our petition was forwarded to you[2] the People of Lebanon in Connecticut have sent for one of our Machine Makers who I suppose will go & assist them in setting up a Manufactory there—you know the state of the one in Worcester [*Massachusetts*] & that there is one in Providence & another in Greenwich [*Rhode Island*]—all these have the benefit of the knowledge & information we have purchased—an increased duty on importation of such articles as are manufactured here will undoubtedly be of public benefit by promoting these attempts, & upon principles of sound policy I think ought to take place but upon a little reflection you will perceive it will be little or no relief *to us*.

ALS, Letters to Goodhue, NNS. Written from Beverly, Massachusetts. An excerpt of this letter, from "I never considered" to "State Govts. for *power*," was printed in *GUS*, 21 April, and reprinted at Norwich, Connecticut; Hudson, New York; and Fredericksburg and Williamsburg, Virginia.

[1] Brackets and an asterisk mark the phrase that begins here to "on any terms," which is omitted from the excerpt printed in *GUS*. This was probably done at Goodhue's insistence, to avoid negative commentary on the value of state securities.

[2] The petition of the proprietors of the Beverly Cotton Manufactory was forwarded by Cabot to Goodhue with a letter on 16 March; see *DHFFC* 8:366–71.

Elbridge Gerry, George Mathews, Rufus King, Lambert Cadwalader, James Jackson, John Henry, and Peter Muhlenberg to Alexander Hamilton

The Subscribers appointed on the part of Mr. Hamilton and Mr. Burke to consider whether there was an honorable Ground of accomodation between the parties in respect to certain Expressions made use of by Mr. Burke in the house of Representatives on Wednesday last, relatively to an Eulogium pronounced by Mr. Hamilton on general Green on the 4th. of July last, having inquired into the Circumstances, and perused the Letters which were interchanged by those Gentlemen on the first instant are of Opinion that nothing more is necessary to an accomodation between them, than a right understanding of each other.

As while on the one hand it appears from satisfactory information, that Mr. Burke did not conceive the letter from Mr. Hamilton to amount to an explicit disavowal of an intention in any part of the Eulogium delivered by him, to cast a reflection upon militia in general, or upon the militia of South Carolina in particular; so on the other from like information it appears to us that it was Mr. Hamilton's intention in that Letter to make such disavowal.

We are therefore of opinion that a proper and honorable ground of accomodation between the Parties will be, that Mr. Hamilton in another Letter to Mr. Burke make an explicit declaration of his intentions as above understood; and that Mr. Burke in consequence of it make to Mr. Hamilton a full and satisfactory Apology for whatever on his part has taken place on the Subject offensive to Mr. Hamilton.

That as considerations resulting from the nature of the precedent in reference to the Privileges of the House, remove the propriety of the Apology in the house questionable, we are farther of Opinion that the Apology be made by Letter.

ALS, hand of King and signed by the committee members, Hamilton Papers, DLC.

Samuel Johnston to James and Hannah Iredell

I am this Evening favored with your Letters of the 16th and 24th. of March, if you have not sent forward my Certificates before this reaches you be so good as to return them to Mr. [*William?*] McKenzie till he hears further from me, it is now doubtfull whether the State Debts will at this time be assumed, under these Circumstances I fear they would be of no Value here had they come to hand a fortnight or three weeks ago I could have made something of them.

I am sorry you think any thing can be troublesome to me which regards your conveniency or the comfort of your Family, I will immediately look out for such a House as you wish to have, had you mentioned it sooner there would have been greater choice, but I hope that one may yet be had which will suit your purpose. I hope my Sister [*Hannah Iredell*] and the Children will come with Mrs. [*Frances Cathcart*] Johnston—I shall be very happy in taking charge of them till you come and will omit nothing in my power to make them comfortable.

I received an Application from [*Clement*] Hall some time ago but not till others had applied, I will take care that his name shall be laid before the President with others which is all I can do for him, you know my resolution to sollicit for no man, indeed after your Appointment, I thank God I have no great anxiety about any other, further than to give my Opinion with Candor when asked, which is a duty which I owe to the President, whom I have every day greater reason to admire. The great object of the funding the Publick Debts is still before the House of Representatives, if our Members come forward in time I have hopes the Assumption of the State Debts will not take place.[1] I am still of opinion that if Congress adopts that measure one of two evils will necessarily ensue, either they will not be able to comply with their engagements or in order to enable them to comply they will be reduced to the necessity of laying taxes which will be oppressive to the people and injure the Government in their Opinion, the House at this time is very nearly divided on the Question. Bloodworth is come to Town this day which I hope will add one vote to the opposition, our Friend Williamson has taken a conspicuous part in this Debate. We perfectly concur in Sentiment.

P. S. to Mrs. [*Hannah*] Iredell

My dear Sister

I am quite overjoyed to hear that I am to see you here I hope you will make it convenient to come with Mrs. Johnston, it will be a fine Season for inoculation. I am sure you will not doubt of my paying the same attention to you and your Children that I would to my own, Kiss the dear little Rogues for me.

ALS, Charles E. Johnson Collection, Nc-Ar. Addressed to Edenton, North Carolina; franked.

[1] Steele did not arrive until 19 April, Sevier until 16 June.

Richard Bland Lee to David Stuart

Since writing the inclosed I have the pleasure of informing you that this day I had the good [*fortune*] of getting a Bill [*Collection Act HR-50*] passed thro' the house of Representatives for further suspending ~~th~~ so much of the Collection Law [*HR-11*] as obliges vessels bound up the Potowmack to come to, and deposit manifests of their cargoes at the mouth of the River. The suspension is till the first day of May 1791. I consulted the Secretary of the Treasury on this subject. He concieved the regulation of no importance to the Revenue; but as a general revision of the Trade laws was in contemplation; he thought I had better apply for the present for a suspension than a repeal of the before mentioned clause.

I have no doubt of the Bill's passing the Senate. And before the first day of May 1791 I have no doubt that the proposed revision will be made and the commercial regulations rendered as uniform as possible thro'out the Union. The papers accompanying this will give the news at home and abroad.

I am sorry to inform you that the President has been unwell for a few days past I saw him yesterday when he was much better.

You mention a prospect of Col. [*Henry*] Lee's being appointed [*to su*]pply Col. Grayson's place. He has not [*bee*]n thought of here. And for many local and perhaps some personal reasons I do not think he has any chance.

From every account unless Col. [*George*] Mason or Mr. [*Patrick*] Henry will accept—Col. Monroe will be the person.

ALS, privately owned in 1981. Addressed to "Abingdon via Alexandria" (Fairfax County, in present-day Arlington County, Va.); franked.

Benjamin Lincoln to Theodore Sedgwick

Your much esteemed favour of the [*torn*] Ulto. came by the last post.

It has been supposed by some that the word "jurisdiction" in the light house law [*HR-12*] would make the ground compleatly a City of refuge and a security against all [*legal*] processes saving those under the union.

I have lately attempted to engage Mr. [*James*] Bowdoin to write in favour of Mr. [*Samuel*] Henshaw I think he would be a great acquisition was he annexed to the revenue officers from his abilities, knowledg in the business, & integrity much might be justly expected from him.

From what I have heard & from what I have seen I have not any reason to believe that a "spirit of bitter animosity" ever ~~in~~ existed in the manner you express I think if it had I should have heard from some quarter or an other a hint of it I never did I assure you.

Great discontent has run through this town & the neighboring ones since monday from a idea that the United States have rejected the State debts—If you was hear you would soon be convinced that the worst of consequences were to be expected in case Congress should finally reject the adoption of those debts—I confess that I am not anxious my self though my future prospects are much involved in the adoption I think it must be done I am persuaded that Congress will be convinced that our well being if not our being depends on the measure.

I will attempt by the next post some observations on the propriety of changing the present mode, in some instances, of collection &c. &c.

ALS, Sedgwick Papers, MHi. Written from Boston.

James Madison to William Short

*** The proceedings of the House of Reps. have related cheifly to the public debt. On the modifications of the domestic part of it the opinions have not been unanimous and on the ~~pro~~ assumption of the State debts proposed by Mr. Hamilton, they are so nicely divided that the result is extremely uncertain. From the aspect of the present moment I rather conjecture that the measure will not take place. With respect to the Foreign debt including the French debts, I have the pleasure to inform you that the utmost unanimity prevails, and I risk nothing in assuring you that certain and effectual provision will be made for it. I hope no doubts are entertained on this head where you are. The very [*lined out*] existence of them would be painful to us here, and if they should lead to any arrangements by wch. the benefit of our ~~justice~~ [*?*] provisions should be lost in any degree to those who have the best of titles to them, our mortification would be inexpressible.

Nothing can prove better the philosophical & republican spirit of the National assembly, than your paragraph on the affair of titles.[1] a late circumstance in Congs. shews that the Senate are not cured of their partiality for their former opinion, and that the House of Reps. retain their vigilance & firmness in counteracting it. The State of N. Carolina, since its accession, has ceded its vacant territory to the U. States. The Deed being executed by her Senators in the Senate, the bill accepting the [*lined out*] cession originated in that House. In the recital the title of *honorable* was prefixed to the names of the Senators. When the bill was taken up in the H. of Reps. the first motion (made by Mr. Page) was to strike out the title. It was agreed to by a very great majority. The Senate did not chuse to maintain a contest on the point, or to submit directly to the amendment. By way of retreat they proposed an amendment to the amendt. by which ~~all~~ [*?*] the naming of the Senators was left out of the recital. In this the H. of Reps. concurred rather than engage in an unseasonable discussion on a point *apparently* of little moment & on which the unsteadfast ~~or~~ insincere opponents of titles would have had a pretext for betraying the cause.

***

We lost Col. Grayson about 3 weeks ago. He was carried off by a Gouty diarrhea, which had been wasting him for 18 Months. It is not yet known who is [*to*] take his place in the Senate. Mr. [*Patrick*] Henry will have the first offer & Mr. [*George*] Mason the next. There are reports that both are willing to undertake the service. I can not believe that either of them is so. Col. Monroe has been spoken of and will probably stand next to H[*enry*]. & Mason but his acceptance is not probable. Who will be thought of after these 3 I can not say. Mr. [*Benjamin*] Harrison & Mr. J. Walker, it is said will not refuse the appointment.

***

ALS, Short Papers, DLC. Place to which addressed not indicated. For the full text, see *PJM* 13:139–41. The omitted text expresses satisfaction with the progress of the revolution in France and that "no fatal consequences are likely to flow"; encloses copy of new Pennsylvania state constitution; and withdraws anything more than a general reference to George James's good character (from Madison's letter of introduction for James, 21 June 1789 [*PJM* 12:253]) upon discovering his trip to Europe was "to be in the character of a Jobber in land."

[1] Short's letter from Paris, dated 17 November 1789, informed Madison that the published debates in Congress had been an inspiration to the French National Assembly's abolition of titles; see *PJM* 12:449.

Nicholas Pike to Benjamin Goodhue

Your Favor of the 20th. Ult. came same safe to hand, for which you have, not only my grateful Thanks: but those of the friends of Mrs. Treat also.[1]

I find there is a considerable number of Candidates for the berth of Colector of Excise here; & the reason I did not make one of the Number was, because I was convinced I should stand no Chance among so many who had more Friends than I could boast of.

Congress, with deference I say it, has *now* departed from the line of Justice, & I find that the Creditors this Way do not intend to reloan their Money on such hard Terms. Had Congress resolved to have paid us what Interest they are now able to do, & the remainder when they shall be able, I believe every Creditor would have been satisfied: but I cannot see the essential difference between their present Resolves, & Tender Acts, if any, the latter have the Advantage; because any thing here is preferable to Lands in the Moon.

I do not love to complain; but when I reflect that the Creditors of Congress have been exerting themselves to establish an efficient Government, & to invest it with Power to do Justice—to do what the Old Congress would have done had they been possessed of the Advantages attending the present Congress, I do think I have a Right, with others, to complain—Why should not I, or any other Person, be paid as soon, altho' I do not rel[*oan*] my Money, as [*one*] who does?

How would such Conduct be reprobated in a private Debtor? Would he not be demolished by the *non-reloaners*? And would not Congress share the same fate, if its Creditors had the same Power over it, as it they have over a private Debtor? I ask your Candor: for I loaned three fourths of the Interest I was possessed of at the Time for the support of Govt., & I am unwilling to be—be—be—shall I say, cheated out of it? I know your sentiments coincide with my own on this Subject, or perhaps I should not be so explicit.

***

Please to present my Compliments to Mr. King, & inform him that I have recd. his obliging Letter, & feel myself under great Obligations to him for his Attention to the business upon which I wrote him.

ALS, Letters to Goodhue, NNS. Written from Newburyport, Massachusetts. The omitted text reports state election returns for governor, lieutenant governor, and Senators.

[1] The petition of the widow Anna Treat, seeking compensation for the death of her son during the war, had been forwarded by Pike (one of her creditors) and presented in the House by Goodhue on 15 February. For more background and text, see *DHFFC* 7:256–58.

Roger Sherman to Simeon Baldwin

I received your letter of the 4th. instant. ~~It~~ The account you give of Society [*church*] affairs gives me more pleasure than any event, Since I left home. I have no doubt but that the State debts will ultimately be assumed—I think it must be for the general Interest in every point of view. probably a question will be taken on it on monday next—It may be well for the circuit court to have some business, but I believe it would not be best to give them Cognizance of a lower Sum, the State Courts will be competent for lesser matters, I wish to hear who are chosen representatives for New Haven & any other Towns. The enclosed paper[1] compleats the year—but as there is to be an Index it will be best to delay binding it till that comes to hand. we have no news here.

ALS, Sherman Collection, CtY. Place to which addressed not indicated.

[1] Probably volume two of *CR*, which covered debates through 1789, published on an unknown date.

George Thatcher to Thomas B. Wait

I dont know how it has happened that yours of the 10th. March, wrote at Biddeford, has remained, till this time, unanswered—Once & sometimes twice a week, I look over my Letters, & notice all that Business, or friendship require an answer.

I am rather of opinion that the Theory you advanced against Mother Hoopers[1] experience is good—but my sentiments, upon education, change, (or advance) so frequently that little dependence can be put on them. Man can arrive to very few general Truths in morals, politics, or Theology—For knowledge, in these subjects, not founded on experience is worth but little; and the longest life is too short, after it is duly prepared to observe, to make many usefull experiments—And the system, founded on the most accurate estimate of facts, will always be objected to by the multitude; because of its novelty—that is, its perfection. Remember what Solon said of his Laws.[2] Now Laws and Constitutions are to a people, what rules of education are to children. It is in vaine to think of educating a child according to the best plan of education—He cannot be educated but in the world we live in; and here your plan & the common one will be like two powers, in mechanics, acting in opposite directions—All that can be expected is to give the former, if possible, a greater momentum than the latter: when this is happily the case, education may be said to be advancing; otherwise it must be retrograde, or stationary at best.

This is not only the case in education, the same is true when applied to morals, politics & Theology—The common opinion is ever at variance with philosophy; and the latter advances to the benefit of the human race in proportion only to its surplus after a deduction of the former.

The clock warns me of its being eleven.

FC, Thatcher Family Papers, MHi. The postscript to this letter was written on 7 April and is printed under that date, below.

---

[1] In his letter to Thatcher, dated 10 March, Wait said that during a recent conversation on education, Hooper "insisted that the Mother had a right to call in the authority of the Father to her assistance—to tell children to do this, or not to do ~~this,~~ that, because the Father will be angry, will chide, or will correct them." Such a recourse, Wait responded, would only secure a "partial ~~of~~ obedience" at the expense of the mother's own authority or the child's affection for the father.

[2] According to his biographer Plutarch (46?–120 A.D.), the great lawgiver Solon once said that he had not given the Athenians the best laws that could be given, but the best laws they could receive.

Newspaper Article

In the Debates which lately took place in the House of Representatives of the United States, on the Memorial of the people called Quakers, respecting slavery, Mr. Scott, Mr. Vining, Mr. Gerry, Mr. Boudinot, and other members, advocated the cause of the memorialists, and vindicated their characters, with great ability, eloquence and liberality, in opposition to Mr. Jackson, Mr. Burke, Mr. Smith, (S.C.) &c. who not only opposed the object of the memorialists, but treated them as a Society, with a degree of acrimony and invective, which ill become *American Legislators*, in particular, and must inevitably lessen that respect the *ingenuity* of their arguments might otherwise have inspired.

[Baltimore] *Maryland Journal*, 6 April; reprinted at Providence, Rhode Island, and Charleston, South Carolina. For more on the Quaker antislavery petitions, see *DHFFC* 8:314–38, 12:718–811 passim.

OTHER DOCUMENTS

Tench Coxe to James Madison. ALS, Madison Papers, DLC. Place from which written not indicated; postmarked. For the full text, see *PJM* 13:141. See also Coxe to Madison, 21 March, and reply, 28 March, above. The papers enclosed related to Spanish wool and Succedanea for Foreign liquors.

Encloses "a further consideration of the affairs of R. Island" (A Citizen of United America, *FG*, 6 April) and copies of two papers, the originals of which were sent to Hamilton; a third relating to "our Navigation" was sixty pages long and Coxe had no one to make a copy.

John Henry, Rufus King, Lambert Cadwalader, Elbridge Gerry, James Jackson, and George Mathews to Alexander Hamilton. ALS, hand of King, signed by committee members, Hamilton Papers, DLC. Printed in *DHFFC* 8:479.

Expresses opinion of signatories, meeting as informal joint committee, for resolving the Burke-Hamilton affair of honor.

Thomas Jefferson to William Short. ALS, Jefferson-Short Correspondence, ViW. Addressed to Paris; marked "Private." For the full text, see *PTJ* 16:318–21. Jefferson wrote the italicized words in code; the decoding is from *PTJ*.

Constitutional provision prevents him from accepting from King of France the customary gift as departing ambassador without Congress's consent, "but I do not chuse to be laid on the gridiron of debate in Congress for any such paltry purpose"; "Page is married here a few days ago, to a maiden lady [*Margaret Lowther*] of about 30. a great poetess"; if Short were in America, he would "without a doubt" be chosen to succeed Grayson; it is said both George Mason and Patrick Henry have declined, Ralph Wormley, Francis Corbin, and Walker seek it, and "we are told" it will be offered to Monroe and he will accept; "*Indeed I wish you had been here 3. years ago. From a view of the stage and the actors I see that you could have been what you please. You would have been sure of returning to Paris now in the character you would have chosen: because you would have been known to the public, would have possessed their confidence which is as necessary as that of the person appointing in a government like ours."*

Henry Knox, Guest List. AN, hand of William Knox, Knox Papers, Gilder Lehrman Collection, NHi. Not dated, but headed "Tuesday next 6th. April." Endorsement in the hand of Henry Knox reads, "List invited."

Includes, among others, the Izards, the Griffins, the Adamses, Cadwallader, Seney, Contee, and R. B. Lee; notes that the Izards and their son declined because of a previous engagement.

John Main to George Thatcher. ALS, Chamberlain Collection, MB. Written from York, Maine; postmarked Portsmouth, New Hampshire, 9 April.

For a pending lawsuit brought by Thatcher, asks him to try to obtain from the papers of the Continental Congress a copy of the commission and/or bond for George Randall's privateer *Sally* (dated 6 August 1781).

Samuel Meredith to Margaret Meredith. ALS, Read Papers, PPL at PHi. Addressed to "Green Hill," outside Philadelphia.

"I have wrote this in a hurry with M[*es*]rs. Clymer & Fitzsimons conversing round me & Mr. C. remarking that the Post is just going out & afraid his letter will miss unless I finish immediately."

Peter Muhlenberg to Benjamin Rush. Excerpt of ALS, *Parke Bernet Catalog* 468(1943):item 170.

"I have delayed writing you, for a considerable time past; as nothing worthy of communication offered, and the fate of the Funding System was rendered more doubtful every day . . ."

Richard Stockton to Elias Boudinot. ALS, American Bible Society Boudinot Collection, NjP. Written from Princeton, New Jersey; franked.

"What are you doing with the funding plan?"; fears "all will not end well"; considers assumption "by far the most important consideration which has yet come before you"; if it passes, "the government is fixed—for ever fixed."

Jeremiah Wadsworth to Harriet Wadsworth. ALS, Wadsworth Papers, CtHi. Addressed to Hartford, Connecticut; franked; postmarked; signed "Your Affectionate father & friend."

"I have been pestered with a bad cold which has much abated"; encloses letter for Aunt Breek.

Joseph Whipple to John Langdon. ALS, Langdon Papers, NhPoA; FC:dft, Sturgis Family Papers, MH. Written from Portsmouth, New Hampshire.

Had Langdon resigned or declared an intention to resign from the Senate, he would have won seven-eighths of the votes for president (governor) of New Hampshire, "but as matters now stand I hope you will not resign this Year"; people complain at Congress's slow deliberations and are impatient for the outcome of the report on public credit; expects commercial treaties and ministerial appointments "will be brought on the Carpet this Session"; office seeking: Langdon's nephew, Henry Sherburne Langdon, for secretary to a European mission; Mrs. Elizabeth Langdon and "little Betsey" are well; "I shoud be happy to hear from you as time shall permit."

William Samuel Johnson, Diary. Johnson Papers, CtHi.

"Visits."

Wednesday, 7 April 1790

Cold High Wind (Johnson)

Abraham Baldwin to Joel Barlow

After the receipt of yours of the 17th Novr. with proposals to me & Reb,[1] I wrote you and included some newspapers by a London ship, which was my last; since then I received the duplicate by Havre [*Le Havre, France*], it was inclosed to [*William*] Duer with one to the girl [*Ruth Baldwin Barlow*], he says he lost them both out of his pocket, mine was brought me a few days afterwards from the Coffee house broken open, the girl's has not appeared, I have not told her of her letter as it would merely encrease her anxiety, the contents of mine were no doubt explored. I had communicated the information contained in it to no one but [*Royal*] Flint, and if any one else appears to possess it I shall know how it was obtained. Hamilton says you have made great sales, he was asked how he knew, and answered that Mr. [*Samuel*] Broome had congratulated him on the occasion in a letter, perhaps he does not know too many particulars. I received yesterday by the French packet, the duplicate of yours of the 12th of Decr. the original has not arrived, also the one of 15 Jany. with one for the girl, which have done me almost as much good as a visit.

I told you in my last in general my determination on the subject. Hamilton has not yet reported on the mode of disposing of the western lands,[2] he will not submit any other business to us, till we have got through his great object of finance. The event probably will be that the business will be put into his hands to sell at a certain rate, which will probably not exceed 20 cents ℔ acre, in his hands, any thing that is thought adviseable will be very manageable. I shall lose no time in getting hold of the Kaskaskia tract opposite the mouth of the Missouri, say two million acres exclusive of two hundred acres which had been agreed by the old cong. to be given to each of the french settlers who have [*been*] on the tract for these twenty years, their number is probably fifteen hundred.[3] If Flint chooses to join the Wabash tract[4] to it, well and good, if not it is as well, his tract has Indians upon it whose title is not extinguished, the other is I believe entirely free of Indian claim.

Your company [*Scioto Land Company*] say they have bargained with [*Nathaniel*] Gorham & [*Oliver*] Phelps for the whole of their Gennesee tract, alias the country of Sullivans Indian expedition south of lake Ontario, whether the cold and snow will be any discouragement to Brabanters[5] is a question, they say they shall send you complete titles to it in a very short time I have given Flint an extract from your letter as to the mode of preparing the business. I wish you to have every chance of doing the most you can for yourself while you are there. If I can get a tract cooked up to your mind, I know you will do the best you can with it, if not it shall be no hindrance to your working for others.

Your two last letters seem to have taken their direction from our proceedings at the last session, you say you saw the acts, journal &c. among the rest a bill for opening a land office, and among the rest probably a speech from Pittsburgh Scott.[6] From the whole you conclude that there is nearly an end to the plan of selling in large tracts, and say we are impolitic &c.

There is no such thing, the business was debated last session, but nothing concluded on. I doubt whether it will be resumed again, in that form. Everybody is in favour of selling in large tracts, rough & smooth, if we can, Scott himself is this session one of its warmest advocates. The other plan seemed to be brought forward from an apprehension that there would be no other way of disposing of the lands, and that was better than none. at the beginning of this session, an Irishman by the name of Hannibal William Dobbyn, petitioned for a large tract, soon after George Scriba[7] the story of which your associates, no doubt told you in their letters, both of them struck as agreeably as possible, and were referred to the secretary to report an uniform mode; all the observations on the subject were as much in favour of that mode as ever they were: And I have no doubt but all reasonable proposals will be accepted.

Some of your observations in these last letters do not appear to arise altogether from our proceedings last session, but in part from the difficulty of manageing a pre-emption in its own nature, and prefer transacting the business for the public, on a commission, if it is properly managed. This is so new as I received it but yesterday, that I have not yet determined what to say to you. I shall think it over thoroughly, but my present impression is, that you may be furnished to try them both. Get as many tracts of private prop. sent to you as possible, which seems rather fattest. and if Hamilton eventually has the matter put into his hands, there is no doubt but anything reasonable may be done.

[*part*] 2 Mr. Barlow

You tell me so many clever things in your letters I have been casting about to find something interesting to tell you in return, but in fact yours is the theatre of events at this time,[8] and we feel ourselves to be but lookers on. You know how anxious I was that you should have all that field of new simple ideas once in your life spread before you, and it was in truth all that reconciled my mind to your expedition, of all periods in the course of our lives, you have probably struck the point most crow[*d*]ed with events, I feel myself greatly compensated for my anxiety if you finally get through with a whole skin.

You have not played Cabogue[9] quite enough till lately, my old letter of "drawing into vision" which you laughed at me about was more to the purpose than you pretended, "my Cabogue thou thy angel I" you contemplate the affairs of this country very differently in your present situation from what you ever would had you been bustling along with us, and in many instances I find very differently from what anybody does here, you frequently hand out to me the end of entirely a new thread. you must leave tracks of all these things, nothing will be so likely to make you do it as talking with me for it is scarcely observable to yourself. Every thing you say is to the purpose, it is the best and probably the only chance.

We have done very little this session except make speeches about Hamilton's plan of finance. I sent you his report long since by way of Havre which I hope you have received. we have been through it in comtee. of the whole and agreed to all his leading principles. We were so nearly equally divided upon some points, that the North Carolina delegates who are now taking their seats, will probably turn it the other way. One fanciful idea brought forward by Mr. Madison, took up a great deal of time, attempting to make a discrimination between original holders & assignees of certificates, it was indeed a wild-goose scheme for so good and so sensible a man. It will not be revived again. Another rugged question is, the assumption of the state debts, it has been carried once, but is now recommitted and will probably be lost. There are many strong reasons in favour of it, the same revenues in the hands of the general government would be more productive, than when divided between them and the state governments, the states cannot let us have the sole use of excise &c. unless we take their debts. It would also have a good effect in establishing the government to have all the creditors look up to them for their pay, and all to have the same uniform provision. The substantial objection is the amount of the state debts is not known, a return of but a small part of them is yet obtained, and many of the states have not closed their settlements with their citizens, to suffer them to pile up accounts against the union ad libitum[10] will not do, and to open the liquidation again in all the states, will be the source of infinite frauds. To assume the whole in the present state of the business, is like plungeing into a gulf where we can see no shore. I am against doing it this session, but if we meet again in the fall, and the secretary obtains a definite return of all the state liquidations which shall bar all further demands, so that we know the amount of what we undertake, I shall be for trying to stagger under it. Our impost and excise will not be equal to it, besides answering all the current calls of the government, but we must do the best we can.

We have past a law for taking a census of the people, and a naturalization law, the prohibition of aliens holding lands was struck out on the motion of Praum,[11] the common law of the several states prevents them; but not in the western territory, it is just as it was before. After two years residence, and taking oaths before a judge they are naturalized, your landholders[12] must apply by squads on their arrival for a bill to naturalize them by name, they hold lands as it is. North Carolina has made a cession again of their western country, which has been accepted; it is said to contain about 16 million acres of land now vacant. It is to be governed for the present like the western territory.

The Commrs. of Vermont & N. York have been together here for several weeks, and adjourned till next summer, it is said the Vermonters had not the necessary powers. Kentucky says nothing about being a state at present. R. Island [*ratification*] convention was together a few days last month, the antis had a majority of 12; they are to meet again the last of next month. what they will dare to do is uncertain, I think we shall dare to manage them pretty soon if they adjourn again without coming to a determination. I have no doubt of our powers on the subject.

Georgia has been selling to some land spec[*ulator*]s. in Virginia &c. 15 million acres of land on the Missisippi, you know the spaniards say it is there by conquest from great Britain, Congress says it is theirs by taking the sovereignty, from the king who held it before, and South Carolina says part of it was in their charter. It is a very tangled business, and was a very imprudent sale on the part of Georgia.

Messrs. [*Rufus*] Putnam and [*Manasseh*] Cutler are in town, Putnam is appointed judge in the room of our friend Parsons deceased.[13] [*William*] Judd tried to get it.

[*William*] Duer has resigned his place of assistant to Hamilton, many reasons are assigned, some say he is going to Europe, he says he was starved out, others mention different reasons.

The girl is very well, she did not know of this opportunity, I send this by the packet, if I find a passenger I will inclose a bundle of news papers.

[*part*] 3 Mr. Barlow

The french packet brought us the speech of the king in the national assembly, & the Presidents speech in return, also the spirited observations of our friend the Marquis to a certain nobleman.[14] we participate in all the politics of our good friends, but I heartily accord with you that it should be at a respectable distance; we shall forget ourselves ig[*re*]giously whenever we intermingle in affairs on the other [*si*]de of the water any farther than by acts of common civility.

Mr. Jefferson has concluded to accept the office of secretary of state and has been with us about a fortnight.

The first circuit court of the United States is now sitting here, Messrs. Jay, & [*William*] Cushing, and the district Judge [*James*] Duane are present. The middle tour is performed by [*James*] Wilson & [*John*] Blair. the southern by [*John*] Rutledge & [*James*] Iredil of North Carolina appointed in the place of old sec[*retary*]. [*Robert H.*] Harrison resigned. The supreme court sat here in Feby. four Judges and the attorney general quondam Govr. [*Edmund*] Randolph attended, Rutledge & Iredil were not here. There is little business but to organize themselves and let folks look on and see they are ready to work at them, this same new government has got some long roots down deep in the soil, I think it will stand a blow bye and bye.

***

The spring ships on their return will give me frequent opportunites I will tell you all the stories I can think of Adieu vive valeq[*ue*].[15]

AL, Baldwin Family Collection, CtY. Place to which addressed not indicated; received 28 May. This letter was written in three parts, probably over a number of days. The omitted text relates to news of family and friends in Connecticut.

---

[1] Baldwin's older brother Dudley (1753–94), a Greenfield, Connecticut, lawyer.

[2] On 20 January, the House referred to Hamilton its June 1789 committee report on public lands; Hamilton reported on the disposition of public lands on 22 July.

[3] A tract of public lands around present-day Kaskaskia, Illinois, which the Confederation Congress designated for sale in the summer of 1788 except for reservations of four hundred acres per family (not two hundred) to be donated to French, Canadian, and other longtime settlers of the area (*JCC* 34:250–51, 467–68). These donations were confirmed under the FFC's Northwest Territory Act [S-17] in March 1791.

[4] By the time of this letter, the claims of the pre-revolutionary Wabash Company were embraced by the United Land Companies of the Illinois and Wabash and spanned much of present-day central and southern Indiana and Illinois. The Company's March 1790 petition to the FFC unsuccessfully offered three quarters of what it claimed by an earlier purchase

from Native Americans in exchange for confirmation of its title to the remaining quarter (*DHFFC* 8:204–7).

[5] Probably referring to inhabitants of Brabant (part of Belgium and The Netherlands), who were among the prospective investors in Scioto lands whom Barlow was trying to attract.

[6] Baldwin refers to Scott's long and well received speech in favor of a land office, delivered in the COWH on 13 July; see *DHFFC* 11:1095–1108.

[7] The petition of Hannibal W. Dobbyn and two from George Scriba, dated 18 January and 2 and 11 March respectively, were referred to Hamilton, whose 22 July report contained uniform provisions for the sale of public lands. For background and texts, see *DHFFC* 8:196–200.

[8] Barlow was in revolutionary Paris at this time, in order to sell Scioto Company land in the Northwest Territory (in present-day southeast Ohio) to European investors.

[9] A cabogue was an itinerant Irish laborer hired to help farmers dig potatoes in the fall. It may be used here as a playful commentary on Barlow's inactivity, either in public affairs or as a land sales agent.

[10] At pleasure.

[11] A family nickname for Baldwin.

[12] Investors in Scioto Company land that Barlow had deeded to the French Compagnie de Scioto to facilitate sales to prospective immigrants.

[13] Putnam was appointed federal district judge for the Northwest Territory after the death of Samuel Holden Parsons in November 1789.

[14] The *Merchant* from Le Havre brought the text of Louis XVI's speech to the National Constituent Assembly on 4 February 1790, Assembly President Jean Xavier Bureaux de Pluzy's speech the next day, and the marquis de la Fayette's (undated) letter "to a certain illustrious character." They were printed in *NYDA* and *NYDG*, 6 April.

[15] Farewell and be happy (Latin).

Aedanus Burke to Alexander Hamilton

Your letter of this day in which you explicitly declare that you had no intention, in your Eulogium on General [*Nathanael*] Green, to cast any reflection on Militia in general, or on any description of the Citizens of South-Carolina, removes all ground of dissatisfaction on my part.

I therefore cheerfully and explicitly retract every thing offensive which I said in the House of Representatives on Wednesday last: in relation to you. And whatever else in any stage of this disagreeable Affair, may have admitted of a Construction wounding to your feelings. And I assure you of my concern that any misapprehension should have given occasion to it. Occurrences of this kind are ever to be regreted, and in an amicable issue, ought not to leave on generous minds any traces of unfriendly impressions.

ALS, Hamilton Papers, DLC.

Edward Carrington to James Madison

I have seen the decision of the House of R. upon the Quaker Memorial, nearly I suppose as the Committee reported. from the lengthy debates however and the Matter of these debates, I had been led to suppose it possible at least that the report was a different one asserting something like a power in Congress to meddle with emancipation. the very circumstance of such a subject being taken up in Congress has given some alarm, and it might have been better that a debate of such a Nature which could not possibly be productive of any kind of effect, had never been entered into at all. indeed ~~it appears~~ from the accuracy of the resolutions as applying to the constitutional powers of Congress over this subject, I am led to suppose that notwithstanding the long debates there was little or no difference of opinion as to what must be the issue of the business—why then were the people of the interested states to be alarmed in consequence of a fruitless discussion? this circumstance before the appearance of the decision had become a subject of serious conversation amongst the people. I doubt not that ~~the satisfaction which the~~ the resolutions will give ~~well~~ full satisfaction as soon as they are generally known—the Assumption of the State Debts remains now a subject of discontent—upon two principles it creates serious complaint. It is by all anti's, and many Fed's considered as leading to the dreaded consolidation—and by all descriptions of Men who think at all it is considered as ~~iniquitous~~ iniquitous from the unequal situations of the States respecting their Debts: of the latter I am one. having already written you pretty fully I will not add more here. whether the constitution is yet so firmly on its legs that it cannot be shocked I will not undertake to decide I am not apt to croak, of this however I am certain, the adoption of this measure without giving to the States the benefit of their respective redeemed Debts will [*have*] considerable effect in abridging the confidence of the people in it.

ALS, Madison Papers, DLC. Written from Richmond, Virginia; postmarked.

Manasseh Cutler to Daniel Story

*** Punctual payment [*for the Ohio Company purchase*] must be made to Congress, or the right of pre-emption will be forfited. *** we have the strongest reason to believe, there is now a Dutch Gentleman in the city who arrived a few days ago from Holland, sent over, on purpose, by the Contractors with B— [*Joel Barlow*] to make enquiry into wt. is done by the S[*ciot*]o. Compy. in providg. for the [*Gallipolis*] settlers,[1] & to know the Value of Con[*tinenta*]l. Securities &c. &c.—We have taken great pains to find out his business. Col. [*William*] Duer told me, last Evg., that he had got full evidence that he wanted to purchase securities if the price suited him. And D—r declared he did not doubt from many other circumstances, that he was come as an agent for those contractors. ***

Judge Put— [*Rufus Putnam*] & I have been here about 6 weeks on the business of the O. Compy. [*Ohio Company*] but as Cong. have been exceedingly engaged & have not decided on the Secry. of the Treasy. report we have not yet preferrd our petition. But we have been making every exertion to engage the interest of members in support of it. I think we have a good prospect of making considerable addition to the funds of the Compy., & of the quantity of land to each share. I dare not, however, promise anything. *** We have prepared a draught for a Charter for the University.[2] But I think it very doubtful whether Congress will act upon it this session. The members to whom I have mentioned it,[3] appear disposed to give it support, &, if [*lined out*] Congress were at leisure to take it up, I presume it would pass without opposition. In the mean time, we hope to be able to make provision for the support of a no. of Schools.[4]

***

ALS, Cutler Papers, IEN. Place to which addressed not indicated. The omitted text relates to the Ohio Company's financial affairs.

---

[1] The syndicate known as the Scioto Associates had purchased fifteen percent of the Ohio Company's shares in land in 1789 as part of a complex scheme to prevent the latter's forfeiture for delinquent payments to the federal government. The Associates, who had expected Barlow to sell large tracts of undeveloped land to absentee European investors rather than smaller tracts to would-be settlers, were left unprepared to accommodate the two groups of emigrés who had arrived in New York City by early May 1790: one under the "agent" John Joseph de Barth, and the other under Charles F. Boulogne. The Associates hurriedly improvised a 150,000 acre settlement centered around present-day Gallipolis ("The City of the Gauls"), only to discover that it lay on a parcel still owned by the Ohio Company. Some emigrés re-purchased the lots, while others moved elsewhere in the Ohio Company's purchase, or simply returned east; approximately one third died of disease. Following the Scioto Associates' default (owing in part to the embezzlement of funds by the broker in Paris to whom Barlow had deeded much of the land), the original settlers unsuccessfully petitioned the House for confirmation of their titles, and in 1795 Congress compensated them with 24,000 acres known as the "French Grant" (Shaw Livermore, *Early American Land Companies* [1939; reprint, New York, 1968], pp. 138–40; *PAH* 6:422n; *Westward Expansion*, pp. 219–20).

[2] When the Ohio Company first petitioned for a land purchase in July 1787, a congressional committee (whose members included future FFC members Benson, King, and Madison) stipulated that "Four complete Townships to be given perpetually for the purposes of an University, be laid off by the Company, as near the centre as may be, so that the same shall be of good land, to be applied to the intended object by the Legislature of the State" (*JCC* 32:312). The congressional order to the board of treasury authorizing the terms of the contract later amended this to reserve only two townships for that purpose (*JCC* 33:400).

[3] Although Cutler had plenteous contacts with congressmen throughout his two months in New York City (21 February to 23 April), his canvassing of members' support for a university may have taken place this day, which his diary indicates he spent "At Congress" (Cutler Papers, IEN).

[4] In addition to its provisions for a university (specified above), the Ohio Company was obligated under the Ordinance of 1785 to reserve one lot (number sixteen), of every thirty-six that comprised a township, for the support of public schools (*JCC* 28:378).

Theodore Sedgwick to Pamela Sedgwick

I have waited till late in the evening hoping to have the pleasure to receive your letter by the northern post, but it is not yet arrived.

Tomorrow I hope the question on the subject of the assumption will be taken. It has been delayed for several days in order to satisfy the pensylvanians on whom the ultimate result will depend. It is to be hoped that they will then be prepared to join us. I will again report to you that no other business will detain me in New York a single hour.

ALS, Sedgwick Papers, MHi. Place to which addressed not indicated.

George Thatcher to Thomas B. Wait

I cannot help noticing the warm expressions you make use of when speaking of certain persons, who, 'twas reported, were about petitioning the President for the removal of a certain Collector;[1] and what would be the consequence to their reputation should they fail of their object; *which I am confident will be the case*—as also the effect of their former conduct—all your language on this subject is strong and passionate. I fear this Language flows from a degree of passion that will produce actions tending more to irritate & provoke, than asswage and reconcile—Remember, resentment cannot be disarmed by harshness of words, or oposition of force—and that angar can only be overcome by soft words.

FC, Thatcher Family Papers, MHi. This is a postscript to a letter dated 6 April and printed under that date, above.

[1] Nathaniel Fosdick, collector at Portland, Maine, whose appointment was strongly opposed by fellow contender Stephen Hall. Hall had also spearheaded Portland's committee petitioning for changes in the Coasting Act [HR-16] earlier in the second session. That petition committee's "former conduct" mentioned later in the letter alludes to a motion, seconded by Hall, to punish Thatcher's inattention by making a feint to forward their petition to Ames instead; see *DHFFC* 8:412–16.

George Lee Turberville to James Madison

Yr. Favor of february tenth did not reach me untill yesterday having been from home six weeks during which I have suffered extremely with a pleurisy—& afterward ~~a severe fit of~~ the Gout—or rather a flying Gout. I am thank heaven now almost recover'd.

Small breaches in Laws are precedents which will be drawn in point in favor of larger & more important ones—and a Government subject to the will only of those in power will be consequential of the patient sufferance of *such breaches* how trivial soever they may appear to be I am still convinced that the Law of the Union is positive in regard to the payment of Specie only in the naval offices for duties—& the Letter to Hudson Muse Collector of Rappa[*hannock River*]. from Mr. Hamilton directs him to receive notes from the Banks—I shall still forbear to comment upon the consequences that may result to the prejudice of the public & of the individuals in the U.S. & shall only add that the secretaries report ~~adds~~ [*lined out*] ~~to~~ encreases my apprehensions of injury from that quarter, I am not unacquainted ~~either~~ personally with that *Gentleman* at the head of that department of the Revenue & still less so with the powers of *his* mind—his acquirements, disposition & character, I tremble at the thoughts of his being at the head of such ~~vast &~~ an immense sum as 86 millions of dollars—and the annual revenue of the Union—The number of dependants on him necessary to manage the great department of Revenue the multitude who will be interested in the funds (in opposition too to the Landed interest of the U.S.) all of whom will in some measure be dependant—or at any rate attached to the principal Officer of the Revenue I profess creates with me apprehensions—that from the complicated nature of the subject I am at a loss to determine whether I ought to foster or to discourage.

I am nevertheless persuaded that the funding business founded upon loans will never answer in America—the example set by Great Britain can never be followd. ~~in this country~~ here untill our Country becomes as ~~numerous~~ thickly populated—as Commercial and as highly Cultivated as G. Britain is—Money there is so abundant & its use so limited that 3 pr. Ct. is better interest than 10 pr. C. in Virginia at least—ready Money will for a long period be worth 7 8 & 10 pr. Cent in this Country. The very purchase of Lands if they remain uncultivated in the Lower Country or any where on the Eastern waters will in 10 years *if sold again* repay the principal & 10 pr. Cent interest—& Cash laid out upon the improvement of the soil will Average 20 pr. Ct. Bills on London are now selling for 12 & 14 pr. Ct. & very skilful merchants are of opinion they will be down to par before 12 Months elapse—our Exports are becoming infinitely greater than our imports—frugality & industry are again becoming familiar & notwithstanding those things specie is scarce—Vast sums are are wanting yet to afford a medium sufficient for the mere intercourse between the holders of soil & those they employ to improve it—taking this veiw of things & recollecting the former want of punctuality in the payments from the public—which cannot easily be eradicated from the ~~public~~ minds of men—is it supposeable that any persons will be found to advance money for the purchase of annuities or to

Vest monies in the funds of the Union for the precarious interest of 6 pr. Centum.

The ~~thought~~ Idea of consolidating the debt of the States with that of the Union is a very unpopular one & for that reason only ought to be laid aside—but I do not think it even political—the debts of Virga. are sinking fast—every creditor appears satisfied—and the monied men are very fond of becoming adventurers & purchasing the State paper Many have made their fortunes by it—why in heaven then shou'd Congress interfere with us? I hope and trust that part of the plan will at least be negatived ~~by Congress~~.

I observe in the secretaries report one Article among many Very exceptionable ones to me—that will be fatal to Virginia 'tis the Tax proposed on Stills—this is a partial law calculated to burthen the southern states & to put a stop to the distillation of brandy & Whisky whilst the Eastern people—mostly resident in Towns are totally exonerated from the Tax—this cannot have escaped yr. Notice.

Touching discrimination—I am entirely of yr. opinion—altho I do not think ~~if it were possible to come at it~~ that the Government cou'd be taxed with injustice if they pay the alienee the bona fide sum he gave for his final settlement, or other state paper with his interest up to the period of reimbursement—'tis admitted that the original holder parted with all his claim when he sold his security but can it be said that when he sold it he expected that its nominal Value wou'd be made good—No—he sold it for what he thought it was worth for what he conceived he conceived his Country woud be able to make good to him & the difference between the nominal & the received value—he sacrificed to the necessities of his Country.

Upon the whole the credit of the Union must be bottomed rather upon what they do in future than upon Quixotic attempts to do impossibilities & to make good what the abilities of their Citizens are inadequate to by aiming at giving real value to their old debts—If they fail in the visionary attempt to pay the nominal amount of their debt—which I am assured they will do—their credit will sink hardly ever to rise again & convulsions probably a revolution will be the consequence.

I am not apprehensive of danger from the doors of the senate being shut—but I am anxious for the Legislature in every instance to conciliate the Affection of the people.

In my next I will give you my ideas touching the measures that appear to me proper to be pursued ~~touching~~ in regard [*to*] the Old debts.

[*P. S.*] Excuse this Scrawl I have not time to copy the Letter.

ALS, Madison Papers, NN. Written from Caroline County, Virginia.

Newspaper Article

The debates of Congress, says a correspondent, are highly interesting, and it is of importance that the people should be made acquainted with them. When they are informed of the reasons which actuate their representatives, they will more readily place a confidence in their determinations. The Congressional Register will record and preserve the debates at full length. But this plan does not appear calculated for a newspaper. Few people can spare time to read the debates in full. A sketch of the heads of arguments would answer every purpose of conveying necessary information, and would not take up the greatest part of a paper, to the exclusion of useful observations on agriculture, commerce, manufactures &c. which in this country ought to be particularly attended to. Would it not, therefore, be adviseable for the printers of newspapers in New-York, who favour the public with the debates of Congress, rather to give a summary, than to attempt them in full?

FG, 7 April; reprinted at Baltimore and Winchester, Virginia.

Other Documents

Peter Allaire, Occurrences from 2 March to 7 April. Mss., Foreign Office 4/7, p. 233, PRO. The Occurrences were dispatches written for the British Foreign Office through the intermediary Sir George Yonge.

"The Southern Members (Georgia South & North Carolina and Virginia) exposed & explained in so pointed a manner the Quakers and those who have the *Rage* of Emancipation that I beleive they will never petition Congress again"; there is not "a Member in Congress, but what thinks himself Capable of Governing this Vast Empire, not a Single Member in either house but what Speechifies for one or two hours, & which makes the public business go on but Slowly."

Andrew Craigie to Daniel Parker. FC:dft, Craigie Papers, MWA. Sent by packet.

The question of assumption will be voted on the next day and no doubt will carry, but by a small majority; "the gratification of the Members from North Carolina was the pretence for re committing" Hamilton's report on public credit; has no doubt of the entire report succeeding.

Benjamin Goodhue to Stephen Goodhue. ALS, Goodhue Family Papers, MSaE. Addressed to Salem, Massachusetts; franked; postmarked.

"We have nothing new in politicks. the question on the Assumption has not yet been taken up expect it will be tomorrow, it will be a hard push, our numbers are nearly equal. but I think it will obtain, I have more hopes then I had a few days past."

Stephen Goodhue to Benjamin Goodhue. FC:lbk, Goodhue Family Papers, MSaE. Written from Salem, Massachusetts. For more on Samuel Carleton's petition for settlement of his accounts, see *DHFFC* 7:555–58.

Benjamin can judge whether state inspection laws are beneficial or not; Stephen wishes they were all repealed; if they were rigidly enforced "it whould be dificult to procure lumber"; a report that assumption has been rejected causes uneasiness; Samuel Carleton wants to know the status of his petition.

Alexander Hamilton to Aedanus Burke. No copy known; acknowledged in Burke to Hamilton, 7 April.

Theodore Hopkins to Jeremiah Wadsworth. ALS, Wadsworth Papers, CtHi. Written from London; addressed to Hartford, Connecticut; carried by Wm. Griffiths.

Sends by the bearer the third number of the *Parliamentary Register* for the present session; sent the first two on 16 March. (An attached memorandum indicates that Hopkins sent Wadsworth fourteen earlier numbers between July and November 1789.)

James O'Fallon to John Sevier. ALS, Draper Collection, WHi. Written from Jonesboro, Tennessee; place to which addressed not indicated. Sevier, who resided in the Holston River settlements in present-day Washington County, Tennessee, did not depart for Congress until perhaps as late as early June, following the formal announcement of his election no earlier than 1 April (*DHFFE* 4:363).

Is en route to the South Carolina Yazoo Company's grant (in present-day central Mississippi and western Alabama) as agent and proprietor, in order to establish there "a formidable Colony"; bears a letter from the company's director, William Moultrie, "with some verbal Messages, proposals & assurances of the company's acquiescence with yr. Request, on the most favourable terms, in case, more especially, you should condiscend to move into the Colony, as a *permanent* Setler"; hopes to confer personally with Sevier as soon as possible.

THURSDAY, 8 APRIL 1790

Warm (Johnson)

George Clymer to Henry Hill

Receiving your letter within these ten minutes, I found on enquiry a packet just on the point of sailing, and got your enclosure to Mr. LaMar thrust into a supplementary bag—the mail having been made up last night—She is the Antelope.

I shall see Mr. [*Samuel*] Meredith at dinner when I shall converse with him about the York county business and write you again.

I remember you once said you envied no man here—Had they all my feelings they would not be the subjects of envy. for nothing is so irksome to me as incessant disputation—unless it be tedious procrastination, and we have them both here in their highest perfection. Yet I suspect there are some people ~~here~~ [*in*] this room very well reconciled to their seats, and would be greatly mortified to be sent back to the comforts of a family or the society of their friends. Such elevation of mind do they feel, sitting on the pinnacle—and such consciousness of their own usefulness and importance. For my own part having neither the elevation nor the consciousness I have no desire but to be at home—When please god I shall be some time or other. Here ~~are~~ being half a dozen lawyers all round me talking up the nature of crimes and punishments[1] I shall conclude with observing that it is my punishment to hear them.

ALS, Signers of the Declaration, MWA. Addressed to Philadelphia; franked; undated, but postmarked on this date. Written from the floor of the House at 11 o'clock.

[1] Clymer wrote during debate on the Punishment of Crimes Act [S-6].

Benjamin Lincoln to Theodore Sedgwick

You say that it is probable that the system of collection will receive many alterations and wish my ideas of those which are necessary to be made.

I will in the first place say that the naval office as the business is conducted is perfectly useless. It seems by the law that it was intended that the Naval officers should be a check on the costings of the duties &ca. Admit that they do attend to that part of their duty and that they absolutely keep regular books as ordered Yet the office I think is of little or no importance. Such is the method pointed out for keeping our accounts of settling them &c. that the different parts are sufficiently ~~by~~ checked by each other—For example we are in the first place to give the united States credit for the amount of the duties upon every seperate consignment once in a quarter we are obliged to render those accounts for adjustment—With this account we send, as a voucher to it, an abstract of the value of the duties on every Cargo imported the different rules placed under different columns all the goods which pay a duty of 5 ℔ Cent in the column of 5 ℔ Cent so of those 7½, 10 &c. in their own colum, as also all the articles which pay ~~to~~ by the pound the gallon or bushell &c. each are placed under seperate columns. When this is done the ~~foot~~ amount of the duties on every cargo are carried out in a seperate line. in one cargo may be comprehended duties of every kind when every cargo is so carried out the amount of them are footed [*summed*]. In order to prove whether they are right we add the duties in ~~the~~ each seperate Columns and bring these foots [*sums*] together we then prove whether these are right by seeing ~~for instance~~ the amount of 5 ℔ Cent on the whole value of goods imported charged with that duty and so through the whole; if we find them right we then compare the foot of the amount of the duties on the several Cargoes with the foot of the duties at the several rates if they agree we then turn to the Ledger and see the sum with which we have credited the public if they all agree it is well if they do not we must look for the errour untill we find it. To make it more plain for I think it important you should under stand it I will give you a short example

	5 ℔ Cent		7½ ℔ Cent		5/8 Cents ℔ Galo.		1 Cent ℔ pound		
	Amo.	Duty	Amo.	Duty	amot.	duty	Amount	duty	Dollars Cents
Cargo Manifest No. 1	100	5	100	7.50	100	18	100	1	31.50
Cargo No. 2—	100	5	100	7.50	100	18	100	1	31.50
Cargo No. 3—	200	10	200	15	200	36	200	2	63.00
	400	20	400	30	400	72	400	4	126—

By this statement we find that the duties on the several Cargoes amount to 126 dollars and the foot of the several rates of duties amount to the same sum

20
30
72
4 } 126—

The amount of the good at 5 P. Cent is 400 dollars 5 P. Cent on four hundred dollars is	20
The amount of the good @ 7½ is 400 Dollars 7½ on that sum	30
400 Galo. @ 18 Cents P. Galo. amounts to—	72
One Cent P. pound on 400 amounts to—	4
	126

by this last act you prove that your several sums were right carried out they serve to check each other and all are a check upon the ledger whence the account rendered is taken I have been thus particular because I hinted that there was a sufficient check upon our accounts without that of the Naval officer I am confident that upon a review of the matter you will be with me in opinion. But a question will arise what can you do with those officers we must not sport with their feelings I say they may be provided for in the farther establishment of the revenue system.

It seems to be agreed on all hands that it will be best to divide the United States into districts and that some person ~~should~~ be appointed in each to superintend the collection &c. We may, I think, with propriety enquire whether this will not multiply officers unnecessarily & thereby cause a clamour for this must be a very responsible officer and cannot undertake the business without a handsom compensation To avoid this it has been a question in my mind whither it would not be best to commit the discharge of the duty of a superintendent to one of the collectors by this mode you avoid the appearance of creating new officers with large salleries and can have the business done, with little additional expence to the mode now in practice, A collector would be able to do a great part of the business in his own office at a time while he was superintending the business of it—He may always add to his number of assistants. I think in this mode of doing the business money might be saved to the United States and the novelty ~~of new~~ arising from creating new officers avoided.

The duties of such an officer should be to receive all communications from the secretary of the treasury and diffuse them thro his distr[*ict*] to receive all questions from the different officers lay them before the secretary—Visit the differen[*t*] ports once a year at the least examine the acct. the mode of doing business &c.—Should appoin[*t*] certain private marks for his district so that wh[*en*] dutiable good were carried from one port to an other it could be know by the office seeing them whe[*ther*] they had paid the duties or not. He might also convey his private marks to the Gentlemen of othe[*r*] Districts and receive from ~~theirs~~ them theirs so that when ever an officer saw property liable to a duty he could instantly tell whether it had paid the duties on importation this would be the means of correcting many. He should receive all the monies from the out post and have a genera[*l*] eye over the whole district.

Their wants an alteration in the collection bill relative to the collectors, half ⅌ Cent for receiving and paying out the money and that only on a part of it is no adequate reward for the risk and trouble.

The bills want various alteratio[*ns*] all of them I trust have been laid before the secretary as they have occurred to the several officers I shall not therefore pretend to mention them I will however mention to you tha[*t*] Coasters may or may not [*lined out*] enter there [*is?*] no penalty on them if they do not.

By the papers received the last night it seems quite uncertain whether the Union will accept the State debts or not if they should not I hope that they will not pass the accounts of the several States ~~untill~~ untill they shall have evinced to Congress that they have established funds sufficient to discharge those debts of the Union which they have undertaken to discharge—This State has charged the Union with a large sum paid to the officers of the continental army they have, its true, given the officers & men certificates of the sums due to them respectively but they have not paid the sum and refuse to make provision for the payment of even the interest I hope they will never have Credit for their charges untill they have evidenced that they paid the money or have secured the payment of it—It may be said that the army have already acknowledged the payment they may have given receipts for the notes which they have received this will not justify the Union in leaving them. The army made a contract with the United States they had no idea when they engaged in the service of the continent that they should have any thing to do with the different States—They finally were referred to the particular States for their pay this was an act of power and one to which the army was obliged to submit—This ought to be considered and the Union should never consider themselves discharged untill the army was paid. They have it now in their power to do this justice either by adopting the State debts or by a refusal to credit the several States for sums said to be paid to their army which in fact have never been paid. It is very easey for Congress to do justice now or at the least to do that which would give very general satisfaction If they do not they will let themselves down in the minds of all *interested* men at the least.

It is said that General [*William*] Heath, who if it was not for his merit in war would have I think little of which to boast, for he is a strange politician, is in the plan of discrimination and I am very apprehensive will encourage some of the officers to petition Congress for a compensation for their losses by the depreciation of their public securities and the want of payment in time by Congress[1]—A number I know will discourage the attempt at this time thinking it very improper to make an application of the kind in this stage of the public business. That the army have a just claim on the public ~~none will doubt~~ from the want of that pay which was promised them none will, I think doubt few I hope however will think this a proper moment to apply, for they are not the only sufferers, were all now to put in their claims who have lost by the old continental money & by public paper it would so embarrass the present measures as to prevent any regular system from being adopted—These observations respecting Heath & those who are with him I wish you to consider as confidential—Indeed the the whole of the letter should be so considered for I have spoken too freely but for the ear of a friend—And my ideas of a person at the head, of the several districts should the Union be thrown into districts would be construed by some as securing a place for my self however your friendship caution will prevent your making an improper use of any part of the letter. You know the world is unkind and should never be intrusted with those things of which they can make an ill use. ~~they should never~~ They must evince that they have a greater disposition to sprinkle the pillow of their fellow men with the soothing essence of the best scented rose rather than to plat it with the most irritating thorns before they should receive our confidence.

If any that before you will have reached thus far you will say to your self that the General has very little to do or he never would write such a plaugy long letter As an apology for my spending so much time in this way I have to tell you that it is a fast day which gives [*m*]e more time than I other wise should hav[*e*] had out of office and you know my dear s[*ir*] that we are more active when we abstain from food than when our stomachs & vessels are loaded. I will not trouble you any farther.

ALS, Sedgwick Papers, MHi. Written from Boston. Two pages of the document are damaged.

---

[1] Heath and Lincoln were among the thirty-seven officers of the Massachusetts Line of the Continental Army who met in Boston on 13 April to discuss what became the petition that Lincoln describes here. For background and documents, see *DHFFC* 7:176–78.

George Thatcher to Sally Barrell

The honor you have done me, as well as the pleasure I enjoyed in reading your favor, is too great not to demand a particular acknowledgment—And I trust your acquaintance with me is sufficient evidence that I have not delighted in viewing the human race as vile & wicked, notwithstanding my sermon to Mr. Barrell[1]—But, in order, to get him in a just train of thinking I myself was obliged to take the wrong side—and I now find it is with him, as my friend Mr. Wingate sais of me; he has frequently, of late, told me, that if he wished to make me a christian he would himself become apparently the deist or atheist—Thus by Mr. Barrell's answers to my sermon on the great wickedness of men & nations, it appears he has undertaken to defend an opposite doctrine; and prove that nations as well as individuals live in the habitual practice of Righteousness; and I have no doubt but that, should I preach him two or three sermons more on the wickedness of the human race, he will be as firm a disbeliever in that doctrine as I am—Is there then, you will ask, naturally a spirit of opposition in men, that leads them thus to oppose what is advanced by one another? I answer this is not the work of nature—for man is born as pure as the angels—If there be any thing wrong in man 'tis the effect of education; and notwithstanding education is yet in its infancy we discover a pretty general disposition, in all people, to take side with the oppressed; and see that justice is done both in restoring the injured to his rights and bringing some pain, at least, to the aggressor—And the greatest danger is that our love to humanity, of which Justice is a branch, will carry us too far in inflicting the punishment.

Mr. Barrell certainly paints well; and if a picture, now & then, has little livelier colours than the original, it will not please the less for it—we see people almost every where trying to add something to nature, by art. I recollect to have seen a painting of the birth of Jesus; but from that I should never have thought the scene was in a Stable.

However Mr. B. might have given a deep colour to his characters in one Letter; in his last he has done them full justice the other way; and made those nations, I had represented the most vile upon earth, both just and amiable.

My friends shall always have access to my Library; & I hope the pleasure you promise yourself in reading some of the Books will equal your expectation; And tho you are pleased to compliment me on account of my good taste in the choice of books; I assure you, in this, you are almost alone—but I am, sometimes, so odd as to estimate a departure from the common road of thinking, a marke of accuracy in judgment.

I shall write to Mr. B. as soon as Congress shall do~~ne~~ any thing that will have a tendency to keep up, in his mind, the good opinion, he seems to have concieved of them—He is gratified, he writes me, in finding that justice & honesty prevail among them—This is pretty well for a man who believes in original sin & the total depravity of human nature—for it clearly implies that he believes also, they have special grace sufficient to destroy the evil disposition of the old serpent.

FC, Thatcher Family Papers, MHi.

[1] In his letter to Thatcher dated 24 March, above, Nathaniel Barrell was pleased to "find you have commencd. preacher and in the common, clerical, orthodox method, have undertaken to prove there never was a Nation supported by righteousness."

An Elector to the Electors of Westchester

THE election for members of Congress approaches, and, at this season, every man feels that he is free, and of some importance in the scale of society. A French philosopher, with a kind of morose satire, and with a degree of envy, observed, that Englishmen were free once in seven years, only a few days during the election. Free electors, beware: that no future reflections of this kind be made on you—If you do not abuse this invaluable privilege, your free Constitution, and your Liberty may be immortal—Exercise your judgment and discernment uninfluenced, and elect no man, whose verbal and meritricious eloquence has supported the new republican doctrine of high wages and salaries, and whose venal and avaricious vote was always in opposition to œconomy—Choose a man whose mind is independent, and keep a *Creaturiam* out of the councils of the nation—Choose a man who is not in the habits of speculation, and who, probably, will not yield his mind to the corrupt influence of avarice, in his senatorial character, and on political questions. If you are not on your guard in your future elections, the world may see the free yeomanry of this country, before twenty years elapse, *hewers of wood, and drawers of water,*[1] to a few in power.

NYJ, 8 April. This article was apparently written in opposition to Laurance's reelection.

[1] Joshua 9:21.

Letter from Boston

We still hope Congress will not finish the session without some decided measures relative to the national debts. If they do *any* thing, they must do *every* thing that we can desire. I am persuaded Congress are not so ignorant of the circumstances of the United States as to imagine a partial system of finance is practicable. Unless the State debts are assumed, no funding system will operate prosperously; and without a prosperous funding system our national government will be but a shadow. In short I dare not predict the consequences of having the public debts long neglected, or partially provided for.

The Creditors of the United States, and of the several States, have not yet lost their patience, or their confidence. I hope they never will lose either; but I imagine if nothing is done for their relief within a few weeks, they will unite in some measures to express their sentiments to Congress in very unequivocal, but respectful language.

Perhaps a Convention of Delegates from the public creditors to meet at New York or Philadelphia, could make some representations to Congress that would facilitate their determinations.

The opposers of a funding system; and in this light I view all anti-assumptionists, are not sensible how large a number of respectable men are holders of the public debt.

The friends of good government—the friends of science; the friends of virtue and honor, mourn exceedingly that Mr. M—[*adison*] has departed so essentially from his federal principles, and that the lustre of his character declines. It is impossible for me to conjecture what can be the occasion he has taken a part so derogatory to his former dignity, and so repugnant to the important interests of his country. I once thought him a very great, and a very good man. I will think so again, when his conduct is more open, public spirited, and accommodating. For the present, I suspend my opinion of him.

GUS, 17 April; reprinted at Baltimore; Fredericksburg, Norfolk, and Winchester, Virginia; and Edenton, North Carolina.

Brutus to Nobody

IN offering your sentiments against the assumption of the State Debts by the United States, you have been very incautious, and furnished means to the enemies of this State to injure it. You have shewn great ignorance of the facts that ought to be brought into view to elucidate the subject; and one of your assertions is so directly opposed to truth, that I am astonished you could be so weak as to make it, to wit, That we should loose the half million we have paid if the rest is assumed. There are two or three men in the State who have long been carefully investigating the nature and situation of our debts, and by their disinterested conduct and perseverance, they have produced a pretty good statement of the debt against the Union, and know and pursue her true interests. They have also corrected, in some measure, the infamous misuse and dissipation of the State funds—and if their compassion which has been too great does not prevent, will I hope bring to light all the tricks and misdoings, of those who trifle with our interests. Our Delegates in Congress are all for the assumption of the State debts, and whatever your insinuations may be, the people know they are better acquainted with the interest of the State than you can be, and have no doubts of their integrity. Beware, Sir, of a mean little policy—You walk on ice and may slip, perhaps fall. Those people who for years past have prevented the State from availing herself of her resources in the western lands, and caused jealousies and suspicions of those who were able and willing to enrich and invigorate the State, are not forgotten; and I intreat you, Sir, to avoid the rock on which they have been wrecked, or rather on which they have cast away the wealth of the State, for I shall not hesitate to correct your misrepresentations. As to your opinion that the National Government will be too energetic, it is dangerous and unfounded, and shews a fear of a personal nature. An open manly conduct, with a proper use of your moderate abilities, will secure you the peaceable possession of the C—r of S—te [Comptroller of State]; a contrary conduct will call for correction.

[Hartford] *Connecticut Courant*, 19 April. Written from Canaan, Connecticut. "Nobody" was the pseudonym of a writer in the [Hartford] *American Mercury*; the piece to which this was a reply has not been located.

OTHER DOCUMENTS

Richard Curson to Horatio Gates. ALS, Gates Papers, NHi. Written from Baltimore; place to which addressed not indicated.

Acknowledges receipt of letter enclosing one to "your friend" White, which he has forwarded; Senator Carroll has been "indisposed" since arriving at New York City; it is said "out of Doors" that Congress will adjourn in June.

Benjamin Franklin to Thomas Jefferson. LS, hand of Benjamin Franklin Bache, Boundaries and Claims Commissions, Record Group 76, DNA. Written from Philadelphia. For the full text, see *PTJ* 16:326.

Refers Jefferson to Adams for more information about the peace commissioners' handling of the Northeast boundary issue during negotiations leading up to the Treaty of Paris (1783).

Jeremiah Hill to George Thatcher. ALS, Chamberlain Collection, MB. Written from Biddeford, Maine.

Regretted not hearing from Thatcher for the past seven post deliveries; "sometimes I was mad—sometimes I scolded, sometimes I swore a little"; acknowledges Thatcher's letter of 28 March and shall be glad to receive Hamilton's report of 4 March on additional sources of revenue; relates town meeting news.

Thomas Jefferson to Governor Charles Pinckney. FC, Jefferson Papers, DLC. For the full text, see *PTJ*, 16:324n.

Has delivered the bonds for South Carolina that the Van Staphorsts committed to his care to Butler and Izard, whom he considered representatives of the state legislature and therefore the most proper depository for those papers.

Marshal Jenkins to George Thatcher. ALS, Thatcher Papers, MeHi. Written from Hudson, New York.

Believes the runaway son of Shearjashub Bourne (enquired about in Thatcher's letter of 1 April, above) is a sailor in his employ; if Thatcher wishes to examine the boy, Jenkins will arrange it when his ship passes New York en route to St. Domingue (Haiti).

Woodbury Langdon to John Langdon. ALS, Langdon Papers, NhPoA. Written from Portsmouth, New Hampshire.

Office seeking: son Henry Sherburne Langdon as secretary to an American diplomat.

Isaac Mansfield to John Langdon. ALS, Langdon Papers, NhPoA. Written from Exeter, New Hampshire; postmarked Portsmouth, New Hampshire, 10 April.

Asks Langdon to support his appointment to a pulpit said to be available in a New York church and to consult with Senator Carroll about the prospects for an appointment as principal of St. John's College in Annapolis, Maryland.

Timothy Pickering to Rebecca Pickering. ALS, Pickering Papers, MHi. Written from Philadelphia; addressed to Wilkes-Barre, Pennsylvania.

The Pennsylvania legislature has repealed (on 1 April) the Wyoming Act, its 1787 law confirming Connecticut settlers' titles in the Wyoming Valley; Morris, Clymer, and Fitzsimons, "all celebrated characters," agree with Johnson, "(whom the people of Wyoming know)," that the 1787 act cannot be repealed; encloses his letter to Johnson on the subject (dated 3 March, unlocated), Johnson's reply (6 March) and a second letter from Johnson (unlocated), for circulation among those interested.

David Sewall to George Thatcher. ALS, Chamberlain Collection, MB. Written from York, Maine; postmarked Portsmouth, New Hampshire, 9 April.

Acknowledges receipt of an (unidentified) issue of *GUS* containing Ames's speech on assumption; reports on state elections; thinks neither Sedgwick nor Strong ought to consider returning for Northampton court.

Daniel Smith to Benjamin Hawkins. Copy of excerpt, hand of William Knox, Washington Papers, DLC. Written from Sumner County, North Carolina (all of present-day north central Tennessee). An endorsement indicates the copy was made by the War Office on 15 May.

Accounts of Creek, Cherokee, and Shawnee aggression planned or conducted in the area, which he has also sent to Josiah Harmar, "together with these few lines"; "my motive for mentioning it to you is to urge the attention of the United States to the defence of this defenceless country."

William Smith (Md.) to Otho H. Williams. ALS, Williams Papers, MdHi. Place to which addressed not indicated. For background and text on the Burke-Hamilton affair of honor, see *DHFFC* 8:476–80.

The "quarrell" between Burke and Hamilton "is accommodated, by arbitration of Six Members of Congress, consisting of both houses"; does not know whether there will be any official notice of this "transaction"; "I have always forgot to mention that Dr. Williamson, has not said anything to me on the Subject mentioned respecting Dr. [*James*] McHenry."

Paine Wingate to Timothy Pickering. ALS, Pickering Papers, MHi. Addressed to Wilkes Barre, Pennsylvania, "To be left at Philadelphia"; franked; postmarked. For the full text, see *Wingate* 2:356–57.

Has delivered Pickering's letter of application as Hamilton's assistant (see *PAH* 6:355–56), enclosed in Pickering's letter of 6 April; was told to reply that the proposal would be considered, if Hamilton's first choice declined the office, "which I do not expect, but should be very glad to see"; hopes to see Pickering in the government and expects it before long; "I have nothing here remarkable to mention to you unless it is that we have done *nothing* yet remarkable"; heard from his family on 17 March that all are well; will be happy to hear from Pickering at all times.

William Samuel Johnson, Diary. Johnson Papers, CtHi.

"Mrs. J[*ohnson*]. sail'd [*to Connecticut*]."

George Washington, Diary. ViHi.

Gerry, Huntington, Cadwalader, Boudinot, Sinnickson, Scott, Gale, Parker, Moore, and Brown dined at the President's.

Friday, 9 April 1790

Fine (Johnson)

Benjamin Huntington to Anne Huntington

By Mr. Emmerson of N[*ew*]. London I send you another Scrawl without News for we have none Our August House is going on Steady Steady and as Slow as Steady In hopes of Rising at some Time or other I had a letter from Harry [*Henry Huntington*] by Capt. Parker in which he says you are in the same State of health as for some Time passd I was in hopes of your gaining health and Strength and am anxious Still to hear that is the Case—cannot the Doctors Contrive Something that will restore the Coats and Juices of your Stomach to a proper temper that your Food might become more nourishing I think that such a Step would put you in a Way to gain Flesh and with it you might Expect Health to be Restored Would you like any Porter or wine or any Thing which I can find from this Place which you fancy would be Palatable ~~for~~ I beleive such things as agree with your appetite will be most Nourishing and Probably tend to correct the Disorders of the Stomach and Replenish the Body with wholsome Juices—But I am writing of things I know nothing of but from my own Reason upon the Subject Pray let me know if you have a Desire for any thing I can find and it Shall be sent I have money and can [*lined out*] Send what you want and have no thoughts of witholding any of the Comforts or Conveniencies which you Desire—When I begin to Write to you I know not how to leave off I have no other way of talking to you and so take the liberty of talking too much as I fear.

Pray let Harry know I have Recd. his Letter with the Inclosed final settlement Certif[*ica*]t[*e*]. and sold it at 7/6 for the Principal and 6/ for the Interest and am to have the Money in Time to send home by Capt. Parker by whom I shall send it with his other Money which I have Recd.

ALS, Huntington Papers, CtHi. Addressed to Norwich, Connecticut; carried by Mr. Emmerson.

Richard Bland Lee to Theodorick Lee

I have this moment received your letter of the 26th. of March. *** You ask me why I advised you not to bring your Servant with you to this City? From this question I suppose you mean to be here in a short time. Slave servants are apt to be spoiled here—and if you mean to travel in the stage the expence of the Journey will at least be doubled. Unless you should mean to go further north my servant could attend on you while you remained in this city. I hope that you will have the land completely surveyed before you leave Virginia.

We have not yet decided the great question concerning [*lined out*] the State debts ~~yet~~. The division on this question will be very near. Tho I think the measure will finally fail.

I find that you are in the plaintive strain complaining of the decay of patriotism and public Virtue Men are by nature alike in all ages. And if they be happy under a government they will love it. And tho' there may be a lukewarmness apparently in quiet times in the body of the citizens; it does not follow that in times of danger the same apathy will exist. It is the nature of man to indulge himself in ease and peace as long as possible. And it is only in trouble some and dangerous times that great displays of patriotism are to be expected. Where every thing is calm and quiet—there is no occasion for—or incitement to extraordinary exertions. This will suffice as an answer to your march reflections.

As to the assumption of the state debts, it will certainly operate injuriously to Virginia, unless the seat of government was so stationed as to diffuse the wealth of the Capital in equal measures to the extremes of the empire. In which case the poison of the measure would be very much diminished. It is very odious to the state of Virginia—from every account we receive from thence.

Col. [*Leven*] Powell mentioned in his last that you were a candidate for the assembly—which I confess was very extraordinary news to me; both because you had never hinted such an intention to me; and because it seemed to be a dereliction of your commercial projects in which I would wish you to persevere, if you have any prospect of making an advantageous establishment in that line.

***

P. S. How do my young horses at Custis look Will they answer for the saddle. The weather here is extremely mild and moist Col. R. H. Lee has just arrived in this City after passing a tempestuous night in the Bay between Elizabeth town [*New Jersey*] & this place.

ALS, Custis-Lee Family Papers, DLC. Addressed to "Sully," Loudoun County, Virginia, "via Alexandria"; franked; postmarked 11 April. The omitted text discusses agriculture, household management, and news of friends.

Letter from Philadelphia

It is in the nature of some people in every community to wish to keep up parties, party names, and party spirit. This is at present particularly instanced in the matter of Federalism. For my own part I have ever been a federalist, upon principles of liberality, and so mean to continue as long as the world characterizes one who is a friend to public unanimity, good order, effective government, and equitable laws. I cannot do otherwise than entertain a contemptible opinion of that man who wishes to allure me to purchase at his shop by the stale bait of federal hats, federal shoes, federal night caps, federal newspapers, &c. &c. It is high time all distinctions of this nature were abolished, especially when it is considered that antifederalism is at present a mere phantom, that can be scarcely said to exist (to any purpose of existence) in the United States. This country, and most certainly this city, has seen so much of the baleful effects of party spirit, that one would imagine every friend to the Union, and every well wisher to the prosperity of America, would, instead of reviving, let these matters of animosity drop into everlasting oblivion.

NYDA, 12 April.

Other Documents

Joseph Barnard to George Thatcher. ALS, Thatcher Papers, MeHi. Written from Portsmouth, New Hampshire; postmarked.

In reply to Thatcher's letter of 28 March (unlocated) asking his opinion on the subject, believes three post offices between Portsmouth, New

Hampshire, and Portland, Maine, "Would be Needless" and not pay the expense; if Congress authorizes the post office to establish one or more along that route, one ought to be at Kennebunk, Maine, with (Benjamin?) Brown as postmaster; would be glad if postmasters could contract with carriers for a three or five or seven year period, for ease and consistency.

William Constable to Joel Barlow. FC:lbk, Constable-Pierrepont Collection, NN.

Information provided by (Samuel?) Broome about western land sales among European investors has convinced Hamilton "to keep the Co[*mpany*]. [*Alexander Macomb's 1787 purchase?*] to the original Contract" (enforcing foreclosure and freeing up land in the Northwest Territory for smaller purchases); "this will make a very material differ[*enc*]e to the Concerned" (George Scriba's petition to purchase at least two million acres).

Marshal Jenkins to George Thatcher. ALS, Thatcher Papers, MeHi. Written from Hudson, New York.

"John Lewes" has confessed his identity as Shearjashub Bourne's runaway son and is persuaded by letters from his father and Thatcher to return home; asks Thatcher to forward more letters for the son and to notify Bourne; awaits Thatcher's "advice & farther Command."

Pierce Butler, Receipt Book. Ms., Butler Papers, PHi.

Paid to James Rivington £15.13.6.

William Samuel Johnson, Diary. Johnson Papers, CtHi.

"Visits."

SATURDAY, 10 APRIL 1790

Night Thundr. Storm (Johnson)

John Baptista Ashe to Richard Bennehan

Inclose'd I send you Some Papers, and will by Next weeks Mail, Send you the event of the grand Question on the assumption of the State Debts, a Question which will if past in the affirmative affect the Citizens of America, more particularly those of the Individual States, who have fund'd already a large proportion of their Security's, more than any Act ever done, and probably ever will be done by Goverment—I feel a Satisfaction in N. Carolina's having Stept into the Union at the Moment she did; for her Delagation I hope will give a favorable turn to this impending load of evil—I ever have, and as late as my leaving Carolina intertain an oppinion, that Debts for Supply's or Services, Shou'd be Assume'd and paid by the Union at large, but when I found Several States had never Sunk, a Shilling, and others but very little, I changed my ground—The Eastern States and, S. Carolina are for including all demands (*when they were immediately local*) under this pretext that they tend'd to a general defence, so that every Privateer fil'd out and taken must be paid for. Instance, *among a thousand similar*, a privateer from Philadelphia, who made seventeen safe Voyages, Captur'd twelve or fourteen Valuable prises, for the use of the owners, and the eighteenth Cruise was taken—I figure to myself the amount of two Million at least, for such claims.

The advocates are oppose'd to a previous liquidation of the Debts alledging that our public Credit was now nearly Sunk, and that an immediate assumption was absolutely Necessary, to raise it as it was a just debt, and ought to be paid, [*torn*] unnecessary that we shou'd know it, this leap wou[*ld*] be we think unpardonable, in the representatives of free People, and one, who are so tenatious of their rights—I am sensible from the disposition of our last assembly, many just Creditors of our state, Stand on unsafe ground, among them a certain Class of Men, whose Interest I feel an immediate attanchment toward, but hope yet, the state will be just, indeed, thus unsafely Situate'd, I am more sanguine in their Compensation, then if their Claims were intermix'd in the common Mass, for obvious it is, that the Group of Speculators, that now hover about us, and watching our Measures, will be the chief dividers, in the Revenue appropriations, and not very doubtfull with me, that they do ~~not~~ influence our Councils, on this important question—I will give you a line now and then, and Shou'd very often, but know they will be [*torn*]ay in getting to hand—And shou'd have sen[*t*] this but it is late & the Mail will close dire[*ctl*]y Mrs. [*Eliza Montfort*] Ashe joins me in best respects to yourself Mrs. [*Mary Amis*] Benehan & family—concluding with requesting you to favor Captain Cain, with those Neusless Papers, after your perusal, and that you will let me hear from you often.

[*P. S.*] excuse this hasty scrawl.

ALS, Bennehan Papers, Nc-Ar. Addressed to North Carolina.

Silas Lee to George Thatcher

Here I am at your table a writing with your dear Wife [*Sarah Savage Thatcher*] ~~to~~ her dear husband—& have just been a Spectator of one of the Most agreeable scenes I ever saw viz.—Sally [*daughter Sarah*] undertaking to teach Sambo [*Samuel Phillips Thatcher*] to read—She in the first place called him to come & read—he would not—she immediately send Eben to get her a rod—Eben brought one—she then took his book & a pin, (after having shook the rod at Sam, & laid it dow[*n*]) pointing at the letters, says "what's that"—Sam made no answer—she repeated it—still no answer—She lays the book & pin ~~down~~ down, takes the rod & says "wont you read"—& falls a whipping of him a few strokes—& then lays by her rod & takes her book & pin again—& again points to the letter, asks, "what's that"—he read one or two ~~words~~ letters & then stopped again—and she was obliged to have recourse to the rod again—then Sam would read a letter or two, & then stop & then she would take the rod—& so they conducted for near a half hour—never did you See a Schoolmistress act her part better—and to see how much they both enjoyed it, was extreemly agreeable—This is children's play—but they are yours, & therefore their little pranks are agreeable to you—they are exceedingly beloved by the writer hereof, & therefore it gives him pleasure to relate those pranks—But this much will suffice.

*** Ma [*Sarah Savage Thatcher*] has something of a cold, but I think it is breaking—Sally & phillips are finely indeed. ***

With respect to the post to penobscot—It is a matter that has quite awaken the Inhibitants, thro whom the Rout must be, viz. Waldoboro & St. Georges—& they have begun [*to*] be very anxious to have such a thing take place—as to the expence of the Rider. Mr. [*Moses*] Copeland says he will procure a good man to ride from Wiscasset for £70 Lawfull a year—& perhaps for £60—I have inquired for a proper person at Waldoboro for post Master, & find that there is a Mr. Stephen Andross, who writes a good hand; as I am told; & is a very honest capable man—at Thomastown where I think the next office ought to be, David Tate Esq. is the best Man, & he I think a very good one—at penobscot Mr. Richard Hunewell a very honest clever fellow, or my Brother John if he should be eligible on acct. of his collectorship.

ALS, Thatcher Papers, MHi. Written from Biddeford, Maine; postmarked Portsmouth, New Hampshire, 13 April. The omitted text relates news of friends, discusses local court news, and asks Thatcher to procure law books for Lee.

William Maclay to John Nicholson

I heartily give you Joy of your riddance of the Troublesome prosecution which you underwent before the General Assembly,[1] & I trust nothing of the kind will happen for time to come. I could say much on this Subject, but must adjourn everything of that kind, for business.

I had your promise a considerable time ago, to give me an Account. how much of the State debt of Pennsylvania was sunk. You will now have leisure, and I will thank you for it. The State of Massachusetts brings forward a demand of upwards of five Millions of a State Debt. about three Millions of which is composed (as I am informed) of the bounties given by their Towns, for the Recruits to the Army. The Class Taxes,[2] and accounts furnished by the Classes, in Pennsylvania, and many other of the States, stand as an equivalent, to this part of the Massachusetts State debt. and with Us and many of the other States, are paid. pray give me all the information which you can on this Subject. The recruiting of the Army, in this way, ought no doubt to form a charge against the Union, in the Account of each individual State. But some Uniform rule ought to obtain, in Cases of this kind. if our State should adopt the Method of Massachusetts. I have no doubt, she could bring forward a Mass of State Debt equally large.

'Tis like I am blamed for corresponding with you, pray then let me have the full advantage of it. By your communicating every information in your power.

Tomorrow it is said the Question will be taken on the Assumption of the State debts. And indeed I sincerely wish how soon it may be put. no Converts will be made on either side, and it has already been delayed shamefully.

I send you this by General [*William*] Irwin to whom I will refer you for the State of Politicks at this time, in New York. I expect to hear from you when you have a Leisure moment.

ALS, Gratz Collection, PHi. Place to which addressed not indicated.

---

[1] Maclay referred to Pennsylvania's investigation of Nicholson's accounts as the state's comptroller general. The initial report of 6 April disclosed nothing more serious than Nicholson's overpayment of three pensioners. A week later the Supreme Executive Council formally disapproved of his overpayments, but failed to unseat him (Robert D. Arbuckle, *Pennsylvania Speculator and Patriot: The Entrepreneurial John Nicholson* [University Park, Pa., 1975], p. 47).

[2] Beginning in 1782 Pennsylvania raised a special tax to support the Revolutionary War. Each county was divided into numbered groups, or classes, of adult males capable of bearing arms. Taxes were assessed in the group, which was expected to cover the taxes of all delinquents in the class.

William Maclay to Benjamin Rush

I have yours of the 6th. and believe I have received all you wrote, in safety. Nunquam desperandum est de republica.[1] We shall certainly do well, and the Cause of Liberty, will be supported always in America I cannot doubt on this head. The Feeble attacks of ambitious Men will only serve to call the attention of Vigilance to the common Weal. and if ever enormities should be attempted it is only to point them fully & fairly out to a discerning public: and the public Voice will, in time, set them right. I do not mean this as an Argument for indolence in Individuals. no quite the Reverse,

When a Man who is conscious of his own rectitude & purity of Intentions sees a false Step taken by Government, he should cry aloud and spare not. quere[2] is he not blame worthy, if he acts differently. But you will expect News from New-York. and not Maxims or precepts. I wish I could give you any thing entertaining to tell you that our proceedings are very slow, would only be repeating what you already know. No Question is yet taken on the Assumption of the State debts. it is expected, that this important point will be settled on Monday next The opposition have gained by the delay and the general Expectation is That it will be rejected, in one shape or other. but Man you know is a versatile Animal. pray let me hear often from you. letters now, and then from Pennsylvania are the only drops of Comfort we receive, in this (to me) disagreeable place.

ALS, Rush Papers, DLC. Addressed to Third Street, Philadelphia; franked; postmarked 11 April.

---

[1] The affairs of the republic ought never to be despaired of.
[2] You ask.

Benjamin Rush to James Madison

I congratulate you upon the prospect of the funding System being delayed 'till the next session of Congress. I hope an election will intervene, before you meet again. Should this be the case, I think it probable that no One of our members who has voted against your motion, & in favor of ~~other~~ the leading principles of Mr. Hamilton's report will be reelected.

I have long deplored the temporary residence of Congress in ~~Congress~~ New york, without wishes corresponding to my bad opinion of that city, to see them in Philadelphia. We thrive & are happy without them. But I am satisfied that the influence of our city will be against the Secretary's System of injustice & corruption. The Quakers & Germans who *now* govern directly, or indirectly ~~the~~ both ~~the~~ our city & State, possess very few Certificates—Of Course Philadelphia will be better ground to combat the System on, than New York. It is a Wider Centre of information to the United states. Nine citizens to the Southward of the Potowmac visit our city, to One that visits New York. Our presses are moreover freer, and we have More ~~visit~~ Widows—Orphans—& Soldiers among us who have parted with their Certificates than any city in the Union. All these will be a heavy Weight in the Scale opposed to the report.

I question whether more dishonourable influence has ever been used by a British Minister (bribery excepted) to carry a measure that [*than*] has [*been*] Used to carry the report of the Secretary. This influence is not confined to nightly Visits—promises—compromises—Sacrifices—& threats, in New

York. It has extended ~~to~~ One or two of its polluted Streams to this ~~very~~ city; the particulars of which you shall hear when I have the pleasure of seeing you on your way to Virginia.

Mr. Fitzsimons ~~was~~ & Mr. Clymer left this city last Jany. as much ~~opposed to a~~ disposed to adopt a Scale of discrimination for the national debt as you have been. Mr. Fitzsimons I thought appeared unhappy while last in town, when spoken to upon his Change of Sentiment & Conduct. He has suffered ~~both in~~ in his Character as a Man of Understanding with our best citizens by becoming the *Midwife* of a System, every principle of which he reprobated when established in our state. I have only to add—to a former Opinion—that not only DELAY, but the *Air* of Philada. will do Wonders for you.

I have just committed to the press a small pamphflet[1] entitled "Information to Europeans disposed to migrate to ~~Am~~ the United States" in which I have dwelt with peculiar pleasure upon the Safety and agreeable prospects of our Country Under her present goverment. The establishment of the Secretary's report can alone contradict the information I have given upon that Subject. It will in seven years introduce among us all the corruptions of the British ~~goverment~~ funding System. The principal part of the information is addressed to cultivators of the earth—mechannics—labourers—Servants—& [*torn*] members of the learned professions. I shall b[*eg*] your acceptance of a copy of it as soon as it published. It is addressed ~~in a letter~~ to a friend in Great Britain.

Your letter in answer to my last came safe to hand.

P. S. I need not hint to you that this letter is confidential.

There will be *four* numbers of Ruricola.[2] To the last will be added, a petition to Congress. They come from One of our most enlightned Citizens, whose name is but little known out of our city.

ALS, Madison Papers, DLC. Written from Philadelphia; franked; postmarked 12 April.

[1] The essay, dated 16 April, was published anonymously as a pamphlet (Evans 22390) and again in the [Philadelphia] *American Museum* magazine of May 1790. It is reprinted in *Rush* 1:549–62. The context indicates that the "friend" to whom it was addressed was a member of the Society of Friends (Quakers).

[2] The four instalments of "Yeoman's Letters" by Ruricola (peasant) ran weekly in *IG* beginning 10 April. The last instalment was published on 1 May and is printed under that date, below.

Newspaper Article

We learn from good authority that an explanation has taken place between Mr. *Burke* and Col. *Hamilton*, on the subject of some expressions used by the former in the House of Representatives, on Wednesday the 31st. ult.

In consequence of which, Col. Hamilton having disavowed any intention in his eulogium on Gen. [*Nathanael*] Greene to reflect on the militia in general or that of South Carolina in particular, as had been apprehended by Mr. Burke, Mr. Burke made a satisfactory apology to Col. Hamilton for the expressions alluded to.[1]

NYDA, 10 April; reprinted at Portsmouth, New Hampshire; Boston; Providence, Rhode Island; New Haven, Connecticut; Philadelphia; Baltimore; Fredericksburg, Richmond, and Winchester, Virginia; Edenton and Fayetteville, North Carolina; and Charleston, South Carolina.

[1] For background and documents on this affair, see *DHFFC* 8:476–80.

For the Independent Gazetteer

I WILL quote a passage from a pamphlet published in the year 1782, on this very subject, entitled, "Proposals to amend the Policy of Government of the United States."[1] (A few copies of this pamphlet may be had at Mr. Spotswood's, in Front-street.)[2] This passage is in page 29 and 30, viz. "The depreciation of money is as a balsam of life to a nation, if it is effected from a merciful disposition in men, (the original creditors) who are willing to compound and lose a part, rather than distress and break up (the insolvent nation, and become slaves, or entail slavery on the posterity of the debtor.) Raising the value of money after it has depreciated and circulated (that is, out of the original creditor's hand, who willingly compounded as aforesaid) is, on the contrary, ratsbane and rank poison. It is engrossed from the public at low rates (the current value) by a few speculators; and to raise it in their hands (as Mr. Gerry would do) is as wicked robbery as house-breaking. All our latter regulations to raise the value of paper money, (observe, after it had circulated at the aforesaid current low value) the stopage of payment of public debts with it, while it yet would have passed, was founded on those views, to cause money to become scarce, that so the publick might be obliged to buy it at full value from a few who had engrossed it for little or nothing. This kind of robbery has always been secretly practised by a few, as well as the vending of tickets, which is of the same kind (of robbery). Let every man in America watch against the least appearance of such theft, as the rankest poison of a state," (that will in time, if not prevented by the laws, let alone encouraged by the laws as on Mr. Gerry's plan, enslave the whole nation.)

It behoves every society and government to guard against their own rulers, elders, ministers, &c. from usurping an authority over their own people, more than to guard and watch against an open enemy.

One plea against our waging war with Great-Britain was, that after we have conquered England, our own rulers will only take their place. To which it was replied, that the devil would be in it, if, after we have conquered England, we should not be able to conquer our own usurping rulers. But as many a true word is spoke thus not in earnest, it has really happened, that the devil was sure enough in the plot that they laid for us. This may be gathered from what is implied in the reasons that many respectable characters gave for their signing the federal Constitution in that Convention, viz. that it was all the choice they had, either to agree to it, or suffer anarchy to take place; and from this we may gather that their bowels yearned for their country, as the woman before Solomon for her child's life;[3] they chose therefore to agree to it, with a view of saving their country again, when government was established, and anarchy (from whose miseries we could not escape) was out of danger, by way of amendments, which happily they had got inserted therein; and it is to be hoped, that the event will prove the wisdom and great foresight of this choice; for if we can once set a precedent of regaining our liberty back from arbitrary power, when they are once in the possession thereof, in a constitutional and civil way, without the sword, then we may begin to lift up our head, and rejoice, for our redemption will then be drawing nigh.

When we look back on the stupid, ignorant state of the people, no farther back than the popery, the fear and pains of the inquisition, which every one endured who dared to attempt the least reformation, and then reflect on the blessings of liberty which we already enjoy, with a prospect before us of greater blessings; and that these blessings are the fruits of the zeal and sufferings of our ancestors, and the price of their blood. Surely on these reflections we will not refuse to exert ourselves in a civil way, in which there is no danger. Every man may exert himself at elections, and help to encrease the minority, who stand for true freedom, in all our councils. If we cannot pay our debt ourselves, without enslaving our posterity with a debt that will always be encreasing, we are insolvent already; and I call it an honorable insolvency, instead of a breach of faith. The mortgaging of the land in security, or selling the vacant territory in large quantities, to private persons, or funding our debt on interest, to be paid by our posterity, all conspire to enslave them, and totally defeat the very object our ancestors had in view, who spilt their blood, and fought for liberty. If we give a preemption right to every emigrant who will move out to the vacant territory, and occupy the land, subject to a reasonable purchase, to be paid in a term of years, without interest, it will bring more money into the treasury, by two to one, than selling it to individuals for what it will now command in ready money.

The present creditors, who are for funding the debt on interest, trust, that when posterity are born with this burthen on their backs, they will know no better than to bear it. They measure times to come by what has been in times past; but they forget that the art of printing is a new invention; for unless they can stop the freedom of the press, our posterity will certainly throw off the burthen, and spoil them, as the Israelites spoiled the Egyptians; and as the oppressed manufacturers and landed interest in England must ere long be obliged to spoil their monied interest—As it is written, "They will fly upon the shoulders of the Philistines (the Indians) towards the west. They shall spoil them of the east, together; they shall lay their hand upon Edom and Moab (our elder brethren, the Esaus, or English, of Canada; and our fathers brothers children of France, under them) and the children of Ammon (the Spanish settlements) shall obey them; the Lord shall utterly destroy this false tongue of the Egyptian sea (domestic slavery) and with his mighty wind (oratory from the mouths of the true patriots of liberty) shall he shake his hand over the river (stream or current of human learning) and shall smite it in the seven streams (sciences) and make men go over dry shod." *See Isaiah* xi. And it is to be hoped, that all this will be civilly and constitutionally accomplished. That flame of liberty which is now so rapidly increasing through Europe, will reflect back to us from whence it kindled. How happily are we situated in favor of liberty! Our success inspired them—their success will inspire us with new life and the zeal of a Nehemiah. Like him they will consult among themselves, and rebuke these new nobility of speculators, landjobbers, &c. and will set a great assembly against them, and cause them to restore these engrossed lands, clear of rents, taxes, &c. *See Nehemiah* v. ver. 1–14.

IG, 10 April. This is the conclusion of an editorial begun on 3 April, above. Isaiah and Nehemiah are books of the Bible.

[1] A thirty-six page pamphlet published in Baltimore, possibly written by George Lux.
[2] William Spotswood (1753/54–1805) was a Philadelphia printer and bookseller ([Philadelphia] *American Daily Advertiser*, 12 April 1805).
[3] I Kings 3:26.

Letter from a New Settler near Fort Laurens

We have wandered about for some time in these vast wildernesses; but God be thanked, are at last settled (more through necessity than choice) in the neighbourhood of Fort-Lawrence,[1] between the three Moravian towns and Newcomers. A very great part of this country is much poorer than is generally imagined. All the way from the Pennsylvania line to Great Sandy, and thence southwesterly to the Carolina line is generally very barren land, and very mountainous, rocky and broken; but from the mouth of the river Sciota, to Fort-Lawrence (every inch of which I have travelled over) between that line and the Ohio, the soil is tolerably good, but generally much broken with sharp hills. From Fort-Lawrence again, to the mouth of Yellow-Creek, and thence northward to the waters of Lake Erie is generally a thin soil, and broken land, not very encouraging to the new cultivator. As to news, I have very little to tell, except what will affect you with melancholy. With the assistance of my eldest son, I have erected something like a house, which is wattled with small saplings instead of being weather boarded, so that when we are sitting at dinner, to a stranger who should look through at us, we might not unaptly be compared to certain wild animals in a wooden cage. To add to our misfortunes, one of our horses has been stolen by the Indians, so that I have only one left. This prevents the possibility of turning up what little ground we have cleared, unless we could catch one of the wild bulls to supply the place of the stolen horse, which I fear would end in our own destruction.

When we first came hither, wolves and panthers were so plenty, that for fear of them, we roosted in the trees many nights together, not daring to trust to our bonfires alone for our security. The anxieties of my dear wife are not the least of my troubles in this remote and unchristian wilderness; she is almost every night dreaming of the Indians, and, mistaking me for one of them, very frequently cries out in her sleep, that I am scalping her. Having no horses to plough, and our strength not being sufficient to do any thing effectual with the hoe, we have concluded to set up a small tavern to get something thereby if possible to make a living. With infinite difficulty two gallons of New-England rum have been obtained from a distance, and with this we have made a beginning. Heaven knows what all this will end in—I am almost discouraged, did I possess the means I would immediately remove further to the southward.

NYDA, 15 June; reprinted at Philadelphia and Baltimore.

[1] Fort Laurens was built in November 1778 on the Tuscarawas River near present-day Bolivar, Ohio.

Other Documents

William Bradford to Elias Boudinot. ALS, Wallace Papers, PHi. Written from Philadelphia.

Susan (Bradford) will be at Elizabethtown, New Jersey, at month's end; "when do you expect to be with us?"; is so tired of the assumption business "that I now pass over the debates about it, as one does over the page of advertisements. Is it possible that any thing new can be advanced? But your next letter I hope will bring me the conclusion of the business"; encloses two bank notes for $120.

Henry Knox to Anthony Wayne. ALS, Wayne Papers, PHi. Addressed to Savannah, Georgia; carried by Capt. Henry Burbeck. Endorsed "private."

All the troops in the President's power to send have been ordered to the Georgia frontier; "it is to be presumed" that Congress will make a proper provision for dealing with the Creeks, but "cannot answer" for how the Yazoo business may affect the opinion of individual congressmen; Georgia's authority to extinguish Indian title to the lands "will probably be further investigated and decided upon"; the federal government will act no further "in the affair of the Creeks" than circumstances dictate.

John Langdon to Joseph Whipple. No copy known; acknowledged in Whipple to Langdon, 23 April.

James Madison to Edward Carrington. No copy known; acknowledged in Carrington to Madison, 30 April.

James Madison to Gustavus Wallace. No copy known; acknowledged in Wallace to Madison, 20 April.

Timothy Pickering to William Samuel Johnson. ALS, Johnson Papers, CtHi. Written from Philadelphia; franked; postmarked 12 April.

Encloses the published dissents to the Pennsylvania legislature's repeal (on 1 April) of its 1787 act confirming Connecticut settlers' titles to Wyoming Valley land.

James Seagrove to Pierce Butler and Robert Morris. ALS, Butler Papers, PHi. Written from St. Mary's, Georgia.

Office seeking: relies on "your friendship" to promote the enclosed application to Washington for any other appointment "in the revenue line, or otherwise, which will better my situation"; his position as collector at St. Mary's "do's not afford me the least support"; asks them to deliver the application, "backing it with your good opinions."

Paine Wingate to Jeremy Belknap. ALS, Belknap Papers, MHi. Addressed to Boston; franked; postmarked 11 April.

Forwards enclosed letter (unidentified), "received by the Southern Mail, I do not know from whom"; no news; the assumption business "labours hard," with Representatives "supposed to be near equally divide[*d*]"; will probably vote on the question Monday (12 April); asks for acknowledgment of Rev. John Clarke's receipt of a letter Wingate sent by the last post.

NYDA, 10 April.

"We are informed the Hon. George Mason has declined the appointment of senator of the United States, by the state of Virginia. The Hon. JOHN WALKER, has since been elected to that important office."

GUS, 10 April. Wister Butler Papers, PHi. Annotated by Butler to indicate the article for which he retained the issue.

Washington's proclamation of 9 April on the Consular Convention with France of 1788.

NYDG, 11 April.

Benson and two others, on behalf of the regents of Columbia College, announced that it will hold an auction (at the Coffee House on 4 May at noon) to sell the right to rent Governor's, or Nutten, Island in the Upper Bay below Manhattan Island.

SUNDAY, 11 APRIL 1790

George Clymer to Henry Hill

I should sooner have followed my letter of Thursday by another but there is a chasm of two days in the going of the post at the latter end of the week. ***

I don't know the exact state of the Presidents health for a day or two past—but it is observed here with a great deal of anxiety that his general health seems to be declining—For some time past he has been subject to a slow fever—[*William*] Jackson seems to think that as soon as the adjournment will let him he will begin a long journey to the southward, which will probably reinstate him, that to the Eastward sometime ago having for a time wrought a very favourable alteration in his health.

In Congress there are two parties assumers and non-assumers, so equally ballanced, that either side seems afraid of a question—this I believe to be the secret of the present chasm in the business of the assumption—but as it must have an end, as well as every thing *eternity* excepted, they talk of some decision tomorrow—But let it end when it will and how it will the ending cannot but be very unsatisfactory.

ALS, Roberts Collection, PHC. Addressed to Philadelphia; franked. The omitted text discusses negotiations for Clymer and Samuel Meredith's purchase of land in York County, Pennsylvania.

John Fenno to Joseph Ward

Your fav. p. post I duly recd. last evening—and with you, most sincerely regret the wretched progress of public business—You see I spur them on as much as I can—More than a week has passed, since it was expected the Question on Assumption would have been taken—but, the friends of the Measure, after *three* Members from N.C. had arrived,[1] and a majority of Pennsylvania had joined Virginia & Maryland, found themselves in the Minority on the Question—this has occasioned the procrastination—(Inter nos[2]) It is said that Virga. & Myland. have agreed to vote for an adjournmt. to Phila. on Condition of Pennsylvania's voting against Assumption—That this Contract has been made is confidently asserted—I much suspect it is the Case [*lined out*] tho' something like an [*lined out*] uncertainty appears to have been entertained by both parties—The Penna. Members have played a vibrating part thro' the whole discussion—New York has been open & candid & will in all events vote for the measure—but *they* do not make it the *sine qua non*[3] respecting a funding System—as some of the Eastern Members appear to—therefore I think the Assumption of the State Debts will not take place this session, but under such Conditions & modifications as will be almost tantamount to a total abandonment of them to their fate with the State Governments—It was expected that the Question would have been determined yesterday, but it was not—however, tomorrow is assigned—and if the question should appear in a dubious situation, I expect warm work—for Sedgwick Wadsworth Ames & Gerry will not let it be lost without some heavy Shots—We must however, have patience—Legislation, is arduous; greatly so—when the Machine is new and designed to effect so many objects—Besides Men, are Men—in a large assembly—there are many *queer* men—and ~~nature~~ some of the absurdest Compositions of Nature are in C[*ongress*]—.

You have depicted some of them very aptly—Your Sketches are almost too free, or else I would make them extracts from the history which I have lately announced, as being on the Anvil[4]—[*lined out*] As soon as this Question on Assumption is over, they will progress with more rapidity—but the terrors of election I fear will fall on them, & produce some mischief—They talk of adjourning by the middle or last of May—to have another Session at the close of the year—therefore, every thing that is to be done respecting funding, must be done before the adjournment or never for the opinions that have been sported in Congress, have created a strange diversity of sentiment among the people—and if the present Session should pass without a System we shall not get one the Next—being so much nearer their demise, the terror before cited will make the majority act very *comically* at least—Your allusion to Grout was much in point—it is enough to rouse stupidity itself—it is said nothing moves him from his design of voting *against* assumption—I thank you for your interest in my success—Mr. Jefferson has given me the publication of the Laws[5]—my subscribers have greatly encreased—and I now do all the senate business[6]—my Debts have accumulated to about 800 Dollars—I have upwards of twelve hundred due—but scattered from Dan to Beersheba[7]—The paper has cost me near 1700 exclusive of my Family—my Receipts have been about 1200—so that if ~~they~~ all my subscribers should pay me, I shall be nearly 500 Dollars the worse for the publication the first year—I reckon now, upwards of a 1000 Subscribers—these if tolerably punctual with my other business, will bring matters upon a ballance another year—after which, barring contingencies, my prospect will be flattering— ***

I [*lined out*] was pleased with your remarks—therefore published them—and they were well received—I shall make some extracts from your last[8]— ***

ALS, Ward Papers, ICHi. Addressed to Boston; carried by Christopher Gore. The omitted text relates news of friends and family. For the full text, see *AASP* 89(1979):359–61.

---

[1] Ashe, Bloodworth, and Williamson.

[2] Between us; i.e., privately.

[3] The necessary condition.

[4] *GUS*, 3 April, above.

[5] Under the Records Act [HR-18], Secretary of State Jefferson was authorized to contract for the publication of all federal laws in five newspapers of his choosing. Fenno's *GUS* was one of the newspapers selected, beginning with the edition of 7 April 1790. This much coveted form of patronage may have been in exchange for Fenno's promise to publish European news accounts from sources contributed by Jefferson, beginning on 21 April. The alliance dissolved by the following September, with *GUS*'s more overtly Hamiltonian stand on public credit and developments in revolutionary France. For an extensive note on this subject, see *PTJ* 16:237–47.

[6] On 29 June 1789, Otis had contracted with Thomas Greenleaf to print for the Senate all bills, secretary's reports, committee reports, simple resolutions, and procedural rules as well as the Senate *Journals*. It was this business that Otis gave instead to Fenno early in the second session (*DHFFC* 4:xxviii).

[7] The northern and southernmost town in the ancient kingdom of Israel, thus "from one end of the kingdom to the other."

[8] Excerpts of letters dated 27 March, 1 April, and 4 April appeared in *GUS*, 14 April, and are printed above.

Benjamin Goodhue to Insurance Offices

I have not wrote you for some time past, because there was nothing before Congress worthy of information—tomorrow is assigned for taking up the question of assumption and from the present complexion there appears a greater uncertainty as to its ultimate decission then ever, for it is strongly suspected by the wavering conduct of the pensylvanians in this bussines who hold the balance and who are not particularly interested in its event, that they mean so to conduct as will best secure to them the residence of Congress in Philadelphia, an object which they would sacrifice almost any thing to obtain, and the almost equal division of the South and North on the question of assumption, gives them a favourable opportunity of promoting such a purpose—under such circumstances is the assumption at present, and probably may put on various appearances before the end of the session.

ALS, Goodhue Letters, NNS. Addressed to Salem, Massachusetts; franked; postmarked.

Thomas Hartley to Jasper Yeates

I received your Favor of the 4th. inst.—and but can this Week give you little in Return—We have been on the Bill for punishing Crimes against the United States & have got through some other Business.

The Assumption or non Assumption of the State Debts will be again agitated to Morrow—how it will terminate I cannot say—but perhaps if we could fund the Debts of the Union—that is more than half of the whole at this Session and suspend the rest it might be well—indeed such Difficulties have arisen—and so many yet may be expected that the latter may be prudent.

The Eastern People say they will not do one without the other and even Talk of going home—perhaps they will not carry their Threats into Execution.

The Situation of our Delegation has become critical—perhaps we may act together—We [*lined out*] have some Matters in view which Oblige us to be more Circumspect—I shall mention them when I see you.[1]

At Carlisle I cannot be but God willing we shall meet at York.

ALS, Yeates Papers, PHi. Addressed to Lancaster, Pennsylvania; franked; postmarked.

[1] Likely a reference to negotiations over the location of the seat of federal government.

Samuel Johnston and Benjamin Hawkins to Governor Alexander Martin

In pursuance of the act of the Legislature of North Carolina "for the purpose of ceeding to the United States of America certain Western lands therein described" we have executed a deed of Cession to the United States: and the same has been accepted by an act of Congress, a copy published by authority you have herewith inclosed [*North Carolina Cession Act*]; and an authenticated one will be sent on as soon as we are able to provide for the government of the ceded lands conformably with the conditions specified in the Cession. A committee of the Senate are assembled for this purpose.

Several of the States have sent up their certifications of the articles, proposed to the Legislatures as amendments to the Constitution of the United States. We know not whether the Legislature of North Carolina ratified them or not, in either case however it is proper that we should be informed of it officially. [*lined out*] The usual con conveyance to Congress is through the President.

We have been applied to and repeatedly by the Vice Consul General of France [*Michel-Guillaume St. John de Crèvecoeur*] to inform him what measures our Legislature took to discharge the Martinique debt.[1] He in the course of conversation remarked that counting on the repeated resolutions of North Carolina since the year 1784 he had taken on himself to inform the Marine Minister that payment would indubitably be made within the last year and that in consequence he was left to provide for the fleet that arrived from the West Indies into our ports out of the monies arising from those promises and some others as ineffectual amount in the whole to a sum nearly equal to their exigencies. His embarrassments were peculiarly great as the revolution in France had caused so great a distrust among the commercial characters here as to render a supply [*by*] the sale of bills too uncertain and expensive to be expended on. We may add that we felt considerable emotion at the delicate manner in which he mentioned his embarrassments and insinuated that probably we meant promises only instead of payment, an[*d*] that although the last general assembly had taken upon them to correct for our errors, yet he was apprehensive when the fleet arrived in the Autumn season he should be again disappointed. If the Executive have power to do any thing in this business we request your Excellency to inform us what assurances we may give.

The Report of the Secretary of the Treasury is still before the house of representatives in committee of the whole, uncertain as to the issue; the proposition for the assumption of the State debt[*s*] which had passed 31. vs. 26. is re-committed 29 vs. 27. and it is conjectured that it will be negatived if the Representatives from North Carolina should be opposed to it. Messrs. Williamson Ashe and Bloodworth are here, and as far as we can judge, are decidedly opposed.

The Judicial power will very soon be extended to our State a Committee is appointed to bring in the bill.

ALS, hand of Hawkins, Governors' Papers, Nc-Ar. Place to which addressed not indicated.

[1] The government of North Carolina accrued a £3099 ($5487) debt for war supplies furnished by the navy department of finance through its colony of Martinique between June

1781 and May 1782. Provisions for paying more than three-fourths of the debt were made in 1783 by warrants issued to the state's agent, who then embezzled the money and was never heard from again. In 1784 the governor promised French authorities that the next revenue collection would be dedicated to extinguishing the debt and the Blount brothers (John Gray and Thomas B.) agreed to serve as the state's agents in the transfer. Because payments in paper money, "public tobacco," and naval stores proved either unacceptable or too costly, the debt still stood at £2151 in 1789, when the governor again promised payment in full, including five percent interest. All but one-fifth of the principal had been paid by 1794, when further payments ceased until the debt was finally declared canceled in 1802 (B. U. Ratchford, "An International Debt Settlement: The North Carolina Debt to France," *AHR* 40[1934]:63–69).

William Smith (Md.) to Otho H. Williams

Yours of the 6th affords me the pleasure of hearing that your excursion to the Westward[1] has been so Successfull, that you are returned in good health, & that all friends are well at Baltimore.

The Value of yr. Military depre[*ciatio*]n. Certificates may perhaps in some measure depend, on the Assn. or non assumption of the State debts, If that measure takes place (which I Still think very doubtful) it must be by some compromise; Such as no extension of time for exhibiting & admitting claims. That the Assumpn. be for a Specified Sum, for each State, not exceeding a certain amot., That Such assumn. for each State be *within*, the amot. reported, so as to leave a Sufficiency for *Special*, State debts. That a clause in the law shall provide, that whatever less may be Subscribed, by the limitted time, then what is assd. Shall be paid over ~~in trust~~ to the State in trust for the non subscribing creditors. That no assumption Shall be conclusive, without the ways & means being in the Same law, And that an equitable ratio for the Settlement of Accots. be agreed upon; Should some Such plan be adopted or an unconditional assumption take place, I apprehend in either case, that State paper & Continl. will be nearly of equal Value. What that value will be must depend on the funds appropriated—the order of the day for Some time past, has been, *the Assumption business*, but has hitherto been postponed from day to day, perhaps both Sides of the question are afraid of the decision, it is Supposed there will not be a majority of more than one either way. So. Carolina declares, that they are unable longer to Struggle under their State debt, assumed for Accot. of the U.S. Massachusetts & Connect. Say the Same, & that they must inevitably become bankrupts if not relieved. I hope this question will be decided tomorrow, when that is done we may again move on.

I thank you for the communications you have made me, relative to yr. tour, & yr. wishes for the restoration of my health. And have only to add that I am as well as I can expect, in a very inactive Situation, & an excessive moist damp climate, which I think one of the worst, I ever experienced, from Serene clear weather we are over cast & raing. in the Space of an hour or two Indeed we have Scarcely two fair days together.

ALS, Williams Papers, MdHi. Addressed to Baltimore. In a letter to Williams the next day, calendared below, Smith said he enclosed newspapers with this letter.

---

[1] Probably to Warm Springs, Augusta (now part of Bath) County, Virginia, where Williams and his family would spend much of the summer of 1790.

George Thatcher to Joseph McLellan and John Fox

Yours of the 27th March came to hand the 7th. inst. on the subject of which I beg leave to observe—when I wrote to Mr. [*Daniel*] Davis the Letter which he shew you, & to which yours is an answer, I had it in contemplation to bring forward, in Congress, a motion for the purpose of authorising the Secretary of the Treasury to take measures necessary to finish the Light-house, at the entrance of Portland Harbor [*Maine*]; and for its support and maintenance out of the Treasury of the United States—But since the Legislature of Massachusetts have adjourned without passing any Law relative to the cession of their Light-houses in general, or of Portland Light-house in particular, I have doubted whether it would be proper to move any Law upon this subject at present—I have consulted with my brethren relative to this matter, & they concur with me, in opinion, that it will be improper for us to take any steps upon this subject before we know the will of our Legislature touching the same—And when this is done, nothing shall be wanting, on my part, to gratify your wishes in having the Light-house compleated & supported under the continental establishment.

FC, Thatcher Family Papers, MHi.

George Thatcher to David Sewall

Since my last the house have been employed in considering the Bill, defining crimes & punishments against the U. States, which was sent them, some time ago, from the Senate; and yesterday they returned it with a few amendments.

It was attempted to insert a clause directing by whom death-warrants should be signed; but it could not be carried—so it is left for the Court before whom judgment of Death is had to issue a Warrant.

On the morrow, I believe, the question of assumption will, again, be taken up—And I am very apprehensive it will pass in the negative. It is said, the Pennsylvanians will vote against the motion; but in case the Massachusetts will hereafter, in this Session, vote with them for adjourning to the City of Philadelphia, they will then agree to the assumption—To the truth of this I cannot vouch; tho I strongly suspect something of the kind is on foot—Now I have told several Gentlemen, in conversation on this subject, that if this be their Trick, I would sweare in my wrath Congress should never settle in the State of Pennsylvania, if my vote could prevent it—I would go to the Delaware, Jerseys or even to the Potomack before I would suffer myself to be Jockied in measures so evidently just, & for the general wellfare, as the assumption.

There is more Locality in the Pennsylvanians, than in all Congress besides; excepting one or two, their mental Horrison closes with the Limits of the State—To them Pennsylvania is the world, & Philadelphia the centre.

Pennsylvania is so situated that it will always hold the scale between the northern & southern States. It is now, and probably always will be the largest manufacturing as well as importing State: Hence, perhaps, it would not be good policy to add to its consequence and means of aggrandisment, that of being the seat of Federal Government.

I well know you view these things on a large and liberal scale; and, justly droping the ideas of States, consider them only as component parts of the great whole; but among the parts of every whole there ought to be observed a certain proportion—An arm, a head, or a leg may be too big for the other parts of the body; and a State may have such influence, from its situation, commerce, manufactures &c. as to disturbe the general System. Are not the United Netherlands merged in politics as well as name into the State of Holland.

The two ~~last~~ nights past we have had very heavy Thunder, sharp Lightning, with much rain—especially last night—The Tempest, for I can call it nothing else, began about ten; and for an hour or better I scarce ever heard heavier thunder, or saw such continued flashes of Light—during which time the rain fell in vast quantities.

Since I have resided in this city, I have noted, that Thunder and Lightning do not have the effect on the general state of air here that they have in our part of the Country—There they generally clarify the air; and after a Tempest, we are almost sure of a clear, serene sky—but the reverse is the case here—I hardly recollect an instance when after a thunder storm the air was more clear, or less hot and sultry than before—The last Summer, Squalls of Thunder and Lightning were very frequent, but the air was generally more sultry after than before.

FC, Thatcher Family Papers, MHi.

George Thatcher to Sarah Thatcher

This acknowledges the receipt of yours of the 29th & 31st March—and brings to you my approbation of your taking a little Girl to live with you—I was delighted last evening in reading, in one of yours, that the little girl begins to be attached to you—next to your affection for me I would have every body esteem & love you—I am always pained to go into a family where a cordial attachment, among all the branches therof, is not evidently percievable—It is not enough for Girls to respect, or esteem the Mistress of a family where they live—they ought to love them—many know no other mother but their Mistresses; and how many of these are at best, but what step-mothers were formerly—ill-natured, difficult to be pleased, & fretfull—but such dispositions, my dear, I know you will never shew to any under your care.

But if you like the little Girl, why do you think of leting her leave you this summer? The general character of the family from which she come, you tell me, is good & honest—This is a recommendation in her favour—if she is ignorant—tis no matter, I had rather that one, who is to live with us, should have all the ignorance of untaught nature about her, than the arts & knowledge of most polished families—And it is easier to teach one, that knows nothing, what she ought to know; than unlearn what she ought never to have known.

But you say she is to return to you again next fall or winter if you want her—perhaps she may be unwilling to return—then you will have the mortification of seeing that she loves somebody else better than yourself; and should she return to you with emotions of joy, will she not be apt to make comparasons, in her own mind, unfavourable to those whom she has left—This may be attended with some disagreeable circumstances—And let me remind you, that if you want a Girl to live with you, and like the one you now have, the sooner she becomes domesticated in the family the better; you may now form her to your own ways, & habits—which will be more difficult when she is older, and has become accustomed to a mode peculiar to the family where she may live—All families, as well as individuals, have their peculiarities. And I am inclined to think a frequent change of families is neither for the advantage of children, or convenience of those with whom they live—I mean more particularly of children who go from their parents for a livelyhood, or subsistance.

However I shall be perfectly satisfied with whatever you may do—I am glad you have taken the poor Girl; you thereby may have released her from the pains of hunger & cold, which are almost the only misery that children know—perhaps, too, the division of food & raiment to the rest of the family will be in greater proportion as their number is lessened.

It now only remains for me to observe, that if you conclude to keep her, you thereby take upon you the duty of father & mother to the child—and whatever you would have another woman do to your children, were they in the situation of the little Girl, do you the same to this unfortunate child—And great will be your reward.

As you live a great way from meeting, I have thoughts of requesting our parson [*Nathaniel Webster*] to call now & then & preach a Lecture to you & the family—or shall I commence preacher myself?

[*P. S.*] Mr. [*Silas*] Lee informed me of the disposition of Dagon, with which I am well pleased.

ALS, Thatcher Family Papers, MHi. Place to which addressed not indicated.

Joseph Wheaton to George Washington

Having had an oppertunity of learning that an additional force is to be aded to the present Establishment of the troops, I am constrained to mention to the President.

The office which the House of Representatives have been pleased to appoint me to, is not altogether that popular Situation nor So profitable to our Country as one could wish to fill.

Having Served in the army from the begining of the war to the end, and having made the duty of a Soldier much of my Study that with the encouragement of many of my Friends in both Houses of Congress, have Considered it a duty I owe my Country to make known my wishes.

If my Services could be made acceptable in the army, it would be the pride of my Heart to perform a duty in which there was full Conviction of rendering Services eaquel to the reward.

I have only to observe, that Should the President view these with a favourable eye I would be happy to resign my present office in favor of Some disabled officer or other person whom the House of Representatives might think proper to appoint as my Successor. This with great defferance is Humbly Submitted to the President.

ALS, Washington Papers, DLC.

Other Documents

Andrew Craigie to Horace Johnson. FC:dft, Craigie Papers, MWA. Addressed to Charleston, South Carolina; carried by Capt. William Elliot.

The prospect of an immediate assumption of the states' war debts is much less positive since Craigie's last letter.

Andrew Craigie to Samuel Rogers. FC:dft, Craigie Papers, MWA.

Morris believes the price of government securities will continue to fall because of the quantity of state securities that will be brought into the market; assumption "meets with great opposition" but is warmly supported and there is not much doubt it will succeed; Hamilton thinks it will pass.

Benjamin Goodhue to Stephen Goodhue. ALS, Goodhue Family Papers, MSaE. Addressed to Salem, Massachusetts.

Cautions about the tonnage that might accrue on their ship returning to Boston; "our Officers can give you information how to proceed if you inquire of them. I suppose they would not demand foreign tonnage by an imperfection in our laws which will doubtless be remedied, but I thought proper just to advise you of it"; complains about Pennsylvania delegation's "wavering conduct" in upcoming decision on assumption; "I am sick of public life."

Benjamin Goodhue to Joseph Hiller. No copy known; acknowledged in Goodhue to Hiller, 6 May.

John Langdon to Joseph Whipple. ALS, Sturgis Family Papers, MH. Addressed to Portsmouth, New Hampshire, with the instruction "Mr. [*Jeremiah*] Libby will be so good as to forward this immediately to Mr. Whipple"; postmarked; franked.

Encloses letter from Treasurer Samuel Meredith stating that an order written out for Whipple to pay Langdon $618 has been lost or possibly stolen; warns against a counterfeit of the order, until the original is found or a second is procured; "there is nothing New."

Robert Morris to Walter Stone. ALS, Stone Papers, DLC. Written from Philadelphia; addressed to Port Tobacco, Maryland.

Left New York City two weeks earlier and would have set out to return that day except for the death of (Thomas) Ridgate; Morris was his largest creditor and was waiting "with uncommon Patience" expecting that he would settle the debt before his death; will not leave Philadelphia until he has dispatched some person to consult with Stone about settling Morris's claims against Ridgate.

Robert Morris to an Unknown Recipient. Combined summary and excerpt of two page ALS, *Parke-Bernet Catalog* 2222(1963):item 181.

"this letter refers to the opposition which Hamilton received because of his radical plans. '*I am happy to learn that Mr. Hamilton will pass by the unmerited insult offered to him* [*by Burke*], *and this he may do, without being subject to the imputations that would in such case be made against a less established character.*'"

Jeremiah Wadsworth to Catherine Wadsworth. ALS, Wadsworth Papers, CtHi. Place to which addressed not indicated.

Hopes Daniel and Decius are recovered; "I am nearly well of my cold we have very wet weather hard Thunder here"; "Uncle Trumbulls" (John and Jonathan) are well.

George Washington to David Stuart. ALS, Ms. W-430, ViMtvL. Addressed to Williamsburg, Virginia; care of Mr. (Thomas) Nicholson; franked; postmarked. For the full text, see *PGW* 5:327.

Believes that, whichever side prevails on the question of assuming the states' war debts, "the Majority will be small *** which, in questions of such magnitude, is to be regretted."

William Samuel Johnson, Diary. Johnson Papers, CtHi.

"St. Pauls."

Richard Henry Lee, Journal. Brock Collection, CSmH.

Arrived at New York City at 8:20 A.M.

NYDG, 13 April.

Gunn arrived at New York City in the evening.

MONDAY, 12 APRIL 1790

Rain (Johnson)

[*John Brown*] to William Irvine

The great question relative to assumption was this day determined in the Negative 31. to 29. Fitzimmons Clymer & Hartley voted in the negative upon Condition that it should if carried be refered to a private Committee. Sumpter Voted in the affirmative—Sedgwick greatly *moved* but little *moving*—pronounced the funeral Oration of his departed friend—Assumption—~~bittly~~ [*lined out*] bitterly lamented its untimely fate—exclaimed against local Politics threatned a disolution of the union &c. &c.

When in Carlisle pray enquire how young Edwards from Kentucke[1] conducts himself.

AL, signature torn off, Irvine Papers, PHi. Place to which addressed not indicated. The writer has been identified by his handwriting.

[1] Haden (Hayden) Edwards (1771–1849), a member of the Dickinson College class of 1792, who had moved with his family to Kentucky in 1780, was later active in the settlement of Texas and the movement for its independence from Mexico. His better known classmate Ninian Edwards (1775–1833) did not move to Kentucky until 1795.

Eliphalet Dyer to Roger Sherman and Benjamin Huntington

I feel my self particularly Oblidgd to You for the sundry letters with the enclosed papers you have been so kind as to send me from New York I also Acknowledge the Receipt of one from Brother Sherman which with yours should have been Answered before this time had not my Constant Attention to the business of the Court (which has engrossed the whole of our time both in the day & Evening to this time prevented) ***

The fatigues are great the Reward Small but as we have mostly particular Laws or rules by which to Regulate our Conduct & Opinions by tho sometimes difficult (Among the great Variety of Causes) in their application. but as to your Politicks it is Very different much more Complex & perplexing ~~its~~ it is—Lanching into a Sea without any sure Pilot or Compass the different Climates manner Education genius & Circumstances of a People, their business & principall employments may & do so differ from Others Ancient or More Modern States & Kingdoms as leaves no Certain rule or plan to Guide direct or absolutely to Relye upon. & the bestness or preference among a Variety of proposals are not to be known but upon Experiment & by its Consequent Effects & opperations and when all is done much Depends upon the humor and the reception it meets with among the body of the People as Candor, prejudice, Confidence, distrust or the like & in the manner of Execution. I freely own I allway felt a much greater Weight & burthen upon me when a Member of ~~some publick Political~~ Congress or Assembly & ~~Suffered~~ much more anxiety perplexity & fatigue Immersed in Politicks than in the Judicial Department. that I Neither Covet or ~~wish~~ envye the places of any of my brethren in that line. I am Sensible you have a Laborious task before you especially in the Secretarys [*Hamilton's*] arrangement, for my own part I have had Neither time or Leisure fully to Examine it, if I had believe I should not thoroughly understand it, I profess no Depth in financeering there are two sides to every question to Weigh & ballance exactly is difficult & when all is done experience will decide and Often Very different from the most Sanguine expectations.

The Discrimination between the Original holders of publick Securitys & the present purchasers or Speculators which you have lately had under

Consideration & the result thereon I rather think is mostly approved by the more Consideration arising from its Impracticability rather than the injustice; for my own part I rather believe in the Scale of real Justice would have turnd in favor of a Discrimination if practicable. The assumption of the State Debts is much more Interesting and Alarming, the People more Divided in Sentiments & opinions. While some seem pleased with the Idea of getting rid of a State Debt (which by its proximity appears in full View) & carrying of it more distant at a greater remove others who take in a larger prospect & have more extensive Views Contemplate the Subject rather as dangerous in the experiment arising from Various quarters, (as follows, The National Debt as at present Stated by the Secretary Sounds Very high to those whose ears have not been accustomed to a higher sound than thousands as applyed to State Debts) and appears Very great at our ~~so early National period~~ first outsells as a Nation & as Compared with any other Nation we have been acquainted with at so early a Period tho the State Debts a great part of them arose on a National account, yet while Continued Seperate and Divided they are not so obvious & perceptible as when accumulated and brot. up into one entire View. I was observing that the several States ~~& the~~ had not been accustomed till Very lately to hear of a publick Debt in which they were Concerned to pay beyond Thousands more lately hundreds added or rather prefixd to the thousands which gave some allarm but when the Word Millions which is the Highest Integral Number the People have been acquainted with & when applied to a Debt they have got to pay prefix to that a hundred & more, it will appear Enormous, Surprise & astonishment & dispair take place, the People will loose all Patience & be discouraged from every attempt to pay the Intrest, much more to Reduce the Principal sum. I conceive we have no Just Idea of the amount of the State Debts especially when they are to be assumed as National, every one will Strive to out do his Neighbor & when to be carried into the general Mass will be Continually increasing with every Species of Claims. Penobscot expedition ill founded & worse Executed,[1] Carolina State Ship built & filled out as a Privateer to enrich the State with her prizes not Suffered to be under the Direction of Congress at Last Scandalously given up to the Enemy by an officer of their own appointment.[2] Virginia Demanding an Enormous sum for unjustly incroaching upon the Indian Territories ~~destroying the peac~~ provoking them to Hostilities & drawing of[*f*] ~~or not~~ their Troops from the National Army or rather not furnishing their Quota to Carry on their land Jobbing and fighting the Indians who would otherwise have been at Peace and quiet.[3] large Demands from the Southern States for their runaway Negroes & Slaves those taken by the Enemy or Shelterd & carried off by them add to these losses by burning of Town houses & every Species of Damage supposed to be done by the Enemy or our own Army Speculators made good for old Continental [*lined out*] Bills beside Numberless private losses Damages—Compensations &c. &c. &c. when all these are Added & placed to the National Debt it will appear so Magnified ~~Untill a~~ to the degree (the Anual expenditures of Government for Support & also Defence increasing in ~~the Whole Amount of~~ the meantime to be paid) that it will baffle every attempt ~~or plan to~~ of our Financier to find ways or Means for funding or fixing & establishing any permanent Security either for Intrest or principal. Our National Credit Sinking abroad failing at Home Speculators like ~~loc~~ Locusts preying on your dying Credit—we fear will be the Consequence, but perhaps you may think these are only Scare crows the imaginations of a gloomy mind Indeed I hope they never will be realised and Submitting to the Wise Determinations of Congress And a Governing Providence.

P. S. as to the Creditors I believe 9 out of 10 will rather Depend on the State to which they belong for payment, & Justice being done therein than to Risque it in that Ocean of Debt which will appear when all is brot. in & accumulated in one National Debt & which will be Continually increasing rather than Diminishing. note if you draw the String on Impost &c. much Faster at present it will break, & Oversett the Whole.

[*P. P. S*] I do not understand a Debt funded irredeemable tho 5 dollars paid annually including Interest which is I suppose to sink one dollar in a year of principal (i.e.) take 2 dollars Clear out of Intrest & then allow, or refund one towards the principal & in that way pay me in a hundred year or rather wrong me out of the whole principal & one pr. Ct. out of my Intrest. it seems to me the word (Justice) was to long hackneyd on the late Subject of Discrimination. that I find it is ~~wholly~~ so ~~omitted~~ much Worn out that it is entirely omitted in the Debates on the funding System: I remark one late Speak[*er*] who says in reply Viz. we might well be Squeamish when forming the Constitution but now we have got it ratifyd & all bound it is time to lay aside all Squeamishness & pay no regard to the Estimate our Constituents will put on the pleasure.[4]

(Caution!)

Compliments of the Court await you.

ALS, Miscellaneous Manuscripts, MHi. Written from Norwich, Connecticut. The omitted text concerns business before the Connecticut Superior Court and responds to Sherman's request to know "what New Points we have determined."

[1] In 1779 Massachusetts launched a costly and unsuccessful attack on British fortifications near present-day Castine, Maine, on the Penobscot River. Despite the fact that Congress had not authorized the expedition, Massachusetts argued for a decade that it should assume part of the cost.

[2] Alexander Gillon, as commodore of South Carolina's state navy during the Revolutionary War, went to France and in May 1780 leased a frigate which he renamed the *South Carolina*. It arrived in American waters in September 1781 and proceeded to take prizes before being

captured by the British in 1782. Dyer may have confused this ship with a merchant ship that South Carolina had earlier sent to France with indigo to purchase war materiel and that had been turned over to the British by its mutinous crew; Burke described both incidents in the same recorded speech of 30 March (*DHFFC* 12:875–76). For extensive background on the *South Carolina*'s cloudy career, which became the basis for an important Supreme Court case, see *DHSCUS* 5:450–53.

[3] Probably a reference to expeditions mounted by Virginia under state militia Gen. George Rogers Clark in 1786 against the Native American villages along the Wabash and Great Miami rivers.

[4] A paraphrase of Gerry's speech of 1 April (*DHFFC* 13:952).

William Maclay to John Nicholson

The Vote on the Assumption of the State Debts, was taken this day & passed in the negative 31 against, 29 for it.

It is still likely that this Matter may come forward in some Shape or other. I must therefore beg of You to give me all the information which You can. particularly as to the amount of the Class Taxes of Pennsylvania and her expenditures for the recruiting of the Army. and whether the whole is not paid. It is clear enough, that the State Debt of Pennsylvania embraces none of these Objects. & I am informed by Mr. [*Joseph*] Howel. That Three Millions of the State Debt of Massachusetts consists of such Materials. I wrote to you Yesterday on this Subject.[1] and shall therefore add nothing now.
[*P. S.*] The Pennsylvanians were divided for the assumption Fitzsimons, Clymer Hartley. against it The Two Muhlenbergs Scot & Hiester—it being in a Committee of the Whole, the Speaker was on the Floor. The Chairman was Judge Livermore of New Hampshire, who we know is against it. Two more members are expected from N. Carolina. those now here from that State, voted in the negative, & consider themselves, instructed so to do.[2]

ALS, Gratz Collection, PHi. Addressed to "Comptroller Genl. of Pennsylvania"; franked; postmarked; received 13 April.

[1] Maclay probably meant his letter of 10 April.

[2] Ashe, Bloodworth, and Williamson.

William Maclay to Benjamin Rush

At Two O'Clock the Question on the Assumption of the State Debts was taken in a Committee of the Whole house. & lost. for it 29 against it 31—The Pennsylvanians divided. for it Fitzsimons Clymer Hartley, against it The Two Muhlenbergs Scot & Hiester—Dismay seized the Secretary's Group. Speculation wiped her Eye. and the Massachusetts men threatned a dissolution of the Union.

Under certain Conditions & limitations, an Assumption might be Acceptable. For instance let the States discharge their requisitions, let the Accounts be settled & assume the Balances. But under the late Doctrine of burning the Books. Assumption would have been political Madness.[1] I am in too much haste to add anything.

ALS, Rush Papers, DLC. Addressed to Third Street, Philadelphia; franked; postmarked.

[1] This letter, primarily as written but with some paraphrasing, was printed with an incorrect date of 10 April as "Extract of a letter from New-York," in the [Philadelphia] *Pennsylvania Mercury*, 15 April.

Roger Sherman, Notes for a Speech

The debates on this Subject have ~~excited~~ given me great ~~anxiety in my mind, not on account of my apprehensions concerning respecting the final division of the question; but~~ concern on account of the threatning Aspect it has on the Government, when I See the house so equally divided in Sentiment, ~~and the members so tenacious of their opinions on both Sides~~ on so important a Subject. and so little ~~disposition~~ prospect of an accommodation.

The Support of public credit by a provision for doing justice to the public creditors was one great object that led to the establishment of the present government, and if it Should fail of doing that justice ~~in that respect~~, it would lose the confidence of many of its best friends, & disappoint the raised expectations of the people in general, both at home & abroad. ~~Nothing can weaken a nation more than divided councils. there fore I think we ought all Studiously to endeavour an accommodation.~~ I consider the debts incurred by the Several States in Support of the War as a part of the national debt. & that a provision for them ought not to be postponed, until a Settlement of the accounts of the States with the United States.

I am sensible ~~there will be Severe~~ that difficulties, and delays ~~will take place in~~ may attend the Settlement of those accounts ~~among the States~~, on any plan that ~~w~~ can be adopted; nor is perfect equity to be expected. but in great national affairs, smaller inconveniencies must be dispensed with. If the States had not by their mutual confidence in each other, ~~and in the Union~~, Surmounted much greater difficulties, than ~~attend the present Subject of debate~~ than these, they never would have accomplished the revolution; but each made all possible exertions in confidence that final justice would be done.

~~I think the question must be decided on Some general~~ [*lined out*] ~~principles.~~ I Shall not now go into a particular discussion of the ~~matter~~ proposition before Committee, every thing that may reflect light on the Subject having been repeatedly Said already. I Shall only State the principles. that induce me to be in favour of the assumption ~~of the State debts incurred by the Several States in Support of the late war~~ of the State debts. Such of them I mean as Shall have been liquidated by the respective States at their just value in Specie. This measure under present circumstances appears to me both just and politic. ~~if not absolutely necessary~~—The assumption is *just* with respect to the creditors whose debts are due for Services & Supplies rendered in Support of the common cause of the Union, & which there fore ought to be paid out of the common funds. and tho' some of the States might provide as well for their creditors, as the united States could. yet that is not the case as to others, & it would not give Satisfaction to assume the debts of Some States & not of others.

The measure will be just with respect to the Several States, because each will bear only its just proportion of the present burthen, and their past exertions will be equitably adjusted in the final Settlement of their accounts. which is already provided for, & any further provision that may be necessary for carrying it into effect; is proposed now to be made.

The policy of the measure will consist in its tendancy, by doing equal justice to the creditors to promote harmony among them, & secur~~inge~~ their confidence ~~& good will to~~ [*lined out*] in the Government; and in allieviating the burthens of a number of the States, who from their Situation & circumstances were necessitated during the war, to make greater exertions, and were Subjected to greater Sufferings & expenditures than the other States: But if those debts are not Assumed those States will be left to Sustain their unequal burthens; or their creditors be left without any provision for Satisfying their claims, either of which must produce great uneasiness & dissatisfaction which will tend greatly to embarrass & obstruct the measures of government. weaken or str[*engthen*]. govt.

It has been Said let those States wait until their Accounts Shall be Settled, & then receive the balances that may be due to them. But why Should those States be Subjected to greater burthens at present than the other States? As it ~~cant be~~ is not known ~~at present~~ which are D[*ebtor*]r. or C[*redito*]r. States, why not bear the burthen [*lined out*] equally until that can be ascertained?

It is Said there is no rule established to determine the quotas of the States, & that it is uncertain whether there ever can or will be a Settlement. I think the rule in the constitution to proportion direct taxes, is an established rule to determine the quotas of the States as to past as well as future expenditures: but if there is to be no Settlemt. I think it a conclusive argument, that the whole public debt Should be assumed by the union. for all the States made great exertions during the war, perhaps as great as their circumstances & abilities would admit, & they have likewise contributed Since the peace toward the payment of the debts contracted during the war. by the united States as well as by themselves individually, and must it not be presumed that each has done its due proportion until the contrary appears, and that can no otherwise appear than by a Settlement of the accounts; & until that is done I can See no good reason why any State Should bear more than its just proportion of the existing debts, whether contracted by the union or the States individually. if incurred for the Common defence.

~~I therefore move that the proposition be amended to read thus. Resolved, that the liquidated debts of the respective States incurred in Support of the late war, ought with the consent of the creditors to be assumed & provided for by the United States; and that any further provision that may be necessary for a Speedy just & final Settle of the Accounts, of the Several States with the united ought at the Same time to be made.~~

AN, Miscellaneous Manuscripts, MHi. With the manuscript are copies of the congressional resolutions of 22 November 1777 and 3 June 1784; for the texts of these, see *DHFFC* 5:859. The dating of this speech is based on comparison with Thomas Lloyd's Notes (*DHFFC* 13:982–84).

Thomas Lee Shippen to William Shippen

You will be surprized at not having heard Sooner of my arrival in this place—a most unexpected and disagreable detention in crossing the bay from Elizabeth town [*New Jersey*] occasioned its being so late, and consequently retarded my writing to you.

My uncle [*R. H. Lee*] is fixed at Mrs. McEwen's where he has Bland as a companion, and I have an excellent room here which Gen. [*William*] Irvine has just left upon the ground floor, and Madison, Heister, Brown and at present Duncan Ingraham[1] as my associates. I am already charmed with Madison. Both before & at dinner yesterday I had a great deal of conversation with him, and I really begin to think that he deserves all his reputation. I went yesterday to the President's where I saw [*William*] Jackson, to Mr. Griffin's where I saw Mary, and drank tea with Mr. White of Virginia where I was introduced to Mrs. [*Elizabeth Wood*] White and 5 sisters & daughters—A large family In the Ev[*enin*]g. I passed 2 or 3 hours at Mr. Izard's where I delivered Mrs. [*Sarah Coxe*] Allen's letter to Mrs. [*Charlotte Izard*] Smith, and received a thousand marks of civility & attention—A great many enquiries too about Mr. [*Andrew*] Allen's and your family. I am now on the wing to breakfast at Mr. V. President's—He breakfasts at 8 and lives 2 miles out of town—I must leave you therefore for the present.

ALS, Balch Papers, PHi. Written in the morning; addressed to Philadelphia; postmarked.

[1] A Philadelphian who settled in Amsterdam and in 1781 became a partner in the mercantile firm of Sigourney, Ingraham, and Bromfield (*Adams* 2:453–54n; *Coxe*, p. 53n).

Letter from Charleston, South Carolina

It is remarkable that almost every place has its epidemical whim once or twice every two or three years. In Philadelphia, I am told, they are all running stark mad for maple sugar instead of sugar from the West-Indies. In your place, report says, the imaginations of the whole city are so intoxicated with the entertainments of Federal Hall, that few can remain at home with any patience (except old women and young children) while the speeches are going on. As to us in Charleston, a universal terror of mad-dogs has lately fallen upon us; and if we may judge from certain ravings in our newspapers, not a few honest citizens have been actually bitten.

NYDA, 24 April; reprinted at Bennington, Vermont.

Other Documents

Josiah Burr to Jeremiah Wadsworth. ALS, Wadsworth Papers, CtHi. Written from New Haven, Connecticut.

Can guarantee delivery of the Osnaburg fabric requested by C. Carroll in New York by early May; has met with Oliver Phelps and has secured deeds in Wadsworth's name for approximately 31,000 acres in the Genessee Purchase.

Joseph Shotwell to Elias Boudinot. ALS, Boudinot Papers, PHi. Written from Bridgetown, New Jersey. For the full text, see *Boudinot* 2:58–59. The author was a founding member of the Pennsylvania Abolition Society in 1789.

Acknowledges brother Elisha Boudinot's successful efforts in lawful manumission of an enslaved Black; "Actions of this Nature certainly merits great applause with Benevolent hearts, and the actors will receive the plaudits of future ages, when the Nabobs of the South will not be entitled thereto."

William Smith (Md.) to Mary "Polly" Williams. No copy known; mentioned in Smith to Otho H. Williams, 12 April.

William Smith (Md.) to Otho H. Williams. ALS, Williams Papers, MdHi. Addressed to Baltimore; franked; postmarked.

The COWH has "this moment" decided against the assumption; "perhaps some modifications may be offerd, that may change the opinions of some members"; "one more vote in favor of the proposition would have carried it, for the chairman [*Livermore*] was on that side."

Michael Jenifer Stone to Walter Stone. ALS, Stone Family Papers, DLC. Place to which addressed not indicated.

Was "attacked on thursday [*8 April*] with an inflamitary fever Sore throat &ca. which confined me to bed till yesterday"; is in Congress at that moment, "Feeble as you may suppose"; believes the COWH will reject assumption.

Letter from Philadelphia. *GUS*, 14 April; reprinted at New London and Norwich, Connecticut; Burlington, New Jersey; and Fredericksburg, Richmond, and Winchester, Virginia.

Is at a loss as to why the funding business has lain over; something about a compromise respecting assumption is reported; "time is passing and I begin to think they will say bye and bye 'it is too late in the session to go thro with such important business as funding the debt, &c.'"

Letter from New York. *PP*, 15 April; reprinted at Wilmington, Delaware, and Richmond, Virginia.

"It was determined in a committee of the whole not to assume the state debts, by a majority of two, 29 for, 31 against it."

Tuesday, 13 April 1790

Fine (Johnson)

Thomas Fitzsimons to Tench Coxe

Since my return to this place nothing has Ocurred worth giveing you the trouble of a letter about till Yesterday When the question on the assumption of the State debts was taken in a Committee of the whole and Negatived ayes 29. Noes 32—it was imprudently pressed as the issue was foretold. yet the advocates for it betrayd all the Marks of disappointment—& passion—that could have been produced from the loss of the most sanguine expectation—What the Effect may be I cannot undertake to determine but from present appearances—there is Reason to apprehend that every thing relateing to finance will fall thro and that we shall end our Session in extreme ill humour. I have long been apprehensive that it would be Impossible to obtain provision for the other parts of the domestic debt without includeing the State debts. I fear my Apprehensions will be realized & another proof furnished that Avarice often disappoints itself—for I consider the opposition to the assumption as a Measure of the holders of Contl. Securitys Who supposed their security would be lessend by the Measure the Correspondence of some of that class with the Members of our house has I am sure influenced their Votes—there were but 3 of the Pensylvs. that Voted in the affirmative. While I lament the probable Consequence, I cannot but Condemn the Conduct of some of the Supporters of the Measure. they have pursued it without discretion and really so as to disgust some Who gave into it more with a View to National Accommodation than from Conviction of the Justice or Necessity of it—the Delegates of Pensylva. had of all others the most reason to Complain: they allways knew the decision depended upon their Vote. Yet have they seen a Combination between So. Co. & Masssts. with New York to disappoint any expectation of the removal of Congress—if my apprehensions shall be realized We shall not be long together the Irritation is so great that it would be Vain to hope for any Union of Sentiment on any other question. You will easily see that this detail is intended for your particular information—I hope My apprehensions may prove groundless—in which case a disclosure of them would be injurious—here is a packet from England Just arrived but I have had no oppy. of hearing any News—there have been later advices than she can bring many days past I took care to put the letters you sent me into the post office to go by the last packet from hence—Inclosed is the Act for Secureing Inventions &c. [*Patents Act HR-41*] not I believe quite so good as it ought to be—the Subject is attended with some difficulty and our Mode of reviseing bills not the Very best to perfect them.

ALS, Coxe Papers, PHi. Addressed to Philadelphia; postmarked; received 15 April. The letter is undated.

Thomas Hartley to Jasper Yeates

I herewith send you a News Paper which can give you some Idea of the Business of Yesterday.

The non assumen of State Debts carried ~~it~~ the Question by a Majority of two in a Committee of the whole to the great Disatisfaction of the Eastern States and South Carolina They now as I expected will prevent any Funding if it is in their Power.

They have began their Embarrassments this Morning—and manage pretty well—and as most of the States who were agst. the Assumption are not great Creditors of the union—they seem to be slow in their Movements.

Our Delegation was divided—3 for and 4 agst. Mr. Wynkoop came to Day which divides us equally we shall perhaps in Time discover who are right.

It is probable that we may get the Business referred to a Special Committee of a Member from each State it is probable in this the Representatives of our State will concur.

I shall go from here on Friday if I am alive and well & unless some Thing unforseen should happen I can give you no more News to Day—I hope we shall meet safely ~~toge~~ at York.

P. S. I write this in the midst of Debate you must make an Allowance for Incorrectness.

ALS, Yeates Papers, PHi. Addressed to Lancaster, Pennsylvania; franked; postmarked.

James Madison to Henry Lee

Your favor of the 4th ult. by Col. Lee was received from his hands on Sunday last—I have since recd. that of the 3d Instant—The anticedent one from Alexandria, though long on the way was recd. some time before. In all these, I discover strong marks of the dissatisfaction with which you behold our public prospects—Though in several respects they do not comport with my wishes—yet I cannot feel all the despondency which you seem to give way to—I do not mean that I entertain much hope of the Potomac, that seems pretty much out of sight—but that other ~~Matters~~ Measures in view, however improper, will be less fatal than you imagine.

The plan of discrimination has met with the reception in Virginia on which I calculated—The towns would for obvious reasons disrelish it, and for a time they always set public opinion—The country in this region of America, in general, if I am not misinformed, has not been in unison with the Cities—nor has any of the latter except this, been unanimous against the Measure—Here the sentiment was in its full vigor, and produced every exertion that could influence the result.

I think with you that the Report of the Secretary of the Treasury is faulty in many respects—it departs particularly from that Simplicity which ought to be preserved in finance, more than any thing else. The novelty and difficulty of the Task he had to execute form no small apology for his errors, and I am in hopes that in some instances they will be dimi[*ni*]shed, if not remedied.

The proposed assumption of the state debts has undergone repeated discussions, and contradictory decisions—The last vote was taken yesterday in a Committee of the whole and passed in the negative 31 vs. 29—The minority do not abandon however their object, and 'tis impossible to foretell the final destiny of the measure—It has some good aspects, and under some modifications would be favorable to the pecuniary interests of Virginia—and not inconsistent with the general principle of justice—In any attainable form it would have neither of these recommendations and is moreover liable to strong objections of a general nature—It would certainly be wrong to force an affirmative decision on so important and controvertible a point—by a bare majority, yet I have little hope of forbearance from that scruple.

Mass. & S. Carolina with their allies of Connecticut & N. York are too zealous to be arrested in their pursuit, unless by the force of an adverse majority.

I have recd. your reflections on the subject of a public debt with pleasure—in general they are in my opinion just and important—Perhaps it is not possible to shun some of the evils you point out, without abandoning too much the reestablishment of public credit—But as far as this object will permit I go on the principle that a Public Debt is a Public curse and in a Rep. Govt. a greater than in any other.

I have mentioned Mr. [*Thomas Ludwell*] Lee to Mr. Jefferson who tells me that he found every place preoccupied, and that he has not thought proper to make changes, where no special reasons existed—Various applications had been made previous to that in behalf of your freind—Several had passed through my hands, some of them from Virginia.

I never heard of the report you mention of the Vice Prest. It is but justice to say that I can not believe it to have originated in fact.

I lament with you the inability which impedes arrangements at the Great Falls [*on the Potomac River*], which would be of so much benefit in a Public, as well as private view—The prospect of aid in this quarter does not strike me as it seems to do you—Money is destined to other projects at this juncture.

Besides I am on no peculiar footing that could favor an experiment, and could never make it less auspiciously than at present. It gives me much concern that it is not more in my power to forward our object.

Copy, Madison Papers, DLC. Place to which addressed not indicated.

George Thatcher to John D. Bourne

I had the pleasure of hearing from you this morning, by Letters from Mr. [*Marshall*] Jenkins; and I rejoice to hear you are alive and well. The Letters accompanying this are from your Father [*Shearjashub Bourne*], mother [*Hannah Doane Bourne*] & friends at Barnstable—who are mourning your absence.

I doubt whether I can present to your mind any more forceable arguments to induce you to return to your friends, than what are, probably, contained in those Letters—But I can assure you, they are very unhappy in your absence; and will receive you with open arms & tears of Joy.

Your Father has desired me to inform you, if I should see you, that he will put you into any Business you may wish to pursue—I shall write to your Father by the next post; & let him know you are at Hudson and well—and disposed to return home.

If you return thro this City, pray call and see me—you will find in Broad street No. 47—should you wish to hear from your Father before you go home, and will send a Letter to me I will forward it to him; and in three or four weeks you will get an answer—should you want money I will supply you.

FC, Thatcher Family Papers, MHi. Sent to Hudson, New York.

George Thatcher to Shearjashub Bourne

Yours of the 20th. March came to hand on the 31st. of the same month; together with seven Letters directed to your son John, & one to Messrs. Folgier [*William Folger*] & [*Marshall*] Jenkins at Hudson—The Letter to Messrs. Folgier & Jenkins I forwarded to them by post, on the first inst. I also wrote them myself—a copy of which Letter is inclosed No. 1.

The next day I engaged a suitable man to enter, occasionally, all outward bound vessells in this Harbour, & to endeavour, if possible to discover whether your son John was on board.

This morning I received two Letters from Mr. Jenkins—No. 2, 3—to which I refer you—since which I have wrote him, see No. 4—and shall forward it to him, by the next mail—I have also wrote to your son, No. 5—And shall forward to him, by the same mail that carries his & Mr. Jenkins Letters, all the Letters you inclosed to my care for him.

Should your son be disposed to return home before I hear or see you—and call upon me I shall lend him any assistance he may want, & it shall be in my power to afford him.

I rejoice at the prospect you & Mrs. [*Hannah Doane*] Bourne have of soon embracing a long lost son; & hope the measures I have taken to assist you in finding him will meet your approbation.

FC, Thatcher Family Papers, MHi. The enclosed copy "No. 1" (Thatcher to Jenkins and Alexander Coffin in lieu of Folgier, dated 1 April) is printed above; enclosures "No. 2, 3" (dated 8 and 9 April, respectively) are calendared above; enclosure "No. 4" (to Jenkins, dated 13 April) is calendared below; and Thatcher to John D. Bourne of this date ("No. 5") is printed immediately above.

OTHER DOCUMENTS

John Dawson to James Madison. ALS, Madison Papers, DLC. Written from Fredericksburg, Virginia. For the full text, see *PJM* 13:149–50.

Virginia's Executive Council named Walker for the interim appointment to replace Grayson in the Senate after both Patrick Henry and George Mason declined; Walker passed through Fredericksburg en route two or three days earlier; his appointment is generally disapproved of and may not be "confirmed" by the General Assembly; no news heard about assumption; it is "universally reprobated" in the state, and expects its passage would "draw some very spirited Resolutions from the next assembly, as it is thought a wanton interferance of Congress and an attempt to hasten a consolidation"; Bland's support of assumption "has raised an opposition to him in his district which I am told will succeed."

Benjamin Huntington and Jeremiah Wadsworth to Governor Samuel Huntington. ALS, hand of Huntington, Smith Collection, NjMoHP. Addressed to Norwich, Connecticut; carried by Capt. Parker; received 22 April; answered 24 April.

They have waited on Postmaster General Samuel Osgood, who consents that the mail carried by Ormsby be entrusted to the stage; he says "the Power given ~~by~~ Mr. [*Christopher?*] Leffingwell under your direction is fully sufficient for the purpose."

James Madison to Edmund Pendleton. ALS, misdated "March," Madison Papers, DLC. Addressed to Williamsburg, Virginia; franked; postmarked. For the full text, see *PJM* 13:148–49.

Reports the defeat of assumption on 12 April; "we hoped that this vote would have been mortal to the project. It seems however that it is not yet to be abandoned. The other part of the Secretary's Report has been studiously fastened to the Assumption by the friends of the latter, and of course has made no progress."

Benjamin Rush to John Adams. ALS, Adams Family Manuscript Trust, MHi. Written from Philadelphia. For the full text, see *Rush* 1:544–49.

Invites him to Philadelphia next spring; "You have many friends in this city—as well as in the State"; "Take care what you say, or write to me. I wish I could whisper the same caution to some other Gentlemen high in power & office in New York. Some of them will find themselves, (if they survive me) turned *inside outwards*"; "I daily hear of Acts & Speeches in New York which mark worse than British degrees of corruption."

George Thatcher to Marshall Jenkins. FC, Thatcher Family Papers, MHi.
Will forward Jenkins's mail to Shearjashub Bourne; requests further attention to Bourne's son, John D., until he receives further instructions or John returns home; encloses letters for forwarding to John; advises taking the packet to Providence or Newport should John choose to return home by sea.

William Samuel Johnson, Diary. Johnson Papers, CtHi.
"Visits."

Marriage certificate for Louis Guillaume Otto and America Frances de Crèvecoeur. AN, in Latin and French, Gilder Lehrman Collection, NHi.
The couple was married this day by Fr. Nicolaus Burke of St. Peter's (Catholic) Church before witnesses who included Wadsworth and Trumbull.

Wednesday, 14 April 1790

Pierce Butler to Edward Rutledge

Before this can reach Your hand I trust You will have embraced your son [*Henry M. Rutledge*], who left us early on Tuesday morning. I fully intended writing to You by Henry had not [*Capt. William*] Elliot deceived me as to the hour of departure. Henry was to have breakfasted and dined with us on sunday; depending on that I defered writing 'till Sunday morning. I was in the act when Henry came into my study in a hurry before eight o'clock and told me Elliot was geting underway. This destroyed my intention. I wished to have given him the best testamonium in my power of his proper conduct while here so far as came to my knowledge from observation and constant enquiry of Doctor Johnston [*William Samuel Johnson*]. He is in truth an amiable Youth, and without flattery every thing that You & Mrs. [*Henrietta Middleton*] Rutledge could wish him. I fancy You will find him averse to returning here; I believe I can guess the reason, but You must try to get it from himself—It is nothing that need make You uneasy: it arises from a mildness of disposition.

Your truly friendly letter of the 28th of March I received last night. We are all infinitely indebted to You and Mrs. Rutledge for Your affectionate solicitude on acct. of my dear Mrs. [*Mary Middleton*] Butler, she has been dangerously indisposed so late as last week. I think as does the Doctor that she is now better: Her long indisposition has sank my spirits; I feel oppressed beyond measure when I look at her & my dear Daughters; indeed it unmans me. I needed all the comfort of Your excellent reasoning in the first part of Your friendly letter.

***

FC, Butler Letterbook, ScU. For the full text, see *Butler Letters*, pp. 27–28. The omitted text discusses Butler's strained finances owing to David Bourdeaux's default, without which he would have had "the heart-felt satisfaction of leaving something of my own to my dear Children, who are infinitely dearer to me than life or any thing but the name of being a just man."

Charles Carroll to Mary Caton

We have so little to do at present that I can't better employ my leisure time than in writing to you.

I hope you are safely got to the Manor[1] with yr. little ones & Mr. [*Richard*] Caton, & Mrs. Rankin, and that you find the country as agreeable as Annapolis.

I have not yet quite got rid of my cold: a little cough remains, but not dangerous, or troublesome; as I do not cough at nights.

Yesterday an important question was decided in the House of Representatives vizt. the assumption of the State-debts: for assuming 29. against assuming 31. I believe the minority will still endeavour to get the State-debts assumed under some limitations & provisions; but I suspect their endeavours will not succeed this Session: and I hope we shall proceed to fund the public debt of the United States without loss of time: however, it is said, many of the minority, who wished the State debts to be assumed by Congress, will oppose funding any part of the public debt, if the State debts are not like wise funded: but these threats will not be carried, I hope, into execution; and if they should, I am confident the party will be too small to obstruct the funding of the debt, (which has always been acknowledged by all, to be the debt of the United States).

You must be sensible this paragraph is more intended for Mr. Caton's information, than yours; for I suppose you know little about our public & State debts, and provided Mr. Caton can extricate himself from Whitsen day[2] you are little concerned about the public debts: these how ever give *us* no small concern, & trouble, and have divided Congress into two parties almost equal.

I cant at present form any opinion when Congress will adjourn: some think about the end of next month or middle of June: I expect that the Session will last till the end of September, and if this Session should terminate in funding the foreign & domestic debt of the Union, I shall not regret its length, tho' I am already tired of my Situation, & wish to be at home, where I could Employ my time more to my satisfaction than in this place.

Mr. O'Neal[3] tells me the late frost has much injured the fruit, peaches, and pears. Let me know whether all the pears and peaches are destroyed: the apples he says, Harry informed him, were not injured.

I hope soon to have a letter from you & Mr. Caton, & to hear that all things on the manor, and at his Farm go on well. Give my complts. to Mrs. Rankin How does She like Dougheragen?

ALS, Carroll-McTavish Papers, MdHi. Written in the Senate chamber.

---

[1] Carroll's Doohoragen Manor, named for an ancestral estate in Ireland, comprised thirteen thousand acres that Charles Carroll "of Annapolis" had accumulated in Anne Arundel County (partly in present-day Howard County), Maryland, by the time of his son's return from Europe in 1765 (*CCP* 1:3–4n). Although Charles Carroll "of Carrollton" distinguished himself from his father by taking the name of another family estate in Frederick County, he used Dougheragen as his country estate until his death in 1832. The manor house, built in 1727 but substantially enlarged since then, is located a few miles west of Ellicott City.

[2] Whitsun Day, the traditional first day of Pentecost, was the seventh Sunday after Easter and fell on 23 May in 1790.

[3] Probably Lawrence O'Neal (1738–1815), planter and sheriff of Frederick County, Maryland, which he had represented from 1780 in the state House of Delegates. His wife Rachel was cousin to Carroll and aunt to Carroll's deceased wife (*CCP* 2:805, 3:1538).

William Few to [*Joseph Clay*]

***

I am happy to learn that our State enjoys peace with the Creek Indians. Congress seems disposed to act on the defensive for the present, and are taking measures to protect the whole frontier of the United States. Three Companies amounting to near two hundred men, with six field pieces and a sufficient quantity of other arms and ammunition have sailed for Georgia and are to be Stationed—one company on the River St. Mary, and another at ~~the Ala~~ Beards Bluff on the Alatamah, and the other at the Rock landing on the Oconee, to be divided into smaller parties as may best protect the inhabitants.

A Bill has passed the House of Representatives for augmenting the Military establishment of the United States to upwards of sixteen hundred men. This bill is now before the Senate, where it meets with much oppossission as to the number of troops that will be necessary. It is the intention of the Secretary at War to establish a line of Posts from the Ohio by the way of the Tugaloe and Oconee to St. Marys river. By the the enclosed papers you will percieve what Congres is doing, and to those I must refer you for News.

ALS, Emmet Collection, NN. Place to which addressed not indicated. An annotation in an unknown hand, probably recording the information from a lost endorsement sheet, indicates it was addressed to Clay at Savannah, Georgia.

William Few to Governor Edward Telfair

I have recieved your little letter, with two Casks of Indigo, which I have deposited in the hands of a Merchant to sell for the highest price, or to retain it until it will command the most. At present good indigo will not sell for more than about 6 shilling this Currency a pound. I have also enquired after window Glass of the size you mention, and there is none such at this time to be had here ~~at present~~, but I have applied to the man who is concerned in the Glass House near Albany, and he has engaged to have the Glass made and sent down within four weeks, I will then take the earliest opportunity of sending it forward to Mr. [*Joseph*] Clay.

By the enclosed papers you will percieve what Congress have done, and are about to do. The [*Naturalization*] Act for admiting Aliens to the rights of Citizens, was much controverted, and various opinions were advanced on the operation, it would Have, and the powers that the Individual States had of granting priviledges to foreigners. It was generally agreed the States might with propriety pass laws to enable Aliens to hold real Estate when they please, and there is no doubt but the regulations of the respective States will govern with respect to the period when foreigners shall be enabled to hold offices under the State Governments. This being admitted the operation of this act cannot be very extensive.

A motion was made in the Senate lately to bring in [*lined out*] a bill to regulate Bankruptcies, but it was opposed and rejected[1] The arguments used in oppossition, were that the other House had taken the business under contemplation and that it would be better for them to originate and bring it forward—By some the principle was objected against, and it was said that it might be attended with consequences highly injurious to attempt to pass any law at present to interfere with the transactions of Debtor & Creditor It was said by others that the insolvent laws of the different States would save the Debtor from the unmercyfull hands of the Creditor, but this I think is questionable—indeed the more I reflect on this interesting subject, the more I am convinced that Congress must enter on the business of Bankrupts and pass some general~~l~~ law that will extend to the relief of honest insolvent Debtors Tho I am inclined to think nothing will be done on that subject during ~~of~~ this session.

Inclosed is a letter from Mr. [*Nicholas*] Eveleigh, the Comptroller of the accounts of the United States on the subject of the late Colo. [*John*] Whites Accounts He tells me that the State of Georgia stands charged with several large sums of money, at different times delivered to Colo. White on account of the State—That the Estate of Colo. White have accounts ~~accounts~~ which will bring the United States in debt which sum due to our State ought to be retained until the heirs of Colo. White settle with or accou[*n*]t to the State of

Georgia for the sums which he has recieved out of the Treasury of the United States, it will be necessary only to order the Auditor to tramsit a Statement of the business and direct that a Caveat be entered against any person recieving the money until those accts. are setled by the Admrs. of Col. White.[2]

Mrs. [*Catherine Thompson*] Few Joins in presenting ~~of~~ our best respects to Mrs. [*Sally Gibbons*] Telfar, and looks forward with pleasure to the day that will commence their acquaintance; but such are the circumstances which must govern our movements, that the time cannot ~~at~~ with certainty be fixed on.

ALS, Telfair Papers, GHi. Addressed to Governor of Georgia.

[1] For more on the unjournalized motion of 22 March, see *DHFFC* 9:225.

[2] For background and texts relating to the settlement of Col. John White's Revolutionary War accounts, see *DHFFC* 7:469–70.

Benjamin Goodhue to Michael Hodge

To my great mortification, the question of Assumption was lost on Monday in the Committee of the whole House by 31 to 29, and from a consideration of the many embarrasments thrown in the way of this bussines I am pretty much persuaded there is little probibility of its obtaining this session, and I am very suspicious it will be the means of postponing the funding of the Continental debt, for the friends of the Assumption are convinced if the one is funded to the neglect of the other, there would be little or no prospect of the State Creditors being attended to hereafter, and for ought they see would be left almost without a remedy, such is the unhappy situation at present of the great object of establishing national credit.

ALS, Ebenezer Stone Papers, MSaE. Place to which addressed not indicated.

William Smith (S.C.) to Tench Coxe

Your letter, accompanied by a packet containing Journals of your Convention,[1] was not delivered to me till a few days ago by Mr. [*Andrew*] Brown, a printer, tho I observed from the date that he must have had it some time in his possession.

I feel myself very much indebted to your kind partiality for the handsome expressions contained in your letter relative to my public conduct; sensible that I am unworthy of such high approbation, I feel a strong desire to merit it & shall on all occasions in public as well as private life so square my conduct as to deserve the testimony of approbation of men whom I esteem & whose applause every one should be ambitious of obtaining. Since you wrote, I am apprehensive some of my observations in Congress on a very unpleasant subject may have excited rather the displeasure than the satisfaction of the citizens of your State[2]—persons not interested in the Subject as we are & therefore under a biass which may induce them to consider it with a very different eye may I fear impute my Sentiments to a want of that general philanthropy which I should be sorry to be thought not to possess: men of candor however who consider political Subjects with an enlarged mind will I flatter myself give me credit for as much humanity and philanthropy as (in the general mass of mankind) falls to my Share: under such impression they will make all due allowance for a delegate from a Southern State, standing in his place in the National Legislature & feeling a strong obligation to justify the conduct of his fellow-citizens to vindicate their character & to protect their property from the intemperate & bigotted zeal of a class of men who seemed to take pleasure in accusing us of infamous & inhuman proceedings & who were pursuing with eager steps the ruin & destruction of our happiness & property: If, acting under the pressure of these considerations & feeling much hurt at seeing the members of the Southern States dragged like Criminals to the Bar of the House to answer for crimes alledged against them by the Quakers & others (whose applications were too warmly supported by some of the members from those States in which Quakers have electioneering influence) ~~wa~~ I was excited to treat the applica~~tions~~nts with asperity, I trust I shall stand justified for it & that it will be attributed to those whose imprudent zeal lead us into a discussion of so disagreable a nature. It was a mortifying thing, I assure you; to see an attempt made to deprive us of our property so soon after we had established a governmt. for the express purpose of protecting it, & in the face of a solemn compact so recently entered into. I have however had the satisfaction to hear that the proceedgs. of the Quakers & the conduct of the Majority of our House in so readily listening to their Memorials & mispending so much time on a subject with which they had no business have been generally reprobated & in no where so much as in Philada. In consequence of this absurd proceeding & the delay occasioned thereby, I very much apprehend a loss of the Assumption of the state debts & with it the Loss of any funding System, at least for the present: we had a majority of five or six decidedly for the measure six weeks ago; had the Committee of the whole then reported to the House & sent the Resolution ~~up~~ to the Senate for their concurrence, as there was then a clear maj'y. for it in that house, the thing wod. have been irrevocably settled, for as the Secretary wod. have been authorized to open Subscriptions had any state creditors Subscribed, it wod. have been out of the power of Congress to have reversed the resolution; instead of which to make a parade of their superior philanthropy & gratify the Quakers to secure their votes at the ensuing election, they must forsooth go into a tedious & angry discussion of the powers of Congress respecting Slavery—after throwing the house into more violent convulsions than it had before experienced & wasting ten days—three North Cara. members[3] arrive & get the business of assumption recommitted; the consequence is that we have lost it—in the mean time somebody had converted one of my Colleagues [*Sumter*] who has voted against it, in direct opposition to an unanimous instruction of the State Legislature—the Members from Pensylva. have been in great measure accessory to this calamity—the Speaker & Scott who voted for it before deserted us the other day & made us lose the vote: there is a report here that your members want to connect the Assumption with the residence & make us vote for Philada. or Germantown that they may join us for the Assumption—I don't say there is any truth in the report & must do the members the justice to say that I have'nt heard a word from any of them which can justify the Assertion—the vote however of the Speaker (who was a few days ago decidedly for the measure) is so very mysterious that it seems to give some countenance to the report—it has altered the good opinion many persons entertained of him before—& Shod. his vote lay the foundation of civil discord in the States he will repent it to his latest existence—we are all in great confusion—the funding business is at a stand—the house about equally divided & drawing violently different ways; the friends to the Assumption think the govt. can't go on without it & that it is idle to fund a debt partially which will raise a host of enemies immedy. agst. the govt. unless therefore members will vote according to their real Sentiments & act openly & fairly & make concessions & not sacrifice the general weal to little state policy, I see no good from our continuing to sit; we may as well adjourn & trust to another Congress.

Mrs. [*Charlotte Izard*] Smith joins me in best respects to Mrs. [*Rebecca Coxe*] Coxe—to thank you for your polite congratulations on the birth of our Son who was inoculated day before yesterday & is very hearty. Please to forward the inclosed by the first opportunity to Charleston. What is become of the Journal of the Convention?

ALS, Coxe Papers, PHi. Place to which addressed not indicated.

---

[1] The published journal of the Episcopalian Convention held in Philadelphia the previous summer.

[2] Smith refers to his speeches attacking Quaker antislavery petitioners and their cause in February and March.

[3] Ashe, Bloodworth, and Williamson.

Oliver Wolcott, Jr. to Oliver Wolcott, Sr.

The question for assuming the State Debts has been taken in a Comtee. of the whole and lost by a majority of two votes—the question will be revived as it is of too much consequence to be lost finally, if it shall be possible to carry it.

I much fear that the various opinions with respect to the public Debt will not soon be reconciled—and that the popularity of the government will be diminished by what shall be adopted.

If the Southern States were prepared for the operation of systematic measures all would be well, this is far from being the case—Many very respectable characters entertain political opinions which would be with us thought very whimsical and the general complection of their sentiments can be but illy reconciled with the plans which have been proposed.

***

ALS, Wolcott Papers, CtHi. Addressed to Litchfield, Connecticut.

Letter from New York

On Monday the question was again taken, on the motion for assuming the State debts; and it was lost by a majority of thirty one against twenty nine. The general subject of the Report of the Secretary has not been taken up since; and what will be finally done thereon becomes more and more uncertain. The opposers of the assumption wish to proceed in funding the continental debt—while the advocates are apprehensive that if a provision be once made for paying the interest of the continental, without the State debts, the latter must unavoidably depreciate much lower than they ever have been, if not die in the hands of the present holders.

[Portland, Maine] *Cumberland Gazette*, 26 April. This is probably from a letter written by Thatcher to the newspaper's editor, Thomas B. Wait.

Letter from New York to Virginia

Last Monday Mr. Sedgwick delivered a funeral oration on the death of Miss Assumption.[1] When this child was born, although her mother only went seven months with her, she was promising indeed—was uncommonly large, appeared healthy, could lisp Papa and Mama, displayed a good set of teeth, and could bite a crust of bread—was fond of molasses, and her principal food was cod's head[2]—her voluptuous manner of living caused her to outgrow her age—was seized with a consumption, which carried her off last Monday.

Her death was much lamented by her parents who were from New-England. Mr. Sedgwick being the most celebrated preacher, was requested to deliver her funeral eulogium. It was done with puritanic gravity. The orator being manly and grave and the language being alternately threatening and soothing, caused unusual sensations—a pause ensued—her southern relations bore the loss with fortitude (except her aunt South-Carolina) reflecting, that if she had grown to womanhood, that her disorder might have been contagious, and a general consumption in the family the consequence.

Sixty-one of the political fathers of the nation were present, and a crouded audience of weepers and rejoicers. Mrs. Speculator was the chief mourner, and acted her part to admiration: She being the mother of Miss Assumption, who was the hope of her family, the picture of herself, and her youngest child. Twenty-nine of the political fathers cried out aloud—Thirty-one bore the loss with manly fortitude, being in full hope of a glorious resurrection, when she might appear again in angelic shape and virgin innocence, unattended by any monstrous appendage.

Her near relations suppose she had a premature death, and intend to try their magic art to raise her from the dead; but as the days of witchcraft are over, and its presumable they have not supernatural powers, it is hoped by those who suppose her death will produce no ill effect, that they will cease their exertions for the present and suffer the dead to rest, lest by disturbing her *manes*,[3] the whole family may be involved in fresh calamitys.

Mrs. Excise may have cause to rejoice, because she will be screened from much drudgery—as she must have been the principal support of Miss Assumption, as well as her mother and all her other relations. Mrs. Direct Tax may rest more easy in Virginia, as she will not be called into foreign service. Madam Impost will have additions to her burthen—she is however well supported, and can better bear it than any other of the domestics, being much of a *woman*, and having the support of Mrs. Luxury and Madam Extravagance, who are *well-born dames*, and above the paltry considerations of economy or reputation.

Fenno's Gazette [*GUS*] of this day will detail the oration. Mr. S—k after delivering the sermon, took his leave for the east to mourn with the rest of the family.

[Edenton] *State Gazette of North Carolina*, 8 May; reprinted at Exeter and Portsmouth, New Hampshire; Bennington, Vermont; Boston and Stockbridge, Massachusetts; Newport, Rhode Island; Hartford, Litchfield, and New Haven, Connecticut; New York City (*NYJ*, 1 June; *GUS*, 2 June); Philadelphia; Baltimore; and Richmond, Virginia. The editors believe this letter was written by a member of the North Carolina delegation, most likely Williamson, who resided in Edenton.

[1] For Sedgwick's speech of 12 April, see *DHFFC* 13:1007–8.

[2] Molasses and cod, mainstays of New England's diet and commerce, allude to that region's support for assumption.

[3] The spirit or ghost of a dead person.

Other Documents

Pierce Butler to Alexander Gillon. FC, Butler Letterbook, ScU. For the full text, see *Butler Letters*, p. 29.

Is making great sacrifices to settle his debt with Hercules Bize; writes in haste; "The question of assumption was lost last Monday by a majority of two."

Benjamin Goodhue to Stephen Choate. No copy known; acknowledged in Goodhue to Choate, 10 May.

Benjamin Lincoln to Theodore Sedgwick. For this letter and background information, see *DHFFC* 7:177.

Describes a meeting of officers of the Massachusetts Line of the Continental Army that led to their petition to the FFC.

Roger Sherman to Simeon Baldwin. ALS, Sherman Collection, CtY. Place to which addressed not indicated. For more on Collins's petition, see *DHFFC* 7:84.

Encloses first 1790 issue of *CR* and *NYDA*; assumption negatived: one absent member (Wynkoop) for it, others said they would not be opposed to it if "properly modified"; expects it will be agreed to; Pitman Collins's petition not reported on yet by Hamilton.

Caleb Strong to Levi Shephard. ALS, Strong Collection, Forbes Library, Northampton, Massachusetts. Addressed to Northampton, Massachusetts.

There will be a clause (in the Mitigation of Fines Bill [HR-45]) "to obviate the Difficulty you complained of in the Impost System, but whether that Clause will be accepted is not certain as there will I perceive be some Opposition to it"; assumption was negatived in the COWH, but it is probable the question "will be taken up again & determined otherwise" or no funding will take place at all in the current session.

William Samuel Johnson, Diary. Johnson Papers, CtHi.

"Visits & Dind. [*Dined at the*] Izards."

[Keene] *New Hampshire Recorder,* 14 April.

Late accounts from New York mention that the members from Virginia and Maryland and some from Pennsylvania are opposed to assumption, the reason being that those states do not have a great amount of debt; but it is expected it will be agreed to; troops are to be raised to defend the southwestern frontier.

THURSDAY, 15 APRIL 1790

Rain (Johnson)

Elias Boudinot to William Bradford, Jr.

I have delayed Writing from day to day all this Week, in hopes of giving you some certainty with regard to our settlement of the Principles of our funding System—but I find it in vain—last Week the Question was taken on the Assumption of the State Debts, when it was lost by the defalcation of one Member, who had formerly voted in favour of it [*Sumter*]—29 ~~agt.~~ for & 31. ~~for~~ agt. it but as the Chairman [*Livermore*] was in favour, one would have turned the Scale—Since that event, all the evils I have so long foretold, are taking Place—The harmony of our House is broken up, and the victorious party, have appeared out of Spirits and have not attempted to call up the Question till this day, when they made a Motion to proceed in the Business. The Temper of the House now broke out, and very express declarations came forth, that it was not to be expected that any funding whatever would be adopted, without being attended by an assumption of the State Debts—The whole Morning till 1/2 past two was spent in disputing, whether the Question should be taken up, and the Yeas & Nays called near the usual Time of adjournment—It was carried, but nothing could be got thro' in consequence of it—In short I fear the worst—It may be voted in the House, but I doubt much if it will be compleated this Session, with out a Coalition—I wish most sincerely, it had never been mentioned.

I wrote you 10 or 12 Days ago & enclosed a Letter for your Coach Maker, begging you to get the Glasses of your Chariot examined by him & certified to me—I shall be much obliged by your sending an Answer as soon as possible, as I keep Hollet out of his Money till I hear from you.

I am sorry that you are so wholly taken up with your Courts. It is to be feared that your Health must inevitably suffer by it—I hope you will at all Events spend a week or Ten days, when you come for Susan [*Boudinot Bradford*], by way of Relaxation—It is as necessary as Application.

I wish you could perswade Mr. [*Ashabel*] Green to come this way—he would be taken great Notice of here.

I lately purchased of a poor woman here, (who was advised to apply to me, as having some Connection with Pennsylvania) a tract of Land in your State—I did it out of mere Charity, not wishing to be troubled with it—Enclosed you have the Deeds—Do enquire into the Value of it at markett—If more than I gave could be obtained for it, I would willingly give the benefit, to the Grantor—I know not who she is, but her Poverty would be relieved by having the full Value.

I begin to wish for a discharge from this Session and to breath a little free Air—I cannot form a guess of the length of the Session—as we are all at Bay.

Our kindest Love to Susan and all Friends—Her Mama [*Hannah Stockton Boudinot*] expects her in all this Month.

P. S. Mr. [*Anthony?*] Cuthbert is here and will not go to your City [*Philadelphia*] till Susan returns.

ALS, Wallace Papers, PHi. Place to which addressed not indicated.

Samuel W. Stockton to Elias Boudinot

***

Pray how long will it be before you get thro' the funding system? There seems to be a design with some people not to fund the public debt at all—and I fear that the protracting it so long & the embarrassments thrown in the way of it by some of the great men in Congress, is very much *decreasing the publick confidence in the new government*, which stood so high at first—I find on reconsidering the *assumption of the State debts*, it has been negatived by a small majority in the H. of Repress. Upon the whole I shall not be very sorry for this—as the *Continental debt* will be so much less as perhaps to induce *funding the Remainder at 6 per Cent*—for the cry is that our present *resources are not sufficient*—and altho' Mass[*achuse*]tts.—tho perhaps might be in such dudgeon, as not to agree to ~~an~~ funding system at all, without the assumption of the State debts, yet it might be carried without them—but they & others would probably after a while come to—I wish there had been a convention of Committees of public Creditors from every State, to *have enforced the speedy funding the public debt*, for unless it is soon done & on honourable terms, Our national character which still totters in the wind, will be blasted for ever—I am now sorry that the State debts were brought forward—and I am also very sorry that the *Quaker memorial* respecting the abolition of Slavery was taken up in the midst of the debates about the public debt—Both these subjects must very much have sourd the tempers of numbers of the members.

I hope you & Mr. Ger—y (whose propositions come to nearly the same thing) will stick to your text respecting the 6 pr. Cent—when you made your proposal which they negatived, you told them—They must in the end come to something like it—& Mr. Gerry's speech on his after motion to same purport, is very much celebrated[1]—even our Treas—r [*James Mott*], when any body talks of Congress *lowerg. the Interest, spits, pulls up his collar, & gets* into a violent passion & says "it wd. be scandalous & shameful & what's more, they *have no right to do it*"—Pray let us hear soon what is the reason of their protracting so long.

***

ALS, Stimson Boudinot Collection, NjP. Written from Trenton, New Jersey. In the omitted text Stockton discusses family health and state courts, and asks Boudinot to forward issues of *CR* and to help settle a financial matter.

[1] Boudinot's motion of 9 March, negatived the following day, was modified by Gerry and moved again on 13 March (*DHFFC* 5:841n, 842n). Gerry defended his motion in a lengthy speech that day before withdrawing it (*DHFFC* 12:701–7).

Thomas Thatcher to George Thatcher

After an Eight months silence I once more set down to write you a few lines, as thinking by this time it is probable you may wish to here from your friends in Yarmouth; tho' you take care not to let them hear one word from you—And if we did not once in a while see your name in print we might possable forgo that ever there was shuch a man as I am now writing to however to do you Justice I veryly believe that your neglecting to write to us, is more owing to the multiplicity of business that you are obliged to attend to, than to any forgetfullness of this your Native place.

But to proceede & give a perticular account of every thing that has happened here since you left the Town; would be too much to be contained in one letter And perhaps more than your Necessary beusiness will Allow you time to read.

I have since you saw me last ben Several time under the Doctors hand, & more than once given for gone with the Consumption, tho' thanks be to God the great giver & preserver of life & health I have stood the whole of the past winter Enjoyed as great a degree of health ~~of~~ as I have for many a year—Tho' at the present time of writing I have my old compaints heavy on me again—My Stomac the Seat of all my disorders is continually Exercised with Sha[*r*]p pain, & has ben so for about 4 Weeks Tho' it is not so bad as I have Several times before Experienced—& As I have put myself under the Same Regimen, that in times past has proved Effectual for a Cure, I am not without hopes that I shall in a Due time find relief.

We ~~must~~ shall all go off the Stage of this world in Such a time, way & manner as will be for the best, & why are we uneasy—For my own part, since I saw you I have lost so many of my friends, that to rejoine their Company I am some times all most persuaded that I am willing to make my Exit—You know that this Town Nevr did abound with people of much Sentiment—So that when you are told that a Colo. [*Enoch*] Hallet, a Lt. Josiah Miller, a William Bassett, & A James Hawes, have ~~left~~ left this world, I trust for a better, You need not think strang that Some of my time hangs heavy, for want of Some company to fetch new Ideas from.

Brothers and Sisters here are all as well as usual, moving round in the old circles—& often get together & hold discours about you, Siting the time when we think it proble you will come & see us &c. &c.

Mr. [*Joseph*] Otis has ben pleas'd to appoint me to do some business for him ~~him~~ in the way of his office—and tho' the profits are very small yet it comes very acceptable at this time as my health will not admid of my doing any things else—He says there is a prospect of his being appoind as an Assistant to the mar[*shal?*] of this Destrict, & if so he will employ me to ride with him through One or Two Towns—which for the Sake of the ride at this time will be very Acceptable—possable if you please you may be a mover in the afare I dont mean for you to do any thing but what is exactly agreeable to your plan of politicks.

The whole profets of Mr. Otises Office is very small I assure you—And what he gets ~~a~~ the greater part comes out of Yarmouth and is very destressing to the poor fishermen—there is about 40 saile that fishes from this Town—they have always the greater part of them ben supplyed with Salt & Store from Providence [*Rhode Island*]—Now the Charge of clearing & Entering together with 6 Cents per Bushel Duties on Salt is very discourageing—& more so if the State of Rhode Island should come into the union before the fishermen can export the fish that they shall catch this summer there & receive the bounty.

I think for the fisher-men of this town to pay 6 Cents a Bushel on 8 or 9000 Bushels of Salt—& if Rhod-Island comes into the union before Next December to loose it will wholley brake-up the business in this place[1]—It has already put a Stop to a numbr of vessels.

You may Say—that if Rhod Island comes into the union—the West-Indian will take off all the fish with other Foreign ports—But that is no help to us we are not Able to Ship fish to any foreign port except it be to Rhod Island—And as we are obligd to pay duties on Salt brought from thence I think it would be well for the fisher men to have Some consideration Some way or other if that State Should come into the union before the Salt that is brought from thence this spring can be wet & the effects carried back & the bounty, which I think is 5 Cent, pr. ~~Bushel~~ is in Can be Recievd—I am no way concerned in the fishery—& what little business I do will wholly stop as soon as Rhod Island comes into the union therefore dont write partially—But feelingly in behalf of my poor Towns men—I am Sensible that no general Law can work for the good of every Individual in A Continent as large as this—but this I will venture [*to*] Say that there is not a Tow[*n*] in the Union According to what the Town is worth that [*lined out*] is so much destrest. by the Duties As the Town of Yarmouth—Especially on Salt & Mollasses.

ALS, Chamberlain Collection, MB. Written from Yarmouth, Massachusetts.

[1] The entry of Rhode Island into the union would change the state's status from that of being treated like a foreign trading entity, thus eliminating the payments received by fishermen who exported salted fish products to Rhode Island under section 4 of the Impost Act. See *DHFFC* 5:942.

Henry Wynkoop to Reading Beatty

Came here on tuesday morning before breakfast, from Elizabethtown point [*New Jersey*]. my leg was somewhat inflamed from the Journey but is now again in a good way of healing, & am in hopes soon to be able to walk to & from the [*Federal*] Hall instead of employing a Coach for that purpose.

***

You will perceive by the papers that the Assumption of the State Debts was negatived in Committee of the whole on monday last, the Gentlemen of New England & those of South Carolina are extremely sore upon it & are anctious for an Accommodation. This day has again been consumed principally upon that Subject without concluding anything. It is wished by the Advocates of the Measure to have the whole Busyness committed to a Special Committee, in hopes thus to produce an acomodation; The House, in short at present is much embarrassed & how they will be extricated, so as to proceed with proper Temper on the great Subject of public Credit, time only can discover, such Situations occasion an inconceivable Anctiety to Minds impress'd with the Importance of this Subject to the future Honor, Credit & Prosperity of our Country.

ALS, Wynkoop Papers, PDoBHi. Place to which addressed not indicated. The omitted text relates to his daughter Anne Raquet's marriage problems.

Assumption of State Debts

Mr. LEAR, Secretary to THE PRESIDENT of the United States, who arrived in town, on Thursday evening from New-York, informs, That on Monday last, the question, *on the Assumption of the State Debts*, was put in the Committee of the whole House, and passed in the NEGATIVE, NOES 31—YEAS 29—Majority 2.

We are, however, assured, that so essentially connected are the various parts of the SECRETARY'S REPORT, that if the ASSUMPTION does not *finally* take place, the *domestick debt* will *not* be *funded.*

[Boston] *Massachusetts Centinel*, 17 April; reprinted at Portland, Maine; Portsmouth and Exeter, New Hampshire; and Newburyport, Salem, and Northampton, Massachusetts.

Letter to a Member of Congress

CRITICAL and perilous as our situation now appears to be; permit me to address you with the freedom & plainness, which from a mind impressed and alarmed might naturally be expected. In the Institution of the federal government, two important objects proposed, and specified, are, "The establishing justice, and ensuring domestic tranquility." Let me then ask, Sir, what has been done for the accomplishment of the former of these objects? and what are our prospects with regard to the latter? By establishing justice, one thing undoubtedly intended (and that not a very inconsiderable one) was, satisfying those demands of the public creditors to which by solemn contract they were entitled. But has any measure of this justice as yet been administered? After spending one whole session, a session of more than six months continuance, all the justice, and all the relief, which this class of citizens received was, a resolution to the following effect: That it highly concerns the honor and interest of the United States to make some early and effectual provision in favor of the public creditors of the union; and that they will early next session take this subject into consideration. The subject has indeed been taken into consideration, but to what purpose? After more than 3 months have been spent in this session, has there any thing effectual been done? Has Congress as yet even determined any thing upon it? Two or three resolves it is that have passed the house, respecting the public securities. But to this hour, do the public creditors know what justice they are to expect? Do they know whether the promises of government to them are to be fulfilled in whole or only in part? Whether they are to receive the full and just sum of their debts, according to contract; or whether they are to look for one third part on the borders of Lake Superior?

The question I hear often asked, Whence it is that Congress spend so much time, and bring so little to pass? The friends of the government have been ready to apologize, from the magnitude of the matters before them—together with the deliberation and debate unavoidably necessary, to bring such matters to a proper decision. In vain however it is any longer to offer this apology. With many it is plainly a fixed, and indeed it appears to be a growing opinion, that the gentlemen of Congress view themselves as in good business—and the more time they spend, the greater will be their own emolument. Sorry, extremely sorry I am, that such unworthy sentiments should be entertained: But since they are entertained, proper I conceive it is that you should know it, and nothing, I am persuaded, but more dispatch and decision in your proceedings, will ever remove them.

We are now indeed told, that upon the question of assuming the State debts, it is doubtful whether there will be any decision the present session. And if this is not decided upon, the probability is, that the whole funding system will be referred to the next session. Is this the way, Sir, to ensure domestic tranquility? It is now about a fortnight since a report was propagated, that the house had taken a vote upon the assumption, and that it passed in the negative. This report had a most sensible effect—and while it prevailed, gave more disquietude to the public mind, than any thing that has taken place since the insurrection in this commonwealth.[1] And indeed it appears to be the settled opinion of the most thoughtful and judicious, that if the tranquility of the United States is to be preserved, the assumption of the State Debts is indispensibly necessary for that purpose. Certain it is that these debts were contracted in a common cause—that the loans advanced, and services performed, from whence these debts arose, were as much for the defence and benefit of the U. States, as those for which the Continental Securities were given. And evident it must be, that by the grant which the States have made to Congress, of the principal sources of revenue, they have deprived themselves of the means of paying the debts they separately contracted; and have put it in the power of Congress to provide for the payment of those debts. The natural conclusion therefore is, that as Congress are exclusively vested with the means of payment, from them the payment ought to be expected. If these arguments, which have been so well stated to your honorable house, have not their effect, to produce the desired conviction; such effects I am persuaded they will have in some of the principal States, as not only to disturb the tranquility of the Union, but even to threaten its very existence. One consideration only, as a reason for this opinion, among many others which might be mentioned, I shall at present suggest—and that is the attempts which will probably be made to defeat the collection of the revenue. In the trading States, many of the gentlemen who pay the duties of impost, are holders of State Securities. Can it then be supposed, that these gentlemen will continue cheerfully to pay these duties, when their own demands are left unprovided for, and neglected? when their securities lie dead in their hands? Surely not. Already, Sir, I see resentment beginning to rise, and should the apprehension once become a reality, it needs no spirit of prophecy to foresee, that a fixed resentment, followed with a correspondent conduct, will certainly take place. Should the assumption be refused, those who have had pleasing expectations of justice from the federal government, finding [*their*] hopes deceived, finding themselves neglected by that government, will think it no harm to disregard their exactions. Evasions, those arts of evasion which have hitherto been thought dishonorable, will be devised and practised—they will be practised till they become common and reputable. And the final issue it is not improbable will be, the forming of combinations to oppose the collection of the revenue—combinations which will terribly convulse the government, if not totally destroy it. Think not, Sir, that because a good government is instituted, and in operation, we are therefore safe; I have, I confess, pleased and consoled myself with this idea; but of late I find my mistake—much I now see is still depending. My fears hitherto have been from those who from the beginning were disaffected to the constitution, and determined opposers of it. They now arise from another quarter. Of the first and best characters, of those who have been most attached to the national government, and warm advocates for it—among these, many there now are, who appear to be exceedingly disgusted. So greatly are their expectations disappointed; and such are the injuries they suffer; that unless the conduct of government should assume a very different appearance, I see nothing but that a most unhappy alienation will inevitably ensue.

What then must be our situation! When the enemies of the government are still numerous, wishing, malevolently and industriously attempting its dissolution—and when a large part of its best friends are disgusted and alienated? A situation so fearful, as strongly dictates the best efforts of wisdom to prevent our making any farther approaches towards it. That such efforts may be made—that your proceedings may assume a more favorable, a conciliating aspect—that the federal government, upon which are all our hopes, may yet appear with dignity, and answer the important purposes for which it was instituted, is the most earnest wish of your very respectful friend.

[Massachusetts] *Salem Gazette*, 27 April. The letter is introduced by a request from C— M— to the newspaper's editor, Thomas C. Cushing, that this copy of a letter to a member of Congress that "lately fell into my hands" be printed. If the letter is real and not an editorial device, Salem's Representative, Goodhue, would be the most likely recipient.

[1] Shays' Rebellion, an uprising of farmers in central and western Massachusetts in late 1786, against court processes brought against them for unpaid debts and taxes. The movement, led by Daniel Shays (ca. 1743–1825), was suppressed by state militia by early 1787.

Other Documents

Pierce Butler to Thomas Parker Butler. FC, Butler Letterbook, ScU. For the full text, see *Butler Letters*, pp. 29–30. The recipient was Butler's nephew and the younger brother of Edward Butler.

Family news; "I never write any thing of a man that I would not repeat in his presence."

Archibald Mercer to John Langdon. ALS, Langdon-Elwyn Family Papers, NhHi. Written from Millstone, New Jersey.

Paterson has written a line asking Mercer to let him or Langdon know when Mercer could call on Langdon at New York; nothing will prevent him from being there about the tenth or fifteenth of May.

Samuel Meredith to Margaret Meredith. ALS, Read Papers, PPL at PHi. Addressed to "Green Hill," near Philadelphia.

There are members enough who prefer removing the seat of government to Philadelphia, but Southern members are afraid that would make it more difficult in the future to move to the Potomac; New England and New York members "are very willing that such doubt should prevail for whilst they do it insures a stay here for at least some Years," by which time a removal will be more difficult than at present.

John Nease to Elias Boudinot. ALS, Boudinot Papers, PHi. Written from Philadelphia.

Office seeking: any new appointment in Philadelphia; "our mutual good friend" Fitzsimons suggested it while recently in town, and Morris encourages him with undoubted sincerity; will also be supported by Williamson, to whom Nease has written on the subject.

David Sewall to George Thatcher. Summary and excerpt of three page ALS from *Collector* 75(1962):item 394. Place from which written not indicated. For background on John Stone's patent petition, see *DHFFC* 8:46–47.

"Reporting a rumor of the 'Building a Bridge over some part of the River that makes N.Y. an Island' for the building of which Capt. John Stone had applied to have exclusive privileges. He gives news of the political scene, mentioning John Hancock, and Samuel Adams and others."

George Thatcher to Henry Sewall. No copy known; acknowledged in Sewall to Thatcher, 5 July.

Jeremiah Wadsworth to Tench Coxe. ALS, Coxe Papers, PHi. Addressed to Philadelphia; carried by Mr. DeWitt.

Mr. DeWitt is involved in the cultivation of mulberry trees with Prince Aspinwall and goes to Philadelphia to sell them; asks Coxe to help facilitate the business.

Poem. *FG*, 15 April.

Mourns the death of Otis's daughter Abigail ("ABBA"), by "Eugenio."

A Citizen. [Boston] *Independent Chronicle*, 15 April.

"A MADISON, a JACKSON, and *others*" who supported discriminating among securities holders "have probably immortalized their memories"; encourages original holders to mass-petition Congress.

NYJ, 15 April. Wister Butler Papers, PHi. Annotated by Butler to indicate the article for which he retained the issue.

Burke's speech of 31 March on assumption.

George Washington, Diary. ViHi.

Adams, Jay, Izard, Dalton, Griffin, and their wives, with Jefferson, Langdon, Butler, and King, dined at the President's; Mrs. King was "indisposed."

FRIDAY, 16 APRIL 1790

Cold (Johnson)

John Adams to John Quincy Adams

***

The Dangers that threaten this Country, are very serious—I see them exactly in the same light with you. be attentive: but cautious and discreet—neglect not your private Studies and proper Business: for the sake of thinking or Speaking or Writing upon public affairs. Uncertainty of sovereignty, is a great Evil and Danger. and wherever there are more than one pretended to it, there is always Uncertainty. Rivalries of Sovereignties involve Rivalries of Men, and produce Jealousies Envy, Resentment and all the Passions incident to such situations. Governors of States compare themselves with the President Senators of States with national senators and Representatives of states with Representatives of the union. and these Comparisons produce Passions and Heart burnings, which will end in Collisions Disputes perhaps seditions. in short, altho the new Government has had all the Influence on public Prosperity that could be expected, the Danger of its Existence grows more apparent. The People have the Power to pull it down, if they Will, but what will be the Consequence? Confusion, Disgrace, and Adversity. in Proportion as the Beneficence of the Govt., appears the Disposition to destroy it, increases.

I take all the Boston Papers[1] and receive some Letters, but your Information will be peculiarly acceptable. I will send you a Newspaper from hence.

***

ALS, Adams Family Manuscript Trust, MHi. Addressed to Newburyport, Massachusetts. The omitted text relates to John Quincy's law business prospects.

---

[1] Boston had four newspapers: two weeklies, the *Boston Gazette* and the *Independent Chronicle* and two biweeklies, the *Herald of Freedom* and the *Massachusetts Centinel.* The latter changed its name to *Columbian Centinel* in June to reflect its national orientation.

James Jackson to Anthony Wayne

I was honored with your favor by [*Capt. Joseph*] Burnham, and altho I do not carry my ideas quite so far as you do, with respect to our disgraceful Cession,[1] yet I equally disapprove of it. I do not conceive it in the power of Congress to touch the right of Pre'emption, nor would I as a Citizen of Georgia permit them to interfere with it. There is however, no fear of their attempting this, as all the leading Characters in Congress are of the same sentiment. and the right of the State thus far is uncontested: but by the powers vested in the Union, I hold that Congress have the Right of holding Treaties & to point out the mode in which this pre'emption shall be obtained. which is a sufficient check. Its impolicy I have very frequently chatted with you on, and I will only add that let [*Alexander*] McGillivray break out again when he will, I believe he will do it with impunity. After a severe labour in our House, and the tightest combatings (not to call it abuse) we got a Bill for the augmentation of the Troops passed[2]—the evident purpose, for ourselves principally. A Coolness in the Senate made it hang, and a letter from our Governor [*Edward Telfair*] I believe will either reject it & or defeat its purposes. I despair of its getting through. I can only say that could I have possessed an idea of such a *pacific information*, I should have spared myself a deal of breath.

Your Pensylvania Friends (the Quakers) have taken up much of our time, and very strenuously pressed the National Legislature for an abolition of Slavery. We were compelled to be severe upon them, and in turn they have been at us in most of the papers—That topic and the Assumption of the

State Debts have brought the House into a deal of ill humor. The latter was rejected in Committee & the principle is daily losing ground (South of Connecticut) both in & out of Doors.

Three Companies of Troops, the whole we could obtain, sailed from this a few days since. and previous to your getting this, no doubt, will have arrived. We had great difficulty in even procuring those. I hope that they will be sufficient at any rate to spirit up the Planters to continue. What might not Georgia be, would she but help herself by salutary regulations—A fatality however seems to attend her, which I am afraid, must be left to remedy itself. I cannot help feeling for that Country [*Georgia*], you & myself have struggled so hard in arms for; and expressing my resentment at seeing her in the Arms of those who (one or two excepted) never lifted a Weapon in her defence.

A Bill is now pending establishing a Government south West of the Ohio (the N.C. Cession) I know not your Sentiments, but I shall talk with Genl. Knox to push you[3]—If that should not pass if the Superintendant of Indian affairs is worth any thing, I shall maneuvre to run you for that.

You must have had fine Weather for it has been delightful here and from general observations the Weather is most frequent of a similar nature—the Range of Mountains serving as a leader or conductor to the Winds either North or south.

Wishing again to hear from you & the State of Politics & Crops.

ALS, AMs 368/16, PPRF. Addressed to Wayne's estate, "Richmond," outside Savannah, Georgia; franked; carried by Capt. Joseph Burnham on the sloop *Friendship*.

---

[1] The Yazoo land sales of December 1789; see George Walton to John Adams, 20 January, n. 3, volume 18.

[2] Military Establishment Act [HR-50a].

[3] Wayne sought appointment as governor of the new territory.

Alexander White to Horatio Gates

I am favoured with yours of 26th. March but a few days ago—I cannot account for the delay of letters, and in some instances I fear the loss—No Man can be more chagrined at the dilatory Proceedings of the House than I am—It is principally owing to the New Project of assuming the State Debts—I call it a new Project because it is a measure which was not contemplated in the Constitution[1] and which the States, or the People at large have not called for ~~it~~ It was long under debate which might well be excused, but since it has been negatived the Abettors of the Measure seem~~ed~~ disposed to throw obstacles in the way of every other Business—more particularly that of funding the Continental Debt—they threaten us with a dissolution of the Union if such a Measure should be carried—I am much obliged by your opinion of my principles, and flatter myself if you were in the Scene of Action, we shall not often differ in the mode of exercising them—I have learnt many things during the present Session which time would not admit of communicating, and perhaps prudence would forbid me to commit to paper—in general, however I may say I am convinced of the necessity of supporting our State Goverments in full Vigour, if we to the South of Potowmack—mean to appear in any other character than Colonies dependent on two or three Great Cities—Mrs. [*Elizabeth Wood*] White and the young Family desire to be respectfully remembered to you Mrs. [*Mary Vallance*] Gates and Mrs. Thompson if she is yet with you, they look forward with anxiety to the Day when they shall reach Travellers Rest[2] notwithstanding the pleasures and gaiety of this place.

ALS, Emmet Collection, NN. Place to which addressed not indicated.

---

[1] On 18 August 1787 the Federal Convention discussed granting Congress the power to assume the state debts. On 22 August the Convention decided not to include such language in the Constitution. Hamilton later claimed that "in a long conversation which I had with Mr. Madison in an afternoon's walk *** we were both of opinion that it would be more adviseable to make it a measure of administration than an article of Constitution, from the impolicy of multiplying obstacles to its [*the Constitution's*] reception" (Farrand 2:355, 377, 3:366).

[2] Gates's estate in present-day Berkeley County, West Virginia.

Hugh Williamson to John Gray Blount

The Certificates you sent came some what too late for a good Market, perhaps they may come in Play hereafter, I wrote you that I should infallibly oppose the Assumption of the State Debts; it appeard to be a measure big with Injustice to N. Carolina and badly as that State has managed its mony affairs I am in Honour & duty bound to prevent the Practice of frauds against it; I confess~~d~~d I had doubts whether the Rage of Assumption could be stayed, but we have now a majority against the measure, and the Certificate Speculators are at a full Stand.

The Bill for erecting a Government in the ceded Territory south of the Ohio has come from the Senate to the House of Representatives, but a Bill we sent from the House of Representatives for raising more Troops [*Military Establishment Act HR-50a*] I fear will be lost in the Senate.

Inclosed is a Subscription Paper, I hope that during the Sitting of the superiour Court at Newbern you will be able to secure 20, 30 or 40 Dlrs. towards this Work,[1] I have nearly finished the Map on a smaller Scale with Improvements, and shall get it engraved within 4 Weeks after I learn that 100 Dlrs. are received towards the Work. You see that no more than one

Dollar is demanded for the Map, a small Price, the Analisis included, but the Mony must be advanced, you know how faithless People are apt to be in attending to the payment of Subscriptions. I wish to be able to give away about 100 of those Maps and Descriptions of the Country. This coming out as the new Govt. is set on foot must affect the public Mind and turn the Current of migrations towards Tenessee.

ALS, John Gray Blount Papers, Nc-Ar. Place to which addressed not indicated.

[1] Williamson had been concerned about the need for a map of western North Carolina, the future state of Tennessee, since at least 1789. He may have begun work on it then. Only in February 1792 did he have the money on hand for the engraving. He gave all of his rights to the map to Matthew Carey, who published it at Philadelphia in September 1793. For Williamson's description of the area, see Of the Extent and Value of the North Carolina Cession, 1 April, above. The map is a foldout at *Blount* 1:278 (*Blount* 2:181, 238, 313).

N. P. to Messrs. Childs and Swaine

UNDERSTANDING that a bill is now before the honorable House of Representatives, for securing to authors the sole privilege of copy-right [*HR-43*], it may not be deemed improper to offer a few hints on the subject.

The law respecting literary property now existing in the state of Connecticut,[1] prohibits a general and reciprocal trade with the neighbouring states in the Union. When an author sells the privilege of printing his work in two or more states, it certainly ought to be explained in the bill now pending, whether each publisher has liberty to sell those copies printed by him in any quarter of the continent.

The act of the state of Connecticut alluded to, prevents the sale of any book in the said state if printed in any other, even under the sanction of the author, provided he has sold the copy-right of it also in that state; consequently a partial sale can only take place, and an author may avail himself of an undue emolument by disposing of the copy-right in each state in the Union.

The licenced printers of books in Connecticut in that case have an unjust advantage over those of any other state, as will clearly appear from the following instance: The author of the American spelling-book sold his copy-right in the state of Connecticut, in Pennsylvania, in New-York, and in Massachusetts. The proprietors in the three last mentioned states dare not send a single book into Connecticut without being liable to a prosecution and damages, which has already taken place in several instances; proprietors in Connecticut on the other hand, send very large quantities into the states where the other proprietors live, with impunity; the injustice and iniquity of this procedure will, it is hoped, be obvious to the honorable framers of the bill now before Congress, and every honest and upright man join in wishing a clause may be inserted therein to prevent such gross encroachments on their rights and liberties in future.

The writer knows not, but this is already explained in the bill;[2] if not, a small amendment might with the strictest propriety be added, signifying that all books printed or to be printed with privilege of copy-right shall have a free circulation and sale throughout the continent.

NYDA, 17 April, edited by Francis Childs and John Swaine; reprinted at Hartford, Connecticut. The author was probably Nathaniel Patten, defendant in an important lawsuit over the distinction between printing and distribution rights before enactment of the first national Copyright Act [HR-43]. In 1783 the Hartford publishing firm of Hudson and Goodwin purchased the sole rights to the first volume of the three part *Grammatical of the English Language* begun that year by the city's noted lexicographer and education reformer Noah Webster. (In 1786 this volume was renamed *The American Spelling Book*, as referred to by N. P. below.) Webster eventually reacquired only those rights to editions published outside New England and sold them to Samuel Campbell of New York, from whom Patten subsequently purchased 1,500 copies to sell at his Hartford bookstore. Hudson and Goodwin sued Patten for infringement of their Connecticut copyright, despite efforts by New England's most famous printer, Isaiah Thomas, to mediate the conflict within the industry. In 1789 the state's supreme court interpreted the Connecticut statute as described by N. P., holding Patten liable for unlawfully selling books with an out of state copyright (James Gilreath, ed., *Federal Copyright Records, 1790–1800* [Washington, D.C., 1987], pp. xx–xxi).

---

[1] The first copyright law passed in the United States, in January 1783.

[2] The Copyright Act [HR-43] was read twice in February 1790 but was not printed before 30 April. N. P.'s professed ignorance of its provisions argues against his residing in New York City.

Other Documents

Aedanus Burke to Mr. T. S. in Baltimore. Copy; Otho Williams Papers, MdHi.

Encloses copies of the letters that Burke and Hamilton exchanged on 1 April, above.

Tench Coxe to George Clymer. FC:lbk, Coxe Papers, PHi. Written from Philadelphia.

Encloses a patent application from George Parkinson to be forwarded to the secretaries of state and war and the attorney general, who made up the patents board established under the Patents Act [HR-41]; Parkinson has "covenanted" with Coxe to make models of the inventions "and that they were invented by him"; requests that time of receipt be endorsed on the application, and that Coxe be notified in Clymer's next letter; Parkinson will comply with any directions from the patents board as soon as Clymer can relay them.

Samuel Goodwin to George Thatcher. ALS, Thatcher Papers, MeHi. Written from Pownalboro, Maine; "To be forwarded by the Post"; postmarked Boston, 9 May.

Describes desperate economic conditions and scarcity of provisions for humans and livestock; suggests Thatcher raise a subscription in New York City for sending relief in a vessel bound for Boston, to be forwarded to Maine by a coaster.

John Langdon to John Jay. ALS, Jay Papers, NNC. Place to which addressed not indicated. For the full text, see *DHSCUS* 2:47.

Repeats invitation to lodge at Langdon's home while on circuit in Portsmouth, New Hampshire; otherwise, recommends William Brewster's public house; hopes Jay will visit with Mrs. Elizabeth Langdon as much as possible.

James Seagrove to George Washington. ALS, Washington Papers, DLC. Written from Savannah, Georgia.

Office seeking: excise officer or some other appointment; mentions Morris and Butler as references.

Letter from London received at New York yesterday. *NYDG*, 12 June (the date on which members of Congress would have seen it).

Encloses a newspaper copy of an Order in Council "pointing out only what articles may be brought here from your States"; some cotton and mahogany have been seized.

Saturday, 17 April 1790

William Ellery to Benjamin Huntington

I have received the three hundred dollars you sent me by Capt. Brown, and the four hundred by Capt. [*Edward*] Peterson; and the letters and news papers which accompanied them.

I wrote a letter to you by the post, after Peterson had sailed for N. York, desiring you to take an order on the Cashier of the bank in Boston for the seven hundred dollars, if you should not have delivered the four hundred to Peterson previous to the reception of that letter, and in ~~that case~~ you had to procure an order for the remaining three hundred on the Cashier of the bank in Boston. If there should be any difficulty in obtaining an order, send the remaining three hundred dollars by the bearer hereof Capt. ~~John~~ [*lined out*] [*Edward*] Peterson.

I have attended to your information respecting the time when the power of the Loan Officers expired, but still I think that an allowance ought to be made for my services and Expenses, posterior to the 31st. of Decr.; for besides the time I expended in the office after that period, an expence of office hire and fuel &c. necessarily accrued.

I beleive I mentioned in my last letter that any act which Congress might think proper to pass, laying duties on the goods, wares and productions of this State should be passed in time to reach this State previous to the sitting of the Genl. Assembly. Lest I should have omitted it I now mention it. You may depend upon it that an Act of that kind would have a considerable effect upon our Antis in general, and probably might induce the General Assembly to request Congress to let the goods &c. of this State pass duty free into the other States, upon its adoption of the Constitution, which ~~you~~ request would greatly influence the conduct of the Convention. The fall of the year is the time when the produce &c. of this State is shipped to the other States, and then Congress will not be in session; where fore if Congress should pass their act in season, the Antis, who I am sure will be desirous to avoid its operation, will be naturally led to make a request similar to that I have suggested.

I repeat it, such an Act passed so as to be here before the sitting of the Genl. Assembly would be highly beneficial.

The Assembly will sit on the 1st. wednesday in May.

If this State should not adopt the Constitution before the next Session of Congress it is probable that this town, the town of Providence, and some other towns in this State may apply to Congress to be received into the Union, and an application may be made before Congress rises, if the Constitution should be rejected by the Convention. Such an application would alarm the Antis and might endanger the Feds, unless the former should apprehend that Congress would protect the latter against any violence which might be offered to them in consequence of their application. If the applying towns should be received into the Union they would ~~be~~ of course be safe under the protection of ~~Congress~~ the United States; but if their application should fail they may be involved in a war with the Antis. In that event would Congress assist the Feds if they should request Assistance? Please to favour me with your opinion, and that of other leading characters in your house on this question.

The non-assumption of the States Debts will I am afraid occasion great confusion in the business of financiering; and disturb State creditors exceedingly. How the States will be able to make provision for the payment of debts due to their citizens, while their revenues are engaged for the public debt I cannot devise; unless they should go into practices like to that of this State. What methods N. Carolina has taken and means to take to pay her

State debt I don't know exactly. I hope She has not used, and doth not intend to use the R. Island sponge.[1]

Ubi longa est fabula, longæ sunt ambages.[2] I recollect that under the old Confederation there was a time when long speeches were thought to retard public business, and therefore all the members of Congress, save one agreed not to speak longer than 15 minutes.[3] While the galleries of Congress are open spouting may be expected; and perhaps the advantages resulting from open doors may more than countervail the loss of time occasioned by protracted declamations. The noble art of amplification may be hereby learned; and that mode of exciting and engaging the passions be acquired which will be necessary as long as men shall be influenced more by passion than by reason. Besides common auditors measure the depth of a man's understanding by the length of his speech, and the printer of the United States gazette [*John Fenno*], which is a matter of infinite importance, will be furnished with ample matter for his paper while speech-i-fi-ca-tion exists.

But I should recollect to whom I am writing, and that a long epistle may be as tedious as a long speech.

ALS, Benjamin Huntington Correspondence, 1772–1790, R-Ar. Written from Newport, Rhode Island.

[1] Wiping out a debt without payment, by the use, for example, of paper money, one of Rhode Island's infamous "practices" alluded to above.

[2] Where the story is long, the ambiguities are ample.

[3] Ellery refers to the 12 April 1778 "Engagement of the members *** to support Order & preserve decency & politeness" (*LDC* 9:403). See also his 21 July 1789 letter to Huntington (*DHFFC* 16:1095–96).

Benjamin Goodhue to Samuel Phillips, Jr.

I have this moment rec'd. yours of the 6th. and will on Monday attend to the objects therein contained—it would give me the greatest pleasure to be able to inform you of the bussines of establishing public credit, being in such a train as to promise success, tis now by the impulsive power of divers and adverse winds in a perfect whirlwind, and its event of consequence uncertain and hazzardous—tis not the coalescence of the members of society in the contents of a Sheet, which is to diffuse those benefits, expected from Civil Government, but its active operations that are to give the impression, and promise us future happiness, as yet I consider we have nothing more to boast of then the first, and no one can tell how far we are to realize any good effects from the latter, by the arrival of the North Carolina Delagates and the secession of the Speaker and an other Pensylvanian, the Assumption was negatived in the Committee of the whole, and they are now attempting to go on with the other resolutions for funding the Continental debt independently of the assumption, and those who are opposed to the assumption at present are collegued together at present for such a purpose, tho' many of them have frequently opposed any funding whatever, and there can be I think little doubt, but after they have got the assumption out of the way, they will abandon their present pursuit and be willing to postpone the whole bussines, and perhaps increase the present impost a little, and appropriate what may be spared to our creditors—this is unquestionably an evil of great magnitude, for I consider the present a golden opportunity of establishing the Government as far forth as its numerous imperfections will admit by interesting a host of Creditors in its support, which we may never again have, but it is an evil in the minds of the friends of the assumption generaly infinitely less ruinous then the funding the one to the neglect of the other, and which after every hope fails us we must acquiese in and endeavour to obtain, the Conduct of the Pensylvanians on this bussines cannot be accounted for upon any other principal, as I concieve then that of o[*b*]taining the residence of Congress, for its evident they do not wish to reject the idea of assumption, but acknowledge the necessity and the impracticability of carrying the one into operation without embracing the other, but they are striving to hav~~ing~~e them taken up seperately suggesting that in that way they beleive it may be so modified as to be agreable to the whole of their delagation, We cannot consent to the seperation but tell them modify the assumption to your liking in connection with the other. and we are content, thus it seems they wish to have the assumption kept alive waving one way and the other as may eventualy effect their favourite object—N. York Delagation is divided the same as Pensylvania on the question, and probably in the prosecution of this bussines, may not be wholy free of mingling a like object of retain'g us in this City—I think I can discover a little of such policy already operating in their conduct, for I do beleive those two Cities would make most shamefull sacrifices for such local purposes, from the time I first heard that Congress were to meet in N. York I dreaded those evils and expected them, and I clearly see that untill we reside in a more Central situation where attempts for removal should be trivial and ineffectual by the action and reactions being so divided as to destroy each others force, that we never shall be able to decide upon any great National concern in which the Northern and Southern States may be divided, simply upon its merits—this is our present unhappy situation, you know I am apt to be gloomy, and have my fears, but I think no one possess'd of a single spark of Amor patria[1] can be otherwise, for most unquestionably it must be found by every discerning and honest mind that if not the existance most certainly the happines of the

Union depends on our decissions in this all important subject—to be, or not to be,[2] to my mind is involved in the question with a depression of spirits ~~for~~ from our political jeopardy.
[*P. S.*] I cannot but lament that Messrs. Sedgwick & Leonard should leave us at this critical period. how can they satisfy themselves or their Country.

By intreaty we have got Grout to vote for the assumption but your friend Windgate *inter nos*[3] is the most perverse and opposed to those great measures calculated to advance our National Govt. of any man I beleive in Congress and by his conduct does great mischief, and is what we should term in Massachusetts a finish'd insurgent,[4] pray dont speak of it as coming from me for we live together and ~~on free oblg. terms~~ agree in every thing but politicks.

ALS, Phillips Family Papers, MHi. Place to which addressed not indicated.

[1] Love of country.
[2] Shakespeare's *Hamlet*, Act III, scene 1.
[3] Between us.
[4] Probably a reference to Shays' Rebellion, meaning an opponent to strong government policy.

John Langdon to Joseph Whipple

Your kind favor of the 6th. Inst. Ive Recd. by which I see the State of N. H. is much divided as to President [*governor*], I am in great hopes J[*ohn*]. P[*ickering*]. will obtain it, as no doubt he is the most Suitable man, it was no Object with me, I only feared it would go out of Portsmouth—I must be as Tender of our Congress as Possable, but I cannot help sayg. that it appears to me at Present the devil is in them of a truth, but the old Patriots and firm men, will I hope soon lay him, and then we shall go on with the Business of the Publick. I thank you for your attention to My Nephew Harry [*Henry Sherburne Langdon*] who I have a high Opinion of and shall do all in my power to Serve him—I have been lookg. for some Station but theres not a single one offer as yet. if any should I shall embrace it—The Treasurer's Order on you is found, it had been mislaid by him—Inclosed you have it, and I wish you to keep the money for my order except so much as Mrs. [*Elizabeth Sherburne*] Langdon may want for her use—When you Receive this let me know it immediately—that I may know that the Order is Safe.
P. S. Tell our Mutual Friend E[*leazer*]. Russell I shall never forget him.

ALS, Sturgis Family Papers, MH. Addressed to Portsmouth, New Hampshire; franked; postmarked 18 April.

James Madison to James Monroe

***

The House of Reps. are still at the threshold of the Revenue business. The assumption of the State debts is the great obstacle. a few days ago it was reconsidered & rejected by 31 agst. 29. The measure is not however abandoned. It will be tried in every possible shape by the zeal of its patrons. The Eastern members talk a strange language on the subject. They avow, some of them at least, a determination to oppose all provision for the Public debt which does not include this, and intimate danger to the Union from a refusal to assume. We shall risk their prophetic menaces if we should continue to have a majority.

ALS, Madison Papers, DLC. Place to which addressed not indicated. For the full text, see *PJM* 13:150–51. In the omitted text, Madison discusses their joint purchase of land in the Mohawk Valley, New York, and a recent visit from John Taylor to settle the transaction.

George Partridge to Jonathan Ames

If anything has happened which has prevented you from selling my mare 'till this time I desire you would convey her to Colo. Leonard's at Norton [*Massachusetts*] as I have promissed her to him in case she is not sold.

It is uncertain whither I shall be at plimouth on Court week ***

I hope to be at home in June at furthest perhaps in may. if Congress should refuse finally to take upon them the Debts contracted by the States ~~in~~ during the War (of which there is some danger) I expect they will rise soon. but I hope we shall be freed from these partial state taxes which has oppressed our people beyond what most of the other states have felt, and which can ~~only~~ be done only by assuming the State Debts.

[*P. S.*] you may send a Letter to the post Office in Boston which will reach me in 4 Days without any expence or trouble you must direct it to George Partridge Esqr. in Congress New York.

ALS, Miscellaneous Manuscripts, NHi. Addressed to Bridgewater, Massachusetts. The omitted text relates to local court cases and business transactions. The recipient was probably Jonathan Ames (1759–1836), who served in the state militia in 1780.

John Sullivan to John Langdon

Permit me to embrace this opportunity to enquire after your heath and ask how matters seem to go on? whethe[*r*] we are likely to have an Indian war? added to a European one—will Rhode Island Join us or perish alone?

I have lately received some letters from Mr. John Carter Printer at Providence he is as high a federalist as he was a whig when you knew him & is perswaded they will Join? he Solicits to be concerned in the post office way he was in for years under Doctor [*Benjamin*] Franklin & conducted to approbation The Doctor is his great Friend but is too far advanced to do him much Service Now I will Esteem it as a very great favor if you will favor him with your friendship at Head Quarters when you see the proper time & as you know the merit of the man I flatter myself that your recommendation will procure the Interest and Influence of the members of this State who are with you; I should not give you this Trouble but I am bound in Justice to his merit to use every effort to serve a man whom I have known in the worst of times & has ever been a True friend to the Interest of his Country and now is an avowed Enemy to antifederalisme paper money and Tender Laws even though countenanced by the Rhode Island assembly.

ALS, Langdon Papers, NhPoA. Written from Durham, New Hampshire.

John Trumbull to John Adams

Thus far I had written when I had the honour to receive Yours of the 2d instant—and having been obliged to attend a fortnight's session of our Court, & severely handled at the same time by a second turn of the Influenza, which is now universal in Hartford, I have had no leisure for an earlier answer.

***

The Ballance, as adjusted by Congress, [*lined out*] between the Legislative & Executive Powers cannot be given up without eventual ruin to the Government. Without the power of Removal, the President is in fact a Cypher—Washington perhaps during his Day might support himself by his personal influence—But a future President must preserve his importance, only by courting the Legislature, & caballing in the Senate or house of Representatives.

As to the advantages to be derived from some appearance of Splendor in the American Court, it is undoubtedly true, that a Medium must be observed—A parsimonious economy, & democratic plainness is as much to be avoided, as the affectation of pageantry & magnificence. Perhaps we have begun rather below the true medium; but should the Government be supported for a few years, & increase in ~~and~~ credit & resources, a sufficient degree of pomp & splendor would naturally be introduced. I conceive there is little danger on this point, & would only observe that it is often better policy to reduce things silently & gradually to their proper situation, especially when they tend towards it by their natural bias, than to give any alarm to the prejudices of mankind by telling them openly what measures may be eventually necessary. ***

I can witness from my own knowlege of the history of your life, that You have not done yourself more than Justice in the account of your exertions, services & sufferings in the public cause—Nor do I believe those services so much forgotten or disregarded as You seem to suppose—That no strong enthusiasm has prevailed in your favor is easily accounted for. An able Negotiator may do infinitely more service to his country, than a General, who fights one successful battle—but he will not be equally the object of the enthusiasm of momentary praise—To raise the enthusiasm of the People, our services must not only be useful, but brilliant—nay 'tis sufficient if they are brilliant, whether importantly useful or not. As a Writer, You never flattered the passions, or adopted the false opinions of the multitude, but have exerted your pen to oppose both. Such a writer as Payne,[1] scribbling to the passions & feelings of the moment, will for that moment be much more applauded, but must content himself with a temporary & decaying reputation—His *Common Sense* cannot now be read without contempt & disgust.

He who serves the public honestly & faithfully must often serve them against their wills—He must often oppose them, because they will often be wrong—and he must expect the attacks of Envy & at times a general combination to depreciate his merit—From this Washington has not been exempt—A Party both in Congress & the Army at one period almost succeeded in an attempt to deprive him of his Commission, on the pretence of his deficiency in military skill.[2] In the choice of V.P. You had certainly no rival—All that could be done by your enemies was to deprive you of a number of votes. Many of your Friends were duped on that occasion—I will inform You how it was managed in Connecticut. On the day before the election, Col. [*Samuel Blachley*] Webb came on express to Hartford, sent as he said by Col. Hamilton &c., who he assured us had made an exact calculation on the subject, & found that New Jersey were to throw away three Votes, I think, and Connecticut two, & all would be well—I exclaimed against the measure, and insisted that it was all a deception, but what could my single opinion avail against an express, armed with intelligence & calculations—So our electors threw away two votes, where they were sure they would do no harm.

By the way is our Secretary H[*amilton*]. a great Politician, or only a theoretical genius—He has great abilities [*to*] be sure—But I doubt his knowlege of mankind—I have never spoken my sentiments on his report [*on public credit*]—but I really fear some parts of his plan are too complicated—& perhaps at this period impolitic as well as impracticable.

I am exceedingly anxious for the present situation of the Public—Many things are indeed wrong—and I believe we must suffer many more evils, before our eyes will be opened to apply the proper remedy—Yet if matters should not be precipitated, all will at last come right. This is no time to desert the public—Your exertions were never more wanted. I shall be happy in knowing your opinions on the subjects You mention. I never had any other Master in Politics but Yourself, & am too old to begin in a new school.

ALS, Adams Family Manuscript Trust, MHi. Written from Hartford, Connecticut. The beginning of this letter was written on 30 March, and is excerpted under that date, above. In the omitted text, Trumbull answers a question about his genealogy, relates what he knows about the Treaty of Paris (1783), encourages Adams to "complete the history of your foreign negotiations," and recalls Adams's radicalism in 1774.

---

[1] Thomas Paine's forty-seven page pro-independence pamphlet *Common Sense* was published anonymously in Philadelphia in January 1776. Its cheap price, brevity, simple prose, and uncomplicated ideology gave it an unprecedented circulation and popularity at the time.

[2] Trumbull refers to the alleged Conway Cabal that tried unsuccessfully to replace Washington as commander in chief in the winter of 1777–78 through a collusion of Congress's board of war, the Lee-Adams coalition, and Continental Army generals Thomas Conway and Horatio Gates, the recent hero of Saratoga and Washington's imputed replacement.

Thomas B. Wait to George Thatcher

***

I see Brother Fenno—(I will do him; or rather myself, the honour to call him *Brother*, notwithstanding he entered at the Cabin window[1])—I see Brother Fenno has begun to publish the Laws of the United States *by Authority*. I therefore conclude that he is to receive a compensation; and if equal services are done by T. B. W. why should not T. B. W. receive equal compensation?

It appears to me that the Laws of ~~Congress~~ the United States ought to be published in at least one paper in every district, by the authority and at the expence of ~~the~~ Congress.[2] If it is expected that the people ~~will~~ should obey the Laws, is it not absolutely necessay that there should be some certain and regular mode of promulging them? At present it depends on the caprice and whim of myself and Brother Printers, as to which, or whether any of the Laws shall be published in our papers.

Do my friend ~~mak~~ use your influence to make [*blotted out*] publication of the Laws, in the ~~province~~ District of Maine at least, *sure and certain*.

ALS, Chamberlain Collection, MB. Written from Portland, Maine; franked; postmarked Boston, 25 April. Signed "I am your friend forever."

[1] Meaning John Fenno entered the printing business in a roundabout way, not having been trained in the business before announcing publication of *GUS*, with encouragement and backing from Federalists in Massachusetts and the seat of government.

[2] The Records Act of 1789 required that the secretary of state ensure publication of federal statutes in only five different newspapers.

Other Documents

William Blount to John Gray Blount. ALS, John Gray Blount Papers, Nc-Ar. Written from Greenville, North Carolina; place to which addressed not indicated; carried by Mr. Baldwin.

If he had been sure that "Williamson's plan of Congress ~~ret~~ purchasing all the Lands West of the Tennessee would have taken place," he would have struck good bargains for land.

Andrew Craigie to an Unknown Recipient. FC:dft, Craigie Papers, MWA. Place to which addressed not indicated.

Believes assumption will pass when revived on the floor of the House or the entire funding system will be defeated for the year.

Thomas C. Cushing to Benjamin Goodhue. ALS, Letters to Goodhue, NNS. Written from Salem, Massachusetts.

Thanks Goodhue for his letters and enclosed newspapers and "communication of intelligence"; they have just heard about assumption's defeat; "people seem almost ripe for a national division of North & South. Perhaps it may be premature."

Elbridge Gerry to Samuel R. Gerry. ALS, Gerry Papers, MHi. Addressed to Marblehead, Massachusetts; franked.

Has asked William Vans to appoint Samuel or their brother Thomas as inspector of the state's excise for Marblehead, "not for the profit of it but to bring you into view, & no exertion of mine shall be wanting to obtain an office for you"; is distressed at Thomas's situation (spells of blindness) and has written him by the same conveyance.

Benjamin Goodhue to George Cabot. No copy known; acknowledged in Cabot to Goodhue, 5 May.

Nathaniel Gorham to Henry Knox. ALS, Knox Papers, Gilder Lehrman Collection, NHi. Written from Charlestown, Massachusetts.

Hopes attention will be paid to "our Indians of the six Nations" in the Indian Trade Bill [HR-51] to keep them in "good temper"; the Southern

Indians tried unsuccessfully to enlist them in "hostilities" the previous autumn; "those overtures will undoubtedly be renewed & if some attention is not paid to them they may be successfull."

Jeremiah Hill to George Thatcher. ALS, Chamberlain Collection, MB. Written from Biddeford, Maine.

"Court Matters are as usual—some righted & perhaps some wronged"; "as *Good* & *evil* went hand in hand at the beginning, so there was and is a Concatenation to Events ever since."

John Hurd to John Adams. ALS, Adams Family Manuscript Trust, MHi. Written from Boston.

Office seeking: although apprehensive that nominations or recommendations for office "might not be so directly in the Line of your Office," has asked for Adams's support in the belief that "a Word from you occasionally might have great avail"; at Adams's suggestion, will write soon to "my Friends" Langdon and Livermore; business in Boston is slow; "our Ship Building Business seems to want a Stimulus from some Quarter to give the Tradesmen of this Town their usual Hilarity"; many speculators there will be "much disconcerted" by the news of Congress's negative of the assumption; "so have we often been baffled when our Expectations were rais'd to the highest."

John Hurd to John Langdon. ALS, Langdon Papers, NhPoA. Written from Boston.

Office seeking: anything in Massachusetts, Vermont, or especially New Hampshire; encloses a copy of his letter to Adams of 17 March; Adams wrote a friend (Thomas Welch, 5 April, above) that Hurd needed no better advocates than Langdon and Livermore; asks Langdon to introduce his name to the President and to mention the matter to Livermore or "shew him my Letters."

James Madison to Edward Carrington. No copy known; acknowledged in Carrington to Madison, 30 April.

Charles Cotesworth Pinckney to Harriott Pinckney Horry. ALS, Pinckney Family Papers, DLC. Written from Charleston, South Carolina; place to which addressed not indicated.

Encloses letter delivered by Henry Middleton Rutledge for Harriott, which Pinckney believes to be in the handwriting of Butler; Mary Middleton Butler was very ill when Rutledge left New York; assumption "is still problematical—The New York Delegates are pointedly against it."

Jacques-Pierre Orillard, comte de Villemanzy to Jeremiah Wadsworth. ALS, Wadsworth Papers, CtHi. Written from Richelieu Street, Paris. The letter that Noailles wrote to Washington (*PGW* 5:346–47), dated 24 April, was evidently shared with Villemanzy in draft form at least a week earlier. Louis-Marie, vicomte de Noailles (1756–1804), Lafayette's brother-in-law and a colonel in the French army serving in America during the Revolutionary War, was an early supporter of the French Revolution as a member of France's Constituent Assembly during the FFC.

Indebted to the vicomte de Noailles for the opportunity to send the letter; asks Wadsworth, who knows "as well as any body" the merits of the French officers who served in the Revolutionary War, to use his "deserved influence" in support of de Noailles's letter to Washington seeking admission of all those officers to the Society of the Cincinnati; "I love you always very tenderly."

Richard Waln to Elias Boudinot. ALS, Boudinot Papers, PHi. Written from "Walnford," Waln's estate near Crosswicks, New Jersey. For the full text, see *Boudinot* 2:59–60.

Asks Boudinot's advice about the legality of two transactions involving the sale of Blacks as slaves in New Jersey.

NYDA, 19 April.

A publicly noticed evening meeting of merchants at the coffee house recommended a ticket of candidates, including Laurance for federal Representative.

NYDA, 20 April.

A publicly noticed evening meeting of mechanics at Mr. Orson's tavern recommended a ticket of candidates, including Laurance for federal Representative.

Letter from Liverpool, England. *NYDG*, 15 June (the date on which members of Congress would have seen it); reprinted at Boston; Poughkeepsie, New York; and Baltimore.

"In consequence of a law [*order in council*] just passed here, no goods can be imported into this kingdom from the United States, but such as are the growth or produce of those states."

Sunday, 18 April 1790

Violent Snow & Rain (Johnson);
Very stormy. Snow fell two or three inches deep, then hard rain (Cutler)

John Adams to Benjamin Rush

***

To The accusation against me which you have recorded in your Note Book of 17th of March last,[1] I plead not guilty. I deny both Charges. I deny an "Attachment to Monarchy" and I deny that I have "changed my Principles Since 1776." No Letter of mine to Mr. Hooper was ever printed that I know of. indeed I have but a very confused Recollection of having ever written him any Letter. if any Letter has been printed in my Name I desire to see it. You know that a Letter of mine to Mr. Wythe was printed by [*John*] Dunlap, in Jany. 1776 under the Title of Thoughts on Government in a Letter from a Gentleman to his Friend.[2] in that Pamphlet, I recommended a Legislature in three independent Branches and to Such a Legislature I am Still attached. But I own at that time I understood very little of the subject, and if I had changed my opinions should have no Scruple to avow it. I own that awful Experience has concurred with Reading and Reflection to convince me that Americans are more rapidly disposed to *Corruption* in Elections, than I thought they were fourteen years ago.

My Friend Dr. Rush will excuse me if I caution him against a fraudulent Use of the Words *Monarchy* and *Republick*. I am a mortal and irreconcileable Ennemy to Monarchy. I am no Friend to *hereditary limited* Monarchy in America. This I know can never be admitted, without an hereditary Senate to controul it. and an hereditary Nobility or Senate in America I know to be unattainable and impracticable. I Should Scarcely be for it, if it were attainable. Dont therefore my Friend misunderstand me and misrepresent me to Posterity. I am for a Ballance between the Legislative and Executive Powers and I am for enabling the Executive to be at all times capable of maintaining the Ballance between the Senate and House, or in other words between the Aristocratical and Democratical Interest—Yet I am for having all three Branches elected [*lined out*] at Stated Periods. and these Elections I hope will continue, untill the People Shall be convinced, that Fortune Providence or Chance call it which you will, is better than Election. if the time should come when Corruption shall be added to Intrigue and Manœuvre in Elections and produce civil War, then in my opinion Chance will be better than Choice for all but the House of Representatives.

Accept my Thanks for your polite and obliging Invitation to Philadelphia. nothing would give me greater Pleasure, than such a Visit but I must deny my self that satisfaction. I know I have friends in Pensilvania, and Such as I esteem very highly as the Friends of Virtue Liberty and Good Government.

What you may mean by "more than British degrees of corruption" at New York and by Sophisticated Government, I know not. The Continent is a kind of Whispering Gallery and Acts and Speeches are reverberated round from N. York in all Directions. The Report is very loud at a distance, when the Whisper is very gentle in the Center. But if you See Such Corruptions, in your Countrymen, on what do you found your hopes?

I lament the deplorable Condition of my Country, which Seems to be under Such a Fatality that the People can agree upon nothing. When they seem to agree, they are so unsteady, that it is but for a Moment. that Changes may be made for the better is probable—I know of no Change that would occasion much Danger but that of President. I wish very heartily that a Change of Vice President could be made tomorrow. I have been too ill used in the office to be fond of it, if I had not been introduced into it, in a manner that made it a disgrace. I will never Serve in it again upon such Terms. though I have acted in public with immense Multitudes, I have had few friends and these certainly not interested ones—these I shall ever love in public or private.

ALS, The Gilder Lehrman Collection, on Deposit at the New York Historical Society, New York [GLC 704]; FC:lbk, Adams Family Manuscript Trust, MHi. For the full text, see *John Adams* 9:565–67. The omitted text includes recollections of the Revolutionary War.

---

[1] In his letter to Adams dated 13 April, above, Rush paraphrased his commonplace book entry for 17 March, in which he recorded a conversation with Jefferson that lamented Adams's growing "attachment to monarchy" since 1776. As proof of this change, Rush mentioned a letter Adams wrote to William Hooper (1742–14 October 1790), a North Carolina delegate to the Continental Congress from 1774 to 1777 (*Rush* 1:546).

[2] In a letter to James Warren in 1776, Adams admitted that he first composed *Thoughts* in the form of "Some Hints" solicited by William Hooper as the latter was about to return to North Carolina to help frame that state's first constitution. Adams said that he wrote out from memory several more, nearly identical copies at the request of fellow delegates to Congress John Penn (1741–88), George Wythe, and Jonathan Dickinson Sergeant (1746–93), before sparing himself any further trouble by finally consenting to have one copy (Wythe's) printed at R. H. Lee's request (*LDC* 3:559).

Benjamin Goodhue to Michael Hodge

I should be happy if I could give you any pleasing account of the state of the great bussines which has so long engrossed the public mind, at present those who have been opposed to the assumption, the most of whom are in heart enemies to any funding sistem whatever, are link'd together in an attempt, to fund the Continental debt, and avoid the assumption, but they will probably be willing if they can avoid the Assumption, eventually to postpone the whole of the Secry.'s report and only appropriate what can be spared from the impost with a little increase of it, to our Creditors—if it should terminate in this manner it is an evil much to be lamented, but infinitely less ruinous then the funding the one to the neglect of the other, for it cannot be immagined, that one Class of Citizens equaly meritorious and for the attainment of a general object can peaceably acquiese in measures which shall deprive them of property to enrich others while they are left destitute, justice policy & humanity forbids us making the attempt—it may at present be said to be in a perfect whirlwind, and no one can say what may be the event, to be or not to be[1] is perhaps involved in the subject.

ALS, Ebenezer Stone Papers, MSaE. Place to which addressed not indicated.

[1] Shakespeare's *Hamlet*, Act II, scene 3.

Nathaniel Gorham to Theodore Sedgwick

*** The loss of the question for the assumption we recd. last Thursday by Mr. [*Tobias*] Lear via Rhodes Island—the Friends of the Govt. are generally much mortified—the Anti's pleased—I am in hopes however that the Senate will ultimately bring things right—It is here considered as a very unfortunate measure the spending so much time with the Quakers & Negroes especially as the Government is prevented by the Constitution from doing any thing effectual for years[1]—those who feal very sore upon the loss of the assumption attribute it in a great measure to this Negro business—perhaps they may be mistaken—at any rate the Government is rather sinking in the estimation of the People—the slow progress they make in business—is allways in the mouth of the Anti's—and used by them with the Country People. & the great expence of the Goverment dwelt much upon—comparisons made between the immensity of business done by our [*Massachusetts*] Legislative & the little or none done by Congress in the same time—the great questions being now agreed upon I hope the business will pass on more spedily *** I observe that was or perhaps is before you a Bill for regulating the intercourse with the Indians.[2] do let it be sufficiently extensive to apply to the six Nations—for if they should joyn those more Southward it would very much increas the expences of Government.
[*P. S.*] Pray write me the character of M. Walker the Virginia Senator—as I have never heard of him before.

ALS, Sedgwick Papers, MHi. Place from which written not indicated. The omitted text relates to Gorham's illness, negotiations with Massachusetts for the return of part of the Genessee Tract, and upcoming state elections.

[1] For background on the Quakers' antislavery petitions, see *DHFFC* 8:314–30.
[2] The Indian Trade Bill [HR-51]. Gorham referred to the first clause in particular, which provided for establishing frontier military posts and making suitable presents to pacify Native Americans.

Benjamin Rush to Elias Boudinot

Last evening at 11 oClock the great and good Dr. [*Benjamin*] Franklin closed his useful life. Great preparations are making to do honour to his memory by his friends in this city. The design of this letter is to suggest to you an idea of Congress shewing by some public Act, their Sympathy in his death, and their respect ~~for~~ & gratitude for his eminent abilities, and Services to his Country. Such a tribute from the United States will serve to rescue republics from the Charge of ingratitude, and may perhaps stimulate Others to imitate his illustrious example. The Old Congress paid a tribute of respect to the memory of Lord Sterling After the peace for his Services during the War.[1] How much more extensive and important have been the Services of Dr. Franklin!

I ~~have written to Mr. Fitzsimons~~ [*lined out*] If you do any thing in this business I beg that you would not let it be known that the hint for it [*came*] from Philadelphia.

P. S. Suppose you consult Mr. Fitzsimons upon the Subject of this letter—but without letting him know you have heard from me, the Acct. of the Drs. Death, or any thing about him.

The Doctor was unable to speak for a day or two before he died—but retained his reason to the last hour of his life. A pleurasy which ended in an Abscess ~~and which if~~ in his lungs cut his last sinew. He expired without a struggle. I have not heard of any thing that fell from him which discovered what his expectations were beyond the grave. My dear Julia [*Stockton Rush*] wished this day that he had left ~~only~~ a short testimony in favor of Christianity. I told her that if he had, he would have overset ~~so~~ much stronger evidences of its truth—for we are told "that not many *wise* are called," & that "the world by *Wisdom* knew not God."[2]

ALS, Signers Collection, Lilly Library, Indiana University, Bloomington. Written from Philadelphia; franked; postmarked 19 April. For Congress's official response to Franklin's death, see *DHFFC* 8:574–95.

[1] William Alexander, whose claim by descent to the title Lord Stirling was never officially recognized by Great Britain, was a prominent lawyer of Basking Ridge, New Jersey, before joining the Continental Army. He rose to the rank of Major General in 1777 and commanded the Army's Northern Department from Albany at the time of his death from gout

on 15 January 1783. On 28 January, the day after receiving Washington's notification of Stirling's death, Congress passed a resolution acknowledging his services; see *JCC* 24:96.

[2] I Corinthians 1:26 and 21.

William Smith (Md.) to Otho H. Williams

Yours of the 10th & 11th I have duly recd. I believe I told you sometime ago, the result of the Quarrell between the Secy. & Mr. B.[1] it was *however* finally Settled by Six Gentlemen, friends to the Parties, the Secy. wrote a letter to Mr. B. declaring that he did not mean any reflection on the Militia in Genl. much less on that of So. Carolina in Particular, ~~wh~~ with which Mr. B. was Satisfied & declared himself Sorry for the expressions made use of in the house (which were certainly very indecent & unbecoming) & for which he ought to have made an appology in his place—Since the accomodation of this business B. Speech has appeared at full length, in Greenleaffs paper,[2] *which I inclosed to you some days past,* If this publication was by consent or with approbation of Mr. B. perhaps the last offence is as great as the first, it is believed that Mr. [*Eleazer*] Oswald now here from Phila. is active in blowing the Coal, be that as it may the printed Speech is much embellished. I do not expect Mr. Secrety. will take any further notice of this business, from every thing I have heard on this Subject, he has conducted himself with Spirit as well as prudence & propriety.

If you find on equiry, that the man who has applied for my brick tenement is trust Worthy, let him have it at the rent you mention, but you will oblige him to take good care of the trees & garden, And he must give it up by the first of Next March, because by that time garden must be made for the Next year, or if I can Sell it at any time he must turn out on reasonable notice & paying him for what he has done.

Before I left Baltimore Capt. [*Clement*] Skerrett applied to me requesting my interest with you to [*lined out*] give him an appointment in your department for the Port of Baltimore, Since my arrival here he has wrote me Several letters on the Same Subject, Stating his poverty & distress, & begging me to recommend him to you for Some appointment, that he may be enabled to Support himself & family—You Know the man I presume nearly as well as I do, & If you think he merits a place that you can give, will appoint him on his application.

A vessell arrived here yesterday from London in Six Weeks, but I have not heard any News She has brot. but that the Prince of Wales is to be married to the Princes[*s*] Royal of Prusia, Mrs. Fitzherbert to retire on a Pension of £5,000. Ster. ℔ Annum.[3] I expect tomorrows paper will probably give us something more important.

This day, the weather is So bad there is no Stiring out; it is at this moment,

& has been all the morning a very Severe Snow Storm & high wind, I think there has fallen as much Snow this morning, or perhaps more than in the same length of time during any period of the winter—I am afraid the fruit is on[*c*]e more gone in Maryland here it is not in danger, the Peaches not yet in blossom which I Suppose is nearly over with you. Tell Robert [*Smith*] I have Some fears for his apples by Capt. White, who was probably out in the last nights Storm. he Sailed from [*here*] on friday about Noon, yesterday he must have had a remarkable fair Wind, which might have carried him into the Capes of Chesapeake, if not he has had a bad night.

Since the question for assuming the State debts has been again rejected, little progress has been made in the funding business, very great opposition will be made to every mode that can be devised, unless there is a consolidation of the whole debts, & various modifications will be offered for a compromise, all of which will probably fail, Nevertheless I am persuaded, a great majority are disposed to pursue every Step in their power for the Support of Public credit, & that nothing can prevent measures for that purpose, unless it is a hope, that those who have hitherto voted against assumption, may be induced finally to comply, rather than risk the whole.

ALS, Williams Papers, MdHi. Place to which addressed not indicated.

[1] For background and texts on the Burke-Hamilton affair of honor, see *DHFFC* 8:476–80. The "Six Gentlemen" who helped mediate a resolution to the dispute were Henry and King of the Senate and Cadwalader, Gerry, Jackson, and Mathews of the House.

[2] Thomas Greenleaf's *NYJ*, 15 April, was alone among New York City's papers to publish Burke's inflammatory speech of 31 March against Hamilton (*DHFFC* 12:915–16).

[3] Maria Anne Fitzherbert (1756–1837) married the future George IV (1762–1830) in 1785. Because she was a Catholic, the marriage was officially a secret and dissolved (to officialdom's satisfaction) by the Prince's marriage to Caroline of Brunswick (1768–1821) in 1795.

George Thatcher to Daniel Little

You have frequently expressed a wish to read Mr. Neckars Thoughts on Religion;[1] presuming, as I did, the [*that*] he, who had shewn himself so great and upright in politics, must be something more than common in his religious notions—I have it now in my power to put the Book into your hands—I have read some part of it with considerable reflection; and shall only say, that his religion is well adapted to a despotic Government; and the circumstances of an ignorant, distressed people—it is addressed to the passions more than the understanding; and as all people are capable of feeling, tho few can reason—the sentiments of the Book, it may be expected, will do more good in tranquilizing the mind of Frenchmen, than accelerating usefull knowledge among Americans.

Having read the Book, be pleased to offer it to our friend Docr. [*Moses*] Hemingway if he has an inclination to peruse it.

FC, Thatcher Family Papers, MHi.

[1] Probably the English version of Jacques Necker's *On the Importance of Religious Opinions* published in Edinburgh in 1789. The first American edition was not published until 1791.

George Thatcher to Sarah Thatcher

Yours of the 3d. & 7th. inst. have come to hand since I wrote you—I forgot to tell you in my last, that brother Joseph [*Savage*] had been in this City & dined with me—He sailed this day week for Georgia, with his Company—where he expects to tarry two or three year—I had a Letter from our Honoured Father [*Samuel Phillips Savage*] last night was a week informing me of the death of Mrs. Jones; & that mother [*Bathsheba Savage*] had been visited with another Parylitic shock—Of these painfull events your last contained a more particular account.

Inclosed is a Bank Bill for Twenty dollars—Mr. [*Jeremiah*] Hill, [*Matthew*] Cobb or any body, who wants to send money to Boston will let you have silver for it.

I have noted what you say about Captain [*Elisha*] Thatchers disappointing you in not sending our molasses—And can only say—that I suppose he is poor—and therefore claims my pity, rather than incurs my censure—I lived at his house when he was in affluent circumstances—~~and~~ he and Mrs. Thatcher were generous—they were kind to every body—the poor found, in them, a friend—I well recollect going with him, myself, one very cold night, after nine oClock, near half a mile, & fetching to his house an old woman—who he feared would perish before morning—I have known him to send victuals to a number of poor people, thro a whole winter season.

The inclosed Bill, together with fourteen, or fifteen Dollars, that will be sent you by Mr. Minot from Boston will help supply your immediate demands—And I shall be able to forward you another Bill soon—I expect to be at home about the last of may.

I have put on Board of Cap. [*Thomas*] Barnard, who is bound to Boston in two or three days—sixty six pounds of Feathers, with the sack, they are in—And on the morrow, if the weather will permit, for it is now a tremendous Storm of Snow & rain, I shall put on board a small chest, containing my books, a piece of ticking, four yards of mersails [*Marseilles*] quilt, & half a yard of muzlen—for yourself—also some of my cloth[*e*]s—I shall give directions for the things to be left at Cap. Thatchers; to whom I shall write, and desire him to forward by some carefull person to Biddeford—I shall also send your Slippers if they are done—Unice Loring spoke to her shoe-maker, about them last-week—she & Betsey [*King?*] send their Love.

As you have flattered me a little on my taste in buying handkerchiefs, I propose to bring you one more when I return—I love to be flattered by my dear wife—But I dont understand what you say about scolding wives.

Keep up your spirits—be always cheerfull—sing & dance.

ALS, Thatcher Family Papers, MHi. Place to which addressed not indicated.

Other Documents

Abigail Adams to Cotton Tufts. ALS, Miscellaneous Manuscripts, NHi. Place to which addressed not indicated.

It is "impossible to Guess when congress will rise"; its agenda is a "Hurculian Labour"; "members of different States think so widely from each other"; "what one member esteems the pillar, the Bulwark of the constitution an other considers as the ruin of his State"; the vote on assumption "has made much ill blood, and as the members are not yet cool enough to persue the subject, they have taken up other business for a few days—from the conversation which I have heard, I believe it will again be brought on, or Congress will rise without doing any thing more upon the subject"; "Gerry has acquired great honour and Reputation upon this Subject, and restored his former credit."

William Blount to John Steele. ALS, Steele Papers, NcU. Written from Greenville, North Carolina; sent by post. For the full text, see *Steele* 1:57–58; for a partial text, see *DHFFE* 4:364.

Congratulations on Steele's election; Hamilton's report on public credit "has no advocates in this State that I have seen or heard of," although he has seen many speculators in Hillsborough, North Carolina, who undoubtedly support it; office seeking: himself for governor of the Southern Territory and John Hamilton for federal attorney for the North Carolina district.

Nicholas Gilman to Samuel Tenney. No copy known; acknowledged in Tenney to Gilman, 3 May.

Benjamin Goodhue to Stephen Goodhue. AL, Goodhue Family Papers, MSaE. Addressed to Salem, Massachusetts; franked.

"As to the funding and assumption bussines, I can say nothing more then this, then that its on the winds and no one can tell where it will light."

Thomas Jefferson to Thomas Mann Randolph, Jr. ALS, Jefferson Papers, DLC. For the full text, see *PTJ* 16:351–52.

Decision not to assume the states' war debts will be brought on again in a different form; experiencing weather as disagreeable as any he has seen.

Richard Henry Lee to Arthur Lee. No copy known; mentioned in R. H. Lee to A. Lee, 19 May.

Matthew McConnell to Andrew Craigie. ALS, Craigie Papers, MWA. Written from Philadelphia; postmarked 19 April.

"Some of our non assumption Members have written that they are able to carry thro', the other parts" of Hamilton's funding plan; "I have had several hints about some of our members and know not what to think, unless that some of them who are right as to the mode of paying the debt may possibly not be so anxious about it as I could wish"; the Philadelphia creditors deceive themselves: they expect the debt to be funded without assumption, "and in case of the worst in the present Congress that they will put in their own men at another Election"; "the much greater part" of them are against assumption and have taken "uncommon pains in writing to their members and making statements"; urges Craigie to suggest to the "assumption Members" that public opinion would become more favorable if they would "exhibit a set of resolutions expressive of their fair just & equitable intentions, to include the leading principles of a settlement, payment of ballances to Cr[*editor*]. state &c."

John Page to St. George Tucker. ALS, Tucker-Coleman Papers, ViW. Place to which addressed not indicated.

Thanks for Tucker's congratulations on Page's marriage; "I had no idea of ever being so happy—Heaven seems to have formed Miss [*Margaret*] Lowther to make me happy!"; "the Wedding tho' private being attended by what they call seeing Comp[*an*]y. has taken up all my Time—Your Brother [*Tucker*] was our principal Brides man."

Abigail Adams Smith to John Quincy Adams. ALS, Adams Family Manuscript Trust, MHi. Written from "Richmond Hill," outside New York City; answered 1 May.

Is preparing to leave "Richmond Hill" and move to a house on Nassau Street during the first week of May; must refer him to their mother (Abigail Smith Adams) and brother (Charles Adams) for news about politics, which "I do not pretend to understand"; "it seems to be a General observation that Congress set day after day and do nothing."

Jeremiah Wadsworth to Catherine Wadsworth. ALS, Wadsworth Papers, CtHi. Place to which addressed not indicated; signed "your affectionate father & Sincere friend."

"You are quite a clever correspondent—I like your laconic letters"; because of the previous night's snowfall and rain he will not leave the house to buy the beans she has asked for; "you say you are all Sick but I hope it is not exactly true."

Letter from New York. [Portland, Maine] *Cumberland Gazette*, 3 May. This is probably from a letter written by Thatcher to the newspaper's editor, Thomas B. Wait.

"The non-assumption of the State Debts, it is apprehended will embarrass the measures for funding the Continental; and we are not without hopes that this embarrassment will be so apparent as to induce the House to make some provision for the State debts."

Monday, 19 April 1790

Cold (Johnson)

John Adams to Richard Price

*** The constitution[1] is but an experiment, and must and will be altered. I know it to be impossible that France should be long governed by it. If the Sovereignty is to reside in one Assembly, the King, Princes of the blood and principal quality will govern it at their pleasure, as long as they can agree. when they differ they will go to war and act over again all the Tragedies of Valois Bourbons, Lorrains, Guise's and Colignis,[2] five hundred years ago.

The Greeks sang the praises of Harmodius and Aristogiton[3] for restoring "Equal laws." Too many Frenchmen after the example of too many Americans pant for "Equality of persons and property." The impracticability of this God Almighty has decreed and the advocates for liberty who attempt it, will surely suffer for it. I thank you sir, for your kind compliment. As it has been the great aim of my life to be useful. If I had any reason to think I was so as you seem to suppose, it would make me happy. For eminence I care nothing. for though I pretend not to be exempt from Ambition or any other human passion, I have been convinced from my infancy and have been confirmed every year and day of my life that the mechanic and peasant are happier than any nobleman or magistrate or king, and that the higher a man rises if he has any sense of duty the more anxious he must be.

Our new government, is an attempt to divide a sovereignty, a fresh essay at "Imperium in Imperio."[4] it cannot therefore be expected to be very stable or firm. It will prevent us for a time from drawing our swords upon each other and when it will do that no longer, we must call a convention to reform it. The difficulty of bringing millions to agree in any measure to act by any rule, can never be conceived by him who has not tried it. It is incredible how small is the number in any nation of those who comprehend any system of a constitution or administration. and those few it is wholly impossible to unite.

***

FC:lbk, Adams Family Manuscript Trust, MHi; copy, in Adams's hand, Waterston Collection, MHi. Sent to Hackney, a borough of present-day London. For the full text, see *John Adams* 9:563–65. The omitted text discusses the ideological origins of the French Revolution.

---

[1] The first constitution devised during the French Revolution, begun by a committee of the National Assembly in July 1789 (but not enacted until September 1791), shared many important features with the U.S. Constitution, the most notable exception being that it provided for a unicameral legislature.

[2] Various noble families of France who contended for control of the government in the fifteenth and sixteenth centuries.

[3] Kinsmen who were martyred following their unsuccessful attempt to assassinate the Athenian tyrant Hippias in 514 B.C. Long after Hippias's expulsion, Harmodius and Aristogiton were honored in drinking songs, statues, and annual sacrifices.

[4] A government within a government.

Elbridge Gerry to Gentlemen of Charlestown, Massachusetts

I am honored with your letter of the 7th instant requesting an opinion "whether an application in the present session of the Legislature would be seasonable, or probably successful" for a compensation for the losses which the citizens of Charleston have sustained "by the late War."

The Sacrifice of your property on ~~that memorable Occasion~~ the 17th of June 1775,[1] was made at the altar of American Liberty; for the patriotic citizens of Charleston had it in their power, by a submission ~~at that period~~ previous to that memorable ~~occasion~~ event, to have saved their property; & this was generally practised afterwards by defenceless communities which were over-run by the enemy; but as such a measure at so critical a ~~moment~~ period would have relaxed ~~thro'out the Continent~~, the Sinews of american Opposition, & might have proved fatal to our liberties, I am clearly of opinion upon every principle of justice & policy that a compensation should be made to them, even admitting that it cannot be generally extended to ~~the~~

~~citizens who were sufferers by~~ similar events in the subsequent periods of the war.

I shall not however at this time enter into a full discussion of the subject, & in answer to your enquiry must candidly acknowledge, that I think an application at present would neither be seasonable or successful. Congress during the greatest part of this session have been deeply engaged in a funding system, & are much divided on the question of the assumption of the state debts. those who are opposed to it, either are or affect to be apprehensive of the inadequacy of our resources, & should your memorial for a compensation be now preferred, they would urge the necessity of relinquishing this or the funding system from the impracticability of effecting both, & the relinquishmt. of the former would ~~be preferred~~ in all probability be adopted as the ~~smallest~~ least of ~~the~~ two evils. should ~~the citizens~~ however if town of Charlestown ~~however~~ be of a different opinion & send forward their memorial, I will do every thing in my power to obtain for them justice ~~for them~~.

FC:dft, formerly at ICarbS.

[1] Out of a pre-war population of 2700, a few hundred residents still occupied Charlestown, at the base of Bunker Hill, when the British army crossed the Charles River to storm the fortifications erected there. Colonial militia added to that number and acted as snipers early in the battle, causing the British to retaliate by setting fire to the town. Gerry seems to imply that the petitioners were among those who had evacuated the town before the battle, thus slowing the British in their attempt to take the town.

Samuel Meredith to Henry Hill

***

Every thing is going on very heavily in Congress, one party very desirous of adopting the States Debts, & unwilling that any other funding System should take place unless accompanied with it, a more moderate one willing that if *they* cannot be funded after previous restrictions, that the other acknowledged debts should; and I believe a small party that are playing a double part with a View of defeating both, these I should hope were not numerous, it may however all turn out for the best, & perhaps in the scuffle Congress may be placed w[*h*]ere I wish in Philada. for the attainment of which I would suffer a good deal—It would take a great burthen off of Mrs. M[*eredith's*]. mind, save considerable expence & raise our property so as to put us in an enviable situation, however in what ever situation we are placed we must try to make ourselves happy & perhaps we shall attain it.

ALS, John Jay Smith Collection, PPL at PHi. Addressed to Philadelphia. The omitted text is an elaborate salutation.

Pelatiah Webster to Benjamin Huntington

***

P. S. As to politicks, I am glad that all Questions on the report of the Secy. of the Treasury are suspended as you advise, tho' I hear that the Assumption of the State Debts was negatived Last Monday which I think was the only Tolerable feature in Said Report for my part I sd. much prefer a Sponge[1] to the risk of it, for I am decidedly of opinion if those who have Earned the money must not have it, 'tis best to pay none of it to any body seven Eighths of the final Settlements were dead, when they were first Issued, & I had rather the other Eighth Shod. follow the Dead Seven, than to have the Country Loaded with an infinite Eternal Tax to pay a parcel of Idle Speculators & foreigners who never Earned any of it—Every Idea of Appreciating Depreciated paper, is absurd & wrongfull with respect to Every body but the original holder for however Sound the promise may be on which the paper depends, when the paper is Depreciated the promise is broken, the Justice is violated, the sin is Committed, & the nature of the thing admits of no reperation, but payment of Damages & if damages are to be paid, common Sense dictates that they must be paid to the sufferers not to those who never Suffer'd. & of Course can have no right to any reperation. Our Citizens will doubtless bear the burden of payment of all the Just public Debt, if the payment can be made to those people who by their merits & Services have really Earned the money, but tis absurd to Suppose that they will crouch quietly under Immense burdens for the payment of enormous Sums to persons whose demands are founded on no merits or Earnings at all—I think the Argts. of Gentn. in Congress on this Subject are the most Extraordinary, ridiculous & puerile that I Ever heard of being offerd. on any Subject in any Assembly of similar Dignity.

P. S. 2d. I beg Leave to add here one observation, which I conceive of the utmost Importance—viz. Our Citizens are tired of Politicks, are engaged in their several Employments, all which tend to enrich & bless the Country, & introduce the Most desirable Tranquility & are of Course Easily Govern'd. because they are disposed to obey a reasonable govt. & wish for the protections of it. What a pity is it then, & how much to be Lamented that the Absurdities of Congress. Shod. force them into remonstrancy, or perhaps more serious opposition to public Measures which must unavoidably fill the Country with wrong & oppress the people with burdens, for no o[*ther*] Reason than to Seperate Wealth from [*torn*] to annihilate the Riches of the nation in[*torn*] [*illegible*] of a few without any Claim of m[*torn*] & to introduce a few monopolies of [*illegible*] [*torn*] fortune, which has already ruin'd Poland[2] Enervated Every Kingdom of Europe, or at Least Lessen'd their power & respectability, & in particular has for Centuries past Subjected France to Mortifications & distresses infinite, & forced them at Last ~~into~~ for a Remedy[3] into the Risks & Miseries of a Revolution—you are welcome to read all this to Congress if you please I hope Truth will not offend them, but if it shod., 'tis no matter how Soon nor how much they are offended—Set me down for an Idiot, if the God of Reason & common Sense does not Support my Sentiments but if he does fight not agt. him—you may be hem'd in with Speculators & See every thing thro' their Mediums, but you may rest assured that the Most Serious people of the best Sense here that I converse with, view the late debates of Congress with contempt & indignation & I have Every Reason to believe that the same Sentiments will prevail thro' the Continent, & will also doubtless be adopted by foreigners. this Crisis most Terrible & alarming & I hope you will allow that it will Justify Strong Language.

ALS, Benjamin Huntington Correspondence, 1772–1790, R-Ar. Written from Philadelphia; franked; answered on 21 April "as soon as Recd." The omitted text replies to enquiries Huntington had made on behalf of "Mr. B." regarding a Philadelphia woman's eligibility for marriage.

---

[1] To wipe out a debt without payment.

[2] The infamous First Partition of Poland among its three neighbors—Prussia, Russia, and Austria—in 1772 made Poland a byword for political impotence.

[3] Louis XVI convened France's long dormant Estates General in 1789 in an attempt to resolve the nation's dire fiscal situation, which had been aggravated in large part by aid to the United States in the Revolutionary War. The meeting of that representative body for the first time in 175 years was the principal catalyst for the French Revolution.

A Subscriber to Mr. McLean

THE love of truth, and the equivocal answer of the Proprietors of the Congressional Register,[1] puts me under the necessity of troubling you once more, in order to prove to those gentleman I was right in complaining of their being too backward in the delivery of the numbers of that work.

Would any one suppose the charge to lay on the numbers remaining of the first session only? No: it applies equally, and more particularly, on the omission of the numbers for the present session; as it is an undeniable fact that, since they jointly undertook that work, they were to deliver numbers weekly (see their advertisement); and that, at the present time, the last number, delivered the 17th inst. does not furnish the subscribers with debates of a later date than the 23d of February.

Moreover, the materials for the remaining part of the first session being ready, no doubt, in the hands of the first proprietor, can by no means be of any weight against their printing, regularly, the weekly numbers of the present session.

I should not have dwelt so much on the subject, which by the bye, may appear trifling to many, but is considered quite in another light by a citizen who expected, by his subscription, to reap nearly the same advantage with those whose leizure admits of their daily attending the House of Representatives. So far have I been disappointed.

Without acknowledging their *unremitted assiduity to the above work*, I have, on first call, answered their *billet-doux* of the 15th inst. which I trust, is to them the most interesting and feeling part of the business.

NYDG, 24 April, edited by Archibald McLean. The date is based on McLean's notice in *NYDG*, 19 April, that he was in receipt of a letter from A Subscriber complaining about *CR*'s slow publication schedule, but was withholding publication pending an interview with the author.

---

[1] Hodge, Allen, and Campbell.

Other Documents

Roger Sherman to David Austin. No copy known; acknowledged in Austin to Sherman, 29 April.

Letter from Kentucky. *NYDG*, 26 May (the date on which members of Congress would have seen it); reprinted at Norwich and Hartford, Connecticut; Providence, Rhode Island; Philadelphia; Winchester, Virginia; and Charleston, South Carolina.

Major (John) Doughty was attacked by Creek Indians near Muscle Shoals, Alabama.

Tuesday, 20 April 1790

Violent Rain (Johnson)

John Carnes to George Thatcher

*** The Assumption of the State Debts is what we earnestly desire, but fear how it will turn, & are ready to trem[*ble?*] imagining that it will nearly overset the Building.

Our Representatives most of them have done worthily, and cannot come under any blame let this important matter turn as it will; but What must be said of Others?

Business languishes in this State, and multitudes are nearly discourged, and will be quite, if Congress dont go into some measures to help Trade. I never knew Complaints to be so universal before.

Our Elections of [*state*] Representatives are near, when perhaps many new Members will be introduced on account of the ill success of the old ones in many matters. Further, Popularity seldom lasts long. People seldom continue long of a Mind.

Pray Sir continue to exert Yourself in the important matter of the Assumption; for who can tell but we may yet carry it? If we shou'd not, I fear, & dread the consequence, & shall be ready to give up all.

ALS, Chamberlain Collection, MB. Written from Lynn, Massachusetts; franked; postmarked. The omitted text discusses state elections.

Governor Alexander Martin to John Sevier

I am favored with yours by Captain Richardson—and have accordingly made out your Commission.[1] as there has been a very important Question in Agitation in Congress the same is postponed I am informed 'til the Arrival of the North Carolina Representatives that is the Assumption of the State Debts, which if carried in the Affirmative appears to be big with Ruin to the Southern States. I flatter myself if you are expeditious you will be [*in*] Time enough for this Business—Congress is supposed to sit 'til July or August before they rise. while you are there, you will please to favor me with your Correspondence on all Such Subjects you think necessary to communicate. I am obliged to you for the Information given me respecting the Indians. I request you to give your Instruction to the Officers of Washington District[2] that in your Absence they and the Militia commit no Hostilities offensively on the Indians—but in Cases of Attack, & Robberies committed they then chastise the Offenders. That they shew particular Friendship to the Chichasaws. my last Accounts from Congress are that the Senate had accepted the Cession of the Western Country from this State, so that the Indian Affairs will be conducted hereafter by Congress should the Representatives accede to the Senate of which there is no Doubt.

ALS, Draper Collection, WHi. Written from "Danbury," Martin's plantation near present-day Danbury, Stokes County, North Carolina. Place to which addressed not indicated. Sevier did not take his seat until 16 June.

[1] Martin's joint commission to the other North Carolina Representatives was dated at Danbury on 27 February, more than a week before Sevier's election (*DHFFE* 4:361). None of the credentials for Representatives exist in House records; for more, see *DHFFC* 8:533.

[2] A large area that in 1790 comprised most of the northeast corner of Tennessee, including present-day Washington County.

Gustavus B. Wallace to James Madison

Yours of the 10th. I receiv'd. Mr. [*James*] Reynolds is now on his way to Newyork from what he inform'd me his partner got the Lists from a Clerk of the Treasury. Since I wrote you he receve'd some other Lists amounting to 3000 dollars due to the offi[*c*]ers of this state. the person that he corresponds with from this place and remits the Soldiers powers of Attorney to is William J. Vriedenburg No. 40 great Dock Street N.Y. What makes this Speculation worse is that he shews a Soldier a list with a smaller sum than is really due him, and gets a power of an Attorney for the whole that is due him with out mentioning the sum. there are Soldiers that have £24 due them and some less but on his list there appears to be none over Six dollars and this he buys for 1/6 or 2/.[1]

We have nothing new here except a report yesterday that Mr. Burk of S.C. had fought Colo. Hamilton a duel and that the latter had fallen.[2] it is Scarcely Credited since I receive'd your Letter.

Tobacco is low from 18/. to 20 Corn 16/. to 18/. wheat 7/ a good prospect for a great Crop of wheat here.

ALS, Madison Papers, DLC. Written from Fredericksburg, Virginia.

---

[1] Reports from Virginia such as this one from Wallace resulted in the Resolution on Compensation Lists, enacted on 7 June; see *DHFFC* 6:2063–70). For more on this issue, see the letters from William J. Vredenburgh to Laurance, May 1790 Undated, below.

[2] The quarrel between Hamilton and Burke concerning the former's alleged disparagement of the South Carolina militia was resolved amicably. For more background and documents on the Burke-Hamilton affair of honor, see *DHFFC* 8:476–80.

A Farmer to the Independent Electors

of the district composed of the counties of Columbia, Washington, Clinton, and that part of Albany that lies east of the Hudson's river

I HAVE this morning seen a piece in Mr. Barber's paper[1] published on Monday last, under the signature of An Advocate for Freedom—whilst he is, with a liberal hand, dealing out his abuses to Congress, and finding fault with what that honorable body have done, I consider him as only exercising the indefeasible privilege of every *disappointed* politician, who is out of office; which is to croak and grumble, and tell the public, that, was he or his friends once more in powers, every thing would be conducted perfectly right, but not till then!

There is not a single expression made use of by this *advocate for freedom*, that comports with his signature, but the freedom he has taken to traduce the character of Mr. Silvester, our present worthy representative to Congress. The policy of this publication seems to have been intended by its author (as I trust every one must easily discern) to consist in its being offered to the public at this late day—that from the remote situation of Mr. Silvester, (who is now at Newyork, attending the duties of the station we last year elected him to) it will be impossible for him to contradict the many falsehoods contained in it, before the day of election.

It would be too great a reflection on the good sense of the citizens of our district to believe that this manner of endeavoring to stab the character of an honest man, without his having it in his power to defend himself, will be of that injury to Mr. Silvester, which this *advocate for freedom* must have promised himself. Such kind of publications are undoubtedly encouraged by a party who must either conceive them of service, or of no service—if they are of no service, it would have been better they had continued in the malicious breast of this *advocate for freedom*; but, if they are of service, what opinion must the honest and dispassionate part of the community have of such measures?

The writer of this piece, for it requires not the power of witchcraft to know who he is, altho extremely biassed at this moment with party pursuits, too much so indeed for a person in his station, has not (for reasons best known to himself) suffered his name to appear to any publication that should recommend Mr. [*Matthew*] Adgate, as a proper person to represent any part of this state in Congress—and what is the more extraordinary, no other person among us has permitted his name to appear to a nomination of Mr. Adgate—and he is held up without any recommendations but fictitious ones; in which a lunatic or other person absolutely incapable, might be recommended without injuring the reputation of any body.

Upon the whole, if Mr. Silvester's character was not established, beyond the reach of calumny, the *advocate for freedom* might possibly, in some measure, for a moment, hurt his reputation, and injure his re-election—But it is well known to every person who has the least acquaintance with Mr. Silvester, that he has for thirty or forty years, uniformly maintained amongst us, the character of a sensible, honest, religious and respectable man—and his friends feel not the smallest degree of reluctance, that his character and abilities should be put in competition with those of Mr. Adgate, at the ensuing election for representative to Congress.

[Lansingburgh, New York] *Federal Herald*, 26 April. Written from Rensselaerswyck, New York.

---

[1] Robert Barber published the [New York] *Albany Register*, 1788–91. The 19 April issue is not extant.

Publishers of the *Congressional Register* to Mr. McLean

The Proprietors of the *Congressional Register* are sorry that *one* of their subscribers should have reason to complain that he has not received a Number of that work since the 28th February last. They apprehend it must have been occasioned by an oversight in the person who delivers them out, as they have published and delivered, in the course of the seven last weeks, Nine several Numbers.

If the Subscriber, who wrote the piece for the *New-York Daily Gazette*, or any other who has not been supplied according to promise, will take the trouble of sending to, or calling upon either of the Proprietors, they can be furnished with those Numbers which they have not already received.

The Proprietors take this opportunity of informing the public, that Three complete Volumes of that work, together with the Acts of Congress, may be had, bound or unbound, at the respective Book-stores of *Hodge, Allen* and *Campbell*, or of *T. Lloyd.*

NYDG, 20 April, edited by Archibald McLean. This letter was written by the publishers Thomas Allen, Samuel Campbell, and Robert Hodge in response to McLean's comment in *NYDG*, 19 April, that he had received a letter of complaint about *CR* from A Subscriber.

Miscellany

*** And here we cannot help contributing our mite of applause to the Hon. Mr. *Williamson*, for his admirable hints in a letter on education, lately published in the *Federal Gazette.*[1] Why should the chop-logic of schools, the musty volumes of antiquity, and the split-hair treaties of modern word-weighers, engross all the attention of the students? ninety-nine in a hundred of whom have no taste for these things; & had they, their after occupations in life would render the acquirements of them as useless as eyes to a mole. Is it not too much confining our knowledge to mere ideas, to empty sounds, instead of things? Rather let us follow the Hon. gentleman's advice; new range education; let experimental agriculture, together with mechanic arts form a part of the system. ***

FG, 20 April; reprinted at New York City (*NYP*, 24 April).

[1] Williamson to Johnson, 14 September 1789, *DHFFC* 17:1549.

Other Documents

Benjamin Goodhue to Samuel Phillips. No copy known; acknowledged in Phillips to Goodhue, 10 May.

Thomas Jefferson to John Adams. LS, Adams Family Manuscript Trust, MHi. For the full text, see Charles Francis Adams, ed., *Works of John Adams*

(10 vols., Boston, 1850–56), 8:496. The letter is identical to Jefferson's letter to Benjamin Franklin of 31 March, *PTJ* 16:283.

Asks for any facts he may remember (as commissioner for the Treaty of Paris of 1783) identifying the river intended as the boundary between Maine and Canada.

Louis Guillaume Otto to Thomas Jefferson. ALS, Notes from Legations, Consular Correspondence, State Department Records, Record Group 59, DNA. For the full text, in French, see *PTJ* 16:354–55. Otto's letters included in *DHFFC* were usually written over the course of days, and even weeks, following the day they were begun. On 30 April Jefferson wrote La Luzerne that Washington had ordered a gold medal and chain as such a testimonial, and that it would be sent as soon as it could be prepared (*PTJ* 16:394).

Reminds Jefferson that (Anne-César, chevalier) de La Luzerne never received any testimonial of satisfaction from the United States for his service as French minister plenipotentiary, as is the custom in Europe; suggests that a land grant on the Ohio River or some other inexpensive testimonial would be easy to obtain if, through Jefferson's intercession, the President communicated to the Senate the attachment that all members of Congress must feel for La Luzerne; were it obtained, Otto would consider it a proof of Jefferson's goodwill if the message were sent on the English packet due to leave on 6 May.

Daniel Hiester, Account Book. PRHi.

Traveled to Harlem by coach and had dinner.

William Samuel Johnson, Diary. Johnson Papers, CtHi.

"Visits."

Wednesday, 21 April 1790

Fine (Johnson)

John Adams to John Quincy Adams

I am not willing you should want Information from the Seat of Govt. but I can do little more than send you a Newspaper.

This Day twelve months I first took the Seat in which I now sett, and I have not been absent one Moment, when the Senate has been sitting, excepting one Day when my own Salary was under Consideration.[1] This Confinement will injure my health, if I cannot soon take a Journey.

Mr. Jefferson has arrived and the offices are all full—The President went yesterday to Long Island for a few days.

The assumption of the State Debts labours, but it is the opinion of many that it will be agreed to at length.

The Circuit Court will sit in Boston soon. The national Courts are proceeding, in all the States. in this City the Circuit Court tryed some Persons for a Species of Pyracy, and passed sentence, but not of death.[2]

The Elections, of senators and Reps. for next year will soon show the sentiments of the People.

ALS, Adams Family Manuscript Trust, MHi. Place to which addressed not indicated.

---

[1] Langdon presided as *president pro tempore* of the Senate in Adams's absence on 7 August 1789 during discussion of the Compensation Act.

[2] For an account of the crime, see William Smith (Md.) to Otho H. Williams, 21 March, above.

William Bradford to Elias Boudinot

"Your letter by Col. Hartley furnishes me with a melancholy picture of the situation of the national Councils. Tho' I have never yet been satisfied about the propriety of an immediate assumption of the State Debts yet I almost wish that the Union temper & dignity of the house had been preserved by the adoption of that measure . . . If the funding of the debt does not take place this Congress, the game is up & public credit will be but a name . . . If the system is not complete now, it is certainly in extreme danger of being permitted to die in peace . . ."

"The people of the different states are by no means so much agitated with these questions nor so anxious about their determination as these gentlemen seem to imagine; much less does their conduct authorise any of their representatives to declare that 'the Union will be dissolved,' or to hold out the threats of resistance. This language however, tho' perhaps the mere ebullitions of resentment, holds us up to the Nations of Europe as a divided people, incapable of coalescing, and, like Nebuchadnezzar's image, ready to be broken in pieces. . . . Dr. Franklin's funeral gave us some occupation yesterday: tho' there was nothing singular but the crowd, which was computed to amount to 20,000 people. I understand the philosopher died very wealthy."

Three page ALS, excerpted in *Parke-Bernet Catalog* 1878(1959):item 2994 (through "die in peace . . .") and *Henkels Catalog* 683(1892):item 65. Place from which written not indicated. The ellipses are in the sources.

Letter from Boston

When it is considered that Congress have a new path to strike out in all their measures—have to reconcile various and contending interests—to regulate the concerns of a nation—to secure public faith, and to choose from a variety of propositions those that shall best subserve the interest, not of a single state, or the trade of a single state (as has been selfishly suggested they ought) but of the great whole; when a generous public thus contemplates, though they may wish greater dispatch, they cannot reasonably expect it. Those who suggest that Congress do not sit more than four hours in a day, &c. make unfair suggestions. It is a rule of the house, that during the hours of session all the members shall be present. Therefore the committees have no time to sit, deliberate upon, and prepare the bills, resolves, &c. committed to them, but in the hours before and after the sitting of the house. If the people wish that their representatives should act with dispatch, the best mode to promote it, would be to stop troubling them, with the innumerable private petitions, memorials, &c. which continually are arresting their attention from the public business.

NYDA, 30 April; reprinted at Albany, New York; Philadelphia; Baltimore; and Edenton and Fayetteville, North Carolina.

Other Documents

Abigail Adams to Mary Cranch. ALS, Abigail Adams Letters, MWA. Written from "Richmond Hill," outside New York City; addressed to Braintree, Massachusetts. For the full text, see *Abigail Adams*, pp. 45–46.

Thought it best to talk to Knox about an appointment for (Joseph) Cranch "before I said any thing to Mr. A[*dams*]. about the place as the arrangments which the Genll. might make would prove more advantageous to him and require his attention on the Spot"; Adams encloses the letter that Knox promised to write for Cranch, regarding work at West Point or Springfield, Massachusetts; asks where she can hire "a Boy of a dozen years"; "Such a wretched crew as N. York produces are Scarcly to be found in any city in Europe. I am so much discouraged by every Body here that I dare not attempt to take one"; must dress for tea that afternoon, when Martha Washington, Lady Elizabeth Temple, Ruth Dalton, Mary King, and several other ladies are her guests.

Benjamin Goodhue to Stephen Goodhue. ALS, Goodhue Family Papers, MSaE. Place to which addressed not indicated.

Sends some clothes, books, and apple tree grafts by boat set to sail the next day; "the propositions for funding the Continental debt independently of the assumption, when they will see this error, I dont know."

Benjamin Huntington to William Ellery. No copy known; docketed on Ellery to Huntington, 19 April.

Benjamin Huntington to Pelatiah Webster. No copy known; acknowledged in Webster to Huntington, 10 May.

Edmund Pendleton to James Madison. ALS, Kennedy Papers, MdHi. Written from Virginia. For the full text, see *PJM* 13:154–57.

Recalls events in Virginia during the Stamp Act crisis; the debate over assumption "has fix'd a Suspicion of a Government by a Junto"; the federal government's power "to make the General Assumption will be questioned, & evils of great Magnitude are to be apprehended"; if it had been limited to debts incurred for the general welfare, assumption could have been less objectionable although still liable to abuse; since beginning the letter, has heard that assumption was rejected, which may lessen the people's suspicions of a junto "when they see it don't constantly prevail"; thinks the "persevering temper of the East" will continue to advocate assumption "in every possible shape."

Thomas B. Wait to George Thatcher. ALS, Chamberlain Collection, MB. Written from Portland, Maine; franked; postmarked Boston 25 April.

(Richard?) Kimball has been riding post between Pownalboro and Portland for no fee, in hopes of a future compensation; thanks for loan of money, to be directed to Boston; asks Thatcher to enquire whether John Fenno procured his print type from a domestic manufacturer and at what price; "so Congress will not *assume* the State debts. I fear their Constituents will *presume* some few things not much to the advantage of that hon[*orabl*]e. Body. *What in God's name have you been doing, Gentlemen?*"

Letter from New York. [Boston] *Independent Chronicle*, 29 April; reprinted at Portland, Maine, and Edenton, North Carolina. Knox's militia plan of 18 January is in *DHFFC* 5:1435–57.

"You would laugh if you was here, to see the parade and farcical dignity assumed by our great gentry in this city. The *militaire* importance, with routs and other imitative follies of the English, are truly ridiculous. The pompous militia plan is emblematical of what some of our new-fangled nobility are aiming at."

Letter from Baltimore. *NYDG*, 30 April. The piece was an extract of a letter received by A Subscriber from an unnamed correspondent a few days before 21 April.

It is reported that the corporation of Georgetown, Maryland (present-day Washington, D.C.) intends to petition Congress to raise and support a company of soldiers to enforce the collection of federal duties, from which the local merchants claim exemption by the state's law of incorporation.

THURSDAY, 22 APRIL 1790

Fine (Johnson)

John Adams, Dialogues of the Dead

Charlemain[1]__Frederick [*"the Great"*]__Rousseau__[*James*] Otis

Rousseau, have you seen Franklin, since he passed the River? or has the Boat been too full of Passengers to bring him over?[2]

Otis. I know not. I have very little Curiosity to know. I ~~care nothing~~ have no solicitude for Steel Rods nor Iron Points. I am very glad his Points were not over my head: They might have detained me in the Regions of Mire, for twenty or thirty years longer.[3] The fluctuating flashes and flourishes of chimical and ~~flu~~ electrical Experiments have no Charms for me. ~~They are as~~ transitory as sparks meteors ~~and Sparks~~, as ~~frieflies~~ fireflies Catterpillars and sea shells. ~~all this is~~ the frivolity and Foppery of Swine. ~~It is~~ Morality! eternal Morality, ~~it is~~ permanent Intelligence, ~~it is~~ the Policy and Divinity of the Universe. ~~That has my Doctor~~ The Intellectual and Moral World. These have ever commanded my Attention and Devotion.

Rousseau. ~~They were mine too~~ And mine—But these are very apt to have the same Effect upon all Men as they had upon us. They ~~produce a little Extravagance~~, often produce a Melancholly then an Extravagance and at last a Delirium

Frederick But had not Franklin a Genius for Morals?

Otis. He told some very pretty moral Tales from the head and some very immoral ones from the heart—~~but his heart~~—I never liked him: so if you please We will change the subject. Populus vult decipi, decipiatur[4] was his Maxim.

Frederick. With all my heart—I never thought any Thing of him, as a Politician. Congress forced me to make a Treaty with him against my Inclination.[5]

[*lined out*] indeed his Philosophy never made any Impression on me—it was chiefly hypothetical and conjectural—I did not think it worth my Notice in my History of my own time.[6] My Attention was drawn to [*lined out*] others.

Otis. Indeed my Pride was not a little flattered at the Notice, taken by so great a Prince of a [*lined out*] Nation which I had so great a hand in forming.

Frederick. Compliments are not the Ton here—if they were I should be at no loss to return yours with Interest. You have not put all our crowned heads to the block. ~~We~~ We have done nothing in Comparison with you. our successors upon Earth must all go to school to your Pupils, who went to school to you. as to myself, I feel small, and humble in your Presence—at infinite hazard, Pains and Anxiety I scattered Blood Horror and Desolation round about me: and indeed ~~was~~ thought myself obliged to do so in self Defence. I was the greatest warrior and statesman in Europe: but if Effects are to be the Measure of Grandeur you should be admitted the Greatest Statesman that ever lived. Your Town of Boston has done more than Imperial or Republican Rome: and your Harvard Colledge, than the school of Caiasius and all the Doctors of the Sorbonne.[7] Even my Brother Charlemain must acknowledge his Inferiority to you.

Charlemain. Very true. I cannot recollect my own Grandeur, my Vast Vienes, ~~by~~ my unbounded designs, and my wonderful success, with out blushing. The detestible Maxim, Mr. Otis which you imputed to one of your Contemporaries, Populus vult decipi, decipiatur, was my Maxim and I owed to it most of my Greatness. Leo [*"the Great"*] gave me the Title of Cæsar and Augustus, and Magnus: and instituted that Superstitious Farce of Consecration, which cheated all Europe for ~~Nine~~ many hundred hundred Years. I, in my turn, transferred to the Pope, the authority which the Roman Senate and People had anciently devised of electing and confirming the Emperors. This infamous Bargain, as contemptible as the Artifices of two [*lined out*] Jockeys, established the temporal and spiritual Monarchies of Europe for ~~near 1000~~ many hundreds of Years. But Providence reserved for you the honour of beginning a system of Policy, which has already almost and will infallibly e'er long totally overturn the whole Conspiracy of Charlemain and Leo.

Otis. Your Majesties do me too much Honour. I lived and Acted it is true in a most important Moment. I was fashioned by Providence as a very proper Wedge to split a very hard Knot. But I was only one of many. ~~Rousseau was~~ our Friend Rousseau had no small share in this Revolution.

Rousseau. I did nothing more than propagate the Principles of [*John*] Lock. And Voltaire himself, whom I never loved nor esteemed very much did as much as I did.

Frederick. The bewitching Charms of Voltaies Wit, and the enchanting

Grace of your Eloquence, made his and your Writings universally read; and as you both filled every Volume and almost every Page with some Recommendation of Liberty and Toleration, your Writings contributed very much to propagate such sentiments among all Mankind. But Reason Wit, Eloquence can do no great Things.[8] Otis began a vast system of Policy which has sett the Reason and the Passions of all Men at Work to promote your Principles.

Rousseau. My Principles were those of Lock. But I swallowed Lock with too little Rumination. Otis's Pupils the Americans have convinced me, that Lock and I, though our Principles of Liberty were good, were totally mistaken in our Ideas of Government, and the Frame necessary to produce and preserve equal Laws.

Otis. This always surprised me. I was enraptured with the sagacity of Lock and the Eloquence of Rousseau—Yet you seemed to me, never to have considered the human heart or the History of the World. how could an observation so obvious, escape You. The Passions of the human heart are insatiable, an Interest imballanced; a Passion uncontrouled, in society, must produce disorder and Tyranny. You have nothing to do therefore to preserve equal Laws but to provide a Check for every Passion, a Reaction to every Action a Centinel to every Interest, which counteracts the Laws.

Rousseau. it is now very plain to me—but like my Master Lock I did not see it, when on Earth.

Otis. Your Error, as well as your Masters, ~~have been~~ may be corrected: but there are other more dangerous still, ~~which have not~~ which may be more difficult to eradicate—and here I cannot acquit your Majesty of Prussia. I fear that some other Errors may do more harm ~~that~~ than the Intrigue of Charlemain, which he just now so candidly confessed and so ingenuously repented. I mean the Resurrection of a future state, and the ~~Ta~~ Tendency to deny or doubt the moral Government of the World, and the Existence of an all perfect Intelligence. This august Company must allow me, to do more honour to Palestine and Jerusalem, than You have done to Boston and Cambridge. These Plans in my opinion would have no merit at all, if they had not respected those. Thou shalt love the supream ~~and~~ with all thy heart and thy Neighbour as thyself, is a Maxim of eternal Phylosophy. it is the sublime Principle of Right order and happiness in the Universe. Affection and Confidence in the Eternal, Resignation to his Will and affection and Beneficence to his Works as far as We are intelligent active and free, must be Truth Duty and Felicity. How then could such Characters as ~~these~~ those in this Company give any Countenance to Encyclopædists,[9] Athiests and theists, in destroying or weakening the Faith of Mankind, in this divine Philosophy?

Charlemain. A confused and uninlightened sense of ~~this~~ these important

Truths really was one of my Temptations to my unworthy Maneuvre with Leo. so much I must say in Palliation of my enormous Error.
Frederick, Rousseau. We both stand convicted.
Frederick—I deserved ~~to be damned~~ the extreams of Punishment at least ~~to suffer long in Purgatory~~ a very lasting Purgation. But am filled with Gratitude equal to my Remorse. Gratitude that Goodness could forgive when Justice might have punished.
Rousseau. I was less guilty than you—Yet I have infinite cause of Gratitude also.
Frederick and Rousseau—if it were permitted We would chearfully return to Earth and undergo the Pains and Anxieties Anxieties of Life once more, if We might have an opportunity of ~~expiating~~ expiating our Faults by warning Mankind against our Errors.

Ms., hand of Adams, Adams Family Manuscript Trust, MHi. Based on a literary device made famous by the ancient Greek rhetorician Lucian (b. ca. 120), this whimsical piece is an imaginary dialogue among Charlemagne, first emperor of the Western Roman Empire; Frederick the Great; Jean-Jacques Rousseau; and James Otis, Jr. Adams annotated "This little thing" on 24 November 1813, indicating that it was written at "Richmond Hill" (or "Church Hill") "in an Evening after the News arrived" of Benjamin Franklin's death. The editors date the document based on indications that news of Franklin's death in Philadelphia on 17 April reached New York on 21 April. "The moment when it was written," Adams concluded, "is the most curious Circumstance attending it."

---

[1] Charlemagne (ca. 745–814) is known as the founding father of Europe for expanding his Frankish Empire into a unified Holy Roman Empire, of which he was crowned first emperor by Pope Leo III, "the Great," in 800.

[2] In Ancient Greek myth, the Styx was one of the rivers of the underworld, across which the ferryman Charon conveyed the dead from the land of the living.

[3] James Otis (1725–83), older brother of Samuel Allyne Otis and Mercy Otis Warren, was a leader of Boston's revolutionary movement until he was injured in a brawl, declared insane in 1771, and retired from public life. He was living in a friend's farmhouse in Andover, Massachusetts, when he was killed by a lightning bolt, hence the allusion to Franklin's life-protecting lightning rods.

[4] "The people wish to be deceived, let them have their wish"; attributed to Giovanni Caraffa (1476–1559), Catholic archbishop of Naples, who organized the Italian Inquisition before his election as Pope Paul IV in 1555.

[5] Franklin signed a Treaty of Amity and Commerce with Frederick's Prussia on 9 July 1785, which was unanimously agreed to by Congress on 17 May 1786 (*JCC* 30:269–85).

[6] *L'Histoire de mon temps* (Berlin, 1788).

[7] Caiasius may be Adams's misspelling of Canisius (1526–97), a prominent Catholic theologian of the Counter Reformation, who founded Jesuit universities throughout Europe. The Sorbonne is the colloquial name for the University of Paris, founded ca. 1255 by the French theologian Robert Sorbon (1201–74).

[8] A paraphrase of Frederick's own *Histoire*; see Adams to Benjamin Rush, 4 April, n. 2, above.

[9] The group of French philosophes who collaborated under the direction of Denis Diderot (1713–84) in the Enlightenment's landmark categorization of modern knowledge published as the *Enclycopédie* (1751–72).

George Clymer to Tench Coxe

The mail being longer on the road than usual it was not till yesterday in the afternoon that I receivd. your letter with the inclosed petition of Mr. Parkinson's[1]—I called with it on Mr. Jefferson this morning and got the receipt of it endorsed /the 22d/—Mr. Jefferson says the law requires the Models &c. to be sent to him before a patent can issue, but that he wishes they may not come 'till the arrival of the Attorney General which would be soon, but precisely when he could not tell Mrs. [*Elizabeth Carter Nicholas*] Randolph being at present ill—The house have got through the secretary's alternatives and will proceed at a slow but I fancy a certain pace in funding the national debt—independently perhaps of the state debts, the assumption after the blow it received the other day not having yet recovered—The house are now in full debate with a cleared gallery—public notice being first given that they were going into the private and secret business of a military establishment.[2]

ALS, Coxe Papers, PHi. Addressed to Philadelphia; franked; postmarked 23 April.

[1] George Parkinson's application to patent his improvements on textile mills.
[2] The House considered the Senate amendments to the Military Establishment Act [HR-50a].

Thomas Fitzsimons to Tench Coxe

Our progress here is so extreamly slow that the Events of the Week will hardly furnish sufficient Reason for troubling you with a letter it may however be well Eno. when nothing better offers that we have done no other Mischief, than Waste our time. & some of the public Mony—Yesterday the three proposals or Conditions rather for receiveing on loan the Continental debt passed the Committee. they stand Agreed to as Reported by the Secy. except that the terms of Redemption in the 2d. & 3d are altered to 6 instead of 4½ dollars. & the Equivalent in the 3d is 33½ dolls. at the end of 7 Years instead of 26½ at the end of 10. an Alteration I contended for as most Acceptable to the Creditors & more beneficial to the U.S.

We have ever since been disputeing about the assumption under Some Modifications proposed and tho I believe that business now hopeless. it will be Argued in the Committee a day or two longer Mr. Madison to day Argued against for an hour & in his Elegant Manner said every thing that Could with propriety be urged [*illegible*] I think something more than words bear the test of examination—And tho I do not know that he made any Proselytes. he has at least Confirmed his Associates & furnished them with Additional

Reasons—some things dropped from him in debate which if Acted upon will be very likely to disappoint altogether the funding System he strongly reprobated excise and as that is a fund relyd on by others if we should divide upon ~~that~~ it We Might disappoint~~ment~~ the Whole—I hope however this will be avoided for tho I shall think it unfortunate that the assumption should not be made I should esteem it doubly so. that none of the debts are provided for & will do every thing in my power to prevent so great an Evil. None of my friends except yr. Self have informed me how the assumption was Considered in Pensylva. & I took my Opinion from the publications & the little Observation I had time to make. my Rule of Action however is if I see my way clear not to be deterred from pursuing it by present Opinions if a Measure is Right it will prove itself so and haveing no Violent predilection for this Kind of life I Value the less a Change in the Opinion of my Constituents. I have long persuaded myself that the honor they Confer is too Dearly purchased.

I hear little indeed about the politicks of the State which in the present Year will be very Important. our Citizens must be unwise if they do not Remember that a Good Governmt. is little worth if not Well Administred—nor should the Genl. Government draw off their attention from their own [*torn*] friends are often late in takeing their [*torn*] but when Roused to Action like [*b*]odys [*torn*] set in Motion they move with Accumulated Velocity—Mr. Clymer has attended to your Commands about which he Called in Mr. Jefferson this Morning. you may depend the business shall not be Neglected.

ALS, Coxe Papers, PHi. Addressed to Philadelphia; franked; postmarked 23 April.

Thomas Fitzsimons to Benjamin Rush

Your favor of the 20 was the first intimation I had of Doctr. [*Benjamin*] Franklins death. tho I had been led to expect it, by prior advices I think it happy that he is released from the painfull situation in Which he has been, for some time past. Now he is gone I have no doubt more Justice will be done to his Character (in his own Country) than was while he lived—in other Countrys he will be Celebrated—the hint you gave[1] has been attended to. And this day the Resolution it put was Agreed to in our house We did not think it prudent to hazard it without previous preparation Which Occasioned its being delayd—the event proved the propriety of the precaution for tho it was not Opposed the Acceptance was not as Cordial as might have been wished his Eastern brethren were not its supporters I have had no oppy. of Inquireing whether the senate have followd our example. the preparatory

Inquirys was first to be made because a Rejection would be dishonorable to all partys. We preferred the Motion in our house being made by some other than a Pensylvanian Mr. Madison undertook it cheerfully & was warmly interested in it, on all this I shall ~~mak~~ avoid Makeing observation but it Suggests some Which all public men in Popular Governments have had occasion at some period of their lives to make.

We progress very slowly indeed with our finance business and I think Your wishes on that Subject stand a good chance of being Realised if they should I shall conclude it to be for the best tho my wishes have been otherwise.

***

ALS, Miscellaneous Manuscripts, PPAmP. Addressed to Philadelphia; franked; postmarked 23 April. A postscript copies verbatim Madison's successful resolution in the House that members wear the customary black arm band in mourning for Franklin's death for one month (*DHFFC* 3:375).

---

[1] Rush's letter to Fitzsimons, 20 April, is unlocated, but it probably included the same "hint" Rush made to Boudinot in his letter of 18 April, above, regarding a congressional tribute to Franklin's memory.

James Madison, Notes for a Speech

Assumption of state debts
1. No security for final balances
2. Criterion of federalis~~t~~m—
—consistent with former argts.
—inconsistency on other side
—distrust of States—[*goes?*] to private debts &c.—
3. Criterion of nationality
—threat from Cont. vs. fedl. Dbts. & Govt.
—offend $^{1}/_{2}$ St[*ate*]s.—especially N. Carolina
no Sts. call for it but S. Carolina
—concentrate debts still more in *one part*
—prolong the national evil of Nat. debt
Sts. can pay sooner
—not true that more funds given up than proportion of fedl. quotas
—case of Genessee lands[1]
4. Not just—proper to know its operation on every State. Virga. Col. Bland
—paid not less during war
—quotas
—paid off Her own debt
—ultimately Creditor

5 yet advance now—& beyond ratio of 1/6
—will pay ~~more than~~ near 1/5 } ratio 1/6
—little more received 1/7
—Massts. pay little more than 1/7 } ratio 1/7 & 1/2
—receive more than 1/5
This disproportion increased by
—drawbacks on salt &c.
—by coasting & land imports
—by probable accumulation of State Dbts.
~~6~~ Col. Bland supposes
1. assumption to look
2. Virga. not to pay after it
Relieve State from 1/7 by imposing 1/5—3 Mil. 5 dr.
plundered—District from due share of 3 by im[*pose?*]
more than share of 5. Million
6. Mode of excises obnoxious
—unequal among Sts. & individls.
~~—unequal to manufacturers~~
—arbitrary & vexatious
—frauds & perjuries, partly.
—Seller charge more than tax
—more expensive in collection
in G. B. 10 Pt. direct taxes less than 3 Pt.
—discourage manufactures
—~~These reasons will soon~~ America has run from one extreme to another—
case of Maryland Constitution
7. Not equalize condition of Citizens
—public debt—a private debt
—internal private debts of Va.
—British debts £1,500,000
—payable at once ~~&~~
—Money s[*ent*] out of Country
—not urged as just tho' accumulated by war
—enforced by estabt. of New Govt.
8 Massts. [*lined out*]—Genessee lands
State of S. Carolina—hard
but 1. instalments
2. tender of lands
3. paper money
4. has full faith in final settlemt.
Distrust of Sts. ☞ sd. Sts. done all they cd.

9. Difficulties
   1—partial subscription of Credrs.
   2. Who & how discriminate nature of debts
   3. Compound Certificates
   4. certificates not bearing interest
   5. paper money of States
   6. private transactions referring to State certificates & State paper money.
   7. Depreciation made up in some States to more of army than in others—
   8. Some States have provided for army in ways not forming an *existing dbt.*
   9. State debts in part unliquidated
      as Illinois claims[2]— if rejected unjust
      if admitted dangerous
   10. Kentucky ~~& Georgia~~ Indian Expeditions since peace
   11. Case of 500,000 drs. liquidd. to Va. by Comsrs.
   12 Is it meant to provide funds now?

Not beneficial to Natl. Govt. in present form
Not just
Not equalizing not practicable
bare majority—

Ms., Madison Papers, DLC. Although Madison did not date these notes, internal evidence shows that they were made for his speech of 22 April (*DHFFC* 13:1156–67, 1171–81, 1182–85). Other figures on the same sheet are being printed with Correspondence: Third Session.

[1] Nathaniel Gorham and Oliver Phelps were forced to renegotiate their contract to purchase the Genessee Tract from Massachusetts, and eventually surrendered their claim to the western two-thirds of the tract, when the state's securities (with which they intended to pay for the land) rose to prohibitive prices in expectation of their being assumed by the federal government.

[2] The Illinois claims were expenses incurred by Virginia in defending the land it ceded to become the Northwest Territory. The dispute between state and Continental commissioners over the value of these claims was finally resolved in May 1788 when the commissioners agreed to award Virginia $500,000 in compensation for the cession (which Madison mentions as item 11 immediately below). The account was not finally adjusted until 1793 (*PJM* 10:353–54n).

David Sewall to George Thatcher

This is to acknowledge the receipt of yours of the 4th. current which was carried forward by [*Joseph?*] Barnard, and came to hand after my last of the 15th. and also yours of the 11th. Instant by the last mail. from Whence and by the Saturday and Monday's Boston Paper I perceieve the ~~Non~~ assumption is for the present lost by a majority of two.[1] It is a measure that sooner or later must take place, or the Foreign and domestick debt of the U.S. will never be honestly discharged. And if I am to put the ques. upon it, No funding System of any kind will take effect this Session If the Pensilvanians are so selfish narrow and Contracted as you Suggest I Wish their understandingins may be enlarged and enlightned. I never Was at Philada. But from my Conceptions of the matter, It is an unsuitable place for Congress to sit in upon more accounts than one—Patience and perseverance are doubtless as necessary for a Statesman and Politician as for Persons in various other Stations in life—and I wish you and others may be afforded ~~with~~ a double Portion of them. The very last letter I Wrote you was in behalf of Mr. [*Joseph*] Hardison—His account of his kinsman returning to his State of Servitude, when he found himself unable to procure Money for his redemption—Brought old Regulus to mind.[2] ***

P. S. I send under your Cover a Letter to Mr. Strong, thinking it possible as N. Hampton Court sits next Week. He may be absent—and should that event happen, & He be absent You may Open it, as Some Ideas may be excited. that may not be from this.

ALS, Chamberlain Collection, MB. Place from which written not indicated. The omitted text relates to local court proceedings.

[1] [Boston] *Massachusetts Centinel*, 17 April, and *Boston Gazette*, 19 April, reported that Tobias Lear had brought the news of the 12 April COWH vote.

[2] In a petition presented in the House, probably by Thatcher, on 30 April, Joseph Hardison sought arrearage of pay for his nephew and legal client, Benjamin Hardison, while captive in Canada from 1777 to 1783; see *DHFFC* 7:402, 418. Benjamin's failure to secure his release from parole reminded Sewall of Marcus Atilius Regulus, the Roman military commander captured by the Carthaginians and sent on parole back to Rome to negotiate a prisoner exchange (ca. 249 B.C.). He successfully urged the Senate to refuse terms, and then returned to Carthage where he died, still in captivity.

Thomas Lee Shippen to William Shippen

*** Well then—first, you want to know how the funding system goes on—never did any system move slower. The assumption of the State debts has been the subject of whole weeks debates, and after two opposite votes upon it, they have put it to sleep for the present, only that it may be brought forth with more strength at some future period. Be it decided in what way ~~you~~ it will, the decision must inevitably as it appears to me produce very considerable convulsions—not so dreadful perhaps as some people imagine, but the public mind has been much agitated, different States see their interests deeply concerned in the measure, and in different ways and must therefore in any event, be, some of them highly dissatisfied. Mr. Sherman introduced some new propositions yesterday tending to an accommodation, upon the principle of a partial assumption of the State debts, to the amount of five millions I think, and apportioning it to the different States according to a ratio of his own. These propositions will probably consume a considerable length of time, and may be in some shape adopted. Indeed it were to be wished I think that some accommodation could be made. There are not wanting members of Congress who declare that there shall be no funding system without the assumption. I never saw more violence, more disorder, or more confusion than the consideration of this subject always occasions in the House. Among the many arguments that the politeness of my friends is continually urging to prolong my stay, I am told that there will certainly be an end of the business in 2 or 3 days and that by staying that time I shall be able to carry you satisfactory accounts. I believe I shall not go before Monday. tho' perhaps I may dissappoint you again; if I do, I will take good care not to come at so unseasonable an hour as before. *** We had a large party at V. Berckel's yesterday[1]—R. M[*orris*]. & R. H. L[*ee*]. sat near without speaking to each other—the former unusually civil to me—I have been busy as a bee in sounding, & feeling pulses, and hope we shall be able to have something done as to changing the place of Congress's residence tho' every thing depends upon the secrecy with which the business is conducted—therefore *bouche couvre*[2]—not a word to any body—for many reasons it is not fit that any body should know any thing about what I write. I am just, come from visiting Otto who brought his new wife to town yesterday[3] and is visited by all the great and small of his acquaintance today—He seems contented—Congress have voted (at least the H. of Representatives) that they will mourn a month for the death of Dr. Franklin.[4] Madison made the motion in a very handsome manner—somewhat to this effect that as D. Frn. had been a citizen whose native genius was no less bright an ornament to human nature, than the exertion of it precious to Science, Freedom, & his Country, Congress desirous of paying that tribute of veneration to his memory which his virtues demanded, would wish &c. There were some *Nos* when the question was put, but the ~~ques~~ house was not divided upon it. The King (as you call our President) was as civil to me as ever—I saw him 3 or 4 times, drank tea with him & Mrs. [*Martha*] W[*ashington*]. en famille &c. &c. He is now gone for the benefit of his health to Long Island—with [*William*] Jackson & [*Thomas*] Nelson where he will stay a week. Sir John [*Temple*] I have only seen for a moment—Lady [*Elizabeth Bowdoin*] T[*emple*]. two or three times—tho' I have been too much engaged to go to their house—The overpowering civility & pressing attentions of the Ministers—V.P. & Congress men are without bounds—Mr. Jefferson is not fixed So that I can only see him in the morng. & at other places than his own house—I see him very often—Madison is charming Our delegates attentive so is Judge [*James*] Wilson who lodges here. They all dined together at [*Samuel*] Meredith's & asked me—My pre engagement to V[*an*]. B[*erckel*]. prevented me from going Robt. Morris was in the same predicament—We both lamented it together—over a bottle of very old Madeira that V.B. drew from his hidden cellar, his *nota interior*[5] on the occasion—*Very great cronies I can assure you*—A conference this morng. in the antichamber of the Senate on the subject of the *great vote.*[6] *not* between members of both chambers but between R.M. & myself We grow sanguine—[*Samuel*] Griffin is our best friend—This day is rendered remarkable by a party of a new kind & called a sans souci[7] party given by Mr. [*Richard*] Platt at his Seat in the Country—50 people there—the invitations to come when you will & go when you please between the hours of 8 in the morng. & 12 at night. Dancing, Music & card playing—breakfast, dinner tea and supper—It is now two o'C. the dancing has been going on ever since 10—and I have not been out yet. Ask my fair inconstant whether she thinks I should have staid as long from a party where she was—I believe I shall go out at 5. with Mr. Smith of S.C. & of with whom I am prodigiously pleased & whose society will be a much stronger inducement than any other tho' *all* the belles of N.Y. are of the party. As we shall probably go out alone—our conversation will be confined to one object—to the enumeration of one person's charms to the consideration of one who never thinks of me but to accuse me & most unjustly, & to be indifferent ~~to me~~ at last. I shall bring you early in the next week the best accounts I can get of Congress—Miss [*Harriet*] Wadsworth is not here—her father is very kind to me—remembers you well—Burr will go on with the divorce[8]—and apprehends no difficulties—These accursed Jews are the Devil—I can get nothing from them but kind words fair promises & artful smiles in lieu of Money which they acknowledge to be justly due—Paterson has paid me & my uncle [*R. H. Lee*] will let me have 40 dollars with which I shall be able to get on—The journey cost me very near the 15 dollars which you gave me—Imagine next the expences of N. York—I think I cannot conclude my letter better or more truly than by assuring you and my belle amie [*Nancy Shippen Livingston*] That tho [*every*] body whom I know or care for here is as kind and attentive and desirous to amuse & make me happy as they possibly can be, I am still unhappy and as anxious to return to you as I could be as in the most disagreable circumstances I could possibly be—that there is no happiness for me, no beauty, no [*torn*] out of Philada.—& that I am as I have always been and must ever continue your own & that no one but Nancy can ever be in any sort your rival in either my Love or esteem. You will forgive me that & love me I hope as much as ever.

ALS, Shippen Family Papers, DLC. Place to which addressed not indicated. The omitted text discusses T. Shippen's relations with an unnamed love interest in Philadelphia.

[1] Franco Petrus van Berckel, or his father and predecessor as Dutch minister to the United States, Pieter Johan van Berckel.

[2] Mouth shut.

[3] Acting French minister to the United States Louis Guillaume Otto married America Frances, daughter of St. Jean de Crèvecoeur, in New York City on 13 April.

[4] For more on the official observance of Benjamin Franklin's death on 17 April, see *PTJ* 19:78–115 and *DHFFC* 8:574–75.

[5] Private stock.

[6] The issue of the removal of the federal government to Philadelphia.

[7] Without tears; i.e., free from cares.

[8] In 1781 Nancy Hume Shippen (1761–1841), daughter and sister of the correspondents, married Henry Beekman Livingston (1750–1831). His behavior towards her caused her to leave the marriage and return to Philadelphia. Aaron Burr handled the subsequent divorce.

Caleb Strong to William Cushing

I recd. your Letter of the 14th. of March and have delayed to answer it untill this Time as I was unable to give you any satisfactory Information on the Subject you mentioned—A Comittee of the Senate was appointed some Time since to bring in a Bill to regulate Processes & Fees in the Courts of the U.S.[1] They requested the Judges of the Sup. Court to furnish them with such Remarks as should occur to them in this Business—The Comittee omitted to come to any Determination, in Hopes that the Judges would prepare a Bill or afford them some Aid in doing it but as the Judges from the southern States were not present, those who attended being unacquainted with the Terms and at the southward were unwilling to propose such as should be used in all the States and thought it might be prudent not to do it at present—This Morning the Comittee have agreed to report—Continuance of the Bill passed at the last Session, to regulate Processes, untill the End of the next Session of Congress—I suggested to them the necessity of making some Provision for the Clerk of the Sup. Court, a major part of the Comittee were of the opinion that 4 or 5 Dollrs. ℔ Day during the sitting of the Court would be as great an Allowance as Congress ought to make—I have conversed with several Gentlemen of both Houses on this Subject and find but few Advocate for a Salary to the Clerk—they generally say that for some Years at least a Person who resides at the Seat of Government ought to be appointed to whom the Fees and perhaps a small per Diem Allowance during the Sitting of the Court will be a sufficient Compensation—from the present Appearances I think there is very little Prospect of such a Salary to the Clerk as will support him, The Idea seems to be that a Clerk of some other Court may very well do the Business of this—I know you will not be pleased with this Representation but I thought it necessary to give it, that you may not proceed on mistaken Grounds, and relinquish a certain Support for what is precarious.

I shall not be able to attend our Court at Northampton and must pray you to present my Respects to the Judges who I think will be satisfied that if I had been directed by my own Convenience I should have attended their Court in preference to any other.

ALS, Robert Treat Paine Papers, MHi. Place to which addressed not indicated.

[1] Courts Act [S-9], presented in the Senate on 23 April.

Henry Wynkoop to Reading Beatty

The Assumption of the State Debts is again the Subject of Debate, as you will perceive by the Newspapers Madison this day spoke in opposition, more than one hour, expect Ames will follow him tomorrow, & possibly on monday a Decission may again take place, I must confess for my part, no Proposition hitherto before Congress has so much embarrass'd my Mind, it is like Sylla & Charybdis,[1] Dangers on every Side & how the Ship will yet with perfect Safety be piloted into Port, Time will discover. The State Debts proposed to be assumed, are those incur'd in consequence of exertions against the common Enemy during the late War. Your Register[2] for last week N. 9 I sent on by Mr. Cornel to Vreden's Berg, shall enquire at Mr. Loyd respecting the others.

Congress have this day agreed to wearing the customary mourning for four weeks, in commemoration of the Merit of Doctor [*Benjamin*] Franklin.

If Your Ground be in Order it is high time Your flax & Oats were in ~~the Gro~~.

[*P. S.*] Have wakked [*walked*] to & from the Hall this day[3] & as yet feel no inconvenience.

ALS, Wynkoop Papers, PDoBHi. Place to which addressed not indicated.

[1] A treacherous rock and whirlpool, respectively, on opposite shores of the Straits of Messina separating Sicily and Italy, named for mythological monsters; proverbially signifying a choice between two evils.

[2] The ninth issue of Volume III of Thomas Lloyd's *CR* was published on 1 April.

[3] During the second session Wynkoop probably resided with Peter Wynkoop on the Bowery, at the northeastern outskirts of the settled part of the city.

Extract of a Letter

It is now in the power of Congress to establish public credit fully and compleatly—the general opinion and wish of the people are strong in favor of it—and very justly—for they feel the accumulation of burthens to originate in a want of confidence in the public engagements—If the present favorable moment therefore should be neglected, who will be answerable for the consequences? If the Representatives of the people think as highly of this matter as many of their constituents, they will never lose sight of the object one moment, till it is accomplished—the people in this quarter wait this event with anxious hopes, and a countenance of solicitude resembling the perilous days of doubtful war—Public credit has begun to decline, and private embarrassments to encrease while this "*one thing needful*"[1] has hung in a state of suspense.

GUS, 5 May; reprinted at Poughkeepsie, New York, and Winchester, Virginia.

[1] Luke 10:42.

Other Documents

John Jay to John Langdon. ALS, Langdon Papers, NhPoA. Written from New Haven, Connecticut.

Acknowledges receipt of Langdon's letter of 16 April "last Evening"; declines invitation to stay at Langdon's house while on circuit in Portsmouth, New Hampshire; will wait on Mrs. Elizabeth Langdon immediately upon his arrival; asks Langdon to forward an enclosed letter to Jay's home.

William Samuel Johnson to [*Peletiah Webster*]. FC:dft, Johnson Papers, CtHi. The recipient is identified by the fact that he had recently written Huntington (19 April, above) and that Webster had previously sent Johnson a series of pamphlets.

A question from Huntington reminded Johnson that he had not acknowledged receipt of several of Webster's essays; "either business or Company has hitherto ~~pre~~ unavoidably prevented it"; has "very little time" to himself; the essays are "particularly useful to be attended to in the present state of our affairs, & I shall endeavour to render them beneficial as far as is in my power."

Henry Lee to James Madison. ALS, Madison Papers, DLC. Written from Alexandria, Virginia. For the full text, see *PJM* 13:157–59.

Is more persuaded than ever that the value of improvements to Potomac River navigation at Great Falls, Virginia, exceeds its owners' and supporters' expectations; a loan of £3,000 needed; "You think money cannot be obtained on loan in N. york—In this you are mistaken—If you would labor for two days as much for yourself & friend, as you have done from early life for the public, the cash would soon be in your possession; or good bills which is the same thing—Hamilton could & would get it for you"; "Set about the matter & you will see how readily it can be effected"; "Why will you not work sometimes for yourself—our object is just & proper & absolutely important to our country."

Robert Morris to Mary Morris. Transcript, Bancroft Papers, NN. ALS offered for sale in *Flying Quill*, June–July 1951, p. 4. Place to which addressed not indicated.

Has not received a line from "my Dr. Friend" (his wife); hopes "my poor little Captain" (Henry Morris) is not sick or Robert or William (his other sons) should have informed him; has heard of Benjamin Franklin's death; "He richly deserves to be happy where he is gone, for he delighted in making happy as many of his Species in this world as came within his circle; indeed that circle had in many instances no other Bounds than the Globe we inhabit"; the letter will be delivered by Mr. Montgomery.

Peter Silvester to Peter Van Schaack. ALS, Van Schaack Collection, NNC. Place to which addressed not indicated. On the endorsement page, in Van Schaack's hand, is the notation, "A Map of the survey on the Partition of the Westerly Part of Gardiner's Patent." The reference is probably to the loyalist George Gardner's estate in present-day Pownal, Vermont, confiscated by Vermont in 1778 (John J. Duffy, et al., eds., *Ethan Allen and His Kin: Correspondence, 1772–1819* [2 vols., Hanover, N.H., 1998], 1:277n). Silvester, who numbered exiled loyalists among his closest friends and family, represented the New York congressional district bordering Pownal. A postscript to this letter was written on 23 April and is excerpted under that date, below.

Directions for planting garden seeds he has sent; "You have heard the great [*Benjamin*] Franklin is no more in this life."

George Thatcher to Stephen Collins. ALS, Collins Papers, DLC. Addressed to Philadelphia; franked; postmarked 23 April.

Forwards legal document and requests others on behalf of Nathaniel Barrell.

Letter from the Intendant at Port-au-Prince, Haiti, to the Vice Consul in Virginia. *NYDG*, 26 June.

An ordinance just passed gives permission for an unlimited time for the importation of flour and biscuit of foreign growth and manufacture.

Friday, 23 April 1790

Fine (Johnson)

Pierce Butler to Alexander Gillon

Thanks to God, the dispenser of every good gift, that He has been pleased to continue to me, amidst all my sufferings & disappointments, two real friends. I feel gratified the more by the warmth and sincerity of their friendship, when I am daily experiencing the perfidy and ingratitude of those who owe me most next to my own Children. I can not express to You my sensibility at the warmth and sincerity of Your attachment & that of my friend Captn. [*Roger Parker*] Saunders. Friends like this sweeten many a bitter draught.

***

I observe the conversation between You and Chancellor R. H. [*Richard Hutson*] My friend if I had the most distant idea or wish of the kind You should be the first, and indeed, with friend Saunders, the only person to know it. It never entered my head. I request You will stop any measures tending to it. I believe if I had wished for it I might have stepped in before a much properer man, Chancellor M. [*John Mat(t)hews*] If I covetted it I would not undertake a business I am so unequal to[1]—I am much indebted to Chancellor H. for his favorable sentiments; be so kind to tell him so, with my compliments. I am always sensible of my friends partiality to me in thinking I am qualified to serve the Union in the line of negociation. If any loans are made it is probable, entre nous, I may have the offer of doing it. Such a hint has been given me: but my friend I have my doubts of any part of the debt being funded: States' debts certainly I think will not be assumed this year, if ever. The friends to assumption are determined if that does not take place to oppose all funding. Parties run high in the lower House; much heat and acrimony. I fear they will break up without doing anything. If the loan should take place, & Your friend have the offer of it can he serve You? Let the above be with Yourself: none of our delegates know any thing of it. ***

Honest Judge Bourke [*Burke*] has just called on me. I made an ample apology for You to him.

I have also explained to the Comptroller of the treasury [*Nicholas Eveleigh*] the nature of the demand against You, but my friend there is a charge in the old treasury books against You, on acct. of some Indico contract. Can I do any thing in adjusting it? the old Treasurer [*Michael Hillegas*] mentioned it to me some days ago. It will be best to adjust it while I am here because I will attend to it. I know a claim will be made on You.

I have told You parties run high in the House of Representatives. Mr. Madison is at the head of the party against assumption; Massachusets So. Carolina and Connecticut joined to obtain the assumption; Pensylvania looking on to avail herself of an opportunity, by throwing herself into either scale, to get Congress to Philadelphia. I am not dissatisfied at a small diversion among the more powerful States. My apprehension was and is that they wou'd or will act the part of Sparta and Athens.[2] This was one powerful motive with me for not being warm in support of the assumption, Yet considering the distress of Carolina it may be better on the whole to get her exhonorated in case of any possible confusion. I shall therefore on this ground, if the question ever comes before Senate, give my vote for it, and also because You, my constituents, have so instructed me.

***

FC, Butler Letterbook, ScU. For the full text, see *Butler Letters*, pp. 32–35. The omitted text instructs Gillon in negotiating the final settlement of a large debt Butler owed to Hercules Daniel Bize. Butler described the terms of the repayment as a "sacrifice to peace of mind, which I have long been a stranger to. If I do not make this sacrifice, I shall sacrifice my life, for my health gives way to the distresses of my mind."

[1] The reference apparently is to a movement in South Carolina to make Butler a commissioner for selling loan certificates to European investors in the event that Congress funded the debt.

[2] The most powerful city states of ancient Greece and their respective allies fought to the point of mutual exhaustion in the Peloponnesian War of 431–404 B.C., ending any hope of Greek unity and autonomy in the ancient world.

Horatio Gates to Jonathan Trumbull

Your obliging Letter of the 17th. Ult., did not come to my Hands until yesterday afternoon. Our post having lately neglected his Duty. inclosed is an answer to your Brothers letter of the same date with Yours, please to present it to Him.[1] Those, I converse with, are displeased at the Violence, and Ill Temper of the lower House of Congress: The Upper, acted with the utmost propriety in their Treatment of The Quakers Petition;[2] the Lower, should consider, that every hour the Legislature Sits, Costs Their Constituents One hundred, & Fifty Dollars! This Time, is too precious, to be thrown away in Wrangling about a measure, they probably, had no right immediately to Decide upon! I foresaw the Assumption of the individual State Debts, would cause much Altercation; but, surely it is not beyond the Wisdom of The Two Houses, to have that matter Equitably adjusted; The Influencing Men in some of the Assemblys of the States, will not like to have a Revenue paid into the General Treasury, which at present they have now so much to say in the disposal of! but I am convinced, The Permanence of The Federal

Government depends almost intirely upon the Assumption; Qualify it, as much as in Justice, you ought to Qualify it; but be sure you make it.

ALS, The Gilder Lehrman Collection, on Deposit at the New York Historical Society, New York. [GLC 6658] Written from "Travellers Rest," Berkeley County, West Virginia; sent by post.

[1] The painter John Trumbull had asked Gates, "my military Parent," whether they would be able to meet at the Society of the Cincinnati's general meeting in Philadelphia the next month for Trumbull to begin studies for his famous painting of General John Burgoyne's surrender to Gates at Saratoga (1777). Trumbull directed Gates to reply under cover to his brother (and house mate), Representative Trumbull (Emmet Collection, NN).

[2] According to Maclay, the Senate spent almost the entire day in intense debate on the antislavery petitions before deciding to take no official action. Beyond noting that they were presented and read, Secretary Otis even departed radically from the customary format of the Senate Journal by omitting any reference at all to the subject of the petitions. In newspaper coverage of the House debate, however, Gates would have read Baldwin's claim that a motion to table the petitions had in fact been made in the Senate, but that "even that was negatived, and they would not blot their paper at all on the subject" (*DHFFC* 9:202, 12:773).

Michael Hodge to Benjamin Goodhue

Mr. Natha. Tracy arrived at this Town in four days from N. York, he brot. us the disagreable tidings of the question for the assumption of the state debts, being negatived by a Majority of two, it is most sensibly felt by the friends of Goverment in this place, they foresee and Shudder at the many evils, which will naturally follow, such a mode of Legislation, it is tho't, by very many, that posponing the funding System for this Session, will be best, it will give the Members time, for reconsideration of the subject. and by mixing with their constituents, may perhaps be enlightned on the Subject, and when they meet again be divested of those Local, partial Views which seems to have been predominant, with too many of the Southern Members.

The Opposers of the Constitution are Exceedingly gratified by it, they promise themselves, that disorder and confusion will imediately follow such Measures, and are not hopeless, but that their old friend Anarchy will pay them a visit again, they really seem to hold up their heads, and to brightnen upon the prospect, it is mortifying, to witness the exultations of so despicable Set of beings, it will I hope, be off but short duration, and a good understanding again subsist among the Members.

We have nothing new this way worthy of communication, a very backward cold spring, presents itself to us, Bread corn is very scarce and dear, in the Eastern parts of this state, with us it is not scarce, but indian corn commands a price of 4/ ℔ Bushel, which the poor very sensibly feels, You will be kind Eno. to continue your communications to us, as it is at this time very desireable, Yours of the 14th Came duly to hand, for which you have my sincere thanks.

ALS, Letters to Goodhue, NNS. Written from Newburyport, Massachusetts.

Peter Silvester to Peter Van Schaack

The question of assumption of State debts has once being determined in favor of it by a majority of 5. since which North Carolina came in & has been determined agt. it as Mr. Skedgwick informed you by a smaller Majority—both sides notice the ill effects a final decision will have either way by a Small Majority & both seem anxious to have something done that will seal [?] the minds of the Generality of the house The assumptionists have taken up the Subject again Upon some what different ground & have Spoken a little upon it Yesterday Madison made a long Speech agt. it in any Shape this Sessions—to day 23d. I expect Mr. Gerry & Ames will come forth largely in favor of it—most of the members of both sides of the house View it in a very important light.

ALS, Van Schaack Collection, NNC. Place to which addressed not indicated. This is a postscript to Silvester's letter to Van Schaack, 22 April, above.

Other Documents

John Brown Cutting to William Short. ALS, Short Papers, DLC. Written from London; place to which addressed not indicated.

From "positive assurances" in private letters received, there is little doubt that Hamilton's funding plan will be adopted.

Nicholas Eveleigh to Philip Schuyler. ALS, Schuyler Papers, NN. Written from the Comptroller's Office. On 13 April 1780 the Confederation Congress appointed its members Schuyler, John Mathews (S.C.), and Nathaniel Peabody (N.H.) as a committee to confer with Washington on the size and management of the Continental Army at its headquarters, centered around the Hudson River highlands. The Committee met from April to August and reported in November 1780 (*LDC* 15:15–17, 618).

Requests final settlement of $12,000 advanced by the treasury to Schuyler as chairman of the Committee at Camp in June 1780.

Sarah Livingston Jay to John Jay. ALS, Jay Papers, NNC. Addressed to New Haven, Connecticut; re-addressed in a different hand to Boston.

Expresses concern for Jay's health, as Wadsworth had informed her the night before that the influenza was very prevalent at Hartford.

Annis Boudinot Stockton to Elias Boudinot. ALS, Boudinot Collection, NjP. Place from which written not indicated; carried by Rev. Dr. William Smith.

Rev. Dr. William Smith and wife leave for New York City; is sure Boudinot will do everything in his power to make the city agreeable to them.

Jeremiah Wadsworth to Barnabas Deane; Jeremiah Wadsworth to N. Shuler. ALSs, Read Papers, MSaE. Addressed to Hartford, Connecticut.

Introduces the bearer, Nathan Read, whose machinery and improvements to the steam engine Wadsworth suggests they might make use of.

Joseph Whipple to John Langdon. ALS, Langdon Papers, NhPoA. Written from Portsmouth, New Hampshire.

They have just heard of the Houses's rejection of assumption; "This is a matter of Surprize to many who conceived well of the Measure, & the more so, as they are told that the Senate are almost Unanimous" against it as well.

Daniel Hiester, Account Book. PRHi.

Paid two shillings for black crape to wear as a badge of mourning for Benjamin Franklin, as resolved by the House.

William Samuel Johnson, Diary. Johnson Papers, CtHi.

"Visits."

Saturday, 24 April 1790

Daniel Cony to George Thatcher

Yours of the 28th. ulto. was received two day's ago. Several Sheets of the Journal of Congress came forward about the 5th. Instant—every Communication from Congress affords matter of entertainment, and is truly gratifying—But the circuitous rout by which your Letters Pass from Portland to Hallowell that tis generally three or four weeks from their date before we receive them.

You Say "Congress go on very Slow" tis veryfying the old observation that "great Body's move slow"—if "Slow" I hope "Sure" also.

Massachusetts was never in a more tranquil Situation than at present. Since I have been concerned with public business—Mr. Hancock & Mr. Adams will be very Unitedly reelected[1]—your name sake [*Josiah*] Thatcher I Suppose will be Chosen a *Senator* for Cumberland County and tis Said that a number of the *good Orthodox People* in Gorham, Portland and else where will vote for him, at the Next Election to go to Congress, for tho' they do not Call in question either your Integrity or Ability yet tis to be feared (Say they) that you are not Sound in the faith, that is you are a little heterodoxical—I hope however that you will by a watchful & Examplary Life convince them that you are a real believer, and in a genuine Scriptural Sense, a *religious Man*, and a *liberal Politician*.

Tis my friend, doubtless of no small importance that our *Legislators, Majistrates*, and other *publick Officers* Should let their Light So Shine before a *peevish World*,[2] that if not to dart rays of Conviction to their Consciences—yet to Silence (if Possible) the *base*, the *Malignant, tongue* of Slander.
[*P. S.*] *Man* & *Beast* in this Eastern Country are realizing at the present day, what may properly be called STARVATION.

ALS, Chamberlain Collection, MB. Written from Hallowell, Maine.

[1] John Hancock and Samuel Adams, or governor and lieutenant governor of Massachusetts, respectively.
[2] A biblical reference to Philippians 2:15.

William Maclay to Benjamin Rush

I have, for upwards of a Week past, had a singular complaint, in the thumb of my right hand. I still hold a pen with difficulty. to this slight cause has it been owing, that you have not heard from me oftner. You have however sustained but small loss by my silence, for little worth communicating has happened since my last to You.

Sherman of Connecticut was pushed forward with some artful propositions. His innocent ~~Manner~~ Aspect and infantile Manner, but ill ~~ill~~ concealed the poison contained in his Proposals.[1] The Secretary's Advocates, now seem disposed to impede and retard business. Thus if You will not let them milk the Cow their own way. they will not suffer her to be milked at all.

I have inclosed You a peice on the assumption of the State debts, which shows the impropriety of it both on constitutional and political Grounds. I will thank You to get it inserted in Hall & Sellers's Paper[2] or any other You may think most proper. A Copy is gone to Baily so you need not furnish him with it. This Measure really only needs to be understood to insure the disapprobation of it.

So it seems death has been with You, and taken away the aged Doctor [*Benjamin Franklin*]. The Representatives in Congress, have put on Crape for him. A Motion in our house to the same purpose miscarried ~~in our house~~. It seems as if some People carried their resentments beyond the Grave.[3]

The Doctor was accused, in his life time, of triming, so as to gain all Men. if he really practised this Art. it has not been with the fullest Success. For there are enemies to his fame. The disposition is a bad One. It is certainly in favour of Virtue. to pay respect to the Memory of great men, to forget their Foibles, if they had ~~them~~ any. & hand down their good qualities, as patterns for Posterity.

I will thank You for a paper, containing the inclosed peice.

ALS, Rush Papers, DLC. Addressed to Third Street, Philadelphia; franked; postmarked 25 April. Copies of the second and fourth paragraphs are in Bancroft Transcripts, NN. The enclosure is printed under 28 April, below; Maclay's diary indicates that he authored it on 22 April (*DHFFC* 9:251).

[1] Sherman's proposal for assumption, including the amount of each state's debt to be assumed, was moved on 21 April and is printed in *DHFFC* 5:858.

[2] William Sellers co-published *PG* with William and David Hall, who succeeded their father in the business in 1772. David Hall, Sr., had run the paper with Benjamin Franklin from 1748 to 1766. Maclay's piece was never printed there, although it did appear in Philadelphia in Francis Bailey's *FJ* and *NYDA* on 28 April and in Andrew Brown's *FG* on 4 May.

[3] The "resentment" Maclay noted was a legacy of the longstanding antagonism towards Franklin by the residual Adams-Lee interest in the Senate. For more on this antagonism and the Adams-Lee interest's influence in the FFC, see Kenneth R. Bowling, "'Good-by Charle': The Lee-Adams Interest and the Political Demise of Charles Thomson, Secretary of Congress, 1774–1789," *PMHB* 3(July 1976):321–22. Accusations of Franklin's "triming" or deceptiveness usually referred to rumors circulated in Congress during Franklin's diplomatic mission in France by anti-French forces in Congress, including future Senators Izard and Lee (Richard B. Morris, *The Peacemakers: The Great Powers and American Independence* [New York, 1965], p. 440; Jack N. Rakove, *The Beginning of National Politics: An Interpretive History of the Continental Congress* [New York, 1979], pp. 251–52).

Benjamin Rush to James Madison

I do myself the pleasure of enclosing you the pamphflet I mentioned in my last letter.[1] I have only to request—that you would not Suffer it to go out of your hands without guarding against the possibility of its finding its way into a newspaper. The ~~edit~~ printer of it insisted upon this request to all the persons to whom I should send it, as the Condition of his furnishing me with a few copies of it. I shall next week send four or five copies of it to Mr. Jefferson.

I enclose you likewise for your perusal Dr. Price's Sermon preached before the Revolution Society in London.[2] It is pregnant with noble sentiments. It suggested to me an idea of your house addressing the national Assembly & king of France upon the present [*lined out*] crisis in their Affairs. Such a national Act of Sympathy may ~~give~~ add Strength to the efforts of the friends of liberty in that Country—It may lead them to adopt a compound [*bicameral*] legislature—& lastly it may encourage the [*lined out*] doubting friends to revolutions in Other Countries to acts of enterprise & patriotism. The United States *kindled* the flame of liberty in Europe. It is highly proper that they should *fan* it.

Your motion in honor of the Memory of Dr. Franklin has added to the number & affection of your friends in this city.

P. S. Please to return Dr. Price's sermon when you have read it.

ALS, The Gilder Lehrman Collection, on Deposit at the New York Historical Society, New York. [GLC 580] Written from Philadelphia.

---

[1] [Benjamin Rush,] *Information to Europeans Who Are Disposed to Migrate to the United States* (Evans 22390), was first published as a pamphlet in 1790 by Carey and Stewart, Philadelphia. It is reprinted in *Rush* 1:549–62.

[2] Richard Price, *A Discourse on the Love of Our Country, Delivered on Nov. 4, 1789, . . . to the Society for Commemorating the Revolution in Great Britain* (London, 1789); republished at Boston in 1790. The London Revolution Society was founded ostensibly to commemorate England's bloodless Revolution of 1688, but actually to support continuing reform in Britain and France.

William Smith (of Boston) to John Adams

It is sometime since I had the pleasure of addressing you but as I know it will not be displeasing to know the sentiments of your countrymen, on the determination of Congress not to assume the State Debts, I wou'd mention them. the State Creditors think they are equally entitl'd to the benefits of the Genl. Government with the Continental Creditors. their property or services were advanc'd for the benefit of their Country at the earliest period, perhaps had they not exerted themselves the Country wou'd have been subdued. they presum'd, when they so readily gave their consent to the adoption of the New Government & agreed to relinquish the funds from which they were paid *their* Interest, that the Genl. Govt. after receiving the resources wou'd have generously provided for their Interest equally with other Creditors. much has been said on the subject of discrimination but in this State, (in the opinion of the Treasurer [*Alexander Hodgdon*]) two thirds of the Debt is in the possession of the original Creditors or become the property of their Heirs. most of them were persons in trade & it is now openly said why shou'd *we*, pay duties to a government, from which *we* are, *not* to receive any benefit. must we increase the Revenue for the benefit of those, who *never* riskt their property till they cou'd purchase into the Funds at an eight of their value—these sentiments are generally expressd. If Congress do not assume the State Debts & fund the whole Debt there is great danger that the publick revenue will sink very considerably. the Publick Papers may puff off the increasing trade of America, but you may rely on it in this State it is on the decline. Our Fishery is discourag'd & is lessen'd One hundred sail this Spring. much was expected from the Carrying Trade. a number of fine Ships were built the last year for that business, & had they met with success Numbers wou'd have been added this season. but wherever we go, we find the Harbours crouded with British Shipping which have the preference. whilst our own Ships sail the Coast from Boston to Georgia beging a Freight.

The British have lately prohibited the importation of any goods even in British Ships which are not the produce of America—Why cannot Congress say, that no Goods, Ware or Merchandize shall be imported in British Ships but what are the Growth or Manufacture of Great Britain surely we have a right to retaliate when it is so much for our Interest. the intention of the British Act is to discourage our Est India Trade, as large quantitys of Cotton have been imported from India & reship'd to Great Britain in British Ships—The scarcity of Specie is very great. all the circulating Cash we can procure goes for Duties & is immediately sent of[*f*] for New-York. & from the slow movements of Congress it is uncertain whether it is to be paid back in *some Years*. the Drafts on our Bank[1] to exchange Notes for Specie to send to New-York. has been so great lately that the Bank has stopt discounting! cou'd not a National Bank be establish'd & their Bills have a Currency thro' the States! this wou'd facilitate the collection of the Revenue & essentially serve the trade of the whole Continent. We are in hopes that Congress will reconsider the subject of assumption & fund the *whole*. by this measure they will unite State & Continental Creditors in the support of one firm energetick Government, & make it their Interest to unite in the regular collection of the Revenue—& put an end to all *partial State* Excise Laws—if this is not done, there will be a very powerful body of State Creditors constantly opposing the proceedings of the Fœderal Government & preventing the collection of the Impost.

ALS, Adams Family Manuscript Trust, MHi. Written from Boston.

[1] The Massachusetts Bank, chartered in 1784.

George Thatcher to Berry and Rogers

Some time ago, at my request, you wrote to your Correspondent, in London, to procure Heroditus' History, translated by Littlebury,[1] which has not yet arrived—I will now beg you to take the trouble of writing your Correspondent, by the first opportunity, and desire him that, in case he has not procured the before mentioned book, he will not trouble himself further about it—but send over Lempriere's translation,[2] if published—However if this latter is not yet published, & not likely to be published, I would then ~~have~~ wish him to forward Littlebury's, whenever he shall be able to find it.

I wish you also to write for Hampton's translation of Polybius[3]—the octave edition—And for Docr. Priest[*l*]ey's Letters to the Jews—part the third—if published.[4]

Be pleased also to remind your Correspondent, that if he shall meet with Plato's works, translated by Sydenham;[5] and Isocrates, translated by Dimsdale.[6] I would have him procure them & send them out.

FC, Thatcher Family Papers, MHi. The recipients were a jeweler and stationery firm in Hanover Square, New York City.

---

[1] Isaac Littlebury (fl. 1698–1710) translated the Greek historian Herodotus (ca. 484–428 B.C.) in two volumes (London, 1709).

[2] John Lampriere (ca. 1765–1824) published a famous classical dictionary (London, 1788) that cited Herodotus frequently, but never published a translated volume of the Greek historian's works.

[3] James Hampton translated the *General History* (2 vols., London, 1762–63) of Polybius, the Greek historian of ancient Rome (ca. 200–118 B.C.).

[4] Joseph Priestly never published a sequel to his two *Letters to the Jews; inviting them to an Amicable Discussion of the Evidences of Christianity* (Birmingham, England, 1786–87).

[5] Floyer Sydenham (1710–87) translated Plato's *Dialogues* (4 vols., London, 1767–80).

[6] The British poet Joshua Dinsdale translated the *Orations and Epistles* (London, 1752) of the Athenian rhetorician Isocrates (436–338 B.C.).

Hugh Williamson to Governor Alexander Martin

The New England Members aided by those of N. York part of N. Jersey part of Pensylvania and S. Carolina are perseveringly determined to adopt the State debts if possible. Hitherto they have been unsuccessful in their several Attempts. I have been obliged, in Order to Shew our willingness to do Justice, to move that a Committee prepare a Bill for making speedy settlemt. of the public Accounts. I am on the Committee and shall not fail to endeavour to have such measures adopted as may put our State on a very respectable footing. I fear Col. [*Abishai*] Thomas and myself will be obliged to apply to the next Assembly to give me Leave to employ two Clerks; They may be obtaind @ 450 Dlrs. ⅌ Annum or 500 Dlrs. I am now convinced that my Duty as Agent requiring that I should fully understand the public Accounts is an Object of more Importance to the State than I had formerly imagined. The general Peace of Society seems to require that great Dispatch should be made in settling the national Accots. Five Continental Commissioners will probably be employed. They will probably be effectually restricted [*lined out*] by Time. The Business must be done, whatever Number of Clerks may be required on their Part, we must keep Pace with them &

be able to correct them if they Err. If such measures should be adopted as may render it advisable for us to employ a Clerk before the Setting of our Assembly I submit to your Consideration whether we might not venture on the Measure. My Hope is that N. Carolina will be a Creditor State to the Amt. of 2,000,000 of Dlrs. The object is too great to be slighted.

Inclosed you have the Outline of my first Argument against the Assumption.[1] I hope the Principles I have adopted will receive your Approbation.

ALS, Governors' Papers, Nc-Ar. Place to which addressed not indicated.

[1] The outline is not with the letter. It probably sketched Williamson's "first Argument" against assumption, on 30 March (*DHFFC* 12:866–69).

Newspaper Article

In the debates which lately took place in the House of Representatives of the United States, on the memorial of the people called Quakers, respecting slavery, Mr. Scott, Mr. Vining, Mr. Gerry, Mr. Boudinot, and other members advocated the cause of the memorialists, and vindicated their characters, with great ability, eloquence, and liberality, in opposition to Mr. Jackson, Mr. Burke, Mr. Smith, (S.C.) &c. who not only opposed the object of the memorialists, but treated them, as a society, with a degree of acrimony and invective which ill become American Legislators in particular, and must inevitably lessen that respect the ingenuity of their arguments might otherwise have inspired.

[Edenton] *State Gazette of North Carolina*, 24 April.

Newspaper Article

In the first of this session of the national legislature, after the President's speech and the Secretary's report were published, so universal were the expectations of the people that public credit would be immediately established, that there was perhaps the most visible and general change for the better ever experienced in any country—the public securities rose rapidly—land greatly appreciated—(more farms were bought and sold in two months, than in five years preceding) all kinds of property seemed to increase in value—money circulated more than it had for many years—many iron repositories, whose hinges had not creaked for a long period, were emptied of their contents, to the great advantage of trade, which evidently appeared to revive, and give industry new vigor—the whole country wore a new pleasing and animated countenance. If these things were the effect of *anticipation* only—what may not the *reality* of *Public Credit* be?

GUS, 5 May.

Other Documents

Aedanus Burke to Anthony Walton White. Place to which addressed not indicated. Printed in *DHFFC* 7:547. For background and related documents, see *DHFFC* 7:543–45, 547–50, 553–55.

Assurances of support for and the success of White's petition for the settlement of his wartime accounts.

Benjamin Goodhue to Stephen Choate. No copy known; acknowledged in Choate to Goodhue, 10 May.

Samuel Griffin to George Washington. ANS, Washington Papers, DLC.

"George Wray of Hampton, Son of the late Collector, wishes to succeed his Father, he is a Young Man of an unblemishd Character, and has Officiated as his Fathers Deputy for the last two Years."

Governor Samuel Huntington to Benjamin Huntington. ALS, Huntington Papers, CtHi. Written from Norwich, Connecticut.

Encloses Joseph Story's power of attorney; hopes Benjamin will be able to obtain the money and clothing due to Story; "it will do the poor Soldier a great kindness, & he asks no more than Simple Justice."

Thomas Jefferson to Ralph Izard. FC, letterpress copy, Jefferson Papers, DLC. For the full text, see *PTJ* 16:376n. The duc de la Rochefoucauld-Liancourt (1747–1827) and Adrienne, Madame de Tessé (1741–1814) were celebrated French philosophes.

Cover letter for enclosed letters of introduction to Lafayette, La Rochefoucauld, William Short, and Mme. de Tessé, for Charles Cotesworth Pinckney's nephew, Charles Lucas Pinckney Horry.

Marshall Jenkins to George Thatcher. ALS, Chamberlain Collection, MB. Written from Hudson, New York.

John D. Bourne departs for Woods Hole (Cape Cod, Massachusetts) the next morning with Capt. Latham Butler, to be reunited with his father (Shearjashub); if convenient, has drawn an order on Thatcher in favor of a New York City merchant, for expenses advanced to Bourne, which his father can reimburse; presumes Bourne will call on Thatcher en route, when he can advise Bourne further.

Caleb Strong and Tristram Dalton to Governor John Hancock. Summary of one page ALS, hand of Strong, *Libby Auction Catalog*(1981):item 5994.

"Regarding the encroachments of the British in Passamaquoddy Bay [*Maine*]."

Thomas Tudor Tucker to St. George Tucker. ALS, Tucker-Coleman Papers, ViW. Addressed to Williamsburg, Virginia; franked; postmarked 26 April.

"We have been doing very little in Congress for some time past, except squabbling about the Assumption of the State Debts, the House being so equally divided upon the Question, that the Minority in either Case submits with a bad Grace. We have assumed & rejected, & the Assumption at present stands rejected, but is perhaps not intirely lost; for, I suppose, it will be brought on again in some new Modification."

The Western Posts. [Boston] *Massachusetts Centinel*, 24 April; reprinted at Bennington, Vermont, and New York City (*NYJ*, 4 May).

The British ministry intends "in the TREATY NOW PENDING," to make provision for purchasing the United States's cession of the western posts; to further the treaty, the British have dispatched the sloop of war *Echo* to New York; citizens need not fear Washington's using his treaty making powers for such a "*humiliating and degrading cession.*"

The Senate's Power over Diplomatic Ranks and Salaries

Jefferson's "Construction of the Powers of the Senate" over diplomatic ranks and salaries (printed under this date, below) was evidently solicited by Washington in anticipation of the House's consideration of the Foreign Intercourse Bill [HR-52]. The second session bill, presented on 31 March but postponed in the COWH as the order of the day until 27 April, followed the recommitment of an earlier Foreign Intercourse Bill [HR-35], which had met with significant opposition. Jackson, Stone, and R. B. Lee led the attack, not only against the proposed expenditures but also against the president's power to fix the salary and grade (minister plenipotentiary or chargé d'affaires) at various European courts without the advice and consent of the Senate. The latter argument focused on the Senate's role in treaty making, the legislature's traditional power of the purse, and the equally traditional fear of executive abuse. Laurance fought these attacks on the same general grounds upon which Jefferson later erected his "Construction" of 24 April: that the only exceptions to the executive's exclusive prerogatives over the conduct of foreign affairs are those specifically enumerated in the Constitution. (Laurance also insisted that the situation was analogous to a department head's control over his clerks and their grade and pay.) Ultimately, the bill was tabled for two months awaiting the arrival of the secretary of state.[1]

Washington's request for Jefferson's formal written opinion was preceded by several informal discussions. The two men discussed the ranks of diplomats on 23 March, the day before the subject was referred to the committee that would propose HR-52. The president's diary entry for 26 March (printed below) summarized a second discussion on foreign service expenditures. "The subject of Diplomatic appointments & on the proper places & characters for Consuls or Vice Consuls" was the subject of at least one more "long conference" on 16 April, possibly the last before Washington's excursion to Long Island from 20 April until his return on the 24th, the date of Jefferson's "Construction."[2]

The document's existence among Adams's papers suggests that Washington also consulted the Vice President, who might have been expected to cast a critical vote on the subject in the frequently tied Senate and who in any case could claim the most foreign service experience of anyone in the administration (Jefferson himself not excepted). Besides Madison, Washington's diary entry for 27 April (printed below) implies that he had also consulted with John Jay, a seasoned diplomat like Adams, presumably before the Chief Justice left to ride the New England circuit for several months beginning on 20 April.[3] Neither Madison, Jay, nor Adams is known to have left any written opinion.

The actual impact of Jefferson's opinion on the final legislation is difficult to assess. The first Foreign Intercourse Bill's reincarnation did not alter its provisions respecting the President's unqualified control over grades or salaries (up to a maximum allowance), and there is no evidence from the recorded debates of the House that the president's prerogative in the matter was brought into question as it had been in HR-35.[4] Only the size of the overall expenditure was in dispute, once again. The Senate agreed with the House's reduction of the expenditure, but eliminated completely maximum allowances for specific ranks, perhaps prodded by Washington's conversation on the subject with Carroll and Izard, described in his Diary entry of 7 May (printed below). There is also the possibility that the Senate compromised to avoid a threatened veto on constitutional grounds.

A version of the stricken language was ultimately reinserted by the conference committee. But another last minute addition suggests that Jefferson did indeed bring some critical influence to bear, even if it was on a provision not directly related to the constitutional concerns expressed in his "Construction." On 27 April, Benjamin Franklin's grandson and trusted secretary William Temple Franklin had reminded Jefferson that outfitting a diplomat's "Establishment" (furniture, carriages, linen, etc.) demanded a sizeable and burdensome initial outlay.[5] Without any prior reference to the matter, the conference committee inserted a clause appropriating money for a minister's or chargé's d'affaires "Outfit" in addition to (but not to exceed the equivalent of) his annual salary.

[1] For the legislative history of HR-52, see *DHFFC* 4:702–7; for the House debate over HR-35, see *DHFFC* 12:69, 71–72, 73–92.)
[2] *DGW* 6:51–52, 62.
[3] *DHSCUS* 2:47.
[4] *DHFFC* 13:1217.
[5] *PTJ* 16:365–66.

George Washington, Diary, 26 March

Had a further Conversation with the Secretary of State on the subject of Foreign appointments, and on the Provision which was necessary for Congress to make for them—the result of which was that under all circumstances it might be best to have Ministers Plenipy. at the Courts of France and England (if any advances from the latter should be made) And Chargés des Affaires in spain & Portugal—Whether it might be necessary to send a Person in this character to Holland—one in the character of Resident—or simply a person well Skilled in commercial matters in any other character being questionable; nothing finally was decided—but it was concluded that the Secretary's information to a Committee of Congress with whom he was to converse on the subject of the Provision to be made, that the Salaries allowed to our Diplomatic characters was too low—that the Grades which wd. be fixed on, to transact our Affairs abroad would be as low as they cd. be made without giving umbrage that therefore, about 36,000 dollrs. might answer as a provision for the characters to the Courts before named—or that it might take forty nine or 50,000 dollars if it should be found that the lower grades will not answer.

Washington Diary, ViHi.

Thomas Jefferson, Construction of the Powers of the Senate, 24 April

The Constitution having declared that the President "shall nominate, & by & with the advice & consent of the Senate, shall *appoint* ambassadors other public ministers & consuls," the President desires my opinion Whether the Senate has a right to negative the *grade* he may think it expedient to use in a foreign mission, as well as the *person* to be appointed?

I think the Senate has no right to negative the *grade*.

The Constitution has divided the powers of government into three branches, Legislative, Executive & Judiciary, lodging each with a distinct magistracy. the Legislative it has given completely to the Senate & House of representatives: it has declared that "the Executive powers shall be vested in the President," submitting only special articles of it to a negative by the Senate; & it has vested the Judiciary power in the courts of justice, with certain exceptions also in favor of the Senate.

The transaction of business with foreign nations is Executive altogether. it belongs then to the head of that department, *except* as to such portions of it as are specially submitted to the Senate. *Exceptions* are to be construed strictly. the Constitution itself indeed has taken care to circumscribe this one within very strict limits: for it gives the *nomination* of the foreign Agent to the President, the *appointment* to him & the Senate jointly, & the *commissioning* to the President. this analysis calls our attention to the strict import of each term. to nominate must be to propose: *appointment* seems that act of the will which constitutes or makes the Agent: & the Commission is the public evidence of it. but there are still other acts previous to these, not specially enumerated in the Constitution; to wit 1. the destination of a mission to the particular country where the public service calls for it: & 2. the character, or grade to be employed in it. the natural order of all these is 1. destination. 2. grade. 3. nomination. 4. appointment. 5. commission. if *appointment* does not comprehend the neighboring acts of *nomination*, or *commission*, (& the constitution says it shall not, by giving them exclusive to the President) still less can it pretend to comprehend those previous & more remote of *destination* & *grade*. the Constitution, analysing the three last, shews they do not comprehend the two first. the 4th. is the only one it submits to the Senate, shaping it into a right to say that "A. or B. is unfit to be appointed." now this cannot comprehend a right to say that "A. or B. is indeed fit to be appointed, but the grade fixed on is not the fit one to employ," or "our connections with the country of his destination are not such as to call for any mission." the Senate is not supposed by the Constitution to be acquainted with the concerns of the Executive department. it was not intended that these should be communicated to them; nor can they therefore be qualified to judge of the necessity which calls for a mission to any particular place, or of the particular grade, more or less marked, which special and secret circumstances may call for. all this is left to the President. they are only to see that no unfit person be employed.

It may be objected that the Senate may, by continual negatives on the *person*, do what amounts to a negative on the *grade*; & so indirectly defeat this right of the President. but this would be a breach of trust, an abuse of the power confided to the Senate, of which that body cannot be supposed capable. so the President has a power to convoke the legislature; & the

Senate might defeat that power by refusing to come. this equally amounts to a negative on the power of convoking. yet nobody will say they possess such a negative, or would be capable of usurping it by such oblique means. if the Constitution had meant to give the Senate a negative on the grade or destination, as well as the person, it would have said so in direct terms, & not left it to be effected by a sidewind. it could never mean to give them the *use* of one power thro the *abuse* of another.

Ms., Adams Family Manuscript Trust, MHi; FC:dft and letterpress copy, Jefferson Papers, DLC; lbk, Washington Papers, DLC. An endorsement, in Washington's hand on the manuscript copy, reads, "Construction of the Powers of the Senate with respect to their agency in appointg. ambassadors &ca. and fixing the grade."

George Washington to James Madison, 27 April

If the weather will permit, & Mr. Madison's health suffer him to go out to day, the Presdt. would be glad if he would give him a call before he goes to the House.

Copy, Sparks Papers, MH.

George Washington, Diary, 27 April

Had some conversation with Mr. Madison on the propriety of consulting the Senate on the places to which it would be necessary to send persons in the Diplomatic line, and Consuls; and with respect to the grade of the first—His opinion coincides with Mr. Jays and Mr. Jeffersons—to wit—that they have no Constitutional right to interfere with either, & that it might be impolitic to draw it into a precedent their powers extending no farther than to an approbation or disapprobation of the person nominated by the President all the rest being Executive and vested in the President by the Constitution.

Washington Diary, ViHi.

George Washington, Diary, 7 May

Exercised in the forenoon, Endeavoured through various Channels to ascertain what places required, and the characters fittest for Consuls at them.

As the House of Representatives had reduced the Sum, in a Bill to provide for the expences of characters in the diplomatic line, below what would enable the Executive to employ the number which the exigencies of Government might make it necessary ~~to employ~~ I thought it proper to intimate to a member or two of the Senate the places that were in contemplation to send persons to in this Line—viz. to France & England (when the latter manifested a disposition to treat us with more respect than She had done upon a former occasion)[1] Ministers Plenipotentiary—and to Spain, Portugal & Holland Chargé des Affaires. and having an opportunity, mentioned the matter unofficially both to Mr. Carroll & Mr. Izard.

Washington Diary, ViHi.

[1] The reference is to John Adams's tenure as the American ambassador to England, 1785–88.

SUNDAY, 25 APRIL 1790

Rain (Johnson)

John Adams to John Trumbull

Your favors of March 30th and April 17 came to hand last night By "the attack in melee" you mean I suppose, that written by Ned Church,[1] a cockfighting cousin and companion of Charles Jarvis a devoted instrument of Mr. H. [*John Hancock*]—Jarvis's mother was a Church. This fellow this Ned Church I know nothing of. I scarcely ever spoke to him in my life—His traiterous brother[2] I knew very well, and the vendue man his father.

I dispair of ever seeing the Ancient Dominion wiser; their stupid and mulish systems have many a time brought America to the brink of ruin. And R. H. Lee as little as you and I think of him as a statesman, is as great as any one I ever knew from that State excepting only Washington yet I am on perfectly good terms with them all.

Mr. Maddison is a studious scholar, but his reputation as a man of abilities is a creature of French puffs. Some of the worst measures, some of the most stupid motions stand on Record to his infamy. I mean that for compelling American ministers at the Peace to communicate every thing to the French ministers, and do nothing without their consent.[3] You hint at suspicions of motives of envy against the Secretary [*Hamilton*]. I would rather hope it is defference to constituents. This is defalcation enough from a character, but not so much as the other. The jealousies and envies of emulation are however the Devil. There are jealousies and envies arising from rivalries for the places of President for the places of Governors of States, for seats in Senates, for offices of State and Judicature; and these passions are increasing to such a degree as to endanger extremely the union of the States: and yet nobody sees them. There is a low hypocricy crept in among us, a solemn dissimulation which will not allow any man to own that himself or any other American has the feelings of humanly nature. An indifference about rank is counterfitted and falsely intended, while the passion for it is eating up the hearts of all men, as the Spartans fox tore out his bowels because he would not own the fox was there.[4] *** Rosseau's examples of the Doge and the Pope are very apposite and very conclusive. They prove incontestibly the efficacy of pageantry. They prove with equal force that this efficacy may be applied to evil purposes. But what is there that may not! Religion and government have both been as ill used as pageantry. Signs do not necessarily imply abuse: they have been applied to good uses as well as bad. If government cannot be had nor laws obeyed without some parade as I fully beleive, we must have some parade or no laws. Is there a Clergyman in Connecticutt who does not wear a band? have they left off the distinction of a red gate and board fence before their houses? Could the people of New England go through the revolution without liberty trees and liberty poles? Was there not as much pomp in escorting delegates to Congress in 1774 and 1776, as in the king of France's tour to Cherbourg?[5] What was all the parade of the Presidents late tour through New England? We practice these things as much as other Country's; our feelings prompt them as forcibly, and we can do as little without them. Was not Mr. Hancock escorted from York town to Boston in 1774 by twelve light horse[6]—a king of England or a Roman Consul had no more. We practice a strange hypocrysy upon ourselves—We ought not to shock the people, but we need not deceive them and ourselves too. Let us be moderate and reasonable but not false. There is a decency in every thing and the common sense of mankind requires an attention to it. There is not in Europe so much attention to it in their common Country churches, as there is in our New England parishes to their meeting houses. Is there a being so low as not to be offended at the thought of worshipping God in a barn or a mean house? Why is plate and handsom vessells at the communion table so much thought of? A common wooden dish and a black bottle would do as well in essence; yet every mortal sees and feels the horrid impropriety of such a thought. Whenever mankind mean to respect any thing they always treat it decently. Why do they build monuments and erect grave stones? Why do they plain and paint a coffin? Why do they cover it with a pall? Why do they march in procession at a funeral? Why do they give gloves? After such grave examples it may seem ludicrous to descend to lesser things; but I mean nothing ludicrous or light. Why do the children call father and mother instead of John and Tom? Why do they call one another Johnny Jemmy and Suzy instead of John James and Sue? In short in the meanest family on earth you will find these little distinctions, marks, signs, and decencies which are the result of nature feeling, reason; which are policy and government in their places as much as Crowns and tiaras ceremonies, titles &c. in theirs—Whenever the people of America shall intend sincerely to have any government, they will treat it decently; but as yet one half of them have no such intention. They have sense enough to know that signs and Ceremonies of a decent kind would soon establish a government, but as they abhor the end, they oppose the means.

I thank you kindly for your anecdote about throwing away votes. Both H—n [*Alexander Hamilton*] and W—b [*Samuel Blachley Webb*] were for me, and I really suspect that they had some real fears that I might have the greatest number of votes. yet in all suppositions it was a corrupt intrigue and an insidious maneuvre.

Our Secretary has however I think good abilities and certainly great industry. He has high minded ambition and great penetration. He may have too much disposition to intrigue; if this is not indulged I know not where a better minister for his department could be found. But nothing is more dangerous, nothing will be more certainly destructive in our situation than the spirit of intrigue. With our delightful symphony of elections of Presidents Governors Senators & & & when intrigue comes in, and is not resisted, we shall have discords of the harshest kinds I fancy I could make a curious rattling in the world by moving an inquiry into the maneuvre in my election. But if it is not repeated it had better be forgotten. If it should be repeated it must be inquired into. The doctrine of throwing away votes is itself a corruption, a base motion in the house or Senate to institute an inquiry would produce a trepidation in many hearts. Throwing away a vote is betraying a trust it is a breach of honour, it is a perjury it is equivalent to all this in my mind. Electors are not despots. They have no discretionary dispensing power—Let Intriguers and dupers both consider this before another election. They may depend upon it they will find in me a man who has patience but will not be a sport nor a dupe. If a repitition takes place I will drag out to public infamy both Dupors and Dupees, let who will be among the number.

FC:lbk, Adams Family Manuscript Trust, MHi. Sent to Hartford, Connecticut. The omitted text describes Adams's role in various diplomatic missions to Europe during and after the Revolutionary War, and his pre-war stance on independence. In acknowledging Benjamin Franklin's recent death, he also protests that he felt "no ill will to his memory but I owe more to truth than to his fame" by attributing his public conduct "neither to the character of an honest man, nor to that of a man of sense."

---

[1] The satirical poem *The Dangerous Vice* ——, by Edward Church.

[2] Edward's brother, Benjamin Church (1734–1777?), one of the earliest leaders of the Revolutionary movement in Boston, turned that role to account as a spy for the British as early as 1774. Exposed and convicted of espionage in 1775, he remained jailed until he was permitted to leave Boston in a schooner that apparently sank en route to the West Indies.

[3] Madison served on a committee (chaired by future New York City mayor James Duane and including future FFC member D. Carroll) that reported a resolution Congress passed unanimously on 4 October 1782, reminding its peace commissioners in Paris that all their

negotiations were to be conducted "in confidence and in concert" with the French ministry (*JCC* 23:638). There is no evidence crediting Madison as the primary author of the report; Adams may have conflated this measure with the resolution that Madison did push through Congress two weeks later, implying annoyance at the commissioners' dereliction of duty and requiring them to report back more frequently (*JCC* 23:663; *PJM* 5:202). In his narrative of the peace negotiations in the omitted text, below, Adams also blames Madison—correctly this time—for his successful motion in Congress on 12 July 1781, revoking Adams's commission for negotiating a treaty of commerce with Great Britain (*PJM* 3:188–89). Adams writes Trumbull that the measure "has hurt this Country more than Mr. Madison ever in his life did it good."

[4] Plutarch's Life of Lycurgus reports this example of how one Spartan youth accepted death rather than acknowledge failure as a fox thief, in a society where successful thievery was a proof of masculinity and prowess.

[5] All the kings of France until Louis XV had their royal privileges confirmed in a ceremony at the important fortified port city of Cherbourg, in Normandy, France.

[6] Hancock resigned his presidency of the Continental Congress, then meeting at York, Pennsylvania, in October 1777. He did not receive a military escort until he reached New York in early November, en route home to Boston (*LDC* 8:132n).

Benjamin Goodhue to Stephen Goodhue

Things remain as to the funding and assumption much the same, as they have done some time past and I suspect one of those days we may be sufficiently tired of the bussines as to refer the whole to next session and see if we can come to gather afterwards in better humour, I hope if the assumption does not obtain the other may not. for I think as do all of our folks, that they never ought to be seperated, do any of the holders of Contin'l. securities think the Secry. [*Hamilton*] has not reported an ample interest for them, I ask this because E[*lias*]. H[*asket*]. Derby between ourselves wrote me in that tone, now I thought that all the holders would jump at the proposal, and pray it might be adopted I am sure they would this way—wish you would tell me the general language on the question of assumption, for Mr. Derby intimated to me that the loosing it would not give so much umbrage as to have the debt of the U.S. funded upon so open a violation of contract as the Secry. proposed, but don't mention it.

ALS, Goodhue Family Papers, MSaE. Addressed to Salem, Massachusetts; franked.

Benjamin Goodhue to Insurance Offices

The Secretary of the Treasury yesterday made his report relative to the several inconveniences in our revenue laws—his report is very lengthy, and he has stated perhaps every inconvenience and hardship that has occur'd, and has proposed remedies, it is Committed to a committee of five, and as I am one, will do every thing in my power for bringing ~~for~~ forward the bills for carrying it into effect as soon as possible [*Coasting Bill HR-89; Collection Act HR-82; Tonnage Act HR-78*]—its a great misfortune we are so much divided upon the funding and assumption, as it not only prevents any decisive measures with regard to those great objects, but greatly unfits us ~~from~~ for attending to any other bussines—propositions are yet before us for specifying the amount from each State to be assumed, with a view of accommodating the subject to those who had heretofore objected to the former proposition as too general and uncertain, but it does not yet appear to have the effect intended, and I suspect nothing can be brought forward that will induce the opponents to relinquish their opposition—what will eventualy be the result is totaly uncertain.

ALS, Goodhue Letters, NNS. Addressed to Salem, Massachusetts; franked.

Arthur Lee to Thomas Lee Shippen

***

I shall by no means deem you enthusiastic, in what you say of Mr. Madison's agreeableness in conversation. I have heard others say the same & as far as I have had experience think with you. It is his political conduct which I condemn. That without being a public knave himself he has always been the supporter of public knaves, & never, in any one instance has concurrd to check, censure, or controul them—That he has had such vanity as to suppose himself superior to all other persons, conducting measures without consulting them & intolerant of all advice or contradiction—That in consequence, he has been duped by the artful management of the rapacious Morris & the intrigueing Marbois. It is possible he may have thought himself right in all this, but in acquitting his intention we hazard the credit of his understanding. ***

I love Genl. Knox & Mrs. [*Lucy Flucker*] Knox & esteem Izard—Mrs. [*Alice DeLancey*] Izard is an incomparable Woman. Remember me to them, if this shoud find you in N.Y. ***

ALS, Shippen Papers, DLC. Written from Alexandria, Virginia. In a few places where the ALS is damaged, missing letters have been taken from a copy in the Lee Family Papers, ViHi.

William Maclay to George Logan

Your letter of the 12th did not reach my hands 'till Yesterday. You have my hearty thanks for it. I find by the public papers, That the Death of Doctor [*Benjamin*] Franklin, which You mentioned as very probable, has actually taken place. he was old and full of days and honors too. he certainly deservd the name of a *Great Man.* how few have arrived at his degree of Usefulness, with all the advantages of expensive educations. his abilities may be said to have been all his own.

The Representatives in Congress have resolved to wear crape, in the usual way, for a Month, as Mourning for him. a motion of a similar kind was made in the Senate, but it miscarried.

Nothing very material has taken place lately in our house. That which appeared to me the most so, was the bill *For regulating the military establishment of the United States* [*HR*-50*a*]. I opposed the Title; and indeed the whole principle of it. For a *Military establishment* is, in fact, a *standing Army.* I wished, at least, to limit it, in point of time to Two Years; the Term fixed by the Constitution, beyond which, appropriations of Money, for supporting an Army, cannot extend.[1] But this we lost, with so small a minority, that we could not obtain the Yeas and nays. The Mutiny bill, in England,[2] on which the regulation of their Army depends, is passed annually. so that tho' they have, in fact, a standing army. Yet in theory, it is only annual. We have not left ourselves the connotation, of opposing even Theory to a standing Army. for the smallness of the number (1216) is nothing to the principle. They are enlisted for three Years. This, and the Clause in the Constitution, which prohibits the appropriation of money for their Support for more than Two Years, at a time. are all the Checks that remain with Congress. I freely confess, my Dear Friend, That no Act of Congress, has given me such deep Vexation. I was by no means fully satisfyed with the reasons offered for the keeping up, and augmenting these Troops. I do not consider it as warranted, in time of Peace, by the Constitution of the United States. and it is directly against both the old and new Constitution of our State.[3] I however have full confidence, in the good Sense of the People of America. And that every thing of a dangerous nature, will be checked before it *arrives* to any hight. altho' this affair has given me much Uneasiness, Yet my acquaintances think nothing of the Matter. and attribute, my opposition, to the Measure, to an over refinement of Republicanism. When the law appears, I scarce think it will escape censure. But if it is animadverted upon, I hope it will be done with temper & decency. I confess many things have been carried In Congress, far from my liking. I have however no right to be pleased in everything. and I hold as part of my political creed. Nunquam desperandum est de republica.[4]

ALS, Logan Papers, PHi. Addressed to "Stenton," Logan's estate in the present-day Germantown neighborhood of Philadelphia; franked. On 1 July 1829, Logan's wife, Deborah Norris Logan (1761–1839), penned a summary of the letter on its endorsement page that concluded "W. McClay. was a man of good sense and a firm Republican for whom my dear Husband always professed much regard."

[1] Article 1, section 8, paragraph 12. For another of Maclay's accounts of this episode, see *DHFFC* 9:249.

[2] First passed in 1689 to punish mutiny and desertion, it remained Parliament's only legislation appropriating money for Britain's army.

[3] Pennsylvania's second constitution, drafted in the winter of 1789–90 but not ratified until September of that year, provided "that no standing army shall, in time of peace, be kept up without the consent of the legislature" (Article IX, section XXII).

[4] The affairs of the republic are never to be despaired of.

Robert Morris to Mary Morris

Your letter of the 21st relieved me from a good deal of anxiety as I had previous to the receipt of it, taken up an opinion that some sickness in the Family had prevented your writing to me sooner.

I am however very happy to know that you are all Well—give my Love to all the Children & tell them to take care of themselves, they are hardly Sensible of the blessings of good Health, as fortunately they have known but little of sickness—I hope Mr. [*Garrett*] Cottringer is quite recovered; if his Illness had continued I must have gone Home which would have greatly interfered with my pursuits here, and I find those pursuits require more care and attention than I expected I cannot get on so fast in the Settlement of Accounts as I wish,[1] The officers having many others to mind as well as mine so that we have constant interruptions and some other difficulties to encounter but I shall persevere untill I get through. ***

The President of the U.S. went last Monday Morning over to Long Island on purpose to get room for Exercise and to change the Air, and Returned last Night, He looked very Ill before he went, I have not Seen him Since his Return so that I dont know wether he has derived much benefit from his jaunt. Mrs. Washington looks as well as ever and by all appearance is as happy as can be, but as to the President I think it would do him good if we could change his place of Residence & bring him to our City, I intend soon to make a new attempt, but this to yourself for the present. *** tell Doctor [*John*] Jones that, remembering his admonitions I did not Kill the Dragon on St. Georges Night[2] altho I sat from dinner untill Ten oClock at night as Merry as Mr. Anybody and as much entertained with Songs of Glee, the St. George's Society here is Numerous and abounds with good Singers and Merry Fellows—And yesterday I took a pretty long Walk by way of Correcting the Humours that might possibly flow from the excess of the preceeding day & Evening. Mr. [*Thomas*] Montgomerie is to set off this Morning but he expects to Travel slowly, He has bought a Charriot & pair of Horses so that He can go at his ease and I suppose he will not reach Philadelphia sooner than Wednesday or Thursday I forgot to give him the invitation to take up his Old quarters but I will Write him a Note this Moment to ask him so to do.

I will Remit you an order of $200, say Two hundred Dollrs. either in this or in my next letter.

ALS, Morris Papers, CSmH. Place to which addressed not indicated. The omitted text relates to household gardening, Benjamin Franklin's will, and news of family friends, including Morris's landlord William Constable and the recovery from an illness of his son John, "an engageing little Creature."

---

[1] For background on Morris's frustrating cooperation with the treasury department's auditor in settling his ten year old public accounts, see *DHFFC* 8:663–65.

[2] The Sons of St. George, the city's oldest existing mutual aid society (founded in 1770), annually celebrated the feast day of England's patron saint on 23 April. George's legendary slaying of a dragon became synonymous for the drinking revelries that still take place on that anniversary in many English speaking countries.

Adam Stephen to James Madison

I reced. the pleasure of your letter, and am greatly obliged for your Sentiments on the assumption of the State Debts—If it could be justly done, it would greatly contribute to the establishment of the Fœderal Government—The N.E. & S.W. parts of our Empire are not like to assimalate, and Should the Devil bring about a dissolution The N. Englanders have such a Coasting Trade that Their imposts and Tonnage into the Southern States would amount to a Large Sum, almost half the Trade of N. England is to the S. States.

The Senate have met with great Applause for not taking Notice of the Quakers Memorial,[1] and people find great fault with your House for wasting so much time and Expence, in a frivoulous manner.

It has disturbed the Minds of our people, and lessened their Confidence in Congress.

We had a Report here that the Se[*c*]retary of the Treasury was killed in a duel,[2] and were all in mourning.

Inclosd. you have the Expostulations of Potowmac. I hope the people of N. England will See their Interest so plainly that they will give instructions to their Delegates in favour of Potowmac—But I have a Suspicion that the Restless Massachusettians, are entering into new plans of Government—They have taken upon them to dictate more Amendment[3]—Our Constitution at this Rate is to change Annually.

N. B. I have inclosd. to Mr. White the Expostulations directd to the Printers of N. England, and would be glad that they had them before they were made public at New York.

[*Enclosure*]

The Expostulations of Potowmac

As my interests were treated with great indifference in an august Assembly, lately, by gentlemen, whose connexions I conceived to be under obligations to me; in duty to myself, I am led to make some observations, which may tend to set gentlemen right—as they seem to have acted on false principles, misled by some designing men. I conceived great hopes of Mr. A—s [*Ames*], from some speeches in the House, in the first part of the session. When virtues of an amiable and exalted nature accompany great talents, they do honor to the man, and are essentially serviceable to his country.

It was commendable in Mr. A—s[4] to endeavor to get acquainted with the different communications with the Western Country, and their distances: It was a misfortune that he fell into the hands of the wrong person: He, being a gentleman of candour, did not suspect the insiduous designs of the informant, and was unluckily taken in. He believed he had his information from a person he might depend on. Had Mr. A—s extended his enquiry, he might have met with my exact portrait, from the place where I first appear on the surface of the earth, to where I am dissolved in the embraces of Chesapeake, in an actual survey made by order of the King, in a dispute between his Majesty and the late Lord Fairfax.[5] Mr. A—s, from his information, was led to declare, that the tide-water on Potowmac was three hundred and four miles from Pittsburgh; now, by the communication lately opened, it is scarcely three hundred miles from Alexandria to Marietta, upwards of one hundred miles below Pittsburgh.

This informant leads Mr. A—s up Susquehanna to Juniatta, then up Juniatta, and Awauch [*a walk*] far o'er the hills to Connomaugh. This communication is a discovery superior to any made by the late celebrated Capt. [*James*] Cooke, in his last voyage. What resembles it most is De Fonte, a river of the West, through which, and some Lakes contiguous, a Dutchman, fond of the marvellous, declared he arrived safe in the Atlantic.[6]

Now, as Mr. A—s was misled by his insiduous informant, and made a diffusive speech on the occasion, which served only to perplex the truth, and bring simple facts into doubt, with people who were strangers to the situation and circumstances of these waters, he, with his informant, whom I shall distinguish by the name of Connomaugh, may have used their endeavours to impress the Members from New-England with the same sentiments; and hence originated the measures so obstinately pursued by the gentlemen of the juncto; because they thought they were in the right: But on re-consideration, they will find themselves misled, and that they had greatly mistaken the interest of the States they had the honor to represent. As this is the case, it is to be hoped that they will have candor enough to acknowledge it; so far from being derogatory, it will do them honor; it would be imitating one of the greatest Princes on earth, in the age he lived. Darius Histaspes was misled by his Prime Minister, Hamon, and was induced by his false and malignant representations to issue a Decree for the destruction of the Jews; but as soon as his Majesty was made sensible he was imposed upon, he had the magnanimity to acknowledge it in a proclamation, and revoked the Decree, as far as the laws of the empire would permit.[7]

Mr. W—dsw—th [*Wadsworth*][8] declares, that being forced, and as it were, dragged by the throat to take the seat of government into consideration, as it has been prematurely brought on, he wished it finished directly; if he did not vote at that instant, he would go into bargaining again: That is to say, as it was prematurely brought on, let it be precipitately discussed! Such reasoning in a senator astonishes; it carries no conviction with it. FORCED, DRAGGED by the throat is harsh language. They speak a good smooth dialect in Connecticut; one of the most elegant addresses presented to the President of the United States, comes from that quarter.[9] The gentleman declares that the people of New-England would think the Union at an end, was the seat of government fixed on Potowmac: It disgusts me to hear the sacred Union mentioned with irreverence. Though that may be the sentiment of an individual, their representative, biassed perhaps by some money concerns in Philadelphia, the wise and considerate people of Connecticut have more understanding. What Mr. Wadsworth means by BARGAINING AGAIN, wants explanation, I hope it is not to be meant that he will bargain for his vote.

Mr. L—wr—e [*Laurance*][10] vindicates the eastern Members from any combination—It would give me pleasure to see him do it effectually: If he consults the interest of his constituents, he will vote for Potowmac, because the commercial and monied men of New-York will be deeply concerned in the funds, contracts, &c. The temporary seat of Congress will continue four or five years longer in New-York, if Potowmac is determined on for what is called the Permanent Seat. He thinks it improper to hold out terrors to the fancy: The proper way to convince is to address the understanding: this is certainly just, where understanding is to be found; but when what little there is, is wrapt up in an impenetrable cloud, and matters pre-judged, what is to be done? It is the duty of gentlemen to point out the dangers of adopting certain measures, and announce them to others who seem to be strangers to the consequence of adopting them.

I am old as the Cumæan Sybile; and, though not disposed to prophecy at present, can tell from experience that slight incidents give rise to great events.[11]

Mr. S—dg—k [*Sedgwick*][12] asserts that the wealth and population of the United States is to N.E. of Susquehannah: It is possible it may be so at present; but not so much as the gentleman gives out. In the exports from Boston, New-York and Philadelphia, it may be observed, that a great part of them are first imported by a circuitous trade; but the exports of the southern states are, in general, the natural produce of the soil, which is one mark of the wealth of nations. Gentlemen acquainted with the former state of Ormus,[13] Alexandria in Egypt, Venice, and Antwerp, will find wealth and population fluctuate and change according to circumstances. My sons are of opinion that the seat of Government on Potowmac, will contribute to their wealth and population; and, as they are the same people with those to the east of Susquehannah, the more populous and wealthy they are, the more they can contribute to the defence and support of Government. It is bad policy to throw any obstacle in the way to prevent their wealth and population. Mr. S—dg—k is not for adopting the constitutional mode of computing our numbers, and warmly declares that the black cattle of New-England may, with equal propriety, be estimated as the black people of the United States. The gentleman may observe that the tax on black people helped the United States through the war;[14] that it has contributed to the support of government since the peace; that their industry increases the wealth of the United States, as they increase our exports. This being the case, neither Mr. S—dg—k nor the horned cattle of New-England, can justly deny that certain attention is to be paid to their numbers.

Mr. S—dg—k, reasoning on the hint taken from Montesquieu, is in favor of Potowmac, as it approaches the mountains, where there lives a set of men as warlike as ever inhabited the mountains of Biscay [*the Pyrenees*] or Wales, whom all the pride and power of Rome could never totally subdue. An exploit performed lately by two boys of the name of Johnston, indicates enterprise, design, and intrepidity, scarcely to be paralleled in history. This is the country for soldiers. As to sailors, I boast of New-England-men; they are the true sons of the ocean; I glory in their enterprising genius, and rejoice in their success—I cherish a number of them in my bosom every winter; their temperance, and attention to business, give a good example to my sons. They open shop on board their vessel; dispose of their cargo (which, in general, consists of the natural produce and manufacture of New-England) for corn and other articles suitable to the West-Indies; carry them to the islands in the spring; barter them there for molasses, that favorite article, and necessary of life in New-England; and, for the most part, return under my wings in the winter.

In the spring, 1776, there were only thirty sea-vessels belonging to me and my brother JAMES (River) and twenty-two of them were commanded by New-England-men. After so great attention given by me to New-England-men, how comes it to pass that they put a river in competition with me, that never cherished a New-England-man in her bosom? This naturally leads me to ask if any of the Delegates from New-England were ever at sea, or concerned in trade? So great strangers do they appear to be to the real interest of their particular states. Do they know that several commercial gentlemen from New-England, are at the present time with me and the other rivers, soliciting contracts to supply the planters with brown linen, blankets and coarse woollens, and shoes for their families? If the seat of Government comes to Potowmac, they will have a great share of the money expended in the administration, and my waters will groan under the pressure of New-England manufactures, which they convey towards the Kentuckey and the territory of the Ohio. Although my sons are not in a habit of going to sea, they have equal merit. This was conspicuous at Eutaw, Ninety-Six, the Cowpens, King's Mountain, and Guilford![15] Hence it is plain, that united, we become a great and mighty people by sea and land; respected by the nations of the earth, and formidable to our enemies.

Mr. S—dg—k asks if a majority was not to govern? My sons are firmly attached to the union; they will bear with patience and strict attention, the conduct of the Delegates from the other states, as far as men of honor and liberal principles can do, consistent with liberty: But they have sense to distinguish between a common majority and an artificial one; nor will they be long governed by a juntocracy.

The same gentleman demands with authority—Are we to be told, that a respectable state would not have joined the union, had they known the proceedings of this House this day? Are Mr. S—dg—k's organs of hearing so delicate, that they cannot bear being impressed with the truth? If the language displeases, remove the cause, and the effects will cease. Let mutual attention and concessions take place, civilities will follow, and matters of government will go on smoothly and with ease.

As it is beyond all doubt, that my waters are, and will be the great thoroughfare to the country west of the mountains; the seat of government on my banks, or near them, will be an inducement to the inhabitants to come cheerfully under the same government, and to be subject to the same laws, and they will be the right arm of the United States: Whereas, were they a separate people, and become hostile, [*blotted out*] the states, [*blotted out*] east of the mountains would be exactly in the same situation to which the French were desirous to reduce them in the year 1753 and 4, when they took post at Læ Beuf, Venango, and Fort Du Quesne.[16] The middle states could not live in peace and safety. The population of the eastern states would avail but little, and the monies now raised would not be sufficient to defend their extensive frontiers. These people and the middle states must be subject to the same government and laws.

If the seat of Government is on Potowmac, the monies expended in the administration will be more equally divided among the states, when every state may have its share there will be no cause of complaint nor murmers. The merchants from Boston to Charleston will have an equal chance of furnishing supplies. The monied men will have equal chance in dealing in the funds, and making contracts with government, when the exigencies of the state require it: On the other hand, if the seat of government is at Germantown, or near it, that respectable city, Philadelphia, is a vortex which will ingulph, absorb, and swallow all the monies expended in the administration; will engross the contracts and command the stocks. To throw great wealth into the hands of a few men, will be dangerous to the states. They, in a short time, will have as great influence in making acts of Congress, as the treasury of England has in making acts of Parliament. Another great consequence of fixing the seat of Government on Potowmac, will be an amazing increase of the trade of New-England; they will have an equal chance of furnishing supplies; they will have a great share of the monies expended in the administration; their monied men will have an equal chance in dealing in the stocks and making contracts, when the public exigencies require it: but above all, they will have ready cash for the manufactures and produce of New-England. In a few years, their imports into the rivers within the Capes of Virginia will amount, annually, to about six or eight hundred thousand dollars, which will be a great object, and next to their fishery, this will be a strong cement to the union: an intercourse so constant, and mutually interesting, between New-England, Virginia, and Maryland, will, in a manner, incorporate the states.

In order to remove some groundless prejudices which Mr. S—dg—k and others entertain against me, I beg leave to mention a few facts that are incontrovertible.

VAN SWEARINGEN died lately, aged 107 years. He had lived seventy-one years on a plantation in Maryland, within two miles of my channel.[17]

Colonel THOMAS CRESSOP died lately upon my bank, aged 109.[18]

A certain DANIEL THOMPSON, born in a cave on the banks of the Delaware, before there was a house built in Philadelphia, died lately on Opeckon, within a few miles of my channel.

JOSEPH EDWARDS died lately, aged 102, who lived on Cape Capon [*Cacapon River, West Virginia*] time out of mind.

HUGH MILLAR is now living in my neighbourhood, aged 97.

DANIEL ROBERTS is now living with me, aged 92.

ROBERT BUCKLES is now living on my bank, aged 90.

PETER BURR nineteen children, eighteen of them on one plantation.

JOHN CONSTANCE, on Cape Capon, has twenty-six children.

BENJAMIN WARREN has sixteen children.

Greater instances of health, vigour, and longevity, are scarcely to be met with in America. Several people born in New-England have lived with me half a century; I cannot tell their age, but their heads are as white as the

Province of Main in the middle of January. I have now finished part of my duty to myself, and am a friend to mankind.

POTOWMAC

Waters of Potowmac, Nov. 20, 1789

ALS, Madison Papers, DLC. Written from Berkeley County, West Virginia. The enclosed broadside, no longer with the letter, is in the Rare Book Room, DLC (Evans 22076). It was authored by Stephen and first published in Martinsburg, West Virginia; reprinted at Alexandria, Virginia. The last section, beginning "Van Swearingen," was reprinted in newspapers at Portland, Maine; Boston; Hartford, Connecticut; and New York City (*NYDA*, 15 May).

---

[1] For more on the Quaker antislavery petitions, see *DHFFC* 8:314–38.

[2] A rumor generated by the Burke-Hamilton affair of honor; see *DHFFC* 8:478–80.

[3] Twelve additional Amendments to the Constitution had been proposed by a Massachusetts legislative committee. They were defeated in the state Senate in 1790.

[4] Ames spoke on 4 September 1789; see *DHFFC* 11:1442–46, 1449–55.

[5] In 1733 Thomas, sixth Lord Fairfax (1693–1781) brought suit against the crown colony of Virginia in order to determine the boundaries of his proprietary claim to Virginia's Northern Neck under the Culpeper Charter of 1688. Based on a survey and rival maps submitted by each party in 1737, the Privy Council defined Fairfax's holdings as everything east of a straight line drawn between the head springs of the Potomac and of the Conway River (the northwesternmost tributary of the Rappahannock River). The so called Fairfax Line was surveyed in 1746 and in 1747 the result was mapped by one of its surveyors, Thomas Jefferson's father Peter (1708–57) (Fairfax Harrison, "The Northern Neck Maps of 1737–1747," *WMQ*, 2nd series, vol. 4, 1[Jan. 1924]:1–15).

[6] James Cook's (1728–79) third and final voyage into the Pacific began in 1776 and included visits to the Hawaiian Islands, Nootka Sound, Alaska, and California. In 1708 an account was published of a 1640 voyage by an alleged Spanish admiral named Bartholomew de Fonte. It claimed that de Fonte had sailed up the west coast of North America and then east to Hudson's Bay.

[7] The account is from the book of Esther in the Old Testament.

[8] Wadsworth spoke on 3 September 1789; see *DHFFC* 11:1414.

[9] The Address was presented to Washington on 17 October 1789 when he was in New Haven; see *PGW* 4:202–3.

[10] Laurance's speeches were delivered on 3 September 1789; see *DHFFC* 11:1407, 1412.

[11] The earliest of the Sibyls. She and her nine books of prophecy resided near Naples, Italy, at the beginning of the sixth century B.C.

[12] Sedgwick's speeches were delivered on 3 September 1789; see *DHFFC* 11:1408–9, 1413.

[13] An ancient city state in present-day Iran.

[14] At the outbreak of the Revolutionary War, various forms of taxes were being levied on enslaved Blacks. In 1777 Virginia, Maryland, and North Carolina began taxing them as personal property rather than "tithables" in the form of a poll tax. Virginia and North Carolina soon reverted back to the poll tax (Robin Leigh Einhorn, *American Taxation, American Slavery* [Chicago, Ill., 2006], pp. 107–8).

[15] Revolutionary War battles in the Carolinas fought in 1780–81.

[16] Forts in western Pennsylvania.

[17] Garrett Van Swearingen (1690–1785).

[18] Thomas Cresap (ca. 1694–1787) who, in 1753, along with the Delaware Indian Nemacolin, blazed the trail from Cumberland, Maryland, to Pittsburgh for the Ohio Company of Virginia.

Letter from Boston

Yesterday the officers of the customs attached Capt. S—t's ship the Neptune,[1] for running goods that were not entered, and other breaches of the revenue laws. It is said more than 10,000 dollars duties had been paid on her cargo.

Unless public credit is firmly established, the revenue will decrease—and of course, many of our expected blessings vanish like a dream.

We still hope some medium may be thought of—some accommodation—that some enlivening ray may illumine our political horizon.

Should the Excise law of this Commonwealth be carried into full execution, it will do more injury to the Revenue of the United States than is at present conceived of.

GUS, 5 May; reprinted at Portland, Maine; New Haven, Connecticut; Charleston, South Carolina; and Augusta, Georgia.

---

[1]Captain James Scott's ship *Neptune* arrived at Boston on 15 April, forty-two days out of London ([Boston] *Massachusetts Centinel*, 17 April).

Other Documents

William Blount to John Gray Blount. *Blount* 2:49.

Thinks a funding bill will pass; "Hawkins says the Knowing ones say it will not."

George Clymer to Henry Hill. Summary and excerpt of three page ALS, *Libbie Catalog* 6 January 1891:item 3160. Addressed to Philadelphia; franked. The ellipses are in the source.

Clymer "writes of his annoyance and disgust at the conduct of public affairs, etc. '. . . The life I have led for a month past having furnished so little to the honour or interest of those who sent me, the petulant pertinacious wrangling and disingenuity and sophistry of that month is not to be matched since the days of the Council of Trent [*Italy, 1545–63*]. I am tired of the scene and wish for a little relaxation to an Algerine galley. . .'"

Bossinger Foster to Andrew Craigie. ALS, Craigie Papers, MWA. Written from Boston.

"People in this quarter" disappointed in COWH's rejection of assumption; the "Warmth" of Sedgwick's speech (*DHFFC* 13:1007–8) on the occasion is easily "accounted for, had his style however been less rash & more Chaste the impression might have been much stronger & ~~might~~ would more easily have reached the heart."

Nicholas Gilman to Jeremiah Fogg. ALS, Signers of the Constitution, Daughters of the American Revolution, Washington, D.C. Place to which addressed not indicated.

Is pleased at his appointment as delegate to general meeting of the Society of the Cincinnati; will probably attend if Congress adjourns "in season"; is disappointed that George Turner left for the Northwest Territory without sending on diplomas for Society members, but will make other arrangements for procuring them; quotes current rates of various types of certificates; has consulted with commissioner of army accounts and reports status of account of Jonathan Ferrar (1753–1827, of Rockingham County, New Hampshire).

Nicholas Gilman to Nathaniel Gilman. No copy known; mentioned in Jonathan Cass to Gilman, 7 May.

Nicholas Gilman to John Sullivan. No copy known; acknowledged in Sullivan to Gilman, 4 May.

Christopher Gore to Rufus King. ALS, King Papers, NHi. Written from Boston; franked. The reference in the last phrase is to Sedgwick's speech of 12 April, published in *GUS* two days later (*DHFFC* 13:1007–8).

News of non-assumption is "very unfavorable" to the people of Boston; failure to fund their debts "would make antifederalists of the town"; sends a bag of West India coffee; "Poor Sedgwick! wonderfully exercis'd! but then he has enjoyd the satisfaction of declaring it to the world."

Henry Jackson to Henry Knox. ALS, Knox Papers, Gilder Lehrman Collection, NHi. Written from Boston.

Boston public creditors plan to petition Congress.

Robert Morris to George Harrison. ALS, Brinton Coxe Papers, PHi. Addressed to Philadelphia. Answered 29 April.

Regrets that Harrison was not able to fulfill William Constable's "plan" (for purchasing Virginia state securities) during a recent journey; "When you Communicate your plan, you shall have the best advice that I am capable of giving on it"; Mary Morris will make arrangements with the overseers of the poor for the orphan or abandoned child that Harrison has mentioned; if Morris's prosperity had continued, he intended to establish a Marine Society for raising such boys and training them for the sea; "perhaps the time may yet arrive when I can put this plan in Motion."

George Thatcher to Jeremiah Hill. No copy known; acknowledged in Hill to Thatcher, 4 May.

George Thatcher to Dudley Hubbard. No copy known; acknowledged in Hubbard to Thatcher, 8 May.

George Thatcher to Moses Levy. FC, Thatcher Family Papers, MHi. Sent to Philadelphia.

Encloses extract (unlocated) of Philip Theobald's letter to Thatcher of 5 March, volume 18, with offer to serve as intermediary in the transaction.

George Thatcher to Philip Theobald. FC, Thatcher Family Papers, MHi. Sent to Pownalboro, Maine.

Returns letter from Theobald to Mary Cobb, enclosed in Theobald's last letter, and requests better directions for forwarding; has written Moses Levy regarding the recovery of Theobald's money from Mr. Hesshuyzen and offering to serve as "medium" for the transaction.

Jeremiah Wadsworth to Harriet Wadsworth. ALS, Wadsworth Papers, CtHi. Addressed to Hartford, Connecticut; franked; signed "Your affectionate friend & Parent."

Glad to hear all are better; directions for sending along Louis (a servant?); "the poor old fellow is honest & good he is intituled to our compassion"; saw Frances Otto (née de Crèvecoeur) the night before.

Monday, 26 April 1790

Theodore Sedgwick to Theodore Foster

I have had the pleasure to receive your favor of the 26. March. Very grateful to me, Sir, are your expressions of affection and regard, because from your general character I am induced to beleive them more than meer compliment—I have an additional pleasure in prospect in the visit with which you have authorised me to flatter myself.[1]

Every man of integrity or humanity will lament the evils attendant on the friends of good government in your state, and there is nothing which would give me more sincere pleasure than again to embrace in in the arms of the confederacy our wandering sister, who I am very confident will soon return to the family, from which she has been led astray by the address and arts of wicked or the delusion of ignorant or misguided men. I have the utmost confidence in her returning good sense and that she will voluntarily relieve us from all those disagreable consequences which might result from her longer continuance in her revolt. There is none so weak as not to perceive that an ultimate seperation between your state and the rest of the nation cannot take place.

Every thing new you will learn from the public papers. Though I have not the happiness to know Mrs. [*Lydia Fenner*] Foster, you will permit me to request you to make my affece. regards acceptable to her.

ALS, Foster Papers, RHi. Place to which addressed not indicated.

[1] Foster's ties to Sedgwick were influenced by their family connection: Foster was the son of Pamela Sedgwick's older half sister, Dorothy Dwight.

Brutus to the Public

ALMOST four months have elapsed since Congress met, the last time, and scarcely that number of Acts has yet passed. The expectations of all descriptions of men are disappointed, and discontent begins to spread among the creditors of the public. The tardiness of our national legislature, the narrow views that govern or divide that assembly, the factions that arise from causes that are trifling and distant from the general interest, are serious and alarming considerations to a people who have placed confidence in the national councils. Let us then examine the conduct of the men who compose Congress, and see whether they have made the public good the great and leading object of their deliberations.

In the first part of the first Session, their attention was directed to national concerns. Party views and little politics did not make their appearance to the prejudice of more important business. Then we saw (and we rejoiced at the spectacle) all parties exerting themselves to devise a revenue system for a great empire, and all parties disposed to make small concessions for the general good. When the great principles of the constitution were agitated, we saw a Maddison, an Ames, a Boudinot, a Benson and other able and eloquent men boldly come forward, and with the manliness of Roman Senators, contend for the establishment of a vigorous Executive, without which our whole government would have been a nerveless body. New-England read the debates, and every mouth was filled with the praises of Congress. Maddison's name was never mentioned but with admiration.

But at the close of the session, what a change! When the question respecting the Residence of Congress came before the house of Representatives, a question that did not materially affect the Union, because at present it is of not one shilling's consequence to the great body politic, where Congress reside, and of still less consequence is it to resolve *now* where they *will* reside hereafter, this trifling question called forth all the narrow selfish passions of the members, it was debated with more warmth of temper than any preceding question had been, however interesting to the United States. Even the cool, modest, temperate M— [*Madison*] was thrown off his guard, and rendered ridiculous by passion. It was moved to postpone the consideration of this unimportant question; but, no; the southern gentlemen urged the question, and it ended in their vexation. The debate however had a pernicious effect—it threw Congress into a ferment, which rendered them unfit to attend, with dispassionate coolness, to the business of the nation.

No sooner had Congress met a second time, than a memorial from the Quakers was presented;[1] and, mostly thro the influence of the eastern and middle states, was taken into consideration. Never was a more foolish, ill timed request, on the part of the Quakers; nor a more rash and imprudent step than the vote of the house to take up the memorial at this session. I can apologize for the zeal of the Quakers, until it becomes so mad and intemperate as to push them in *the face of their own interest.* But when men, with eyes open, take the most direct means to defeat their own purposes, I hardly know whether to pity their weakness or despise their obstinacy. Congress however deserve censure; for they knew, that, by the Constitution, nothing of consequence could be done in favor of the memorial, and it was their *duty* (and *policy* called loudly for the measure) to have dismissed it with an answer of ten lines. Instead of this, a question that affects *the interest of one part of the union most materially*, while with respect to the *other*, it is *little more than a question of speculation* or mere morality, a question therefore not of a general nature enough to demand the time and attention of Congress at this juncture, this question I say must be dragged before the house to set the whole into an uproar of faction and finish the business which another unimportant question had begun at the close of the last session.

A liberal enlightened people can forgive little errors in their legislators; they can pity and overlook a charge of lying, made in a fervid passion; but can they forget *repeated* acts of *public* folly? Will they not censure most freely the representatives who consent to trifle away the time of Congress? Will not these men be answerable for the factions that prevail in Congress, and the consequential delay of public measures?

The Report of the secretary is an object of inconceivable magnitude, and the assumption of the debts of the several states is an event that will sooner or later take place. Some of the gentlemen who oppose it, do not yet foresee the consequences of rejecting it. I am bold to say this, because it is most candid, for if they do foresee the final consequences, they cannot be honest men and friends to the general government. That vote of Congress which finally rejects the proposition for assuming the State debts; *will shake this government to its center.*

The public creditors compose a numerous and respectable, as well as the most wealthy part of the States. Whenever *better* provision is made for *some* of them than for *others*, a jealousy will spring up that will produce discordance between the States and the general government. Should the time ever arrive, when the creditors of the United States receive their interest in specie, and their paper shall approach to its nominal value; and should the State creditors, at the same time, receive but a small pittance for the interest of their money, and the principal remain at 3, 4, or 5 shillings on the pound, the general government will become as unpopular as that of Great Britain before the war; it will be deemed meritorious to elude the revenue laws; and the officers of the customs will be shunned and detested as a set of harpies. I boldly assert, that unless Congress shall assume the debts of the several states, their government will loose the confidence of our citizens in general; and unless the national government has their confidence, *the revenue will not generally be collected.* Do Congress forget that their revenues are collected in the *several States?* Do they forget that unless they protect the rights of *all* the citizens, the *neglected* will have recourse to the *nearest government* for redress; a government over which they have more influence? Do Congress forget, that their laws, thus become unpopular, will be feeble and inefficient? This is the prospect even with the most peaceable acquiescence in the partial measures of our national government.

But if the creditors of the several states, whose claims to justice stand on the same ground as those of the union, should ever combine together for the support of their demands, *it lies in their power to sever the union.* This is not said *in terrorem* by an interested person—I am not a creditor for a shilling, either of the *United* or of *particular States.* I offer only a dispassionate opinion on a very solemn subject, and sincerely hope that more enlarged views of national policy will produce a change of measures. The design of the national government was to *equalize the burdens of the war,* to *unite the interests* and *the powers* of the individual states, for the purposes of *common good*; the man therefore that attempts to prevent this *equality* of *burdens*, forfeits his claim to the *common protection*; and I flatter myself the gentlemen who oppose the *assumption*, will not have the face to ask for *money or forces to guard their frontiers from the Savages.*[2]

[Hartford] *Connecticut Courant*, 26 April; reprinted at Boston and New York City (*NYDG*, 30 April). The author's pseudonym was synonymous with freedom loving tyrannicides, from the sixth century B.C. consul who legendarily founded the Roman republic, to Julius Caesar's assassin, Marcus Brutus (ca. 85–42 B.C.).

---

[1] For more on the Quakers' antislavery petitions, see *DHFFC* 8:314–38.

[2] Opposition to assumption was strongest in the delegations of Virginia, North Carolina, and Georgia, three states with extensive western frontiers that were experiencing hostilities with Native Americans.

A Card

A DISTRESSED officer presents his compliments to Messrs. Wadsworth, Gerry, Smith and Vining, and begs to interest the same feelings and eloquence, which they lately exercised in Congress in behalf of Baron Steuben,[1] in his favor. He served his country faithfully for seven years during the late war. A year after the peace he sold his certificates for 3/9 in the pound, to pay some debts he contracted for the support of his family. He now humbly solicits the charity of a few dollars to pay his house-rent. The honor of Congress he conceives is concerned in relieving his wants, for they never can suffer one of those men, to whom they owe the existence of the government, from which they derive their power and consequence, to end his days in a gaol, or a poor house.

FG, 26 April; reprinted at Boston and Baltimore. The title refers to the calling card used in society when paying visits.

---

[1] For more on Gen. Frederick William Steuben's petition for compensation and the resulting Steuben Act [HR-60], see *DHFFC* 7:201–46.

Other Documents

Thomas Jefferson to Henry Lee. FC:letterpress, Jefferson Papers, DLC. For the full text, see *PTJ* 16:385–86.

The more equitable distribution of public offices is another reason for moving the seat of government to a more central location; partisans of assumption of the state war debts are nearly equally divided in Congress; it will probably be some time before it is decided; the question's fate in the Senate is not yet known.

Richard Henry Lee to Thomas Lee Shippen. ALS, Shippen Family Papers, DLC. Place to which addressed not indicated. For the full text, see *Lee* 2:509.

Is not surprised that Shippen is drawn so precipitously back to Philadelphia; "the numerous beauties, the many friends, the gaities & amusements of the Metropolis [*New York*] have no charms for you"; forwards enclosed letter; will keep [*Edmund*] Burke's "Philippic" "for the amusement of some friends here," but will return it later.

Peter Muhlenberg to Benjamin Rush. Combined summaries of one page ALS from *Parke-Bernet Catalog* 468(1943):item 170 and *Carnegie Book Shop Catalog* 101(1943):item 857. Franked.

Encloses copy of speech by Madison; mentions possible adjournment.

David Sewall to an Unknown Recipient. ALS, Miscellaneous Manuscripts, NHi. Written from York, Maine; place to which addressed not indicated. Internal evidence suggests the recipient was a resident of Boston and probably a judge (such as John Lowell).

Strong has written that Chief Justice Jay and Justice William Cushing are to ride the eastern circuit that spring.

Samuel W. Stockton to Elias Boudinot. ALS, Stimson Boudinot Collection, NjP. Written from Trenton, New Jersey; sent by post.

Has not yet heard reply from his letter of the previous week; "unless you do something of consequence and that *speedily too*," regarding funding, "we shall all starve to death"; public opinion in Philadelphia and elsewhere recognizes an "absolute necessity of its being completed this session or the public credit & national character will be in danger of sinking forever."

Oliver Whipple to John Adams. ALS, Adams Family Manuscript Trust, MHi. Written from Portsmouth, New Hampshire; answered 18 May.

Office seeking: appointment as federal excise collector for New Hampshire when the office is created; the New Hampshire members of Congress, being all natives of the state, already have their circle of connections to provide for; Langdon, "my Friend & Neighbour," will support him; Livermore is "a good Man," but will support his own friends; asks Adams to speak to Langdon and mentions Dalton, King, Thatcher, Goodhue, Partridge, and Leonard as other references; fondly recalls the four months he spent as a student-boarder in Adams's father's house.

[Charleston] *State Gazette of South Carolina*, 26 April.

Izard has been replaced as a delegate to the state constitutional convention.

TUESDAY, 27 APRIL 1790

Snow & Cold Rain (Johnson)

John Brown to George R. Clark

Your favor of the 30th. Jany. came to hand this Morning—The Act of Congress which you will find inclosed [*Patents Act HR-41*] contains all the information I can give you relative to obtaining a Patent Right for the Discovery you have made—Several applications for Patent Rights for supposed improvements in Navigating of Boats have been made but as yet no Patents have issued—*Mr. Jefferson* has accepted the appointment of Secretary of State & is now in the discharge of the duties of that Office Your favor of the 20th. August signifying your willingness to favor the World with a Narative of your Campaigns in the Western Country gave me as well as many of your friends in this quarter great pleasure I hope you have not relinquished a work which would make so important an addition to the History of the Revolution—*Mr. Madison* will chearfully undertake to revise & arrange the collection of facts should you please to put ~~them~~ it into his Hands but begs you to desend in the recital even to minutiæ.

Acts have passed & are passing the present Session of Congress for carrying into effect a new System relative to Indian Affairs—The plan is—to encrease the number of Regular Troops & milatary Posts upon the whole extent of our frontiers—to quiet the hostile Indians by Treaties—to establish a commercial intercourse with them under proper regulations & upon such liberal principles as to supply them with Goods &c. upon terms more advantageous than offered by British or Spainards—& thus establish a permanent peace upon the foundation of Interest & friendly intercourse—I inclose you a few of the late Gazettes they will inform you of the News of this place.

ALS, Draper Papers, WHi. Addressed to "Bear Grass," outside present-day Louisville, Kentucky.

John Brown to Harry Innes

Your very agreeable favor of the 15th. March was handed to me a few hours ago for which I return you my sincere thanks—I immediately waited upon the Treasurer of the U. States [*Samuel Meredith*] & presented your Dft. for payment—being desirious to inform you of its fate by the next Western Mail which sets out in an hour from this time Your application differing from the Mode established by the Treasury department occasioned some difficulty but I had influence enough with the Secretary to prevail on him to issue a Warrant for the Money which I shall receive tomorrow & shall with great care & chearfulness endeavour to appropriate ageeably to your wishes If I cannot in a few days purchase a good Bill on Richmond or meet with a safe Oppy. of sending the Money I will inclose your letter & advise Colo. [*James*] Innes to draw upon me for the amt. The Books you wish me to procure shall be forwarded shortly to Mr. Hoops also the money to Mr. Dobson Printer[1]—The Secretary of the Treasury recommend it to you to execute & forward a Power of Atty. to some person in this place authorising to receive your salary from time to time as it may become due—Mr. [*John*] Beckley or myself or both will chearfully undertake that trust.

I am unable to express the pain I felt on reading the long list contained in your letter of the Masacres & depredations of the Indians committed upon the defenceless Inhabitants of Kentucke. I have from time to time communicated to the President & Secy. at War all the information which I have recd. from you & my other friends in the District upon this Subject urging earnestly the necessity of adopting immediate measures for the protection of our frontiers Some step for that purpose would have been taken place long since had not the President been in daily expectation of the passage of such Acts by Congress as would enable him to adopt a general System relative to Indian affairs & therefore was unwilling to have recourse to temporary expedients—Finding greater delay relative this Business in Congress than he had expected he has issued orders for a certain number of Scouts to be kept in service in each of the Counties in Kentucke (Fayette excepted) giving to you instead by the Commanding Officer or Governor of Western Teritory a superintending power over the Business[2]—This alteration I suggested not doubting but it would be more agreeable to the people of the District & consequently that you would excuse the trouble—The Dispatches upon this subject were forwarded to you by last Post—The plan proposed for the defence of the frontiers is to encrease the Number of Regular Troops & of Military Posts—to quiet the Hostile Indians by treaties—open a commercial intercourse with them under proper regulations & upon such liberal principles as to supply them with Goods &c. upon better terms than they can procure from the British or Spaniards & thus establish peace upon the foundation of Interest & friendly intercourse. The Act for increase of the Troops [*Military Establishment Act HR-50a*] has passed—total 1200—The Report of the Secretary relative to support of Public Credit still under consideration. Resolutions providing for the funding of the foreign & Domestic Debt have passed the House & a Committee appointed to bring in a Bill for that purpose The Commtee. of the whole was yesterday discharged from the further consideration of the Resolution relative to the assumption of the State Debts You will find part of the debates upon this subject in the Gazettes I herewith inclose—No amendments proposed this Session to the Judicial Act—some of your objections to it were suggested when on its passage & all of them merit serious attention when the subject is again taken up—tis acknowledged by all that the Act is very objective & requires considerable alterations & amendments—if it is taken up this Session the alteration of the [*lined out*] Terms of the Court for Kentucke which you propose shall be attended to—I do not expect an adjournment will take place before July.

The letter from the Directors of the Kentucke Manufacturing Society[3] to which you refer me has not come to hand nor have I recd. any letter from them except the first by Mr. Yeizer tho have written three or four to them advising of my proceedings in executing their commands—requiring further instructions more money &c. I have regulated my conduct by their letter by Mr. Yeizer have procured all the Necessary Machinery &c. employed a Manager, & Manufacturers & yesterday returned from Philada. to which place I found it necessary to repair in order to make final arrangements for the transportation of the whole to Kentucke The whole will move from Philada. about 5th of May The ~~amount of the~~ outfit including Machinery traveling expences of Manager & family & Manufacturers—& price of a Boat amounted to 530 Dollars the expence of Waggonage not included the amt. of which I could not assertain as the articles were not cased & packed, but from the enormous price of Grain it will come very high—the deficiency of money I must advance—I wish you to communicate this information to the other Managers as I have not time at present to write to them—If the engagements I have entered into would permit I would defer forwarding Manager &c. untill I hear further relative to the delay you apprehend from the distruction of the Crop of Cotton last season But the arrangements I have made are such that (accidents excepted) you may expect the whole in Kentucke early in June—I have some thoughts of sending on with them 200 or 300 lbs. of West India Cotton to give employment untill the new Crop comes in—My Sentiments relative to a Seperation I will give you in my next not having time at present This I write in my place in the House during a warm debate[4] therefore will offer no other appology—I expect to return to the District in August probably through the Wilderness[5]—sho[*uld*] be extremely happy to have the pleasure of seeing Mrs. [*Elizabeth*] Innis in Virga. pray present my most respectful Complts. to her—I had the pleasure to see Mrs. Shields in Philada. the day before yesterday she was perfectly well & looked handsomer, than [*torn*] her before [*torn*] [*w*]ill return to Kentucke in the fall.

Tell me as a friend how Br[*other*]. James [*Brown*] makes out—present me to him as I cannot write to him by this Post.

P. S. Pray forward the Letters herewith enclosed The Laws of Congress will be forwarded to you by the Manager also Journals of last Session John Walker has taken his seat as Senator vice Grayson whose place I fear will not shortly be supplied—in him our loss was great.

ALS, Innes Papers, DLC. Addressed to Danville, Kentucky; franked.

---

[1] Thomas Dobson (1751–1823), a native Scotsman and Philadelphia publisher.

[2] The orders were first relayed by Knox to Governor Arthur St. Clair and Gen. Josiah Harmar on 3 March, and authorization to Innes to call out up to eight scouts per county followed on 13 April. The orders were rescinded in July (*PGW* 5:235n).

[3] The Kentucky Society for Promoting Manufactures sought to establish a cotton factory at Danville (Patricia Watlington, *The Partisan Spirit: Kentucky Politics, 1779–1792* [New York, 1972], pp. 192–93). Brown probably refers to Engelhard Yeiser, a prominent merchant of Baltimore at that time, who was involved in the encouragement of Maryland's textile

industry and had acquired substantial tracts of land in Allen County, Kentucky, by the time of his death (before 1808).

[4]The day's debate in the COWH over ways and means for discharging the public debt, during which many Southern members opposed a proposed excise on distilled spirits (*DHFFC* 13:1214–17).

[5]The Wilderness Road through Cumberland Gap connected the Great Valley of Virginia to Kentucky. Innes was active in the effort to improve the road.

Thomas Fitzsimons to Tench Coxe

Our finance business has taken a Complection within these last two days Which gives Reasonable ground to hope that we shall get thru it Speedily the Conduct of the Gent most Anxious for the assumption of the State debts: has been such, since that proposition was Negatived, as proved beyond a doubt that they meant to oppose Every provision for the other part of the debt and besides their general declarations to that effect, they Contrived to waste our time in Useless disquisitions, Merely to force the other part of the house into their measures. ~~I have had my~~ on friday papers were Called for Which would take many days to Obtain & in short we were wasteing our time & the patience of our Constituents—I had my Apprehensions that those who opposed the Assumption Might divide upon the Ways and Means. & that we might be intirely disappointed of means to fund the debt Yesterday I called upon Mr. Maddison for an Explicit declaration upon that Subject and upon being satisfyd that he would concurr in the funds. Reported by the Secy. I Moved that the Committee should be discharged from the further Consideration of that part of the Secys. report which Respects the assumption (for the present). this it was seen would ascertain the Strength of Party in the house. Which meant to provide for the [*lined out*] debts independant of the States from those who did not & if Agreed to would enable us to go on with that business—after a Considerable degree of opposition the Motion was Agreed to And in Consequence We Compleated our decisions upon the terms of funding & this day have Agreed to the funds Recommended by the Secy. Committees are appointed to bring in bills for both purposes. And I expect they will soon be Ready to report them. I expect further Opposition from the Assumptionists but have great Confidence that the Measure will be Agreed to—I do not even give up ~~our~~ the expectation of Assumption but I thot. it improper to Couple it with the other ~~but~~ & Rather let it rest upon its own Merits—the Eastern & So. Carolina Members have pursued it with heat and indiscretion—I think the Opposers have Considered Local opinions Rather than Genl. principles—if however the Measure is as Good as I suppose it will serve itself—And an Observation of one of my Colleagues ought to have great Weight—Viz.—that as the house was Nearly divided it would be Safer to postpone because if we Agreed the Case would be Irremidiable whereas it can hereafter be Agreed to if found proper.

As our progress may have an Effect upon the price of Public securitys. I wish you to make it known in Substance, for the Information of our Citizens.

I have added the Articles Reported & Agreed to.

[*P. S.*] I see that the inclosed states the transactions of yesterday—today we Agreed to the funds recommended by the Secy.

ALS, Coxe Papers, PHi. Place to which addressed not indicated.

Hodge, Allen, and Campbell to Archibald McLean

THE publishers of the *Congressional Register* are sorry to trouble the public with an answer to the puerile piece signed A SUBSCRIBER, which appeared in this paper on Saturday last. Had the person who thought himself aggrieved by not receiving the numbers of that work regularly, come candidly forward with his name, they would personally have waited on him, and explained the matter sufficiently to his satisfaction; if there was any irregularity committed in publishing, who could redress the grievance? Certainly not the public; consequently he could have no other view in having recourse to a newspaper, but to injure that publication, which is already too well established to be affected by the splenetic pen of any anonymous scribbler.

Had he read our advertisement, *and could understand what he did read*, he would there have seen that we promised to give the public one number weekly; this we have more than strictly complied with, having for several weeks given two numbers at one time: Whether the first or second session of Congress ought to be first finished, we leave to the discernment of unbiased subscribers.

The *subscriber* ought to have made himself better acquainted with the subject, before he had shewn *his love to truth* by the assertion of a *falsehood.*

The materials, for the remaining part of the first session were not ready, the editor had them to copy for the press from his M.S.S. occasionally as wanted by the compositors; the task though seemingly light, is by no means easy to write a sufficiency of matter to keep five journeymen constantly employed.

We have every reason to doubt that the person who wrote that piece is not a subscriber to the *Congressional Register*, nor a citizen, as he wishes to represent himself. Our numerous list of subscribers, both at home and abroad, are principally composed of the first characters, and gentlemen who would have despised to trouble the public with an ill grounded and unjust trivial complaint.

The publishers are certainly obliged to such gentlemen as pay their accounts regularly; but conceive it would have discovered a more *honest* disposition in the *subscriber* had he assumed less merit to himself in discharging a just debt; and much more would it have been to his credit had he not exposed to the world his discontented and peevish disposition.

The encouragers of the Debates of Congress are respectfully informed, that No. I. of Vol. IV, containing debates on the Assumption of the State Debts, with a half sheet of the Acts passed this present session, is just published, and for sale at the Book-stores of Hodge, Allen, and Campbell.

NYDG, 27 April. The letter is a continuation of the publishers' response of 20 April, above, to the complaint of A Subscriber to Mr. McLean, 19 April, above.

Samuel Johnston to James Iredell

I am favored with yours of the 3d and 7th Instant. this is intended to meet you at Savannah, after receiving your directions to procure a House for you, I rented another having before taken one which I intended for myself, they are neither of them such as please me altogether, but being in a low state of health, altogether unacquainted with the Town and not caring to give too much trouble to my Friends, I took such as I could get with the least trouble, tho I examined at least twenty. when you come, you may take your choice of them, in the mean time if it is agreeable to Mrs. [*Hannah*] Iredell we will all live together.

The Bill for extending the Judiciary to North Carolina is not yet brought in, the Plan proposed by the Committee is to say the Circuit Courts to be held at Newbern & Hillsborough alternately, begining at Newbern on the 18th of June and 8th of November, the District Courts to be held at Newbern the first monday in April, July, October and January whether it will pass in this form is altogether uncertain, I will give you the most early information.

The Committee of the whole were yesterday discharged from any further Consideration of the Report of the Secretary of the Treasury so far as relates to the Assumption of the State Debts and a Committee of five appointed to report a Bill for Funding the ~~Foreig~~ Debt of the United States agreeable to the Secretary's Report.

The Gentlemen who are in favor of the Assumption are very sore and impatient under their defeat, they will probably endeavor to bring the measure forward again. I scarcely think that they will succeed this Session, if they do it will be with so small a majority, that in my opinion, if the measure was even less exceptionable than this appears to be in the estimation of many, it had better be laid over to another Session than be now adopted ~~in the~~ contrary to the opinion and Judgment of so respectable an opposition.

I enclose you the papers of yesterday and this.

I hoped to have had Letters this evening by the post from my Friends at Edenton [*North Carolina*] but am disappointed. I shall in the course of the next fortnight look out with great impatience for our Families.

ALS, Iredell Papers, NcD. Addressed to Savannah, Georgia.

William Maclay to John Nicholson

I have been looking for a letter from you by every post for a Week past. and now begin to believe, that 'tho' You were not killed in your late engagements, That You must be dead of Your wounds, or I should certainly have heard from You before this time.[1]

The house of Representatives, after having been almost Stationary in business, made some rapid Movements Yesterday. I have inclosed You the result. and will thank You for any thoughts that may occur to you upon it. The State debts being rejected, The information which I wrote last for, may not now be so necessary. But as I have received many Useful Communications from You, I beg for a continuance of your Correspondence.

We hope to finish the session, some time next Month, and wish to adjourn to Philada. both points are however as Yet uncertain.

[*Enclosure*]

Mr. Nicholson,

May inform me what amount of Indents belong to the State of Pennsylvania. are they not equal to the interest of the New Loan, for four Years, at least? pray do not forget to send me a line on this Subject—another Committee has been appointed this day to bring in a bill for the new impost. &ca. so that now the Danger seems to be, that of too much Haste.

ALS, Gratz Collection, PHi. Addressed to "Comptroller Genl. of Pennsylvania"; franked; postmarked; received 30 April. The enclosed note included a column clipped from *NYDA*, 27 April, that reports the resolutions on funding passed in the COWH the day before; see *DHFFC* 5:860–61.

[1] For Nicholson's political troubles, see Maclay to Nicholson, 10 April, above.

James Madison to Governor Beverley Randolph

Information having been received here that some persons acquainted with the appropriation made at the last Session of Congress in favor of the officers & soldiers of the Virginia & N. Carolina lines of the late army, are taking advantage of the claimants who are ignorant of that provision, by purchasing their claims for very inconsiderable proportions of their amount, it became a question whether any remedy could be applied to so flagrant an imposition. Several difficulties arose from the established rules of office, from which the Secretaries of the Treasury and at War did not think they should be justified in departing, and from the uncertainty and inconveniency of obtaining an interposition of Congress. The result has been that redress would be most attainable by the aid of the Executives of the two States, and that the nature of the case authorized an expectation that they would readily afford it. The mode suggested is that fit persons be appointed to procure powers duly authenticated from all such as may have alienated subsequent the act of appropriation, together with evidence concerning the circumstances under which and the persons to whom the alienation shall have been made; and that in virtue of those powers, there may be some fit person at the Seat of Government to make claim on behalf of the Soldiers and exhibit the evidence collected. When the matter shall be thus prepared, if there shall appear indications of fraud or undue advantage, a suit may be instituted against the officer who will be authorized to pay the sums due (for which pecuniary aid will not be wanting) and the fraud may in this way be ascertained and redressed. It is supposed that the mere institution of a suit will beget a disposition in those who may have taken the advantage to better their title by additional compensations to the parties injured, and that the appearance of such an investigation may deter from like practices in future. It is thought also that if the same persons should be authorised to obtain powers from those who may not have alienated, it may render the payment of the money more convenient.

Inclosed herewith are copies of the names and claims of the Officers & Soldiers of the Virginia line, which may facilitate the arrangements for obtaining the requisite powers from them. It is said that the persons who are taking advantage of their knowledge of the appropriation, in order to proceed with more certainty, possessed themselves of like copies from some office here, but we have not been able as yet to trace the fact.

ALS, Gratz Collection, PHi. Place to which addressed not indicated.

Governor Beverley Randolph to James Madison

The act of the present Congress to prevent the exportation of goods not duly inspected, according to the laws of the several States [*Inspection Act HR-48*], although it secures the execution of the state inspection laws, will not, I fear, procure to the States every benefit, which might be derived from it. By the Constitution of the United States, the several States are Authorized to lay such duties upon Exports as may be necessary for executing their inspection laws.[1] Great frauds may be committed in the collection of this Revenue unless the Officers of the Customs are used as checks upon the Inspectors.

In this State a tax of six shillings pr. hogshead is laid on all Tobaccos exported.[2] This tax is to be paid by the Exporter to the Inspectors, who are to render annually an Account upon Oath, of all Tobaccos shipped from their respective Warehouses. In order to take away all temptation to purjury and to ensure to the State the full amount of the tax, the inspection laws direct, that the Inspectors shall by every boat or other Craft, loaded with Tobacco, send a list of the Marks, weights, &c. of every hogshead of Tobacco then delivered, which lists every Master of a ship is to lodge with the naval officer by whom his ship is cleared. This proceeding will, I suppose, be continued under the Act of Congress, but the check will not be complete unless the Collectors are directed to return the Manifests delivered to them by the Masters of ships, to the Executive or some Officer of the State, in order that they may be compared with the Accounts rendered by the several Inspectors. Permit me to request your assistance in procuring the establishment of such a regulation, either by Congress or the Secretary of the Treasury, if his powers will reach the object.

LS, Madison Papers, DLC. Written from Richmond, Virginia.

[1] Article I, section 8, paragraph 2.

[2] "An Act to Amend and Reduce the Several Acts of the Assembly for the Inspection of Tobacco, into one Act" was passed in May 1783 (Hening 11:240–41).

John S. Sherburne to John Langdon

I have so long delayed replying to yr. last obliging favor that I am satisfied I can make no sufficient apology for the neglect—Your goodness I'm persuaded will however admit such as I have —The Courts for this month have been constantly & now are sitting, most of that time I've been from Town, but constantly intending to write next post, till next post was gone & by such delusive self promises have spun out the Delay to the present moment—their offence being forgiven to the offenders in all other cases, I am willing to promise an amendment in future.

The true friends of Govt. regret the loss of the motion for Assumptn. in the house, altho the Anties rejoice at it—notwithstanding so much time spent in your funding scheme, we are apprehensive 'twill all be in vain—people sorrowfully complain of your slowness—the samples we have had are not much in favor of yr. dispatch, however energetic you may be—with so much still undone, & so many matters requiring immediate attention. I think Congress, if they consult the general good, must necessarily sit thro' the summer—this doctrine I know will not suit your feelings. but judge if it is not necessary—Mr. Lear you have heard before this has become duplex homo[1]—Mr. Lewis is still here & at yr. house. I believe he finds his residence in Town very agreable—Shd. Congress continue siting, we hope soon to see you, don't let my example prevent yr. writing, but heap coals of fire, by yr. good works—Inform us how affairs go on, & if there is any probability of the Secys. plan, in any part being adopted this Session.

ALS, Langdon Papers, NhPoA. Written from Portsmouth, New Hampshire.

[1] A compound man, meaning two made one in marriage. Tobias Lear married Mary Long in Portsmouth on 18 April, during several weeks' leave from his duties in Washington's official family (Stephen Decatur, Jr., *Private Affairs of George Washington* [Boston, 1933], p. 128).

Roger Sherman to Simeon Baldwin

You will see by the enclosed paper the progress Congress have made within a few days—The business of the Assumption of the State debts is postponed for the present 5 or 6 of the members in favour of it are now absent so that it would not be safe to risque a vote till they return—I believe there is a majority in favour of it. Roger wrote last Post that his mother[1] & he expected to set out for this place the middle of this week—so that I have not wrote to either of them. I was informed that my son Isaac was here this week & enquired for me but I did not see him—if you write by the next Post please to Inform me whether John & he are at New Haven [*Connecticut*].

The Secretary of the treasury has not reported on Capt. Pitman Collens's Petition he has been constantly employed in complying with orders of the House on public matters. nor has he reported on the memorial of the President & Fellows of Yale College[2]—Please to present my love to Mrs. Baldwin[3] & write how she does—I have heard nothing as to her health since I came from home.

ALS, Sherman Collection, CtY. Place to which addressed not indicated.

[1] Sherman's wife, Rebecca Prescott Sherman.

[2] For more on Pitman Collins's petition on a Revolutionary War claim, and that of Yale College for a remission of impost duties, see *DHFFC* 7:84 and 8:362–64, respectively.

[3] Sherman's daughter Rebecca.

William Smith (Md.) to Otho H. Williams

When I wrote you last, I omitted to mention, that the Secy. has at last reported on the defects & objections, to the Impost & Tonage laws.[1] The Report, contains forty Seven pages, & in general provides for many of its deficiencies, but from a Cursory reading I am not Able to Say much on the subject, or to give you the information you might wish—I would therefore only observe that he recommends to Congress, that they ought to wave their Claim to the duties arising from the 1st of Augst. untill the officer's were organized at the respective districts. that permission be allowed for owners or Masters to Report their inward Cargoes for exportation, without landing. That ten boats be employ'd to prevent Smuggling wh. he computes will cost 18,000 dollars ℔ Annum. disaproves of the 10 ℔ Cent discount for prompt pay. And Says that in his opinion, the compensation to the Officers, are in many instances inadequate to the Services required, & Unless further provision, in some cases are made, it cannot be expected that Characters Worthy of trust will continue to be employed. That some have already offered their resignations, & only continue untill they know what will be further done; Our house have appointed a committee to consider this Report—Goodhue, Wadsworth, Lawrence Fitzsimons & Lee. ~~they~~ Secy. has reserved many communications, which he proposes to lay before the committe relative to those Acts.

As I understand you intend a Visit to N. York shortly, I think you had better contrive your business so, as to be here while this report is under consideration, I expect it will be proceeded on with as little delay as the length & importance of the Subject will admit.

The assumption of the State debts, has been again rejected & a committee appointed to Bring in a Bill for funding the debt of the U.S.—But the assumption will be again brot. forward, modified under restrictions, & limitations. Although I am convinced a very considerable part of the debts contracted by the several States, are proper Charges against the U.S. I much question, if they are assumed Under any shape this session.

ALS, Williams Papers, MdHi. Addressed to Baltimore. Smith wrote on the inside address sheet, "at this moment is a very heavy fall of Snow in this City."

[1] For the secretary of the treasury's report, see *DHFFC* 4:437–56.

Michael Jenifer Stone to Walter Stone

I inclose you a paper which will shew our Friends that at last we have Started and progress—I can farther inform you that we are now on the "ways and means" and it appears to me we shall Speedily adopt those recommended by the Secretary. The difficulties are not all over—But I fondly hope we may rise from that disgrace which I fear we have been thrown by our unreasonable delays and inconsistencies—However let it be remebred that as yet there never has been a General Sistem revenue or finance in America—Nor in any Country Similarly Situated.

I request that you will attend to my Dividends in the Potowmack Company. I had thought of something to request of you when I began this Letter but have forgot it—I hear that Tobacco is high in London Please to Collect and Ship all you Can for me.

I am Still in very poor Health—Tho' I believe I am getting better—I have been joked here about my Complaints and they have been said to be the effects of *Love.* But I give you my word that the Sex has not been the Cause—and that I have Stated them truely—I only mention this that you may be authorized to contradict any report—I find so much said about me in my own Country that are not true that I am Cautious.

ALS, Stone Family Papers, DLC. Addressed to Charles County, Maryland.

Nathaniel Wells to George Thatcher

Having a little leisure and in some degree recovered my health, I acknowledge the receipt of sundry letters from you since the commencement of the present Session of Congress in one of which the Report of the Secretary of Treasury was inclosed for which I am much obliged to you and am sorry that there is no prospect at present that his plan in all its substantial parts will be adopted by tho' I have reason to believe that it will be done sooner or later as it appears to me to be well formed for restoring the credit & promoting the Interest of the United States as a Nation. I was much disappointed upon hearing that a majority of the house of Representatives had determined not to make provision for the payment of the debts contracted by the particular States In the prosecution of the late War and am at a loss to conceive the reason why the Representatives from Newhamshire and some other States are in opposition to that measure, Can it be because they imagine that the States represented by them will be gainers by rejecting that part of Mr. Hamiltons Plan—It appears to me if things are duly considerd to be impossible. It may be said that their State debts are less in proportion than those of other States which may have the appearance of truth and I would ask how it happens that that the State debts of Newhamshire, for instance, is less than that of Massachusetts, perhaps they may reply and say that they have attended more to the Rules of Œconomy than the Government of Massachusetts have done which may possibly may be true but I would ask how much has been saved in that way. It must be answered not a large sum and the Question still remains why is the State debt of Massachusetts much larger in proportion than that of Newhamshire and the true Answer as it appears to me must be this, that in the course of the War more was required of Massachusetts than their proportion & less of Newhamshire and to the sum required of Massachusetts may be added the several sums advanced by them pursuant to particular applications and recommendations of Congress &c. In the year 1780 according to the best of my recollection Massachusetts was directed by Congress to raise Eleven Regiments of Soldiers while no more than two Regiments were required from Newhamshire in which case Massachusetts furnished one Regiment which Newhamshire ought to have procured in order to have done as much in proportion as Massachusetts did. In raising that Regiment Massachusetts expended about forty thousand Pounds and hired Soldiers belonging to Newhamshire which Expence most surely Newhamshire ought to repay, besides Cloathing & provision were procured by Massachusetts for the continental army in the same proportion for which they also ought to have an allowance By the Rule established every State is to contribute in men & money in proportion to their Numbers making a certain allowance for black servants and every State is to be credited with their Advances drawing Interest, now if the Expences of the War should be settled according to that Rule or upon any other equitable principles, may it not be made to appear evidently that several hundred thousand pounds advanced by Massachusetts must be repaid by Newhamshire or some other State and I may go farther & say if that Rule is to be strictly adhered to it is in my opinion probable there is near as much due to Massachusetts as the whole amount of their State debt so that I think that Massachusetts has less reason to wish for the assumption of the State debts than many other States in the union I suppose that in the course of the War Newhamshire did not advance for the benefit of the united States more than three quarters so much in proportion according to the rule before mentioned as Massachusetts did, If it should be supposed that Newhamshire fell short in advancing their proportion so much as thirty thousand pounds a year the sum will amount to Two hundred and forty thousand pounds which may be considered as part of their State debt. The difference between taxes imposed upon the citizens of Newhamshire & those [*of*] Massachusetts was striking and was much noticed by the people of Newhamshire. The citizens of Massachusetts during the War bore their unequal burdens with great degrees of patience in full confidence of a future adjustment according to the rule prescribed however for my part I should be willing to have an adjustment upon the principles of equity without insisting upon the rigid observance of that rule. tho I am fully satisfied that such an Observance would operate greatly in favour of Massachusetts, I have made use of the State of Newhamshire as one instance in order to make it appear where a State debt is apparently small yet in reality it may be comparatively very great by adding thereto such sums as ought to have been advanced by them in the course of the War. The observations respecting Newhamshire may be found to be applicable to several other States in the Union. If any doubt should still remain in regard to the proportion which ought to paid by each I must refer you to the proportion in which they are now severally represented in Congress in which Newhamshire is to Massachusetts as *three* to *Eight* but if it should be supposed that Newhamshire have too many Representatives yet if you don't think that they have more than one third more Representatives in proportion than Massachusetts my Observations will be found to be strictly true, It is suggested by some that no adjustment according to the rule prescribed is ever intended to be carried into effect but I am not at present disposed to hearken to such dishonorable suggestions and I don't apprehend that it would ever been thought of had it not have been difficult otherwise to have accounted for the part which the representatives from some States have lately taken. The only doubt which ever existed in my mind in regard to the expediency of assuming the State debts arose from an uncertainty of the Ability in Congress to make provision for payment of Interest without the Aid of direct Taxes and it appeared to me inexpedient for the general Goverment immediately to impose such Taxes but from the operation of the impost Act and by considering to what an amazing Extent Excises may be carried by the general Government without any considerable detrement to Trade I am at length satisfied that ample provision may be made for paying the interest of the national debt including therein the particular State debts without the assistance of direct Taxation with which the people by immoderate Exercise are become weary and now stand in in need of relaxation, for my own part I must confess that I see no Way of paying State Interest without State Excises which may often interfere ~~with~~ with Excises laid by the general Government, State Excises greatly embaras the Trader especially the fair and I dont imagine that it is possible by any State Act to prevent a multiplicity of Evasions in regard to the payment of Excise duties. In short I am of the opinion that an an Excise upon any particular article under the direction of the general Government which would produce ten thousand pounds in any particular State would not produce in the same State under the direction of the particular Government thereof more than three quarters of that sum so that in the collection of State Excises there will be a loss at the Rate of 25 ⅌ Cent and at the same time the fair Trader will be greatly injured. I am not at present possessed of a single State Note and have no apprehension that the particular debt of this State is larger or even so great as those of the other States in general after making the proper deduction therefrom according to the Rule prescribed or any other equitable principles (which I hope will done

soon & at farthest within the course of the present year) yet I most ardently wish that the debts of the united States and particular States contracted for the same common cause may be speedily placed and rest upon the same common funds as such a measure will in my opinion greatly tend to do general Justice & produce that union and harmony between the several States and their citizens which may be considered as ~~so~~ essential to their Welfare & happiness as a Nation If provision should be made by the general Government for discharging the State debts the business of the State Legislatures ~~which~~ would be much lessened and great Expence saved to the particular States without much if [*of?*] an addition to the business or expence of the general Government.
[*P. S.*] My Kindest Regards to Messrs. Strong Dalton Goodhue Sedgwick Ames &c.

ALS, Chamberlain Collection, MB. Written from Wells, Maine.

OTHER DOCUMENTS

Orchard Cook to George Thatcher. ALS, Foster Collection, MHi. Place from which written not indicated.

Office seeking: excise collector; admits his personal acquaintance with Thatcher is small; mentions Silas Lee and the most respectable gentlemen of Lincoln County, Maine, as references.

Thomas Jefferson to William Short. ALS, Short Papers, ViW. Place to which addressed not indicated. For the full text, see *PTJ* 16:387–89.

Walker and family arrived in New York the day before; many think his interim appointment will not be confirmed by the Virginia legislature.

James Madison to Mann Page. No copy known; mentioned in James Mercer to Madison, 12 May.

Lewis Morris to Lewis Morris, Jr. ALS, Signer Collection, N. Written from "Morrisania,"in present-day Bronx, New York; place to which addressed not indicated.

"The State of South Carolina has but an indifferent representation except Smith and Tucker ~~they~~ the others are no great things Judge Burke from his intimacy with Huger I should Suppose him a bad man he is ignorant Some few weeks before the Legislature broke up I was in the Same house with Huger, as he was Obliged to move his lodgings and he with a number of other members of Congress came to Mrs. McEwen's you may judge my Situation."

Edmund Randolph to James Madison. ALS, Madison Papers, DLC. Written from Williamsburg, Virginia. For the full text, see *PJM* 13:180.

Has been anxiously awaiting word from Madison's conversation with the President regarding his continued absence from the seat of government owing to his wife's illness; must resign if his presence is indispensable.

Joseph Whipple to John Langdon. ALS, Langdon Papers, NhPoA. Written from Portsmouth, New Hampshire.

Acknowledges receipt of treasurer's order for $618 due Langdon; regrets that its lack of an endorsement prevents his authorizing the charge; suggests Langdon alert the treasurer not to allow the sum to be drawn by anyone until properly endorsed.

George Washington, Diary. Washington Diary, ViHi. The day before, Washington had appointed 2:45 P.M. as the time for receiving the Address of the Virginia General Assembly congratulating him on his election as President (*DGW* 6:68). For the address, dated 28 October 1789, and Washington's reply, see *PGW* 5:349–52.

"At the time appointed, Messrs. Lee & Walker (the Senators from Virginia) attended, & presented the Address as mentioned yesterday & received an Answer to it."

Wednesday, 28 April 1790

Snow & Rain (Johnson)

Elias Boudinot to Benjamin Rush

Your letter of the 18th. announced the death of one of the first of our fellow citizens [*Benjamin Franklin*]—his loss, is great to your city—state—our country and to the world—although at the same time, we ought to be thankful, that he was continued to so good an old age, for the common benefit of mankind.

The public papers will inform you of what Congress has done to testify their respect for the memory of so worthy a fellow citizen—We have been blamed for this measure and the Senate refused to follow our example, as being improper for a citizen who was not in a public character at the time of his death. I confess the objection appears to me a weak one—Poor republics have no other means of shewing their grateful remembrance of important services but by testimonies of this sort, and I think too great attention to those of the deceased cannot be shewn. There can [*no*] injury arise from the precedent, as I doubt whether he has left his equal behind, in point of usefulness to his country.

Had the Doctor left a death bed testimony in favor of religion, it might have brought many of our pretended Deists to some serious consideration: for I do believe that a man who has the reputation of great wisdom and an uncommon insight into the works of nature, dying calmly and with apparent satisfaction, has a tendency to lull those of a careless turn of mind, or whose interest it is (in their own conceit) that a future state should be a mere fable to rest in the wisdom of this world without even turning a serious thought, to the concerns of futurity.

We have at last got into the funding system and have agreed on the ways and means, but the measure yet goes on so heavily that I still fear the issue.

Your Aunt [*Hannah Stockton Boudinot*] joins me in most affectionate love and respect to our neice [*Julia Stockton Rush*] and her little brood.

If any particular anecdotes of the Doctor, should transpire, I should be obliged by a repetition of them. This year seems to be marked by the deaths of great men—cullen—Howard—Joseph[1] and a Franklin—Oh how great is the advantage of the true Christian—usefulness in this life, so far from being the brightest gem in his brighter character, it is but an emblematic figure of that holy activity which shall increase through an endless eternity.

Transcript, Bancroft Papers, NN.

[1] Dr. William Cullen (1710–90), Rush's teacher at Edinburgh and the acknowledged head of Britain's medical establishment; probably John Havard (1726?–90), British prison reformer and essayist; Joseph II (1741–90), considered the epitome of enlightened despotism for his ecclesiastical, economic, and legal reforms, including the abolition of serfdom, while Holy Roman Emperor (1765–90).

Daniel Davis to George Thatcher

I have Recd. yours enclosing Fabres State Notes Notes,[1] with the mark of the beast set upon them by the Treasurer of New York—Damn the Knave who counterfeited them.

I sincerely acknowledge my fault in neglecting to write you so often as I ought—one reason that has prevented me, was a fear that I should give you more trouble in answering my Letters ~~that~~ than you could comfortably away with, considering the numerous correspondents that you are obliged to attend to—In the course of the last session of our Legislature I was much occupied by the business with which we were incumbered—I don't pretend that a love for the publick, or a ~~Con~~ desire to discharge my duty conscientiously, prompted me to this Attention; but being perfectly ignorant of the mode of doing business in the general court, it became necessary in order to Save me from ridicule—This is my apoloy for not writing you more frequently when at Boston.

I find the wise acres of your Legislature are in what you & I should call here, a petty Damnable hobble—What will be the end of these things remains a secret in the brest of of providence—But I am much inclined to Conjecture that it will be confusion & ruin the whole Israel of God—If I was of your House, I would see the Gentry in opposition to the assumption *tetotled* & *rididled* before I would fund the Debt of the Union upon any terms, unless that of the States was equally well provided for.

ALS, Foster Collection, MHi. Written from Portland, Maine; addressed to Thatcher "In the federal House of Representatives"; franked. This letter was continued on 1 May and is calendared below. The salutation reads, "Dear Jack," perhaps employing the nickname for "Jonathan," as the stock New England character was known in American slang, or perhaps more specifically a reference to Thatcher's well known pseudonym "Crazy Jonathan" during the ratification debate.

---

[1] Possibly state certificates belonging to Peeter Fabree, residing in Portland, Maine, in 1790.

Benjamin Goodhue to Stephen Goodhue

*** I can hardly tell you how the affairs go on with respect to the Assumption and funding bussines, the opponents of the Assumption taking an advantage of the absense of 5 or 6 of our side, have passed resolutions for funding the Continental debt and say nothing about the assumption, and have agreed a bill shall be brought in for the purpose with the Excise &c. as proposed in the Secrys. report, seeing they were determin'd to push the matter upon their majority, there was no opposition to them at present, and let them proceed, till we find an opposition may answer some purpose, I am heartily sick of our national politicks, for I am convinced they are not honest, and wish to over burthen the eastern States.
[*P. S.*] please to give the inclosed papers to the printer after you have read them.

ALS, Goodhue Family Papers, MSaE. Addressed to Salem, Massachusetts.

Jeremiah Libbey to John Langdon

Knowing that the Public Affairs Occupy your Attention, and, that you are often receiving Letters from your friends, has prevented me from the pleasure of writing to you sir, for fear of Interrupting you from more Important matters than is within my sphere—but having seen the Post Office Bill as reported to the House,[1] brot. my promise (fresh in my mind) of writing to you on the subject of a Post to the back parts of this State. I observe by the Bill, the Post Master General, with the Consent of the President, may Farm, any of the Cross Roads, for a Number of Years, whether a Post from Portsmouth to the upper part of this State would be Considered as a Cross Post, I cannot determine—as we several times Observed the design of Establishing posts, was for Communication for the Benefit of Commerce, and raising a revenue, and that it ought to be as equal as possible—is that the case with New Hampshire? we now have a post at the Public expence about Eighteen Miles in this State, how much is paid by the Inhabitants towards defraying the Expence of the Riders is known—That part of Massachusetts, called the Province of Main, has a post from this to Portland, at the Public expence, and I am told have also one from Portland, fifty miles further east, at the same expence, how much is paid by the Inhabitants on that rout, may also be known, and by comparing the distance travelled, & the Expence paid, by the Public, with the amount paid by said Inhabitants, a Judgement may be formed, whether they are allowed, or Indulged with a greater proportion of Posts at the Public charge, than New Hampshire.

I mention that part because I am better acquainted with it than any other, perhaps there are circumstances attending that rout, that may make it more equal, than some may Imagine.

If it should be found on examination, that New Hampshire can be Indulged, with a post from this to the Back part of this State, it would serve the State greatly, with respect to farming it, that is out of the Question, If by farming is [*lined out*] meant that the Person Contracting is to receive no pay from the Public, for tho' the rout is of Consequence to the Inhabitants, the Business at Present will not pay the Expence, and whether under all circumstances New Hampshire is entitled to any additional post in the State, at the Public expence, must be determined by those whose province it is.

I have mention'd this Subject according to my promise, and in Confidence to you sir—must beg it as a favour it may not be known I have had any thing to say about it—as it might be tho't meddling with matters I had no business with.

P. S. please to present my best regards to our good Friend Mr. [*Ebenezer*] Hazard how does he do? is he yet had any provision made him by the Public for his ___.

ALS, Langdon Papers, NhPoA. Written from Portsmouth, New Hampshire.

[1] The Post Office Bill [HR-42] was reported to the House on 23 February; one hundred copies were ordered printed the next day (*DHFFC* 6:1655–56, 1664–71).

Robert Morris to Mary Morris

I received last night my Dear Friend your letter of the 25th and am always happy in knowing of the good Health of yourself & the rest of my Family. I am glad you got the poor Miserable Foundling so well disposed of and hope it may be better taken care of than it would have been without its Brutal Parents.[1]

Mr. {*William*} Constable's little Boy John is very Ill indeed, two Doctors have been in Consultation over him a little while ago, one of them Seems to Augur Ill of him, but the other Doctr. {*Charles*} McKnight says he will do well enough, the Parents are very gloomy to day and full of apprehension. I hope he may recover for He is really a charming little Boy, I observe you had given me an account of Doctr. {*Benjamin*} Franklin's will different from the reality which is a pity as I had spoken confidently on the Subject relying on the Authenticity of the information which you had received I was at Court Yesterday to see the President who has been riding on Long Island all last week & he has regained his looks, his appetite & his Health, I tell him we must remove him to Philada. where he will have room enough to Ride as far as he pleases without Crossing to any Island for the purpose I am to dine there tomorrow when I shall see Mrs. Washington also.

Genl. Knox sets out for Philada. next Friday and will call to see you & as the Cincinnati meet there on Monday[2] I hope there will be some Gayeties for them to partake of at Philadelphia You can give them a Tea Party.

I suppose Mr. {*Thomas*} Montgomerie is with you by this time, He has been very unfortunate in Weather I intended to have sent you an order for $200 in this letter but I have not yet received it, my next will bring it.

ALS, Morris Papers, CSmH. Written in the evening; addressed to Philadelphia.

---

[1] The abused "foundling" remains unidentified, but Morris's active interest in the child's safekeeping accords with what seems to have been his special sensitivity to the plight of orphans. Morris himself was an illegitimate child, orphaned at age fifteen, who took responsibility for a brother (Thomas) and at least one acknowledged illegitimate daughter of his own. In 1775, he publicly supported the school established in Philadelphia by Ann Brodeau upon her immigration from England with her illegitimate daughter Anna Maria (who in 1790 married the famous inventor and abolitionist, Dr. William Thornton). Mrs. Brodeau's became the city's finest school for young girls, numbering among her pupils Morris's own daughters as well as on occasion, it is believed, the illegitimate children of the elite (*DHFFC* 14:766; C. M. Harris, ed., *Papers of William Thornton* {Charlottesville, Va., 1995}, 1:xlviii, xlix; *PGW* 6:576). The editors wish to thank Elizabeth Nuxoll, former editor of the *Papers of Robert Morris, 1781–1784*, not only for providing some of this information but for suggesting its synthesis to form a fuller picture of how Morris's profound sense of philanthropy was engaged during the time of the FFC.

[2] Under the Society of the Cincinnati's 1787 constitution, meetings of the general society were to be held at least once every three years on the first Monday in May.

Merchants and Traders of Philadelphia to the Pennsylvania Delegation

A meeting of the merchants and Traders of Philadelphia was held this morning at the city Tavern for the purpose of considering the expediency of ~~introducing~~ enacting into a law the two propositions that have been brought before congress by our eastern Brethren.[1] The subject was deemed of great importance and was therefore agitated wth. freedom tho with much moderation. There seemed to be very little doubt or hesitation upon ~~the subject of~~ the first proposition concerning the additional duty of 10 ⅌ Cent. on goods from such ports as do not admit our Vessels. The second was attended at first with more diversity of Opinion, tho you observe it was finally adopted and with a good deal of Unanimity. It was argued that Maryland & Virginia which are two very principal Southern States, had laid a dollar ⅌ Ton upon British Ships by their separate legislatures, and had continued that tonnage till the regulation of trade was committed to congress, ~~and~~ also that the duties on shipping in So. Carolina must have been on a medium nearly as high as they will be when the additional fifty cents shall be laid, for our Vessels which then paid about 33⅓ Cents, now pay but six. It was also urged that both these addl. burdens on foreigners might be mitigated by treaty, and that they would provide something to concede in favor of well disposed foreign Nations who might incline to confirm to us an old benefit or to do away ~~a~~ an injurious restriction. It was also observed that different treatment had been recd. from foreigners and that this would enable the President & Senate to return ~~it~~ the favors of the friendly effectually by mitigations & yet in such a way as not to give unnecessary offence. Upon the whole the Merchants have thought ~~fit~~ it safe to approve the ~~measures~~ propositions, because they knew that the united wisdom of our Country would be exercised upon the subject before it could become a law, and that if the day fixed for the operation of the Act should be a little removed there might be time for foreigners to avoid the ~~Burdens~~ Inconveniencies, if disposed to act kindly by us, and if not that they really ought to bear them.

Some of the principal Merchants in the passenger trade stated to the Committee after the meeting, that considerable ~~inconvenience fell~~ expence & hardship fall upon them by being obliged to pay tonnage twice in the River Delaware. Once when the~~ir~~ passenger Vessels stop at New Castle or Wilmington ~~and aga~~ to land their passengers, which is ~~often~~ generally desired by them & [*lined out*] again upon their coming up to this town where they have to discharge their goods & are intended to [*lined out*] load for Europe. this is a manifest hardship & we beg leave to recommend the remedying ~~wh~~ it in the bill which ~~will~~ may contain the abovementioned regulations.

FC:dft, hand of Coxe, Coxe Papers, PHi. Coxe listed among an unspecified number of signatories only himself, James Ross (1729–1800), John Nixon, and John M. Nesbitt (ca. 1730–1802).

[1] The petition of the merchants and traders of Portsmouth, New Hampshire, presented in the House on 26 March, was the basis for the two proposals alluded to in this letter and formally recommended in a House committee report of 16 April (*DHFFC* 6:1970–72). The proposed dollar per ton increase in tonnage was ultimately included in the Trade and Navigation Bill [HR-66], which did not pass the House.

William Smith (Md.) to Otho H. Williams

The inclosed paper will show you the State of the funding System. The Resolutions therein contained passed Unanimously, yesterday in the Committee were reported & received by the House with very little debate, & all in the course of a few hours. a committee appointed to bring in a bill in conformity thereto.

Notwithstanding this rapid progress, & the Small opposition that has been made, I expect the Assumptionists will come forward when the bill is brot. in—many of their friends are absent on furlow,[1] & daily expected—Continues a very heavy Snow with rain at intervals.

ALS, Williams Papers, MdHi. Place to which addressed not indicated.

[1] Cadwalader, Leonard, Sedgwick, and Trumbull had leave of absence from the House.

Michael Jenifer Stone to Walter Stone

I received your Letter of the 22d. I am much better in Health—go about and seem to be getting well—The Influenza has appeared to the Eastwards and has arrived at this City—with very mild Simptoms. I have nothing new having written to you often and long. I Know no more of what passes in Maryland that if I was at the Antipodes.

P. S. I am pleased with Johnsons appointment[1] and hope he will accept—as to the others to be sure there is not a fit one—who are the most unfit perhaps the [*Executive*] Council may have to Judge.

ALS, Gratz Collection, PHi. Addressed to Charles County, Maryland; franked; postmarked.

[1] Thomas Johnson was appointed chief judge of the Maryland General Court on 20 April (*DHSCUS* 1:71).

[*William Maclay*] to Messrs. Printers

WHOEVER will pay attention to the acts of the old Congress, both during the war and since the peace, will find, that the public demands, for the exigencies of the general government, were managed by requisitions, charged on the different states, in a ratio, that was supposed to bear proportion to their abilities, for the time being, carrying on the face of each requisition, an express reference to a final settlement, and a direct assumption of any balance which an individual state might advance, more than her proportion should be found to be, on a general adjustment of the accounts.

As all debts contracted and engagements entered into, under the confederation, were confirmed by the new constitution, it may be justly demanded, by what authority, any *ex post facto* law can now be passed, altering the arrangement for settlement, or in any wise impairing the force or effect of former engagements? The hope and firm belief of a final settlement, when ample justice would be done to the advancing states, gave confidence to the exertions of the union. The state debts which stand charged on the funds of individual states, are the most effectual pledges to secure this settlement. For should the general assumption of the state debts take place, agreeable to some late proposals, the debtor states, which are believed to be, by much, the most numerous, would check every motion for settlement, as it must be contrary to their interest. We are informed that this was actually the case in Holland, and that the city of Amsterdam never was reimbursed the sums which she advanced, beyond her proportion, during the revolution of the United Provinces.[1]

The states being charged with their respective debts, may be regarded as a fortunate circumstance in facilitating a final settlement, and equalizing the accounts—thus when any state is deficient in her requisitions, let a portion of her state debt remain upon her, equal to such deficiency; in this manner the general burthen will be distributed agreeable to the principles on which the debt was contracted. Innovation will be avoided, and the public expectation complied with. Whereas a general assumption of the state debts would deprive Congress of a simple and easy mode of obliging the delinquent states to make up their deficiencies and have a direct tendency to prevent all settlement whatever. The evident consequence of which, would be, the punishment of the creditor states for their superior exertions, and the rewarding the deficient ones for their delinquency.

NYDA, 28 April; printed in *FJ* the same day; reprinted in *FG*, 4 May, over the signature "A Federalist." The identification of the author is based on Maclay's diary entry of 22 April, and Maclay to Rush, 24 April, above.

[1] The United Provinces was formed by the Union of Utrecht in 1579 by the seven northern provinces of the Spanish Hapsburg holdings that made up present-day Belgium and The Netherlands. After renouncing allegiance to Spain in 1581, the United Provinces fought a war until its independence was declared by the Treaty of Westphalia in 1648. Amsterdam was the capital of Holland, the most important of the United Provinces.

Letter to New York

I understand the President has been indisposed lately—this is grievous intelligence, but such as I expected to hear—it is extremely difficult for a person of the best constitution, and in the prime of life to preserve a flow of health with such an infinity of care and solicitude on their mind—but in life's advance—and when the constitution begins to feel the shocks she early received in the public service, if intense application to public business is superadded at *this period*, the pillars of life will be undermined; and this I understand is the cause of the late indisposition; for your city is undoubtedly one of the healthiest situations in the United States, combining every advantage of climate, air and water.

A life so precious, should be watched with the eyes of Argus;[1] Health so important, should be nurtured with the vigilance of Angels. Constant exercise in the open air, and perpetually diversifying the scene, are as necessary as the circulation of the vital fluid. That habit of application must be broken thro—or the Hope of the western world will fail.

I ask pardon for a deviation from my proper line; but to the prayers of millions, the most active attention should be added for the preservation of a life, which everyone *feels*, but no one can express the importance of.

GUS, 8 May; reprinted at Bennington, Vermont.

---

[1] According to Greek legend, Argus had one hundred eyes.

Other Documents

Abigail Adams to Mary Cranch. ALS, Abigail Adams Letters, MWA. Written from "Richmond Hill," outside New York City; addressed to Braintree, Massachusetts. For the full text, see *Abigail Adams*, pp. 46–47.

Has had the most severe attack of rheumatism and fever that she has experienced for several years; weather is uncommonly wet and cold; snowfall in the past two weeks has exceeded that of the entire preceding winter; "our House has been a mere Hospital ever since Saturday last"; enquires about employing a house servant from Boston, whose terms will be three dollars per month and smallpox inoculation; complains that it is impossible to find male or female servants in New York City who do not drink; "I have at last ~~light with~~ found a footman who appears Sober, but he was Born in Boston"; no one can recommend a boy for hire; pays five dollars per month to her housekeeper, who oversees the servants and makes tea for "my publick Evenings"; "the chief of the Servants here who are good for any thing are Negroes who are slaves. The white ones are all ~~forigeners~~ Foreigners & chiefly vagabonds."

Stephen Goodhue to Benjamin Goodhue. FC:lbk, Goodhue Family Papers, MSaE. Written from Salem, Massachusetts.

People are discontented with the increase of government officers, their salaries, grants, and the slowness of business; assumption would "quiet" them; "Courtly appearances what is Called great pay here and a great ~~Show of~~ Pomposity doth not agree with Republican Tempers here while the people are groaning under heavy burthens as they Call it & the public Creditors not provided for."

Richard Henry Lee and John Walker to Governor Beverley Randolph. ALS, hand of Lee, Signers of the Constitution, Pierpont Morgan Library, New York City. Place to which addressed not indicated. For the enclosure, see *PGW* 5:349–50. The governor transmitted the letter and its enclosures to the Virginia legislature on 18 October when it next met (LS, Executive Communications, Vi).

They presented the congratulatory address of the Virginia House of Delegates to the President the day before, enclosing his reply.

Samuel Phillips Savage to George Thatcher. ALS, Chamberlain Collection, MB. Written from Weston, Massachusetts; franked; postmarked Worcester, Massachusetts, 29 April.

Reads that "the President of Congress" has ordered federal troops to Georgia and presumes Capt. Joseph Savage will be among them; asks "on what design, *if it may be known*"; requests forwarding of letter to Joseph; Savage's wealth is chiefly in government securities, which is as beneficial as gold to a miser—"they do to look on"; asks if there is an expectation of anything being done to fund the debt that session; "people begin to clamour, but more than I think there is reason for"; is startled by the growth of "local Spirit" in Congress; has not heard lately from Sarah (Thatcher).

Governor John Sullivan to Nicholas Gilman. Listing of ALS, *Henkels Catalog* 1074, pt. III(1913):item 459.

George Thatcher to Jeremiah Hill. No copy known; acknowledged in Hill to Thatcher, 6 May.

George Thatcher to Thomas Robison. FC, Thatcher Family Papers, MHi.
Reports House resolution on new duties; the resulting bill (Duties on Distilled Spirits [HR-62]) will probably undergo "some modification; &, perhaps, the sums will be reduced"; the bill will not pass in under three or four months, "but this is only an opinion."

Lund Washington to George Washington. ALS, ViMtvL. Written from "Hayfield," near Alexandria, Virginia. For the full text, see *PGW* 5:353–54.
Has heard from a neighboring merchant that George Mason, in refusing the appointment to fill Grayson's Senate seat, criticized the Republican Court's pomp and ceremony, by which, without Washington at the head, "those Damnd Monarchical fellows with the Vice president, & the Woman [*Abigail Smith Adams*]" would "ruin the Nation"; George Mason has read "some poem" satirizing Adams, "& was so pleased at it, that he took two copys of it in his own hand writeg."

Letter from Rhode Island. *GUS*, 12 May; reprinted at Bennington, Vermont; Stockbridge, Massachusetts; Hartford, Connecticut; New York City (*NYDG*, 13 May); Richmond and Winchester, Virginia; and Charleston, South Carolina.
Rhode Island politics; "most of the *country* towns are as opposed to the Constitution as ever"; "the *seaports* are all federal"; if the Constitution is not adopted at the convention "(which I very much doubt) necessity will drive the seaports to measures of a most serious nature, measures which will pave the way for a dismemberment of this unhappy state."

Thursday, 29 April 1790

Rain (Johnson)

Amicus to John Adams

I have ever considered the Assumption of the State Debts by Congress, as a Measure necessarily flowing from the Adoption of the Constitution of the United States: That on it, the Stability, the Respect, if not the Existence of the Government, would essentially depend. Little did I suppose, that the Gentlemen composing the house of Representatives of Congress, would determine this Subject, upon the narrow, selfish Principles, as it respects State,

& State; and put out of Sight its great Importance as it relates to the United States. When I considered the many Sources of Disunion, the Difference of Climate, Habits & Manners, between the States composing the Union, I looked upon the Debts of the several States as a happy Circumstance, wch. Congress would gladly seize upon, as a cementing Principle, to give Energy & Stability to a Government, otherwise weak from a Thousand Causes: Little did I think, that some characters, which I have heretofore respected, and revered, would have exposed their little Souls, before the great Theatre of the World, on a Subject, that must lead Mankind to suppose them under a criminal Defection to the very Government, they exercise.

The more I reflect upon the Plan of the Secretary of the Treasury, the more I am satisfied with it: and instead of his being thrown out of Office, like the Ministers of England, when their Plans are not supported by a majority in Parliament the People of the United States will feel themselves interested in it, and will support the Man, for the sake of his Measures.

The Public Creditors of the United States are too respectable a Class of Citizens in all the States, not to have a very strong powerful Influence, especially when there is a Disposition in the people at large, seeing that the honourable Discharge of their Debts, is perfectly within their Power, to second their Views. For the great Body of the People of every Country, when not corrupted, possess the Principles of Honour, & Honesty, in the highest Degree, and there is nothing but absolute Inability will induce them to depart from these Principles. It is for this reason that the faith of public Engagements has been always more sacredly preserved in free, than arbitrary Governments.

But perhaps the Gentlemen of the house of Representatives may cunningly cover their Opposition to the Assumption of the State Debts under the Idea of the contract's not being originally made by Congress, but this Subterfuge is too shallow: The Debt was contracted in a common cause, for common Purposes; Congress possess the whole, & only means, whereby it can be discharged, and therefore a partial Discharge will never give Satisfaction. And what will become of the Government of the United States, without the Confidence *of* the People! in a non-Entity very Shortly. For will the People rest satisfied with one Class of the public Creditors being paid, while another Class, equally meritorious, shall have no Provision made for their Demands? If there is a distinction of Debts, there will of course be of Creditors: If the State Creditors are referred to the State Governmts. for the discharge of their Debts, the Powers of Congress must be retrenched at least so far, as to put it in the Power of the several States to fullfill their Engagements, nor will the State Creditors rest satisfied with any thing short of it.

From this Source then, will there immediately rise up an opposition to the Government, the State Creditors who might have been made instrumental to its Support already begin to clamour agt. it, and will very shortly be in open Opposition to it. Whatever appearance, these observations may put on, it may be depended on, I am in no wise interested in any public Securities whatever. I can ~~look~~ judge therefore, of the probable Effect of Congress, not assuming the State Debts, with some Degree of Impartiality. And it is with much concern, I foresee, that the Well wishers to the Government of the United States have every every thing to apprehend, if the late measures of Congress are persisted in.

It appears to me there is now an excellent Opportunity for the President to express his Sentiments upon the Secretary's Report. The Members of Congress having taken Sides upon this Business, will hardly relinquish their Opinions to one another unless by the judicious Interference of the Supreme Magistrate; whose conciliating advice and Influence might prove salutary upon this occasion. It may be said that the Presidt. may be charged with Impropriety in interfering ~~upon this Occasion~~, perhaps so; but it will be only by Those Members of Congress, who at present are blinded by their Passions & Prejudices, and who find their Vanity gratified in the supposed Success of their narrow, selfish Designs. I am the more anxious for the President's Opinion at this time, as a new choice of Representatives is just at hand; ~~the Presidents~~ His Opinion therefore would be something like an appeal to the good Sense of the People, ~~will be either rejected or confirmed~~ whereby to regulate their next choice of ~~Representatives~~ Persons to represent them. In England, if a Dispute takes place between Parliament, & the King's Ministers, the King either gives up his Ministers, or dissolves the Parliament, if the latter, it operates as an appeal to the People, whether they will vindicate the Measures of his ministry by choosing fit Persons to ~~overthrow or to~~ enforce them ~~or not~~. By such an appeal the classic Principle of the Government ~~is~~ tried, as the reaction of ~~the President's Opinion~~ the Principle, in case there is a coincidence of Opinion, between the People & [*lined out*] Persons administering the Government, will give~~s confidence~~ permanency & Stability to it. Every Government ought to reflect the general Opinion, for when the Measures of it, counteract it, the great end of Government, is perverted, and the public are constrained to accept the narrow, selfish Views of a few Individuals, instead of their own enlightened, & extended Sentiments. The frequent Election of Representatives is hereby rendered necessary to pull down those, who through mistake or Design, act contrary to the general Opinion, and to elevate such, who are better qualified to discern, & to enforce it.

The great public have had before it, the funding System of the Secretary to the Treasury. The Public Creditors did not at first seem satisfied with the Reduction of Interest from six to four per Cent: but it is left optional, whether to subscribe to the Propositions of the Secretary, or not. The public felt, that from unavoidable Circumstances, the Credit of the Securities had sunk to a very low price: to raise them at once above par, wch. would have been the Effect of funding the Debt at six per Cent Interest would have been an injustice to those, who have parted with their Securities; to have reduced them to their Value, as sold in the public Market, or to have made a Discrimination between the Original Holders, & present Possessors, would be an injustice to the Present Possessors by not indemnifying them for the Risk they had run, & ~~destructive to~~ would by prostrating public Credit. For if the Securities are not to be wholly owned by the present Possessors, will the public market give credit to the Notes of Congress in future? it is plain it would not. For the Notes being made transferable, the public Market will give the Principal, as long as, or whenever the annual Interest is punctually discharged. What then would become of this Principle, if a Discrimination between original Holders & present Possessors was to take place? It wd. be forever lost, and utterly out of the Power of Congress to retrieve it. But the advantages of the Secretary's Propositions, do not stop here, the Reduction of Interest promises us the Benefit of the Circulation of our own Debt. For if there was a great Temptation to Foreigners to become the Purchasers of it, wch. wd. have been the Case if it had been funded at six per Cent, the People of the States would in a few years have possessed but few of their own Securities, and the Monies raised by the Duties for the payment of the annual Interest, would be transported out of the Country, to its great Loss & Injury.

A Perfect System of Finance taken in the present State of the Debts of the united States, is not to be expected. A compromise of Opinion upon this subject, something like the one produced by the Secretary, will probably give general Satisfaction. The Faith & credit of the united States may be preserved, whilst there is some Regard paid to the public Opinion, in consequence of the very great Depreciation of the Securities, in medio tutissimus ibis.[1]

Every thing it appears to me stands suspended upon this important Question. If Congress assume the State Debts, Peace, Tranquility & a firm Government, will be the Result. if not, a weak, and an ineffecient one, or perhaps no Government at all, may be the Consequence. The Choice lies before Congress—Honour, or Disgrace; I hope they'll ~~prefer~~ accept the first, that we may not be again exposed to the Inconveniences of a State of Anarchy & Confusion but if they prefer the last, may the Stigma of Defection rest upon those men, who seem disposed to sacrifice the Government to their narrow, selfish & contracted Views.

ALS, Adams Family Manuscript Trust, MHi. Written from Massachusetts. "Amicus" means "friend" in Latin.

[1] Safety lies in a middle course (Ovid).

William Smith (S.C.) to Edward Rutledge

In one of my Letters [*from Mr.*] Tench Coxe of Philada. is this paragraph which I insert for your information & that of the Agricultul. Society:[1]
"I am well assured that a Mr. Oswald Eve[2] (or a son of his) formerly a Captain of a Vessel out of Philada. has invented a very valuable machine for ginning Cotton in New Providence where he now resides. As the Bahamas are near to your State it would be a trifling Expence to send a person thither for it. A couple of Guineas a peice for a dozen Gentlemen would probably do it. If you speak or write of it, let it be cautiously & confidentially, as it may occasion some difficulty. The Machine will always be worth more than the cost, if the Patent-Office should be opened before it arrives. The person sent shod. take great care about the mode of procuring one, & of shipping it, tho there is no Law, I believe, to prohibit the exportation of such things from thence."

Please send me by the next oppty. the Plan & rules of the Santee Canal Company, & any other ~~navigatn.~~ rules which the other Compy.[3] may have published, with the Laws incorporating them (if convenient)—Mr. Coxe has written to me for them.

I have sent your newspapers to [*Christopher*] Gadsden, with a request to forward them to you at Columbia." my respect to Genl. [*Charles Cotesworth*] Pinckney.

AL, incomplete, Smith Papers, ScHi. Addressed to Charleston, South Carolina; franked. This is the conclusion, perhaps a postscript, of what has survived of the manuscript.

---

[1] The South Carolina Society for promoting and improving agriculture and other rural concerns was founded in Charleston in 1785. Izard, a charter member, served on the society's executive council. Butler was also a member, and Jefferson the first honorary member (Chalmers S. Murray, *This Our Land: The Story of the Agricultural Society of South Carolina* [Charleston, S.C., 1949], pp. 32, 38, 49; *Butler Letters*, p. 76).

[2] Joseph Eve of Nassau on the island of New Providence is credited with the invention of a cotton gin and obtained a British patent for it five years before Eli Whitney's cotton gin was patented (George C. Rogers, "Letters of William L. Smith to Edward Rutledge," *SCHM* 69[April 1968]:114n).

[3] Smith was a principal investor in two inland navigation companies in 1790. The first was chartered in 1786 to build a canal from the Santee to the Cooper River, which then flowed into Charleston. The second (1787) aimed to extend the Santee's reach further inland by clearing its tributaries, the Wateree and Catawba rivers, up to the North Carolina border. Sumter was an early investor in the latter, and Izard (Smith's father-in-law) invested in both, even envisioning a great commercial entrepôt named "Izardtown" at the eastern end of the Santee canal (Joseph S. Davis, *Essays in the Earlier History of American Corporations* [1917; reprint, 2 vols., New York, 1965], 2:142–48, 335; George C. Rogers, Jr., *Evolution of a Federalist: William Loughton Smith of Charleston (1758–1812)* [Columbia, S.C., 1962], pp. 131–34).

Henry Wynkoop to Reading Beatty

You will perceive by the Debates of Congress that this week has been more propitious to Busyness than some time past, that the State Debts are put out of View for the present, A Committee appointed to report A Bill making Provision for the public Creditors, agreable to the Principals established, and also one for A Bill to lay aditional Duties on certain enumerated Articles, since which the House has been perfectly harmonious and the files are clearing off fast, see nothing at present which will be likely to embarrass except the return of the Assumption Affair, which will inevitably be brought forward again.

***

Several Members of Congress are unwell Mr. Madison this morning was said to be dangerous, the Air is as damp raw & disagreable, as must necessarily endanger the Lives of many people, from such Scituation, good Lord deliver us.

ALS, Wynkoop Papers, PDoBHi. Place to which addressed not indicated. The omitted paragraph concerns a personal financial matter.

Other Documents

Silas W. Arnett to George Washington. ALS, Washington Papers, DLC. For the full text, see *PGW* 5:357.

Office seeking: attorney for North Carolina district; mentions Williamson by name and other North Carolina Representatives as references.

David Austin to Roger Sherman. ALS, Sherman Collection, CtY. Written from New Haven, Connecticut; postmarked. The enclosed receipt, signed by Austin as agent in New Haven on 27 April, was for a $250 certificate issued by the register of the treasury to Amos Morris and Joel Northrop (Ms., Sherman Collection, CtY).

Acknowledges receipt of certificate for lottery prize with thanks for Sherman's "great care, & attention" in securing it; requests any political information "which you Judge interesting to me"; thinks it impossible to liquidate the different evidences of national debt by the same ratio, admitting himself "to be Interested in this matter, having a considerable sum in the [*17*]75 Emition" ("old emission" money); thinks that the former Congress's grand committee report (of 18 March 1780, in *JCC* 16:262–66) "would come as near to Justice as any measure I can think of at present."

Pierce Butler to Frances Butler. FC, Butler Letterbook, ScU. For the full text, see *Butler Letters*, pp. 35–38. The verse quoted is from Alexander Pope's *Epistles to Several Persons* (1732).

Has written to her three times since her last letter to him; Mary Middleton Butler "has been exceedingly indisposed all the Winter. She is still confined to Her bed. I am full of anxiety about Her": complains about his nephew Edward's "self interest and sordidness" in their business dealings together; "How unlike my Angelic Brother [*Sir Thomas*]! 'Tis education that teaches the tender mind;/ As the Twig is bent the Tree's inclin'd."

Robert Morris to Mary Morris. Listing of ALS, *Libbie Catalog*, 3 February 1892, item 1386.

South Carolina Delegation to the Commissioners for Settling Accounts Among the States. No copy known; mentioned in William Davies to Governor Beverley Randolph, 20 June 1790, as being an addendum to the Commissioners' Report of 30 April.

Seeking an additional gross claim of $3,000,000.

William Samuel Johnson, Diary. Johnson Papers, CtHi.

"Dined [*at the*] Presidents."

George Washington, Diary. ViHi.

Senators Strong, Johnson, Paterson, Morris, Carroll, Lee, Walker, Johnston, and Gunn, and Representatives Sturges, Benson, Floyd, Schureman, Vining, Smith (Md.), Bland, and Sumter dined at the President's.

[Providence, Rhode Island] *United States Chronicle*, 29 April.

By latest accounts from New York, assumption "appears every Day less probable," despite many members trying to bring on the question; many will oppose all funding of the domestic debt unless assumption is agreed to.

Letter from Rhode Island to A Philadelphia Merchant. *PP*, 19 May; reprinted at Stockbridge, Massachusetts; New York City (*NYDG*, 21 May; *NYP*, 22 May); Edenton, North Carolina; and Charleston, South Carolina.

Many think Rhode Island will adopt the Constitution next month "though in my opinion it is a very doubtful matter"; criticizes some of the convention members as illiterate and common laborers.

FRIDAY, 30 APRIL 1790

Fine (Johnson)

Daniel Benezet to Robert Morris

My Son [*Daniel Benezet, Jr.*] has sent me his Petition, with desire that I would forward it to some Gentleman in New York, have taken the Liberty to inclose it to you, with Request that you will please to hand it to the President so soon as a Law is past respecting that Business.

I have wrote to Messrs. F. A. Muhlenberg, Cadwalader, Patterson & Sinnickson & spoke to Mr. Fitzsimons on the Subject, & inform'd them that I have settled my Son at Egg harbour [*New Jersey*], have built him a Grist Mill & Saw Mill &ca.—he has had a good Education & from his prudent Conduct seems to have gain'd the Respect of his Neighbours the Legislature of Jersey have lately appointed him to the Commission of the Peace in Gloucester County—I will be ready to give any Security that may be required.

Hope you will excuse my giving you this Trouble.

LS, Washington Papers, DLC. Written from Philadelphia; franked; postmarked. The enclosed application from Daniel Benezet, Jr., to Washington, undated, is calendared under 3 May, the date it was forwarded to Washington.

Edward Carrington to James Madison

I have this moment come to Town and am favored with yours of the 10th. & 17th. Instant for which I beg you to accept my thanks. I am exceedingly happy in the majority having shifted sides upon the subject of the assumption of the State debts because I am certain that no measure could be carried in Congress more productive of discontent; nor do I think that any could be taken under consideration in which the States are so dissimilarly situated. much as I wish to see an establishment for the support of public credit, I would rather relinquish it altogether for the present session, than see involved with it so fruitful a source of dissatisfaction, especially as the best supporters of the Government in States that have redeemed considerable portions of their debts, would be compelled to assent to the propriety of the complaint. could the States be admitted as Creditors in the scheme upon their redeemed securities, the measure would perhaps be satisfactory to a majority of the Community. all the true freinds of the Government would unite in defending it, and might be too weighty for its enemies, who would make it a topic for popular clamour, but the proposition as it has been contended for, could not but add to the Enemies of the Govt. many of its friends as a discontented party. to say that upon a final adjustment of Accounts all things will be set right is ~~saything~~ saying nothing that ought to be satisf[*ac*]tory, because leaving the attainment of general justice to depend on that issue is throwing the hazard on the States alone who have been paying their debts, while, to consider them as Creditors for their redeemed securities can ultimately injure no part of the Union: in case there should be no settlement the paying States will nevertheless receive the benefit of their honest exertions should they be considered as Creditors, and should a settlement take place they can receive no more. but leave them on the footing proposed ~~thesy~~ their receiving justice must depend absolutely upon an adjustment of Accounts—at present, and always hitherto, this adjustment has been held an object equally interesting to all the States: yet the prospect of effecting it is desperate; and I presume that to interest some States in deferring it forever, which would be the case with all the non-paying States under the proposed measure, could have no tendency to better the prospect of a final settlement. as to the permanent Seat of Government I have always, since the fatal vote of 88,[1] expected that it would long hang as a clog upon every important measure, and that it would at last, unless the fixture is too long deferred, be placed at the pleasure of Pensylva.

I am much obliged by your observations upon the establishment of the Marshals office. it at present subjects me to expence without a [*lined out*] prospect of a Shillings emolument. and after the sitting of the Court at Charlottesville, duties will be required which I am satisfied cannot be executed for many times the amount of ~~which~~ what the Laws of the State authorise the officer to receive.

Your desire to have the Act concerning the Census [*Enumeration*] faithfully executed induces me to inclose you a Copy of my advertisement upon that subject in which you will see my arrangement for appointing assistants. perhaps I have undertaken more labour in the business than was contemplated when the compensation was fixed, but less would not have given to myself a satisfactory assurance of proper assistants.

I still think that an oath is necessary to the faithful compliance of the people ~~to~~ with the requisites of the Census Act. the Assistants may compel every one he calld on to make him a return by means of the penalty, but it is not probable he will be able to discover any concealments of parts of families & there is no doubt but that many evil disposed persons will endeavour to impress upon the minds of the people, ideas that their future taxes will be governed by the numbers they shall now return. our Commissioners of Taxes collect the number of tithables by means of an oath, so that, as to Virginia, it will not be a novelty to require one. if it is viewed in a different light in other States, I suppose the alteration will not take place, but I shall have much less confidence in the effect of the Act as it stands, than I should were the alteration made—in order that my assistants may know with certainty whom t[*h*]ey are to call on I shall injoin it as one of their duties, to take from the Commissioners Books in the several Counties, copies of the lists of tithables which are now collecting & will be compleat before August. these lists will shew them every family: and I shall further injoin it as a duty that these lists be returned to me with ~~their~~ the other proceedings for my better satisfaction of the faithfulness with which they have executed their several Trusts. in order that the measures may be as well patronised as possible I have inclosed copies of my advertisement to the Gentlemen of the different Counties who were in the last assembly requesting the favor of their aid to my assistants in impressing upon the minds of the people the importance of faithful returns, and this I have done without respect to the political sentiments of individuals.

ALS, Madison Papers, DLC. Written from Richmond, Virginia. Carrington's advertisement, dated 26 March, was printed at Richmond by John Dixon and in several newspapers. It is in the Madison collection of printed material, Rare Book Room, DLC.

---

[1] A reference to the 13 September 1788 vote to name New York, "the present seat of Congress," as the seat of the new federal government. Both Carrington and Madison voted "aye," giving up their summer-long struggle to name Philadelphia instead.

William Maclay to Tench Coxe

I have received yours of the 27th & return You my hearty thanks for it and the inclosures. We will endeavour to obtain a republication of the ~~pe~~ peice which respects our State at this place.[1] But what is of more importance, We will get it translated and published in Germany, by Means of Doctor Kunzee [*John Christopher Kunze*], with whom we lodge, and who is fond of things of this kind.

The House of Representatives, have been more rapid in their Movements this week, than Usual. and we now hope an End of the session, with the Month of May. This seems a pretty general wish. There is another, in which many of your Friends, are not less fervent, and that is an adjournment to Philada. It will certainly be right to try this Measure, As even a miscarriage can place Us in no Worse situation, than we now are. We do not hear any Complaints in point of health, from your quarter; we seem to have a second edition of the influenza in this place. Madison and many other Members of both houses confined, or at least complaining, perhaps it may be general. or soon become so. Genl. Hiester & Genl. [*Peter*] Muhlenberg are both laid up with it.

I shall be happy to hear from You at all times.

ALS, Coxe Papers, PHi. Addressed to Chestnut Street, Philadelphia; franked; postmarked 2 May.

[1] "Notes Concerning the United States of America," [Philadelphia] *American Museum* 8(1790):35–42.

John Meals, Georgia State Debt

Georgia State Debt April 30th 1790		£	s	d			
Governor's & Speakers warrants							
Reported by the Comtee. on Finance Jany. 1787							
to be then outstanding					12,849	6	2½
Governor's issued in 1787		19,431	19	5¾			
Speakers —— in January 1787	1547.0.4						
—— in July 1787	927.14.8	2,474	15				
					21906	14	5¾
Governor's in 1788		15991	14	10¾			
Speakers —— in Jany. 1788		1,252	17				
					17,244	11	10¼
Govrs. warrants in 1789 called anticipd. wrts. all of which except £105 in favour of D[*avid*]. Hillhouse contractor		13715					
Do. drawn payable in final settlements for supplies &c. for the Indian treaty		11,730					
Do drawn for the support of the civil list, for contingencies, and special appropriations of the legislature		11,687	3	3			
Speakers Jany. 1789	2036.12.10						
—— Decr. 1789	1285.1.6	3321	14	4			
					40453	17	7
					92454	10	1½
Govrs. & Speakers wrts.							
Destroyed Jany. session 1788		26,131	9				
Jany. session 1789		19,660	6	1½			
Novr. session 1789		13,115	12	5			
Now in the Treasury		1,528	15	2			
anticipation warrts. of Executive of 1787 —— Do.		8250	15	2¾			
warrts. and orders of Executive for final settlements Do.		11,730					
					80416	17	10½
Leaving outstanding					12037	12	3½

Item	Date	Amount	Subtotal	Outstanding
Paper Medium				
Emitted in August 1786			50,000	
Destroyed by Comtee. of Finance				
	Jany. 1787	20,000		
	Jany. 1789	5,000		
Now in the Treasury		1,205.3. 5¼		
			26205 3 5¼	
Leaving outstanding				23,794 16 6¾
Ticket Emission 9th Feby. 1786			1145 4	
Destroyed by Comtee. of Finance				
	Jany. 1788	1004.8.10		
	Jany. 1789	12.4.5		
	Novr. 1789	4.5		
Now in the Treasury		7		
			1027 18 3	
Leaving outstanding				117 5 9
Audited certiffs.				
Amount issued by John Wereat Esqr.			285763 3 5	
Destroyed by Executive in				
	May 1786	151,883.18.5		
— by comtee. of Fin.				
	Jany. 1787	22,160. .5½		
— Do.	Jany. 1788	15,933.3.9		
— Do.	Jany. 1789	19,192.3.6		
— Do.	Novr. 1789	6,575.9.2½		
Now in the Treasury		7,464.7.11¼		
Leaving outstanding, (exclusive of Audits issued by Jno. Wilkinson & Jno. Gibbons Esqrs. former Auditors, of which I do not find that any returns have been made; but Mr. Wereat says they do not amount to any thing considerable				62554 ½
Gratuitous Certiffs.				
Issued as ꝑ Cheque in the office of the Secy. of State			6,555	
Destroyed by Executive in				
	May 1786	2637.18.6		
— by Comtee. of Finance in				
	Jany. 1788	749.0.3		
— Do. in Jany. 1789		451.15.		
— Do. in Novr. 1789		25.0.		
			3863 13 9	
Leaving outstanding				2691 6 3

Funded Certiffs.			
Issued as ⅌ checque in the Treasury office exclusive of Interest		74,426 14 8½	
Destroyed by Executive in May 1786	523.16.9		
— by Comtee. on Finance in Jany. 1787	7,200.11.7½		
— Do. Jany. 1788	736.14.9¼		
— Do. Jany. 1789	22,930.15.4¼		
Novr. 1789	2445.3.6¼		
Now in the Treasury	1322.19.8½		
		35160 1 8¼	
Leaving outstanding		39,266 12 11	
on which may be computed 5 yrs. Interest @ 7 ⅌ cent		13,743 6 5	
			53,009 19 5¼
Treasury certiffs. by George Jones Esqr.			
Issued as ⅌ account in the treasury books		6,393 11 9½	
of which recd. in payment at the treasury by G. Jones	1063.1.5		
— Do. by J. Meals	4790.12.11		
		5853 14 5	
Leaving outstanding			539 17 4
Treasury certiffs. by John Meals			
amount issued		1911 15 1½	
Recd. again in payments at the Treasury		1286 7 9	
Leaving outstanding			625 7 4½

The Treasury certificates issued by John Martin and Seth John Cuthbert Esqrs. formerly Treasurers cannot be ascertained. Mr. Martin I believe issued very few. many of Mr. Cuthberts have been taken up and the holders of those outstanding have been notified by the Auditor 8 or 9 months ago, to report the sums and dates to Mr. [*Joseph*] Clay & myself; but the amount yet reported is very inconsiderable.

Of O'Brien & Wades certificates many are yet outstanding the time for liquidation is long since elapsed, but the amount issued cannot be ascertained.

Certificates issued by the Executive of 1782 ⅌ cheques in the office of the Secretary of the state (If any of those have been taken up and destroyed they are included with the gratuitous certificates, therefore I extend the whole amount) £ 1,726.18.9

Total 157,097.3.9½

Ms., hand of Meals, Abraham Baldwin Papers, GU.

Ezra Stiles to Abraham Baldwin

A Captain Peter Pond[1] of Milford has been absent for seventeen years in the Indian Furr trade between the West end of Lake Superior & the Western [*Pacific*] Ocean. on this tract and up to the 64 degree of Latitude, a Furr trade Company in Canada have established 21 Factories garrisoned with 800 troops to collect all the Furrs. Capt. Pond resided in 1774 in the Sources of the Mississippi beyond Capt. Carver's residence,[2] and afterwards 3 years in the 64 degree of Lat. Thus he has had great opportunity of knowing the rates of Indian population in this territory; which he assures me to be much in the same manner of scattered Sachemdoms, as between Mischilimackinack[3] and the Atlantic Ocean. He judges he never saw ten thousand Indians. I had long wished to know this, of which we never before had any satisfactory information. He showed me a Map of the territory across to the pacific ocean & indeen [*indeed*] over to Kamschatka [*Russia*]. He was probably within 150 or 200 Miles of the Western ocean; and indeed freely heard by Indians from those shores, as well as from the Shores of the American Hyperborean [*Arctic*] Ocean.

Copy, hand of Madison, Madison Papers, DLC. Baldwin's reply of 3 June, below, indicates this letter had an enclosure for forwarding to a Mr. Holmes. This copy's existence is proof of Madison's early interest (although at an undetermined date) in the potential of an all-water route to the Pacific Ocean, such as that sought by Lewis and Clark's corps of discovery in 1804–6.

---

[1] Pond (1740–1807) was a native of Milford, Connecticut, who became a fur trader in Canada after serving in the French and Indian War. Penetrating further northwest than any other White trapper, he was the first non-Native American to explore the Athabasca basin (1778), where he established a fur trading post. The next year he persuaded a group of Montreal investors to establish what became in 1783 the North West Company, the Hudson Bay Company's rival in western Canada. In 1785 he explored the Great Slave Lake in Canada's Northwest Territory and, after meeting Native Americans who claimed to have seen Capt. James Cooke's ships in the present-day Gulf of Alaska, conceived of trading furs westward to the Pacific rather than along the two year route back to Montreal. Pond returned to Connecticut permanently in 1787 and left it to his protege, Alexander Mackenzie, to discover the Great Slave Lake's outlet to the "American Hyberborean Ocean." (For a reproduction of Pond's map, see William H. Goetzmann and Glyndwr Williams, *The Atlas of North American Exploration* [Norman, Okla., 1992], pp. 112–13.)

[2] Jonathan Carver (ca. 1732–1780) explored the northern Mississippi and as far as two hundred miles up the Minnesota River from present-day Minneapolis in 1766–68, recording his exaggerated discoveries and sometimes plagiarized observations in his famous *Travels* (London, 1778).

[3] Michilimackinac, at present-day Mackinac Island, Michigan.

OTHER DOCUMENTS

William Samuel Johnson, Diary. Johnson Papers, CtHi.
"Dind. [*Dined at the*] Daltons."

NYDA, 30 April.
"We hear" that the day before, Strong was added to the Senate committee on the Rhode Island Trade Bill in lieu of Butler, "excused at his own desire; his colleague being on the committee."

APRIL 1790 UNDATED

George Beckwith, *Notes of Conversations with Different Persons*

[*With Alexander Hamilton*]

[*Hamilton:*] *** My communications with You, You will of course always consider to be informal; but on this particular point I think I speak the sentiments of the majority of those, who are to conduct the affairs of this country; as to my own part my ideas naturally extend to objects, which I hold to be favorable for the general interests of the States, in which view I contemplate a connexion with You, and further than they may have that tendency, I certainly should not go, but with us different gentlemen may view this matter in different lights; the President of the United States I am inclined to think considers this subject in a favorable one. Mr. Jefferson, the Secretary of State, who lately returned from Paris on his private affairs, the condition of France not requiring his presence, and who did not know of his appointment until his arrival in America, is of opinion, that the struggle for freedom in that country will be successful, and when completed, that it will be productive of great commercial benefits to the States; from the influence of the Marquis de la Fayette, who is greatly attached to this country, as well as from that general bias, which those, who guide that party, have always shewn towards us. From these considerations I am the more strongly disposed to view the present time as particularly favorable for the consideration of a commercial Treaty.

As to Spain no doubt the navigation of the Missisippi does attract the attention of discerning men with us, and it is looked forward to as the probable source of coldness, possibly of difference with that court at a future period, but it does not appear to me, that it could come under immediate consideration. With regard to Your Court having a Minister here I am clear, that would be a measure, which would give general satisfaction, the particular rank might depend on the pretensions of the gentleman in question for that station; high appointments in our situation would not be thought eligible; I am not versed in diplomatic distinctions, but am led to think that a Minister Plenipotentiary is of a scale adequate for the purposes of both countries, concluding that a parity of rank would be proper for each.

[*Beckwith*] I am authorized farther to say, that it is for Your consideration whether in the present stage of this business You may judge it expedient to make any further communications to Lord Dorchester.

[*Hamilton*] I cannot at this moment determine, whether it may be proper to communicate further with Lord Dorchester on this subject, or to carry it forward through a regular official channel.

Mr. Jefferson arrived last night, and these matters are in his department. Pray how long do you intend to remain here?

[*Beckwith*] Until about the middle of April.

[*Hamilton*] It is probable that before that time I shall have it in my power to give You some information on this point.

We observe a paragraph from a London paper, that mentions Lord Hawkesbury and Mr. [*Lord*] Grenville being engaged in the framing the outline of a Commercial Treaty with us, pray in what official station is His Lordship?

[*Beckwith*] His Lordship has presided at a Committee of the Privy Council for commercial affairs.

In continuation

[*Hamilton*] Nothing has happened since I had the pleasure of seeing You, to render it requisite for me to change my opinions on the different subjects touched upon in that conversation.[1]

A Treaty of Commerce with Great Britain is generally wished, and the full consideration of the subject is desirable. The reciprocal appointment of Ministers is also very agreeable, the particular grade is a secondary consideration, and may be readily accommodated to the mutual convenience of both countries.

N. B. Mr. [*Hamilton*] added something with respect to the States having sent a Minister to our Court,[2] which we had never acknowledged, and hinted, as if it was expected, that it was for us to make the first offer; I replied that the condition of the States at that time had been such, as to have rendered it impracticable for a Minister from *us* to have remained at New York, and if otherwise, from the nature of their then Government he could have been of no service.

In Continuation

[*Beckwith*] I have requested to see You as the time is drawing near when I intend returning to Quebec; I conceive it to be necessary and not improper for me to remark that I take it for granted, the different communications,

You have been pleased to make to me, flow from that source, which under Your present government, is alone competent to make them.

[*Hamilton*] I am not authorized to say to You in so many words, that such is the language of the President of the United States; to a gentleman, who has no public character such a declaration cannot be made, but my honor and character stand implicated in the fulfilment of these assurances. The gentlemen at the head of the different departments may not have precisely the same way of thinking on all public concerns. I therefore speak with the greatest caution on all points in which they have a direct share, but where it respects the President to whom this must have reference, I can speak with more precision. I can say this, that his mind is perfectly free from any bias whatever on this subject and that he is ready to go into the discussion of every thing unsettled between the two countries.

[*Beckwith*] If I comprehended You the last time I had the honor of seeing You You suggested some difficulty in the appointment of a minister to us.

[*Hamilton*] Yes I did so, we have had a Minister at Your Court. You did not send one in return, we should find a difficulty in taking the lead again in such a nomination.

[*Beckwith*] I am sorry to observe the disputes upon Your northeast frontier relative to the boundary, and the publications in Your newspapers on the subject.[3]

[*Hamilton*] Yes, that matter ought to be settled as soon as possible, as some accident may possibly happen.

[*Beckwith*] It is to be hoped, that Your government most interested in this matter (Massachusets bay) will not become intemperate.

[*Hamilton*] I think it right to remark to You in this place, that a degree of moderation and good sense, has been conspicuous in the conduct of the Eastern Governments since the peace, which has not been equally so to the southward of Pensylvania; at the different periods, in which I have been a member of Congress under the late Constitution, I have had frequent occasions to observe this, and at first I acknowledge with some surprize; cool, plain good sense, determines their decisions without either animosity or partiality; it is not so much so, I am sorry to say to the southward, and I have been frequently led to consider the cause; I am inclined to think that the sentiments of one or two gentlemen in the southern States, whose characters give them influence, has led to this, they have been esteemed men of superior capacity, And certain causes have induced them to keep alive distinctions neither wise nor proper; but these persons are not at present in office, and possibly the private circumstances of too many of our southern planters, and their dread of the operation of the federal Courts, may also have an influence.

[*Beckwith*] As enthusiasm cannot suppose that with respect to *us*, there exists the smallest necessity to compel the consideration of commercial subjects, with the States, and however embarrassed You may still continue in many respects, as candor must admit, that Your situation is better, than it was two years ago, I should hope if there shall be any discussions on this subject they will be entered upon with temper and candor.

[*Hamilton*] It is the duty of every man in Office to do so; we have still much to do, but the foundation is laid, and our difficulties are chiefly owing to ourselves; it will require time, but in the course of things we must become a very considerable people.

I have ever thought it undesirable, that we should be *courted* by one power in Europe only; I do not mean this in the common acceptation of the word, but that our connexions should be more extended.

[*With Other Persons*]

1. [*Johnson*] There are two parties in our Legislature, both have it in view to form a friendly connexion with Great Britain, differing in their ideas as to the means; the one is desirous of very moderate measures on our part, and the shunning every thing, that may wear the appearance of commercial warfare, observing that although Great Britain has excluded us from her American and West India possessions, yet that She has granted us certain advantages in her ports of Europe, that in Asia She treats us with kindness, that hers is the best market for our exports, and that, if we are intemperate we may naturally look for an alteration in these points: the other is of opinion, that prompt and spirited resolutions are best calculated to effect this purpose, and that the interests of the States essentially require them; these gentlemen think that in placing all the maritime powers of Europe under similar restrictions, and treating their shipping in our ports precisely as they treat ours in their American and West India possessions, or in excluding them from ours, if they shall continue to exclude ours from theirs, the States in such a struggle will have the best of it; for one of two things must happen; either some European power will give way in order to form an advantageous treaty with us, to the disadvantage of the others, or if not, we shall consume less in future, set seriously about the introduction of domestic manufactures and take our chances for a market for our raw materials. Such is the language of the two parties; which may finally preponderate I cannot tell, but those, who are the advocates for strong measures carry with them an air of popularity.

We have many important points to discuss during the present sessions, respecting our internal finances, and I doubt whether any steps will be taken by the Legislature upon the foregoing subject. A commercial friendship with You is I am persuaded very generally wished; but I think the great difficulty in the way is, that Your navigation Act is so very important to Your naval greatness, that You will not be disposed to break through so essential a part of it, as to give us a share in Your West India trade, and this is what we want. I have not a doubt, but that the Federal Courts will give the most perfect satisfaction in their proceedings, yet I am sorry to say, that Your creditors must unavoidably lose great sums, many of their debtors having little to pay; I hope however in many instances, that the Creditors are in possession of the paper securities, which altho' low at the time they got them, have had a great rise lately, and may be expected still to increase in their value; it is remarkable that the present Chief Justice (Mr. John Jay) was the minister for foreign affairs, who reported the various infractions of the Treaty of Peace, by the State Legislatures, and is it possible to suppose, that what he openly acknowledged in his political character, will not equally affect his decisions on the Bench, either in trials at law or in equity? for the powers of the supreme Court are those of Your Courts of Chancery, King's bench and Exchequer; it unites the whole; we wished to have them distinct for obvious reasons, but when we formed our present government it was not practicable to effect it, from some of the States having been wholly unused to a Court of Chancery, and having imbibed very false ideas on this point.

Our boundary with You to the eastward is a subject of difference and has been so for years past; Mr. Adams when in London presented Memorials on the subject, two of our Commissioners, who signed the Treaty of Peace, being in this Country, they were called on by the late Congress to declare, which was the real boundary, they said, that Mitchel's map lay on the table, in which one River Saint Croix only is laid down, that the late Mr. [*Richard*] Oswald retained this map, on which as they think some traces were made, and they say, that the river, nearest to the river St. Johns was in contemplation At that time,[4] and with respect to the Islands the Treaty expresses, that all such as are within a given distance of the Coast, shall follow the fate of the boundary line, excepting they shall have been previously granted by Nova Scotia; they are valuable for the fisheries, but I am inclined to think that on an investigation, they will be found to have been so granted. I have inquired into the extent and nature of the land in dispute, and from the best information I find, that the distance between the two rivers bearing the same name does not at their mouths exceed Ten miles, but increases considerably as You ascend them, being an object of one hundred and twenty Townships each of six miles square, a large proportion of which is good land.

The boundaries to the southward are also in contest with Spain;[5] the conduct of this Court since the peace has been so marked by want of plan and system, that we are quite at a loss to know her real intentions; she first of all would not suffer our western people to navigate the river Missisippi; latterly Mr. [*James*] Wilkinson, a man of consequence in that country, and formerly a General Officer in our Army, has made a contract with the Intendant at New Orleans, in consequence of which he has permission to store and to sell his exports; how long this indulgence may last I cannot tell; for the present it gives much satisfaction, but our people will not rest contented until they shall acquire a port of their own on the Missisippi, by the means of which they may trade with the rest of the world, as the Atlantic States do.

The opposition of Rhode Island to the present confederation is founded in dishonesty, they want to cheat all the world by depreciated paper money.

We shall probably increase our military establishment this spring, in order to protect Georgia, and perhaps to carry on the war against [*Alexander*] Macgillevray and the Creek Indians; our Commissioners [*at Rock Landing*] could have settled the matter with that tribe last summer but he would not hear of it, his views extend to commercial objects, and to the establishment of a free port, he is a man of ambition, and has formed a plan in conjunction with a spanish house, in which a house in London has a share,[6] as to our adopting any hostile measures against You, or with a view to seize the Forts by Arms,[7] I can assure you it is not in our contemplation at present; there may be individuals in the house of representatives who have such wild ideas, but I do not think there is a single member in the Senate who would not reprobate such a proceeding, *and without our approbation no such measure can be undertaken.*

We know that you have put the Forts in repair.

Our Western territory requires Troops for its security, and the hostile disposition of certain Indian Tribes, those of the Wabash nation particularly render this the more necessary.

In Continuation

Mr. Jefferson considers the revolution in France as compleated, and he declares it will be productive of great benefits to the states, he is greatly too democratic for us at present, he left us in that way, but we are infinitely changed, and he must alter his principles; I think this gentleman's ideas are not friendly to the formation of a commercial treaty with you, nor are those of Mr. Adams our Vice President more so, although from very different reasons, otherwise things go on well; in the consideration of this subject in this country, Mr. Jefferson would become the official minister, this would be an unfavorable channel; we are poor and expensive appointments will not answer the condition of our finances. Will you send us a Minister? perhaps we shall not wish to send a second time without assurances of this nature, or your taking a lead in it; it would be a popular measure and tend greatly to set everything in motion in a good humoured way.

In Continuation

The idea of opening free ports in the Bahama and Bermuda Islands has been mentioned for sometime, at first we thought it very desirable, but it has occurred lately, that it will affect the price of the articles shipped from our ports, as there must be a double freight, the fact is we would rather carry to the West Indies.

We have ideas of insular possessions, two of our East India Men fell in with two Islands on their voyage to China, which they think were never discovered before, but they did not take possession of either.

In Continuation

The present period is infinitely more favorable for the consideration of every matter unsettled between us and Great Britain, as well as for the contemplation of a treaty of commerce, than any that has preceeded it; I am however still doubtful how far our demands may not exceed the value of our consumption.

To narrow the idea as much as possible, we on our part have to say, we will lay a heavy duty on your imported productions, say fifteen or twenty ℔ cent for instance ad valorem, and we will prohibit British Ships from clearing out at our ports excepting to Great Britain or Ireland; with these restrictions we will come to market; this we have to give up for the freedom of navigating to your islands, or possibly a qualified freedom.

I think a dispassionate investigation might fix this great matter to the common advantage, but there are difficulties; You are a great manufacturing people, we wish to be a manufacturing people, you have an immense carrying trade which is the source of your greatness and naval power, we also wish to have a share in this trade, we have the materials for shipping, seamen in abundance and enterprize, but to think that you will cut away the prop of your own grandeur or touch it lightly is unreasonable and absurd.

The President in his heart leans to France, his obligations to that Court he can never forget.

Mr. Jefferson is a republican and a frenchman.

Mr. Maddison who is in great favor with the President, is still more partial to a French Interest.

I think if a minister shall be sent from us to you, especially if charged with extensive powers for specific purposes, the choice may be looked for in a narrow compass. Mr. Adams, Mr. Jay, Mr. Hamilton, Mr. Jefferson, Mr. Maddison, General Knox or perhaps Mr. King, although this gentleman would have been more likely to succeed to such an appointment a year ago, than at present.

If *Mr. Adams* should be the person, I am sure things would not go well.

If *Mr. Jefferson* I should fear it.

If *Mr. Jay or Mr. Hamilton*, I should think well of it.

If *Mr. Maddison*, I should expect little.

If *General Knox*, I should be certain of it.

If *Mr. King*, I should think favorably of it.

The impost and Tonnage support our present government, the former operates as a bounty upon our manufactures, we look forward to the time when they shall become so matured, as to enable us to prohibit foreign importations, and to support our Government by an excise on our own manufactures, on this as well as on many other points, we follow your ideas and profit from your experience.

Our present wish is to adjust all our differences with you by amicable negotiation, we have talked this over lately in the Senate,[8] and as the easiest and cheapest mode we should prefer . . .[9] by a reciprocal appointment of Arbitrators, or in any other equitable manner, or if this shall not be thought eligible, by the appointment of Commissioners in Europe, as to the Forts, if after we shall have complied with the spirit of the treaty they shall still be retained, in that event doubtless, we shall become very restless and dissatisfied. I am sorry to remark the late frequent publications in the news papers of Massachusetts relative to the disputed boundary as it produces warmth and animosity.[10] It is a question frequently discussed with us, whether it is our real interest to make great exertions in the establishment of manufactures or not; and on this point we are much divided in opinion.

I think it is our interest to establish that species of manufacture, distinguished by the late Lord Chatham [*William Pitt the Elder*], by the appellation of the domestic manufacture, and that beyond this we ought not to go for many years.

10. [*Paterson*] To the Southward of Maryland the expected operation of the federal Courts has given the most serious alarms, in these states the Merchants and Planters are greatly indebted to the Merchants of England, and to be sure for years past a spirit of Government has been manifested equally dishonest and unjust, this must now cease; peculiar as it may seem a more democratic opinion prevails in that district, than in the middle and eastern states, where the science of Government is better understood. Mr. Jefferson is a proof of this, he is a man of some acquirements, extending even to elegant literature, but his opinions upon Government are the result of fine spun theoretic Systems, drawn from the ingenious writings of Locke Sydney and others of their cast,[11] which can never be realized; such opinions very probably are the favorite ones with those who now conduct the revolution in France; I am far from thinking that the troubles in that great Kingdom are over, and I doubt whether it will be found practicable to rule that high spirited nation, with a single Assembly, thwarted as it will be by a dissatisfied Clergy and nobility.

***

13. [*Mr. Telfair, a merchant from Great Britain*][12] No possible exertions either of Mr. Jefferson or any other persons can enable France to promote the essential commercial interest of the States, she has no market for the

raw material of this country compared to Great Britain and Ireland, and were the merchants of France in the complete possession of the trade of this Continent to-morrow, they could not retain it three weeks. They are a set of Pedlars, nothing more. The States are naturally anxious to form a treaty of Commerce with us, by which in truth they wish to get certain advantages, without giving up anything further than we now enjoy (their consumption) but we want nothing further, nor do I believe that they are in a condition to carry matters to extremity with us by restrictive regulations, whatever Mr. Jefferson, Mr. Maddison and that party may insinuate to the contrary. Let us examine this, say these gentlemen. "We will prevent the shipping of Great Britain clearing out from our Ports for any other foreign possessions, and if this shall induce her to impose restraints or duties on our shipping in her ports in Europe, we shall go further; in the event of a war shall assist the fleets of France, for instance in every respect; whilst those of England shall not even be allowed to refit in any of our harbours"—such is their language. Mr. Maddison has used those very expressions to me, to which I replied such behaviour by the law of Nations would be construed actual hostility.

***

I am assured that the Legislature here have it seriously at heart to adopt more honourable as well as more prudent measures than heretofore with respect to the Indian tribes in general, to protect them in their lands from future depredations, and when soil shall be wanted, to purchase it fairly, hitherto great abuses have prevailed.

14. [*Scott*] In the year 1770 there were thirty families only settled beyond the Allegany Mountains, excepting a few stragglers, left by your Troops at Fort Pitt [*Pittsburgh, Pennsylvania*] in the year 1763—now Pensylvania has four counties upon the Western waters represented by nine members in her Assembly and containing upwards of Seventy thousand souls. Virginia has three populous Counties exclusive of the district of Kentucky, in which there are seven Counties and upwards of one hundred thousand souls. There are besides several thousand people in the Federal Territory, which is beyond the Ohio River—and in all a regular dispensation of Justice, such an exertion in a vast wilderness never was made before—Kentucky is a growth of twelve or thirteen years and the annual accession of people, beyond the Allegany Mountains is incredible. Our general advancement in this New World is by no means a favorable object with the Atlantic states as they think our prosperity will be at their expence, that it lessens the value of their landed property, checks the prospect of raising a revenue by taxation and ruins the rising manufacturing interest, they are therefore little solicitous about our obtaining an export for our produce, and I may say, they wish we may not. added to these considerations is the question now before our house, which involves the selling the lands beyond the Ohio, at an estimated value, in

lieu of a portion of the public debt,[13] this is greatly opposed by certain gentlemen, who are either personally or from their connexion already possessed of large tracts in that Country, which they wish to dispose of advantageously, and for this purpose are anxious to keep the lands belonging to the public unsettled, these gentlemen have great weight in our house, and I am not certain whether they may not succeed—they prevented the establishment of Land Offices [*Land Office Bill HR-17*] in that Country the last Session, which created much uneasiness with us—these circumstances lay the foundation for a separation of interests and have induced men of reflection with us, who look forward to the importance of an export, and to the possible effect of these measures, to contemplate the necessity of a foreign connexion, this from our situation must be either Great Britain or Spain, although the Provinces of the latter power are more favourably situated for us.

At present the Governor at New Orleans [*Esteban Miró*] and his friends carry on an illicit commerce with us which is very advantageous paying our people in dollars—we find it impracticable to remount the rivers without infinite labour and prefer the selling our Wheat, flax, Hemp and Tobacco with the flats on which it is transported and afterwards taking passages for the Havanna [*Cuba*], from whence as opportunities offer, our People return to Philadelphia, or to the Chesapeake Bay, where they procure woollens, and other European and West India Articles, or return beyond the mountains with their money and buy what they want nearer home—this circuit is usually compleated in from four to six months, and the precise time generally depends on the delays in the shipping.

The expence of transporting merchandize from Philadelphia to the back Countries of Pensylvania on the Ohio, in covered waggons and the insuring the property from damage is no more than one guinea ℔ hundred weight, which in fine goods is a mere trifle, in woollens of the second quality may be estimated at about two per cent., but in sugars, liquors and wines is some thing higher, yet when the cheapness of house rent, fuel, and the difference of taxation is considered, the retailers with us, can in fact afford to sell nearly as cheap as in Philadelphia. Baltimore in Maryland is fifty miles nearer and the roads equally good. Our great difficulty is in the means of exporting, and what we want is a commercial deposit near the mouth of the missisippi, with merchants of enterprize and property, to buy our raw materials, and to give us good bills with which we may be enabled to buy foreign productions, at Philadelphia, Baltimore and other places, most contiguous to the back Counties. the fashions of Philadelphia find their way in three months to Kentucky.

The Indians in the western Territory we estimate at about five thousand fighting men; the disorders in general are perpetrated by a number of stragglers from the different tribes, who are settled on the Wabash River, they are not publicly countenanced by the Indians although privately connived at; their first object generally is, to steal horses to carry away their peltries towards the close of the Hunting Season, and if they happen to be discovered by any of the settlers, they murder them to ensure their retreat.

The Strength of the Indians is towards the missisippi. there the Creeks, Chickasaws & another tribe [*Chocktaws*] united, can bring fifteen thousand men into the field, Macgillevray who is at the heart of the Creek tribe, when he first arrived in Georgia after the peace presented a very modest petition to the Legislature requesting to have his fathers lands restored to him; this they denied, on which he immediately went to the Creek Nation and threw himself into their protection, they received him kindly, and he has waged war with Georgia ever since, his mother was of this tribe, his father a Scotch trader. this conduct of Georgia has by their own account, already cost them fifty such estates as they refused to return, and Macgillevray declares, that if he had chosen to do it, he could easily have taken Savannah, and destroyed the whole State, and that it is in his discretion to do so whenever he pleases; this in truth is the case, but being a man of strong sense and foresight, he is aware that an act of this nature would spread such an alarm in the continent, that we should raise a large army, destroy the whole Creek Country and drive the Indians beyond the missisippi. These tribes have carried off at different times a great number of Negroes from Georgia, they retain them in bondage, have compelled them to plant corn, to raise vegetables of different kinds and in a word to introduce agriculture, which these Indians have in consequence acquired a taste for, a taste the more necessary from their comparatively dense population, and favored by the fertility and mildness of their climate.

***

Copy, Colonial Office 42/67 pp. 238–62, PRO. The ellipses are in the source. These conversations are part of a compilation of transcribed conversations sent to Lord Dorchester at Quebec, who in turn sent them to Lord Grenville in London on 27 May 1790. Beckwith identified his interviewees by a numbered code, the key to which was provided in a separate document. Hamilton was "No. 7," Johnson was "No. 1," Paterson was "No. 10," Mr. Telfair, a British merchant in New York City, was "No. 13," and Scott was "No. 14." Other important interviewees in the FFC included Schuyler, Jay, Knox, Ames, and R. H. Lee. For an exhaustive treatment of Beckwith's role in the FFC, see Julian P. Boyd, *Number 7: Alexander Hamilton's Secret Attempts to Control American Foreign Policy* (Princeton, N.J., 1964). The dating of these conversations is based on three factors: their placement following the text of Beckwith's conversation with Hamilton on (22 March); and Beckwith's assertion (see Beckwith to Hamilton, 22 March, above) that he intended to stay in New York until mid-April. The words "In Continuation" in the text probably indicate a change of date.

---

[1] See 22 March, above.

[2] John Adams served as the first American minister plenipotentiary to Great Britain from 1785 to 1788. Britain did not accredit an equally ranked diplomat to the United States until

the appointment of George Hammond (1763–1853), who served from 1791 to 1795. A successor to Adams was not appointed until 1792.

[3] For documents providing background for the ongoing boundary dispute between Canada and the Massachusetts district of Maine in 1790, see *DHFFC* 2:359–87. See also n. 10, below.

[4] The American commissioners who signed the Treaty of Paris (1783) frequently insisted that the principal, if not only, map used during their negotiations was the famous map of North America by Dr. John Mitchell (d. 1768), first published in London in 1755. The copy known as "King George's Map" was the one annotated by Richard Oswald (1705–84), the London merchant who served as sole British commissioner at the negotiations. No maps were attached to the final treaty (Richard B. Morris, ed., *John Jay: Unpublished Papers, 1780–1784* [New York, 1980], p. 383).

[5] Spain refused to recognize the thirty-first parallel as the southeastern boundary of the United States, claiming territory north to the junction of the Yazoo and Mississippi rivers, an area that included the important town of Natchez.

[6] When Great Britain relinquished its colonies of East and West Florida to Spain at the end of the Revolutionary War, McGillivray asked the British firm of Panton, Leslie and Company to stay on as the Creeks' primary supplier of European goods. His friend William Panton agreed, on the condition that McGillivray became a partner to lobby Spain for trading privileges. Spain sought to regulate the Creek trade under the Treaty of Pensacola (1784) and appointed McGillivray commissary to the Creeks. Panton and McGillivray's firm subsequently enjoyed a monopoly on trade passing to and from Creek markets through the ports of St. Marks and Pensacola, Florida (*McGillivray*, pp. 24–26).

[7] Article VII of the Treaty of Paris (1783) required Great Britain to abandon all the forts, posts, and arsenals it held on what the treaty defined as United States soil. Yet Great Britain retained possession of these posts, and consequently the strategic borderlands they controlled, until Jay's Treaty of 1794 finally negotiated their turnover effective in 1796. These posts were: Oswegatchie (present-day Ogdensburg), Oswego, and Niagara in New York; Presque Isle (present-day Erie), Pennsylvania; and Sandusky, Detroit, and Michilimackinac (in present-day Michigan). Although the British ministry claimed the forts were being held pending the United States' fulfilment of its own treaty obligation to reimburse British creditors, other reasons included Britain's desire to maintain a buffer zone between its former Native American allies and the States, and to exploit the possibility of western settlers seceding from the United States and offering Britain commercial access to the Mississippi in exchange for protection (A. L. Burt, *The United States, Great Britain, and British North America from the Revolution to the Establishment of Peace after the War of 1812* [New Haven, Conn., 1940], pp. 82–105).

[8] The Senate discussed the Northeast Boundary Dispute on 10, 15, and 24 March.

[9] In the margin next to the ellipsis is written: "Expressions of personal civility [*are*] omitted."

[10] For an example of outraged public opinion on British encroachment along the border at Passamaquoddy Bay, Maine, see A Correspondent, [Boston] *Massachusetts Centinel*, 20 March.

[11] Like John Locke, the Whig martyr Algernon Sidney (1622–83) influenced American social contract theory with his *Discourses Concerning Government* (1698).

[12] Perhaps a relation of the Telfair from Georgia whose suicide on 19 June caused such a stir in New York City; see *DHFFC* 9:298 and Sedgwick to Pamela Sedgwick, 19 June, below.

[13] The resolutions that the COWH was considering at the time provided public creditors with an option to receive part of their payment in public lands.

Letter from Rhode Island

From a tolerable exact calculation, the number of men, women and children in and belonging to this state, may now amount to about 60,000 people. Out of these could be mustered (upon urgent occasion) about ten thousand fighting men, including boys from 15 years old, and upwards. Besides these, should the state be attacked *ab externo*,[1] a very large proportion of the females would turn out (like the heroines of France[2]) in support of the honor and independence of their country. There is hardly any such thing as forming a proper idea of what might be effected by such a host of people, when thoroughly exasperated, especially if headed by such able men as Dr. T. [*John Taylor*] and some others I could mention. As to unanimity, no doubt a prospect of certain danger would soon put an end to our intestine divisions, and unite us in one common cause.

NYDA, 9 April; reprinted at Hartford, Connecticut, and Philadelphia.

---

[1] From without.

[2] The women of Paris were credited with one of the most dramatic developments in the French Revolution when they marched to Versailles on 5 October 1789 to demand from the king and National Assembly a decree lowering the price of bread. The mob, soon augmented by thousands of men, stormed the palace, forced Louis XVI to assent to the Assembly's Declaration of the Rights of Man, and induced him to accompany them back to Paris, from which time he became a virtual prisoner of the revolutionary forces.

Letter from Rhode Island

If Congress would lay a duty on the produce and manufactures of this state, to take place before the 22d of May, there would be little doubt of the adoption of the Constitution. If this is not done, we shall remain in our present disagreeable situation all the year. The duties on tonnage, affects only the friends and well wishers to the federal constitution, while the opposers of it, exult at our misfortune.

NYDA, 22 April; reprinted at Stockbridge, Massachusetts; New London, Connecticut; Burlington and New Brunswick, New Jersey; Philadelphia and York, Pennsylvania; Baltimore; and Edenton, North Carolina.

Letter from the West

ON the eighth of January I landed at *Limestone* [*Maysville, Kentucky*]. This is a place that at some future day cannot otherwise than become a place of great consequence, not only from the nature of the surrounding country, but also from its landing place, which on account of the boldness of its water is far better than is commonly met with in these parts. The buildings at present in *Limestone* are trifling, I may say they consist of about twenty places (scarcely to be called houses) where a few families may be rather said to stay than live, this place being the resort of the principal part of the settlers traveling towards the fertile country of Kentucky. Such is the famous town of Limestone. About four miles from hence is the much talked of town of Washington, through which passes the great road leading to Lexington. Washington is the capital and county town of Mason, and contains 119 houses. It is laid out in a township of little more than 900 acres of land, with 192 in-lots, containing half an acre each and the rest in out-lots of five acres each. One of the magistrates, who is an experienced surveyor, informed me that this town lies a few minutes above the 38th degree of N. latitude. On a south course from Washington, or nearly so; and at about the distance of 40 miles stands Bourbon, the capital of the county of the same name. About 20 miles further on is the celebrated town of Lexington in Kentucky, From all that I have seen, heard, or known of Kentucky, it may with great propriety be rated amongst the first and finest countries in the world. The central part of it is in lat. 38, and is about 250 miles in length (from east to west) and about 200 miles in breadth. I need not mention the boundaries, as Fitch's map[1] will at once show them to you. This tract of country was formerly known to the Indians by a name importing, *The dark and bloody ground*,[2] on account of the many bloody wars among the various tribes of Indians in former ages, when the possession of it was disputed with as much violence as any territory has ever been in Europe.

On the 13th of March I arrived at the Miami river, about three quarters of a mile below the junction of the little Miami with the Ohio. By turning to the map you may see the very spot where I have erected my little cabin on the banks of the fair Ohio, a river not less celebrated through America then deserving of every elogium.

A little below me is the town of *Columbia*, in and about which, according to the account rendered his excellency on the 4th of January last, are 500 inhabitants, 150 of which are supposed capable of bearing arms; and two companies of militia are organized for Columbia. About six miles below this (on the Ohio) is another town originally called Licken or Licking. It afterwards received the name of Losanteville, but upon Governor [*Arthur*] St. Clair's coming down and expressing his disgust at these outlandish names,[3] and desiring the inhabitants to give their town a name that he could pronounce and write, they have named it CINCINNATI. It is a county town, and has one organized company of militia. About seven or eight miles still lower down is another town called *Southbend*, from the bend of the river. It is, as yet, a very small and insignificant place. Seven miles from hence is the town of *Northbend*, where the Hon. Judge [*John C.*] Symmes resides. Since this, a town is laid out, by order of the proprietors, on the point of a neck of land lying between, and formed by the Ohio and great Miami, and, as I am informed, has received the name of the City MIAMI. I have been down at the settlement, but have not explored the ground; yet know that it is sufficiently high, and as broken and rough as New-York was at its first settlement. This will contribute to the health of the place, which bids fair to be considerable for trade, lying between two such important rivers as the Ohio and the Great Miami. This last mentioned river is navigable for boats and shallops upwards of 170 miles from its mouth, and I am informed the British have transported their cannon and stores up and down these waters in the late war.

About twelve miles from the city of Miami, there is another settlement going on, and town founding by the name of COLDRAIN [*Colerain*]. There is a creek a small distance from Cincinnati called Millcreek, which empties into the Ohio: 12 miles up these waters there is another settlement going forward. Nine miles up the Little Miami is what is called *Evaults station*, with perhaps about 20 fighting men on it. About the middle of last July I accompanied Major Stites,[4] with four other gentlemen, to the seventh range of townships, in order to explore that range and lay out a town on the waters of the Great Miami, near the confluence of the Tiber and that river. We found the ground intended for a town to be high and firm, and in point of elegance far exceeding our most sanguine expectations. This town is one mile square, with two streets of 100 feet in width, running half a mile from the center. All the other streets are 66 feet wide. In each of the great quarters of the town is a park containing four acres, reserved to the public forever and never to be built upon, but to be appropriated to shades, walks, &c. This seventh range is well watered, and the water excellent. There are also several prairies, or great meadows, in this range, interspersed with forests. One of them contains 2000 acres, and is generally verged round with honey locust, and is full of thistles from one end to the other, which you know is a convincing proof that the soil is rich and warm. The first settlers may go on with at least one thousand head of cattle, there being grass enough both to summer and winter them. [*25 May printing ends here*]

I SHALL now give you a few particulars from my Journal, and then proceed to say something of Indian affairs.

Numbers of horses since our coming to these parts have been stolen by the Indians. On the 4th of April two of surveyor [*John Reading?*] Mills's attendants were killed, when on duty about 39 miles to the Northward of this settlement. A cat-fish was taken the other day, weighing 58 pounds, four feet long and eight inches between the eyes. Altho' of such a size the taste and flavour of these cat-fish are excellent, and if ever these parts should become the seat of general government, the officers will find the Miami and Ohio cat-fish incomparably superior to those offered them by the Philadelphians. Last summer we laid out the city of *Venice*, in the seventh range, 43 miles north, a few minutes east, of the mouth of the little Miami.

Since that we have built Fort Miami, and Fort Columbia. Cincinnati is now head quarters for the army, and is also fixed upon as the most convenient spot for the public stores.

On the fourth of January 1790, his excellency governor St. Clair arrived at Cincinnati. The next day but one, after, the gentlemen from the different towns waited upon his excellency, when Judge Symmes purchase was created a county, by the name of the county of Hamilton, the civil and militia officers were also nominated, and on the 6th, sworn in.

I now come to Indian affairs, which appear to be in a very unsettled situation. The horses that have been stolen from the settlements in and about Columbia, and from the waters of the little Miami amount at least to six hundred pounds in value. Our public boats have been fired on. Lee's station has been attacked and several killed. Conady's station, about 18 miles above Washington, has also been attacked. There were nine men in that station, six women, and some children. Two of the men were killed, the rest with the women &c. carried into captivity. Boats have been frequently taken as they were coming down the river, and the people killed or taken prisoners. Mr. [*John*] May of Kentucky lately fell a victim. Sometime ago the Indians made prisoner a Mr. Thomas, up Cabbin creek; they have since (to his great mortification) made use of him as a stool pigeon, to decoy the boats ashore, which he is obliged to do, to prolong his miserable life. It was the lot of this unlucky wight to be forced to decoy the boat in which Mr. May was; and they were nearly ashore when an Indian was discovered. Mr. May then made every possible effort to work the boat off to the channel, but in this attempt both he and a young woman were killed. The boat, with a considerable property, and the rest of the passengers, then fell into the hands of the savages. Besides Mr. May's property, which was considerable, there was on board to the amount of 500l. belonging to Col. [*Thomas*] Hart of Baltimore.

Yesterday a boat arrived here (at Columbia) that informed us that as six boats were coming down the river (the two sternmost about 10 miles above the mouth of the Siota [*Scioto*]) they were pursued by the Indians. The two were fastened together, but upon the approach of danger they all got into one and cast off the other in which were the cattle. This the Indians boarded and carried off. The other four did not pass without being attacked, in which was killed one man, one horse, and nine wounded. The Indians have sent off their booty to their towns by a few men, and keep their ground on the river with their main body; it is also said, they have sent for two hundred warriors more to line the river. This account has been received by a prisoner who made his escape.

From all this it appears, that if something effectual is not soon done to put a stop to their proceedings, privateering will become a considerable business on the Ohio. In a word, were it not for the name of peace, we might as well have actual war.

The depredations of the Indians have been carried on so long that Congress could not but have had official information before now. We therefore cannot help persuading ourselves that at this instant they are making arrangements, if not movements, for the protection of their remote citizens. Either the ministers of the war department have been seized by some strange lethargy, or some of the states are actuated by narrow and interested motives, neglecting the citizens of these happy western climes and suffering them to fall victims to savage cruelty, and thus deter other settlers from coming down, hoping thereby, perhaps, to induce them to settle on their cold barrens of the north. However that may be, it is evident the same attention is not paid to the protection of the persons and property of our citizens, and those in the vicinity of the government. Congress would without delay wage war with any power upon earth that would dare to molest those of the last description, and yet they suffer the distant members of the Empire to be robbed, murdered, scalped, and carried into captivity by an insignificant herd of tawny banditti, whose whole united force would be an object almost below our contempt, were *the dogs of war* once let loose upon them. Let them only send a regular force among us and the Indians will soon be found to be no more than an atom.

NYDA, 25, 26 May (the dates on which members of Congress would have seen it); first part reprinted at Charleston, South Carolina.

---

[1] In 1785, the inventor John Fitch drew, engraved, and sold in Philadelphia a map of the Northwest Territory, based on his personal observations as a surveyor and prisoner of war in the Ohio River Valley in the last years of the Revolutionary War. He produced one hundred copies for sale at one crown apiece, "cheap [*and*] Portable," he wrote in his autobiography, "to any who wanted to go to the Woods" (John T. Faris, *Romance of Forgotten Men* [New York, 1928], pp. 186–91).

[2] "Kain-tuk-ee," legendarily coined by the Chickamauga (Cherokee) warrior Dragging Canoe in the aftermath of a meeting with Anglo-American settlers in 1775 (Theodore Roosevelt, *Winning of the West* [New York, 1905], 1:229).

[3] "Losanteville" was a combination of "L" (for the Licking River, Kentucky), "os" (Latin for "mouth"), "ante" (Latin for "opposite from"), and "ville" (for "town").

[4] Benjamin Stites (d. 1804), a native of New Jersey, served as a captain in a western Pennsylvania militia unit during the Revolutionary War. He first explored the Ohio River valley in 1787, and late the next year led the first White settlers to what became Cincinnati.

Other Documents

John Adams to Thomas Welsh. FC:lbk, Adams Family Manuscript Trust, MHi. Sent to Boston. In Adams's letterbook this item is located between letters dated 4 and 5 May; it may have been written on one of those dates.

Office seeking: John Hurd for an office in New Hampshire or Vermont; acknowledges Welsh's letter of 21 March, enclosing one from Hurd (of 17 March?), who "cannot have better advocates than his friends" Langdon and Livermore; inquires about commercial conditions in Boston.

James Madison to Ambrose Madison. No copy known; mentioned in James Madison to James Madison, Sr., 2 May.

Letter from London to Philadelphia. *FG*, 27 May; reprinted at Boston and Northampton, Massachusetts, and New York City (*NYDG*, 31 May; *GUS*, 2 June).

Rejoices at the state of America; she "has many warm friends in this country"; "Great things hath God done for America, and greater things no doubt he hath in store."

May 1790

Saturday, 1 May 1790

Fine (Johnson)

Abraham Baldwin to Joel Barlow

Yours of the 15th of Feby. & 9th March have been received since I wrote you. The girl [*Ruth Barlow*] is in very high spirits on the subject of the voyage nothing could please her better. [*Andrew*] Craigie is going the last of this month, with the large parchment [*map*] of the Gennesee [*tract*] for your disposal. Guile[1] formerly tutor at Cambridge Colledge, with his lady, will sail from Boston for London about that time, Craigie & your girl talk of joining them for the sake of company.

Hamilton has just got your letter,[2] I have not seen him since, but am sure it will suit him, it opens a sett of prospects new to him, this subject has hitherto been kept much out of his view. I told [*Royal*] Flint in general terms that you had written Hamilton on the subject, then, says he, the whole scheme is blown, for he will raise the price of the land, I told him there was no danger that you should say any thing about the price, but that I believed you was right in getting the business into that train; the fact is our friend's itch for speculation is boundless, and he wished to do all that was done, but I believe his scope is large enough as it is. Hamilton has not reported his plan for the disposal of lands, I suppose his anxiety for having us finish the business of finance, prevented him from bringing forward any other business. I expect he will soon let us see it, as the other business is in so great forwardness. The assumption you see is laid aside for the present all the other parts of the report have been agreed to, and bills to carry them into effect are ordered to be brought in. The senate is much attached to the assumption, and I expect will not consent to have the business progress without it. I should not be disappointed if the session should close without doing any thing material on the report. But I send you all the papers, you may read and judge for yourself.

I would not thank the creditors to *modify* the debts as proposed, perhaps it will be as well to pay the current interest, and as much of the old interest as we can, and let the debt stand as it does.

I have but three minutes notice of this opportunity. I will write you more fully by one of the London ships, I write this by a brig for Havre [*France*], and send you a course of papers as you direct, which will tell you more than I can. I expect we shall adjourn early in June, when I shall travel homeward, probably this house will not meet again during the period of this appointment.

I have found three decent ladies who are just engaged to sail with Watson[3] for London the 7th Inst. I have written the girl that they are going, that the ship and the Capt. are such as I have great confidence in, and that if she chooses to step into the stage and be here in the Thursday or Saturday's stage, she can step right aboard and have every thing in fine order for the voyage; but I do not expect her as I recollect, you say in your letter to me, that you have told her in your letter to her, to wait till you write again which would be in a few days. Of course I suppose she will scarcely think of going till she gets your other letter.

AL, Baldwin Family Papers, CtY. Place to which addressed not indicated.

---

[1] Benjamin Guild (or Guile) (1749–92) graduated from Harvard in 1769 and served as an itinerant Congregational preacher before accepting a tutorship at Harvard, 1776–80. In 1784 he married Elizabeth Quincy and spent the remainder of his life as a Boston bookseller, on occasion traveling to England to restock his inventory (*Harvard Graduates* 17:161–66).

[2] Probably the (unlocated) letter of 9 March mentioned in Baldwin to Barlow on 8 May, below, on the subject of public lands.

[3] *NYDG* advertised freight or passage available on the ship *New-York*, under Capt. Thomas Watson, bound for London about 5 May.

George Clymer to Tench Coxe

T'other day I lodged you drawings[1] with Mr. Jefferson, but not having had the [*Patents*] act lately in my hands don't call to mind the further steps necessary to be taken by you—you however have it—You will recollect what I said that Mr. J. wish rather you should wait for the arrival of Mr. [*Edmund*] Randolph before any thing further was done.

We are both surprised and vext to hear there are frequent conversations at Philada. on the certainty of the return of Congress—were any such scheme on foot this [*lined out*] imprudence would block it—for god's sake silence all such prating blockheads.

You will percive from the papers the fate of the assumption—It was necessary forcibly to detach it from the report, for while there it lay a dead weight on the indispensible business of the Union—You may have seen my name in the list of voters agt. the seperation—this is a mistake of a printer and of a kind so common as to be greatly complained of[2]—We wish to hear the ultimate opinions of the Merchts. with regard to the proposed measures of tonnage &ca.

ALS, Coxe Papers, PHi. Addressed to Philadelphia; written on "Saturday Nt."; franked; postmarked 2 May.

[1] The designs for water powered spinning machines, provided by Coxe's business partner, George Parkinson; see Coxe to Clymer, 17 January, volume 18.
[2] Clymer's vote to discharge the COWH from further consideration of assumption is correctly recorded in *DHFFC* 3:379–80.

Samuel Johnston to George Washington

The following is an Extract from Genl. [*Isaac*] Gregory Collector of the District of Camden's Letter to me.

"Respecting a Surveyor for Currituck Inlet there is no person that lives on Crow Island but Herbert. I am told the people dont like him, Mr. Samuel Jasper is the only man that I think will answer, who lives on Knot's Island, within Six or Seven miles of the Inlet, I have sent Mr. Thomas Williams, who is Surveyor for Port Indian Town, down to the Inlet, he informs me that he can do all the Business for both Ports himself by attending at Mr. [*Thomas*] Younghusbands one day in a Week—there are very seldom any other than coasting Vessells which come in at that Inlet."

I believe the above state of facts may be relied on.

ALS, Washington Papers, DLC.

Robert Morris to Thomas Jefferson

Mr. Morris presents his Compts. to Mr. Jefferson & is sorry he had not the pleasure of meeting him Yesterday at either of the reciprocal calls on each other, When Mr. Morris came to reflect on the Persons to whom the Consular appointments might be desirable, He could recollect but few, and even of these He has set down two Americans that He is not sure of, Mr. Geo. Harrison & Mr. Edwd. Hall, they are Young Gentn. of good Character and if desired mr. M. would Consult them on the Subject.

[*Enclosure*]

For Consuls

Dublin	Mr. Philip Wilson
Cadiz [*Spain*]	Mr. [*John*] Welsh of the House of Dominick Terry & Co.
Lisbon	Mr. Stephen Moylan
St. Martins Isle of Rhe [*France*]	Fr[*ançois*]. Baudin

Marseilles	Estienne Cathalan
Bourdeaux	Mr. [*John*] Mason of Virga. Mr. Geo. Harrison of Philada. Edwd. Hall of Maryland
Cowes Isle of Wight	Mr. a Nephew of Strachan Mackenzie & Co.
Hamburg-Denmark	Mr. John Parish

AN and Ms., Miscellaneous Letters, Miscellaneous Correspondence, State Department Records, Record Group 59, DNA. Another list filed with this AN indicates that at a later date Morris withdrew Hall and Harrison as candidates for consul at Le Havre, France.

John C. Symmes to Elias Boudinot

I make no doubt my dear sir of your receiving multiplied accounts of Indian hostilities in all parts of this country, no corner escapes their ravages, murders, piracies, & robberies both on land and the rivers are every day perpetrated by the savages I believe of every western nation however some of them may pretend to peace & friendship—The fact indubitably is that the young men of every nation & tribe embrace every occasion of going to war, It is the only path to honor & repute among them—They have no ambition for wealth—they have no thirst for science, They have no value for a man of moderation & virtue, they have no means of acquiring so much property as a state of nature demands but by plundering their neighbours the white people—They are Idle in the extreme and yet they must live, they must have arms & ammunition but know not how to attain it so easily as by war & theft—they kill men and take their rifles—they steal horses & sell them at Detroit & to British traders for blankets & amunition And can nothing arouse government to avenge the nation of these insults—must the people of the Western country forever submit to these provocations. Will nothing but vain treaties suffice; when repeated experiments shew us the futility? Pray sir turn your eyes to the blood-stained banks of the Tenesse, what is the voice of the blood our late worthy friend major Doughty and those brave slaughtered soldiers with him?[1] was he not going to the Indian country with the olive branch in his hand? From the Missisipi to the Big Beaver, not a village, not a neighbourhood but can point you the place where & name you the person, and give you the time when one or many of its inhabitants fell victims to savage barbarities—I will not attempt an enumeration of these murders for they really are not to be counted up by an individual This you may rely on my good sir tho whatever may be pretended to the contrary, the Indians are generally hostile through all the western nations—they may pretend peace, but their safety dictates this, that they may war with impunity.

Chiefs of the Shawanaese, Wiandots, and Delawares have been with me at different times in the preceeding year; I always endeavoured to inculcate harmony & friendship with them, & at no inconsiderable expence of property—they always promised fair—but how have they kept their promises? In the space of one year past they have killed nine men at Miami [*Ohio*], made three prisoners, and stolen upwards of fifty horses from the settlers on the [*Symmes*] purchase and is this the treatment which they bestow on those with whom they avow to live in peace, what then must be their depredations against the district of Kentucky, inhabited by a people who from the long and settled inveteracy borne against them by the Indians are called the big-k[*n*]ife, against whom not a single Indian will hessitate to [*te*]ll you they wage eternal war?

I flatter myself that by this time you begin at least to pause, & to doubt whether it may not be true that the [*I*]ndian tribes are hostile as nations.

I left Miami on the 19th of last mo[*nth*] have been but twelve days from home a visit to my daughter Mrs. Short,[2] and by the enclosed you will see that one of our citizens at Northbend [*Ohio*] has been killed by the Indians, and that in sight of the houses and within the midst of the City limits as I remember the place & very stump where the Indians lay. I learn that many settlers have fled to Louisville from Miami on this occasion.

Give me leave my dear sir to conclude by saying that nothing but a formidable campaign carried into the heart of their country will ever give us peace.

ALS, Bamberger Collection, New Jersey Historical Society, Newark. Written from Lexington, Kentucky; carried by Capt. [*Abner*] Howell. The enclosure is unlocated.

---

[1] Although reports circulated widely in the East beginning as early as May (see Letter from Kentucky, 19 April, above), the official account of the incident Symmes mentions was not received by the Washington administration until 2 July. On 22 March, while proceeding under a white flag of truce down the Tennessee River to a conference with friendly Chickasaw representatives, Major John Doughty and no more than fifteen other soldiers were ambushed by approximately forty Cherokee, Shawnee, and Creek warriors. Despite suffering eleven casualties, including five fatalities, Doughty and his party were able to elude the attackers after a four hour chase and escaped down the Tennessee, Ohio, and Mississippi rivers before reaching safe haven at New Madrid, in present-day Missouri (*DGW* 6:83–84).

[2] Maria Symmes (b. 1762) married Maj. Peyton Short of Kentucky in 1790.

George Washington, Diary

Mr. Alexr. White, Representative from Virginia, communicated his apprehensions that a disposition prevailed among the Eastern & Northern States (discoverable from many circumstances, as well as from some late expressions which had fallen from some of their members in the Ho[*use*].) to pay little attention to the Western Country because they were of opinion it would soon shake of[*f*] its dependence on this; and in the meantime, would be burthensome to it. He gave some information also of the temper of the Western Settlers, of their dissatisfactions, and among other things that few of the Magestrates had taken the Oaths to the New Government not inclining in the present state of things and under their ideas of neglect to bind themselves to it by an Oath.

Washington Diary, ViHi.

Yeoman's Letters, Letter IV

Friends and Fellow-Citizens,

IT behoves us to view our situation with firmness and attention. We have, in addition to our own immediate state taxes, an expensive general government to support; we owe a foreign debt which *must* be paid; and we have an impost and tonnage already established which may produce annually about a million and three quarters of dollars—here let us arrest the progress of taxation *for the present year.* Perhaps it will be asked, what is to be done with this money? I answer, introduce economy and moderation into every department: A great saving can and *ought* to be made in the salaries of officers, and in the pay of Congress.

		DOLLARS
I will state the amount of duties and tonnage as now accruing under the late law of Congress, as per Secretary's Report,		1,800,000
From this I will deduct for expences of collecting $2\frac{1}{2}$ per cent. instead of 5, as allowed by the Report,		45,000
Nett income		1,755,000
This sum I will suppose appropriated as follows:		
Foreign debt, 10,070,000—interest per contract will average $4\frac{3}{4}$ per cent.		476,996
Certificate debt, 16,947,000—pay half the year's interest, 3 per cent.		508,410
Loan Office debt, 10,436,000—pay half the year's interest, 3 per cent.		313,080
Services of the current year, estimated in the Report,	507,410	
From this may be deducted out of the civil list at least	50,826	
		456,514
		1,755,000

Here let the matter remain, and permit a new election of Representatives to take place before we proceed further. Let the people at large have time to consider the subject: let us know, by actual experiment, the exact amount of the income of the United States: let us feel the effect of the present law before we lay fresh burthens. Let all the western lands be brought to market, and the product applied to pay off such arrears of interest as shall, from a fair investigation, be found due, and also as much of the principal of the foreign debt as it will accomplish. In the mean time leave the several states at liberty to manage their own private debts.

It would certainly be the wish of every honest man honorably to fulfill his engagements; but in the present case there are two points to be kept in view; *first*, the ability of America to satisfy all who may have claims upon us, and *next*, a knowledge of the amount of the true, honest and just debt which we ought to pay. Perhaps upon a close scrutiny it will be found, that an excess of certificates have been granted without just foundation; that a large amount of interest is payable for loans in Continental money which was not really worth one *third* or a *fourth* of the sum it was estimated at. We are not in a condition to gratify every man who wishes for a share of public monies. Our load is already heavy under the *present* impost—we cannot bear much more; if an additional impost or tax *must* be laid, we wish to nominate the men who shall decide upon the quantum and the manner, for we had no conception at the time of our sending Representatives to Congress that they would have run their hands so rapidly into our pockets: we now plainly perceive that a majority of the present Members have views very different from those of their constituents. Let us tell our Representatives that we sent them to Congress to relieve, not to oppress us, that if by a collision of argument meeting argument, they should have wrought each other into a belief that the honor of the United States can be no other way supported than by the sweat of the industrious mechanic, and laborious Farmer, let them at least give us an opportunity of shewing our assent; let them, I repeat it, forbear all additional taxes until after the next general election of Congressional Representatives—what will be the result of such an election I well know—you, my countrymen, know it too—a very general change will take place. Wrapped up in the pleasures and luxuries of New-York, our Delegates perhaps have forgotten their laborious fellow citizens in the various parts of this extensive continent, and conceive that we shall find the means to pay, as readily as they seem disposed to levy on us, but they will most certainly soon discover, that neither our ability nor our inclination will keep pace with their hopes.

Much has been said of the honor of fulfilling contracts, and of the infamy and disgrace attendant on a breach of public faith; let us beware then how we promise and let those take the consequence to themselves who shall generate the cause of unstable councils; for should the proposed burthensome system of taxation be even carried into effect for the short remaining period of the present representation, we certainly shall not hold ourselves bound to continue it, we will exert every nerve to elect men who will repeal such grievous laws, and thereby instruct future Legislators to move guardedly on the great ground of Continental taxation. We know this may prove a terrible disappointment to those who thought they had built their nests on high; but the American people are too wise and too determined to sit quiet under such precipitate measures. If foreigners have bought at second or third hand into our funds, we can only say we are sorry for them—they ought to have studied the true state of American politics before they embarked their fortunes amongst us; the failure of our promises in the case of the Continental money might have taught them to fear that the same necessity would probably compel us to pay off a considerable part of the domestic debt in the same manner. This is an event which may be accelerated by the very means taken to avoid it; should the people be oppressed beyond their ability to bear it, there may be a danger of their rejecting the whole debt, and applying the devouring spunge. Of this there need be no fear so long as our rulers study the real resources and true interest of their country.

It is essentially necessary that we know the full and *true* amount of our debts; and for this purpose I would propose that the securities of every sort and description be directed to be brought in, and exchanged for some new uniform kind of paper, to be struck for that purpose. I would ask whether we have any tolerable grounds for supposing that we possess an accurate knowledge of the whole Continental debt? if we are uncertain on this head, as we most assuredly are, with what propriety can Congress continue to encrease our taxes? Is it meant that those which first come to light shall be first paid, and that the distant and uninformed creditor shall wait for payment to a future day? If this knowledge is still to be acquired, why are we to be called on to pay so long before it will be wanted? Will it not require a year or more to ascertain the just amount, and will it be prudent or justifiable to keep such a sum, either idle in the Treasury, or subject to private management? Surely the money ought to rest in our own pockets until we know the quantity wanted, and the purpose to which it is to be appropriated. Has the word *confederation* such a charm inherently in it as to transform want into plenty, and individual poverty into public riches? Is it only for Congress to give forth the mandate, and the wealth of the whole continent is to fly to their coffers? Friends and brethren, we require a short respite from taxation, let that respite be whilst we are obtaining information of the true state of our affairs. The old government is deceased, the new government is become administrator—How do we act in private life? Do we not always take twelve months to advertise for all persons to bring in their claims? If long experience has dictated this as a just and a necessary measure in private estates, surely it will equally apply to the public. But the greater extent of country which the public administrators preside over, will demand an extension of time.

There is one reason for delay in this business which is unanswerable. The various certificates now afloat have many of them been in existence for several years. I ask what sort of security have you that those securities may not come forth beyond the supposed amount? What certainty have you that there is not an inundation of counterfeits of every description, some of them so well executed as to elude the most accurate eye, nay, some of them struck from the identical forms, and surreptitiously obtained by loungers about the offices where they were deposited, to which it would be easy to affix a name with passable accuracy. If report is to be depended on, the counterfeits in the various denominations may amount to a sum that would stagger belief. And some of those very counterfeits may be amongst the securities recited as *cancelled* and registered, whilst the genuine are still abroad. A minute account and investigation of *all the paper* in the United States is immediately necessary; and this too, before one farthing additional tax is laid on this groaning country. We find that some counterfeiters have lately been arrested in Worcester and Springfield.[1] In France, so much were they alarmed at the idea of counterfeits, that the value of their National Bank stock sunk, upon a late discovery of an imitation of their *Caisse d'Escompte* (or bank notes:)[2] How cautious then ought we to be in previously ascertaining the quantity of the circulating paper. It is evident that the present Congress admit the possibility and danger of counterfeits, otherwise, they would not have given such great encouragement to Mr. Francis Bailey, of Philadelphia, for his ingenious mode of providing against *future* counterfeits.[3]

I promised in my first letter to give you a copy of a petition to Congress, agreed to by a respectable number of citizens in our neighbourhood; if approved of, you are requested to copy it from this paper, and procure signatures, which, if sent to the Philadelphia Post-Office, sealed up and directed to any of your Representatives in Congress, it will become their duty to present them. You will also find it necessary to keep a copy of the names. You will recollect that the following gentlemen are your Members in the Lower-House: Messrs. George Clymer, Thomas Fitzsimmons, Thomas Hartley, Daniel Heister, Peter Muhlenberg, Frederick A. Muhlenberg, Henry Wynkoop, and Thomas Scott.

As this petition has met with the approbation of a number of judicious men, who are true Federalists, and staunch friends to the liberties and happiness of their country, I have no doubt of its being very generally signed.

To the Honorable the Senate and Representatives of the United States of America

The Petition and Remonstrance of the Inhabitants of , in the state of Pennsylvania,

Humbly sheweth,

THAT your petitioners, attached to the interests, honor, and happiness of America, have inquired into your proceedings with much anxiety. That sensible of the want of an efficient government, they cheerfully acceded to the New Constitution, which granted those powers you now possess. That your petitioners have already felt the weight of the taxes arising from the advanced prices on various imported articles; and receiving information that you are meditating to levy new taxes, by way of impost, excise, and duties on home manufactures, and also to introduce a Stamp Act amongst us, amounting in the whole to more than two millions and a half of dollars, annually, in addition to the heavy burthens we already bear, they pray that *you will withhold further taxation until after the next election of Representatives*, when the sense of the people may be fully and fairly taken on so important a measure, and your petitioners may be able to judge, how far they can bear an addition to the load they have so long sustained.

Your petitioners also pray, that you will immediately take measures for ascertaining the *full and just* amount of all the Continental and state debts, that all the public paper be called in by a limited time, in order to determine whether there are not an abundance of counterfeits in circulation; and that some uniform kind of paper be returned to the proprietors, properly marked and checked, in such manner as to detect and prevent future counterfeits; by which step the next succeeding Congress may be able to decide upon those measures, which the *gross amount* and the *nature of the case* may call for.

This petition, so reasonable, so just, and so necessary, will surely meet with attention and support.

IG, 1 May 1790; signed Ruricola (Latin for peasant, or yeoman). Three earlier essays by Ruricola appeared in *IG* on 10, 17, and 24 April. On 10 April Benjamin Rush apparently sent the first Ruricola piece to Madison, noting in the letter, printed above, that the fourth and final piece would include a petition to Congress. He described its author as one of Philadelphia's "most enlightened citizens." The editors assume that this was not George Logan of Germantown whose letters To the Yeomanry of Pennsylvania, signed A Farmer, were appearing in *IG* at the same time.

---

[1] Perhaps a reference to the counterfeiting ring led by Francis Crane and his brother Adonijah.

[2] The Caisse d'Escompte, founded in 1776, was actually a private banking firm that kept the accounts of the French government and had the right to issue notes. It was nationalized

by order of France's National Assembly in November 1789 and became the forerunner of the Bank of France.

[3] Bailey received no special "encouragement" for his anti-counterfeiting print types, beyond Congress's postponing the Bailey Bill's provisions for a private patent and referring the matter to the committee on the Patents Act {HR-41}. For background and texts, see *DHFFC* 8:73–84.

Other Documents

Daniel Davis to George Thatcher. ALS, Foster Collection, MHi. Written from Portland, Maine; franked. Concludes a letter begun on 28 April, above.

News of York County (Maine) court; "But while you are taken up at New York with the weightier Matters of the Law, they will be unentertaining to you"; regards to "Brother Ames."

Stephen Goodhue to Benjamin Goodhue. FC:lbk, Goodhue Family Papers, MSaE. Written from Salem, Massachusetts.

"I think prudence is Necessary in all Governments the tempers of the people appear to be Sour"; family is well.

Marshal Jenkins to George Thatcher. ALS, Chamberlain Collection, MB. Written from Hudson, New York. Printed in *DHFFC* 8:428.

Explains petition that would result in the Jenkins Act {HR-67}.

John Langdon to John Sullivan. No copy known; acknowledged in Sullivan to Langdon, 24 May.

Roger Sherman to Simeon Baldwin. ALS, Sherman Collection, CtY. Place to which addressed not indicated.

"Mrs. {*Rebecca*} Sherman & Roger {*Sherman, Jr.*} arrived about noon this day, they had a comfortable Journey. I received your letter by Roger & Shall write again Soon I have enclosed this days paper. Isaac {*Sherman*} arrived here last Saturday—and I believe he will find employ in an office. I{*n*} haste. {*P. S.*} *** I Should have wrote John {*Sherman?*} by this Post but was not quite prepared to give him the information he wants."

Daniel Hiester, Account Book. PRHi.

Shared a hack with Madison on "single 4 mile round" of Manhattan Island.

William Samuel Johnson, Diary. Johnson Papers, CtHi.

"Visits."

NYDA, 4 May.

Seney married Frances Nicholson in the evening in a ceremony conducted by Rev. William Linn.

Letter from Winchester, Virginia. *NYP*, 18 May; reprinted at Wilmington, Delaware.

"The rage for Kentuckey already appears conspicuous. Though the weather for some time past has been extremely cold for the season, it has not prevented a number of families from setting out for the land of promise. If the emigrations thro' the spring continue with the same rapidity they have begun, we may venture to predict they will equal if not surpass those of any former year."

Sunday, 2 May 1790

Fine (Johnson)

Fisher Ames to John Lowell

Since I have been engaged in the business of this second session, I have considered my letters as a tax upon the time of my friends, They have been a transcript of my own mind, and accordingly have expressed my disgust against measures and my presages of the consequences. Like a valetudinarian, I have vented my spleen, and given useless pain to my friends—But since the assumption has been rejected I think I perceive that my friends are grown as valetudinary as I am. It has not been often [*torn*] fortune to be a simple spectator of public affairs—At this time, I am almost sure you will feel as strong a sense of the hazard to which the Govt. may be exposed by our being so long doing nothing and at last doing wrong, as any person whatever. Those who see most clearly into the principles of Govt. & the human character will most disapprove the non-assumption. You are acquainted with Mr. Madison, and of course you know that he possesses a most ingenious mind, and extensive learning. He has long been deemed a champion for the Constitution—I think you will be surprised therefore to read his Speech[1] against the assumption, pronounced the week before last—He spoke more than an hour, and seemed to have framed his argument with great care—The reasoning is specious, but will not bear a strict examination. He speaks of the assumption as increasing & perpetuating the *evil* of a debt—This word *evil* is always in his mouth when he speaks of our debt. He affirms that without assuming the debt may be paid more easily & speedily—North Carolina & R. Island have an expeditious mode—The former has a law for calling in their paper at 4/ in the pound. and yet their members talk of the *exertions* of that state to keep up her credit—[*Mr. M*]adison says too that New Hampshire, under the Confedn. wd. have had to pay $^{1}/_{20}$ of the debt—taking the present ratio of representation as the rule of contribution—& that she actually pays to the impost but $^{1}/_{100}$ Therefore that state saves $^{4}/_{5}$ of her quota, & may take that saving & apply to her state debt. He reasons in the like manner about Connecticut & some others. Peter Pindar[2] ought to answer this argument. It will not bear a serious refutation—He is totally silent on the topic of settling State a/cs. [*accounts*]—but enlarges on the burden that Virginia will bear—a creditor by the war—more forward than Masstts.—instead of being repaid she will be obliged to advance more, & for states wch. have been delinquent—she consumes more too than other states, & has paid more since the peace towards her debt & to the union—This will have an inflammatory effect in Virginia—and as the Committee of the whole was discharged, soon after this speech, from the assumption, no opportunity was given to refute such bold vague & groundless assertions.

I see that the public mind is irritable in Boston. I have some fears that they will be intemperate. The enemies of the Govt. seem to be making use of the peevish humour of it's friends to wound it—I wish that the Antis could be made to clamour for the assumption more & agt. the Govt. less.

They scold about our tardiness, & perhaps with some reason—But last week was a very industrious one, & as much was done as I ever knew in any Assembly—Delay has often been wished by the public for it's own sake—in order to gain friends, or to have them return to Congress—and it has been the necessary consequence of those exertions which were made to carry measures conformably to their own wishes—No charge can be made with worse effect—for base people will readily believe that the members trifle away time to get more pay, because they feel conscious that they would do it themselves. People are least of all placable towards their own vices when practised by others—It strikes too at the root of popular confidence.

It give me the truest satisfaction to hear that the District Court has proceeded with so much popularity. Brother [*Christopher*] Gore's account of the term at Salem makes me hope that the Judicial will gain ground while the Legislative is certainly losing it—I have not wished to *impose* upon you the burden of an unprofitable correspondence But if you would sometimes favour me with a line, it would be highly acceptable. For I think I value the share which you have been pleased to allow me of your friendship as I ought—I shall no longer deserve when I cease to value it.

[*P. S.*] I hear that your Neighbour Heath is trying to stir up the Officers.[3] I hope in vain—Is the assumption liked by our state rulers any better since it was rejected? If they shd. approve it, & it shd. pass finally, they will be estop'd.

[*P. P. S.*] I had sealed the Letter before I thought to answer yr. Quere respecting New Emission Money. It is very doubtful what the Secry. [*Hamilton*] will report.[4] I understand he is not ready to report yet. It is intimated that large sums are in some of the state treasuries wch. it is feared, if allowed as U.S. debt, wd. be issued into the market. On the whole, I incline to think his Report will be less favorable to that paper than was expected sometime ago. Congress seems to be little disposed to call them the debt of the U.S. The point was started lately in the House & it seemed to be the opinion that the N. Emission shd. be left to the States to provide for: Congress havg. only engaged to pay in case the states shd. be made unable by the War. However, a further assumption seems probable & in that event, the New Emission wd. be wrap'd up with the other paper. I suspect the Secry. meaning to recommend the latter measure delays his Report.

ALS, American Manuscripts, MB. Place to which addressed not indicated. The second postscript is a fragment found in the Ames Papers, MDedHi. Internal evidence indicates that it was written after 23 April and before 11 May (see n. 4). The editors are placing it here; however, it could well belong with another letter, especially a non-extant one to Thomas Dwight, many of whose letters from Ames are found in the same collection as the fragment.

---

[1] Madison's speech of 22 April; see *DHFFC* 13:1171–81, 1182–86.

[2] The pseudonym of John Wolcott (1738–1819), a London physician whose satirical verses became widely popular.

[3] For more on William Heath's role in the April 1790 meeting of veteran officers of the Continental Army's Massachusetts Line, which some feared would reignite the debate over discrimination, see *DHFFC* 7:176–78.

[4] On money received from or paid to the states, ordered by the House on 23 April and submitted on 11 May; see *DHFFC* 5:888–910.

John Baptista Ashe to Governor Alexander Martin

I inclose you some papers one of them containing a report of ways and means I think extravagantly of it and I yet flatter myself a majority of Congress will think with me; Duties thus high will induce smuggling consequently lessen rather than increase revenue the Tax on Stills I consider as a very partial and iniquitious one, as it operates peculiarly oppressively on the Citizens of Virginia and North Carolina and on that class least able to bear taxation—Those measures have been induced by the Assumptionists presuming if the revenue could be brought to exceed other demands an assumption of the State debts would take place—in the first Instance I sincerely wish it may never happen but I Assure you Governor I dispond every day more and more ever seeing of our finances equal to the exigencies of our Government We have men in our House eternally forming or proposing an increase of officers and augmentation of Salaries and were they at Liberty every shilling of revenue would be exhausted by those moths—I expect we shall adjourn in the course of next month and probably to meet at Philadelphia I hope this will not be effected, once they get us there adieu to the Potomack.

Copy, Governors' Papers, Nc-Ar. Place to which addressed not indicated.

Thomas Fitzsimons to Tench Coxe

I thank you for Your favor by post. its purport will be as Safe with me as if it had not been Communicated I think a good Opporty. will soon present of bringing the two Gent. you Mention to an Explanation. that being done the test will Lye with thier friends—I have allways Supposed that the funding of the public debt would very much divide the people of Pensylvania and I shall not be in the Smallest degree disappointed, if such of their present representatives as take an Active part in that measure forfeit their interest by it. I only fear the business cannot be Accomplished as Effectually and Liberally as it ought for the other Consequence. I have Very little solicitude. the man Who in times such as these can *allways* retain the Good opinion of the Multitude: must he have much more flexibility than I should wish to Possess—in public life to Act with Independance must (for the Moment) be Unpopular. We have been so Industrious this last Week as to Clear our *files* table of every bill & report—the revenue bills are prepareing with the Post office &c. and will soon be brot. forward Several of our Members have been absent but I suppose in the ensuing Week we shall be all assembled—some Essential Improvements will be Made in all the revenue laws—from the experience of their operation—great Opposition will be made by those favorable to Assumption. I find the People in Boston are Calling Meetings With a View no doubt to remonstrate—as soon as any thing is decided on the point You Advert to I will Communicate it.

ALS, Coxe Papers, PHi. Addressed to Philadelphia; franked; postmarked.

Benjamin Goodhue to Michael Hodge

The Committee on the report of the Secry. relative to amendments in the revenue laws, have gone through most of his observations, and have given it him to report bills which he will do as soon as possible, the old bills will be repealed, this is thought will be more intelligible then having additional acts, the Committee agreed upon the most material amendments, but I could not get them to adopt every one suggested by my friends in Massachusetts—there has nothing turn'd up relative to funding and assumption since my last, the Committee I suppose will soon bring forward bills, founded upon the resolutions agreed to on that subject when it will again come into consideration and I cannot but flatter myself with a hope, that the funding of the Continental debt upon the excises &c. independent of the assumption will appear so hazzardous a project as to induce them to abandon the attempt, and be the means of bringing about an accommodation.

ALS, Ebenezer Stone Papers, MSaE. Place to which addressed not indicated.

William Maclay to John Maclay

Another Sunday had overtaken me without any time being appointed for our leaving this place. after having staid so long, I cannot without reluctance think of coming away without giving my Vote and assistance to get Congress out of this place. three Weeks are now talked of as the time during which we will have to stay in New York. I shall most certainly quit it without any Reluctance.

***

Bobey [*Robert*] Harris is gone home a considerable time ago. You will hear from him in all probability, long before You receive this letter.

Remember me to all Your Sisters and to your little Brother Billey.[1] You all wish me home. and it is a Wish in which I am equally fervent with any of You. May the good God guard and protect Us and give Us an happy meeting.

ALS, Dreer Collection, PHi. Addressed to Sunbury, Pennsylvania. The omitted text relates to farming and husbandry.

[1] Besides John, Maclay's children at the time of the FFC consisted of daughters Elizabeth (1772–94), Eleanor (1774–1823), Mary (1776–1823), Esther (1778–1819), Sarah (1781–ca. 1832), and Jane (1783–1809), and son William (1787–1813).

James Madison to Edmund Pendleton

***

You were right in predicting that the assumption would not be abandoned as long as new shapes could be devised for the measure. I understand that the leading advocates persist in declarations of their hopes of final success, and that new experiments are in agitation. Since my last a vote has passed by a large majority separating that part of the Secretary's plan, from the provision for the federal debt, and bills have been ordered in for the latter alone. This will embarrass the efforts in favor of the Assumption, but will not defeat it, if by any means a majority can be made up on that side.

Something like the Influenza is revisiting this part of America. It seems to be less severe than it was last fall, though nearly as general. I have been confined for some days with that & the effects of the medicine I took for it, but am at present pretty well again.

ALS, Madison Papers, DLC. Place to which addressed not indicated. For the full text, see *PJM* 13:184–85. The omitted text thanks Pendleton for reminiscences of the Stamp Act in Virginia.

Frederick A. Muhlenberg to Tench Coxe

Your favr. of the 29th. ult. together with the Note on Gelston & Saltonstall[1] was delivered to me yesterday-Morning. On Tuesday the Bank receives Notes for discount & the Result is made known on Thursday. I shall take Care to have it done, & from what I hear I believe there is no Doubt but that it will be discounted, shall therefore expect Your further Directions.

Last Week [*torn*] Business went on rapidly, even [*torn*] Numbe[*r*] of Reports from the differen[*t*] [*torn*] and tomorrow we shall have the funding & Revenue Bill[2] reported & read the first Time. How the great Business will terminate is at present difficult to ascertain, the Assumption of the State Debts having hitherto in some Measure been the Conditio sine qua non[3] with the Eastern States, whilst others perhaps would rather see the whole present System destroyed than consent to the same. Individual Members also declare that Mr. Maddisons first proposition, when this Business was taken up,[4] or something like it, was gaining Ground in every State to the Southward of this, and that such would be the Number of Converts, that if the System was not adopted at this Session, something very different would take place the next. The friends of the Assumption have hitherto been silent, but I expect when all their Forces are collected there will be another serious Struggle, should they fail I dont know the Consequence, but should they join those who are against the present System in toto, their Number would be formidable. I confess as I long as have been in public Life, I have never yet found as great [*di*]fficulties in any Business as A[*ssumption*] [*torn*] matter I find the Assumption Question of the utmost Importance, its binding Quality cannot but have the best Effect, whilst the peculiar Situation of some States—the deranged State of the Accounts of individual States with the U. States—the many and unauthorized Claims—& perhaps the Impracticability of ever coming to a just & proper Settlement present almost insurmountable Obstacles. I hope however that there will be a Majority for funding the foreign & domestic Debt this Session, & that if nothing more can be done that the Question on the Assumption will be deferred to the next. In the mean Time the Commissioners for settling the Accts. may proceed, & perhaps Members be better prepared for a Decision.

We have again revived the Question on a Removal,[5] & not without hopes of Success. We anxiously wait for the Arrival of Mr. Basset—as the Question is first to be put in the Senate.

It is probable, from the present State of Business that we may close the Session in 3 or 4 Weeks & agree to meet again some time in the fall [*of*] the Year. [*several lines torn and missing*]

The Members of the Convention at their next Meeting[6] will have considerable Weight in determining who is hereafter to be the chief Magistrate of our State, and I suppose no final Determination will take place until that Time.

Your publication[7] I shall transmit to Hamburg together with some other Materials on similar Subjects which I have collected—there to be ~~published~~ entered in a political Journal which is published once a Month & circulates thro out all Germany, and whose Author is a friend and Schoolmate of mine.

ALS, badly torn at fold on all pages, Coxe Papers, PHi. Addressed to Philadelphia; franked; postmarked.

[1] David Gelston and Gilbert Saltonstall were partners in a New York shipping firm.

[2] The Duties on Distilled Spirits Bill [HR-62] was presented on 5 May, the Funding Bill [HR-63] on 6 May.

[3] The necessary precondition.

[4] Madison's unsuccessful proposal to discriminate between original and subsequent assignees when funding government securities.

[5] Removal of the seat of government, taken up on a motion in the Senate on 24 May, ten days after Bassett's return.

[6] The second and final session of Pennsylvania's state constitutional convention convened on 9 August. During the four weeks it met, state politicians privately discussed several candidates for the first gubernatorial election under their new constitution, scheduled for October. F. A. Muhlenberg and Morris were leading possibilities until September, when they joined Clymer and Fitzsimons in supporting the unsuccessful candidacy of General Arthur St. Clair (*DHFFC* 9:192–93n).

[7] "Notes concerning the united states of America, containing facts and observations relating to that country, for the information of emigrants. Ascribed to Tench Coxe, Esq.," [Philadelphia] *American Museum* (1790).

William Smith (S.C.) to Tench Coxe

I wish the Members from your State were as zealous for the Assumption as you are; we only want their assistance to effect it & their voting against us lost the question—two of them, Scott & the Speaker were with us formerly, but they aftds. changed sides. The Majority triumph in our defeat & are endeavouring to hurry on the funding System, without the State debts: some of the States will consider this as a very unjust treatment & I am persuaded the Creditors of those States will do every thing they can to defeat the collection of the Impost & that the Govermt. will never be settled without the Assumption: If you or any of your friends have any influence with those Gentlemen you will do essential service to the Union in pressing them to vote for the assumption. I hope there was no foundation for the report respecting the Seat of Govt.[1]—time will however ascertain the truth or falsity of it. there certainly appears in some gentlemen who have hitherto advocated the assumption a disposition to keep ~~up~~ back that measure, without rejecting it altogether, & the knowledge of such a Question's depending on their votes may hereafter tempt them to derive some essential benefits from the power they possess: a gentleman who from the beginning had expressed himself of opinion that the Assumption was indispen[*sibl*]y. necessary to a funding System was however seen to exult at it's being lost—he is now endeavouring to carry on the revenue System by every possible means, & yet holds out the idea that he is a friend to the Assumption—such conduct will create suspicions & may almost justify them—the temptation is great & perhaps irresistible. Virginia & No. Cara. oppose the measure because they say it will be injurious to them on accot. of the great advances they made during the war & their prodigious exertions since the peace to discharge their debts—let the Accounts be first settled, say they, & pay us our ballances & then you may assume: they are perpetually vaporing about the immensity of their Claims & crying out against the injustice of making them pay a proportion of the debts of other states which have been deficient during the war & since the peace: unfortunately for them the Report of the Commissrs. of Accounts which has been presented to the House throws a ridicule over their claims which they can never get over: Virginia has not made good a single claim & the Commrs. have reported that it is not in their power to liquidate their accounts they are so confused & unsupported; among the Vouchers is a claim for a *Horse* valued at 400,000 *dollars*, which at 40 for 1. would be 10,000 dollrs.—ab uno, discite omnes[2]—this little anecdote cannot fail to afford peculiar satisfaction to Massachtts. & So. Cara. as the *Virginian Horse* will be a good Counterpart to the Penobscot Expeditn. & the So. Car. Frigate. The Claims of No. Cara. are arranged by the District Commissrs. under the following Heads; irregular, inadmissible, unsupported, unauthorized, improper, &c. &ca.: Some of the Eastern States, I am told, have made claims nearly as extravagant as the Virginian *Bucephalus*,[3] viz., charging for *calves in embryo* &ca. while poor So. Cara. sinking under a load of debt, incurred every farthing of it by the war, plundered by the ~~enmy~~ enemy of half her property & just beginning to breathe again after her struggles, has modestly claimed even less than the amount of her debt, & has charged nothing to the U.S. for her fortifications, cannon, armed vessels, obstructions in Rivers, militia, bounties &c. &ca. to the amount of millions: She must now be left to fund that debt, amounting to 5 millions & pay an immense revenue to the U.S. for the Interest on the Continental debt, of which She does not hold 50,000 dollars: is this *equal Justice—common & general* welfare, *promoting harmony?* don't you think our people must be great lovers of order & tranqy. if they acquiesce in such measures?

The Secretary has not made his Report on the subject of a National Bank; I can give you no information respecting it at present.

I have written to Charleston for the rules of our inland navigatn. Compy.[4] & will transmit them when received. I have also written to one of my friends, who is a cotton planter & a member of the Agricul. Socy. on the subject of the Machine you were so good as to give me notice of.[5]

Our old acquaintance Parson [*John?*] Bissett was here a few days ago & was so good as to send me a Copy of the Journals,[6] another of which I recd. from you the day after, & I return you thanks for it: my friend Dr. [*William*] Smith informed me at Philada. that I was appointed a member of the Standing Committee, but I see [*William*] Brisbane's name on the Journal—I imagine there must be some error, as the Dr. mentioned it to me, immedy. after the Committee had been appointed.

I condole sincerely with your unfortunate brother & yourself for the death of his lady.[7]

Our little boy [*Thomas Loughton Smith*] has been inoculated since my last—& is thank god recovering—Mrs. [*Charlotte Izard*] Smith is well & desires to join me in best respects to Mrs. [*Rebecca*] Coxe.

After I had read your papers on the Assumption & Rhode Island[8] which I did with considerable Satisfaction, I gave them to a Printer—they have been all published here. I wish you wod. continue to write on the Assumption, as I am persuaded your Labours will be productive of much good to the Community & may contribute to secure the blessings of that Govt. we all rejoiced at the establisht. of, & which without that measure may be dissolved in anarchy & state contentions.

Your Paper respecting Pensylva.[9] is recd. & I will give it to the Printer the first time I can see him. it will be productive of much benefit to that State, as the advantages detailed in it cannot fail to encourage emigration to it—as a friend to the Union, & a well wisher to every part of this great Empire, I rejoice at the amazing improvemts. Penya. is daily making—as an American, I am gratified with the growing prosperity of that State because I am Sensible that the opulence of each state adds to that of the others. I have lately heard from Geneva that another revolution is about to take place[10] which will induce all the Exiles to return home, a general oblivion being promised them. I will however send one of them to Geneva & get Mr. Izard to send them to Flanders, where there is less prospect of peace.

ALS, Coxe Papers, PHi. Place to which addressed not indicated.

[1] At least as early as 4 April (when Maclay reports it), the Pennsylvania delegation considered proposing to trade its votes on assumption for South Carolina's and the northern delegations' support for an adjournment to Philadelphia. By mid-June Coxe himself was strenuously advocating a similar bargain, but for a permanent seat of federal government on the Susquehanna River (*DHFFC* 9:235, 291).

[2] From one example, you may see them all.

[3] The favorite horse of Alexander the Great, who established a city in India to honor the site of its death during battle in 326 B.C.

[4] The Santee Canal Company.

[5] Probably Joseph Eve's cotton gin; see Smith to Edward Rutledge, 29 April, above.

[6] Of the Episcopalian Convention held in Philadelphia in the summer of 1789.

[7] Grace Riche Coxe, wife of Coxe's older brother John (1752–1824), died on 17 April.

[8] Likely "A Citizen of the United States" on assumption and the two part "paper" entitled "To the People of Rhode Island and Providence Plantations" and signed "A Citizen of United America." The first article, originally printed in *FG* on 8 April, appeared in *NYDG* on 12 April and *NYDA* on 21 April. The two articles on Rhode Island, originally printed in *FG* on 8 and 12 April, appeared in *NYDG* on 10 and 15 April. The first nom de plume was a favorite of Coxe's and the second is a variant probably designed to make a statement about unity to Rhode Island.

[9] "Notes concerning the united states of America, containing facts and observations relating to that country, for the information of emigrants. Ascribed to Tench Coxe, Esq.," [Philadelphia] *American Museum* (1790).

[10] Smith had spent the years 1773–78 as a student in Geneva and no doubt retained many contacts there. It is not clear what rumor may have reached him from Geneva, probably concerning an easing of tensions between the revolutionary forces ruling France and the mostly aristocratic, reactionary émigrés (exiles) who began to flee across the border to Geneva en masse after the fall of the Bastille in July 1789. In 1790, Flanders (part of present-day Belgium, France, and The Netherlands) consisted of Austrian Flanders in the east and French Flanders in the west. Contributing to its destabilization at the time was the influence of both Revolutionary France and the subversive "Patriot Party" active since 1785 across Flanders' northern border in the United Provinces (present-day Netherlands).

George Thatcher to Sarah Thatcher

You did right in borrowing money of friend [*Jeremiah*] Hill—and I would have you borrow again if you need, & if he will lend—but I hope before this time you will have received enough from me to repay him, & some besides for your own use.

I have two of your Letters before me that came to hand since I wrote last—The first informs me of your being unwell, & the other of your being on the mending hand—This affords as much occasion of rejoicing as the other of grieving.

I am almost impatient to get home, and hope it will not be longer than the last of this month before I see you.

I cannot close this without telling you that Captain Chadwell got home the night before last, after being absent more than three years.

ALS, Thatcher Family Papers, MHi. Place to which addressed not indicated.

George Thatcher to Thomas B. Wait

Last evening I enjoyed the pleasure of reading yours of the 17th. & 21st. of April & to the speculative part of the former, will, at this time, only observe—leaving the full discussion of the question to some future opportunity, when I may have more leisure to write, and your mind is duly prepared to read, what I may have to advance on the curious subject.

Because I said, man can arrive at very few general truths in morals politics & theology, you seem to conclude, that a man whose duty & interest it is to be a politician ought not to employ two thirds of his time in the study of morals and theology—Strange! In this, my friend, you are certainly wrong—but your error results from not seeing two or three facts—and these too before your eyes! If two thirds of mans actions are the direct effects of the morality & theology taught in every country—if from the begining of the first empires down to the establishment of the Constitution of the United States, religion has been the source of more misery to the human race, & one of the greatest obstacles to the formation of good Laws, shall you think a politician is out of the line of his duty in examining the various systems of theology &, as well as the principles of morals—as they have been & still are taught in the world?

Public utility is the only measure of the goodness or badness of human actions—and tho all actions that tend to the public good are, by some, called religious; yet there are a great part of the very religious & pious actions of men that are good in no sense of the word—that is—do not advance the general happiness of man.

According to my analysis, there is nothing more distinct than good actions and those that are religious.

The seven sacriments of the catholics are ridiculed by the protestants—the ceremonies of the Church of England are, by some of the dissenters,[1] esteemed no better than the fooleries of ancient Greece & Rome—and many religious actions of the dissenters are, by other sects, still farther dissenting, accounted of no substantial use to the public—Yet those are all religious actions, & those who attend to & perform them are religious people—But do not all agree that, for parents to instruct their children in a punctual discharge of the duties they owe to themselves, to the magistrate & the Laws of their Country are part of a good education—and that the actions flowing from such instruction are good actions?

What is it that makes a religious man? Is it a punctual discharge of his political & moral duties? no—He must do something more in ~~every~~ all Countries—He must observe the ceremonies established by the priests—Now ought not a politician, whose object is the *greatest possible happiness of the greatest number of individuals*, to inform himself of the effect these ceremonies have on society—and whether there be any natural connection between the observance of them & this great object—The diversity of religious ceremonies among different nations is visible—this diversity is also equally perceivable among different sects in the same nation—All nations are not equally happy—are the individuals of each sect, in the same nation, and under the same Laws, equally good members of society? If you say they are—of what avail then is their religion? do not different religions produce the same effects? If you answer in the negative, from what does this arise, but their difference of religious tenets—for all other things are equal—What then is of more importance to a politician than to know the different religions & their effects on nations and individuals? But I have rambled too far—this is a copious subject, & in my opinion it has been hitherto but imperfectly understood—Hereafter I will examine it farther.

FC, Thatcher Family Papers, MHi.

[1] An umbrella term for Protestant sects (sometimes called the "Free Churches") that refused to conform to a government-established church. In Thatcher's lifetime it was applied more specifically to Baptists, Quakers, Moravians, even Methodists, and eventually Unitarians.

Other Documents

Elias Boudinot to John Edwards Caldwell. ALS, Stimson-Boudinot Collection, NjP. Place to which addressed not indicated. On the endorsement sheet, Boudinot wrote, "N. B. this rough Copy being mislaid was not sent, but the enclosed was in its stead," referring most likely to his letter to Caldwell dated 17 May, below, in the same vein.

Illustrates Boudinot's latitudinarianism, while cautioning Caldwell against too rash a decision to convert to Catholicism; "I am satisfied that the Grace of God, is not confined to Sect or Party"; "The longer you live, and the more you Converse with Mankind, the more you will be convinced that God has in every Nation, those who love him & keep his Commandments."

Benjamin Goodhue to Stephen Goodhue. ALS, Goodhue Family Papers, MSaE. Addressed to Salem, Massachusetts; franked.

Encloses a newspaper; has just then encountered "your sister" (Stephen's wife's sister, Rebecca Prescott Sherman) and their son (Roger, Jr.), who arrived the day before; the general expectation is that Congress will adjourn some time next month.

James Madison to James Madison, Sr. ALS, Madison Papers, DLC. Place to which addressed not indicated. For the full text, see *PJM* 13:183–84.

Encloses newspapers containing news of the House; discusses sale and price of tobacco; "the influenza or something like it but less severe has revisited this quarter of the Union," and an attack of it has kept him home for several days; he is largely recovered and will be able to resume his seat the next day, "or at least shall be able to do it"; if there is no important business there, may take two or three days off "for exercise & recreation"; requests weather reports from home; has located theology books for a friend to purchase; is happy to hear his mother (Eleanor Rose Madison) is recovered.

Robert Morris to Tench Coxe. ALS, Coxe Papers, PHi. Addressed to Philadelphia; franked; postmarked.

Has given a "carefull perusal to the Paper that came enclosed" (subject unknown) in Coxe's letter of 27 April (unlocated); most of it meets his approval, except for one point which ought not to have been included and which they will discuss when they meet next.

Robert Morris to George Harrison. ALS, Brinton Coxe Papers, PHi. Addressed to Philadelphia; franked; postmarked; answered on 6 May.

Has taken the liberty (see Morris to Jefferson, 1 May, above) of supplying Harrison's name in a list of consul nominees, which Jefferson had asked of him; the list did not specify a post and declared that Harrison was not aware of the recommendation; "the Consuls have no Salarys, the office is deemed Honorable and gives rank in Foreign Country's, it can only be made profitable by Commercial operations and Consignments"; writes (Garrett) Cottringer by the same post to "Continue to Relieve your pecuniary necessities," although "We have been hard Run and the Sun has hardly shined since you left us."

Philip Schuyler to Nicholas Eveleigh. FC:dft, Schuyler Papers, N.

Replies to Eveleigh's letter of 23 April, received on 30 April, regarding the accounts of the Committee at Camp in 1780; Schuyler was absent when the committee dissolved, but he believes its accounts and proceedings may have been delivered to the other members; he will write "without delay" to John Mathews on the subject, and will "advise you of the result as soon as I receive his Answer."

George Thatcher to John Avery, Jr. No copy known; acknowledged in Avery to Thatcher, 13 May.

Monday, 3 May 1790

Cloudy (Johnson)

Edward Carrington to James Madison

I am sorry to be troublesome to you, but upon further examination of the Census [*Enumeration*] Act, it appears to me that the penalties under which alone the people are compellable to render their returns truly, are without any practicable means of recovery: this will render them entirely nugatory unless a remedy is applied before the commencement of the business: as this act Stands, together with that of last session for the Judiciary establishment, all these penalties will be exclusively within the Cognizance of the district Courts to which it will be impossible for the assistants from the distant parts of the Country to resort for such small Sums, of which they are only to have half nor indeed will they in cases of false returns be able to establish their Suits without witnesses. this will soon be understood by the people, and the penalty will cease to operate on their minds—I am of opinion that it is absolutely necessary to give the State Courts concurrent jurisdiction with the district Courts in these penalties, or none will ever be prosecuted for. I think I am right in my conception of the State of this matter, but refer you to the parts of the two acts from whence it is formed: In the ~~judicary~~ judiciary act Sec. 9, you will see that the district Courts are to have "exclusive original Cognizance of all Suits for penalties and forfeitures incurred under the Laws of the United States": In the Census Act Sec. 6. the penalty for not rendering to an Assistant a true return is "twenty dollars to be sued for and recovered by such assistant, the one half for his own use, and the other half for the use of the United States." In the small States it may be practicable to enforce these penalties, but in the large States, the matter will be considered in a different light, and they will effect nothing. I take the liberty of submitting this circumstance to your judgement—if you have the same idea of it that I have, I will thank you to take such measures for a remedy as to you shall seem best.

ALS, Madison Papers, DLC. Place from which written not indicated; postmarked Richmond, Virginia, 6 May.

William Ellery to Benjamin Huntington

I have received your letter by Capt. [*Edward*] Peterson with the draft upon the bank in Boston for 300 dolls. which completes the sum of 1000 Dolls. I am much obliged to you for your attention to that business and now send you by Col. [*William*] Peck eight Dolls.—which I hope will be satisfactory.

Our Genl. Assembly will meet here on Wednesday next. If they should do any thing worthy of notice I will give you an account of it. The Antis will have a considerable majority, and from them no good thing is to be expected.

I am sorry that it was not convenient for Congress. to take measures with this State which might have had an influence on the Assembly, and of course on the Convention. It is my opinion still that the Convention will adjourn again unless you do something which will touch the interest of the Anti's before the Convention meets; which will be the last monday in this month.

You did not answer ~~the las~~ that part of my last letter which expressed a desire to be informed whether upon ~~the~~ a failure of the application ~~of~~ which the Federal towns might make to Congress to be put under the protection of ~~Congress~~ The United States, Congress would defend them against any violence which might, in consequence of such application, be offered to them by the Antis? For my part I do not imagin that the Antis would resent such an application in a hostile manner, nor should I fear them if they should; but among the Feds there are some prudent men who would wish to be sure of a favorable issue to their application; or of protraction if Congress should not think it political to receive our federal towns into the Union.

I should be glad to know when it is probable Congress will rise.

Present my regards to my friends in Congress.

ALS, Benjamin Huntington Correspondence, 1772–1790, R-Ar. Written from Newport, Rhode Island.

Gouverneur Morris to Robert Morris

***

I am very sorry indeed to learn that our friend Maddison has adopted such singular Ideas respecting the public Debt. This thing will prove injurious to him because it will give a Handle to those who may wish to call his Judgment in Question and the World is so formed that Objections on that Ground are frequently more fatal than upon that of Morals. I think that on this Occasion he has been induced to adopt the Opinions of others for I cannot beleive that his own Mind would so much have misled him. I am very very sorry for it because I think he is one of those Men whose Character is valuable to America.

I have read with Pleasure your Memorial to the two Houses of Congress Persevere my dear friend in the setling of all Accounts with every Body. Let no Disappointments or distressful Incidents damp the Vigor of your Mind. Look up & hope and the Time and Chance which happen to all must at last happen right.

FC:lbk, Gouverneur Morris Papers, DLC. Written from London. The omitted text relates to private business transactions, economic conditions in Europe, and arrangements for hiring a clerk "should I be placed any where for a certain Period of Time which you will know." For background on R. Morris's petition, see *DHFFC* 8:663–75.

George Nicholas to James Madison

Your favor of the 27th. of Feby. is now before me.

The last act of the Virginia assembly on the subject of a seperation[1] seems to have given general satisfaction. The opposition to that measure still continues but as far as I can hear the bulk of the people are in favor of it.

Spain takes great pains to seduce our people to remove to their country. I have myself seen letters from the Governor of New-Orleans [*Esteban Miró*] to certain characters who had talkd of going down the river stating the advantages that would result to them from such a step.

The depredations of the Indians have been of a more striking nature this spring than formerly, but not to a greater amount. They have taken several boats, *attacked a few of the troops and stolen the officers horses.* These last have opened their eyes which have remained so long shut they no longer consider them as brethren and declare them the aggressors. Their conduct has been the same for ten years, and the only change that has taken place is in their attacking the property and persons of these men who I suppose are the servants of government and not the objects they wished to protect. If these Gentn. now change their language to government it will prove very sufficiently that what I suggested in my former letter was true: that they disregarded the interests of Kentucky entirely and ~~and~~ only thought of that of the other side of the river.

Those persons who are best acquainted with Indian affairs say nothing will be effectual unless a war is carried into their country. If such a measure should receive the sanction of government the troops that can be spared from those now in the Western country with the militia will be sufficient to carry it into execution. But if this arrangement should be made the command of the expedition shd. be given to some person in the district [*Kentucky*]. Genl. [*Charles*] Scott, Col. [*Benjamin*] Logan or Col. [*Isaac*] Shelby appear to be the characters best suited to conduct it: if I was to make a choice it would fall on the last Gentn. Mr. Brown is better acquainted with them than I am. The people would go with pleasure and we could furnish every thing necessary but the military stores and wait until it was convenient for Government to pay us.

You are now engaged in the most important deliberations. I do not like the assumption of the state debts. It is too much like consolidation and every thing that was denied by the friends to the new government, when it was under consideration.

Discrimination is a tender subject; upon the best view I can have of it I should have voted against it.

The funding system is dangerous. I think the people should always be called on to make payment as far their abilities extend; this system was introduced into England when the government doubted it's own strength and popularity: I hope that is not the case here. A government that relies for support on it's creditors and not on the affections of the people cannot be durable. And yet I find this one of the arguments relied on in favor of this system.

A happy selection of characters appears to have been made to fill the public offices. The Western country consider their interests as safe in the hands of Mr. Jefferson.

I wish success to all the attempts that have been made in favor of liberty. It will be a greater honor to this age to have it hereafter said that it best understood and asserted the rights of man, than to have to have repeated of them ten times as much as ever was said of the age of Lewis 14th. or Augustus.[2]

ALS, Madison Papers, DLC. Place from which written not indicated; franked; postmarked Richmond, Virginia, 10 June.

---

[1] "An Act concerning the erection of the district of Kentucky into an independent State," passed on 18 December 1789.

[2] Louis XIV (r. 1643–1715) and Augustus Caesar (r. 27–14 B.C.) reigned over a "Golden Age" in France and Rome, respectively. The arts and sciences flourished but civil rights languished under their absolute rule.

Samuel Tenney to Nicholas Gilman

Your favor of April 18th. is now before me. & I am to thank you for the concern you express in it on account of my loss by a fellow, in whom I should now blush to have it known I ever confided, did I not find myself in very respectable company. At the time of Odlin's absconding I thought my loss great & felt it severely, though I flatter myself I bore it philosophically. But since the fate of the important question on the proposition for the assumption of the State Debts. I view it as much less considerable. You are as well acquainted with the wretched policy of this State as any man. Calculating their future proceedings with regard to their creditors by their past transactions & present apparent disposition, they have no just reason to estimate their securities at a very high rate. But this does not now concern me, for I am not of the number. With respect to State Securities Fate, by the ministry of Odlin,[1] has already done me its worst.

I consoled myself a while for this loss by thinking that my *finals* [*final settlement certificates*] were in a way to become valuable. But the fair prospect, which some time since opened upon the federal creditors, has of late been much obscur'd; & I will frankly confess to you that many of us begin to suspect that our interests, together with the honor & happiness of the nation, ~~is~~ are destin'd to fall a victim to the infernal Demon of public discord. They reason in this manner. From the present prevalence of party spirit & from the small progress hitherto made in the important business of establishing the national credit, which, as you observe, all allow can be done only by funding the national debt, there is little prospect that the system in contemplation for the purpose will be brought to a favorable conclusion by the present Congress. The present is, however, as good and probably better than that by which they will be succeeded. If then the funding System is not completed & put in execution before a new choice, they have little ground for expectation from any future Congress. But you may enquire why they expect the next Congress will not be as good as the present. I answer You are sensible that the federal interest in Massachusetts & Newhampshire has heretofore but barely preponderated. The large salaries Congress have assumed to themselves & given their officers & servants although justified by most men of liberal minds & extensive views—& their slow progress in business, have afforded the opposers of the Constitution copious themes of declamation, by which they have at least maintaind their numbers, & probably gain'd some accession of strength. The non-assumption of the State Debts will in Massachusetts throw a considerable weight into their scale. This interest, in New England, are in general, I imagine, pointedly oppos'd to all important patriotic measures. You know they are as mischievous as

Hell, & you may depend upon it, I believe that they will, at the next election of members, be as busy as Death. I hope, in this instance, I shall find myself among the *croakers*—but I shall be agreeably disappointed if there are not, in the next Congress from this State & ~~the~~ Massachusetts, two Anties to one federal member.

It does not appear from anything I have seen that Congress fully enter into the liberal views of the Secretary relative to the modification of the *federal debt*. The proposition they have adopted may be agreeable to many of those who hold large sums & are dispos'd to speculate in Lands. But the mass of public creditors. who possess but some few *hundreds* or at most *thousands* of dollars, will esteem their proportion of lands, laid out the Lord knows where, as unworthy of their attention, & consequently will think themselves ungenerously depriv'd of one third of their demands. The only method then by which Congress can preserve even the appearance of justice & generosity (& this ought by no means to satisfy them if the substance be neglected) will be to adopt at least two of the Secretary's three first propositions, or others similar; & to give transferrable debentures for the land, on interest till taken up; which interest may be in lands at a certain premium per 100. acres—If, in addition to this, Congress should order the Commissioners, that may be appointed to dispose of the federal Lands, to receive these debentures at a little higher rate than funded securities, their depreciation might be prevented, a ready market provided for them, & their holders secur'd. I found my ideas of the necessity Congress ~~in~~ is under, in the present case, of making propositions to the public creditors, that shall be substantially fair & generous ~~from~~ upon what passes in my own mind, & upon a certain principle in human nature, which always makes a man, particularly one of a generous spirit, revolt at the idea of having an honest claim on his neighbour modified to his disadvantage without his free consent.

I had written thus far before I saw the proceedings of Congress on the 20th. of April. The propositions there adopted fully come up to my ideas of justice & liberality: & I have to ask pardon for mistaking a mere deferrence of the secretary's alternatives for a positive rejection. The proposition to have two thirds funded immediately & the other third in seven years, at an annual interest of 6. per cent, must, I apprehend, be quite satisfactory to all, who are dispos'd to relinquish any part of their present claim: All we are call'd upon to give up by this ~~plan~~ [*illegible*] plan is two per cent for 7. years; & he who would not do that for sake of securing the remainder of both principal & interest would, in my opinion, make but a bad calculation.

My paper admonishes me that it is time to finish my letter.

ALS, Chamberlain Collection, MB. Written from Exeter, New Hampshire.

[1] A John Odlin of Concord, New Hampshire, resigned his state militia commission in late 1790, perhaps as a consequence of the unspecified irregularity mentioned here.

Other Documents

Daniel Benezet, Jr. to George Washington. ALS, Washington Papers, DLC. Place from which written not indicated. For the full text, see *PGW* 5:360.

Office seeking: revenue officer at Egg Harbor, New Jersey; mentions Senators Morris, Paterson, and Elmer, and Representatives F. A. Muhlenberg, Fitzsimons, and Sinnickson as references.

Mary ("Polly") Hetfield to Elias Boudinot. ALS, American Bible Society Boudinot Collection, NjP. Place from which written not indicated; written on Monday evening; franked.

Hopes she will not be mortified by the Boudinots' absence from her wedding Wednesday evening (5 May); has always looked up to him "as my Father"; they may either take the stage that leaves from Paulus Hook ferry between four and five in the afternoon, or a horse will be sent to the ferry to pick them up, and they may return as early the next morning as they wish.

James Madison to Benjamin Rush. Two page ALS, *Parke-Bernet Catalog* no. 468(1943):item 151. The ellipses are in the source.

". . . Your hint as to addresses from the H. of Rep. to the National Assembly was perfectly new. I am far from thinking that such a measure might not be formed as [*to*] do credit to this Country and good to both . . ."

Robert Morris to George Washington. AN, Washington Papers, DLC. For the enclosed letter, see above.

Covers application of Daniel Benezet, Jr. for revenue officer at Egg Harbor, New Jersey.

George Thatcher to Shearjashub Bourne. FC, Thatcher Family Papers, MHi.

The bearer, Bourne's son John, leaves for Woods Hole (Cape Cod, Massachusetts) at noon, having called on Thatcher earlier that morning and previously on the evening of 1 May; Thatcher has given him ten dollars to procure some things; encloses letter with an order for payment, which Thatcher has discharged on Bourne's behalf.

Joseph Whipple to John Langdon. ALS, Langdon Papers, NhPoA. Written from Portsmouth, New Hampshire.

Has told Mrs. Elizabeth Langdon that any sum of money she needs is available to her from Langdon's compensation, payable out of Whipple's customs office; "I find the information intimated in one of my letters respecting the Senate's being in favor of the Non Assumption was wrong— Mr. [*Tobias*] Lear informs me that much the greater part of that patriotic Body are of a different Opinion."

Oliver Wolcott, Jr. to Oliver Wolcott, Sr. ALS, Wolcott Papers, CtHi. Addressed to Litchfield, Connecticut.

Has been confined by the influenza; Congress is proceeding with more zeal than usual and will probably adopt the principles of Hamilton's report on public credit, except for assumption; the ultimate success of that measure would depend on "the verdict of public opinion"; about a hundred French émigrés have arrived (for Ohio's Gallipolis settlement), "with the national cockade in their hats, fully convinced that it [*is*] one of their natural rights, to go into the woods of America and cut down trees for a living."

Daniel Hiester, Account Book. PRHi.

Attended "Monday Club" or mess day with the Pennsylvania delegation at Fraunces Tavern; Maclay indicated that James Wilson attended (*DHFFC* 9:259).

George Washington, Diary. ViHi.

"the Secretary of the Treasury called upon, and informed me that by some conversation he had had with Mr. King (of the Senate) it appeared that there was a probability the Senate would take up the [*Yazoo land*] Sales by the Legislature of Georgia, and the Affairs of the Indians which would be involved therein in a serious manner, and gave it as his opinion that if this was likely to be the case, it might be better for me to let the matter originate there, than with the Executive."

Proceedings of the General Society of the Cincinnati. Society of the Cincinnati, Washington, D.C. The same source noted Hawkins's absence from the session convened on 4 May.

Among those in attendance at the Society's triennial general meeting convened in Philadelphia that day were Wadsworth, Hawkins, Gunn, and Mathews.

Tuesday, 4 May 1790

Fine (Johnson)

Nathaniel Barrell to George Thatcher

*** I am sorry to find by yours such an opposition to the assumption of the state debts, as I know it must proceed from injustice in the opposers—it is said Maddison has lost himself in the opinion of many great and vertuous men, & has done more injury by his chicane, & cunning, than he can ever repair—when I find disinterested persons, who have no connection in continental or state securitys expressing these Noble sentiments, I cannot suppose their inducement proceeds from any thing but the love of Justice, and I am pleasd there are such men yet existing among us, and tho they are but few, and but seldom heard, yet I am obligd to consider them as the salt of the earth.

ALS, Chamberlain Collection, MB. Written from York, Maine; postmarked Portsmouth, New Hampshire, 5 May. The omitted portion discusses Thatcher's assistance in Barrell's legal dispute with Stephen Collins.

Jeremiah Hill to George Thatcher

Yours of the 25 Ulto. is received—the Manifest of your Cargo, when the Coaster arrives, shall be duly attended to.

You tell me the Secretary has reported his Observations on the Collection & coasting Acts—Mysteries you know I don't deal in, of course I wished a little specimen of the Business, as a copy[1] at that Juncture was not attainable—when at Biddeford you said that you thought it probable, the officers of the revenue would, instead of fees, have a Salary, I will give you a short specimen which perhaps may be of some service in the discussion of the business if pertinent at that time—You recollect I told you of the Uneasiness at Scarborough with Mr. [*Edward*] Emerson & Others at the Entry of the first Vessel after the Congressional Laws took place[2]—They wanted to enter as usual under the States Laws, that is, to enter on their own Terms, that is, be allowed nullagus &c.—In consequence of my insisting on a proper Entry they have never entered in this District since Quid tum?[3]

ALS, Chamberlain Collection, MB. Written from Biddeford, Maine; postmarked Portsmouth, New Hampshire, 5 May.

[1] Hamilton's report, dated 23 April, was never ordered printed.

[2] The Collection Act [HR-11] defined the districts and officers for executing the Impost Act [HR-2] and the Tonnage Act [HR-5], effective 1 August 1789.

[3] What then?

James Jackson to Caleb Swann

I can give the secretary of War no positive information of the numbers of the Militia in actual service from 1775 to 1782. the statement below as near as I can guess may be supposed the amount.

For the Year 1775 I believe that the State of Georgia had one thousand Militia constantly in Service and which number were continued until the spring of 1776 I am led to this belief from the parties I know of my own knowledge to have been called out, the frontier situation of Georgia the struggle with our internal Enemies the defence of the Country against the Florida Banditti[1] & the expedition agt. Savannah under Commodore Barclay.[2]

For the Years 1776 & 1777 the Militia in actual service may be computed at 750 exclusive of two Battalions of Minute Men which were in service untill July 1778 of 750 each and a state regiment of Horse supposed 250 with three additional troops of 40 Men each under the command of a Major.

In the Year 1778 exclusive of the State Corps, there were two thousand Militia in actual service for nearly six Months.

In 1779, 1780, 1781 & 1782 the Militia may be computed at 750 constantly in service for the whole period; as the state during this time was totally ravaged by the enemy & the Citizens of Georgia never quit the Field altho compelled to abandon not only their homes but frequently their state this is likewise exclusive of the Georgia Legion[3] raised in 1781 by order of Genl. Greene.

ALS, James Jackson Papers, GHi.

[1] Gangs of marauding Seminoles and Loyalists, formally under British military command based at St. Augustine, East Florida.

[2] In February 1776, HMS *Scarborough*, under Capt. Andrew Barkley, arrived off Savannah, Georgia, to procure rice for British troops besieged at Boston. Finding the Savannah River obstructed by militia forces who also mounted an artillery defense of the town, Barkley rescued the royal governor-in-exile Sir James Wright, aborted an amphibious assault, and seized two transports loaded with rice before returning to Boston in late March (*Naval Documents* 4:443–44).

[3] The Georgia State Legion was a special troop, outside of the regular Continental Army establishment, authorized by Gen. Nathanael Greene in June 1781. It consisted of two hundred men to be enlisted for ten months under the command of Jackson, whose rank as lieutenant colonel was confirmed by the Georgia legislature on 21 August (*PNG* 8:325).

Warner Mifflin to George Thatcher

Just accept this as a Token of my friendly remembrance of thee, my esteem for thee is considerable, as it is disinterested, I want no favour from Goverment as to any thing pecuniary, I desire the promotion of righteousness, upon solid grounds, and the Welfare of Mankind universally—This is the hight of my Ambition if I know myself.

It has been said that I acted as I did[1] to gain the favour of the delegates of Congress to carry points, in a Political Line, this I leave to the Judgment of the members, who were pleased to give me their Company I am not uneasy thereat knowing my Motive, and shall be pleased to have similer oppertunities with many of you again, feeling indeed great respect towards many—I shall be oblig'd to thee to Visit me in return with a few lines—I am Ashamed of my little piece of paper but having several Letters to write this evening, I took this just to let thee know I had not forgot thee.

P. S. please to remember me kindly to thy Coleagues at thy Lodgings & my acquaintance in thy freedom.

ALS, Chamberlain Collection, MB. Written from Kent County, Delaware; carried by Bassett. The salutation reads, "Respected Friend."

[1] Mifflin refers to his strident lobbying on behalf of Quaker antislavery petitions to Congress between 6 February and 25 March.

Benjamin Rush to James Madison

Your proposition for doing justice to the late Army of the United States[1] becomes both popular & practicable in proportion as it is contemplated. Many people are Converts to it, who at first considered it as impracticable & impolitic. Among these I have reason to believe is A Gentleman from South Carolina [*Smith*] who bore a decided part in the Opposition to you on the floor of Congress. He is a Correspondent of our mutual friend's Mr. Coxe.

The principal design of this letter is to request that Mr. Coxe may not be made acquainted with my Opinions respecting the funding System, nor even with our having exchanged letters upon the Subject. He is devoted to the Secretary's principles and plans—and I have harmonized with him upon so many subjects than I did not wish to hazard an interruption of our friendship by letting him know how heartily I reprobated the whole of the Secretary's report.

ALS, Madison Papers, DLC. Written from Philadelphia.

[1] Rush is referring to Madison's proposal of 11 February for a discrimination between final and original holders of public securities.

David Sewall to George Thatcher

Yours of the 25th. ulto. came to hand this morning—and of the 18th. last Week—I am sorry Mr. Sedgwick appeared so warm upon the determina. of the question of non assumption in the Committee[1] for it answered I suppose no Valuable purpose—But am more sorry that He and Leonard have left the Ground[2] at this particular Crisis When their Voice would be as much and more necessary, that at any other period—however as N. Hampton S[*upreme*]. J[*udicial*]. C[*ourt*]. is now over as also Mr. L.'s probate Court—I suppose they may be back again time enough for the passing any Bills upon the funding System—Unless there be an assumption of the State debts or a very Considerable part of them upon good Father Shermans Plan[3] or some similar one, (and Whose charackter I have had favourably represented some time since) A financier of but small abilitys will very soon discover the ways and means inadequate for providing *even the Interest* for the foreign & domestick debt—The clashing of Revennue Systems, of the several States will so militate with the Revennue System of Congress as to injure each other—and make them unproductive for their respective purposes—And another disagreable Consequence is The clashing & thwarting expectations of the different Creditors of the Union & the States, ~~Which~~ Whose Credits originated for precisely the same Common purpose Will bring on something which Time alone can fully determine the end of—The Bill to secure to authors & Inventors the Benefits of their Inventions [*Patents Act HR-41*] has been published in our Papers—If you can send me that respecting Crimes & Punishments [*Punishment of Crimes Act S-6*] it will be both more Novell and usefull—as I must, the beginning of next month Try the unhappy Persons in Portland Jayl—I am not a little Surprized at Capt. Stones Petition,[4] and wish you to send me a Copy of it, *Nobody here can* believe the Truth of some parts of it—and there are *many* that *know* 'em to be otherwise—If my leisure permits between this & tomorow noon, I may Write something particular on the Occasion—If I should not, there is in Thomas Massa. Magazine *for March last, I think* a true publication respecting major Saml. Sewall's being the Original *Inventor* of driving Piles &c. &c.[5] the greater part of ~~Which~~ what is therein related came within my own certain Knowledge and observation.

[*P. S.*] I forwarded some time since an authority to recieve the nullaged Salary for 1789—Which I think you mention as having come to hand When it is convenient you will be so good as to procure and forward a draft on the Massa. bank— ***

ALS, Foster Collection, MHi. Written from York, Maine; postmarked Portsmouth, New Hampshire, 5 May. The omitted text relates to local weather and politics.

[1] The reference is to Sedgwick's dramatic lamentation upon the defeat of assumption in the COWH on 12 April; see *DHFFC* 9:241, 13:994, 1007–8.

[2] Sedgwick was granted two weeks leave on 12 April; Leonard obtained three weeks leave on 16 April.

[3] As a substitute for the defeated resolution on assumption, Sherman on 21 April moved a resolution would have provided for immediate payment of the continental debt while defining the states' war debts by their liquidated specie value according to specified evidences of debt, and pledging their future payment upon a modified schedule that was in almost every state's case lower than the amount prescribed in Hamilton's report, with the difference payable upon a final settlement with the United States (*DHFFC* 5:858n).

[4] John Stone's petition for a patent for his method of driving wooden piles in the construction of bridges was presented in the House by Thatcher on 15 February; see *DHFFC* 8:46–47, 49–50.

[5] Isaiah Thomas's monthly *Massachusetts Magazine* for March 1790 (p. 143) contained a piece written by "A. B." that credited Maj. Samuel Sewall of York, Maine, with the idea of driving wooden piles for bridges, a method first demonstrated by his Charles River Bridge (1786) and said to have been fraudulently claimed as Stone's invention.

Other Documents

Tench Coxe to James Madison. ALS, Madison Papers, DLC. Written from Philadelphia. For the full text, see *PJM* 13:188.

Asks Madison to engage a room for him in Mrs. Dorothy Elsworth's boarding house, preferably one with a southern exposure; intends to arrive, without his family, on Saturday (8 May), to assume the position of assistant secretary of the treasury; just that day received Hamilton's letter offering the post, "but as the matter had best come to the world from him you will be pleased to consider this information as confidential."

Thomas Perkins to Nathaniel Appleton. ALS, Appleton Papers, MHi. Place to which addressed not indicated.

A bill is being proposed for the support of public credit; some think assumption will be reintroduced to meet approval when the bill is presented; "there are many who differ, little can be learnt from our Rep's. they are not at all communicative, tis generally thought the Cont'l. Debt will be funded tho' the State debts should be rejected."

Benjamin Rush to John Adams. ALS, Adams Family Manuscript Trust, MHi. Written from Philadelphia.

Having read Adams's last (18 April, above), "I shall make no material alterations in your political Character"; introduces Tench Coxe.

John Sullivan to Nicholas Gilman. ALS, MS 29, University of New Hampshire, Durham. Written from Durham, New Hampshire.

Thanks Gilman for sending the warrant for his salary and "attention to my affairs" and continuing "your kind offices" (collecting his salary?) with the enclosed power (of attorney?); is convinced that assumption "would not be injurious but beneficial," but will "submit to my Superiors who are on the Ground" and will "acquiesce in their Decision."

Proceedings of the General Society of the Cincinnati. Society of the Cincinnati, Washington, D.C. For the full text of the society's address, see *PGW* 1:952.

Mathews, Gunn, Hawkins, and Wadsworth appointed to a committee to present an address to Washington and inform him of his reelection as president general of the Society of the Cincinnati.

Wednesday, 5 May 1790

Fine (Johnson)

George Cabot to Benjamin Goodhue

An invincible indolence of disposition derived from nature & confirmed by habit has prevented my acknowledgement of the receipt of your favor of the 17th. ultimo.

Having settled it as an irrefragable truth, in my own mind, that the National Govt. cannot go on without assuming the state debts, I cannot discharge myself of anxiety for the peace of our Country until that object is attained—while my pride is gratified to see all New England united in their efforts & wishes to establish this measure I am at a loss to account for the conduct of some other men whom I have been accustomed to think well of—I can't reconcile Mr. Maddison's present conduct with his ~~first~~ former principles—I conclude that his principles now do not guide him or he has changed them—he was once sensible of the folly of such a divided Sovereignty as left the Supremacy no where—& he woud then have thought that the powers which must be exercised by the States in providing for their own debts are such as belong to a Supreme Govt. only & cannot be safely left to subordinate ones—while Congress are acting so unworthy of themselves & of the great trust reposed in them, it is to be apprehended that the antifederalists may seize the opportunity of attaching all the State Creditors to their cause by providing honestly for them—if they shou'd do this in the the State Legislatures the Genl. Govt. wou'd be ruined irrecoverably—the only security that remains seems to be that the Members of Many of the State

Govts. will not do honestly even to carry their own points against the National Govt.—thus we have more to hope from the vices than the virtues of men in some cases—"all Nature's difference keeps all Nature's peace"[1]—I hope you will not be wearied out by the perplexities that attend these great questions—the welfare of the Community certainly depends upon your success—this idea will animate you to persevere & if you die to fall in the last ditch.

ALS, Letters to Goodhue, NNS. Written from Beverly, Massachusetts.

[1] From Epistle iv, l. 56 of Alexander Pope's "Essay on Man."

Andrew Craigie to Daniel Parker

*** The assumption of the state Debts remains undecided. The absence of many members who are in favor of it has induced a Delay—but it will be brot. into discussion again in a few Days—Congress are much divided on the subject and it is not certain that it will take place the present sessions—Very few however doubt of its ~~finally~~ taking place the next Session and it is my opinion it will this. Mr. Hamilton in a conversation I had with him the other Day seemed to have very little Doubt about it He thinks the Senate will add the Assumption to the Bill should the House not provide for it—& there is no no doubt a majority in the senate are in favor of it. The whole difficulty in the Business may be fairly imputed to Mr. Madison whose politicks this sessions have disgusted many of his best friends. *** I lodge in the house with Mr. Strong Mr. Ames Mr. Sedgwick & several other Members of Congress[1] Mr. Strong informed me last Evening that he had not the least Idea that the funding System would be carried without the Assumption—Mr. Elsworth who is a leading Man in the Senate says it can never happen that Govt. cannot with safety attempt to fund one Debt without the other. ***

FC:dft, Craigie Papers, MWA.

[1] Mrs. Sarah Smith Loring's boarding house on Broadway.

Thomas Fitzsimons to William Jackson

I have as you desired Annexed the Names of some persons that appear to me, to be Eligible as Consuls at particular places and have thot. it Necessary at the Same time to add some Remarks Which you will make the proper Use of. I suppose there are some of those & others who will be Named that have Never applyd and where that is the Case I think it ought to be mentioned least the President might be Induced to appoint persons who might decline Accepting—any further Information in my power to give You May Command.

[*Enclosure*]

Cadiz [*Spain*]	R[*ichard*]. Harrison the Character of this worthy Man is too well Known to require Recommendation I doubt of his acceptance.
Oporto [*Portugal*]	there is a Very respectable Portugeeze Mercht. at Philada. who was Mentioned some Connection of his there. I have Wrote for the Name & Character.
Teneriffe [*Canary Islands*]	[*Francisco*] Sarmento. a Spaniard. Marryd at Philada. & settled at Teneriffe he has Acquired a great share of the American business of excellent Character. And has applyd for this appointment.
Madeira [*Islands*]	Mr. [*Henry*] Hill was formerly very desirous of this appointment. whether he is so now I cannot answer or whether the present Agent means to return if not & Mr. Hill is still desirous he is sufficiently Known.
Fayal [*Azores*]	There is a Respectable family there of the Name of Street one of whome [*John*] applyd to me while in the former Congress they are Known to Mr. Morris I have written to a friend at Philada. to Know whether it would still be Acceptable.
Dublin [*Ireland*]	Jos. Wilson formerly Resident at Philada. and allways Attached to this Country his Character is unexceptionable but I do not Know whether the appointment would be Acceptable I will write today to his friend at Philada.
Marseilles [*France*]	F. Haller Nephew to the Banker Haller of Paris this Young Gent. was some time at Philada. and Employd by me at Augustine his friends wrote for him & Established him in a Very Capital House at Marseilles. I am not however Warranted to say he would Accept tho I believe he would haveing allways expressed strong attachments to America.

ALS, Washington Papers, DLC. An annotation by Jefferson on the last page reads, "Sarmento, Street, Wilson, Haller"; an annotation in another hand reads, "Treasury of the United States New York May 4 1790."

People of Holstein to Samuel Johnston

We the Subscribers being chosen by the Inhabitants of the Teritory ceded to Congress by the State of North Carolina, & fully impower'd [*lined out*] to Request in their Names, your Assistance on their behalf in the Particulars hereafter to be mentioned; are imbold'ned from Your well known Patriotism, and the particular Respect by You in Charactor of first Magistrate, paid to the Interest of this so Infant Country; hoping You will in the high Office You now fill, further evince to us that Friendly Disposition and Respect to our Interests, which we have heretofore expereanced.

In the first Place Your Committe prays Your Assistance and Influance which we have no Doubt will be in Proportion to Your Abilities in making such Appointments as our Member Genel. Severe [*Sevier*] Shall recommend and Your honorable Body may think necessary for the well-Governing this Country.

Secondly and in a more Particular Manner We request Your Assistance in the Appointment of a first Magistrate as a Matter of the highest Importance to this Country, and begs leave to recommend to You and through Your Assistance shall hope for Success, in having the honorable John Severe, Appointed Governor and Commander in chief in and over this Country And in the Name of the People we beg leave to assure You that no other man upon the Continant the Presidant of the United States, (not excepted,) can give as general Satisfaction to the People of this Country, in that Office as the Person to You recommended.

The Reasons will naturely Suggest Themselves, We have been Uniformly a Frontier, constantly imbroiled with our Savage Neighbours, The Senews of civil Government—so long unbrac'd, Party Heats and Civil Commotions not Yet Asswag'd, so that a long Acquaintance must be essential, to govern a People Martial in their Nature and heretofore in a kind of Anarchy.

ALS, hand of James Rea, Hayes Collection, NcU; signed by "Joseph Hardin Chairman" and "James Rea, C. C."; docketed "People of Holstein," by Johnston. Written from Greenville, Tennessee; carried by Sevier. The Holstein settlements comprised present-day northeastern Tennessee.

Peter Muhlenberg to Thomas Jefferson

Being prevented by Your indisposition from paying my Respects to You in Person—I beg leave to inform You, that I am requested by some Gentlemen in Philada. to mention Mr. [*James*] Collins to You, as a Gentleman well Qualified, to act as a Consul for the United States in Ireland, if such an Appointment shall be thought necessary. Mr. Collins is a Native of that

Kingdom, & Certificates of His Abilities, & Qualifications, will be forwarded in a few days, To The President of The United States.

ALS, Washington Papers, DLC.

Samuel Phillips, Jr. to Benjamin Goodhue

Your repeated favors I have receivd. and am very greatly obliged for your very friendly attention to the matters of business I mentiond. to you, as well as for the recommendations of a public nature; as to the former, upon the information you gave respecting screws,[1] have sent [*torn*] endeavor to procure them at Bridgwater—and have written the enclosed for Mr. [*Samuel?*] Hodgdon, ~~to~~ whom you recommended to me, to whom must ask the favor of you to superscribe it as I have not his christian name.

I deeply lament the situation of our national concerns, but tho' in perplexity, we must not be in despair—We have been saved, as a people, almost by miracle, in numerous instances, even from the beginning—*This we ought more sensibly to feel & acknowledge*—at the same time to observe two things—we must take "perseverando"[2] for our motto, while we remember *that the beginning of contention is as when the letting out of water.*[3] Our Friend Sedgwick, in my humble opinion, was sudden, warm & ~~I think~~ imprudent[4]—The sentiment he advanced, looks too much like the forlorn hope[5]—I think it is much too early to have resort to it; my believe is, that you will yet succeed, *if we are not too ungrateful a people to be established as a Nation*; I am strengthed in this belief, by the information of your success with Mr. G—t [*Grout*], for he is one of the last, from whom I shd. have expected it; the majority against you is very small, far less than it was in the negative, in the Convention of Massachusetts, fo[*torn*]ering the Constitution, for ~~many~~ several weeks after their first meeting;[6] but time, patience, perseverance, calmness, manly reasoning in public, and private influence—(I dont mean unworthily used) produced a surprizing change—The advantage you have in the argument, is vastly in your favor; but dont let us forget that when the passions are raised, the door to conviction is barred. my letter is called for, and I can only promise to write again soon.

ALS, Letters to Goodhue, NNS. Written from Andover, Massachusetts; franked; postmarked Boston, 6 May.

---

[1] In Phillips's papermaking mill at Andover, Massachusetts, layers of wet paper and absorbent felt would have been collected into piles called posts and subjected to repeated squeezing by a screw press in order to dry.

[2] It must be persevered in.

[3] Proverbs 17:14.

[4] A reference to Sedgwick's emotional lamentation over the defeat of assumption, pronounced on the floor of the House on 12 April; see *DHFFC* 9:241, 13:1005, 1007–8.

[5] The "forlorn hope" (from the Dutch term for "lost squad") referred to the body of volunteers in the first ranks of a desperate military maneuver.

[6] The Massachusetts convention that ratified the federal Constitution sat from 9 January until 7 February 1788.

Other Documents

Pierce Butler to John McQueen. FC, Butler Letterbooks, ScU. For the full text, see *Butler Letters*, pp. 39–41.

Recently paid Fitzsimons £83 on a bill drawn to provide a loan to McQueen in 1783 and requests repayment of the loan, "never being more circumscribed in my finances than at this time"; the House has been "long occupied with the finances & money arrangements of the union. The question for assuming the States Debts was lost"; "It is questionable whether they are disposed to fund any of the Debt"; invites McQueen to visit Congress; think they will not be able to adjourn before the end of June; "I hope that by means of the troops gone to Georgia You will plant in peace & security & make a large crop"; wife Mary Butler has been ill all winter and is still bedridden.

Samuel Penhallow to John Langdon. ALS, Langdon Papers, NhPoA. Written from Portsmouth, New Hampshire.

Acknowledges notification of Langdon's failure to procure him an appointment; speculates whether an earlier application might have been successful; thanks for his "assurances."

Post Office. *NYDG*, 5 May.

Until next 1 November, mails to the eastward will leave three times weekly, and to the southward every weekday at 7:30 A.M.; "merchants and others" are reminded to be precise in their addressing, "as there are many towns and places in the United States of the same name, and some in Europe similar to those in America."

[Portsmouth] *New Hampshire Spy*, 5 May.

"The State of New-York has already commenced an electioneering campaign for federal Representatives."

THURSDAY, 6 MAY 1790

Fine (Johnson)

Benjamin Goodhue to Stephen Goodhue

*** the bills for funding the Continental debt and the bill for increasing the impost on certain Articles together with a heavy excise on distill'd spirits have been read once without debate and are to be taken up for a second reading on Tuesday, and I am suspicious they are determin'd notwithstanding all our opposition and the ill consequences attending such measures to push it through, you cannot be more sick among you of our proceedings then I am, for I sincerely wish myself at home where I should not have my mind so perpetualy worried as it is by being here.

My love to Fanny [*Frances Goodhue*] &c. and hope they will soon be well through the measles.

[*P. S.*] The post now goes 3 times a week. ***

ALS, Goodhue Family Papers, MSaE. Addressed to Salem, Massachusetts; franked; postmarked. The omitted text relates to their joint mercantile transactions.

Christopher Gore to Rufus King

I have been writing to our mutual friends Dalton and Ames—on the subject of attempting a delay to ~~the~~ fund~~ing~~ that part of the debt called Continental, until the State debts shall be assumed—I suppose that these gentlemen think such measures adviseable—but I am well convinced that the attainment of their wishes, altho in my own opinion truly important, if not indispensably necessary to a good system of finance, ~~can be~~ will not in any degree compensate~~d~~ for [*lined out*] a delay of funding that part of the debt which is more immediately obligatory on the nation—the people were disappointed & dejected at the non assumption—but all orders of men, in the populous towns, are outrageous, in their exclamations, against Congress, for delaying to fund the continental debt—they say their money is taken from their pockets, and from trade in general, to be locked up in the chests of the treasury, or spent by the immediate officers of Government—unless something is speedily done by Congress to throw the money from the custom houses among the ~~the~~ people at large, I am really afraid that the collection of duties will be as unpopular, as under the british government—the evils complaind of are perhaps not real, & very probably not imputed to the right cause—but a general belief that the ~~non~~ delay to fund the debt takes so much money out of circulation and that the doing this woud revive their trade and business has the same effect as if absolutely true—I write these things to you because I fear that some of our f[*riends*] feel the object of assumption so important to Massachusetts, as to be in danger of hazarding too much for the prospect of attaining it.

ALS, King Papers, NHi. Written from Boston; franked; postmarked.

Jeremiah Hill to George Thatcher

I sincerely thank you for yours of the 28 Ulto. not only for the information respecting the Assumption, but more also for the several Libels published to be tried before the District Court in the City of New York, several of which respected Coasters. I mean to poste it up in my office *in Terrorem*[1]—The old Proverb is, he that spareth the Rod hateth his Son[2]—so winking at the little things may lead a wayfaring Man to run a Risque, exceeding two hundred Dollars or 400 Galls. & thereby forfeiting his all, where in his extremity he will be tempted *to bite off his Mothers Nose*[3]—I have often told you the plague I had with the Coasters—this paper has given me more *Light* than any one thing I have ever met with—The Secretarys Report [*on defects in revenue laws*] still lies heavy in my Mind.

ALS, Chamberlain Collection, MB. Written from Biddeford, Maine; postmarked Portsmouth, New Hampshire, 7 May.

---

[1] As a warning.

[2] Proverbs 13:24.

[3] A reference to an Asian proverb in which a son mutilates his parent when he must face the consequences of having been over-indulged in his youth.

Joseph Hiller to Benjamin Goodhue

I feel myself indebted to you and thank you very cordialy for your kind favour of the 11th. April. we are anxious the substance and effect of the Report you mention,[1] from its bulk it is hoped that it embraces all the important alterations and improvements that were necessary.

I have not yet been necessitated to demand foreign tonnage of an american Vessel, but should a case occur here like those mentioned in your letter it will be a satisfaction to have received the information you give me and shall follow your advice.

That restraint that has been observed in the high departments of office respecting directions in cases where law and reason appear to be opposed, has operated very inconveniently and I wish it may not always be continued. I have asked advice in a number of cases and am left to form my own decisions.

But I console my self with the idea, that if the natural motion of the machine is not impeded it will free itself from many offensive obstructions.

The murmers and discontents incident to the descendents of Britain are not new to your ears, and tho' they must be very disagreable, and are rendered still more so for want of a united exertion to remove the ground of them; yet we reflect with some satisfaction that tho' such disunions may be the natural product of ~~of a government of~~ a government like ours, they are commonly temporary, and not always disadvantageous.

You have the domestic occurances of the day from those who can feel the beating of the pulse in this part of the great body with so much more accuracy than I can that my observations need not be obtruded. *** Capt. [*Bartolomew*] Putnam, sometime since mentioned the situation of Mr. Needhams Vessel[2] as ~~a proof~~ an Instance of the inconvenience arising from there being no specified time when a vessel shall begin to unload. I should be glad of your observations on this subject & also on the method of procuring payment from the owners or masters of Vessels having Salt or Coal, to Inspectors detained more than fifteen days after beginning to unload. and whether the~~y~~ subjects are noticed in the Secretarys Report.

ALS, Letters to Goodhue, NNS. Written from Salem, Massachusetts. The omitted text relates to a pending revenue fraud court case.

[1] Hamilton's report to the House on 23 April, on difficulties encountered in executing the impost and collection acts and recommended remedies (*DHFFC* 4:437–56).

[2] Daniel Needham was master of the schooner *Polly*, owned by the Salem merchant Benjamin Needham. Weeks before, it had returned from the Turks Islands, Bahamas ([Massachusetts] *Salem Gazette*, 13 April).

Roger Sherman to Simeon Baldwin

I received your letters of the 26. April & 3 May. I now enclose the last paper, & No. 55. & 107.[1] Mr. Fenno could not find one of 47. but Says he thinks he has one & if he finds it I shall have it. Roger [*Sherman, Jr.*] has had Some thing like the influenza which confined him two days but he is growing better, has walked about the City Yesterday & to day. It has been cloudy uncomfortable weather perhaps Mrs. [*Rebecca*] Sherman will not come home quite So Soon as She at first expected. She is well—We want to hear from the family, whether Betsey & the rest are well—I Expect the question of assuming the State debts will be taken up when Some absent members return. & I hope it will be agreed to under Some modification with a good degree of unanimity—Business has progressed very fast in Congress for a week past. I hope the session will close by the first of June.

ALS, Sherman Collection, CtY. Place to which addressed not indicated.

[1]The issues of 21 October 1789 and 21 April 1790, respectively, of John Fenno's *GUS*. Number 47 was the issue of 23 September 1789.

Letter from a Member of Congress to a Gentleman in Boston

A Committee of Senate, to whom was referred a Consideration of the Provision proper to be made in the present session respecting Rhode-Island, have reported, that all commercial Intercourse between Rhode-Island and the United States should be prohibited after the First of July next—and that a Requisition be made on Rhode-Island for 27,000 Dollars, to be paid into the public Treasury before the First of August next, Monday is assigned for a consideration of this Report. It is universally agreed, that the public Good requires a decisive Line of Conduct towards these People.

[Rhode Island] *Providence Gazette*, 15 May; reprinted at Albany, New York, and Norwich, Connecticut.

Other Documents

Pierce Butler to Simpson and Davisson. FC:lbk, Butler Papers, PHi.

Believes Congress will not adjourn until July; the House has been occupied with the public debt, and has rejected assumption for the present; trusts there will be peace in Georgia because of the federal troops sent there in April.

George Clymer to Henry Clymer. ALS, John Work Garret Library, Johns Hopkins University, Baltimore. Addressed to Market Street, Philadelphia; franked; postmarked. Written in the evening.

Discusses error in accounting of tax payments past due; "Were I at home 10 minutes I could make every thing clear by knowing what papers to lay my hands on"; has received (wife) Elizabeth's letter, but has no time to answer her that day; "the influenza or what is the same an extreme bad cold has laid up a great many people here, I believe a third of Congress have been seized with it."

Elbridge Gerry to Samuel R. Gerry. ALS, Gerry Papers, MHi. Place to which addressed not indicated; answered.

Shocked by the contents of Samuel's letter of 26 April, which he received in Congress, even though he had not been without apprehensions regarding their brother (Thomas); "such repeated strokes are very heavy on me" for "the recollection of former affections produces habits of regret which constantly distress me"; but they must submit to the decrees of the

"Author of our existence" and trust "that our dear friend has 'exchanged this world for a better'."

William Samuel Johnson to Samuel W. Johnson. ALS, Johnson Papers, CtHi. Addressed to Bermuda.

Has just heard that a vessel finally sails the next morning for Bermuda, "& now after impatiently waiting so long I am so engaged in Company & business that I can write but a very short Letter"; is in good health; family news.

James Madison to Edmund Randolph. ALS, Madison Papers, DLC. Place to which addressed not indicated. For the full text, see *PJM* 13:189.

Received Randolph's letter of 27 April "this instant"; had ceased writing under the assumption that Randolph had already left for New York; considering the cause (wife Elizabeth Randolph's illness), no criticism can be made of his continued absence, nor is resigning a necessary alternative; further efforts will probably be made to include assumption with funding, but they do not threaten to be successful, and the federal debt will be funded as Hamilton has proposed; has been confined nearly a week with a minor relapse (of dysentery) and with the influenza that is generally afflicting New York.

John Nixon to Thomas Fitzsimons. ALS, Fitzsimons Letters, PHi. Written from Philadelphia; franked; postmarked 7 May. The right margin of the second page is obscured by binding.

Thanks for sending the treasury warrant; "Commercial Gentlemen" generally were surprised to read in the newspapers about the petition of Philadelphia's manufacturers of cordage (presented 29 April; see *DHFFC* 8:365); the business was "managed very privately indeed"; expects the city's merchants and ship carpenters will "in a day or two" come forward with a similar petition, "which will be no doubt forwarded to you"; has been requested to mention the subject to Fitzsimons, "altho' I do not think there is much danger of a hasty determination in your great house"; thanks for the information regarding the timing of the new duties.

William Samuel Johnson, Diary. Johnson Papers, CtHi.

"Visits."

George Washington, Diary. ViHi.

Senators Wingate, Maclay, and Walker, and Representatives Gilman, Ames, P. Muhlenberg, Wynkoop, Page and his wife (Margaret), Smith

(S.C.) and his wife (Charlotte), and White and his wife (Elizabeth) dined at the President's; several others were invited but were prevented by illness from attending.

Equity. [Boston] *Independent Chronicle*, 6 May.

"If the sentiments of a MADISON, and others had been adopted in a *discrimination*," an act for funding the debt might have already been achieved, justice established, and "*love* and *good will* conspicuous among the citizens at large"; quotes from Sedgwick's 12 April speech after assumption was defeated in the COWH; the citizens of Massachusetts should instruct their Representatives to the Second Congress to permit the funding of the state debt by leaving to the state the necessary resources, "without *discouraging trade*, or *unreasonably burdening the People*."

Letter from Alexandria, Virginia. *NYDG*, 14 May.

Two hundred Frenchmen have arrived en route to settle in the Western Country; a much larger number is hourly expected; hopes their reception and the fertility of the soil will induce thousands to emigrate to "this Land of Peace and Plenty."

Letter from a Member of Congress to Newbern, North Carolina. [Edenton] *State Gazette of North Carolina*, 4 June, from non-extant [New Bern] *North Carolina Gazette*, 27 May; reprinted at New Haven, Connecticut; New York City (*GUS*, 19 June; *NYP*, 26 June); Philadelphia; Baltimore; and Richmond, Virginia.

"The business of Congress moves with tardy advances, the assumption has taken much time and is not yet fully decided. Our worthy friend, Doctor Williamson, has done himself great honour in opposing the measure, and on every occasion merits the confidence of his constituents."

FRIDAY, 7 MAY 1790

Rain (Johnson)

Jonathan Cass to Nicholas Gilman

*** I beg for the honor of Justice that the present Congress will not sufer their times to expire without funding the debt of the United States if they do my faith in the public Credit will almost expire with it Great efforts are making by the dishonest intriguing to Git an artifical Majority in Favour of new men & mesuers [*measures*] I call it artifical because I cannot suppose that a Majority of our Countrymen unpersuaded or unprijudiced would wish to see dishonesty sancioned by authority. I saw in a letter to your B. N. [*Brother Nathaniel*] of the 25th instant [*ultimo*] that you ware not altogether a Stranger to the reflections made by some against your *political Character* it is not in their power to do you much injury in the opinion of those who who think & see for themselves. but as it is a selfish motive in them there is every stimulous to industroy for such people and of Course something ought and may be don to counteract their plans otherway, they may for a moment hurt the reputation of Good men and thereby work themselvs into Congress which is compleatly answering their purpose Tho you are not without friends in this Quarter yet a line from some know fair Character in or about Congress to Genl. [*John*] Sulivan or any other sutible person to be Communicated ~~at~~ in a proper maner at June Court "for that is the time they will lay their plans" may be necessary to put the matter in a fair light If my proposition should appear two officious pray impute it to the want of Judgment in those delicate matters my Chief motive is to Counteract a set of men whose principles I obhor Mr. ~~S—H.~~ S. Sh. [*Samuel Sherburne*] is the man that is Straining every nerve to get into Congress the next election, and as he has become a member of the the State Legislator I am not without my fears that he will accomplish it.

I understand Congress has ordered 400 men to be raised but as Genl. Knox has so many friends to provide for in Masschusetts I I am doubtful New Hampshire will not be thought of for a Major but if the detayls are made right New Hampshire may furnish 100 men out of 1200 and one Major out of 7 field officers which I suppose will be the propotion calculating the infintry and artilery that are now in service But if a Majority can not be had, I should not refuse a Captaincy. As I intend to go into that Country in a future day with my family I think a military appointment "to which I make my self beleve I have some Claim" will not only be pleasing but profitable to me. I therefore beg it as a particular favour that if agreeable to your feelings you would use your influence with Genl. Knox or who ever has the ordering of the matter to Call on New Hampshire for a Major & a Surgeon. I suppose there will be much ~~difil~~ dificulty in the mater for doubtless many applycations will be made as soon as the order of Congress is known, pray Give me your opinion on by whom and how the appointments will be made.

ALS, Lewis Cass Papers, MiU-C. Written from Exeter, New Hampshire; postmarked Portsmouth, New Hampshire, 10 May. In the omitted text, Cass claims an inability to pay a debt to Gilman because the low value of securities has reduced his available finances, which the restoration of public credit will enable him to put "in a bater train."

William Maclay to Benjamin Rush

Your's of the first I have received and placed the inclosed peice in the same channel which I have heretofore used with Success.[1] Tho it is possible it may be now rejected, as it bears hard on the Arguments of One of the Representatives. and this with the Yorkers is deemed a critical time, When they would even risk the safety of Union, rather than loose a Vote on the Subject of Residence.

Our Proceedings are slow beyond all bearing. and instead of pursuing the great subject of finance, there is even some, by Business, to take Congress off. I fear indeed, my friend, that we will tire the Patience of our Constituents. but I hope they are better employed, than in taking any notice of Us Whatever. The Spring is very backward at this place. And let me add very Unhealthy. The influenza is almost Universal, and has been in some instances Mortal. The President of the U.S. is so affected by it as to have nearly lost his hearing. The effect this place has had on him is visible to every one. such a change has taken place on him in the last year, as seems plainly to say the Measure of his life, will not fill his first Presidency. The Warmest advocates of New York, admit the change, but charge it to the Cares of Government. Cares no doubt he has. but what are they to those, which must formerly have oppressed his mind. when the doubtful die of American fortune, often spun on the dubious point of chance & contingency?[2] and Yet health never forsook him. In short we must snatch him from this place, or we shall loose this palladium of our new Constitution and with him perhaps the Constitution itself. Mr. [*Tench*] Coxe has this day come to Town (as is said) to enter on the duties of his new appointment, at the Treasury.

ALS, Rush Papers, DLC. Addressed to Third Street, Philadelphia; franked; postmarked 9 May.

[1] Maclay had had at least two pieces published in *NYDA*, one as recently as 28 April, above. In addition, although his authorship cannot be proven by documentary evidence, the content and tone of at least two pieces that were printed in *NYJ* appear to be Maclay's; see Machiavel, 4 March, and A Janisary, 18 March, above.

[2] That is, during the Revolutionary War.

Governor Beverley Randolph to James Madison

I have the Honour to acknowlege the receipt of yours, of the 27th. Ultimo. Upon inquiring into the subject of the 4 months pay and Subsistence due to the officers and soldiers of the Virginia line, I am informed that the privates are not possessed, of any evidences of their Claims.

The officers, have received warrants for the pay but have no acknowlegement from the public, for the subsistence due them. In this Situation I suppose Congress, may direct the Officer who shall be intrusted with money to discharge these claims, to pay the Sums due to the original claimants only, or to persons duly authorized by them. Speculations may be further guarded against by obliging such persons as may apply for payment under powers of attorney from the original claimants to produce satisfactory evidence that the money received, is to be applied to the benefit of the original claimant only; If you think a measure like this will sufficiently protect the rights of this worthy Class of citizens, you will no doubt take the steps necessary to regulate the business.

But should there be any impropriety in it, or should any difficulties arise in obtaining the establishment of it, I shall be much obliged to you to communicate them to me. You may be assured that the Executive will unite with you in your endeavours to secure the Interests of men, who are so much entitled to the attention of their Country. It will be certainly proper that the appropriation which has been made in their favour, should be communicated to the claimants.

FC, Executive Letterbooks, Vi. Written from Richmond, Virginia. On this date Bland introduced a resolution directing the secretary of war to cause lists of officers and soldiers of the Virginia and North Carolina lines who were due pay from the United States to be published in the newspapers in those states. See *DHFFC* 6:2063–70.

[*Abishai Thomas*] to Governor Alexander Martin

*** A Bill [*Settlement of Accounts HR-69*] is now preparing by ~~be laid before~~ a Committee of the House of representatives in aid of former resolutions[1] to compleat a settlement, and I believe Congress are now serious as to that matter, which heretofore I have had my doubts concerning, and am fully perswaded that had the assumptionists of the state debts succeeded ~~in~~ their plan was never to settle, ~~indeed such~~ but having lost their object in the first instance they give into the other measure in hopes of conciliating the minds of gentlemen of the other side & of bringing about an accomodation whereby they will finally obtain the assumption, to this I do not know whether we could have any solid objection, but in the present posture of affairs I am confident our state must have been a sufferer, in this sentiment I am happy to inform you—our members were also unanimous and that it was through their exertions & unanimity that the measure was defeated— ***

Draft, hand of Abishai Thomas, Governors' Papers, Nc-Ar. The omitted text relates to Thomas's activities and pay as commissioner for settling North Carolina's accounts with the federal government and apologizes for not writing sooner.

[1] For the Confederation Congress's ordinance for settling the accounts between the United States and individual states, adopted on 7 May 1787, see *JCC* 32:262–66.

Other Documents

Robert Morris to Gouverneur Morris. No copy known; mentioned in William Constable to G. Morris, 7 May, Constable-Pierrepont Collection, NN.
A "very long letter respectg. Lands."

William Samuel Johnson, Diary. Johnson Papers, CtHi.
"Degrees given [*at Columbia College*]."

George Thatcher, Notes on the Steuben Bill. Ms., Thatcher Family Papers, MHi. Undated. Based on internal references to the published *House Journal* and Thatcher's implied intent to defend himself for various unrecorded votes on this controversial subject, the editors believe these notes were written during his reelection bid to the Second Congress. See *DHFFC* 7:245n.
Thatcher voted against an amendment by Boudinot granting back pay of $7,000 while leaving blank a proposed annuity amount.

Saturday, 8 May 1790

Fine (Johnson)

Abraham Baldwin to Joel Barlow

I wrote you ten days ago[1] by a brig for Havre, and sent you all the late papers, addressed to the care of our Charge Mr. [*William*] Short. If you have got that, the present will contain nothing but old stories. One new story though to begin with, which might as well have been omitted if Misfortune would have permitted: the day after I wrote, a vessel arrived here with 90 of your colons[2] which they picked up at sea, just on the point of sinking five feet water in the hold. [*Royal*] Flint will probably tell you the story, I have not seen the agent who was in town but a short time, they all went immediately over to Amboy [*New Jersey*] to recruit a little and keep together till they can embark for Alexandria [*Virginia*].

General [*Rufus*] Putnam, who by the bye is appointed judge vice [*Samuel Holden*] Parsons deceased, is in town and is to go on with them. it is surprising so little has been said on the subject of these folks, it has not been mentioned in any of the papers, and scarcely any body appears to have heard of it, the few who mention it say they were going to settle at Alexandria. It is one joust of fortune, and unlucky to begin with, but she will do as she pleases, and our allies ought to know it by this time, and set it down in the proper chapter, true colons will not be discouraged by these trifles.

We have had a very warm variable winter, and a cold backward spring; vegetation now looks promising, the wheat which many supposed was injured by the open winter has now put on a very favourable appearance and so far as I have heard has not been injured at all.

The season has brought on the influenza again which raged so much last fall, it is more mortal now than it was then; a dozen of our house are now down with it, but I believe we shall lose neither of them. The enclosed from your girl [*Ruth Baldwin Barlow*] will probably tell you she has had a short turn of it, but is almost well. I told you in my last the different opportunities all of them favourable for her voyage which presented themselves together. She has determined on the Ship London Capt. Woolsey,[3] her Greenfield [*Connecticut*] connections make him feel like a relation, that is a sufficient reason for a preference, and I believe the ship and the Captain are as good as any she could have chosen; she seems in high spirits on the occasion, and with good reason is pleased with the prospect of the tour.

The progress of our politicks has been very slow, the debate on the assumption of state debts has been almost infinite, the N. Carolina members turned the scale against it, but they are still trying to cook the dish so as to make it more palatable, and intend to bring it forward again: The report of the secretary, except that article, has been agreed to with but little alteration. The fourth and fifth alternatives which he proposed to offer to the creditors viz. annuities, tontine &c. were struck out. After agreeing to the principles of his report, bills were brought in to carry the same into effect; the one for funding the debt was reported yesterday. the additional revenue for the purpose is the law[4] annexed to his report, which the Comtee. reported to the house with scarcely an alteration. We shall go upon these two bills next week, what will be the fate of the business is not yet certain. I can scarcely believe our house will agree to so high an impost, after all that was said against high duties last summer. The whole summer was spent in fighting down the duties then proposed, and yet no one then thought of going to half the amount now proposed. The subject was just the same then and as fully in view of the mind at that time as now. There are so many under-tows in the business now it is hard keeping the reckoning or telling where we shall land. I am sure they take too strong hold, there is not sufficient occasion to warrant it, our folks are many of them surely in a fever. It is probable to me the senate will hold us back as they did last summer: many of them are for the assumption, it is to me probable that if the assumption is not made a part of the plan, they will put the whole business over till next session.

The Secy. has not said a word yet about the land business he has got your duplicate of the 9th of March, and I am told is much pleased with the arrival of these allies,[5] but his ministerial wisdom and reserve grows upon him, and he says little on any subject.

Our great and good man [*Washington*] has been unwell again this spring, I never saw him more emaciated, he has been out for a ride on Long Island for ten days, and since his return appears manifestly better.[6] If his health should not get confirmed soon, we must send him out to mount Vernon to farm it awhile, and let the Vice [*Adams*] manage here; his habits require so much exercise, and he is so fond of his plantation, that I have no doubt it would soon restore him. It is so important to us to keep him alive as long as he can live, that we must let him cruise as he pleases, if he will only live and let us know it. His name is always of vast importance, but any body can do the greater part of the work that is to be done at present, he has got us well launched in the new ship.

Yesterday I got your package of Revolutions de Paris [7] &c. it is all news. we have now and then newspaper extracts, but it does not form the ideas in the mind. I am feasting upon them, and will afterward let every body that can read french, have a cold cut.

There will now be frequent opportunities by the London ships, I will write as the spirit moves by each of them. I shall go up after the girl as soon as she lets me know she is ready, and shall see every thing properly fixed. Woolsey will sail in about three weeks. We shall probably adjourn by the beginning of June, I do not expect there will be another meeting during our reign.

yrs. affly. viva valeq[*ue*].[8]

AL, Baldwin Family Collection, CtY. Place to which addressed not indicated.

---

[1] This letter is endorsed as no. 25; no. 24 is actually dated 1 May, and is printed under that date, above.

[2] The "colons," or colonists, were the vanguard of French emigrés bound for the Scioto Company's settlement of Gallipolis, in present-day Ohio.

[3] *NYDA* advertised the *London*'s passage to London, sailing from New York under Master John Woolsey, in early May.

[4] Duties on Distilled Spirits Bill [HR-62].

[5] Another reference to the Gallipolis settlers, "allies" in Hamilton's campaign to promote immigration to the West, especially from abroad "rather than at the entire expence of the Atlantic population" (Hamilton to Arthur St. Clair, [19 May 1790], *PAH* 6:421–22).

[6] Washington escaped New York City and toured Long Island for exercise from 20 to 24 April, in order to complete his recovery from an apparent bout with influenza contracted in late March or early April. But on 9 May he developed a bad cold that deteriorated into a relapse, confining him to bed, near death, from 10 May until at least 20 May (*PGW* 5:394–96).

[7] *Révolutions de Paris* was a periodical published in Paris in 1789–90 by Antoine Tournon (1760?–1794), in support of the revolutionary movement.

[8] Farewell and be happy.

Thomas Hopkins to George Thatcher

I beg leave to lay before you a grievance which I labour under, in consequence of the Impost act, which subjects our produce removed from one state to another, in American bottoms, to pay duties.

Some months since, I shipped on board the sloop Portland packet of Portland, Joseph McLellan junr. Master, from hence, bound to Georgia, a quantity of foreign goods; on the outward bound passage he had occasion to touch at a foreign port, before his arrival at Georgia, in consequence of which said master had to enter said goods there, & pay the duties as coming from a foreign port, he then sold those articles & took in pay 400 lbs. of Indigo, and touched at a foreign port on his passage home; on his arrival here, I had to give bonds for the payment of 72.64 dollars foreign duties—thus I have *already* paid double duties on the *same* goods, & am under bonds to pay near half the value of the returns I have for them, the *third* time.[1]

This is the case I would lay before your honour, beg you will use your utmost influence, to procure an abatem[*ent*] of said duties, so far as the same has operated to the injury of others in similar circumstances.

ALS, Chamberlain Collection, MB. Written from Portland, Maine; addressed to "Josiah Thatcher," apparently confusing Thatcher with the state senator of that name; franked.

[1] Hamilton had recommended a solution to this problem in his report to the House on 23 April, which was referred to the committee that reported the Collection Act [HR-82]. Section 23 of that act, which resolved the problem, was added by the Senate on 26 or 27 July.

Benjamin Huntington to William Ellery

By Col. [*William*] Peck I Recd. your Letter of the 3d Instant with the Eight Dollars which you say you hope will be Satisfactory. But I assure you sir that I should be greatly dissatisfied with myself was I to yeld ~~so far~~ to [*lined out*] Avarice as to sell the pleasure I took in Serving you *for Eight Dollars*; Enough, Indeed to reward a mercinary Agent but I did not act in that Capacity. I did the service as a small act of kindness to an old friend and am happy to hear your money has all arrived safe and when you have any further commands which I can Execute with Equal facility I shall be happy to Serve you I have Returned the same Eight Dollars by Col. Peck which I hope will (with the bearer) arrive safe.

You are sensible I cannot give an official nor even an Authentic answer to your Question "Whether upon a failure of the application which the Federal towns might make to Congress to be put under the protection of the United

States, Congress would defend them against any Violence which might in Consequence of such application be offered to them by the Anties?" This is a Question which Congress alone could answer, but I have no doubt of their Doing it because I know there is a Number of that Body who would Justify such an Application and I believe very few who would Refuse Relief to their Friends the Feds when under an apprehension of an Enemy. I suppose the Anties would Charge such applicants with Treachery ~~and Rebellion~~, as should apply to be Received into the union which they would Construe as an Attempt at the Subversion of the Constitution & State of Rhode Island but they must be better assured of Success than their own Strength would Warrant, before they could with Prudence take measures to Punish the Federal Parts of the State as Traitors the Consequence of the measure might be very serious I Cannot Suppose it will be proper to Commence an Application of that Nature ~~but~~ unless at the Begining of a Session of Congress—at Present there is a Prospect of Rising in the Course of a few weeks and it might be fatal to the Feds if Congress should not be in Session during the whole Progress of the Business—We have so many Merciful men among us who chuse to wait to see the Result of the Next Session of your Convention,[1] that I am not Certain they will agree to any Coercive measures with the Little Sister untill they are convinced of her finale Obstinacy Much debate has been in the House the Present Week on account of the Petition of the Barron Stubend[2] Praying for further Pay and Allowance for his Sacrifices of Emoluments in his own Country when he left it to Come to America. ~~but~~ It has not yet been fully decided on as to the Sum he is to Receive but it is Certain that he is much in debt and a Small Sum will not Maintain him. he has been the Companion and Confidant of a King[3] & dwelt in the Shade of Royal Dignity so long that he cannot be persuaded to live with much Family Œconomy.

ALS, Benjamin Huntington Correspondence, 1772–1790, R-Ar. This letter, to be carried by William Peck, was not sent, according to Huntington's notation on the endorsement sheet. A postscript dated 12 May is calendared under that date, below.

---

[1] Rhode Island's ratification convention, recessed from 6 March, reconvened at Newport from 24–29 May.

[2] For the petition of Frederick William Steuben, see *DHFFC* 7:203–46.

[3] Steuben's preferment under Prussia's King Frederick the Great included service on the royal staff as aide de camp and in the suite of the Prussian ambassador to Russia (1761–63). There was some controversy surrounding his discharge from Frederick's army following its general demobilization in 1763; he left Prussia to serve as chamberlain of the Prince of Hohenzollern-Hechingen, 1764–77, and never returned (John McAuley Palmer, *General von Steuben* [New Haven, Conn., 1937; reprinted 1966], pp. 38–56).

Other Documents

Abigail Adams to Mary Cranch. ALS, Abigail Adams Letters, MWA. Addressed to Braintree, Massachusetts. For the full text, see *Abigail Adams*, p. 50. Dating is based on internal evidence.

Since her last, has diagnosed her family's illness as the influenza, from which she is mostly recovered; only Mr. Adams has avoided an attack of it; asks Richard Cranch to send a large mirror, for which "Richmond Hill" is ideally suited, "having all the Rooms Eleven foot high."

William Bradford to Elias Boudinot. ALS, William Linn Folder, Miscellaneous Manuscripts, NHi. Written from Philadelphia, "Friday Night"; carried by Hartley. Notation on the endorsement sheet, dated 22 November 1862, indicates it was sent by John W. Wallace to Frank Southwick, of Albany, New York, to illustrate a collection of autographs; a copy remains in the Wallace Papers, PHi.

"I am pleased to find you looking forward to the time that will give you a residence nearer to your Children," but "I would not wish it purchased by the sacrifice of any more essential interests"; commends Boudinot's "plan of life" for retiring from the bar; expects that the seat of government's removal to Philadelphia would allow them to enjoy Boudinot's company "a considerable part of the year," since "after the great objects of Govt. are arranged you would not be so engrossed as you are at present"; regards to (mother-in-law) Hannah Boudinot and (wife) Susan Bradford.

Stephen Goodhue to Benjamin Goodhue. FC:lbk, Goodhue Family Papers, MSaE. Written from Salem, Massachusetts.

"There appears to be Some defects in the laws respecting trade, under the incumbrances trade now labours under a person must be almost mad either to enter into it or persue it"; thinks nothing will quiet the minds of the people as much as assumption of the states' war debts; "as to the interest proposed I think the most of the people whould be Satisfied that are holders, I am Confident if it was higher the great body of the people whould murmur there are but few holders of Continental Securities here Compared to ~~the~~ State holders Continental Securities appear to be principally in the Middle States"; "I wish there was more Member's in Congress acquainted with Trade under the present imbarisments trade Cannot flourish"; wonders whether a land tax would not be more "politick," so merchants would not "bare all the burden" themselves; a great part of the "Inhabitants of the Trading Towns are in poverty & wretchedness for want of employment, which is not the case in the Country"; "give our love to Brother Sherman & Wife [*Rebecca Prescott*] if She be in New york tell them we are Comfortable"; Fanny and the children are well.

Dudley Hubbard to George Thatcher. ALS, Chamberlain Collection, MB. Written from Berwick, Maine; postmarked Portsmouth, New Hampshire, 17 May.

Is trying to amass a private library and asks Thatcher to procure certain book titles for him; pledges to pay the money back during the summer; no local news to report of interest to New York; Berwick's town meeting has just elected Thomas Cutts as state representative, "a striking Instance of the impudence & instability of the town."

Samuel Kennedy, Jr. to Elias Boudinot. ALS, Gilbert Collection, College of Physicians, Philadelphia. Place from which written not indicated.

His father, Boudinot's deceased friend, Dr. Samuel Kennedy, Sr. (1720–87), invested his landed estate worth £1500 for loan office securities; "would humbly Crave your friendship" in getting Congress to grant him four tracts of 640 acres each in the Northwest Territory, as compensation for that loan; asks "whether ever there will be an allowance made for continental Currency."

Richard Henry Lee to Thomas Lee Shippen. ALS, Shippen Family Papers, DLC. Place to which addressed not indicated. For the full text, see *Lee* 2:510–13.

"I have had a most dangerous attack of the Influenza in my Lungs & Head which has nearly destroyed me—I am much recovered, begin to ride out, but yet very unwell."

Theodore Sedgwick to Nathaniel Gorham. No copy known; acknowledged in Gorham to Sedgwick, 15 May.

Theodore Sedgwick to Benjamin Lincoln. No copy known; acknowledged in Lincoln to Sedgwick, 17 May.

Theodore Sedgwick to Mary Otis Lincoln. No copy known; acknowledged in Lincoln to Sedgwick, 18 May.

Theodore Sedgwick to Pamela Sedgwick. No copy known; acknowledged in Pamela to Theodore Sedgwick, 13 May.

Theodore Sedgwick to David Sewall. No copy known; mentioned in Sewall to Thatcher, 20 May.

Caleb Strong to David Sewall. No copy known; mentioned in Sewall to Thatcher, 20 May.

A Correspondent from New York. [Philadelphia] *Pennsylvania Mercury*, 8 May. The duties referred to were those agreed to by the House on 27 April; see *DHFFC* 4:548–50.

"Assures us, that the additional duties agreed to in the House of Representatives, are not intended to take effect for a considerable time."

[Massachusetts] *Salem Gazette*, 18 May; reprinted at Hartford, Connecticut.

"Mr. WADSWORTH, of Connecticut, in the late debate in Congress on the Assumption of the State Debts, made use of the following language: "I confess, Sir, I almost begin to despair of the Assumption of the State Debts—*and with that I shall despair of the National Government.*"

Report of the Commissioners for Settling Accounts between the United States and Individual States

The Articles of Confederation provided that "all charges of war and all other expences, that shall be incurred for the common defence or general welfare, and allowed by the United States . . . shall be defrayed out of a Common Treasury." What charges the United States would allow became the focus of the settlement from the beginning. By the time it was completed in 1793 the federal government had gradually moved away from requiring strict documentation, as it had under the Articles, to an equity based system.

The final Ordinance on the subject adopted by the Confederation Congress on 7 May 1787 provided for three commissioners who had complete authority to decide which expenses to accept and which to reject. In September 1788 it elected John Taylor Gilman of New Hampshire, William Irvine of Pennsylvania, and Abraham Baldwin of Georgia as the commissioners.[1] The latter was elected to the FFC and resigned from the Commission as soon as Washington took the oath of office as President; two days after Congress passed the Settlement of Accounts Act [HR-13] on 4 August 1789, Washington nominated John Kean of South Carolina to fill the vacancy, and the Senate approved Kean for the position on 7 August.

On 23 April 1790 the House adopted an order, moved by Madison, to the commissioners for settling accounts between the United States and individual states that they report "the amount of such claims of the States as have been offered to them since the time expired for receiving claims, specifying the principles on which the claims are founded, and distinguishing them from other claims."[2]

William Davies, in New York City as commissioner for settling the continental accounts of Virginia, had previously expressed his doubts about whether the report would fairly account for Virginia's claims. In a letter to Governor Beverley Randolph, written the day before Madison's motion, Davies predicted that state's irregular accounts would suffer from the commissioners' impatience to form some idea of the overall state of continental accounts, "especially as two of the gentlemen are strong assumptionists, while General Irvine, who has been uniformly favorable to the claims I have put in, leans wholly to the other side of the question. Every thing being more or less influenced by that object," Davies feared that Virginia's opposition to assumption could have "had some operation on the temper of two of the Commissioners."

Davies's fears were evidently realized when the commission's report was received, read, and tabled by the House on 30 April. It was signed by Gilman and Kean, but not Irvine, who was out of town. Not well received by House members, particularly southerners, the report was not ordered printed. Neither the cover letter nor the report, nor copies of them, exist in House Records—a rare, if not unique, occurrence for reports. Also uniquely, the House suppressed publication of the report in the press. Both documents were probably destroyed in the 1790s before House Clerk John Beckley had the executive branch reports transcribed into bound volumes. The report still existed in the third session when Beckley provided [*John Taylor*] Gilman with an authenticated copy on 10 February 1791. It ran six pages in length; pages three through six, discussing the accounts of the states south of Pennsylvania, are extant and were printed with the legislative history of the Funding Act in *DHFFC* 5:862–67. The contents of the report, except the portion on Virginia pages one and two, are summarized in notes made by James Madison, printed below.

The Virginia delegation took particular offense at the report and on 8 May Davies sent the delegation an analysis of the report's comments on Virginia's accounts. On 21 May Davies sent a copy of this letter to the governor of Virginia, along with an extract from the report and his own statement and explanation of the claims of Virginia against the United States for advances and supplies during the Revolutionary War.[3]

---

[1] *Purse*, chap. 10.
[2] *DHFFC* 3:377–80.
[3] For additional commentary on Virginia's reaction to the report, see *PJM* 13:190–92.

James Madison, Summary of the Report of the Commissioners for Settling Accounts, [30 April–20 June]

N. Hampshire. rate of depreciation settled by law after Mar. 18. 80. from 40 to 120 for 1. Actual rate do. in new emissions as 4 to 1.

Besides the State bounties, bounties by towns classes & individuals are charged the amount of £115,683.12–8 = Dollars 385,612

Massts. depreciation settled by law after Mar. 18. 80. from 40 to 160 for 1.

do. new emissions, as valued by State Commissioners. extends as far as 5 for 1.

Amt. of Penobscot claim £116,282.6—10 =

amount of bounties to 3169 men for 3 years or war at £128.9.6. lawful specie—£407,137.5.6

do. for bounty *&c.* for service in Canada & N.Y.—& in 76 for 3 years & during war } 243,773.19.10

Amt. of bounties for 3 Months, 5, 6, 9, do. and for deffit. & indefinite services dollars 1,688,965, ~~of which~~ of which 727,347 dollrs. for 3, 5 & 6 months—& in 80 & 81—extended at 40 for 1.

Mileage charged

R. Island— scale extends no farther than Continental—payts. after Mar. 18. 80 are rated at 40 for 1—New Emission depreciated as far as 8 for 1.

getting stock off Island charged—

enlistments for 3 months, [*lined out*] & [*lined out*] bounties charged—in 80, 81, & 82. and extended at 40 for 1.

Connecticut. scale extends no farther than continental—No New Emission issued—but a state currency—of which the rate was a contest between Commissioner. of U.S. & do. of State

For defence of sea coast—charged at Specie £312,485.18.4 =

loss of baggage charged—Committee service, charged—Bounties for short levies charged—

N. York— scale no farther than the continental—actual depreciation much higher—By laws of Feby. & Mar. 1781. rated

	at 75 for 1. & of May 1784 old money made receivable at 120 for 1.—New emission rated as specie.
	Bounty to Militia charged at Specie 597,170.30 dollars—extended @ 40 for 1.
N. Jersey.	scale extends as far as 150 for 1. & as far as it applies claims reduced by it. New Emission reduced by a scale extending to 3 for 1.
	518,469 67/90 ~~specie~~, charged in specie recd. for interest pd. in paper on debt of U.S. (this to be deducted in consequence of the funding bill which credits N.J. pro tanto)[1]
	Stoppages—(by U.S.) charged 45,000 drs.—quer. if actually pd. by State to individls.
Pennsyla.	Legal depreciation extended to 75 for 1. actual to 225 for 1.
	Actual do. of New Emission extends to 5 for 1. This much affect claim
	further claims intimated to a considerable amt.
	Naval armaments for bay & river charged at Dollrs. 449, 928.72, specie.
	Whole charge for recruiting army—only 282,154.3. & enlists. long. Compare this with this with like claim of Massts.
Delaware—	Scale of depreciation extends no farther than July 80—then @ 64 1/2 for 1.
	The whole recruiting charge only Dolrs. old emiss. 90,615 = to Specie and 7965.38
Maryld.	Scale extended to May 81. then 280 or 7 State dollrs. for 1
	total claim as made by State. Dolrs. speci 4,000,000 Drs. old emission 10,000,000
	Contl. dollrs. 812,985.74 = & Specie & Speci Drs. 40,244.88—form the whole charge for recruiting army—
N. Carola.	Rate of depreciation in 1781—725 for 1.
	No New Emission issued
	Claims considered by Genl. Board as vague &c. &c. & a mere conjectural statement
S. Carola.	little use of Cont. Money—no new Emission
	State scale extends to May 1780—then 52 for 1.
	further claims intimated
	Dolrs. speci 57,531.7 charged for equipping ships to procure cloathing—

	specie dolrs. 4,400,000 stated Apl. 27, 1790, pending assumption by Senators & Reps—as to be added to claims [*lined out*] reported by general board—(note 2,900,000 thereof, for fortifications, vessels sunk &c. armed vessels & for defence of Charleston & sea Coast).
Georgia.	few payments in Contl. money after Mar. 18. 1780 No New Emission State scale extends to June 1780, then 80 for 1.

Ms., hand of Madison, Madison Papers, DLC. These notes may have been made at the time he and William Davies were reviewing Virginia accounts in mid-June 1790. See Davies to Governor Beverley Randolph, 20 June, below.

[1] For so much.

William Davies to the Virginia Delegation, 8 May

The Commissioner for settling the Continental Account of the State of Virginia having seen the report of the two Commissioners of the General Board to the House of representatives begs leave to remark to the Senators and Representatives of Virginia,

That altho' it is not very evident how far the information called for by the House, rendered it necessary for the two Commissioners to go into a discussion of the conduct of the State Commissioner, yet candor would seem to have required that they should so far have possessed themselves of facts, as not to ascribe to him transactions with which he was wholly unconnected, being in no measure concerned with the public accounts till the period for presenting claims had expired, nor having ever had any communication with the district Commissioner [*Davies*], till within one month prior to his leaving the State with the papers. It is true that with an intention of defining more precisely the claims of Virginia, the State Commissioner after his arrival here did propose a recurrence to certain books and papers for that purpose. But when he found that the period limitted by the General board was too short for the object, that some of the public officers were unwilling to part with documents which had been officially committed to their charge, and that no general principle of ascertaining the depreciation had been adopted, so as to have universal operation thro' all the branches of the account, it became obvious that the measure was not only impracticable for want of time, but unnecessary, as little more certainty could be hoped for as to the amount of the just claims of Virginia than already appeared in the General statements which had been presented, which were formed on principles of as much accuracy as the occasion would admit, or as could have been expected after so extensive a destruction as that of near five years vouchers. The Commissioner of Virginia therefore, resumed the employment in which he had been engaged, of collecting evidence to supply the loss of vouchers, and of completing the statements from the books and papers which had been left by the district Commissioner. These statements have since been regularly delivered, partly to the Auditor of the Treasury [*Oliver Wolcott, Jr.*], and partly to the General board; tho' from the expression of the two Commissioners, "that no other or further specification was made," it should seem that this circumstance was wholly unknown to them: And indeed, from the terms in which they speak of the books opened by the late district Commissioner [*William Winder*], it would appear that they were not acquainted with the existence of two other books delivered at their office, in which the whole of the advances from the Treasury from the 13th of September 1775 to the 4 of January 1781 are distinctly stated and have actually undergone the examination of former Commissioners from Congress.

The remarks made by the two Commissioners on the vouchers they have specified, are so wholly incongruous to the modes and principles by which the State of Virginia settled with her citizens, that it is difficult to affix to them any definite meaning that can apply to the subject. It may be sufficient therefore to give some explanation of the nature of these vouchers. No. 396 was granted under a law which entitled the citizen furnishing the article to be paid in six months after date with interest and depreciation: This depreciation had no referrence to the scale, as the two Commissioners seem to suppose, for that was not formed till more than 12 months afterwards, but was ascertained at the commencement of every quarter by the grand jury of the General court, making the price of Tobacco the standard. No. 431 & 437 were given under laws which allowed no depreciation, but entitled the holder to prompt payment at the Treasury or authorised him to pay the voucher to the collector in discharge of an equal amount of his tax at the rates fixed in the laws: And as there is nothing in either of these vouchers which respects or in any degree militates with the scale of depreciation, it is difficult to discover for what purpose they are introduced. No. 680, 685, 741 & 745 are all of them for horses impressed under special restrictions, and the depreciation on the specie value ascertained from time to time by temporary regulations similar to what has been before mentioned. Everyone of these vouchers as well as those which have been before specified were given to the citizens and settled by the State, some time before any scale of depreciation was established and while no other payments but paper were made at the Treasury. This circumstance will at once account to the two Commissioners why the scale could not govern in the settlement with the individuals, as well as why specie certificates were turned into Continental money, "the necessity of which" to them it seems, "was not apparent." After all, it is humbly conceived that the principles and modes by which the State adjusted the claims of her citizens are not in ordinary cases so properly the objects for the enquiries of the General board, as the proofs, that these claims were actually adjusted and assumed.

That it will "be necessary to consider from whence the amount charged arises, and the rate by which depreciated paper has been reduced to specie, as it will materially affect the real specie value of the claims," are truths not likely to be denied; and if the introduction of Voucher No. 445 was only to shew the powers of calculation and to prove that an article charged at a depreciation of 40 for 1 is rated fifteen times as high as at 600 for 1. it is probable the House will not think the information either new or very important. If however it is meant to insinuate that exorbitant prices were allowed to the citizens, the original letters, ready to be produced from the commanding Generals of the southern troops, complaining of the restrictions imposed by the government of Virginia on this head, will evince the caution and even parsimony of the State: And if we consider that the temporary rates of depreciation by which these claims were adjusted, were almost always fixed some time before the settlements were made, it will be evident that the payments to the citizens, and of consequence the charges against the Union, must in like manner in all these cases be invariably below the appraised value of the articles furnished. But if it is meant that the claims are vague and indefinite for want of reduction by some scale, it may be sufficient to reply that they are stated as they were actually settled with the individuals, neither claiming 40 for 1 when the State settled at less, nor relinquishing the claim if it should be allowed to others.

Upon the whole, if the two Commissioners in framing their report, had it in contemplation to criminate the conduct of the Commissioner of Virginia, it may be doubted whether the occasion was proper, or the object pertinent to the views of the House: Or if their design was to discredit the accounts of Virginia, the vouchers do not appear to have been well chosen for the purpose, nor duly understood by them; neither is it improbable that at least an equal number of doubtful charges might have been selected with equal ease from the accounts of any other State. More enquiry would have afforded the two Commissioners better information, and would probably have induced them to have avoided "a discussion," which they profess to have been "highly disagreeable to them," and which the concurrent sense of the House has pronounced to be unfit for the public eye.

Copy, signed by Davies, Executive Papers, Vi. This copy was enclosed in Davies to Governor Beverley Randolph, 21 May, below. An additional manuscript version, copied for inclusion in Governor Randolph's letter to Washington, 4 August, is in Miscellaneous Letters, Miscellaneous Correspondence, State Department Records, Record Group 59, DNA.

William Davies to Governor Beverley Randolph, 21 May

In consequence of an order of the House of Representatives that the Commissioners of the General board should report the amount of the claims of the several States, Mr. [*John Taylor*] Gilman & Mr. [*John*] Kean, Genl. [*William*] Irvine being absent, tho't proper to report No. 1. which Mr. Madison calls a libel on the State. North Carolina and Georgia are also stigmatized, but their vengeance seems more particularly directed at Virginia. How far their own speculations may have influenced their conduct, cannot be ascertained, but their zeal for the assumption is well known. The House were so little pleased with the report, that they would ~~neither~~ not suffer it to be read and ~~several members~~ on the request of Mr. Fitzsimmons, with the general assent of the members, the printers & short hand writers were desired not to publish it. I was at that time confined to my bed with sickness, but as soon as I was able I delivered to the Senators & Representatives the remarks No. 2, a copy of which I also furnished the General board. I have at the request of the Representatives made a Statement of the claims of Virginia, with explanatory remarks, No. 3. There is, however, no certainty in the business, as there has been no system observed in forming the accounts since Mr. [*Leighton*] Wood was employed in it. Indeed, the change of Agents from time to time has of itself proved injurious, and I cannot now find any of the treasury settlements prior to the establishment of the board of Auditors, tho' by letters of Mr. Wood to different persons now in my possession, it is evident he has had them long since ~~the destruction~~ Arnold's invasion.[1] Having in vain searched for them when in Virginia, and made applications respecting them to Mr. Wood without success, I have no expectation of procuring them, unless possibly Mr. Wood & Mr. Smith by conferring together may be able to determine where they are—I have been for some time past engaged in stating the specifics, as by my last letter I had the honor to inform you. The difficulty of connecting vouchers & accounts which have been wholly dissorted, is very ~~tiresome~~ considerable, every person who has had the handling of them, having changed the numbers and deranged them so as to answer their purposes according to the objects in view at the time. I have been also engaged in extracting from the account of payments at the Treasury, all the charges for the army, navy or militia: this is nearly compleated; but the specifics, will take some time yet to finish them—I have enclosed copies of the vouchers to which the two Commissioners refer in their report; the indorsements in red ink I have had made for their better explanation to you. The papers marked B to which the two Commissioners refer, I have not been able to get, but suppose they mean the general accounts presented to Mr. [*William?*] Winder, one of which together with the protest they allude to, were presented to your Excellency at the time of the transaction—As there is a bill now before the House with respect to a continuance of the General board, it will be necessary the papers from Williams's & [*Samuel*] Eskridge's districts should come forward as soon as they are in readiness; a part will be better than none.

Some time ago, I think it was in March, I requested £20 on account of contingencies of office, payable to Stott & Donaldson. My order in their favor does not appear to have come to hand, and I have been put to some little inconvenience on account of it. I will thank your Excellency to honor my draft in their favor to that amount, when presented.

Not knowing of the present opportunity till an hour ago, I have written in much haste which I hope your Excellency will excuse, being desirous to save the postage of so large a packet.

[*Enclosure No. 1*]

The Claims of Virginia

On this head the board feel themselves much at a loss to say any thing satisfactory, because they have not received from the district Commissioner any abstract that will give a precise idea of what the State does claim, nor can they obtain from the Agents of the State of Virginia a specification of her claims in any other than general terms and those so couched as to conclude little or nothing, nor can the Commissioner of Army accounts give any statement from the papers in his Office, nor the Auditor from the papers in his office relative to specific supplies—Thus situated the Board feel themselves compelled to go into a discussion highly disagreeable to them.

In some measure to comply with the order of the house it will be necessary to make a statement of facts, and a few observations which may enable the house to form some opinion of the claims of this State.

It appears that numerous papers were exhibited to the district Commissioner by the Agents of Virginia without being accompanied by any specification of their amount or purport, or without being arranged or methodized as the Ordinance of Congress contemplated—these the district Commissioner proceeded to arrange under a variety of heads in two folio Volumes now in this office, in order as the board conceive to have a more perfect idea of what the claims of the State were. The time limited by the act of Congress for receiving claims being nearly expired, a difference of opinion arose between the district Commissioner and the State Agents about the claims, the nature of which difference of opinion as stated by the Agents of Virginia, the house will see from the protest marked A, which is all the evidence the board has upon the subject; the Agents then withdrew many books and papers, and exhibited certain papers which they call the claims of the State, copies whereof accompany this report marked B but which are stated so generally, and appear to have been formed so much from conjecture that the board cannot say what their amount is, or in what kind of Money they are made. The Agent of Virginia then came to this place and on the 5th. of May 1789 applied to the board for their interposition so that the papers might be received, at the same time requesting that no precise time for the delivery of the papers might be fixed or if a time was specified that it might be so long as to enable the State to send on the papers without inconvenience—Thus the matter was untill the month of November last, when it was represented by the Agent of Virginia, that no precise statement of the claims of the State could be made without having the unlimitted use of the books and papers which had been brought on by the district Commissioner—finally on a specification of certain books and papers by the Agent of Virginia it was agreed that he should have the books and papers requested, but they together with all the books and papers which had been tendered in due time to the district Commissioner were to be returned (without the addition of any new claim) on the first of February last, and if possible with a precise statement of the claim of Virginia—when this time arrived further time was again requested, but the board were of opinion that they were not authorised to grant the request, on which the books and papers were delivered into this office, but no further or other specification than those papers which have been before mentioned was made—it must also be observed that the Agent never availed himself of the books and papers which he had requested the use of, which had been granted with a view of having an exact statement of the claim of the State exhibited.

In the books mentioned before to have been opened by the district Commissioner for the arrangement of the Accounts of this State, under the heads of specifics, Cavalry, State Cavalry, State Hospital, provisions, Clothing, forage and a great number of other heads, we find entered, claims to the amount of 23,074,188 2/90 Dollars in paper money, and 537,435 25/90 Dollars in specie, in several instances the district Commissioner has classed these claims under the heads of Unsupported, Unascertain'd, Irregular &c. This amount cannot be viewed as the whole claim, because no part of the States expenditures before 1780 is entered in these books.

The depreciation in this State was fixed by Law in December 1781 at 1000 for 1. It will appear from the documents herewith transmitted No. 396—431—445—437—448—680—685 & 741, that some articles have been charged at 600 for 1—it will also appear that the depreciation established by Act of Assembly was not so great at the time the voucher is dated as it is charged at in these books, as for instance, the depreciation in June 1781 by law is 250 for 1, voucher 448 is given in that month for a sum in specie which is charged at 600 for 1—if it should be said that this is occasioned by the money not being paid when the certificates were given, and that an intermediate depreciation had taken place, then it will appear necessary that the receipt of the Individual should be produced to ascertain the precise time when the payment was made, not only to fix the value of the money, but to determine the period when interest is to commence in favour of the State. The necessity of turning specie certificates ~~into~~ into Continental money is not apparent.

The Agents of Virginia, declare in their protest, page 10th, "that the general accounts formed as before recited, are lodged with him (the district Commissioner) and are upon every principle of justice claimed as a sufficient, and under the circumstances before mentioned, a proper specification on the part of the State of the general amount of her advances in behalf of the United States"—if by this is meant that the figures on those papers which are marked B, represent specie sums, it will then be necessary to consider from whence they arise, and if from depreciated paper, the rate by which they have been reduced to specie will claim attention as it will materially affect the real specie value of their claim, this will more fully appear if any given sum is taken into consideration for instance Voucher No. 445 is for 400,000 Dollars if the Continental scale is used in reducting this sum (the lowest rate being 40 for 1) the value then would appear to be 10,000 Dollars, whereas the actual rate of depreciation being 600 for 1 the sum ought to be no more than 666 2/3 dollars and which is the appraised value of the horse mentioned in this voucher; from this instance the house will perceive, that as the rate of depreciation by which any sum is reduced is less than the real rate of depreciation, so is the claim increased beyond its real specie value and in the instance above stated (if that was the rate of depreciation) the claim would be increased fifteen times the real amount in specie.

With respect to the state of the evidence in support of these claims, the protest of the Agents goes so fully into that matter as to render it unnecessary to say any thing upon the subject.

(Here follow remarks on the accounts of North Carolina, South Carolina & Georgia, the report then proceeds.)

The House will please to distinguish between the claims immediately before this board, and those which are in the Office of Army accounts because the observations which accompany the foregoing statements are intended to apply to those claims only which are in this office.

They will also please to observe that where old emission money was paid after the 18th. of March 1780 on account of the army or militia, the Commissioner of Army accounts has estimated it at the rate of 40 for 1. This may materially affect the real Specie value of the Claims.

[*Enclosure No. 2*]

William Davies to the Virginia Delegation

[*See the preceding letter of 8 May in this section.*]

[*Enclosure No. 3*]

Statement of the Claims of the Commonwealth of Virginia against the United States for Advances and supplies on Account of the late War. Viz.

		£—	—	—
Amount of payments made at the Treasury from April 19th. 1775 to Jany. 1777		459,844	16	5
"	" from Jany. 1777 to Sepr. 1st. following	341,929	15	8
"	" from Sepr. 1777 to 31st. Decr. 1780 reduced by the State Scale	575,837	10	6
"	Specifics supply'd under Requisitions of 25th. feby. & 4th. Novr. 1780	757,497	3	9
"	Warrants granted by the Auditors of Accounts subsequent to January 1st. 1781, which have been sunk by Taxes or otherwise discharged; the paper payments reduced by the State Scale	456,446	14	11
"	Bounties paid by Counties and Classes, under Recruiting Acts of Spring 1779, 1780 & 1782—and fall of 1780	158,673	5	7
"	Certificates issued to Officers and Soldiers for Pay and Depreciation of Pay	986,830	7	6
"	" " for Militia services as ℔ Pay Rolls	231,670	17	8
"	Lead supplyed from the Mines	15,000	"	"
"	for Waggons and Teams, and drivers furnd. by County's, and Clothing by classes, under Act of Fall 1780	21,000	"	"
"	Paper money on Account of Old Emission Requisns. of Congress, Paid in 1785 £ 615,985.16. " " 1786 1,319,863. 8.			
"	Acres of Land—as ℔ Account of Bounties			
"	of Interest on the several sums above			
	Virga. Curr[*enc*]y. £			

The above exclusive of Interest—Land—and payments in Paper Money, Amounts to £4,004,730.12. —Or 13,349,102. Dollars.

ALS with Ms. enclosures, Executive Papers, Vi. Signed by William Davies; place to which addressed not indicated. Additional manuscript versions of most of this letter and all enclosures were copied for inclusion in Governor Randolph's letter to Washington, 4 August, and are in Miscellaneous Letters, Miscellaneous Correspondence, State Department Records, Record Group 59, DNA. For the text of the Randolph letter, see *PGW* 6:185.

[1] In December 1780 Brigadier General Benedict Arnold undertook his first campaign following his defection to the British, when he led a raid of 1200 troops and Loyalists up the James River as far as the Virginia capital of Richmond, which they burned after occupying it from 5 to 7 January 1781.

SUNDAY, 9 MAY 1790

Fine (Johnson)

Jeremiah Hill to George Thatcher

Sunday being a day set apart for relaxation to the mind as well as the body, to meditate upon, and investigate such things as the Cares of the Week discard. I therefore dedicate ~~of~~ a few Hours to the above purpose and as a theme to these meditations I have made choice of an Extract of a letter from West-Jersey dated April 19—printed in the Independent Chronicle May 6. 1790. being the 22d. Vol. No. 1123. Page 3d & column 2.[1]

"A CURIOUS INFANT" &c.

In the first place it is necessary to explain the Text which I shall do as briefly as possible. antiently it was mightily in fashion to speak in Parables, and it is still in fashion to speak figuratively, the Reader, being at liberty to put such an Interpretation upon it as to him seems fit *A curious Infant*, this is figurative of the Constitution of the United States. your Ideas will naturally point out the fitness of the Comparison. it being in the *neighborhood of West Jersey* will of course apply to the City of New York,[2] *Teeth of considerable Length* will very aptly represent the large Powers of Congress. *the upper & lower Gums* the two Branches of the legislature, *the Mother who could not endure the pain of suckling it*, the Anxiety of the People *the drawing the Teeth or filing of them*, the Various Propositions by the Uneasy for *Shaysing*[3] the Government or introducting a Catologue of *Amendments* but the more thoughtful concluding this Operation too *severe* & concluding still *to nourish the Infant with the Milk of Cattle* must of course mean that the more thoughtful are for changing the Legislature after the expiration of their present two Years upon the next Election & let the old ones return to live on the *fat of the Land*.

Having gone thro' the explanitory part of the Text Time would fail me to speak of Adam, of Nimrod, of Abraham, of Melchisadeck, of Jethro, of Moses of Joshua, of Samuel, of Saul, of David, of Solomon, of Jeroboam, of Jehu, of Gideon, of Nebuchadnezer, of Cæsar Augustus, of Herod, of Pilate or of Felix but shall leave you at present to reflect on what has been said and make the improvment at a *more convenient Season*.

I am, my dear Sir, without Partiality & without Hyporcricy
Your Friend.

N. B. Aunt Hooper gave me some of the leading thoughts or my pericranium would never have ran wild at this rate—Parson [*Nathaniel*] Webster is sick to day and cant preach. quid tum?[4] why stay at home & write.

ALS, Chamberlain Collection, MB. Written from Biddeford, Maine; postmarked Portsmouth, New Hampshire, 11 [?] May.

[1] Nature does, undoubtedly, at times commit, what to us appears to be mistakes, in her animal as well as vegitable economy. A Child was lately born in this neighbourhood, with teeth of considerable length, both in its upper and lower gums. As the mother could not endure the pain of suckling it, proposals were made to have the whole set of teeth drawn; others imagined that filing them down might answer the purpose. Neither of these operations, however, have been carried into execution, as being thought rather too cruel as well as too severe, for an infant of so tender an age to undergo. The parents have concluded to let these premature teeth remain and if possible, nourish the infant with the milk of cattle.

[2] Hill would have more appropriately interpreted this as Philadelphia, the birthplace of the Constitution as well as the commercial and cultural center of West Jersey.

[3] A reference to Shays' Rebellion.

[4] What now?

Samuel Johnston to James Iredell

***

The Act for extending the Courts to North Carolina [*North Carolina Judiciary Bill S-10*] is still before the House of Representatives, I am told they have made some alterations but have not heard in what particulars, one however I am told is to have one of the Circuit Courts held at Salisbury instead of Hillsborough, as it stood when it went from the Senate, as soon as it passes I will send you a Copy of it, I scarcely think you will receive Official Notice of it in time to hold a Court in North Carolina this Circuit.

Business goes on pretty smoothly since the Question of Assuming the State debts has been laid aside and they are busily engaged in finding ways & means for establishing Funds, I fear they will find it difficult to accomodate this business so as to avoid Censure & Murmuring from some quarter or other.

I am not much pleased with the House I have taken for you nor yet with my own, but as they are only taken for one year, we may suit ourselves better hereafter, I am getting one of the Houses in order to receive our Families and shall look for them with great anxiety after the expiration of this Week.

I find it very expensive being here, tho I observe as much Economy as I can consistently, I ~~live at the~~ have lived at the rate of £400 ℔ Annum. for myself & Servant, tho I have not expended more than £10 for Cloaths for both of us in the time. I sincerely wish you an agreeable Journey and that we may see you here in good health as soon as you can make it convenient.

ALS, Iredell Papers, NcD. Place to which addressed not indicated. The omitted text relates to family news.

Other Documents

William Samuel Johnson to Robert Charles Johnson. ALS, Johnson Papers, NNC. Place to which addressed not indicated; franked. Written at 4 P.M.

Wife (Anne Beach Johnson) and daughter (Charity) arrived just that minute by boat as far as Kip's Bay and overland thereafter; all are well, although "Half the Town are ill with the Influenza, and many have died"; does not know what advice to give regarding public securities; thinks "they will soon be better, tho' the House of Representatives proceed heavily, & we almost despair of the Assumption of the State Debts. But I leave it to you to Bargain ~~of~~ as you can."

William North to Benjamin Walker. ALS, Smith Collection, NjMoHP. Written from Duanesburgh, New York. (Page married thirty year old Margaret Lowther on 27 March. To tickle a trout is to beguile it into being caught by the naked hand. The phrase appeared in William Wycherley's [1640–1716] play, "Love in A Wood, or St. James's Park.")

"What a fine fellow to tickle a trout that old lecher Page is?"

William Short to Thomas Jefferson. ALS, Jefferson Papers, DLC. Written from Paris. For the full text, see *PTJ* 16:417–19.

The king of France is to write to the king of England to coordinate the establishment of a uniform standard of weights and measures; regarding Short's own desire to succeed Jefferson at Paris, hopes Madison is too indispensable at New York to take the post.

George Thatcher to Sarah Thatcher. ALS, Thatcher Family Papers, MHi. Place to which addressed not indicated.

Asks if a bible, left at Boston for rebinding, has been returned home; acknowledges her letter of 25–28 April, and will procure the requested fabrics; King's wife (Mary Alsop) was delivered of a daughter a few days earlier, and all is well; "The Influenza has been & still is prevelent in this City—I have had a light touch of it, but am recovered—and in pretty good health."

Mary Thatcher to George Thatcher. ALS, Chamberlain Collection, MB. Written from Boston; franked; postmarked.

Seeks Thatcher's assistance in determining how David Kirkpatrick of York, Pennsylvania, disposed of his estate.

Jeremiah Wadsworth to John Chaloner. No copy known; acknowledged in Chaloner to Wadsworth, 16 May.

Jeremiah Wadsworth to Harriet Wadsworth. ALS, Wadsworth Papers, CtHi. Addressed to Hartford, Connecticut; franked; postmarked.

Returned from Philadelphia on 7 May, leaving "uncle John" (Trumbull) there; Laurance and wife Elizabeth (McDougall Laurance) are both sick with influenza, the latter "confined & in ~~a~~ some danger"; "Jack" may accompany Wadsworth home in May, "if I can come"; Dr. (Samuel or John) Bard says son Daniel's case is "easy & certain"; friends in Philadelphia urge Harriet to visit; Daniel is "very much liked" by Mary White Morris and family.

William Samuel Johnson, Diary. Johnson Papers, CtHi.

"St. Pauls. Mrs. Johnson arrivd."

Monday, 10 May 1790

Fine (Johnson)

Stephen Choate to Benjamin Goodhue

I receivd. your kind favours of the 14 & 24 of april Last, am Sorry to hear you Complain of depression of Spirit. though I can easely Conceive your Cituation to be truly. exerciseing indeed. but Steady Perseverence in a Good Cause, often Produces important Consequences beyound our expectations. I acknowledge I have been troubled, in the same manner, for a Considerable time passed, the unhappy devisions in Congress, have tended, much to Lessen the Confidence, of the People at larg in that important Body, and Some from whom better things might be expected, are exceeding imprudent, in their remarks on the doings of the General Government. we have enemies enough, without, our friends Joining them—on hearing that, the Question of assumption was lost. I found my Self much dejected, for before that Period I was fully convinced, of the absolute necessity of the measure, and I Still entertain a hope that things will take a more favourable turn by & by; at any rate I hope Congress will not adjourn and Leave matters in their present Situation relative to Public Credit. if they should I fear fatal Consequences will follow—a Strange indiferency has taken hold of the minds of many, on whom we have heretofore had dependance for the Support of Goverment. this gives great oppertunity for the buissy [*busy*] tribe to prosecute their hurtfull scheems to advantage—I have Long wished for a Settled State of Government. wheither I shall Live to see the day or not. is uncertain— but this I am sure of, that, I most ardiently Desire that, this People, whose prosperity, has for many years, been an object, which has engrossed most attention, may not be prevented by their own folley. the objection, against Providing Sufficient funds for the establishing public Credit, founded in the want of ability—appears to me altogeather absurd, especially, while we observe the Prodidgous Sums of money that have been Spent wantonly by our people, Since the peace. I dont expect things will go well with this Nation, unless we adhear to the Principls of Justice and Righteousness, Please to excuse my Delay in writing. and rest assured that it is not oweing to forgetfullness, or want of Regard. but partly owing to my not haveing any thing of importance to Communicate, and partly, for want of time, the last mentioned reson may seem strange, but so it has happened, that, for several months passed, I have been exceedingly crouded with buissiness, of one kind or other, perhaps as much so as in any Part of my Life. I supose you have been informed befor this time, that, the same Gentleman [*Governor John Hancock*] that filled the Chair the Last year, is Chosen again, and that, Mr. [*Samuel*] Adams is elected Liet. Governer. I believe it is not Certainly known abroad as yet, who are elected Senators for our County, the anties, I Believe, did pretty much as they Pleased, in the affair of elections, as but few others, paid much attention to the Subject. however it is Reported that four that were in the Last year are Chosen again, the Truth perhaps will be known in a few days—Please to Continue your favours, as they are Very Grateful to me.

ALS, Letters to Goodhue, NNS. Written from Ipswich, Massachusetts.

Abiel Foster to William Plumer

My Ideas of the Assumption of the State Debts, I have already forwarded to some of my friends in New Hampshire, and as soon as I can find time to commit them once more to Paper, I shall transmit them for your consideration.

Although your opinion, relative to funding the the other debts of the United States, nearly corresponds with the Opinions of certain Gentlemen here, who have passed for great Characters; yet I confess myself unable to think, either with them, or with you, on that interesting subject. You will please Sir to remember, that all the debts which it is proposed to fund, have already undergone a liquidation by a Scale—by a Scale, not the most favorable to the public Creditors, and have been reduced to the lowest Specie value—The evidences have been given, that the sums specified therein, were due, and payable to the creditors, or bearer in Silver or Gold—And Government has, in these cases, received a full, and perhaps, in some instances, more than an equivalent—No sufficient reason, can therefore be assigned, why the Creditors should submit to a reliquidation of their claims—an attempt to compel them to such reliquidation, would, as I conceive, not only be in it self, highly unjust; but would fix on the Goverment a Stigma, which would destroy all future confidence in its promises & engagements. However from the train of your reasoning, I am induced to believe the foregoing, is not precisely your Idea of the matter in question: your wish seems to be rather, that a discrimination should take place between the original holders, and those who have purchased below the nominal Value—this I infer from what is stated in your Letter of the injustice of calling on the Soldier, who sold at two Shillings & six pence on the pound, to pay the present holder twenty shillings on the pound: But it may be asked, where is the injustice in this case? Was not this the understanding between the parties at the time of the contract? Did not the seller obtain the market price? and did he not chuse to take this, rather than run the risque of keeping his security longer? And was there no hazzard to the purchaser, of loosing the whole of the purchase Money? It perhaps, depended on nothing less, than the change of the *then* Goverment, whither he would ever receive any thing for the securities he bought; and this you are sensible must have been a great contingency.

It may be further observed, that many of the Officers and Soldiers of the late Army, sold their certificates at six shillings & eight pence on the pound; and afterwards purchased a like sum, from the first purchasers, at two shillings & six pence on the pound, making to themselves the *difference,* in clere profit by the transfer & repurchase; And if Goverment were to interfere, in the cases which are so circumstanced, it may be a serious question, whether it will do more justice, or injustice by such interference—I beg leave to state another case relating to the subject which falls within the compass of my knowlege—Many of the Towns in New Hampshire, in the course of the late War hired their Soldiers, giving them from one, to two hundred Dollars for every Year they served in the Army, and took Orders to draw, to their own use, the Wages of those Soldiers—they now hold the same, which are due from the United States to those towns—And as those towns, have long since, fully compensated the Soldiers for their services; would it be right in the general Goverment to reduce the Value of those certificates in the hands of the towns ~~who~~ which have paid so dearly for them? I presume not. And if it be right, that Goverment should make a discrimination in the public Debt, in cases of ~~tra~~ transfer; it must have an equal right to interpose in all the bargains of individuals, and where it may so happen, that a Citizen has sold property on credit, when it was low, that the purchaser should be compelled to pay a larger sum, when from a change of circumstances, the same property will bring more; and yet I believe it has been the general Opinion, that Goverment has no just right of interference in this case.

You state however, that the experiment hath been tried in respect to the old Money—that has been liquidated by a Scale—In answer to this, I observe, that all sums which have been lent to the Goverment, to carry on the War, in Paper Money have been reduced by the Scale to the Specie Value—The sums proposed to be funded are not the nominal sums lent, but the value of those sums liquidated to specie, compaired by the Scale, at the time the Money was furnished. In blending the existing liquidated debt, of the United States, with the old Continental Money, it appears to me, you have United things, in their nature, quite different—The present liquidated Debt, is the specie Value of services rendered, or supplies furnished, by individuals to Goverment; But in the cases you state of the old money, the holders have furnished one Bushel of Wheat for twenty paper Dollars, in some instances, and in other instances, but one bushel of Wheat for one hundred & twenty of those Dollars—And it will not be contended, that he who holds one hundred & twenty Dollars of the old Money, for which he has furnished only one Bushel of Wheat, is equally intitled to have that number of hard Dollars funded, as he who hath furnished one hundred and twenty hard Dollars, or another, who hath furnished Paper Money sufficient to purchase one hundred and twenty Bushels of Wheat—These are shortly, my Ideas of funding the public Debt—a subject very intricate, and which requires great investigation.

I believe it will not be an easy matter to make a bad choice of President out of the three persons you mention as Candidates[1]—for my own part, I have an high opinion of the integrity, and abilities of each of the Gentlemen, and shall acquiess, in which ever of them, my fellow Citizens, or the legislature may fix upon.

I hope the business of this Session will be compleated, & ~~and~~ adjourment take place early in June—The nature & difficulty of the subjects to be considered, and the variant Opinions which have taken place amongst the Members have much delay'd the progress of Congress: I hope however, that the last of the Session will give greater dispatch to business.

I am happy to find you are elected into the Legislature of New Hampshire, and wish it may be in my power to see you at the June Session in Concord.

ALS, Plumer Collection, New Hampshire State Library, Concord. Place to which addressed not indicated.

[1] Josiah Bartlett, John Pickering, Joshua Wentworth, and Nathaniel Peabody were the leading candidates in New Hampshire's gubernatorial election, which Bartlett won on 5 June.

James Madison, Abstract of Duties

Treasy. Dept. May 10. 1790 A. H. [*from Alexander Hamilton?*]
Abstract of duties which have accrued on the Tonnage of Foreign & Domestic Vessels from Sepr. 1 to Decr. 31. 1789

States	Foreign Tonnage Dolrs. Cents	American do.	Total
N.H.	469.50	339.30	808.80
Massts.	4829.37½	3855.60	8684.97½
Connect.	618.8	722.47½	1340.55½
N. York	8739.87½	1496.66½	10,236.54
N. Jersey	83.50	224.31	307.81
Penna.	11,587.64	1515.6	13,102.70
Delaware	603	122.96	726.96
Maryland	4,994.5½	1723.88½	6722.94
Virginia	11,210.93½	1423.30½	12,634.24
S. Carolina	4,630.59	453.84	5,064.43
Georgia	2600.17	126.65	2726.82
	50,366.72	11,990.5	62,356.77

	Foreign	American	
~~2/50,366~~			
~~25,183~~	50,366.72	11,990	3996
	2	16 2/3	
	100,733.44	71,940	
		119,90	
		7992	
		199,832	

Ms., Madison Papers, DLC, hand of Madison. These notes were probably used in preparation for Madison's lengthy speeches of 13 and 14 May in favor of discriminatory tonnage duties; see *DHFFC* 13:1273–1333.

Andrew Moore to James Breckinridge

I have just receivd your Letter and agreeably to your request have inclosd a Copy of the Secretarys report [*on public credit*]—I sent a Copy On its first Publication to Capt. [*Henry*] Bowyer—I am Surprizd He did not receive it—As the others which Accompd. it Arrivd safe at Staunton Mr. Brown receivd a Letter from you a few days ago—I then Wrote you a full state of the Business before us—It will be unnecessary now to repeat it—A [*Funding*] Bill is now before us Nearly as it stands in the Inclosd report ~~Except That It~~ The first Second & third funding Propositions have been agreed to And a Bill is now before us in Conformaty to them—The two latter have been amended by changing the rate at Which The Principle may be redeemd to Six dollars per Annum Including both Principal & Interest—The Proposition for Assuming the State debts has been rejected—It will again be brought forward—But what its fate will be is uncertain—I intend offering at the next Election And shall be obligd to Such of my friends as think me Worthy their Trust for their Interest—In Order to avail myself of the Days post I must Close this—I will Write to you again in the Course of the Week.

ALS, Rockbridge Historical Society Collection, ViLxW. Addressed to Botetourt County, Virginia.

Louis Guillaume Otto to Comte de Montmorin

***

The Representatives from North Carolina who were opposed to Congress's assumption of the debts of the individual states, Sir, have made so much commotion that they succeeded in winning a majority against that motion, so that the individual state legislatures will continue as before in raising taxes and will consequently retain an important branch of sovereignty that it is in the interest of Congress to assume exclusively to itself. The friends of this consolidation have not yet, however, given up hope of succeeding on a third attempt. While waiting, time passes. Five months already have slipped by without Congress being able to definitively act on the public debt, the creditors of the government are getting restless, some of them accuse members of that assembly of prolonging debates just to enjoy the use of their pay which is six dollars per day. They are in session three hours at a stretch at the most and do not seem eager to satisfy the impatience of the public who begin to be tired. The diligence of the French National Assembly is often pointed out to them as an example, without effect.

As for the militia plan, which I spoke about in Dispatch No. 16 [*20 January*], Congress embraced public opinion in leaving it entirely aside. Constant in its principles of moderation and restraint, Congress has contented itself with ordering the raising of 1216 men, including officers as well as soldiers, who will be enough to protect the border for this year.

Copy, in French, Henry Adams Transcripts, DLC. Received 2 July. Otto's letters included in *DHFFC* were usually written over the course of days, and even weeks, following the day they were begun.

Josiah Parker to George Washington

In consequence of the resignation of Mr. [*George*] Savage Collector at Cherrystone [*Virginia*], I take the liberty to recommend Mr. Nathaniel Wilkins to fill his vacancy. Mr. Wilkins is Gentleman of good Character & I know he is qualified for the appointment & lives near the port. whether it will be worth his acceptance or not I am not to determine haveing no request from him or any other for the appointment.

ALS, Washington Papers, DLC.

Samuel Phillips, Jr. to Benjamin Goodhue

***

We are very anxious respecting our national concerns; Those who were opposed to the Constitution begin to triumph; Their reflections are aggravating; I have no better opinion of some of them, than to believe that they would rejoice to see us divided, distracted & ruined; it lies with the present Congress, under Providence, to prevent it; There is great danger that the next election will not be disposed to act on so liberal a scale as the present; The general dissatisfaction which prevails with the compensations allowed by Congress, which is considered, by some at least, as one cause of their slow progress, will I fear have an unfavorable influence upon the next election; & Rhode Island may come in presently; we cannot, we dare not despair of success to attend the *well judged* perseverance of the advocates of the assumption; there are two many members of Ability & Integrity to be out-generald—or overborn by those who are less discerning or less attatched to the prosperity of their Country, and if they keep steady & *calm* they will prevail; In some very special cases, *private conferences* have had more effect than public debates: there may be reasons, founded in the constitution of the human nature, why it should be so—be this as it may, the fact is uncontrovertable, and surely no pains will be thought too great to be taken for the accomplishment of so important a work—But every thing that savors of passion must be avoided; Are you satisfied that Mr. D[*alton*]. of the Senate is friendly to the measure? it has been hinted to me, that he is not: if the House should accede, it may not be amiss to give some attention to that quarter: You will be good enough to excuse the freedom I take—a consideration of the powerful incentives to warmth, which attend the situation of the minority, puts me on suggesting the great need of caution on that head; I am confident it would disserve us; warmth begets warmth, and where that takes place, there is not so much attention to the merits of the question, as to the obtainment of victory; There will yet appear magnanimity enough in a majority of Congress, to consider the United States as one great family, & to view every measure as *highly important*, which has a tendency to keep them such; If a number of passengers on board a ship [*lined out*] in a tempestuous Ocean, in danger of an immediate wreck, were so to exert themselves for the general safety, as to loose all

~~concern~~ attention to their separate interest, should the vessell arrive safe in harbor, and a fierce contention arise about the share of loss that each should sustain, would it not infer a very gross reflection upon their characters? had They hesitated for deliberate consultation, in the hour of danger, upon the necessity & expediency of this or that particular sacrifice, the whole might have been lost & not excepting the passengers themselves—and shall those who discover the ~~greatest~~ most active zeal on such occasions, be the greatest sufferers? Such a line of conduct in the present case, would afford great encouragement to the Tyrants of the earth, as it would throw another great discouragement to an attempt for emancipation: Much more is to be said in favor of the sufferer, when there ~~has~~ is no pretence of prodigality or profusion on his part; This extreme, our brethren in Congress do not think the Gentlemen from Massachusetts inclined to at present or did not in the time of establishing compensations; but they are as much inclined to it now, as the Legislatures of the State have been in the different periods of the war, if proper allowance be made for the difference in circumstances; if in the Penobscot expedition, they were thought injudicious, had the event been otherwise the measure would have been denominated very differently; That it was not very injudicious, or at least to an inexcusable degree as *circumstances appeared at the moment*, may be argued from the readiness with which private Gentlemen, risqued their own property; but admitting the charge of imprudence in a degree, for a moment, how far is a part to suffer, on that account, when an ardent zeal for the general Safety, was the cause of it? but I shall weary your patience; If I have not done it already; excuse me.

[*P. S.*] If you put Mr. Seller's letter into the Post Office, will thank you to pay the postage & charge me.

ALS, Letters to Goodhue, NNS. Written from Andover, Massachusetts. In the omitted text, Phillips asked Goodhue to procure and forward a screw for the paper mill at Andover, Massachusetts.

George Thatcher, Notes on the Steuben Bill

When the two last motions were put[1] & carried Mr. Thatcher, hapned not to be present; therefore his name does not appear on the Journals—But he came into the House just as the names of the members were called & read from the Clerks Table And He then moved the House that he might be permitted to put his name on the Journals with the noes, for he had always been decidedly against the Barons pretended Claims—but it was observed that ~~he not being~~ as he was not present when the questions were put, he had not a right to have his name on the Journals—It was against a standing Rule of the House.

Ms., Thatcher Family Papers, MHi. Undated, but based on internal references to the published *HJ* and Thatcher's implied intent to defend himself for various unrecorded votes on this controversial subject, the editors believe these notes were written during his bid for reelection to the Second Congress.

[1] For the recorded votes on the failed motion to grant Steuben an annuity of $2706 and the successful motion to grant $2000, see *DHFFC* 3:403–5.

Pelatiah Webster to Benjamin Huntington

I duly recd. your favr. of 21st. Ult. & note Contents, on the doctrine of Discrimination I dont See much difficulty in framing a rule that will come fully view to Justice viz. debit every original creditor with all the certificates which were paid to him, at the price or Exchange which they were worth in Market at the Time of Delivery, & redeem or pay them at the Same Excha. to any body that brings them in to the Treasury with Interest of the same Excha. & pay the residue of the Debt with Interest to the Original creditor—I know not that Congress have any business to Make any declarations abt. the Justice or frauds of buyers or Sellers of Certificates—Whatever advantages may arise from different Opinions, & the disputations & discussions arising from them, I cant conceive any benefits resulting from Opinions or decisions that the payments of Debts ou[*gh*]t not to be made to the persons out of whose Merits & Earnings they originally Grew, but that they must be defrauded, & the payment made to people who never had any Merit or Earnings whatever. all the Authority of the first dignity can never make such decisions go down, or carry them into Effect & Every Step in any Such Attempt will be big with Absurdity, & of Course meet with Embarassments Innumerable, & must finally End in smoke if not fire, & I Wonder that any body can wonder what the matter is, when they See Such Absurd propositi[*ons*] constantly runing into Gross confusion & Chaos of [*torn*]te, & inchoherent Sentiments Inclose you my Essay on the Culture of Silk &c. Which I hope you will like Somewhat better then my silken Arguments on the subject of Discrimination.

ALS, Benjamin Huntington Correspondence, 1772–1790, R-Ar. Written from Philadelphia; franked; postmarked.

Brutus to the Public

FOUR months have elapsed since CONGRESS met, the last time, and scarcely that number of Acts has yet passed. The expectations of all descriptions of men are disappointed, and discontent begins to spread among the creditors of the public. The tardiness of our national legislature, the narrow views that govern or divide that assembly, the factions that arise from causes that are trifling and distant from the general interest, are serious and alarming considerations to a people who have placed confidence in the national councils. Let us then examine the conduct of the men who compose Congress, and see whether they have made the public good the great and leading object of their deliberations.

In the first part of the first Session, their attention was directed to national concerns. Party views and little politics did not make their appearance to the prejudice of more important business. Then we saw (and we rejoiced at the spectacle) all parties exerting themselves to devise a revenue system for a great empire, and all parties disposed to make small concessions for the general good. When the great principles of the constitution were agitated, we saw a Madison, an Ames, a Boudinot, a Benson, and other able and eloquent men boldly come forward, and with the manliness of Roman Senators, contend with the establishment of a vigorous Executive, without which our whole government would have been a nerveless body. New-England read the debates, and every mouth was filled with the praises of Congress. Madison's name was never mentioned but with admiration.

But at the close of the session what a change! When the question respecting the Residence of Congress came before the House of Representatives, a question that did not materially affect the Union, because at present it is of not one shilling's consequence to the great body politic, where Congress reside, and of still less consequence is it to resolve *now* where they *will* reside hereafter, this trifling question called forth all the narrow selfish passions of the members, it was debated with more warmth of temper than any preceding question had been, however interesting to the United States. Even the cool, modest, temperate M___ [*Madison*] was thrown off his guard, and rendered ridiculous by passion. It was moved to postpone the consideration of this unimportant question; but, no, the southern gentlemen urged the question, and it ended in their vexation. The debate however had a pernicious effect—it threw Congress into a torment, which rendered them unfit to attend, with dispassionate coolness, to the business of the nation.

No sooner had Congress met a second time, than a memorial from the Quakers[1] was presented; and, mostly through the influence of the eastern and middle states, was taken into consideration. Never was a more foolish, ill timed request, on the part of the Quakers; nor a more rash and imprudent step than the vote of the house to take up the memorial at this session. I can apologize for the zeal of the Quakers, until it becomes so mad and intemperate as to push them in *the face of their own interest.* But when men, with eyes open, take the most direct means to defeat their own purposes, I hardly know whether to pity their weakness or despise their obstinacy. Congress however deserve censure; for they knew, that, by the Constitution,[2] nothing of consequence could be done in favor of the memorial, and it was their *duty* (and *policy* called loudly for the measure) to have dismissed it with an answer of ten lines. Instead of this, a question that affects *the interest of the one part of the union most materially*, while with respect to the *other*, it is *little more than a question of speculation*, or mere morality, a question therefore not of a general nature enough to demand the time and attention of Congress at this juncture, this question I say must be dragged before the house to set the whole into an uproar of faction and finish the business which another unimportant question[3] had begun at the close of the last session.

A liberal enlightened people can forgive little errors in their legislators; they can pity and overlook a charge of lying, made in a fervid passion; but can they forget *repeated* acts of *public* folly? Will they not censure most freely the representatives who consent to trifle away the time of Congress? Will not these men be answerable for the factions that prevail in Congress, and the consequential delay of public measures?

The Report [*on public credit*] of the Secretary is an object of inconceivable magnitude, and the assumption of the debts of the several states is an event that will sooner or later take place. Some of the gentlemen who oppose it, do not yet foresee the consequences of rejecting it. I am bold to say this, because it is most candid, for if they do foresee the final consequences, they cannot be honest men and friends to the general government. The vote of Congress which finally rejects the proposition for assuming the State debts, *will shake this government to its centre.*

The public creditors compose a numerous and respectable, as well as the most wealthy part of the States. Whenever *better* provision is made for *some* of them than for *others*, a jealousy will spring up that will produce discordance between the States and the general government. Should the time ever arrive, when the creditors of the United States receive their interest in specie, and their paper shall approach to its nominal value; and should the State creditors, at the same time, receive but a small pittance for the interest of their money, and the principal remain at three, four or five shillings on the pound, the general government will become as unpopular as that of Great Britain before the war, it will be deemed meritorious to elude the revenue laws; and the officers of the customs will be shunned and detested as a set of harpies. I boldly assert, that unless Congress shall assume the debts of the several states, their government will lose the confidence of our citizens in general—and unless the national government has their confidence, *the revenue will not generally be collected.* Do Congress forget that their revenues are collected in the several *States?* Do they forget that unless they protect the rights of *all* the citizens, the *neglected* will have recourse to the *nearest government* for redress; a government over which they have more influence? Do Congress forget that their laws, thus become unpopular, will be feeble and inefficient? This is the prospect even with the most peaceable acquiescence in the partial measures of our national government.

But if the creditors of the several states, whole claims to justice stand on the same ground as those of the union, should ever combine together for the support of their demands, *it lies in their power to sever the union.* This is not said *in terrorem*[4] by an interested person—I am not a creditor for a shilling, either of the United or of *particular States.* I offer only a dispassionate opinion on a very solemn subject, and sincerely hope that more enlarged views of national policy will produce a change of measures. The design of the national government was to *equalize the burdens of the war,* to *unite the interests and the powers* of the individual states, for the purposes of common good; the man therefore that attempts to prevent this *equality* of *burdens,* forfeits his claim to the common *protection*; and I flatter myself the gentlemen who oppose the *assumption,* will not have the face to ask for *money or forces to guard their frontiers from the Savages.*

Boston Gazette, 10 May. Brutus, a popular pseudonym connoting a defender of civil liberty, may refer to any one of several quasi-legendary and historical figures of ancient Rome. The most famous were the Brutus who expelled the last king of Rome to establish the Republic in 510 B.C, and Marcus Brutus (85 B.C–42 B.C), "the tyrannicide," who assassinated Julius Caesar in 44 B.C.

[1] The antislavery petitions of the Philadelphia and New York Yearly Meetings of Friends (Quakers), and the Quaker-sponsored Pennsylvania Abolition Society (PAS). For more, see *DHFFC* 8:314–38.

[2] The two Yearly Meetings' petitions asked Congress to impose humane regulations on the slave trade in American ships, under the Constitution's commerce clause (Article 1, section 8, paragraph 3). Only the PAS's petition urged an abolition of slavery itself, under the Preamble's general welfare clause. The trade in general was protected until 1808 by Article 1, section 9, paragraph 1, and Article 5.

[3] The location of the seat of federal government.

[4] As a warning.

Other Documents

Nicholas Eveleigh to John Langdon. ALS, Langdon-Elwyn Family Papers, NhHi. Written from the Comptroller's office at the Treasury Department.
Finds that Langdon's accounts as contractor with the secret committee of the Continental Congress and Congress's commercial agent in New Hampshire "are rendered with great regularity and correctness"; poses two or three questions for clarification of the accounts.

Eliphalet Fitch to John Adams. ALS, Adams Family Manuscript Trust, MHi. Written from Kingston, Jamaica; addressed "the Honble. John Adams &c. &c. &c.," with a note referring Adams to the following postscript:

"I do not know what Title to give to Men in America; and beg your Candour in that respect."

Sends goods from his estate as a gift; has arranged to send Adams a packet of pamphlets related to the slave trade, for forwarding to Washington if he thinks appropriate.

John Hoomes to James Madison. ALS, Madison Papers, DLC. Written from Bowling Green, Virginia. For the full text, see *PJM* 13:195. For background on the Twining petition, see *DHFFC* 8:241–46.

Has reason to believe that Nathaniel Twining's stage line for delivering mail between Virginia and Savannah was the cause of Twining's financial ruin; asks Madison to render Twining and his petition before Congress any possible service.

Oliver Whipple to George Thatcher. ALS, Chamberlain Collection, MB. Written from Portsmouth, New Hampshire.

Office seeking: excise collector for Portsmouth district; venerates Thatcher's "Character & rising Fame"; "I know your Influence is great, and altho' you are not a Representative of our State, yet your Recommendations will prove effectual"; Langdon will not be unfriendly but Livermore has "Friends & Dependants" who will claim his influence; Foster and Gilman are good men, but not acquaintances; Adams will not be unfriendly; King, Dalton, Goodhue, Partridge, and Leonard "will if you desire it recommend me to the President"; letter will be delivered by Lear.

Daniel Hiester, Account Book. PRHi.

Attended "Monday Club" or mess day with the Pennsylvania delegation at Fraunces Tavern.

[Worcester] *Massachusetts Spy*, 13 May.

Leonard passed through Worcester en route to New York.

TUESDAY, 11 MAY 1790

Fine (Johnson)

William Ellery to Benjamin Huntington

***

I find by the news papers that the Senate have appointed a Committee to consider what provision should be made respecting this State ~~during~~

at the present Session of Congress. If any measures should be taken before the meeting of the Convention which would make the Antis feel that their interest would be affected by holding out, it might induce an adoption of it this month; otherwise the Convention in my opinion will adjourn again. The Antis had it in contemplation at the late Session of the Assembly to pass an Act recommending it to the several towns in the State to call town meetings for the purpose of taking the sense of the people whether the New Constitution should be adopted or not. This would have taken the business out of the hands of the Convention and again remitted it to the people. They found upon sounding some of the Federal Deputies, that such an absurd proposition would fail of success, and therefore dropped it. Not a word was said in the Genl. Assembly respecting the New Constitution until the Lower House had agreed to an adjournment, then one of our Deputies ~~desired~~ moved that the sense of the House might be taken whether the Governour [*Arthur Fenner*] should be requested to call the Assembly provided the Constitution should be adopted by the ensuing the Convention, which he ventured to say he did not doubt would be the case. should be respected. Some of the Antis sneered, but no objection was made to his motion. He was desired to wait upon the Upper House and acquaint the Governor with the sense of the Lower House. He did and his Excellency said that, in either of these events, he would immediately call the Assembly. The intention of the gentleman who moved the question was to feel the pulse of the Assembly if he could, and to provide in case of [*an*] adoption that Senators should be appointed to attend Cong[*re*]ss before it should rise, and if rejected to consult what measures should be taken to prevent the mischiefs. which might follow from a rejection.

If Congress should pass any act respecting this State, as I hope they will before the meeting of our Convention, I would be obliged to you if you would send me an authenticated copy of it immediately.

Will Congress defend the Feds if they apply to Congress for protection, and the Antis should [*torn*] war with them on that account?

When will Congress rise? How goes [*torn*] business? The application[1] of the Quakers f[*or the aboli*]tion of Slavery I find has created ill blood among you[*torn*] No application made by a religious Society as such ought ever to be countenanced by Congress. If the Question had been asked the applica~~tion~~nts whether their petition was founded on religious or political principles, ye would have found that they were moved by religious motives, and that politics was a secondary consideration in their minds, and if ye think as I do ye might have got rid of them on that ground.

They will come again I expect. If they should I hope Congress will tell them that they have nothing to do with their religious matters. The non-assumption of the State debts will be the cause of future trouble, as the question on that subject has been a cause of uneasiness in the present Congress.

Business proceeds best when there is a good understanding among those who are to execute it.

They who come hither from New York say that there are contentions among you. Where every man has his text, and every man his [*illegible*], the preaching and music will not be edifying. Hoping for the perfect establishment of peace among the brethren, and of the New Government.

ALS, Benjamin Huntington Correspondence, 1772–1790, R-Ar. Written from Newport, Rhode Island; franked; postmarked; answered 22 May. The omitted text relates to state politics, including the still unlikely (to Ellery) ratification of the Constitution.

[1] For more on the Quakers' antislavery petitions, see *DHFFC* 8:314–38.

Thomas Hartley to Jasper Yeates

I arrived here on Sunday, and find that I came in Time to act on some of the most important Business.

The Funding System will come on again to morrow. Parties have become much more moderate, than when I left them and there is a probability that the Debts of the union will be funded this Session.

The Assumption of the State Debts will I immagine be postponed. If the Measure shall be found necessary to be adopted—I wish it were possible to have the Balances of the several States fairly stated first.

A number of Gentlemen are very sanguine in their Expectations of adjourning to Philadelphia—The New Yorkers are a little frightned—and indeed they hold Congress upon such a feeble Tenure that they must be under continual Apprehensions—I must confess that our Prospect for the Adjournment is much more favourable than I had expected.

I will send you a News Paper which mentions what Congress were about yesterday.

ALS, Yeates Papers, PHi. Addressed to Lancaster, Pennsylvania; franked; postmarked; answered 28 May.

James Madison to Governor Beverley Randolph

On the receipt of your letter on the subject of the Inspection law of Virginia, I communicated the matter to the Secretary of the Treasury.[1] He sees no impropriety in his giving the requisite instruction to the Custom-

House officers and having promised to do so, I shall decline an application to Congress.

Since the late separation of the State debts from the national, the House of Reps. has been cheifly employed on objects of the inferior kind. Bills are now brought in for the intended provision for Public Credit. They correspond in substance with the plan of the Secretary so far as it relates to the National part of the debts. If the assumption of the State debts should not be revived as we apprehend may be done, it is probable that a little time will now close the deliberations of the House of Reps. on the subject which has so long occupied them.

I inclose the papers of this morning.

ALS, Executive Papers, Vi. Place to which addressed not indicated; "read" 5 June.

[1] Randolph to Madison, 27 April, above. As a result of Madison's communication with Hamilton on the matter, the Secretary sent a circular to the collectors and surveyors of Virginia on 18 May (*PAH* 6:419–20).

Alfred Moore to Samuel Johnston

You are ext[*r*]emely kind in writing to me & telling me of those things that engage the mind at New York; I am pleased to learn the consequence of Judge Burke's ill temper & indecency to Mr. Hamilton.[1] I am yet more pleased at the success you have had against that part of the Secretary's report that proposes to assume the State debts—nothing has engaged our minds in this State more than this business I have not heard one word in its favor—I have not one word to say myself that can amuse you & make some return for the entertainment your letters have given me— *** There is a dismal void here in the removal of yours & Mr. [*James*] Iredell's family.[2]

If I should see Mr. [*William J.*] Dawson I will put a few guineas into his hands that I may avail of your kindness to procure me a few books—I will at the same time give him a memorandum.

Typescript from ALS, Hayes Collection, NcU. Written from Edenton, North Carolina. The omitted text relates state judicial news and includes a list of four guineas worth of books for Johnston to purchase.

[1] For background on the affair of honor and the barely avoided duel between Burke and Hamilton, see *DHFFC* 8:476–80.

[2] Frances Cathcart Johnston and her sister-in-law Hannah Iredell sailed from Edenton, North Carolina, on 12 May, en route to New York. They were accompanied by Johnston's young cousin, William J. Dawson.

George Thatcher to Abijah Poole

I have got Land-warrants for you and the Gentlemen,[1] in whose behalf you wrote me & forwarded powers of Attorney—I shall bring them with me, on my return; which will be about the middle of June.

The Warrants are for Land that is or shall be appropriated, by Congress, out of the Lands belonging to the U. States, for the purpose of paying the bounties to the Officers & Soldiers of the late Army of the United States.

The Lands in the eastern part of the Massachusetts are the property of that Commonwealth; & therefore the Secretary of the war department could not give warrants for locating your Lands in that State.

The Officer for setling the Army Accounts [*Joseph Howell*] informs me, that the Officers of the description with yourself & those in whose favour you wrote, are barred from receiving their years pay, because their Claims were not lodged in his office in season—But for more particulars relative to this subject I must refer you to the statement of Mr. Howell, inclosed in my last.

FC, Thatcher Family Papers, MHi.

[1] William Stanwood, Samuel Thomas, John Lemont, and Richard Mayberry (Poole to Thatcher, 20 March, above).

[*Fisher Ames*] to [*Jabez Bowen or John Brown*]

I think the Period cannot be very remote when the People in general in your State will discern, that a Union with us *is necessary to their own Interest.* The Idea of a perpetual Separation cannot I am sure find Place in the Mind of one reflecting Man. There has been no Instance in the History of Mankind, where two contiguous and unconnected States have existed for a Length of Time in uninterrupted Peace, *and the Sources of Contention in the present Case would be numerous.* If we are ever to be united, Delay would manifestly be injurious as well to Rhode-Island as to the other States. Many Questions, in which the Interest of your State will be deeply concerned, are yet to be decided. By the Accession of North-Carolina you stand alone, if it is probable that will continue to be the Case, the Safety of this Government, and the Collection of its Revenue, may require *that Measures disagreeable to your Citizens should be adopted.* If such are adopted I am sure it will be with Reluctance.

[Providence, Rhode Island] *United States Chronicle*, 20 May. The identifications of the author and recipient are based on George Benson to Sedgwick, 21 May, below. The letter is undated; the editors are printing it here as Benson indicated that two letters from Ames arrived in Providence at the same time as Sedgwick's letter to him, below.

[*Fisher Ames*] to [*Jabez Bowen and John Brown*]

Our Accounts from your State are not very favourable as to the Fate of the Constitution with you; but be the Event what it may I am glad a Convention has been called, and that the Constitution is before them, as the Result of it will enable us to determine what to depend upon; if the Constitution is rejected in direct Terms, or if the Convention again adjourn without Acceptance, which, after so long a Time to reflect on the Subject, *will be only a delicate Mode of Rejection*, the Government here will be justified even to the discerning People in Rhode-Island, in pursuing Measures *that in other Circumstances might be thought severe*, but I hope your Expectations of an Adoption will not be disappointed.

[Providence, Rhode Island] *United States Chronicle*, 20 May. The identifications of the author and recipient are based on George Benson to Sedgwick, 21 May, below. The letter is undated; the editors are printing it here as Benson indicated that two letters from Ames arrived in Providence at the same time as Sedgwick's letter to him, below.

[*Theodore Sedgwick*] to George Benson

The local Situation of your State, its commercial Advantages and Pursuits, the Energy and Enterprize of its Citizens, combined in Consideration with its former Connections with the Nation, will render it impossible that an ultimate Separation should take Place.

It being now generally believed that your Convention will reject the Constitution, the Measures to be pursued in that Event are in the Contemplation of the Senate. It is probable the Result will be, that all commercial Intercourse between Rhode-Island and the United States will be interdicted, as well by Land as Water; and that a Demand of immediate Payment of the Interest at least, perhaps the Principal, of her Proportion of the National Debt. While Humanity will regret the Evils to be produced by these Measures, their Necessity I am persuaded will justify them to the Candour even of those who may be the principal Sufferers. These Evils, which I am confident you will believe I ardently wish may be avoided, are the least that can be done under the present Circumstances. They may be averted, and I will not altogether despair, that Rhode-Island will yet, before it is too late, know and pursue the Things which belong to her Peace and Happiness.

[Providence, Rhode Island] *United States Chronicle*, 20 May; reprinted at New York City (*GUS*, 2 June). The identification of the author is based on Benson to Sedgwick, 21 May, below.

Caleb Strong to Theodore Foster

The Senate is employed in framing a Bill for prohibiting all Intercourse with Rhode-Island by Land or Water, after the first of July; and also to require the Payment of your Quota of the Debt without Delay.

If Congress should begin to coerce your State they must proceed; and I should suppose that your Opposers would readily see the Prudence of preventing Coercion, by an immediate Return to their Federal Duty. What is now before the Senate, and which is supported by a Majority perfectly disposed to bring your State into the Union, ought to be made known in your State. The People in the back Parts ought no longer to be deceived with the Idea, that the Condition of single Independence is an eligible one. I sincerely wish your Efforts may succeed on the 24th.[1]

[Providence, Rhode Island] *United States Chronicle*, 20 May; reprinted at Exeter and Portsmouth, New Hampshire; Boston; and Litchfield, Connecticut. The identification of the writer and recipient is based on George Benson to Sedgwick, 21 May, below.

---

[1] The opening of the second session of the Rhode Island ratification convention.

A Patriot to a Certain Great Body

May it please your most agreeable HIGHNESSES

HAVING the utmost concern for your personal ease as individuals, and regarding *the labor* you have undergone, in being obliged to spend your time in tiresome debates upon questions of *no importance to yourselves*, but of the highest consequence to your constituents—I say, regarding the labor of debating upon any public question as a public evil, and, considering the establishments of offices and departments a business entirely out of your province, I would seriously recommend, that a committee of five be appointed to bring in a bill, which you can ratify in *ten minutes*, to empower the S—y of the T—y to nominate and appoint all the executive officers of the United States, and all their clerks and assistants.

By this means you will save the trouble of edging clauses into bills every day, such as that which allows him to apportion, the number of clerks that are to be allowed to each of the commissioners who are shortly to be appointed to settle the accounts of the individual states with the United States. One good stout sweeping clause like that here recommended, by which the S—y will have it in his power to increase his influence, as he would have the nomination of one or two thousand needy clerks, who would support his systems and give their votes at every election in every part of the United

States, would fully answer my intention; and it is to such a clause as this you will all owe your future preferment—for if your constituents should not re elect you, you will be elected, nevertheless, that is, by the S—y, into a *snug birth* of 1500 or 2000 dollars per annum.

Should you neglect this wholesome advice, I now warn you to take care of your persons, fortunes, and characters, yourselves—as I shall not give you any further advice, but leave you the resentment of the aristocratic junto.

NYJ, 11 May. The editors are publishing the piece because the similarity of its ideas and rhetoric to William Maclay's diary and newspaper articles suggest he may be the author.

A Berkshire Farmer to Mr. Andrews

THE Question in Congress for the Assumption of the State Debts is a subject of much conversation in this County, but not so well understood as I could wish; and as the speeches of two of the honourable Members of our Delegation have thrown great light upon this important subject (I mean Mssrs. SEDGWICK and GERRY) I wish you to insert them in your Paper. The Assumption, Sir, of the State Debts, is of the utmost consequence to the Landed Interest in this Commonwealth. I am therefore desirous that it should be fully understood, that the good people of Massachusetts may know whether the Delegation from this Commonwealth have consulted the true interests of their constituents, by voting unanimously for the Assumption, or not. It is to be presumed that those Gentlemen have had the fullest information, from the length of time the matter has been under discussion, before they determined. I would ask my fellow citizens, if it is not more probable that this subject has been better understood by our Members of Congress, than by anonymous writers, who, by their opposition to the General Government, contemplate their own importance.

[Stockbridge, Massachusetts] *Western Star*, 11 May; edited by Loring Andrews. Immediately following this piece is a reprinting of Sedgwick's speech of 24 February, taken from *GUS* (*DHFFC* 12:534–40). The *Western Star*, 18 May, continued with the promised printing of Gerry's speech of 25 February, taken from *NYDA* (*DHFFC* 12:556–60).

OTHER DOCUMENTS

Madame de Bréhan to Thomas Jefferson. AL, in French, Jefferson Papers, DLC. Written from Paris; received 14 October. For the full text, see *PTJ* 16:424–25.

Asks to be remembered to "our friend" Madison, who she hopes might succeed Jefferson as minister to France.

Henry Chapman to Zachariah Collins. ALS, Papers of Stephen Collins and Son, DLC. Addressed to Second Street, Philadelphia; carried by Mr. Backhouse.

Among the vessels arrived at New York City that day is Morris's ship *Federalist*, returned from Canton (China) under Capt. (Richard) Dale and reported to be carrying 1800 chests of Hyson tea, which should help relieve Morris's financial problems.

Benjamin Goodhue to Stephen Goodhue. ALS, Goodhue Family Papers, MSaE.

"I have nothing new to tell you, we have done nothing of consequence since my last, except what I think a profusive grant of money to a man [*Frederick William Steuben*] who has already received 50,000 Dollrs. in specie and spent it."

Stephen Goodhue to Benjamin Goodhue. FC:lbk, Goodhue Family Papers, MSaE. Written from Salem, Massachusetts.

"Salt is dull here at 10/ it is easy to discover who pays the impost when the aditionall one ~~the~~ takes place it will be easyer to discover"; "The merchants are exceeding Sour"; "as our business is decaying & we are exceeding poor & obliged to live accordingly I hope we Shall not be obliged to quit the Town or Starve"; "give our love to Sister [*in-law Rebecca Prescott*] Sherman if She be at New York."

Jeremiah Hill to George Thatcher. ALS, Chamberlain Collection, MB. Written from Biddeford, Maine.

Regards to Langdon; "I want a Custom House boat in this River these d—d Coasters are to many for me, & as law less as the D—l is full of wickedness—*quid tum* [*what now*]? a Custom house boat may bring them to a sense of their duty—may be so kind as to mention it again to the Secy. [*Hamilton*] multiplicity of Business may have put it from his Mind."

Louis Guillaume Otto to Comte de Montmorin. Copy, in French, Henry Adams Transcripts, DLC. Received 2 July. Otto's letters included in *DHFFC* were usually written over the course of days, and even weeks, following the day they were begun.

Describes the arrival and expectations of the French immigrants to the Scioto Company's lands in the Ohio Valley; from the most important among them he has received requests to be presented to the president, which he has managed to avoid doing; thinks the Bordeaux packet has been lost at sea, so that he has to rely on the irregular schedule of merchant ships, but since American affairs offer so little of interest to the politics of Europe, that inconvenience will not be felt.

Michael Jenifer Stone to Walter Stone. ALS, Gratz Collection, PHi. Addressed to Charles County, Maryland; franked; postmarked.

Gossips about New York City courtships; the city has been "extremely Sickly"; he again suffers from a cold; is pained to report that Washington is ill with a "severe attack" of influenza.

Jeremiah Wadsworth to Catherine Wadsworth. ALS, Wadsworth Papers, CtHi. Addressed to Hartford, Connecticut; franked; postmarked. Signed "Your affectionate friend & Parent."

Is too busy to write to anyone but her; discusses the difficulty of procuring clothes for her brother Daniel; "the Beaux here have so much ocasion for their legs [*pants?*] that they will not spare them"; has delivered Harriet's letters; consultations with "several Medical Men" assure him of Daniel's speedy recovery; "I am impatient to be at Home but the business of the House is such I dare not leave it at present"; influenza rages.

Wednesday, 12 May 1790

Warm Shower (Johnson)

Thomas Fitzsimons to Benjamin Rush

***

I suppose it Never was Expected by the friends of Mr. Morris or Mr. [*F. A.*] Muhlenberg, that personally they would use interest or influence, to *Obtain* the Government.[1] for my own part I should deem them Unworthy of the Station if they could Stoop to Solicit it—if their fellow Citizens think them the most Eligible—they ought to give the one Most fitting their Suffrages. I should hope either of them had as many personal friends as woud do all that was Necessary—in Recommending them I am not to learn that the Republicans[2] are wanting in *painfull* industry—or that the Success of their Measures for some years past has been oweing to the Zeal and Activity of a few—it would be too great a Reflection, however, on their Good sense and Patriotism to suppose that they were so lost to a Sense of their duty as Citizens of a Republic—to admit a Man they have so unfavorable an opinion of as the present President [*Governor Thomas Mifflin*] to obtain the [*lined out*] High station of Chief Magistrate at a time when the happiness of the state depends So much upon a different choice—for myself—Electioneering Never was my talent nor would my present situation [*lined out*] admit of my bestowing any Considerable portion of my time to it—in fact—I have no interest or influence in that part of the State where either could be made Use of— *** we have labored to little or rather bad purpose if on any occasion we decline takeing some part in the affairs of our Country for of all governments Republics must be the worse when we suffer them to fall into the hands of Improper people—I have heard the Little arts Made use of by the Present Candidate [*governor*]. they are, they Must be too Little to answer his purpose. I have Never yet entered into any particulars with the Gent. here I will take an oppy. of doing it and the liberty of Communicateing to you hereof ***

I will tell Mr. [*Tench*] Coxe what you desire and shall be extreamly glad if his News paper persecuters Remain Silent. I knew of the Secys. intention to appoint him[3] sometime Ago haveing been Consulted upon that Occasion—Indeed I was surprized at his Accepte. tho no doubt he had considered that himself—You must know that ~~it is Con~~ his Appointment is Considered here as a Complimt. to Pensylvania—I learn from him that You are very Much Employed in the duties of your profession—it is a Very laborious one—& I wish & hope one More Suited to your Case & Interest may before long be substituted—the people here are Sickly—few haveing Escaped the present Epidemick—I am fortunately one of that few—as Yet—what you Suggested in a former Letter about an Address to the National Assembly of france is farr above ~~our Ideas~~ the Meridian of our body. which is not Composed of the *Greatest* Spirits in the Nation it happens fortunately that we Mould things into a tolerable shape before we send them out but the means by which that is accomplished is Neither prompt nor Sublime—the ~~proposal~~ hint therefore has gone no further than to 2 or three friends.

Nothing is yet *finally* done with respect to the funding System, but I expect the Continental debt will be provided for in the Manner Agreed to in Committee of the Whole—I have heard from difft. quarters, that I am threatned with dismission for my Conduct. but this will not deter Me from doing what I beleive to be right & if I Err upon this Subject it will not be for want of time & Reflection—I hope you will receive this long dissertation as an Answer to your two last & a proof that Nothing which comes from You is disregarded by me, because Independent of my Opinion of your Judgement I have the Utmost Reliance on your friendship.

ALS, Gratz Collection, PHi. Place to which addressed not indicated. The omitted text relates to state election politics and Rush's involvement in it.

[1] Politicking for the October 1790 election of Pennsylvania's first governor under its new constitution began at least as early as January. F. A. Muhlenberg and Morris were considered

leading candidates until they joined Clymer and Fitzsimons in declaring support for Arthur St. Clair in September 1790. The incumbent Thomas Mifflin won the election with ninety percent of the vote (Harry Tinkcom, *Republicans and Federalists in Philadelphia, 1790–1801* [Harrisburg, Pa., 1950], pp. 33–40).

[2]The state political party that spearheaded the movement to replace the Pennsylvania constitution of 1776.

[3]Hamilton offered Coxe the post of assistant secretary of the treasury on 1 May, although the formal appointment was dated 10 May. Fitzsimons had served as chairman of the unofficial congressional committee whose investigation of unethical conduct probably precipitated the resignation of Coxe's predecessor, William Duer, in late March or early April; see House Investigation of William Duer, March 1790 Undated, above. At least one "News paper persecuter" declined to remain silent in the anticipated backlash against Coxe's appointment: alluding to Coxe's imputed loyalism during the war, a satirical fantasy published in Philadelphia's *Independent Gazetteer* on 12 June depicted Coxe as Hamilton's successor in a cabinet that included Loyalist expatriates and the arch-traitor Benedict Arnold (*PAH* 6:401; *Coxe*, p. 152n, 158–59n; *DHFFC* 9:259).

Benjamin Huntington to William Ellery

Since Writing the foregoing The house have Passd a Bill to Give Barron Stubend 7,000 Dollars, to Pay his Debts and 2000 Dollars ℔ Annum during life for his Services &c. &. in full of all Demands.

By the N. York Packett of the [*torn*] you will See, the Senate have appointed a Committee on the 28th of April to Consider what provisions will be proper for Congress to make in the Present Session Respecting the State of Rhode Island—Nothing has yet come from that house [*lined out*] on the Subject nor have I heard of any thing proposed by the Committee on the Business of their appointment.

ALS, Benjamin Huntington Correspondence, 1772–1790, R-Ar. This is a postscript to a letter dated 8 May, above. The letter was not sent, according to Huntington's notation on the endorsement sheet.

William Maclay to Benjamin Rush

I have just received yours of the 10th, ~~and~~ the Observations containd in it are just and Striking. But what is there in the power of Six or eight People, in this place. It is with You in Philada. It is with the Mass of the People to determine. The Gentlemen You allude to, do not mean to oppose each other. But I believe they wait for the public Voice to determine, who shall be taken up. This perhaps is best. The question is a delicate one, too delicate for me to touch. I live with one of them as with a Brother. The other I sit every day beside in habits and intercourse of Friendship.[1] I will not wound either by a proposal, which for aught I know, might hurt either of them In a very sensible Manner. Philada. Lancastor & York are the points which if United, will insure Success in this Business. A Consultation, might be proper; but this cannot well be accomplished before the Meeting of the Convention.[2] This was a Subject on which I had almost determined never to blacken paper, but to you I could not excuse the rudeness of leaving a letter unanswered. The City of Philada. is justly considered as one third part of the State. how much respect ought to be paid to them in the Choice of a Chief Magistrate is Obvious. Altho' I have endeavoured to serve Philada. in everything in my power, with a zeal almost bordering on enthusiasm. Yet I well know how ready discontent is to foster on any one, Where a charge of medling can be brought forward. thoughts of this kind had determined me to be quiescent at the next election, or at least to confine myself to our poor County of Northumberland, where I will be happy to Cast my mite into the Treasury for the Common good.

In the Mean time should anything happen here which it will be Useful for You to know. You shall hear from me. A Word from the Bible. *the Race is not always to the Swift.*[3] The President of the U.S. is very poorly, the Whole Town, or nearly so, is sick and many die daily.

[*P. S.*] The Muhlenbergs both busy & beg their Compliments to You.

ALS, Rush Papers, DLC. Addressed to "third Street," Philadelphia; franked; postmarked 13 May.

---

[1] Maclay lived with F. A. Muhlenberg at the home of the Muhlenberg brothers' sister [*Margaretha Henrietta*] and her husband, the Lutheran minister Dr. John C. Kunze, at 24 Chatham Street. "The other" refers to his Senate colleague, Morris. Both were talked about as candidates to oppose Thomas Mifflin in the Pennsylvania gubernatorial election.

[2] The second meeting of Pennsylvania's state constitutional convention met between 9 August and 2 September 1790.

[3] Ecclesiastes 9:11.

Philip Schuyler to Catherine Schuyler

I wrote you this morning by Capt. Jacob Wendell, but lest a long passage should prevent his Arrival, and that you might be Alarmed by accounts from hence, I repeat that I was violently attacked by the Gout on Sunday, attended with a high fever—but my friendly Medicine, plenty of way [*whey?*] and keeping my bed until Yesterday afternoon has perfectly restored me.

The bill in favor of Baron [*Frederick William*] Steuben meets with Objections in the Senate, and I doubt If It will pass so favorably to him as It came from the other house.

ALS, Schuyler Papers, NN. Place to which addressed not indicated.

Roger Sherman to Governor Samuel Huntington

The daily publication of the proceedings and debates in Congress. is the only apology that I can make for neglecting to write oftener to your Excellency. The session has been protracted beyond my expectation.

The funding the national debt has occasioned considerable debate, but the principles are now settled by the House of Representatives, and Bills are reported, for extending the revenue, and for funding the immediate debts of the United States.

It is expected that the assumption of the State debts will again come under consideration, Massachusetts. & South Carolina are so involved in State debts, that it will be impossible for them to provide for paying the interest without laying such excises as will be very prejudicial to the collection of Impost, and be a grievous burthen upon commerce, these States from their particular circumstances during the war were necessitated to take upon them much more than their quota of the common expence. Connecticut is likewise burthened beyond her just proportion. The Secretary of the Treasury Supposes that ~~that~~ Sufficient provision may be made for the whole debt of the united States including that part contracted by the individual States, without resorting to direct taxes or general excises. if so, I think it would be a great relief to the States.

I think all possible Savings ought to be made in the expenditures of public money, and the revenue applied to discharge the debts. A Bill lately passed the House, in favour of Baron Stuben, making him an allowance of a Sum to pay his debts and an annuity for life—many of the members Supposed that the united States were obliged by Contract to grant him a larger Sum for his Sacrifices & Services. All appeared to be of opinion that he had rendered great Services to the united States by introducing discipline & Œconomy in to the Army, and therefore were willing to provide for his comfortable Support for the remainder of life, but it was thought by a Number of the members that the united States were not indebted to him by contract, and that a less annuity would have been sufficient.

***

I have Some expectation that Congress will end the session by the beginning of next month.

P. S. Congress have made great progress in business for a fortnight past.

ALS, Dearborn Collection, MH. Addressed to Hartford, Connecticut; franked; received 14 May; answered 9 June. The omitted text describes Sherman's reckoning of the balance due to the state from his unsettled accounts as Superior Court judge. Claiming "It is impossible for me to raise money to pay that debt at present," he suggested an offset from the money the state owed him as delegate to Congress from 1775 to 1780 or 1781, and enclosed an (unlocated) "Short resolve" to that effect, which the legislature might consider adopting. The letter's endorsement sheet is annotated in the hands of the state House and Senate's clerks, attesting that each house had voted negatively on "whether this house would take any order on this Letter."

Other Documents

Elbridge Gerry to an Unknown Recipient. Listing of one page ALS, *Parke-Bernet Catalog* 1843(1958):item 19.

Rev. James Madison to James Madison. ALS, Madison Papers, DLC. Written from Williamsburg, Virginia. For the full text, see *PJM* 13:196–97.

Acknowledges Madison's letter (date unknown), favored by Edmund Randolph; congratulations on the motion for discrimination, which all but very few agree with; "The Disappointments of the best Politicians are not perhaps less frequent than those of other Men; but they must console themselves with having erected Lights, which tho' the unwary Mariner may not avail himself of at present, will, most probably be of future Utility"; encloses two letters, one of which—to Samuel Seabury (Connecticut's Anglican bishop [1729–96])—one of the other members of Congress may forward; Edmund Randolph hopes to return to New York City very soon.

James Mercer to James Madison. ALS, Madison Papers, DLC. Written from Fredericksburg, Virginia. For the full text, see *PJM* 13:197–98.

Entrusted with responding to Madison's 27 April letter to Mann Page, regarding an applicant recommended by Johnson to fill a teacher's vacancy at the Fredericksburg Academy; asks Madison to await news of another candidate's formal acceptance of the job offer before declining Johnson's recommended applicant, on behalf of the Academy; reports on the progress of "our Infant Seminary."

John Telles to Robert Morris. ALS, Washington Papers, DLC. Written from Philadelphia; franked; postmarked.

Office seeking: recommends John Street as vice consul at Fayal (Azores); Street will wait on Morris at New York if necessary.

Thursday, 13 May 1790

Cool (Johnson)

John Avery, Jr. to George Thatcher

Your kind favour of the 2d. instant I have had the pleasure of receiving and am glad to hear that you have got through most of your business—All Eyes are waiting upon you to see the result of your determination upon the public debt—there are so many interested that I do not wonder at their impatience—may you give satisfaction is my sincere wish—We are a comical set of Beings—never pleased—however do right and leave the event—If you can serve my friend I wrote you about, shall be glad—Inclosed you have this day's paper in which you will find the debates of the Halifax House of Representatives *truly spirited*[1]—there seems to be a spirit of liberty pervading the whole World—may they go on and prosper is my sincere wish—Should be obliged to you to deliver the inclosed—Please to give my respects to all friends.
P. S. Please to give my respects to Mr. [*Nathan?*] Dane, if he should be in New York and tell him that I recd. his kind favour and have mentioned the matter he desired to Mr. Eayres.[2]

ALS, Chamberlain Collection, MB. Written from Boston.

[1] Boston's *Independent Chronicle* of this date carried excerpts from the journal of Nova Scotia's House of Assembly, covering the conflict that erupted the previous March over the House's prerogative to refuse to consider His Majesty's Council's amendments to a revenue bill.

[2] Joseph Eayres was a Boston housewright in 1790.

John Brown to Elias Boudinot

I take the liberty to address you from my Acquaintance with you as well as the Mutal Benefit which may Arise from a Releif On the subject, The Indians Are determined on all sides for war Against the Subjectes of the Goverment of America You have Probibilly heard of the many depredatons committed by them, this Winter & spring, they have taken boats at every Oppertunity through the Winter And Attacked a Station Eighteen miles above limestone[1] killed & took every Person which was fifteen Old & young they Assembl'd in March Past near the mouth of Sioto in a large Party they took by Report Seven Boats before they was broak up, Consequences appeared so serious that General [*Josiah*] Harmar with a detachment of his

Troops & a body of Militia from Kentouke marched to rout them, which was done tho without Action as they fled before he reach'd the Place—they are Continually Killing & Sculping both here & in Kentoucke we have lost five Killed [*lined out*] from this Place Since I came to it Our Settlers are very much dishartened & without something done soon, I am fearfull that the Stations or Towns which is without Troops will be broak up we have lost Two Persons since the 21st. of April & their signs very frequent you Very likely have heard of the Tragedy of Major [*John*] Doughty death who was killed while treat with them with the Masseecree of Two thirds or more of the People[2] Mr. Seydamm [*Cornelius Sedam*] Made of with a few men who was fortunate enough reach the Boat, as did Doughty but was Shot on Getting in Capt. [*Jonathan*] Hart Who was out bringing in an other Part of the Indians was met by the Perpetrators which gave him the whole Account he has like wise made his Escape, within one Week Four boats Stop'd a few miles Above lime Stone in Consequence of a very dark foggy night one of which was taken with Eighteen Souls in three only made their Escape the Other boats cut loose made their Esape on board of which was one Continental Officer with Eight Soldiers, I would therefore Pray your Interposition & Influence in our Behalf; & As One of the Gardians of Our Country knowing your Power & Influence in the Goverment, with your famed Humanity[3] to Mankind in General I will hope Much from you.

You have heard so much of the Good Quallity of the Soil Climate of this Country that a Repetition will be unnecessary I will only say that with *Peace* it Excells all Others in my Opinion our City Plot has a number of fine Springs on it which not frequently found near the River & bids fair with Proper Encouragement to make the most Populace Place from the mouth of the Ohio to its Source your Block[4] Excell's all, every Given away lot is taken on it if you wou'd sell a Peice in the Center for a Tan Yard I wish you wou'd favour me with the Terms as it may be a means of Giveing us a Usefull Mechanick for it is the most Eligeble spot on the Plot, we are Bounded on the Ohio & Miami Rivers both with the City Plot, the Portage of the Miami will be of Great Use tho a Rapid Stream for the Country on the North west Excell's this Purchase if Possible I am told Congress is about to Open a Land Office for the Sale of that Country Shou'd it take Place If you think me Worthy I shou'd be Glad of the Surveyors & Regesstering Office Your Influence to such an appointment with the President Or Secretary of the Treasury (whose Province it is) will be always Greatfully Acknowledge'd, & as I intend in [*torn*] this Country my chief Residence I think the fa[*torn*] If I can Tender you any Service here shall all [*torn*] ready to obey your Commands Make my Respects to Mrs. Boudinot with all my Acquaintance in Elizabeth Town.

ALS, Brown Collection, ICHi. Written from the banks of the Great Miami River, at North Bend, Ohio; carried by Mr. Board. John Brown was a former resident of Elizabethtown, New Jersey.

---

[1] Near present-day Maysville, Kentucky.

[2] For background on Brown's mistaken account of Doughty's rumored death, see John C. Symmes to Boudinot, 1 May, n. 1, above.

[3] In the context of the apparent abduction of settlers, this may allude to Boudinot's highly praised role as Washington's hand picked commissary of prisoners (and de facto head of intelligence gathering) in 1777–78.

[4] In March 1788 Boudinot spent £200 on a half interest in John C. Symmes' forty thousand acre tract at the mouth of the Great Miami River, part of the latter's million acre purchase between there and the Little Miami River, up the Ohio River at present-day Cincinnati (George Adams Boyd, *Elias Boudinot, Patriot and Statesman* [Princeton, N.J., 1952], pp. 149–53).

William Ellery to John Adams

Immediately on the receipt of your letter of the 28th. of Febry. last, I returned an answer to it. Since that time I have not had the pleasure of receiving a line from you, which induces me to apprehend that my letter miscarried; especially as you promised to be a better correspondent in future.

Our May session began and finished the last week. The Antifederal prox succeded. The Antis have ten majority in the Upper and five majority in the Lower House. However the Feds had the address to bring a good Fed. and a moderate Anti into the Supr. Court, and to obtain several other points in the election of officers.

The New Constitution was not made a subject of debate during the Session. At the close of it, after the Lower House had agreed to adjourn to the second monday in June, one of our Deputies observed that the Convention would meet on the fourth monday in May, and would then without doubt adopt the Constitution, in which event it would be necessary that the Assembly should be immediately called to chuse Senators &c. and therefore moved that the sense of the house should be taken, that the Governour should be requested to convene the Assembly on that occasion. Some of the Antis sneered, but none of them objected to the motion, or said a word about the Constitution. The Assembly will be convened agreeably to the motion; which was partly designed to feel the pulse of the majority. In the Session it was whispered out of doors by some of the Antis that something would be done to pave the way to the adoption of the Constitution. On the last day (Saturday) a bill was brought in, which was said to originate with the Governor [*Arthur Fenner*], empowering debtors to discharge Judgments obtained against them on specific Contracts; either in the articles specified in the Contracts, or by specie amounting to their value at the time Judgments should be obtained. Notwithstanding the bill was in favour of the debtor, the consideration of it was referred to the next Session by a majority of four. The Feds, viewing it as a stepping stone, voted that it should be acted upon immediately; the Antis perhaps for the same reason voted ad referendum.[1] It is said that the framer of the bill was much disappointed; but we cannot certainly tell what Antis mean by what they say. They have endeavoured to amuse Congress as well as the Federalists of the State.

What the result of the Convention will be is conjectural. Some suppose that the Constitution will be adopted with recommendatory amendments; some that it will be adopted conditionally; and some that the Convention will adjourn again. It is the universal opinion that it will not be absolutely rejected. I cannot conceive that even the Antis can be so absurd as to vote for a conditional adoption; for they know that such an adoption is and will be considered by Congress as tantamount to a rejection; and I have not faith enough to embrace the first supposition.

It has been intimated to me that the Governor would favour the adoption if he could be satisfied that his friend [*Ebenezer*] Thompson, who is now Collector of the Impost for the Providence district, could hold that office under the Federal Government; and the Governour has great influence among the Antis. Mr. Thompson was a violent Anti; but it is said he has lately become a Fed. How this is I don't know; but I beleive interest has a mighty effect on the opinions of Men.

I find by the News papers that the Senate have appointed a Committee to consider what provisions will be proper for Congress to make in the present Session. If any thing should be done which would wound the interest of the Antis it might have a good effect.

If the Convention should adopt the Constitution the interval between the time that Congress can receive the ratification and their rising will be so short that there will be little or no opportunity to apply for offices, and as Exitus in dubis est[2] give me leave to intreat you to renew your applications on my behalf to the President of Congress [*Washington*], and to address those whom he may consult with on such occasions, that I may be appointed Collector of this district. The known Character of the present Custom house officers will prevent their being candidates; and without disparaging others who may solicit for that office I beleive I may venture to say that my pretensions are equal at least to any of them.

ALS, Adams Family Manuscript Trust, MHi. Written from Newport, Rhode Island.

[1] That it be further considered.
[2] The result is in doubt.

Pamela Sedgwick to Theodore Sedgwick

I was made happy this Morning my dearest Love by the receipt of your Letter of the 8th Instant—the weather was so very bad here the week after you left us that I was excesively anxious on account of your Health Thanks to a Gratious Providence you Got along in Safety and are now Better—Mr. [*Silas*] Pepoon Tels us It is very Sickly in N. York. I pray you may not get a relaps—let me here from you every Post I beg and dont forget to tel me how you doe—and weather your Cough has Left you. Robert [*Sedgwick*] continues much as he was when you left us. the Blisters[1] ware laid on last week but I think have made no Perceiveable alteration—Parson Bacon is Elected For Stockbridge[2] and it is said much elated because he shall now have I[*t*] in his power to oppose the Assumtion—The Little Girls ware pleasing Themselves with the Idea of Coppy~~y~~iing P[*eter*]. Pinder For you Tomorah but unfortunately for them The Post goes Tomorah Morning accept their Intention.

ALS, Sedgwick Papers, MHi. Written from Stockbridge, Massachusetts.

[1] Any one of several typical applications, such as the Spanish fly, intended to promote an inflammation of the skin, leading to a discharge of the "ill humors" blamed for several kinds of disorders, including fevers, measles, diarrhea, and kidney diseases.

[2] John Bacon succeeded Sedgwick in the Massachusetts House of Representatives.

Hugh Williamson to Governor Alexander Martin

You was long since informed of the Part I had taken on the Question of assuming the State Debts. Hitherto we have opposed successfully but we have been obliged to support our Opposition by the Necessity of settling Accounts first and assuming afterwards if we should then be so minded. Uniformity requires that we should promote proper Measures for the Settlement and the Interest of the State certainly requires it. The Committee of which I am a Member has nearly prepared a Bill for making a final Settlement, and fixing a Rule for the Quotas.[1] It is proposed that all Services shall be charged including Forts & armed Vessels, not cruisers.[2] That all the militia shall be charged at specie continental Price, all Articles furnished in the same manner. This will naturally cover our ~~Char~~ Expences for the Ship Caswell[3] & [*enlistment*] Bountys Guns. It will also make it necessary for us to look sharp after our militia Rolls. Most of them as You know have been paid off with depretiated mony and if that Mony should be valued according to the Scale of our State it would be worth little, the other Plan will give us a substantial Credit. I had weighty Objections to admitting Charges for Forts and Galleys, but it appeared that some of the States have already been authorised by Congress to charge their Forts, this gave countenance to the Claim of other states doing the same. The Militia Business is clear, for North Carolina must doubtless gain by the proposed regulations on that Head.

This Scheme you see if adopted will oblige us to restate the whole of our Accounts. A painful Business but the Play will be worth the Candle I think we must gain a Million of Dollars by the difference of Systems. I promised you formerly that while serving in Congress I should not lose sight of the States Accounts. You see I have not forgot the Promise. As soon as the Law passes & congress adjourn I think it will be necessary for Col. [*Abishai*] Thomas or myself to come to the State to expedite the collecting such new Vouchers as may then be thought necessary. I have to request that in Case we are hampered in Point of Time and one or two Clerks should be found absolutely necessary, you will be so good as authorise us to employ them until the meeting of the Assembly. This Question in my Opinion claims the Attention of the Executive.

ALS, Governors' Papers, Nc-Ar. Place to which addressed not indicated.

---

[1] Settlement of Accounts Bill [HR-69].

[2] By "cruisers," Williamson must have meant simply privateers, since they were also armed, but privately, and not state owned.

[3] The *Caswell* was one of two ships supplied by Virginia to jointly defend Ocracoke Inlet and the Albemarle Sound under an agreement with North Carolina. It became part of the North Carolina state navy in early 1778 and served until it sank at Ocracoke in 1779 (Charles O. Paullin, *The Navy of the American Revolution* [1906; reprint, New York, 1971], pp. 456–59).

Other Documents

Mary Cotton to John Langdon. LS, Langdon Papers, NhPoA. Written from Boston; marked "Answered."

Asks Langdon to recommend that Smith (S.C.) "& Lady" (Charlotte Izard Smith) use her boarding house during their summer tour through Boston.

Benjamin Goodhue to Stephen Goodhue. No copy known; acknowledged in Stephen to Benjamin Goodhue, 20 May.

Stephen Goodhue to Benjamin Goodhue. FC:lbk, Goodhue Family Papers, MSaE. Written from Salem, Massachusetts.

Sorry that Benjamin is worried about the prospect of funding without an assumption; trade and the Eastern states are in the minority, and cannot be disappointed because they expect always to be so; "your discharging what you think is your duty is Sufficient"; reports on the family's recovery from measles, and on state elections.

Joseph Hague to John Adams. ALS, Adams Family Manuscript Trust, MHi. Written from Williamsburg, Virginia. Joseph Hague and his brother John, an artisan in Alexandria, Virginia, pirated from their native Great Britain the innovative technology for constructing spinning and carding machines in 1774–75 and again in 1788, for which they received premiums and patent protection from Pennsylvania (David J. Jeremy, "British Textile Technology Transmission to the United States: The Philadelphia Region Experience, 1770–1820," *Business History Review* vol. 47, 1[Spring 1973]:24–52).

Describes his importation from Great Britain, and reproduction, of wool and cotton spinning machines before the Revolutionary War; asks Adams's assistance in procuring a patent; has written also to Representative Brown.

Rufus King to Robert Southgate. Summary and excerpt of three page ALS, *Carnegie Book Shop* 256(1961):item 284. The ellipsis is in the source.

"Interesting letter concerning the education of his half-brother Cyrus [*King*]. Prefers that he attend 'the College in this City (Columbia), then by sending him to Cambridge [*Harvard College*] . . .' ."

Sarah Livingston Jay to John Jay. ALS, Jay Papers, NNC. Addressed to Jay on circuit in Portsmouth, New Hampshire; franked by Dalton; postmarked. A reference to Lady Elizabeth Temple's weekly Tuesday evening reception as "yesterday," indicates that the letter may have been begun on 12 May.

Dalton, accompanied by his wife (Ruth Hooper Dalton), visited that morning and offered to frank her letters to Jay, and she intends to accept his offer.

James Madison, Notes on Navigation and Trade, and Notes for a Speech in Congress. Ms., Madison Papers, DLC. For the full text, see *PJM* 13:198–211. These will be printed in Correspondence: Third Session, 1789–91 Undated.

Theodore Rogers, Zabdeil Rogers, and Samuel Woodbridge to Benjamin Huntington. ALS, all signatures in the same unidentified hand, probably that of one of the signers, Washington Papers, DLC. Written from Norwich, Connecticut. This letter was enclosed in Huntington to Washington, 17 June, below.

Office seeking: the bearer, Samuel Snow, as surveyor of Providence, as soon as Rhode Island has ratified the Constitution.

Theodore Sedgwick to Pamela Sedgwick. ALS, Sedgwick Papers, MHi. Place to which addressed not indicated.

Is very well since arriving in town, except for "my common complaint," lack of sleep; "this is more or less the case as I have frequently told you when I am from home"; the measure (Trade and Navigation Bill) considered over the previous three days—on discriminatory tonnage duties—met with "violent opposition from the southward," but passed in the COWH by two to one; news of family friends; success in procuring household goods she requested to be sent; is disappointed by lack of letters from home, fearing his "best friend has an intention of puting in practice her threat."

George Thatcher to David Sewall. No copy known; acknowledged in Sewall to Thatcher, 20 May.

FRIDAY, 14 MAY 1790

Cool (Johnson)

Richard Henry Lee to [*Thomas Lee Shippen*]

It will be a fortnight tomorrow since I have been *almost* wholly confined to my Room with a severe stroke of the Influenza that had nearly dispatched me to that Country from whose Bourne no Traveller returns—I thank God that my present state of health, tho feeble, is yet such as promises to be good in a reasonable Time with proper care— *** Is the "Widow of Malabar"[1] realy a thing of genius & entertainment? or does your Theatre in a spirit of Politeness state it so? I rely on your judgement as a Critic Sound, if not severe—When I propose you to get it for me & if you will stake your taste upon it—The enclosed supposed you might be here—The plaguy Influenza Cough sticks faster than a blister, for the latter has quitted me but the former yet distresses—Is your whole Soul absorbed—Absolutely engrossd, so that you cannot write but of Love, & to your Love—Love does not forbid friendship from sliding in for a Moment or so—Under this idea I may hope an answer—My best affections where you know they are due I pray you to present.

ALS, Shippen Family Papers, DLC. Place to which addressed not indicated. The unnamed recipient is addressed as "dear Cousin," a salutation Lee sometimes used with his nephew. For the full text, see *Lee* 2:513–14. The omitted text concerns personal business.

[1] A romantic play set in India, translated by David Humphreys in 1790 from an earlier French play. It became part of the Old American Company's repertoire with its premiere in Philadelphia on 7 May (*FG*, 6 May).

OTHER DOCUMENTS

John Brown to John Francis. ALS, Henry A. L. Brown Deposit, RHi. Written from Providence, Rhode Island; place to which addressed not indicated.
Has heard that a congressional committee (on the Rhode Island Trade Bill) called on Rhode Island to pay $27,000 and "Cut of[*f*] all Communications with us" after 1 July; asks Francis, when passing through New York, to talk with Morris and others regarding a discrimination in the treatment of Rhode Island Antifederalists and Federalists; asks Francis to petition Congress to allow them (Brown and Francis) to enter a ship at New York or Philadelphia on the same terms as United States citizens.

John Dawson to James Madison. ALS, Madison Papers, DLC. Written from Richmond, Virginia. For the full text, see *PJM* 13:215–16.
Virginia's council has taken steps to facilitate the federal government's payment of arrearages to soldiers of the Virginia line of the Continental Army, and will "readily cooperrate with you in any plan which will render a service to this class"; rejoices to hear about assumption's defeat, but laments the Senate's treatment of R. H. Lee's motion to open that chamber's doors to the public; considered Lee's and Grayson's letter to the Virginia legislature (28 September 1789; see *DHFFC* 17:1634) "a very imprudent thing," but expects the Senators to report fully on the failure of Lee's motion; Parker has written him that a motion to adjourn to Philadelphia will probably succeed; has heard that Arthur Lee will run for R. B. Lee's seat, and Giles for Bland's seat, while Benjamin Harrison will probably defeat Griffin.

Samuel Meredith to George [*Clymer*]. ALS, Dreer Collection, PHi.
Clymer has key to chest containing some of Meredith's indents, "in case of need"; wishes for the speedy recovery of Clymer's health.

George Thatcher to David Sewall. No copy known; acknowledged in Sewall to Thatcher, 20 May.

Thomas B. Wait to George Thatcher. ALS, Chamberlain Collection, MB. Written from Biddeford, Maine.
On a quick and spontaneous visit to Thatcher's house, "Sister Sally [*Sarah Thatcher*] is now at the table with me, and is also writing to ~~our~~ her husband and my brother"; news of friends.

SATURDAY, 15 MAY 1790

Pierce Butler to Edward Rutledge

*** My dear Mrs. [*Mary Middleton*] Butler is much the same, one day a little better; again a relapse: my hopes and fears are constantly alive. I am nearly a slave to her situation.

Our excellent President is dangerously indisposed at this moment. I give You the very words of his Physicians; of which body he has four attending him.[1] His disorder is a peropinumany—Too much hangs on the life of this good man. The House of Representatives are not the best united body at present—what effect the loss of him, who unites all parties would have I need not say to You.

Nothing has been done in the funding system for some time. I am of opinion that the States' debts will not be assumed this session. I have had my doubts on this subject; they are not only too lengthy to trouble You with at present, but of that nature that I should feel reluctant to commit to paper, not that I would hesitate to entrust them with you, but I wish not to have cause to entertain them myself. Under my present impression I am led to believe that if [*South*] Carolina was not peculiarly circumstanced with respect to her load of debt it would be her best policy to be opposed to the measure. Circumstanced as our State is, and instructed as our Legislature have thought fit to place me, I shall assuredly vote for and support the assumption; but I believe posterity in Carolina will not thank me for it, or approve the measure; yet I have made up my mind, with some hesitation, to do so. There are strong arguments for it, there are to my mind very strong political causes involved in the measure: I should say consequences.

We are again threatened with an encrease of 50 cents on foreign vessels. The measure was well opposed by our Representatives. Madison carried in the committee a discrimination in favor of the French. I think the Senate may be brought to reject the whole. Our gentry voted for the discrimination with a view of frustrating the whole, as Pensylvania, who favored the first, will vote against the [*Trade and Navigation*] bill rather than irritate Britain, so that it is possible it may be lost *for this session* in the House of Representatives without coming up to Senate.

You will see by the prints what We are about to do with Rhode Island. I am for doing something, but not at present for going the lengths the [*Rhode Island Trade*] bill holds out. Our declarations and our actions will not very well accord—We the zealous supporters of civil liberty!

FC, Butler Letterbook, ScU. For the full text, see *Butler Letters*, pp. 41–43. The omitted text discusses Rutledge's assistance in the settlement of Butler's accounts as surety for Daniel Bourdeaux's debts.

---

[1] The four physicians who attended Washington during his recovery from peripneumony (pneumonia) were Samuel Bard, John McKnight, and the former British army surgeon John Charlton, all of New York City, and the Philadelphian Dr. John Jones, who was summoned to consult with them on 13 May (*PGW* 5:395).

Nathaniel Gorham to Theodore Sedgwick

Your favour of the 8th. came safe to hand—I belive you must have misconceived of some expressions in my Lettre or I think you would not appear to be hurt by it—as I am afraid you was, by your answer. I very probably might not express myself as I intended—but you may depend my Dear Friend—that I had not then or now an Idea in my mind toward you but those of the most sincere Friendship & regard—Your valedictory speach upon the loss of the assumption (if I may so term)—betrayed no marks of warmth of a wan[*t*] of patience—& altho it might not strictly speaking, be in order, every Body was pleased with it.

A Virginia Federalist is perhaps not exactly defined or made certain—but I am glad to hear that Mr. Walker is not an Anti.

Be so kind as to send the enclosed to Mr. Smith & remember your Letters are allways considered as a favour.

ALS, Sedgwick Papers, MHi. Written from Charlestown, Massachusetts.

Roger Sherman to Simeon Baldwin

Enclosed is a news Paper and a letter from Salem [*Massachusetts*] for Mrs. Sherman.[1] Betsey [*daughter Elizabeth*] may open it, if it comes to hand before She gets home. Roger will probably be at home tuesday evening. I have been a little unwell for two day be feel better this afternoon, I have been able to attend Congress have no news but what is contained in the—I shall want to know as soon as may be when Mrs. Sherman gets home & the particulars of their Journey.

P. S. Col. Ely's Petition for compensation[2] is rejected by the Senate they were furnished with information that the State of Connecticut had made him such compensation as the[*y*] supposed him to be intitled to—I have not enclosed Mrs. Sherman's Letter.

ALS, Sherman Collection, CtY. Addressed to New Haven, Connecticut; franked; postmarked.

[1] The letter to Rebecca Prescott Sherman from Stephen and Martha Prescott Goodhue, which Representative Goodhue forwarded under a cover of this date, below.
[2] For John Ely's petition and the Ely Bills [HR-49] and [HR-56], see *DHFFC* 7:320–25.

[*David Daggett,*] A Republican to Messrs. Printers (No. 1)

I despise the idea of railing against public men and public measures without any just cause—I equally despise the man who dares not speak his sentiments openly against an iniquitous administration.

I was a strong advocate for the adoption of the new constitution—I still think it an excellent form of government—but the conduct of Congress I am far from applauding.

Many and various advantages (we were told) were to result from this new system—we were all invited to lend our aid in organizing an establishment which should secure lasting benefits to every class of men—The merchant was told that he would no longer lament the languishing state of commerce—The arbitrary exactions of foreign nations were to be provided against and the mercantile interest to be regarded with the most scrupulous attention—Fourteen months have already elapsed since Congress met—and what measures have been adopted tending to promote the public weal? or rather, what measures have been neglected? I am at a loss to determine which deserves most censure their acts of *omission* or of *commission.* Instead of seeing commerce rendered more flourishing, we have heard of nothing but *heavy duties* already imposed and still more grievous, in contemplation. These exactions, we confess, are necessary when we view the enormous salaries given to the officers of Congress. That our legislators and judges should be honorably paid, and that every man employed in the business of Congress, should receive an adequate compensation, I do not deny, but I seriously contend, that the wages given, in many instances, are not only utterly inconsistent with the finances of this young empire, but highly unjust—comporting better with the luxury and prodigality of some dissipated court, than the simplicity and œconomy which ought to characterize a republican Congress. The salaries of the President—Vice President—Judges of the Supreme and District Courts and the wages of Members of both Houses of Congress, I pass over—observing only that there is no proportion between the income of a Judge of the Supreme Court and that of a District Judge—observing also that an allowance of six dollars per day for every twenty miles travel of each member while coming to or returning from Congress, is an unreasonable compensation—each of those gentlemen, if traveling on his own private business, would perform a journey of twice that distance every day—and will not those patriots be as diligent for the public as for themselves? Each Chaplin of Congress is to receive at the rate of 500 dollars per annum during the sessions of Congress—for what? why, for praying five or six times in each week. Is not this unparralled? Allow them to pray 300 times in each year (a calculation much too large) they will then receive 1 dollar and 66 cents for each prayer. Suppose their prayers 15 minutes each (which is allowance sufficient in a house where they dispatch business so *rapidly*) and then consider that this duty is altogether *professional* with the Clergy, and is not their compensation extravagant? Who among us, my fellow citizens, can, with laborious industry, earn, in 24 hours, the sum which a Chaplin receives for 15 minutes employed in a devotion so pleasing to his pious heart?

The Secretary of the Senate and Clerk of the House have each a salary of 1500 dollars per annum–and two dollars per day during the session of that branch for which they officiate—Suppose the session continues six months in each year, their income will be little short of 1900 dollars each per annum. And for what is this sum given? for performing service which any man may perform, that can be taught to *read* and *write*—their business is as mechanical as that of making a horse-nail. An hundred men may be found in each state in the Union equal to the business of Clerk to either House of Congress. The Serjeant at Arms—the Door-keeper and assistant Door-keeper, each receive about as much as is given to the second Officer in the state of Connecticut. Congress thought it beneath their dignity to create an office worth less than 500 dollars per annum. The duties and exactions must indeed be great, where such a multiplicity of officers are to be paid such extravagant wages.

Shall I be told that the Southern members in Congress, being accustomed to give great salaries, influenced the compensations above mentioned? I answer, the New-England states will contract to furnish clerks, door-keepers, sweepers, &c. at one half the sum allowed by Congress.

But it has been said we cannot judge of the duties of these several officers, and therefore are incompetent to determine upon the quantum of their pay. We know, even in Connecticut, the ordinary mode of *praying*, the usual method of *reading* and *writing*, the manner in which our servants *keep* our doors, and the most natural mode of *sweeping*.

The fact is, such disposition of the public money is no more nor less than sporting, wantonly sporting with the property of the subject—The people at large consider it in this point of view, and common sense declares their opinion to be just. "Brethren, these things ought not to be so."

[New Haven] *Connecticut Journal*, 19 May. This is the first of ten essays that appeared in this newspaper during the late spring and summer of 1790; the first nine numbered essays bear the dates 15, 22, and 29 May, 7, 14, and 25 June, 10 and 19 July, and 16 August. Most of the essays were reprinted at least once; one appeared as many as nine times and another was reprinted as far away as Fredericksburg, Virginia. Together they constitute the most sustained newspaper attack on the FFC. "Frederick" responded in the *Connecticut Journal* of 26 May; a more vigorous counterattack appeared in the same paper over the signature "Gallio," written by Sherman's son-in-law Simeon Baldwin and published on 30 August. Gallio elicited the final, unnumbered reply from A Republican on 6 September. All of these documents are printed under their dates, below and in volume 20.

By August it had become apparent to many readers that A Republican was seeking Sherman's defeat in the second federal election scheduled for 20 September. A Real Republican & Farmer, writing for Hartford's *American Mercury* of that date and citing sources "best acquainted with the *local politics of New Haven*," identified A Republican as a local attorney, "the known friend, follower, and trumpeter" of another New Haven attorney with "an unconquerable desire" to sit in Congress. Pierpont Edwards, a leader of the New Haven bar, had already emerged as Sherman's outspoken rival in the election, and fellow lawyer David Daggett was known to be his "Tool" (Henry Channing to Daggett, 22 November 1790, Daggett Papers, CtY). A short poem in the *Connecticut Journal* of 9 August mocked the congressional aspirations of A Republican's "*eager Master*," while "Frederick" scoffed at A Republican's pretensions to a seat in the state legislature, where Edwards was already in his third year as Speaker of the House but where Daggett would not win a seat until 1791. Daggett's and Edwards's efforts yielded mixed results. In the at large election of the five man delegation, Sherman and Edwards came in first and second place respectively.

Other Documents

Abraham Baldwin to Joel Barlow. AL, Baldwin Family Collection, CtY. Place to which addressed not indicated.

"Your girl" (Ruth Baldwin Barlow) will be in New York City ready to sail for Europe in about four days; "none of our finance questions are yet determined, it is very doubtful how they will go, they depend entirely upon undertows as a sailor you know what that is"; one hundred more French "colons" (colonists) have arrived at Virginia, for Scioto Company lands; it has been reported that Maj. (John) Doughty was attacked going down the Ohio but Baldwin does not believe it; will send newspapers by the first conveyance to London.

Tench Coxe to Benjamin Rush. ALS, Rush Papers, PPL at PHi. Addressed to Philadelphia; franked by Hartley; postmarked.

Expresses concern for the country if Washington's "continued health" is not possible; Adams, who was not at home when Coxe called, returned the visit and received Rush's letter; "He was very easy and unreserved," expressing esteem and affection for Rush, and demonstrating "considerable knowledge" about Pennsylvania affairs; found the Adamses "delightfully situated on the North [*Hudson*] River" (at "Richmond Hill"), with Mrs. (Abigail) Adams engaged in needlework, "like a Philada. matron"; she "appears to be a lady of observation and information," much recovered from a recent indisposition; has not yet seen Burke, who returned a visit when Coxe was out; Hartley said there were "some clamours" in Philadelphia over Coxe's appointment (as assistant secretary of the treasury); "there is considerable apprehension about defects in taking the census in several parts of the Union"; send mail to Coxe under cover sheets addressed to Hamilton or Hartley.

Elbridge Gerry to James Sullivan. No copy known; acknowledged in Sullivan to Gerry, 1 June.

Benjamin Goodhue to Rebecca Prescott Sherman. ALS, Sherman Collection, CtY. Addressed to New Haven, Connecticut; franked by Sherman; postmarked.

Forwards a letter just received from Stephen Goodhue, enclosing "his and Sisters [*Martha Prescott Goodhue*] love to you expecting that you would have been here when his letter arrived."

Christopher Gore to Rufus King. ALS, King Papers, NHi. For a partial text see, *King* 1:387. Written from Boston.

Congratulations on the birth of King's daughter (Caroline); hopes she inherits her parents' virtues; sends bourbon, coffee, and a quintal of fish; "the Chief Justice hath delighted the people of Massachusetts—they regret that Boston was not the place of his nativity—and his manners, they consider, so perfect as to believe that New York stole him from New England."

Jeremiah Hill to George Thatcher. ALS, Chamberlain Collection, MB. Written from Biddeford, Maine; postmarked Portsmouth, New Hampshire, 17 May.

Discusses limitations on the authority of Holy Scripture and the need to interpret revelation rationally; reports on local elections to the state legislature.

Sarah Livingston Jay to John Jay. ALS, Jay Papers, NNC. Addressed to Jay on circuit in Portsmouth, New Hampshire.

King called on her the previous evening; "he has a little daughter [*Caroline*] in addition to his flock."

Frères Lanchon to John Langdon. LS, printed, Langdon Papers, NhPoA. Written from L'Orient, France; addressed to Portsmouth, New Hampshire.

Writing to their correspondents at large, the mercantile firm reports on the state of France's economy and the revolutionary government's liberalization of trade regulations and its impact on promoting trade in certain enumerated commodities; hopes that the changes in the United States' and France's new constitutions help cement relations between the two countries.

Richard Henry Lee to Thomas Lee Shippen. ALS, Shippen Papers, DLC. Place to which addressed not indicated. For the full text, see *Lee* 2:514.

"I must begin by assuring you that I am yet much too unwell to write with any care to myself"; arrangements for procuring and shipping some iron to "Stratford Hall," Virginia; "N. York is at present a perfect Hospital—few are well & many very sick—Among the latter is unfortunately placed our most worthy P[*resident*]. of the U.S.—You know how strong my private predilections are for P[*hiladelphia*]. You know how very sincerely I love many there or at German-Town—Therefore you ma[*y*] well suppose that the cause must be very potent that will with-hold my voice from what will [*lined out*] promote her prosperity."

Philip Schuyler to Volckert Douw. No copy known; acknowledged in Douw to Schuyler, 20 May.

Alexander White to an Unknown Recipient. ALS, *The Collector* 90 (May 1895), p. 95. This is likely the letter dated "1790," probably to Mary Wood, listed in *Henkels Catalog* 24 October 1894, item 506.

"The President has the influenza or some similar disorder—so as to confine him to his bed—these two days past."

[Boston] *Massachusetts Centinel*, 15 May. The Virginian mentioned is likely Madison, but Moore and Brown are also possibilities.

"MARRIED—At New-York, Hon. JOSHUA SENEY, Member of Congress, to Miss FANNY NICHOLSON, of that city. *The Miss Nicholsons have been very fortunate—in attracting the attention of the Rulers of The Nation. One of them* [*Catherine*] *was some time since married to the Most Hon.* WILLIAM FEW, *of the Senate—and another, we are told, is now addressed by a very worthy member from Virginia. Nor are these Ladies more fortunate than meritorious.*"

[Providence, Rhode Island] *United States Chronicle*, 20 May.

"*A Gentleman, who arrived in Town from New-York just as this Paper was going to Press, has favored us with the Gazette of the United States, printed in that City on Saturday last* [15 May], *from which the following is copied*"; prints the Rhode Island Trade Bill.

Sunday, 16 May 1790

Cool (Johnson)

John Fenno to Joseph Ward

***

I perceive that great uneasiness exists respecting the delays of Congress—many of them however, are unavoidable—and tho' the reasons of others are at present involved in clouds I doubt not you & other anxious friends to Govt. will see that there is no intentional delay—& will be convinced by the members that all is right—The serious, & almost equal division on the essential point, Assumption, occasions all the difficulty—the majority is not perfectly satisfied in the decisions that have been made—and the minority think *all* is suspended on the Question—Mr. Madison's very long Speech is the last that has been made on the Subject (it will appear in my next paper)[1] and contains many extraordinary assertions—this led Ames to call for Documents[2]—some delay unavoidably ensued—they are now before the House—and the reverse of the picture must be exhibited—Madisons Speech must be dissected—The Assumptionists think they will carry the point, finally, by a handsome majority—all the rest will speedily follow—and as they talk of adjourning by the last of this month, & very strongly—they must make dispatch.

The talk is of adjourning to Philadelphia to meet there in Dec. next—~~I am sorry that the new married man, appears to want ballast,~~[3]—you should tread on his toe—My Compliments & Mrs. [*Mary Curtis*] Fenno's to him; & please to present our Congratulations—I will mention what you hint to Col. Trumbull—the idea had occurred to me but I believe it is entirely too late—as that piece was finished I think before he left England—pray is not Col. prescot dead? All the portraits in his pieces are taken from the life as far as possible—or from pictures drawn from the life[4]—You say the apologies will not do—I assure you, that persons here on the spot (not merely the Citizens who are interested) do not find so much fault as those at a distance—and it is my sincere opinion that there is not an influential member in the

House that wishes to protract the Session unnecessarily—but this Subject of funding is attended with innumerable difficulties—There are however delays that I cannot account for—last Wednesday was assigned to take up the funding bill—the Tonnage business [*Trade and Navigation Bill*] however was taken up, & unexpectedly has consumed the Time ever since—however, this is in the line of Revenue and I think a good, & popular System will be adopted—Meantime I think the members are coalescing with respect to assumption—the Fundg. & Ways & means Bills[5]—so that when they are taken up, a mutual understanding will prevent much more collision.

Our beloved President is alarmingly sick with a pleurisy[6]—expectorates blood—& has a very high fever—he was a little better last night—May God be gracious to the united States in sparing his life.

Thro' divine goodness my Family is at present in tolerable health—we have had attacks of the disorder of the day but are recovered—Mrs. Miles was taken very ill yesterday with a pleuresy—& is very sick—Very few persons have escaped, & numbers have died. ***

ALS, Ward Papers, ICHi. Addressed to the Land Office, State Street, Boston; postmarked. The omitted text relates to the recent death of Ephraim Fenno's father, other family news, and local and national news. For the full text, see *AASP* 89(1979):361–63.

---

[1] *GUS*, 19 May, reprinted Madison's lengthy speech of 22 April from *NYDA*, 26 April; see *DHFFC* 13:1171–81.

[2] Ames was one of the introducers of the House orders of 23 April seeking several reports (*DHFFC* 5:859–60). The specific report he sought was the one received from the secretary of war on 11 May (*DHFFC* 5:876–88).

[3] This heavy strike out of more than a line of the manuscript was probably done by Ward or some later reader, to avoid the risk of publicizing a perceived indiscretion of Fenno's. The newlywed's identity is not known.

[4] Ward appears to have suggested some alteration to the composition of John Trumbull's famous painting, *The Battle of Bunker Hill*, perhaps involving Ward's distant kinsman, Gen. Artemas Ward (1727–1800), commander-in-chief of Massachusetts militia during the battle, for whom Joseph served as aide-de-camp, 1775–76. The first of Trumbull's monumental series depicting critical moments in the Revolution, *Bunker Hill* was completed while Trumbull was still a student at Benjamin West's London studio in early 1786. Col. William Prescott (1729–95) commanded the colonial forces at the battle on 17 June 1775 and the 7th Continental Regiment the next year.

[5] The House had last considered the Duties on Distilled Spirits [HR-62] and Duties on Wines [HR-64] bills on 5 May.

[6] Pleurisy is an inflammation of the membranes encasing the lungs. It sometimes appears as a complication of pneumonia or influenza.

Elbridge Gerry to John Wendell

I have two of your esteemed favours unanswered, one without date [*24 March*] & the other of the 2d of April—the indisposition of myself &

family, & a constant attention to business when in health, have induced me of late to suspend answers to all the letters of my friends; indeed the measure has been indispensible, for the influenza has disqualified me a great part of the time, from attending to any business. but I am not less sensible, from these circumstances, of your friendship & kindness, & am happy to find that any part of my political conduct meets the approbation of my friends—I am not surpriz'd at my not hearing of Capt. Philips, because (entre nous) I have not been twice at my Collegues lodgings since my return from Massachusetts, & not much oftner before I went there, but how Mr. [*James?*] Thompson missed him I cannot conceive for he is a member of a lawyers Club & must as I supposed get information of every person of note in the city. certain it is he took much pains to find him out, but I am happy to hear that altho he failed of success you sustained no injury thereby.

The late decissions of the House respecting an increase of foreign tonnage [*Trade and Navigation Bill*] &c. will remove your difficulties on that score; but I must confess to you that I think the subject is not well digested or understood.

I agree with you that the conduct of Congress in scaling the old emission was a partial bankruptcy, but they ought to extend it no farther if they can possibly avoid it. had they not taken the measure at that time they must have given up the contest, & nothing but such a necessity could be considered as a justification or even an apology for their conduct. their desperate situation at that period led them no further than to violate their faith as it respected the old emissions, for which the publick never had *value* received; & What would be the effect if they were now to extend the violation to other parts of the debts, when there is not the plea of necessity or of their not having recd. the full amount of them?[1]

I observe your hints respecting a lottery, bank &c. & am not ripe for an opinion on the subjects. each of them will require great tho't before they can be matured. indeed the questions relating to the assumption, & revenue for funding, engross our whole attention, & I question whether we shall be able to compleat them to public satisfaction this Session. I feel the force of your observations respecting [*lined out*] of a [*lined out*],[2] & as soon as our present business is finished will attend to it, altho it [*lined out*] lies principally in the department of the Secretary of the Treasury. sure I am that the fiscal operations of the union cannot proceed, without some artificial or real increase of money. I sincerely wish you was a member of the House, which of the two branches is I think to be preferred for variety; but you would find it [*as*] everyone must who attends to business a slavish employment.

ALS, Gratz Collection, PHi. Addressed to Portsmouth, New Hampshire; franked; postmarked 18 May. Gerry enclosed a letter to Wendell from a Mr. Randall.

[1] Under a March 1780 plan to resolve the problem of the devaluation of continental currency, Congress revalued it at forty dollars to one specie dollar. It was to be known as the old (emission) currency and withdrawn from circulation ("sunk") through state taxation. The act virtually repudiated the old money, reducing its legal value from two hundred million to five million, which amount was to be withdrawn by the spring of 1781. For every forty dollars thus withdrawn, two dollars in "new issue" paper money would be circulated. Although the plan did not work, the value of the old currency expired in the spring of 1781 as planned—except for speculators willing to pay one dollar (or less) in specie for five hundred dollars in currency. Each dollar of new emission, or money of 1781, was regarded as equal to forty dollars in old currency rather than one specie dollar as planned (*Purse*, pp. 51–52, 64–66).

[2] These two strike outs were probably done later by Wendell or someone else.

Benjamin Goodhue to Stephen Goodhue

Yours of 28th. Ultimo 1st. and 8th and 11th. instant have receiv'd, your sister [*in-law, Rebecca Prescott*] Sherman set out for N[*ew*]. Haven on Thursday last, and I have forwarded the letter you inclosed Mr. Sherman has the influenza but not bad, the President has that or rather a pleuresy so that his Physicians look upon him a very sick man and are not a little apprehensive of the event. I hope our Children are well through the Measles, ***

[*P. S.*] I wish you to write me often—I am sensible of the decline of trade and bussines in our qua[*rter*] and consequently the increase of poverty. I have a long time seen this coming, and I think the Town of Salem and our other Towns have seen their best days, and am grieved at the reflection, but I do not know how to help it, as to the fisheries I do not know what can be effectualy done for them. I hope the Government will do what little they can, but I fear people expect more then is in their power—I had I think rather enjoy but little in private life then much in this station where my mind is perpetualy haunted with disquieting considerations. I don't mean by this to blame you. for mentioning the distresses of my townsmen.

ALS, Goodhue Family Papers, MSaE. Addressed to Salem, Massachusetts. The omitted text relates to private commercial concerns.

John Page to St. George Tucker

I write now merely to shew you that I will write to you whenever I can—I look upon myself as largely indebted to you—not only for your friendly Congratulations on my Marriage & for Your Verses on that Occasion but for your quis quæ quid[1]—I received these very critically, they were handed to me whilst in Bed with my Bride, for they reached me the Morning after I was married—I have been so pestered by damn'd Ceremonies & hurried by Business that I have not had Leisure to write an Answer to quis &c. but your own was excellent—I have not Leisure now to copy the few Trifles I have for you—I wish you had sent me the Errata in Dodsley I would have them added[2]—The Whole city nay whole Countries around us, have been & still are suffering under the Influenza, or Catahral [*catarrhal*] Fever as now [*blotted out*]—it is as infectious as the Plague—Mrs. [*Margaret Lowther*] Page & myself have had it slightly, we did not lie by for it—some are very ill—Your Brother [*Thomas Tudor Tucker*] has had it mostly—the President has had it, & is now ill of a Peripneumony his Life was yesterday despaired of—He has 4 Physicians attending him I went last Night to inquire how he was, & had the Pleasure to find that his Disorder had taken the happy turn—& I am this Minute informed by my Boy whom I sent for Information, that he is a great deal better—My Wife unites with me in best Wishes to you—Oh Tucker how I wish you were blest with such a Wife as I am! What Mr. Bracken[3] has said of us in his latin Verses addressed to me on my Marriage is literaly true.

"Consociantus—Dextræque Animique"—
and, "Nil sibi jam metuunt, pariter nil ferre recusant,
"Vir Sponsa felix, Sponsa beata Viro."
"—tibi Numine fausto"
"Ipse Deus Sponsam fert, propriamque dicut."[4]

I am called off my dear Tucker therefore Adieu.

ALS, Tucker-Coleman Papers, ViW. Addressed to Williamsburg, Virginia; franked; postmarked. Tucker wrote the following on the address sheet, perhaps as a note to himself about some point included in a subsequent, unlocated letter to Page: "An original, ~~voluntary, free~~ written Social compact, freely, voluntarily, & solemnly entered into by the people of the U.S. by which ~~every~~ the Citizens of the U.S. have reciprocally bound themselves & the States to each other, and to the general Government, & by which the General Government is bound to ~~every Citizen~~ to the several States, and to every Citizen of the U.S."

[1] Tucker, his brother the congressman, William Nelson, and Page sometimes exchanged light hearted observations on public and personal subjects in verses variously entitled with these Latin interrogatives. None by St. George on the subject of Page's marriage has been located.

[2] Over the previous three months, Page and Tucker had been exchanging a "Dodsley"—either a volume by the British writer Robert Dodsley (1703–64) or a volume of the correspondents' own verses composed in his style.

[3] John Bracken (1745–1818) was the Anglican minister of Williamsburg, Virginia, and master of the grammar school at the College of William and Mary there, from approximately 1776 until the position was eliminated in 1779 (*John Marshall* 2:67–68).

[4] "United—both in hand and in spirit" and
"They reap nothing for themselves, nor do they refuse to produce,
A happy husband, a beautiful maiden."
"— by an auspicious command,
God himself proclaimed the union, and indeed declared it His own."

Joseph Pierce to Benjamin Goodhue

I thank you for the several Letters you have written me—many are fully of your opinion "that if the Domestic Debt be now funded & provided for—and the Assumption of the State Debts postponed that nothing but the most violent Convulsions will induce an assumption hereafter"—there are however some who think if both were now to be done that worse consequences would ensue, for say they the collection of duties will be much lessen'd after two or three years—a deficiency must follow—and to make that up recourse must be had to a dry Tax—and in some States perhaps where never any has been which may produce generaly the same consequences as the morrisses Taxes[1] did in this State some years since—indeed you have a choice of difficulties—and the bussiness is hard—we are at a distance and know very little what you have to struggle with—I am not surprised that you are tired of a political Life.

I have understood that bussiness is so brisk in N. York that the City is like a bee hive—if so—Boston is a perfect contrast—for never was business known to be so dull—as a Town we are growing poor rapidly—if you were here you would be surprised.

ALS, Letters to Goodhue, NNS. Written from Boston; place to which addressed not indicated.

---

[1] Although Massachusetts ultimately ratified both the 1781 and 1783 Amendments to the Articles of Confederation that empowered the federal government to collect a five percent impost (tariff) as proposed by Superintendent of Finance Robert Morris, the state was a hotbed of opposition to Morris and his entire financial program.

Philip Schuyler to Stephen Van Rensselaer

The post was already returned when Your favor of the 9th Instant was delivered me.

The conduct of the family you mention has cast an indeliable stain upon them.[1] It is much to be lamented that people in a station of life which should put them far above what is mean low and unworthy should suffer themselves to be made ~~the~~ instruments of by a set who only despise them, and who would not have had recourse to them unless with a view to render them subservient to their designs. I fear Mr. Sylvester will be the victim of their operation as well as [*Leonard*] Gansevoort & Schuyler.

The President has been dangerously Ill for some days past with a violent fever and inflamation on the lungs he has had some ease last night. and is apparently relieved. we have however still very seriously to apprehend the result.

Tomorrow another attempt will be made in the house of representatives in favor of the debts contracted by the Individual states. The Issue is very problematical, appearances are rather unfriendly to it.

No motion has yet been brought forward to remove the seat Government, but we apprehend that If the assumption is not carried, that the South Carolinians may (in order to Obtain that Object which is so important to them) negotiate with those who wish the removal. If so we shall lose congress, unless all the Members from our state would vote for the assumption which would supercede the necessity of a negotiation on the part of Carolinens, and would be more agreable to them, as nothing but the magnitude of the Object of promising relief from their debt would induce them to assent to a removal.

***

ALS, Schuyler Papers, N. Place to which addressed not indicated. The omitted text concerns the birth of a child.

---

[1] Van Rensselaer's letter is unlocated, but the family he referred to was undoubtedly the Livingstons, a vast clan whose acreage extended as widely as their influence in the state's "popular party." Despite their intermarriage, from about this time and throughout the 1790s, the Schuyler-Van Rensselaer family alliance and the Livingstons were adversaries in a fight for political control over the upper Hudson River valley. John Livingston, cousin of Chancellor Robert R. Livingston, unsuccessfully challenged Silvester in the second federal election in 1790, while the Livingstons' coalition with the incumbent George Clinton helped to narrowly defeat the John Jay-Stephen Van Rensselaer ticket in the state's gubernatorial election two years later.

George Thatcher to Sarah Thatcher

By a Letter of yours I received some time the begining of the week past, but which I have now lost I learn you had agreed with a woman at the falls [*Biddeford*] to take Phillips [*Savage*] to school, and that he was to dine at Esqr. [*Tristram*] Jordan's—I like your plan very well, & hope he will be attentive; I would have no pains spared to make him willing to go to School—I wish you had told me who the Mistress is & where she keeps her school—As he must pass the Bridge two or three times a day, it give me some uneasiness lest he should fall into the river—if you think there is any dander [*danger*], I would have you desire the Girl that lives at Mr. Jordans to see him safe across the bridge—drowning always strikes me with more horror than death in any other form—I scarce ever look upon the water but it brings to my affrighted imagination the image of a drowned corps!

Yours of the 2d. inst. came to hand last evening—In this you say Philips goes to school like a good boy—Teach him my dear, to be punctual in going and returning—and dont let him loiter & play by the way, without leave—You will desire our friend Mercy, to be a little particular to him when he dines there—He was in a good habit when I left home, & behaved prettily at Table—He had nothing of that kind of bashfullness so disagreeable in children before company—Habituate him to a manly regularity—dont let him catch & pull for what he wants—Whenever he drinks, teach him to take a decent notice of the company. above all things, my dear, dont countenance him in geting birds eggs—picking up little Turtles, and ~~small~~ young birds—But rather let him know that they are all capable of pleasure and pain—and that it is as painfull & [*lined out*] cruel to hurt them as it is to cut off his finger, or carry him or his sister Sally [*Sarah*] away from his mama.

To inspire a child with attention to school & his book, endeavour to create a notion that if he learns to read, write &c. he will be able to procure himself such things as he most wants—By the next mail I will send him a Book—which he must learn to read by the time I return.

It is usual to teach children some catachise or other—If there were any that held up to the view of children plain, simple ideas I should have no objection to your teaching him to repeat them—provided they said nothing about the Devil, or that dredfull place, where it is usual to tell children they will go if they are wicked—I am a mortal enemy to the Devil & all such notions—But I have no objection to your learning him & his sister the Lords prayer—this is simple, & contains no frightfull pictures—away with such from the minds of children; thousands have been hurt & none profited by them.

As soon as I can procure some Bills on Boston Bank I will send money to Mr. [*Thomas*] Dakin & desire him to get some sugar & other things you wrote for, & send them to Biddeford—Your Gown & Linnen for the children I will bring with me.

ALS, Thatcher Family Papers, MHi. Place to which addressed not indicated.

Original Communications from New York

As to the ASSUMPTION OF THE STATE DEBTS, the question will come on again in a few days with redoubled energy. I think it must, and will take place. Mr. MADISON made the last speech on the subject[1]—it was lengthy, and contained many very *extraordinary assertions*; in short, granting his statements to be facts, which are doubted, they fairly erased from the mind every idea respecting the importance of the Eastern States, more particularly *Massachusetts*. But Mr. AMES called for documents—this has occasioned some delay—they are at length produced—and the *other side* of the piece will now be exhibited. Mr. MADISON's long harrangue must be dissected. Justice must be done to those to whom it is due—and I trust the enemies of *Assumption* will be changed to friends—the wandering brought back, and the *consistent* confirmed.

I always anticipated the greatest difficulties in effecting the FUNDING OF THE DEBT. Many of those who oppose the *Assumption*, are opposed to any plan of *funding* whatever—their scheme is to make annual grants for the payment of interest, according to the State of the Treasury from year to year. I know people are uneasy—but you know that a *few* persons can make a great deal of noise; and the publick Creditors should not be too clamourous; for if *Congress* does not provide for them, they are gone—you know there is not a great majority of the people, in favour of paying them; or rather there is nearly a majority that would without scruple apply the *sponge*.[2]

I never have seen any thing that looked like a wanton mispense of time—nor do I think there is a member of Congress who wishes to protract the session one moment unnecessarily. The great division upon the subject of *Assumption* has occasioned the delay. Those *against* the measure I think are not perfectly satisfied in the decisions that have been made; those *in favour* of it think every thing depends on it, and therefore hold on. And I hope have at last got the business in such a train as to secure a handsome majority. This is an important work, and when done, ought not to be done over again very suddenly.

The Quaker Memorials were an unlucky business. However, it served to ascertain points, which may be of great use at a future day.

[Boston] *Massachusetts Centinel*, 22 May; reprinted (all or in part) at Portland, Maine; Worcester, Massachusetts; Newport, Rhode Island; Hartford, Connecticut; New York City (*NYDG*, 29 May); Philadelphia; and Baltimore. Although several individuals acted as "correspondents" for Benjamin Russell's *Massachusetts Centinel*, the fact that the first paragraph repeats verbatim certain phrases from Fenno's letter to Joseph Ward of the same date, above, is further proof that Fenno was one of those correspondents. These "communications" are either a separate letter Fenno may have written that day to Russell, or a compilation of several letters, including one from Fenno. Like Ward, Russell was a patron: he had been Fenno's first employer in the printing trade, delivered the press with which Fenno began his *GUS* in New York City, and was that paper's Boston distributor (*DHFFC* 10:xxxiv–xxxv; 15:568).

[1] Madison made his last "lengthy" speech on assumption on 22 April (*DHFFC* 13:1171–81).

[2] To wipe out a debt without payment.

OTHER DOCUMENTS

John Chaloner to Jeremiah Wadsworth. ALS, Wadsworth Papers, CtHi. Written from Philadelphia.

Discusses brokered exchange certificates for Wadsworth.

Benjamin Goodhue to Cotton Tufts. No copy known; acknowledged in Tufts to Goodhue, 3 June.

Theodore Sedgwick to Thomas Dwight. No copy known; acknowledged in Dwight to Sedgwick, 20 May.

Theodore Sedgwick to Pamela Sedgwick. ALS, Sedgwick Papers, MHi. Place to which addressed not indicated. The closing reads, "I am dearest and best beloved of my heart, sincerely ever your affecte."

"I have not dared to mention to you before, the sickness of the president. Last Monday he was violently seized with a pleuresy, and the malignity of it encreased with its progress. About five oClock in the afternoon yesterday, the physicians declared that they had no hopes of his recovery. But about six he began to sweat most profusely, which continued untill this morning and we are now told that he is entirely out of danger, if he should not relapse. The danger in which his life has been gives additional evidence how very dear and precious it is to all ranks of people."

George Thatcher to Jeremiah Hill. No copy known; acknowledged in Hill to Thatcher, 23 May.

Jeremiah Wadsworth to Harriet Wadsworth. ALS, Wadsworth Papers, CtHi. Addressed to Hartford, Connecticut, in care of Peter Colt; signed "Your affectionate father & Sincere Friend"; franked.

Expresses assurance of Daniel's recovery; "the President has been dangerously ill for several days with a Violent Peripeniming [*pneumonia*] but is better today—my own health continues good."

William Samuel Johnson, Diary. Johnson Papers, CtHi.

"St. Pauls."

Monday, 17 May 1790

Cool (Johnson)

Elias Boudinot to [*John Edwards Caldwell*]

*** Our New Government succeeds beyond Expectation—Our Country increases in every advantage of Life—Peace is within our Walls & Prosperity on our Borders—The Arts & Sciences are in a very flourishing State and Agriculture is extending its Blessings far & Wide—The Western Country blossoms like a Rose & affords a happy Assylum for all the oppressed of the Earth. Plenty of the finest Land ~~on Earth~~ in the Universe may be bought there for about Eight [?] Livre an Acre, which will constantly produce from 20 to 30 Bushells of wheat [*lined out*]—In short we want nothing, but Gratitude to a gracious God and to live conformably to his Laws & Example.

***

FC, Boudinot Family Papers, NjR. A postscript dated 27 May is printed under that date, below. The recipient is identified from the context. The omitted text illustrates Boudinot's latitudinarianism: while cautioning Caldwell against too rash a decision to convert to Catholicism, "I wish not to limit the Spirit of God, whenever I behold his work, was it on the Heart of an Inhabitant of Indostan"; offers to furnish letters of recommendation if Caldwell goes to Edinburgh to study medicine; conveys most affectionate regards to the marquis de Lafayette.

Thomas Crafts to John Adams

***

Commerce & Business in general here is extreamly dull, perhaps it was never more so except at the time of the Port-Bill[1]—Business is supposed not to be so brisk & florishing as it has been for several Years past and many suppose it is in consequence of the large sums of money locked up in the different custom houses and by that means keept out of Circulation or for ought we know sent to the Seat of Government—You ask if no Benign influence has as yet been felt in Consequence of the new Goverment—The not assuming the State Debts has had a most disagreeable and banefull Effect here, and I am perswayded has made more persons disaffected to the New Goverment, then any other matter could possably have done. The long time Congress spent in disputing on the Quakers petition in favour of the Negro's[2] & the warmth with which it was supported by the Eastern Members has given great unesiness to many Persons—It being said here that was the cause of sowering the minds of the southern members against an Assumtion of the State Debts—The Price of of Bills of Exchange have fallen here 10 pr. Cent that is they were 5 pr. Cent above parr & are now 5 pr. Cent below parr. But it seems this was more by accendent. (The great demand for Grain from Europe) then from any benign Influences of the New Goverment And this has opperated rather against this Town, as large sums of Money, in addition to what is already Shut up has been sent to New York Philida. &c. to purchase Bills—You inquire if the Ship Carpenters are Employ'd I answer that they are wholly out Business as are most other Tradesmen, And I assure you the Situation of this Town is truly Melancholy and Distressing. The sound of the Ax or the Hammer is hardly to be heard in any part of It—The Tradesmen almost totaly discouraged. No

Work to be done, High Taxes & no prospect of Relief—You will see by Little attention paid to the Choice of Representives[3] but 200 Voters. Then more then 20 Candidates—No list presented or prepared & when called upon to Vote in general answerd they care'd not who were Chosen, they could not be worse off and that it was not probable they should be better distress & poverty being thier portion & they appear to me to be quite Discouraged.

Cannot something be done to Encourage the Cod & Whale Fisheries—
Must the Ship building be wholy Annihilated in the Eastern States—
Must the Assumtion of the State Debts be giving up for this Sessions—
Will not Congress take some measures that the monies collected for Imposts may be brought into Circulation again as soon as posable.

ALS, Adams Family Manuscript Trust, MHi. Written from Boston. The omitted text relates to Martin Brimmer Sohier's application for an army commission.

---

[1] The Boston Port Bill, one of Great Britain's Intolerable Acts of 1774, closed the port to commercial shipping pending compensation for damages from the Boston Tea Party.

[2] For background on the antislavery petitions to the FFC, see *DHFFC* 8:314–38.

[3] Until 1831, Massachusetts' state representatives were elected every May at least ten days before the beginning of the "political year" on the last Wednesday of the month.

Benjamin Goodhue to Michael Hodge

Your favr. of 7th I have recd. for which I thank you—We have adopted certain resolutions, relative to an increase of Tonage on Foreign Vessels which are put into the hands of a Committee for reporting a bill [*Trade and Navigation Bill*], agreably to what you see in the paper—an increase of tonage on foreign Vessels is a matter of the highest importance to our Eastern States, but whether it be proper to make such a discrimination between foreigners is a question on which there is a great division of sentiment—to me it is not so very material, provided our Navigation is encouraged, whether the tonage is on all foreigners or constructed so as to operate principaly on the British, the object I consider as attained in either case for the British are our principal rivals in the carrying bussines, all I hope is that it may not be the means of loosing the whole—the funding and assumption bussines remain as it has done for some time past, I still flatter myself with success, to be or not to be, I think is much involved in the question, I am proportionately affected with its issue.

[*P. S.*] The President has been so unwell as to cause much apprehension for the event of his illness, but today is much better.

ALS, Ebenezer Stone Papers, MSaE. Misdated 7 May; place to which addressed not indicated.

Benjamin Goodhue, by Joseph Wright, 1756–93, oil on canvas, 1790. Goodhue brought this painting with him when he returned to Salem, Massachusetts, at the end of the Second Session. He inscribed on the back "Sept, 13 1790 this picture is acknowled'd a strong Likeness" (Margaret C. S. Christman, *The First Federal Congress, 1789–1791* [Washington, D.C., 1989], p. 267). (Courtesy of the New York Society Library and the Frick Gallery.)

New York May 7. 90

Dear Sir

your fav.r of 7th I have rec.d for which I thank you—We have adopted certain resolutions, relative to an increase of Tonage on Foreign Vessels which are put into the hands of a Committee for reporting a bill, agreeably to what you see in the paper—an increase of tonage on foreign Vessels is a matter of the highest importance to our Eastern States, but whether it be proper to make such a discrimination between foreigners is a question on which there is a great division of sentiment,—to me it is not so very material, provided our Navigation is incouraged, whether the tonage is on all foreigners or constructed so as to operate principaly on the British, the object I consider as attained in either case for the British are our principal rivals in the carrying business, all I hope is that it may not be the means of loosing the whole—

the funding and assumption business remain as it has done for some time past, I still flatter myself with success. to be or not to be, I think is much involved in the question, I am proportionately affected with its issue—

yours &c—

B Goodhue

M Hodge Esqr.

Benjamin Goodhue to Michael Hodge, 17 May, ALS, p. 1. Through letters to Salem's insurance officer (Hodge), Goodhue informed an important hometown constituency about the latest proposed legislation bearing on tonnage and shipping, such as the Trade and Navigation Bill discussed here. Internal evidence proves Goodhue misdated the letter. (Courtesy of the Peabody Essex Museum, Salem, Massachusetts.)

Thomas Hartley to Jasper Yeates

It is agreed that the Funding Business will be taken up to Morrow—I immagine that the union Debt will be carried on & funded—tho' I am sure that every Attempt will be made agst. it without ~~the~~ a Provision is annexed concerning the State Debts we must do the best we can.

We complain of the British Policy in shutting their Ports in the West Indies[1]—and consider ours open to all Intents and Purposes as to them and also for his witholding the Posts.

We have brought in a Bill[2] aimed at her which is supported by a considerable Majority and some spirited Conduct has been discovered—We hope it will lead the British Court to relax in ~~their~~ her commercial Regulations &c.

The President has been very ill—but happily now is on the Recovery—we anxiously wait for the Reestablishment of his Health—but I fear his Constitution is much impaired & we cannot promise ourselves that he will live many years.

All was gloomy until the happy Change yesterday Morning was announced.

This City is very sickly—I hope my Freinds in Pennsylvania will escape the second Addition of the Influenza.

ALS, Yeates Papers, PHi. Addressed to Lancaster, Pennsylvania; franked; postmarked 18 May; answered 28 May. Probably enclosed the note dated 18 May, below.

[1]British Orders in Council dating back to July 1783 closed ports in the British West Indies to American ships, forcing American produce to be carried on British ships. Other trade regulations between the United States and British possessions in North America and the West Indies were contained in the act of 28 Geo. III, c. 6 (1788).

[2]The Trade and Navigation Bill.

Theodore Sedgwick to Pamela Sedgwick

Since I came from home as yet I have not recd. a single line from any of the family. A very disagreable suspence and anxiety is always the result of such a situation. Was you sensible how painful it is you would not permit it to exist. I do not know but I shall be obliged to retaliate in order to bring you to a compromise.

The papers in the ancient dominion of Virga. are constantly paying an attention to my conduct in the house.[1] Among others the paper which contained the inclosed was forwarded to me from an unknown hand. It is a pitty that the writers should take so much pains, because very few of them have reached me. I am told however that the writers have invariably treated me with respect and that their strictures have been conveyed in decent language.

Should the assumption be finally lost, the session I presume will not continue many days longer. We have, however, at present as fair a prospect of success as we have had for some time past. There are some converts, and I hope no apostates. Present, tender affection, duty, respect &ca. as due from your ever sincere and affece.

ALS, Sedgwick Papers, MHi. Addressed to Stockbridge, Massachusetts.

[1] The reference is to Sedgwick's widely reported "conduct" on the floor of the House following the COWH's vote against assumption on 12 April. Anti-assumptionist commentaries roundly criticized his alarmism on the occasion. The most inventive of these was a parody of Sedgwick's "funeral oration on the death of Miss Assumption," originally published in North Carolina on 8 May but addressed as a "Letter from New York to Virginia," dated 14 April and printed under that date, above.

John Steele to Governor Alexander Martin

A great variety of business at present ocupies the attention of Congress, and tho' the sessions commenced with the year, there is little probability of adjourning previous to the 1st of August.

The President is dangerously ill of a pectoral complaint, the opinion of the faculty is against a recovery: Before this attack he was engaged in extending his appointments to the several departments of No. Carolina and the ceded Territory, but the secrets of his cabinet are retained in such absolute darkness, that were I to attempt to give you information, it woud be mere conjecture. If this stroke shou'd unfortunately prove fatal, the Vice President will [*be*] in office, by virtue of his present appointment, untill the 4th. of March 1793. An event melancholy indeed. Shou'd it happen, perhaps it wou'd have been better for the United States, that Genl. Washington had never been chosen; for relying on his virtue and abilities, Congress have in repeated instances, by law vested him with powers not delegated by the constitution, which I suppose woud have been intrusted to no other man.

These powers, can never be recalled, without the consent of his successor in office or an union of Sentiment, which in these factious [*times*] is not to be expected.

The assumption of the State debts we are told, will be brought forward next week in a new dress. This is intended either to gull some of the more moderate members; or by delaying the progress of public business constrain some of the Georgians or No. Carolinians, (who are anxious to return,) to obtain leaves of absence: Or the Eastern Members have been tampering with the Pennsylvanians, by offering the permanent residence of Congress to Philadelphia. This surmise, I have taken occasion to speak of to those who are most zealously attached to the interest of that City, holding out as a threat that if they did desert us, we shou'd most assuredly desert them: so that eventually Philadelphia might loose more by the bargain, than she wou'd gain.

A bill[1] has lately been passed the senate, and sent to us for concurrence, designed to prohibit any further intercourse with Rhodeisland, untill [*she*] shall ratify. It is tyrannical and arbitrary in the highest degree, and the author of it,[2] indeed the senate by passing it, seem to have lost sight of that political connection which once existed and of that sperit of moderation, and mutual forbearance, which ought forever to subsist between governments related as they are to us, as well as between individuals. That state, tho' comparatively small was not backward in the late Revolution, she performed essential services in the common cause; she sustained important sacrafices, and is therefore entitled to respect. How far in her present politicks she has bee[*n wron*]g? Or how far right? are questions which time only c[*an de*]cide.

I hope the bill will not pass our house, if it shou'd, there will be a proof given to the world, of the sandy foundation of all human friendships, or political connections.

ALS, Steele Papers, NcU. Addressed to "Governor etca. etca. etca., North Carolina"; franked; postmarked 18 May.

[1] The Rhode Island Trade Bill.
[2] Senator Carroll.

Michael Jenifer Stone to [*Walter Stone*]

I only write to inform you that I have again the Influenza or a Complaint much like it—But Slightly.

The President has been Ill—So that his life was despaired of—Influenza Pleurisy and Peripneumony all at Once—He Spit Blood—had a Violent Fever—&ca.

He is now better—But is not yet out of bed or out of danger. Tell Mr. [*William?*] Craik I shall write him fully when my Spirrits return.

Give my Love to all Friends—I can place 300 Dollars in the Hands of Luper.

ALS, Stone Family Papers, MdHi. Place to which addressed not indicated. The editors base their identification of the recipient on the fact that the only extant letters that Stone sent to his district in 1790 were to his brother Walter, and the similarity of the closing to those in other letters he wrote Walter.

Other Documents

Samuel Langdon to John Langdon. ALS, Langdon Papers, NhPoA. Written from Hampton Falls, New Hampshire. The writer (no relation to the Senator) was issued the first copyright in New Hampshire in July 1791 for his *Observations on the Revelation of Jesus Christ to St. John* (Worcester, Mass., 1791).

If Congress has not passed a general copyright act, asks "if you will do what is necessary to procure a Patent for me"; will repay any expenses; encloses the title page; wishes him "all divine direction in the Counsels of the Senate."

Benjamin Lincoln to Theodore Sedgwick. ALS, Sedgwick Papers, MHi. Written from Boston; postmarked 18 May; franked.

Encloses order (bill of exchange) for Andrew Craigie as part of a financial transaction involving Sedgwick; "I hope the State debts will be embraced by the union I fear the consequences if they are not—I think however that we must fund the domestic debt and rely on the justice of Congress hereafter. Pray tel my friend Mr. Ames that I would have wrote ℘ this post but did not know what to say on the politicks of the day."

Daniel Hiester, Account Book. PRHi.

Attended "Monday Club" or Mess Day with the Pennsylvania delegation at Fraunces Tavern. (Maclay indicated that the delegation ate from 3:30 until about 4 P.M. and then spent the next five hours in conversation he described as a "Scene of Beastial Ba[*w*]dry" [*DHFFC* 9:270].)

Tuesday, 18 May 1790

Fine (Johnson)

John Adams to Oliver Whipple

With much pleasure I received your favour of March [*April*] 26th It brought fresh to my memory the many hours we spent together in the chamber where I first saw the light of the sun. I beleive there are few persons who run through a public career, especially one that interests the passions of the people; without finding persons to recollect prophecies that great things would one day be his lot. The political path in which I set out in life must lead either to destruction or to great success. As I know there ~~are~~ were not wanting persons to predict that I should rise high, and among these were men of merit; so on the other, I beleive there were many more who prophesied that I should ruin myself, family and Country, and reach nothing but infamy. I am not sorry as you may well imagine that the prognostications of the latter sort are not fulfilled.

The representation of your independent and respectable circumstances gives me much pleasure. The sense of Congress seems to be so much against many missions abroad, that I apprehend you could find no chance from that branch, in which so many have already been employed with reputation who are not out of office.[1] I really think you will find no office better than a lawyers office—Mine I know, while I held it, was the best office I ever enjoyed. As executive department by the constitution is wholly in the President I make no promisses to any one and interfere as little as possible in appointments. I should however have much pleasure in concurring with the friends you mention, in recommending you as far as the public service may justify.

FC:lbk, Adams Family Manuscript Trust, MHi. The ALS sold as item 25123 in the 16–17 April 2007 *Heritage Auction Galleries* sale.

[1] Whipple sought appointment as an excise officer or a diplomatic secretary.

Paine Wingate to Jeremy Belknap

I have received your favour of the 7th instant, and delivered your enclosure to Mr. [*Ebenezer*] Hazard. I am very happy to hear that you are recovered from your late indisposition, and lament with you the premature death of our valuable friend Mr. Hilliard.[1] The influenza has been a general & grievous complaint this way. I have been visited with it more favourably than most, & am now pretty well. I grow languid however with my confinement here & most heartily wish to return home. You ask when this will be? It is very uncertain. I please myself with the hope that Congress will adjourn some time in June or the beginning of July; but if I was to judge by the business already done I should not expect it before the end of our political existence. The house of Representatives have not yet taken up the bills relative to the funding system, but I think they will this week. It is very uncertain what will eventually be done in this business. I make no dependence on any decisions already made. I cannot undertake to give you any further information on this matter but must refer you to the newspaper accounts. The bill for encouragement of literature has passed both houses with no material alterations from that which I sent to you. I mentiond what you supposed needed an amendment respecting abridgements &c. & the Gentlemen of the law said it was similar to the British Statute & had always been construed in a sense sufficient for the securities of another.[2] I enclose to You the [*American*] Museum & a newspaper.

ALS, Belknap Papers, MHi. Place to which addressed not indicated.

---

[1] Rev. Timothy Hilliard, a New Hampshire native and Harvard graduate of 1764, was pastor of the First Church (Congregational) of Cambridge, Massachusetts, from 1783 until his death on 9 May 1790 (*JQA*, p. 23n).

[2] The Copyright Act [HR-43], passed on 17 May, contained no special provisions extending to copyrighted works protection from abridgements. This and other principal features of the law were patterned on the British Statutes of Anne of 1709 (8 Anne c. 19).

Letter from a Member of Congress to Providence, Rhode Island

It has been very difficult to persuade Congress or the Public to believe that your Majority intend to stand out. It is a jest, to pretend to single Independence. What then can be their Object? The Minority cannot expect to dictate a Form of Government to the Majority. A real or affected Dislike of the Constitution has not appeared to me a sufficient Reason for refusing to adopt it. Absolute Independence, if your People could support it, would be a bitter Curse to them. To maintain it, even a short Time, against the other States, would require such Exertions as would exhaust and distress them more than their Contributions to the Union perhaps for a Century—and, after all, a Breath would destroy it; for if they could support it, by foreign Aid, it would be ten Times worse. In that Case, the Work of Ruin would be sooner accomplished, as both Friends and Foes would work at it. It is a strange Thing to talk of an Independence against the Union, which cannot be maintained a Minute longer than the Union shall permit. Is it not inconsistent and absurd to say, we cannot live with you as Fellow-Citizens under one Government, but we are willing to live near you under a separate one, which your Will and Pleasure may demolish? The less your People like the Constitution, the more strange this Language and Conduct will appear. Whatever is bad in it, or pretended to be in it, you will suffer—and whatever is valuable and you will be deprived of, if you make yourselves Strangers to the Union. As Citizens, you would be entitled to the Privileges, and secured by the many Checks upon the Powers of Government. While you keep out of the Union, you have no Claim to these. Your People therefore say what amounts to this—the Government is under several Restraints—but still we do not think it safe to live under—but without any of these Securities we chearfully consent, nay insist upon living exposed to the Operation of this Government. I do not know whether I have explained the Idea I have endeavoured to convey, so as to make it intelligible. To my Understanding, however, there seems to be a singular Absurdity in the Reason given for refusing to adopt the Constitution. We are afraid of it, say they; but we are not afraid of that, and worse.

I have been informed that infinite Pains have been taken to embitter the Minds of your People against their Brethren in the twelve States. I can easily conceive that it is very unpleasant to tread back the Steps which have been taken in a wrong Path, and that the human Mind readily assents to any Story which will justify a Man in his own Eyes. We ought not to expect, that even honest and discerning Men will escape being deceived under Circumstances which make Truth undesirable. Your people refused to have any Thing to do with framing the Government, and afterwards to adopt it. That soon created a Distinction between them and the Union—what was hastily begun, was passionately maintained. Self-Love would certainly justify itself—supposing themselves perfectly in the Right, as People ever do, and that they were going to be oppressed by the Union, they have been open to a Thousand Deceptions, and afflicted with a Thousand groundless Fears. In this situation of Things, some will find it convenient to help deceive others, perhaps being themselves deceived. I have been trying to account for the Refusal of your State to join the Union, on such Principles as will throw the least possible Censure upon the great Body of your Citizens who have supported that Refusal. When we judge of the Motives of great Bodies of Men, we cannot exercise too much Candour. But whatever Reason may have guided your State in rejecting the Union, it is a Subject of perfect Astonishment among all Ranks of People in this Quarter, and I believe extensively through America. It is constantly asked, what does your State mean to do? How far is the present System to be carried? It seems to be expected that the Constitution will not be adopted, and that the Convention ought to be considered as a Measure of Evasion. Formerly, it was thought impossible that you should continue long in a State of Disunion, and that you might be let alone. Now a very different Sentiment seems to prevail.

Congress is about funding the Debt, and the Creditors are impatient to have it accomplished, as you may suppose. The People at large seem to wish for it too, because they expect, and I believe justly and with good Reason, that a funded Debt will favour the Circulation of Money and active Property. Two Things are asserted in Regard to your State, which do Violence to these Hopes—That you are collecting Duties into your State Treasury upon imported Articles, which are consumed chiefly by the People in the Union, so that you escape paying your Share of the common Debt, while you actually tax your Neighbors, who are obliged to pay it—and further, that your State will nearly destroy the Collection of the national Duties, by favouring the illicit Passage of dutied Goods.

Measures which will oblige your State to pay its Part, and secure our

Citizens from paying to your Treasury, and at the same Time will secure the Revenue from Loss, by smuggling through your State, seem to be indispensible: The Creditors and People at large will concur to call for them. The former will not consent to go unpaid, nor the latter to pay for others. Justice requires that your State should pay its Part; and your Legislature will not be able to find any Pretext of Complaint, as by their Letter to the President they have consented to the Principle, and given Assurances that they were getting ready to pay; nor can your People, of Right, claim the Trade and Privileges of Citizens, if they prefer the Condition of Strangers. Upon these Principles the Senate of the United States have nearly completed a Bill to forbid all Intercourse with Rhode-Island; and to demand about 27,000 Dollars without Delay: This has passed hitherto by a great Majority in the Senate. The House of Representatives have not expressed any Opinion on this Subject; but my Conversation with Individuals has led me to this Opinion, that the Demand of Money is thought to be unexceptionably just—and that Duties on the Articles of the Growth or Manufacture of Rhode-Island which the Senate cannot impose constitutionally, as Bills for Revenue must originate in the House, ought to be laid. Whatever Reluctance Congress may have discovered heretofore to a System of Rigour in Regard to you, the Necessities of Revenue will soon force them to it. Your People could not object to Duties upon your Produce as cruel and unjust—and have they weighed the Operation of such Duties? While this City is growing so fast, a large Sum will be paid for your Lime. A moderate Duty would put an End to the Trade. The Breweries of this Place and Philadelphia furnish an increasing Vent for your Barley. Your Cheese, Butter, &c. find their *best,* and many of your Articles their *only* Market in the States. A Preference will be given to the Articles of the like Kind produced in the States, and you will admit that it ought to be so. What unknown Blessings attend your State of Disunion, to balance these grievous Inconveniences, I know not. I do not believe that any such exist. Now in the Name of Peace and Union, which your Accession would make perfect, is there no Possibility of keeping Mens' Passions quiet long enough to bring these Things before their Eyes? Is there no one among the good Men who still oppose the Constitution, and who alone will be heard with entire Confidence, who will shew how much better he loves his Country than his Party, by warning his Friends of these Evils, by showing how weak, how useless and unavailing, how pernicious and dangerous, any further Opposition will be? Though such a Man may wear the Name of an Antifederalist, and be ever obnoxious to the adverse Party, I shall not hesitate to pronounce him a Patriot, the Benefactor of his Country, the Preserver of its Peace and Honour. Men may overcome or despise the Passions of other Men, but it is the Part of true Magnanimity to overcome one's own—and if your Opponents should yield to the Duty which they seem manifestly to owe their Constituents, they will go far to refute an Opinion which many have adopted, that they do not care what may become of the Interest of the Public in future, if they can only make Shift to keep in Power. I confess I feel an Anxiety upon this Subject—I long to see the Union complete—to see your State joining with the others in those Measures which I verily believe will make our Nation the most respectable in the World. We are Brethren—the State of Discord and Alienation is unnatural, and ought not to last a Day longer than may be necessary to employ honest Men of both Parties to put an End to it.

[Rhode Island] *Providence Gazette*, 29 May. It is uncertain which member of Congress wrote this letter, but it was probably one of the Massachusetts delegation (or Adams), which was involved in an apparently orchestrated campaign to persuade Rhode Island to ratify the Constitution; see the letters from Ames, Sedgwick, and Strong, 11 May, above.

Other Documents

Edward Fox to Andrew Craigie. ALS, Craigie Papers, MWA. Written from Philadelphia; postmarked 19 May.

Understands that the report of the commissioners for settling accounts "has given great offence, and that there is likely to be some very serious business in consequence"; Continental creditors are "in high spirits at the thoughts of every thing being completed this Session"; left New York in company with Wynkoop, who said "there is reason to suppose that the N. Hampshire Senators are for Philadelphia" (as the seat of government).

Stephen Goodhue to Benjamin Goodhue. FC:lbk, Goodhue Family Papers, MSaE. Written from Salem, Massachusetts.

Reports on the children's recovery from the measles and the good health of friends and family; quotes prices for goods they hope to sell; "I hope you Remember it [*is*] Specie you are dealing with & not old Continental [*money*] & that we are republicans ~~and expect~~ we earn our money here exceeding hard and find prudence Exceeding Necessary, the Anties do not appear to be disappointed while the reverse appears on the other side I hope you will not make your Self uneasy Discharge a good Conscience let the event be as it will"; "the Season is Cold & backward."

Thomas Hartley to Jasper Yeates. ALS, Yeates Papers, PHi. Place to which addressed not indicated; written at 3 P.M.; probably enclosed in Hartley to Yeates, 17 May.

The President is better; "there are strong hopes of his Recovery"; "we have strong Expectations" that both houses of Congress will agree to convene the next session at Philadelphia; encloses newspapers.

John Langdon to Joseph Whipple. ALS, Sturgis Family Papers, MH. Addressed to Portsmouth, New Hampshire; franked; postmarked.

Has been too unwell to write; "the President, has been very near Death, but this day all Symptoms are very favorable."

Richard Henry Lee to Thomas Lee Shippen. ALS, Shippen Family Papers, DLC. Place to which addressed not indicated. For the full text, see *Lee* 2:515–16.

Received Shippen's letter of 14 May "this day"; very painful to write in his current state of weakness; "respecting the removal of Congress, "refers Shippen to his letter of 15 May; is informed by some of the attending physicians that the President was "dangerously ill," but took a favorable turn on 15 May and his recovery is no longer in doubt.

Mary Otis Lincoln to Theodore Sedgwick. ALS, Sedgwick Papers, MHi. Written from Boston; carried by Tobias Lear. Lincoln's husband, Benjamin Lincoln, Jr. (b. 1756), died on 18 January 1788, leaving her unprovided for with two infant sons.

"Unfaigned thanks" for letter of 8 May "and one previous"; "The sums you mention having payed to General [*Benjamin*] Lincoln (my good father) when previous to the 18th of Jany. 1788, which was the fatal period to my temporal felicity"; "the sum due on the Note I have Given by you to Our frind Dr. [*Aaron?*] Dexter is £180 ~~£ M~~ our Mony. I am gratifyed to hear that you have received it but The purchasing publick securities with it is not the object as it is still uncertain wether they will be addopted. if they are not I must pettition ~~you~~ your *High mightiness* for a *pension*"; is ashamed to beg for alms, "which a pension however is but *little* superior to"; congratulations on "the late addition to your little flock."

Benjamin Rush to Tench Coxe. ALS, Coxe Papers, PHi. Written from Philadelphia. The Roberts whom Rush mentions is probably John Roberts (ca. 1721–78), a Quaker miller whom Rush befriended and unsuccessfully defended when he was convicted of high treason and hanged for collaborating with the British during their occupation of Philadelphia (*Drinker*, p. 2205; David Freeman Hawke, *Benjamin Rush* [Indianapolis, Ind., 1971], p. 228).

Washington's "complete recovery cannot be expected while he remains in New York"; describes at length how "the Sea Air is poison to weak lungs when it is *combined* as in New York with the Air of the land"; will vouch for all those facts connecting the seat of government question "with the health & life of our beloved President"; Morris is openly supported for governor of Pennsylvania, although he can expect "more opposition & more calumny" from the friends of F. A. Muhlenberg if both men remain candidates; "Old Mr. [*John?*] Roberts used to say *banked* Meadow was no *real* estate. Perhaps there is as little *real* friendship in other kinds of *Banks* as there is real ~~Security in a~~ property in banked meadows. Read this Sentence to Mr. Maclay."

George Thatcher to Nathaniel Barrell. No copy known; acknowledged in Barrell to Thatcher, 27 May.

William Samuel Johnson, Diary. Johnson Papers, CtHi.
"Charles [*Johnson*] returnd."

NYJ, 18 May; reprinted at Boston and Northampton, Massachusetts; Hartford, Middletown, and New Haven, Connecticut; Baltimore; Winchester, Virginia; and Edenton, North Carolina. Carroll moved for and then chaired the Senate committee on the Rhode Island Trade Bill, Ellsworth drafted the bill, and Morris presented it. The article may have been stimulated by the publication of the bill in *GUS* and *NYDG*, 15 May.

"A correspondent observes, that he is surprized a certain member of the S__ had not taken pains to enquire the national disposition of the Rhode-Islanders previous to his originating a *certain Bill*—for, says he, it is sufficiently ascertained, that they are disposed, *like hogs*, to *run back* in proportion to the attempts to *drive them forward*."

Wednesday, 19 May 1790

Cool (Johnson)

John Adams to William Ellery

I have received your favor of the 13th. as I did that of [*illegible*] in due season—One wishes to be informed of all facts in which the public is interested: but the detail of Rhode Island manœuvres is distressing. The Senate yesterday passed a [*Rhode Island Trade*] bill, which cutts off all communication with Rhode Island, if she chooses such a solitary selfish and unsocial system. The bill passed by a great majority, and the Senators appear very decided in this business. I would send you a copy of the bill, if I had one, but it is not necessary to send to town to get one, because the newspapers have already contained the substance of the bill, and the true bill as it passed will be with you in the gazetts before this letter.

If the inland part of your people are so abandoned as to refuse still to ratify the Constitution, there will be no part left for the Seaports, but to do what I think they ought to have done long ago, meet and adopt the Constitution for themselves and petition congress to be received and protected. Your views and wishes I have communicated to several gentlemen in confidence, but not to the President. He has been very ill and unable to attend to business. It is a rule with me to meddle as little as possible in appointments; and I know not who are candidates for the office you speak of at New Port. Whenever my opinion is asked concerning any candidates within my acquaintance I always give it according to my best judgment—I presume that the applications of your Antis, are made to other men, to such as they have consulted with already too long—Your [*ratification*] convention meet next monday—Our bill cannot pass the house soon enough to reach you till many days after. I sincerely hope that your people will adopt the Constitution and send us an account of it before the bill passes the house. I know not the character of the Governors [*Arthur Fenner*] friend Mr. [*Ebenezer*] Thompson but possession you know is eleven points and if there is not any pointed objection against him, it would not I presume be difficult to gratify the Governor.

FC:lbk, Adams Family Manuscript Trust, MHi. Sent to Newport, Rhode Island.

John Adams to Benjamin Lincoln

I have duly received but not duly answered your favor of April 3d. It is a misfortune that a man can never be spoken to by a projector without being misunderstood or misrepresented I told Mr. Forbisher [*William Frobisher*] that if he expected any thing from the general government,[1] he must apply to it by petition. But I never told him, that I had the least suspicion that the general government would ever do anything for him. How should they? He is in possession of no secret; if he was an inventor or discoverer he has long since made his art public, he therefore cannot obtain a patent. One is harrassed through life with an hundred of these dreamers who will never take no for an answer. If he will beleive that Congress will assist him why does he not petition? I have no such faith; if the state would not assist him, why should the Continent? We have been much allarmed, at the sickness of the President; but thank God, he is better and recovering fast. The house do not harmonize in the right system, so well as we could wish: but the prosperity of the Country, has been so greatly promoted by the government, that I hope we shall not throw it away. The Massachusetts have appeared to me to waver as much as any State: but the elections this year I hope are more favorable.

FC:lbk, Adams Family Manuscript Trust, MHi.

[1] For his improvements to the making of potash.

Richard Henry Lee to Arthur Lee

Since my arrival here I have written to you twice and have received as many letters from you—I think you mention to have written one letter that I have not received, to wit, in answer to mine of the 18th [*April*]. Your letters to Mr. Dorchmer & Mr. [*Abijah?*] Hammond have been delivered, and I wish they may have the proposed effect. But your commissions of Gallantry have not yet been executed, & perhaps never may, at least in the precise way that you mention. Having been brought nearly to my Grave by a severe illness, I feel very little disposed to Gallantry—I do most perfectly agree with you, that Men (not Government) are wanted—I have long thought so, but now I know it—This goes by a young Gentleman & you know how careless, now a days, such are. So that for politics I must refer you to the enclosed papers—I hope to hear from you frequently & I will endeavor to be equally communicative.

[*P. S.*] If you had not learnt every body as well as you have, I would say, are you not Astonished to be informed that the Marked Resolutions in the daily Advertiser of the 18th. instant[1] should be so opposed as probably to frustrate them altho 'tis certain a parcel of Scoundrel Speculators went directly after the appropriation of last September & cheated the Soldiers out of 27,000 dollars for less than a penny in the pound—And tho the Money is yet in the ~~money is yet in the~~ pub. Treasury—& these resolves only calculated to prevent the fraud from being carried into effect.

ALS, Lee Family Papers, Special Collections, University of Virginia Library, Charlottesville. Place to which addressed not indicated.

[1] The House resolutions on the discharge of arrearages to soldiers of the Virginia, North Carolina, and South Carolina Lines passed on 17 May and, as amended by the Senate, became the Resolution on Compensation Lists (*DHFFC* 6:2063–70).

James Madison to Edmund Randolph

The President has been *critically* ill for some days past, but is now we hope out of danger. his complaint is a peripneumony, united probably with the Influenza. Since my last I have found that I did not go too far in intimating that the cause of your delay would forbid the smallest criticism on it. I earnestly pray that you may no longer have occasion to plead that apology.

In consequence of ~~the~~ a petition from N. Hampshire[1] the subject of our comercial relation to G.B. has been revived. A majority of the H. of Reps. seem disposed to make a *pretty bold experiment*; and I think it will meet with a very different reception ~~from~~ in the Senate from the measure tried at the last session. If it fails it will be owing to a dislike of the preference to Nations in Treaty.

The debt is not yet funded. The zealots for the Assumption of the State dbts. keep back in hope of alarming the zealots for the fedl. debt. I understand that another effort is to be made for the assumption. Motives are felt I suspect which will account for the perseverence.

ALS, Madison Papers, DLC. Place to which addressed not indicated.

[1] For the petition of the merchants and traders of Portsmouth, New Hampshire, presented in the House on 26 March, see *DHFFC* 8:253–54.

Anthony Wayne to the Pennsylvania Delegation

~~On this day twelve months~~ On the 19th of May, & on the 4th. July 1789, I did myself the honor of addressing you upon the subject of the South western territory of Georgia, & suggesting the expediency, as well as good policy for Congress to accept of the Cession then in their choice,[1] [*lined out*] & also the Establishment of a Government, under the Federal authority, similar to that which Genl. [*Arthur*] St. Clair presided over to the West for I clearly foresaw, that unless that business was taken up at an early period, the Opportunity wou'd be lost—~~as it was natural to expect~~ [*lined out*] as it ~~is~~ was not in the Nature of them that so invaluable a territory wou'd ~~will not~~ remain long Vacant. on the Contrary the interprising genious, & adventurous disposition of the Americans, wou'd naturally cause great Numbers to turn their attention from a Cold worn out & Sterile Land—to a Country abounding with every advantage that a happy Climate, luxuriancy of soil, & Navigation can afford!

This idea is now verified, & the emigration will be great & rapid, from every quarter of the Union—as well on account of the rigorous Judiciary Act, and Process Law [*Courts Act S-4*], as from other causes & Considerations.

Wou'd it not therefore be prudent proper ~~&~~ wise, ~~& expedient~~ for the General Government to accept of the Jurisdiction—altho' the greatest & most valuable part of the Land may be disposed of. ~~shou'd that, together with a limited Cession of territory eventually be offered—under similar Conditions, by the State of Georgia contained in the North Carolina Cession?[2] permit me to urge the expediency of an immediate acceptation~~, for ~~shou'd~~ that Country is possess'd & settled, unsanctioned by Congress—the Genl. Government may find it a more difficult business to extend her Authority over that Quarter at a future day, than if settled in the first instance under her ~~Authority~~ Auspecious & protection? ~~for~~ Settled it inevitably will be in a very short time, either with—or without that sanction! & the acquisition of inhabitants will be great, from the causes already mentioned, as well as from the distubances which seem to pervade the Continent of Europe!

I pray you therefore, as you regard the peace & happiness of America, not to let slip an Other Opportunity (shou'd it eventually offer) of extending the Jurisdiction of Congress to the South Western boundary of the United States? even if the Conditions were less favorable to the Genl. Government, than those mention'd in the North Carolina Cession of territory!

Shou'd the Legislature of Georgia at their meeting in June come into a measure of this Nature I may probably have the honor of paying you a Visit in New York, in the course of a few weeks.

[*P. S.*] I shall proceed to Augusta to try to prevail upon the Legislature to come into this Measure—for shou'd it be much longer Neglected I shall not be the least surprissed to hear of Overtures to & from the Spanish Nation—who probably may not be very much Aversed to an Acquisition of Several thousand Inhabitants Not subjects of the United States.

FC:dft, Wayne Papers, MiU-C. Written from Richmond County, Georgia.

---

[1] On 1 February 1788, Georgia's legislature passed an act ceding a portion of her western land claims to the U.S. government. The cession offered a territory encompassing roughly the southern halves of present-day Mississippi and Alabama, in exchange for (among other things) a credit of $171,428 against Georgia's federal quota, equivalent to what the state claimed to have spent "quieting the minds of the Indians and resisting their hostilities," and a guarantee of her remaining territorial claims, presumably to prevent concessions to Spain or various Native American nations. On 29 May 1788, Georgia Delegates (and future FFC members) Baldwin and Few formally presented the cession to the Confederation Congress, which rejected the offer two months later. Considering the cession "clogg'd with Conditions which were not thought proper to be acceded to," Congress proposed instead that Georgia enlarge the area to be ceded, adjust the sum to be credited, and abandon its demand for territorial guarantees. State legislators took no formal action on Congress's rejection for well over a year; not until November 1789 did they form a committee to draft another act of cession. Considering Georgia's inexorable drift towards an Indian war it was incapable of winning without federal aid, such a delay cannot be attributed to unmindful neglect. In conjunction with Wayne's efforts in May and July 1789, the delay suggests rather that some important Georgians considered the 1788 act of cession valid, at least until the state sold much of the same land to various Yazoo companies in December 1789 (*JCC* 34:320; *LDC* 25:297; Lamplugh, p. 66).

[2] For the ten conditions that North Carolina placed on its cession of western lands, see *DHFFC* 6:1545–47.

Other Documents

Pierce Butler to Thomas Fitzsimons. ALS, Roberts Collection, PHC.

Is awaiting money from bonds he has in South Carolina, which he will turn over to Fitzsimons as soon as possible; "my Crop was so small as not to admit of any paymt. from it."

Joseph Hardy to John Langdon. ALS, Langdon Papers, NhPoA. Written from the treasury department.

Certificate for the balance due to Langdon on the settlement of his "Commercial Accounts" (as Continental agent for New Hampshire and/or contractor for the Secret Committee of Trade) is available to be picked up at the treasury office.

John Langdon to John S. Sherburne. No copy known; mentioned in Sherburne to Langdon, 28 May.

James Monroe to James Madison. No copy known; acknowledged in Madison to Monroe, 1 June.

Daniel Sewall to George Thatcher. ALS, Chamberlain Collection, MB. Written from York, Maine; postmarked Portsmouth, New Hampshire, 19 (?) May.

As executor for a widow to whom Daniel Hooper owed money, which Hooper says Thatcher had promised to loan him by 1 May, Sewall asks if and when Hooper might have the money; asks if Thatcher had any opportunity to speak with Governor John Hancock "respecting the matter we conversed upon last October, at Biddeford."

William Samuel Johnson, Diary. Johnson Papers, CtHi.

"Billy [*Samuel William Johnson*] arrivd. [*from Bermuda*]."

John Sevier, Journal. Claiborne Collection, Ms-Ar. This journal, which details Sevier's 1790 trip to New York, includes his expenses en route.

Left for New York City at 10 A.M.

THURSDAY, 20 MAY 1790

Rain (Johnson)

John Adams to William Smith (of Boston)

Your agreeable favour of the 24th of April, was brought to me in season and I thank you for it, though my thanks are not in good season. Your sentiments concerning the assumption of the State debts, the encouragement of American navigation and the establishment of a national bank, are conformable to those of about one half the Continent and contrary to those of the other half. How shall we contrive to make the Clocks all Strike together? Virginia begins to be convinced of the necessity of uniting with the States on this side of her, in measures to encourage our shipping, and give it an advantage over foreigners; but your cousin of Carolina [*William Smith (S.C.)*], who is one of the most Judicious men in the house, is you see quite an enemy to such measures. The Carolinas and Georgia, I suppose will be longer in their conversion than Virginia has been. It may require a more United people and a stronger government to take those Steady measures, necessary to support our navigation: but my sentiments on this point are no secret to Congress. I wrote them continually from England: and I still think for us to build man, and maintain twelve hundred ships for a foreign nation, out of the labour of our husbandmen is very ill contrivance for the interest of Agriculture, whatever our friend Smith may say.

Division of sentiments about everything—some inclining to the French, some to the English; one party to the south and another to the north; one sett advocates for the interest of Agriculture; another for those of commerce a third for those of manufactures—every party pushing their own principles too far, and opposing others too much—How few minds look through the mighty all, with a steady eye, and consider all its relations and dependences! How few aim at the good of the whole, without aiming too much at the prosperity of parts? These questions have occurred ever since I was born, and will as long as I live, or you either. The turbulent manœuvres of a faction in the Massachusetts weaken and embarrass us,[1] as much or more than Rhode Island. I despair of New England: They upon principle tie the hands and destroy the influence of every man who has any chance and any desire to serve them. So says and so feels, by cruel experience yours.

FC:lbk, Adams Family Manuscript Trust, MHi. Sent to Boston.

[1] Adams probably meant the supporters of John Hancock and Samuel Adams.

Fisher Ames to George R. Minot

It is a long time since I have heard from you. I wish to be assured by your own handwriting, that you have escaped the influenza, or if not, that you are well over it. The most dismal accounts of the prevailing sickness of the people in Boston have been given here. Our friend, Dr. [*Aaron*] Dexter, I am told has been very ill, and is but half recovered. I hope this is not true. You are going to be busy soon with the General Court, and after that kind of duty shall have begun, I shall despair of getting a word from you.

All my letters from our State assure me that Congress is becoming unpopular, and losing confidence as well as reputation. The impatience of the creditors to have their debt funded without delay has been mingled with the murmurs of the *antis*. I think I can see the policy of the latter, in forbearing to complain of the assumption as a piece of usurpation, and making use of the angry creditors to help their cause against the government. I was lately made apprehensive that the creditors were going to agree on a memorial, praying that the debt might be immediately funded, whether the assumption should be agreed to or not. Such a step would have blown up the whole assumption, and probably the funding system with it. But that memorial seems to be laid aside, and I am glad of it. For the cause of assuming the State debts has derived aid from the opinion, that the advocates of that measure would not suffer it to be separated from the funding system; but if the creditors at Boston had expressed a willingness to submit to such a separation on any terms, the aid of those who have been lugged along, *vi et armis*,[1] to approve of the assumption, would be withdrawn. We are now in committee on the bill for funding the debt, and debating about the old [*emission*] money. I am not sure that it is prudent to introduce it in this place. The success of any provision for the old money is problematical, and as it is now objected that it will delay and embarrass the funding business, it is attended with increased difficulty, to get the rate fixed at the scale of forty for one, which would confirm the promise made by the old government.

The assumption is not less to be hoped for than it has been for several weeks past. Mr. Sherman is indisposed, but in a day or two will renew his motion for assuming certain fixed sums. The success of it would be certain, if the Pennsylvania creditors[2] were well disposed towards it. But they consider it as dividing their loaf with others, and they wish to have it all. I am surprised that men, who are to depend on government should be careless as to arguments, which seem to prove how much its strength will be impaired by a divided revenue system. They seem to be secure as to the permanency of the government, and mindful of nothing but the property of the debt. I hope we shall not finish the session without funding the whole debt; if not the whole, then as much as we can. For if we should not fund at all, I am apprehensive that the popular torrent, at a future session, would be found to be strong against funding. It might be said, we ought not to promise more than we know we can perform; that of consequence, temporary appropriations would be safe, and adequate to every purpose of justice, and the old game of preying upon the creditors would be played again. Without a firm basis for public credit, I can scarcely expect the government will last long. I own, my dear friend, I am sometimes ready to despond, when I think how great hazard attends those measures which are essential to its being. The President has been dangerously sick, and though much better, is still very weak. This circumstance has added something to our gloom. I hope in a few days, however, that I shall be able to say, the assumption is agreed to.

Ames 1:77–79.

[1] By force of arms.

[2] Ames singled out the Pennsylvania creditors because they were a powerful, vocal lobby; indeed, both petitions Congress received prior to passage of the Funding Act, urging the immediate payment of bona fide evidences of debt, originated in Pennsylvania. See *DHFFC* 8:258–68.

Thomas Dwight to Theodore Sedgwick

There was real anxiety among your friends here on account of your absence from Congress—I told them you was not without a very reasonable excuse, and that your state of health was the only cause of the excursion—in your favr. of the 16th. by which I am greatly obliged, you do not mention your vertiginous headachs—I sincerely hope your journey has r[*e*]lieved you, and that you have left them behind you—had you not better frequently ride out in the morning and evening on horseback for the benefit of the May air? in cases like yours it will often restore when all other prescriptions fail—I am not without my fears for the consequence of these vile dizzy pains of the head which have so much tried your patience, pray for Heavn's sake take care of them—You request me Sir, to inform you what will be the complexion of our State Legislature this year—I am not fully informed on this subject—tis said that the County of Worcester will be worse represented than ever—this cannot be the case, unless they have chosen men, out of their County, or supplied themselves with Legislators by a Goal [*jail*] delivery—it is also said that much pains have been taken there to render the assumption unpopular—and that this is thoroughly affected if so—Mr. G—t [*Grout*] will leave you at another trial of the question—In this County [*Hampshire*] the assumption, I am sure, is very generally popular—I hope it will not be otherwise. ***

You have probably heard that Jno. Bacon is chosen [*state*] Rep. of Stockbridge by a very small majority—my brother [*Josiah*] writes that they shall instruct him (if possible) to support the assumption of the State debts—I wish this may be affected, if it were only for the sake of embarrassing the hero in his political warfare.

P. S. Be so good as to make my respectful compliments to all your houshold.[1]

ALS, Sedgwick Papers, MHi. Written from Springfield, Massachusetts. The omitted text reports further on state elections.

---

[1] Late in the first session, Sedgwick and Partridge settled into quarters at Sarah and Eunice Loring's new boarding house on the Bowling Green at Number 4 Broadway, and they probably continued to reside there throughout the second session.

Stephen Higginson to Alexander Hamilton

Since I had last the pleasure of writing to you, I have learnt with uneasiness, that some gentn. in Congress have had an Idea of stopping the progress of the funding System, with a view to compell an assent to the assumption of the State Debts. This Idea demands a very careful & cool attention before it be practised upon. The situation of things is to me critical & important. shd. the question of assumption be carried over to another Session a fermentation will certainly be excited in this & other States. how great & extensive no one can now tell; but should both go over, & the whole body of public Creditors remain without any provision, an irritation much more general & violent may be apprehended—those in Trade also will very generally receive like impressions in the latter case; &, deprived of the usual supply of Cash, by the collection of Duties & looking upon the money, may be led into combinations, & openly refuse any farther paymts. the prospect of success should be very clear, before such a measure be taken. if gentn. can be assured of this, it may be well to attempt it; but very rough points may be created by it, &, from the feelings & views before discovered in the discussion of that question, will be the probable effect. it strikes me, that in the present temper of the house, the question may be brought on with much more advantage after the funding System, & the ways & means are settled. having perfected that business, & being strongly impressed with a Sense of the necessity of such a provision for the proper Debt of the union, gentn. must feel interested in giving it a free & successful operation. They will then be much more likely to perceive the obstructions & interferences, which must arise from the provisions, which the States must make for their respective Debts, than they are now, while the whole Subject lies open, & every thing is viewed in theory only, & in a complicated state. when they come to simplify their Views, & critically attend to the means they shall have provided, they will feel the force of objections That have now no weight. They will naturally wish their own measures to have freedom & success; & upon their own principles, & by the help of their own feelings, may then be drawn into measures they had before opposed. if some member was to suggest to them, that by a mutilation of your plan, They alone must respond for the success of their System, it would have much effect. These reflections having made an impression on my own mind, I have suggested them to Mr. Ames & Mr. Strong, for their consideration. the question is a nice & important one; it involves many difficulties, & good men are divided about it. ***

Our delegates in Congress will be earnestly solicitous to gratify their Con-

stituents; & believing the representations they may receive, will perhaps be impelled to press the Subject with much warmth & to an undue degree.
***

ALS, Wolcott Papers, CtHi. Written from Boston. For the full text, see *PAH* 6:422–26.

Benjamin Lincoln to Fisher Ames

Such appears to be the state of politicks in your neighbourhood and in Congress it self that I may hardly venture a sentiment on the important objects before your house as I am so much a stranger to the arguments for and against the propriety of adopting or rejecting them—Whether the Union should or should not embrace the debts of the several States is a question of importance and much depends on a proper issue of it—Among the opposers I consider the stubborn old tories, the haters of the present constitution, the men averse to the payment of the public debts by any body or in any way what ever and those whose ~~only~~ importance is nourished and kept a live by an opposition to national measures.

How ~~shall~~ the designs of those men shall be counteracted is the question to be determined—Can it be done by refusing to fund the domestic debt independent of the several State debts. I doubt, for who suffers by the omission not the class of creatures above mentioned If we could make those feel & those solely I should subscribe to the idea most cordially but that is not the case few of them compared with the citizens at large will become sufferers if the domestic debt should never be funded Yea most of them would be gainers—What than will be the consequences if we too ridgedly pursue the idea of rejecting a provision for funding the domestic debts untill we can fund the several State debts also.

I say we shall I think very essentially wound our own cause injure & sour our friends & please and gratify our enemies—There ~~are~~ is a large proportion of the marcantile interest in the united State who are holders of the securities of the Union they have long waited for the arrival of that moment when they should receive the interest on such security and have lately been pleasing themselves with the idea that such interest would in a most convenient manner come in and of the payment of those duties which they are daily ~~paying~~ discharging Besides they have painted in their minds the real advantages which would be derived from that dissemination of [*lined out*] cash which would be the natural consequence of such a system but if instead thereof ~~if~~ the measure should be clogged, the debt remain unfunded & no provision made for the payment of the interest These very best of Citizens will be disappointed and they will magnify in their own minds the evils which will necessarily follow a locking up all the cash which shall be collected by the operation or the revenue system untill the time shall arrive when the interest may be paid Will they not say that we had better be without a constitution *"if the friends of it have not Spirit enough to administer it as it was framed"*—If we secure these valuable Citizens and fix them by the strong cement of Interest to the general Government we shall then have secured such an augmentation of strength as will perfectly establish the constitution—But on the other hand if we neglect the necessary measures and in consequence thereof we throw them into the arms, already opened to receive them, of the disaffected the wicked will triumph and stand high on the chagrine & ruins of those of a very different character.

It appears to me therefore sir that we risk too much when we make the assumption of the State debts the unaltrable condition of our funding the ~~State~~ debt of the Union I feel the importance of an assumption of the State [*lined out*] Debts my little all is in the Notes of this State I have not one continental security Yet I think I had better hazard the loss of them that [*than*] do that which shall sap the foundation of the Union. Let us progress as fast as we can and [*lined out*] do those acts of justice which to perform was the declared intention of the people when they established the constitution these objects should not yeild to any other How far it may be right ~~to make~~ to make the establishment of those debts depend on any conditions ~~for the performance of certain contracts not known by the constitution~~ whatever I leave others to determine.

FC:dft, Lincoln Papers, MHi. Written from Boston.

Louis Guillaume Otto to Comte de Montmorin

The system of embarrassing and of gradually reducing the commerce and navigation of Great Britain makes rapid progress in this country, and this disposition alone demonstrates sufficiently the great influence which the politicians of Massachusetts continue to exercise on all minds. Every impartial man must agree that in the present situation of the United States the abundance of their products and the extension of their agriculture ought to induce them to receive without distinction the ships of all the nations which need their produce and to establish among them the greatest possible competition. Congress is going to follow an altogether contrary course. It judges that there are still too many foreign ships in its ports and it seems to wish to discourage them or at least to make them pay very dearly for the advantage of frequenting its shores. The tonnage paid by foreigners from the month of September till December 31 of last year had risen to 50,000 dollars while that of American ships only amounted to 11,000. This proportion of five to one has not seemed large enough yet to the merchants and navigators of the North. Those of Portsmouth in New Hampshire have presented a petition[1] begging Congress to double the duty of fifty cents per ton paid by foreigners and to prevent the latter from carrying the products of the United States to any country where American vessels are not admitted. This last request is particularly directed against the supply trade carried on by the English for their Antilles, of which the Americans are extremely jealous. They state, in fact, that Jamaica could not subsist without the United States; and they conclude that in prohibiting the exportation of their products in English ships, they will wrest from Great Britain the permission to carry them there themselves or else they will force her to sign a treaty of commerce the terms of which they will decide. The measure is bold and the success at least doubtful. The first proposal made of it in the House of Representatives has caused great excitement. The Southerners have represented with bitterness that their interests were again going to be sacrificed to the personal views and insatiable greediness of the people of the North; that the inhabitants of the South were not navigators; that it was important to them to attract buyers from all parts of the globe and that, if the English paid better than the others or bought in much greater quantity, they were proportionately more agreeable to them; that the maxims of a commercial jealousy so much spoken about by the writers of Europe, where many men and much wealth were compressed in a small space of land, did not suit America where labor is lacking in an immense land and where it is a question rather of *producing* than of *trading*; that England was much too proud to accept the law of a newborn power which she had so much reason to humiliate rather than to respect; that, besides, under the present regime and without the proposed increase the English already paid greater duties in America than the Americans paid in England; that at all times nations had stood for the right to regulate the commerce of their colonies according to their own convenience and that the usefulness of the products of the United States to the Antilles produced a reciprocal advantage which it was necessary to expand rather than to restrict; that it was absurd to wish to renounce a commerce because one could not carry it on completely; that the English usually paid in cash—counting the products which they exported—and that far from discouraging those exportations, it would have been a good policy to facilitate them by all sorts of means. These arguments and an infinity of observations and replies have occupied the House for several days. Finally the Southerners, seeing that their adversaries were as usual inflexible and the strongest, proposed for the purpose of amendment: *"to exempt from the new tonnage the ships of nations which have a treaty with the United States."* The Northerners rather than lose their motion have consented in it and the new duty of one hundred cents per ton has been enacted by a majority of thirty-one to thirteen.[2] I ought to point out, My Lord, that on this occasion several members told me that they regretted that by the terms of their commercial treaties they were obliged to let the Dutch and Swedes share in the favors which they had the intention of granting to France. These favors are, however, purely nominal; because for sixty English ships, scarcely two French and one Dutch are found in American ports. But if some encouragements of this kind could be kept up for several years, they would undoubtedly produce a perceptible effect with regard to our navigation.

Congress attended also, My Lord, to the commerce of the United States with the savages. It has decided[3] that people can trade with them only by means of a permit from the Superintendent of this Department which will purchase merchandise wholesale to have it resold by its agents to the savages at retail. Besides, any individual is forbidden to buy lands from the savages, which from now on can be acquired only under the authority of the United States. Any hostility committed by an American against a savage will be severely punished. By the same act,[4] the lands of the West are divided into two great governments, one of which is to the north of the Ohio and the other to the south. The governor [*William Blount*] of this last division has just been appointed by the President. The savages are with regard to the United States what the Barbaresques [*Barbary pirates*] have been till now with regard to the Powers of Europe. They could be exterminated if absolutely necessary; but in an expedition of this kind, there would be everything to risk and nothing to gain. Besides the savages have for themselves the right of an immemorial possession. It is generally agreed here that the American emigrants established on the frontiers are the scum of mankind and infinitely more ferocious, more perfidious and more intractable than the savages themselves. One seldom knows the crimes by which these adventurers provoke the vengeance of the savages, but the particular governments and Congress do the best they can to check them and one must render especially to the Federal Government the justice of saying that it has always treated the savages as neighbors whose rights should be respected. It is for this purpose that it no longer permits that private persons trade with them without being previously known and registered by its officers. It declares besides that all the separate treaties for lands belonging to the savages will be null unless sanctioned by Congress. It is in these treaties that they tried to entrap the good faith of these simple men either by intoxicating them or by making them believe that Congress proposed to exterminate them and that they could not think too soon of evacuating the lands bordering the United States. On the other hand, some savage imposters calling themselves chiefs of a nation often disposed of lands which did not belong to them; and after having consumed the brandy which was the price of it, themselves excited their compatriots against the buyers. The measures are so well taken at present that these irregularities and the hostilities which resulted from them are no longer to be feared, and the troops stationed on the frontiers to check the Americans rather than the savages will maintain the good harmony between the two parties. One can cite as a new proof of the moderation of the general government the commission which the President of the United States just gave to an intelligent officer [*Marinus Willett*] to go to the Creeks and to engage some chiefs to come to New York in order to end by a formal treaty the dissensions which have existed for so long a time between them and the Georgians. He had sent to them last year three plenipotentiaries who, after long and expensive negotiation, were able to obtain only an equivocal and not very honorable truce for the United States. The President, who does not change his principles easily, wants to try the medium of negotiations a second time; and if he succeeds in getting some savage plenipotentiaries to come here, he is too adroit to let them leave without having obtained and signed a permanent peace. The governors of the different states through which these plenipotentiaries will travel have been requested by the President to receive them with the greatest distinction and to drill the militia before them so as to give them a high opinion of the resources and of the population of the United States.

O'Dwyer, pp. 429–32. Otto's letters included in *DHFFC* were usually written over the course of days, and even weeks, following the day they were begun.

---

[1] For this petition, dated 11 March and presented in the House on 26 March, see *DHFFC* 8:353–54.

[2] Apparently the vote of 13 May on Madison's proposed amendment to the first resolution of the committee report that led to the Trade and Navigation Bill (*DHFFC* 6:1971n).

[3] A system of trading districts, each superintended by a military officer, was proposed in the Indian Trade Act, presented in the House on 14 May (*DHFFC* 5:988–90).

[4] Actually, by the separate Southern Territory Act, passed on 10 May (*DHFFC* 6:1901–2). Blount's nomination under this act was not made until 7 June and agreed to the next day (*DHFFC* 2:79).

Charles Christopher Reiche to John Adams

These Conjectures, Arguments, and Plan which I have the honor to transmit, have given great satisfaction to almost all, who have read them, when they were first published by me in a weekly german paper, which I have established here, on moral, historical, political and economical arguments.[1]

As a plan, contrary to that proposed by me, hath already been adopted by the Hon. the house of Representatives in Congress, and, by sickness and other incidents, I have been prevented from laying these Conjectures before that house; so I do give me the honor to apply to Your Excellency, who being the President of that august Body, where the adopted plan now lies for approbation, will, I trust, and most humbly entreat, graciously be pleased to pay some attention to the plan here subjoined, and either return the same to the subscriber, or make such other use and application thereof, as Your well known wisdom, and patriotism will suggest.

ALS, Adams Family Manuscript Trust, MHi. Written from Philadelphia. The enclosure can be found on reel 601 of the Adams Papers. In his fifty-some page handwritten "Conjectures, Arguments, and Plans for the Funding of the Public Debt of the United American States," Reiche argued against a funding system on the grounds that it would promote war, economic inequality, private and public immorality, and an outflow of American wealth to Europe without promoting American agriculture, commerce, or manufacturing. Instead, he believed, the debt should be paid off immediately by assessing every American family 1/24th of its wealth, excepting an estimated 110,555 families whose wealth was less than $500. Implementing his plan, Reiche concluded, would make the federal government a colossus that could not fail.

[1] Charles Christopher Reiche published the *General Postboothe* from January through June 1790, and *The Neue Philadelphische Correspondenz* from October to his death at Philadelphia in December 1790. His conjectures appeared in the *Postboothe* on 19, 23 February and 2, 9 March.

George Thatcher to Sarah Thatcher

Yours of the 11th. inst. which came to hand the evening before last, was very pleasing, and that for many reasons; but for none more than that it informed me of your being well & happy; & wished for nothing more than my return—this also is uppermost in my mind. I am homesick, and nothing but being at home with our dear children will effect a cure.

Your account of the Tea-party you had the night before, with our two little angles [*angels*], was too pleasing a scene, to view at a distance, not to cause a sensation of grief that I could not be present to enjoy with you the most delicious feelings the human heart is susceptable of. The account of Phillips going to school like a good boy; and Sallys seting at the Tea-table like a little woman are too pleasing to pass over without assuring you I promise myself very much from your attention to them in these little things—I call them little things because the world calls them so; but in my view they are causes of future good behavior, which is every thing.

I send to Phillips a little Hieroglyphick Bible[1]—at present I am sensible it may not be of much service to him; tho it may excite his curiosity, & thereby diminish, in some degree, that reluctance most children are apt to contract towards that book. I could wish to impress on the minds of children an idea that the Bible contains many pleasing, curious things, and usefull truths. I would not convey ~~an idea~~ a notion of its being sacred or holy;

according to the sentiments generally entertained of it—otherwise than every thing may be called sacred & holy that is usefull; and in this view, the Bible will be sufficiently raised above all other Books—As a History it is the most ancient, and the best attested of ancient history—As to its morality & Religion it contains principles the most pure and simple.

At what age, and the particular manner children should read the Bible I am not yet agreed in my own mind. This is a subject worthy of the attention of instructors—and as all parents ought to be the first instructors to their children, I shall contemplate this matter at all leisure moments & by the time our dear children are able to read understandingly, will endeavour to put my thoughts into some regular order for their use.

In turning over the leaves of this Book, I have discovered, in several places, something designed as a picture of the Devil—As I disbeleive the existance of such a creature, and am fully convinced the general notion of him as taught in the pulpit, in schools and in common life, is injurious to the progress of usefull knowledge and sound morality, I could wish it was obliterated, and recommend it to you to cover those awfull shapes with a blank leaf of paper—I have not time, or I would do it myself—Children & women ought to have pleasing images presented to their minds.

ALS, Thatcher Family Papers, MHi. Place to which addressed not indicated.

[1] A version of the Bible published by Isaiah Thomas in Worcester, Massachusetts, in 1788, representing select scripture passages through almost five hundred illustrations (Evans 20961).

Henry Wynkoop to Reading Beatty

Left home between 10 & 11 on monday & came here at 12 on tuesday, had an agreable ride & good Compay.

We have been greatly alarm'd for the Safety of the President, but happily he is again out of Danger, owing, I am inform'd, more to the natural Strength of his Constitution than the Aid of Medicine, the Disorder being seated in the Lungs, an uncomon Discharge taking place afforded immediate Releif, am not without Hopes we shall be able to rescue him from a third Attack arising from Disorders occasioned by the cold Damps of this place and prolong his Days by breathing the more temperate & salubrious Air of Pensylvania.

The Bill providing for the payment of the National Debt [*Funding Bill*] is now under Discussion, in Committee of the whole & the funding the old Continental money yet in the Hands of individuals is the Subject of the Day.

The House have this day agreed to meet at 10 in the morning, an Omen this predictive of an Adjournment being not far distant, as the Committee Busyness, which otherwise consumes the mornings is nearly disposed of.

***

ALS, Wynkoop Papers, PDoBHi. Place to which addressed not indicated. The omitted text relates to private business transactions.

Other Documents

Edward Carrington to James Madison. ALS, Washington Papers, DLC. Place from which written not indicated; enclosed in Langham to Madison, 1 June. For the full text, see *PJM* 13:222–23.

Office seeking: military appointment at Point of Fork (present-day Columbia), Virginia, for Maj. Elias Langham, "whom you lately saw at New York."

Francis Child to Samuel Johnston. FC, Treasurers' and Comptrollers' Papers, Nc-Ar. Written from Hillsboro, North Carolina. The enclosure is in the Hayes Collection, NcU.

Encloses "an Account of all the Certificates issued by this State, as well as the Account of all those that have been taken [*lined out*] in by taxes or otherwise," per Johnston's request of 7 March.

William Constable to Joel Barlow. FC:lbk, Constable-Pierrepont Collection, NN.

The question of assumption "has agitated Congress much, & I think it is not impossible that the whole funding System might be laid over 'till next Session."

Tench Coxe to Michael Jenifer Stone. ALS, Coxe Papers, PHi.

Has remitted $441 from the U.S. treasury to his former partner (Nalbro Frazier) and brother Daniel Coxe at Philadelphia to be credited to Stone's account at the Bank of North America, and has requested from them an additional $60 "necessary to make up your Balance."

Samuel W. Dana, Asher Miller, and George Phillips to Jeremiah Wadsworth. ALS, Washington Papers, DLC. Written from Middletown, Connecticut; enclosed in Wadsworth to Washington, 7 August. For a partial text, see *PGW* 6:215n.

Office seeking: recommends William Walter Parsons as revenue officer in Hartford County, Connecticut.

Volckert Douw to Philip Schuyler. ALS, Schuyler Papers, NN. Written from "Green Bush," near Albany, New York.

Will either travel to New York or send down his "Indian Accounts," as Schuyler requested on 15 May.

Stephen Goodhue to Benjamin Goodhue. FC:lbk, Goodhue Papers, MSaE. Written from Salem, Massachusetts. For background on the proposed library for Congress, see *DHFFC* 8:653–62.

Private commercial transactions; "be Pleased to Send me word *** when it [*is*] likely Congress will rise Fanny [*Frances Ritchie Goodhue*] & Benja. are well of the Measles Stephen hath not had them yet Fanny & the ~~rest of the~~ Family are well—the colds are going of[*f*] Nothing new here we Se[*e*] a motion in the house to purchase a library for Congress which Seems to puzzle us ~~as Cash appears plenty and a disposition to do Justice it will be extended to all~~."

William S. Grayson to James Madison. ALS, Madison Papers, DLC. Written from Dumfries, Virginia; postmarked. For the full text, see *PJM* 13:223–24.

Office seeking: appeals to Madison as "the only effectual friend [*from*] which I dare hope for any thing"; his father (Senator Grayson) left his affairs in a "ruinous situation" at his death; the expense would not allow the younger Grayson to accept Monroe's offer of "friendly assistance" in studying law; all his father's personal property and fifteen thousand acres is already mortgaged; asks Madison's intercession with Washington and Knox for a commission in the military force of twelve thousand said to be forming for the defense of Georgia and the frontier; asks about the necessity of coming to New York, or any other method of proceeding.

James Lovell to John Adams. ALS, Adams Family Manuscript Trust, MHi. Written from Boston; carried by Leonard Jarvis.

Office seeking: Adams may refer advantageously to the bearer, Leonard Jarvis, for an answer to his questions regarding local public opinion of the new government; recommends him in any of the government's "Arrangements," especially for his knowledge of commerce and revenue in eastern Massachusetts; he "will probably suggest useful Hints" to Hamilton in that regard.

James Madison to Thomas Jefferson. AN, Jefferson Papers, DLC. The editors of *PTJ* dated this document based on Madison's citations to pages of the second draft of Jefferson's report, completed around 20 May (*PTJ* 16:649n;

DHFFC 8:484). For the full text, see *PJM* 13:226–27. For additional documents and background to Jefferson's report, see *DHFFC* 8:482–503.

Queries concerning Jefferson's report on weights and measures.

Edmund Randolph to James Madison. ALS, Madison Papers, DLC. Written from Williamsburg, Virginia. For the full text, see *PJM* 13:224–25.

Wife (Elizabeth Carter Nicholas Randolph) is recovering from her miscarriage, and the entire family will be returning to New York with him without delay; asks Madison to inform Coles and Hawkins; Virginians are against assumption almost unanimously, and Antifederalists praise those Congressmen who opposed it; the arguments posed in Madison's speech (of 22 April), the "difficulty of receding" should assumption be an error, and the threat of consolidation, make him happy with the vote of the Virginia delegation; asks that enclosure be forwarded.

David Sewall to George Thatcher. ALS, Chamberlain Collection, MB. Written from Portsmouth, New Hampshire; postmarked 21 May. For background on Stone's petition, see *DHFFC* 8:46–47.

Acknowledges Thatcher's letter of 13 May, enclosing John Stone's petition; has met Justice Jay, is pleased with him, and finds Thatcher's description of him to be perfectly just; reports on local elections to the state legislature.

John Witherspoon to James Madison. ALS, Witherspoon Papers, NjP. Written from Perth Amboy, New Jersey. For the full text, see *PJM* 13:225. Madison forwarded the enclosed letter to Thomas Pleasants, Jr., who informed him on 10 July that it was a fraud (*PJM* 13:225n).

Encloses a letter sent to Witherspoon from an Episcopalian or Roman Catholic clergyman in Nova Scotia unknown to him, for forwarding to a Mr. Sterling Pleasant of Mecklenburg County, Virginia, whom he does not know; asks Madison to forward it.

Pierce Butler, Receipt Book. Ms., Butler Papers, PHi.

"To J[*ames*] Robardet, for tuition for his 3 daughters, @ 2 guineas each / quarter £ 14.18.8."

NYDA, 20 May.

Floyd lost his reelection bid.

Letter from a Person Returned from the West. *NYDA*, 2 June. The editors believe the colorful letter is a fictional contribution to the debate over immigration to the West.

Cautions potential western settlers against the "disasters and misfortunes, mishaps and misgoings, disappointments, fevers and agues, and almost whatever else on the dark side of the matter you choose to mention."

Friday, 21 May 1790

Fine (Johnson)

George Benson to Theodore Sedgwick

I now do myself the pleasure to acknowledge the reception of your very acceptable favr. of the 11 inst. which reach'd me on friday last, the very important and no less pleasing Contents I immediately imparted to several particular friends, who express'd great pleasure in the intelligence and Conceiv'd it advisable that most of the Letter should be publish'd, and as your Worthy Colleague Mr. Ames whose friendly attention we gratefully feel had written to Govr. [*Jabez*] Bowen & Mr. Jno. Brown by the same opportunity, and Mr. [*Theodore*] Foster having not long since received a Letter from Mr. Strong, several extracts of Corresponding import are Publish'd in the News Paper, which I have now the honour to transmit you.[1] The bill[2] which appears to be design'd as a Wholesome but severe applycation to the Political Maladies of this State arriv'd in Town several days after I recd. your Esteem, & favour, and is also inserted in the Paper—We are extremely anxious to hear the result of the debates, which have probably before this period decided the important Point. The Letter with which you favour'd me, with the others on the same subject, have furnish'd a topic of much interesting Conversation, and it is with ineffable satisfaction I assure you that the Contents have made a very alarming impression, on the antifederal minds, it is very obvious that no Occurrence has produced effects so apparently auspicious to our wishes, and we are now inspir'd with the most sanguine expectations that the Convention next week will adopt the Constitution, and receive us from that Deplorable state into which the Malignant Policy and Reverseness of the Anties, have plung'd us, and, also avert the more Deplorable evils which appear impending, tho' I Confess we rather enjoy than regret the expected operation of the Prohibitory Bill, as the inveterate Enemies of the Federal Government will then suffer in the Common Calamity—hitherto the restraints have been partial, and unhappily felt &

lamented by those only, who have long and ardently wish'd & endeavourd for an occassion to the united states.

I Cannot sir do ample Justice to those Grateful sentiments of my heart which your Obliging kindness has impress'd, as so long time had elaps'd since I assum'd the liberty to address you, I was painfully apprehensive that you consider'd me, as Presuming on an acquaintance too transient, to warrant the freedom I exercis'd; and I am now embarrass'd for language, in which to express, how much I admire the Delicacy of your apology, with how sensibly I feel the favours you have done me. will you my Kind sir be so obliging as to inform my truly estimable friend Mr. Ames, that my best and grateful respects Court his acceptance, and permit me to subjoin that our most Judicious and Discerning Characters—Justly Conceive—Mr. Sedgwick and Mr. Ames, as having the most Distinguish'd Claim to the exalted Character of Enlighten'd, and Eloquent Statesmen, and as the most influential advocates for the interests of the Eastern States—if it was not very ungraceful, for an *alien* to Censure—I should *expatiate* where, I only *hint*—but, in reference to a Gentleman [*Leonard*] in the Massachusetts representation—some Persons, *not very Captious*, Cannot forbear Complaining in the language of sacred Writ—"*one to his farm*"[3]—but I hope the good man will return to his seat in season to *signify* his affirmative to the assumption of the State Debts, should that Question be finally negativ'd—it will be productive of Evils more injurious to the Federal Government than the defection of many *Rhode Islands*—but the alarming Consequences of a *non assumption* you have fully, solemnly, and irrefutably, stated to Congress in sentiments and language, which should be recorded in "Letters of Gold"[4]—tho' they are more indelibly engraven on the grateful hearts of the numerous state Creditors, where they will erect a Monument to your Fame, that shall flourish unimpair'd, "When Statues and Triumphal Arches, shall moulder in the Dust."[5]

ALS, Sedgwick Papers, MHi. Written from Providence, Rhode Island.

---

[1] All four letters alluded to appeared in the [Providence, Rhode Island] *United States Chronicle*, 20 May, and are printed under 11 May, above.

[2] The Rhode Island Trade Bill, also called the "Prohibitory Act" below.

[3] Matthew 22:5, in the parable about the subjects who refused the king's summons to be guests at his son's wedding. Officially on leave for three weeks beginning 16 April, Leonard missed the debate and votes on the issue of assumption.

[4] A practice associated with early Muslim illuminated writings of the Near East and later adopted for certain early Christian texts to denote special significance.

[5] A paraphrase of the famous sermon "Government the Pillar of the Earth," delivered in Boston in 1730 by the noted Congregational minister Benjamin Coleman (1673–1747).

Samuel Emery to George Thatcher

You know I am watching the motions of your Honbl. Body & sometime since observed you was on a Committee to Bring in a Bill for regulating the manner of haveing the Laws & judicial proceeding of one State so as to make them take effect in other states[1]—Now the matter I wish you to inform me is this whether this Law of yours (for I perceive it has passed) has any reference to poor Devils in my situation whither this will have any effect on persons having taken out a Certificate of Bankruptcy in one state, so as to discharge him from his debts in another state—If you think it has any relation to the business I will be very much oblige to you for your opinion on the subject & if you have a Copy of the Bill (if not perfect) please to send it me the very first post—I am in an unhappy situation, as I can neither stay at Home or go abroad in peace or for any profit till something is done. Write me immediately if only one Line.

[*P. S.*] If you have not the Act by you please to tell Mr. Otis he would oblige me particularly by sending me a Copy unless it is published in the United States Gazette [*GUS*].

ALS, Chamberlain Collection, MB. Written from Boston; postmarked 20 May.

[1] The Authentication Act, passed by both houses on 10 May.

John Page to St. George Tucker

I thank you for your Letter from Winchester [*Virginia*] which came to hand yesterday—I shall pray for your safe Return & an agreable meeting with you at Rosewell—I hope you mean to surprise us with a Wife. it has been said here that you had Mrs. Brent in View—Mrs. [*Margaret Lowther*] Page unites with me in best Wishes &c. to you & yours—I can not yet discover when we shall adjourn I shall dread carrying my dear Wife through our sultry Suns 430 Miles—As to the *dissecting Bill*[1] which you mention I did my best to get the detestable Clause stricken out & used the very Arguments which were used afterwards by the Physicians in Philada. in their Address to the Assembly which was about to insert that Clause as New-York has done[2] in a Bill stupidly copied from this Bill of our wise Senate the Physicians Petition succeeded & the Clause was stricken out—but no Notice was taken by the Retailers of our Debates here even of the Names of the Members who ~~moved~~ made & seconded the Motion—Your Brother [*Thomas Tudor Tucker*] renewed the Motion in the House which I had made & the Committee of the Whole but in Vain—the Novelty of thing & the

Weight of the Senate prevailed It was affirmed by me that it was introducing a new mode of Punishmt. which was therefore unconstitutional, that it would disgust our Constituents, wound the Feelings of the unfortunate Friends &c. of Persons executed; degrade Anatomy making it infamous to be dissected, & placing respectable Professors of Anatomy on a footting with Executioners—& that all this was to be done to no good Purpose for the Experiment had long been made in England & did not prevent Murders it, only tended there make Dissections so odious that few Persons were willing to suffer their Relations to be dissected that besides it appeared ridiculous for Congress to make such an Innovation in our ~~penal~~ Criminal Laws to take Effect only the little Spots of Territory they were to hold their Light houses—Docks & their 10 miles Square.

I write this in great Haste by yr. Son The[*oderick Randolph*]. let me entreat you to keep him in Virga. & sooth him he is so unhappy here, & so little can be learned in this City that I think you will injure him greatly if you send him back. This is the last Place in the U.S. ~~that~~ to which I would send a Young Man for an Education.

ALS, Tucker-Coleman Papers, ViW. Place to which addressed not indicated.

---

[1] The Punishment of Crimes Act [S-6], the fourth clause of which empowered courts to order that the corpses of executed convicts be dissected by surgeons.

[2] The New York legislature passed the so-called Anatomy Act ("An Act to Prevent the Odious Practice of Digging up and Removing for the Purpose of Dissection, Dead Bodies Interred in Cemeteries or Burial Places") on 6 January 1789, in response to the "Doctors Riot" of the year before, which was sparked by rumors of grave robbing by local physicians. The new state law criminalized grave robbing, but authorized judges to allow physicians to conduct anatomy lessons on the corpses of executed murderers, arsonists, and burglars.

Other Documents

Wallace Alexander to John Steele. ALS, Steele Papers, Nc-Ar. Written from Salisbury, North Carolina. For the full text, see *Steele* 1:59–60.

Office seeking: any office of consequence in the state's back country; forgot to mention it before Steele's departure; is one of his strongest advocates; all is the same there as when Steele left.

William Davies to Governor Beverley Randolph. Printed with documents on the Report of the Commissioners for Settling Accounts between the United States and Individual States, 8 May, above.

Theodore Foster to Theodore Sedgwick. No copy known; acknowledged in Sedgwick to Foster, 1 June.

Theodore Sedgwick to Pamela Sedgwick. ALS, Sedgwick Papers, MHi. Addressed to Stockbridge, Massachusetts; carried by Dr. Hyde.

"My health is as well as could be expected, in the poluted air of New York"; longs for the country and domestic life; household management.

John Cleves Symmes to Elias Boudinot. Summary of six page ALS, *Henkels Catalog* 731(1894):item 182.

Relating to Indians in the Northwest Territory, their depredations, and the uselessness of converting them to Christianity.

Governor Edward Telfair to Georgia Delegation. FC:lbk, Executive Council Journal, G-Ar. White served as colonel of the Fourth Regiment of the Georgia Line from 1777 until he died of wounds in 1780. For his widow's petition for the settlement of his accounts, see *DHFFC* 7:469–70.

Transmits copy of Georgia's claim against Col. John White, which the delegation is to have retained out of the settlement of White's accounts with the United States and credited to Georgia.

NYDA, 21 May.

Laurance and Benson were reelected.

Saturday, 22 May 1790

Fine (Johnson)

Pierce Butler to Weeden Butler

I am greatly in arrear to You—since my letter of the 4th. of April I have been favour'd with three from You one of Feby. the 2d. the others of March the 1st. I am very thankful and sensible of Your kind attention—Every individual of my Family participate in the satisfaction arising from Mrs. [*Weeden*] Butler's recovery—I am not so fortunate as You My Dear Wife [*Mary Middleton Butler*] is still greatly indisposed.

*** We are just at the point my last letter to You left Us—Still meditating on the best mode for arranging Our Finances Next Week will I think fix it In a Governmt. like Ours time must be given to every individual of the Legislature, who wishes it, to come forward and offer his sentiments on the best mode of taxing his Constituents—It is not a small Extent of Country inhabited by People of similar manners or modes of thinking the manners of the Northern & Southern States differ much time must be given to Assimilate—It will come round—we are going on very well—though we had nearly felt a temporary Embarassment by the precarious Situation of Our worthy President whose life hung on a thread last week He is now out of danger thank God— *** Our [*Benjamin*] Franklin is no more We have lost a Man of great mental powers.

My Boys [*Thomas Butler*] latter letters are well written I am quite pleased at Your Statement that he begins to feel his footing let him often my Dear Sir, look back at it—I mean the Grammar Rules, which are, and must be Our foundation His Exertions must be Continued and Constant He must raise to himself a Name or he may as well not Exist—I like his desire to Draw—Indulge him in that or anything else as You see proper You say truly when You remind me that I gave to You a Charte-blanche—He is in Your hands—Shape Him.

I thank You for placing me among Doctor Rutherferds Subscribers—I like his History much—It gives me pleasure That he is geting free of his incumbrances.

***

You are very good in troubling Yourself to Advertise for the House keeper—She, if good, will be Acceptable, for the worst Servts. I have met with are in New York.

ALS, Butler Papers, Uk. Place to which addressed not indicated; answered 2 August, "when Tommy wrote to Mrs. B. and I enclosed Miss F. B.s [*Frances Butler*] Letter from Ireland to the Major." The omitted text relates to foreign news and mutual friends.

Benjamin Goodhue to Michael Hodge

You'l find we have been some days on the funding bill, and have rated the old money at 100 for 1 the House were almost equaly divided between that and 75 and if the bill should finaly pass its not improbable the latter may obtain—we shall try again in a day or two to annex the assumption to this bill and form a part of it, whether it will obtain is uncertain for tho' we have as we suppose gain'd the other two Jersey members,[1] by intreaties &c. yet I have my fears least the question of temporary residence which I hear is to be brought forward in the Senate will throw the whole bussines as it were in the winds to be hurld about, as that current may affect it, its a humiliating reflection that so important a subject should any way depend on so paltry and local considerations—but so it is and our being so nearly divided unfortunately gives an opportunity to a very few persons to practise such unworthy measures with success—I consider this attempt will be our last serious effort for this session, if we fail we I mean our delegation are pretty much of this decided opinion that the evil of a postponement of the whole funding will be incomperably less then an independent funding upon

the excises &c. as is proposed, by the former our hopes are kept alive by a well grounded expectation that all will go right next session, by the latter as we apprehend certain confusion must ensue and the assumption for ever lost, unless the magnitude of the confusion should coerce a remedy, which at best is a horrid one—to me our path has always appear'd plain and easy before us, and nothing is wanting but to be divested of local and inconsiderable considerations to pursue it.
[*P. S.*] my respects to the Gentlemen of Newburyport.

ALS, Ebenezer Stone Papers, MSaE. Place to which addressed not indicated.

[1] Schureman and Sinnickson.

John Steele to Joseph Winston

I am now writing you a letter which it is very doubtfull whether it will ever reach you, or not—The distance is so great, the people so inquisitive for news, that it is a very common practise to break up letters by the way.

The President has been dangerously ill, but is now on the recovery, if we should unfortunately loose him, the vice President by virtue of his present appointment wd. take the chief majistracy untill the 4th. March 1793.

This I contemplate as an event melancholy indeed—and if it shou'd take place shortly, perhaps it wou'd have been happy for america, that General Washington had never been chosen. Relying on his virtue and abilities, congress have by law vested him with powers not delegated by the Constitution, which I suppose they wou'd have intrusted to no other man—These powers cannot ~~now~~ be recalled at any future period without the consent of his successor in office, or an union of Sentiment, which in these factious times, is not to be expected.

A bill[1] has lately passed the Senate, and sent to us for concurrence which is designed to prohibit any further intercourse with Rhodeisland, untill she shall ratify. It is tyrannical, and arbitrary in the highest degree, and the author of it,[2] indeed the Senate by passing it, seem to have lost sight of that sperit of moderation, and mutual forbearance which ought forever to subsist between Governments, related as they are to us, as well as between individuals.

It is certain that little state was not backward in the late Revolution, that she performed essential services, that she sustained important sacrafices and is therefore entitled to respect.

How far she is wrong in her present politicks? Or how far she is right? are questions which the unerring wisdom of the deity is only capable of deciding.

I hope however the bill will be rejected in the house of Representatives, if it shoud not, and be finally passed into a law, it will be a public testimonial given to the world of the slender foundation of all human Friendships, or political connections.

Last thursday I made a motion that a committee shou'd be appointed to take up the amendmts. proposed by No. Carolina, and to report what further amendments were necessary to be recommended to the several states—after some debate the motion was ordered to lie on the Table untill next monday, when I shall again revive it. What the event will be God only knows.

I have just written a letter to Mr. Howzer [*George Houser*] which together with this contains all the news worth relating. Be pleased to read his letter, and in return give him the reading of this.

ALS, Steele Papers, NcU. Addressed to Dan River, Stokes County, North Carolina; franked; received and forwarded by Jno. Sibley on 22 June.

---

[1] The Rhode Island Trade Bill.

[2] Carroll proposed and reported the bill in the Senate, but the manuscript bill is in Ellsworth's hand.

Michael Jenifer Stone to Walter Stone

I have received your Letter and immediate after reading it I did as you requested—I shall persue your Opinion—I think you are right.

The Influenza is an amazingly irksome Disorder—I have been plagued off and on for a month—I have almost habitual Sore Eyes—And you may beleive me I am very temperate in Every thing—I have my Wine of the best kind and separate—and I do not drink more than 6 Quarts in 4 Weeks—And the people in the House[1] tell me I shall Starve—I find also that I *dare* not live generously—If I do I am tortured with the Head Ache—However I think I shall soon get *well.*

The President is mending so Slowly that it is three Days now since the Doctors pronounced him out of Danger and he is not yet (unless within a few Hours) out of Bed—I shall bring forward on Monday a motion "that both Houses address him upon his recovery and advise him to seek his Health in any part of this Continent he may think ~~it~~ likely to find it in"[2]—This I believe will be necessary—because I am Satisfied was he sure to die he would not quit his *Station*—His life is as dear to the Interests as to the affections of America. I had a very pretty little Horse in virginia—a Cub Colt—I have a Curiosity to Know what has become of it. Saml. Sterret is married and leads his wife in Triumph towards Home on Monday[3]—I have been in a round of Gay Company since Thursday Night and it will continue till Monday—Today we dine at Sir John Temple's who is some way connected and very intimate with the [*Tobias*] Lears Family—The Beautifull and accomplished Miss Aspinwall is to be married to Col. Platt[4]—who is an old Homely &c. Speculator—But said to be a Generous Honest Man.

I think it will be very imprudent in you to have any thing to do with Widgate's affairs—No doubt the Creditors will be much dissapointd and of Course Dissatisfied &ca.—[*William*] Craik having little to do may be Enabled to manage it to his advantage.

I have written to Fred[*erick Stone*] & Shall write to Col. [*John Hoskins*] Stone.

ALS, Stone Papers, MdHi. Place to which addressed not indicated. The editors identified the recipient from the salutation "Dear Brother," which Stone often used with Walter and the fact that their other living brother is mentioned in the letter.

---

[1] Stone probably still resided at Mrs. Mary Dobiney's at 15 Wall Street, where he had lived with Bassett, Cadwalader, Contee, R. B. Lee, Moore, Read, and Seney during the first session.

[2] There is no evidence that Stone proposed this motion.

[3] Samuel Sterret married Rebecca Sears in New York's Trinity Church on 20 May.

[4] Richard Platt married Sarah Aspinwall in New York City on 5 September 1790.

George Thatcher to Thomas Thatcher

***

Now for Politics—

The House of Representatives are about funding the Continental Debt—and propose to redeem or call in the old paper money at one hundred for one—but whether this will be compleated this Session or not till the next I cannot determine.

Your observations touching the situation of Yarmouth & the other Towns on the Cape are very just—I have often contemplated their circumstances—and being well acquainted therewith, mentioned this subject to Mr. Partridge, your Representative—I really fear the fishery, thro our State, will decay—and tho we shall endeavour, this Session, to do something, in Congress, for their encouragement I apprehend it will not be enough to make them flourish.

The Senate have passed a Bill[1] cuting off all communication with Rhode-Island—and subjecting every vessel that goes from the United States to that State; or from that State to any port, creek or harbour in the U. States, to forfeiture—A[*l*]so demanding Twenty five thousand dollars of that State to be paid into the Treasury of the United States—But I am very certain this Law will never pass our House—I shall notice some other parts of your Letter hereafter.

FC, Thatcher Family Papers, MHi. Sent to Yarmouth, Massachusetts.

[1] The Rhode Island Trade Bill.

Hugh Williamson to John Gray Blount

I am greatly disappointed as to the sale of the Certificates you sent me. It happens that Col. [*Abishai*] thomas is intimate with two of the chief Brokers in this Town and he had some Time ago consulting their Safety informed them of the Date of our suppressed Certificates; of this Circumstance I had no suspicions or Information untill some days ago that I was consulting him about the properest Broker to be employed. He then told me that himself had given such Information as would necessarily prevent a Sale. Mr. S[*amuel*]. Johnston has some Certificates of our State I will see whether he is able to sell them & may possibly continue some mode of passing off those of [*17*]86.

Congress Yesterday in a Committee of the whole fixed the Scale of old continental Bills @ 100 for one to be funded—Securities are now @ 8/9 at this Rate old Bills are worth in Specie about 1 Dlr. for 212. Green's Rects.[1] are of the same Value, cannot you buy any at the old Price of 800 for 1 or 700, 6 or 500. still there would be a Profit. The Speculators as you may guess by the inclosed are not pleased with N. C. for her Conduct respecting the Assumption.

The Presidents late Illness has prevented several Bills from being sent up for his Approbation. In the Court Bill for our State I have so managed it as to have all the Courts to sit at Newbern. I hope it will pass without alteration. We lost our Bill by a heterogenious Tack that was appended to it in the Senate.[2]

ALS, John Gray Blount Papers, Nc-Ar. Addressed to Washington, North Carolina.

[1] Shortly after Gen. Nathanael Greene (1742–86) assumed command of the Continental Army in the South in late 1780, he complained to the North Carolina board of war that Continental certificates were not as widely accepted as the state's certificates. To increase the circulation of the former, he recommended that the county commissaries responsible for provisioning the army during its operations throughout the state be allowed to purchase goods with state certificates and then accept from Continental quartermasters the Continental certificates as receipts for those purchases. The board of war delegated to the state's commissary general the powers Greene recommended and dissolved in January 1781 without the state legislature's taking up the question (*PNG* 6:598, 7:54–55n).

[2] The North Carolina Judiciary Act [HR-68], presented in the House on 21 May by a committee (including Williamson) to which the matter had been recommitted when the "lost Bill," the North Carolina Judiciary Bill [S-10], was defeated by disagreement over the inclusion of New Hampshire's district court (*DHFFC* 6:1552–56).

Oliver Wolcott, Jr. to Oliver Wolcott, Sr.

I have been all this morning attempting to write you some account of the progress of affairs here, but have been continually interupted; I hope you will therefore excuse the scrawl of one moment.

Congress are debating a bill for funding the public debt, exclusive of the State debts, of which I despair of a settlement—there is however a strong current to be opposed, and the success of any measures may be considered as dubious—I am not certain that the gentlemen who embarrass this subject are not as honest men, as those who are endeavouring to establish some system.

The truth is, that the goverments of most of the States were so entirely prostrated at several periods during the war, that it is impossible to arrive at any considerable certainty, in adjusting the mutual claims of the States—it is also the case that desultory regulations, and knavish and weak persons who have been impowered to establish debts against the public, have increased the public burdens, very improperly—the avidity of speculators has also excited a resentment which, though not strictly rational, is in a great degree excusable.

These circumstances create different sentiments both with respect to the justice of the debt & the obligations of government to discharge it—and as a political tie of union, the arguments which recommend a funding system to one party, disgrace it in the opinions of another.

The people of this country do not appear to me to harmonise in sentiment, in governmental subjects; they have the same general interests, but when the details of systems are examined & the operation of particular laws discussed; almost insuperable difficulties are presented.

The President has been exceedingly unwell, had the fears of those acquainted with his situation been verified, the consequences would have been exceedingly alarming.

What is most wanted here, is stability & political knowledge, there are men of great abilities and extensive science—but they are in some instances, prone to indulge their minds in fanciful theories of republican liberty—some few, mistake cunning for wisdom.

The office which I hold is the most burdensome under the government; but I shall execute it in the best manner, which I can—what degree of success I may expect, is intirely uncertain.

ALS, Wolcott Papers, CtHi. Place to which addressed not indicated.

[*David Daggett,*] A Republican to Messrs. Printers

THE citizens of Connecticut are under peculiar embarrassments. A decayed commerce has been attended with barren crops for many years past— "The labour of the olive has failed and the fields have yielded no meat."[1] In a state so dependent on agriculture this circumstance has created evils of an alarming nature. The cry of distress has been heard from every class of men, and none are exempt from this general calamity. Nor, are these complaints without foundation—the people do not clamour in vain. Can the merchant enjoy the same pleasure in seeing his vessel enter her port, when, with her whole cargo, he cannot raise cash sufficient to satisfy the collector, as he once did in viewing her returning from every voyage laden with a generous reward for his industry? Tell me, ye farmers, if ye have the same peace and prosperity within your dwellings, while the constable continually knocks at your doors for taxes, or is driving your oxen and fatlings to the sign post to sell at public auction, as when you "sit under your own vines and fig-trees and had none to make you afraid."[2]

The merchant, in addition to these embarrassments, groans under an excise law of this state—a law as oppressive as impolitic, as unjust as partial. The West-India islands, to which he trades, also subject him to heavy impositions. I was told by a merchant of reputation (who employs only one vessel) that he pays annually in the island of Cape Francois about 200l. to ob[*illegible*] with him, that he should conform to the laws of the Island, while at the same time, his property lay under the guns of an armed vessel, and would have been seized any moment for the least violation of law. Of all the merchants who resort to that island, this exaction is made, and this becomes a heavy burden upon the mercantile interest—this evil might be remedied by the appointment of an agent for the United States, to reside at Cape-Francois.

These circumstances, with the heavy duties already imposed by Congress, render the navigation of Connecticut rather a curse than a blessing, and induce all concerned in this branch of business, to wish that a general conflagration might at once destroy that species of their property, which is now devoted to a lingering death. If the three last cargoes imported into New-Haven, had been cryed thro the streets for sale, there would not have been ready cash enough raised to pay the duties. Under these embarrassments, we look up to the new constitution and those who administer it, for relief—And what do we obtain in answer? why, an *additional duty*—"when we ask bread they give us a stone."[3] It is argued however, in favour of this enhanced duty, that it can be paid—that the revenue will be greatly increased—or, at least, that it will prevent the importation of distilled spirits into this country and thus secure to us an important benefit. I answer, that duty will not be paid nor the revenue encreased, for the merchant will smuggle or quit commerce. I presume there is a greater quantity of cash paid now, for the duty of rum, than if it was double—when the impost shall completely sweep away the profits of the trader, he may as well hazard his property, by running goods, as see it going to certain yet slow destruction, by the grievances under which he labours. It is said, the prevention of the importation of ardent spirits, &c. is an object greatly to be wished—the enhanced duty will effect this purpose if no other. But are we to lose the W. India trade entirely? How will the farmer dispose of his horses, cattle, lumber, &c.? And shall the merchant feel, at once, the entire loss of his property? It may be said, let your vessels bring home the avails of their cargoes in cash—the answer is obvious we cannot carry on a commerce, with those islands, upon such principles—we must invert the avails of our property in their produce or quit the pursuit.

Combatting these difficulties, the merchant can but wish that his vessels might be fitted out as *privateers* instead of merchantmen, and the husbandman is almost induced to pervert the scripture, and pray that his *plough-shares* might be made into *swords*, and his *pruning-hooks* into *spears*, and that this whole nation might *learn* war *still more.*[4]

Shall I be told that Congress have not had time, as yet, to lend their aid to the interest of agriculture, manufactures and commerce? If so, I will answer next week and endeavour to tell you to what they *have* had time to attend.

[New Haven] *Connecticut Journal*, 26 May. For information on this series and its author, see the location note to A Republican to Messrs. Printers (No. 1), 15 May, above.

---

[1] Habakuk 3:17.
[2] Micah 4:4.
[3] Matthew 7:9.
[4] Isaiah 4:3.

Other Documents

Nathan Dane to Samuel Phillips, Jr. ALS, Dane Papers, Beverly Historical Society, Massachusetts. Addressed to Boston; postmarked 25 May. The Settlement of Accounts Bill [HR-69] that Dane describes was not presented until 27 May, five days after the date of this letter.

Discussion of issues of the settlement of state accounts, particularly that of Massachusetts; "a bill is reported by a Committee for continuing the board and adding to it the Secretary of the Treasury and the Comptroller and for enlarging the ground of claims so as to admit at once those for particular as well as those for general defence—what will be done I do not know—there is at present a degree of languor and discord pervading the measures of the union."

Nicholas Gilman to Oliver Peabody. No copy known; acknowledged in Peabody to Gilman, 7 June.

Benjamin Huntington to William Ellery. No copy known; acknowledged in Ellery to Huntington, 7 June.

John Steele to George Houser. No copy known; mentioned in Steele to Winston, 22 May.

John Steele to Henry Knox. FC, Steele Papers, Nc-Ar. For the full text, see *Steele* 1:45–46.

The commission on which he served, for treating with the Cherokee in May–June 1789, stored the unused gifts at William Davidson's; reminds Knox that the gifts, being chiefly woolens, would soon be spoiled; offers to assist in making any arrangements for their disposal, upon his return to North Carolina as soon as Congress adjourns.

Sunday, 23 May 1790

Fine (Johnson)

Benjamin Goodhue to Stephen Goodhue

*** I mean to discharge a good conscience, but yet I can't but feel a great degree of uneasiness at things going as they do—some times I have hope with regard to the assumption at other times I despair—I suppose it will be renewed again this week for the last time, if we fail, it is the very decided opinion of our delegation that the whole funding bussines should be postponed as a far less evil then funding the other as is proposed *** We go on slow theres no knowing when we shall get up, the members appear tired and want to adjourn. they generaly say the last of June but I fear not so soon, tho' I rather suppose they will at all events soon afterwards.

ALS, Goodhue Family Papers, MSaE. Addressed to Salem, Massachusetts. The omitted text relates to private commercial transactions.

Benjamin Goodhue to Insurance Offices

We have been for some days on the bill for funding the Continental debt and have rated old money at 100 for 1. tho' I am not without hope if the bill should get through it may eventualy be put at 75. for the house were almost equaly divided between that and 100—the assumption will again be tryed to be annexed to this bill and form a part of it, but whether it will obtain is wholy uncertain, if it rested upon the justice and policy of the measure independently of partial and local considerations, which too much affect our national legislature, there could be no doubt of its success—should it fail it may be the means of postponing the whole bussines as being a less evil then funding upon the excises in the manner as is proposed without the assumption—should this be the issue I take it for granted the present revenue would be appropriated as far it would go towards paying our Creditors, and perhaps in future there might be a better agreement upon this important bussines.

ALS, Goodhue Letters, NNS. Addressed to Salem, Massachusetts; franked.

Jeremiah Hill to George Thatcher

Misteries you know are matters that I do not deal in, though the Mind is always anxious to to pry into every thing, that appears mystical in its way, yet being under rational restraint acquiesces to the Incumberance, like the Sun in a foggy Morning, till its piercing rays physical dispel the thick Mist, and then the Mistery becomes a Revelation—The inclosed Letter whose Seal has been broke came to me Yesterday inclosed in your Letter of the 16th. inst. this is a mistery and as my *Noodle* cannot dispel the *Mist*, I wish the loan of your *Telescope*—I have now to thank you for the papers you inclosed me—As to the Inspectorship you mention, I cant say any thing about it, as I do not know the Emoluments that will arise in the business, but If I may be allowed a Conjecture it will be very trifling in this District however I think you are a competent Judge of the Business—Mr. [*Matthew*] Cobb has imported in his Schooner a small Cargo of Wines, which is all that has ever been imported in this District since the Revenue Laws took place, If you should think this Office not worth our Friend [*Joshua B.*] Osgoods attention or better provision could be made for him, as I know you wish to help him, I would mention Samuel Emery the Young Man who lives with me, he being in the way a small matter will be worth his notice, and I assure you he makes good improvements in the Office, I have appointed him my Deputy & in my Absence he has done exceeding well. However I am not anxious if friend Osgood can be accomidated.

I view the Liberty of the Press in a republican Government in the same light I do the Doctrine of original Sin in the moral world as a physical Evil, for as evil is the Mirror through which we see good actions, so whoever a republican Governments exalts, the Liberty of the Press debases, which

Debasement only serves to shew the Lustre of the Exaltation, Evil is a natural Attendant on the Moral World, in the same manner the Liberty of the Press is a natural Attendant on a republican Goverment & both answer the same good purpose in their several Stations. I think there is a great deal of propriety in making a Distinction in the Revenue Laws between nations in commercial Treaty & those that are not, of course I like the *bold stroke* your house has made—Rhode Island appears to me to be in a fit of Lunacy. I am rather Jeasous [*jealous*] whether *Physic* will answer any good purpose except the *Physician* is directed to let a *little Blood* which the Doctors commonly allow to be very good in such disorders.

ALS, Chamberlain Collection, MB. Written from Biddeford, Maine; postmarked Portsmouth, New Hampshire.

Richard Henry Lee to Charles Lee

*** Our President is so well recovered from a dangerous illness as that he proposes tomorrow to ride out if the day is good. We have had a most Morbid season in this City, and it still continues—many have fallen sacrifices & myself had nearly gone to visit my fathers. I thank God that my health & strength are greatly restored. *** When I was here in the year 1787[1] I desired Mr. [*Thomas*] Greenleaf the Printer of the N. York Journal to send Me his News paper—he says he has regularly done so ever since, & to your care as desired—He has accordingly charged me with 3 years Gazettes—I told him that I had not received them, nor did I believe that you had—He still insisted on having sent them, but said that on writing to you, if you replied to me that they had not come to you, he would give it up—Tis certainly hard on him, if he sent them; and certainly hard on me who got them not, to pay for them—However, if you have received them I will pay for them with great pleasure. Let me know, if you please, how this is? *** The Secretary of the Treasury tells me that he has written a Circular Letter stating that when Vessels go from one district to another in the Same State and call or come to a part of the District where no Collector or N[*aval*]. Officer *resides*, that they are at liberty to land goods without going to the Office for a permit—This you know was ever my opinion—But now, I suppose, Vessels going up & down Potomac from one district to another will be in no difficulty about landing our Things at Nomony,[2] witht. going to Yeocomico for permit.

***

P. S. Where is your brother Harry, & how does his Mrs. Lee—I want to write to him, but have understood that he was at some Springs in the Western Country.[3]

ALS, Emmet Collection, NN. Place to which addressed not indicated. The omitted text relates to family news and Lee's household management. For the full text, see *Lee* 2:518–20.

[1] Lee attended the Confederation Congress in September and October 1787.

[2] Nomony Bay, near the mouth of the Potomac River.

[3] According to both Morse's *Geography* and Jefferson's *Notes on the State of Virginia*, the most reputable medicinal springs in Virginia's "Western Country" were Warm Springs and nearby Hot Springs located in Bath County (then part of Augusta County). They were visited most frequently in July and August, for treating skin ailments and rheumatism. The "Men's Bathhouse" at Warm Springs dates to 1761, while the first public accommodations at Hot Springs (known as Little Warm Springs during the Revolution) were available as early as 1766. The lesser known Sweet Springs lay an additional forty-two miles south in Botetourt County. Henry "Lighthorse Harry" and Matilda Lee probably stayed at one of these.

Richard Henry Lee to Thomas Lee Shippen

I am very thankful to my dear Nephew for his favor of the 20th. instant—The enclosed shall be sent by tomorrows post to Ludwell.[1] I went yesterevening to the Presidents and was introduced to his Chamber (the first it seems, since his illness, except his Physicians & his family) I found him sitting in his easy Chair, where he had been greatest part of the day—his countenance expressed a clearness that shewd the Morbid matter which occasioned his malady had been well removed—he has had no return of fever since the first left him which is now 8 or more days, and on Monday he hopes to ride out in his Carriage—So you see that all danger of relapse seems now removed—Now for Phila., Many circumstances have concurred to render it probable that our Adjournment will be to meet at Philadelphia—I shall certainly Vote for it, and so I think will my Colleague [*Walker*]—I believe there is a majority in S—e and I am told that no doubt remains of the other H—e—However, as intrigue may defeat the most probable prospects, it is prudent not so to speak of this matter as that the account may come from you here—Success will be more sure by the proposition coming on witht. previous room for Cabal, and the thing be yet very fair as both Houses will be ~~very~~ full from this time. ***

ALS, Shippen Family Papers, DLC. Place to which addressed not indicated. The omitted text relates to family and household management. For the full text, see *Lee* 2:517–18.

[1] Ludwell Lee (1760–1836), the Senator's second son.

William Maclay to Benjamin Rush

Sleeping or waking for a week past, I have scarce thought of any thing but a removal of Congress to Philada. to relate all our small difficulties & delays would be to write a Volume. This Week we will certainly try our fate. It is agreed on all hands that we will try our fortune first, in the Senate. we are, or what amounts to the same thing, *affect to be*, confident of Success. This You know to be politically right. And Yet (aside) we have our Doubts and difficulties. Were I a roman catholic I would say, Ora pro nobis.[1] but we have your best Wishes and that amounts to the same thing. tomorrow will perhaps be the day. may it be a lucky One.

ALS, Rush Papers, DLC. Addressed to Third Street, Philadelphia; franked; postmarked 24 May.

[1] "Pray for us," a frequent refrain in the Catholic liturgy.

Robert Morris to Mary Morris

Your affectionate letter of the 20th. arrived Yesterday and I am rejoiced to find that the Influenza let you off more easily than has generally happened; The Cough however remained, and I observe that Cough lasts a good while and is a troublesome kind of Cough, therefore I shall be glad to learn that you are entirely freed of it, and Bob [*Robert Morris, Jr.*] also, I hope William [*Morris*] & the rest will have no more of it, Thomas [*Morris*] is gone to the Passaic Falls [*New Jersey*], He and young McGivan set out yesterday to Walk it and I suppose they will not be back untill this Evening [*torn*] this you will [*torn*] that he keeps clear of the Infl[*uenza*] [*torn*] your humble Servant The President is [*torn*] all that is now wanting is the recovery of his Strength, for the Fever is gone and the disorder Conquered. I did not see Doctr. [*John*] Jones yesterday so that I dont know whether he intends to Set out to day or not, but I find our Neighbour Wm. Bell does & if he sees you before this letter gets to hand he will tell you that I am in perfect Health. as the President will live and Continue a blessing to this Country we will spare ourselves the trouble of thinking of a Successor, I certainly ought to feel gratefull to those who honoured me with their approbation in the manner you mention, but they must have forgot that the Constitution gives Succession to the Vice President untill a New Election at the end of the Presidents four years—God forbid that there should be any Vacancy during my Life for I never wish to see any other then Geo. Washington fill the Presidential Chair. I am sorry that our Neighbour Mrs. Stewart[1] has been so Ill as you mention, however she will recover, for She has too much Sense to die whilst young and you may tell her that I not only *say* but *think* so—present my Compliments & good wishes to Genl. [*Walter*] Stewart also—I should have been at home with you this day if the New Jersey Senators had been here on Friday but they were both absent, and we durst not risque a certain Question without them, it is a great pity, [*torn*]t *babling* about it does great mischief [*torn*] Yesterday the Yorkers took Serious al[*arm*] and are now Circulating several Story's some true & some false, in the hope of defeating our plans. I shall not give them much time, for if there is a full Senate tomorrow I intend to Move ~~in Senate~~ "That The next Session of Congress shall be held in the City of Philadelphia" and if all prove true to what they have said, we shall carry it ~~in Senate~~.

The Members of the other House Say they are Sure there, but I am not so Confident, having too often experienced that Political Men indulge in loose Conversation, and Act totally different when brought to the Test. I rather however incline to the opinion that we shall now Succeed; altho our long stay in this place has fixed many strong attachments; at Head Quarters;[2] amongst the members of both Houses; and amongst all the Executive officers; and the Citizens; many of the latter are more attentive than I apprehend ours in Philada. will be if we come there. You will readily conceive therefore that it is not an~~y~~ easy matter to remove a Body of Men Composed as we are, and the greater part of whom are not only Contented but pleased with their situation.

As to the reports and opinions [*torn*] from hence [*torn*] different Gentn. that occasion[*torn*] they are not worth a farthing, they ask ea[*ch*] of us our Opinions & none of us like to discourage the expectation of removal, therefore the answer they generally get, is that we shall carry it, & from those who are Sanguine themselves, they get answers that encourage very sanguine expectations & these are reported on their return to Philadelphia as Certainty's. You have however found how vague and uncertain such Reports prove and must have learnt not [*to*] place Confidence in them. I shall be happy, if next Week I can give you a pleasing account of the event of my intended Motion, and untill you hear from me, make yourself easy I dined yesterday at Mr. Daltons, Mrs. [*Ruth Hooper*] Dalton was particularly kind and attentive in her enquiries about you, Hetty [*Ester Morris*] & Maria [*Morris*] So that I think you have made a strong Impression on her She is a kind & Worthy Woman, Mrs. LeBlois [*Ruth Dalton Deblois*] did not appear She is ill with the Influenza. Today Mr. [*William*] Constable Mr. Chalmers [*John Chaloner*] & my self intend for Morrisania, it is a fine day and yet I dont feel fond of the Jaunt.

However I may deserve or not your encomiums upon my Philosophical Temper, now trained to patient endurance of Misfortune. I can assure you that I am charmed with your reflections because they have a [*torn*] that will prove usefull to yo[*u*].

Belie[*ve me m*]y Dearest Creature when I do m[*ost*] Seriously assure you, that the bitterest Moments of my present Life are those in which I contemplate You as the Partner of misfortunes ~~for~~ of which I am not only the

Victim, but in Some degree perhaps Culpable in not having guarded better against them. I am however Striving to retrieve them if I succeed all will be well again, If I do not I hope at all events to retain sufficient Firmness to do the best that is possible for me to do. Adieu, I want to see You & will as soon as I can.

ALS, Morris Papers, CSmH. Place to which addressed not indicated. The salutation reads "My Dearest Friend."

[1] Deborah McClenachan (1763–1823), daughter of Blair McClenachan, a Philadelphia merchant and wartime business associate of Morris, married Walter Stewart in 1782. The couple ranked high among Philadelphia's upper class.
[2] I.e., Washington's house.

Philip Schuyler to Stephen Van Rensselaer

I did not receive your favor of the 16th Instant until It was too late to return an Answer by the post—I sent the letter directed for General [*James*] Gordon on Thursday morning.

The papers will have advised you that Mr. [*Samuel*] Townshend is returned a representative in Congress for the Long Island district. this man is dying, and at a future Election It is supposed the Contest will be between [*Ezra*] L'hommedieu, [*Thomas*] Treadwell & [*John*] Van Der Bilt. If both the former are Candidates, the latter will probably succeed. Our friend Mr. Benson is returned for the Dutchess district—Mr. [*Cornelius*] Schoonmaker for that of Ullster & Orange General Gordon succeeds Mr. Rensselaer—whether Mr. Sylvester or Mr. [*John*] Livingston ~~are~~ is Elected, it is not yet decided. hitherto the ballots stand favorable to the former. I shall call at the Secretarys office to Morrow for the Commissions, and send them up.

Notwithstanding all the Chicane and opposition to the Assumption of what are improperly called the States debts, I believe they will be Assumed and that the decision will be tomorrow or on tuesday at farthest.

The bill to compensate Baron Steuben meets with so much opposition in senate. that If It passes at All, the Allowance will be greatly reduced.

The President is again on his legs, he was yesterday able to traverse his room a dozen times. he has been dangerously Ill. If he had expired we should in all probability have been in great confusion.

I have either had the Influenza or a severe cold Attended with a fever & cough, I am nearly recovered of the latter & of the former not a Symptom is left.

ALS, Schuyler Family Papers, Albany Institute of History & Art, New York. Place to which addressed not indicated.

Pamela Sedgwick to Theodore Sedgwick

Thank you my dearest Love for your favour By Mr. Ashman[1] am Told that your health is much mended wish you to indeavour to Court Sleep at the Proper hours for That Refreshment, as I think its friendly Influences on the Constitution are very necessary to Comfortable health—I hear not a Word my Love of Congress being About to Rise—am affraid you will not be home so soon as the Time propoesd.

In Short I am Tired of Liveing a Widdow and ~~a~~ being at the same Time a Nurse—sometimes I am all most in the mind—of quiting here and Paying You a Visit in New York—we here no more of the funding Sistem I hope however it will not be Given up this Session—Antifedderalism—I am Told is daily Gaining Ground Perticulilarly in the State of N. York Mr. [*John*] Bacon Goes to Boston ~~I am Told~~ with high hopes of effecttually opposeing the assumtion—I cannot get So much Resolution as to neglect wholly To write and Trouble you with my Letters but for the futer they shall be short I am ever my dearest friend more your obliged and affectionate than can be expressd.

ALS, Sedgwick Papers, MHi. Written from Stockbridge, Massachusetts.

[1] Probably one of the Mohicans, a Christianized Indian tribe centered at Stockbridge. John and Justus Ashmun of Blandford, Massachusetts, were listed in the 1790 census.

David Stuart to Richard Bland Lee

I am extremely concerned at the intelligence of your last letter, respecting the President's illness—I hope the strength of his Constitution will yet get the better of it—His death at the present moment, would in my opinion be more fatal to the government, than at any former period, since its comm[*ence*]ment—I am just returned from attending the District Court at Williamsburg The minds of people in general, appear to me to be more than alienated from the government, in consequence of the obstinacy with which the assumption of the State debts is pursued; in open defyance to the Constitution as they think, and most certainly to every principle of equity—They appear to be much exasperated. It has been observed, that since this subject has been in agitation, a number of vermin from the Northward, have been posting through the Country purchasing up, indiscrimately, all evidences of public debt—Hence it is concieved, that while publick benefit is made the pretext of the measure, private views are the real source of it—The uncommon warmth and asperity with which it is contended for, I think justifies the suspicion—So much personality and menacing are not commonly observed where the public good is the only object of pursuit with both sides—Be assured, it furnishes great cause of triumph to the opponents of the government and when an opportunity offers, will be used by them, in detaching those who have formerly been zealous in support of it from a further continuance of their exertions—If the measure should unfortunately be carried, in spite of your exertions, you may calculate on the best grounds, that Virginia will never acquiesce in such an infraction of the government—She allready feels the utmost contempt for the bullying conduct of Massachusetts, and will remember to a late day, the ingratitude of South Carolina—My ideas of Mr. Maddison's discrimination plan, agreed perfectly with your explanation of it—I am more convinced than ever of its inpracticability, and injustice—One circumstance which recommended the government strongly to me, was, that it provided against all legislative interference in contracts—The frequent instances in which these had happened, were a source of disgust to every person of property, and led them strongly to espouse a government which would protect them in future from such wanton exertions of power—And it be pretended that it was not a legislative interference—But it is done with, and I shall not take up your time further upon it—I dare say you will consider it as a proof of the aversion entertained towards the assumption, when I inform you that Mr. Maddison who was so harshly spoke of, for his plan of discrimination, has done away all the prejudices which the illiberal and interested had concieved against him on that score, and is become extremely popular for his conduct respecting the assumption—I am sorry to find our Senators have been as unsuccessfull in their attempt to have the doors of the Senate opened, for the admission of all who chose to hear the debates of that House—The manner in which the application has been rejected, is not less mortifying, than the rejection itself[1] We hear that some bargain is [*on*] foot, between Pennsylvania, and the Eastern States, respecting the seat of Government founded on the assumption business—Considering the temper of mind, in which the Eastern States are in, at present, from the agitation of that question, it will be an unfortunate moment for taking it up.

ALS, Custis-Lee Papers, DLC. Written from "Abingdon," Fairfax County (remains of the house in present-day Washington National Airport, Arlington County), Virginia.

---

[1] R. H. Lee's motion of 29 April was rejected overwhelmingly, with only himself, Walker, and Maclay voting in favor, after (it was reported in Virginia) two days of debate. See Stuart to George Washington, 2 June, below.

George Thatcher to Thomas Hopkins

Your Letter, dated Portland May 8th. and directed to the Honorable Josiah Thatcher Esqr. member of Congress at N. York, was handed to me a few days ago; and, presuming it was designed for me, I opened it—And shall observe—That the inconvenience & hardship you complain of, I think will be remidied, in a bill, that has been directed to be reported to the house, for amending the Revenue Laws, so far as to exempt Goods of American Growth, sent to a foreign port and returned unsold, from paying foreign duty.[1]

But it is the opinion of respectable merchants that foreign Goods exported from the U. States to a foreign Market, & thence to the U. States again, cannot be exempted from duty without great hazard of frauds on the Revenue.

FC, Thatcher Family Papers, MHi. Sent to Portland, Maine.

[1] Hamilton had recommended such an exemption in his report to the House dated 23 April, which was referred the same day to the committee that reported the Collection Act [HR-82] on 8 July. On 26 or 27 July the Senate added the exemption as article 23 of the amended act, passed on 2 August.

George Thatcher to Sarah Thatcher

I forgot to inform you in my last, I had sent your slippers to the care of Mr. [*Thomas*] Dakin—I would have you desire some friend to take them; they are wraped in paper, but they must be taken good care of, or they will get dirted—as soon as you get them let me know how they sute—and whether you like them, and if you wish it I will bring you another pair.

I have wrote to Captain [*Elisha*] Thatcher and requested him to call upon Mr. Larkin,[1] the man whith whom I left the Bible to be bound, and forward it to you—I dont see how you have been able to keep house so long without the Bible—it is certainly the most necessary peace of furniture in a house—I have always deemed it such.

Last evening I received yours of the 15th. inst. In which you ask why I say nothing about returning home—it is because I cannot tell exactly the time of adjournment—but I am pretty confident it will not exceed three or four weeks—I never wanted more to be in the Country—that is at home—in my Life, than I do at this time.

If we shall adjourn so that I can get to York [*Maine*] about the time of the seting of the Court in June—what think you of meeting me there, at Mr. [*Nathaniel*] Barrells, or Mr. [*Joseph*] Tuckers? Mrs. [*Sally*] Barrell, in a Letter I was honored with some time ago, proposed I should meet you there on my return—I have returned her no direct answer to this because it must be too uncertain to depend upon—If [*Joseph*] Barnard rides in his stage—will it not be an agreeable ride for you? or will the heat of the season—as well as *other reasons*, make it inconvenient?

I hope the inclosed Cambrick will be agreeable to your wishes—I gave fifteen shillings £ money for it—Your Gown & Linnen for the Children I shall bare in mind when I get to Boston.

Kiss our dear Children for their papa—& tell them he expects to find one of them [*Samuel Phillips*], on his return, a man—& the other [*Sarah*] a mere woman. I want to enjoy the pleasure of seeing them seting with us at the Table—and behaving with propriety.

ALS, Thatcher Family Papers, MHi. Place to which addressed not indicated.

[1] Benjamin (ca. 1756–1803) and Ebenezer Larkin (ca. 1767–1813) were Boston bookbinders and sellers.

Henry Van Schaack to Theodore Sedgwick

How comes it that I have not had a line from You since you got down to New York? I hear that you have wrote to others. The news from Newyork is truly bad—The President very ill—maddisons plan of discrimination of Tonnage carried.[1] The House unstable we see little now ~~not which~~ from Congress but squabbling reconsidering &ca. &ca.—all this leads to ~~distroy~~ lessen, if not distroy, the confidence of the people in the new Government—These local prejudices will distroy I fear the present Union—I have long had my doubts as to the policy of being in Government connection with the southern folcks—I dread a seperation and ~~I also~~ almost equally fear a connection—The complection of the house at present has a bad aspect—God mend the bad & keep the others good. Your Speech [*of 12 April*], after the assumption of the State Debts has been rejected, has done you yeomans service—you are generally considered as a friend to your State and my fears of your being re-elected are now vanished. *Bill Lyman* is talcked of as a Candidate for Congress not in this County but in Hampshire—However I have no apprehension from that quarter. I long for a lengthy letter from you.

[*P. S.*] When do you talck of breaking up? I wish you could reason the Southern Members into measures that wod. promote the full operation of the Government—If this cannot be Effected what is to become of us? The proceedings of Congress of late do not seem as if they were the result of Such foresight as one wod. have expected in this enlightened age. These *frequent* reconsiderations forebode no good—[*blot*] will be long before your Laws will be like those of the Medes & Persians.[2] I want to see you upon Paper again. Is the Senate a firm body? Is there a great or small majority for right measures.

ALS, Sedgwick Papers, MHi. Written from Pittsfield, Massachusetts.

[1] The 14 May House resolution that resulted in the Trade and Navigation Bill (*DHFFC* 6:1972).

[2] Laws that are unalterable.

OTHER DOCUMENTS

Thomas Bee to George Washington. ALS, Washington Papers, DLC. Written from Columbia, South Carolina. For the full text, see *PGW* 5:417.

Office seeking: to succeed William Drayton as federal judge for the South Carolina district; had asked Izard and Butler to put his name forward (in the fall of 1789), but they were prevented by the President's absence from New York; they can provide recommendations.

William Constable to Gouverneur Morris. FC:lbk, Constable-Pierrepont Collection, NN.

Price of North Carolina debt certificates has fallen to the southward but still higher in New York; "as hopes are still entertained that the Assumption of the state Debts will take place this Session"; R. Morris and Constable are going to Morrisania "it being Sunday."

John Fenno to Joseph Ward. ALS, Ward Papers, ICHi. Addressed to the Land Office, State Street, Boston; carried by (William?) Bradford. For the full text, see *AASP* 89(1979):364.

Hopes that "dreadful" delay on assumption issue will bring "*good* out of *evil*"; there is no talk of addressing the permanent residence question, but fears there will be an adjournment to Philadelphia; it is expected that old emission money will be set at seventy five for one, and new emission money will be considered as state debts; doubts Congress can possibly adjourn before the middle of June.

Thomas Hartley to Jasper Yeates. ALS, Yeates Papers, PHi. Addressed to Lancaster, Pennsylvania; franked; postmarked.

The President is thought to be out of danger; the House has made some progress on funding; motion for adjourning to Philadelphia is expected to be made in Senate the next day; "If present Appearances continue I believe we can really carry it in our House"; will write more the next day or the day after, and also to Adam Zantzinger.

Philip Schuyler to John B. Schuyler. ALS, Schuyler Papers, NN. Addressed to Albany, New York. Schuyler's infant grandson died within days of his birth.

Received John's letter of 15 May on 20 May; "My health is restored, except that I am not yet quite freed from the cough which is here the invariable attendant on the Influenza, but am mending daily. It is expected that the funding system will be compleated in the Course of the next week, and that Congress will rise in a few days after that—I am exceedingly Anxious to return to my family, and shall make the best of my way up"; congratulations on the birth of a son.

Theodore Sedgwick to Pamela Sedgwick. ALS, Sedgwick Papers, MHi. Place to which addressed not indicated.

Laments Ephraim Williams's decision to leave Stockbridge, Massachusetts; "the business is protracted beyond my expectation. a few days will give us more certainty of the time when congress may have a power of adjourning."

Theodore Sedgwick to [*Ephraim Williams*]. ALS, Sedgwick Papers, MHi. Place to which addressed not indicated. The recipient is identified by internal evidence and a reference in Sedgwick's letter to Pamela of this date.

Laments Williams's intention to leave Stockbridge, Massachusetts, and promises to write further on the subject.

George Thatcher to Jeremiah Hill. No copy known; acknowledged in Hill to Thatcher, 30 May.

Jeremiah Wadsworth to Harriet Wadsworth. ALS, Wadsworth Papers, CtHi. Addressed to Hartford, Connecticut; franked.

Is very well, except for "a little Head ach"; talked yesterday with Johnson about the latter's son, Samuel William, just returned from Bermuda; "I told him I thought the Young Gentlemen should be carefull to be acquainted before they made love"; believes Johnson will put his son "safe in your way"; wishes to return home, "but can't at present"; Daniel (Wadsworth) continues in bad health.

William Samuel Johnson, Diary. Johnson Papers, CtHi.

"St. Pauls."

From New York. [Boston] *Massachusetts Centinel*, 29 May; reprinted at Exeter, New Hampshire, and Salem, Massachusetts. The editors believe this quotes or paraphrases a letter from Fenno, based on similarities with his letter to Ward on this date, calendared above.

"THE PRESIDENT is recovering fast—several acts now lie ready for his signature. There is a talk of holding the next session at *Philadelphia.* I think the *Assumption* will finally take place—this it is which has occasioned them. As the funding system advances, Continental Securities rise—Finals are 9/. Indents, 7/."

MONDAY, 24 MAY 1790

Cool (Johnson)

Abraham Baldwin to Joel Barlow

The reb [*Dudley Baldwin*] and the girl [*Ruth Barlow*] are both with me I have so much to talk with them that I have but little spare talk for the absent, and I find your frenchmen,[1] [*Royal*] Flint &c. have fogged you up with so many letters, that there cant be much left for me to say, or much leisure for you to hear it. your last was the 9th of March, since the receipt of it I have written you three times, to Havre with a bundle of papers, to London by [*Capt. Thomas*] Watson, & ten days ago by a Bristol brig, I shall send you now the continuation of the papers, which will tell you all the public talk here both true and false, at any rate there is not much left to be told after our printers, and much of that ought to have been left untold. It is probable our session will last a month or six weeks longer, *modify* has been our whole business, and nothing finally determined on as yet; the two bills viz. funding, and the excise or additional revenue to support it are now before us: the issue is as problematical as ever; infinite anxiety in individuals, they fill all the papers, and from the public face of things one would suppose there was nobody else in the country, they labour like men at days works to accomplish their business, but I hope and trust it will be found that there are disinterested men enough to give a proper decision. There never can be again such a jumble of affairs crouded up all to the same point. The land business has lain perfectly quiet, the secretary is so anxious to get his report on finance finally decided on that he will not report on any other business referred to him till he is particularly ordered.[2] I fear he will delay reporting on a general plan for the the disposal of lands till it will be too late for us to act upon it. There is some talk of having another session in the fall, but if we do not rise till the beginning of July, it is not probable to me there will be any meeting till after another election. We have by concurrent resolution[3] explained the puzzle when the President, members &c. are to be considered as commencing their office, and whether our commissions shall expire together or be governed by the dates of our respective appointments, the decision was very strong that the period is the fourth of March, and that we all commenced on the same day. We have been much alarmed by the danger of loosing our President. he is now in a fair way, and is nearly free from the disorder.

Rhode Island convention meets today, the whigs say they will reject if they dare, you will see the act which has passed the senate,[4] and which will probably pass into a law if they do not prevent it by a pretty speedy adoption. It will never do to let them remain in this situation, they will prevent the collection of a great proportion of our revenue, you know my maxim, that the great Sachem called society has his natural rights as well as other folks, and that whatever is necessary to his preservation, perfection and happiness, is as good as any of the rest of the laws of nature. If their place of existence was more remote from ours, we might let them have their own way in safety, but in our present situation, self preservation requires us to *modify* them, sic utere tuo ut alienum non ledas.[5] In fact I have no doubt of organizing the government over their heads at once, as it is over the rest of us, let them bounce, it would give us little trouble.

I talk politicks with you because I have nothing better to talk, I have been very anxious to bring your thoughts on the land business to a point, but it has not been possible, at present it is doubtful whether it will be done this session. If the Secs. plan was brought forward, we could tell in a minute whether it would be best to let you negotiate for the public altogether, or whether to weave in some private jobs, he is very wrong in keeping it back but it cant be helped. your colons [*colonists*] seemed well satisfied with the reception they met, they express great respect for you and appear well pleased with the country.

Ever since my plan of having the girl sail with Captn. [*Thomas*] watson, I have been looking out for a maid used to the seas but it is impossible to find one that unites the qualities of maid and sailor so as to be depended on. The one we have got in every respect seemed the most promising, but in all probability will be as stupid as a drunken hog on the whole passage, and in fact I consider as of no account, but it was the best that could be done. All the service in such cases must be done by those who have their sea legs aboard, the cabin boy steward mate, & Capt. will do all that is ever done. I should not have thought it worth while to put you to the expence, but as there was no other lady on board, and the talk of the women here was that she must have a girl, she will answer that purpose as well perhaps as another, for I know it is principally the name of it, upon the whole I thought it was best.

I have written too much for a man to read that has got so much talk to do, and will fill up my story when you will be more anxious to hear.

AL, Baldwin Family Papers, CtY. Place to which addressed not indicated. The letter closes "viva valeq[*ue*]"—live and be happy.

[1] The French settlers of Gallipolis (Ohio) also frequently referred to by Baldwin as the "colons," or colonists.

[2] The House first ordered Hamilton to report on a general plan for the sale of western lands on 20 January; his report was not received until 22 July.

[3] Actually a joint committee report, agreed to in both chambers (with one inconsequential amendment in the House) by 18 May, and forwarded as "a resolution of the House . . . for the information" of the states' executives, on 9 August (*DHFFC* 4:659–60).

[4] The Rhode Island Trade Bill.

[5] Exercise your rights in such a manner as not to injure another man's rights.

Pierce Butler to Roger Parker Saunders

Since my last letter to You I have been favored with two from you; both without date. This, I conclude, will find you returned from giving to Carolina the best of Constitutions.[1] A great blessing to States or Individuals. We shall all thank You; I mean ye that have secured to us by your labours equal rights, equal security of property, and personal liberty. I am told there were many Constitutions made to your hand. Political Reformers are not the scarcest class of Men in America.

We have done little or nothing in Congress since I last wrote to You. State Debts unassumed as yet; the funding Bill had the last reading this day in the Committee of the whole of the House of Representatives; and this day Mr. Morrace [*Morris*] made a motion in Senate to adjourn at the end of the Session to Philadelphia; that is that the next meeting of Congress shall be there. This, the State Debts and the funding Act, have furnished ample seed for Intrigue and cabal to those who choose to exercise themselves in that way. If Elliott does not sail tomorrow I may be able to write you the issue.

I observe what you say respecting a total removal to Georgia. I cant but think well of it. You will save greatly by it and be the sooner an independent Man. Dependence on the will of others is a great curse. I shall never know happiness while I owe a shilling. I trust you have by this day got me clear of [*Hercules Daniel*] Bize.

***

Our good President has been dangerously ill with a perepneumiary. He is now better. I shall soon renew my application to him for your Uncle; and shall submit to lay myself under a personal obligation to him to accomplish my wish. I will go even further than I did for Coll. Evely [*Nicholas Eveleigh*] for whom I so well succeeded. If I fail in my application for Mr. [*John, Sr.*] Parker I never will apply for any other.

FC, Butler Letterbook, ScU. For the full text, see *Butler Letters*, pp. 43–45. Carried by Capt. William Elliott. The omitted text relates to ongoing financial disputes with Butler's nephew, Edward Butler.

[1] On 3 June South Carolina's constitutional convention, meeting in Columbia, ratified the state's third constitution since 1776.

George Crowninshield to Benjamin Goodhue

Give Me Leave to Address You Again, We feele Agreved, & with Ought Redress form Your bodey. The former Tonage Layed On Our Coasting trade, which Puts Us Much belo the Strange Nations that Visit's Us, A Small alteration in the Act Would Remadey the whole Viz. Either Read *Or* in the Roome of *And*[1] Or Else A Short Resolve to Amend the Same I would Comment On it, but I Suppose You would Smile to hear A Plebean, Dictating A Patritian, & therefore Rest the Same to You, who Are Appointed to think for Us. but Belive Me Friend Goodhue, I Never Saw, Eaven in Our worst times A Greater Dissatisfaction Amongst High, & Low, As at this time.

Another Eavel is this, A Vessell Arives with Goods Subject to it Dutey, & Permitted to be Exported & Recive A Drawback, Your Officer, Enters & takes Bond to Pay the Dutey in Six Months, & on the Morrow the Marchant Clears the Same Goods for A Fairer Market, with All the Propper Documents in that Case Made & Provided for, the officer obbliges him to Bond for the Producing A Certificate in 6 Months, the Marchant Produces A Certificate in 3 Months, & Notwithstanding He Avous it Good, Yet He Demands the Duties for His Bond, & Sues if Not Paide in 6 Months, Alltho the Voucher is Brought in 3, Holds the Money till the 6 Months Bond for sd. Certificate is Oute, & then Returnes Saide Money A Gain, when we Say the Certificate is Evidence in Law, (*I Meene Common Law*) to Cansell the Bond for Payment, & Ought to be Recived As Such, & be Assured Sr. the People feeles As tho they Cannot, & I be Live well Not, Put Up with it, & for My Part I Cannot Sea Any Advantage to Congrass On that Head, & As Congrass Gains Nothing I think Friend Goodhue the Good Will of the trading Part to that August Body, is better Kept, then Lost, I Have Looked into the Law on that Head, & think Your Officer is Rong, & we All wish You would Order Your Financeer [*Hamilton*] to Emediately Direct Accordingly, for when People Gets Over Loded, they then will Make A Stand, & I feere A Grate One, A few Alterations will Allways Pleas the People, You Know Very well, Thier is Sum few More Alterations Might be Made, but As You Are On the Committee for those things[2] I Know Your Good Sence will Point them

Oute to You Pray Pay Emideate Attention, to those two Matters As Soone As May be, they Are Easily Alltered, & Now Give Me Leave to Say I thank You for Your Coind Letter, Sometime Past, I Now Say I Have Every Proper Document Against Capt. Harden & Sufficiant to Demand the Property of Congrass & Shall Some waite On that body for Redress of Grievenceses[3] Having Nothing to Ad, Only to tell You thier is A General Uneasyness, which Some times Small Sparks Blow in to Grate flames, which in Our Case May God Evert.

ALS, Letters to Goodhue, NNS. Written from Salem, Massachusetts.

---

[1] The reference is to section three of the Tonnage Act [HR-5], which required that vessels engaged in the coasting trade be built in the United States and be owned by a citizen thereof in order to be exempt from tonnage duties.

[2] Goodhue served (with Laurance, Boudinot, Fitzsimons, and R. B. Lee) on the committee formed on 23 April to consider alterations to the various revenue laws. He submitted the committee's proposed Tonnage Act [HR-78] on 22 June and Collection Act [HR-82] on 8 July.

[3] Crowninshield's grievances dated back to January 1781 when the brig *Elizabeth and Nancy*, of which he was part owner, was confiscated in the Caribbean by the Continental Navy frigate *Confederacy* under Capt. Seth Harding. Crowninshield and his co-owners had equipped their vessel with a double set of registration papers to evade British capture as a prize ship, but Harding used its (fake) British registry as grounds for claiming it as his own prize, awarded by a French admiralty court on St. Domingue (Haiti). Crowninshield and his partners were unsuccessful when they petitioned the Confederation Congress for compensation in August 1781, and they did not petition again until the Third Congress, when the matter was tabled (Memorial to Congress, August 1781, item 42, 2:118–21, PCC, DNA; *JCC* 20:1013; *Petitions Submitted to Congress, 1789–1795*, Energy and Commerce Committee, 99th Congress [Washington, D.C., 1986], p. 335).

Robert Morris to George Harrison

I am indebted for your favours of the 6th & 15th. Inst. immediately after the receipt of the first I withdrew your Name from the list of Consuls, in fact my View in placing it there was more to make it Familiarly known at Court than from any expectation that such an appointment would suit *** I am at a loss in my attempts to decypher the last Paragraph of your last letter, but I very freely tell you that if I can, in a Consistent and proper manner be instrumental to the making "your Fortune" or "promoting your happiness" I shall Chearfully nay gladly do it, It would seem however by what you say, that you Conceive the thing you wish for would be desirable for one of my Sons, as yet I have taken no thought of them beyond the perfecting their Studies and getting them well qualified to enter into this World of Trouble on such terms as may enable them to gain & keep Elbow room—You may therefore Speak out, I shall if you & they ever come in Competition with equal pretensions give them the preferrence but I do not see how the Competition can arise, at least for some time to come ***

ALS, Brinton Coxe Papers, PHi. Sent to Philadelphia. In the omitted text, Morris discussed private business transactions and at one point made reference to someone arriving "in Philadelphia (where I long to be)."

William Smith (S.C.) to Edward Rutledge

I wrote you by [*Thomas*] Snell—[*William*] Elliott sails tomorrow & I wish to give you Some account of our proceedings since my last—We have taken up the Funding Bill & have nearly got thro it in a Committee of the whole—we intend moving a Clause providing for the State Debts—the Success very uncertain—if the measure is lost, it will not be for its demerits, but thro Some out-of door management—I am pretty Sure the removal to Philada. is to be connected with it—I have been just informed by a Jersey Member,[1] who is an Assumptionist, that the Assumption must not be connected with the Funding Bill, but that that Bill must be allowed to pass seperately to quiet the Continl. Creditors & that we must make provision for the State Debts by another Bill; this he told me after a long conversation with Fitzsimmons—the plain English is that the Assumption must be kept back till the close of the Session & then we shall be made to understand that unless we vote for Philada., the State debts will not be provided for. Should any of our party vote ~~out~~ agst. the Assumption on this principle we must lose it; we have had a consultation & have firmly resolved to bring on the Question & endeavr. at all hazards to insert it in the funding Bill. The only material alterations we have made hitherto is ~~altering~~ raising the price of the Lands from 20 to 30 Cents.[2] Sumpter has been Sick for some weeks but has contrived to crawl out to day, under the idea that the question was to come on that he might vote against it: his vote lost it in the Committee of the whole on the Resolutions.

I am very anxious to hear the result of your Labours at Columbia; I hope you'll fix the seat of Govt. in Charleston by the Constitution, at least for a term of years.[3]

Do attend to the sending on our Claims; millions depend on your exertions on this point. The good management of other States has given them a decided advantage over us in their Claims; if Some people would employ their time in attending to this business instead of writing Essays on Governmt. & making Constitutions, they would fulfill the duties of their Stations more profitably for the society: the first their abilities are equal to; the last they had best leave to abler heads.

The President continues mending—he was in great danger when I wrote last & was at one period given over by some of the Physicians—our alarm has been great, equal to the danger to be apprehended from such a calamity.

The R. Island [*ratification*] Convention meet to day—the Bill[4] from the Senate (which past by a majority of two to one in that house) is ~~fixed~~ to be taken up this day week in a Committee of the whole; by that time we shall learn what they intend doing—it may work upon them Successfully. The two houses have fixed Some ~~principles~~ points which were rather ambiguous under the Constitutn. viz.; that the H. of R. changes *totally* every Second year dating from 4th. March 1789, conseqy. That the No. Cara. Members hold their Seats only for a year, instead of two, as they affected to beleive; that the President & V. Presd. are to be only elected from 4 years to 4 years, even should ~~they~~ both P. & V.P. die within that period; & we have appointed a Committee to bring in a Bill determining what Officer Shall act as Presidt. in case of the death of both P. & V.P.[5]—opinions are divided between the Chief Justice & the Secretary of State—they will be much influenced I fear by the persons holding those offices, instead of the nature of the Offices themselves. I think the Secy. of State the proper officer; the C. Just. wd. be improper because it would blend the Judiciary & the Executive. The two Houses were pretty unanimous ~~on these several points~~ in their determination.

AL, incomplete, Smith Papers, ScHi. Place to which addressed not indicated.

[1] Probably either Boudinot or Cadwalader, the only pro-Philadelphia New Jersey congressmen who were also consistent supporters of assumption.

[2] The per acre value of the land offered as an equivalent to one third of a creditor's subscription to the national debt, according to one of the alternatives offered to creditors under Hamilton's original funding plan and under the Funding Bill as first presented to the House on 6 May; see *DHFFC* 5:914.

[3] The South Carolina constitution, ratified on 3 June by a convention held in Columbia, fixed the seat of state government there, subject to removal by two thirds vote of each house.

[4] Rhode Island Trade Bill.

[5] These "points" were agreed to in a House resolution on 18 May (*DHFFC* 3:416), when the said committee was appointed. The committee did not report in the second session, but was revived in the third session. Three bills were introduced, but none passed until the Second Federal Congress (*DHFFC* 4:656–63).

John Sullivan to John Langdon

Your favor of the first Instant, reached me yesterday by which I feel myself much obliged and gratified: I am convinced that you have a hard task in Congress; but such is the fate of things, & cannot be avoided; Your acts are good, well digested, & wisely calculated to build up a new Government;

and though some may be uneasy it is only because they have Eyes & See not & Ears but hear not.[1]

Judge Jay[2] will before this reaches you have no Doubt have informed you that your family are in good health ***

I am very much mortified to hear that the President of the united States is Indisposed; may god preserve him for the good of a rising Empire and for the benefit of the world in General. I am much pleased that we are not threatned with any foreign attacks and that the Little speck in Creation *Rhode Island* can do us but litle hurt even if the old Spirit prevails; my own Indisposition prevent me at this moment from writing you upon a number of points which were in my mind when I began this Letter you will therefore permit me to Conclude ***

ALS, Langdon Papers, NhPoA. Written from Durham, New Hampshire. The omitted text comments on the ill health and deaths of individuals in New Hampshire.

[1] Jeremiah 5:21.

[2] Chief Justice Jay was in Portsmouth to preside, with district court Judge Sullivan, over the first federal circuit court session for the district of New Hampshire on 20–21 May (*DHSCUS* 2:68–71).

Mercy Otis Warren to Elbridge Gerry

Though we have neither of us receved a a line from you since Mr. Warren's return from New York[1] I have not a doubt but it will give you pleasure to hear from your plimouth friend, more especially as I can now inform you my dear partner is nearly recovered from a very dangerous Illness. his very fatiguing journey in the late inclement season produced complaints of an ~~unna~~ alarming nature & threatened a speedy period to his useful life, but a fit of the Gout though an unwelcome visitor is sometimes a salutary friend ~~to us~~, gives us hopes that he will kick away with one foot those appearances that have greatly alarmed my mind, as he does with the other the unmerited abuse to the unjust detention of his property that would wound the feelings of any man of less philosophy & Conscious virtue than himself.

You who have witnessed his long services & sufferings in the Cause of his Country: who have seen his exertions & his labours through the best period of his life: when he sacrificed health ease and convenience without reward: will suffer me to complain a little—nor will you wonder if you should discover some risings of indignation when the claims of common justice have been denyed & the small pittance of hard earned wages rather cruelly withheld.

But I could despise all pecuniary considerations notwithstanding the Equity of the demands had not his sacrifice of time & property in the public cause have put it out of his power to assist effectually a family of sons ~~eddu~~ educated & quallified for any bussiness who from these Circumstances and the malignancy of party yet stand unemployed while those who can claim nothing, either from thiere own or the merit of their ancestors are amply provided for.[2]

But I forbear after asking why the plums of Gratitude are all directed to the military line. were not the patriots in the legislature & other departments as indefatigable, as necessary, as meritorious & as much endangered as those in the field—& if a Warren sacrificed the happiness of Domestic life & relinquished various private departments in bussiness (that gave an income sufficient to answer the convenience & to gratify the Ambition of his family, from the principles of advancing the Fredom of his Country & the liberties of mankind:) is he not as much entitled to the consideration of his Country & the Gratitude of his fellow citizens as a [*Frederick William*] *steuben* or any other soldier of fortune or foreign nobleman?

But we do not ask a stipend or liberal donation. we only request our own—a *property* advanced for the public weal—& the scanty pittance of wages due for laborious duty—for the payment of which the public Honour & equity was plegeed: & which every honest man in Government must blush to see withheld from a faithful servant of the united states.

You will, sir, pardon my emotion when you contemplate not only the feelings of the wife & the mother: but the woman who has suffered much in the Great struggle for American liberty both in her repose: in her connexions: in her health & her fortune.

[*P. S.*] Mr. Warren desires me to tell you, after his best regards, that as soon as health is a little more confirmed, he shall write you himself & thank you for your late strenuous exertions that justice might be done him: as well as for every other Instance of friendship.

Photostat of ALS, Gerry Papers, DLC. Written from Plymouth, Massachusetts.

---

[1] Warren's husband James went to New York on 25 March and probably stayed at least until 3 April, when his petition for depreciation allowance for wartime services on the navy board was presented to the House and referred to Hamilton. For Warren's unsuccessful petition attempt, see *DHFFC* 7:1–4.

[2] Of Mercy and James Warren's five children (all sons), two were actively seeking federal appointments at this time. Winslow (1760–91), a failed Boston merchant, was finally appointed a lieutenant in the Second Regiment of the federal army on 4 March 1791, and was killed exactly eight months later in Gen. Arthur St. Clair's defeat by the Miami Indians in the Northwest Territory. His younger brother Henry (1764–1828), who had served under Gen. Benjamin Lincoln during Shays' Rebellion and briefly in 1790 as his clerk while Lincoln was collector at Boston, would not receive a revenue appointment until the Jefferson administration (*DHFFC* 2:514, 16:753, 1198; *PGW* 3:104–5, 7:40; Rosemarie Zagarri, *A Woman's Dilemma: Mercy Otis Warren and the American Revolution* [Wheeling, Ill., 1995], pp. 109, 124–30, 139).

Other Documents

Henry Chapman to Stephen Collins. ALS, Collins & Son Papers, DLC. Addressed to S. Collins & Son, Merchants, Philadelphia.

"An universal opinion prevails here that Congress will adjourn to meet at Philada. a sort of compromise between the friends of this measure and that of assuming the State debts it is thought will effect both."

Andrew Craigie to Elnathan Haskell. FC:dft, Craigie Papers, MWA. Place to which addressed not indicated; carried by Capt. William Elliott, of the Charleston, South Carolina, packet ship *Maria.*

Difficult to form an opinion respecting the fate of assumption, which is again before Congress, which is nearly equally divided; believes it will succeed, or the entire funding business will be postponed until the next session; (Theophile) Cazenove is purchasing a large amount of South Carolina securities for Dutch investors.

Theodore Sedgwick to [*Ephraim Williams*]. ALS, Sedgwick Papers, MHi. Place to which addressed not indicated. The recipient is identified by internal evidence and by a reference in Sedgwick's letter to Pamela Sedgwick, 23 May.

Continues his argument against Williams's decision to leave Stockbridge, Massachusetts; unprofitable law practices are common throughout America, owing to the poverty of the people and "the relaxed state of the government"; but "The times must be submitted to—they will be better"; assumption is again before the House; "what will be the event is to me uncertain, though I confess I am not at present pleased with the appearance."

Daniel Hiester, Account Book. PRHi.

Attended "Monday Club" or Mess Day with the Pennsylvania delegation at Fraunces Tavern (Maclay indicated he arrived at 3:30 P.M. and that the dinner was already almost all eaten [*DHFFC* 9:275]).

Item 187, p. 56, PCC, DNA.

Boudinot borrowed General Washington's "Sentiments on a Peace Establishment," dated 2 May 1783. (For the Sentiments, see John C. Fitzpatrick, *Writings of George Washington* [39 vols., Washington, D.C., 1931–44], 26:374–98.)

Letter from New York. [Winchester] *Virginia Gazette*, 5 June. The letter was probably written by White.

"THE PRESIDENT OF THE UNITED STATES is so far recovered as to ride out in his carriage; and has notified the committee of Congress appointed to present bills for his assent, that he is ready to receive such as have passed the two houses, and are waiting his approbation."

NYDA, 24 May.

Van Rensselaer lost his reelection bid.

TUESDAY, 25 MAY 1790

John Adams to Thomas Crafts

I have received with a mixture of pleasure and gloomy melancholy your favour of the 17th. What motives the eastern members can have to support the silly petition of Franklin and his Quakers,[1] I never could conceive: but it was not that conduct which sowered the minds of the Southern members against an assumption of the State debts. The seat of Government is more likely to have had such an effect on some minds. What is the reason that bills should be ten or twelve per Ct. below par here, and only five at Boston The demand from Europe for grain would not alone have produced so great and sudden a change in the price of bills. The sudden rise of stock which was certainly occasioned by the new government contributed a great share to this symptom of prosperity. If no measures could ever be carried in the State Legislature to encourage the fisheries I leave you to Judge whether it is probable that bounties can be obtained from the general government.

Ships before the revolution were built upon British capitals. There are no capitals in Boston I fear not such as consist in credits to the nation or the State or employed in speculations in the Stocks. The carrying trade is the only resource for ship building. The English are in possession of this. They not only have ships ready, but they own the crops for the most part. To dispossess the English from this business requires a system of measures and a course of time and our people are so fickle and unsteady, that it is doubtfull whether they would bear with patience the trial of a fair experiment The Massachusetts a few years ago, made a navigation act,[2] which if it had been preserved to this day would in my opinion have found full employment for her shipwrights: but Mr. [*James*] Sullivan and Parson [*Josiah*] Thatcher, I heard in London became declaimers if not preachers against it and it was repealed. If Congress should make a similar law, it will be opposed by powerful interests who will continually grumble against it and there is neither vigour nor constancy enough in the government, I am afraid, to persevere. That Congress will take some measures to bring into circulation the monies locked up, I cannot doubt. This must be done—I am assured that considerable sums of money are ordered to America from Europe, so that I hope we shall not have so great a scarcity of money long. The State debts I fear will not be assumed this session.

Without a national government and steady measures we shall never be prosperous, and there is too powerful a party in Massachusetts against both. I hope we shall see better times. but my hopes are not sanguine.

FC:lbk, Adams Family Manuscript Trust, MHi. Sent to Boston.

---

[1] For the antislavery petitions of the Pennsylvania Abolition Society (signed by Benjamin Franklin) and the New York and Philadelphia Yearly Meetings of Friends (Quakers), see *DHFFC* 8:314–48.

[2] The Massachusetts legislature's Act for the Regulation of Navigation and Commerce, passed on 23 June 1785, excluded British shipping from carrying exports, restricted the state's imports to three ports of entry, and, in addition to high tonnage duties, imposed double impost duties on foreign shipping. Finding the provisions inefficacious without the cooperation of her sister states, Massachusetts suspended the act indefinitely on 5 July 1786.

Pierce Butler to Alexander Gillon

***

I purposed making this a long letter but totally contrary to my expectations [*Capt. William*] Elliott has just [*sent*] me word that he will possitively sail this day. Business thickens on us. yesterday Mr. Morrace [*Morris*] moved in Senate that when Congress do adjourn, it shall be to meet at Philadelphia. This is just what I expected, as I informed you in my last letter. The question is to be debated this morning. Much Bustle and Intrigue. Your friend smiles and looks on. Strange combinations and party work! which I intended to have sketched out in this letter had not Elliott deceived me in point of time. It shall be the subject of another letter. The funding Bill had the last reading this day in a Committee of the whole. An attempt was made by Messrs. Gerry. Wm. Smith [*S.C.*] & Sherman to incorporate the State Debts. They did not succeed. They mean to try it again I am told when the Bill is before the House.

There is some manouvering to connect Assumption and Seat of Government. It puts me in mind of a measure of old Capt. [*Thomas*] Buckle's during the war: He had got in some Gun Powder from Statia[1] which, as you may suppose, was in demand. He happened to have some old Bibles or Testaments from a former trade, which he connected in sale with the powder. Just so are the Assumtionists doing with the future Seat of Congress. Parties as I informed you in my last begin to take stronger hold and measure out their Ground. As yet I have kept free of all—When you have closed with [*Hercules Daniel*] Bize and secured me from [*Daniel*] Bourdeaux's creditors, my mind will be more at ease to become more active. I shall be glad to know what you have done in Convention.[2] I suppose Governor [*Charles*] Pinckney had a Constitution cut & dry for you, as Doctor Ramsay expressed himself respecting Congress and the general [*federal*] Convention. When our Legislature were debating about the number of Members to be sent to Convention he told them that *one* wou'd answer, for that Congress had a Constitution *Cut & dry* for them which he thought a good one.

FC, Butler Letterbook, ScU. For the full text, see *Butler Letters*, pp. 45–47. Carried by Capt. William Elliott. The omitted text discusses Butler's ongoing financial distress as guarantor of a defaulted loan from Hercules Daniel Bize to Daniel Bourdeaux, and expresses concern that Butler's 23 April letter may have been tampered with by hands other than James LaMotte's, to whom he addressed it (in addition to a duplicate sent via Philadelphia.)

---

[1] St. Eustatius, a Dutch island in the West Indies, was a center of the trade in contraband between Europe and the United States during the Revolutionary War.

[2] South Carolina's state constitutional convention.

Nathan Dane to Governor John Hancock

I improve the first opportunity, after having obtained any considerable degree of particular information respecting the claims of the several States, and the state of the business on which I am sent here,[1] to inform your Excellency of the situation of that business and of the general State of those claims—from which you will be able to form a general opinion as to the relative advances of our State.

It is about sixteen months since the Board of Commissioners entered upon the business of their appointment, and their Commission will expire in less than two months from this time—I believe they have taken a general view of the advances of the several States to the Union; but I do not find that they have made any considerable progress towards a final adjustment of the accounts—But it does not appear to me that the little progress made is to be imputed to any Special difficulties in the business; but to several other causes—the claims of some of the States are brought forward in a very irregular and confused State, whereby the regular officers in the Treasury department who have power to pass upon such claims as are sanctioned by Acts of Congress, and supported by proper vouchers, have been very much retarded in executing the part of the business assigned to them; and then circumstances have impeded the proceedings of the board; and the Commissioners of the board have been in a situation to do business but a part of the time Since they met—not long after they met, one of them resigned, and another gentleman was appointed,[2] & has occasioned a vacancy in their proceedings of seven or eight months—want of health also has retarded their proceedings—and Congress pretty early in the present Session took this Subject into consideration; since which time, the Commissioners of the board have been so far waiting for the determinations of Congress that they have not lately established any general principles; being uncertain whether new principles on which to settle these accounts will not be adopted; and they have, I believe, for sometime past been in daily expectation that Congress would decide on this subject.

It is said the questions, whether the commission of the board shall be continued; the number of Commissioners be encreased, and the grounds of admitting claims enlarged are before Congress; and the settlement of the accounts depends altogether upon the adoption of the necessary measures for effecting a final adjustment by that honorable body.

I am very sorry to find that claims have been lately irregularly exhibited by ~~sever~~ two or three States, whose claims regularly presented are not very considerable; and that a settlement in this State of the business is now proposed to be made, partly, on new principles—not that I think Massachusetts can be injured by any unsupported claims made by other states, or by the principles or modes of settlement now proposed; provided a Settlement can be made in a reasonable time—But the States which have made advances beyond their proportions, may be essentially injured by adopting such various modes for settling the accounts, and such delays as will finally prevent any settlement—three years ago the present board of Commissioners and the principles whereon to settle the accounts were unanimously established by Congress after repeated attempts for near two years preceeding to agree in an Ordinance for the purpose—Commissioners were sent to the respective States to receive and arrange their claims, and there claims are now generally collected & prepared for settlement—I think that Massachusetts will press for a conclusion of this business, and for the adoption of measures from which a fair and Just settlement will Speedily result—the advances made by individual States to the union, have been made on the solemn engagements of Congress, that there should be a future adjustment; and an equalizing of the burdens of the late war among them—nor probably, will the most material Causes of discord among the States, and the greatest embarrassments to general measures be removed, until the accounts of the several States against the United States shall be equitably and Justly settled—Massachusetts has a particular Interest in a fair and early settlement of the accounts—under these impressions I shall esteem it my duty, in behalf of that state, to make exertion to promote such a settlement—If the door be again opened for the states to bring in further claims, and the grounds of admission extended,

Massachusetts, I suppose, as well as other States, may find further charges against the Union, but if we are to Judge from things past, this may eventually prevent any settlement—To add the Secretary and Comptroller of the Treasury, as proposed by a Committee,[3] to the Commission, may have a like effect—these officers must have too much other business to attend to, to be able to examine these voluminous accounts so as to effect a Settlement in any reasonable time—No measures are yet taken to settle the quotas of the States the present Session of Congress; so as to determine what proportion of the charges of the war each State shall bear—this is a matter of great importance, and, perhaps, if not settled before the amount of the respective claims shall be assertained, it can be done afterwards, but with the greatest difficulty—Since I arrived in this place I have been able to collect a pretty full statement of the claims of the several States against the United States; and as no quotas have been settled, all payments made, supplies furnished, and services performed by the respective states to and for the United States on requisitions and otherwise, are considered as advances—the aggregate advances of all the states charged by them since the commencement of the war and lodged in the offices amount to upwards of 75 millions of Specie dollars, near one fourth part of which have been credited on requisitions &c. and the residue constitute, at present, the unallowed claims—It is to be observed that from these aggregate advances are to be deducted upwards of ten millions of dollars loaned or advanced by Congress to the several States; this leaves the balance of State claims against the Union at 65 millions of Specie dollars nearly—It is probable that when these claims shall be examined there will be considerable deductions made—In some cases the charges being of so local a nature as not to be proper to be admitted in the general account—in some cases there is no evidence to prove the payments charged were made; in some no evidence to prove they were made for continental purposes; and in others the charges must be reduced.

In the foregoing Statement I have omitted some after claims exhibited by South Carolina, &c. to considerable amount; because these have been put in wholly out of season, are in gross sums, and without vouchers; have altogether the appearance of conjecture, and respect heads of charges on which their claims included in the Statement appear to be large.

Of these aggregate advances of 65 millions Massachusetts exact proportion is not known; because the quotas of the States have not been settled; probably not less than eight nor more than ten millions—as the Claims stand the State of Massachusetts appears to have advanced large sums over and above [*lined out*] ten millions and her advances appear to be 14 millions and a half of the 65 millions; and on the balance there is probably seven or eight years Interest due—then, probably, will be considerable deductions from all the claims, and from those of Massachusetts among the rest—if the deductions from her claims are only in proportion to those on the whole they will not effect the ratio, or in any considerable degree the balance— whether they will be greater of [*or*] less, it is impracticable, at present to determine—It appears to me, however, that the claims of Massachusetts are better supported by vouchers than the claims of the states in General, particularly those of the Southern States; and her claims may not suffer so great a diminution on account of high charges as the claims in General; but they may not be so generally sanctioned by Acts of Congress—the claims of Massachusetts may be much effected by the settlement of the governing principles, in a few instances, perhaps more so than those of any other State—as in the cases of payments made on requisitions of old money after the 18th of March 1780—and in advances in the [*Ne*]w Emission, and in the cases of depreciation to her line of the army, bounties and the sea coast men[4]—It is of great importance to Massachusetts in these Cases, in a particular manner, to have right principles adopted; about which very different opinions appear to prevail—but if a settlement be made much less favourable to the State than there ought to be, which is not to be presumed, there must still be a large balance due to her—there are several important circumstances to Strengthen & confirm this opinion—Massachusetts has credit for payments on the requisitions of Congress made for Specie and paper, for much more than her proportion. So far as the claims of the States have been admitted, they Stand much in her favour—By the actual returns of the army it appears that Massachusetts furnished, on an average, throughout the war, near three tenths of the regular army of the United States; and not far from her proportion of the militia called into service; and that she paid her troops for a larger portion of time than the States in general—It also appears that Massachusetts since the war commenced has assessed and collected much heavier taxes than the States in General; all which taxes, deducting the small expences of the civil list, must have been applied towards the purposes of the war; and all, with very triffling exceptions, in the Common cause and now the State owes about one million and an half of dollars more than her proportion of the several State debts.

Though the accounts and claims of Massachusetts are better arranged than those of the States generally; and the State appears to have better vouchers in most cases—Yet I find a great number of objections made, and many more will be probably, made to her charges on account of the deficiency of vouchers—these objections will effect the State so much, that they ought, if practicable, to be removed. as it will be very difficult to do this by writing, from time to time, to the proper officers in the State for papers ~~vouchers~~ &c. and this mode will be expensive on account of postage I think it will be necessary for me to remain here a few weeks to endeavour to get measures adopted for settling the accounts on Just principles, and to collect all the objections of any importance to the vouchers of the State, and then return to it to collect all such regular or circumstantial evidence as can be of service in supporting the charges objected to.

ALS, Miscellaneous Legislative Papers, M-Ar. Place to which addressed not indicated. Endorsements indicate the letter was received on 1 June and read in both the Massachusetts Senate and House on 2 June before the latter referred it on that date to a committee preparing instructions for the state delegation relative to assumption.

---

[1] On 4 March, just weeks after Nathan Dane's election as state senator for Essex County, Massachusetts, Governor John Hancock appointed him agent "to arrange & enforce" Massachusetts' claims against the United States, "& as far as you may find it expedient to support & advocate the same" before the commissioners for settling accounts with the states, in accordance with a resolution of the state legislature passed on 23 February (Dane Manuscript Collection, Beverly Historical Society, Massachusetts).

[2] Baldwin resigned on 30 April 1789 and John Kean was appointed in his place on 7 August, although he did not assume his post for several more months.

[3] The proposal was in the Settlement of Accounts Bill [HR-69] that would be presented to the House by a select committee on 27 May (*DHFFC* 6:1873–74).

[4] The men who, since colonial times, had guarded the coasts of Massachusetts and other colonies.

Benjamin Goodhue to Stephen Goodhue

*** We brought forward to day the matter of assumption to be connected with and form a part of the funding bill but they would not decide on it, but bent their whole force to throw it out from such a connection which they effected—we urged there ought to be an inseperable connection, they said they ought to be seperate—those who opposed us were two parties, those who are in every view opposed to the assumption, and a few Pensylvanians who tho' they wish for an assumption yet wish to have the other debt funded first and then let the assumption help them in obtaining their favourite object of removing to Philada. this appears to be the language of their conduct such is the disgracefull situation of this bussines and what it will end in no one can form the least judgement—neither can I form an opinion when we shall adjourn—I believe they are all tired of worrying and would be glad it was over.

[*P. S.*] you mention the library it was one of Gerrys follies it will come to nothing. I hope you did not think I approved of such extravagant absurdities.

My love to Capt. [*Bartholomew*] Putnam. I have just recd. his letter but have not time [*to*] write him.

ALS, Goodhue Family Papers, MSaE. Addressed to Salem, Massachusetts; franked; postmarked. The omitted text relates to private commercial transactions and news of friends and family.

Stephen Goodhue to Benjamin Goodhue

*** Stephen hath had the Measles very full and Very bad we feared yesterday he whould not ~~live~~ have lived ~~thru~~ through the day the Measles was turning and he was very much oprest at his Stomach and exceedingly Stufed but he grew better in the evining and remains better & the Measles appears to be mostly turned and we hope the worst is over with the Measles and I think he will recover[1] he hath been very much Stoped in his head for this two or three months and unwell at times Fanny & the rest of the family are well as are all friends Shall write again next post.

FC:lbk, Goodhue Family Papers, MSaE. The omitted text relates to private commercial affairs.

[1] Benjamin's nine month old son Stephen died on 31 May.

Governor John Hancock to Elbridge Gerry

I have been informed that Mr. Hamilton in his Revenue System has proposed revenue Cutters—Should his plan be adopted by Congress permit me to recommend Capt. John Foster Williams of Boston, a Gentleman, that was in service of this State during the late War & behaved with great reputation & is the Eldest Navy Officer of this Commonwealth—If you can render him any service when the appointment shall take place you will serve a worthy man.

LS, formerly on deposit at ICarbS. Written from Boston.

Benjamin Huntington to Anne Huntington

Your kind letter of the 19th with the Post Script of the 22d Instant was this Day Recd. at the hand of Capt. Perkins which with the unfavourable News I have by the Norwich [*Connecticut*] People concerning your health is *Affecting indeed*; but don't let this trouble you I have Pleasure Even in the Pangs of Sorrow when felt for the beloved Object of my Esteem and Affection—Pardon (my dear) these Emanations of an Anxious heart and let your Confidence be in him who was dead and is alive & lives forevermore—The dreary road of Man to Bliss is through this Vale of tears.

The Time will come when the King of Terrors shall loose his frightful Form and his deadly Sting Shall hurt no more Then shall we have Beauty for Ashes and the Oyl of Joy for the spirit of heaviness—All the Days of our appointed Time will we wait, till our change comes—If you should go before I am sure to follow when I have Accomplished as an Hireling my Day—Man cometh forth like a Flower & is cut down he fleeth like a Shaddow and continueth not[1]—May the Lord be your Strength upon the bed of languishing[2] and when flesh & heart shall fail may God be the Strength of your heart and your Portion forever and though we are Sorrowful now yet may our Sorrow be turned into Joy—When the Great Redeemer was Scourged by wicked men and Suffered on Mount-Calvery The Chastisement of our Peace was thier upon him & by his Stripes we are healed, to this only Source of our Salvation can we look for that Peace which the world cannot give nor take away. May God Almighty grant you all Joy and Peace in Believing.

We have lived many years in great Harmony and I hope & Trust not without that love which is beyond the Power of Death to Extinguish—I have the most grateful Satisfaction in your Love towards me at all Times, that it has been with that ardent affection which has its Foundation in the Purest Principles of Conjugal Friendship and Fidelity improved by the Precepts taught us by our great Lord and Master; But I most sincearly lament my own Defects of Duty towards you and have in the whole Course of our Connection been Mortified that I had it not in my Power to Render your Life more happy—A kind Providence has been Sufficiently Bountiful and we have abundant Reason of Thankfulness—Accept (*my dear*) of my tender and most hearty acknowledgement of all your kindnesses and to our Children who have (for ought I know) grown up in Virtuous Habits under your Parental Assiduity of Care and Government.

I hope and expect to see you in the course of a few Weeks and in the mean Time must commit you to the kind Protection of the Father of spirits.

I Should come home Immediately to see you for a few Days if for the least, but cannot Sustain the Idea of another Parting.

ALS, Huntington Papers, CtHi. Place to which addressed not indicated. The letter is signed, "your faithful Friend & Consort." A postscript dated 29 May is calendared under that date, below.

---

[1] Job 14:2.
[2] Psalms 41:3.

Richard Henry Lee and John Walker to Governor Beverley Randolph

In consequence of information being received here that a set of unprincipled Speculators had by false statements fraudulently purchased up the rights of the Soldiers of the Virginia and No. Carolina Lines for arrears of pay in 1782 and 1783; the resolves that we have now the honor to enclose were introduced, and have passed Congress. Altho the Presidents consent is not yet signified, having not the least doubt but that they will be approved, we take the liberty of thus early forwarding them to your Excellency. We are induced to this from a consideration of the wonderful and vicious activity of the Speculators, and the very great dispersion of those who may yet fall Victims, in some measure, to the arts of wicked men; unless the soldiers receive speedy and effectual intelligence of the provision coming forward immediately, in their favor.

It was a fortunate circumstance that this speculation had not been so far carried into execution, as to have drawn from the Treasury the appropriated money, which furnished an opportunity to Government of so regulating the issues, as that the money should only be paid to the honest proprietors.

The general proceedings of Congress are so well detailed in the public papers, as to render it unnecessary here to trouble your Excellency with a repetition of them, but if any thing should occur that it is proper the Executive of our Country should be informed of, we shall not fail to forward immediate intelligence.

ALS, Executive Papers, Vi. Place to which addressed not indicated; read 5 June. The recipient is identified by internal evidence. The enclosure is unlocated.

James Madison to Governor Beverley Randolph

Previous to the receipt of your favor on the subject of the arrears to the Virginia line, a proposition for remedying the abuses which have taken place, had been made and was under consideration. It has since passed the two Houses in the form which corresponds with the idea suggested by you. I take the liberty of inclosing a copy, though it has not yet been submitted to the President. As soon as it shall have had his sanction, it will be made known to you by the communications required from that source.

The President has lately been dangerously and almost desperately ill. It is with very peculiar pleasure that I am enabled by a favorable turn in his complaint ~~enables me~~ to acquaint you that he is now not only out of danger, but so far advanced in his recovery as to be able to ride out.

We had flattered ourselves that the project of assuming the State debts was laid aside, at least for the present Session. The measure was however revived upon us yesterday, and it is probable that some time will be again spent upon it. We hope this is the worst that is to be apprehended; but the zeal & perseverance as well as the number of its advocates, require that we should not [*lined out*] be too sanguine in our calculations.

ALS, Executive Papers, Vi. Addressed to Richmond, Virginia; franked; postmarked. The enclosure, a copy of the Resolution on Compensation Lists certified by Beckley, is in the same location.

Governor Alexander Martin to [*Samuel Johnston and Benjamin Hawkins*]

I was favoured with your Letter of the 11th Ulto. a few days ago with sundry Inclosures particularly an act of Congress for accepting the Deed of Cession of the Western Lands by you made to the United States[1]—which I shall do myself the Honour to lay before the Legislature at their next meeting.

I was informed by some of the Clerks at the adjournment of the assembly that the ratification of the articles proposed by Congress as amendments to the Constitution of the United States by the Legislature of this State had early in the Session been sent forward to Congress before my coming into the administration; and gave myself no further trouble about it—but thinking that a duplicate of the Cession act should go forward lest the original might miscarry I sent to Colo. [*James*] Glasgow for the Exemplification, and he accordingly transmitted me the same with an authenticated Copy of the ratification act you mentioned which I have done myself the honour to inclose to the President of the United States.

Respecting the Martinique Debt the Executive are empowered to discharge it, but the Assembly have appropriated some very uncertain Funds for this purpose. Blackledge's Debt[2] and the monies arising from the Sales of the public damaged Tobacco which are first to be drawn upon to discharge it in part; Blackledge being indulged with stay of Execution for 6 months which is near expiring to make payment, has prevented any thing being done on this business until this time—when this day I sent out a notification to the Council to attend me at the Rockingham Springs[3] on the 24th day of June next to advise on certain proposals made by divers Merchants on this subject who will be bound to discharge this debt without delay, but as the Vice Consul General [*Michel-Guillaume St. John de Crèvecoeur*] has signified he is to provide for the French Fleet expected in the fall out of these monies with necessaries, he intends I presume the same be paid to him; please to inform me how far he is authorized for this purpose & whether a payment to him will discharge the State of North Carolina from a debt due to the Government of Martinique this State having had repeated applications to make payment to the Administrators of that Island who are supposed to reside there: this seems a necessary enquiry, however delicate the subject may be, please to know, if the Monies are not to be paid to him, to what person, and the place, where they are to be paid, that the proper instructions be given to the person who shall transact this business. Perhaps provisions or some other productions of the State may be wanting for the fleet, that would be an easy remittance for our Merchants. Your communication on the above I request may be as expeditious as possible [*lined out*] and forwared to Mr. [*Joseph*] Grammar the Post Master in Petersberg that I may lay them before the Council.

In the mean while Assure the Vice Consul General of France that the Executive ~~of this State~~ entertain a high sense of the long indulgence this state hath met with from the Government of of Martinique; that notwithstanding attempts have been twice made to pay this debt which unfortunately have failed, the utmost exertion will be used to extinguish it as soon as possible at such time and place, as advice shall be given as afore said.

A report prevails which is relied on that the proposition for the Assumption of the State debts is rejected: This seems to give general Satisfaction to our Citizens, the more especially when they are told, it was effected by the means of the Senators & Representatives of this State in Congress.

FC:lbk, Governors' Papers, Nc-Ar. Written from Rockingham, North Carolina. The recipients are identified by the fact that this letter is a response to their letter of 11 April.

[1] For the North Carolina Cession Act, see *DHFFC* 6:1544–48.

[2] In 1787 Richard Blackledge, Jr. "borrowed" sixty thousand pounds of public tobacco stored in his warehouse, which he encountered some difficulty paying back over the ensuing years (*Blount* 1:358–59).

[3] The site of a health spa in eastern Rockingham County.

Governor Alexander Martin to [*Hugh Williamson*]

Your Letters of the 6th. 7th. and 20th of March with the 24th. of April last I have duly recived and am much obliged to you for the Public as well as private communications you have been pleased to favour me with—Agreeable to your request I directed the Comptroller [*Francis Child*] to furnish you with all the Certificates that have been taken up by the sales of Vacant Lands—of Confiscated property—or by Taxes, also the amount of the Certificates in circulation distinguishing those of 1786, and enjoined since to be as perticular as possible on each article and transmit the same to you by Express, to the post Office should he not have all immediate opportunity he being nearer Petersburg than myself intends in Person to effect this business—I am told he is gone on to Petersburg himself that his dispatches to you may be safely delivered to the Post Master no doubt by this time they have reached you.

Our Citizens appear much ~~pleased~~ satisfied with the exertions you have made in the House of Representatives to negative the proposition of the assumption of the State Debts by Congress, which proposition should it take effect seems to portend ruin to those States which have not redeemed their State Certificates—The Arguments you offered on that body seem to be conclusive and should it be carried against you I think you have done Justice to this State in the firm opposition you made—However a Report prevails and is relied on that this proposition is rejected which gives us the greater pleasure as the same is said to be effected by the means of our Senators and Representatives in Congress. As the Council is shortly to sit on the subject of the Martinique Debt[1] which the Senators inform me the Consul General of France [*Michel-Guillaume St. John de Crèvecoeur*] wishes to receive to enable him to supply with necessaries the French Fleet expected to the Northward in the fall—I shall do myself the ~~pleasure~~ Honour to lay that proposition on your last letter respecting a Clerk before them, and make no doubt they will advise me to recommend the measures you suggested of employing one, especially as you are to receive no pay in the agency Service during your taking a seat in Congress—but some difficulty will remain how his pay is to be remitted to him.

FC:lbk, Governors' Papers, Nc-Ar. Written from Rockingham, North Carolina. The recipient is identified by the fact that Williamson had requested a clerk to assist in the settlement of North Carolina's accounts with the United States.

[1] See Johnston and Hawkins to Governor Alexander Martin, 11 April, n. 1, above.

Josiah Parker to George Washington

Since I had the honor of transmiting to you the resignation of Archibald Richardson Surveyor of the Customs at Suffolk I have received a letter from Willis Riddick Esqr. representative for Nansemond County recommending Mr. [*Benjamin*] Bartlet as a proper person to fill the vacancy—as I have the firmest reliance on Mr. Riddicks honor and integrity I can hazard a recommendation of Mr. Bartlet in preference to Mr. Lawson.

ALS, Washington Papers, DLC. The salutation line reads, "Sire."

George Thatcher to Nathaniel Wells

We are now making the last effort for an assumption of the State debts; but I rather fear it will prove as ineffectual as former exertions—The opposers of the measure seem to have arrived at a state of mind that all arguments are useless, having made up their judgments—When this is the case as to any subject, a postponement is the wisest measure—And it begins to be the wish of several Gentlemen, who are warm advocates for the assumption that the whole funding Business may be put over to another session—should this be the case, I hope Congress will adjourn by the middle of next month—otherwise I am fearfull we shall run far into the summer.

The inclosed motion was brought forward in committee, yesterday, by Mr. Gerry[1]—And is now the subject of debate—I do not expect any question upon it to day.

We are again like to be troubled with a question on the place where Congress shall set—for yesterday, it was moved, in the Senate, that Congress at their next Session shall meet in Philadelphia—We are now realizing the inconveniences, I foresaw, when Congress in the year eighty nine [*1788*], was about to fix the place at which the Congress, under the new Constitution, should convene—Then I was clearly of opinion that Congress meeting in this City would become a subject of much altercation; and mingle itself in many important questions—This has been the fact, & I apprehend it will continue so till Congress go farther south.

I shall thank you for the earliest information of any measures the Legislature may take touching the State debt—From some information, it is apprehended the [*Massachusetts*] Legislature will disapprove of the assumption of the State debts by Congress; and we are told that some influential men, who are in [*the General*] Court, are very much set against the measure—You will readily see what a disagreeable situation this will put us in—as the whole Representation from Massachusetts have again & again voted in favour of the assumption.

FC, Thatcher Family Papers, MHi. Sent to Boston.

[1] In the COWH debate on the Funding Bill on 24 May, Gerry moved the insertion of an additional nine sections that would have provided for an assumption of the states' war debts. The COWH rose that day without taking further action. For the text of Gerry's motion, see *DHFFC* 5:874–76n.

The Motion

STILL the public good designing,
Hear the motion made by —:[1]
"To-morrow when we meet again,
Let it be at th' hour of ten."
He, no slave to love or beauty,
Constantly attends his duty:
'Xcept it be the hour of pray'r,
You never see Jack's empty chair;
Punct'al or to speak or vote,

His example all men quote.
Next morn, when business came before 'em,
The Speaker could not find a quorum:
And Jack, with most consistent grace,
Among the *last*, to fill his place,
By help of *Sergeant and his Mace.*

NYDG, 25 May.

[1] Before adjourning for the day on 20 May, the House agreed to a motion by Vining to move the daily hour of meeting from 11 to 10 A.M. (*DHFFC* 13:1372).

Other Documents

Andrew Craigie to Daniel Parker. FC:dft, Craigie Papers, MWA. Sent to London; carried by Ruth Barlow.

Congress is so equally divided on assumption that he cannot calculate its success with any certainty, but will not part with any South Carolina certificates because he thinks it will pass.

Thomas Dwight to Theodore Sedgwick. ALS, Sedgwick Family Papers, MHi. Written from Springfield, Massachusetts.

Reports on state elections; if other counties had voted as correctly as Hampshire County, the state's politics "would be on a much better footing."

Certificate of Richard Bassett. ANS, by William Killen, Records of the Supreme Court, DNA. Written from Dover, Delaware. Killen provided this document to Bassett, who filed it in support of his application to be admitted as a counselor to the bar of the Supreme Court on 2 August. For the full text, see *DHSCUS* 1:544–45.

Certifies that Bassett had practiced law in Delaware for at least twelve years.

Wednesday, 26 May 1790

Fine (Johnson)

Governor Beverley Randolph to James Madison

I am much obliged by your attention to the Business of the Inspection Laws of this State. I will thank You to request the Secretary of the Treasury to furnish me with a Copy of his Instructions to the Custom House officers on that Subject.

I had Hopes that the Decision of the House of Representatives upon the assumption of the State Debts would have been final. No Proposition has been before Congress since the operation of the New Government which has been more generally disliked than that has been in this State. Should the measure be at length adopted I fear it will give great Disquiet to the People & perhaps produce some warm animadversions from the Legislature.

Accept my Thanks for the News Papers which you were so obliging As to inclose to me. I shall always be glad to receive such communications as you may think proper to make.

ALS, Madison Papers, DLC. Written from Richmond, Virginia.

John Samuel Sherburne to John Langdon

Yr. kind promptitude in replying to my letters, which are ever written in much haste as almost to be illegible demands my warmest acknowledgments—We observe with great pleasure that our petition[1] is like to be productive of such general benefit to the commercial interest, the statement of the Treasurers of the foreign & domestic shipping is astonishing. I shd. before have thought, such a disproportion incredible—We last week held our Circuit Court in Town, every one is enraptured with the Chief Just[*ice*]. his excellent charge by his permission I have had printed in a pamphlet & as he informed me he had not before delivered a copy to any one, I suppose you cannot yet have them among you, I have therefore inclosed one for you,[2] & another for that Counter part of Presdt. Washington my respected friend Mr. Lear. wh. please to deliver him with my compliments—Such general sickness has never before been known among us— ***

ALS, Langdon Papers, NhPoA. Written from Portsmouth, New Hampshire; postmarked. The omitted text discusses state politics and the health of mutual friends.

---

[1] The petition of the Merchants and Traders of Portsmouth, dated 11 March, related to trade policy; see *DHFFC* 8:353–54.

[2] Chief Justice Jay delivered the same "charge" (or instruction of duties) to the grand juries of each of the courts he opened during the spring 1790 Eastern Circuit: at New York on 12 April; New Haven, Connecticut, 22 April; Boston, 3 May; and Portsmouth, New Hampshire, 20 May. Sherburne was apparently responsible for the first publication of Jay's charge, in pamphlet form, by George Jerry Osborne of Portsmouth (Evans 22587). With some variations among them, several newspapers from Portsmouth to Philadelphia reprinted the speech, beginning on 27 May. For a transcription of Jay's original autographed draft, see *DHSCUS* 2:25–30.

One of the Gallery to Mr. McLean

IN your Gazette of yesterday, I observe a sort of *jeu d'esprit*,[1] evidently pointed at a certain member of the House of Representatives [*Vining*]. Lest this humble attempt at wit should be taken for the truth, I will beg leave to state the facts, which seem to have awaked the author's drowsy muse.

The member alluded to, on Thursday last made a motion that the house should meet at 10 o'clock, for the remainder of the session, in order that the business of the public might be expedited.

On Friday morning, before the house came to order, Mr. B—t [*Boudinot*], in a jocular way, desired the Sergeant at Arms to call for the member who had made the motion for meeting at ten o'clock; but he appeared in the house a few minutes after ten, whilst the Sergeant at Arms was gone in search of him.

These are the facts; and I may, with candour, add, that there is not any member more attentive to the public good, or more independent in his principles, than the gentleman alluded to by the *poet*; and with regard to his abilities, it is to be presumed, that he did not wish to level himself so far as to reply to any indelicate insinuations like those which appeared in yesterday's Gazette.

NYDG, 26 May, edited by Archibald McLean.

[1] The "witticism" was The Motion, 25 May, above.

Frederick to Messrs. Printers

THE writer of the piece signed *A Republican* in your last paper has touched upon a state subject, and has even repeated the same dull words that had been before blunted against justice and the public opinion. They met the disgrace of contempt at their birth and fell into the dirt, and have now no other life or efficacy than to support the din of vulgar murmur, and I presume their utterance in the present instance was only to obtain vulgar applause. I think he is of a different persuasion; but men of his cloth are not in the habit of preaching according to their faith. I don't imagine him to be over squeamish at receiving six dollars upon occasion—indeed six dollars do not gratify him in an ordinary case. I would ask that lawyer whether his *wages* for saying *here* at the county courts are not equal to a chaplain's salary? And does *he* concede that he possesses abilities or merit superior to the members of congress, or the divines in general? His literary performances do not pro[*ve it*]—and as to his services at the bar, the state of Connecticut may well accord to the annihilation of three quarters of his profession. Nay, I aver, that the annihilation of three quarters of that race, and the destruction of their overgrown influence is *necessary* to our liberty & happiness. I call upon the people to *look* to their liberties—they are not in danger from congress—that august body is to the extent of its constitutional capacity their *guardian*—its members are the men of our free choice—they are the *best* of our citizens—and they ought to be well rewarded for their abilities, their virtue and their important services. But the liberties of the people are in *danger from the lawyers*—they are a present oppression and will soon become an intolerable aristocracy, if measures are not speedily taken to deprive them of their exorbitant influence over the people and controul of the legislature. The great interests of the state are agriculture, commerce, and manufactures—the legislature ought therefore to be composed of men who are acquainted with and concerned in these subjects. What have the lawyers to do with them, or what right indeed have they to pretend to a seat in the legislature? They have, it is true, one concern about all the property in the state; which is to *argue* the proper owners out of it and get themselves into possession. But God forbid that such a shame and calamity should ever happen to us.

[New Haven] *Connecticut Journal*, 26 May. For information on the subject of this attack, see A Republican (No. 1), 15 May, above.

Other Documents

Benjamin Contee to Governor John Eager Howard. No copy known; mentioned in Contee to Howard, 8 June.

Royal Flint to Enos Hitchcock. ALS, Miscellaneous Collection, RHi. Place to which addressed not indicated. For further background on Hitchcock's petition, see *DHFFC* 8:32, 34.

"Though the people of this place do not often purchase books," Flint expects brisk sales of Hitchcock's book (*Memoirs of the Bloomsgrove Family*); Hitchcock's petition (for copyright protection) "will I presume be presented by Mr. Ames" and "I shall pay every attention possible to that"; the fate of assumption is as doubtful as ever; "the parties on the question are nearly equal in strength, and there are some among them, wavering characters, who change their opinion often, or rather who have not any decided opinion at all"; the House will probably concur with the Senate on its Rhode Island Trade Bill "without material alterations."

Benjamin Huntington to Governor Samuel Huntington. Summary and excerpt of one page ALS, *Parke-Bernet Catalog* 1802(1958):item 167. Addressed to Hartford, Connecticut; franked; postmarked. The ellipses are in the source.

"Acknowledges receipt of his letter '*containing a hint of my not being totally forgotten in my native country*' and that he received a copy of the number of votes for nomination; informs him that the House voted to receive '*the old Continental bills at seventy five for one. . . .*'"

James Madison to Governor Beverley Randolph. ALS, Executive Papers, Vi. Addressed to Richmond, Virginia; franked; postmarked; received on or before 5 June. For the full text, see *PJM* 13:229; for Hamilton's enclosed circular letter to the collectors and surveyors of Virginia, dated 18 May, see *PAH* 6:419–20.

Encloses instruction of the secretary of the treasury on Virginia's tobacco inspection law, which was given to Madison to forward.

Fontaine Maury to James Madison. ALS, Madison Papers, DLC. Written from Fredericksburg, Virginia. For the full text, see *PJM* 13:229–30. Neither of the petitions mentioned in this letter was presented to the FFC.

Having heard that the people of "the Lower Counties" of the Rappahannock River collection district have petitioned Congress to remove the naval office to Urbanna, the inhabitants of Fredericksburg and neighboring Falmouth have solicited Maury "to request you will so far Interest yourself as to have the Business delayed" until they can present their own petition through Madison; asks for a line as soon as is convenient.

NYDA, 26 May.

Silvester was reelected.

Thursday, 27 May 1790

Rain (Johnson)

Nathaniel Barrell to George Thatcher

Yours of 18th. inst. is now before me by which I am reminded of my faults—I ought to have inform'd you on receipt of your kind letter with thanks for your care in procuring what I requested of you from Mr. [*Stephen*] Collins—you certainly judg'd right in preferring the accot. under [*John*] Sullivans hand to a Copy, and you may rest assur'd I mean to comply with your engagement to Mr. Collins & return it so soon as the purpose is answerd.

I am far from thinking all the opposers to the assumption of the State debts are influenc'd by motive[*s*] of injustice—but when I see a man coolly and deliberately in a lengthy studied elaborate speech, exhausting all the powers of rhetoric to support a fallacious argument and carefully warding off every thing like truth—perverting the sacred palladium of Nations—when I see this oration fully, clearly, & masterly answer'd—its fallacy pointed out to demonstration, and its baneful effects guarded against—when after a months silence I again find this *Oratorical hero* [*Madison*] pursuing his nefarious plan, and in a still more labord harangue, misrepresenting the States—I say my good friend will not all this justify a mans being a little off his guard, and for a moment, in the heat of resentment, loosing sight of that prudential rule which leads men to dress their Anger in language that cannot offend?[1]

I am willing to think with you that some of the opposers as well as the supporters of the assumption persuade themselvs they are right in the measure they advocate but I dare not say even should it be for the wellfare of the united states, it consequently is just, for let the event be as it will beneficial or otherways it still is just, or unjust, and cannot be alterd, tho to appearance it may be doing good or evil—will any honest man say that an act of justice shall not take place because it may not be (to present view) for the wellfare of the United States? Aristides I think it was, oppos'd [*de*]stroying the Spartans fleet because it was unjust, tho it was manifestly for the general benefit of the Athenians to do it[2]—will you say he did [*lined out*] wrong? that it was an error or a vice in him so to do? any one would think from what I have said upon this subject that I was deeply interested in the speculateing business and possessd largely of the various state securitys—but I can assure my friend I dont know that I am directly or indirectly in possession or reversion owner of ten dollars in this way in the world—I know the assumpt[*ion*] must & will take place eventually and the sooner this is done the more will it be for the~~ir~~ interest of the United States—and in so doing, Congress will establish justice & promote the interest of the Union—which is all that induces me thus to express my mind to you who it is with pleasure I consider my my friend.

ALS, Chamberlain Collection, MB. Written from York, Maine.

[1] This is probably a reference to Sedgwick's speech of 12 April.

[2] According to Plutarch's life of the Athenian statesman and general Aristides (530?–468? B.C.), after repulsing a Persian invasion at the battle of Plataea in 479 B.C., the Athenians' leader Themistocles urged that they destroy the arsenal of their Greek allies, including the Spartans, in order to become supreme masters of Greece. Aristides persuaded the Athenians that nothing could have been more advantageous, or more unjust.

John Fenno to Joseph Ward

Yesterday the House agreed that old Conti[*nental money*] should be funded at 75 for one—The funding bill was passed this day & ordered to be engrossed for a 3d. reading on Monday—The propositions for Assumption [*lined out*] offered by Mr. Gerry were this day bro't forward by Mr. Boudinot in the form of resolutions—I *now* think that no assumption will take place this Session—the majority are silent, but determined—It was moved in the House this day by Mr. Fitzsimons that Congress meet, & hold their next Session in Phila. A Similar motion was agitated in the senate yesterday—it is supposed that it will be negatived in the Senate—it is to be determined next Thursday—The president is so much better, that he signed four Bills yesterday—I have only time to say that we are well.
P. S. Let [*Benjamin*] Russell have the News in this which you may see proper to communicate.

ALS, Ward Papers, ICHi. Addressed to Land Office, Boston; postmarked.

James Madison to [*Ambrose Madison*]

I have this moment your favor of the 16th. The enclosed papers will shew you that the project of assuming the State debts is revived & likely to employ further time I hope we shall be able to defeat it, but the advocates for it are inconceivably persevering as well as formidable in point of numbers. The bill for funding the other debt is gone thro' and will pass the 3d. reading in the H. of Reps. in substance as reported by the Secretary of the Treasury. I inclose a bill for regulating the navigation & trade in such a manner as either to bring G[*reat*]. B[*ritain*]. to reasonable terms or to try the consequences of her refusal. The [*po*]licy of the measure is daily gaining friends. It will probably pass the H. of Reps. by a very large majority. and the Senate are much better disposed on the subject than at the last Session. I conjecture it will succeed there also.

The President has been at the point of death, but ~~is~~ now rides out and is getting well fast. The influenza has made great havoc on the health of [*torn*] I am quite restored myself. Col. Bland

AL, incomplete, Madison Papers, NN. Place to which addressed not indicated. The recipient was identified by the salutation "Dear brother." The enclosures are unidentified and unlocated.

James Nicholson to John Barry

Dale seting out in the morning gives me an opportunity of leting you Know how our Affairs stand with Congress.[1] Colo. Hartley (who is our Main Stay) has promised with the assistance of the Judge[2] & Mr. Stone, to watch a favourable opportunity & to bring the business on before the House the two last Gentlemen has come forward in a very friendly & sincere Manner & I have acquiest in Resting the matter solely with them, only requesting they may not let it be prolonged over this Session as I was of oppinion we should never have more freinds then in the present Congress, they have Consented so to do & there the Matter Rests as present, They are now Jockeying about the Assumption business & the Removal of Congress & I hope while they are about it they may make a Compromise & Include our small affair in their Bargain, upon the whole I am not very Sanguine. I suspect (& from pretty good Authority) your Philada. friends are not the Most Strenious in the business. I think a Letter from you Joging their Memory would be of service. Mr. Morris you will have an opportunity talk to him & beg him to press the Matter froward when he returns.

Since you left us Mrs. [*Frances Nicholson*] Seney has been so Alarmingly Ill that I have not had Spirit to do any thing, but I thank God she seems mending.

[*P. S.*] Give my Love to Murray & Polly [*Alexander and Mary Murray*], for further particulars refer to Dale. some of my friends Advised against delaying the Matter, but as those Gentlem. above has Undertaken in so friendly a manner I could not do otherwise, Altho' against my own Sentiments, I shall be glad to hear from you, directing under Cover to ~~Colo.~~ the Honble. Wm. Few.

ALS, Barry-Hayes Collection, Independence Seaport Museum, Philadelphia. Addressed to Strawberry Hill near Philadelphia; carried by Capt. Richard Dale.

---

[1] Richard Dale (1756–1826) fought under Nicholson as a lieutenant in the Continental Navy. After the war he engaged in the China trade, and at the time of this letter had just returned from Canton as captain of the *Federalist*, owned by Morris. For the petition of navy and marine officers referred to here, see *DHFFC* 7:438–43.

[2] Probably Burke, who was often referred to by this title and who, like Hartley and Stone, had served on the committee that reported favorably on Nicholson and Barry's petition, and subsequently (but unsuccessfully) defended it in House debate.

Henry Wynkoop to Reading Beatty

Yours of Sunday last received yesterday, the President is so far recovered as again to attend to Busyness & ride out. On monday last the Motion for fixing the next Meeting of Congress at Philadelphia was made in the Senate by Mr. Moris & seconded by Mr. Langdon, which lay on the Table until yesterday when it was again brought forward & postponed to that day week, to afford time for RodeIsland to send forward their Senators, the Votes stood 13 for the postponement & 11 against, thus you see our sanguine Prospects of going to Philadelphia are at least rendered precarious, tho' we will not consider it as lost yet, *Perseverando*, ~~in the~~ You know was the Motto of one of our Continental Bills.[1]

The Assumption of the State Debts was again brought forward as You will perceive by the papers, but was rejected as part of the funding Bill, which this day has been compleated, so far as to be engrossed for a third reading on monday next; this done Mr. Fitsimonds introduced the folowing Motion, *That Congress meet & hold their next Session in Philadelphia*, this was seconded from various parts of the House & now lays on the Table, what will be it's fate time will discover, many Gentlemen are yet sanguine, while others wear long faces upon it; The coming in of Rode-Island is yet precarious, as the Communications from thence are various in Opinion, some Gentlemen conceiving they will adopt the Constitution while others are possitive in Asscertions to the contrary.

Coll. Bland is extremely Ill, & what is somewhat remarkable, I beleive is the only Gentleman from Virginia, who prefers this place to Philadelphia.

Mr. Boudinot in the form of Resolutions agreable to what is contained in the Report of the Secretary & the propositions of Mr. Gerrey of monday last, again this day brought forward the Assumption of the State Debts, these now lay on the Table.

The Adjournment of Congress cannot yet be ascertained much Bu[*s*]yness is yet depending & little probabillity that it can possibly take place before some time in Ju[*ly?*].

I send You Child's paper [*NYDA*] of this day, containing the Speeches of Sherman & Boudinot on Mr. Gerry's proposition of last monday, but the Cream of that Debate is in the Speech of Ames not yet published, as that probably will appear tomorrow, shall send it to You on monday.[2]

ALS, Wynkoop Papers, PDoBHi. Place to which addressed not indicated.

---

[1] "It ought to be persevered in" was one of the most popular among the more than one hundred moralistic mottoes to appear in the insignia printed on American paper money during the Revolutionary War. *Perseverando* appeared on various denominations of Continental currency between 1775 and 1780, and on the currencies of nine states in 1780 (Eric P. Newman, *The Early Paper Money of America* [Iola, Wis., 1990], pp. 26, 42, 481).

[2] Francis Childs's *NYDA*, the only newspaper to provide an original account, cited the length of Ames's speech of 25 May as an apology for not publishing it until 29 May (*DHFFC* 13:1432–46).

Newspaper Article

ON Thursday the 27th ult. Commodore [*Alexander*] GILLON mentioned in the [*South Carolina constitutional*] convention, that there had been a subject agitated in Congress, the propriety of the Convention taking notice of which he submitted to their consideration. It was this, a number of quakers, presented a petition to Congress praying for their interference on the subject of slavery.[1] The memorial was not indeed successful, but our delegates felt themselves exceedingly alarmed at the manner in which it was debated. Though not successful in the first instance, yet as the Quakers were a persevering people, their conduct ought to be carefully looked after, and every precaution made to prevent five millions in property being sacrificed to their prejudices. We came into general government under a belief that our property would be protected, and gentlemen taking this into consideration, might, perhaps, think it necessary to let the general government know their sentiments.

[Charleston] *State Gazette of South Carolina*, 3 June; reprinted at Boston; Newport, Rhode Island; New York City (*NYDA*, 2 July) and Poughkeepsie, New York; and Philadelphia.

---

[1] For the petitions, see *DHFFC* 8:314–38.

OTHER DOCUMENTS

Elias Boudinot to [*John Edwards Caldwell*]. FC, Boudinot Family Papers, NjR. This is a postscript to a letter begun on 17 May, above.

"Our worthy President has been most dangerously ill, but is on the recovery—We were much alarmed, but God has had Mercy upon Us."

Royal Flint to Manasseh Cutler. ALS, Cutler Papers, IEN. Addressed to Ipswich, Massachusetts; postmarked; answered 14 June.

Approximately six hundred French immigrants have arrived at Alexandria, Virginia, en route to their settlement at "Gallipolis" (Ohio); "Some of the leading characters among them" have come to New York and discussed their plans with Hamilton and several members of Congress; "there is a good disposition in Congress towards the proposed settlement," and there will be an order for some federal troops to be stationed near the Kanawha River (West Virginia) for their protection.

Benjamin Goodhue to Samuel Phillips, Jr. No copy known; acknowledged in Phillips to Goodhue, 1 June.

Stephen Goodhue to Benjamin Goodhue. FC:lbk, Goodhue Family Papers, MSaE. Written from Salem, Massachusetts.

Stephen (Benjamin's son) is recovered from his measles, but remains weak; other family and friends are well; "nothing New to Inform you of the murmurs much as heretofore"; the [Boston] *Massachusetts Centinel* hints at assumption's likely passage, "which Seems to Chear the minds of People a little"; "excise upon Excise ~~upon excise I hope~~ will make it exceding troublesome"; the fishing season is promising.

Thomas Jefferson to William Short. FC:letterpress copy, Jefferson Papers, DLC. The ALS was auctioned by Sotheby's in April 2008. For the full text, see *PTJ* 16:443–45. A postscript was written on 28 May, below.

Has been suffering a "periodical headach" for almost a month and has been unable to attend to any business, "public or private"; at the same time "we have been very near losing the President," who, suffering from peripneumony, "was pronounced by two of the three physicians present to be in the act of death"; the public was greatly alarmed, which "proves how much depends on his life"; thinks Trade and Navigation Bill will pass; there is a great majority for it in the House; his hope of obtaining concession to export salted provisions to France, which he asks Short to pursue, was an inducement to the bill; motion before the Senate regarding the next session of Congress meeting in Philadelphia will probably be carried in both houses.

Benjamin Lincoln to [*John Adams*]. ALS, Adams Family Manuscript Trust, MHi. Written from Boston. The recipient is identified by the letter's location and its continued discussion of the subject of Frobisher's request for federal compensation for his improvements to the making of potash; see Lincoln to Adams, 3 April, above.

"Your ideas of [*William*] Frobisher are the same with ours here We shall I think hear little more from him"; encloses Cotton Tufts's order on Adams, and requests a draft for it, or a receipt by the next post; reports on state legislature.

James Madison to John Dawson. No copy known; acknowledged in Dawson to Madison, 5 June.

James Madison to [*Eliza House Trist*]. Transcript (of ALS, privately owned in 1961) from *PJM* 13:231. The recipient is identified by the editors of *PJM* and from the letter's closing.

Commiserates with her bout of influenza, which has "spared very few in this place," but from which he himself is totally recovered; Bland is extremely ill with influenza and other complaints, and his recovery is improbable; Jefferson is over the worst of his headache fit and hears by letter from Williamsburg, not from Edmund Randolph, that he is still detained there by his wife's health.

Stephen Mix Mitchell to Oliver Ellsworth. ALS, Petitions and Memorials, House Records, DNA. Printed in *DHFFC* 7:423. Related to Seth Boardman's invalid petition claim.

William Smith (Md.) to Otho H. Williams. ALS, Williams Papers, MdHi. Addressed to Baltimore. The Baltimore Company was founded in 1731 to mine and refine iron ore. Its founding partners included Senator Carroll's father and two cousins (*CCP* 1:101n).

Hopes Williams has arrived back at Baltimore in restored health; encloses newspapers of the day; believes the Funding Bill will be engrossed that day, and that assumption, which had "another tryal" that failed since Williams left New York, will be brought on again in some form; discusses the Baltimore Company's ongoing legal challenge to Senator Carroll's ownership of meadows at Pimlico, outside Baltimore.

William Samuel Johnson, Diary. Johnson Papers, CtHi.

"Billy [*Samuel William Johnson*] saild."

Friday, 28 May 1790

Cold rain (Johnson)

John Dawson to [*Tench Coxe*]

***

The rejection of that part of the Secry's. plan which proposes an assumption of the state debts has given much pleasure to all classes of people in this state, except the speculators in N. Carolina certificates, which number is small—the bad policy as well as injustice of this proposal, ought to have prevented so tedious a debate, & I am persuaded that the more the subject is developed, the greater the difficulties will be found—Madison's conduct has renderd him very popular: he will be reelected in September, without any opposition—we hear that some of your members voted in favour of the plan, contrary to the decided interest of your state & the opinions of your most enlighten'd citizens, because the[*y*] thought it more *fœderal*—I suspect the word has a very different signification on the north & south sides of the Potomac.

The gentlemen from the East appear warm, & to have lost that strong attatchment to the union—if a removal to Pennsylvania, which my friends write me is in contemplation, can be secur'd. it can probably bring them to a right way of thinking, & render combinations sometimes ineffectual.

Poor Grayson's death still fills me with sorrow—in him we loose an agreeable acquaintance—the public and upright & able servant—he possessd genius, learning & a general knowledge of men & things—more particularly was he acquainted with the characters & anecdotes which go to make up the history of american transactions for the last twenty years—he possessd with his other agreeable qualities much good nature—was friendly in the highest degree—& moreover was an honest man—where is there in the circle of our friends & acquaintance another with fewer faults & more agreable & valuable accomplishments—it became the duty of the executive to fill the vacancy in the Senate untill the meeting of the legislature—the eyes of every member were immediately fix'd on P. Henry esqr.—the appointment was put of[*f*] for some days, while I sent to him—read an extract from his letter in answer to mine; then judge of the heart of this much abus'd man, & the principles by which he is actuated.

"I beg you to accept my most grateful acknowledgements for your Kind offer to fill the vacancy in our fœderal Senate, by appointing me to it—but my mind recolls at the idea of accepting it—I cannot find those dispositions in my breast which *I* deem necessary for all the confidential servants of the present goverment—some of its leading principles are subversive of those to which I am for ever wedded, while its practices seem equally at variance with republican sentiments. cou'd I believe that my poor efforts woud work a change, I woud sacrifice every thing & go there—but the utmost which I see possible to effect is now & then to impede some of the lesser movements of the system, which the radical errors of it will remain, & be nurtur'd by a determind majority—at present therefore I am convinc'd I coud do no good—whether the time for purging away the vices of our general goverment will ever come is very doubtful—I expect it not in my day, & whenever it shall arrive it will be attended with so much hazard, that its friends will hesitate & perhaps desert from attempts to reform—notwithstanding all this and more, I do not despond—&c. &c.—(complimentary) give me leave to assure you that I thank you, & with the sincerest gratitude am sensible of the high obligation I have to you for your goodness—but feeling as I do the impediments I have described [*seal*] you will see the propriety of my remaining in a private station."

This letter was written with the freedom & sincerity of a friend & I communicate it to you with the confidence of one, in order to show what kind of an animal of Virginia [*an*] Anti is—let it remain with you.

I never approvd of the letter written by our Senators to our last assembly[1]—but I hold it to be the duty of the present members to communicate fully the conduct of that right honble. body, on the motion of Mr. Lee for opening the doors—I think as a Fœderalist to enthusiasm cannot approve of it.

***

ALS, Coxe Papers, PHi. Written from Richmond, Virginia. The recipient's identity is based on the letter's location and the handwriting of the endorsement. The omitted text discusses the Pennsylvania constitutional convention.

[1] For Grayson's and Lee's letter of 28 September 1789, see *DHFFC* 17:1634–35.

John Parrish to James Madison

The evening ~~we~~ myself & Friends left New York[1] thou gave it as thy op~~p~~inion the subject ~~that induced Friends to~~ on which our relig[*iou*]s. Society had address'd Congress had better not be revived during the present Session unless some Instances should appear that any of the States were in the Practice of fiting out foreign Vessels for the African trade or American bottoms to supply foreigners with slaves which appears by the Voat of the House as entered on the Journal Congress have it in their Power to prevent with out infringing on the Constitution; Inclosed I have sent a list of the Vessels cleared out from the State of Rhoad Island by which it appears there is 10 now in the trade with those that are fiting out and from divers information there is reason to believe that several other States are not clear in these respects, we were informed by the Skipper of the boat when we left New York who appeared to be a man of Voracity that he knew of 14 that had been latterly fited out of New York altho Road Island dose not come with in the Jurisdiction of Congress and therefore no remedy can be applyed to them at presant Yet for the Honour of Your August body which will be Viewed by foreign Nations may it never be said that the Americans have so little sence of true Liberty as the Author of the fragment has allready that after haveing establishing their own Liberty they continue to make deperdations upon others. And as thou had a short Bill Essayed to present to the House[2] and if past into a Law would at least tend to discourage this Inequitious commerce and perhaps [*that*] is going as far at present as can be done with safty, from a persuasion that thy Influence is such that the matter may be accomplished before the House Rises I have embraced the presant oppertunity to request thy deep and weighty attention to a Subject that appears to me of as great Magnitude and in its affect and Consequences as serious and Intrersting as ever came before any body of men, it would be a Melancholy consideration to reflect that even one Vessel load of this unhappy race of people should be torn from there native shore from all that is near & dear to linger out their Lives in a state of Unconditional Slavery when perhaps a little exertion in the presant critical Juncture might prevent, and allso save the people Called Quakers the trouble of Interfeering at the next Session on this very disagreeable tho Necessary Business which I hope might be compleated by a motion from a Member of Your own Body which would be a real sattisfaction to thy Assured friend.

ALS, Cox-Parrish-Wharton Papers, PHi. Written from Philadelphia. Enclosures unlocated.

[1] Parrish had joined a delegation of ten other Philadelphia Quakers in promoting anti-slavery petitions to Congress in February and March 1790; the four who remained until the end left New York on 25 March. For more, see *DHFFC* 8:314–38.

[2] Possibly an unknown revision of the Slave Trade Bill [HR-30], originally presented by Parker on 19 September 1789, postponed until the second session, and never acted on again. According to Parker, his bill aimed to lay the constitutional maximum impost of ten dollars on Blacks imported for slavery (*DHFFC* 10:643).

Hugh Williamson to George Washington

While you are considering of a proper Person for Governor of the Territory ceded by North Carolina I take the Liberty of requesting that you would be so good as to enquire whether Mr. William Blount would not probably discharge that Trust with Honour to himself and advantage to the Public. Those People who had most of them been separated from the State for some Years,[1] have been torn by Factions and very disorderly; Some address will be required in governing them and I think there is not any other man who possesses the Esteem and Confidence of both Parties so fully as Mr. Blount, for some of the Leaders of both Parties have assured me that they knew no Man in whom they could be so fully united.

It is true that Mr. Blount has a considerable Quantity of Land within the ceded Territory, but he has none to the Southward of it, and he must be the more deeply interested in the Peace and Prosperity of the new Government. Perhaps it is because I have many Relations and some Land there, given me by the State, that I am the more anxious to see it prosper.

Mr. David Campbell, who lives near Holsten and is an assistant Judge under the State of N. Carolina, [*lined out*] of a fair Character and respectable Abilities, appears to be a proper Person for a Judge.

Mr. Howel Tatum formerly a Continental Officer, now a Lawyer in that Country, whom I have ever considered as a Man of Honour and respectable Abilities might be a proper Person to Discharge the Duties of Secretary.

ALS, Washington Papers, DLC.

[1] Williamson referred to the separatist movement known as the "state" of Franklin. Resentful of North Carolina's initial cession of their land to the United States in early 1784, settlers sought to avoid territorial status by declaring their independence and seeking admission to the union as a pre-existing state. The pro-independence faction, led by future FFC member Sevier, resisted re-annexation by North Carolina (which repealed the cession in late 1784) and negotiated their own treaty with local Cherokee in early 1785. But the Franklinites' title to most of the "state" was nullified later that year by the Treaty of Hopewell, by which the Cherokee ceded the Cumberland River basin to the United States in exchange for guarantees to their possession of the upper Tennessee River watershed—which constituted most of Franklin. This act, and a series of legislative reforms by North Carolina, led most of the secessionists to disavow the movement, which died by late 1788 (*Westward Expansion*, pp. 203–6). By asserting in this letter that Blount held no lands south of the ceded territory, Williamson may have been assuring Washington that the candidate would experience no conflict of interest in helping the federal government stem illegal white settlement of Cherokee lands along the southern reaches of the Tennessee River (in present-day northern Alabama).

Other Documents

Joseph Ellis and Franklin Davenport to Jonathan Elmer and William Paterson. ALS, Washington Papers, DLC. Written from Perth Amboy, New Jersey; carried by Daniel Benezet.

Office seeking: Daniel Benezet, Jr., for collector at Perth Amboy, New Jersey; mentions Morris, Fitzsimons, "and the other Gentlemen from Pennsylvania" as further references.

Thomas Fitzsimons to Benjamin Rush. Summary of two page ALS, *Parke-Bernet Catalog* 499(1944):item 119, and *Carnegie Book Shop Catalog* 259(1962):item 185. Addressed to Philadelphia; franked; postmarked 29 May 1790. The "business" referred to was whom Pennsylvania Germans would likely support in the October gubernatorial election.

Pertains to civic affairs, transactions in Congress, and the attempt to move Congress to Philadelphia, mentioning "that the bill for establishing the permanent & temporary seat of Government of the U.S. has passed"; "there is to be a meeting of the German Clergy in Phila. on Sunday or Monday next when I believe the Genl. [*P. Muhlenberg*] intends to attend and there the business I expect will be settled."

Thomas Jefferson to William Short. FC:letterpress copy, Jefferson Papers, DLC. For the full text, see *PTJ* 16:443–45. This is a postscript to a letter dated 27 May, above.

Notes the withdrawal of the Senate motion to convene at Philadelphia for the third session and the impossibility of the success of a similar one in the House.

John Samuel Sherburne to [*John Langdon*]. ALS, Langdon Papers, NhPoA. Written from Portsmouth, New Hampshire; postmarked. The recipient's identity is based on internal evidence.

Had not enclosed copies of Chief Justice Jay's charge as he promised in his last letter (26 May), because they were not printed yet; encloses two in the current letter, one of which he asks to be presented to "our amiable friend," Tobias Lear; if the state legislature decides federal officeholders cannot serve as legislators, he may have to return, under cover to Langdon, his commission as United States attorney.

George Thatcher to David Sewall. No copy known; acknowledged in Sewall to Thatcher, 13 June.

William Samuel Johnson, Diary. Johnson Papers, CtHi.

"Visits."

George Thatcher, Notes on the Steuben Bill. Ms., Thatcher Family Papers, MHi. Undated; the editors believe these notes were written during his reelection bid to the Second Congress, based on internal references to the published *House Journal* and Thatcher's implied intent to defend himself for various unrecorded votes on this controversial subject.

Thatcher voted to agree with a Senate amendment to strike $7,000 back pay.

SATURDAY, 29 MAY 1790

Cool. Rain (Johnson)

Henry Marchant to John Adams

'Tis done—'tis done—The Constitution this Day was adopted by Our State Convention, by a Majority of two—Never were Days of more anxiety, Labor and Assiduity, Hope and Fear, than the last six—It is a happy Circumstance that the Convention was adjourned to this Town, where we had the largest fœderal Interest, and little Influence of the Country Anties—The late Act [*Rhode Island Trade Bill*] passed by the Senate of Congress was an Instrument which we weilded with much Success and Execution: Nothing could be more timely—It would take a Quire of Paper to give You the entertaining particulars of this Week: But I know not how soon an Oppertunity may offer to New York—Therefore to Business.

Congress may soon rise, and may find it necessary to make the Act proper to the Introduction of this State into the Union, before Our Members may be able to reach Congress—Our Assembly will sit three Weeks from next Monday.

The Senators may be chosen then; The Representative cannot be, till four Weeks after. I have therefore inclosed You the Revennue Act of this State;[1] passed as nearly as possible to that of Congress—Here you will find all the Ports marked out and well described, and every Thing necessary for forming Your Acts or Bills—Names for officers I dare say have gone forward in Abundance long ago, and are in the Care and Charge of one Member or another. But if Satisfaction cannot yet be had on that Subject, or not untill Congress should rise—The Act may provide for this State, That the President have the intire Power of Appointment; at any Rate, untill Congress meet again.

I don't know but I am impertinent in this Business; but my Wish is to advance the publick Weal, and to give every Aid in my Power, that the wheels of Government, and Revennue, may be in Motion—what is well You may retain; You have been used to refine; The Dross You may throw away.

Upon this happy Occasion I congratulate You Sir, And thro' You Sir, I desire to congratulate the President, Our fœderal Head and Father; Congress and all well Wishers to the building up Our grand fœderal Cause and Government—With sincere Respects to Mrs. [*Abigail Smith*] Adams, Compts. to the Family and all Friends, without Time to add, having come this Moment out of Convention, and amidst the din & Noise of Bells, Huzzas and Guns.

P. S. Amidst my hurry I had forgot to acknowledge the Honor done me by yours of the 20th. of March, which would have been answerd before, but that I was tired of Conjectury, and wished for something substantial to communicate—Part of Yours will hereafter require further attention.

ALS, Adams Family Manuscript Trust, MHi. Written from Newport, Rhode Island. An alienated fragment within the Adams Papers was apparently enclosed in this letter. Marked "N.B." (*Nota Bene*, or "note well") on the reverse, it reads:

> private
> There is some Reason to presume that Mr. H—l [*David Howell*] and Mr. B—d [*William Bradford*] of this State have made some Interest for the Place of D—t J—e [*District Judge*] The latter under the Friendship of Judge L—d [*Leonard*] of T—n [*Taunton, Massachusetts*] now in Congress—If Incouragement to either, should be early given It may become a delicate Matter afterwards to do what might be most wished.

The dating of this fragment is based on the fact that the next known letter from Marchant to Adams (7 June) mentions Bradford as being already well along in lobbying for the U.S. district judgeship that Marchant also, and successfully, sought.

[1]The Rhode Island legislature passed an act on 9 May 1789, imposing the same duties as those that might be imposed by any future revenue act passed by Congress and appointing the same categories of officers to collect them. In September it passed an additional act designating the collection districts.

Judith Sargent Murray to Winthrop and Judith Sargent

***

The ground upon which New York is built, was originally very unequal, but, with incessant labour, and industry, the hills have been thrown in to the Vallies, and it is now a fine extensive tract, nearly level—Everything in the City of New York, seems upon a larger scale, than in the Town of Boston—and I am told it covers a full third more ground. The streets are longer, and more capacious, and their is an air of thriftiness, as well as elegance about the buildings far surpassing any thing I have ever yet seen. The streets of New York are paved with more exactness than those of Boston, many of them are arched, and to obviate the inconvenience of pavements, to the stranger, they are generally raised on each side, several inches above the surface, and smoothly laid with brick, over which you may pursue your way, with much ease—The houses are principally of Brick and Brodway presents a pile of buildings, in the centre of which, the President resides, which are indeed truly magnificent—The Citizens of New York have erected many public buildings, no less than twenty Churches, among which are Episcopalians, presbyterans, Quakers, dutch Institutions, Roman Catholicks, and Jews The Columbian University is a spacious structure, presenting in Front no less than sixty windows—The Hospital, Bridewell and Work house, figure respectably, and I am told are under excellent regulations—St. Paul's Church Towers with mingling elegance, and grandeur, and is fronted by a Monument, sacred to the memory of General Montgomery, adorned with military insignia &c. &c.[1]—But my attention was principally attracted by the Federal Edifice ~~is~~ Its very air majestically descriptive, seems to designate it consecrated to National purposes, and it is of course interesting to every genuine American—Almost entirely unacquainted with the terms of Art, the attempt to delineate, may draw upon me an accusation of arrogance yet I will nevertheless hazard a slight sketch Its situation is pronounced ill judged—It is however erected at the head of broad street, of which it commands a complete view—an elegant church [*Trinity Church*] is nearly finished upon its right, and upon its left, a good street [*Wall Street*] of a thrifty appearance winds its way—The Federal structure is magnificently pleasing and sufficiently spacious—Four larg pillars in front, support an equal number of columns, with their pediment—A large gallery also, presents, in which in the presence of Almighty God, and in view of a numerous Concourse of people, the illustrious, and immortal Washington, took his oath of office, being thus solemnly inaugurated, and cloathed with powers, which we doubt not he will continue to exercise, with augmenting celebrity to himself, as well as for the public weal—Thirteen Stars, the American Arms, crested with the spread eagle, with other insignia in the pediment, tablets over each window, which tablets are filled with the thirteen arrows, surrounded with an olive branch, are among the principal ornaments which emblematically adorn, and beautify the front of the Federal Edifice—The entrance introduces into a square room, which is paved with stone, from which we pass on to the Vestibule in the centre of the pile—This Vestibule is lofty, it is floored with marble and highly finished, with a handsome iron Gallery, and a sky light richly adorned—From this Vestibule we proceed to the floor of the Representatives' Room, and through arches on either side, by a public staircase on the left, and a private one on the right, to the senate Chamber, and other apartments—The room appropriated to the Representatives is spacious, and elegant—It is worthy the respectable assembly now convened there—it is sixty one feet deep—fifty eight feet wide, and thirty six feet high—its ceiling is arched and I should have called its form Oval, but I believe the technical term is octangular—four of its sides are rounded in the manner of arches, which adds much to its beauty, and gracefulness—the windows are large, and wainscoted below, interrupted only by stoves, which I think are four in number—above are columns, and pilasters, with entablatures variously disposed, and in the pannels between the windows, trophies are carved, and the letters U.S. surrounded with Laurel—The Chair of the Speaker is opposite the principal door—and it is elevated three steps, the chairs of the members form around it a semicircle—a writing stand properly furnished, is placed before every chair. In one piece a number of these stands are connected, which piece forms a segment of a circle—upon the right and left of the speaker, are semicircular compartments, in which are tables for the accommodation of the Clerks—Over the great door, and fronting the Speaker two Galleries are erected—The lower Gallery projects considerably—This is commonly, during the Sessions of the Assembly, filled by gentlemen, and the upper Gallery is appropriated to Ladies—Besides these galleries, a space upon the floor, separated by a bar, may be occasionally occupied by visiting individuals—This apartment is furnished with three doors, exclusive of the principal entrance, all of which are conveniently disposed—The chairs, curtains, and hangings in this room, are of light blue harateen, fringed and tasselled, and the floor is elegantly carpeted—We have received many civilities from Mr. Goodhue, who introduced us into the upper Gallery, where we attended the debates of Congress, for near four hours—the scene was truly august, and as I threw my eyes around, taking a view of the Delegates of America thus convened, a solemn air pervaded my bosom—a new, and undefinable sensation originated a kind of enraptured of veneration, and I prepared to listen with most profound attention—But shall I own a truth—Let it be however be in a whisper—my reverential feelings considerably abated, as I observed the apparent negligence, of many of the members—a question of much importance was agitated, and investigated by the several Speakers—and that with a warmth, ~~an~~ and energy, which would have done honour to a Demosthenes, or a Cicero, while, with all imaginable sang froid, gentlemen were walking to, and fro—their hats occasionally on, or off—Reading the News Papers—lolling upon their writing stands—picking their nails, biting the heads of their canes, examining the beauty of their shoe Buckles, ogling the Gallery &c. &c. yet we were fortunate enough to hear some of the best Speakers, among whom were Mr. Maddison, Mr. Ames, Mr. Sedgwick, Mr. Jackson, and Mr. Vinning—From the stairs upon the left hand of the Vestibule, we reach a Lobby that communicates with the Iron Gallery, which leads on one hand to the door of the Representatives Room, and on the other to the Senate Chamber—The Senate Chamber is pleasingly decorated—the pilasters &c. are ~~are~~ highly ornamented, and amid the foliage of the Capitals, a splendid star makes its appearance, surrounded with rays, while a small medallion is suspended by a piece of drapery, with the interesting letters U.S. in a cypher—The ceiling presents a sun, and thirteen Stars, which appear in its centre—The Chimnies are finished with American Marble said to be equal for the beauty of its shades, and high polish, to any found in Europe—The Presidential Chair is, of course, stationary at the upper end of the senate chamber—It is elevated several steps from the floor, and placed under a superb canopy of crimson damask—The chairs arranged semicircularly, as in the room of the Representatives, with the window curtains, and hangings are also of crimson damask, and the floor is richly carpeted—From the throne, or chair of state, his highness, the Protector of the Union, delivers a speech at the opening, and close of a Session which doth not much vary either in form, or manner, from those delivered by a british Sovereign, we differ essentially in nothing, but in name, and it is possible the time is not far distant, which may invest us with royal dignities—There are in the Federal Edifice, many other apartments, besides those of which I have attempted a sketch, guard rooms, Committee Rooms, and a handsome library—In the room of audience, we were shown portraits of the reigning King, and Queen of France, which are very fine Paintings—One side of the Federal Edifice is furnished with a platform railed in with iron, which affords an agreeable Walk, and the cupola is in good taste, highly ornamental, producing a very pleasing effect and seeming to give a finishing to the whole—An elegant statue of Lord Chatham [*William Pitt the Elder*] once distinguishing a principal street in New York, and in a spacious square, majestically towered an equestrian figure of George the third King of Great Britain—But alas! such hath been the ascendancy, shall I say of Gothic animocity, as to procure their destruction—New York exhibits no promenade, equal to the Mall [*The Common*] in Boston—But we intend visiting the orangery, and the seats on the north river, on our way home, and we already know this River abounds with beautiful imagery—The North or Hudson's River, rolls its waters along its Banks—the sound divides it from long Island—Straton [*Staten*] Island is in view, with many other less considerable Islands—Thus variously are the Land, and water prospects displayed—New York, however suffers in the lack of *good water*—Every family not residing in the Bowery, being obliged to purchase tea Water &c. &c. New York is undoubtedly a populace, and opulent City; many of its streets reminded me of the picturesque views, which we have so often admired upon paper, at present the seat of Government, it may be considered as the Metropolis of America, but it is probable it will not retain this distinction—During our attendance in the Federal Edifice, a removal was proposed, seconded, and laid upon the table Philadelphia, and New York are rival Cities—The Southern Members are for convening in Philadelphia The question hath been frequently agitated, until it has become annexed to the most important National concerns—I am told there is an agreement between the Southern, and Eastern Members—If the Eastern delegates give their voices in favour of one question, the Southern Gentlemen, will aid them in another! If this information be correct, will not that august Body depart (while engaged in this kind of dangerous and unbecoming traffic,) much from their dignity? Is it not bartering the public weal? Yet Members of Congress are but Men.

***

Ms., Murray Papers, Ms-Ar. For the full text, see *Murray*, pp. 88–101. Like many of Murray's letters, particularly those describing her travels, this letter presents problems. The ALS is not extant, the copy is written on paper not manufactured until after 1790, and large portions paraphrase an article that appeared in the June 1789 issue of the *Massachusetts Magazine* (reprinted in *DHFFC* 15:33–35). Furthermore, Murray was a creative writer and some of her description may be colored by that fact. Indeed, Janet Carey Eldred and Peter Mortensen in *Imagining Rhetoric: Composing Women of the Early United States* (Pittsburgh, 2002), pp. 75–88, argue that Murray believed, in effect, that it "falls to the Republican Mothers to instruct the new nation in the art of plagiarism."

---

[1] General Richard Montgomery (b. 1738) died leading the unsuccessful assault against Quebec on New Year's Eve 1775. Within weeks, Congress voted £300 for a monument to honor the first and highest ranking Continental Army general killed during the Revolutionary War. In Paris, Benjamin Franklin procured the services of noted sculptor Jean Jacques Carrieri (1725–92), and the first monument commissioned by the United States government

was erected under the west portico (on the Broadway side) of St. Paul's Chapel by November 1787. Peter Charles L'Enfant supervised the work, adding ornamentation of his own design that critics derided as tawdry and more appropriate for the stern of a French packet. Montgomery's remains were removed from Quebec in 1818 and re-interred under the monument, which remains to this day (*Iconography* 5:1222, 1599, 6:36).

Jeremiah Olney to Philip Schuyler

I am happy to inform you that my fears Communicated to you in my last Letter Respecting the Result of the Deliberations of our Convention, on the Subject of the New Constitution are at an end, the Convention having this day adopted Said Constitution by a Majority of Two Votes—Much in the form as was done by the State Convention of New York,[1] permitt me my Dear Freind to Congratulate you on this Happy event, our Genl. Assembly are to Convene on the Second monday in June Next when the Senators will be Chosen who will go forward Immediately to Congress—~~I propose my Intention is to be in New York~~—perhaps the appointment of the Revenue officers will not be Made untill the arrival of our Senators, but Shoud it take place before? ~~I~~ permitt me Dr. Sir to Request your Interest with the President, in favour of my appointment to the office of Collector for the ~~Port~~ District of Providence &c. the appointment I have from the President to pay the Invalids on the 5th of June next[2] prevents my going Immediately on to New York, however I hope to Compleat this business & ~~be there~~ have the pleasure of Seeing you by the 15th or 20th of June—Colo. Barton takes passage in the Packett that Sayles this Evening for New York,[3] he has An intention of opposing me as Collector, I mention this that you & my Freinds may be prepared to Counteract him.

FC:dft, Domestic Letters, Miscellaneous Correspondence, State Department Records, Record Group 59, DLC. Written from Newport, Rhode Island.

---

[1] Like New York's convention, which also ratified by a margin of only two votes, Rhode Island's ratification was accompanied by a series of proposed amendments to the Constitution. Among these were radical proposals unique to Rhode Island, including the adoption of laws and regulations to effectually prevent the importation of slaves as soon as possible and the requirement that after 1793 all amendments to the Constitution would be ratified by eleven of the original thirteen states. See *DHFFC* 3:570–77.

[2] Hamilton notified Olney on 4 February that the President had appointed him to pay Rhode Island's invalid pensioners under the terms of the Invalid Pensioners Act [HR-29].

[3] Col. William Barton was entrusted by the convention's president David Owen with delivering notice of Rhode Island's ratification, but not, significantly, the formal certificate of notification. For the suspected motive for withholding the certificate, see Henry Marchant to John Adams, 7 June, below.

Josiah Parker to the Representatives of Accomack County, Virginia

Not hearing who is elected I do not know to whom to address myself personally—not hearing from you induces me to suppose a miscarriage of my letters—hence I have changed the direction.

Inclosed is some papers which will give you a feint Idea of the proceeding of Congress. on my return Shall transmit you a Sett of our Journals which will shew you the Share of business assignd me by Congress. Presumeing that my conduct has merited the approbation of my Constituents. I request you will inform the Citizens of Accomack, that I again offer my services to represent them in Congress at the Election to be held on the first Monday in Septr. next. do me the favor to acknowledge the receipt of this.

ALS, John Cropper Papers, ViHi. Place to which addressed not indicated. The county's representatives to the upcoming session of Virginia's House of Delegates were John Cropper, Jr. and Thomas Custis.

Theodore Sedgwick to Pamela Sedgwick

I fear I shall be obliged to inhale the poluted air of New York a much longer time than I expected. A week from next monday is now assigned as the time to take again into consideration the assumption of the state debts. This time was agreed upon by the friends of the measure because Wadsworth was unexpectedly called home to see his sick son [*Daniel*], and poor Bland now lies at the point of death. This gentleman is the only man we have with us from the state of Virginia.[1]

***

I fear now the session of congress will continue 3 or 4 weeks longer, though madison says he expects it will be concluded in a few days. This I presume cannot be the case. As if we had not at present sufficient causes of dissention, the pensylvania members have brought forward again the question of adjourning to Philadelphia. This at least is a great task of patriotism.

As yet the little girls have sent me no transcripts of Peter Pinder. Tell them Papa says that they are idle, lazy gypsies.

Adieu, best beloved of my soul.

[*P. S.*] I have the pleasure to inform you the president still continues geting well, though his disorder has greatly emaciated him.

ALS, Sedgwick Papers, MHi. Place to which addressed not indicated. The omitted text relates news of family friends and of his visit to Sarah Wentworth Morton a few evenings earlier.

[1] Meaning, the only Virginia congressman who favored assumption.

Theodore Sedgwick to Pamela Sedgwick

Your kind but short letter of the 23rd. I have had the pleasure to receive this evening, and I cannot go to rest without first acknowledging my obligations to you for it. It gives me the most sincere pleasure to be informed that dear little Robert [*Sedgwick*] still continues to grow better. From present appearances I can't but indulge a hope that a steady pursuit of the course you are in will produce the desired effect. Could I indulge the hope one part of your letter would seem to inspire of seeing you in this town, my tedious absence would be less irksome to me.

I am not surprised, my love, that you are uneasy with your lonely situation. The reflection is inexpressibly painful to me. I mentioned to you in the letter I wrote this day the uncertainty of the time of adjournment. I am this evening informed that Mr. Madison says congress will not continue together but a few days. his influence, if he is in earnest will be considerable. I am by no means certain I should not join him, so great is the perplexity of proceeding under our present circumstances.

I have waited till within a few days with regard to the settlement of my public account[1] hoping to find a season of leisure. Dispairing of that I am now attending to the business, which requires more time than I can spare with comfort to myself. I do endeavour, my Love, to get my necessary rest, but sometimes fail. Will you be so kind as to be very perticular as to yourself on this account.

I shall write the misses each a few lines tomorrow. tell Master Theodore his papa would thank him for a little letter—kiss my other sweet little ones for me. I hope I shall see my little lisper [*Henry Dwight Sedgwick?*] in his waistcoat and overalls when I get home.

I have a letter from my Brother [*John*] in which he says my mother [*Ann Thompson Sedgwick*] is dangerously ill. I regret with pain that I did not visit her when I was at home.

ALS, Sedgwick Papers, MHi. Place to which addressed not indicated.

---

[1] The accounts related to Sedgwick's service as a commissary of supplies for the Continental Army's Northern Department, 1775–78 (Richard E. Welch, Jr., *Theodore Sedgwick, Federalist* [Middletown, Conn., 1965], pp. 24–26). Charges that Sedgwick had defaulted on public funds advanced for his commissary purchases dodged him throughout the first federal election; see *DHFFE* 1:723–27. An intriguing denouement is provided in a letter dated 2 January 1794 from Samuel Lyman, Sedgwick's principal opponent in the first federal election, to Georgia Representative Baldwin, with whom Lyman had studied divinity at Yale. Lyman claimed that sometime during the second or third session of the FFC, Sedgwick "most grossly imposed upon" his "particular Friend," Auditor of the Treasury Oliver Wolcott, Jr., to receive $14,000 in duplicate receipts that Sedgwick had already applied towards his outstanding account, "in order thereby to deceive and defraud the Public." Lyman's source was evidently Oliver Phelps, who was one of Commissary Sedgwick's contractors, partnered with

him as a government contractor in 1782, and speculated with him in western New York State lands during the FFC. While wishing to maintain his anonymity, Lyman suggested that Baldwin share the letter with Connecticut Representative James Hillhouse "to make good use of the Information" (Baldwin Papers, GU). Some of Sedgwick's army supply accounts are in box 9, folder 27, Sedgwick papers, MHi.

George Thatcher to Nathaniel Wells

The Bill for funding the continental debt, exclusive the State debts, passed, the last week, to be engrossed, and will be read the third time on the morrow.

On motion, by the opposers of the assumption, the Committee of the whole was discharged, on wednesday, from any farther consideration of the Bill for providing for the national debt, so far as it relates to an assumption of the State debts—This motion was carried by a junction of those who are adverse to an assumption in any modifycation whatever, & such as are in favor of an assumption, but wish to have it in a Bill by itself—and disconnected with the provision for the Continental debt—It now only remains to be decided, whether the former, or latter description makes a majority in the House.

The propositions, inclosed in my last, being severed from the Bill then under consideration, were, on thursday, moved in the House and a motion was then made by the anti-assumptionists, that they be taken up on the first monday of December next—the designe of this motion was evidently & professedly to put an end to the whole object of the mover of the propositions [*Boudinot*]—However, after some little debate, it was agreed they should be taken up on monday week—but we cannot conclude from this, that they will be adopted—some, perhaps, & I have no doubt of it, voted for taking them up, who, nevertheless, will, on the final question, be against them.

I ought to have observed that by the Bill for ~~providing~~ funding the continental Debt—it is provided that the old emission of paper money shall be considered as part of the public Debt, & redeemed at seventy five for one.

The motion, made in the Senate, for meeting of Congress, the next Session, at Philadelphia did not meet so favourable a reception as the mover [*Morris*] expected—the members being divided, he withdrew it—The same motion has since been made in the House by Mr. Fitzsimmons—And at the same time Mr. Butler, from South Carolina, gave notice to the Senate, that on monday, (tomorrow) he should move for leave to bring in a Bill fixing the Seat of permanent residence of Congress—What will be the event of these two motions I will not say—but I am rather of opinion they will terminate in one Bill for fixing the permanent Seat, & till that shall be prepared, Congress to reside at N. York.

FC, Thatcher Family Papers, MHi. Sent to Boston. The reference to "(tomorrow)" suggests that at least part of this letter was actually written on 30 May.

[*David Daggett,*] A Republican to Messrs. Printers (No. 3)

THE old maxim is "Great bodies move slowly," but that must be a *very* great, unwieldy and useless body which does not move *at all.*

In my last I promised to attempt telling you to what business Congress have had time to attend.

Immediately after the meeting of Congress in March 1789, came up the *great* question of ascertaining the mode of communicating messages, &c. from the house of representatives to the senate[1]—This question drew forth many specimens of eloquence—and Chesterfield's whole doctrine upon the subject of making bows and obeisances[2] was digested by the committee appointed for the purpose and incorporated into their report—I accidentally happened in the gallery when this report was read—an interesting debate ensued (for it was an *interesting* question) and the subject was discussed as tho' the fate of an empire had depended on the issue. After much time and altercation, it was agreed that the messenger from one house to the other, should *walk, bow* and deliver his *papers* or *verbal messages*, in the ordinary form of doing such business—and so this *great* and *momentous* affair ended without creating much party-spirit and with the *trifling* expence to the Union of 1000 or 1500 dollars.

One great event usually accompanies another—very soon the subject of giving a *title* to the President came upon the carpet[3]—It was warmly contended, on one side, that titles were fashionable in all polite nations—that supreme magistrates were destitute of all essential qualities without them, and that his "HIGHNESS" would sound better than simply "The President." On the other hand, it was urged, that the idea of giving titles was too monarchical or aristocratical for this young empire, and that a spirit of republicanism ought to characterize all our proceedings. It was finally left where the constitution had expressly placed it, that the first magistrate should be called "The President of the United States," and the wisdom of that body should have informed them of this fact long before.

A report of a committee which allowed a greater compensation to the members of the senate than to the representatives, soon engaged their attention, and called up speakers from all sides of the house[4]—At length they concluded, that they were equal in power & dignity to the senate, & determined that there should be no difference in their pay.

Before Congress had made provision for the payment of a single creditor, or were the proprietors of a single foot of land, we find them in a *severe engagement*, upon the question where the seat of government should be fixed. While foreign benefactors were despising us for our ingratitude in neglecting to make provision for the repayment of money generously loaned, and while the widow and orphan, the bankrupt soldier and the defrauded officer, were looking, from the depths of their distress, for relief, our federal legislature were attempting to plunge still deeper in debt, by purchasing a sufficiency of territory and erecting suitable buildings for their permanent residence. Federal-hall and New-York were theatres on which they could not display themselves with sufficient lustre.

This subject agitated the feelings of every member—various places were pointed out as being the most proper for the accommodation of this illustrious body, and the advocates for each place described it's excellencies in all the flowers of language. To the Potowmac, as answering the description which Milton [*in Paradise Lost*] gives of the garden of Eden, Congress was politely invited.

"In this pleasant soil
It is a far more pleasant garden God ordained;
Out of the fertile ground he caused to grow
All trees of noblest kind for sight, smell, taste;
And all amid them stood the tree of life,
High eminent, blooming ambrosial fruit
Of vegetable gold."

It might be demonstrated that the discussion of this subject cost the United States more than 5,000 dollars.

A recess of Congress was proposed some time in the month of August—The merits of every question ought to be fairly tried, and therefore no adjournment could take place, till the conveniences and inconveniences were clearly stated, and several days spent in hearing the cogent arguments on one side and on the other—business was so urgent and came with such weight upon their minds, that they were mortified at the idea of quitting it.

At the meeting of Congress in January last, an insuperable obstacle against proceeding, presented itself—The difficulty was to determine whither the matters then begun and pending should be resumed in the stage they were left, or taken up de novo or *anew*—much time was spent upon this very *important* point—It strikes me that this question is similar to the following—suppose a company of joiners having framed and raised a house, should be obliged to quit it for a week, and on their return, should spend a month in debating whither the frame should be again taken asunder or the house covered in it's then situation.

The memorial of the Quakers relative to African slavery, has been agitated the present session, with great spirit and warmth—fine-spun speeches, of one, two or three hours in length, containing the most bitter invective and virulent abuse against that innocent and humane society, and arguments of equal prolixity, to exonerate from those aspersions, employed Congress for whole days and weeks—many of those declamations are handed us in the papers—We might admire the talent at satire which is so conspicuous and the happiness of the sentiment and expression, if the observations had been pertinent to the subject; but now we are only surprised at the patience of that body in sitting there hours to hear an harangue no more connected with the business before the house, than a description of the mode of marrying on the Cape of Good Hope, or a picture of Mahomet's Paradise.[5]

The petition of Baron [*Frederick William*] Steuben has cost the Union more money than he demanded—so that if nothing is allowed him, the subject pays his proportion of all he requires.[6]

Col. [*John*] Ely's memorial, after enduring a most severe trial in the committee and the house, was finally passed—the Senate have negatived it for this substantial reason, because he has already received a full compensation by this state—This fact could not be ascertained, tho' we had five members on the floor, till a sum far exceeding his expectation had been expended in discussing the memorial.[7]

The consideration of the Secretary's report, I agree, is a matter of the first magnitude, and therefore ought to have engrossed the undivided attention of Congress—yet nothing decisive is determined relative to the national debt—The question whither the State debts ought to be assumed, has been largely discussed, upon the merits of this I give no opinion—I must however doubt if it be prudent, to *consume* much time in considering whether debts ought to be *assumed* which I *presume* Congress cannot discharge till it *resumes* the œconomy and wisdom of the Congresses of 1775 and 6.

These several topics Congress have had time to dwell on. I omit the time which has been wasted in *expiring* speeches upon questions already decided. Congress have also had time to *appoint a committee to select a library for their education*—Of this a word or two next week.

P. S. Please to inform the writer in your last, under the signature of FREDERICK,[8] that I must be excused at present from answering him—I am now dealing with superiors, viz. the Congress of the United States—when I shall quit them and descend to address myself to their door-keepers and sweepers, he and his very *pertinent, candid*, and *liberal* observations may chance to be noticed.

[New Haven] *Connecticut Journal*, 2 June; reprinted at New York City (*NYJ*, 15 June) and Philadelphia. For information on this series and its author, see the location note to A Republican to Messrs. Printers (No. 1), 15 May, above.

[1] For this issue, see *DHFFC* 8:783–87.

[2] Philip Dormer Stanhope, Fourth Earl of Chesterfield (1694–1773), commented on etiquette in letters to his illegitimate son that were published in 1774.

[3] For this issue, see *DHFFC* 8:729–35.

[4] See Salaries-Legislative Act [HR-19], *DHFFC* 6:1833–45.

[5] For these petitions, see *DHFFC* 8:322–38.

[6] For the Steuben petition, see *DHFFC* 7:203–46.

[7] For the Ely petition, see *DHFFC* 7:320–25.

[8] See Frederick to Messrs. Printers, 26 May, above.

Other Documents

John J. Bleecker to Philip Schuyler. ALS, Schuyler Papers, NN. Written from Albany, New York.

Asks Schuyler to make enquiries at the comptroller's (Nicholas Eveleigh) office about the status of an unsettled Indian department account from 1778, involving Timothy Edwards and Volckert Douw.

Bartholomew Burges to John Adams. ALS, Adams Family Manuscript Trust, MHi. The enclosure is unlocated.

Was honored by Adams's offer some time earlier to "present to your friends in Congress" any memorial Burges might prepare, "pointing out the eligibility of the Americans establishing factories in the East Indies, and of striking up Commercial treaties with the Indostan, and other Asiatic powers"; was to have done so as soon as he secured some income from a second edition of his book (*A Short Account of the Solar System* [Boston, 1789]), the profits of which he was subsequently swindled out of; has come to New York City to promote his published proposal, which he encloses, for opening "a private Marine Academy" and "a Marine Intelligence Office" where "Captains of Vessells of all denominations should be supply'd with Charts" and other nautical aids, and for preparing "an Edition of large Terraquious Globes," which would "have a Tendency towards promoting useful Knowledge in this Empire"; solicits Adams's and Washington's patronage.

Thomas Fitzsimons to Benjamin Rush. A ghost of Fitzsimons to Rush, 28 May, mistakenly created by *Carnegie Book Catalog* 157(1951):153.

Theodore Foster to Caleb Strong. No copy known; acknowledged in Strong to Foster, 3 June.

Benjamin Goodhue to Samuel Phillips, Jr. No copy known; acknowledged in Phillips to Goodhue, 3 June.

Benjamin Huntington to Anne Huntington. ALS, Huntington Papers, CtHi. Place to which addressed not indicated. This is a postscript to Huntington's letter of 25 May, printed above.

Has purchased for her: calico fabric, shoes, flour, coarse linen, and a coffee mill; "I Shall not think it Strange if you dont write often to me nor would I have you make any Exertions of that kind I cannot Desire it."

Benjamin Lincoln to Theodore Sedgwick. ALS, Sedgwick Papers, MHi. Written from Boston; postmarked 1 June.

A large number of invalid veterans in Massachusetts still need to have their cases examined; Congress is right to set a deadline for the completion of the business, or the state legislature "will be greatly harrassed by applications."

William Paterson to Governor William Livingston. ALS, Livingston Papers, MHi. Addressed to Perth Amboy, New Jersey; carried by Robert Hoops.

A bout of Influenza kept him sick at (New) Brunswick for more than two weeks, prior to returning to Congress a day or two earlier; will draw up and send a writ for a local judicial procedure; Congress has not yet received New Jersey's ratification of the Amendments to the Constitution.

Theodore Sedgwick to Samuel Henshaw. No copy known; acknowledged in Henshaw to Sedgwick, 3 June.

Theodore Sedgwick to Henry Van Schaack. No copy known; acknowledged in Van Schaack to Sedgwick, 5 June.

George Thatcher to David Sewall. FC, Thatcher Family Papers, MHi.

Wrote Daniel Hooper sometime in February that he might be able to help "on the subject you mention" (a loan of money) upon Thatcher's return "which I supposed would be in may if I recollect"; when in Boston last, began a conversation with Governor John Hancock "leading to yourself and another Gentleman," and dined with him the next evening, but the large company prevented them from talking up the subject again; will try to talk to the governor again en route home.

Daniel Hiester, Account Book. PRHi.

Paid for *CR* through 24 May.

Letter from New York. [Portland, Maine] *Cumberland Gazette*, 29 May. This is probably from a letter written by Thatcher to the newspaper's editor, Thomas B. Wait.

"The Bill for funding the Continental debt, exclusive of the State debts, will to-morrow be read a 3d time, and pass without opposition. Some who have opposed the assumption and funding the State debts in the same bill with the Continental, have declared in favour of the measure, provided the advocates would permit the Continental debt to be funded by itself, and bring forward propositions for the assumption and funding the State debts in a bill by themselves. These propositions were laid on the table on Thursday, & will be taken up on Monday week."

[Philadelphia] *Pennsylvania Journal*, 2 June.

A letter from New York of this date indicates that the question of adjourning to Philadelphia will be taken up on 2 June, and that "the opinion of the best judges in New-York" is that Congress will agree.

Letter from Lexington, Kentucky, to Winchester, Virginia. *NYMP*, 15 June (the date on which members of Congress would have seen it). Received at Winchester, 1 June; the letter must have been written before 29 May.

A group of Indians came into the neighborhood the day before, killed several whites, took several children prisoner, and carried off some horses; much trouble is expected this summer "as the savages appear to be determined on every barbarity and mischief in their power."

SUNDAY, 30 MAY 1790

Cool (Johnson)

Abigail Adams to Cotton Tufts

I received your kind Letter of May last week I was very sorry to hear that you and your Family had not escaped the prevailing Sickness. the disorder has universally prevaild here. not a single one of our Family, except mr. Adams has escaped, and polly [*Tailor*],[1] it was very near proving fatal too. We Have been in very great anxiety for the president, during the state of suspence, it was thought prudent to say very little upon the subject as a general allarm might have proved injurious to the present state of the Government, he has been very unwell through all the spring. labouring with a Billious disorder but thought, contrary to the advise of his Friends that he should excercise [*it*] away without medical assistance; he made a Tour upon Long Island of 8 or ten Days which was a temporary relief, but soon after his return he was seayd [*seized*] with a voilent plurisy Fever attended with every bad symptom, and just at the Crisis was seayd with Hiccups & rattling in the Throat so that mrs. Washington left his room thinking him dying The Physicians apprehended him in a most Dangerous state. James powder[2] had been administerd, and they produced a happy Effect by a profuse perspiration which reliefd his cough & Breathing, and he is now happily so far recoverd as to ride out Daily, I do not wish to feel again such a state of anxiety as I experienced several days I had never before entertaind any Idea of being calld to fill a place that I have not the least ambition to attain to. the age of the two gentlemen being so near alike that the Life of one was as probable as that of the other; ~~and~~ but such a Train of fearfull apprehensions allarmed me upon the threatning prospect that I shudderd at the ~~prospect~~ view. the weight of Empire, particularly circumstanced as ours is, without firmness without age and experience without, a revenue setled, & establishd, loaded with a Debt, about which there is little prospect of an agreement, would bow down any man who is not supported by a whole Nation & carry him perhaps to an early Grave with misiry & disgrace. I saw a Hydra Head before me, envy Jealousy Ambition, and all the Banefull passions in League. do you wonder that I felt distrust at the view? yet I could not refrain from thinking that even a Washington might esteem himself happy to close his days before any unhappy division or disasterous event had tarnishd the Lusture of his reign.

For the Assumption of the debts you will see in the papers a wise and judicious speach of Father Sherman as he is call'd, and a very able & lengthy one of Mr. Ames's.[3] all has been said upon the subject that reason justice, good policy could dictate. I hope it will yet take place. but Mr. M[*adison*]. leads the Virginians like a flock of sheep. if congress should rise without assuming, I perdict that the next year will not be so tranquil as the last, let who will hold the reigns.

***

ALS, Adams Family Manuscript Trust, MHi. Addressed to Boston. The omitted text discusses Tufts's management of the Adamses' financial affairs at home, including one expense that Abigail wishes "had been laid out in paper securities, then one might have had a *chance* of some benifit from it," and the Harvard College commencement of the Adamses' son Thomas.

---

[1] A local girl whom Adams took with them from Braintree, Massachusetts, to serve as house staff at "Richmond Hill" and later at Philadelphia (Page Smith, *John Adams* [2 vols., Garden City, N.Y., 1962], 2:769, 808).

[2] James' powders (oxide of antimony and phosphate of lime) were first prescribed for fevers in 1747, to induce sleep and perspiration (*Drinker* 1:594).

[3] Both speeches were delivered in the COWH on 25 May; see *DHFFC* 13:1419–24, 1432–46.

Thomas Fitzsimons to Benjamin Rush

In my Last letter I accounted Candidly for the delay of Writeing to you. and the Gent. to whome I promised you I would write. I hope My Reasons were satisfactory for I should think myself Very unfortunate indeed if ~~my~~ any part of my Conduct should subject me to the Imputation of duplicity much less that of Sacrificing or Makeing a Cats paw of a friend.[1] my policy is not of the Machiavelian Kind and tho bred a papist I have never Subscribed to the Doctrine (said to be held by the Jesuits) that evil might be Committed if good was to result from it. ~~I~~ My experience on the Contrary has satisfyd Me that tho duplicity may be usefull for a Moment it is pernicious in the end.

I suspect that the delay of this business may be Very injurious to our Views but even under that Conviction it is absolutely Necessary that the Sense of the 2 Candidates[2] here should be so explicitly declared as to leave no room for doubt between their friends—and You cannot be surprized that there should be some hesitation in Makeing it—the Speaker has been flattered by his friends with hopes of Success. I suppose it must have been very flattering to him and it Required time & Solid Reason to induce him to Relinquish ~~a dignifyd~~ a prospect so very dignifyd and honorable as that of ~~of~~ the first Government in the Union. my share in this business has been Uncommonly delicate. I Know myself to be considered as Warmly attached to Mr. Morris—and Might therefore be subject ~~myself~~ to the suspicion of pressing The Speaker to Relinquish upon the expectation of promoteing the Views of the other. that was not my Motive yet it was Necessary I should conduct myself so as not to give Color to the imputation. I have been thus lengthy in ~~m~~ the Reasons for my Conduct as well to satisfy you for the present, as with a View to prevent any hasty suspicions in future—I may with truth add here that the delicacy of our situation here with Respect to the question of Residence has Rendered an incessant attention to that Object Necessary ~~And~~ which Combined with other public duties and a Necessary attention to some private ones furnishes Me with Abundant Occupation every hour in the day—We Mean to try our question of Removal tomorrow—it was deferred on friday at the Request of some friends—Who it would not be prudent to disoblige tho we were not convinced that their Advice was Salutary—to day being Sunday—I have time to write to Mr. [*George*] Latimer & Mr. McGiffin—I mean in a day or two to do the Same to [*William*] Lewis & [*Richard*] Peters. I saw the former the Morng. I left town,

& mentioned the subject to him he Appeared to receive it with Cordiality and I have no ~~doubt~~ Reason to doubt his sincerity if application could be made to Peters in the Way you have hinted, I am sure it would be most Effectual—but as I ~~have~~ do not admit the propriety of personal applications from the Candidates. I would not Recommend it I think the man Capable of Soliciting an office under our Governmt. except it be a pecuniary one ~~is~~ may be presumed to do it for his own Sake. And I hold it to be One of the great Errors of the people to expect Solicitations for What ought to be given [*seal*] Very different grounds—as soon as I [*seal*] from the Speaker sufficient authority to declare his Renunciation I will extend my Correspondence & Communicate to you every step I take in the business—you may Rely that your Communications to me are as Sacred as honor Can Render them and that they Never shall be made use of with[*ou*]t. Your Approbation. if our attempt tomorrow Suceeds you shall hear of it by next post if not I shall probably be too much Chagrined to write on the Subject.

ALS, The Gilder Lehrman Collection, on Deposit at the New York Historical Society, New York. [GLC 3408] Addressed to Philadelphia; franked; postmarked 1 June.

[1] To use a friend to do one's dirty work, as in the fable of the monkey who persuaded the cat to use its paw to pull some roasted chestnuts from the fire.

[2] The two candidates at New York City being considered for the governorship of Pennsylvania were F. A. Muhlenberg and Morris.

Benjamin Goodhue to Stephen Goodhue

I recd. yours of 25th. last Eve'g. and from your information am very apprehensive we may loose our Infant [*Stephen*], but I hope otherwise *** as to our politicks We are as we were, the question for having our next sessions in Philada. will come on tomorrow, and the great bussines must stop till that is decided, and there is no such thing as crouding it out—there is not any doubt but there is a majority in Congress for the assumption if it could be taken up on its own merits, but we are so circumstanced that We cannot obtain it without the aid of some of the Pensylvanians, and the N. Yorkers, and how to act in so critical a case is extreamly difficult, it surely is altogether immaterial whether we set here or Philada. to the people at large—if by going to Philada. we could get rid of any future vexation on this score and at the same time not offend the Yorkers, so as to make them turn about, (which is much to be fear'd) We might be in happier circumstances—its difficult to manage.

ALS, Goodhue Family Papers, MSaE. Addressed to Salem, Massachusetts; franked; postmarked. The omitted text relates to their joint commercial transactions.

Benjamin Goodhue to Michael Hodge

The bussines of funding and assumption, remains much the same as it has for some time, there is not the least doubt, but there is a majority in favour of the Assumption if it could be taken up simply on its own merits, but that banefull question of residence is so darling an object with the Pensylvanians and N. Yorkers that it mingles itself disgracefully in every great national measure and its impossible to croud it out, a motion is now before us that our next meeting shall be in Philada. and they mean to bring it on tomorrow—it is most assuredly of little or no consequence whether Congress set in Philada. or N. York to the Union at large, but its our great misfortune it should be made so by those two States, to that degree as to impede our public bussines, and ever will till the subject is some how or other, put more at rest then it is at present. whether by being in Philada. which is more central, that truly desirable object would be more likely to be attained, is I think the only question on which the merits of removal ought to rest. but we are circumstanced so peculiarly at this time, that its difficult to act without offending the members of the one State or the other in such a manner as to affect another question, and its certain the assumption cannot obtain without the aid of both—the Pensylvanians disclaim any connection between the two questions, and say it shall not affect their votes—what we have extreamly to regret is that the great National bussines must give place, to comparatively such paltry and local policy, and that its out of our power to avoid it.

Our passions would lead us to be revenged on such disturbers of our tranquility, if it could be done without sacrifising our policy and judgement which latter I conceive we should never part with.

ALS, Ebenezer Stone Papers, MSaE. Place to which addressed not indicated. All but the concluding sentence appear virtually verbatim in a letter of the same date from Goodhue to the Insurance Offices of Salem, Massachusetts (ALS, Goodhue Letters, NNS).

Christopher Gore to Rufus King

The Assumption has been again attempted, and lost—I sincerely hope no other delays will attend funding the continental debt—very dangerous consequences are to be apprehended to a future system of funding—it is verily true, that the doctrine of discrimination now finds advocates, among many, who have heretofore been consider'd as rational men, & men of understanding—what shoud you think of Judge [*Francis*] Dana's Genl. [*William*] Hull's and some others, equally important, advocating such doctrines in the most public, & unequivocal manner—these things are true.

and it is likewise true, that a spirit of opposition to the revenue laws has been created, and is increasing—People say, for what purpose do we pay our money into the Collector's chest—none of it returns—and what can oblige us to visit the Custom House, on an arrival? the most substantial men, in point of property, & hitherto, the firmest supporters of the present constitution, in Salem, have publicly exp[*ressed*] such sentiments, if not the very words.

These things, my dear friend, make me truly anxious that some men shoud be bound to this government by strong pecuniary ties, and which ties are not obvious to the public view—suppose a possible [*lined out*] event, the dissolution of the President, woud not, unless some chain, of more, & stronger links than now binds the union, shoud hold us together, the American People cease to exist as a nation—and let me ask what other chain so binding as that of involving the interest of the men of property in the prosperity of the Government.

ALS, King Papers, NHi. Written from Boston; postmarked.

Samuel Henshaw to Theodore Sedgwick

***

To morrow I intend moving for a Commee. to consider & report the most eligible method for choosing a Senator & Representatives to Congress.

I wish your opinion on the Subject, & hope it will reach me the Evening that this will arrive at N. York.

We are told from N. York, That the Assumption is certain, & that the majority will be considerable—I hope the account is true—and I rejoice that my Friend deserves so much of his *Country* for the part He has taken to effect it—And I have no doubt but *their* approbation & Gratitude will be expressed in their future conduct towards him.

How is the President's Health? and has Mr. Comptroller [*Nicholas Eveleigh*] had an opportunity to display his talents before him? Will Gerry & Goodhue assist you to promote the appointment of your Friend? I hope it will not be necessary for me to come on to N. York; least I should be again disappointed; but if it is, I will come.

P. S. Since writing this Letter, I am told, there are private letters in Town which announce, that the assumption is lost! Good God! how unstable are all human things—But I will forbear 'till I know the truth.

ALS, Sedgwick Papers, MHi. Written from Boston. The omitted text relates to state legislative business.

Frederick A. Muhlenberg to Benjamin Rush

I had last Week already taken down the Heads of a long Letter to You, which containd an Abstract of my public Life since its Commencement in the year 1779, & which involved a considerable part of the History of our [*Pennsylvania*] republican Party from that Time to this; but on reflection I have thought proper to withold it for the present & until I have the pleasure of seeing You, when I can give a fuller Detail of it. This much I will only say at present, that it hurts me that I cannot find Cause to thank those for any preferment in public Life, whose Cause I have ever espoused & faithfully served to the utmost Extent of my Abilities. Some times indeed my Conscience seems to upbraid me with Ingratitude to those whom from political principles according to my Judgment I was bound to oppose, but who notwithstanding have ever shewn more friendship to me than the former, for notwithstanding 10 Years Experience I am not yet politician enough to sacrifice every tender feeling or moral Obligation & I hope I never may be so consummate a one. Besides my own Example, I can quote the Treatment You have hitherto met with from those you so faithfully served. I lament it exceedingly & the more so when I cannot even to this Day discover a serious Disposition of rendering any Services to You, amongst those very People whose Battles You have successfully fought. I do not mention this to pay You a Compliment, they are the Sentiments of my Heart & correspond with the Opinion of other real friends of yours. The Transactions between Mr. Morris and myself concerning the next [*gubernatorial*] Election, & the Letter I wrote to Mr. Fitzimmons on the Subiect, I presume You are fully acquainted with. The reasons why I declined are set forth, they are the true ones, & such as I think will satisfy my friends & justify me in the Step I have taken. I sincerely wish the other Object, that of running Mr. Morris *success* fully may be as easily obtained. I confess I entertain great Doubt of it for however successfully we could heretofore carry Mr. [*John*] Dickinson—that Business was confined to one County only. this branches over the State, & is new to us & therefore uncertain. My own Wish never extended itself to that arduous Station—my friends first started it without my Knowledge, had I been previously consulted I should as readily have given my Opinion then as I did now. I think I stand a Chance, unless again opposed by my republican friends, of being continued in my present Situation, if so I desire no more. How far this may govern the Opinion of my friends, & I still flatter myself I have a few both in Town & Country I will not pretend to say. I am in their Hands & submit to their Decision. Should they ever think fit to leave me out of all public Employments I shall not regret it, for I am frequently disgusted with public Life & public Affairs my Heart pants for the tranquil Walk & domestic Happiness of private Life. The papers inform You of our proceedings in Congress. To morrow Week another Trial of Strength will take place on the Question of assuming the State Debts. The Bill for funding the foreign & domestic Debts is now engrossed, & ready for a third Reading & passage in our House. I am not yet reconcild to it, & can never consent to all its parts—that of funding the indents or Interest especially. The more I contemplate the whole System, and the more I hear it discussd, The more I must disapprove of it, & I seriously wish the whole Business might be put off, until the next Session—that Congress would now adjourn visit their Constituents—hear their Sentiments & return early in the fall of the Year to their Duty. Our Hopes of getting to Philada. were in some Measure frustrated in the Senate, by the Defection of several, whom we had a right to expect to be on our Side. But the Motion is withdrawn in that House, & is now on our Table. Tomor[*row*] it will be discuss'd in our House, & the prospect is good. At all Events we as pennsylvanians are determined, & I think consistent with our Duty to leave this place, & should we even be obliged to travel further South for a while. I need not tell you how improper a place New York is in every Respect, to be the Seat of Goverment. The funding System has in my Opinion contributed not a little to make it the most improper place on the Continent—I am sorry that too much undue Influence already prevails—Mr. McClay & Brother [*Peter Muhlenberg*] are well.

ALS, Miscellaneous Collection, PHi. Addressed to Philadelphia.

Philip Schuyler to Stephen Van Rensselaer

***

A motion is before the house of Representatives. to Adjourn Congress to Philadelphia If Messrs. Floyd Rensselaer & Haythorn could have been brought to Decide in favor of the Assumption of the state debts, we should Indubitably have retained Congress here for many years. but as the business now stands many who are anxious for the assumption, will rather than lose that favor the Motion, which I believe will be carried in both houses, perhaps we may retain Congress for four years by fixing the permanent seat, either at Delawar in the vicinity of Trenton [*New Jersey*], at the Susquehanna or Germantown [*Pennsylvania*], we wait for the decision of the motion in the house of representatives, before we can decide ~~on~~ ultimately on the plan we shall pursue.

I have a letter from Colonel [*Jeremiah*] Olney of providence of the 25th Instant. the Rhode Island Convention had convened on the preceeding day, and the appearances of an Adoption were very Slender. The Town of

Providence have in town meeting resolved that ~~unless~~ If the state does not Acceed to the constitution, that town will entreat the protection of Congress and seperate from the state. It is believed New port will do the like.

***

The President is so far recovered as to ride out in a carriage, but his constitution is much injured, and It will require great care to keep him up.

My health is restored, and I feel myself rather better than I have been for years past.

ALS, Smith Collection, NjMoHP. Place to which addressed not indicated. The omitted text relates to family news, including the loss of Schuyler's grandson (also Van Rensselaer's nephew), and state elections.

The Economy of Congress, exemplified in the Case of Baron Steuben

BARON STEUBEN had most liberal appointments during the war—pay as a Major General 166 dollars per month—pay as Inspector General 84 dollars per month—and 300 dollars per month for his table, &c. Got his commutation, and every allowance belonging to his rank—He, however, soon got out of money, & Congress made him a further grant of 7,000 dollars, on the 27th of September, 1785, which is expressly in full for all sacrifices and services; so that he had then cost us, exclusive of grants made to him by particular states, near 50,000 dollars specie. But here he has got in debt again, and flies to Congress for relief. The Senate was full, and divided on every question, and our President [*Adams*] uniformly gave his vote in favor of the Baron. The result is, that he has got a *pension, for life, of two thousand five hundred dollars per annum.*

IG, 5 June; reprinted at Portsmouth, New Hampshire; Newburyport, Boston, and Springfield, Massachusetts; Litchfield and New London, Connecticut; New York City (*NYJ*, 11 June); Trenton, New Jersey; Wilmington, Delaware; Baltimore and Georgetown, Maryland (present-day Washington, D.C.); and Edenton, North Carolina. The editors believe that this is a letter from Maclay to John Nicholson. It was written by a Senator, and Maclay, from Pennsylvania, was deeply involved in the issue. Nicholson is the likely recipient because he, unlike Benjamin Rush, to whom Maclay also wrote, used *IG* as his mouthpiece. For more on Frederick William Steuben's petition to the FFC for compensation, see *DHFFC* 7:201–46.

OTHER DOCUMENTS

Abigail Adams to Mary Cranch. ALS, Abigail Adams Papers, MWA. For the full text, see *Abigail Adams*, pp. 48–50. Addressed to Braintree, Massachusetts.

The influenza has been very violent and mortal particularly on Long Island; it is thought Congress will sit until July and then adjourn to

Philadelphia; "it would be a sad business to have to Remove. besides I am sure there is not a spot in the united States so Beautifull as this upon which I live [*'Richmond Hill'*], for a summer residence."

Jeremiah Hill to George Thatcher. ALS, Chamberlain Collection, MB. Written from Biddeford, Maine; postmarked Portsmouth, New Hampshire, 31 May.

Discusses religious prejudices; "I am glad to hear of the resurrection of the dry bones [*Ezekiel* 37:4] of old [*Continental*] paper Money"; "I want to enquire after the Post office Bill [*HR*-74] and my good friend *Amendment* to the Collection [*HR*-82] & coasting [*HR*-89] Laws."

Thomas Jefferson to Thomas Mann Randolph, Jr. ALS, Jefferson Papers, DLC. For the full text, see *PTJ* 16:448–50.

Madison has just received a weather diary from Orange, Virginia, with which Jefferson has compared his own observations from his short stay at Monticello; the fate of the House resolution to convene next session in Philadelphia is uncertain; the assumption of the states' war debts may prevail; the Trade and Navigation Bill will probably pass; Bland is dangerously ill.

George Thatcher to Sarah Thatcher. ALS, Thatcher Family Papers, MHi. Place to which addressed not indicated.

Has not received a letter from her since his last; will not insist on her writing more than once every week or every two weeks; is sending twenty dollars to Thomas Dakin for delivery "to any body who shall call for it in your name—or lay it out as you shall direct"; enquires about son Phillips and daughter Sally; "I am anxious to take them into my arms, & give them a thousand kisses"; in a few days will send home some books "adapted to catch the attention of Children"; encourages Sally's reading lessons.

Oliver Wolcott, Jr. to Oliver Wolcott, Sr. ALS, Wolcott Papers, CtHi. Addressed to Hartford, Connecticut.

"Nothing of consequence has been accomplished in Congress, the question of assumption will be revived, but from present appearances it will not suceed—whether any provision will be made for the Debt except to divide what monies can be collected on account of the current interest may be considered as uncertain."

William Samuel Johnson, Diary. Johnson Papers, CtHi.

"St. Pauls."

Letter from Boston. *GUS*, 5 June; reprinted at Elizabethtown, New Jersey; Philadelphia; Baltimore; Richmond, Virginia; and Savannah and Augusta, Georgia.

"Unless we can effect a repeal of the excise laws, or if Congress does not interfere in our favor, we shall experience as dull a summer as ever we did during the contest with Britain; If the excise was equal throughout the union, we should acquiesce in it most cheerfully; by what I can learn our East-India voyages will turn out bad this year."

Letter from New York. [Boston] *Massachusetts Centinel*, 5 June.

"To-morrow we shall have the question to remove to *Philadelphia*. It seems probable that the Southern Members will be the principal combatants on this question. The President is well."

MONDAY, 31 MAY 1790

Cool (Johnson)

Tench Coxe to Tench Francis

Tis probable that before this reaches you you may have heard that the house of Reps. have determined that the next session of Congress shall be in Philada. by a Majority of 38 to 22, exclusive of the Speaker who would have made 39. New York was tried before & stood at 35 against & 25 for—& Baltimore upon a proposition in its favor in another form had a Majority of 14 against it—The Senate is now the place—A very judicious N. Carolinaman assures me both their Senators will be with us—and the Opinions seem much in our favor. Several things will operate for Us—so large a Majority of the Representatives—the fear of a proposition for the *permanent* Seat in Pennsa.—and some other considerations will ~~of~~ affect the votes of the southern people. I wish Mr. Morris was here. A Number of modes of informing him by the different stage routes have been vigilently attended to, and I trust he will be here by ten or eleven to morrow.

Rhode Island is in the Union. Their Convention adopted the Constitution on Saturday at 5 OClock by 34 to 32. Touch & go you will say, but they are in—we have time to fix this matter in the Senate before their Senrs. can be here.

I have troubled you with this line convinced that both points interest you much.

ALS, Coxe Papers, PHi. Addressed to Philadelphia; postmarked 1 June.

Roger Sherman to [*Simeon Baldwin*]

Enclosed is the last Gazette [*GUS*] & the Index to the first volumn. You will See that it is to be prefixed to the papers & make a Title Page. No. 47 [*17 March*] is not to be had So that the others must be bound with out it— The house have this day resolved, that the next session of Congress Shall be held at Philadelphia. I dont know how it will fare in the Senate.

The Assumption of the State debts is Assigned for next monday—The funding Bill is engrossed, and will probably pass the House to morrow It is expected that Congress will rise next month, but is uncertain what time.

ALS, Sherman Collection, CtY. Place to which addressed not indicated. The recipient's identity is based on the handwriting on the docket.

William Smith (Md.) to Otho H. Williams

I Recd. on Saturday last, a letter from Colo. Smith inclosing one to you, accompanied by Sundry papers from your Brother;[1] the papers, relative to the contract, I deliverd this morning, to the Auditor [*Oliver Wolcott, Jr.*], who says he will state & Settle the Accots. & furnish me, with a transcript for your government but he added that you had recd. a payment in advance, & he was of opinion, there would not be any money due on that Accot.

The powers of Attorney for receiving the Soldiers pay, being in Mr. [*Robert*] Elliots name, *only* cannot be negotiated, without a power of Attorney from him. [*lined out*] I urged that you, had transacted business of a Similar Nature, *when here*, & that I only represented you, on this head To which the paymaster replied, that you acted under a general power of Atty. from Elliot & [*Elie*] Williams, but those powers being from Eliott alone, *that could not be admitted* even were you on the Spot. If therefore I can Serve you in this business, Mr. Elliot must transmit to me his power of Atty.

The question was taken this forenoon on the adjournment of Congress from this City to meet for their Next Session at Philada.—I offerd Baltimore as a Substitute for that City, which was Supported by a respectable Number of friends, but Unfortunately for Poor Baltimore, the Representatives from Maryland were devided, Gale, Carroll, & Contee for Philada.—the other three for Balto. & So the question was lost, it is now resolved in our house that the next Session Shall be held in Phila. for which I finally voted, on failure of the other question—A Bill was brot. into the Senate this Morning for fixing the Permanent Seat leaving a blank to be filled up, & Congress to Sit here Untill a certain time, I dont know how long—perhaps it may all end in Smoke.

P. S. Inclosed you have yr. Brothers letter wh. S[*amuel*]. Smith directed me to open, if you were gone.

ALS, Williams Papers, MdHi. Addressed to Baltimore.

[1] Williams's brother, Elisha Otho ("Elie"), had received an army contract with the federal government in September 1787. Both Samuel Smith and Elisha O. Williams forwarded mail to Otho H. in care of Smith (Md.) under the impression Williams was still at New York City, where he had spent much of that month.

Henry Wynkoop to Reading Beatty

This day the Proposition for meeting & holding the next Session of Congress at Philadelphia was taken up in the House of Representatives, A World of maneuvering as usual was introduced for the purpose of embarrassing but the Freinds of the Measure were prooff against every Attack & by two oClock the Question was farely brought before the House, when the Votes stood 38 for & 22 against it, so that we had a majority of 16 on the floor & the Speaker makes 17. I beleive I told You in my last that the Convention of Rode Island were sitting; they met last monday, Debated until Saturday, when at 5 oClock in the afternoon the Question on the Adoption of the general Government was put, ~~when~~ 34 were for & 32 against it, perhaps by Saturday next we may expect their Senators; Thus You see Doctor, it is hot work here, our getting into Pensylvania now entirely rests with the Senate, with whom the great majority in the House of Representatives, must have an Influence, two more Votes in that Body previous to the coming in of Rode-Island does the Busyness. Spent sunday at Ackqueekenonk[1] & Newark, Freinds all tolerably well except Peggey Cummings, who was last evening better.

Do let me know precisely how Mama [*Sarah Newkirk Wynkoop*] is & let me not be deceived with flattering Representations, but let me know the wor[*s*]t, I can make the best of it myself, the various Accounts hitherto received give me uneasyness.

ALS, Wynkoop Papers, PDoBHi. Place to which addressed not indicated.

[1] Aquakinunk (present-day Passaic), New Jersey, lay half way along the road from Newark to the Great Falls of the Passaic River, "one of the pleasantest roads for a party of pleasure in New Jersey" (Jedidiah Morse, *The American Geography* [Elizabethtown, New Jersey, 1789; reprint, 1970], p. 283).

Horatio to Mr. McLean

In your Gazette of Saturday last, you have inserted, under the Boston head, a piece said to be *Original Communication from New York*,[1] expressed in terms highly disrespectful of Mr. Madison. Could I suppose that those *original* communications from New-York, sent to the printer of the *Massachusetts Centinel*, were the sentiments of a politician, or a scholar; it would give me little trouble to refute what shadow of reasoning they contain. But, convinced as I am, that the piece is the effusion of a person, who, instead of attending to the trade which he has assumed, commenced politician some 10 or 12 months since, and has endeavoured to spread his lame opinions over the continent.[2] Under this impression, I feel myself degraded in stooping to take notice of any thing which may have fallen from the pen of such a writer.

It may not, however, be improper to make a few remarks in a general way. *And first*, I am authorised by some of the most respectable members from the Eastward, to declare, that they are disgusted with the writings of the person who is supposed to be the author of those *original* communications; neither do they approve of his officiousness in advocating the assumption of State debts, because they have digested their own plans, and they have no desire to hurt the feelings of any of the Southern members, which must be the intention of the inflamatory pieces that are so often trumphed up from the *same sink* of impertinence.

It is the distinguishing privilege of the citizens of a free government to examine the conduct of those, who are entrusted with the administration of public affairs; to weigh, with impartiality, the actions of their representative, to whom the important task of deciding on the lives and properties of their fellow citizens has been committed; and to ascertain, with justice and precision, whether they deservedly possess, and or have wantonly violated the confidence of the people. The language of panegyric might be exhausted, were an adequate encomium conferred upon men who, actuated purely by a regard for the public welfare, have expended their time and exercised their talents for the purpose of promoting it; while, on the other hand, no terms are sufficiently strong to reprobate the measures of those false patriots and writers, who, abusing the credulity of the people, make use of their confidence only to deceive them.

The authority of these indisputable truths will support me in giving the lie direct to the following assertion of the New-York communicator. "You know there is not a great majority of the *people*, in favour of paying them (*i. e.* the public creditors) or rather there is nearly a *majority* that would *without scruple*, apply the sponge."[3] Was there ever such an insult offered to a nation! This scribler has the effrontry to say in the face of the world that a *majority of the people* of America are dishonest men. Whether the above quoted paragraph does not express it in direct terms, let the people judge; and condemn the baseness of the assertion, together with its *author*, to eternal contempt and infamy.

It would be well for the supporters of this scribler, that they consulted their duty, rather than the gratification of their resentments; they would not then have insulted the public by calumniating that legislature which the voice of their country had invested with authority, nor would they have been reduced to the wretched necessity of reviling a particular man, because he did not so far degrade the majesty of the people as to consult the interests, or be influenced by the opinions of any party, but studied the happiness of all.

The following words of the piece to which I allude—"The public creditors should not be too clamorous; for, if Congress does not provide for them, they are gone." As they convey no clear ideas, so I am certain they were suggested by none. But had the folly of the author alone, weak as he is, furnished a subject of censure and complaint, his labours might have passed unnoticed; they might have sunk neglected into those vast depositories of political compositions, the bare perusal of which, will instruct mankind: that to write, and to be informed, are widely different, and that no greater curse can possibly attend the descendants of Adam, than to be governed by men, whose prejudices, interests, and follies; not reason, constitute the rule of their lives, and guide of their actions.

The baneful spirit of aristocracy, or, in other words, the interest of the *few* in opposition to the interest of the *many*, appears clearly, as the light of heaven, in the sentiments which are attempted to be spread over the United States by the same person who uttered the assertion "that a majority of the people would, without scruple, apply the sponge;" an assertion as insolent as it is ill grounded, by involving in one general undistinguished censure, both government and people. Mr. Madison, and all the members who wished to postpone the assumption in order to collect the sense of their constituents, are villified for speaking the sense of the people, and the people (happy contradiction) are in their turn abused for having confided in their representatives. But it seems that the author of the libel esteems it perfectly unnecessary for members to ground their conduct upon the opinions of the people and posterity will scarcely believe that only 12 or 14 years after the establishment of a government, which had for its basis the common equality of all its citizens, a party should be found at once sufficiently weak and sufficiently hardy to stigmatize a member of the house of representatives for having conducted himself agreeably to the most popular opinions of his countrymen.

NYDG, 31 May, edited by Archibald McLean; reprinted at New York City (*NYP*, 1 June) and Philadelphia. Horatio Cocles, the most famous Horatio in the ancient world, legendarily held back an invading Etruscan army singlehandedly in the fifth century B.C. The author may have had the lesson of that story in mind by choosing the name.

[1] Printed under 16 May, above.

[2] The editors believe that the author of the "Original Communications" was John Fenno, publisher of the pro-administration *GUS*.

[3] To cancel or wipe out debt without payment.

Other Documents

John Brown Cutting to John Adams. ALS, Adams Family Manuscript Trust, MHi. Written from London. Cutting's letter to Jefferson is unlocated (*PTJ* 16:415n).

Encloses newspapers; understanding that Congress meant to adjourn sometime in May, he writes via Boston; has written fully to Jefferson on the impressment of American seamen; will forward in a separate letter any European news arriving the next day.

Jeremiah Olney to [*Henry Knox*]. ALS, Knox Papers, Gilder Lehrman Collection, NHi. Written from Providence, Rhode Island; answered 18 June. The recipient's identity is assumed from the letter's location. For a partial text, see *DHFFE* 4:416.

Office seeking: collector for Providence; regrets he cannot "be on the Ground myself" by attending at New York, like his competitor William Barton.

Henry Sherburne to Henry Knox. ALS, Knox Papers, Gilder Lehrman Collection, NHi. Written from Newport, Rhode Island; answered 6 June. For a partial text, see *DHFFE* 4:416.

Office keeping: collector at Newport; solicits Knox's interposition with such as he thinks best, particularly Schuyler, Langdon, and Gunn, "with whom I have had a personal Acquaintance"; cannot expect much help from Rhode Island's Senators, who will probably be antifederalist.

John S. Sherburne to [*John Langdon*]. ALS, Langdon Papers, NhPoA. Written from Portsmouth, New Hampshire. The recipient's identity is based on internal evidence and the letter's location.

If his election to the state legislature is opposed on grounds of his appointment as federal attorney for New Hampshire, asks Langdon to deliver the enclosed letter to the President, resigning that office; "I will take care to give you seasonable information on the subject"; thinks he will not be disqualified by the dual office holding, but if so, "I can with truth say that my resignation has gone on"; Langdon's family continues well.

Roger Sherman to Rebecca Sherman. ALS, Sherman Collection, CtY. Addressed to New Haven, Connecticut.

Has recovered his health; hopes Rebecca's return journey (from New York) has mended hers as well; the President has returned to normal health and has renewed his invitation to dinner for the following Thursday; will send household goods, and asks to be sent "my Nankeen Cloths & Striped Jacket, & 1 pr. white Silk Stockings"; hopes to be home in about three weeks.

Gideon Wanton to Pierce Butler. ALS, Washington Papers, DLC. Written from Newport, Rhode Island.

Office seeking: naval officer of Newport; asks "to interest your self in my continuance," although he is unknown to Butler, or "any gentlemen" of the Senate.

William Samuel Johnson, Diary. Johnson Papers, CtHi.

"Visits."

Letter from New York. [Winchester] *Virginia Centinel*, 16 June. White was probably the author of this letter.

"A Resolution has this day passed the House of Representatives, purporting that the next meeting of Congress shall be at the city of Philadelphia—by a majority of 16—viz. 38 to 22."

May 1790 Undated

Benjamin Goodhue to Stephen Goodhue

I have a little more hope of the assumption eventualy then I had, but I am decidedly of opinion there ought to be no funding without it, and I beleive this is the opinion of all our delagates and most of others who are friends to the assumption, this won't please perhaps some of the holders of Certificates, but it is just and it is true policy—if the assumption and funding takes place, the proposed duties will undoubtedly follow, this is certain, but my fears are they may push the high duties and excises for funding the Continl. debt without the assumption, which will for aught I see end in confusion and ruin.

ALS, Goodhue Family Papers, MSaE.

William J. Vredenburgh to [*John Laurance*]

In perusing Mr. Bland's report respecting arrears of pay due part of the Troops of Va. and N.C. Lines,[1] should it pass agreable to his report, I, as well as others, shall be greatly injured and the Door of Justice shut against me. I am one of those that Speculate in all kinds of Pay and Public Securities, due to officers or Soldiers of any line or State, and have now by me Sixty Assignments amounting in the whole by the Paymaster General's [*Joseph Howell, Jr.*] account to 1800 dollars. These assignments are in my favor, regularly executed before a Justice of the Peace and would have been paid long since—but there were a few [. . .] that had not come to hand, which I waited for and not wishing to trouble the Paymaster to settle them in small amounts. The above assignments are all that I have or Expect to have—out of which there are several of the Same persons pay that is claimed by other persons in this city and which I shall probably lose as those persons' claims are prior to mine. The objections I have to Mr. Bland's report are 1st. He requires the Transfer to be Executed before two Justices. Mine are before one. 2. A representative [*of the original claimant*]—I am only assigne and attorney. 3d. [*that the transfer be for*] A certain [*specified*] Sum. Mine are for all the pay found due. 4th. Payment to be made within the States of Va. and N. Ca. Mine are from the Paymaster Genl. for the time being.

I hope you will Excuse the Liberty of thus addressing you and that you will be of the opinion that Mr. Bland's report, as it now stands, ought not to pass into a Law, or any other that will destroy my right to those Assignments.

PTJ 18:621–22, from a transcript in E. Ruell Smith, Note Book II, pp. 23–24. The ellipses are in the source. The bracketed words are from the committee report. The editors of *PTJ* identified the likely recipient based on the fact that Vredenburgh was his constituent. This probable identification is supported by Laurance's speech on 24 May (*DHFFC* 13:1389). The document is undated, but as Vredenburgh makes specific references to points appearing in the House committee report's resolutions of 14 May, the editors believe that it is likely that it was written between this date and 17 May, when the House agreed to the resolutions. A third letter from Vredenburgh on this subject is printed under June 1790 Undated, below.

[1] For the report of the House committee that Bland chaired, see *DHFFC* 6:2068–69. It led to the Resolution on Compensation Lists (*DHFFC* 6:2063), in which an exception was made for secondary claimants who had the certificates in their hands prior to the adoption of the Resolution.

William J. Vredenburgh to [*John Laurance?*]

Mr. *Bland* states that a *list* of Names of officers and soldiers of the Va. and N. Ca. Lines having pay due them, had been obtained from a Public Officer and Assignments of their pay fraudulently obtained.[1]

Several gentlemen and Myself of this City some time last fall employed a Person in Va. to purchase a certain number of Officers' and Soldiers' arrears of Pay and Bounty of Lands, due to them from the U.S. We obtained a list from a Gentleman that had one a long time before . . . and we heard of Numbers of persons that have purchased their pay in Richmond and Carolina. It is impossible to know what particular office Mr. Bland alludes to.

I believe there have been many copies in Circulation and received from different channels. How far Mr. B. can support his assertions, I know not. I have no doubt that frauds have been committed in buying and selling soldiers' pay—and where there has been one instance of soldiers being cheated there have been fifty instances of soldiers cheating. I bought Soldiers' Bounty Lands at the same time as I bought their pay by different assignments. I presented the powers for the Land to the Secty. of War who without hesitation issued the Warrants.

Out of the few claims that I have lodged in the Paymaster Genls. [*Joseph Howell, Jr.*] office I find there are several that are claimed by others.

There are many persons in this speculation unconnected with each other and have no doubt but the greater part of the claims are purchased already &c. &c. Is it any strange thing for soldiers or even officers to sell pay due them, which they can not get and which has been due them many years? Have not the soldiers and officers of the present Army on the frontiers and Elsewhere been obliged to sell their pay at a very low rate? Some have assigned the whole to receive a 3rd, 4th, or 5th part immediately. Those very assignments have been presented to the Paymaster Genl., Examined and 1/3 part of the sum due actually paid and the rest will be shortly. The officers lately gone to Georgia[2] were impatient waiting to receive *the due to them* for their past services, chose to sell their claims at a low rate. If Mr. Bland wished to prevent the Officers and Soldiers selling their pay or lands he should have got Congress to have passed a Law for the purpose several years ago.

We have a higher opinion of the Wisdom and Justice of Congress than to believe that they will be guilty of so bare faced a piece of injustice as to pass a law agreeable to the notions of Mr. Bland.

The law now in agitation is a down right Ex post facto Law which the Constitution forbids being made.[3]

PTJ 18:621–22, from a copy, Vredenburgh Papers, Skaneateles, New York, in 1971. The document is undated but refers to the House committee report of 14 May. The editors believe it is likely that it was written between that date and 17 May, when the House passed resolutions reported by the committee. See also the location note to the previous document.

---

[1] The unnamed public officer was accused by Bland on the floor of the House on 17 May. The officer's identity became a major point of contention in the much broader scandal that erupted in 1792 over the activities of James Reynolds. Jefferson believed then that Reynolds, Vredenburgh's agent in Virginia, had been furnished with the list by Hamilton's assistant

secretary William Duer (see The House Investigation of William Duer, March 1790 Undated, above). When the scandal escalated in 1797, Hamilton's successor Oliver Wolcott wrote that the "infidelity" had in fact been committed sometime later in 1791 by a register's office clerk, whom Wolcott immediately dismissed, still without divulging his name (*PTJ* 18:649, 652–53).

[2]The two principal groups of settlers in upcountry Georgia following the state's establishment of a land office in February 1783 were from Virginia and North Carolina. Many Continental Army veterans, including heroes such as Nathanael Greene and "Mad Anthony" Wayne, contracted "Georgia Fever" during their military tours of duty in the state (George R. Lamplugh, *Politics on the Periphery: Factions and Parties in Georgia, 1783–1806* [Newark, Del., 1986], pp. 32–33).

[3]Article I, section 9, paragraph 3.

Letter from Rhode Island

Do not blame us all with too much severity for what may appear to you in our conduct absolute perverseness and obstinacy. Wherever ignorance and prejudice prevail, both those vices will also abound. Where numbers of the representatives of the people have been collected from the dregs of the people, what better is to be expected than opposition to what they have been taught to believe contrary to their interests. No one person out of fifty thinks or reasons for himself, and a few artful and interested knaves have found means to keep this little state in a ferment for a long time past, and probably may do the same in some degree, for a considerable time to come. I predict, however, that their reign is almost at an end. *Illiterate hirelings* certainly cannot much longer find a place in our public bodies. The meeting of the convention at Newport, the latter end of May, augurs well to the federal cause, and evidently shows that the main weight is coming into that scale. Paper money is the real cause of all the remaining opposition and the dread of being obliged to pay past debts with solid coin, is at the root of antifederalism. Hundreds of villains will run away the moment a majority adopts the new constitution.

NYDA, 26 May; reprinted at Baltimore and Easton, Maryland.

Letter from England

SINCE I wrote you last I have been in London, about the ____________ which I informed you was detained here by the Collector; he alledging she was not navigated according to law. As you are much concerned in American vessels, I think it necessary to give you a particular account of this transaction, and also to inform you of some very alarming proceedings going forward, on this side the Atlantic, against American shipping in general. You are acquainted that the British Navigation Act, requires, that the master and three-fourths of the mariners on board all foreign vessels trading to England, be subjects of the country the ships belong to. Now it is necessary that the Captain and three-fourths of the mariners of every American vessel coming to England, should be subjects of America at the time independence was granted by England. When the __________ arrived here, she had 14 people on board, out of which number the Captain and 10 of the people were really Americans, the remaining three were Englishmen, who had become citizens since the war—according to the present construction of the British navigation act, she had one more real American on board than the law requires, but 5 of the above number were apprentices, which the Collector would not allow to be numbered as mariners, the vessel was in consequence detained till he had the opinion of the commissioners of the customs; but this being too difficult a question for them to resolve, it was referred to the Attorney-General, and after detaining the vessel 7 weeks, with her cargo on board, he gave his opinion that she was navigated according to law. I wish to remark, that apprentices on board English vessels are always allowed to be mariners by the collector, underwriters, and every other person. When an American vessel arrives here, the collector has all the crew up to the custom House and makes them swear *where they were born, how old they are, how and where they have been employed, &c.* in short, it is a species of inquisition which the collector has instituted against the Americans only, as he makes no such enquiry of the vessels belonging to any other foreign nation, and I am sorry to add that this partial conduct of the Collector is approved of by people in power, for I saw a letter from [*Charles Jenkinson*] Lord Hawkesbury, who particularly mentioned it; this letter was in answer to one wrote him by the merchants of this place, desiring something might be done for the benefit of British shipping, to counteract the 10 pr. cent discount, on all goods imported into the United States in American vessels: He recommends that the merchants here should reduce the freight of their vessels, which he says would be only for a short time, and that by *their exerting themselves against American vessels, and by the collector's being particularly strict with them,* in a short time it must have a good effect, and that as soon as he had gained the necessary information in the business, he promised that something should be done. I have also been informed, that the merchants here have wrote out to America, giving positive orders not to stop any goods on board American vessels; and without something is done in this business, the sooner you set them on fire the better. You will also take notice, that a British subject becoming a citizen of America since the war, cannot hold any part of an American vessel.

The above facts are undoubted, coming from the very best authority.

GUS, 30 June. For the republication history of this piece, see p. 1864.

Letter from Ireland

A private letter from Ireland, received at this office, communicates a disgraceful account of the contracted persecuting policy of their parliament. Tho' the legislature hath at length rescinded the code of penal laws, still liberty is shackled, and the Catholic is excluded from any share in the formation of laws, intimately connected with his property and his life, while he continues to worship the Creator of the Universe according to the suggestions of his conscience, and that form of divinity handed down from a long line of illustrious ancestors.

The writer of the letter alluded to, which we may probably on some future day publish at large, having expatiated with a degree of enthusiasm on the liberties of America, and the excellence of our federal constitution, pathetically laments the distance of that day which he has appointed for planting his family and removing a colony to the land of freedom and virtue—where, alone, the tyrants of the old world may learn lessons of magnanimity, moderation and wisdom! He seems not to entertain a shadow of doubt of introducing, into our Western Territory, a most respectable, useful and numerous class of emigrants, should the prayer of his memorial receive a favorable ear from the Congress of the United States.

NYP, 1 July (the date on which members of Congress would have seen it).

Other Documents

Daniel Hiester, Account Book. PRHi.

Attended Pennsylvania delegation dinners at Fraunces Tavern at least three times that month.

Letter from New York. [Massachusetts] *Salem Gazette*, 1 June; reprinted at Portsmouth, New Hampshire.

"Tho' the Assumption of the States Debts has been again negatived, its advocates, do not despair—they are determined to bring in a bill for the purpose separate from that which includes the Continental Debts; and in this way they are promised support."

June 1790

Tuesday, 1 June 1790

Warm (Johnson)

John Adams to Henry Marchant

Your obliging Letter of the 29. Ult. was brought to me Yesterday at my house, and as there happened to be a few Friends with me, we joined in Wishing Happiness and Prosperity to Rhode Island with great Cordiality. This morning the President did me the honour of a Visit and I had the Pleasure of congratulating him on this pleasing Event and presenting to him your affectionate Respects.

Congress I conjecture will wait the arrival of your Senators, before they pass any Act.

My hopes of the Blessings of Liberty from this Government, are much increased Since Yesterday. United We Stand but divided We fall. Join or die. these were our Maxims, twenty five or thirty years ago, and they are neither less true nor less important than they were then.

The renovation of that Union, which has acquired such renown in the World, by tryumphing over Such formidable Ennemies, and by Spreading the Principles which are like to produce a compleat Revolution both in Religion and Government in most parts of Europe; cannot fail to res[*tore*] respectability to the American Name, and procure us Consideration among nations.

I earnestly wish to see your Senators here and your Representative in the other house and I cannot but hope that you will be one of the former.

ALS, Miscellaneous Manuscripts, Special Collections, Wellesley College Library, Wellesley, Massachusetts. Place to which addressed not indicated.

William Ellery to John Adams

The grand question is decided. The Constitution was adopted last saturday by a majority of two. On this auspicious event I most heartily salute you.

The ratification will in a few days be transmitted to the President; and I presume federal Officers will be soon appointed for this State. I am greatly obliged to you for the interest you have taken in my views and wishes, and hope that it will be continued, and extended as far as is consistent with the rule you have prescribed to yourself.

I had been informed that the President in his appointments paid a regard to the old Law adage;[1] and therefore I gave you a strong hint that the characters of the Collector and the other custom house officers for *this* district are objectionable. I wish that the offices of the United States may be filled with respectable characters, and I think I may venture to say that any office I may be honoured with will be discharged with fidelity.

Some of the Antifedl. Delegates after the Constitution was adopted declared that upon their return home they would use their influence with their Constituents to reconcile them to the New Government.

I hope that they will, and that peace, order and happiness may be restored to and established in this distressed, distracted State.

ALS, Adams Family Manuscript Trust, MHi. Written from Newport, Rhode Island.

[1] Possession is nine-tenths of the law.

Benjamin Goodhue to Samuel Phillips, Jr.

The question of residence which has been the bane of this Session, and had it not disturbed us in so disgracefull a manner, there can be no doubt, we might long before this have effected all our bussines long before this and been at home, was yesterday determined in our House in favr. of Philada. and is now before the Senate where the decission is very uncertain—there were suspicions that the Pensylvanians had bargain'd away the Assumption with the Southern members for their object and those suspicions are not yet intirely eradicated previous to the questions being taken up I waited on the Pensylvanians who totaly disclaimed such a bussines and declared their abhorrence of such a measure, but how far such declarations are founded in truth, their future conduct must prove in those circumstances, knowing it was impossible the assumption could ever obtain without some of their aid, I judged it advisable and with the advice of some friends, that it would be best for our delagation to divide on a question which in itself is immaterial, in order that we might not make either N. York or Pensylvania our declared enemies in the great object of assumption accordingly we divided, but the event proved that Philada. would have been carried without our aid—it is truely humiliating to be placed in such a situation, and dishonorable that our public measures should be impeded and their success any way depend on so insignificant a consideration but so it is and the circumstance grieves me beyond measure—but as we could not help it I have taken such part in this bussines as would place the assumption in the least hazzard—if the question of residence was once out of the way, I have no doubt but we might terminate our sessions before a great while, and perhaps to our liking, but this must depend upon the character which the Pensylvanians may establish by their future conduct—strange it is that since the vote for Philada. has obtained, some of the N. Yorkers have discover'd a lukewarmness towards the assumption so that there is no great difference of character.

[*Thomas*] Barnard will sail the last of the week with your Screw[1] which I hope may answer, as I am totaly ignorant how it should be I depend intirely on him who makes it, with directions to make such a one as he has made for others.

ALS, Phillips Family Papers, MHi. Place to which addressed not indicated.

[1] A machine for Phillips's papermill at Andover, Massachusetts.

Stephen Goodhue to Benjamin Goodhue

I received your's of the 25 of May I am Sorry to Inform you that [*Benjamin's son*] Stephen Died yesterday about half after Nine of the Clock in forenoon [*lined out*] on the Measles leaving him a Violent Sore mouth Set in but we flat[*te*]red our Selves he whould recover till Saturday. I hope we do not forget that the Lord gave. we Shall bury him to morrow & Carry him to the tomb in the Usual way in a Chase. Fanny bares the loss with exceeding great Christan fortitude & Resignation I think much more So than She whould if you where at home with the family. he was a Very promising Child When you left home about four weeks ago he had a Violent fit Since which he hath appeared to fail and had ~~one~~ another about ten days ago but not so Violent the fits Very much damped his Mothers expectations Conscerning him ***

FC:lbk, Goodhue Family Papers, MSaE. Written from Salem, Massachusetts. The omitted text relates to private business.

Richard Henry Lee to Thomas Lee Shippen

Your letter of the 28 of May found me in great grief, it having arrived about two hours after the death of our much valued friend Colo. Bland, who departed this life this forenoon after a painful illness of 11 days—It must be so—"Good dyes immature and at its death bequeathing endless pain"[1]—Altho I thought our prospects of meeting at Phila. the next Session were well founded, experience hath *so far* proved that I was mistaken—To some of your friends[2] I gave it as my opinion, that to prevent the success of intrigue, it would be better not to bring forward the motion until the time of adjourning was come; they thought otherwise, and on the motion being made in Senate, you lost it by a majority of two—For Phila. were N.H. half of Jersey Mr. P—n [*Paterson*] being against—Pensylva.—Delaware, Maryld. and Virginia—Against you, Massachusetts—Connecticut, N.Y.—half Jersey—N.C. S.C. & Georgia—A bill was then proposed for fixing both Temporary & Permanent Seats—but in the mean time the House of Representatives passed a Resolve with a Majority of 16 to meet at Phila. the next Session—Their Resolve & our Bill are both now before the Senate—No Man who has sense enough to ballance a straw sees not that the effect of the Bill will operate solely to the purpose of keeping Congress here, where now that Rhode Island has acceded to the Constitution, it will probably remain for 40 years to come. Those, who thro motives of ambition &c. choose to hazard everything, will I suppose continue to come here, and for me they are welcome to do so. Had our poor friend Bland been well the whole Representation of Virga., in both houses, would have been for Phila.—All but him so voted, & he poor Man was ill in bed—I spoke to Mr. Staats Morris as you desired—He said that he had received your letter & that he had answered it—He is now gone to South Carolina having sailed for Charleston Town a week ago. I will write to you shortly about our friend A[*rthur*]. L[*ee*]. and in the meantime I will thank you for your attention to the bracelets, and the Iron. To all our freinds both at Phila. & German Town I send my love.

P. S. Let me know quickly if you receive this letter & when—for as Heaven & Hell are now moved to keep us here, & my sentiments are well known, curiosity may be prompted to know what I write to you on the subject—This letter will go from hence tomorrow morning the 2d. June.

ALS, Shippen Family Papers, DLC. Place to which addressed not indicated.

[1] From "Night IV: The Christian Triumph" in *Night Thoughts* (London, 1742–45) by the British poet Edward Young (1683–1765).

[2] That is, supporters of Philadelphia.

James Madison to James Monroe

Your favor of the 19th. of may has been duly received. The information relating to your little daughter [*Eliza K. Monroe*] has been communicated as you desired. I hope she is by this time entirely recovered. Your friends in Broad way[1] were well two evenings ago.

I have paid the money to Taylor, and hope you will take the time you intimate, for replacing my advances on your account.

The assumption has been revived and is still depending. I do not believe it will take place, but the event may possibly be governed by circumstances not at present fully in view. The funding bill for the proper debt of the U.S. is engrossed for the last reading. It conforms in substance to the plan of the Secretary of the Treasy. You will have seen by late papers that an experiment for navigation & commercial purposes has been introduced.[2] It has powerful friends and from the present aspect of the H. of Reps. will succeed there by a great majority. In the Senate its success is not improbable, if I am rightly informed. You will see by the inclosed paper that a removal from this place has been voted by a large majority of our House. The other is pretty nicely balanced. The Senators of the 3 Southern States are disposed to couple the permanent with the temporary question. If they do I think it will end in either an abortion of both or in a decision of the former ~~favor~~ in favor of the Delaware. I have good reason to believe that there is no serious purpose in the Northern States to prefer the Powtomac, and that if supplied with a pretext for a very hasty decision, they will indulge their secret wishes for a permanent establishment on the Delaware. As R.I. is again in the Union & will probably be in the Senate in a day or two, The Potowmac has the less to hope & the more to fear from this quarter. Our friend Col. Bland was a victim this morning to the influenza united with the effects & remains of previous indisposition. His mind was not right for several days before he died. The President has been at the point of death but is recovered. Mr. Jefferson has had a tedious spell of the head-ach. It has not latterly been very severe, but is still not absolutely removed.

ALS, Madison Papers, DLC. Place to which addressed not indicated. The recipient was identified by the letter's content and the handwriting of the endorsement.

[1] In his letter of 19 May (unlocated), Monroe had probably enquired after the Gerrys, who lived on the corner of Broadway and Thames Street. Gerry and Monroe had formed a strong friendship while serving in Congress in 1784–85; they both courted daughters of wealthy New York City merchants and married within weeks of each other in early 1786.

[2] On 17 May Madison presented the Trade and Navigation Bill.

James Nicholson to John Barry

A few days since I wrote you by [*Richard*] Dale and gave a detail of our Business there before Congress.[1] I have now to inform that this day our friend Mr. Stone made a motion that it should be made the order of the day on Friday next, which was Seconded by Mr. Laurence and met with no opposition. It is probable some interferrance of other business may put it off to another day, otherwise I should Surgest the propriety of your being here, but as the difficulty of Keeping you a few Additional days from Mrs. [*Sarah*] Barry is so great I shall decline requesting it, but when I can certainly Know the day (which expect will be shortly) I mean to give you timely notice & then leave the matter to yourself, Mr. Seney has this moment Surgested to me the Necessity of your Attendance. Cap. [*Seth*] Harding yesterday informed me Mr. Huntington[2] had promised him to Second the Motion in bringing the business froward, so that (if he can be believed) we have at least our Earstern friend, Indeed I have some reason to think we shall have several which we did not expect from that quarter.

The death of Colo. Bland has put a Stop upon all Publick business for two days at least. had that Misfortune not have happened, by this time it would have been determined weather the next Congress met in Philadelphia or not New York lost it yesterday by a majority of 10 & Philada. carried by 15 or 16, So that at present you can distinguish little esle [*else*] but long faces in our Citizens, and of Consequence your friends all a Tiptoe, but as it is not the first disappointment they have met with, perhaps it may not be the last, I Confess I should not be Surprised at their passing through your City & going down to the Disspised Baltimore, but I assure you I am not amongst the Politicions nor do I care half as much as I have done upon a Semilar occasion.[3]

You will see by the Papers the Adoption of Rhode Isld. for which happy Event I think all the well wishers of this Country ought heartily to rejoice.

I am sorry that Friday was made the order of the day for bringing on our business. Sailor like I have no good oppinion of any thing undertaken for them on that unlucky day, and should we not Succeed & should you not be here, I shall certainly attribute it to those Combined Circumstances. Mrs. [*Frances Nicholson*] Seney & Mrs. [*Frances Witter*] Nicholson I thank God are much better.

ALS, Emmet Collection, NN. Place to which addressed not indicated.

[1] For the Petition of the Officers of the Late United States Navy, see *DHFFC* 7:438–43.

[2] Huntington resided at Harding's boardinghouse, 59 Water Street.

[3] Perhaps a reference to Nicholson's having served as one of the five commissioners for supervising the conversion of New York's city hall into Federal Hall in 1788–89.

Louis Guillaume Otto to Comte de Montmorin

The plan of which I had the honor to give you an account in my Dispatch No. 22 has at last been accomplished. The Northern Senators who have long desired to have a more powerful party and who have regarded with indignation Rhode Islanders' dislike for the new American government, succeeded in having a Bill passed to break off, on 1 July next, all communication with the small state of Rhode Island by land and by water, on pain of seizing the ships, wagons, and merchandise, a monetary fine, and imprisonment. In addition the Bill authorizes the President of the United States to ask Rhode Island for the payment of its quota of the public debt. So vigorous a measure, at the moment when the federal government is still in its infancy, astonishes the public; only five Senators opposed it; they thought that Congress had not the least right to use force against a state that conformed strictly to the articles of the old confederation and that committed no other wrong than that of not relishing the innovations that they wished to introduce; that this force could produce a much different effect than that which they appeared to pursue and that, far from intimidating it, could fortify and even justify that state in its opposition; that, moreover, menaces of this type must be followed by coming to blows; that the poverty and exhaustion of the public treasury would render [the policy] illusory and that before thinking of subjugating it would be necessary to ascertain the means of undertaking [it] effectively, but even supposing the possibility of success the measure would always be unjust in itself and would dishonor from the start a government founded on equity and on the voluntary consent of the people. The dissenting Senators accordingly asked that their protest be inserted on the Journals, but the majority opposed that and delivered the Bill to the House of Representatives. That House affected to consider the Bill as threatening and postponed the discussion until the fifteenth in order to leave the Rhode Islanders time to ward off the blow that was aimed at them. In the interval the Convention of Rhode Island that had already adjourned re-assembled in the greatest consternation and ratified the Constitution almost without debate by a majority of only 34 against 32. This new victory gained by the people of the North is useful for the Confederation in that it reunites the 13 Republics that previously composed the body politic of the United States, but it infinitely displeases the Southern States, which will henceforward have two more votes against them in the Senate and whose interests were already too neglected by Congress. On the other hand, it is certain that Rhode Island had no time to lose; Newport and Providence, the principal cities of that state, had already authorized their delegates to treat separately with Congress in order to assent to the Confederation.

This ratification, Sir, finally completes the new government of the United States and makes of it a much more formidable body than she was under the old system. From this moment on, the United States can be considered as an homogeneous nation that receives its laws and its impetus from a common center, which is no longer, as in the past, a Congress of delegates without power and without force, but a Government of three well organized branches and whose powers are clearly defined by a *written* Constitution, which gives it a great superiority over that of the English. It is true that there yet remain here, as in some federal monarchies, some separate bodies whose pretensions obstruct the supreme power, I speak of the legislatures of the individual states. The Americans regret, too late, not having thought to make a new division of their territory at the beginning of the revolution, a measure so happily taken and executed in France in order to destroy the little tyrants and local prejudices of the different districts. The moment has passed, the individual legislatures, so jealous of their independence and even of their Sovereignty, will prevent this government from expanding in a way that, without them, she would not fail to do in a few years.

It is a result of that jealousy that even Rhode Island proposed amendments and appended them to her ratification of the new Constitution. These amendments number about 20, of which I have the honor, Sir, of submitting to you the most important: "The United States will guarantee the Sovereignty of each individual state and all the powers which are not expressly delegated by the Constitution. The Congress will not interfere in any way with the redemption of paper money currently in circulation in any State. The judicial power of Congress will not extend to criminal cases against a State, nor to claims of a particular individual against a State. The consent of eleven [*of the original*] states will be necessary to introduce a new article into the Constitution. The Congress will not impose any poll tax. It will not impose any direct tax without the consent of 3/4 of the individual legislatures. It will not maintain a standing army in time of peace. It will not make any loan without the consent of two thirds of the two Houses. It will prohibit as soon as possible the importation of slaves. The Legislature will be able to recall their Senators when they think it fitting." This last amendment, Sir, would be the most dangerous to accept because it would damage the liberty of debate in the Senate, but the amendments of Rhode Island will be like those proposed by the other States, one looks upon them simply as the means that were employed to gain a majority in the Conventions and the Congress will always be sufficiently occupied to have a valid pretext not to take them into consideration. Besides there is always in Congress a party strong enough to obstruct the stretching of powers which are assigned to them by the Constitution and although it is generally agreed to brush aside all deliberation on amendments to the Constitution it acts in a manner which leaves undecided the questions that concern them. When the government takes on a certain stability it will be easier to return to amendments and experience will shed more light on such a delicate question.

Copy, in French, Henry Adams Transcripts, DLC. Place to which addressed not indicated; received 25 September. Otto's letters included in *DHFFC* were usually written over the course of days, and even weeks, following the day they were begun.

Samuel Phillips, Jr. to Benjamin Goodhue

Your kind favor of the 27th. ulto. has just come to my hand, for which I am greatly obliged to you, tho' the contents are of a nature truly alarming and the conduct of the Pensylvanians, according to your apprehensions is truly astonishing—I hope you will find yourself mistaken in your conjectures, for they had no reason to doubt the disposition of the Massachusetts members, from a review of their conduct when the subject of residency was under discussion before—As I have but a few minutes before the mail will be closed, I must attend to your question on the expediency of consenting to the funding of the Securities of the U.S. without the assumption—if the former is to encroach upon the resources on which the States depend for ~~latter~~ the payment of their own debts, I should be very slow in consenting to it—if this should not be the case, I am at a loss to determine on an answer—You, on the ground, can form a much better judgment of the probable consequence of a postponement—should the opposers to every funding system take you at your word & say hereafter, as you once refused a provision for the domestic debt of the U.S. we will adhere to that determination; such a Resolution would chagrin us; but I hope this is not possible; our prospect is truly gloomy, should you finally fail in the attempt to carry the assumption, (for I cannot yet consider the case as desperate) even tho' the excise should be left entire to us, for the difficulties in the way of the separate States attempting to regulate an excise, are daily encreasing; such are the embarrasments ~~in the way~~ attending the collection of our present excise, that many are zealously striving for a repeal of the act, altho' it obtained but the last session of the last General Court [*legislature*].

The Governour [*John Hancock*] to day made his Speech to the Genl. Court—said much about the [*torn*] expressed a doubt of the propriety of Cong[*ress*] assuming the debts of the several States, withou[*t*] [*torn*] application or consent—nevertheless, sugges[*t*] that an advantage might arise from the transfer and submitted the propriety of instructing our Senators & Representatives on the subject; I hope to be able to send you his speech by the next post. Dont yet be discour[*aged*] pray persevere with calmness & firmness [*torn*] hope to the last.

[*P. S.*] Will give an Order on Mr. [*Samuel*] Osgood in my next for pay for the Screw.[1]

ALS, Letters to Goodhue, NNS. Written from Boston. The last page of the document was torn, probably when the seal was broken.

[1] For Phillips's papermill at Andover, Massachusetts.

Theodore Sedgwick to Theodore Foster

I have had the pleasure to receive your favor of 21st. of may.

You will now please to accept my most candid congratulations on the happy result of your convention. Every true american will pertake in your joy.

Permit me, sir, to suggest the great importance of having your state represented in senate at as early a period as may be. To the commercial States in general, and to your's which is peculiarly so in particular, the funding the debt, & thereby providing a medium of commerce, is immensely important. It is not improbable that this consideration may be a foundation of opposition in some parts of the united states. The assumption is so indispensible a part of the funding system that I have no apprehension that any men who can discern the obvious interest of Rhode island will oppose it; I shall therefore most cordially welcome your senators here.

ALS, Foster Papers, RHi. Addressed to Providence, Rhode Island; franked; postmarked.

James Sullivan to Elbridge Gerry

I believe that I am many Letters behind what I conceive to be my duty, but I hope you will take my almost continual absence from home as an apology. I have yours of the 15th before me and am not a little distressed on the idea of the great uneasiness which I anticipate between the united States and our Commonwealth on account of the collection of Impost by the Latter between march and august 1789 and what is worse still I can devise no way to remedy the evil. my mind is too apt to anticipate ills and I Sincerely hope this will be an instance of it.

We have been Expecting an assumption of the state Debts and are frequently disappointed I have been rather averse to it but when I found ~~I~~ that our Legislature would make no provision for payment of the Interest of our State Debt, I became a Convert. for I resolve all into the Interest of the great whole and can see no possible way for Congress to get along with a System of finance which absorbs all the resources and leaves the Creditors of the several States in an awful discrimination [*?*] now, without any hope of Justice unpitied and unreleived by their own States.

The Governor [*John Hancock*] has made a Speech today. it is said he is [*in*] favour of an assumption and in Such a way as he hoped to induce the General Court [*legislature*] to instruct for the measure, the Effect ~~would~~ is uncertain. I will forward it next post.

ALS, Extra-illustrated copy of B. F. Stevens's *Facsimiles*, volume 6, Special Collections, NjP. Written from Boston.

Letter from Stockbridge, Massachusetts

Considering what human nature is, as exhibited in the history of the world, there is too much reason to believe, that, as those states which have done the least will be the greatest creditors, they will not be over anxious to promote a settlement of accounts. Many other facts will tend to produce the same effect; and it would be easy to shew that an ultimate adjustment of the accounts is a contingency too remote and uncertain to be relied on for that justice; which this state, in particular, hath a right to demand. Massachusetts is now indebted about five millions five hundred thousand dollars, which is more than two millions beyond her equal proportion—South-Carolina is nearly in the same situation. On the other hand, that state of New-York has purchased in the public funds, and that principally by the sale of confiscated property, to such an amount, that by it, she can discharge all the debts she owes, and with the residue more than support all the expences of her civil government. The majority of the New-York delegation, therefore, deserves praise for being so strongly impressed with a sense of justice, as to be in favor of the measure of the assumption. There is every reason to believe, that if the debts are not assumed, our taxes will become intolerable, our commerce will be materially injured, and of consequence our contiguity to the state of New-York must give an irresistable energy to a spirit of emigration, which will immensely depreciate the real property of the commonwealth, and ultimately, be the ruin of those who have done most in their country's cause.

NYDA, 11 June; reprinted at Philadelphia.

Letter from Kentucky

The general government by this time, I should think, might be convinced of the folly and absurdity of Indian treaties. They only serve to tie up our hands, whilst our enemies, under pretence of not being able to restrain new, lawless and vagrant tribes, are allowed to let loose upon us all the horrors of the most savage, cruel war that ever was submitted to by any people on earth, who had courage and ability to defend themselves. However disagreeable the alternative may be, Congress must either go to war or lose their Western, at least this part of their Western Territory.

[Winchester] *Willis's Virginia Gazette*, 10 July; reprinted at Portland, Maine; Concord and Portsmouth, New Hampshire; Boston, Northampton, Springfield, and Stockbridge, Massachusetts; Newport, Rhode Island; New York City (*NYDG*, 29 July (the date on which members of Congress would have seen it); *NYP*, 31 July; *NYJ*, 3 August); New Brunswick, New Jersey; Philadelphia; and Charleston, South Carolina.

Other Documents

John Adams to Thomas Brand Hollis. FC:lbk, Adams Family Manuscript Trust, MHi. Sent to Westminster, London. For the full text, see *John Adams* 9:568–69.

His duties leave little time for personal correspondence; sends a "small paket" giving some idea of Congress's proceedings; "I am situated on the majestic banks of the Hudson, in comparison of which your Thames is but a rivulet"; "Never did I live in so delightful a spot."

John Adams to Alexander Jardine. FC:lbk, Adams Family Manuscript Trust, MHi. Sent to Woolwich, near London. For the full text, see *John Adams* 9:567–68.

Would prefer studying the science of government; but his life is destined for a much less agreeable labor; discusses balanced government.

William Constable to Gouverneur Morris. FC:lbk, Constable-Pierrepont Collection, NN.

Debt certificates continue to rise in price, although believes that the whole funding business may be laid over until the following session; both houses of Congress employed on the residence question, "& parties run so high that nothing can be done—our Friend [*Robert Morris*] is the prime Mover."

Jacob Cuyler to Philip Schuyler. ALS, Schuyler Papers, NN. Place from which written not indicated.

Has sent Volckert Douw receipts and such certificates "as you have some Time since directed me to make out" regarding the accounts of the Indian department; discusses New York state election results for (Albany?) and Montgomery counties.

Elbridge Gerry to Samuel R. Gerry. No copy known; acknowledged in Samuel R. to Elbridge Gerry, 21 June.

Elbridge Gerry to Henry Marchant. No copy known; acknowledged in Marchant to Gerry, 12 June.

Elias Langham to James Madison. ALS, Madison Papers, DLC. Written from Point of Fork, Virginia; franked; postmarked Richmond, Virginia, 4 June.

Encloses Edward Carrington's letter to Madison, 20 May, above; office seeking: manager of the military magazine or arsenal for Virginia, if his previous request is not successful; people there are satisfied with the government, except for "the propos'd plan for diciplining the Militia"; congressional news arrives very late; crop reports; office seeking: Howell Lewis as a captain in the federal army.

Pamela Sedgwick to Theodore Sedgwick. ALS, Sedgwick Papers, MHi. Written from Stockbridge, Massachusetts. The remainder of this letter was written on 4 June and is calendared under that date, below.

Rejoices in Washington's recovery; regrets that "union of Sentiment" has not yet permitted Congress to adjourn; "The Season is now Inviteing for a Country Life the Earth for some days has Been covered with the most delitious Verdure and I most sincerely regret your being Buried in a citty."

Theodore Sedgwick to George Benson. No copy known; acknowledged in Benson to Sedgwick, 18 June.

Abishai Thomas to John Gray Blount. ALS, John Gray Blount Papers, Nc-Ar. Addressed to Washington, North Carolina; postmarked. For the full text, see *Blount* 2:60–61.

Trusts that assumption will again be defeated at its third trial in the House on the following Monday, as there appears to be a majority of five against it, but believes the matter will be revived "*ad infinitum*" until it passes; is happy at North Carolinians' general approval of their congressmen's "decided part" against the measure; his housemate Ashe asks "why Don't you send his Tob[*acc*]o."

George Thompson to James Madison. ALS, Madison Papers, DLC. Written from Fluvanna County, Virginia; postmarked Richmond, Virginia, 10 June. For the full text, see *PJM* 13:235–37.

Is lately returned from Kentucky and has traveled the western frontiers of Virginia, Pennsylvania, and North Carolina; reports details of the "murders and outrages lately committed by the Indian Savages in those parts," including an attack on his party going down the Ohio River; "Pray Sir what does Congress mean to do with those Creatures?"; "america ought not to exist as a nation unless she chastises" them; would not be understood to dictate when he declares that in one year ten thousand men could kill or drive them all out of the country.

Oliver Wolcott, Sr. to Oliver Wolcott, Jr. ALS, Wolcott Papers, CtHi. Written from Hartford, Connecticut. Wadsworth had taken an unofficial leave in order to return to Hartford because of his son Daniel's health.

Intends to write Oliver, Jr. another letter in a few days via Wadsworth; is happy to hear from Wadsworth that Oliver, Jr. and family are well.

NYJ, 8 June. The address, dated 4 May, is printed in *PGW* 5:451–52.

Gunn, Hawkins, and Mathews presented Washington an address from the triennial meeting of the Society of the Cincinnati.

The Death of Theodorick Bland

On the morning of 1 June, Representative Theodorick Bland died in his lodgings at Mrs. McEuen's boardinghouse, 32 Broad Street.[1] At least since late April, Mrs. McEuen's had also been home to several of Bland's colleagues in the FFC: Paterson of New Jersey, Huger and Tucker of South Carolina, and perhaps most reassuringly, Bland's fellow members from the "Ancient Dominion," Senators Lee and Walker, and Representative Page with his new bride, Margaret. That afternoon, Jackson rose on the floor of the House to relate the news of Bland's death. While Virginia's Senator Grayson had died less than two months earlier, without ever returning to take his seat in the second session, Bland's was the first death of a member while attending at the seat of government, and the first death of a member of the House.

The House responded quickly to that unprecedented event with a series of official measures: unlike the Senate, which paid no official notice whatsoever to Grayson's death, Representatives resolved to wear the traditional mourning ribbon of black crepe on their arms or hats for one month (as they had voted to do in honor of Benjamin Franklin five weeks earlier); Virginia's delegation in the House was ordered to superintend preparations for the funeral; and the entire House would attend it. The day after Bland's interment, Speaker Muhlenberg officially notified Virginia's Governor Beverley Randolph of the news.[2] These proceedings are documented in *DHFFC* 8:474–75.

Bland's death was reported in *NYDA*, *NYDG*, and *GUS* on 2 June. In adjoining newspaper columns, the New York State Society of the Cincinnati inserted instructions for their participation in that afternoon's funeral for their fellow member. It was the first state funeral to be mounted by the new federal government, and the committee of Virginia Representatives may have needed all the time at their disposal to plan the interdenominational ceremony; anticipating their absence, Morris wrote his wife on the morning of the funeral that the major business before the House would be suspended, the Virginians "having undertaken to direct Respecting the Funeral." Additionally, Walker assumed responsibility for posting notice that local creditors' demands on Bland's estate would be paid.[3]

The interment took place in the presence of Congress, the executive officers of the federal government, and much of New York society. The site—the burial ground of Trinity Church, with its famous two hundred foot spire completed barely six months before—crowned the view down Wall Street from Congress's home at Federal Hall. Serving as pall bearers were Virginia's entire congressional delegation except for Moore and Page, joined by South Carolina's Tucker, who was the older brother of Bland's friend and brother-in-law, St. George Tucker. Congress's Episcopalian and Presbyterian chaplains jointly officiated, with Rev. William Linn sermonizing on the scripture passage, "Certainly brethren your time is short."[4]

Even without the veil cast by the interval of so many years, it would be difficult to diagnose the precise cause of Bland's death based on contemporary accounts of his general health alone. Bland himself was an Edinburgh-trained physician who described his condition during the FFC as a variety of vague symptoms. For the last twenty years of his life, "gout" was his major complaint. Its cause and progress were poorly understood in the eighteenth century, but its symptoms were common enough that Bland's self-diagnosis is credible. Gout occurs when high concentrations of uric acid eventually precipitate out of the blood and crystallize in the body's peripheral joints (wrists and ankles), causing swelling, burning sensations, and sometimes recurring paroxysms throughout the duration of the flare up, which usually was no more than a few weeks. Besides these crystals, gout can also produce kidney stones which, over time, may result in kidney failure. Except for those extreme cases, gout is not directly fatal in itself.[5]

On 19 May 1789, Bland suffered from an attack that witnesses (none of them doctors) described variously as a fit, a seizure, or a stroke that was either "apoplectic epileptic or paralytic." Although this may have been evidence of epilepsy, Bland described the ailment in terms more familiar to him, as a "Gout in my head." His health is not mentioned again until March 1790, although Washington later recalled that Bland's general ill health had prevented him from attending any of the presidential levees during the session. On 9 March Maclay noted that Bland was so weak that he had to be carried into the House chamber that day to cast his vote for assumption in the COWH.[6]

It was this ongoing, underlying condition that gradually weakened Bland's system to the point where he was finally carried off by an infection that was as incidental as it was virulent: the influenza. As with any epidemic, the flu that ravaged New York City in the late spring of 1790 chose its victims irrespective of status or rank; many members of Congress were bedridden by it, while Washington lay near death for several days in mid-May. Washington's case was extreme. Like the gout, the strain of flu that New Yorkers complained about rarely proved mortal, "except," noted former Postmaster General Ebenezer Hazard, "when accompanied by other Disorders." Bland's generally debilitated state after twenty years of battling gout precisely describes that condition, so that there is little reason to question the consensus among his peers that Bland died of the flu. He suffered for eleven days—the last several of them spent in dementia.[7]

[1] Madison to Monroe, 1 June, above.

[2] *DHFFC* 3:375, 13:1167. For the House actions mourning Franklin, see *DHFFC* 8:574–76.

[3] *NYDG*, 2 June; Robert to Mary Morris, 2 June, below; *NYP*, 10 June.

[4] *NYDG*, 2, 3 June; *NYDA*, 3 June.

[5] The editors are indebted to Mark Dexter for his research into Bland's health for a George Washington University seminar on the FFC.

[6] Wynkoop to Reading Beatty, 20 May 1789 and Madison to Eliza House Trist, 21 May 1789, *DHFFC* 15:602–3, 606; William Davies to Governor Beverley Randolph, 22 May 1789, Executive Papers, Vi; Bland to John Randolph, 11 June 1789, Tucker-Coleman Papers, ViW; Washington to David Stuart, 15 June, below; *DHFFC* 9:215.

[7] *PGW* 5:393–99; Hazard to Jeremy Belknap, 5 June, Ellsworth to Abigail Ellsworth, 7 June, Richard Henry Lee to Thomas Lee Shippen, 1 June, and Madison to Monroe, 1 June, all printed above or below.

Newspaper Article

☞The Members of the New-York State Society of the Cincinnati, are requested to assemble at the City Tavern, this afternoon, at half past four o'clock, to attend the FUNERAL of Colonel THEODORIC BLAND, deceased, late a Representative from Virginia in the Congress of the United States, and a Member of the Cincinnati.

The usual mourning is to be worn for the space of twenty one days.

Members of other State Societies of the Cincinnati, now in this city, are also requested to honor the society with their attendance.

NYDG, 2 June; signed by John Stagg, President.

Newspaper Article

Yesterday afternoon, the remains of the late honorable THEODORICK BLAND, were deposited in the family vault of John [*James?*] Nicholson, Esq. in Trinity-Church burial ground.[1] The Senate, House of Representatives, Executive Officers of the United States government, and several of the most respectable officers and citizens of New-York, attended upon this solemn occasion. Bishop [*Samuel*] Provost performed the usual ceremony of reading funeral service; and the Rev. Mr. [*William*] Lynn delivered a discourse from these words: "*Certainly brethren your time is short.*"[2]

We cannot presume to determine on the merits of this discourse; but we will venture to express an opinion, that it was one of the most rational and unaffected that we have ever heard.

The funeral was conducted with the utmost plainness of ceremony, such as was suitable to republican mourners.

NYDG, 3 June.

[1] *NYWM*, 5 June, reported more specifically that Rev. Linn discoursed from 1 Corinthians 7:29: "But this I say, brethren, the time is short."

[2] Bland's remains were reinterred in Congressional Cemetery, Washington, D.C., in 1828.

Newspaper Article

Yesterday afternoon were interred in Trinity Church yard the remains of the Hon. THEODORICK BLAND, Esquire. The Honorable the Congress of the United States and the society of the CINCINNATI, together with a great number of respectable citizens attended the funeral, paying all that respect that was so justly due to this amiable character.

The Honorable *Richard H. Lee, John Walker, Isaac Coles, Samuel Griffin, Richard B. Lee, James Madison, Josiah Parker*, and *Thomas T. Tucker* Esquires, supported the pall.[1]

After the corps[*e*] was carried into the church, his Reverence the Bishop, read prayers; after which the Reverend Dr. Lynn delivered a most excellent sermon, peculiarly adapted to the occasion.

A short account of the Hon. Theodorick Bland, Esq. *deceased, one of the Virginia Delegation.*

Mr. BLAND was a native of Virginia, and descended from an ancient and respectable family in that state. He was bred to physic, but upon the commencement of the America war, having been educated in very liberal principles, he quit the practice, and took an active part in the cause of his country. He soon rose from a volunteer to the rank of Colonel, and had the command given him of a regiment of dragoons. While in the army, he frequently signalized himself by brilliant actions. In 1779 he was appointed to the command of the *Convention troops* at Albemarle barracks in Virginia,[2] and continued in that situation till some time in 1780, when he was elected to a seat in Congress. He then resigned his commission of Colonel, and continued in Congress three years, the time allowed by the confederation; after the expiration of this term, he again returned to Virginia, and was chosen a member of their State Legislature. On the great question of the Constitution, Mr. Bland was opposed thereto, as supposing it repugnant to the interests of his country [*Virginia*], and was in the minority that voted against the ratification. When the Constitution was at length adopted, Mr. Bland, acting in conformity to the character of a good citizen, submitted to the voice of the majority, and became a candidate to represent the district in which he lived, in the Congress of the United States. He was elected without opposition, and has had the honor of representing them in the first Congress under the new Constitution. Mr. Bland's character in the present Congress has been such as to merit the warmest esteem of his countrymen in general. In his character, he was honest, open, and candid, and bore an universal good character in his intercourse with mankind.

NYDA, 3 June. All or part of the newspaper notice of Bland's funeral and the accompanying "Short account" of his life was reprinted at Windsor, Vermont; Exeter, New Hampshire; Boston and Salem, Massachusetts; Litchfield, Connecticut; Burlington, New Jersey; Philadelphia; Baltimore; Richmond and Winchester, Virginia; Edenton, North Carolina; and Charleston, South Carolina.

---

[1] Moore and Page were the only members of the Virginia delegation who did not serve as pall bearers; Tucker was the older brother of Bland's friend and brother-in-law, St. George Tucker.

[2] The Convention troops were the five thousand man force General John Burgoyne surrendered at Saratoga, New York, in October 1777, according to an agreement or "convention" with Continental Army General Horatio Gates. After a brief internment in Boston, they were marched to Charlottesville, Virginia, where they were held from 1779 to 1780 before being moved elsewhere in Virginia and Maryland. The half who did not die or desert were not released until the war's end.

[*Margaret Lowther Page,*] On the Death of Col. Theodorick Bland

On the DEATH of Col. THEODORICK BLAND
THO borne *alike* on Time's unresting bier,
All claim from *some* the tributary tear;
Yet grief *superior* should bedew the grave,
Where rests the *wise*, the *patriot*, and the *brave!*
Oh! skill'd alike in *Councils* to preside,
Or in the *Field* the martial band to guide,
Long shall Virginia mourn the fatal blow,
That laid her *Warrior* and her *Statesman* low!
Long call to mind, while gratitude inspires,
The Man, who warm'd by Freedom's sacred fires,
The tranquil joys forsook of social life,
To wield the sword in scenes of sanguine strife!

His country's good, his first, and only aim,
Undaunted, firm, in *every* view the same!
  Nor shall his mourning friends forget to tell;
Or on his gentler virtues fail to dwell.
Wit, Grace, Politeness, Dignity and Ease,
And all that in th'accomplish'd Man can please,
Insur'd applause, and in the milder sphere
Of sweet domestic bliss still made him dear!
The faithful Husband—(now, alas! no more!)
His weeping widow deeply shall deplore!
Th'indulgent Master—many a work-worn slave
With grateful tears his memory shall lave!
But ah! how vain each human power to charm
Mute now his *Tongue*—unnerv'd, alas! his *Arm!*
Hush'd are his lays, that once so sweetly flow'd,
On him the Muse her choicest gifts bestow'd,
His smallest praise, so high his fame was held
His *life* alone, his tuneful strains excell'd!

GUS, 5 June; reprinted at Charleston, South Carolina. In his letter to St. George Tucker, 6 June, below, Page identified his wife as the author of this anonymous piece. A noted poet, she is identified as "a LADY of this city" in the attribution to a poem on Washington's recovery printed in the same column as her poem on Bland.

WEDNESDAY, 2 JUNE 1790

Cool (Johnson)

Thomas Hartley to Jasper Yeates

I received your Favor of the 28th. ulto. by Mr. Hough—I went immediately with him to General Knox and introduced him also to Major [*William*] Jackson at the President['*s*] the several Letters from General [*Edward*] Hand were delivered and I did every Thing that was proper for me—I fear from what appears that there is no vacancy in the Military Line, but his Name is put down and possibly might be reached before very long.

But General [*William*] Irvine thinks that it would be better to try to bring him in as a Clerk in some of the Offices where he will get between 400 and 500 Dollars a Year—I wish he could be provided in the latter way.

We on Monday carried it in our House by 38 agst. 22 that the next Meeting should be at Philadelphia—The Resolution was sent up to the Senate but I hear they have refered it to a Committee of three two of whom are for staying here and one for going to Philadelphia—Rhode Island has adopted the Constitution and her Senators will be here to Morrow or next Day—and I suppose of Course we shall be ankored here again—In our House we really did wonders—we cannot answer for the other.

We this Day passed the Funding Bill of the Debts of the United States.

As it is possible [*lined out*] we shall not get away from New York—Public Affairs will be in a disagreeable way I wish I may not be mistaken.

ALS, Yeates Papers, PHi. Addressed to Lancaster, Pennsylvania; directed in Hartley's hand, "To be put in the Post Office at Philadelphia"; franked; answered 7 June.

Robert Morris to Mary Morris

I arrived safe here yesterday about 12 oClock and found that a hue & Cry had been sent after me, and altho I came quite as soon as I had promised or as was necessary, yet Such was the anxiety and impatience of our People here, that several had written letters and the Speaker sent an Express to meet me—I came however at the moment without having received one of the letters or seen the Express, where He passed me, we cannot Conceive. You will have heard that The Motion for holding the next Session of Congress in Philada. was carried by a large Majority in the House of Representatives on Monday and sent to the Senate yesterday for Concurrence, it was then postponed as Major Butler had brought in on Monday a Bill for establishing the permanent Residence of Congress which was also postponed untill this day, and I think it is probable that both these questions may be again postponed untill tomorrow, on account of the Death of Colo. Bland as the Virginia Delegation will probably be absent, having undertaken to direct respecting the Funeral, but this is only Conjecture, you will perceive that I arrived at a Critical Moment and my attention was immediately called upon, so that I have been deeply engaged in preparing and Canvassing, but I am far from being sanguine.

The Bill for fixing the permanent Residence is introduced for the purpose of amusing and deceiving our Weak Bretheren, and in the hope of Slowing up the whole business of Residence, and I find several of the Senators preaching in favour of the Bill. even Some of those on whose Votes we depend for Success. However if we do not carry the question *Now* I begin to think we Shall carry it before the Session is over.

The New Yorkers are alarmed seriously at the present State of things and abuse me, I am told, most confoundedly as the Contriver of the mischief.

If we do but finally succeed I can bear the abuse therefore you & all Pensylvania may depend on the utmost exertions that I am capable of—Rhode Island has adopted the Constitution and as they will soon send in Senators it is probable that attempts will be made to postpone all Questions of Residence untill they come forward & then N. York will feel Secure but how all these Considerations will work or how they will end, I cannot undertake to pronounce, time must disclose the Events. Tom [*Morris*] is well, we met Mr. & Mrs. [*George*] Harrison Mr. & Mrs. Ab[*raha*]m. Ogden &c. &c. at Brunswick [*New Jersey*] on their way to Bethlehem [*Pennsylvania*]. Mr. & Mrs. S[*amuel*]. Ogden and all their Family were well, I got my business done with him.

ALS, Morris Papers, CSmH. Addressed to Philadelphia.

David Stuart to George Washington

The accounts of your recent illness having just reached this place on my return, I delayed writing, 'till I could again congratulate you on the reestablishment of your health; which I now do most sincerely, both on your account, and on that of your Country—I fear much, that the great change which has been unavoidably made, in your accustomed mode of living, by your office; has been the cause of both the attacks you have so unfortunately been subject to—I have understood, that you had some intention before your late illness, of visiting Virginia this Summer for your health. I hope you will now think it indispensably necessary.

***

I shall now endeavour to give you, all the information I have been able to collect during my journey, respecting the present temper of mind of the people of this State; so far as I can judge, from those I mixed with, and from what I could hear—I could wish indeed, to speak more favourably of it; but it appears to me, that the late transactions of Congress, have soured the Public mind to a great degree, which was just recovering from the fever ~~with~~ which the Slave business[1] had occasioned, when the late much agitated question of the State debts came on—With respect to the Slave business, I am informed by Mr. [*Thomas*] Lomax, whom I met on his return from Pittsylvania [*Virginia*], that great advantages had been taken of it in that distant quarter, by many who wished to purchase slaves, circulating a report that Congress were about to pass an act for their general emancipation—This occasioned such an alarm, that many were sold for the merest trifle—That the sellers were of course much enraged at Congress, for taking up a subject which they were precluded by the Constitution from medling with for the present, and thus furnishing the occasion for the alarm wch. induced them to sell—As the people in that part of the Country were before much opposed to the Government, it may naturally be supposed, that this circumstance has embittered them much more against it—as to the assumption of the State debts, I scarce think it would be a measure generally acceptable on any principles—On such as have been contended for, I hardly think it would be acquiesced in by this State—How far indeed, a certain degree of shame or obstinacy natural to the human mind, which acts as a constant check on every rising disposition to depart from a cause or side once resolutely espoused; would continue to operate, I know not—But setting this aside, I think I should not be far wrong in saying, there would be as nearly an unanimity of opinion for an opposition, as perhaps could ever be expected on any subject—There is I think in general, [*lined out*] in consequence of these two instances, a strong apprehension, that the predictions relative to the grasping at power by unwarrantable constructions of the Constitution will be verifyed—On these two subjects at least, it is observed by most, (for there are some who after a proper liquidation, and allowance of credit to the States, for what has been paid, approve of the Assumption) that the Constitution appeared so clear, as to be incapable of misconstruction, by those who wished to make it a rule and guide to their conduct—At any rate on a subject of such importance, which may be considered as doubtfull in any shape, under the Constitution, it would at least have been prudent [*lined out*] in the Members, to have consulted the general sentiment entertained of it, in their respective States—But it really appears, as if they were so charmed with the plenitude of their powers, as to have considered this as a degrading step—a strong suspicion too is entertained, from the number of Speculators, who have been traversing the State purchasing up State Securities, that there is a good deal of selfishness mixed with the plan—And this perhaps causes it to be viewed with more particular dislike—Mr. Maddison's conduct on this business has gained him great popularity, even among those, who were illiberal enough, to pass severe censures on his motives respecting his discrimination plan.

As I passed through Richmond, the news of the rejection of the motion made by Mr. [*R. H.*] Lee, for opening the doors of the Senate, agreeable to his instructions from our Legislature,[2] had just arrived—It occasioned much disgust—But the manner of the rejection seemed to be as offensive, as the rejection itself—It being said, that after speaking two days ably on the subject, without recieving an answer, the question was called for and lost; no one voting with him but his Collegue, and Mr. Maclay. It is supposed, it will be productive of an application from our Legislature, to the other States calling on them, to join them in similar instructions to their Members—It is a pity the public wish (as I believe it to be) in so trivial a matter, cannot be gratifyed—The slowness with which the business is carried on, is another cause of complaint—Congress it is said, sit only four hours a day, and like School boys observe every Saturday as a Holy day. If this be true, it is certainly trifling with their Constituents in the extreme, who pay them liberally, and have therefore a right to expect more diligence from them—It is the more unfortunate as it is represented at the same time, that they generally live for two dollars a day—I have now, gone through the Catalogue of Public discontents; and it really pains me much, and I believe every friend to the government, to think that there should be so much cause for them; and that a spirit so subversive of the true principles of the Constitution, productive of jealousies alone, and fraught with such high ideas of their power, should have manifested itself at so early a period of the Government—If Mr. [*Patrick*] Henry has sufficient boldness to aim the blow at it's existence, which he has threatened, I think he can never meet with a more favourable opportunity; if the assumption should take place on the principles on which it has been contended for; and I understand that tho' lost at present it is to be again brought on—But I doubt much, whether he possesses so adventurous a spirit—It will be the fault of those who are the promoters of such disgustfull measures, if he ever does, or indeed any one else—I believe it has ever been considered as a maxim in Governments recently established, and which depend on the affections of the people, that what is rigidly right ought not to be the only standard of conduct with those who govern—Their inclinations & passions too, must be consulted more or less, in order to effect ultimately what is right. How much more ought this to be done when it rests solely on a construction of their powers, whether a measure in contemplation ought to be carried into execution or not?

A member of the [*Executive*] Council, who wrote privately to Mr. Henry, to know if he would accept of the office of Senator in Congress, if appointed, shewed me his answer, in which he declines it, and says he was too old to fall into those aukward imitations which were now become fashionable—From this expression, I suspect the old Patriot has heard some extraordinary representations of the Etiquette established at your Levees. Those of his party no doubt think they promote themselves in his good opinion by such high colouring—It may not be amiss therefore to inform you, that Bland is among the dissatisfyed on this score—I am informed by good authority, that he represented, that there was more pomp used there, than at [*the Court of*] St. James's, where he had been, and that your bows were more distant & stiff—This happened at the Governor's [*Beverley Randolph*] table in Richmond—By such accounts, I have no doubt the party think to keep alive the opposition and aversion to the Government, & probably too, to make Proselytes to their opinions.

You have no doubt heard of the number of vessells, we have had this winter at our Ports in this State. It is mortifying to think how fiew of them have been American—one of the great benefits expected from the operation of the general Government was an encouragement to our own vessells; and I think Maddison's plan of the last year would have had the desired effect—It seems to give pleasure, that something of that sort is now in contemplation[3]—I mean to the Americans, for it will excite a great clamor among the British factors, as it did before—as I think I must now have fatigued you, I will conclude.

ALS, Washington Papers, DLC. Written from "Abingdon," Fairfax County (in present-day National Airport in Arlington County), Virginia. The omitted text relates to private legal matters and the management of Washington's estate.

[1] The antislavery petitions presented to Congress in February and debated the following month; see *DHFFC* 8:314–38.

[2] On 16 December 1789 the Virginia legislature instructed Grayson and Lee to use "their utmost endeavours" to obtain "free admission" to the Senate for the public (*Acts Passed . . . Virginia, Begun October 19, 1789* . . . [Richmond, Va., 1791], p. 45).

[3] Madison proposed discriminatory tonnage rates aimed at the British and at encouraging the United States' carrying trade under the first session's Tonnage Act [HR-5] and the second session's Trade and Navigation Bill [HR-66].

Paine Wingate to Samuel Hodgdon

I have just received your favour of May 31st. and have delivered the two letters you enclosed. I also acknowledge the receipt of several letters from you heretofore, which did not require any direct answer from me, which however have been duely attended to with pleasure. I am happy to hear that Mr. [*Timothy*] Pickering and family were lately well. I shall not be disappointed or displeased, if the annuity given to the Baron should excite general disgust.[1] I think it an inexcusable abuse of the public money. How the house of Representatives voted you will see by the newspapers. In the Senate, when every member was present we were equally divided. The Vice President decided in favour of the Baron. I hope the conduct of this business will be generally known & not soon forgotten. This day the Senate have had under debate the vote of the other house that the next session of Congress should be at Philadelphia. To defeat this the permanent residence was again brot. in to view by a bill offered by Mr. Butler. A motion was made to commit the bill which tryed the sentiments of the house, as it might naturally be presumed that those who were for going to Philadelphia would oppose the entering on the question of permanent residence. After some dispute the Senate, all present, were equally divided & the Vice president determined in favour of committing which will delay the business for some time. How it finally will issue is very uncertain. It may possibly depend on the vice presidents vote. If Mr. Paterson should be for Philadelphia & Mr. Hawkins who has not yet I believe declared his sentiments, Philadelphia would prevail, but all is uncertain. You may well suppose that New York is not wanting in exertions & they will if possible delay the business until Rhode Island Senators come on whom they calculate upon in their favour—This day the President made his nominations for officers in the milatary establishment. All those in the present service are nominated & the additional officers are from Maryland & Southward of that State. This day the funding bill came to the Senate from the other house. It is nearly as has been published in the newspapers. What alterations may yet be made in it I cannot tell I have given you this very hasty letter which I hope you will excuse.

P. S. I have nothing special to write to Mr. Pickering at present; but if you write to him please to let him know that I desire my love to him & family & that I am well, as was my family 14 days ago.

ALS, Pickering Papers, MHi. Place to which addressed not indicated.

[1] Frederick William Steuben's $2500 annuity, granted under the Steuben Act; see *DHFFC* 7:201–46.

Letter from New York

The House of Representatives have agreed to adjourn to Philadelphia, which resolution was before the Senate this day; and they have agreed to refer the question of adjournment and that upon the permanent residence, to a committee: the committee are—

Butler of South-Carolina, Dalton of Massachusetts, Johns[*t*]on of North Carolina—said to be for New-York.

John Henry of Maryland, R. H. Lee of Virginia—said to be for Philadelphia.

We are therefore sanguine that the business will NOT be concluded in the Senate until the Rhode-Island Senators come forward: when we expect a decided majority in favor of New-York.

IG, 5 June. A different version of this letter appeared in *PP* the same day. One version or the other was reprinted at Portsmouth, New Hampshire; Boston and Northampton, Massachusetts; Philadelphia; Easton, Maryland; Edenton, North Carolina; and Charleston, South Carolina.

Warner Mifflin to Members of the House of Representatives

REQUESTING your favourable attention to, and candid consideration of my religious concern, on account of that cruelly oppressed part of our fellow men, the people of Africa; feeling my mind deeply affected with the injuries they suffer; and much interested in the national character of America, my native country, which I sincerely desire may, by a disinterested adherence to public justice, and the common rights of men, be dignified with distinguished lustre as a light to surrounding powers and empires; not content with acknowledging in the pomp of verbal expression, that it is *righteousness which exalteth a nation*;[1] but more nobly testifying to the sacred verity of this interesting position, by the real exercise of unfeigned public virtue.

I trust I am entitled to credit from the candid and liberal spirited, when I say, it was not the desire of honor or applause from men that induced me to leave my home and near connections, for near two months, to solicit your attention to the violated rights of humanity;[2] but a sense of duty I owe, not only to this injured people, but also to my country and countrymen; to whose sincere welfare this great cause of common right has an essential relation—a cause which I firmly believe to be of at least equal importance with any that has ever come under the deliberation of your body. And it is therefore my fervent request that no motives of unsound policy, no partial or inferior considerations, may divert you from giving it that serious and unprejudiced attention it rightfully claims.

If we not only acknowledge, but really believe the Almighty Disposer of events to be just and equal in all his ways, and that he assuredly takes cognizance of human actions; from him we have reason to expect *that* measure to be meted to us, that we measure out to others.

Let rational reflection have free entertainment, unobscured by the fascinating influence of political subtleties, and surely the simple feelings of an honest mind will shew the absurdity of national declamation against the cruelties of a vindictive Indian foe in the western parts of this continent, while on the same floor of our federal assembly, the more savage barbarity, exercised eastward, is vindicated with the heated zeal of self interested partiality.

Weighing things of public concernment in this unequal balance, is I believe productive of what, abstractly viewed, must appear a strange incongruity—that the same men, when turning their attention to the sufferings of their countrymen in our cold northern climes shall find their spirits susceptible of an animating warmth; yet, on turning their view to the sultry regions of Africa, shall become as it were instantaneously changed into a frozen insensibility: Under the prevalence whereof, though unkind reflections have been personally aimed at me, and ungenerous aspersions thrown out against the christian community [*Quakers*] whereof I am a member, I may with truth and reverence acknowledge, that I believe it has been through divine favour that my mind has been preserved free from resentment against those, who, for want of better arguments, have manifested so much littleness of spirit. And I desire not to be so unreasonable as to cherish any unfriendly sensations towards those who have done our religious society so much honor as, by reviling us, to hope to defend the cause of injustice and violence. Good will towards them & all men, is the ground of our perseverance, in seeking the relief of the oppressed; wherein, if we have been stedfast, we have, we apprehend, been influenced by a religious sense of duty, and consciencіously shewn all due respect to government, and a disinterested concern for the public weal; towards which we believe it in the power of peaceable men, under the government of the blessed gospel principle, to contribute as amply and effectually, as any who affect to consider us, and disingenuously endeavour to represent us, as useless to civil community, because of our dissent from that faith and confidence in the arm of flesh which is congenial with the degenerate spirit of ambition and strife, and which is set up in the world above that true christian faith, which is evidenced by the peaceable fruits of righteousness, meakness, brotherly kindness and charity—tempers truly noble and amiable; and irreconcileable with the vindictive spirit of war, or with the sordid and dishonest practice of trading in the life and liberty of our fellow men.

When a religious body of people are scoffingly and opprobriously reviled for their professed belief in, and adherence to that divine christian principle, which both teaches and enables to overcome evil with good, does it not become the soberly considerate and well meaning, impartially to reflect whether such scoffers and revilers do not, either blindly or wilfully, reproach the christian religion? If as a people resigned to divine disposal, confiding in divine protection, and manifesting a consistent care that instruments of violence be not found in our habitation—that attentive diligence be exercised to improve the opportunities afforded to promote mercy, equity, peace and harmony among mankind: If a patient pursuit of this line of duty be considered offensive to those maxims of political expedience, idolized by the wisdom of this world, I am not ashamed to acknowledge myself one of that class of offenders—nor think myself dishonoured by the haughty contempt of those who found their boast of usefulness in the world on their attachment to the exercise of arms, or what in their creed is stiled military virtue.

And as a member of that religious society, who as a body adhere to our christian self denying testimony against war and strife, however some individuals under our name may have departed from it, I think it not impertinent, on this occasion, to remark a peculiar want of candour in our adversaries; who, when endeavouring to lessen us on account of our attachment to the precepts and example of the blessed Prince of peace, are scarce ever known to do us the justice of acknowledging, that whatever persecutions we have suffered for conscience sake, we have never been found justly chargeable with engaging, or being concerned in any plots, conspiracies or insurrections against any government which divine providence has permitted to be set over us; but have laboured, at least equal with any other body of people, for the support of civil order, peace and concord. So that, with due submission, I do conceive, notwithstanding the unreasonable censures of despotic spirits, who contend for slavery, and thereby evidence a contracted narrowness of sentiment respecting equal liberty and the rights of men, we have never forfeited our just claim to the attention of the legislative and executive powers of government, when, in compliance with duty, we are induced to offer, or urge to their consideration, our sense and religious concern, respecting those public objects which effect the well being of either our christian community in particular, or that of civil society in general.

And although it ought to be acknowledged, your house of Representatives, as a House, and generally in your more private capacity, paid a friendly and favourable attention to our yearly meeting's address on the African trade, and gave a kind reception to the committee who attended therewith; yet in contemplation of what occurred during the public deliberation and debate on the subject, and the state in which the matter was left, I have thought as one of that committee, it might conduce to the satisfaction of my own mind thus to communicate to you, respectively, as individual members of the federal body what has presented to my view on the occasion—believing it to be clearly in the power of the Legislature of the United States, greatly to obstruct the purposes of avarice in the pursuit of this iniquitous traffic, if not to put an effectual stop thereto, without infringing the constitutional right of any branch of the confederation. And am free to add, that the honor of the countries you represent, the public weal thereof, the public voice of the people, and the interesting nature of the case, loudly demand of you as a duty of first consideration, in fulfilling the important trust reposed in you, to exert vigorous endeavours, to the utmost of your power, to remove the foul guilt and reproach from our land.

That thus you may fill your eminent station with encreasing dignity, and that an increase of social concord and happiness may be experienced throughout the extent of the countries you represent, as the effect of your wisdom and public virtue, is the unfeigned desire of Your sincere friend.

[Philadelphia] *American Museum* 8(October 1790):156–58; reprinted at Portland, Maine. Although Mifflin's open letter to congressmen is not known to exist in manuscript form addressed to any particular member, Thatcher enclosed it under a cover letter to Thomas B. Wait dated 6 November (printed under that date, below), in which he states that he had the letter in hand two days prior to leaving New York City at the end of the second session in August, well before its first known printing. Thatcher's cover letter, which appeared with the republication of Mifflin's letter in Wait's *Cumberland Gazette*, 22 November, describes the "considerable acquaintance" the congressman developed with the Quaker antislavery petitioner in the spring of 1790. Perhaps that friendship accounts for Thatcher's apparently singular treatment.

---

[1] Proverbs 14:34.

[2] Mifflin was among the delegation (or "committee" as he refers to it later in this piece) that represented the Philadelphia Yearly Meeting of Friends (Quakers) when its antislavery petition was under consideration early in the second session. The eleven member delegation

arrived in New York around 6 February, when they joined six counterparts from the New York Yearly Meeting; after 16 February, only a remnant of four continued at the seat of government until 25 March. Mifflin was unquestionably the most active of these early lobbyists; for details about their activities, see William C. diGiacomantonio, "'For the gratification of a volunteering society:' Antislavery and Pressure Group Politics in the First Federal Congress," *Journal of the Early Republic* 15(1995):169–97.

Other Documents

Pierce Butler to R. Coghlan. FC, Butler Letterbook, ScU. For the full text, see *Butler Letters*, p. 48.

Will be pleased to continue the correspondence Coghlan has begun; from reports of a war between Britain and Spain, suspects Coghlan will soon be promoted to command of a regiment; encloses newspapers.

Matthew Harrison to Charles Biddle. ALS, Biddle Family Papers, DLC. Addressed to Philadelphia; postmarked 3 June.

The Senate committee, to which was committed that day the House resolution that Congress hold its next session in Philadelphia, consisted of a majority who favored New York City, "and from what I can learn it is generally thought they will be for staying where they are."

Samuel Pintard to Elias Boudinot. ALS, Boudinot Family Papers, NjR. Addressed to No. 12 Wall Street; place from which written not indicated. The letter is docketed as being undated but received on 2 June. Like Pintard's letter of 22 June, below, it was probably written from Hempstead, Long Island, no more than a couple of days' delivery away. Lewis Searle Pintard (d. 1818) graduated from Princeton in 1792 (*Princetonians, 1791–1794*, pp. 208–11).

Asks Boudinot to direct son Lewis Searle Pintard's studies in preparation for transferring to Columbia from Princeton, which he considers "a Grog Shop *** by no means so well regulated as the barracks of the foot Guards."

John Steele to Thomas Jefferson. ALS, Jefferson Papers, Missouri Historical Society, St. Louis. For the full text, see *DHFFC* 8:472.

Requests that the House committee on Amendments to the Constitution be furnished with any information about ratification by the states.

William Samuel Johnson, Diary. Johnson Papers, CtHi.

"Col. Bland Buried."

Advertisement. *GUS*, 2 June.

Sale of Boudinot's home ("Boxwood Hall") in Elizabethtown, New Jersey; directs enquiries to him at 12 Wall Street.

GUS, 5 June; reprinted at Carlisle, Pennsylvania.

"We hear" that a bill for establishing the permanent seat of federal government was referred to a committee of five; a motion to refer the House resolution for holding the next session at Philadelphia was referred to the same committee by the casting vote of the Vice President.

From New York. [Boston] *Columbian Centinel*, 16 June.

The commissioners for settling accounts between the United States and individual states have agreed to credit Massachusetts the expense of the Penobscot expedition.

THURSDAY, 3 JUNE 1790

Cool (Johnson)

John Brown Cutting to John Adams

I inclosed You a few days ago a parcel of printed papers some of which I conceived might contain interesting intelligence especially if the dispute ~~with~~ between Britain & Spain shoud terminate in hostilities, as in such an event the government of the United States woud at least be involved in discussions of considerable importance to our country with one or both of those nations.

Among the rest you have an authentic copy of the memorial or narrative of Mr. Mears on the seisure of the british vessels in Nootka sound[1]—as also a sketch of the debate in parliament occasion'd by the message of his britannic majesty on that affair. You will not however obtain from the sketch an adequate conception of the high tone in which the minister [*William Pitt "the Younger"*] spoke. It was thoroughly understood on all sides of the house—(I speak this from having been an auditor) that in unanimously promising his majesty national support against the insult of Spain the minister on his part was pledged to obtain not only pecuniary reparation for the confiscated property and for the insult offered to the british flag, but also a full dereliction from the Court of Spain of its claim to exclusive sovereignty over the coast in the vicinity of Nootka Sound and on the northwest coasts of America and of exclusive navigation and commerce in those seas. A categorical answer to a demand of this sort is pretended by the Court of London to be expected from Madrid by the return of a messenger sent with it just four weeks ago. Meanwhile the warlike preparations in every port and corner of the Island are most vigorous and extensive. Ever since the summer of 1787 Spain has been putting her fleets in the most formidable condition. Nor can one believe that the mere menace of Britain will make her under such circumstances yield the point in contest. In such a crisis it was natural for both nations to turn their eyes on France with considerable anxiety. The late discussion and determination in her national assembly of the great constitutional question whether the power of declaring war shoud be lodged with the Legislature or be confided to the Executive was doubtless hasten'd by this anxiety.[2] The settlement of this point in favour of the Legislative body is conceived by many here as decisive that the french nation will take no part in a war between Spain and Britain. But a more erroneous conclusion never was made. The military spirit of the nation is more alive than ever—and if a majority of its representatives shoud after public discussion and debate decree to go to war, it woud be carried on with more vigour than ever. A partial sale of the ecclesiastical remains for a paper curency has opend a resource of finance that in case of state necessity might be vastly amplified. And as to the supposed hazard that Spain might interfere to attempt a counter revolution in France the idea is already scouted by the partisans of the reform—Two points only are wanting to produce a decree of the french national assembly for war. 1. A persuasion that the spanish have justice on their side ~~and 2d.~~ in the present quarrel and 2dly. That it is for the interest of the french that the mines of South America shoud not become british property. I expect to see both positions established by fact and argument shoud Britain manifestly overstep the limits of equity in her claims. In the interim the naval preparations in the ports of France will keep pace with those in the ports of Britain.

From the moment that a spanish war was publicly known to be impending—the people of the United States began to rise in the estimation of all ranks of men here. Instead of being considered as heretofore a sort of republican banditti enemies to kings and good order on land, and on the ocean ~~a~~ one grade above the algerines only—in the course of a very few days we became popular in the City and bearable I am told even in the Cabinet: The unkind behaviour of Cap. Hendricks an american navigator at Nootka sound—in not quarreling with the Spanish Commodore [*José Martinez*] was overlooked: and the leading Editors of the ministerial newspapers have now orders to affirm that the offer of a treaty offensive and defensive between Britain and America is already dispatchd across the atlantic. The principal inducement to an acceptance of such a treaty on the part of Congress—is a guarantee of a free navigation of the river Missisippi—a participation of some farther indulgencies as to the west india traffic—an adjustment of all disputed boundaries and a speedy surrender of the posts.

I wish the present juncture cou'd be improved for the adjustment of some criterion whereby our seamen might be discriminated from british seamen and consequently exempted from the outrages of the british press gangs. The great point to be guarded against on our part is the first violence of having our mariners forced from on board ~~their~~ our ships under a pretext that they are britons—To do away all colour for committing it some palpable species of prima facie evidence is wanted—such as being immediately produced might stare every officer of a press gang in the face and leave him without excuse if he ventured to depart from the orders of the Admiralty-Board by which he is even directed to take no foreigners. A few days after I had memorializ'd the Lords of the Admiralty and almost exacted by dint of diligent and remonstrating assiduity the liberation of those six crews or parts of crews which had been impress'd, Mr. Governeur Morris to whom I had communicated my toils and their termination sent a note to the duke of Leeds and asking for an hours conversation with him—stated verry forcibly to him the pernicious effect that impressing our mariners must have on the commerce of Britain. The Duke listen'd to him, thanked him, & seemed to believe him and said orders shou'd be issued and measures taken to prevent the american seamen from being impress'd in future. But there are real difficulties in the business that general commands of this nature do not meet. As a zealous citizen I do wish some effectual remedy to such a national mischief and indignity coud be devised. No moment can be more favourable for attempting something of the sort than the present. The perfect protection of our mariners from being impressed or impeded is just now a desirable object to the commercial part of this nation. In former wars when the british seamen were press'd to mann the navy—the merchants coud generally procure Swedes Hollanders and other european seamen to supply their places—but at present all those foreign seamen are engaged by their sovereigns [*lined out*] or by their fellow subjects—and the~~ir~~ british merchant will be compeld to resort to the United States for american seamen in lieu of them.

As I send this letter one post later than that by which the mail is conveyed to Falmouth—it is necessary for me to close it immediately to obtain the chance of its reaching Mr. [*John, Jr.*] Rutledge at Falmouth.

ALS, Adams Family Manuscript Trust, MHi. Written from London. The news of Great Britain's preparations for war arrived in the United States via the Falmouth (England) packet on 18 June.

---

[1] Intent on enforcing Spain's exclusive territorial claim to northwestern North America, between May and July 1789 two Spanish warships under José Martinez detained and then seized three British merchant ships and a modest trading post built in 1788 in Nootka Sound, on the west coast of present-day Vancouver Island, British Columbia. The ships and the post were the property of a trading firm headed by the former British naval officer and explorer John Mears (1756?–1809), who was among those taken captive to Mexico. Although they

were soon released, no restitution was offered for the damages and treatment Mears described in an inflammatory memorial submitted to the British Home Secretary William Grenville on 30 April 1790. The scene in Parliament described by Cutting took place on 6 May, when Prime Minister William Pitt "The Younger" announced the government's preparations for war against Spain. The packet ship carrying this news arrived in New York on 18 June, thirty-six days out of Falmouth, England. The implications of the Nootka Sound Affair for American domestic and foreign policy were far reaching, as its many subsequent references in congressional correspondence suggest. Even as American merchants anxiously anticipated the profits that would accrue from supplying interrupted trade, American diplomats in Europe warned of the renewed threat of their seamen's being impressed while ashore during Britain's "hot press" for its own naval forces. Following an ultimatum from Pitt's government on 5 July and his intensified diplomatic overtures towards France (as well as more covert ones towards the United States), Spain ended the Nootka crisis by yielding on all points in dispute, according to the Treaty of El Escorial signed on 28 October 1790 (John Rutledge, Jr., to Jefferson, 6 May, *PTJ* 16:413–15; *NYDG*, *GUS*, 19 June; *DHFFC* 13:1611; Howard V. Evans, "The Nootka Sound Controversy in Anglo-French Diplomacy, 1790," *Journal of Modern History*, vol. 46, 4[Dec. 1974]:609–40).

[2] In the early months of the brinkmanship sparked by the Nootka Sound crisis, Spain relied on tipping the scales against England by invoking the terms of the Family Compact of 1761, which bound the Bourbon crowns of Spain and France to a policy of mutual mobilization. Despite initial reports that France would abide by the Compact, as much out of dynastic obligations as its traditional anglophobia, the revolutionary National Assembly used the occasion to annul the Compact on 22 May 1790 (Evans, "Nootka Sound Controversy," pp. 609–23).

John Fenno to Joseph Ward

It seems a *very* long time since I heard from you—thro divine goodness we are all well—I most sincerely hope that no sickness or misfortune has prevented your writing.

The funding bill passed the House yesterday & was Sent up to the Senate—I enclose you a Copy—we have been a good deal agitated at a vote of the House to meet the next session at Philadelphia—the business however appears to be arrested in its progress, in the Senate—it has been referred to a Committee to whom a Bill respecting the permanent Residence is committed—It is expected that the funding bill will receive some amendments—among others, I expect~~ed~~ a Clause in favor of the assumption whether such a Clause will not defeat the funding bill altogether I really feel uncertain—It is possible that at the *close* of the session, those in opposition may be more reconciled—but matters appear to me in so precarious a state as to their final Issue, that I was never more puzzled—every appearance either pro or con, as to funding, immediately affects *stock*—Finals are now up to 9/6 and Indents were this day sold at 7/6—in consequence of the pass~~age~~ing of the Bill—but should it receive a check in the Senate, they would immediately fall—& should the funding System be postponed to the next Session—they will be down, down, down—Tell Mr. Russell if you please, that I congratulate him on his appointment to print the Laws[1]—He will I suppose be informed of it by a Letter from one of his Friends by this post.

I want to write you many things—but have not time—My Love to Mrs. [*Prudence Bird*] Ward & Compliments to Mr. Harbach—Mrs. [*Mary Curtis*] Fenno's also.

It is rather a cloudy time with us—but the Sun will break out—and I really expect that Congress will attempt to set matters right before they rise. [*P. S.*] Post is in—and no Letter.

ALS, Ward Papers, ICHi. Addressed to the Land office, Boston. The address sheet includes the notation, "the Conductor is requested to Deliver this with his own hand." The editor Benjamin Russell either paraphrased this letter or quoted a different letter from Fenno in his [Boston] *Massachusetts Centinel*, 9 June, from which it was reprinted at Portsmouth and Exeter, New Hampshire; and Portland, Maine.

[1] Benjamin Russell's *Massachusetts Centinel* was one of five newspapers selected by Jefferson to publish and circulate federal statutes under the Records Act.

Samuel Henshaw to Theodore Sedgwick

I have this moment recd. your's of the 29 ult.—and hope that, at the same moment, you recd. my last—I thank you most sincerely for your kind exertions—I hope & almost venture to believe, that they will be effectual, notwithstanding all the Letters Mr. [*Leonard*] Jarvis has taken with him to the contrary—I could easily procure a Cart load, if necessary.[1]

I am happy to find that Messrs. Gerry & Goodhue continue my Friends.

A proposition to instruct our Members in Congress to enforce the assumption of the State debts is *now* in debate before the [*Massachusetts*] Senate—we shall undoubtedly have it before the House to Morrow—[*John*] Bacon & [*Thompson*] Skinner oppose it warmly—but I have no doubt, but it will pass by a very large Majority in each House.

We have not yet determined the Mode for chusing federal Representatives. I rather think they will vote to choose by districts as before, except ~~only~~ that a second voting shall determine the choice—At any rate or Mode, I will for one drink of humble grog ensure your re election—This is serious.

I will this evening see what Genl. L. [*Benjamin Lincoln*] will do.[2]

If I write one line more I shall not send by this post.

So farewel my dear Friend.

ALS, Sedgwick Papers, MHi. Written from Boston; franked; postmarked.

[1] Henshaw sought an appointment under the proposed Duties on Distilled Spirits Bill [HR-62].

[2] An unsigned note in Benjamin Lincoln's hand and endorsed by Sedgwick, "Genl. Lincoln 3. June 1790." reported: "The house I think is a pretty good one & will act probably

with the senate." Lincoln probably gave the note to Henshaw that "evening" and the latter enclosed it in his letter.

Benjamin Huntington to Governor Samuel Huntington

Your Excellencys Favr. by the last Post was Duely Recd. which adds to the many Instances of Obligation arising from Favourable Notice from your Excellency—The Innovations attempted by Certain Characters, to be brought into the laws of our State, If I have been rightly Informed are not so favourable to Democratical Government as the many Miss Informed Gentlemen may apprehend[1] I think they are not Immediately very Dangerous but in Process of Time the State will find that Important Characters Placed in the General Legislature and finding themselves under the unfavourable Circumstance of an Exclusion from all Places of Honor or Profit in their own State will in the first Place make use of all Intrigue in their Power to obtain Elections to Continue themselves in the General Government either in Congress or in Some of the Lucrative Departments, they will consider themselves less Attached to the State and more Interested in Promoting an Aristocratic Power I cannot think it good Policy to Exclude the Members of Congress from holding any Office in the States because it cuts off a Connection which if kept up would always form a very harmonious Tye between Congress and the Assemblies of the States, but if Destroyed, the Members of Congress will Consider themselves of Superior Rank and tho' their next Election will in most Cases be a Check upon their Conduct yet they will no longer be under this Check than the feel their Dependence and this Dependence will be wholly avoided whenever they can make themselves Independent by Securing Appointments Independent of the People whom they will consider as an unfriendly Mobb.

In the next Place it will be natural for men, who have been in Place and Respected by their Neighbours, to feel themselves Degraded when Declared by law Incapable of their former Honors and obliged to live nine or ten months in the Year among their former Neighbours under the Mortifying feelings of a legal Disability they will not feel themselves under the Same obligation to Support the State Government as if they were capable of a Share in Such Government and in some Instances be Seditious—They will be Considered by the Populace as [*lined out*] Objects of their Just Jealousy as having too much Power in their hands & This Jealousy will Seldom fail to be Increased by the Suggestions of Designing People and the Distance between the General Government and that of the State be Increased in Proportion to their Alienation from each other I have no Personal feelings of this Subject & have Suffered nothing to my own mortification in Consequence of any

Neglect nor Shall I as long as I think my Reputation is untouched but mean to be understood as Regarding the Subject Generally The Inclosed Papers will Show the Business in Agitation here at Present (Saving only that the Subject of Removing to Philadelphia is in the Senate, Referred to a Special Committee). We have the Official News of the Accession of Rhode Island and a Bill is in agitation to Extend the Laws of the United States over the State of Rhode Island.

ALS, Gratz Collection, PHi. Addressed to Hartford or Norwich, Connecticut; franked; postmarked; marked "private"; answered 4 July.

[1] The attempt to exclude members of Congress and other federal officials from seats in the Connecticut legislature. The House passed the bill in the last week of May after striking only the provision that excluded federal officials, but the bill was negatived by the Council of Assistants (Connecticut's upper chamber) two weeks later ([Hartford] *American Mercury*, 31 May, 14 June).

Richard Bland Lee to Theodorick Lee

Since my last I have the distress of informing you that we have lost a very dear and valuable relation Col. Bland,[1] who departed this life on the 1st Instant. Yesterday the last honors were paid to his remains by the Congress—officers of the general government, of the State government, the [*Society of the*] cincinnati and the respectable Citizens of the town.

In my last I explain'd my Conduct to you on the subject of amendments. Since which I have received a letter from Col. [*Thomas*] Blackburn which has drawn from me a more minute explanation. I could wish that this could meet with an extensive circulation among my Constituents. I am anxious to return to Virginia in order to vindicate myself from the aspersions of my enemies. I hope we shall adjourn in July.

R. Island has adopted the Constitution. ***

ALS, Custis-Lee Family Papers, DLC. Addressed to "Sully," R. B. Lee's plantation in Loudoun County, Virginia, by way of Alexandria; franked; postmarked. The omitted text relates to the sale or mortgage of land for which Lee wanted £200 "immediately." No response from R. B. Lee to Blackburn has been located.

[1] Theodorick Bland's father, Theodorick Sr. (b. 1720), was the younger brother of Richard Bland Lee's and Theodorick Lee's paternal grandmother, Mary Bland Lee (1704–64).

Samuel Phillips, Jr. to Benjamin Goodhue

I cannot yet perswade myself to give up the idea of your final success in the business of assumption—if you should not succeed before the Bill goes up to the Senate, may not hopes be entertained from that quarter—In the State Legislatures there have been instances, where the Senate have been the means of preventing great evil, & sometimes of effecting important measures—you have witnessed the salutary consequences of the deliberations & wisdom of the Senate of the U.S. in more instances than one; I trust our Friends in that body have not been unemployed, in respect to this great subject, while the House has been labouring thus seriously to prepare the work for them, and I have more faith in the success of private conference than of public debate, in certain cases, especially where the populace have warmly interested themselves in the question or where it is expected they will do it; It is not common to find a man who has zealously engaged on either side of a question, (especially if viewed of great moment) before a numerous assembly, to receive conviction of his error, or, if he feels it, to possess candor enough to acknowledge it—and the longer a man has persevered in his argument, the more improbable is the change, for his pride becomes more & more interested ~~to~~ in maintaining the ground he has taken, by every hour's continuance on it & by every public exertion to defend it—The prospect is not, even at this hour, so discouraging as it was for weeks, in respect to the adoption of the Constitution itself, and I am apprehensive, if the Convention of this State had continued together till this day, their *public debates* would not have produced an acceptance of it; some were influenced by serious & often repeated private interviews, some by the expectation of personal honor or profit, perhaps some by the timely aid of the first magistrate;[1] In the present case, it cant be desired that the P—t of the U.S. should do any thing improper in itself, or that would endanger his popularity but would there be any thing amiss in his taking ~~occasion~~ a proper season to witness to one or two *proper* persons *the relief he has felt* in *seasons* of the *greatest distress*, from the exertions of Massachusetts ~~as well as~~ & a few others, to forward men & supplies; *Then*, There was no hesitation on our part, in order to be ascertained of the time & manner of payment—our language was, every thing that is in the power of our hands we will do; if we finally succeed there cant be a doubt but Congress will be as ready to do us justice as we are to make the advance.

Thursday eveng.—I have just come in from Senate, where we have been considering the report of a joint Commee. relative to the assumption[2] A copy of that Report & a minute of the proceedings of Senate, I herewith send you, as well as the paper which contains the Governor's Speech[3]—I am informed there is no do[*u*]bt but a majority of the House will be in sentiment with the Senate—should this be the case, one of Mr. Maddison's arguments must loose some of it's force[4]—I hope the result will go on by the next Post, tho' such delays often attend~~s~~ the settlement of forms, in large public bodies, that it is difficult to say when any business will be compleated.

I have just received your kind favor of the 29th. Ulto., and am very happy to find that the Pensylva. have not made the bargain with the southern Gentlemen, which was feared—I dont see how any dishonorable imputations can be cast upon those Gentlemen, who before voted to go to Pensylva. if they should again express the same sentiment; but to have it in the power of an enemy to say that there was a bargain in the case, would be unfortunate—cannot the Gentlemen of that State be perswaded of your good disposition towards them—they may be sure we had rather go there, than advance farther south and ~~they~~ we can't expect to remain long at New York—As to agreeing to the city of Philadelphia rather than the place before concluded on, I have little to say, for I am ignorant of the comparative advantages & disadvantages—saving that in general, large populous places are unfriendly to deliberation & dispatch. having been detained at Senate, to an unusual hour must ask you to excuse me from fulfilling my promise in regard to Mr. [*Samuel*] Osgood till the next post.

ALS, Letters to Goodhue, NNS. Written from Boston.

[1] A reference to Governor John Hancock's critical intervention during the Massachusetts ratification convention; see John Trumbull to John Adams, 30 March, n. 4, above.

[2] The resolution of the Massachusetts legislature is printed under 4 June, below.

[3] Hancock's annual message to the Massachusetts legislature in Boston on 1 June is described in Phillips's letter to Goodhue of that date, above. Phillips probably forwarded the text of the speech from the [Boston] *Massachusetts Centinel*, 2 June, as no other Boston printing was available before the date of this letter. The only New York City printing (*GUS*, 9 June) was in the form of extracts taken from the [Boston] *Independent Chronicle* of 3 June.

[4] In a speech on 22 April, Madison argued that the Massachusetts legislature's failure to instruct its state delegation on the subject of assumption was evidence that it did not support the measure (*DHFFC* 13:1174).

Caleb Strong to Theodore Foster

I have this Moment recd. your Letter of the 29th. of May—We had before the very agre[*a*]ble News of the Adoption of the Constitution by your State and I am happy to be informed of the Probability that the State will be represented in the Senate in a very short Time, and I hope and trust the Persons chosen will be Men of enlightened Minds & liberal Policy, should they be of a different Character they may oppose an Assumption of the State Debts which to me appears necessary to the Peace & Happiness of this Country.

The House a few Days since sent us a Resolve that the next Session of Congress should be holden at Philadelphia, previous to this a Bill had been brought into the Senate to fix the permanent Residence of Congress—The Bill & Resolve are both committed in the Senate & the Comittee will probably report to morrow or on Monday—an Effort will be made to fix the permanent Residence on the Potomack—you will undoubtedly wish that your State may be represented when this Question is settled—if they are the Senators must be here soon.

ALS, Foster Papers, RHi. Addressed to Providence, Rhode Island; franked; postmarked.

Cotton Tufts to Benjamin Goodhue

I received Your Favour of the 26th. Ulto. and must readily confess that my Delay in writing has furnished you with some Cause to reprove me for Inattention. I can however assure You that the old Proverb Out of Sight, out of Mind will not apply on this Occasion—for I have often thought of my Friend, his Scituation, the Mortifications He must meet with from Delays as well as the numerous Embarrassments that has and probably will arise in the Prosecution of the Business of Congress—I have indeed had sympathetic Feelings altho I have not so often expressed them in writing as I could have wished to have done—But in Vindication of myself I have to say That for some Months [*lined out*] Time & Attention has been so much engross'd in the Business of my Profession in consequence of the general Prevalence of the Influenza & Meazles in my Vicinity, that I have had scarce any Leisure—I am now released and again called to unite with our State Physicians in administring to the Body Politic, but here Administrations how ever judicious will, I fear, fail of Success—From year to year We jog on—we prescribe, alter our Prescriptions, lay them aside, prescribe anew throw them away—resume the old ones, but effect no Cure, indeed we too much resemble those who make great Pretensions to Skill, promise much but instead of curing the Patient, either protract the Disease or put Him beyond Recovery—I hope Your Administrations will meet with better Success—There are, ~~So~~ it is apprehended, some Appearances that indicate too great a Similarity between our State and Fœderal Physicians—I will not undertake to run the Pararell—To get rid of the Payment of the just Debts of Government has been an object with many in our Legislature for some years past—How it is in yours I will not pretend to say. It is said, That Our present Court [*legislature*] is much better than the former ~~one~~ We may therefore have some Hopes that our affairs will wear a better Aspect, Our Senate is as well filld as could be expected—The Report of a joint Committee in Favour of instructing the Senators from this Commonwealth in Congress to move in Congress for the Assumption of our State Debt, and to convey to the Representatives from this State the Sense of the Legislature on this Subject, was considered & accepted by a large Majority 17 for & 7 against—it passed this afternoon & will be sent to the House in the morning—there will be many opposers to it there, but it is the opinion of those who are in the House & best acquainted with the Sentiments of their Members, that they will concur with the Senate—We have had before us this day a Bill for ceding our Light Houses to Congress—The greatest objection made to it was respecting Jurisdiction—That to give entire Jurisdiction to Congress would be parting with a portion of Sovereignity which we had no authority to do and which by our Oaths we were bound to preserve—also with such a Jurisdiction vested in the General Government, the State could have no authority to arrest a Debtor or Criminal in any of the Places thus ceded to the Fœderal Government, the former objection made no great Impression, the latter was considered of so much Weight as to produce a Commitment of the Bill—and with some small amendments it will pass ~~in~~—as I have Opportunity, shall take the Liberty of transmitting to you an Acct. of such Proceedings in the Court as I think would afford you Satisfaction to be acquainted with.

ALS, Letters to Goodhue, NNS. Written from Boston.

Other Documents

Abraham Baldwin to Ezra Stiles. ALS, Stiles Papers, CtY. Addressed to New Haven, Connecticut; franked; postmarked; received 5 June.

Will forward letter to Mr. (Abiel) Holmes, enclosed in Stiles's last, at Savannah, Georgia; trusts that Peter Pond's information (about western North America) "must be highly gratifying to the many who wish to know every thing about this country," and that it will be carefully studied; reports Rhode Island's ratification, by which she "takes her place in the old circle of her friends"; "their delegates are daily expected."

Andrew Craigie to Daniel Parker. FC:dft, Craigie Papers, MWA. Sent by packet; part of letter copied and sent to Samuel Rogers.

Almost impossible to say what will be the issue of the debate on assumption, scheduled to be taken up the next Monday and decided.

Jeremiah Hill to George Thatcher. ALS, Chamberlain Collection, MB. Written from Biddeford, Maine.

Office seeking: William Vaughan asks to be considered; also, "our friend" Joshua Bailey Osgood, for "the Inspectorship you mentioned a few posts since," under the Duties on Distilled Spirits Bill [HR-62]; he ought to be pitied and helped because of his poverty, "if consistant with the good of the great whole."

David Howell to Thomas Jefferson. ALS, Miscellaneous Letters, Miscellaneous Correspondence, State Department Records, Record Group 59,

DNA. Written from Providence, Rhode Island. For the full text, see *PTJ* 16:451–53.

Office seeking; encloses packet of pamphlets (James McVarnum, *The case, Trevett against Weeden* . . . [Providence, R.I., 1787; Evans 20825]) to distribute to Adams and others; asks that contents of the letter be shared with Adams.

Thomas Jefferson to John Steele. FC, Domestic Letters, Miscellaneous Correspondence, State Department Records, Record Group 59, DNA. For the full text, see *PTJ* 16:470–71. The report of the House committee that Steele chaired on this subject (*DHFFC* 8:472–73) repeats Jefferson's letter almost verbatim.

Reports the legislative proceedings in six states (New Hampshire, New York, Pennsylvania, Delaware, Maryland, and South Carolina) on the proposed Amendments to the Constitution.

John Langdon to John S. Sherburne. No copy known; acknowledged in Sherburne to Langdon, 14 June.

George Mason to John Langdon. ALS, Langdon Papers, NhPoA. Written from "Gunston Hall," Fairfax County, Virginia; carried by Joseph Fenwick.

Introduces Joseph Fenwick, his son John's business partner in Bordeaux, France, who is visiting the principal merchants of the Eastern states en route to Boston or Portsmouth for his return to France; solicits letters of introduction on his behalf; office seeking: Fenwick for consul at Bordeaux; asks Langdon to introduce Fenwick, whose application has already been sent to the President, "to some of your Friends in the Senate."

Frederick A. Muhlenberg to Governor Beverley Randolph. LS, Executive Papers, Vi. Printed in *DHFFC* 8L475.

Notification of Bland's death and burial, enclosing extract of House proceedings on the occasion.

Richard Platt to Jeremiah Wadsworth. ALS, Wadsworth Papers, CtHi. Addressed to Hartford, Connecticut; postmarked.

Sorry to hear of the "indisposition of your Son [*Daniel*] which caused your return home"; Elizabeth McDougall Laurance "is reduced lower than when you left the City—I fear her stay with us, is but very short—she has moved out to the Hill" (Bunker Hill); asks help in procuring a cow and a fieldhand.

Sir John Temple to Francis Osborne, Duke of Leeds. ALS, Foreign Office 4/8 pp. 252–53, PRO.

"Tomorrow being His Majestys Birth I shall have to dine with me, as usual, The Vice President of Congress (Mr. Washington is not Well enough to come) The Great officers of state, The Treasurer, the Secretary of State, the Secretary at War. The Chief Justice of the United States. The Speaker of the lower house of Congress. The Episcopal Bishop [*Samuel Provoost*]. the Members of Congress, and all his Majestys officers of Navy & Army (and they are not few) that are here."

George Washington to Marquis de la Fayette. FC:lbk, Washington Papers, DLC. For the full text, see *PGW* 5:467–69.

The government is in operation despite "thorney questions" remaining, which he hopes Congress will settle prudently; federal appointments to office give "perfect satisfaction to the Public"; it is thought Congress will recess for the summer.

Letter from London to Philadelphia. *NYMP*, 7 August (the date on which members of Congress would have seen it).

There will be no war between Spain and Great Britain.

Friday, 4 June 1790

Cool (Johnson)

Governor John Hancock to the Massachusetts Delegation

The expediency of Instructing the Gentlemen representing this State in Congress or ~~to make application~~ to make ~~any~~ an application to that Honble. Body on the Subject of assuming the debts of this Commonwealth have been the subject of Debate this day ~~before of~~ by the two branches of the Legislature and I have only ~~now~~ Time to enclose their Resolution just this moment passed in complyance with their request—Upon hearing that Congress have it in contemplation to determine upon this important Question relative to the Assumption of the State debts the beginning of next Week; It was thought advisable to send it by Express that you might have the earliest notice of their Sentiments—It being so late in the Evening and the Express now waiting ~~you I can't~~ [*lined out*] ~~I have not~~ my Time ~~to~~ [*lined out*] will not admit of being explicit upon this ~~important~~ Subject ~~but~~ [*lined out*] as I would wish [*lined out*].

[*Enclosure*]

The Committee of the two Houses appointed to consider, whether it is expedient to Instruct our Senators & Representatives in Congress, or to make any other application to that Honourable Body on the subject of assuming the Debts of this Commonwealth, submit the following ~~Report~~ Resolve— E[*leazer*]. Brooks pr. Order.

WHEREAS it appears to this Court that the Debts of the several States in the Union being contracted for the Common defence, ought to be a common charge and Assumed by, & provided for by the United States of America; And Whereas it further Appears that such Assumption is necessary to secure to the United States the [*lined out*][*co*]llection of their own Revenues, to equalize the burthens of the several States, and to releive the People from the oppressive, & too frequent ~~unjust~~ operation, of large direct Taxation— THEREFORE RESOLVED That his Excellency the Governor be requested as soon as may be, to write to the Representatives of the People of this Commonwealth & communicate to them the sentiments of the Legislature on this subject, and also to write to the Senators of this Commonwealth in behalf of the same, to instruct them to apply to Congress to Assume the Public Debt of this Commonwealth and make provision for the payment of the same as part of the Debt of the union: it having been incured in consequence of the War between the United States and the Kingdom of Great Britain.

FC:dft, signed by Hancock, Resolves, 1790, M-Ar. The ALS of the letter has not survived, so it is unknown whether Hancock sent separate letters to the Representatives and to the Senators; they responded separately (Hancock to the Legislature, 14 June, Miscellaneous Legislative Papers, Senate, M-Ar).

Governor Beverley Randolph to James Madison

Your favour of the 25th. of May inclosing a resolution of both Houses of Congress, on the subject of arrears due to the Virginia Line, has been received. So soon as the Resolution shall be officially communicated to me, you may be assured that the Executive, will take every possible step to prevent impositions upon the claimants.

I have lately received a letter from Colonel Davies, inclosing a report from two of the Commissioners, appointed to settle the Accounts, of the individual States, with the United States; made in consequence of an order of the House of Representatives, directing them to report the amount of the Claims of the several States.[1] This Paper discovers such a Temper in the Judges as does not inspire us with confidence that their Judgments will be grounded upon Strict Principles of equity. Although their conduct on this occasion has not met with the countenance of the House of Representatives, we are uncertain whether that honorable Body, disapproved it, merely as not complying with their requisition, or that they were dissatisfied with it, as conveying improper Reflections upon this State, and her agents. If there be no impropriety in it I should be much obliged to you to communicate to me the sentiments of the members who Spoke on the subject. I confess I was the more surprized at this report when I saw a fair Statement of the Claims of Virginia against the United States to a very large amount, which Statement I conceive must have been known to the Commissioners. We are rejoiced to hear of the Presidents recovery.

LS, Madison Papers, DLC. Written from Richmond, Virginia.

---

[1] William Davies, Virginia's commissioner for settling Virginia's continental accounts, sent his letter with enclosures on 21 May; it is printed under the headnote on the Report of the Commissioners for Settling Accounts, 8 May, above.

William Smith (Md.) to Otho H. Williams

Yours of the 29th ulto. afforded me a great deal of pleasure in hearing that you were Safe arrived at Baltimore, your health, restored, and all your little family well.

I regret much, that I cant have the pleasure of seeing you all, before your departure for the [*Warm*] Springs, especially the Boys [*Robert and William*] who I ardently long to see, I have therefore only to Anticipate the Joy of Seeing you all return Safe & in good health; May God bless & preserve you is my most Sincere prayer.

***

You will have Seen by the papers, that our house have agreed to hold their next Sessions at Phila. the Same day, that our resolution on that head, went to the Senate, a Bill was brought into that house to fix *the permanent residence*, with a View I apprehend to Secure the temporary residence in this City *for Some time*, & perhaps to defeat Philada.—Whatever are the Views of the friends to N. York Some good may come from it to us, it Seems Potomack Baltimore, & Susquehanah, are all Spoke of in the Senate for the Permanent Seat. and although, I am not very Sanguine on this head, I have however a distant hope, that, betwixt two great contending, rival Cities, something may turn up in our favor.

ALS, Williams Papers, MdHi. Addressed to Baltimore. The omitted text directs the management of some personal business transactions.

John Steele to George Washington

A sincere desire that the office of district Judge for No. Carolina, may be bestowed upon a worthy character induces me to offer you my opinion at present. I have been told that Colo. [*William R.*] Davie's name has been mentioned to you already. he is unquestionably better calculated for the office, than any other man in the State; but acquainted as I am, with his practice as an attorney, his plans, and his prospects, I have reason to believe that he would not relinquish such profitable pursuits for so small a salary. Samuel Spencer Esqr. has been also mentioned, I presume for the same office; he is a good man, at present one of the judges of that state, not remarkable for his abilities, but nevertheless deserves well of his country. Colonel John Stokes, has not been mentioned, but I am authorised to transmit his name to Your Excellency as a Candidate for the same Office.

This Gentleman is a native of Virginia, descended from a very respectable family, was a Captain in the Sixth Regiment of that state in the late War, continued in service untill Colo. Beaufort was defeated in So. Carolina,[1] when unfortunately he lost (among other wounds) his right hand.

He then setled in No. Carolina, has practiced the law ever since, with reputation, and success, has been frequently a member of the State legislature wherein he supported a very respectable, and honorable rank, both as a man of business, and a man of abilities, was a member of the Convention and very instrumental in bringing about the ratification of the Constitution, is at this time Colo. Commandt. of a Regt. of militia Cavalry, and additional Judge of the supreme Court of Law and Equity in that State. Notwithstanding the loss of his right hand, few men write better than he does with the other, and is extreamly capable of business.

With respect to the Candidates for any other office within that State, or the ceded territory if my opinion, or any information from me, are necessary they shall be given with candor, and impartiality.

ALS, Washington Papers, DLC. Received 5 June.

[1] Col. Abraham Buford's decisive defeat by Lieut. Col. Banastre Tarleton at Waxhaws, South Carolina, on 29 May 1780.

Nathaniel Wells to George Thatcher

Your Letters of the 25th & 29th of last month were this Week recd. in the first of them you observe that you have been informed that a number of the principal Members of the general court [*legislature*] are opposed to the Assumption of the State debts by the general Government but I am satisfied that you have been misinformed for upon enquiry I find only a small Number in opposition to the Assumption a Resolve has this [*day*] been passed the General Court in favour of the Assumption by a considerable majority in both houses in the Senate 24 Members were present 17 of which were in favour of the Assumption & 7 against it, in the house as I am informed 123 members were present & 83 of them in favour of the Measure and the residue against it the Resolution of the Legislature will be sent forward by the next Post, there is great opposition in Boston & Salem against State Excises and what effects the opposition may produce time only will discover, The Merchants do not complain of the impost duties because they operate uniformly thro the several States in the Union and they say they are willing to submit to uniform Excises as thereby they will not be distinguished from the citizens of the other States and will enjoy the same commercial advantages with them If the debt of this State is not assumed a State excise will be indispensibly necessary in it to a considerable amount which will undoubtedly produce discontent and uneasiness which it may be difficult to subdue I am inclined to think at present if Congress should pay no regard to the interest of the several States considered in their seperate capacities yet if they attend to the National Interest respecting their Revenue they finally will be disposed to adopt such measures as will render State Excises unnecessary as I conceive that they will be found upon a fair experiment greatly injurious to the Revenue of the united States and possibly may produce such Effects as after making the experiment can not be easily remidied I think there will be a strong temtation to smuggling in case of State Excises in order that goods may be sold as cheap in this as in the neighbouring States and it may by many b[*e*] thought justifiable, there will be a division between the State & continental Creditors the former in favour of State Excises and the latter in favour of those imposed by the general government and when the people of this Commonwealth in general consider how much is raised in it by continental Excises and at the same time are under the necessity of providing for payment of a large State debt which ought to be provided for by other States in the Union in part at least as I suppose every one will readily acknowledge. *** there is as great a Scarcity of Provision in the eastern Country [*Maine*] in general as perhaps was ever known owing to the great drought and early Frosts the last season and the astonishing Number of Devourers I mean the Grasshoppers which were vastly more numerous than was ever before known.

ALS, Thatcher Papers, MB. Written from Boston; franked. The omitted text reports on the deaths of friends.

Henry Wynkoop to Reading Beatty

Those sanguine expectations, express'd in my last respecting an adjournment to Philadelphia have since been somewhat allay'd by the Proceedings of the Senate, which You will see in the papers, however ~~our~~ do not yet despair of Success, the popularity of the Measure in the House of Representatives & the respectabillity of the minority in the Senate, must undoubtedly accomplish it in some Shape or other, I send You [*Francis*] Childs paper [*NYDA*] of this day, by which You will perceive how the Shoe pinches, the Newspaper Wiffets [*whippets*] are barking they snarl & shew their Teeth, so much for the Treatment the Pensylvanians received here last Fall, for which tho' I beleive our Newyork Brethren are now sincerely penitent; Their superior Adress saved our 100,000 Dollars & I hope by the time this Matter is ended our Reputation will be saved also.

The funding Bill passed the House yesterday, that making provision for the Settlement of the Accounts between the United States & individual States is now under discussion, hope this will in some measure quiet the Minds of the Advocates for the State Assumptions, I learn by [*son*] Nicholas's Letter received this day that my family are much indisposed, wish You therefore to visit them as Doctor & direct what may be proper for them. Hope to be at home on sunday week, unless Busyness prevent.

ALS, Wynkoop Papers, PDoBHi. Place to which addressed not indicated.

A Country Correspondent to Mr. Greenleaf

I just now arrived in town, Mr. Printer, and as I was walking up Wall-street I heard a man say, as how Congress were about making a great *balloon* out of *continental certificates* and *public securities*; that they were filling of it as fast as they could with *inflammable air*; that in about a fortnight it would be nearly inflated; and that the great *hall*, which cost you *Yorkers* about £.30,000, was to be then suspended to the balloon, with all its animate and inanimate contents, and set down near the new goal [*jail*] in the city of Philadelphia. Now, Mr. Printer, I wish you would explain this affair; for my part, I have heard of balloons, but I never knew that they could be made to carry such great bodies.

NYJ, 4 June, edited by Thomas Greenleaf; reprinted at Poughkeepsie, New York; Richmond and Winchester, Virginia; Edenton, North Carolina; and Augusta, Georgia.

OTHER DOCUMENTS

William Constable to James Seagrove. FC:lbk, Constable-Pierrepont Collection, NN.

Morris "is so Embarrassed with a thousand Perplexities that He can do nothing—He spoke Handsomely of You, but fair words is all He can afford—with respect to the Contract for supplying the Troops" (in Georgia); William Duer is out of office "at his own instance I assure you, such is the natural fickleness of his Temper that He cannot Remain any where or pursue any scheme long"; believes the assumption of the states' war debts will not take place that session.

Tench Coxe to Benjamin Rush. ALS, Rush Papers, PPL at PHi. Addressed to Philadelphia.

In a "respectable circle," Coxe mentioned Rush's "medical hint" about towns' unhealthy proximity to sea air; two or three characters "in our interest applied it in a moment" to New York City; "I observed, it attracted a good deal of Mr. Madison's Attention, whom I find a charming companion on these as well as political subjects."

Sampson Fleming to an Unknown Recipient. FC, Fleming Letterbook, 1782–90, NN.

The Rhode Island Senators "are expected speedily."

Dominick Lynch to Daniel Carroll. AN, Washington Papers, DLC. Written in the morning. The note is undated; the editors supplied the date based on Lynch to Tobias Lear, 4 June (*PGW* 5:471).

Office seeking: John D. Street of Philadelphia for American consul at Fayal in the Azores; asks Carroll to speak to the President and Jefferson.

Robert Morris to Gouverneur Morris. No copy known; acknowledged in Gouverneur to Robert Morris, 31 July.

Samuel Phillips, Jr. to Benjamin Goodhue. ALS, Letters to Goodhue, NN. Written from Boston; franked; postmarked 6 June.

Hopes the Massachusetts legislature's recent instructions urging assumption will not embarrass but "aid you, and afford you fresh spirits"; the consequences of not assuming are difficult to predict because the state excise is unpopular in Boston and he believes many other places; the legislature will resist doing anything until the assumption question is settled; complains that other states have been "fattening on our spoils"; asks Goodhue to manage financial transaction with (Samuel) Osgood regarding purchase of a screw (for a papermaking manufactory); wishes "your long & painful labours in this trying juncture may be crowned with success"; trusts Congress will have passed a funding system before Rhode Island's delegation arrives.

Pamela Sedgwick to Theodore Sedgwick. ALS, Sedgwick Papers, MHi. Written from Stockbridge, Massachusetts. The first part of this letter was written on 1 June and is calendared under that date, above.

Begins to think Congress will sit through the entire summer, in which case she will be tempted to go to New York; daughter Eliza left that morning to pay last respects to Sedgwick's mother (Ann Thompson Sedgwick) in Cornwall, Connecticut; enquires of the prospects of nephew Theodore Sedgwick's commissioning in the federal army; son Robert's leg continues to heal and it is next to impossible to keep him on his crutches; "I have promissd. him that Doctr. [*Richard*] Bailey or Pappa will bring him a Bag of Sugar Plumbs If he will be good."

Michael Jenifer Stone to Walter Stone. ALS, Gratz Collection, PHi. Addressed to Charles County, Maryland; franked; postmarked.

Acknowledges Walter's letter; "I shall get the things for the Girls" (brother Thomas's orphaned daughters?).

William Samuel Johnson, Diary. Johnson Papers, CtHi.

"Dind. [*Dined at*] Sr. J. Temple's."

FG, 5 June; reprinted at Baltimore.

"By a letter from an eminent character in New-York, dated yesterday morning, we learn that notwithstanding all the exertions of the citizens of New-York and their delegates to the contrary there is every reason to expect that Congress will adjourn to meet in this city [*Philadelphia*]. The measure was to have been brought before the senate yesterday."

SATURDAY, 5 JUNE 1790

Hot (Johnson)

Fisher Ames to John Lowell

Sometime ago, a resolution passed the house for preventing payments on the assignments of pay given by the soldiers of the North Carolina line of the late army, unless they shd. be acknowledged before *two* magistrates. It was said that the Soldiers had been cheated, having recd. only 1/ or 2/ in the pound, and being ignorant of the amot. of what they assigned. This was said to be necessary in order to prevent the success of the fraud, by annulling the assignments already made. The pay was appropriated during the last session, and remains in the hands of Mr. [*Joseph, Jr.*] Howell. It is probable that roguery was practised in many instances. But the pay was assigned, chiefly, many years ago, and no money being in the treasury, the purchasers have not recd. their dues. The land warrants, however, in many instances have been del[*ivere*]d. on these assignmts. So that the Assignments are so far good and have taken effect, and for the residue are made void This was vigorously opposed in the house as a violent invasion of private right, as meddling with judicial power, as partaking of that discrimination which the house had disapproved &c. &c. In the Senate, an amendment was proposed to authorise the delay of paying the assignees untill enquiry could be made as to the nature of the transaction—and if fraud appeared, suits to be bro't. at the public expence to try the case legally—if none, to be paid—It was not carried, however, and the resolution passed in Senate by the casting vote of the Vice Prest.—which I am rather sorry for, but I believe it was entangled with some point of order, otherwise I cannot conceive of his assent being given to it. This seems to rest in some obscurity. The president has not signed and sent the Resolution back, tho the ten days are almost expired—I wish he may put his negative upon it, with his reasons. obsta principiis,[1] may be his motto without any loss of popularity, and as this resolution is the first act of encroachment by Congress. I should approve his doing so as a measure equally useful and proper. His delay makes it probable that it will be negatived.[2] You have seen Chf. Justice Jay. I think you will have had cause to esteem him. our worthy friend Geo. Cabot speaks highly of him. I am truly gratified to hear that mr. Jay is pleased with New England. I will not try to root that sort of prejudice out of my heart—while I feel so sensibly the weight, and the vexation more than the weight, of public business, during a session the most embarrassing that can be concieved, I have been in the best state to enjoy the excellent society of mr. Cabot—I am more sensible of our need of him *in* the Govt. and I trust he is more than ever sensible of his good fortune in being *out* of it.

ALS, Ames Papers, NcD. Place to which addressed not indicated. The recipient was identified from the closing salutation.

[1] Resist the first beginnings, or, root out evil at its first appearance.

[2] Washington signed the Resolution on Compensation Lists on 7 June (*DHFFC* 6:2063–70).

John Baptista Ashe to George Washington

Having been this evening inform'd you wish to have the opinion of the N. Carolina Representatives of Persons proper to fill the offices of the Government South of the Ohio, Also those of the Federal Judiciary in No. Carolina, I beg leave to give mine Sir and will do so with candor and disinterest'dness, Colo. William Blount, who I may presume you are acquaint'd with, has long and on various occasions had the confidence of the People of that Country and who in private life has ever conduct'd himself with firmness & independence and is a Man of Abilities and business, therefore do think Sir, he wou'd fill the office of Governor with as much dignity, and Satisfaction to the Citizens who he is to preside over, as any one within my knowledge.

Colo. Robert Hayes, an Old and Valuable Officer in our late Army, of the rank of Lieutt. who has been living in that Country Several years has been a representative from it, in the Legislative body of the State of No. Carolina Several times, I conceive Sir, wou'd fill the Office of Secretary of State with propriety; Mr. David Campble [*Campbell*], a Mr. John McNairy, and Mr. Howell Tatum, the Offices, of Judges the two former I have no personal knowledge of, they act in those capacities in that Country at present under appointments of No. Carolina—The latter gentleman was an Old Captain in the late Army, and probably may be known to you sir, he now practices the Law in that Country and is considerd clever at his profession is a Man of great application And of a fair and unimpeach'd character As a States Attorney I wou'd Mention A Mr. Edward Jones, a young Gentleman, who I not well acquaint'd with, but who I have often heard Spoke of, as a young Gentleman of Merit and an enlighten'd understanding As a Federal Judge, I beg leave to Mention Mr. John Stokes, who Mr. Steel tells me, he express'd his opinion of, to you this day, and as Federal Attorney Mr. John Sitgreaves, a Gentleman who has practis'd the Law for some years past in No. Carolina, tho' not so brilliant in Abilities, Stands as a favorably as to rectitude of Mind as any of his profession in perfect obedience to your wish sir—I have been more prolix, than I wish'd to have been and which I hope will excuse me to you.

ALS, Washington Papers, DLC.

Timothy Bloodworth to George Washington

With the utmost defidence I proceed to exercise priviledge founded in Your indulgence, that of Mentioning Carrecters to fill offices, created by the Adoption of the Constitution, & Cession of the Western Country [*Tennessee*], By North Carolina. this subject are more irksom, as I consider it out of the line of my Duty, and only warrentable by Youre permission. through this Chanel I venture to mention Coll. William Blount, as a Carrecter which I have reason to Believe, would afford satisfaction to the Inhabitants as a governer. thiss Belief is founded in the attention paid to him by their Members. & the people Electing him a Member for the Last Convention.[1]

For Judges David Campble [*Campbell*], at present Judge in that place also Mr. Robert Hayworth Howel Tateham [*Tatum*] secretary. th[*ese*] are carrecters with whom I have no personal acquaintance for States Attorney in the western Country Mr. Edward Jones. with this Gentleman I have a personal acquaintance, he supports a good Carrecter, & has been twice return'd for the Town of Wilmington. with respect to Judge for North Carolina, Mr. Samuel Spencer one of our State Judges, has ~~expres~~ express'd his Desire to fill that station. several Gentlemen have signifyed their Desire to be appointed States Attorney. Viz: mr. Arnot [*Silas Arnet*], Mr. Hambleton [*John Hamilton*], Mr. John Hay of Fayetteville & som of my Colliegues have Mentioned Mr. John Sitgraves, who is a gentleman of Carrecter & represented the State in Congress in the Year 1785 Pleas to excuse the Liberty I have taken.

ALS, Washington Papers, DLC.

[1] The second North Carolina convention to consider ratification of the federal Constitution.

John Dawson to James Madison

I have been favourd with your letter of the 27th. ulto. enclosing some papers for which I request that you'll accept my thanks.

I hope that the speculations on the officers and soldiers who were to the South at the close of the war have not been so extensive as you apprehended, and that the plan adopted[1] will prevent the injury & do justice to this meritorious class of our citizens. Our clerk has already made known their claims in the public papers, & as soon as we receive the resolutions *officially* we shall take such steps as appear necessary to obtain the desir'd end.

The zeal & perseverance of the friends to the assumption are realy astonishing & can only be equalld, in my opinion, by the absurdity, ill policey, & injustice of the measure. All attempts will, I trust prove equally unsuccessful; altho I do not like the time at which Mr. Fitzsimons introduces his resolution for adjourning to Philadelphia, as we have heard that a private negotiation is going on between the members from the eastern & middle states—"assume the debts & we'll go to Philadelphia—or stay where we are"—& as, from what I saw last August, I well know those tricks are sometimes play'd.

We hear that Colo. Bland is very ill—Shoud he live I am realy apprehensive that he woud not be reelected, there is such a clamour raisd against him because he voted in favour of this assumption[2]—Mr. [*Patrick*] Henry was in this town [*Richmond*] a few days ago—He had determind not to come to the assembly but hearing of this plan earnestly requested the people to elect him, which the[*y*] accordingly did.

In some of the papers I observe that Nath. Twining had presented a memorial to Congress, & that a report had been made, in part favourable[3]—This man is indebted to me about £300—which I have actually paid by the sale of my property at a very low rate—as Security—In April (I think) as he pasd through this state on his way to N. York. I had him arrested—he then told me of this claim against the continent, & gave me the most pointed assurances that my money shoud be paid—I scarc[*e*] need observe to you, that you'll render my a very singular favour by attending to this business, & securing me as far as possible, either in cash or whatever he may receive—the enclosed note which you'll please read & present, will authorise the payment of any money, & the nature of the debt will I hope induce him to attend to it.

I shall ever be happy in having an opportunity of rendering you similar, or any services.

[*P. S.*] The land patents left by Mr. Twining with me have remain'd in my hands unmolested since, & may at any moment be had.

ALS, Madison Papers (under date of May 1789), DLC. Place from which written not indicated. The date is estimated by the editors of *PJM*, based on internal evidence.

[1] The Resolution on Compensation Lists, signed by the President on 7 June, took measures to prevent fraudulent speculation in pay arrearages for Virginia and North Carolina Revolutionary War veterans.

[2] Bland was the only member of the Virginia delegation to support assumption; see Madison to Edmund Randolph, 14 March, volume 18, and *DHFFC* 14:887.

[3] For Nathaniel Twining's petition for remission of fines accrued for breach of "contract to carry mail" and the Twining Act, see *DHFFC* 8:241–46.

Ebenezer Hazard to Jeremy Belknap

***

I did not at the time, nor do I yet, approve the Application made by the Quakers to Congress,[1] or rather the manner in which it was conducted: if, as I understand, the Quakers meaned no more than to request Congress to lay the African Trade under such Restrictions as the Constitution allowed, there certainly was nothing improper in it, & it ought to have been done: I believe this was all that was intended; but one of the Petitions mentioned *Abolition*,

& this alarmed the Southern Members, & excited violent Opposition, which was accompanied with a degree of Illiberality & personal Invective that was truly distressing to those who had the honor & dignity of the Union at heart. Congress might, & ought to have imposed a Duty of 10 Dollars pr. head on all negroes imported; they might have restrained our own Citizens from going to Africa for Negroes, & carrying them to the West Indies, & they might have hindered Foreigners from fitting out in our ports for the African Trade: all this might have been done; but the Southern Members affected to believe that a total prohibition of the Importation of Slaves was wanted, & that those already amongst us were to be liberated, & ~~they~~ some of them made a terrible Outcry, and became abusive: they abused the Quakers generally, & an Individual of them (then in the Gallery) by name [*Warner Mifflin*]. Such Conduct was infamous. The Application of the Quakers was ill-timed, & discovered more Zeal than Knowledge: they discovered, in my opinion, a forwardness, & Obstinacy, & Stubborness in the Business, which were unbecoming: they are too prone to these things. I belong to the Society here;[2] but have not attended their meetings lately, for I was constantly saddled with an undue Proportion of Business; & though I will cheerfully do my Share on such Occasions, I do love to do more, while others are idle. I have not heard that our Society intend to make such application as you mention, though it is possible they do: if it will stir up Controversy it ought to be avoided, especially in the present Situation of our Affairs. I do not know D. Howel's Character, though he has been a member of Congress.[3]

The Influenza has raged here as well as with you, but has not proved mortal, except when accompanied by other Disorders: my family have had very little of it.

***

Congress—I hate to say anything about them, for I can say nothing good.

***

ALS, Belknap Papers, MHi. Addressed to Boston.

---

[1] The antislavery petitions of the Yearly Meeting of Friends (Quakers) of Philadelphia and New York, and of the Quaker-led Pennsylvania Abolition Society, presented in Congress on 11 and 12 February; see *DHFFC* 8:314–38.

[2] New York's Society for Promoting the Manumission of Slaves was founded in January 1785. John Jay was its first president, while others among its front ranks included Schuyler, Hamilton, Aaron Burr, James Duane, and Robert Livingston (*PAH* 3:597; Walter Stahr, *John Jay: Founding Father* [New York, 2005], pp. 237–39).

[3] Belknap wrote Hazard on 7 May that David Howell, as its president, had asked the Abolition Society of Providence, Rhode Island, to lend its weight to the New York Manumission Society's intention to submit an antislavery petition at the next session of Congress (ALS, Belknap Papers, MHi). New York and Rhode Island did join four other state abolition societies in an unsuccessful petition attempt in December 1791.

Richard Henry Lee to Thomas Lee Shippen

I am this moment favored with yours of the 3d. instant for which I thank you—The business of the Seat remains much as when I wrote you last—Your friends did on Wednesday the 3d. [2 *June*] oppose the Committment of the Bill for fixing the Permt. & Tempory. Seat of Govermt. to a private Committee, because it would produce delay, & because the subject was of a Nature fit only to be discussed in a Committee of the Whole Senate where it must go at last—The Members for & against Phila. were then tried, & the Senate divided 12 for & 12 agst. the Commitment Mr. Patterson voting with us—The Vice P. sent it to a private Committee where it has remained ever since. What was apprehended is verified and delay alone is the consequence—3 Members of the Committee being agst. you—Mr. Henry & myself Are overruled [*?*] in every proposition for reporting—Thus we shall probably remain until the Rhode Island Senators arrive & then the business will no doubt be pushed, and end as you may judge. I fear you have little to expect from N— C— [*North Carolina*] or from G— [*Georgia*].

My family at Chantilly, & that of Stratford have been severely visited with the Measles—they are, I thank Good all recovered or in a good way.

ALS, Shippen Family Papers, DLC.

William Maclay to Benjamin Rush

For this whole week have we wared with the influence of New York, on the Subject of removing Congress to Philada. three times were the Senate divided 12 & 12 and our President uniformly voted against Us. The main Question has not however been Yet put. and the Business is in the hands of a Committee. The object of the Yorkers is to get the Matter delayed untill the Senators from Rhode Island come in. by whose Means they hope to fix Us here for ever. In the mean While both public papers and private Conversations, are filled with every sarcastic cut, biting Jibe & sophisticated [*lined out*] argument, That invention can furnish, on the Occasion.

Some of our Friends here, altho they despise all low Scurrility, think that the Philada. Papers should not be altogether silent on the Occasion, & this thought makes Us naturally turn our Eyes upon You. to aid You in this I inclose the notes which I prepared for the debates of Monday and Tuesday last. I beg you to make the best Use of them which you can,[1] they are poor helps I own, but you know I never was averse to offer my mite in the Cause of the public, and this I consider not as the Cause of Philada. or new York, but the Cause of The Union at large.

The funding bill, the accursed thing which I fear, future Generations will hate, is come up to Us. and Monday is assigned for it. and long as we have been here I fear we are not Yet ready for it. There is no certainty of the time Congress will break up. Indeed many Members do not seem to wish it. This is far from being the Case with your most sincere Friend.
[*P. S.*] Excuse the roughness of this Scrawl, and the inaccuracy of the notes, I cannot now copy either of them, the Subject of removal occupies every Moment of my Time.

ALS, Rush Papers, DLC. Addressed to Philadelphia.

[1] Rush used the notes to write the newspaper article printed under 16 June, below; see also Maclay to Rush, 18 June, below.

John Murray to Benjamin Goodhue

Indulged by your condescending goodness to me and mine, I take the liberty to inclose you a Packet which I have to request, you will send on as soon as possible, directed as before.

You will, my dear Sir, be so obliging as to let me know by a line, directed to the care of Mr. Thos. Fitzgerald Mercht. between front & Second street in Market street when the President will leave new York. I am told he is expected this way very speedily. I am concerned to know in as much as the Convention[1] of which I am a member is determined to present him an Address with a Copy of our proceedings,[2] a printed Copy of these proceedings will also be presented by order of the Convention to every Member of the Senate and House of Representatives. but as these proceeding will make some noise in the religious world, I have to request you will keep the subject of this *wholy to yourself* till the business is concluded. it is proposed by the Convention that a Committee from their Body wait on the President. but it is thought that on my return to newyork on my way to the eastward will be time enough, and then, your humble servant being one of the Committee, may present it. I should if this may be the case but we must be governed by the Presidents movements. a line from you therefore on this subject will be a considerable addition to the many favors already conferred on Your ever obliged Friend.

ALS, Letters to Goodhue, NNS. Written from Philadelphia.

[1] Murray was attending a convention of seventeen clergy and laymen, representing the Societies of Universal Baptists in Pennsylvania, New Jersey, Virginia, and Massachusetts, and meeting in Philadelphia from 25 May to 8 June to draw up plans for their new church's government.

[2] *Articles of Faith, and Plan of Church Government, Composed and Adopted by the Churches*

Believing in the Salvation of All Men . . . (Philadelphia, 1790), which was also reprinted in several newspapers at the time. Although he did not attend the Convention, Benjamin Rush espoused Universalist beliefs and played a leading role in helping to edit and arrange this publication. The Convention's (undated) congratulatory address to Washington was presented on 9 August during Murray's return to Massachusetts through New York City (George W. Corner, *Autobiography of Benjamin Rush* [Princeton, N.J., 1948], p. 185). For the address and information about its presentation, see *PGW* 6:223–24.

Nathaniel Rogers to John Langdon

***

If it would not be thought presuming I would ask why Congress are so anxious about the State debts before they have provided for those of the Union why not leave the States to pay their own Debts or at least wait till they desire Congress to do it for them what has N. Hampshire [*lined out*] to do with Massachusitts extravagance at any rate let the Assumption alone till the Acco'ts. are properly & equitably settled but I forbear. wisdom is with you & will direct the best but we ignorants can't help thinking which perhaps would be in a different way if we had the same information as you have at N. York.

***

ALS, Langdon Papers, NhPoA. Written from Concord, New Hampshire. The omitted text apologizes for being too busy to begin a correspondence, regrets not hearing from Langdon, and reports on local health conditions and on state elections, including an (unlocated) list of state senators.

Epes Sargent to Benjamin Goodhue

I have looked forward to the period for the exportation of dried cod fish,[1] with a degree of anxiety which I took the liberty to express to the Secretary [*Hamilton*] in a Letter to him of the 11th Feby. it is arrived with all the difficulties I expected, and those encreased. 'tis probable there will go from this port not less than 80,000 Qts. [*quintals*], the weighing this article at 1 Cent will cost 800 dolls., besides the charge of Inspection, I know of no way to avoid this expence, with any safety to myself, other modes might be adopted than what the law points out which might satisfy me personally; but that the whole transactions may appear clear, and explain themselves, when I am removed, it must be actually weighed inspected, and supervised by the Surveyor. I have turned it every way, and no other will satisfy me, but such as I conceive is warranted by Law, should it appear on practise inconvenient and expensive, 'tis for the Legislature whose Power is paramount to all other, to rectify and correct their own doings.

Should there be a likelihood of the bounty undergoing a different modification, either by assuming the shape of a bounty on the Tonnage of Vessells and men employed in the fishery, as in the British whale fishery, or be altered, or abolished you can best judge; but should it stand permanent, I submit it to your ideas of justice, if the considerations as provided by the act will be in any measure for the services of the officers; there is no provision at all for the Surveyor; and if to the allowance already made to the Collector, which is calculated in most sparing and moderate quantity, added to the severe encrease of duty there will be an abridgment of 50 dolls. from his present allowance; the calculation being made on 80,000 Qts. at 5 Cents will, with the weighing and Inspection amount to 5,000 dolls. at 1 ℔ o/o [*percent*] be 50 dolls., no Commission being allowed on money other than what is payed into the Treasury: it is true there is demandable 40 Cts. for a Bond & 30 Cts. for a permitt, but you will not conceive this intended as commensurate to the additional weight of care and responsibility.

Your attention to the public interest and as connected with it the safety of its Servants, will if you see fit, encourage you to attempt such legislative relief as may be judged sufficient to sett all right.

ALS, Letters to Goodhue, NNS. Written from Gloucester, Massachusetts.

[1] The Impost Act had provided for a five cent per quintal bounty on exported dried (salted) or pickled fish in lieu of a drawback on imported salt; the Coasting Act [HR-16] contained a provision suspending collectors' payment of this bounty to exporters until 1 June 1790.

Peter Silvester to Peter Van Schaack

I received yours of the 27th. ult. with a letter enclosed for Europe which I have delivered in good hands to be put on board the packet—a few days now will determine whether our present Sessions will be of much longer duration or not & whether All or which of the debts will be now funded that is to say the foreign, Domestick, & the State debts so called. yesterday our house were wholly agitated upon a motion for the removal of the temporary seat of Govemt. from hence to Philadelphia at their next Sessions—it was carried for philadelphia—how this will go in the Senate I know not—had Rhode Island come in the union before it probably might have fixed the temporary seat here for awhile with more certainty. at any rate I am glad they are come in. I congratulate you on this occasion a larger majority than two, would have been more agreeable—*** Bensen has promised me several times to apply in behalf of Mr. Dirk Gardinior—I reminded him of it Yesterday when he was to dine with the Vice president where he would see Colo. [*William Stephens*] Smith.

ALS, Van Schaack Collection, NNC. Addressed to Kinderhook, New York. The omitted text relates to procedures in a pending lawsuit.

John Trumbull to John Adams

***

Man is a strange being. His vice & depravity is every where seen—but his folly & dishonesty is no where so conspicuous, as in a popular assembly. Every man who pretends to form an opinion for himself & impose on others, chuses his party, & takes his side, from motives of passion, interest or ambition. When this is completed, he employs what reasoning talents heaven has given him in the subsequent stage of the business, in forming arguments to justify his opinions. Nothing can be more ridiculous than to hear us then pretend to be governed only by reason, & spend hours of debate in acting the farce of rationality.

We are alarmed at the present situation of affairs in Congress. Of the Senate we hear little—but in the House of Representatives every thing seems conducted by Party, Intrigue & Cabal. We constantly hear of bargains between Members from different States for Votes on the most important questions—If State policy & local attachments are to continue their predominating influence—if they are to govern, or if not govern, to embarrass, the affairs of the Union—we may bid adieu to the hopes of a Fœderal Government. One half of the People, as You truly observe do not wish to have any Government, & I believe we may add that the other half are not disposed to agree upon its form.

As to our debate on signs & ceremonies, I fully subscribe to their efficacy in government; but I firmly believe that from the present temper of the People, none of any significance or importance could at present be established or imposed without occasioning the most serious alarm. We might almost as safely introduce the Papal ceremonies in Religious worship. We neither fear God nor regard Man, but in a manner wholly democratical. But should the government continue, signs, ceremonies & external parade will naturally & gradually be introduced by the people themselves, who, as You justly observe, are equally fond of them, as the rest of mankind.

Our Clergy have shed their wigs & laid aside their red gates & board fences—They retain no mark of distinction but the Band on Sundays. At the same time they have lost nine tenths of their dignity & influence. I do not however ascribe this chiefly to the loss of the sign, but am [*of*] opinion that from the cooperation of other causes, the wig & the dignity naturally fell together—for when the Dignity was gone, the wig was unable to support itself.

I hinted, in my last letter, some dissatisfaction at the Secretary's reports. I will explain myself. He recommends the immediate Assumption of the State-debts, & yet discards all idea of direct Taxation. When, in the name of Common Sense, are direct Taxes to be wanted, when can they with propriety be demanded, if not now? Does he mean to give them up forever, & lose the most important resource of the Empire? Is he ignorant that direct Taxation to a moderate amount is the strongest link in the chain of Government, & the only measure, which will make every man feel that there is a Power above him in this world? Does he fear the unpopularity of the measure? Is it more unpopular than the Assumption? Would not both be advocated and opposed from the same quarters? Ought not both to be proposed together? And has he not by discarding direct Taxation furnished the opposers of the Assumption with their strongest argument—that his proposed resources will fail him?

A direct Tax of one Cent on the Pound according to *our lists* once laid & submitted to by the People, as I have no doubt it would be, would establish the Fœderal Government.

I have a very high opinion of the Secretary—but must think that in this matter he has either gone too far or not far enough—and that if both measures could not be ventured at once, a small direct tax would be of more importance to the Government, than the immediate assumption of the State Debts without it.

The Secretary was warmly your Friend, & wished as much as any man in the States for your election to your present office—but, if the representation of Col. W. [*Samuel Blachley Webb*] may be depended on as to the part he took in that affair,[1] he was duped by the Antifederalists. I hope he has no inclination to intrigue, & am sure both in that affair, & in his opposition to [*Governor George*] Clinton's ~~reel~~ re-election, he displayed no extraordinary talents for it. He absolutely scribbled against Clinton on topics calculated to make his enemy more popular. Let him keep to his Fort[*é*]—Sterling abilities & Independent Honesty, joined with indefatigable industry.

I have to thank You for the Defence of the American Constitutions,[2] & the two Pamphlets, which I received by Col. Wadsworth. *** Fame has certainly ben very liberal to [*Benjamin*] Franklyn in his lifetime—but I doubt She will hereafter reclaim a great part of her donations. I could never view him as the extraordinary Genius, either in Politics or Literature which he has been called. Except his invention of Electric rods, I know no claim he has to merit as a Philosopher. He certainly never rose to high eminence as a literary character, & tho' always busy in politics & party, seems not to have been well versed in the Science of Legislation, or the Theory of Government.

Maddison's character is certainly not rising in the public estimation—He now acts on a conspicuous stage, & does not equal expectation. He becomes more & more a Southern Partizan, & loses his assumed candor & moderation. Indeed no man seems to have gained much reputation in the present session of Congress. Even Ames, who succeeded to King as the temporary Idol of Massachusetts, & whose praises were so much trumpeted forth in the last session, seems to be losing part of his Votaries.

Our Legislature seem determined to make no provision for the State Debt. We insist that we have paid beyond our proportion already, which I believe is true—but I suppose other States talk in the same strain. The State debts must be assumed by Congress, or they will never be paid—& before the period of their assumption, will probably in many of the States be so much depreciated as to afford Maddison & his adherents, new arguments for a discrimination.

Since I began writing we have the news of the accession of Rhode-Island to the Union. I hope it may prove a just subject of congratulation—but fear their members will join you full fraught with State politics, & a tolerable infusion of Antifederalism. The real friends to an efficient Government are so few, that we have reason to dread any accession to the number of its opposers.

ALS, Adams Family Manuscript Trust, MHi. Written from Hartford, Connecticut. The omitted text reports Trumbull's instrumental role in convincing the state Assembly that its excise was unpopular and antifederal and ought to be repealed, and discusses political theory and events in France.

---

[1] Webb served as Hamilton's messenger in a successful last minute appeal to Connecticut's presidential electors to "throw away" two of their votes for Adams, for fear that his votes for President would equal Washington's; see Trumbull to Adams, 17 April, above, and *DHFFE* 2:47.

[2] The first and second editions of Adams's *Defence* appeared in 1787 and 1788 respectively.

Henry Van Schaack to Theodore Sedgwick

I am favord with your two *short* letters informing me of the assumption business being brought forward. I wish the matter had been in such a train as that you could have given me hopes of success—I fear the Pensyvanians will Join the opposition when the Votes come to be counted. we will hope for the best. Doctor [*Erastus*] Sergeant called on me yesterday all was well at Stockbridge—Eliza and her Grandmama [*Anne Thompson Sedgwick*] go to the Pool this week[1] We shall see them when they return—Perhaps you will be here to attend them home—I hope not, for in that case the assumption I suppose will be lost—The longer you stay away the greater the prospect of success.

[*Ebenezer*] Kingsley of Beckit and [*Joseph*] Chaplin of Washington are gone to put—Their Speculations have brought on their ruin—so much for speculation.

Colo. Rowley[2] just from Boston—nothing new there—at Springfield the talk is that S[*amuel*]. Lyman is to be held up as a candidate for the House of Representatives in the union—General [*David*] Cobb also—I shd. Suppose the opposition to you must fail; for I cannot learn from any quarter in this County but that you are a Man of the *People.* It will be well that it shod. be known in Time that you *will serve if* the *people will chuse you.* It seems doubtfull with some whether you will again sacrifice domestick quiet for public warfare—I have almost taken upon myself to say that you will not quit the Helm before the Ship is Safe moord in the Harbour—Say yourself to me what is meet and needful. It is better to take time by the forelock.

Your family I shod. suppose wod. wish you to Relinquish some of your other Relations in compliance with what your family may desire may probably also wish you to decline In this situation of things it shod. be known from you What is to be done. The language I use favors that you will Serve if chosen.

[*P. S.*] Remember me to Silvester Strong and Benson.

The Presidents recovery has diffused general joy among us.

If you want me to write you [*torn*] better paper you must furnish me w[*ith*] some If not I am content [*torn*] Scribbling shall go on such paper as [*torn*].

Since the preeceding your favor of the 29th of Last month is come to hand. I thank you for being so particular—what reply will you get to "unfounded facts monstrous premisses and inclusive deductions" I long to see what will come [*lined out*] next.

The Pennsylvanians make a grim figure upon the Political Stage—From all I can hear and see there does not appear efficiency of character in them.

When I expressed to you in my letter a wish to see you appear in the Debates it was merely to gratify my own curiosity I had not heard any inclination that you was falling into indolence—no body that knows you in public or private life will suspect you of laziness. God Grant you and the rest who are for the assumption abilities and strength to carry this important business to a happy conclusion. Untill that object is accomplished I shall have my fears and doubts about the Government. I will hope for the best. When I contemplate your Vinnings Your Pennsylvanians I dread that this business will not terminate to your and my wishes.

ALS, Sedgwick Papers, MHi. Written from Pittsfield, Massachusetts.

---

[1] The famous medicinal resort at Lebanon Springs, New York, just over the state line from Pittsfield, Massachusetts, at the foot of the Berkshire Hills.

[2] Nathan Rowley (1760–1821) of West Springfield, Massachusetts.

William Vernon to Jeremiah Wadsworth

I was honored with your answer respecting a sum of Money, that I received at Parr emitted by your State in 1780 adviseing me to hold it untill, your Genl. Assembly should provide for the Payment thereof or an efficient Government was established, and some mode prescribed for Liquidating State debts, accumulated by the War. That happy moment hath taken place, and should esteem it, as a fresh instance of your friendship, in further adviseing me, what measures to pursue, in obtaining payment for the principal of upwards of £1100—& Ten years interest thereon?

Our long refractory State has, at length, by the unremitted assiduity of the minor & patriotick part of the Inhabitants, effected the Adoption of the Constitution, in Convention, on the 29 Ulto., by the small majority of Two only, that gave inexpressible pleasure to the Persons of property, and a fatal stab, to Paper-Money robbers and Legislators. You will doubtless see many applicants for Offices, under the Genl. Government some that have no pretences either, from their attachment to the Constitution, or their merits: others perhaps, supported by the recommendations of the Merchants & Traders of the state; which in my humble opinion, ought to have little weight or consideration in the appointment; for this well known reason: that is even proverbial, as to the state of Rhode-Island. viz. That smuggleing is justifiable, because the Penalty warrants the measure, for the resque by seizure—upon this principle, many instances might be given, where Legislators, that have passed Revenue Laws, have openly, saved more then half their Duties on importation of Goods—Therefore, it cannot be inconsistent with their interest to recommend Persons for Revenue officers that, perhaps may connive at frauds.

If a firm zealous attachment, a steady uniform perseverance, in the service of the United states, through the War. If sustaining the Loss of great property in the cause? If integrity, probity, disinterested, impartial views in serveing the American revenue, is a recommendation to Office—No Man stands fairer then Doctr. David Olyphant; whom the Inhabitants of Newport, can have no objection too—being a respectable Free-holder for some Years.

I am perswaded Sir, from those and other motives, That I have not mentioned, he will merit your Interest, in the appointment of Collector for the Port of Newport.

ALS, Wadsworth Papers, CtHi. Written from Newport, Rhode Island.

V. to N.E. N.Y. P. and C.

Dear Sisters,

SOME time ago I saw your familiar epistle addressed to me;[1] and am at a loss to say, whether the perusal of it gave me more pleasure or pain. If wit, and elegancy of style, produced the former, the prejudices and illiberalities it contained, naturally created the latter. As I have not the vanity to hope to rival you in what is pleasing and agreeable, I shall rest contented with the humble task of endeavoring at least, to equal you in what is not so—and to excel you in candor, wherein you seem to be the least eminent.

Admitting, then, that my purse is low, my farm[2] untenanted and out of repair, myself in debt—pray, my dear sisters, did not this bankruptcy proceed from my exertions to protect and defend an extensive neighbourhood, who first cried out, "Help! murder! &c.?" Or, are these sufficient reasons, why injustice should be done to me? If your purses are full, your farms in good repair, yourselves clear of debt, (which by the bye I fear is not true) your sons and servants mannerly and wise, the arts and sciences, and large cities flourishing among you—what a reproach is it, my dear sisters, that the unprejudiced world do not add liberality, justice and gratitude, to the long catalogue of your endowments!

How can you say, that my servants or people have insisted that the general farm-house should be placed in my particular farm? However evidently just this might be, they have, as far as I can learn, endeavoured to avoid even the appearance of topical prejudices. This, I know, you will deny: and were Omnipotence (with whom you seem to sport) to declare, in articulate sounds from on high, that with his finger he pointed out the place where this general farm-house ought to be, when he made the fair, the beautiful, the central, the grand river Potowmac—I fear, my dear sisters, that, influenced by self-interest, you would deny your assent, and attempt to outvote Him.

It is with pleasure I give you credit for one instance of candor and gratitude, blended together in one of your servants—who acknowledged, that the Potowmac was by far the most proper place for the general farm-house; although he himself being under obligations to the lower part of the particular farm to which he belonged, could not do otherwise than vote with his neighbours.[3]

My servants, B. and D. perhaps have erred, in writing me the exceptionable letter[4] you refer to; and had I answered it, or given them my thanks for it, this would have been my apology, That I knew not what you might possibly be doing in the dark. Why, then, these sarcasms on me? Be liberal—be candid, as you are eloquent, and the whole world will give you credit—which is surely to be preferred to that which is now given you by only a small interested part of it; and which, even by those few among yourselves, who consider justice as wisdom, is thought to be more than you deserve.

And after all your disparagements of my sons and servants, there is at least one characteristic trait in their principles, which, I trust, sets them at least one grade above some of you, with all your imaginary advantages: They are not so taken, they are not so bewitched by the fascinating charms of pomposity and monarchical parade. In this they display a superior firmness—in this they triumph.

I give you no thanks nor credit for your superlative commendations of my son George [*Washington*]—which he neither needs, nor loves: And could one tenth part of the fulsome hyperbolical panegyricks which are continually erudacted upon him, be possibly gulped at the same time, it could not fail to create a loathsome nausea.

I will conclude with a piece of advice, which, like the Pope's blessing, can do you no harm: The next time you take up to your agreeable, but rather too reprehensive, pen, stick close to, and follow, your own beautiful and witty style: Add to it, the candour of a Scott—the justice, integrity, and disinterestedness of a Madison—the firmness and gentilesse of a Butler—the honesty and independency of a Tucker, a Burke, or a Jackson—the conscientiousness of a [*Daniel*] Carroll, or a Boudinot—the princely liberality of a Vining—and, lastly, the oratorical excellency, if possible, of an Ames: but—avoid, by all means, his, and your own, speciousness, illiberality, prejudices, and contracted policy.

IG, 5 June; reprinted at Portland, Maine; Boston; Georgetown, Maryland (present-day Washington, D.C.); and Richmond, Virginia.

[1] The Familiar Epistle from N.E., N.Y., P. & C. to V., printed under 14 January, volume 18. An earlier response to the Epistle, entitled "Virginia to New-England, New-York, Pennsylvania, and [*South*] Carolina," probably written by a different author, is dated 10 March and printed under that date, volume 18.

[2] The pieces employ the word "farm" as a metaphor for state.

[3] The reference is to Scott's speech of 4 September 1789; see *DHFFC* 11:1447–49.

[4] B. (William Grayson) and D. (Richard Henry Lee) enclosed the proposed Amendments to the Constitution and expressed their fears about the new federal government in a letter to the Speaker of the Virginia House of Delegates dated 28 September. For that and a joint letter to Governor Beverley Randolph of the same date, both widely reprinted over the subsequent six months, see *DHFFC* 17:1634–35.

Other Documents

Elbridge Gerry to Governor John Hancock. ALS, The Monroe, Wakeman, and Holman Loan Collection of the Pequot Library Association on deposit in the Beinecke Rare Book and Manuscript Library, CtY.

Office seeking: has conferred with Hamilton and has reason to believe that he will recommend John Foster Williams to the President as commander of any cutter that may be authorized under the revenue system; congratulations on Hancock's reelection as governor of Massachusetts.

Elbridge Gerry to James Sullivan. No copy known; acknowledged in Sullivan to Gerry, 20 June.

Stephen Goodhue to Benjamin Goodhue. FC:lbk, Goodhue Family Papers, MSaE. Written from Salem, Massachusetts.

Benjamin's son Stephen was buried on Wednesday; wife "Fanny" would be consoled by his presence, but does not require it.

Benjamin Huntington to Governor Samuel Huntington. No copy known; acknowledged in Samuel to Benjamin Huntington, 4 July.

William Irvine to Anne Callender Irvine. ALS, Newbold Irvine Papers, PHi. Written in the afternoon; place to which addressed not indicated. The conclusion of this letter was written on 8 June and is calendared under that date, below.

Is in suspense over the value of certificates as affected by the uncertain fate of the funding bill, but "I will have the best intelligence every hour, and must be governed accordingly"; there must be another attempt in the Senate to remove the seat of government to Philadelphia in two or three days, since Rhode Island's Senators are due in perhaps a week; thinks eighteen months or two years is the longest that the Settlement of Accounts Bill, soon to be completed, will authorize the board of commissioners; is being solicited to serve in Congress "by some influential persons, of the Western Country—I wish to keep good terms in that Country, there at least some of our Children, must reside & make their way."

Robert Morris to George Harrison. ALS, Brinton-Coxe Papers, PHi. Addressed to Philadelphia; franked; answered 8 June.

Will meet to converse privately in about a month; "We are trying hard to bring Congress to Philadelphia but the Success is yet doubtfull."

John S. Sherburne to John Langdon. ALS, Langdon Papers, NhPoA. Written from Concord, New Hampshire; answered.

Reports Josiah Bartlett's election as president (governor) of New Hampshire and the state legislature's vote permitting him to retain his dual offices as federal district attorney and state representative; asks Langdon to bring his federal commission when he returns home; "the subject of yr. last relative to the district Court shall be duly attended to."

NYDG, 5 July. Wister Butler Papers, PHi. Annotated by Butler to indicate the article for which he retained the issue.

"On the Subject of the New Tax 1790" (House debate of 2 June, on the committee report on ways and means).

SUNDAY, 6 JUNE 1790

Hot (Johnson)

Benjamin Goodhue to Stephen Goodhue

Yours of 1st. instant came to hand last Evg. and gave me the sorrowful news of the death of our Infant [*Stephen Goodhue*], he surely was when I left home a fine boy, but as you inform me he was subject to fits, which I did not before know, perhaps they would never have left him through life, but we must acquiese in the supreame wisdom and direction of the Great Governor of the Universe and believe he does right. I have wrote Fanny most ernestly that she would not suffer it to prey on her spirits, pray urge her to it, for if it should I should be doubly unhappy—I am glad you have got the [*ship*] Lydia so near sailing. hope she may do well, you may I think expect the [*ship*] Fanny in a month from this time, when I hope to be at home or soon after, for I think the question of residence which has been the cause of our delays is brought to a crisis and must in a day or two be determined, and then our bussines will doubtless be expedited and soon come to a close, how is uncertain, I mean the assumption, I have my hopes and fears and sometimes one predominates and sometimes the other.

[*P. S.*] tell Capt. Shallaber I sent his last letter on to Philada.

ALS, Goodhue Papers, MSaE. Addressed to Salem, Massachusetts; franked; postmarked.

Benjamin Goodhue to Michael Hodge

The question of residency which has too much mingled itself with public measures, and occasion'd a delay in our bussines, will probably be determined in the Senate in a day or two, when I suppose the bussines will be expedited, and an end soon be put to our session, how it may affect the assumption is uncertain, for neither the York or Pensylvania members care any thing about it compared with the residence of Congress and which ever may be disappointed may feel indisposed to the assumption, to the people of N. England it is surely indifferent whether we sit in one City or the other, and no reason can be given why we should fight the battles of either, perhaps it is our policy not to affront either if it can be avoided—as the R. Island Senators are soon expected, whose presence may put a new face on this bussines, both as to residence and assumption, I conclude this week may render certain what has been so long doubtfull, what the issue may be is as uncertain as can be conceived. God grant it may be favourable.

ALS, Ebenezer Stone Papers, MSaE. Place to which addressed not indicated.

James Madison to John Parrish

I have been favored with yours of the 28th May and am much obliged by the friendly communication. The number of Vessels employed in the Trade to Africa is much greater than I should have conjectured. I hope it will daily diminish and soon cease altogether. This hope is the better founded since the return of Rho. Island under the jurisdiction of the Union. Should the evil still go on, it continues to be my opinion that the interposition of the Genl. Govt. ought to be applied as far as may be constitutional; as I am persuaded it must be your's that such a remedy ought in prudence to be foreborne in case it be not absolutely necessary. At present I not only flatter myself that the necessity may not exist, but apprehend that a revival of the subject in Congs. would be equally unseasonable & unsuccessful. Future opportunities cannot be more and will probably be less so.

ALS, Cox, Parrish and Wharton Papers, PHi. Addressed to Philadelphia; franked; postmarked.

Louis Guillaume Otto to Comte de Montmorin

The laws of Congress concerning commerce have naturally brought up the question of establishing consuls in several parts of the world where the American flag is allowed. But without awaiting a decision from the legislature on the salary and functions of these officers, the President appointed some to Cadiz, the Madeira Islands, Liverpool, Dublin, Bordeaux, Nantes, Rouen, Marseilles and Havre de Grace, that is to say, one to Spain, one to Portugal, two to Great Britain, and five to France, which indicates a desire to have more and closer relationships with the Kingdom of France than with the other countries of Europe. But we do not have reason to be equally satisfied with the appointment of two other consuls, one to St. Domingue [*Haiti*] and the other one to Martinique. I could not resist, Sir, expressing my surprise to several Senators, whose concurrence is necessary for all nominations made by the President. They replied that they believed this matter was agreed on by both the [*French*] Court and Mr. Jefferson and that it appears to them, besides, as wholly natural that there should be an American consul in a French port where the American flag is allowed. I observed to them that this admittance was not founded on any treaty and that it even contradicted the principles that are generally accepted by all nations possessing colonies overseas, that the right to appoint consuls supposed an entirely free trade, that the American trade with our islands was only tolerated and that at any time the Government could revoke the decree that allows Americans to sail there, that moreover it would have been more proper to first make an arrangement with the Court to learn its opinion on the admittance of a foreign consul because without this formality we could fear that the two consuls in question would not be recognized by the governors of our colonies. They insisted on the principle that a nation could send consuls wherever their flag was allowed and that if it ever happens that Americans were no longer admitted to our islands, the mission of the consuls would stop *ipso facto*. I therefore no longer objected and limited myself, Sir, to giving you an account of this consular establishment, unique in its kind and which, in the present disturbances in our colonies,[1] could justify among our colonists pretensions that are not compatible with their submission to the Mother Country. It has not been possible until now to nurture in the minds of the Americans reasonable ideas about the relationships that exist between the Antilles and their Mother Country. Even Mr. Jefferson, who is so fair and clear-sighted on other issues, is highly prejudiced towards his country, to the extent that he considers as absurd the restrictions that are put on trade in our colonies. Mr. Jay has been obstinate and I am afraid Mr. Jefferson could be as well. Mr. [*Conrad-Alexandre*] Gérard said jokingly to the President of the [*Continental*] Congress: "if you absolutely need 'Sugar Islands,' we will give up one to you as long as you leave us alone in the other ones!" "That is not what we need," replied the American. "We leave you, without any regret, the honors of sovereignty. We will limit ourselves to trade!"[2] This quote is the only way they think here of the Antilles and they even want to convince us that it is in our best interest to leave their trade entirely free. Those views have reached, if it were possible, the highest point of absurdity since Congress, in their own ports, employs every means to impede foreign vessels in favor of the American flag. So that they preach free trade abroad while they practice at home the very example of restrictions and prohibitions. The appointment of two consuls to St. Domingue and Martinique may eventually provide a new opportunity to correct their views on these issues, if as I believe this appointment absolutely contradicts the principles. But the diffidence I have always had for my opinion has caused me to be very temperate in my conversations and to offer more doubts than severe remonstrances.

Copy, in French, Henry Adams Transcripts, DLC. Received 25 September. Otto's letters included in *DHFFC* were usually written over the course of days, and even weeks, following the day they were begun.

[1] In the late winter of 1789–90 France's National Assembly was debating the future of slavery in its Caribbean colonies, where the institution helped insure that sugar and coffee exports made St. Domingue (Haiti), in particular, the wealthiest European colony in the western hemisphere. The threat to the islands' status quo heightened class and racial antagonisms, with white separatists raising the specter of secession unless Paris granted them more political autonomy over race relations. Otto may have been anticipating the fresh "disturbances" that erupted in the aftermath of the famous "Decree of 8 March," which was interpreted as granting voting rights to free blacks.

[2] Gérard's conversation likely took place with John Jay, whose position on trade policy while secretary of foreign affairs (1784–89) Otto just alluded to, and with whom Gérard had engaged in futile negotiations over consular affairs throughout his tenure as first French minister to the United States, which nearly coincided with Jay's term as president of the Continental Congress (1778–79). There were further opportunities for such a conversation when Gérard returned to Europe on the same ship that carried Jay to his new appointment as American minister to Spain, on a voyage during which damaging sea conditions forced them to put in at Martinique for several weeks in December 1779.

John Page to St. George Tucker

I have only Leisure to tell you that I received yours by the last Post, announcing your safe return Home, with the Satisfaction it ought to give to your warmest Friend—that your Brother [*Thomas Tudor Tucker*] is now perfectly recovered; & no Pains shall be spared by me to endeavour to prevail on him to accompany me to Virga. Inclosed you will find 2 of Fenno's Papers sent you on Account of the little Piece written by my dear Wife on the Death of our deceased Friend.[1] I added to it the Piece which you have in our Dodsley—One of the Papers may at a proper Time be no unwellcome present to Mrs. [*Martha Dangerfield*] Bland—I recommend in this Paper to yr. particular Notice the No. VIII Dis. on Davila,[2] as I did last year a Production of the same infatuated Author[3]—Such Pieces ought to be lash'd & hunted out of a Gazette of the U.S., I have more than once endeavoured to hold up this Strange Character to the World[4]—but have not Leisure to follow him in a proper Manner through all his windings & turnings although I track him constantly, come in sight & always cry out tally hoo!

ALS, Tucker-Coleman Papers, ViW. Place to which addressed not indicated.

[1] The poem "On the Death of Col. Theodorick Bland," written by Margaret Lowther Page and first published in John Fenno's *GUS*, 5 June, is printed under the headnote on Bland's death, 1 June, above.

[2] John Adams's *Discourses on Davila* was a series of thirty-two essays on political theory published serially in *GUS* between 28 April 1790 and 27 April 1791. Written in response to the democratic excesses of the French Revolution, the dense and largely plagiarized work's

most enduring legacy may have been in prompting Jefferson to sponsor the first American printing of Thomas Paine's *Rights of Man* as a rebuttal (Joseph J. Ellis, *Passionate Sage: The Character and Legacy of John Adams* [New York, 1992], p. 148; *PTJ* 20:290–91).

[3] Adams's *Defence of the Constitutions of the United States* had been published at Boston, New York City, and Philadelphia; see Page to Tucker, 23 July 1789, *DHFFC* 16:1110.

[4] See, for example, "Fountain of Honors," published in *NYDA* on 22 May 1789 (*DHFFC* 15:614).

Theodore Sedgwick to Pamela Sedgwick

I have not this week recd. a syllable of inteligence from home. Indeed, my love, it renders me very unhappy whenever my expectations of receiving a letter from you are disappointed. The little time I expect now to be from home, I hope my good, dear lovely wife will not again subject me to endure so much pain.

The President is again well, and the last time I saw him was in good spirits. He has determined that the new Troops to be raised shall be procured in the states of Maryland, Virginia and N. Carolina. This was done in order to prevent their jealousy of the northern states from being further stimulated. Theodore [*Sedgwick III*] is then again disappointed. I wish he had a little spirit to put himself forward. Indeed had I not depended on providing for him in this way I would have sent him to Jennisee [*the Genessee tract in New York state*]. I wish when I return home I may not find him idling away his time.

Your friend Mrs. [*Susan Kemper*] Jackson is in town, I shall call on her and drink tea this afternoon, I have not yet seen her. Doctor [*David*] Jackson is in company with her he will have her here some time. I shall promise myself some pleasure in her company. The void I feel from having no person in whom I am greatly interested, to converse with gives an uneasiness which at some times greatly depresses my spirits. ~~I was~~

I am as yet some what uncertain when congress will adjourn, be it however as it may I will not stay here longer than thro this month, unless the business then before congress shall be more important than I can at present imagine.

ALS, Sedgwick Papers, MHi. Place to which addressed not indicated.

David Sewall to George Thatcher

While Mrs. [*Sarah Savage*] Thatcher is preparing Breakfast I have borrowed her Pen Ink and Paper to Write a line having called this morning on my returne from Portland. I find your little folks. very Well and Social, and if one may form an Opinion from appearances, your Family will probably increase.[1] my Portland Court that has bore upon my Mind is now over—and to give you the result two of the Three [?] persons in Jail were Indicted for a Piratical Murder on the high Seas—one as Principal in the first degree & the other as being present aiding & Willingly abetting &c. the other Prisoner was taken as a Witness—The Jury found one Guilty and Acquitted the other[2]—on yesterday I Pronounced Sentence of Death upon him fixed the Time of Execution to friday the 25th. of June Instant and have Ordered a Writ under the Seal of the Court to have it performed between 3 & 5 P.M. of the 25 June—And have inclosed a Copy of the Process to the President of the U.S. that, in case an application is made for a Pardon or Respite of Sentence to a future day—He may be acquainted Seasonably of it[3]—That letter I directed to be put in the Portland Mail, and will arive at the same time with this— ***

ALS, Chamberlain Collection, MB. Written from "your house at Biddeford," Maine, in the morning.

[1] George Thatcher, Jr., was born on 7 September.

[2] Thomas Bird, a British born mariner on the American sloop *Mary*, was indicted for shooting and killing the ship's master John Connor off the coast of West Africa on 23 January 1789. Hans Hanson, a Norwegian immigrant, was indicted on the lesser charges. For background on the case, see *PGW* 5:478–81.

[3] Sewall, who believed Bird's case was the first instance of a capital conviction since the establishment of the federal courts under the new Constitution, enclosed a copy of the entire legal proceedings in a letter to Washington on 5 June. In reply to Washington's enquiry, Chief Justice Jay advised against a pardon, and Bird was hanged according to sentence on 25 June.

Abigail Adams Smith to John Quincy Adams

*** to turn our attention to one [*subject*] in which you and myself ar some what interested—I mean the question of removeall of Congress to Philadelphia—which is to be decided in Senate in the Course of the week and which you will doubtless hear has passed the House in favour of that City—it is Supposed that the Senate will be equally divided—and that the V. P. will decide the question and I can tell you it will be in favour of going to Phila. and I presume to add from a mistaken opinion respecting some certains matters things, oppinions, and influential, Characters, it will be a disadvantage to Charles to be changeing his office[1]—and particularly as he has become very steady and attentive to his Studies and is very happy in his circle of acquaintance here—but private interest we are taught to believe should be sacrifised at the alter of Publick good—how they are in this instance Connected I do not see—for it is a Bargain as much as if such a sum was stipulated for the removeall—I mean with the magority.

ALS, Adams Family Manuscript Trust, MHi. Addressed to Newburyport, Massachusetts; carried by Charles Storer; postmarked Boston, 24 June. The conclusion of this letter, dated 16 June, indicates that the extreme heat of the previous week had prevented Smith from copying it, and that she was finally sending it off in care of Storer, who had been visiting them for a few days.

[1] Adams's son Charles had been studying law under Laurance since September 1789.

Caleb Strong to Samuel Phillips, Jr.

I have just seen a Letter from a Member of the [*Massachusetts*] House of Representatives in which the Writer suggests that the Genl. Court have not been duly informed when Mr. Daltons Seat will be vacated in the Senate—Mr. Dalton and I soon after the Lots were drawn[1] wrote to the Governour [*John Hancock*] to inform him of that Event and supposed he would send the Letter to the two Houses, if he has not the Letter probably miscarried or was mislaid—I shall not have Time to consult Mr. Dalton before the Mail closes—but perhaps it will be sufficient for me to say that Mr. Dalton is in the third Class whose Seats will be vacated next March—I can hardly think this Information is necessary but if it is, and will be thought of sufficient Authority be kind enough to communicate it to the two Houses.

ALS, Colburn Collection, MHi. Place to which addressed not indicated.

[1] On 15 May 1789, the day after the Senate was divided into three classes, one Senator from each drew lots on behalf of his respective class to determine whether they would serve two, four, or six years, ensuring that thereafter one third of the seats would be up for election every two years, according to the terms of Article I, section 3, paragraph 2 of the Constitution. See *DHFFC* 1:45–47.

George Thatcher to Josiah Thatcher

Mr. [*Nathan*] Dane informs me that, at the last Session of our Legislature, there was a report of a Joint committee respecting a cession of the Light-houses, in the Commonwealth, to the United States—which he thinks will, in this Session, be taken up & passed upon in some form or other—wherefore I take the liberty to observe that it is the opinion of the Secretary of the Treasury, with whom I have conversed on this subject. that a general cession of an unfinished Light-house, to the United States, will not authorise him to proceed to finish it, as it does to keep one in repair & furnish it with lights—I therefore submit it to your consideration, in case a cession of the Light-houses to the Union, takes place, whether it will not be proper, in the Act of cession, to make particular mention of the unfinished State of the Light-house, on Portland-point [*Maine*], & request that it may be compleated at the expence of the United States.

If Mr. [*John*] Fox or Mr. [*Daniel*] Davis is at Court I will thank you to mention to them the contents of this Letter.

FC, Thatcher Family Papers, MHi.

George Thatcher to Sarah Thatcher

The account you give me, in yours of the 29th. may, which came to hand last evening, of the manner Phillips [*Thatcher*] received his book[1] pleases me highly—By his readily turning to the picture of the Devil, as soon as the book was put into his hand, shews the force of the impression that had before been made on his mind by that image—this being the case its of no service to try any longer to keep him from viewing those pictures—If these impressions are hurtfull to very young minds, the injury has already commenced, and not to be remidied by attempting to prevent his looking at them—I should rather take no notice of his turning to them—but let him view them as he does other curious figures—An attempt to prevent his seeing them, by concealing, or covering, will, as you justly observe, only excite his curiosity—and fix the ideas more forceably on his mind—Children are like women—they have a wonderfull curiosity for investigation—This increases in proportion to the attempts made to keep them in ignorance—I think I have heard you say that your anxiety to come at the knowledge of certain things was never greater than when you saw others trying to keep you in ignorance—Remember how you have contemplated the possible ways & means of geting out of the chimney—this I am sure you never would have thought of if going out of the chimney was as easy as to pass from one room to another.

You complain at my not fixing a time to return—you must not be impatient, my dear—I am as anxious to return as tis possible for you to be—And I am determined to get leave of absence in this month should Congress not adjourn by the latter end thereof—But there are yet some things before Congress of too much importance to leave, as one vote may turn the question—I will mention one—viz. the assumption of the State debts—This you must get our friend [*Jeremiah*] Hill to explain to you—He is skilled in making rough places plain, and crooked paths streight.[2]

I am sorry to hear our dear Phillips is unwell—I fear it will prevent his going to school—which I would not have him neglect on any account—Pray encourage him all in your power—and leave no means untryed, if not to make him love, to make him not hate & averse to going to school—It can hardly be expected that children should be pleased with the restraint and compulsion attending their school hours—all that can be done is to create so many agreeable sensations in their going, & returning from school, as to make them forget the pain resulting from two or three hours confinement—and their attending to their Book when they read—Continual & unrestrained motion is as agreeable to children as quietude & rest to old age—Their powers, & faculties ~~of children~~ expand by a continual activity & exertion—I well recollect when I went to school, tho more than twice or three times as old as Phillips, I even hated the school considered in itself, but delighted in the many pleasures resulting from going to & returning home—such as playing with my school mates—runing jumping &c. &c.—And for the sake of these I endured the pain of school-confinement & attention.

I had intended to have got some little books, yesterday, to inclose for Phillips—but it sliped my memory—one is for himself—& the others for him to give to his school-mates—Children who go to the same school, should love one another—half the pains that are taken to make children fight & hurt one another, would fill their minds with love & benevolence—& become a noble spring of action forever after.

ALS, Thatcher Family Papers, MHi. Place to which addressed not indicated.

[1] The Hieroglyphick Bible that Thatcher mailed home for his son Phillips on 20 May.
[2] A paraphrase of Luke 3:5.

Other Documents

Thomas Fitzsimons to Benjamin Rush. Summary of ALS, *Parke-Bernet Catalog* 499(1944):item 116.

"On political and civil affairs; and informing Dr. Rush of transactions in Congress."

John Frothingham to George Thatcher. ALS, Chamberlain Collection, MB. Written from Portland, Maine; the salutation reads, "Brother Thatcher." For the enclosed petition (LS, signed with a mark, Miscellaneous Letters, Miscellaneous Correspondence, State Department Records, Record Group 59, DNA), as well as background on Bird's case, see *PGW* 5:478–81 and David Sewall to Thatcher on this date, above.

Begs Thatcher to present immediately the enclosed petition to President Washington from Thomas Bird, for pardon or commutation of his death sentence for murder.

Benjamin Goodhue to Insurance Offices. ALS, Goodhue Letters, NNS. Addressed to Salem, Massachusetts. Abbreviated version of his letter to Hodge of the same date, above.

Thomas Hartley to Jasper Yeates. ALS, Yeates Papers, PHi. Addressed to Lancaster, Pennsylvania; franked; postmarked.

The motion to adjourn to Philadelphia "hangs in the Senate and I fear is rather in a bad way—in our House we behaved well"; "To Morrow I immagine will produce some Important Events"; will write again soon.

Henry Hollingsworth to George Washington. Written from Elkton, Maryland. ALS, Washington Papers, DLC. For the full text, see *PGW* 5:484–85.

Office seeking: commissioner of loans for Maryland; "am Imboldened to offer myself through our worthy Senators."

Thomas Jefferson to Tench Coxe. AN, Coxe Papers, PHi.

"Mr. Jefferson's compliments to mr. Coxe: he [*torn*] the liberty of requesting him thro' mr. Madison t[*torn*] partake of his little dinner to-day. he shall be happy if mr. Coxe can do it, and pardon his asking him to so unceremonious a one."

Thomas Jefferson to Martha Jefferson Randolph. ALS, Jefferson Papers, MHi. Place to which written not indicated. For the full text, see *PTJ* 16:474–75.

Acknowledges Randolph's letter of 28 May, received on 5 June; it is thought the Senate will be equally divided on whether to concur with the House vote to remove to Philadelphia; suffers lingering effects of severe headache; is going sailing with the President (to Sandy Hook, New Jersey) for three or four days and hopes any seasickness will carry off the remains of the headache.

Thomas Jefferson to William Short. ALS, Jefferson Papers, ViW; received 19 October. For the full text, see *PTJ* 16:475–76.

It is thought the Senate will be equally divided on the question of convening the third session in Philadelphia, and that the issue will be decided by the Vice President, who will himself be divided between his own inclination and the unpopularity he would earn by obstructing the wish of such a great majority; the opponents of removal are trying to draw out the time to postpone the vote until the arrival of Rhode Island's Senators, in about ten days or two weeks; the Count de Moustier writes that he is coming back to New York City, although he would not find a single friend there.

Theodore Sedgwick to Samuel Henshaw. No copy known; acknowledged in Henshaw to Sedgwick, 13 June.

John Swan to Michael Jenifer Stone. ALS, Washington Papers (misdated 8 June), DLC. Written from Baltimore.

Office seeking: begs leave to introduce William Barton of Rhode Island, who wishes an office under Congress, his state having adopted the Constitution.

George Thatcher to Jeremiah Hill. No copy known; acknowledged in Hill to Thatcher, 12 June.

William Samuel Johnson, Diary. Johnson Papers, CtHi.

"St. Pauls."

Letter from Boston. *GUS*, 12 June; reprinted at Philadelphia; Baltimore; and Fredericksburg, Virginia.

"If the State debts are not assumed, distrust, dissatisfaction, and murmuring will be the inevitable consequence in Massachusetts—God grant, that that open and patriotic policy which led America through a solemn war, may yet take her by the hand, and extricate her from the embarrassments under which she now labors."

Letter from New York. [Rhode Island] *Providence Gazette*, 12 June.

"The Accession of Rhode-Island to the Union is a most propitious Event—it completes a great and glorious Work, and will open the Way to such a Revolution in that State, as will, I trust, obliterate all Remembrance of former Times."

MONDAY, 7 JUNE 1790

Rain (Johnson)

Pierce Butler to John Houston

I was some days ago favored with Your letter of the 12th of May. It is too true that Your Governor has done as You mention—he did repeatedly and in strong expressions discourage the sending of Troops[1]—The Eastern Senators, who wished not to go to the expence of sending Troops to Georgia, caught at the information, & availed themselves of it to lessen the number, otherwise You wou'd have had many more. The President has the best inclination to afford You effectual support, but he can not of his own accord raise troops, & We are assured you do not desire them. I never had so much difficulty in Sennate as to get these troops. I fear You must make much of what You have got, unless [*Alexander*] McGuilverry sends down the Indians, so as to assault the soldiery—then our *honor* will be called on: this is the expression made use of. If Your Governor attemps to send Commissioners to treat with the Indians Congress will interfere. I foresee no good to Your country from the measures of the Yazoo Company.[2] You will have heard before this reaches You that Major [*John*] Doughty was sent with some soldiers to take post at the bent of Tenessie, provided the Choctaws & Chickesaws approved & promised support—We are yet ignorant of the event—there is a flying report of his being cut off. If not true, & that the above named Indians promise support to the post 400 Soldiers will be immediately sent there. It is not improbable that they will have some instructions respecting the Yazoo lands; I am inclined to believe they will, & that the Company may find themselves disappointed.

No attack is meditated on the Creeks unless they commence hostilities again. With respect to the Spaniards, tho' I do verily believe they are active & with Panton & Forbes[3] at the bottom of the business of Indian measures, yet We are not, at present, in a situation to demand a different conduct; indeed it would be a fruitless attempt in Senate, so cautious are our Eastern Brethren. We must then, in Georgia, submit for the present to Our fate. If the Indians break out again I am sure the President will call out the Militia—but while Your own Executive says you are in profound tranquility what pretext is there for asking for more force than you have? Nothing in my power has or shall be left undone to serve Georgia, but I can not contend succesfully against such statements of Your Executive.

We are like to have a long and perhaps not a very cool session. The future residence of Congress now agitates both Houses. Mr. Morris moved in Our house & Mr. Fitzsimmons in the other to adjourn to Philadelphia—I moved a postponement & carried my motion—I next day moved for leave to bring in a bill for fixing the permanent residence of Congress—I had leave & brought in the bill, which, together with a resolve of the house of Representatives is with a commee. of Sennate, Your humble servt. chairman. The Senate are equally divided; I believe in this business Mr. A[*dams*]. will turn the scale. The funding bill has passed the house of representatives & is now before Sennate. I enclose it with this. If I was near You I would communicate some matters that I should not like to venture to commit to paper least this letter might share the fate of one I lately wrote to Captn. [*Roger Parker*] Saunders on my own affairs, it was opened and my name forged to a draught on my Factor. I shall be glad to have the earliest information from You of what passes in Georgia. I must here observe to You that even the opposers to the Yazoo company, such as Mr. [*Nathaniel*] Pendleton, in all their letters to this quarter advocate the right of Georgia to sell the lands; this strengthened the party in favor of the measure, and discouraged Your friends.

***

FC, Butler Letterbook, ScU. Sent to Savannah, Georgia. For the full text, see *Butler Letters*, pp. 48–50. The omitted text relates to private financial transactions with John McQueen.

[1] Georgia's Governor Edward Telfair was one of the voices assuring federal authorities that the abiding peace on the Creek frontier did not merit a reinforced military presence; see his letter to the Georgia delegation, 22 February, volume 18. Gunn used such assurances to protest the augmentation of the federal army intended by the Military Establishment Act [HR-50a] (*DHFFC* 9:243, 245).

[2] The Yazoo companies' purchase of Georgia's western lands.

[3] William Panton (of Panton, Leslie & Co.) and John Forbes, a business associate at Mobile, West Florida (present-day Alabama).

Tristram Dalton and Caleb Strong to Governor John Hancock

We have just had the Pleasure to receive your Excellencys Letter of the 4th. of June, inclosing a Resolve of the General Court of the same Date, in which you are requested to give us Notice that we are instructed by the Legislature to apply to Congress to assume the Debt of Massachusetts and make Provision for the Payment of the same as part of the Debts of the Union—We shall with great Cheerfulness comply with the above Instructions, our private Sentiments on this Subject perfectly coinciding with those of the General Assembly—The Justice and the Policy of this Measure we have long been convinced of, and we pray your Excellency & the General Court to be assured that no Endeavours on our part will be wanting to effect an Object so interesting to the State we have the Honour to represent, & so necessary to the Peace and general Prosperity of the Union.

ALS, hand of Strong, Miscellaneous Legislative Papers, M-Ar. Place to which addressed not indicated. Hancock received this reply on 12 June and laid it before the legislature on 14 June (Miscellaneous Legislative Papers, Senate, M-Ar).

William Ellery to Benjamin Huntington

By some bad conduct of the Post master at Little Rest [*Rhode Island*] your letter of the 22d. of May did not come to hand timely enough to be answered in my last of the 1st. of June. This is not the first time that he has been guilty of mal-conduct. It has been repeated, and the Post master of this town has complained of it, but he is still continued in office.

I am happy to find that there is so much harmony in Congress. Little bickerings will some times take place in all public bodies, and a warm debate now and then ~~like a tempest~~ clarifies and gives a spring to the mind, as a tempest doth to the air. By a vessel lately from N. York we are told that your house by a majority of ten had voted for an adjournment to Philadelphia. Will this produce an Assumption of the State Debt? Shall you have time this Session to do any thing with the copper coinage? We are plagued with coppers of various stamps various weights and of various adulterated metal. In short we are so glutted with them that a penny will purchase four of them. In the course of five or six weeks much business may be done, especially as Congress will be soon aided by our Senators. We shall not have a Representative chosen for this Session.

Our Genl. Assembly sits this day by special vocation. By the best information I can obtain the famous Jonathan Hazard of South Kingstown & Theodore Foster of Providence will be appointed Senators. The last is a Fed, and brother in law to our Governour [*Arthur Fenner*]; and probably by that connection, and his own political principles will get in. The Antis will have one of their kidney, and Jonathan I think will make the largest vote. They are strong enough to chuse whom they please. By the Constitution the members of the Legislature must take the fœderal Oath before they can proceed to business. It will tickle me to see some of the __ gnaw the file. In general they will make no bones of it. But there are some of them who will look confounded sour on the occasion. I have inquired about the state of the minds of the country party since the adoption of the Constitution, and by what I can find they are composed. I don't doubt but that in a short time they will become good Feds. From the members of the Genl. Assembly I shall be able to obtain the best information in this respect.

I have said so much about myself in former letters, and am so confident of your friendship, that I shall only beg leave to mention now that the time will soon arrive when my fate will be determined.

My friend The Honble. Henry Marchant is proposed for District Judge in this State. I don't know whether you are acquainted with his character or not. Father Sherman is. He was several times a Delegate to Congress under the late Confederation, has long practiced and is well versed in law, and, which is saying a great deal of a lawyer, is an honest man. In a word he i[*s in*] every way qualified to fill that office with reputation. your influence in his favour will be well bestowed and will ad[*d*] to the obligations you have already conferred.

P. S. When the ~~State~~ public debt is funded a sort of District Loan off[*ice*]r. may be appointed to receive subscriptions &c. and I may be possibly be thought of as a suitable person to be the Loan offr. [*lined out*] ~~then~~ then in that event. If it should be in contemplation to appoint such officers, and it should be ~~thought~~ thought that such an office might be agreeable to me it might operate against my views of the Collectorship. To prevent this I would inform you and desire you would inform Mr. Ellsworth, and Mr. Sherman that such an appointment would not suit me, one half so well as that of the Collectorship.

Present my regards to Col. Partridge, [*A.*] Foster, Baldwin Gerry &c. &c. &c., and tell them that now standing on ~~of~~ federal ground, and clapping my wings I most heartily salute them.

The Ratification of the Constitution will be presented to the President by our Senators.

ALS, Benjamin Huntington Correspondence, 1772–1790, R-Ar. Written from Newport, Rhode Island; franked; postmarked; answered 2 July. A second postscript to this letter was written on 8 June, below.

Oliver Ellsworth to Abigail Ellsworth

There is mortality enough everywhere to remind us that we are but dust. Congress last week attended the funeral of one of their own members [*Bland*] who died of the Influenza.

I send on by Sally Root,[1] who goes today some muslin for Nabby [*Ellsworth*] a pattern for a gown & coat. It is as fine probably as she would wish, but plain. I was told by some ladies here that striped was not now so fashionable as it had been & that I must get plain or spriged, no matter which it was but fine. The price was 8 dollars.

The reason for my omitting to send you the newspapers for some time was, that having changed my lodgings my papers did not find me.

Rhode Island is at length brought into the Union, & by a pretty bold measure taken in Congress which would have exposed me to some censure[2] had it not produced the effect which I expected it would & which in fact it has done. But all is well that ends well. The Constitution is now adopted by all the States, and I have much satisfaction & perhaps some vanity in seeing at length a great work finished for which I have long labored incessantly.

Typescript, Ellsworth Papers, CtHi. Place to which addressed not indicated. The letter opens "Dear Mrs. Ellsworth" and closes "Your affectionate friend."

---

[1] Possibly Sarah (1773–1857), daughter of Jesse Root (1736–1822), a noted lawyer of Hartford, Connecticut, and Ellsworth's former law teacher.

[2] Ellsworth was a member of the Senate committee that drafted the Rhode Island Trade Bill, the introduction of which on 13 May was the "bold measure" he refers to.

Daniel Hiester to John Nicholson

The Committee of the Senate have reported a bill for the permanent residence of Congress to be on the banks of the Potowmac, and on the resolution for the Temporary Seat, they have remarked, that the places are so few and the subject so fully in the view of the Senate that they forbear giving an opinion—This afternoon there was a meeting of Gentlemen of the Senate that are friendly to Philadelphia. I suppose to concert a plan, as the business is to be brought on tomorrow, Governor Johnson [*Samuel Johnston*] and Mr. Few are both sick; should either of them be away when it is decided, and Mr. Patterson vote as he has done once before (which however is doubtfull) the determination will be favourable.

The Bill for Settling the Accounts of the different States [*HR-69*], with the United States was again before the House of Representatives today and is nearly gone through—The Commissioners will be encreased to five, a majority of which to be competent to any decision, They will have a much greater Latitude than was given by the Ordinance of the old Congress,[1] which confined them to what was authorised by the different resolutions of that body; They are now to be authorised to take in all the expences incurred for the defence of any Particular State or for the United States.

The Gent[*lemen*]. of Massachusetts have received Instructions from their Legislature, now in Session, to insist on the Assumption of the State debts, We may therefore expect they will make another very vigorous effort.

ALS, Nicholson Papers, PHarH. Addressed to Philadelphia; received 9 June; "Answered wrote 2 letters 14th June."

[1] The Ordinance of 7 May 1787; for more information, see Report of the Commissioners for Settling Accounts, 8 May, above.

Thomas Jefferson, Memorandum for George Washington on North Carolina and Southern Territory Nominations

North Carolina

District Judge.

Colo. [*William R.*] Davie is recommended by Steele.

Hawkins sais he is their first law character.

Brown sais the same.

Samuel Spencer.

Steele sais he is a good man, one of the present judges, not remarkeable for his abilities, but deserves well of his country.

Bloodworth sais Spencer desires the appointment. but sais nothing of him.

John Stokes.

Steele names him at his own request. he is a Virginian, was a Captn. in the late war, lost his right hand in Beaufort's [*Abraham Buford*] defeat. practises law in S. Carolina with reputation & success; has been frequently of the legislature, was a member of the [*second North Carolina ratification*] Convention, a federalist, is now a Col. of militia cavalry, and additional judge of the Supreme court.

Hawkins has understood he is a worthy man.

Ashe names him.

District attorney.

[*John*] Hamilton. named by Bloodworth.

Hawkins sais he is now under indictment for extortionate fees & will be silenced.

Hay [*Robert Hays*]. named by Bloodworth.

Hawkins sais he is an Irishman who came over about the close of the war to see after some confiscated property. he has married in the country.

[*Silas W.*] Arnet. named by Bloodworth.

Hawkins sais he is a N. Jersey man of good character.

[*John*] Sitgreaves.[1]

Hawkins sais he lives in Newbern where the courts are held. he is a gentlemanly man, and as good a lawyer as any there.[2]

Ashe sais that Sitgreaves is not so brilliant in abilities, but of great rectitude of mind.

Bloodworth sais that Sitgreaves is a gentleman of character and represented the state in Congress in 1785.

South-Western government

Governor.

[*William*] Blount.[3]

agreed to be the properest man by Williamson, Hawkins, Bloodworth & Ashe.

Secretary.

Howel Tatham [*Tatum*].

Williamson sais he was formerly a Continental officer, is now a lawyer, a man of honor & respectable abilities.

Bloodworth names him, but sais nothing of him.

Brown thinks him illy informed, & more a man of dress than of business.

Robert Hayes.

Bloodworth only mentions his name.

Ashe.[4] says he has been a representative several times, & an offic[*er*].

[*Daniel*] Smith.

Brown considers him as the ablest & best character there.

Hawkins considers him as a very good & able man. he was a leading character in the opposition to Sevier, and so would not be a very agreeable appointment to Sevier.

Judges.

David Campbell.

Brown thinks him not a well informed lawyer, but honest. he is now judge.

Bloodworth & Ashe name him only.

Williamson sais he is of fair character & respectable abilities.

Howel Tatham [*Tatum*].

see what is said of him above for Secretary.

Ashe proposes him as a Judge, and sais he is of great application, fair & unblemished character.

John McNairy.[5] Ashe only names him.

Attorney.

Edward Jones.

Ashe proposes him. he has heard that he is a young gentleman of merit & enlightened understanding.

Bloodworth sais he is of good character, has been twice returned for the town of Wilmington.

Ms., hand of Jefferson, Washington Papers, DLC. This list was probably compiled at Washington's request. The editors base their dating on the fact that Ashe and Bloodworth did not send their recommendations to Washington until 5 June and he submitted his nominations to the Senate on 7 June.

[1] On the draft in the Jefferson Papers, DLC, there is a check mark after this name.
[2] The draft reads, "Genteel man, and as good a lawyer as any or more."
[3] On the draft in the Jefferson Papers, DLC, there is a check mark after this name.
[4] The draft reads, "Ashe proposes him for Secretary."
[5] On the draft in the Jefferson Papers, DLC, there is a check mark after this name.

North Carolina Representatives to George Washington

Being informed that John Skinner Esqr. of North Carolina has expressed a Wish that he may be favoured with the Appointment of Marshal for that District, We beg Leave to represent that Mr. Skinner not only sustains a fair Character but holds a very respectable Rank in the State; From his Integrity,

Firmness and good Understanding we believe that he is well qualifyed for an honourable Discharge of the Office and that his appointment would give general Satisfaction to his fellow Citizens.

ALS, hand of Williamson, Washington Papers, DLC; signed by all North Carolina Representatives except Sevier, who was not seated until 16 June. The letter is undated; the editors are printing it here because of its relationship to Jefferson's Memorandum of this date. The omission of the office of marshal in that document suggests this letter predated it.

John Page to St. George Tucker

Recollecting this Moment that I have not said a Word to you respecting the Piece which you sent me[1] to insert in the Museum I have snatched up my pen to inform you that as it was from your Account & other Reports improper for me to appear in that Business, I gave it in Charge to Mr. Scott of our House, who is Presidt. of a Society at Fort Pitt[2] similar to the one in Virga. & Philada. for the Abolition of Slavery. Adieu.
[*P. S.*] written at my Seat in the [*Federal*] Hall.

ALS, Tucker-Coleman Papers, ViW. Place to which addressed not indicated.

[1] Tucker's proposal for promoting the abolition of slavery is printed as an enclosure to his letter to Page, 29 March, above. The [Philadelphia] *American Museum* apparently never published the piece.

[2] Scott served as president of the Pittsburgh based Washington (County, Pennsylvania) Society for the Relief of Free Negroes and Others Unlawfully Held in Bondage.

Oliver Peabody to Nicholas Gilman

I have received Yrs. of the 22d of May—Thank you for the Statement of the proceedings respecting the removal of the district Courts from Exeter to Portsmouth[1]—I am not at all surprized at the conduct of the Great Man [*Langdon*] in the Senate, the rancour he has discovered towards Exeter, is not new; to injure us, would be pleasing to him, even if his interest, which is his dearest object, should be effected by it—We feel ourselves under great obligations to you for your exertions on this occasion, but have some fears that we shall not be able to reward you properly, however that may be, the exertions of your friends will not be wanting—I suppose your Good friends L[*angdon*]. & L[*ivermore*]. will do all in their power to remove the Offices from us, & that they are now endeavoring to lay a plan not only to remove the Offices, but the Circuit Court now established at Exeter to Concord, this plan has leaked out of [*John Samuel?*] Sherburne— ***

I am surprized at the impudence of the Petitioners of P.[2] in setting forth that the adoption of the Constitution of the U.S. was effected by their exertions, tis *false*—more was done by Exeter, than any town in the State. *** I cannot conclude without observing that 'tis very extraordinary, that Mr. Wingate should stand alone in the Senate, on that clause in the N. Carolina Bill, to what cause is it owing that he has not even the appearance of influence? Had he ever any? [*lined out*] If he had how has he lost it? I should be mortified in being of a body where I had not the appearance of influence, when I could not carry one with me—His abilities far surpass Langdon's, & a consciousness of that, to me would make the circumstance more painful.

ALS, Chamberlain Collection, MB. Written from Concord, New Hampshire. The omitted text relates to state elections and legislative affairs.

[1] As proposed under the fifth clause of the North Carolina Judiciary Bill [S-10]. The House struck out this clause.

[2] The Petition of the Merchants and Traders of Portsmouth, New Hampshire, presented on 26 March; see *DHFFC* 6:1970–71.

Governor Beverley Randolph to Richard Henry Lee and John Walker

I have had the Honour to receive your favour of the 25th. of May covering the Resolutions of both Houses of Congress on the Subject of Arrears of Pay due the Officers and Soldiers of the Virginia and North Carolina Lines. The Executive had some Weeks ago communicated to these deserving Citizens their rights, and appointed an agent here to receive Powers of Attorney from such as could not conveniently attend in Person, in order more effectually to secure the Money to their own use. So soon as the resolution of Congress shall be officially communicated, the executive will take such farther steps as may be requisite to prevent speculations upon the Claims of the Soldiery.

FC, Executive Letterbook, Vi. Written from Richmond, Virginia.

Philip Schuyler to Jeremiah Olney

Accept my best thanks for your communications and permit me to congratulate you on the Accession of your State to the union, an event which affords General satisfaction to all who truly estimate the interest of what are called the eastern states in which I trust that of New York may be fully included. the prospect which we have of soon be strengthned by Vermont will give us an Ascendency which the Superior exertions of all north & East of the Delawar entitle us to.

I am happy to inform you that Colo. Barton's Aim was not the Office which we wish you to enjoy he has I am Informed sollicetted the place of Surveyor had he attempted the other I have every reason to believe his hopes would have been disappointed, for tho I have no explicit assurances that you will be nominated to It yet I have such as do not leave me in the least doubt but that you will have It—and as the Bill for appointing revenue Officers in Your state will pass both houses to Morrow I hope by next post to Congratulate You on the Appointment.

[*P. S.*] If the Gentlemen to the senate from your state should not have left you before the receipt of this, and that you are on such a footing with them as to offer them introductory letters to this place, please to favor Colo. Hamilton and me as the ones.

ALS, Shepley Collection, RHi. Addressed to Providence, Rhode Island; franked.

Governor Edward Telfair, State Debt

In the treasury	£56,702.16 viz.
Gold & silver	0. 5.2
Paper medium	1422. 0.9
Anticipd. warrants	8225. 8.4
Govrs. warrants	1250. 7.11
Speakers Do.	710.19
Audited certificates	9844.13
funded Do. includg. Interst.	2121.15
State emission	10. 8.3
gratuitous certificts.	15. 0
Treasury do. by S. J. Cuthbert	125. 9
Do. by George Jones	89.18
Do. by John Meals	416. 3
final settlements	32469. 5.8
	56702.16
outstanding	
Govrs. & Speakers warrants	11,630. 7.4
Paper medium	23,577.19.2
State emission of Feby. 9th 1786	113.17.6
audited certiffs.	61,173.14.7
gratuitou[*s*] Do.	2676. 6.3
funded Do. including 5 years interest	53,009.19.5
Treasury do. by George Jones	519.17.4
Do. by John Meals	625. 7.4
Do. by Executive of 1782	1726.18.9
amounting to	155,074. 7.10

& there is due and owing to the state by returns and estimates the sum of £355,468.2 leaving a surplus in favour of the state of the sum of £200,393.14.1.

Ms., hand of John Meals, Abraham Baldwin Papers, GU. This copy was prepared from Telfair's message to the Georgia legislature, dated 7 June and read on 9 June.

Jonathan Trumbull to William Williams

I have to acknowlege the receipt of two favors from you—the one under 28th May—the other the 4th instant—for which I thank you—as also for the particular information they contain. I am very glad, on the whole, that you have repealed the Excise Law—its operation I have observed to have been very disgustfull to great parts of the people—& particularly so to that Class of Citizens, on whom in future, we must perhaps principally depend for the security & collection of our revenue—besides it would be sanctiong. other neighbourg. States in a like Establishment who would have it in their *power* by a diversity in the mode, to prey upon poor Connecticut—& what would be their *disposition*, we have already had too fatal an experience.[1]

Your exclusion Bill[2] I think had better have been left to the people—it is their prerogative—& they are generally very good Judges of the matter—as has been frequently seen from their Choices.

***

I think it very probable that Mr. [*William*] Imlay will have the appointment of Commisrs. of Loans in our State—I will certainly write to him in behalf of M. Porter—should he have employ for a Clerk, Mr. Porter will serve him with as much Integrity & Attention as any one can.

Congress is still progressing slowly in their business—a Bill makg. Provision for funding the national part of the Debt, has passed thro' our House—& is gone to the Senate, nearly on the principles of the Secretary of Treasury, The Assumption of State Debts is to be the Subject of Tomorrows Consideration—what will be the Issue is uncertain—I have my fears & I have my Hopes—& scarcely can tell which preponderate—We are again troubled with the foolish Question of Congress removal from this place—you recollect what agitations we suffered last Year on this point—& the same, in spite of all endeavours to the contrary, must be gone over again—& that before we have decided on the great Objects of the national Consideration before the present Sessions—*O Homines & Mores*[3]—& what is still worse it will interrweave it self into the decision of all important Questions—which should each be decided on their own merits—so are we circumstanced—my support is Faith & Patience—with a hope that the final Event may issue in general Good.

ALS, Trumbull Papers, CtHi. Place to which addressed not indicated. The omitted text relates to state politics.

[1] Perhaps a reference to New York's 1787 law providing that foreign goods shipped from Connecticut to New York were dutied four times higher than American goods.

[2] Connecticut's bill for excluding members of Congress and federal officials from the state legislature.

[3] Oh, the men and manners!

[*David Daggett,*] A Republican to Mess'rs. Printers (No. 4)

CONGRESS have appointed a committee to select a library. It is indeed laughable to see that illustrious body, in the midst of the greatest national questions, attending to the purchasing of books for their *amusement* or *instruction*. Did we, my fellow citizens, choose men to represent us in congress who are yet to be instructed in first principles? Or is it not sufficient that we already pay them six dollars per day, but must we allow them a considerable sum for tuition and books? If a library should be procured, it would be expedient also to furnish them with an instructor, and to establish a system of education. The supreme legislators of this empire, in this way, may be enabled to transact their business more satisfactorily to their employers. I confess it is a novel idea that men should alternately give law to a nation, and be pupils of a preceptor, yet from their proceedings they appear to have much to learn. If the expence of an instructor should be considered an obstacle, perhaps their clerk might be prevailed upon to read daily lectures to them—add 500 dollars to his present pay and I suspect he would consent to this additional trouble—and who would doubt the propriety of thus encreasing his salary from 19[00] to 2400 dollars, if, by that measure, congress could be properly educated. It may be doubted whether the United States would willingly incur the expence of erecting and maintaining an academy for their representatives—I presume ways and means can be proposed which will obviate this difficulty. An *additional duty* or *a direct tax* would answer the purpose. If cash should be requisite to purchase the library, let congress draw bills on France or Holland—*those nations owe us large sums for money which they borrowed of us during their late war with England.*

In the course of their education, I think congress should devote much time to the study of Rhetoric, Mathematics and Natural Philosophy—These sciences will enable them to determine the exact number of tropes and figures necessary in a congressional declamation, also to calculate the *solid content* of a speech of three hours in length which has neither *weight* nor *depth*, also the *quantity of words* and the *height of voice* requisite to constitute an argument of weight.

The Bible is a book to which they may frequently advert, there they will find such sentiments as these "I will make thy officers peace and thine exactors righteousness,"[1] also, "Moreover thou shalt provide out of all the people able men, such as fear God, men of truth, hating covetousness."[2] Particularly let them thoroughly read and digest the whole book of Job, a book which contains such an excellent lesson of *patience*, for surely no men (THEIR CONSTITUENTS EXCEPTED) have more need of the exercise of that virtue than the members of the house of representatives, who are obliged to spend whole days in hearing harangues upon questions which might be decided in half an hour. *Dr. Franklin's works*, especially that part of them called "The way to wealth," should be read every day, nay I think it would be expedient that the following passages from that ingenious author, should be printed on a large type and pasted up in the representatives chamber, "Drive thy business and let not that drive thee."

"Never leave that till to morrow which you can do to day. If you were a servant, would you not be ashamed that a good master should catch you idle? Are you then your own masters? Be ashamed to catch yourselves idle, when there is so much to be done for yourself, your family and your country."

When questions are in agitation about fixing salaries, let the members cast their eyes upon these lines, "It is as truly folly for the poor to ape the rich, as for the frog to swell in order to equal the ox."

"Vessels large may venture more,
But little boats should keep near shore."[3]

When the debate grows warm about the removing the seat of government, let silence be commanded, while the clerk reads the following old fashioned lines,

"I never saw an oft removed tree,
Nor yet an oft removed family,
That throve so well as those that settled be"

The Progress of Dulness,[4] a poem, written some years since, in this state, appears to convey in its very *title*, a strong precedent to justify the manner in doing business in congress. This book may answer the purpose of quieting conscience when it shall flash conviction on their minds for delaying the most important concerns of the nation, to discuss the most trifling questions.

[New Haven] *Connecticut Journal*, 9 June; reprinted at Boston; New York City (*NYJ*, 18 June); Elizabethtown, New Jersey; Philadelphia; and Fredericksburg, Virginia. For information on this series and its author, see the location note to A Republican to Messrs. Printers (No. 1), 15 May, above.

[1] Isaiah 60:17.
[2] Exodus 18:21.

[3] Published in 1757, Benjamin Franklin's *The Way to Wealth* was a compendium of sayings from his annual Poor Richard's *Almanack*.

[4] John Trumbull's (1750–1831) verse satire on education at Yale was published in three parts during 1772 and 1773; characters included Tom Brainless, Dick Hairbrain, and Harriet Simper.

Letter from Philadelphia

Many of our citizens seem half mad with joy at the prospect of this city becoming the temporary, if not the permanent seat of the general government. Some are brushing away the cobwebs from their parlour windows; others projecting galleries in the state-house, another set proposing bell-ringings, &c. &c. &c. For my own part I view a removal hither in a different light from the multitude, who I am convinced will soon find, in case of a removal, that they will be very little, if at all, benefited by such an event taking place. Our landlords, remarkably severe and avaricious, are only watching some such opportunity to squeeze exorbitant rents from the industrious tenant; and our markets (at present low) would soon take a rise in every necessary article of life. These evils would sensibly affect the most useful members of the community, while the real advantages of a governmental residence would be confined to a very few. You may depend that the more disinterested people here wish Congress to remain where they are, at least for a number of years, were it only to acquire the character of stability. The truth is, *vanity* is too much our failing already and the residence of Congress would be a feather in our cap, that I fear would spoil us entirely. As far as I can find, no sound reasons have yet been assigned for removing hither: it would be even, at present, a sort of ingratitude to New-York: for

Has she not, to her utmost, strove
For fear the Congress should remove—
Put some things up, pull'd others down.
And *rais'd* her streets thro' half the town—
Have you not built, with toil and sweat
And made the Federal Hall complete,
Pull'd down your fort[1] to give them air,
And mov'd your guns—the Lord knows where!

NYDA, 10 June; reprinted at Portsmouth and Exeter, New Hampshire; Boston and Northampton, Massachusetts; Hartford and Norwich, Connecticut; Philadelphia; Baltimore; Winchester, Virginia; Edenton, North Carolina; and Charleston, South Carolina.

[1] Fort George stood at the foot of Broadway just below the Bowling Green and above the Battery. At this time it was being leveled to construct a residence for the President of the United States.

OTHER DOCUMENTS

Joseph Clay to Abraham Baldwin. FC, Clay Letterbook, GHi. Written from Savannah, Georgia.

Letter is being delivered by Clay's son (Joseph, Jr.), who goes to New York City for his health; refers Baldwin to him for news.

William Ellery to John Adams. ALS, Adams Family Manuscript Trust, MHi. Written from Newport, Rhode Island.

Office seeking: Henry Marchant for federal judge of the Rhode Island district; his selection over William Bradford would satisfy Federalists generally.

Woodbury Langdon to John Langdon. ALS, Langdon Papers, NhPoA. Written from Portsmouth, New Hampshire.

Has not heard from John "for some time"; reports on health of friends and family; state politics; so many British carriers are discouraging the state's exports to the West Indies; hopes he will not resign his Senate seat and thinks "you will repent of it if you do"; one reason is that "some very undeserving Persons are endeavoring by every undue method to take your place"; encloses a letter for forwarding; John's family is well.

James Manning to John Henry. ALS, Washington Papers, DLC. Written from Providence, Rhode Island.

Office seeking: the bearer, Benjamin Stelle, as naval officer for Providence.

Henry Marchant to John Adams. ALS, Adams Family Manuscript Trust, MHi. Written from Newport, Rhode Island. In closing the letter, Marchant indicates he had kept it open until noon of the next day, 8 June, hoping to include the latest news about the state legislature. For the full text, see *DHFFE* 4:420–22.

Suspects that the state ratification convention's president, David Owen, failed to send the ratification to the President immediately, to prevent the administration from choosing federal office holders until the state legislature had appointed Senators whose influence the antifederalists might rely upon for appointments; encloses his application to Washington for district judge, with a copy for Adams's perusal, with request that he deliver it if appropriate; has been informed that he is supported by many in and out of Congress; recommends William Ellery for collector at Providence, Walter Channing for naval officer there, William Channing for district attorney, and Jabez Champlin for marshal.

Henry Marchant to George Washington. ALS, Washington Papers, DLC. Written from Newport, Rhode Island. A copy was enclosed in Marchant to Adams, above. For the full text, see *PGW* 5:488–90.

Office seeking: federal district judge for Rhode Island; mentions Ellsworth, Sherman, Jay, and particularly Adams, "with whom from a student at Law; I have enjoyed the pleasure & honor of an Acquaintance," as references.

James Monroe to James Madison. ALS, Madison Papers, DLC. Written from Fredericksburg, Virginia. For the full text, see *PJM* 13:241.

Introduces the bearer, (Muscoe?) Garnett, who is visiting New York for business reasons; asks Madison to convey to friends that daughter (Eliza K. Monroe) has recovered her health.

Jeremiah Olney to Alexander Hamilton. FC, Olney Papers, RHi. Written from Providence, Rhode Island. For the full text, see *PAH* 6:458–59.

Office seeking: collector at Providence; has written to "my Worthy Friends" Schuyler and Knox, "who have given me ~~their~~ assurances of their Friendship & Influence in promoting my Wishes."

Hugh Williamson to John Gray Blount. ALS, John Gray Blount Papers, Nc-Ar. Addressed to Washington, North Carolina; franked. For the full text, see *Blount* 2:62–63.

Encloses list of certificates Blount had sent him; believes some of them will not prove valid; advises selling them to brokers, some in New York City and some in Philadelphia, and not in their numerical order, which "bears rather a suspicious Appearance"; offers to forward the certificates to brokers under a cover letter Blount may supply; mentions the possibility of using some of the proceeds to pay the French consul (for North Carolina's Martinique debt).

Daniel Hiester, Account Book. PRHi.

Attended "Monday Club" or Mess Day with the Pennsylvania delegation at Fraunces Tavern; Maclay indicated that all the Senators who were friendly to the removal of Congress to Philadelphia were invited and that eleven attended (*DHFFC* 9:285).

TUESDAY, 8 JUNE 1790

Warm (Johnson)

Abraham Baldwin to Daniel Lyman

Your favour of the 3d Inst. with the enclosure of the additional string in our union was very grateful, and was a treat to our news-mongers, being the first copy received at this place.[1]

The President is out of town on a party of pleasure for a few days,[2] the anxiety of every body respecting the present state of his health has compelled him to break off from business, and to pay some attention to himself. as soon as he returns I will pay attention to every thing which you request. It is impossible to form any opinion of what will be the result, you have taken all the measures necessary and proper on the occasion the rest he will keep to himself till his duty draws it into view.[3]

The senate has just sent us down a negative to our vote of adjournment to Philadelphia. what will be the next move on that pretty question is uncertain; many gentlemen will feel uneasy till matters are put in some train that may eventually give them a more central situation.

ALS, Miscellaneous Manuscripts, The John Carter Brown Library at Brown University, Providence, Rhode Island. Addressed to Newport, Rhode Island; franked; postmarked.

---

[1] The first published text of Rhode Island's act ratifying the Constitution was a broadside printed in Providence on 31 May (Evans 22847). Lyman had enclosed either the broadside or the *Newport Mercury* of 3 June, which also printed the act. Official notice of the ratification, which took place on 29 May, was not sent to the federal government until 9 June. Washington received it on the evening of 15 June and transmitted it to Congress the next day. For the documents, see *DHFFC* 1:355–62.

[2] Following his brush with death from pneumonia in May, Washington's convalescence included a fishing trip off Sandy Hook, New Jersey, from 6 to 9 June.

[3] Lyman sought a revenue appointment by letters of application to Washington in March and May, and by supporting letters in February.

Stephen Choate to Benjamin Goodhue

After repeated debates on the Bill for ceeding to Congress, the light houses, within this Commonwealth, it passed this day by a considerable Majority and is gone down to the house, for Concurance, its fate not yet known;[1] there is also a report of a Joint Committe, before the Court. relative to the Choice of one Federal Senator. and representatives, to Take their Seats in congress, the first of March next, how the public pulse will beat, is at present Uncertain. we are anxious here about, the Determination of Congress on the Question of assumption. I Cant, but repeat, my wish, that, the present Session of Congress, may Continue untill this buisness is Completed—if no provision ~~of~~ of this kind is made, I conceive it will tend grately to lessen the Confidence of many of our worthy citizens in the Justice and imparchality of that honourable body. I am Sorry to Say that, this confidence, which is So important, to the well being of our Nation is two much impaired allready, it appears from the Late descisions of your house, that a Desided Majority are in favour of moveing farther to the Southward. I wish to be informed, whiether, there must not be a Concurrance of the Senate, in questions of this kind, and if So, what, the prospects are, in the other house—as we see nothing of the Debates in the Senate, we are not able to Collect any thing of their Sentiments, on this Subject. I dont expect, any thing, will be attempted by the Genl. Court [*legislature*], this Session, respecting the State Debt. but, if nothing is done, by the General Government, for the relief of State Creditors, it will render it impracticable for the General Government, to Collect, their revenue in this State, to any Considerable degree, for from what appears I think the merchant and Trader, will reluct, exceedingly at paying so much money for public uses in Case there was an equal distribution among the Creditors of Goverment, and much more so, if it is to be partially applied, to the benefits of some Creditors, while others are neglected by Goverment. I have been Long Convinced, that, in a free Goverment. it is absolutely necessary, that, a good Degree of imparchalliety ~~must~~ be preserved, relative to money matters. otherwise the foundations, of such a Goverment, will Soon Falter, if not utterly give way. it is needless to make further observations on a Subject, in which I believe, wee are perfectly agreed. Shall only add, that, I conceive it highly Probable, in case the assumption does not take place, that, this Goverment, and Some others in the Union, in like Circumstances, will, make vigerous exertions, to obtain Justice for their immediat Creditors, even if it should tend to injure the revenues of the General Goverment, the Principle of Self preservation is a Powerful and persevering, Principle, and it is my wish that Legeslators may at, no time forgett it. I find perticular information from Gentlemen, with whom I am intemately acquainted is much more Satisfactory, than what is received through the channel of the public prints. therefore hope you will continue your wonted favours.

ALS, Letters to Goodhue, NNS. Written from Boston.

[1] By the act for ceding its lighthouses and other navigational aids (Ch. IV, 10 June 1790), Massachusetts ceded a total of eight lighthouses: one in Boston; one in Portland, Maine; four in Essex County; one in Plymouth; and one on Nantucket.

Benjamin Contee to Governor John Eager Howard

I am this moment hond. with yrs., of no date, in which the rect. of mine of 25th Ulto.

I am now able, with great satisfaction, to inform you of the Presidents having greatly recovered from the dangerous state of illness he was lately in—he has resumed the duties of his Office—and I believe now experiences no worse effects from his disorder than a consequent debility.

The funding Bill, as I believe I informed you, has passed this House.

A Bill, for the Settlement of accts. between the U.S. & individual States [*HR*-69] is about to pass.

A Committee is just appointed to confer with a Committee of the Senate on the business necessary to be finished during the present session of Congress I heartily wish an adjournment could immediately take place—it may very possibly in a few weeks—the Committee will probably Effect [*?*] a day.

ALS, Etting Collection, PHi. Addressed to "Governor of Maryland"; franked; postmarked.

Benjamin Contee to George Washington

Being informed you are about to fill up your nominations of Consuls for the United States, I beg leave to mention *Alexander Contee*; who has requested my application in his behalf, for the *consulship at the port of London*. Delicacy forbids my saying much of a Brother, and might restrain me likewise from doing him Justice, But I persuade myself that if your appointment for the above port is not allready provided, It will not discredit your choice to place his name in the nomination, as consul for that port. He has resided in London since the year 85, and for the most of the time at the Head of a mercantile House; He is expected to arrive soon in Maryland, but with intention to return to England in the fall.

Forgive me, Sr., for the trouble I occasion you. I thought it best to do it in this mode as it leaves less room for that embarrassment consequent on applications—and places you in a less arduous situation than personal application would.

It does also favor my own deffidence nevertheless if I thought a personal application would be more expressive of respect, I would not hesitate to make it.

ALS, Washington Papers, DLC. Written on "Tuesday morning."

Rufus King, Notes in Senate

Mr. Lee moved to postpone the Bill introduced by majr. Butler for the establishment of both permanent & temporary residence, to take up a resolution sent from the house that the next Session of Cong. shd. be in Philadelphia—a motion was made to postpone the whole subject till tomorrow—the Senate being equally divided (mr. Johns[*t*]on & mr. Few being both absent,) the Vice president voted against the postponement—mr. Johns[*t*]on & mr. Few being notified of the question, attended—mr. Johns[*t*]on came with his night cap and wrapped in many Garments, attended by Doctrs. Bard & Romaine,[1] and having a Cot with a Matras in the antichamber to repose on—by general consent the resolution was taken up—and negatived 13. to 11—the report of the Committee was afterwards taken up & the first clause, which asserted the propriety of fixing the permanent Residence at this time, was negatived by the voice of the vice president—the report being laid aside a motion was made to fill the blank in the Bill with Potomack as the permanent Residence—this was negatived as were also Baltimore and Wilmington—a motion to postpone the bill a fortnight, as also another motion to postpone it indeffinitely, were negatived—finally congress adjourned—previous to negativing the Resolution Mr. Butler told me that Mr. Schuyler & myself must vote to fill the Blank in the Bill with potomack, as they cd. not vote against the Resolution—I agreed so to vote—and finally voted accordingly.

Ms., King Papers, NHi. For Maclay's account, see *DHFFC* 9:286–87.

[1] King probably referred to Samuel Bard (1742–1822) rather than his father, John Bard (1716–99), who opened a medical practice in New York City with Samuel in 1767. Nicholas Romaine, a Columbia College professor of medicine, had an office at 156 Queen Street (*New York*, pp. 93–94).

Massachusetts House Delegation to Governor John Hancock

We had the honor yesterday, soon after the meeting of Congress, of receiving by express your letter of the 4th, inclosing resolutions of the same date passed by the honorable Legislature, & communicating their "sentiments" on the assumption of the state debts.

It affords us the highest satisfaction, whilst united in our opinions of the justice, policy, & necessity of the measure, to receive such solid support as results from the sanction of that honorable body: and We beg leave thro your Excellency to assure them that We shall continue our unremitted exertions, whilst there is prospect of success to attain this important object.

A majority of the House have passed a seperate bill for funding the residue of the debt of the United States, and as we have information that a proposition will be made in the Senate, to annex to that bill a clause for assuming the state debts, we have not tho't it advisable to renew the consideration of the subject, altho it was an order of the House for yesterday.

ALS, hand of Gerry, signed by all eight Representatives, Mss. LI, Boston Athenaeum. Received 12 June. Precisely when this letter was alienated from M-Ar is unknown, but it was offered for sale by Walter Benjamin in *The Collector*, January 1893, p. 57.

Benjamin Rush to Tench Coxe

***

A Change of nearly all our delegates will it is said take place at our next election. Different reasons will operate with different parties; & in different parts of the state—But a majority unite in reprobating the assent of our members to that part of the funding System which rejects discrimination. If this measure is *right*, it will be the first one that ever was so in the United States to which a majority of our citizens were opposed. ~~to it~~ Mr. Madison is next to G. Washington in the estimation & confidence of the people, chiefly for the part he took in the controversy upon that Subject.

Jno. Adams has fixed his character for ever in the United States. In One of his letters to me ~~to~~ he gives a decided preference to Philada. and [*lined out*] commends as a reason for that preference, "our noble libraries." When we view the height from which this ~~po~~ man has fallen, and the ~~ig~~ insignificance to which he must descend After his four years expire, we are led to cry out "titles! poor human Nature"!

***

ALS, Coxe Papers, PHi. Written from Philadelphia.

Benjamin Russell to Benjamin Goodhue

The obligations under which I remain for your repeated good offices, needed not any further instance to impress my mind with the most lively emotions of gratitude—Your last favour has laid me under obligations which I know it will never be in my power to discharge; and the very flattering terms in which you have been pleased to communicate the intelligence, demands a return which I am unable to make; If the strictest regard to punctuality, and accuracy, in discharging my duty—if a constant zeal to [*pr*]omote the best interests of the United States (as far as my feeble abilities extend) can be an earnest of my gratitude; these you may depend shall invariably mark my conduct. In advocating an efficent government, I did no more than discharging a duty which I conceived I owed my country—whose safety & happiness I ~~conceived~~ thought essentially depended on its establishment; and the approbation of one liberal and understanding man, is a sufficient satisfaction for the calumny of a thousand blind and ignorant zealots.

Your correspondents, no doubt, inform you of all political events, this way. This day, a Bill for ceding the Light-Houses in this State, to the United States, came down for concurrence from the Senate—as also, A Bill prescribing the times, places and manner of holding elections. Thursday is assigned for the latter—and tomorrow for the former. The Counties of Nantucket and Duke's County, are added to Suffolk, in the formation of the first district.[1] Judge [*David*] Sewall will be in town in a few days, and will take his seat in the House; Mr. [*Abraham*] Holmes, seconded by Mr. [*John*] Gardiner, moved for a time to be assigned for the consideration of the eligibility of any persons holding a seat in the Legislature who enjoy any offices under the United States. The subject will have a free and full discussion.

The subject of Assumption occupies the whole attention of the people this way—and the happiness of Massachusetts they think is suspended on the issue. The murmurings against Congress, are only a relapse of the disease, which has prevailed, at times [*in?*] this country, ever since its establishment—and while they think that the general sentiment of the People, ought [*lined out*] to have attention paid to it, the Frinds to order and good government feel happy that the unreasonable clamourings of restless demagogues, and ignorant State-Quacks, have no influence on Congress.

ALS, Letters to Goodhue, NNS. Written from Boston; franked; postmarked 10 June. A postscript, probably written on 10 June, is calendared under that date, below.

---

[1] Massachusetts, the only state to pass joint resolutions rather than an act for regulating its first federal election, continued that method of proceeding with the second federal election. The state Senate sought to redistrict the state by separating the single district embracing Hampshire and Berkshire counties into two distinct districts, and consolidating two others by combining Dukes and Nantucket with Suffolk County, and Bristol with Plymouth and Barnstable counties. The proposal was defeated in the House on 18 June, and the provisions left essentially as they were for the first federal election ([Boston] *Independent Chronicle*, 24 June).

George Thatcher to Sarah Thatcher

I have this day put on board a packet, bound to Boston, some books—among which are two or three Law-books for Mr. [*Silas*] Lee—And two, in particular, for yourself & the family—They are the sermons of the celebrated Docr. Blair[1]—I have often heard you complain for the want of proper family books—such as are practical & may be read with advantage to children & domestics—And more especially on sundays.

I have a great opinion of reading, you know, tho I care but little about praying—I would have every body read at certain times in a day, if absolutely necessary business do not take their whole time—People who live at a distance from meeting houses—or who choose to tarry at home on sundays, ought to make a duty of spending some part of the day in reading—I would extend this not only to heads of families, who should read to servants and children—but to servants & children themselves—And the next question is what books shall they read? I need not here mention the Bible—for it is in every body's hand—& I am of opinion it is sufficiently run over by most people—I have only to wish it was duly attended to & understood—next to this people read sermons & books on religious points of which I am rather inclined to think there is not more than one in a thousand but what rather darken the understanding and shut the mind against receiving usefull information than otherwise—And the real reason I have not bought more family books is because I have not met with any that I thought would on the whole be usefull—I have no idea of a book's being usefull, otherwise than it becomes a means of instruction—devotional books, so much recommended by people in general, I look upon hurtfull—And ninety nine sermons out of an hundred are either of this kind, or treat of questions & points of no more consequence to mankind than it is to know whether Adam & Eve were exactly of the same height or the former half an inch taller than the latter—The Sermons I now send you, I have not read—I am told, however, that they are plain discourses on virtue & morality—they point out the duties of men in the various relations they may exist in Society—that their general tendency is to make people contented with their situation—and to view all things as good—I have no opinion of books that hold up the things of this world in a sorrowfull dress—and paint the world itself as a dungeon—a place of misery & wretchedness—If any thing is wrong it certainly springs from some erroneus step in our education—all things are good as they come out of the hands of God—evil results solely from ourselves—of what infinite importance then is education—& how much has every one to answer for who has the charge of others committed to them.

ALS, Thatcher Family Papers, MHi.

[1] Dr. Hugh Blair (1718–1800) was a noted Scottish Presbyterian divine famous equally for his literary criticism as for his series of popular sermons published in four volumes (1774–94) in which he espoused a liberal position opposed to strict Calvinist doctrine. The first American edition was published in New York in 1790.

George Thatcher to Nathaniel Wells

The Bill for setling the accounts between the U. States & the individual States [*HR*-69] has engaged the attention of the House for seven or eight days past, and is not yet compleated—Upon this subject there is a great contrariety of opinions; and when a principle is acceeded to, it seems more the result of necessity than a proper agreement in sentiments.

Mr. Peas[1] arrived here yesterday morning about ten oClock, with dispatches from the Governor [*John Hancock*][2]—He also brought papers containing the Governors speech to the two Houses at the begining of the Session—The principle held up in this speech, that an assumption of the State debts ought to be founded upon a previous request, & transferral of a right for that purpose, from the States, I fear will be made use of, by those who are ~~opposed~~ adverse to an assumption, as an argument against the measure—at least till the other States signify their consent.

The Bill for making provision for the Continental debt was yesterday taken up in the Senate, & debated—but I beleive no amendment was made to it—It was proposed by Mr. Elsworth from Connecticut, to strike out the clause that funds the old paper money at 75 for 1—& insert 100 for 1—but it did not then take place.

I have some doubt whether the subject of assumption will be taken up in the House before it has been tried in the Senate—should the Senate propose it, as an amendment to the funding bill, I think it will meet a more favourable reception in our House—However every thing touching the Funding system is precarious—Some are absolutely against it—others are opposed to its passing this Session; & I beleive some may be brought to oppose it for more special, & perhaps, party reasons. since writing the above the Bill for setling Accounts between the U. States &c. &c. has passed to be engrossed & read a third time—& the Senate has non-concured the Resolution of this House for meeting the next Session at Philadelphia.

I rejoiced at hearing Judge [*David*] Sewall was chosen a member of the Legislature—And as I am of opinion his being a district Judge, under the General Government, is neither a Constitutional, or a prudential disqualification, I shall grieve if the House refuse him a seat[3]—If he is at court be pleased to make my Compliments to him—I shall write him as soon as I know where a Letter will find him.

FC, Thatcher Family Papers, MHi. Place to which addressed not indicated.

---

[1] Levi Pease operated a stagecoach between Boston and New York City.

[2] Besides Governor Hancock's speech to the legislature on 1 June, Pease brought the Massachusetts legislature's resolutions on assumption and its "sentiments" addressed to the state delegation; see Hancock to Massachusetts House Delegation, 4 June, above.

[3] On the grounds that his federal judgeship made him ineligible to hold a state office.

Joseph Willard to John Adams

I take the liberty of enclosing a petition to the National Legislature, from the Convention of the Congregational Ministers in this Commonwealth, by a Committee of the Body, upon a very important subject, viz. that of preventing incorrect editions of the Bible from being published among us. The Committee have desired me to request your Excellency to take the charge of this petition, and to introduce it, at such time, as you may judge most expedient. They have full confidence in your Excellency, that you will do every thing in your power, that the American editions of that sacred Book, which contain the foundations of our holy religion, and for which, they are persuaded you have the sincerest regard, may come forth as correct as possible.

The Committee, by the direction of the Convention, are preparing letters to be sent to the Ministers of the various denominations of Christians, in the United States, requesting them to join in applications to the Congress, in this important business; and they hope, that the cause of true religion will be subscribed by these exertions.

ALS, Adams Family Manuscript Trust, MHi. Written from Cambridge, Massachusetts. For background and the enclosed petition, presented in the Senate on 14 June, see *DHFFC* 8:306–8.

Important Decision

Yesterday, we are informed, the Senate proceeded to consider the resolution of the House of Representatives, respecting the holding the next session of Congress at Philadelphia: after a full discussion of the subject, on taking the question the resolution was negatived by a majority of two, 13 to 11. It is said that the advocates of the resolution were so exceedingly anxious to have it determined, that two of the members opposed to it, though very much indisposed, were constrained to attend, one of the gentlemen being so unwell that he was carried to the Senate Chamber.[1] It must be pleasing to the citizens of New-York to reflect that many of the members of the House of Representatives who voted for Philadelphia have confessed that they should leave this city with regret, where they had received such polite and hospitable treatment, but that they thought it incumbent on them to give their sanction for a situation nearer the centre of territory; we have reason, therefore, to flatter ourselves that the determination of the Senate will not prove unsatisfactory.

NYDG, 9 June.

[1] Few and Johnston were induced to attend the Senate proceedings of this day, although both had been staying at home sick. Johnston was brought "in a Sedan" with his nightcap on; an accompanying bed was set up for him in an adjoining committee room (*DHFFC* 9:286).

Cassius to the Connecticut Courant

By the public papers printed in New-York, I find, to my astonishment, that Congress are at the old play of *cross purposes*—of *Residence*, both *temporary* and *permanent*, whilst the great business of the nation either is suffered to *stand still*, or *retrogrades*. That different sentiments should obtain in such a body as Congress are, and difficulties arise about public measures, and the best means of effecting the objects of our national government, is not to be wondered at; but that the principal part of their time should be *wasted* in *wrangling* about the place of their residence—about funding their debts, and providing the ways and means of establishing sufficient funds for paying the current expences of government, and the annual interest of their funded debts, without determining *ultimately* and *unalterably* any thing thereon, is truly astonishing and incredible. What patient animals do they conceive their constituents to be, to suppose they will sit quietly under the administration of such a government, which costs them so much money to so very little purpose. If the interest of the northern and southern states are so totally *opposite* and *incompatible* as will admit of no coalition, no compromise, where from *mutual concessions mutual benefits* will accrue to both parties; we had better separate at once, before we become the jest not only of foreigners but of ourselves. If the southern states cannot exist but under the benign influence and smiles of the British government, let them return to their former bondage, and quietly partake of the *leaks* and *onions*, which they enjoyed under the former dominion of those generous masters! Let *Virginia* and *Pennsylvania cabal* about the *Seat* of *Government*—about having the *first slice* of the *loaves* and *fishes*;[1] of what consequence is this dispute to the rest of the states, or even to *ninety nine* in the *hundred* of the citizens of those states. The business of Congress may go on as well at *New-York* as at *Philadelphia*; as well at Philadelphia (were Congress and their public offices there) as at New-York. But surely no wise man would propose moving thither, unless some benefit adequate to the *expence* and trouble that this removal must occasion, would result from the measure. It might accomodate Mr. M—s [*Morris*] and Mr. F—ns [*Fitzsimons*], who could in that case enjoy the solace and company of their families and friends; or attend to private business and speculations, whilst they were paid for attending the public business of the nation. What other good is to arise out of the removal, neither they or their friends, or even their *toad-eaters*, have (as far as I recollect) ever suggested. Those who know what trouble and expence it will be to remove all the public offices, books and vouchers; what a delay at this critical stage of public business, and for no apparent cause; cannot suppress their indignation at this wanton waste of time in Congress—this egregious trifling with the interest of their constituents. It is most convenient for the four New-England states, New-York and Jersies, that Congress should hold their sessions at New-York. The delegates from Georgia and South-Carolina, will probably always choose (in time of peace) to come *by water*, whether Congress remain at New-York or remove to Philadelphia; in that case they must prefer New-York as being the safest and shortest navigation. As far as we are interested in European connections and politicks we must prefer New-York. It is true that the encrease of population and wealth may be expected to take place in the *middle* States, and indeed in some of the Southern, over that of the Northern States; and at some future period—Some *twenty* or *thirty* years hence it may be necessary to remove the seat of Government to the *extreme* parts of *Pennsylvania* or on the banks of the *Potowmac*, that *River* of *Rivers*, whose salutary waters would wash out all our *political leprosy*. But why should we hasten this business before the time—why *run before Providence*? what has Philadelphia done for the United States, or for the *honor* of *Congress*, that they should run *mad* to get thither? will they enjoy more *freedom* of debate—more advantages, to *consult* and *promote* the *public weal*—more *personal safety*—or more of the *good things* of this life there than at New-York? Or is it expected the *name* of *Philadelphia*, like a spell, will introduce more candor to their debates; more *union*, more *brotherly love* in our national Legislature than what appertains to that honorable body in their present place of residence; if so, God speed their journey: But if no such good is to be expected from removing thither, (and if we may judge from the conduct of their own legislature, whose members have been subjected to personal abuse and violence—have been compelled to attend their duty by a mob, there is not) then let them quietly attend to the duty of their stations where they are. If the *delegates* from *Philadelphia* cannot make it convenient to attend Congress in New-York, why then *Pennsylvania* must be content to forego their services, and endeavor to make up the loss in the best manner they can—the *Union* will not be in much danger from shifting two or three men. These are my sentiments, Messieurs Printers, and the declared sentiments of most of the people with whom I have conversed on this subject.

[Hartford] *Connecticut Courant*, 12 July; reprinted at New York City (*NYDA*, *NYDG*, 15 July; *NYP*, 17 July) and Danbury, Connecticut. Cassius was a popular pseudonym for political writers, the best known being Caesar's assassin Cassius Longinus (d. 42 B.C.).

[1] Matthew 15:36; Mark 8:6.

OTHER DOCUMENTS

Pierce Butler to James Seagrove. No copy known; acknowledged in Seagrove to Butler, 8 August.

William Ellery to Benjamin Huntington. ALS, Benjamin Huntington Correspondence, 1772–1790, R-Ar. This is a postscript to a letter begun on 7 June, above.

Encloses letters to Adams, Ellsworth, and Sherman indicating Ellery's preference for appointment as collector at Newport, Rhode Island, rather than loan officer for the state; asks Huntington to tell King that Ellery received his letter "this instant (June 8th.) after I had sealed my letter to him, and that I have not time to write another"; "our Senators will be chosen this week, and will I suppose proceed to Congress."

William Irvine to Anne Callendar Irvine. ALS, Newbold Irvine Papers, PHi. Place to which addressed not indicated. The first portion of this letter was written on 5 June and is calendared under that date, above.

The Senate has rejected the House resolution for adjourning to Philadelphia; despite a renewed attempt in the House, "I think it is all over at this time"; the House has passed the Settlement of Accounts Bill [HR-69], but does not know what the Senate will do with it, since "they some times take the liberty of differing from the Representatives."

Gouverneur Morris to Le Couteulx and Co. FC:lbk, Gouverneur Morris Papers, DLC. Written from London; sent to Paris. The recipients—more specifically Laurent Le Couteulx—were an old Norman family of financiers with offices in Paris, Rouen, and Cadiz, who were employed as bankers to the United States during Morris's tenure as superintendent of finance, and occasionally as his (and Wadsworth's) personal bankers thereafter (Beatrix C. Davenport, ed., *Diary of the French Revolution* [2 vols., Boston, 1939], p. 4n; *PRM* 1:124n, 7:262n).

Both his letter of 28 May and this one enclose letters to Le Couteulx and Co. from Robert Morris, who "is mistaken in the Idea that you cannot hold Lands in Newyork for I believe that Matter is already settled" by the Franco-American Treaty of 1778.

Samuel Osgood to William Smith (Md.) FC, Letterbook A, Records of the Post Office Department, RG 28, DNA.

Acknowledges receipt, the evening before, of Smith's "note" and the accompanying recommendation of "sundry Gentlemen" of Baltimore for

(George) Keeports as postmaster of Baltimore; regrets he has already appointed Alexander Furnival to the post.

William Seton to [*Richard Curson?*]. No copy known; quoted in Richard Curson to Horatio Gates, 12 June (ALS, Gates Papers, NHi).

"The motion for removal came on this day in the Senate and was carried against it 13 to 11—so it cannot come on again this Year. Had the Rhode Island Members been here It would have been more hollow—Some are of opinion this will affect the funding Bill, and that the House will not agree to it."

John Swan to Michael Jenifer Stone. Misdated; see calendar under 6 June, above.

Josiah Thacher to George Thatcher. ALS, Thatcher Papers, MeHi. Written from Boston.

Thanks for sending "a Continuation of the Journals of Congress"; reports state legislative business; office seeking: was informed a few days earlier that Thatcher was enquiring about candidates for a federal excise collector at Portland, Maine, if Congress should provide for one; recommends the state's excise collector there, Ebenezer Mayo.

Oliver Whipple to John Langdon. ALS, Langdon Papers, NhPoA. Written from Portsmouth, New Hampshire; postmarked Portsmouth, 14 June; Langdon wrote "Answer'd" at the bottom of the first page.

Acknowledges Langdon's letter of March; office seeking: excise; mentions Adams, Dalton, King, Thatcher, Goodhue, Partridge, and Leonard as references, "but on you Sir I principally rely"; congratulations on Rhode Island's ratification; although "eleventh hour Christians," they might atone for their "Back Sliding"; office seeking: recommends John Carter as naval officer and Jabez Bowen as collector for Providence, Rhode Island; Langdon's wife (Elizabeth) and sister (Elizabeth Barrell) are well.

[Columbia, South Carolina] *Columbian Herald*, 8 June. Wister Butler Papers, PHi. Annotated by Butler to indicate the article for which he retained the issue.

South Carolina constitution.

From New York. [Boston] *Columbian Centinel*, 16 June; reprinted at Portland, Maine; Portsmouth, New Hampshire; and Northampton, Massachusetts.

Before the Senate took up consideration of the Funding Act the day before, (Levi) Pease delivered to Massachusetts' Senators the state's resolutions on assumption and a letter from Governor John Hancock; "the receipt of these papers gives much satisfaction, and they will make impression."

WEDNESDAY, 9 JUNE 1790

Cool (Johnson)

Thomas Hartley to Jasper Yeates

Yesterday the Senate negatived our Resolution for our next Meeting at Philadelphia—by a Majority of two—I could never say much as to the Senate tho' some of our Friends were very sanguine.

However the Game is not totally lost I was so much used to Defeat in the Army—that I can rally without much Difficulty.

We presented a new Resolution in our House—I would have discussed it to Day but the Speaker declared by the Rules that it must lay upon the Table until to Morrow.

The New Yorkers are alarmed again—all is afloat—they offer to give the Permanent Residence to Pennsylvania—Temporary Residence at New York for only two Years—but this is all Deception—we must go on Steadily with the Virginians—Temporary is all we can aim at, at present.

The Troops wear a tollerable good Countenance & we have still somewhat to hope.

I inclose you a News-Paper.

ALS, Yeates Papers, PHi. Addressed to Lancaster, Pennsylvania; franked; postmarked; answered 20 June.

Philip Schuyler to Catherine Schuyler

I have the pleasure to Inclose you three letters from our Dear Angelica [*Church*], one for you, a second for our dear Margret [*van Rensselaer*], and a third to me—you will participate with me in the pleasure I experienced in the perusal.

Yesterday the Senate negatived the resolution of the house of representatives to remove to Philadelphia, but the danger is not yet over. It will be brought on again, in another shape. If however all the representatives from this State could be brought to Act in concert we shall defeat our opponents.

Baron [*Frederick William*] Stuben who will take Albany in his way to

Montgomery County will leave this to Morrow, I shall write you or Margret a line by him.

Cornelia [*Schuyler*] Improves wonderfully, and my little Caty writes me so charmingly that I am equally pleased with both. why will not my son Rensselaer compleat the happiness. pray urge him to It.

We are all well.

ALS, Washington-Biddle Correspondence, PHi. Addressed to "near Albany"; franked; postmarked.

Michael Jenifer Stone to George Washington

I have taken the Liberty to inclose a Letter from Major [*John*] Swan[1] recommending Colonel [*William*] Barton—I had not the pleasure of being known to that Gentleman untill the present. But I am intimately acquainted with Major Swan and have the fullest confidence in his recommendation of Col. Barton.

ALS, Washington Papers, DLC.

---

[1] Swan to Stone, 5 June, calendared under that date, above.

L. to Mr. Fenno

NOTHING evinces more forcibly the high value of a federal government, founded on the great democratic principle of representation, than the conduct of the House of Representatives of the United States. Its members extend their paternal care equally over every part of this great empire—nothing escapes their minute researches to benefit every part of the Union—While many regulations in the collection laws shew how attentive they have been to avoid oppression; they have uniformly manifested an ardent desire to accommodate all their constituents, by assigning numerous ports and districts for the convenience of commerce—nay, in some instances, this disposition seems to have led them almost to sacrifice that security, which the due collection of the revenue requires. These observations are corroborated by a late transaction.

The committee recently appointed for the purpose of bringing in a bill for extending the revenue laws of the United States, to the State of Rhode-Island, reported that foreign ships, and all vessels coming from China or the East Indies, should be limitted to the port of Newport—the size of that State would lead one to suppose that one port was fully sufficient for all its purposes of foreign commerce; but such was the desire of that body to extend the advantages of commerce to all ports that were in a capacity of enjoying and benefiting by them, that they added the port of Providence, on the motion of Mr. Sedgwick, who assigned this reason, in favor of it, that he had been informed by a worthy and intelligent gentleman from that State, that it was the wish of some of its inhabitants. What could justify the foregoing remarks more fully?

Americans! while you employ such men as agents, regard not the malevolence of the snarling and insiduous—creatures who live in faction, and exist upon the vapors of a foul imagination—who may be traced like the snail upon the rock, by the slime of defamation they leave behind them?

GUS, 9 June, edited by John Fenno.

Newspaper Article

Yesterday a gentleman attending in the gallery of the Federal Hall, had his pocket book stolen out of his pocket, containing a number of papers, and about 30s. in money. Fortunately the owner had a little before taken out of his pocket book a sum to a large amount and deposited it at home. The pocket book and papers were in the afternoon found on the battery, the money gone. This is a convincing proof that political knowledge is not the *universal* motive to attend in the galleries.

NYDA, 10 June; reprinted in some form in every New York City paper and in Boston and Northampton, Massachusetts, and Hartford and Norwich, Connecticut.

Memnon to Messrs. Goddard and Angell

I OBSERVE, by the proceedings of the Lower House of Congress, that three of our delegates, Messrs. *Carroll, Contee,* and *Gale,* voted against Baltimore being the temporary residence of Congress; so that our members were equally divided upon, what may be properly termed, a mere state question—The jealousy which the Patowmac interest entertain of Baltimore, induced people, generally, to expect the two former gentlemen would sooner vote for Boston, or Charleston; but Mr. *Gale* has hitherto been considered a friend to Baltimore, therefore *his* voting against it, was as unexpected as Mr. *Stone*'s voting for it—I consider it as very immaterial to the welfare of the United States at large, *at present,* whether Congress sits at New York, or Philadelphia; therefore it is to be regretted, a question of such a nature should be brought forward, tending to irritate the members of Congress against each other, and to call into action every local prejudice and jealousy, which ought to be confined to the state governments, and carefully excluded (if possible) from the federal government—Perhaps national considerations may have rendered a removal from New-York necessary; If so, the people at large are ignorant of them, and they should be communicated—Maryland, as a state, is not interested in increasing or diminishing the prosperity of either Philadelphia or New York—Applicants for offices, or persons having business with Congress (which are not one-twentieth part of the inhabitants of this state) certainly could reach Philadelphia sooner than New York; but that is an object of very little consequence, indeed, to the body of the people—Report says, the Pennsylvania delegates have bartered with some from the eastward, to vote for assuming the state debts, if they will but vote for the removal of Congress to Philadelphia. Probably, the report was originally groundless, framed and propagated to answer some party purpose; but if the Pennsylvanians should now advocate the assumption of the state debts, after having hitherto opposed the measure, many people may consider it as a confirmation of the truth of the report. The Maryland delegates formerly voted for New-York, as the temporary residence of Congress, in preference to Philadelphia; and though they may have good reason for *thus shifting their ground*, yet most of their constituents are ignorant of them, and wish for information.

[Baltimore] *Maryland Journal*, 11 June, edited by William Goddard and James Angell. Memnon was a rarely used pseudonym perhaps intended to compare the vote on 31 May against choosing Baltimore as the place where the FFC would hold its third session with Achilles's murder of this mythic Ethiopian prince during the Trojan War.

Other Documents

Robert Aitken to George Washington. ALS, Washington Papers, DLC. Written from Philadelphia. For the full text, see *PGW* 5:493–95.

Office seeking: printer and stationer to Congress, or any other employment suitable for a printer; had considered petitioning Washington for a copyright on the Bible; mentions Morris, Boudinot, Gerry, and unnamed others as references.

William Constable to Gouverneur Morris. FC:lbk, Constable-Pierrepont Collection, NN.

Refers Morris to R. Morris's letter (no copy known) sent by the same conveyance for the news of "Politics, Residence & Removal the bone of Contention still."

Governor Arthur Fenner to George Washington. LS, Washington Papers, DLC. Written from Newport, Rhode Island; signed by Fenner, deputy governor Samuel Potter, and eight (of ten) members of the Rhode Island legislature's upper house, the Council of Assistants (James Arnold, Thomas G. Hazard, Benjamin Watson, James Congdon, Thomas Hoxsie, John Cook, John Harris, and Peleg Arnold). For the full text, see *PGW* 5:497–98.

Office seeking: Theodore Foster for naval officer at Providence, Rhode Island; the application is not to be considered as made in the signatories' legislative capacity.

Governor Samuel Huntington to Roger Sherman. Listing of one page ALS, *Flying Quill*, May 1952, p. 18.

"On legislative matters."

William Samuel Johnson, Diary. Johnson Papers, CtHi.

"Mrs. Johnson sailed [*for Connecticut*]."

Thomas Rodney, Journal. NjP. Probably refers to William Killen, Jr. (b. 1767), son of Delaware's chief justice.

Young William Killen intends to apply to the Delaware members of Congress for an army commission.

THURSDAY, 10 JUNE 1790

Rain (Johnson)

Pierce Butler to James La Motte

I yesterday received your kind favor of the 29th of May covering Your acct. The precariousness of the conveyance of this letter prevents my writing fully; besides since the rascally usage of the letters of the 25th of April I am almost detered from writing—Unfortunately I wrote more explicitly then than I ever did before, so that the Villain who opened these letters & forged my name has got a full knowledge of my affairs; surely such a Rascal deserves hanging—yet I do not wish him to suffer death on my account.

***

I have lately run my eye over your acct. I am persuaded that every thing you have done was influenced by regard for me. There are two charges I wish to have altered. The expences or disbursements for M. Ville[1] are greater than suits me at present I wish them lessened; indeed I do not just now wish to expend one shilling more on the improvements; because I can not afford it. With regard to the pullies, locks &c. we must do without them at present I can not afford to buy them, neither do I wish to buy them in Charleston. Let things then remain as they are—I never bought in 3 years so great a quantity of medicines as you mention; We must œconomise. My kind Nephew [*Edward Butler*] took effectual steps to distress me; He as well as P—[2] may yet have reason to be sorry for their ingratitude to me. I will write You more at large by the first good conveyance.

FC, Butler Letterbook, ScU. For the full text, see *Butler Letters*, pp. 50–51. Sent to Charleston, South Carolina. The omitted text discusses financial negotiations with Hercules Daniel Bize.

[1] "Mary Ville" was the 1168 acre rice plantation on the north bank of the Ashley River, about twelve miles upriver from Charleston. Butler bought it as his family's primary residence in 1786 and named it after his wife Mary Middleton.

[2] William Payne was a servant of the Irish branch of the Butler family before coming to America with Edward Butler around 1768 and becoming Pierce Butler's clerk. Like Edward, he involved Butler in some serious financial embarrassments (*Butler*, pp. 49–50; *Butler Letters*, p. 157n).

Elias Hasket Derby to Fisher Ames

I have two ships arrd. from Canton Capt. Magee & Nichols the impost on the Chargoes will Amount to a large Sum of Money, but as they as are as yet not unloaded I cannot assertain the exact sum It is all in Teas, and as their is eleven or twelve Vessels ~~arri.~~ Mostly large arrive and on their way from Canton for different parts of the Continent they will import teas enough for three years consumption; and I can see no way of raising Cash from this stock even to pay the wages of the Seamon who have been this long voyage, in less than three or four Months; And I must sacrifice one half of my trading property. if I should push the sales of my tees to raise the Money to pay the Impost. I thefore have sent on a petition to Mr. Goodhue to lay before Congress in order that I may have liberty of paying the impost as I may raise the case from the Stock imported, beeing well persuaded that Congress never intended that any law that they pass'd should tend to nearly ruin a Citizen, whose intentions were honest toward Government, by obliging him to dispose of his goods at a certain loss to pay Government their dues, when by waiting time it may be an Advantage to the Citizen, & no detriment to Revenue I wish you to see the Petition, and if you think it reasonable, as I doubt not you will your influence in the house to have the prayer of ask granted will oblige.

FC:lbk, Derby Shipping Papers, MSaE. Written from Salem, Massachusetts. For background on Derby's petition, see *DHFFC* 8:403–11.

Benjamin Goodhue to Stephen Goodhue

The Assumption has yet had no decission but I think the chance of its obtaining this session is very small, and the funding the other very uncertain, for the question of residence which has for the whole time been connected with assumption in the minds of many unworthyly, is not yet settled and I fear will not be so as our object may be affected—the resolution for meeting next session in Philada. which sometime past went from our House to the Senate, was there negatived, and they are renewing it to day in our House—on the whole there is such caballing and disgracefuly mixing National with local questions, that I am heart sick of our situation. I feel ashamed of the body to which I belong and therefore wish you not to proclaim our disgrace.

ALS, Goodhue Family Papers, MSaE. Addressed to Salem, Massachusetts; franked; postmarked.

Benjamin Hawkins to Daniel Smith

I have to acknowledge the receipt of two of your favours of the 22nd. of december and 8th of April and I should have written to you long ere this but delayed to do so untill I should be able to inform you of the measures that would be taken in relation to your country. The [*North Carolina*] Cession being now accepted, the act establishing the government passed, and the officers appointed, (all of which you will be informed of by the Secretary of State), you will proceed in the government conformably therewith.

Accept my congratulations on your being appointed Secretary you will see by the papers the other officers. The Sallery is 750 dollrs. ℔ annum paid quarterly.

You may rest assured that although you are no longer a part of the State of North Carolina yet I shall not cease my endeavours to contribute my mite to the prosperity of your country. I had an abundant share of Odium for my deposition evidenced to be servicable to them at Hillsborough [*North Carolina*] in 1784 and I believe I was the only one perfectly disinterested in my endeavours, as well as entirely regardless of what was said of me. I hope your governor [*William Blount*] will be with you soon, you all know his character well, and how much he is interested in your particular welfare.

Let me advise you to impress as early as possible on your Citizens the necessity of attending to their home manufactures your relative situation with the commercial part of the United States is such that this is indispensable to your prosperity. You can raise fruit trees of all sorts, grapes of all sorts for wine—salt Iron and clothing of cotton flax Wool and silk. You never can have much money, but you have facility in acquiring the necessaries and comforts of life from the richness of your soil and mildness of your climate unknown to any other country in my recollection. Recommend therefore by your own example the raising nurseries of fruit trees and having them planted throughout your whole Country. I have often lamented the unaccountable inattention of our people to the raising the comforts of life One hour devoted only weekly to the planting vines, trees and garden stuff is quite sufficient to stock any plantation with an abundance of these things.

The information from your country respecting Majour [*John*] Doughty seems so much corroborated by several letters as to have but little room to hope that the Chickasaws have been misinformed, however I confess I am somewhat incredulous, on the present occasion, and trust that on this you have sufficient grounds to contradict the report of the defeat the boat may have been driven back, But the major being a soldier and those under his command prepaired for action and particularly the design of the boat, it would require a party more numerous than the one named by you to defeat him.

ALS, Draper Papers, WHi. Place to which addressed not indicated.

Daniel Hiester to John Nicholson

I have been Honoured with your favour of the 7th. The Bill for settling the Accounts of the different States [*HR-69*] was Printed, but during a debate of several days was almost entirely changed. Yesterday it came in engrossed but was recommitted to a Select Committee to make some alterations. There will be two additional Commissioners and the Powers of the Board, and the objects of their Settlemt. will be greatly enlarged. The Invalid bill will pass towards the Close of the Session, when all the Petitions of those that have Petitioned this Session to be put on the Pension list are decided on.[1]

This whole day was taken up on Colo. Parkers motion to adjourn to Philadelphia without deciding on it; The friends to Philada. Carried the motion for taking up the business by a majority of five, and negatived the Motion for committing it to a Committee of the whole. I doubt whether it will even be decided to morrow, for Procrastination is evidently the design of the [*New*] York Interest—they were left so much in Possession of the debate, that they at last complained of not being answered.

ALS, Nicholson Papers, PHarH. Addressed to Philadelphia; franked; postmarked 11 June; received in June and answered. Hiester wrote "In full Confidence" on the cover page.

[1] Both the first session's Invalid Pensioners Act [HR-29] and the Invalid Pensioners Act [HR-80] that was presented by Hiester on 29 June and signed on 16 July were simply

annual reauthorizations for paying the pensions inherited from the Confederation. State governments continued to regulate the pension rolls under strict federal statutes limiting the eligibility of claims. Hiester's legislation altered the status of no petitioners during the FFC, although some individual claims were allowed under a few private or omnibus bills. For more, see *DHFFC* 7:332–434.

Richard Henry Lee to Patrick Henry

My ill state of health, the inclemency of the season appointed for the meeting of Congress, which in this place is most severely felt by all, and absolutely destructive to valitudinary people, prevented me from reaching Congress, before the 20th of April.[1] {Previous to my arrival here, the Cession of North Carolina had been accepted, and legalized by both houses; and a temporary government established there, similar to that west of Ohio, This system included the appointment of a Governor of that district, who by the same system is also Indian Agent and authorized to transact all affairs with the Indians in a more extensive and absolute manner than such Agents have been heretofore authorized to do.

This then being an Office of great consideration and importance, you may easily see that it would be earnestly sought after, and attainable chiefly by the interest of such as were in office here from that State which had made the Cession.} as well as by those from Georgia, who were hostile to General M—n [*Joseph Martin*]. {On my arrival here, and finding your two letters[2] that had been here some time before; I immediately carried Governor [*Alexander*] Martin's to the P—d—t [*President*][3] The event has been as I apprehended, that your friend would fail, for Mr. Wm. Blount, of N. Carolina, (heretofore in Congress, from that State) has been appointed Governor of the ceded Territory—And, as I have observed above, that appointment includes the Indian Agency. Thus this business has been terminated. I should have given you this information sooner, but quickly after my arrival here, I was, with many others, taken extremely ill so that my life was put in danger, and I was confined for near a month.} The effects of this malady are still upon me, and my weakness so considerable, as to render writing painful to me. With my letters, I found one from you to Colonel Grayson, which I secured, and now return to you, presuming, that you designed it only for the inspection of the friend to whom it was addressed.[4] It is impossible, for me to describe the scene here, and shall I content myself with saying, that every thing met with in my former life is mere trifling, compared with this, and you know that I have been in very stormy legislative scenes. The active and persevering efforts of those who have engrossed the public securities for little or nothing, not content with that advantage, must have six per cent forever, on the full nominal value of their possessions; so that a vast monied interest is to be created, that will forever be warring against the landed interest, to the destruction of the latter; and this evil, great as it would be, by funding the debts of the United States only, is to be increased ten fold, by the assumption of the state debts. By this plan the monied and the political speculator, will both be gratified; the former, by the way I have already stated, and the latter, by possessing the general government, with the sole cause, and consequently, with the whole power of taxation, and so converting the state legislatures into mere corporations. That this will be the consequence of funding the continental and state debts, amounting to about eighty millions of specie dollars, there can be no difficulty in foreseeing. There appears to be no prospect of further amendments to the constitution this session, and I own 'tis my wish that the amendments generally, as proposed at the last session, had been adopted by our legislature; for although there is much force in your observations, upon that subject, yet when I consider one great object of declarations beyond which government may not go, to wit: that they inculcate upon the minds of the people, just ideas of their rights, it will always be hazardous for rulers, however possessed of means, to undertake a violation of what is generally known to be right, and to be encroachments on the rights of the community; besides that by getting as much as we can at different times, we may at last come to obtain the greatest part of our wishes. It would probably contribute as much to this end, if at the ensuing election of representatives, instructions were given by the people of those districts that send influential members here, to exert themselves to procure such additional amendments as have not yet been made. Such bad use has so often been made of my letters, that I am sure, the bare hint of this, is sufficient to secure your remembrance, that when I write to you, 'tis always in confidence. I shall be at all times happy to hear from you.

Patrick Henry 3:420–22. The portions of the letter within curly braces come from a partial transcript of the ALS in the Draper Papers, WHi, which varies significantly from the W. W. Henry transcript.

[1] Likely a mistranscription of 12 April, the day Lee took his seat (*DHFFC* 1:283).
[2] Dated 29 January and 8 February, volume 18.
[3] The letter is calendared under 18 January, volume 18.
[4] The letter, of undetermined date, has not been found.

Richard Henry Lee to Arthur Lee

*** The letter you mention to have written declaring yourself[1] and desiring I would write to {*Martin*} Picket & others I have not received—I got one from you desiring me to inform our Cousin R. B. Lee that *he* had declared you prematurely (which he denies having done) but in that you seem not fixt about standing yourself—However I will write to Colo. Picket shortly—Since my illness, a feebleness is left behind that renders writing hurtful to me. The President has certainly been dangerously ill, but he is fortunately recovered so well as to attend to business, and has been for 3 or 4 days past at the Hook [*Sandy Hook, New Jersey*] for benefit of the Sea Air & amusement—This place however, seems not favorable to his health any more than it is to most of the Southern Members of Congress—Yet we have been defeated after a strong attempt to remove from hence [*to Philadelphia*]—16 majority for it in the H. of R. & in the Senate 12 for & 13 against—The Assumption has been frequently rejected in the other House, yet it is to be again pushed—The funding Bill is with us which proposes to fund the old Continenl. money at 75 for one—Tis probable that we shall make it an hundred for one—And instead of Land & the various alternatives for paying the debts of the U.S.—it seems probable that all will be refused but the simple plan of paying with money the interest at 4 pr. Cent & part of the principle, leaving the Land to be sold by Land Office & the money applied to the debt—you will see that our Old friend S. Adams still retains his attachment to the State Governments by his Speech in one of the inclosed papers[2]—Have this republished in the Alexandria paper, & get Ludwell [*Lee*] to send it to Davis in Richmond to publish it in his paper[3]—We have no news here—the Packet brought none, but a probability of the War continuing in the N. of Europe.

***

ALS, Lee Family Papers, ViU. Place to which addressed not indicated; sent to Alexandria, Virginia. The omitted text discusses the health of family in Virginia and directions for Cassius (a servant?). For the full text, see *Lee* 2:525–27.

[1] As a candidate for R. B. Lee's congressional seat in Virginia's second federal election.

[2] Samuel Adams, close collaborator of the Lees in the earliest days of the Revolution, addressed the Massachusetts legislature upon being sworn in as lieutenant governor on 28 May. The speech, as reported by Boston papers on 29 May and reprinted, for example, in *NYDG*, 5 June, reiterated Adams's conviction that Massachusetts was a free, independent, and sovereign state.

[3] Augustine Davis's [Richmond] *Virginia Independent Chronicle.*

Roger Sherman to Henry Gibbs

I received Your letter of the 14th of last month—I was just about that time taken ill with the Influenza which continued about fifteen days. I am now in good health—I congratulate you on the addition to your family—my family were well the last I heard from them, a few days ago Mrs. Sherman and I design to come to Salem this Summer if Congress does not detain me too long. I expect the session will end this month.

There are Several important matters unfinished, the Act for funding the National debt has passed the house, and is now before Senate—Business has been Interrupted by a motion to hold the next session at Philadelphia, which passed the House & has been negatived by the Senate—but is revived again in the House of Representatives—I Suppose the Rhode-Island Senators will be here in a few days, as the Assembly of that State are now in session.

The members from the Eastern States are willing that Congress Should remove to the centre of the Union as Soon as a permanent Seat of government Shall be established & prepared—The assumption of the State debts is not yet finally decided on.

ALS, Gibbs Family Collection, CtY. Place to which addressed not indicated.

George Thatcher to Dummer Sewall

Inclosed you have a Bill lately reported to the House, for establishing Post-Roads, and Post Offices, thro' the United States [*HR-74*]. Some of the members of the committee, who reported the Bill, were for stoping the mail at Portland—By returns, from the Post-Master-General,[1] it appears that the net income of the Transportation of the mail, for the last quarter, from Portland to Wiscassett, did not exceed one Dollar & about forty cents—whereas there were paid to the Mail Carrier twenty five Dollors, for that quarter—From these facts some of the committee were of opinion that the settlements & Business, east of Portland, were of too little consequence for the United States, to be at the expence of establishing a Post-Office east of Portland—And it was with difficulty I could prevail on them to report a continuation of the mail to Wiscassett—which you see by the Bill, they have done. I am very sensible how anxious the people, who live up Kennebeck River, are to have the Mail Line extended to Hollowell—and I really wish they could be gratified—but I see no prospect of it at present—And I am fearfull, that if I should attempt to extend the Line to Hollowell, it will bring on a more strict scrutiny into the expences of Transporting the mail east of Portsmouth [*New Hampshire*], when it will be found that the whole of that part of the Line, & every part thereof, is a continual expence to the General-Post-Office; & thereby the House may be induced to stop the mail at Portland.

It seems to be the designe of the House so to regulate the Transportation of the Mail as to make the proceeds of the Post-office contribute to the national Revenue—Hence you will observe, by the Bill, the Post-Master-General is restrained from establishing, or continuing any Roads, other than such as are established by the Law, whereby the Revenue, arising from the General Post Office, may be diminished—However, it will be my endeavour, and I flatter myself I shall succeed, to continue the Transportation of the mail, once a week, to Wiscassett—And should this be the case I shall propose to the Post-Master-General, the establishment of a Post-Office at Bath—I have conversed with him upon this subject, & he is of opinion an Office ought to be keept there—And if it be agreeable to you I will mention you to him for Deputy post-master at that place—The profits cannot be much—but the duty will neither be troublesome, or expensive; and some conveniences may accrue to the post-master—If I recollect, the high-road, from Brunswick to Bath, passes near by your house: But if you think it will be inconvenient to be post master—I will thank you to mention to me some suitable person—There is now before the House a Bill for laying an excise on Spirits [*HR-62*]—it is not certain this will pass into a Law this Session; but if it does, there will be wanting an officer, at Bath, denominated an Inspector—his Compensation will rise from a certain per-cent on the money collected, and as he will be confined to the district of Bath, you can form a better judgment of the amount of what may be his compensation than I am able to do—I will thank you to recommend some trusty person for this office. The Business at Bath, I suppose, will not be very extensive, consequently, I am rather of opinion the duty of his office will not interfere with his attending to his private affairs—provided they do not call him a great deal from home.

FC, Thatcher Family Papers, MHi. Sent to Boston. With the exception of Portsmouth, all places named are in Maine.

[1] Samuel Osgood's returns, reported to the House on 27 April, are at *DHFFC* 6:1674–81.

George Thatcher to Sarah Thatcher

Some little Books for [*son*] Phillips will accompany this—one or two will be eno' for him—and if [*daughter*] Sallys curiosity is excited she will think one, at least, belongs to her—the rest Phillips may dispose of among his little school-mates—Tell him his papa sais he must read night & morning, as well as at school—And he must mind his school-mistress & do every thing she tells him to do.

He must strive to read as well as any of his school-fellows—indeed I shall expect, when I come home, to find he is able to read away like a man in his new Books.

Tell him his papa expects to hear he is a good Boy about going to school—and that after school is done, he returns directly home; and does not stop to play, unless he has leave.

I have no Letter to acknowledge—but look out for one this evening—and I hope to hear you are in pretty good spirits, and the dear children, who by your last, were ill with a cold, are geting better—I am extreamly anxious to be with you, & am determined to get leave of absence by the first of July—If Congress do not adjourn by that time.

ALS, Thatcher Family Papers, MHi. Place to which addressed not indicated.

Stephen Wilson to William Smith (Md.)

As I am proprietor of the first parcel of Goods siezed in England under the Construction of the Officers of the Revenue in that Country put upon the Laws restricting the Intercourse between our States & them, the Members of our Insurance Office have requested me to send you the following extract of a letter I have received from my friends Messrs. C. Kensington & W. Coningham of London to whom the article was consigned; it was 42 Bales of Cotton Wool I shipped on the British ship Virtuous Grace from James River. "We cannot concieve why this Country should be inclined to admit Cotton Wool &ca. ~~from all places & refuse it~~ from all other places & refuse it from America—It is said our Government have an Idea that it would encourage America in her Trade with India & assist her in being a carrier for this country—We have done every thing in our power to explain this matter which we stated very fully in a letter to Mr. [*William*] Pitt—We added that it must irritate the people of your Continent very much to find themselves excluded from vending Cotton &ca. here, & yet every other country in the World permitted to do it—& that it was not improbable, your Government would retaliate by laying heavy imposts on British Ships enter[*ing*] your Ports—We fear no remonstrance will avail, & that the Law will remain as it now is." It is unnecessary to make any Comment upon it as you will see the matter in a fuller view than I can take of the subject.

ALS, Jefferson Papers, DLC. Written from Baltimore.

An American to Mr. Greenleaf

ATTENDING in the gallery of the House of Representatives yesterday, I was forcibly struck with the propriety and justness of the remarks of many members, and of the impropriety and weakness, not to say selfishness of the observations of others. To see a body of men, of the picked and chosen of the land too, enjoying such big salaries, and entrusted with such momentous and important concerns, trifling away their time, about the most trivial affairs—affairs which no way concern the union; and at a time too when a jealous public is watching their motions, and eagerly searching to find faults, and cry aloud—I say to be the silent spectator of such conduct, gives pain to the honest heart, and excites sensations that are distressing to every lover of his country.

NYJ, 11 June, edited by Thomas Greenleaf. The subject of debate was the removal to a temporary seat of government.

Letter from New York

As to the *assumption*, it appears dubious. The Continental Debt is in a fair way of being funded—and if the subject of residence does not generate a sourness of temper, we have hopes the session will terminate with *eclat*. It would be a happy circumstance if the permanent situation was once determined—as it would prevent the politicks of the States from being contaminated by local considerations arising out of this business. This subject will, I expect come on again tomorrow. I somewhat expect the permanent residence will be agreed upon.

Congress talk of rising by the last of JUNE. They have, however, much to do previous to that time.

[Boston] *Columbian Centinel*, 16 June; reprinted at Portland, Maine; Portsmouth and Exeter, New Hampshire; and Northampton, Massachusetts.

OTHER DOCUMENTS

Elias Hasket Derby to Benjamin Goodhue. FC:lbk, Derby Shipping Papers, MSaE. For the full text, see *DHFFC* 8:6–7.

Paraphrases letter from Derby to Ames of this date, printed above.

Thomas Fitzsimons to Benjamin Rush. Excerpt of three page ALS, *Parke-Bernet Catalog* 499(1944):item 118. Place to which addressed not indicated.

"You have already heard that the Senate negatived our resolution [*regarding holding the third session of the FFC at Philadelphia*], and no doubt the circumstances attending it. . . It was curious to see the New York Senators & Doctr. Johnson of Connecticut voting for Potomack while the senators of Virga. & Maryland voted against it. . . I have no doubt but Hamilton is the main spring that gives motion to all this business. . ."

Benjamin Goodhue to Samuel Phillips, Jr. No copy known; acknowledged in Phillips to Goodhue, 15 June.

Henry Hill to Benjamin Goodhue. ALS, Letters to Goodhue, NNS. Written from Philadelphia. The enclosure to Boston concerned Franklin's bequest of

£1000 to the city of Boston (his birthplace) for the education of young men. Hill was one of the executors of Franklin's will.

Thanks Goodhue for forwarding a packet to the selectmen of Boston and asks the same favor for an enclosure addressed to the president of "the Philosophical society established in New England" (the American Academy of Arts and Sciences?).

Louis Guillaume Otto to Comte de Montmorin. Copy in French, Henry Adams Transcripts, DLC. Otto's letters included in *DHFFC* were usually written over the course of days, and even weeks, following the day they were begun.

Details about the large group of French immigrants who were planning to settle on the Scioto River; reports that the President has ordered federal troops stationed on the Ohio River to accompany them to their settlement and station themselves between the settlers and the Indians.

Benjamin Russell to Benjamin Goodhue. ALS, Letters to Goodhue, NNS. Written from Boston. This postscript to Russell's letter of 8 June has been dated 10 June on the basis of internal evidence and the letter's postmark from Boston on that date.

Reports the lighthouse cession bill has passed (the Massachusetts legislature); the "eligibility business" (dual federal-state office holding) was postponed that afternoon until the arrival of Judge David Sewall, "(the object of the motion)"; speakers' sentiments suggest that the redistricting bill for U.S. Representatives will leave the districts substantially the same; the two houses of the legislature will probably elect the U.S. Senator the following week; "There are several who look up to it; and are, I think, manœuvring accordingly."

George Thatcher to John Fox and Daniel Davis. FC, Thatcher Family Papers, MHi. Sent to Boston.

Office seeking: asks their opinion on Thatcher's preference for John Frothingham over William Vaughn or Samuel Pearson as federal excise inspector under the Duties on Distilled Spirits Bill [HR-62] then before the House; as its profits will probably not support a family, believes the job suitable for someone with other "business not incompatable with the Duties of Inspectorship."

Jeremiah Wadsworth to Nehemiah Hubbard. ALS, Gratz Collection, PHi. Addressed to Middletown, Connecticut; franked; postmarked. Elijah Hubbard (ca. 1744–1808) also lived in Middletown.

Announces Hubbard's election to the Society of the Cincinnati and reminder to deposit one month's pay in final settlement certificates as dues before the next meeting at Hartford, Connecticut, on 4 July; asks that the same information be relayed to Elijah Hubbard.

Jeremiah Wadsworth to Catherine Wadsworth. ALS, Wadsworth Papers, CtHi. Place to which addressed not indicated.

Rejoices to hear of Daniel Wadsworth's continuing recovery; has sent a cask of oranges, to be divided with John Chester.

Jeremiah Wadsworth to Harriet Wadsworth. ALS, Wadsworth Papers, CtHi. Place to which addressed not indicated. Dating is based on its partial legibility and on the letter's placement in the collection.

John Trumbull gave him her letter the evening before, with news that the family was well; will attend to her memorandum; sends love to family; asks to be sent some cotton; arrived very well early on Wednesday evening.

William Samuel Johnson, Diary. Johnson Papers, CtHi.

"Dind. [*Dined at*] Mr. Smith's."

NYDG, 11 June.

Apologizes for any inaccuracies in the account of the day's debate, as "the Galleries being crowded with spectators, rendered it difficult for us to hear precisely what the members said."

Friday, 11 June 1790

Warm (Johnson); *Very calm & pleast.* (J. B. Johnson)

Fisher Ames to Thomas Dwight

I recd. your esteemed favour by the post last Night, and thank you for it I am exceedingly interested in the information contained in it respecting our amiable friend I hope Mr. B.[1] is a man of merit. If he is not possessed of a great deal, he will not deserve her. for I think she is a most excellent woman. I wish I could go to S[*pringfiel*]d. and satisfy my curiosity in regard to this subject. I will not say that I have no other reason for the most impatient desire to see you there You say. "I ~~have~~ recd. your's inclosing one for *your* F[*rance*]s." I wish *I* could claim property there. I am going ~~tomorrow~~ this afternoon to visit Passaick Falls in N. Jersey. with a Party. and I write now because I wish you to know the events of this day by the next post—which I shall not return in due season to write ~~unless~~.

You have seen that *we* are sold by the Pensylvns. and the assumption with it. They seem to have bargained to prevent the latter on the terms of removing to Philadelphia It became necessary to defeat this corrupt bargain. we had voted in the House for Philadelphia The Senate disagreed. The motion being renewed in the house, we have opposed it, first so as to gain time, and next to baffle the scheme *in toto.*[2] Yesterday it rained, and Govr. Johns[*t*]on, who had been brought, in a sick bed to vote in Senate agt. Philaa. could not be safely removed in the rain. It was supposed that if the Resolve to remove could be urged thro' the house and sent up while it continued raining, that it wd. pass in Senate They called for the question—but Gerry & Smith [*S.C.*] made long speeches & motions, so that the question was not decided till this morning Rather than gratify the Pensylvns. and complete their bargain at the same time, *we* voted for Baltimore, which passed by ~~one~~ two majority to the infinite mortification of the Pensylvns. Philadelphia was struck out, & as by the rules of the house it could not be inserted again, it is a complete overthrow. But my dear friend we gain useless victories. I care little where Congress may sit, I wd. not find fault with Fort Pitt [*Pittsburgh, Pennsylvania*], if we could assume the debts and proceed in peace and quietness. But this despicable Grog shop contest, whether the taverns of N. York or Philaa. shall get the custom of Congress, keeps us in discord & covers us all with disgrace. How this resolve will fare in Senate, I know not. I trust the attempt will be made to turn it into a question of *permanent* residence—That would make the friends of the Assumption the umpires and enable them to dictate their own terms. I am however almost in despair of Success. Yesterday it was moved in Senate to tack the assumption as an Amendment to the Funding Bill. But Morris, Langdon, & another, declaring that they liked the Assumpn., said that they would not agree to it as part of that Bill, lest the Bill should be lost by it, whereas the Pensylvns. have both in their own power and there is no ground for pretending danger to the Bill, if *they* are disposed to vote for it Their declaration is plain proof that *Philadelphia* stands in the way of the State debts It is a shameful declaration for men to make who have so solemnly asserted thier zeal for the Measure. Langdon is a partizan for Philadelphia. It is barely possible for any business to be more perplexed & entangled than this has been. we have ~~fasted~~ fasted watch'd & prayed for the cause. I never knew so much industry and perseverance exerted for any cause. Mr. Sedgwick is a perfect slave to the business—Mr. Goodhue frowns all day long and swears as much as a good christian can about the perverseness of Congress.

We are passing the Ways & Means Bill [*Duties on Distilled Spirits HR-62*] we do so little, and behave so ill in doing that that I consider Congress as meriting more reproach than has been cast upon it.

I am gratified to know that your [*Connecticut*] river is becoming important. I wish you could, by faith, or otherwise remove the rocks from its bed.

I am pleased to find our General Court [*legislature*] so much better than it was. But their sense as expressed by their vote[3] will not help us to carry the assumption—It furnishes the others with a plan to delay & get the sense of the other states which cod. not be in the like strain—my regards to friends. The first week of leisure, or rather of respite from urgent business will carry me to Springfield.
[*P. S.*] The Pensylvns. have hurried the removal of Congress, because R. Island Senators are expected daily to join the New Yorkers.

ALS, Ames Papers, MDedHi. Written "In the Federal Hall"; place to which addressed not indicated.

---

[1] "Our amiable friend" was Mary Worthington (b. 1760), whose younger sisters Hannah and Frances would soon marry Dwight and Ames, respectively. "Mr. B." was the prominent loyalist emigré and Canadian officeholder Jonathan Bliss (1742–1822) who married Mary in Springfield, Massachusetts, on 11 July 1790.

[2] In its entirety.

[3] The Massachusetts legislature's vote of 4 June resolved to convey to the state's congressional delegation its "sentiments" in favor of assumption.

X to Mr. Greenleaf

THE *assumption* was the bastard of eastern speculators, who have lost their puritanical manners, and who have even laid aside the troublesome cloak of religion, which was the antient dress of their ancestors, and was established by the laws of the colonies. The S—y [*Secretary*] condescended to act on this unworthy occasion, the part of *Doctor Slop*,[1] who, by the exertion of all his obstetric skill, and by the dexterous application of the *forceps*, forces this unfortunate brat into the world. He pronounced, with all the conceited gravity of the profession, that though the child was bruised and injured by the *violent delivery*, yet it possessed great appearances of constitution and stamina, and ordered nurse G—y [*Gerry*] to feed it on *molasses* and *boiled pumpkin*, and to bathe the body with *Yankey rum*. This opinion from a man learned in the obstetric art, who could even *conceive himself* and *deliver himself*,[2] gave great joy to the anxious eastern family—as the parents were *Presbyterians*, there could be no sponsors,* but yet the parish officers insisted that these lewd and licentious parents should give security for its maintenance, and should equalize the burden of support. R[*oger*]. S[*herman*]. of the family of C— [*Connecticut*], who has a lewd christian name,[3] and Mr. L[*angdon*]. of the family of [*New*] H[*ampshire*]. became securities, gave their bonds, and their vanity induced

*Mr. S— [*Smith*], of S.C. who was an episcopalian, wished to be God-father, but the presbyterian formality would not allow it.

them to confess publicly their illegitimate connections. This unfortunate child was presented at the baptismal font by Granny F—z—ns [*Fitzsimons*], and Mr. S—ck [*Sedgwick*], who is gifted with canting talents, officiated as priest, baptized the infant, and his name stands recorded on the parish book, as *Alex—der* [*Alexander*] *Assumption*. The Methodists have reason to regret, that politics engross the talents, and that forensic eloquence employs the *sing-song* voice of the baptising priest, who would have been a *shining candle-stick* on the altar, and a leader of the canting tribe, and the champion of *Moorfields*.[4] He finished this joyous ceremony by a long Presbyterian prayer. He invited all the blessings of heaven on this unfortunate illegitimate. He solemnly invoked all its vengeance against any who should hurt the hair of its head.

Short is the interval between the cradle and the grave!

The child of promise, who would have redeemed the eastern states from poverty and despair, is now no more—The parents are disconsolate, and in the ravings of their grief, they fulminate terrible threats, because they suspect that the infant was strangled by a Dr. W— [*Williamson*].

Poor infant! In your passage to this world you suffered exquisitely. In the month, you experienced little tender care, and storms growled over your cradle. Granny F— forgot her duty in her intrigues about your future nursery, and where the allowance for your support should be paid[5]—Your life did not leave you in gentle sighs, and by unperceived degrees—your birth and your death were both attended with calamitous circumstances of violence—Many a long life has not experienced such woe—Party threw thorns in your cradle—vinegar and worm wood in your food. The contention of party always disturbed your slumbers, and your ears never heard the soothing sound of sweet *Lullaby*. Rest sweet babe! in sure and certain hope of a joyful resurrection.† You are now removed from the injury of man, and enjoy the tranquility of the grave.

There has been some contention about the place of burial, which is determined in favor of Boston. The infant will be enbalmed, and is to pass through Connecticut, attended by their representation, and the village bells are ordered to express their bell metal grief in funeral tolls— The bearers, it is supposed, will be composed of speculators, in and out of *C—ss* [*Congress*].

†Granny F— as has applied to the grief of the parents, which is always superstitious, and has contracted to raise the child, by a secret charm, if they will vote to move the national treasury to Philadelphia. He represents to them, that the child is not dead, but *sleepeth*. These people know how to make good bargains, and I have no doubt, but we shall see, the next session, the ascension of the child, who was dead, and is now alive.

The coffin is to be adorned, not with plated ware, but with state certificates, and a concise character of the child will be taken from the report [*on public credit*], and inscribed on the tomb stone.

NYJ, 11 June, edited by Thomas Greenleaf; reprinted at Portsmouth, New Hampshire; Boston, Northampton, Springfield, and Stockbridge, Massachusetts; Hartford and Litchfield, Connecticut; Philadelphia; and Richmond, Virginia.

[1] The ignorant physician who delivered the title character in the novel *Tristram Shandy* (1760–67) by Lawrence Sterne (1713–68).

[2] Perhaps an allusion to Hamilton's having been born out of wedlock.

[3] "Roger" was introduced via Norman France from Germanic roots meaning "famous with a spear." This perhaps is the source for its slang usage, common throughout the eighteenth century, as both a verb (to have sexual intercourse with a woman) and a noun (penis).

[4] An eighteen acre park just outside London's downtown City that by the mid-eighteenth century had become a playground of sin including such entertainments as prostitution, bear baiting, dog fights, and organized violence. It was also a "molly market" or cruising area for illicit homosexual activities.

[5] A reference to efforts to remove the seat of the federal government from New York City.

Other Documents

John Adams to Thomas Brand Hollis. FC:lbk, Adams Family Manuscript Trust, MHi. For the full text, see *John Adams* 9:569–71.

Has been too busy to write; discusses political theory.

Joseph Anderson to George Washington. ALS, Washington Papers, DLC. For the full text, see *PGW* 5:510–11.

Office seeking: judge of the Southern Territory; mentions Paterson and Read as references.

John Brown to John Adams. ALS, Adams Family Manuscript Trust, MHi. Written from Providence, Rhode Island. For the full text, see *DHFFE* 4:406–7.

Office seeking: recommends Jeremiah Olney, William Peck, and William Allen as revenue officers at Providence, Rhode Island; congratulates Adams on Rhode Island's ratification; hopes for the election of at least one Federalist Senator, thinks it unlikely; the ratification itself would not have passed "had it Not beene for the Rod which was prepaird in Your House which was to Scourge us on the 1st. of July" (the Rhode Island Trade Bill).

Elbridge Gerry to Mercy Otis Warren. No copy known; referred to in the docketing of Warren to Gerry, 24 May, as the reply.

James Hutchinson to Albert Gallatin. ALS, Gallatin Papers, NHi. Written from Philadelphia; addressed to Fayette County, Pennsylvania; carried by Dr. (Robert) McClure.

Reports in detail transactions in Congress since Gallatin left Philadelphia; "it is said that Mr. Madisons speech" (of 22 April; see *DHFFC* 13:1171–85), "which is much admired, encreased the Majority against the Assumptionalists, but the measure has been continually loosing ground as it become more and more understood"; "Madison's influence is much encreased"; believes Morris rather than F. A. Muhlenberg will be chosen to run against Thomas Mifflin for governor.

Robert Morris to Alexander Hamilton. No copy known; mentioned by Maclay (*DHFFC* 9:292) as stating that Morris "would be walking early in the Morning on the Battery, and if Col. Hamilton had anything to propose to him [*regarding an assumption-seat of government bargain*], he might meet him there as if by accident."

Pamela Sedgwick to Theodore Sedgwick. ALS, Sedgwick Papers, MHi. Written from Stockbridge, Massachusetts.

Local news of friends and family; daughter Catherine Maria "is finely Grown and is now the Beautifull Likeness of her Pappa"; has just learned of Sedgwick's indebtedness from bankruptcy of (Nathaniel) Kingsley; asks if it is possible to "Indemnify your Self by the way of Mr. [*Oliver*] Phelps"; the children divert themselves by devising means for helping their father pay his debt; "at one time Thay determined to get your bond and destroy it but being Convinced that would be very dishonest—Frances Said she would sell her Clothes and Give the money to Pappa and then she and Eliza would go to Yoke Farm and have a dairy and get their Living by Seling Cheese and Butter but then she should not like to go to Market with It."

Theodore Sedgwick to Pamela Sedgwick. No copy known; mentioned in Theodore to Pamela Sedgwick, 14 June.

Oliver Wolcott, Sr. to Oliver Wolcott, Jr. ALS, Wolcott Papers, CtHi. Written from Litchfield, Connecticut.

Regrets that Congress has voted to remove to Philadelphia; "It has been said that an Assurance from some Members at concurring in Voting to Assume the States Debts has facilitated this Determination to alter the Place for the next Session."

SATURDAY, 12 JUNE 1790

Rain (Johnson); *a rainy day* (J. B. Johnson)

William Ellery to Benjamin Huntington

The Genl. Assembly, after idling away a whole week, have just now chosen ~~the~~ Senators; the act directing the mode of chusing the Representative, will not admit of our having a Representative in Congress this Session. Our Senators were requested by the Assembly to procede on to Congress as soon as possible, and they both declared that they would be ready to go on the last of next week; so that you may expect that they will take their seats by the middle of the week after. They will I presume be both against the removal of Congress to Philadelphia; but they will be against the Assumption of the State debts.

Our Senators are William [*Joseph*] Stanton of Charlestown, and Theodore Foster of Providence. The first is a violent paper-money man, and was an obstinate Anti to the last, the other is a Fed and a modest, ingenious man. The first was opposed by Jonathan Hazard who was prime conductor of the paper money system, and, until a few months ago, as bitter an Anti as Stanton; but finding that the Constitution must be adopted sooner or later, and desirous of being a Senator he became a trimmer. He thought he was sure, in consequence of his long and faithful services, of the Antis, and hoped by a moderate conduct to gain the Feds over to ~~its~~ his interest; but by his trimming he incurred the enmity of his old friends, and the Feds were not strong enough to give him any effectual aid if they were disposed to do it. The last was opposed by ~~the late~~ Mr. [*Jabez*] Bowen who was formerly deputy Governour, and is a staunch, warm Fed. Mr. Foster by being brother in law to our present Governour [*Arthur Fenner*], and a moderate man had the voices of the Antis with him, and so carried the election. All things considered the election has turned out as well as could be expected. Mr. Stanton will oppose an Assumption of the State Debt; because it ~~is~~ will be agreeable to the party who put him in, as well as his own opinion, and his instructions, and Mr. Foster I believe will be guided by his instructions.

During the Session the Genl. Assembly passed an Act incorporating a society for the Abolition of Slavery similar to the Act passed not long since by the Legislature of Pennsylvania.[1]

The principal part of the Session was taken up upon this question whether the members of the Assembly were obliged by the Constitution and the [*Oath*] Act of Congress made conformably thereto to take the Oath of Allegiance to ~~the~~ the United States previously to their proceeding to business, This took up two days. The Feds contended earnestly for it, the Antis did not object to it absolutely; but either because it was a disagreeable pill, or because they had not arranged the business of the election, or both, they insisted that it might be put off to the next Session, and they did not chuse to have the Oath crowded down their throats. However they finally yielded, and all the members of both houses swallowed it. Much time too was employed about the ~~bill~~ act directing the mode of chusing Senato[*rs*] and the Representative; especially that part of it which respec[*ts*] the choice of the latter. I have not time to give you an account of the debate on this subject. The Feds desirous that the people might be represented in the present Session of Congress wished that the Act might be so constructed that the Candidate who had the largest number of votes in his favour should be the Representative—the Antis contended that he ought to have the majority of all the votes, that if no one of the candidates had that majority at the first voting in Town Meetings, there should be another trial, and if the election was not then decided in that manner, that the two who had the greatest number of votes should be returned to another ~~Town~~ meeting of the towns as the sole subjects of choice; and that the first ~~Town meetings are to be held~~ voting for Representative ~~is to~~ should be at the Town Meetings to be held on the last week in August, when we chuse Deputies for the last half of the year. The Antis succeded; and therefore it was that I said that our mode of chusing our Representative would not admit of our having a Representative in Congress at their present Session.

This will be handed to you by Mr. Walter Channing of this town who is a good Fed, and a sensibly worthy man, and my friend, and therefore permit me to recommend him to your notice. Don't forget me—I know you won't.

I am in great haste for I expect Mr. Channing will sail this night.

ALS, Benjamin Huntington Correspondence, 1772–1790, R-Ar. Written from Newport, Rhode Island, in the evening; carried by Walter Channing; answered 2 July.

[1] The Providence Society for promoting the abolition of slavery, founded in February 1789, was incorporated by the Rhode Island legislature on 7 June 1790. The Pennsylvania Society, founded in 1775, reconvened in 1784 and formally reconstituted in 1787, was incorporated in 1789.

Benjamin Goodhue to Michael Hodge

It would give me inexpressible satisfaction if I could communicate any thing which has taken place, that would serve to brighten our prospects to future honour and happines, at present the reverse is the appearance and we are encircled with clouds and darkness—the future residence of Congress has a long time past been secretly the cause why we have not accomplish'd the great bussines, the public has justly expected from us, it has now burst forth and in the conflict between N. York and Pensylva. in which no other states are much interested, the great concerns of the Nation are suspended and put in extream jeopardy, what this will issue in is extreamly uncertain—I have only to lament our situation in which all important public measures must give place to paltry and local considerations.

ALS, Ebenezer Stone Papers, MSaE. Place to which addressed not indicated. Goodhue's letter to the Salem Insurance Offices of this date repeats this letter almost verbatim (ALS, Goodhue Letters, NNS; addressed to Salem, Massachusetts; postmarked 13 June).

Thomas Hartley to Jasper Yeates

***

The Temporary Residence was yesterday voted in our House to Baltimore—but the Senate have not yet acted upon it—The New Yorkers will strive to keep it of[*f*] until the Rhode Island Senators arive—In Short in this sort of Business no man can be certain of any Thing—The New Yorkers are certainly an artful intriguing People and they have attached themselves to the Eastern States—the Southern States are broken and divided and I am rather inclined to think there will be some Manœuvre or other to defeat the Resolution in the Senate—The Conduct of Mr. Smith ~~of~~ & Mr. Seney of Maryland (the same two Gentlemen who voted for the Proviso[1] in the Bill for fixing the permanent Seat on Susquehanna—which was the Pretext for its Destruction) prevented our carrying the second Vote for Philadelphia. These Gentlemen have much to answer, if we should be fixed here in Consequence of their Obstenacy—we are at this Moment much broken in our Politics.

An attempt was made in the Senate to annex the Assumption of the State Debts to the Bill funding the Debts of the union—but it was negatived by a Majority of 15 to 9.

On Monday we proceed in the Ways and Means—tho' we may {*lined out*} expect great opposition in the final Passage of the Bill.

I shall strive to leave this as soon as I can—give my vote against an unqualified Assumption. I have had much Trouble and pain of Mind for these three weeks past—and I fear all to no Purpose.

The Defeat in the Senate was a great Misfortune to Pennsylvania—this is a gloomy Day—I seem as if I was imprisoned—To apprehend that Congress will be detained here is a disagreeable Consideration.

ALS, Yeates Papers, PHi. Addressed to Lancaster, Pennsylvania; franked; postmarked 15 June; answered 20 June. Although Hartley's date looks like "11 June" and cataloguers have dated the letter as 10 June, internal evidence indicates that the majority of it was written on 12 June. The omitted text discusses friends and neighbors.

[1] The Proviso was an amendment to the first session's Seat of Government Bill, moved by Gale and agreed to by the House on 17 September 1789. It required that the Pennsylvania and Maryland legislatures pass acts guaranteeing the navigability of the Susquehannah River from any site chosen along it for the seat of government, down to the Chesapeake Bay. Because this threatened to redirect central Pennsylvania's trade away from Philadelphia in favor of Baltimore, the proviso facilitated the creation of a bloc that succeeded in striking the Susquehannah from the bill altogether, which ultimately helped to defeat the bill (*Creation of DC*, pp. 150–57; *DHFFC* 6:1866n).

Jeremiah Hill to George Thatcher

Yours of the 6th. inst. was received by this days post—as the sun dispells fogs in the morning, so Revelation clears up Mysteries—the facts stated respecting Miss Thatchers Letter being inclosed to me, answers the same purpose as tho' you had lent me your mystical Telescope. Thank you kindly for the loan of your theological observing Glass, I have a tolerable good one of my own, and after taking a few Observations I will with your leave lend it to our Parson [*Nathaniel Webster*], he sees but poorly with *spectacles*, and having *trod* a great way in error, I fear whether he will, without better Glasses, be ever able to tread *back* to the Union of truth; except we fix him on *Stilts* & make him tread back *mechanically* as some *folks write Letters.*

ALS, Chamberlain Collection, MB. Written from Biddeford, Maine; postmarked Portsmouth, New Hampshire, 14 June.

Henry Marchant to John Adams

Yesterday I was honored with yours of the first Instant—I am this Moment late in the Evening, after a most tiresome Week, returned Home; Having completed the Business of choosing [*federal*] Senators—With all Our Efforts we could not get the Anties to agree to a speedy Choice of a Representative—They have put it off to the last of August. So that if Congress should be continued in Sessions, the representative cannot be there till the middle or last of September—I presume we might as well choose now to meet you till the fourth of March next—We were two Days, before we could get the Stomachs of the Anties in any Condition to swallow the Oath prescribed by the Constitution and the Act of Congress—The Canditates for Senators were at first numerous, but like the weaker Blossoms they fell off at length to four; and we pushed them so hard, as to oblige them to put up a Federal ~~Mr.~~ Theodore Foster Esqr. as good a Man as we could wish, save his Connection with Our Govr. [*Arthur*] Fenner whose antie Principles have given Us great Trouble—Mr. Foster is the Son of your late Judge [*Jedidiah*]

Foster of Massts. He has had a liberal Education, regularly studied the Law, has been in Practice, but too modest and diffident for a Speaker at the Bar. He has ever been a good Fœderal, and an honest virtuous man—He married Govr. Fenners Sister [*Lydia Fenner Foster*], and that has been a Restraint upon Him, and as he goes by his Influence I presume it is required of Him to promote if possible a Number of unworthy Anties to Revennue Offices—which if he should not succeed in, as I trust he will not, I do not imagine he will be much mortified at. Setting this Aside You'd find him all You can wish—Indeed as to the Question of Assumption altho' his Heart is fully agreed, He will not venture I fear to agree to it; so extremely unpopular is the Measure here from Ignorance and self Will—Joseph Stanton is the other Senator—Antie up to the Brim without one Quallity to ballance it.

***

ALS, Adams Family Manuscript Trust, MHi. Written from Newport, Rhode Island; carried by Walter Channing. For the full text, see *DHFFE* 4:424–25. The omitted text discusses Adams's encouraging Marchant to run for the Senate ("the most respectable Body on Earth") and recommends Walter Channing for naval officer at Newport. Foster and Stanton were elected on 12 June and on the same day Rhode Island loaned each of its new Senators $150 "to enable them to take their seats in Congress" (*DHFFE* 4:423).

Henry Marchant to Elbridge Gerry

I was yesterday honor'd with yours of the first Instant—Your Wishes had been antiscipated so far as respected Our procuring as speedy a Meeting as possible of the Genl. Assembly to determine on the Appointment of [*Rhode Island's federal*] Senators &c. We met on monday last and broke up but this Eveng. We have appointed Theodore Foster Esqr. Son of the late Judge [*Jedidiah*] Foster of Massts. A Gentleman of strict Honor and good Sense, and a good Fed—but under some Restraint from his Connection with Our Govr. [*Arthur*] Fenner, having married his Sister [*Lydia Fenner Foster*], and being appointed by His Influence—I presume the Senators will both be for the Continuance of Congress at New York; and against the Assumption, tho' utterly against the Wish and better Knowledge of Mr. Foster as to the latter Object. But I fear he will not have sufft. Resolution to support him agt. the amazing Prejudice and Opposition here to the Assumption—Our Anties tho' opposed to every Thing good, yet expect to procure Appointments for Their Friends; and for obtaining which Our Senators will be charged to use Their utmost Exertion—But it is hoped they will meet their just Disappointment—As to the other Senator Joseph Stanton Jr. I would not take the Trouble to speak of Him—This will be handed you by my Friend Mr.

Walter Channing a Gentleman of good Sense, Abillities, strict Honor and Virtue, and from whom the best Information can be had and relied upon It is the wish here that He may succeed for the Naval Office for this Port—I shew your Letter to Mr. [*William*] Ellery—We wish Our Friends may remember those of us who have been fellow Labourers thro' every trying Scene.

If any Opposition should be to either of us—We expect, it will be chiefly by Applications to Genl. Knox—But I conceive we have too much the good Wishes of that Worthy Character, to have His Influence agt. us—I shall ever consider myself as honored by any Communications from you Sir.

ALS, Gerry Papers, MHi. Written from Newport, Rhode Island; carried by Walter Channing.

William Smith (of Boston) to John Adams

I have to acknowledge the Rect. of your esteem'd favor, of the 20 Ulto. Our Genl. Assembly are now in Session. their Conduct thus farr has been perfectly Fœderal, how long it may continue is uncertain. I am sorry that the assuming the State Debts & funding the Continental Debt are so long delay'd. so long as we are kept in suspence we are a prey to Speculators as most of our circulating Cash is employ'd in trading in paper. 'till the Debt is fix'd but very little other Business can be carr'd on. I do not find in the funding Bill any provision made for the New Emission Money, which runs on Interest & which Congress pledg'd their Faith to redeem & pay the Interest annually, provided the State neglected to make provision. One Years Interest *only* has been paid. I have a considerable sum in this kind belonging to my father's Estate, which has lain for a number of Years. Our Court [*legislature*] has given up the Light Houses in this State to Congress; it will be necessary for Congress, soon to make the Law regulating Pilots &c. at present the Pilots of this port are under no controul. shou'd this Law be bro't forward, the Marine Society of this port,[1] wou'd be happy to render their services to put the Pilots on a proper footing.

ALS, Adams Family Manuscript Trust, MHi. Written from Boston; franked; postmarked 13 June.

[1] The Boston Marine Society was founded in 1742 and chartered in 1754 in order to share knowledge of the sea and to provide mutual aid to member seamen and their families. Although membership was originally restricted to sea captains, Adams was made an honorary member in 1769. The FFC passed no law regulating pilots, leaving it to the states under the Lighthouses Act [HR-12], passed in the first session. Beginning in 1791, the Marine Society appointed the commissioners who appointed the Boston Harbor pilots. In January 1791 it petitioned the FFC to establish a chain of marine hospitals; see *DHFFC* 8:309–11.

George Thatcher to Meletiah Jordan

Yours of the 12th. February is now before me, but it did not come to hand till some time about the 20th of May—and I should have answered it before, but I waited to see what probability there is of your port being made a port of Delivery for vessells owned by foreigners—And I have the pleasure of informing you, that, in a day or two, a Bill [*Collection Act HR-82*] will be reported to the House making Frenchmans Bay [*Maine*] a port of Delivery for Vessells owned by foreigners—And before this Session ends the Law will be compleated—as soon as this is done, I will send you a copy—I beleive you may rest perfectly easy on account of there being any complaints against you as Collector—I am confident none have been made to the President, or the Secretary of the Treasury—I should know it if any had been made I have no doubt but your conduct as Collector is well approved of.

I dont know but there will be wanting an Officer at Frenchmans Bay, called an Inspector, to collect the excise, if one shall be laid, at that port—And if the excise Law [*HR-62*] passes I shall recommend to the president—either Coll. Leayant, Coll. [*Eleazer?*] Crabtree, or Cap. Phillip Hoskins as suitable for that office—The profits of office cant be very great—but worth something—If an Officer be wanting at Union River [*Ellsworth, Maine*], I have thought of recommending Mr. Theodore Jones.

I hope to get home in season to attend the Court at Penobscott [*Maine*] in the fall, when I shall be glad to see you, if you have any business there; but it is possible I may not be there, so that I would not wish you to take the trouble of coming on purpose to see me; for if you have any thing in particular, you wish to mention to me, you may write a Letter & send it, & if I should not be at Court, let it be given to Mr. [*Silas*] Lee—& he will bring it to me.

I want to make some enquires about the ports at and below Penobscott—and know whether the people, in general, are pretty well accommodated—And whether any, & what alterations in the revenue Laws, will be usefull in those places.

FC, Thatcher Family Papers, MHi.

George Thatcher to Warner Mifflin

Your favour of the fourth of the fifth month [*May*] came to hand some time ago, & would have been acknowledged before this time had I known how to have got a Letter to you.

I assure you, my friend, I was much pleased when I found you had not altogether forgot me; and exceedingly gratified at your telling me "your esteem for me is considerable"—If our short acquaintance rendered me deserving your good will, it shall be my endeavour hereafter to become more so.

I can acquit you of entertaining any ambitious, pecuniary, or interested motives in the application you, & your Brethren, made to Congress.[1] I conscientiously beleive the happiness of your, and my fellow-creatures, and a real sense of duty were your only motives—And my most ardent wish is, that you and the friends of Humanity may be enabled to persevere in the glorious cause of general freedom untill we see the whole human Race equally partaking of its Blessings.

Despare not, my friend, we have the sure word of prophesy declaring that Righteousness will finally prevail, & nations shall live in peace—This sentiment is animating—and the prospect ravishing. What feelings can be more delicious than those of beholding the happiness of others springing from our Labour & Toil!

I dont know that I shall ever see you again—but you have my wishes for your health & happiness—I shall always be happy to hear from you; and should you, or your friends ever pass into the eastern part of Massachusetts [*Maine*], I expect that you call and tarry with me.

When you see the Gentlemen who were of the Committee,[2] with you, tell them I respect them, & hope their endeavours will be abundantly success[*ful*] in this world—I know they will be rewarded in a better.

FC, Thatcher Family Papers, MHi. Sent to Kent County, Delaware.

---

[1] Mifflin was one of the eleven man "committee" (as Thatcher called them) who brought the Philadelphia Yearly Meeting's antislavery petition to the FFC in New York City the previous February. All but four of them—including Mifflin—stayed for more than another five weeks after the petition was presented and referred to committee on 15 February. For background on the petition attempt, see *DHFFC* 8:314–38.

[2] For the names, see John Pemberton to James Pemberton, 11 and 16 February, n. 3 and n. 1, respectively, volume 18.

Hugh Williamson to Governor Alexander Martin

Your's of 25th May came to Hand two days ago. The System for settling the Accounts of the several States with the U.S. is hitherto agreed to in Congress. The Committee reported. The Report was taken up and some Days spent in considering and modifying it. The whole is recommitted or referred to a select Committee of which I again happen to be a Member. We are again ready to report and hope the System will in a few Days be passed to the Senate. According to this Plan two other Commissioners are to be appointed who doubtless will not be ready for some Time to enter on the Duties of their Office, In the mean while nothing will be done effectually by the others. During this Interval I expect to have Time to come to the State for Papers respecting such other Expences not hitherto charged as we may be at Liberty by the Ordinance to charge.[1] I have duly attended to the mode in which other States have raised their Charges & hope to profit by their Example in being able to state good and reasonable Charges the Amot. of near half a Million Dlrs. above what we have hitherto charged. If a Clerk should be wanted it cannot happen before [*Sep*]tember next. Nothing that I can do myself shall be referred to other People. The Business is [*too*] important to be submitted to Substitutes in the great Outlines of it.

The Address of the President is simply

The President of the United States.

Neither Senators nor Representatives have any legal Titles. A Bill was sent from the Senate respecting the N. Car. Cession and the Names of our Senators who had executed the Conveyance were inserted with the prefix of *the Honourable.* but the Appendage was struck off in our House. A Law lately passed respecting de Steuben in which we would not agree to call him *the Baron.* For we hold it that no Man in our Laws shall have a Title since the President has none. This Rule however does not extend to common Parlance or common writings for as I have observed I wish our State was safely deliverd of the Martinique Business which has given us so much Trouble.

ALS, Governors' Papers, Nc-Ar. Place to which addressed not indicated.

---

[1] Adopted by the Confederation Congress on 7 May 1787; *JCC* 32:262–66.

A Citizen of the Union

THE very extraordinary proceedings of some of the citizens of Philadelphia, in attempting, so often, to destroy the harmony of the Union, by the constant revival of their claim to force Congress into their capital, in hopes of securing a permanent residence, deserves to be noticed by all the friends to good government. Had Congress met at Philadelphia the 4th of March, 1789, I believe it will be admitted that the citizens of New-York would not have required their Members to render themselves odious, by any attempts which could have had the least tendency to interrupt the progress of the new constitution; but it seems as if the people of Pennsylvania think they can drag Congress where they please—how consequential! The indecent conduct of some persons in refusing to delay the question of adjournment for only a few days, is not unknown to the public: it was modestly requested by the temperate friends of peace and harmony; but, no, the furious partizans insisted on an instantaneous decision; and two amiable Gentlemen were dragged out of a sick bed,[1] in order to stem the torrent of ill-timed zeal, and influence: the aged Johnston appeared, like a second Chatham,[2] at the risque of his life, to oppose the zealous junto. O! Philadelphia! thou that killest and stonest thy Patriots, how can ye expect that the great Legislature of United America, will subject themselves to the well dressed mobs of *gentlemen*? Remember, that in 1788, the house wherein five of the Members of thy own Legislature lodged, at the mid-night hour, when all were fast asleep, except a mob of __ was not the windows and doors of the house destroyed, and the lives of your Representatives threatened with instant destruction?[3] For what? Because the *genteel* mob did not approve of the conduct of these five Members. So will it be if the same *gentlemen* should disapprove of the conduct of any particular Member or Members of Congress from the northern and southern States; and thus we should have club-law established over the United States. Forbid it ye Fathers of our country—nor suffer a Continent to become a mere article of speculation for the ambitious __ to cheapen down, as they would, a chest of tea, or any other article of traffic.

NYP, 12 June.

---

[1] Few and Johnston. For more on this, see *DHFFC* 9:286.

[2] William Pitt "the Elder" (1708–78) became the first Earl of Chatham in 1766 for leading Britain's ministry to success as secretary of state (1757–61) during the French and Indian War. Despite a history of gout and mental illness that largely curtailed his public appearances, on 7 April 1778 he attended the House of Lords to deliver a highly anticipated speech against recognizing American independence. When he rose to respond to an opponent, he suffered a stroke from which he died one month later.

[3] This is in reference to a disorderly crowd that gathered outside Alexander Boyd's boarding house on the night of the October 1787 Assembly election (Robert L. Brunhouse, *The Counter-Revolution in Pennsylvania, 1776–1790* [Harrisburg, Pa., 1942], p. 206).

Maxims for Representatives

No man can be safely trusted with the important concerns of a country, who is deficient in knowledge, principle, or industry—who is extremely avaricious, or under the controul of ambition. He must be firm, laborious, but not obstinate, nor jealous, nor too much concerned about his *own* honor. He must express many ideas in few words, as long speeches, (even when excellent) generally displease some of the hearers. He must be undisguised, open, candid, and attentive to his opponents—always manifesting a disposition to accommodate. Never aim to carry a point by any means which the most impartial minds will not approve—and never triumph in success. Study to avoid hurting the feelings of his opponents—while he brings strong arguments against his opinions, clothed in soft and respectful language. No appearance of *cunning* should stain his political character—mankind associate the ideas of cunning and roguery together—and whenever a measure is effected by mere cunning, its opponents will ever after view its advocates as dishonest men—it ought therefore to be constantly impressed upon his mind that finesse, craft and cunning, are miserable expedients, and commonly issue in defeat and loss of character. Moderate abilities, if exerted only in the strait line of truth and honor, with a single eye to the public good, will save the nation, and render the plain honest statesman the delight and glory of his country. But the artful and designing, however learned, are always *seen through*, and detested. Although this hath been the fate of cunning men in all times, yet all times to come may expect to be *curst* with such characters.

GUS, 12 June; reprinted at Windsor and Bennington, Vermont; Salem, Massachusetts; Newport, Rhode Island; New York City (*NYDG*, 22 June); and Philadelphia.

Other Documents

Nicholas Evertson to John Cotton Smith. ALS, Helen E. Smith Collection, NHi. Addressed to Sharon, Connecticut; carried by George King (1754–1831, a merchant at Sharon).

Sedgwick advocated assumption "with singular animation" in debate.

Benjamin Goodhue to Stephen Choate. No copy known; acknowledged in Choate to Goodhue, 24 June.

Benjamin Goodhue to Samuel Phillips, Jr. No copy known; acknowledged in Phillips to Goodhue, 19 June.

Thomas Jefferson to David Rittenhouse. FC, letterpress copy, incomplete, Jefferson Papers, DLC. ALS in private hands in 1954 is source for printed text in *PTJ* 16:484–85.

Session will close as soon as money bills are got through, and that will be soon.

John Pintard to Elisha Boudinot. ALS, Boudinot-Pintard Papers, NHi. Addressed to Newark, New Jersey.

Acknowledges Paterson's delivery of Boudinot's letter; "I have in vain attempted to find a clue to the measures of our state [*New York*] in Congress" relative to the seat of government question, "But as observed I have little influence with our members, & there is something too humiliating in my present situation to run after them"; has "with the rest of our citizens been much agitated by this weeks debate"; "R. Morris has carried his manœuvres with the utmost indecency & barefacedness & has hurt his cause more than all that we c[*oul*]d. do"; suggests that (Anthony) Cuthbert may be induced "from friendship" to buy Elias Boudinot's Elizabethtown, New Jersey, estate ("Boxwood Hall").

Benjamin Russell to Thomas Jefferson. ALS, Miscellaneous Letters Received Regarding Publishers of the Laws, Miscellaneous Correspondence, State Department Records, Record Group 59, DNA. Written from Boston.

Goodhue and Ames have informed Russell of his appointment by Jefferson to publish the laws of the United States in his newspaper ([Boston] *Massachusetts Centinel*); requests directions for discharging this duty.

Letter from New York. *PP*, 15 June; reprinted at Baltimore and Georgetown, Maryland.

"Should Rhode-Island not be represented in the Senate in two or three days, it is very likely that Baltimore will be the seat of Congress at the next session."

Letter from Abington, Washington County, Kentucky. *NYDG*, 30 July (the date on which members of Congress would have seen it), from a non-extant Norfolk, Virginia, newspaper dated 24 July; also reprinted at Providence, Rhode Island; New York City (*NYP*, 5 August); Philadelphia, Carlisle, and York, Pennsylvania; Wilmington, Delaware; Norfolk and Richmond, Virginia; and probably elsewhere.

Reports Indian depredations in the area; asks if the federal government "will submit to these outrages."

SUNDAY, 13 JUNE 1790

Rain (Johnson); *A great deal of rain, in showers* (J. B. Johnson)

Joseph Barrell to Samuel B. Webb

Your favors of 3d & 8th. Inst. Ive receved in both of wh. you seem surprized at my having given up the Idea of Assumption of the State Debts, and express Your rising hopes on that subject, but Letters from our delegates in Congress, recived by last post seem to speak a different language, and intimates that local principles wch. ever were, and ever will be dispised by great minds, have so far got into Congress that we must expect they will do many things wch. they themselves in the hour of reflection, will Condemn most heartily—will it be beleved in future that Virginia & Pensilvania, have cudled up a bargain, and the former to obtain a point wch. they ought to be ashamed of, have engaged to gratifye the Latter at the expence of the Union, and to remove Congress into a situation the most humiliating, if they can reflect on what has past already[1]—and that the Latter, because the Senate have acted for themselves and not agreed to the darling Object, will now oppose tooth and nail, the Assumption of debt wch. they owe, if they owe any? But so it is, and should the Senate (as you seem to intimate) reject the funding Bill, because they cannot obtain the Assumption and in Consequence the Congress should rise after the expence of so much time and money—if the People should be quiet under such conduct, judge you the figure they will cut in the eyes of the world.

*** We expect the Columbia in all this month,[2] many people here say the Duties on her Cargo ought to be remitted as the first Adventure of the kind, and was commenced before the formation of the present government, I wish you would sound round amongst the members, and propose it from yourself not from us, and if there is any prospects of success in an honorable way, We shall apply.[3]

ALS, Barrell Papers, CtY. Written from Boston and postmarked there; answered 18 (June?). The omitted text discusses friends and Webb's management of funds for the purchase of state debts. For the full text, see Worthington C. Ford, ed., *Correspondence and Journal of Samuel Blachley Webb* (3 vols., New York, 1893), 3:161–62.

---

[1] The residence of Congress in the populous commercial city of Philadelphia during the Revolutionary War resulted in jurisdictional and political conflicts with Pennsylvania, whose State House (Independence Hall) served as the meeting place for Congress as well. The most famous conflict occurred in late June 1783, when Continental Army soldiers refused to accept furlough without a settlement of their accounts and marched on Philadelphia to ask the state to assume the federal government's payment of those debts. When an armed demonstration of approximately three hundred troops surrounded the State House on Saturday, 21 June, to negotiate with the state's Supreme Executive Council meeting there, Congress was hastily called into special session in order to challenge the threat to its dignity and authority by both the soldiery and the state government. Dissatisfied when state authorities peacefully defused the crisis without clearly asserting congressional supremacy in federal-state or civilian-military relations, the Confederation Congress adjourned to Princeton, New Jersey, never to return to Philadelphia (*Creation of DC*, ch. 1, and Kenneth R. Bowling, "New Light on the Philadelphia Mutiny of 1783," *PMHB* 101[1977]:419–50).

[2] The Boston based *Columbia* returned from its three year long, 49,000 mile voyage to Canton, China, on 9 August 1790. Barrell was the chief investor (joined by John Marsden Pintard and the son of Elias Hasket Derby, among others) in the historic enterprise. Although it was not a financial success, the voyage helped to establish America's China trade and was the first circumnavigation of the globe by an American vessel (Margaret C. S. Christman, *Adventurous Pursuits: Americans and the China Trade, 1784–1844* [Washington, D.C., 1984], pp. 34–35).

[3] Barrell and his associates never petitioned the FFC for a remission of impost duties, but Elias Hasket Derby submitted a successful related petition on 23 June; see *DHFFC* 8:403–11.

Benjamin Goodhue to Stephen Goodhue

*** as to the assumption I see but very little prospect of its obtaining this session if ever—for the cursed residence which has for months past mingled itself with that object and been the sole cause of the delay, has now burst forth, and in the conflict between N. York and Pensylva. without whose joint efforts the assumption cannot obtain, it may probably fall a victim, they are each of them more fond of residence then assumption and make a hobby horse of it to answer their purposes, such is our disgracefull situation.
[*P. S.*] I suppose Baltimore will be negativd by the Senate as Phila. has been.

ALS, Goodhue Family Papers, MSaE. Addressed to Salem, Massachusetts; franked; postmarked. The omitted text discusses joint mercantile ventures.

Benjamin Hawkins to Governor Alexander Martin

I received on friday evening your favour of the 25th of may and upon consulting Mr. Johnston who was sick and confined to his bed, I immediately communicated the contents to Mr. [*René Charles Mathurin*] De la Forest the Vice Consul general of France and requested him to answer the two paragraphs respecting the Martinique debt, his answer you have herewith enclosed—The bill for funding the debts of the United States is now before the Senate, having been past by the house of representatives, a motion has been made to blend the assumption of the State debts with it, and on a motion to commit this to the same committee to whom the funding bill was committed it passed in the Negative. However the advocates for this measure are determined to persevere untill they succeed in some shape or other They are numerous, and respectable in point of property and Abilities, They urge that the thing is in itself just, that the division in Congress proves that there is but a small majority against it, That they can see no difference why a man who has a continental claim should be prefered mearly because, it was settled by a commissioner of the United States, and that a man holding a state certificate, for his services or property done or furnished to the United States should for that cause only be excluded, and even taxed to make the first good while his is perishing in expectancy on State promises.

I wish the post was so near your residence as to enable us to hear from you frequently, If news-papers had a general circulation through our country [*North Carolina*] we could very readily give that information which is absolutely necessary for our fellow citizens but in the present situation it is impossible.

[*P. S.*] I observe you mark your letters *Free.* the governors of the States have no authority, by the present arrangemts. of the post office to Frank letters.

ALS, Governors' Papers, Nc-Ar. Place to which addressed not indicated.

Samuel Henshaw to Theodore Sedgwick

I thank you for your favour of the 6th. Inst. I believe with you, That instructions to Senators & Representatives are generally very prejudicial—They have a tendency to prevent freedom of Debate—liberallity of Sentiment, & rectitude of conduct. No Man, in a deliberative Assembly, ought to feel himself under the least possible Bias to act contrary to his real Judgment; but this often happens when a person is fettered with Instructions.

The Instructions of this Govt. to their Senators in Congress, to enforce the assumption of the State Debts, would never have passed, had they not beleived, from the observations of Madison[1] & some others, that such instructions from so important a State, might influence a few doubting Members, at least, to vote in favour of the proposition—Besides it was thought, that such instructions would give new strength & courage to our Members, and justify them in perpetually urging the Measure.

I reprobate that part of the Govr's. Speech[2] to which you allude; and thought at the time it was delivered, That if State Instructions were requisite to sanctify the assumption, it would be urged, that then Congress ought to wait untill they receive such Instructions from each individual State—For if according to the Speech, Congress ought not to assume the Debt of this State without their consent, they ought not to assume the debt of any other State without their consent also.

And [*John*] Bacon made great use of this Idea in his opposition; and extolled the Speech as the best ever made—But it was said in Reply, That Congress ought & would, take it for granted, that no State was against the Assumption unless they instructed their Members to oppose it. And on supposition that some of the States did so instruct their Members, yet unless a Majority did it, it ought to take place. And if it does not, I would not give a six pence for either federal or State Government.

We have not yet agreed on the Districts for Fed. Reps. [*Thompson*] Skinner is zealously endeavouring to disconnect Berkshire & Hampshire—We tell him that Berkshire have not the least reason to complain—For they have had the Representative from their County & probably would have—He replies it is true: But asks, who chose him? Not Berkshire but Hampshire—The fact is, and every body now beleives it, that He thinks if the Western District remains as it was, you will be chosen—if altered, He will be the Man.

But all his wishes & schemes will prove abortive. I have no fears—Not the shaddow of a doubt.

I wish you could make my calling an election as sure as yours is.

I intend to go home the last of this week; therefore write me next at N[*orth*]. Hampton.

What for a figure did my Freind [*Leonard*] Jarvis make at New York? Did Mr. Secretary H[*amilton*]. think him to be the Necker of America? And will He fill some important place in the Revenue Department?

Have you ever heard any thing said concerning Govr. Bd. Letter?[3]

ALS, Sedgwick Papers, MHi. Written from Boston.

---

[1] In a speech of 22 April; see *DHFFC* 13:1174.

[2] Governor John Hancock's speech before the Massachusetts legislature on 1 June.

[3] Former Massachusetts Governor James Bowdoin wrote Washington on 20 March in support of Henshaw's obtaining a federal revenue office (*PGW* 5:254–55).

Thomas Jefferson to George Mason

I have deferred acknoleging the reciept of your favor of Mar. 16. expecting daily that the business of the consulships would have been finished: but this was delayed by the President's illness & a very long one of my own, so that it is not till within these two or three days that it has been settled. that of Bordeaux is given to Mr. [*Joseph*] Fenwick according to your desire. the commission is making out & will be signed tomorrow or next day.

I intended fully to have had the pleasure of seeing you at Gunston hall on my way here. but the roads being so bad that I was obliged to leave my own carriage to get along as it could, & to take my passage in the stage, I could not deviate from the stage road. I should have been happy in a conversation with you on the subject of our new government, of which, tho' I approve of the mass, yet I would wish to see some amendments, further than those which have been proposed, and fixing it more surely on a republican basis. I have great hopes that pressing forward with constancy to these amendments, they will be obtained before the want of them will do any harm. to secure the ground we gain, & gain what more we can, is I think the wisest course. I think much has been gained by the late constitution; for the former one was terminating in anarchy, as necessarily consequent to inefficiency. the House of representatives have voted to remove to Baltimore by a majority of 53. against 6. this was not the effect of choice, but of the confusion into which they had been brought by the event of other questions, & their being hampered with the rules of the house. it is not certain what will be the vote of the Senate. some hope an opening will be given to convert it into a vote of the temporary seat at Philadelphia, & the permanent one at George town

[*Maryland, present-day Washington, D.C.*]. the question of the assumption will be brought on again, and it's event is doubtful. perhaps it's opponents would be wiser to be less confident in their success, & to compromise by agreeing to assume the state debts still due to individuals, on condition of assuming to the states at the same time what they have paid to individuals, so as to put the states in the shoes of those of their creditors whom they have paid off. great objections lie to this, but not so great as to [*lined out*] an assumption of the unpaid debts only. my duties preventing me from mingling in these questions, I do not pretend to be very competent to their decision. in general I think it necessary to give as well as take in a government like ours. I have some hope of visiting Virginia in the fall, in which case I shall still flatter myself with the pleasure of seeing you.

FC, letterpress copy, Jefferson Papers, DLC. Place to which addressed not indicated. For the full text, see *PTJ* 16:493–94.

Richard Henry Lee to Thomas Lee Shippen

I have received your letter of the 10th with a letter enclosed for Count [*Paolo*] Andreani—I have been twice to search for him in vain—Being as you state him an Agreable, he is so sought after that there is no finding him—I have been obliged to leave your letter for him, with my compliments, in the hands of Mr. Maddison who lodges in the same House—We have tried every method without effect, for holding Congress at Phila. next Session—It turned out as I feared—And now, after trying your place again, it failed in the H. of R. and they have sent up a Resolve for meeting next at Baltimore—What will be the success of this, I am sure I cannot tell—But I am sure that I heartily wish to get from hence— ***

ALS, Shippen Family Papers, DLC. Place to which addressed not indicated. For the full text, see *Lee* 2:527. The omitted text discusses personal business.

James Madison to James Madison, Sr.

My last was to my brother A[*mbrose*]. and acknowledged [*the*] receipt of the [*weather*] Diary. I inclose one for the month of April [*whi*]ch you can compare with your own for the same month. I inclose also a few grains of *upland* rice, brought from Timor by Capt. Bligh lately distinguished by an adventure which you must have seen in the newspapers.[1] He was returning from a voyage of discovery in the South seas, and turned out of his ship with a few others by a mutinous crew, into a long boat which continued more than 40 days at sea. A little rice of which the inclosed is a part was all that he saved out of a fine collection. It will be best to give the grains their first vegetation in a flower pot of rich earth, and then shift the contents of the pot into the ground so as not to disturb the roots. A few of the grains may be tried at once in the garden in a strong soil.

You will see by the inclosed Newspapers that the seat of Govt. has been again on the carpet. After a variety of questions which the state of the votes as you will at once remark do not truly explain a very unexpected result has happened in favor of Baltimore. It is possible that a like fortuitous one may take place in the Senate, but it does not appear probable. It is much to be apprehended that the final event will not square with the pretensions of the Potowmac, tho' in the chances to Which this question is liable, it may possibly turn out otherwise. I am anxious to hear the progress of my mothers [*Eleanor Rose Conway Madison—"Nelly"*] health, and that of my sister Nelly.[2] I hope yours continues good. Mine has been reestablished for some time. [*lined out*]

ALS, Madison Papers, DLC. Place to which addressed not indicated.

[1] The samples of upland or "dry" rice were collected by Capt. William Bligh (1754–1817) while en route home to England after his successful rescue from the mutiny on H.M.A.V. *Bounty*. The British scientist and political economist Benjamin Vaughan had acquired the collection from the noted naturalist Sir Joseph Banks within days of Bligh's return to England and forwarded them immediately to Jefferson, from whom Madison evidently received them (*PTJ* 16:274–76).

[2] Eleanor Conway Madison (1760–1802) married Isaac Hite in 1783 and resided in Frederick County, Virginia.

Louis Guillaume Otto to Comte de Montmorin

The popularity of Mr. Adams, Vice President of the United States, is falling lower and lower. The monarchical ideas that he is always spreading in his speeches and in his writings excite the indignation of some and the contempt of others. Superstitiously prejudiced in favor of the English constitution, he floods the gazettes with his political dreams about the creation of Lords and the royal prerogative. As Vice President he likes to consider himself as heir apparent of the American Presidency and his principles are distrusted the more the motive making him act is clearly seen. In his publications the austere republican who at the beginning of the Revolution preached equality of conditions in the streets of Boston is no longer recognized. His conversations manifest his decided contempt for the people and his desire to introduce an hereditary nobility, he who had formerly written against the establishment of the order of Cincinnati as prejudicial to the equality of conditions. He was satisfied up to now to set forth only the theory of his principles, but he is beginning to apply them in writing some commentaries on the conduct of the National Assembly of France under the title of *Discourses on Davila.* He told me one day with his customary modesty: "I see well that I will have to make another trip to France in order to explain to them my book which they have not rightly understood." This book is a pretended apology of the American Constitutions, in which he gives excessive praise to that of England. Dr. [*Richard*] Price having written him "that it was to be desired that the National Assembly had turned this book to a better account," he has had that flattering letter printed.[1] Finally, one cannot take more trouble than Mr. Adams does to make himself disagreeable to the greatest number; and the public, tired of his diatribes, begins to harass him with lampoons and epigrams. It appears certain at present that he will never be President and that he will have a very formidable competitor in Mr. Jefferson who, with more talents and knowledge than he, has infinitely more the principles and manners of a republican. There is only one voice with regard to this estimable citizen who ought to be particularly dear to us by the affection he never ceases to show for France and by a sort of enthusiasm which he communicates to persons in office for everything which concerns us. Knowing the great influence of the gazettes, he continues to discredit those of England and he even employs a writer to translate and have printed the most authentic news of France,[2] especially that which can contribute to make the nation loved. It is remarkable, My Lord, and in case of a war it would be very satisfying to know that all the executive officers of the United States, I do not exclude even Mr. Adams, are by taste or by their personal ties with the French strongly predisposed towards our nation; and, as long as the interests of their constituents will permit them to act, disposed to render us service. I have never doubted the good intentions of the President, although his reserve is always extreme and sometimes icy. Mr. Jefferson, Secretary of Foreign Affairs, Mr. Knox, Secretary of War, Mr. Hamilton, Secretary of the Treasury, all forming the Council of the President, are deeply imbued with the necessity of maintaining consistent and very amicable relations, with the Kingdom; the establishment of five American consuls in France to two in England is a recent proof of it.[3] The influence of Mr. Adams is almost nil. As to Mr. Jay, he limits himself scrupulously to his functions as Chief Justice which cause him to travel very much and prevent him from taking any part in politics.

It is demonstrated more than ever, My Lord, that nothing can impair the respect and affection of Americans for their President although there are several traits in his character which are not entirely agreeable to some of his compatriots. If it depended only on Mr. Adams, the President would affect the whole display of royalty, but his good sense keeps him in limits, which could be restrained more without harming his dignity. One sees him with regret in a coach with six horses, accompanied by his aides-de-camp on horseback and followed by the Secretaries of State [*department heads*], taking a drive in the country. The choice of his aides-de-camp who perform the functions of gentlemen of the chamber is at least bizarre;[4] not one of them is esteemed and as the President is a perfect judge of men there is reason to believe that he is so badly escorted only to convince the public that he does everything by himself and that no one holds the pen for him nor the staff of command. Almost all his letters are written in his hand and notwithstanding his great reputation as statesman and warrior, he does not disdain that of a pure and elegant writer. He seems in all things to wish to resemble Caesar whose *Commentaries* are constantly on his table,[5] but in several respects he is much above his model and the public hardly notices some little blemishes that human nature has left on one of its masterpieces and which the American patriot likes to cover with a thick veil. Although great and generous in public, he gives in private the example of the frugality and economy which ought to reign in a household. He is usually up and dressed at five o'clock in the morning; he wakens his domestics, looks over his house and stables, giving the orders necessary for the day's work himself. From there he goes into his office where he is busy until noon. He rides horseback with his aides-de-camp, dines at two o'clock and returns to his office at five where he remains till nine, his bedtime. Dignity, foresight, circumspection, love of work, perseverance, all are united in this great man; and as he has the prudence necessary to display only the qualities proper to his situation, one is tempted to believe that he possesses all those which it would be useless and even dangerous to show. Nobody has ever been more impenetrable than General Washington; even the people who constantly surround him know his way of thinking only by the orders he gives. The mystery which envelops him makes his demeanor so icy that with the exception of the days of public audience[6] his house is deserted and it can be said that he enjoys all the advantages possible excepting the comforts of friendship, which seem incompatible with his rank in public and which he does not seek even in private. Judging by the decline of his health, one would say that he is unfortunate. It is certain that the constraint in which he lives, either by choice or by necessity, can leave him no other joys than those of a satisfied ambition; but even this flower is not without thorns.

The funds for foreign affairs being fixed definitely at 40,000 dollars,[7] Congress has proceeded, My Lord, to the determination of the salaries of ministers and chargés d'affaires who will probably be the only employees of the United States in foreign countries. It has granted to a minister 9,000 dollars, making 47,250 L. tournois per year, and half of that sum for a chargé d'affaires. The first year will be carried at twice as much because of the expense of travel and settling. Probably the nominations will follow closely this act of the legislature, but it is impossible up to now to guess the subjects who will be employed. The candidates are numerous and in view of the modicum of funds there will be few posts to give. The minister's first year alone will absorb nearly half of the sum allocated by Congress. The Government employs at this moment only two chargés d'affaires, one in France and the other in Spain.[8]

O'Dwyer, pp. 432–35. Otto's letters included in *DHFFC* were usually written over the course of days, and even weeks, following the day they were begun. Place to which addressed not indicated; received 26 November.

---

[1] Price's letter to Adams, 1 February (ALS, Adams Family Manuscript Trust, MHi), was excerpted in *GUS*, 12 June.

[2] Jefferson himself translated the extracts from The Netherlands' *Gazette de Leide* that he, by pre-arrangement, provided to John Fenno for republication in the latter's *GUS* beginning in April 1790. In exchange for government patronage, Jefferson relied on Fenno to disseminate more balanced (that is, non-British) newspaper coverage of the French Revolution that was forwarded by his diplomatic contacts in Paris and The Hague. During the same period Jefferson also supplied Fenno with extracts from letters he received from John Brown Cutting in London. This alliance broke down in early August, when Fenno's editorial policy signaled a decidedly anti-French shift. For more, see *PTJ* 16:237–47, 255n, 262n.

[3] On 7 June, the Senate consented to the nominations of consuls to five ports belonging to France (Bordeaux, Nantes, Rouen, Hispaniola, and Martinique) as well as Liverpool in England and Dublin in Ireland. The vote on Washington's nominations to the additional ports of Cowes on England's Isle of Wight and France's Havre de Grace were postponed and not agreed to until 17 and 22 June, respectively.

[4] Otto's phrase "aides-de-camp" is a military term for the personal staff Washington employed while wartime commander in chief and again as President. During the second session of the FFC, this "official family" consisted of his nephew Robert Lewis, William Jackson, Thomas Nelson, and, most importantly, David Humphreys and Tobias Lear. Humphreys was the only one of the five who had actually served as one of Washington's aides-de-camp during the Revolutionary War. Their general duties were to serve as messengers and secretaries capable also of receiving and entertaining company. Humphreys also filled some of the present-day functions of bodyguard and speechwriter.

[5] Julius Caesar's famous "Commentaries" *On the Gallic War* was his first-person chronicle of Rome's final conquest of Gaul (present-day France, the Low Countries, and Germany west of the Rhine) between 58 and 50 B.C. The first English edition, printed in the late sixteenth century, was followed by many others, but no American edition existed by 1790. There is no evidence that Washington's personal library included an edition of Caesar's work.

[6] By this point in the weekly cycle of the "Republican Court," public levees were held at the presidential mansion on two occasions: Washington's open-door audience on Tuesdays between three and four o'clock, and Martha's usually crowded levee on Friday evenings between eight and eleven o'clock. Friday night's guests would be introduced by either Lear or Humphreys and then enjoy cake, ice cream, lemonade, and an appearance by the President himself (*DHFFC* 9:21n; *DGW* 5:451n; Washington to David Stuart, 15 June, below).

[7] Under the terms of the Foreign Intercourse Act [HR-52], introduced on 31 March but not enacted until 1 July. The specific money amounts Otto mentions were arrived at by a conference committee that did not report until 23 June, indicating that the letter was not sent until just before he began his letter of 24 June.

[8] William Short at Paris and William Carmichael at Madrid.

Philip Schuyler to Catherine Schuyler

This morning I received Mr. Robertson's letter of Wednesday last announcing the Intentions of Jacob & Cuff. I believe we shall in future have so much trouble from these fellows and so little service, that I believe It would be best to part with them—and If you approve of It, I wish you to advertise them for sale and to get what you can for them—& If those who may Incline to purchase them cannot pay the money to take bonds with security payable a year hence.

If I can find a purchaser here I will sell them on condition that you have not sold them before.

I do not think It will be prudent to take them out of Goal [*jail*], but of this you are the best Judge as being on the spot.

The question about the removal still agitates Congress on Friday a resolution passed in the house of representatives to go to Baltimore—this I believe will not pass the Senate—but unless some compromise takes place relative to the permanent seat of Congress, I appehend the next meeting will be at Philadelphia.

I shall purchase and send the tea and sugar by the first safe conveyance.

We are all well.

ALS, Schuyler Papers, NN. Place to which addressed not indicated.

David Sewall to George Thatcher

My last was Wrote from your domicilium at Biddeford [*Maine*] *** As I find Congress is to sit, at Philadelphia the next Session & of course I suppose a removal of the Treasury and other offices—I inclose an Authority to apply for Salary[1] for *two quarters* in case You should remain there, until 1st July which is now at no great distance—a draft upon the massa. Bank will be agreable—The Complection of the G. Court [*legislature*] is much better I am told than the last—The Choice of a Senator I hear as to be made this Session, as mr. Dalton Term, will expire before they may have another opportunity of doing it Seasonably—and a Time & manner of Chusing Representatives for the next Congress will also be Setted before the Court Rises which will probably be in the Course of next Week—This is all I can at present Communicate.

P. S. ***

The Capital Trial[2] in my Court has been attended with some expence already. and the Marshall must be at Some more in Carrying the Judgt. into Execution—The Gaoler has also applied to me to know how When & Where he is to recieve Compensation for the Prisoners Subsistance, &c. I want your Sentiments on that head—Those little matters I early suggested, & if my memory serves me I forwarded a rough draft of a Bill—But more Important matters have put the matters of such small magnitude out of Sight—Some way I think ought to be devized for these small matters or the attendance of Jurors &c. will soon be deemed Bothersome.

N. B. in case thou [?] should come off before July—you will only apply for one quarter Salary—from What you said when you sent me the last draft I thot. it could do no harm to put in *two* quarters.

ALS, Foster Collection, MHi. Written from Boston; franked; postmarked. The omitted text relates to local news and business of the Massachusetts legislature, including mention of instructions on assumption of state debts and cession of lighthouses.

[1] Sewall's salary as federal district judge for the Maine district of Massachusetts.

[2] Of Thomas Bird, hanged for piracy on 25 June.

George Thatcher to Sarah Thatcher

Having wrote you by every mail, for almost a fortnight, you must not expect me to say more than just to tell you I am well, & last evening received your Letters of the fifth & sixth June, together with Judge [*David*] Sewalls, wrote at our house—I wish I could have seen our dear children as they were trudging off to meeting—[*daughter*] Sally, I fancy, was all in a hurry—her brother [*Samuel Phillips Savage*] will be more sedate, & I guess less sprightly—I am very much pleased with your account of Sally's reading—Pray omit no means to make her attend several times a day to her Book—For if she reads willingly, it will induce Phillips to look into his Book also—and if you can create a sort of emulation between them I think they will both learn the faster—To encourage them, once a day, tell them they must try which can read the best—but be carefull that they pronounce their letters distinctly—and dont let them hurry—Half a dozen words pronounced slowly & with propriety will do them more good than a dozen lines hudled over in a confused, indistinct manner.

Tell them they must try all in their power to see which can read the best to their papa when he comes home—I want to hear what they do with the books I sent to Phillips—whom he gives them to, & whether he is pleased with keeping them—or gives away all but one or two with pleasure—At my return I will bring each of them some more.

In a few days I will send more money to Mr. [*Thomas*] Dakin & desire him to get the things you mentioned in a former Letter—For tho I hope to be at Boston in three weeks or less, yet I shall be in too great an haste to attend to the geting them myself—And, perhaps, Mr. Dakin can get, & send them down by the time I return, & I think tis probable you need them.

I am very sorry to hear of Silas' [*Lee*] illness—and fear he will live but a little while—I hope, however, they will be blessed with one *little baby* before he goes off—you know I want much to kiss one of Tempe's [*Temperance Hedge Lee*] children—If Silas dies, Tempe & her baby shall live with us—I will be their father & you their Mother.

ALS, Thatcher Family Papers, MHi. Place to which addressed not indicated.

George Thatcher to Nathaniel Wells

Since my last your favour of the 29th. May & 4th. inst. have come to hand—I have nothing to write you, but discouraging prospects touching the assumption. One day last week, while the funding Bill was before the Senate, Mr. Strong produced the instructions of the Legislature, & a motion was made for amending the Bill by adding thereto a provisional clause for the State debts, which after some debate was negatived: Mr. Langdon & R. Morriss, who have ever professed themselves warm advocates for the measure, made each of them a strange sort of an exculpatory speech and concluded against the motion—but intimated that it was their opinion, the State Debts should be provided for in a seperate Bill—which Game had before been played off in our house, & begins to be very well understood. I beleive, however, a Bill, for this purpose, will be brought before the Senate—But I have no expectation of its being agreed to. This Transaction, with one that took place a few days, ~~ago~~ before in the Senate, respecting a permanent seat of Residence of Congress, convinces me there is an agreement, or a good understanding, in the minds of some members, to make the assumption serve as a pack-horse to carry Congress to Philadelphia. When the Bill for fixing the permanent seat of Congress was before the Senate, a motion was made to fill the Blank with some convenient place on the Banks of the Potomack—This place has been vigorously contended for, heretofore, as the only proper place for Congress to reside at, by the Virginians, Marylanders, & some others—but on this occasion they voted against the motion—and argued that Congress ought now to remove to Philadelphia, & let the seat of permanent Residence alone for the present—The like took place, on fryday in our house. The Pennsylvanians, ever uneasy and envious at Congress being in New-York, like the old serpent at the felicity of the first pair in Pardise,[1] could not rest ~~easy~~ quiet at the Senate negativing the Resolution for meeting the next Session at Philadelphia—On Thursday a motion was made in the house, by Mr. Parker from Virginia, whose representation, on this occasion, were mere tools to the Pennsylvanians, that the next meeting of Congress should be in the City of Philadelphia—This motion, tho but a day or two before non-concurred in the Senate, was now again urged on by the Virginians, Pennsylvanians & three or four from Maryland, with all the hurry & dispach, that could have taken place, had the salvation of the United States been at hazard—And it was with the utmost difficulty the standing rules of the House, or that decency and decorum due to the entreties of a considerable minority, could prevail on the Advocates of the motion to put off taking the question till the next day; and had not the day been far spent, much after the usual time of adjournment, a postponement would not have taken place—However the House adjourned; and the next day (fryday) a motion was made for striking out *Philadelphia*, & to insert Baltimore—This amendment was then opposed, with the same vehemence, & by the same persons, that, a moment before, had urged the original motion—But unluckily for them they could not make use of the same arguments—they had all along contended that N. York was not a proper place for Congress to set at, being too far east—And that we ought to take a more central situation—But every thing must bend to serve a purpose; and what was reasonable before is nonsense now. It was observed, by those who were against removing at all, for the present—that if Congress must go—we ought to go as near the center of the United States as accommodations could be provided, which might as well be done at Baltimore as in Philadelphia—And if Congress was in Baltimore, they might rest quietly many years; whereas should a removal be made to Philadelphia; its uncentral position would be the cause of continual uneasiness—and exertions, bargains & intreagues would always exist till Congress went farther south—However, on taking the question for striking out Philadelphia & inserting Baltimore, those who had contended so much for a central position, particularly—the Virginians, Pennsylvanians & some of the Marylanders—also two from Georgia & the member from Delaware were against the amendment; but it was carried by a majority of two or three—And on the Resolution as amended, with Baltimore, it was carried by a majority of fifty two against six—What the Senate will do with it—whether they will concur, or non-concur—is left to their future determination.

This question about Residence has been the Demon of the present, & a great part of the last Session—And it ever will prove a haunting Ghost till it is laid by fixing a permanent seat of Government—but where this ought to be few are agreed in opinion. And it certainly must be a subject of regret to those who have been friends & supporters of our new Government to see the time of Congress, & the Treasures of the U. States lavished in party disputes about a question that Reason & sound policy seem to point out as what ought to be variable for a century to come!

I read in a Boston paper an application from General Towns in Massachusetts to the Legislature for a repeal of the State excises—what these will lead to I dont know—neither can I point out what steps are the wisest to be taken at this time—But I am rather inclined to think with you, that a pretty high excise on spirits should be laid by the State—so high, perhaps, as to prevent an additional one being laid by Congress.

Ought I to suggest, or even think—that no argument will have more force with Congress, in favour of an assumption, & continental provision of the State debts, than the difficulties, that must attend the collection of the general Revenue, arising from State excises? When these difficulties are felt, many who now oppose, from selfish, will then, from the same motives, advocate the assumption.

P. S. The inclosed copy of returns from the war office will serve to give you some idea of the comparative exertions of the several States during the war[2]—Having satisfied yourself, you may deliver it to Judge [*David*] Sewall—I wish to have it again—There was a motion in the House to have this statement, & some other documents of a like nature, printed, but it was lost.

FC, Thatcher Family Papers, MHi. Sent to Boston.

---

[1] Genesis 3:1–5.
[2] For this report of the secretary of war, see *DHFFC* 5:876–88.

Other Documents

Abigail Adams to Mary Cranch. ALS, Abigail Adams Letters, MWA. Addressed to Braintree, Massachusetts. For the full text, see *Abigail Adams*, pp. 51–52.

She is tormented by "apprehension of a removal from a very delightful situation"; "To be every session disputing upon this subject [*the seat of government*], & sowered as the members are, is a very unpleasant thing."

Royal Flint to Enos Hitchcock. ALS, Miscellaneous Collection, RHi. Place to which addressed not indicated. For background on Hitchcock's petition for copyright protection, see *DHFFC* 8:32, 34.

To encourage sales of Hitchcock's book (*Memoirs of the Bloomsgrove Family . . . Containing Sentiments on a Mode of Domestic Education* [2 vols., Boston, 1790]), advises him to address a set each to Mrs. (Sarah Livingston) Jay, Mrs. (Lucy Flucker) Knox, and Mrs. (Charlotte Izard) Smith; regarding Hitchcock's petition, there is no hope at present; Congress is "in an ill-humour about the removal to Philadelphia, and about the assumption. In such a state of ferment, men (even the best) do not feel disposed to encourage literary productions."

Alexander Hamilton to Robert Morris. ALS, privately owned in 1995. Misdated on the docket as 14 June.

"I called upon you this afternoon to communicate a letter I have received from Mr. G. Morris. I shall be at home all the Evening if it should be convenient to you to pass my way."

Thomas Jefferson to Francis Hopkinson. FC, letterpress copy, Jefferson Papers, DLC. Place to which addressed not indicated. For the full text, see *PTJ* 16:490–91.

It is doubted whether the Senate will concur with the House's vote to remove to Baltimore; "I am only a passenger in their voyages, & therefore meddle not."

Thomas Jefferson to Richard Peters. ALS, Peters Papers, PHi. Place to which addressed not indicated.

"notwithstanding Friday's vote for Baltimore, some tell us we shall still have the pleasure of sojourning with you at Philadelphia. we shall soon see."

William Samuel Johnson to Samuel William Johnson. ALS, Johnson Papers, CtHi. Addressed to Stratford, Connecticut; franked; postmarked.

Discusses family news and his legal practice; notes that a bill has been submitted and paid, but Charles (son Robert Charles) "has I suppose by this time lost it into the all-insolving Vortex of Speculation"; encloses letters to Samuel William from his friends.

William Widgery to George Thatcher. ALS, Ransom Collection, Litchfield Historical Society, Litchfield, Connecticut. Written from Boston.

Had expected a line from Thatcher until Dr. (Daniel) Conant disclosed that Thatcher didn't know where Widgery would be; asks Thatcher's opinion on assumption; it is thought that if Massachusetts abolished its excise, Congress would assume its state debt; the state will be again divided into districts for the choice of federal Representatives; there is "talk of Choosing a Seanator, a berth for which there are many Suiters—I think Best to Keep Dalton in—this may be put off till the winter Sessions."

William Samuel Johnson, Diary. Johnson Papers, CtHi.

"St. Pauls."

Letter from New York. *FG*, 17 June; reprinted at Portsmouth, New Hampshire; Annapolis and Baltimore, Maryland; and Fredericksburg, Richmond, and Winchester, Virginia.

"The dispute about the residence of Congress is the only subject of conversation here. I wish it was settled—for it is too evident, that an eye to it influences the votes upon many questions, and in some instances produces delays or decisions, that are both injurious and dishonorable to our country."

Letter from New York. [New London] *Connecticut Gazette*, 18 June.

"*Congress is wasting time about the place of adjournment to sit at their next meeting, but whatever may be their present opinion or idea, they will meet at New-York.*"

Letter from New York. [Providence, Rhode Island] *United States Chronicle*, 1 July; reprinted at Portsmouth, New Hampshire, and New York City (*NYJ*, 9 July).

"The Senate have thrown out the two Alternatives in the Funding-Bill—and 4 per Cent. only on the Principal of the Continental Debt, it is thought will be the most that will be obtained. The Indents are struck out of the Bill, by the Committee, and Western Lands only are appropriated for their Discharge. *Old Continental* is reported at 100 for 1."

MONDAY, 14 JUNE 1790

Warm (Johnson); *Very pleast.* (J. B. Johnson)

Jabez Bowen to John Adams

I most sincearly Congratulate you on the accession of Rhode Island to the Union by this event The Chain seems compleat, may our publick deliberations be conducted with that wisdom as shall insure Happiness to this great Nation.

I have just returnd from attending our Genl. Assembly. Convened on purpose to Ele[*c*]t Senators and prescribe the mode of Choosing the Representative. Your Humble Servant was a Candidate for a Senator, but was not able to obtain; the whole of the Paper Money and Antifederal Intrest being oposed to him. Theodore Foster Esqr. who is appointed is and has been Federal. but being Brother in Law to Govr. [*Arthur*] Fenner we fear will be totally against the Assumption. Joseph Stanton the other Senator is a full blooded Anti and a strong advocate for paper Money. hope they will both be for promoting The General good when deteached from their old Connections.

I have wrote the President of the United State praying him to appoint my Son Oliver Bowen to the place of Navel Officer for the District of Providence he is about Twenty two Years of Age has had a Liberal Education and at present attends an apothecarys Shop. The U. States owe me nearly Twenty Thousand Dollars which I lent them in the Years 1776 & 77. which puts it out of my power to provide for him at present. Theodore Foster Jr. was the Navel Officer. by his appointment as a Senator it will become vacant, if you will be so kind as just to second my application to the President shall esteem my self under many Obligations to you Therefor.
P. S. The Bill which originated in the Senate for stopping intercourse with Rd. Island [*Rhode Island Trade Bill S-11*] & The Demand for 27. Thousand Dollars. were the procuring Causes of the Adoption of the Constitution.

ALS, Adams Family Manuscript Trust, MHi. Written from Providence, Rhode Island.

Abiel Foster and Benjamin Huntington to George Washington

We hope its not disagreeable that we mention the Hone. William Ellery of Newport as a good man for a Commissioner of loans or a District Judge, or a Collector of the Duties for the Port of Newport in Rhode Island His Character is well known from past services in, & under various appointments from the late Congress He was commissioner of Loans at the Adoption of the Constitution and will doubtless give Satisfaction in any of the Abovementioned Offices.

ALS, Washington Papers, DLC.

Theodore Sedgwick to Pamela Sedgwick

Imediately after I wrote you on friday last I set off for a jaunt to Pesaic falls [*New Jersey*]. We dined on the other side the river and afterwards had a delightful ride as far that evening as Hackingsack [*New Jersey*], The company was composed of Benson, Smith of S. Carolina, Ames, Mr. [*Martin?*] Hoffman whom you know, and Mr. Nicholas Low. The exchange of the poluted air of the city, for the sweet fragrance of the country, the delightful verdure, luxuriance vegitation, the enchanting musick of the birds, the prospect of well cultivated fields and the good humour of the company gave me a flow of spirits which I have not enjoyed since I left the bosom of my family. The evening passed delightfully, and I was refreshed by an undisturbed repose during the night, which I rarely experience. The next day we went to the falls, which are indeed worth veiwing. The stream glides gently on over the surface of a smoth rock till it comes to a fissure of from one to fifteen feet over and about as it is said eighty feet deep, into this opening it enters and descends dashing against each side of the opening with furious violence. The roaring of the water is heard at considerable distance, and adds greatly to the pleasing horror which the scene inspires. The water as soon as it reaches the bottom takes the direction of the aperture in the rocks and is hurried throgh it till it comes to an opening. This stoped at the distance of 12 or 15 rods by a high shore and a basen is formed where the water is reduced to a dead calm. This place is said to be unfathomable. From it the water takes a direction nearly the same as before the fall, and glides gently down between its banks. The water in quantity is probably about equal to our [*Housatonic*] river at Stockbridge. Below the fissure into which the column of water enters, are three or four others of unequal width from twelve inches to three feet, and of about 70 or 80 feet deep. From every appearance one would be inclined to suppose that it is not as it was created. Into one of these rents I was determined to enter and desend to the bottom, hoping to have got a veiw of the water as it was falling. I went down to the bottom but I could not gratify my wish in going down, not being able to take the veiw I had promised myself without going into water more than knee deep, which I dare not do as I had made myself exceeding warm in the descent. The other gentlemen prefered being above, and indeed I found the assent very fatiguing. During the time we were making our veiw and indeed the whole day it rained violently, which deprived us of part of our pleasure. after dinner we went down to Newark [*New Jersey*], where the whole company was treated with great hospitality. We were not permitted to go to a tavern; and the the gentry of the village seemed to exert themselves to make us happy The distinction shewn to me perticularly though flatering, was yet painful. On sunday I went to meeting and we returned home in the evening. The Tour I find has been of great benefit to my health. Indeed I cannot and I will not submit myself much longer to the continuance in this painful situation.

Will you my dear love tell Mr. Woodbridge that it will be necessary for him to procure some good wine for the New York commissioners who will be there on the 5th. of July.[1] He can get it of MacMechen of Kinderhook [*New York*].

I am happy to have it in my power to inform you that I have at last settled my defaulter account.[2] There is a very considerable ballance due to me which I am affraid it will never be in my power to realise.

I have some time since written Mr. [*Ephraim*] Williams on the subject of his removal—he has as yet returned no answer.

ALS, Sedgwick Papers, MHi. Place to which addressed not indicated.

[1] Commissioners appointed by New York and Vermont were scheduled to meet at Stockbridge on 6 July, as part of the ongoing negotiations for settling land title disputes as a condition for Vermont's admission to the union. The meeting was postponed indefinitely to either New York City or Bennington, Vermont, when only one of New York's commissioners proved able to attend ([Stockbridge, Massachusetts] *Western Star*, 6, 13 July). For background on the negotiations, see *DHFFC* 16:1114–15n.

[2] See Theodore to Pamela Sedgwick, 29 May, second letter, n. 1, above.

John Samuel Sherburne to John Langdon

I have had the pleasure of yours of the 3d. inst. from which I imagine you will be surprised at the contents of my last from this place. altho I think the choice will be agreable to the people, & I hope to you—There has been a matter in agitation in this Court [*legislature*] in which I am much interested, & which you will much oblige me by speaking to the Secretary of the Treasury about, tho' without mentioning my Name, By a resolve of the old Congress of June 11th. 1788—The States are to have credit on their general account with the U.S. for all sums paid to Invalids Pensions to 1st. Jany. 1782—& for sums pd. after that period to 1st. Jany 1788—they are to have credit on the Specie requisitions.[1] This State instead of payg. their invalids in specie requisitions have paid them with Notes & Certificates of their own worth on an average about 6/ in the pound, but have charged the Congress with the full sum in Specie—Complaints have often been made to Congress, & they have written this State on the subject but in vain—The Secy. of the treasury some time since demanded an Account of the payments & their kind, & also their receipts, by which the whole matter is fully explained to him, & he has wrote the President [*governor of New Hampshire*], that for the paper paid to the Invalids, the State will *only* be credited its value in the market at the different times—of course the Invalids will be paid the difference between the value of the Notes &c. & Cash. this will make a difference to me of £500 or 600—You will oblige me by conversing with the Treasurer on the Subject, & save yourself from the imputation that is cast on the State by their unrighteous conduct—Our Court seems now deeply sensible of the injustice, but are at a loss what steps to take—I wish some measures might be adopted to ascertain the value of the paper given to the Invalids, & that orders might be given Mr. [*Joseph*] Whipple to pay them the difference—Our Light house will be ceded to Congress this Session, & I hope the Fort[2]—Shd. an officer of Invalids be appointed to the command with full pay—the offer wd. not be disagreable to me.

Col. Hoit[3] informs me that some troops are to be raised in this State for the use of Congress, shd. a field officer be appointed, he requested me to name him to you—for the service they are intended perhaps no person wd. better answer, & that might in some measure better Enable him to pay you—We are under great obligations for yr. exertions relative to the tonnage I hope it will answer the intended purpose.

ALS, Langdon Papers, NhPoA. Written from Concord, New Hampshire.

[1] The resolution can be found in *JCC* 34:210.
[2] The lighthouse and Fort William and Mary at the entrance to the harbor at Portsmouth, New Hampshire.
[3] Nathan Hoit (d. 1820) of Moultonboro, New Hampshire.

William Smith (S.C.) to Edward Rutledge

I suppose your mind is so engaged by the important & interesting business before you in Convention[1] that you feel less impatience to learn our proceedgs. than on another occasion. My Mind has been of late considerably distracted between the business at Columbia (of which some disagreable accounts have reached us) & the Subjects which have been under our consideration here; the questions of Assumption, Residence, funding &ca., have not yet received such a determination as to quiet our apprehensions; negotiations, cabals, meetings, plots & counterplots have prevailed for months past without yet ripening to any decision, & I am sorry to say that such ~~measures~~ transactions have more influence on the public business then fair argument & an attention to the general good. It would take more time than either of us can at present spare to give you a detail of the negotiations which have lately taken place; in former letters I anticipated them in some respect; the policy of Pensya. & those who are anxious to remove Congress to Philada. has been to keep off the question of assumption & we have not yet felt strong enough to hazard it; the other party have not suffered us to take any question on it in the House but have detached it from the funding bill which they have carried thro & sent to the Senate, where it is now under consideration & where we hope the assumption will be inserted: they then took up the Bill laying the increased duties on Spirits & establishing the Excise [*HR*-62]; this Bill is now before us & will be opposed with great violence if the assumption does not succeed: those who are anxious to fund the continental debt are very apprehensive of losing the Excise, as they think sufficient funds cannot be obtained without it; on the other hand the friends of the Assumption are disposed to make that apprehension subservient to their wishes; in this we are supported by the Virginns. & North Carns. who are strongly opposed to an Excise; if we are strong enough to strike out the Excise the funding Bill will be in Such jeopardy that we may expect much less opposition to the Assumption, & there is a great probability we shall Succeed.

The fear of losing Congress has induced the three obstinate antifederal members from this State[2] to relax in their opposition to the Assumption—to court New England & South Carolina, on whose good will they depend for retaining Congress at New York, they have nearly pledged themselves to vote for the assumption; the day the vote passed in our house for removing to Philada. we had a meeting; New Engd. New York & myself: there those three gentlemen promised that with some trifling modification they would vote for the question and had so much at heart; we have also gained the two Jersey Members who voted against the Assumpn. by agreeing to a clause in the funding Bill which is advantag[*eou*]s. to their State.[3]

ALS, Smith Papers, ScHi. Place to which addressed not indicated. In a postscript dated 29 June, Smith indicated, "I wrote the above some time ago but have hitherto had no opportunity—yours in haste."

---

[1] South Carolina's constitutional convention, convened in Columbia, adjourned on 3 June.

[2] Floyd, Hathorn, and van Rensselaer.

[3] Schureman and Sinnickson. The clause in question was a proviso moved by Boudinot on 20 May and added at the end of the third section of the Funding Bill. It provided compensation to states that had paid interest on any of the various classes of certificates to be funded (*DHFFC* 5:870, 9:299).

An American Citizen to the Congress of the United States

CONFIDENT that the public good is the ultimate object of all your deliberations, and that true patriotism directs all your measures, I shall venture to address you on a subject of no small importance to the United States. Should my remarks appear to be just, I entertain too high a sense of your wisdom and candor, to suppose you capable of rejecting an useful hint, merely because it comes from an anonymous author.

The encouragement of literature by laws, securing copy-right to authors and proprietors of books, &c. has been long wished for; and it is with pleasure your constituents behold a law lately enacted by you for that salutary purpose. With respect to this act, however, I would remark, that a question may arise, whether it is not, in some degree, an *ex post facto*, and consequently an *unconstitutional act*, so far as it secures to authors and proprietors the copyright of books, &c. *already published.* Let us suppose a printer considerably advanced in preparing an edition of some of those books, which have lately made their appearance amongst us—when he began he violated no law; for none to prohibit the undertaking existed.

What then is to be done? Is he to lose his property and incur fines, by means of an act passed after the supposed offence? If actions, which were void of all criminality at the time they were committed, may be punished by a subsequent law, where will the principle end?

I would further beg leave to suggest the propriety of securing copy-right to those, who may be at the pains and expence of translating literary works from foreign languages. Were this encouragement given, we should soon have many valuable books translated in America, and published in our own language. But, while every person has it in his power to rob a translator of the fruits of his useful toil, we must, I fear, be still dependent on Great-Britain, for the literature of all the nations in Europe. The thought is too degrading. In your wisdom, Gentlemen, is it not possible to devise some mode of securing to American translators the sole right of disposing of their works?

Permit me, in the last place, to ask, whether the benefits of the law in question are designed to be extended to the female sex? And if so, whether the words "author," "him," "his," &c. will be sufficient to express this idea? Though I have no disposition to cavil at words, perhaps some of our ingenious gentlemen of the bar may be differently inclined; and may deny that these words can be applied to a lady.

FG, 14 June; reprinted at New York City (*NYDG*, 18 June).

[*David Daggett,*] A Republican to Mess. Printers

AND what important business now engages the attention of Congress? Why the *great* question about changing the seat of government. In the lower house it was determined to remove to Philadelphia—this was non-concurred in the senate.

New-York have been at very great expence to provide suitable accommodations—justice and gratitude therefore demand that congress should continue there for the present. But is it not truly surprising to see that illustrious body again involved in this question? Can it be important to the union, whether their legislature sit in New-York, or remove to Philadelphia? And shall we pay them 500 dollars per day for discussing this subject every session of Congress?

The people care not in what place the seat of government is fixed, but they look, with indignation, at the party spirit and narrow politics which induce the agitation of this question. 'Tis of less moment to the subjects *where* congress spend their time, than *how* they spend it; and we can but declare it childish nonsense, to delay the important interests of the nation to determine whither the southern, can out-vote the northern states. Besides, such disputes may be attended with the most alarming consequences. We cannot expect peace, happiness or respectability, when our national council is torn with perpetual jarrings and discord. All questions which are to be decided by local prejudices, are to be avoided, as containing the most deadly evils. The dignity of Congress, and the interest of our country is concerned in their being reprobated, and I shall take the liberty of doing it without fear or restraint.

In a former publication, I attempted to tell you to *what* business Congress have attended; let us now see *how much* of their time is actually employed in any public concern; on five days out of seven they sit from eleven o'clock till three—a space of four hours per day, or twenty hours per week, which constitutes less than one seventh of their time. In no nation like ours was there ever such a mispence of time. In ancient Greece or Rome, it was not uncommon to see their forum crouded by day light in the morning, and their deliberations continued till late at night. Cicero, and Demosthenes, those illustrious patriots, were ever vigilant and industrious, regarding with a watchful eye the public good. Cincinnatus, on the same day, quitted his plow and assumed the command of the Roman army; he was not ashamed to be found employed in the labour of the field, when his voice or sword was not necessarily employed for his country. And is it because we exceed Greece and Rome in opulence and political grandeur, and because our national situation is so flourishing, that our legislators devote so small a portion of their time to the public? Is it answering the general expectation, to see them rolling from street to street in their coaches, while a system of laws is to be established for an empire? If to visit the play-house is more profitable than to devote their time to the interest of the nation, we have the pleasure of seeing many of the members employed much to our advantage. And here I can discover one motive which induced a vote in the lower house to remove to Philadelphia: The play-house has been, for some time, vacant at New-York, and the performers are at Philadelphia.[1]

Upon the subject of the employment of time, I would observe, that eight hours for business is neither unusual nor unreasonable. If we hire a mechanic or a husbandman, and he should employ only four hours per day in our service, should we not think ourselves egregiously injured? Nor is there a member of congress who would think eight hours too much when devoted to his own emolument. Nay they require of us *twenty* hours for their own use each day. But let us consider it in another point of view; suppose congress now sit 9 months in a year, their pay will then amount to 112,000 dollars pr. ann. in this calculation I make no mention of travel to, and from Congress, nor of the wages of the whole host of attendants upon Congress, "numerous as the sand upon the sea-shore."[2] If eight hours were employed instead of four, the business would be dispatched in one half the time, and of course 66,000 dollars saved to the union; a sum too large to be sported with, especially when the "sweat of your brows,"[3] my countrymen, must pay it. It would be more to our honor, as a nation, if this 66,000 were saved, and applied to relieve the distress of the widow, and the orphan, whom we have wickedly robbed, and whose "cries have entered into the ears of the Lord of Sabaoth."[4] The divine precept is, "Six days shalt thou labour, and do all thy work, but the seventh day," &c.[5] Congress seem to have abrogated this precept, and substituted the following for their own conduct, "One seventh part of your time shall ye labour and do all your work, for the nation, and the other six parts shall ye attend to all your amusements." We would prefer the command, as given originally from Mount-Sinai.

P. S. Tell Frederick[6] that in Proverbs the 26th chap. and 4th verse,[7] he may read my excuse for not answering him.

[New Haven] *Connecticut Journal*, 16 June; reprinted at Norwich, Connecticut, and Philadelphia. For information on this series and its author, see the location note to A Republican to Messrs. Printers (No. 1), 15 May, above.

---

[1] The John Street theater, a crude wooden structure between Broadway and Nassau Street, was New York City's only theater from 1767 until 1774, and again from 1785 until the Old American Company moved to Philadelphia, where it began a regular theatrical season in the fall of 1790 at the newly remodeled Old Southwark theater at South Street between Fourth and Fifth.

[2] A paraphrase of Genesis 22:17.

[3] A paraphrase of Genesis 3:19.

[4] James 5:4.

[5] Exodus 20:9–10.

[6] See the piece so signed, 26 May, above.

[7] Answer not a fool according to his folly, lest thou also be like unto him.

Letter from New York

The resolution of the House of Representatives for the adjournment to Baltimore, was sent up this morning to the Senate, and after a short debate was postponed til this day fortnight.

Rhode Island Senators were elected last Wednesday, Mr. [*Jonathan*] Hazard and Mr. Foster. They are expected here this day or to-morrow, and are said to be both in favor of New-York.

PP, 17 June. The letter was written in the afternoon. Virtually identical letters appeared in newspapers at York, Pennsylvania; Baltimore; and Alexandria and Fredericksburg, Virginia.

Letter from Berlin, Maryland

I was informed that you had been making inquiries respecting the success of the Potowmac company, in making that river navigable, and the prospect of rendering the different waters that fall into it, from the upper country, useful in bringing produce into it, on its way to market through the Great Falls, at a future day. It is with much pleasure I can inform you, that there are not less than twenty five boats many of them of considerable burden, daily employed from Fort Cumberland [*Cumberland, Maryland*] and other places above this, carrying tobacco, flour, hemp, &c. to the Great Falls; new ones constantly appearing, and, from every information, a great number on the stocks. The navigation is already very easy, and extremely useful, and there remains not a doubt of its being shortly made more so, and that the transportation of country-produce down, and imported articles up the river, will be as moderate and safe as could be wished. To this I must add, that a boat with six people in her, on Monday last, came to this place through the Shanandoah, from near Staunton [*Virginia*]. Their business was to explore that river and down into Potowmac, and report to the gentlemen who employed them, whether it was practicable to improve the Shanandoah, so as to make the navigation of it into the Potowmac useful. They informed me it could be done very easily, and would report accordingly on their return. The people of this neighbourhood are preparing a petition to the next Assembly for an inspection of tobacco; no doubt it will be granted, and in the course of a short time we shall have a great inspection of the finest tobacco.

[Alexandria] *Virginia Gazette*, 24 June; reprinted at New York City (*NYDA*, 5 July); Philadelphia and York, Pennsylvania; and Charleston, South Carolina.

Other Documents

Elias Boudinot to William Bradford. No copy known; acknowledged in Bradford to Boudinot, 17 June.

John Brown Cutting to John Adams. ALS, Adams Family Manuscript Trust, MHi. Written from London.

Encloses, sent via Boston, newspapers and George III's speech on the dissolution of Parliament; general European war expected; reports Britain's vigorous naval mobilization on the "pretext" of the Nootka Sound affair, with Prussia, Poland, Turkey, Sweden, and The Netherlands allied in a "hostile confederacy" with Britain against Russia, Austria, Portugal, Denmark, and Spain; no person of sense thinks Britain is risking such a widespread war because of Nootka Sound alone; would not be surprised by British naval advances on the Baltic, the Mediterranean, and the West Indies before September; will write more via Gravesend (England) the next day.

Alexander Hamilton to Robert Morris. No copy known; mentioned by Maclay (*DHFFC* 9:293) as stating that Hamilton "cannot think of negotiating about the temporary Residence. That his Friends will not hear of it."

Benjamin Huntington to William Ellery. No copy known; acknowledged in Ellery to Huntington, 21 June.

John Manley to John Langdon. ALS, Langdon Papers, NhPoS. Written from Boston. For the full text, see *Langdon*, pp. 110–11. Manley never petitioned the FFC.

Requests support for his intended petition to Congress for compensation for service (in the Continental Navy); also requests a letter of recommendation to Washington, whom he intends to visit.

Governor Charles Pinckney to James Madison. ALS, Madison Papers, DLC. Written from Charleston, South Carolina. For the full text, see *PJM* 13:242–43.

Acknowledges Madison's letter with enclosures, per John Deas; apologizes for neglect in writing, but intends to maintain a correspondence; encloses a copy of the new South Carolina constitution and describes some of its provisions.

Thomas Robison to George Thatcher. ALS, Chamberlain Collection, MB. Written from Portland, Maine; franked.

Recalls their last conversation, when he endorsed Thatcher's suggestion of recommending John Frothingham for federal excise officer at Portland, Maine; as he understands that Washington's policy is to retain state officers if not objectionable, he recommends the present state excise collector at Portland, Ebenezer Mays, instead, and Frothingham for "that place" at Stroudswater, Maine, currently held by Mr. Frost, who is expected to die soon.

Philip Schuyler to Jeremiah Olney. No copy known; mentioned in Schuyler to William Allen, 16 June.

Jeremiah Wadsworth to Thomas Seymour. No copy known; acknowledged in Seymour to Wadsworth, 19 June.

Regards Seymour's replacement of William Imlay as commissioner of loans for Connecticut.

George and Martha Washington to Abigail and John Adams. AN, Adams Family Manuscript Trust, MHi.

Invitation to dinner on Thursday (17 June) at 4 P.M.

Daniel Hiester, Account Book. PRHi.

Attended "Monday Club,"or Mess Day, at Fraunces Tavern with the Pennsylvania delegation; Maclay indicated that he did not attend until 5 P.M. but stayed until after 8 P.M. (*DHFFC* 9:293).

PP, 14 June.

"A gentleman who arrived in town last Saturday, from New-York, informs, that the House of Representatives of the United States, had resolved, on Friday, to hold their next session at Baltimore, but that it was expected the Senate would not concur."

NYDG, 15 June.

On a motion, the Senate's consideration of the House resolution to adjourn to Baltimore was postponed for two weeks, by a vote of 13 to 11.

GUS, 19 June.

Jackson presented an address from the Hebrew Congregation of Savannah, Georgia, to the President.

TUESDAY, 15 JUNE 1790

Hot (Johnson); *Very warm* (J. B. Johnson)

Thomas Dwight to Theodore Sedgwick

On your assurances, in regard to the assumption, we are led to have a more sure and certain hope of its taking place ultimately—I congratulate you on the conduct of our General Court [*legislature*] in this business—to me I confess so much was unexpected—the speech of Govr. H.[1] foreboded no great good, but he is not always the best judge of the general sentiments of the people. His doubts whether Congress has ~~any business~~ right to assume without the interference and consent of recommendation of the several Legislatures of the States, is really a striking demonstration of the profundity of his political wisdom.

The failure of [*Ebenezer*] Kingsley has swept our little parish of property to the amount of 2500 dollars specie, among the losers are Colo. [*Jonathan*]

Smith—Jona. Dwight—Alex Bliss—and a widow White besides others—I cannot but believe, that the fellow carried off large sums in paper or specie—for almost every man in the Counties of Hampshire & Berkshire who had money or paper is his creditor—I have been informed that you was surety for him in a bond for a very considerable amt. that you had taken a mortgage for your security—but Genl. [*Caleb*] Hyde of your Countey was here the last week and informs me that the lands ~~of~~ which were conveyed to you were attached for large sums, by several different persons, before your deed was upon record—is all this true God forbid.[2] It is matter of astonishment to all of us, how or by what kind of address Kingsley got so much property and from so many persons, into his hands without having his credit in the least doubted or suspected.

When will Congress adjourn? as much as the people talk of compensations—I cannot believe that yours has so many charms with it as to make your confinement to publick business for so long a time easy and agreeable to you—this kind of life to be sure has its pleasures, but to a man who takes an active part, and feels interested in the event of national conduct and politicks, it has its thousand vexations—For all your labors I wish you may have the blessings of the people and late find your reward in Heaven—for the latter you stand at least as good a chance as the former—the body of the people are not prone to gratitude.

I have been preaching—forgive me I am not apt to do it; having no great confidence in my abilities for such a work.

ALS, Sedgwick Papers, MHi. Written from Springfield, Massachusetts.

---

[1] Governor John Hancock's speech to the Massachusetts General Court on 1 June (printed in [Boston] *Massachusetts Centinel*, 2 June). That body subsequently passed a joint resolution instructing the state's Senators and urging the House delegation to support assumption; the resolution, sent under a cover letter by Hancock, is printed under 4 June, above.

[2] In 1788, Ebenezer Kingsley, Joseph Chaplin, and Stockbridge tavern keeper Anna Bingham (1745–1829) borrowed for one year $11,000 worth of final settlement certificates and indents from Thomas Jenkins (1741–1808), a wealthy merchant from Hudson, New York. Sedgwick pledged to Jenkins to "hold himself *fully* bound *with* them, by any contract *they* should form on the subject." Kingsley and Chaplin "failed" a little over a year later, without repaying (undated memoranda, Sedgwick-Van Schaack Correspondence, MHi; *DHSCUS* 6:176–78, 183n). Sedgwick's surety may be related to a deed for land Kingsley conveyed to Sedgwick for $1,000 on 20 April 1790 (Sedgwick Family Papers, MHi).

William Ellery to Elbridge Gerry

The New Constitution being adopted by this State I can now with propriety request your influence that I may be appointed Collector of the Southern District in this State.

In my former letter I think I mentioned the office of District Judge as the object of my wishes. I have since relinquished that Idea, because I thought myself better qualified for the office of Collector than of a Judge, and that our mutual friend Mr. [*Henry*] Marchant would fill the Judge's chair with reputation to himself, and with honour to the United States.

I am not unacquainted with mercantile business, and I was a Naval Officer of this State when it was under the British Government.

If by your influence and that of my other friends I should be so happy as to obtain my wishes I shall endeavour to conduct myself in such a manner, as not cause you or them to regret their recommendation.

Our Senators I expect will be at New York by the middle of next week. One of them (Mr. Foster of Providence) is a modest, ingenious man—the other (Mr. Stanton of Charlestown) I am not acquainted with; but he is not perfectly esteemed by my acquaintances.

They have no instructions from the Legislature; but I imagin they will both consider themselves bound by the third article of the amendments proposed by the Convention to oppose the assumption of the State Debts. Indeed the latter is so strongly attached to the party who procured the Act forfeiting the State Securities[1] which should not at the periods prescribed by that act be exchanged for paper bills at par, that, the article alluded to aside, he would without doubt be against the Assumption. As some of our State securities have been exchanged for paper bills, and the rest are forfeited the Inhabitants of this State in general are averse to that measure; but they whose securities have been so unrighteously forfeited will never sit down contented with their losses.

As long as the State Debts are unassumed we shall not enjoy peace in this State. The holders of State securities will strenuously endeavour to obtain an administration which will do them justice, and the sticklers for the forfeiting act will as strenuously contend for a legislature that will support that act. and I presume that the State Creditors throughout the Union will never be at ease until the State Debts are assumed. These considerations alone, if there were no other in favour of it would induce me to wish for an Assumption. I recollect that under the Old Confederation there were sometimes opposite sentiments on very important subjects; but that perseverance in what was well founded was finally successful.

~~By~~ The act passed at the late Session of our General Assembly prescribing the mode of chusing a Representative[2] has rendered it impossible that the people should be represented in this Session of Congress.

Please to present my regards to Col. Partridge and all the gentlemen of your State, to father Sherman, old [*Abiel*] Foster, and all my old congressional acquaintances.

I should be happy in a more frequent epistolary intercourse with you.

ALS, The Gilder Lehrman Collection, on Deposit at the New York Historical Society, New York. [GLC 1497] Written from Newport, Rhode Island.

[1] "An Act for paying off the whole of the State Securities," passed in March 1789.

[2] According to Rhode Island's first federal election law, enacted on 12 June, town meetings were to vote on 31 August and the returns submitted to the subsequent meeting of the state legislature. Any runoff would take place ten days after the legislature's adjournment (*DHFFE* 4:409–10).

Richard Bland Lee to Theodorick Lee

Your friendly letter from Alexandria [*Virginia*] of the 6th. Instant arrived some days ago: but I was so unwell at that time that I could not immediately answer it. Your line of Conduct relative to me is perfectly affectionate and proper.

I am glad to hear that the prospects of a wheat crop have very much improved, and that the other crops are in as promising a way as could be expected I wrote to you some days ago to sell ~~my~~ the lot of land in possession of Mr. Sears, and to remit to me the money. I had written to Mr. W[*illiam?*]. Lane offering it to him. tis of importance to me to receive £200 Virginia money before I leave N. York—which I begin to apprehend will not be till the middle of July or ~~begin~~ first of august. But the sooner this object can be accomplished the more important will be the service to me. Write to me your prospects on this business immediately and excuse ~~this~~ the trouble I have imposed on you. Perhaps this money may be borrowed for a few months—which would give time to make a better bargain. These transactions had better be as private as possible.

I have purchased in the New-York lottery[1] two tickets for you to wit. No. 9332 & No. 9333 and two for Mr. Robert Carter Vizt. No. 9334 & 9335—which I will either forward by letter or bring with me to Virginia as may be desired.

A Removal of ~~the~~ Congress to another place as a temporary residence has been attempted. Philadelphia was the object. It was first carried in the house of Representatives, and failed in the Senate. It was again attempted in the house of Representatives and there failed. Philadelphia being struck out of the Resolution and Baltimore inserted. The Resolution in favor of Baltimore then passed by a vote of 53 against 6. This great majority was produced by the New-York intere[*s*]ts—voting for Baltimore to frustrate the hopes of Philadelphia—their votes added to the votes of those who were anxious for a more southern position produced so unexpected an event. This Resolution was sent to the Senate and would have passed yesterday if the Senators of either of the three southern states had acted in concert with their Brethren.

~~As~~ The Consideration is now postponed for a fortnight—in which time the R. Island Senators will be here—and machinations may be formed to defeat totally the object: either absolutely—or by a compromise which may establish the permanent seat of government in a station very unfriendly to the Southern Interests.

Inform me whether a side board—two dining tables two card tables, and a small chest of Hyson tea have yet arrived at Sully.

Deliver the inclosed to Mr. [*George?*] Shivelley.

[*P. S.*] The newspapers will have informed that our very valuable Relation Col. Bland paid the debt of nature on the 1st. Instant—and that every proper respect was paid to his remains.

ALS, Custis-Lee Family Papers, DLC. Addressed "By way of Alexandria" to "Sully, Loudoun [*County*], Virginia"; franked; postmarked.

---

[1] Government sponsored lotteries were a prominent feature in the economy of the early Republic, despite some moral opposition. The Lottery of the United States had helped finance the Revolutionary War, and even Hamilton's report on public credit recommended a type of lottery—the tontine—as an alternative for subscribers to the public debt. Lotteries were resorted to in postwar New York City, as elsewhere, to help finance public works and public charities. On 4 March 1790, the New York City Common Council adopted a lottery scheme to raise £7,500 to help defray the outstanding debt from its largest public works project to date: the conversion of its City Hall into Federal Hall in 1788–89. On 15 March it advertised the sale of 25,000 tickets at forty shillings each, of which 8,346 tickets drew prizes ranging from one £3,000 award to 7,950 £4 awards. Drawing commenced on 5 August and ran until 3 September. On 27 August the Council approved a second lottery to defray an additional £5,500 of the debt, with drawings to commence on 3 January 1791 (*Iconography* 5:1262; *NYDA*, 15 March, 6 September).

Abraham Ogden to Elias Boudinot

***

You may recollect that in February last you was so obliging as to present a Petition to Congress from [*James*] Perry & [*Thomas*] Hayes[1]—It was then refer'd to the Secretary of the Treasury—From that Time it has slept in his Office.

My Clients Messrs. Perry & Hayes are extreamly pressing upon me for the Result of this application—Upon that Result, the Commissioners in England[2] will report on the Claim of Perry & Hayes to Parliament—And until it is known the Commissioners decline making any Report—In August next the Door is closed agt. any future Reports from the Commissioners in England.

Under these Circumstances, I hope the Secretary will be induced to report upon this Petition without further Delay—The Petitioners have suffered great Loss & Injury—The United States are bound by the Treaty [*of Paris,*

1783] to make Restitution *They* are Foreigners, & have therefore Claims upon the Policy as well as the Justice of the United States—Will you be so obliging as to call on the Secretary & let me have his Answer.

If it be necessary in the further Progress of this Business—I can call the Attention of Sedgwick, Ames, Smith (S.C.) & Benson to the Petition—But I hope you will need none of them—The Secretary's Report taken up in Congress by you will readily pass the House.

The Fate of this Petition I have much at Heart—Let me intreat the Favor of your fostering it, in it's Way to & thro', Congress [*torn*] You know well, that it is founded in Equity or I should not thus address you on the Subject.

ALS, AMs 779, PPRF. Written from Newark, New Jersey. The omitted text describes Ogden's frustration with Boudinot's failure to provide assistance to their clients at a legal hearing in New Jersey on 11 June.

---

[1] For background on Perry and Hayes's petition for compensation for supplies impressed during the Revolutionary War, see *DHFFC* 7:83–84.

[2] Great Britain's American Claims Commission examined £10,360,000 worth of claims from 3,225 claimants during investigations conducted in England and Canada between 1783 and 1789, finally awarding £3,033,000 to 2,291 Loyalists as compensation for services rendered, or property or income lost during the Revolution (Hugh E. Egerton, *Royal Commission on the Losses and Services of American Loyalists, 1783 to 1785* [Oxford, 1915], p. xl).

Samuel Phillips, Jr. to Benjamin Goodhue

Your Favor of the 10th. instt. I have just recd. received & for this as well as the last preceeding & many others return you many thanks; your doubtful apprehensions for the fate of the assumption, are alarming—if it dont take place at the present Session, will not the prospect of it's success be still less at the next; on account of the accession of R. Island, that's being the *last* Session before a *new election*, and the attempt that will be made to obtain instructions from the Legislatures of other States; what will be our ~~Situa~~ fate, in case of a failure, it is hard to predict—In the last session of the G[*eneral*]. Court [*legislature*] the excise was lowered 2/3 or thereabouts, but ~~ma~~ provision made for a more compleat & general collection; At the present Session, Petitions are presented from Boston (with 1070 signers) Salem & the prencipal trading towns, haveing upward of 1600 subscribers in the whole, & consisting of as respectable people as any in them, for opulence & influence, urging a repeal of the excise act—a Commee. of both houses to whom these petitions have been committed, reported in favr. of a repeal; This afternoon is the second that has been spent in discussing the question in Senate; two or three previous questions which have been taken, shew that there will not be a greater majority, than of one or two, on either side—if a repeal should be the result, it will be from a conviction, that [*lined out*] it will be impracticable to carry the act into effect, and the members from the Country say it will be in vain to think of discharging the Interest of the public debt by direct taxes, what then is to be the consequence?

The observations you have an Oppy. of making are enough to awaken all your resentment, but you will have wisdom & fortitude enough to suppress those feelings, and patience yet to persevere as well as to engage others to unite their endeavours with yours—and if ever the point is carried, it must be by other means, than by exertions of eloquence in the face of crouded Galleries—what do our Brethen expect or desire of us? do not the Returns from the public Offices, shew our exertions in the time of the war? Have not we gone so far in taxing the people since the war, as to hazard the existence of the Government, in the late [*Shays'*] Rebellion? and what would have [*been*] the fate of the other Goverments, if the Scale, which for some time was in equilibrio, had turned against us? and were there taxes to defray the expence of our internal Govt.? the salaries of our public Offices will determine this.

ALS, Letters to Goodhue, NNS. Written from Boston.

Thomas Thompson to John Langdon

I was in Boston the other day when the Court [*legislature*] pass'd an act to give up the light Houses to the United States (ours I suppose will follow their example) this being the Case—it naturally follows that Commissioners or Inspectors of Lights Buoys, Beacons piers &c. &c. will of Course be appointed—for certain districts—New Engd. will doubtless form one—and those persons should be men experienced in nautical—and Marine affairs who should be every way Compentent to Judge of the Properiety of placing lights Buoys &c. &c. of the repairs attending &c.—and viset in a small vessel every port and Harbor on the Coast within their department.

As Self Intrest, in some measure Governs all mankind, and more or less Influences their conduct—you will readily observe that I mean to recomend your Humble Servant to be one of those very Commisoners; and am confident, if it were in your Gift. I should have the appointment (were their any such) and I flatter myself, that my experience and abilities would enable me to discharge the trust with properiety and advantage to the public (I cannot think the lights &c. ought to remain under the directions of the Collectors?) you are in every respect a Competent Judge of all those matters therfore needless to sugest to you the properiety of such an arrangement being made soon as posible for the good and Safiety of Trade & navigation—This or some other place, you must procure me before you leave Congress or I am a lost man to my friends and the Community for at present I cannot, nor do I see any way to mentain my Famely in which I am moste Compleatly blessd *** my only wish is to live with my famely *constantly*, next House to Mr. Langdon *** I have a great mind to come to [*New*] York but suppose you may have set out for home before I could reach that City? you ask the news? here—A dull malencholly Silence reigns—throut the Town—a Sperit of Intrigue, Injustice, pivat party and Self Intrest pervades the Genl. [*Court*]—at Concord [*New Hampshire legislature*] of whom you have better Information from other hands then I can give you—I wish you were more united, and more decisive in Congress—then you appear to be—otherwise I think you must have a long Sessions—however we hope it will end with Honour and advantage to the public—for my own part I am satisfyd to confide in the wisdom, Honour and Integrity of that great National assembly.

P. S. You will pardon me for Trespassing on your time.

ALS, Langdon Papers, NhPoA. Written from Portsmouth, New Hampshire. The omitted text relates the personal and financial circumstances that caused Thompson to request the appointment.

Jeremiah Wadsworth to George Washington

I am requested by Captn. William Littlefield and his friends to Name him to You as a proper person to be appointed Marshall for the district of Rhode Island I should not have complied with this request if I had a shadow of doubt of Mr. Littlefields fitness for the office.

ALS, Washington Papers, DLC. Littlefield had mentioned Wadsworth as a reference in an application to Washington, 24 September 1789 (ALS, Washington Papers, DLC).

George Washington to David Stuart

***

Your description of the public mind, in Virginia, gives me pain. It seems to be more irritable, sour & discontented than (from the information I receive) it is in any other state in the Union, except Massachusetts; which, from the same causes, but on quite different principles, is tempered like it.

That Congress does not proceed with all that dispatch which people at a distance expect; and which, were they to hurry business, they possibly might; is not to be denied. That measures have been agitated wch. are not pleasing to Virginia—and others, pleasing perhaps to her, but not so to some other States; is equally unquestionable. Can it well be otherwise in a Country so extensive, so diversified in its interests? And will not these different interests naturally produce in an assembly of Representatives who are to Legislate for, and to assimilate & reconcile them to the general welfare, long, warm & animated debates? most undoubtedly; and if there was the same propensity in Mankind to investigate the motives, as there is for censuring the conduct of public characters, it would be found that the censure so freely bestowed is oftentimes unmerited, and uncharitable—for instance, the condemnation of Congress for sitting only four hours in the day. The fact is, by the established rules of the House of Representatives, no Committee can sit whilst the House is sitting; and this is, and has been for a considerable time, from ten o'clock in the forenoon until three, often later, in the afternoon before & after which the business is going on in Committees—If this application is not as much as most Constitutions are equal to I am mistaken. Many other things which undergo malignant constructions wd. be found, upon a candid examination, to wear other faces than are given to them. The misfortune is, that the enemies to the Government—always more active than its friends, and always upon the watch to give it a stroke—neglect no opportunity to aim one—If they tell truth, it is not the whole truth; by which means one side only of the picture appears; whereas if both sides were exhibited it might, and probably would assume a different form in the opinions of just & candid men who are disposed to measure matters by a Continental Scale. I do not mean however, from what I have here said, to justify the conduct of Congress in all its movements; for some of these movements in my opinion, have been injudicious, & others unseasonable, whilst the questions of Assumption—Residence—and other matters have been agitated with a warmth & intemperence; with prolixity & threats; which it is to be feared has lessened the dignity of that body, & decreased that respect which was once entertained for it. And this misfortune is encreased by many members, even among those who wish well to the Government, ascribing in letters to their respective States when they are unable to carry a favourite measure, the worst motives for the conduct of their opponants; who, viewing matters through a different medium may, & do retort in their turn; by which means jealousies & distrusts are spread most impolitickly, far & wide; & will, it is to be feared have a most unhappy tendency to injure our public affairs—which, if wisely conducted might make us (as we are now by Europeans thought to be) the happiest people upon Earth. As an evidence of it, our reputation has risen in every part of the Globe; and our credit, especially in Holland, has got higher than that of *any* Nation in Europe (& where our funds are above par) as appears by *Official* advices just received. But the conduct we seem to be pursuing will soon bring us back to our late disreputable condition.

The introduction of the (Quaker) Memorial, respecting Slavery,[1] was to be sure, [*lined out*] not only an ill-judged piece of business, but occasioned a great waste of time. The final decision thereon, however, was as favourable as the proprietors of that species of property could well have expected considering the great dereliction to Slavery ~~by~~ in a large part of this Union.

The question of Assumption has occupied a great deal of time, & no wonder; for it is certainly a very important one; and, under *proper* restrictions, & scrutiny into accounts will be found, I conceive, to be just. ~~The~~ [*lined out*] ~~Congress~~ [*lined out*] The Cause in which the expences of the War was incurred, was a Common Cause. The States (in Congress) declared it so at the beginning and pledged themselves to stand by each other. If then some States were harder pressed than others, or from particular or local circumstances contracted heavier debts, it is but reasonable when this fact is ascertained (though it is a sentiment I have not made known here) that an allowance ought to be made them when due credit is given to others—Had the invaded, and hard pressed States believed the case would have been otherwise; opposition in them would very soon, I believe, have changed to submission; and given a different termination to the War.

In a letter of last year[2] to the best of my recollection, I informed you of the motives, which *compelled* me to allot a day for the reception of idle and ceremonious visits (for it never has prevented those of sociability and friendship in the afternoon, or at any other time) but if I am mistaken in this, the history of this business is simply and shortly as follows—Before the custom was established, which now accommodates foreign characters, Strangers, and others who from motives of curiosity, respect, to the Chief Magistrate, or any other cause, are induced to call upon me—I was unable to attend to any business *whatsoever*; for Gentlemen, consulting their own convenience rather than mine, were calling from the time I rose from breakfast—often before—until I sat down to dinner—This, as I resolved not to neglect my public duties, reduced me to the choice of one of these alternatives, either to refuse them *altogether*, or to appropriate a time for the reception of them—The first would, I well knew, be disgusting to many—The latter, *I expected*, would undergo animadversion, and blazoning from those who would find fault, *with*, or *without* cause. To please every body was impossible—I therefore adopted that line of conduct which combined public advantage with private convenience, and which in my judgment was unexceptionable in itself. That I have not been able to make bows to the taste of poor Colonel Bland,[3] (who by the by I believe never saw one of them) is to be regretted especially too as (upon those occasions) they were indiscriminately bestowed, and the best I was master of—would it not have been better to have thrown the veil of charity over them, ascribing their stiffness to the effects of age, or to the unskilfulness of my teacher, than to pride and dignity of office, which God knows has no charms for me? for I can truly say I had rather be at Mount Vernon with a friend or two about me, than to be attended at the Seat of Government by the Officers of State and the Representatives of every Power in Europe—These visits are optional—They are made without invitation—Between the hours of three and four every Tuesday I am prepared to receive them—Gentlemen—often in great numbers—come and go—chat with each other—and act as they please. A Porter shews them into the room, and they retire from it when they please, and without ceremony. At their *first* entrance they salute me, and I them, and as many as I can talk to I do—what pomp there is in all this I am unable to discover—Perhaps it consists in not sitting—To this two reasons are opposed, first it is unusual—secondly, (which is a more substantial one) because I have no room large enough to contain a third of the chairs, which would be sufficient to admit it—If it is supposed that ostentation, or the fashions of courts (which by the by I believe originates oftner in convenience, not to say necessity than is generally imagined) gave rise to this custom, I will boldly affirm that *no* supposition was ever more erroneous; for, if I was to give indulgence to my inclinations, every moment that I could withdraw from the fatigues of my station should be spent in retirement—That they are not proceeds from the sense I entertain of the propriety of giving to every one as free access, as consists with that respect which is due to the chair of government—and that respect I conceive is neither to be acquired or preserved but by observing a just medium between much state and too great familiarity.

Similar to the above, but of a more familiar and sociable kind are the visits every friday afternoon to Mrs. Washington where I always am—These public meetings and a dinner once a week to as many as my table will hold with the references *to* and *from* the different Departments of State, and *other* communications with *all* parts of the Union is as much, if not more, than I am able to undergo, for I have already had within less than a year, two *severe* attacks—the last worse than the first—a third more than probable will put me to sleep with my fathers; at what distance this may be I know not. Within the last twelve months I have undergone more, and severer sickness than thirty preceding years afflicted me with, put it altogether—I have abundant reason however to be thankful that I am so well recovered; though I still feel the remains of the violent affection of my lungs—The cough, pain in my breast, and shortness in breathing not having entirely left me. I propose in the recess of Congress to visit Mount Vernon—but when this recess will happen is beyond my ken, or the ken I believe of any of its members.

AL, damaged and incomplete, ViU; missing text, including the last three paragraphs, from FC:lbk, Washington Papers, DLC. Addressed to Virginia.

---

[1] See *DHFFC* 8:314–38. The COWH report on the petitions simply summarized Congress's limited powers to regulate the slave trade.

[2] Portions of Washington's letter to Stuart, 26 July 1789, describe his efforts to develop a presidential protocol (*PGW* 3:321–27).

[3] Stuart's letter to Washington, 2 June, above, disclosed that Bland was said to have described the President's levees as more stiff and full of pomp than those at Great Britain's Court of St. James's.

Hugh Williamson to John Gray Blount

Having seen the Appointments lately made you will presume that my Mind is relieved from any Anxiety respecting our Western Territory. The Cession being accepted and Govt. established I am now only to consider how the Current of Migration shall best be turned towards the Tenessee Govt. that so the Value of our Land may be improved or increased. Lieut. Long at Halifax to whom I sent a Subscription Paper for the Map has sent me no Answer. Your Brother Jacob [*Blount*] got none at Edenton from Newbern & Wilmington I have not heard but fear that little is done. Wish nevertheless to publish the Map and Analisis, describing the best mode of going to that Country and to whom Application is to be made for Land—For the present general Complaint is that Emigrants when the[*y*] arrive, say at Kentucke, cannot find Land, unless perhaps at a very extravagant Price.

I hope that you will agree to serve at least in the next Genl. Assembly of our State. You see by late Appointments how many useful Members are removed. Perhaps some disappointed factions Incendiary may, among new Members [*lined out*] who are incautious, attempt some Mischief. My Object is if possible to have Justice done the State in settling her Accots. An Office is soon to be disposed of in the State, which Col. [*Abishai*] Thomas wishes to obtain; in this Pursuit he certainly is right, but if he gets that Office, who is to mannage our Accounts? In fact I would rather hold on by the Charge of the public Accounts than give up that Trust for a Seat in next Congress. I hope that in Congress I shall during this Session have served the State essentially on the Head of its Accounts, and that future Occasion for similar Exertions will not occur. If Thomas goes out I should wish that the State would allow me to employ one Clerk or two @ 500 Dlrs.; for every one of our Accounts must be stated over in a new Mode else we shall lose near one Million of Dlrs. under the Head of Militia Claims. I perceive that every State will have one or more Agents here & they are sending forward Men on whose Steadiness and Abilities they have most Dependance; to be a meer Accountant is not sufficient. If the State employs an Agent incapable of supporting a System, meerly because such Agent may serve cheap, they must be saving units & losing Thousands. The Continental Agents have £900 ℔ Ann. in Specie, we have only £760 in Paper. Under all those disadvantages I would try to finish the Work. I wrote the Governor that I should keep my

Eye steadily on the Accounts of the State though I had accepted a Seat in Congress but should not expect any Pay from the State for any Services I might render while serving in Congress. In fact the Service in Congress is to a Person who takes such Portion of the Burden as I do, a most painful Drudgery, having done what I had much at Heart, I would now retire of Choice provided no twist is given to the other Office. You will nevertheless consider that what I have here said is only intended for your own Information.

ALS, John Gray Blount Papers, Nc-Ar. Place to which addressed not indicated.

Paine Wingate to Jeremy Belknap

I have not time to write to you but a line. I have this day recd. the enclosed ~~the~~ letter which with pleasure I forward to my respected friend. The Senate have spent this day in discussing the funding bill but have come to no decision. It has been moved to strike out the several alternatives & to propose a loan of 4 pr. Cent. & pledge the faith of government to those who *do not* subscribe ~~to~~ that their old contracts shall remain good—What will be the result I cannot tell, & do not think it worth while to conjecture. I am weary of dissentions & disputes. I hope very soon to be released from the task of being here; & to have the pleasure of seeing you & the rest of my friends well on my return.

ALS, Belknap Papers, MHi. Addressed to Boston; franked; postmarked.

Letter from Guilford County, North Carolina

I have just received papers from Petersburgh [*Virginia*], which inform me of the proceedings of Congress relative to this date. The courts to be held exclusively at Newbern[1]—this is strange indeed! but not more so, than that every office of importance should be bestowed upon men living in Edenton, Newbern and Halifax. Is this because the President has been imposed upon, and induced to believe that Wilmington, Fayetteville, Hillsborough, Salisbury and Morgan districts afford no characters worthy of public confidence? Or that men are recommended to the President, not on account of abilities and integrity, but on account of their local situations? Is it because the people in the Eastern parts of the state are better born? Or that we, merely for the sake of Federalism, have been simple enough to allow them both the Senators?[2] If it has been alledged that we are not as well attached to orderly and regular government, you can correct the mistake. If it has been said, that people in these districts which are now neglected, and disclaimed, are not the majority of the state; the fact relative to our seat of government will be a sufficient answer, for it is fixed at Fayetteville, in defiance of the *Eastern Junto*, and shall remain there forever. If it has been said that we are not the strength of the state—Lord Cornwallis, has given an unequivocal answer, when he said that the Western part of North-Carolina contained the bravest, and most rebellious set of people, that he had ever met with in America.[3] If our Senators are not disposed to recommend any man among us that has been opposed to the constitution for an office, they might at least recollect that we have some men of real abilities who were uniformly federalists, and who interested themselves, from the beginning in order to establish this government.

We have been informed that a committee of the house of representatives have reported an alteration in the main post road,[4] so as to make it pass by Fayetteville, through the centre of the state, and that the house will probably concur. This would be highly pleasing to us, but if the Senate acts uniformly, they will reject it also. We have been told that it is a prevailing maxim in that *most honorable body*, that the ease by which people may be governed, is in exact proportion to their ignorance. Our senators I hope will never subscribe such damnable opinions. If the disposition of the locality so early discovered, should continue, we must submit to it, but time will afford us a remedy.

NYDA, 7 July; reprinted at Philadelphia; Baltimore; and Edenton, North Carolina.

[1] Under the North Carolina Judiciary Act.

[2] North Carolina's principal base of Federalism was the tidewater northeastern counties, including Johnston's home county of Chowan. Hawkins's Piedmont county of Warren, which had been overwhelmingly Antifederalist in 1788, joined the Federalist majority supporting ratification of the Constitution in late 1789.

[3] Until its surrender at Yorktown in late 1781, the British army under Charles Lord Cornwallis (1738–1805) suffered the most serious setbacks of its southern campaign in battles either in North Carolina or with North Carolina troops, including King's Mountain, Cowpens, and Guilford Courthouse.

[4] Under the Post Office Bill [HR-74].

Other Documents

John M. Binford to John Steele. ALS, Steele Papers, Nc-Ar. Written from Northampton County, North Carolina. For the full text, see *Steele* 1:62–63.

Office seeking: superintendent of federal revenue for North Carolina; as he is already well known to Steele, considers letters of recommendation unnecessary; mentions Ashe as reference.

Pierce Butler to James Seagrove. No copy known; acknowledged in Seagrove to Butler, 8 August.

William Constable to Gouverneur Morris. FC:lbk, Constable-Pierrepont Collection, NN.

Has some "serious Apprehension" that the session will end without more than a temporary provision for the public debt.

William Samuel Johnson to Anne Johnson. ALS, Johnson Papers, CtHi. Addressed to Stratford, Connecticut; written in the evening; franked.

Has nothing new to report; everyone is well; Morgan and Edwin (servants?) "make out to cook for us very well, but the latter runs away almost daily as soon as Dinner is over & Gilly is not returned from Fish Kill" (New York).

John Langdon to Nathaniel Rogers. No copy known; acknowledged in Rogers to Langdon, 3 July.

Ebenezer Mayo to George Thatcher. ALS, Chamberlain Collection, MB. Written from Portland, Maine; franked.

Office seeking: federal excise collector for Maine district; supposes approval of the proper candidate rests with Thatcher.

Nathaniel Phillips to George Washington. ALS, Washington Papers, DLC. Written from Warren, Rhode Island. For the full text, see *PGW* 5:523.

Office seeking: surveyor for ports of Warren and Barrington, Rhode Island; Foster and Stanton are in possession of a recommendation on his behalf, signed by inhabitants of Warren, ratification convention delegation, and state legislators from Barrington.

David Meade Randolph to Thomas Jefferson. ALS, Washington Papers, DLC. Written from Presquile, Virginia; postmarked Richmond, Virginia, 16 June. For a partial text, see *PTJ* 16:509.

Office seeking: William Heth for commissioner of loans and for Randolph to succeed him as collector at Bermuda Hundred; his application for that office, when it was first being considered, vainly relied upon the friendship of several members of Congress; his friend Walker has forwarded him a copy of the Funding Bill, which prompted "the above sentiments."

Stephen Sayre to Henry Knox. ALS, Knox Papers, Gilder Lehrman Collection, NHi. Written from No. 10, Great St. Helen's, London.

By the same conveyance, has written to "my old friends" Izard and Floyd, regarding propositions for the improvement of naval vessels; asks that Knox consult with them on the subject "& lend them your assistance";

"They may not think proper to give you any trouble in the matter, unless you are kind enough to mention it to them."

George Thatcher to Shearjashub Bourne. No copy known; acknowledged in Bourne to Thatcher, 24 June.

Simeon Thayer to George Washington. ALS, Washington Papers, DLC. Written from Providence, Rhode Island; addressed care of T. Foster. For the full text, see *PGW* 5:528–29.

Office seeking: revenue officer or marshal in Rhode Island.

John Sevier, Journal. Claiborne Collection, Ms-Ar. (This journal, which details Sevier's 1790 trip to New York, includes his expenses en route.)

Arrived at New York City at 9 P.M. and lodged at "Stair Ferry" (probably named for the stairs where the Elizabethtown, New Jersey, ferry docked).

NYP, 17 June.

Public examination in Latin and Greek at Malcolm Campbell's Grammar School (at the foot of Cortlandt Street) attended by Johnson as president of Columbia College.

Wednesday, 16 June 1790

Fine (Johnson) *Warm, & fine wind* (J. B. Johnson)

Joshua Brackett to John Langdon

I understand there is a Commissioner with a Salary of eight hundred Dollars a year, soon to be appointed by Congress, for the State of N. Hampshire and I think you must be devoid of all resentment, if you suffer the office to be kept at Exeter, or the Officer to be taken out of that Town, if it is by any means in your power to prevent it; considering that people have always been against, and ever opposed you—and I think, you cannot have forgotten the mean and spitefull reflections lately cast upon you in Congress, by a member [*Gilman*] from that Town—his Brother [*Nathaniel Gilman*] I suppose is a Candidate for it—but I hope, you will use your utmost endeavours in the Senate, and your Influence with the President not only to prevent him, but to have your Brother [*Woodbury Langdon*] appointed to the office—he wants it—'twould do him good—he could attend to it without any Interference with his other bussiness; besides he is well qualified for it, & would be agreeable to the people—I have likewise been informed, you intend to leave Congress before the adjournment, & resign your Seat in the Senate—this I think unadvisable—& hope on due consideration you will see it in the light I do—to be highly impolitic; & give up, all thoughts of it—The loss of your abilites would not only be ruinous to this State, but very prejudicial to the whole union—your family are in health, and conduct well—your bussiness may be carried on without you—the hay shall have my attention therefore I hope you will continue till this Session is finished, for there was a good deal of mischeif done last year, by your leaving Congress before the rest of our Members—The expediency of your resignation *at all*, we shall have Leisure to investigate on your return.

***

Tho I have not been favoured for a long time with a line from my *old acquaintance*, I have had the pleasure of hearing by Mrs. Langdon of your wellfare 'tis reported here, that you are grown very fat & portly— ***

ALS, Langdon Papers, NhPoA. Written from Portsmouth, New Hampshire. The omitted text relates to state politics.

Newspaper Article

The question concerning the temporary residence of Congress has been viewed in different lights. While some consider it as of the utmost importance, others conceive it to be a matter of total indifference. Perhaps a medium between the two will be right. That the seat of government should be near the centre is on all hands admitted. No one wishes Congress to remove to Savannah or the province of Maine. But whether they should sit at New-York, Philadelphia or Baltimore, is a point upon which we cannot so readily agree. That Philadelphia is nearer the centre of population than either New-York or Baltimore can easily be shewn. On each side of it the number of senators is equal. The representatives from the eastward are 27 those from the southward are 30. To the eastward of New-York there are but 8 senators and 17 representatives, while to the southward there are 16 senators and 42 representatives. To the north and east of Baltimore there are 16 senators and 36 representatives, to the southward but 8 senators and 23 representatives. As representation is in proportion to population Philadelphia appears to be the most central situation. But if it can be shewn that a residence at Philadelphia will be less expensive to the union, it will be a more powerful argument in favour of this city. From New-York and beyond it the number of members which will come to this city is 33. The mileage from New-York to Philadelphia will be 30 dollars to each member every session. This will amount to 990 dollars. But on the other hand mileage of 30 dollars each will be deducted from 52 members to the southward, which will be 1560 dollars. Deduct from this 990 dollars and the remainder is 570 dollars saved to the union every session by a residence in Philadelphia. Allowing two sessions per annum, the annual saving will be 1140 dollars. Upon a comparison with Baltimore it will appear that the annual saving will be 720 dollars.

There is another circumstance worthy of notice. A number of our citizens from different parts of the states are obliged to visit the seat of federal government, to transact business of different kinds to attend the federal court; to solicit a mitigation of fines and forfeitures; to apply for patents for useful inventions; to make applications for different appointments under the general government; or to transact business at the treasury or in the war office. A central situation will be found most eligible on this account. New-York is too near to the northern extremity. The interest of the southern states requires the seat of government to be removed further south; and at the same time it is the interest of the eastern states that it should not be removed as far as Baltimore. Philadelphia is the medium which will suit the interests of both extremities of the union.

A want of confidence in Congress will be the certain consequence of staying, in an improper place; as it will be apparent, that this must be the fruit of undue influence, and if such influence is successful in a case of such moment, it may be expected to govern in every one.

Affecting to establish the permanent residence at a future day, does not go to remedy present inconveniences. It is saying to the sick man, wait two or three years and you shall be cured, to the hungry man, next year I will give you bread.

The inconveniences exist, and a free legislature ought to remedy them.

To fix the permanent residence by contract is unjustifiable in every point of view. It is treating the public like an unhappy person, locked up in a spunging-house;[1] stay here six or seven years, and consent to let us pillage you, or you shall not get away at all. Is this language fit for, or treatment proper to be offered to freemen?

The intercourse between New-York and the United States, is principally by water. All connection with the agricultural interest of the union is cut off, or nearly so. The inhabitants are merchants, or very generally engaged in some kind of speculation or other. If the members of Congress are to go by sea to the Federal residence, and be cooped up in an island, perhaps Bermudas will be found to be a more eligible situation than New-York. The members of Congress ought to travel to the federal residence by land. Thus they would become possessed of a knowledge, not only of their own state, but of the United States in general. And the residence should be fixed in a central position, to promote and facilitate this object.

FG, 16 June. This piece was composed by Benjamin Rush from notes Maclay sent him in a letter dated 5 June, above. See also Maclay to Rush, 18 June, below.

[1] In England, a house where persons arrested for debt were temporarily confined and "sponged" of their valuables before being sent to prison.

Letter from Baltimore

On my return to town, yesterday, I was favoured with your letter of the 10th inst. Before I got here, the vote of our senators, on the subject of the permanent residence of Congress, had reached the town. It gave more dissatisfaction to the citizens of Baltimore than I can express; indeed I never witnessed so general a sentiment, in the citizens, on any former occasion; in every company, at every corner, the subject of conversation was, "Have you heard how our senators have deserted us?" So universal is the disgust at their vote, that I verily believe, if the election of senators to represent Maryland was to take place to-morrow, there is scarce a man in Baltimore would give either of them a vote.

From Mr. C. [*Charles Carroll*] the citizens say they did not expect much, knowing his partiality to Annapolis; but they looked for a different conduct from Mr. H[*enry*]. There are two or three friends of his here, who try to excuse him, by saying that the proposals for fixing the permanent residence of Congress, first on the Patowmac, and then, when that was lost, in Baltimore, were not serious, but meant only to distract, in order to keep Congress in New York. Some gentlemen here, who have been in Charleston, say that Mr. B[*utler*]. who you mention to have brought in the bill, is much regarded and esteemed as a man of candor and independence, and a very influential man there. His colleague, Mr. I[*zard*]. they say, is also esteemed as a very independent man.

Supposing that Mr. B. had intended a parliamentary deception, yet that does not excuse the conduct of Messrs. C. and H. because, if the bill was meant to distract, they could not lose more by voting for it than by aiding to reject it; and if it succeeded, the advantages would have been great to this town. In short, the citizens will believe nothing else than that they betrayed them. I do not wish so ill to either of the gentlemen, though, as well as many others, a sufferer by their conduct, as to desire to see them here; so great is the ferment and so strong the passion of resentment, that I am persuaded they would meet with some insult. Is there no chance of retrieving the error?

I am sure, if these gentlemen expect to live happily in Maryland, they ought to try to bring on this business once more. As to the conduct of the Vir—n—a senators, people say, they expected nothing good from Col.

R. H. L[*ee*]. whose uncertain sophistic conduct is well known throughout America: the other gentleman [*Walker*] is a stranger to us.

Our crops of wheat have mended much by the late rains; I think we have a fair prospect of plenty.

NYDG, 22 June. The letter is preceded by the following: "Mr. [*Archibald*] McLEAN, You are requested to insert the following in your independent and impartial paper, whereby you will oblige A CUSTOMER."

OTHER DOCUMENTS

Jeremy Belknap to Ebenezer Hazard. ALS, Belknap Papers, MHi. Written from Boston.

Has answered David Howell (president of the Providence, Rhode Island, Abolition Society) "expressing my doubt of the propriety of addressing or rather *admonishing*" Congress on the subject of slavery.

John Brown Cutting to John Adams. ALS, Adams Family Manuscript Trust, MHi. Written from London. The ellipsis is in the source.

Encloses a couple of newspapers; impossible to predict events from day to day with any reliability, but it is probable a general European war will follow Britain's alliance with Prussia; France, whose fiscal credit is becoming respectable again, offers to mediate between Britain and Spain for an end to the Nootka Sound crisis; "Our country will be equally courted by both sides . . . and will I trust profit from the present crisis."

John Fox and Daniel Davis to George Thatcher. ALS, Chamberlain Collection, MB. Written from Boston; franked; postmarked 17 June.

Office seeking: Ebenezer Mayo as excise collector and Bezilla Delano as keeper of the Portland Head lighthouse; estimates it will take almost £400 to finish the lighthouse, including furnishing its lantern; requests he write as often as possible.

Robert Morris to Gouverneur Morris. No copy known; acknowledged in Gouverneur to Robert Morris, 31 July.

Philip Schuyler to William Allen. ALS, Adams Family Manuscript Trust, MHi. Place to which addressed not indicated.

Acknowledges Allen's letter of 10 June received the day before; the office Allen solicited (surveyor at Providence, Rhode Island) has already been given to William Barton; regrets the inability to offer "my best exertions, which would have been freely bestowed, inforced by those of my friends"; will "most willingly interfer in your favor" for any other office Allen may seek; informed Jeremiah Olney of his appointment as collector at Providence on 14 June, via Newport by sloop.

William Thornton to John Vining. ALS, Fitch Papers, DLC. Written from Philadelphia. For the full text, see *DHFFC* 8:62–63.
Recommends John Fitch, who has petitioned for a private patent act for his invention of steam powered navigation, "to whom can he apply with more propriety than my Friend Vining?"; "May the Smiles of the Gods be yours, the Goddesses always smile on you."

William Samuel Johnson, Diary. Johnson Papers, CtHi.
"Examn. Candids. [*examined candidates at Columbia College*]."

John Sevier, Journal. Claiborne Collection, Ms-Ar.
Took his seat in the House in the morning.

NYDG, 17 June.
"We hear that the Senate of the United States have now under their consideration the funding bill, in which, it is reported, they have made some alterations. At present there are high debates upon the subject of funding the interest at 4 per cent, and strong objections made to any reduction of the original contract, either under the denomination of capital or interest."

THURSDAY, 17 JUNE 1790

Hot (Johnson)

William Bradford to Elias Boudinot

Your letter of the 14th. inst. surprized me greatly by the account it gave me of the intended report on the funding bill. It was generally beleived that if the Senate should propose any alterations they would be in favor of the public creditors. The disappointment therefore being the greater has shocked the public mind, & I am told that Certificates are sinking fast in their value. When the principles of public faith are once departed from, it is difficult to know where the incroachments may stop, & all confidence is lost. But the prospect these measures give us of a still lengthened Session, & of the possibility that the whole system may fail, is to many a distressing consideration. I am concerned for several defendants in suits brought by their british Creditors. Some of these have the greatest part of their property in the hands of the public & their ruin is inevitable if they shall be forced to sell their Certificates. Congress first forbid them to remit or pay their creditors during the war—then they borrow their money & promise them the principal with 6 ℔ Cent—Then they stipulate that the british Creditor shall meet with no impediment in recovering his debts—& while his suit is proceeding under this article, Congress are debating whether they shall ~~pay~~ pay, not the Debt, not the arrears of interst—but whether they shall pay the usual interest on money that is withhelden from those whose families have been ruined for want of it. Our friend, Isaac Wickoff is one of these—he is now confined in Gaol on mesne process.[1] He offers 24/. in the pound payable in certificates—of which many cost him specie dollar for Dollar. We have some hopes of procuring a compromise for him—but if we cannot, he must, in prison, abide the decision of Congress. The late accounts make such a compromise much more difficult.

***

Patty leaves us in the morning and will be the bearer of this letter. Polly Bradford,[2] whose health is very precarious & whose life probably depends Upon [*blotted out*] change of air & gentle exercise, will accompany her at least as far as Elizabeth [*New Jersey*]. Susan [*Boudinot Bradford*] writes to her Mamma [*Hannah Stockton Boudinot*], with whom we expect you will be when this reaches you.

I wrote to you & Capt. [*Anthony*] Cuthbert by Monday's mail.

ALS, Wallace Papers, PHi. Place from which written not indicated. The omitted text relates to clients' financial affairs and household management.

---

[1] Literally, an intermediate process, between the commencement and the final execution of a lawsuit. Usually referred to the writ "capias ad respondendum," by which a defendant was ordered held as surety of his appearance in court. Wikoff (d. 1814) was a Philadelphia merchant. During the Revolutionary War he was engaged as a contractor by Congress's Secret Committee (*Rush* 2:676n; *LDC* 4:156, 208).

[2] Probably Mary Bradford (1750–1805), who married William Bradford's older brother Thomas in 1768.

William Floyd to George Washington

Agreable to your Request I wrote for a Machine for gathering Clover Seed, it is now arrived, and is at the Store of Mr. David Gelston in front Street, Subject to any orders you may please to give concerning it.

If no Oppertunity Immediately presents to Send it to Virginia, Mr. Winkoop Requests that a Joyner may have it for this Day and tomorrow as a patern to make one by.

ALS, Gratz Collection, PHi.

Theodore Foster to Dwight Foster

I Received your kind Congratulations on the Adoption and Ratification of the National Constitution by this State which you communicated in a very Laconic Epistle by Brother Peregrine—Accept mine for yours in Return. This Event compleats a Revolution in Favour of Government as astonishing as any mentioned in History exhibiting the American Character in a more respectable Point of View than that of most other Nations in that their Coolness Prudence and Wisdom have erected a Fabrick of Government on the Broad and solid Foundation of the Public Liberty in a General Election of the People at Large so curiously compacted as that the Vox Populi may be heared and attended to in every Part of the Magnificent Dome. in such a Manner as to be productive of the General Good without the Confusion ever attendant on Perfect Democracy—A Form of Government which one of your Massachusits Representatives has Justly compared to a Volcano which conceals the Fiery Materials of its own Destruction.[1] The New Constitution knits and weaves the States together by a firm and Strong Web but it leaves them so much of separate Independency as that they Serve as a controuling Balance upon each other. and upon the whole United productive and preservative of the General Liberty of every part of the Empire and of all the Individuals that compose it.

May Gracious Providence grant that the Halcyon Days of Peace Tranquility and Happiness may arise and be enjoyd by our Dear Country under a Wise, a Just, and a Prudent Administration of the General Government ~~for~~ May that Almighty Power whose Goodness has so remarkably overruled all things for the General Good of our Country direct the Councils of the Union to the Adoption of such Measures as shall promote Secure and insure the Liberty Happiness & Safety of all the People who are worthy of those best Blessings of Heaven.

I have become more interested in the Adoption of the Constitution than I expected. I have not Time to give you an History of the Circumstances and Causes which led to my Nomination as a Senator to represent this State in Congress. But Such a nomination did take Place and was Successful on the Part of those who brought it forward—The Governor issued his Warrants for convening the General Assembly for the Special Purpose of appointing the Senators and taking Measures for a Representation of this State in Congress. They met on Monday last Week at Newport—A Number of Candidates appeared in the Different Parts of the State. Those most talked of were George Champlin in the County of Newport—Jonathan Hazzard and Joseph Stanton in the County of Washington—Job Comstock and Thomas Holden in the County of Kent and Daniel Owen Peleg Arnold Benjamin Bourne Jabez Bowen and my self in the County of Providence.

The Election finally fell on Me and I expect to Morrow or Next Day Deo volente[2] to Set out for New York.

ALS, Foster Papers, MHi. Written from Providence, Rhode Island; addressed to Brookfield, Massachusetts; carried by "our Brother" Peregrine Foster; received 18 June.

[1] Ames made this remark in the Massachusetts ratification convention on 15 January 1788 (*DHROC* 6:1192).

[2] God willing.

Benjamin Goodhue to Stephen Goodhue

The assumption as you have long known has been so disgracefully connected with the future residence of Congress, that it has been impossible for us to seprate it—since the Pensylvs. have been defeated in carrying us to Philada. the Virginians and other Southern members who have their hearts fixed on being able in some future time of having the permanent seat on the Patowmack, are much alarm'd least we should join the Pensylvs. and fix at this time the permanent seat some where in Pensylva. to the eternal loss of the patowmack—under these apprehensions, Madison at their head has made us private proposals, that they will assume under some modification provided we will abandon the idea of fixing the permanent seat, and have an Act pass'd empowering the President in 1792 to adjourn to Philada. and leave the permanency to future contingences—We are in great hopes this may some how or other be improved to the attainment of the assumption, and are in better spirits on that head then we have been for some time.

You may shew this to some persons, tho' I wish it may not be public, in the present infant state of this bussines, for it may fail notwithstanding the present pleasing prospect.

[*P. S.*] Give the inclosed to some person going to Beverly [*Massachusetts*].[1]

ALS, Goodhue Family Papers, MSaE. Addressed to Salem, Massachusetts; franked; postmarked.

[1] Goodhue's correspondent at Beverly was probably George Cabot.

Benjamin Goodhue to Michael Hodge

I cannot refrain from just mentiong. to you that from certain circumstances, there is reason to believe the Virginians and others who have been so much opposed to the assumption begin to be alarm'd with the critical situation of our affairs without it, and have privately come forward to us with propositions which I am in hopes may lead to an accommodation on that subject, things have not yet got into such a state of maturity as to be able to form any accurate judgement as to its issue, but it has revived our almost expiring hopes—if we attain the object at last I am confident my political happines will exceed anything I have ever experienced, for it will be in a ratio of the magnitude of the object and the innumerable difficulties we have incessantly encounter'd to obtain it.

ALS, Ebenezer Stone Papers, MSaE. Place to which addressed not indicated; recipient identified by the handwriting on the docket.

Benjamin Huntington to George Washington

The Inclosed letter to me is Signed by Gentlemen of Character who have a better Acquaintance with Capt. [*Samuel*] Snow Than I have[1] But I am happy to say in his Favour That from the Acquaintance I have with him which was in the way of Business I always found him a Man of honor and Good Conduct and think him Capable of Executing the Office of Marshal for the District of Rhode Island to the Satisfaction of the Public & hope he may be appointed.

ALS, Washington Papers, DLC. This letter is misdated 7 June in *PGW* 5:458n.

[1] The enclosure, Rogers et al. to Huntington, 13 May, is calendared under that date, above.

Richard Henry Lee to Thomas Lee Shippen

I find by your last that you had not received my last when yours was written—In mine I had given you a precise statement of the business relative to the Seat of Government—It is an affair in which I have been so much agitated & so often disappointed by the very extraordinary detours of the friends to this place, that the very thought of it realy sickens me, and I now write on the subject merely to oblige you—And now I can only say that my best belief is, that we shall be chained here for a great length of time—The present question is, whether we shall adjourn to Baltimore—but this, like the rest, will, I think, terminate in staying here, which God in his infinite mercy forbid—Give my love to my much esteemed friend your father [*Dr. William Shippen, Jr.*] and say that I have presented his order to Mr. Wincoob [*Wynkoop?*] who promises to consider of it & thinks he will provide the money before we adjourn, which seems now to promise not to be before September—The present great dispute is, whether the debts of the United States shall be funded at 4 or at 6 per Cent—The former is your friends opinion, & there is some reason to think it will prevail.

[*P. S.*] If the funding Bill succeeds, the Salary proposed for the State

Commissioner of Pensylva. is 1500 dollars annually—Mr. [*Thomas*] Smith will have my Vote.

Turn over.

ALS, Shippen Family Papers, DLC. Place to which addressed not indicated. The salutation reads, "My dear Cousin." A second postscript is dated 19 June, below.

James Madison to James Monroe

You will find in the inclosed papers some account of the proceedings on the question relating to the seat of Government. The Senate have hung up the vote for Baltimore, which, as you may suppose, could not have been seriously meant by many who joined in it. It is not improbable that the permanent seat may be coupled with the temporary one. The Potowmac stands a bad chance, and yet it is not impossible that in the vicissitudes of the business it may turn up in some form or other.

The assumption still hangs over us. The negative of the measure has benumbed the whole revenue business. I suspect that it will yet be unavoidable to admit the evil in some qualified shape. The funding bill is before the Senate, who are making very free with the plan of the Secretary. A committee of that body have reported that the alternatives be struck out, the interest reduced absolutely to 4 per cent., and, as I am informed, the indents be not included in the provision for the principal.

PJM 13:246–47, from Madison, *Letters* 1:520.

Peter Muhlenberg to Benjamin Rush

Some circumstances, that have lately risen induce me to write you a few lines this Morning in The House to request your Sentiments on a subject which is like to involve the Pensylvn. Delegation in some difficulties; I do not wish that any of my Colleagues should know I have wrote you on the subject, and if you please to give me your sentiments They shall remain inter nos[1]—The removal of Congress from this place becomes every day more necessary, The reasons are obvious to every one that is acquainted with the Politics carrying on—It is now establishd *beyond a doubt* that the Secretary of the Treasury guides the Movements of the Eastern Phalanx; They are now ready to sacrifice every other object, provided They can thereby gain the assumption of the State Debts, They now offer a Carte blanche[2] for the Permanent Seat, provided we will join in carrying the assumption, and permit the temporary Seat to remain here for two Years longer—The difficulties arising with me, which prevent my joining in the measure are these—I can not reconcile it to my feelings to vote for a measure which in my *opinion* is unjust, in order to obtain a doubtfull good—I have likewise so bad an opinion of N. York Politics, that I really believe, if, at the expiration of the two Years residence in this place, The Southern Members should come forward, and propose to the Yorkers, to remain two years longer Provided the Permanent Seat should be fixt on the Powtomac, That the Yorkers would accede to the proposal—The Southern Members have some suspicion that a measure of this kind is in agitation and in order to counteract it, propose to fix the temporary Seat in Philada. for 10. 15. or 20 Years, provided the Permanent Seat shall then be on the Potowmac—The Southern Members have hitherto acted with great Candour on this occasion, and I am more inclind to accede to their Proposal, because no Conditions are annext that may be thought dishonorable, and because in the course of 15 or 20 Years, Circumstances may alter cases. It is needless to enlarge; This short sketch will fully explain the predicament in which we stand. I will only add, that the different interests are so equally pois'd, that Pensylva. can turn it, in favor of either.

ALS, Gratz Collection, PHi. Addressed to Philadelphia; franked; postmarked.

[1] Between us.
[2] To confer absolute freedom of action on someone; a blank check.

Josiah Parker to James Madison

A Charte Blanche is offered to the Pennsilvania Delegation respecting the permanent & tempore Seat of Congress if they consent to the Assumption of the State Debts as reported by the Secy. of the Treasury—A meeting has been on the Subject. Genl. M. Genl. H. & Mr. S[*cott*]. would not consent—this is from indubitable authority.

AN, hand of Parker, Madison Papers, DLC. At the top, Madison wrote "Handed to me by ''; he also identified "Genl. M. Genl. H." as P. Muhlenberg and Hiester. The note is undated and was probably written soon after the meeting that the Pennsylvania delegation held on 15 June (*DHFFC* 9:294). It is printed here because of its relationship to the previous document.

Theodore Sedgwick to Pamela Sedgwick

This day I have written you two letters the one I sent by the way of Springfield [*Massachusetts*] and the other by the way of Kinderhook [*New York*]. They were both written in the house. I was anxious to make you quiet on the subject of Kingsley and Chapman.[1] Though it is now so late as half past eleven oClock I cannot retire to rest untill I have in a few lines addressed the dearest object of my tenderest affection. Till this moment I have not had a particle of leisure since the adjournment. I spent two or three hours this afternoon with the Presidt. who treated me with a familiarity I have never before experienced, and with a confidence which was highly flatering to me. The substance of the conversation I may hereafter relate to you. The affairs of this country are drawing to a crisis. A very few days will determine what will be the future complexion of the Government. I have much stronger hopes than I have for some time entertained of a favorable issue. I cannot now be explicit. I will write you again on saturday. Till you receive my next you must suffer the pain of suspence which I have long endured.

Shall I purchase you a glass and carpet for your best room? and of what kind? May Heaven render you as happy as your virtues merit.

ALS, Sedgwick Papers, MHi. Addressed to Stockbridge, Massachusetts; carried by Mr. Lush. Stephen Lush (ca. 1753–1825) was an Albany lawyer.

---

[1] A reference to Sedgwick's entanglement in Ebenezer Kingsley's and Joseph Chaplin's bankruptcy.

Henry Sherburne to Henry Knox

***

Our Senators will be on their Way (in a few Days) to New York; Mr. Stanton you'l find to be a man highly tinctured with Anti principles, and filled with the most exalted Ideas of the Landholders Consequence, but as he is a man of much Modesty & Condecension, I flatter myself he will do (after spending some time with you) right. Mr. Foster will do all in his power to promote the Interest of the Union, with a proviso, that he does not deviate from any of the determined plans of his Brother [*Arthur*] Fenner our present Governor, by whoes Influence he obtained his appointment. This Gentleman possesses a good heart, has genuine Federal sentiments, a full share of sensibility, and is a man of Liberal Education.

***

ALS, Knox Papers, The Gilder Lehrman Collection, on Deposit at the New York Historical Society, New York. [GLC 2437.04629] Written from Newport, Rhode Island. The omitted text relates to office seeking. For the full text, see *DHFFE* 4:431.

George Thatcher to Josiah Thatcher

This acknowledges the receipt of yours of the 8th. inst.

Mr. [*John*] Frothingham, [*William*] Vaughan & Saml. Pierson have been recommended to me as suitable persons for Collectors of Excise, under the General Government, should an excise be imposed—And it being indifferent to me who shall be appointed to that office, provided he be capable and honest, I have wrote to Messrs. [*John*] Fox & [*Daniel*] Davis, who I suppose are at Court [*legislature*], for their advice.

Should an Excise be laid, the officer who collects it will be called an Inspector And there will be one at each port of Delivery—their Compensation will arise from a certain per cent. on the monies collected—Hence as there will be three or four in the County of Cumberland [*Maine*], their respective emoluments will be far short of what the Collector receives under the State Revenue.

I cannot say that I am perfectly satisfied at the great number of petitions from Towns & Individuals to the Legislature of Massachusetts, for the total repeal of the Excise Laws—I fear the people, should a repeal take place, will not find their expectations answered—For if the state debts are not assumed, by the Union, Massachusetts must raise money to pay the interest on their Domestic debt, by an excise, or a direct Tax—But if the assumption does take place a continental Excise must be laid, I believe fully equal, & perhaps higher, than the present state Excise—so that in either case I fear the people, not finding a Diminution of their Taxes, will attribute their disappointment to the ill opperation of the General Government—unreasonable expectations always bring on disappointment—disappointment genders discontent & uneasiness, & these are the forerunners of cabals & insurrections.

As to the assumption of the state debts, & the prospect of success this session I can only say—it is an event we are most anxious should take place—And within twenty four hours it seems to grind pretty well; and bids fair to get the Grist thro before we rise—However a few days will enable me to be more certain hereon.

If I mistake not a sheet of the [*House*] Journals containing pages 65. 66. 67. & 68. was omitted in the list I sent you—I therefore inclose it, with a continuation.

FC, Thatcher Family Papers, MHi. Written to Boston.

A Public Creditor to Mr. McLean

A CORRESPONDENT, whose fortune it is to be interested in the success of the funding system, would beg leave, through the medium of your paper, to offer to the public an observation or two relative to that subject.

Having a few weeks of leisure on hand, and as well to gratify a desire of visiting the seat of federal government, as the better to watch over his interest, he indulged himself in a tour to N. York.

During the investigation of the important subject of funding the public debt, in the House of Representatives, he heard, with pleasure, all the arguments that ingenuity, candour and patriotism could urge for and against the measures reported by the Secretary, exhausted; and, possessing the same opportunity and materials as other people to form opinions upon, he confesses himself highly entertained with the discussion, and perfectly well satisfied with the decisions.

But since the business has been transmitted to the Senate, all is involved in mystery, doubt and uncertainty. Last week he found his property reduced 20 per cent—this week, raised—to-morrow, probably, knocked down lower than ever; and all this effected by causes totally impenetrable to him. If he inclines to purchase, a few *knowing ones* can inform him the Senate have agreed to such a proposition, and stocks must rise 25 per cent.—then, on the other hand, if he inclines to sell, they can tell him, with an evil-portending shrug, *the Senate have stricken out this, and put in that—doubtful whether any thing will be done—and stocks are down in consequence of it.* Thus, unfortunately, his property is bandied about at pleasure; and not having the honor of an acquaintance with Mr. [*King*], Mr. [*Morris*], General [*Schuyler*], Colonel —, &c. he cannot possibly explore the reason. Thus circumstanced, to provide against the consequences of unfavorable measures, or to profit by those that are more propitious, is totally impracticable, till the alarm is spread and all is over.

It is a position clearly understood and well established, wherever the principles of free government are, that all avenues to legislative debates and proceedings (especially such as relate to revenue) should be equally open to every member of the society they legislate for, because every individual is immediately interested in those deliberations; and surely the United States will not form a disgraceful exception.

With the greatest deference, therefore, to the exalted wisdom of the federal Senate, the observer humbly proposes that they adopt one of the two following plans. 1st. That their proceedings be kept profoundly secret, until they are delivered to the press for publication; or, 2d. (which is much to be preferred) that they open their doors to the promiscuous admission of citizens, at least whilst they are determining on bills, &c. relating to revenue and public debt. This would be *fair play*; and a departure from these propositions will be losing sight of that jewel, and must inevitably be attended with unfavorable suspicions, if not partialities and public discontents.

The honorable Senators will, no doubt, read these observations: they neither express nor intend any foul imputation to that respectable body; but, with some degree of anxious solicitude, cast upon them to give the above subject a serious and solemn reflection; and although this is but the appeal of an individual, it undoubtedly contains sentiments warmly entertained by very many.

NYDG, 19 June, edited by Archibald McLean.

Other Documents

Elbridge Gerry to James Sullivan. No copy known; acknowledged in Sullivan to Gerry, 18 July.

Benjamin Goodhue to Samuel Phillips, Jr. No copy known; acknowledged in Phillips to Goodhue, 22 June.

Thomas Jefferson to John Steele. FC, Domestic Letters, Miscellaneous Correspondence, State Department Records, Record Group 59, DNA.

Has received the act of North Carolina legislature ratifying all twelve proposed Amendments to the Constitution.

John Langdon to Woodbury Langdon. No copy known; acknowledged in Woodbury to John Langdon, 25 June.

Jeremiah Wadsworth to Catherine Wadsworth. ALS, Wadsworth Papers, CtHi. Place to which addressed not indicated.

Is very well; will send some muslin soon.

Friday, 18 June 1790

Cool (Johnson)

George Benson to Theodore Sedgwick

I have this day done myself the Pleasure to address you by our Mutual Friend Theodore Foster Esq. and this instant received your esteem'd favor of the 1st Curr[*en*]t. I cannot account for its detention as it came ℘ Mail—you are no doubt before this appriz'd of the names & Characters of the Gentlemen who are Elected senators from this State—Collo. Stanton is avowedly in the Antifederal interest, and adverse to the assumption—but from Mr. Foster we hope and expect *better things*—his liberal and Cultivated Understanding—his Probity—his Zeal for the Public good *all all* Conspire to excite the most Confident expectations that his Conduct in this most interesting Business will realize our fervent Wishes—I know that strong wishes have a latent & very forcible influence on the Judgment—but Mr. Foster *will not* Cannot disappoint us—and We reap much Consolation from the ascendency Which your respectability and influence must acquire with him—he is so distinguished for an Amiable Moral Character that he is very Popular—but his sagacity must have discern'd that the Anti-interest is on the Ebb—the adoption of the Constitution is such an effectual Check to their Mad Career, that many of the Party will 'ere long revert to that obscurity from which perhaps they would never have emerg'd had they not avail'd themselves of the Popular Frenzy—on the Contrary the Men he esteems—the Men who esteem his Virtues will gradually recover that influence to which their respectability entitles them.

Your exertions sir on the important subject of Funding & particularly the assumption has and will I trust forever endear you to the Eastern states—while your Patriotism is universally acknowledged—The Trumpet of Fame is uplifted in your favour and her Eulogiums were never more properly apply'd.

As the Mail is on the Point of Departure I can only but very sincerely subjoin my ardent Wishes for your happyness, that a grateful Country will ever remember & reward your Distinguish'd services—and that after having long enjoy'd her Applause & Honours you May receive the Transporting Plaudits of that Adorable Being whose "Favour is better than life"—in great haste.

ALS, Sedgwick Papers, MHi. Written from Providence, Rhode Island; franked; sent "℔ Mail." Quote from John Wesley's *Notes on the Bible* (1754–65), on Psalm 84:11.

John Brown to Harry Innes

I send you herewith inclose[*d*] [*torn*] of Law Books which at your request I purchased [*at?*] this place & forwarded to Mr. Hoops in Philada. The Book are something dearer than formerly [*torn*] to the 10 ℔ Ct. Impost but believe the[*y*] are as cheap as could be procured any where in this Country [*torn*] Genl. [*Richard*] Butler from Fort Pitt [*Pittsburgh, Pennsylvania*] is now here & pr[*torn*] should they be at that place on his return [*torn*] them sent on to you by first safe Oppy. ope[*ns?*] [*torn*] I forwarded 100 Dollars part of your D[*illegible*] by [*torn*] Griffin to Colo. [*James*] Innis sometime past have written to J. C. Owings informing him of the Ball[*ance*]. in my hands & directing to draw on me for it—In the same Box with the Books have sent a Canister of the last imported Tea which please to present [*torn*] together with my most respectful Compliments.

I am fully of opinion that the Rules to regulate [*torn*] mode of proceeding in the District Court for Kentucke [*torn*] in your last you inform me you have framed for [*torn*] purpose are necessary & proper, but I cannot [*a*]ltogether agree with you in opinion respecting the Jurisdiction of that Court—The Judicial Powers of the General Government are defined in the Constitution but those powers will remain a dead letter unless Congress shall establish [*Cour*]ts to carry them into effect. This they may do either [*in wh*]ole or in part—They may distribute the exircise [*torn*] powers among such inferior Courts as they [*choo*]se to establish—having established District [*and Cir*]-cuit Courts & assigned to each their respective Jurisdictions they cannot by construction extend their Jurisdiction to omitted Cases—these must remain in their original State 'till Congress by a Legislative act shall constitute a Court with Power to take [*torn*] of them to extend the powers of the Courts already constituted—The Court for Kentucke having the Jurisdiction of both a Circuit & District Court a Citizen of one State may sue a Citizen of another in that Court in all Cases in which either of those Courts has cognizance—But I do not find that one Citizen can sue another of the same State for Debt or Tort in either of those Courts—In my last either to you or my Brother [*James*] I mentioned that the alterations to the times of holding that Court which you had [*torn*] to me as proper had been made but this informa[*tion*] was premature as the Bill [*North Carolina Judiciary Bill (S-10)*] was unexpectedly [*rejected*] by the Senate at the Third reading.

I cannot express the pain it g[*ave me*] to read the long & alarming account of In[*dian*] depredations contained in your last lett[*er. I*] immediately communicated the contents to the [*torn*] & Secretary at War but being at the same time informed of the march of Genl. Harmar & Genl. Scott[1] they concluded that it was unnecessary [*to*] take any other measures untill the result of that expedition was known—I have been very p[*torn*] laying before the President from time to time your letters & all the information I receive from my friends in Kentucke relative to Indian hostilities indeed the only authentic information he receives upon the subject is through me—He has repeatedly declared to me his readiness immediately to direct an expedition against those Indians who commit depredations upon the Ohio & in Kentucke pro[*vid*]ed it could be assertained to what Tribe or Nation they belong but of this we in this quarter are wholely [*ign*]orant your letters as well as those I have received [*from?*] others being altogether [*si*]lent on this head [*I wi?*]sh you would be particular relative to [*any?*] information you may have on this Subject in your next [*torn*] favor me with your Sentiments respecting the practicability of extirpating or driving off that Banditti living on the heads of the Kentucke The officers are appointed & measures are now taking for the raising of an aditional number of Troops for [*the protec*]-tion of the Frontiers & I expect that a new & more effectual System for the regulation of Indian affairs will be carried into operation in the course of the present year.

As yet it is altogether uncertain when Congress will adjourn as great part of the Business cut out for the present session is still unfinished Some expect & indeed I myself think it probable that we shall adjourn in July to meet again [*in the?*] fall—A Bill providing for funding the foreign & domestic debt, of the U. States agreeably to the plan reported by the Secy. of the Treasury, for that [*torn*] has passed the H. of Rep[*resen*]tatives & is now before the Senate—The further consider[*ation of*] the important question relative to the assum[*ption of*] the State Debts has been postponed for the prese[*nt*] but expect it will be called up agai[*n*] [*torn*] tho do not apprehend that it will be [*pa*]ssed this Session—We are now engaged in passing a Bill providing for the Settlement of the accounts between the U. States & the Individual States [*HR-77*]—also in providing [*ways*] & means [*Duties on Distilled Spirits Bill HR-62*] it is expected that for the [*torn*] only have recourse to additional Duties on Tonnage & an additional duty on distilled Spirits Wines Teas & Coffee—a Resolution for holding the next Session of Congress in Philada. was a few days ago brought forward by the Representatives of Pennsylvania & carried by a large Majority—it is now before the Senate & they I am told intend to annex to it a resolution establishing the permanent [*se*]at—I expect this Business will end as on former occasions [*with a?*] determination to continue in this place especially as Rhode Island will be represented in the Senate this [*torn*] [*wee*]k having adopted the Constitution on the 29th May [*I wro*]te to the Managers of the Cotton Factory[2] by the last [*wes*]tern Mail informing them of my embarrassments [*torn*] in the arrest & confinement of Mr. Walsh [*whom?*] I have employed as a Manager & who had set out for Danville together with his family: a sufficient number of Manufacturers & all the necessary Machinery As yet I have neither heard from Mr. Rhea [*lined out*] [*torn*] [*under whose dire?*]ction the Waggons & people went [*torn*] from Mr. Walshs wife therefore am still uncertain whether they have determined to proceed or to return nor can I take any further steps in this Business before I hear from them—I expect to have it in my power to write to you more fully by next Post.

The Presidents life was lately dispaired of by all in this place but it is with great pleasure I can assure you of his recovery—Perhaps the happiness [*of*] a Country never depended so much upo[*n the*] life of one man as that of America does upon his.

I at present intend to return [*to Ken*]tucke as soon as Congress adjourns which [*will*] probably be before the Election in S[*eptember*] again offer my Services to the Distr[*ict*] if some other Candidate more acceptable [*torn*] not appear—I should be glad to hear [*torn*] the ~~change~~ present state of my

Intirest [*torn*] & whether my presence at the Election will be indispensably necessary—pray write me without reserve your Sentiments upon this Subject & let me know what effect the exertions of my Woodford *Friends*[3] have had to lessen the confidence of the people of Kentucke.

ALS, Innes Papers, DLC. Place to which addressed not indicated. The outer margins of the document are badly damaged.

[1] On 7 June, Knox ordered territorial Governor Arthur St. Clair and Brigadier General Josiah Harmar to organize a punitive "expedition" against war parties of the "Wabash tribes," also known as the Miami Confederacy, consisting of the Miami and hostile elements among the Shawnee and Cherokee who occupied the headwaters of the Maumee, Miami, and Wabash rivers in present-day central Indiana. Preparing a force of 1500 Kentucky and Pennsylvania militia and approximately four hundred federal army troops took all summer; it was not until late September that the two pronged invasion departed from Fort Washington (Cincinnati, Ohio) and Fort Knox (Vincennes, Indiana). The latter force returned early owing to a lack of supplies, while a detachment under Harmar's larger force suffered a decisive defeat on 22 October. Brown apparently expected Brigadier General Charles Scott of the Kentucky militia to play some role in Harmar's "march," although Scott did not take the field against the Wabash tribes until the 1791 expedition (Richard Kohn, *Eagle and Sword: The Federalists and the Creation of the Military Establishment in America, 1783–1802* [New York, 1975], pp. 100–106, 111–12; *PGW* 5:376–77n).

[2] The Kentucky Manufacturing Society.

[3] Thomas Marshall, a major political rival to Brown, emigrated from Virginia to Buckpond (in present-day Versailles), Woodford County, Kentucky, in 1783. The father of the future Chief Justice and a longtime colonial legislator, Marshall rose from major to commanding colonel of the Third Regiment of the Virginia Line before resigning in 1777 (Elizabeth Warren, "John Brown and His Influence on Kentucky Politics, 1784–1805," Kentucky State Historical Society *Register* 36[1938]:63; *PJM* 1:228–29n).

Daniel Hiester to John Nicholson

I have recd. your favour by post and now enclose you the Bill for settling the Accots. between the United States, and the several states just published anew and will be taken up next Monday.

There is now every Appearance that the Senate will strike out all the Alternatives in the funding Bill and reduce the Int. on the whole to 4 ℔ Ct. and set the lands apart for a sinking fund—The Arrearage of Interest will probably be funded although a very formidable opposition has as we are informed has been made—A British Packet is just arrived and says that a War is on the Point of being declared by England against Spain.

ALS, Nicholson Papers, PHarH. Addressed to Philadelphia; carried by Col. (Francis) Mentges; received 19 June.

Governor Samuel Huntington to William Samuel Johnson and Oliver Ellsworth

You will receive herewith enclosed, an Act of the Legislature, by which You are fully authorised to cede to the United States, the places where the Light-house, Piers, Buoys, &c. are erected in this State.[1]

It is the desire of the General Assembly, that such cession be made, conformably to, & within the time limited by the Act of Congress relative to this subject.

The business hath been delayed from a doubt existing, whether the State had a Title to the lands & places where the Light-house is erected; but after considerable search, I have discovered that the State have a good title, by purchase of the lands & place at the time the Light-house was first built.

During our late sessions of Assembly the proposed Amendments to the Constitution were again brought under consideration & adopted at the Council Board but the house of Representatives rejected the two first Articles & adopted the residue & the subject remains in that situation at present.

The communication by the public papers is so frequent & full, that it is presumed, You are already informed of the general events of our Election, & procedings of the Legislature in their last session.

LS, Johnson Papers, DLC. Written from Norwich, Connecticut.

[1] Passed on 2 May 1790.

[*Neil Jamieson*] to Josiah Parker

Finding a disposition in some enlightened members of Congress, and particularly in your two worthy Colleagues, Mr. Madison and Mr. Page, to give such encouragement to American Shipping as will soon appear to be absolutely necessary (unless a majority of the Legislature should think the carrying business and all the advantages, riches, and consequence, resulting therefrom, unworthy their Attention, and mean to throw 'em away upon Gt. Britain) I have made free to address you on the subject, confiding in your good sense and prudence, not to make an improper use of any information I may be able to afford thereon, and that you will keep it entirely to yourself if you deem it unworthy communication.

First. In confirmation of Mr. Page's observation. "I believe it the interest of the Southern States that Ship building should be encouraged to the utmost extent in the United States. The fine timber they have would then be sold to advantage in the form of Ships, instead of being destroyed or thrown away under the name of lumber, or in trifling staves: much I know has been destroyed in Virginia, much wasted in staves. Sir, it is their interest that their Sister States should carry for them instead of foreigners."[1] I beg leave to ask, on the supposition of the Southern States determining that American Shipping and the carrying trade was unworthy their attention, what inconvenience might they not experience, what loss would they not suffer, in case of a war between Great Britain and France, their produce for several years at least, until American Ships could be built, must either be transported to Europe in English, or French bottoms at a war freight, or by neutrals at nearly the same freight? I would also ask when the rise in freight becomes an object to a man to invest his money in vessels, where are the seamen to come from, every power in Europe becoming every day more jealous of her own? Is it not evident that if it was generally perceived that Congress was steady, and determined to support the Shipping interest, we should in a few years have a sufficiency to carry half our produce to market and in case of a rupture between Great Britain and France could soon build as many as would transport the whole to the most eligible market?

I should not have troubled you with this letter was I not conscious it was in my power, and of course my duty, to furnish you with some information on this subject, founded on facts worthy your attention as a Legislator.

You are not unacquainted with the situation of the lower parts of this State respecting timber suitable for Ship building, but as my business has led me to pay more attention thereto than perhaps any other man in the State, I can tell you from experience that the quality is excellent, but diminishing very fast in most places convenient for Ship building. In 1765, I was supercargo of the Ship Hicks of 500 Hhds. [*hogsheads*] built at Newtown in Princess Ann [*County, Virginia*], and then eighteen year old, and had never been repaired; there is now a vessel of 400 Hhds. burthen belonging to Whitehaven I'm informed is sound and good, that I had built by Mr. Hope[2] at Hampton in the year 1775—the above facts are sufficient to establish my assertion respecting the quality.

I have this day examined two quarterly returns from the Collector's Office of this Port, the first commencing the 17th. Augt. and ending the 31st. December 1789—the other commencing the 1st. January and ending the 31st. March 1790—by which I find that 8,012,600 Staves and heading have been shipped in the above time, 60,500 of which only was Shipped to the French West Indies—the rest of coarse white oak Lumber, chiefly, nearly equal to 16,000 tons, and 20,000 Trees, sufficient to build 134 vessels of two hundred tons each. The quantity of the produce shipped in the above time I calculate at 41,166 tons @ 60/ this currency pr. ton (a low freight) is £123,493—the value of the produce shipped, estimated by the Collector's return 769,781 dolrs. or £230,910—not twice the amount of the freight. I make no doubt you know how scarce good white oaks are become contiguous to the water, the difference between hawling one mile or seven, is perhaps equal to twenty shillings pr. ton. There has not been a square rigg'd. vessel built in this District since the adoption of the present Constitution except a small Brig by Mr. Hope, and the Brig I lately built of 600 Hhds. I am about to set on two others of nearly the same size, but unless the present policy of Great Britain can be counteracted by Congress, perhaps I had better set fire to them; if American bottoms are well supported many Merchants will follow my example of building, (in short I shall probably be concerned with many therein). If not, in a few years we shall have neither Timber, Carpenters, nor Sailors: the following extract which you may rely on as fact, proves my last assertion. "Since I wrote you last I have been in London about the U—s who I informed you was detained here by the Collector, he alledging that she was not navigated according to law; as you are much concerned in American vessels I think it necessary to give you a particular account of this transaction, and also to inform you of some very alarming proceedings going forward on this side the Atlantic against American Shipping in general. You are acquainted that the british navigation Act requires that the master and three fourths of the mariners on board all foreign vessels trading to England be subjects of the Country the Ships belong to, now it is necessary that the Captain and three fourths of the mariners of every American vessel coming to England should be subjects of America at the time Independence was granted by England. When the U—s arrived here she had fourteen people on board, out of which number the Captain and ten of the people were really Americans, the remaining three were Englishmen who had become citizens since the war. Now according to the present construction of the british navigation Act, she had one more real American on board than the law requires, but five of the above number were apprentices, which the Collector would not allow to be numbered as mariners; as such the vessel was detained till he had the opinion of the Commissioners of the Customs, but this being too *difficult a question* for them to Resolve, it was referred to the Attorney General, and after detaining the Vessel seven weeks with her cargo on board, he gave in his opinion that she was navigated according to Law. I wish to remark that apprentices on board English vessels are always allowed to be mariners by the Collector, Underwriters and every other person. When an American vessel arrives here the Collector has all the Crew up to the Custom House, and makes them swear *where they were born, how old they are, how and where they have been employed &c.* in short it is a species of Inquisition which the Collector has instituted against the Americans only, as he makes no such enquiry of Vessels belonging to any other foreign nation, and I'm sorry to add that this partial conduct of the Collector's is approved by the people in power; for I saw a letter from Lord Hawkesbury who particularly mentioned it. This letter was in answer to one wrote him by the merchants of this place, desiring something might be done for the benefit of british Shipping, to counteract the 10 p. C. discount on all goods imported into America, in American vessels; he recommends that the Merchants here should reduce the freights of their vessels, which he says would be only for a short time, and that by *their exerting themselves against American Vessels, and by the Collector's being particularly strict with them,* in a short time it must have a good effect, and that as soon as he had gained the necessary information in the business required, he promised something should be done. I have also been informed that the Merchants here have wrote out to America giving positive orders not to ship any goods on board American Vessels, and without something be done in this business the sooner you set them on fire the better. You will also take notice that a british subject becoming a Citizen of America since the war cannot hold any part of an American vessel. Whatever may be the effect of the above information I beg my name may not be mentioned."[3]

The above facts being undoubted and coming from the very best authority, we have only to draw the conclusions naturally resulting therefrom.

The first and most obvious of which is, that the people of Great Britain from the Merchant to the Minister, foreseeing the advantages that will accrue to America from a proper attention and support of her shipping interest, and concluding that she will attend thereto, are determined if possible to prevent it, and throw every obstacle they can in way to effect it. The second is the deep laid scheme of reducing the freights for a time, 'till they have annihilated the American shipping, so as to make the Southern States pay dearly for their selfishness, credulity, and inattention to the general welfare of the States of which they are members. The third is the attempt to consider apprentices as no part of the Crew and thereby counteract the only mode we have of raising American Seamen, and reaping that trifling share of the trade to Britain which [*we*] possess. The fourth is, that Congress is not to expect any exertions from the Southern merchants any more than from the Southern Delegates to counteract the attempts of the british merchants, as nine tenths of the former are dependent upon the latter.

I shall conclude with observing that if the carrying trade was secured to American subjects, the profits thereon, even at the present low freights, are sufficient to allure monied men to place their cash in Shipping, and as a proof that Great Britain cannot afford to carry our produce on the same terms that America can, if the trade was secured to herself I give you the following example and proof.

The Brig Friends is allowed to be as strong a vessel as ever entered the Thames, and sails fast. She measures 341 tons, carries 600 Hhds. and cost £3253.13.2½ this currency, having the advantage of a freight to Europe as soon as fitted, she earned on her first voyage £965.14.10 Sterlg. on her second she will probably earn 970 do. That's £1935.14.10 sterlg. within the year, and if, as well employed, may be a clear ship in three years. A British ship of same burthen and as good, would cost at Bristol, or Whitehaven, or London thirteen pounds to thirteen Guineas pr. ton, that is £5660.4 this currency say @ 33 1/3. I have but 14 people and 5 of them apprentices, and can sail on as low terms as any british ship, reckoning the interest and insurance on each, you will find it will take double the time to clear a british ship that it will to clear an American; and when the latter are built faithfully, out of young seasoned timber, I verily believe they will last near or full as long.[4]

Does not the extract I have transcribed for your information strike you with the propriety of the following remark of Mr. Madison? "There are cases in which it is better to do nothing, than not do a great deal."

FC, hand of state department clerk George Taylor, Madison Papers, DLC. Written from Norfolk, Virginia. The cause of retaliatory trade legislation made use of this letter when Parker quoted it during the COWH debate on the Trade and Navigation Bill on 29 June (*DHFFC* 13:1616–17), and when extracts were extensively reprinted (noted below). The identification of the author is based on internal evidence that he was a resident of Norfolk, Virginia, and the owner of a brig named *Friends*. Jamieson, a native of Scotland, had been a fixture in Norfolk's mercantile community from the late 1750s until 1776. Although closely allied politically with Parker (to whom he was also related by marriage), Jamieson broke with Norfolk's revolutionary leadership shortly after the outbreak of war and settled under British protection in New York City, where he operated a dry goods store by 1785. He remained there until at least 1786, during which time he served as the trusted go between for Jefferson in Paris and Madison of Virginia (*PJM* 8:128, 247, 249–50n). The absence of Jamieson's name from New York's 1789 city directory supports the conclusion that he had relocated to Norfolk by that time. He eventually returned to Great Britain. For a more extensive case made for Jamieson's authorship, including the discovery that in 1769 he owned a Norfolk brig named *Friends*, see *PTJ* 16:521–22, 528n.

---

[1] Page's "observation" is quoted from his speech of 11 May printed in *NYDG*, 14 May (*DHFFC* 13:1262).

[2] George Hope (1749–ca. 1822) was a ship's carpenter in Virginia's Norfolk-Portsmouth area.

[3] A lengthy quote from the beginning of the letter to this point later appeared as an Extract of a letter from a gentleman in ——— England, to his friend in America, in *GUS*, 30 June, *NYDA*, 1 July, *NYWM*, 3 July, and *NYP*, 10 July, and was reprinted at Boston, Salem, Northampton, and Worcester, Massachusetts; Newport and Providence, Rhode Island; New Haven, Connecticut; Burlington, New Jersey; Philadelphia and Carlisle, Pennsylvania; Alexandria, Richmond, and Winchester, Virginia; and Charleston, South Carolina. The printings do not provide the "U——s" given in the Madison Papers' transcribed copy as the first and last letters of the name of the ship being written about.

GUS's printing of this extract may have been a factor of Jefferson's short lived "alliance" with the paper's editor, John Fenno, described in Louis Guillaume Otto to Comte de Montmorin, 13 June, n. 1, above; Madison certainly availed himself of its timing when he moved his substitute Trade and Navigation Bill on the same day (*DHFFC* 6:1972–73n).

[4] The preceding paragraph was printed verbatim and the two paragraphs before it were closely paraphrased in *GUS*, 3 July. This is further evidence that Parker and/or Madison probably collaborated with Jefferson in ensuring that Fenno publicized this letter to an extent

and according to a timetable that would maximize its impact on the debate on the Trade and Navigation Bill.

William Maclay to Benjamin Rush

Thanks to You my dear sir for Your letter of Yesterday, with the inclosed paper.[1] But how could You make so great a Mistake about the Mileage. The Members of Congress have mileage for returning as well as going to the Residence of Congress. the Double distance between New York and Philada. gives a mileage of 60 doll. to each member and of Course operates a disadvantage of 2280 Doll. Annually to the Treasury in case of Two Sessions being held each Year. It was right in the original paper which I sent to You. and in that light I Stated and supported it in the Senate.

The adjournment to Baltimore stands postponed to Monday Week, The Rhode Island Senators will be with us in that time, and we have no chance of carrying it. Here however I never will be contented. and the whole Tenor of my conduct shall be a constant endeavour to get away. The funding bill is not Yet passed, we have waited some days, for the bill with the Ways and means, As many Members consider them as insuperable. But the Very Goddess of Slowness seems to have possessed Congress. It is a fact that our Wages are too high, to permit Us to do business expeditiously. The Spending of Six dollars ℔ day in Taste agreeable to the modes of New York. will leave a Man but little time to bestow on business. Pay and Business operate in an inverse ratio. the less of the former the more will be produced of the later, in the political laboratory.

ALS, Rush Papers, DLC. Addressed to Third Street, Philadelphia; franked; postmarked 21 June.

[1] Newspaper Article, *FG*, 16 June, above, attributed to Rush with some collaboration by Maclay. Rush's cover letter enclosing the paper has not been located.

Walter Stone to Robert Morris

I have had none of your favors for Some time—It is my Intention to go to London & I did propose to depart in a Ship wch. are loaded here but fear it will not be in my Power, so that my Journey will be postponed for some time. It is not my *Wish* to banish myself from my own Country, yet it is probable my *Interest* may oblige me to reside in London, to make the Residence as agreable and as usefull as in my Power, I have contemplated a public appointment. my ambition is very humble, and if we had a commercial Treaty with Great-Britain, I should aspire no higher than the lowest

Grade of Consul—If an officer under Congress is to be sent to that Court, whether Resident, Charge des affaires &c. and you think me better qualified than any other applicant you as *a Senator* will prefer me, not regarding our *Friendship* futher than as it has led to a thorough acquaintance with me. I never expected or wished any appointed heretofore contented with my own occupations, but I confess I have so warm an attachment for the Dignity of my Country that I have been sometimes mortified that all the public officers have not been of those Charactors who from their respectability, Situation and fortune were best entitled, and it has disgusted many Men who have thought themselves neglected, because they Were not at New York to enforce their pretentions, it is however impossible that General Washington and the Senate can be acquainted with every Man and much must depend upon the opinion & recommendation of others.

I have not written to any other Person on this Subject committing myself entirely to you knowing you will do what you may consider your Duty as a Senator and no further. I have not mentioned it to Michael,[1] knowing his aversion to my going to England at all, I presume he would be the more opposed to any Situation that might fix me there. It is equally painfull to me to be seperated from him and my other Relations, but I have such Prospect of advantage held out to me, that I think it my duty to myself and others who depend on me, to embrace the opportunity.

ALS, Washington Papers, DLC. Written from Port Tobacco, Maryland.

[1] His brother, Representative Michael Jenifer Stone.

John Walker to Alexander Donald

Yours of the 9th Inst. with its inclosures is just come to hand. The bill you speak of, has not yet appeared before the Senate,[1] nor do I know what will be the fate of it, when it does. Your imagination seems to be warmed when you speak of it, & your apprehensions of the mischief that will ensue appear to be rather high coloured. My opinion at present is, that all discriminations of that kind are impolitic & disadvantageous to the Trade of our Southern States; yet my mind is ever open to conviction, & while I have the honor of Seat in the American Councils, I hope & trust, that no considerations of private friendship, nor any "easiness of temper" will so far prevail with me as to warp my judgement.

Congress is still agitated with assumption & Seats of Government, & nothing conclusive done in either, yet I am not without a hope that all will end well; & were these two distressing subjects once removed, I see nothing else to disturb our future tranquility.

By a British packet this day arrived after a short passage, the News is, that the British are going immediately to loggerheads with Spain, in consequence of the capture of some British Vessels ingaged in the pe[*a*]rl fishery on the coast of California [*Nootka Sound*]. The particulars I have not yet heard, but what I have related, I had from Mr. R. Morris, who has received letters by the Packet.

We are all in good health & Salute our friends in Virginia with every good wish.

P. S. Just as I was concluding my letter, I saw another from London of may the 6th, which sais the Press[2] was so hot, that every Ship from Graves end to London was swept in one night.

ALS, Gratz Collection, PHi. Addressed to Richmond, Virginia; franked; postmarked 20 June.

[1] The Trade and Navigation Bill then being debated in the House, which would have imposed higher tonnage duties on vessels of nations with which the United States did not have a commercial treaty.

[2] Impressment of seamen into the British Navy.

Newspaper Article

We are informed that there has been lengthy debates in Senate (the funding bill being yet under their consideration) upon the subject of funding the indents, and respecting the alternative proposed to the public creditors. Some members have argued against the ability of the United States to pay 6 per cent.; nay, it is said that they have declared their doubts whether the country is able to pay 4, or even 2 per cent. at present; and that many of the present holders of certificates, who became so by speculation, will have more than justice done them at 2 per cent.; and respecting the contract, there is not any between government and this description of creditors.

On the other hand, it is contended that it would be highly degrading to the United States to attempt any reduction of the original contract, as government is a party, and the most powerful party in this bargain; the creditor is the other party, but weak and laying at the mercy of the stronger party, who now assumes the privilege of becoming a judge in its own cause. This is like an armed man attacking one that is unarmed, and cannot be vindicated either upon principles of policy or justice.

The debates in Senate are conducted with such good order, and the abilities of the Senators so highly esteemed, that it is greatly to be regretted, the loss the people sustain in not being allowed to see those debates made public.

NYDG, 18 June; reprinted at Portland, Maine; Boston; and New York City (*NYJ*, 22 June).

OTHER DOCUMENTS

Paul Allen to George Washington. ALS, Washington Papers, DLC. Written from Providence, Rhode Island; delivered by T. Foster. For the full text, see *PGW* 5:531–32.

Office seeking: naval officer for Providence; mentions T. Foster as reference.

Pamela Sedgwick to Theodore Sedgwick. ALS, Sedgwick Papers, MHi. Place from which written not indicated.

Silas Pepoon recommends Theodore not be uneasy about Nathaniel Kingsley's bankruptcy, as "their is some Mistery in this Business"; asks whether enquiries can be made for finding employment for (nephew) Theodore Sedgwick; all are well; hopes for his return soon.

John Sevier, Journal. Claiborne Collection, Ms-Ar.

Won a guinea from Parker playing whist.

PP, 21 June. The editors believe this was written by a member of the Pennsylvania House delegation.

"The funding bill is not yet come from the senate: it has been committed to a select committee: that committee has reported: Strike out all alternatives—fund the principal, without indents or back interest at four per cent: Continental money 100 for 1. These amendments have been the subject of debate in senate (Committee of the whole) for Tuesday and Wednesday—nothing determined: Yesterday other business occupied the whole day. I don't learn what they have before them today. The House of Representatives are this day in the way and means: The bill will go heavily on [*Duties on Distilled Spirits Bill HR-62*]."

SATURDAY, 19 JUNE 1790

Timothy Bloodworth to Governor Alexander Martin

Your favour of the 28th of May came safe to hand. Your charge of negligence are Justly founded, whose origin was Inattention & not disrespect, togather with a firm persuation that You received every necessary information from the Senators whose duty compels them to correspond with the executive & the representatives more perticularly with their Constituents, shall notwithstanding at all ti[*mes*] be happy to correspond. With respect to Business of the Union it Lyes in such broken fragments that I am not able to give You satisfactory information. when I took my seat on the 6th Aprill, the house was engag'd in the Assumtion of the States Debts. & the Delegation of North Carolina (as You have heard) gave a turn to the Business, but the Advocates for the measure are not easily beat from their ground, altho twice defeated, they stil return to the charge in hopes of success from perseverance. how the matter will end remains Uncertain, a Bill for that purpose is now in the order of the Day, & has been for sometime past, but I presume the[*y*] are apprehensive of an infavourable decision, is the reason the[*y*] permit it to rest for better prospects. the Bill for funding the Debts of the Union is now before the senate, & is likly to undergo som alterations. in consequence of which, the certificats have pd. six pence in the pound among the speculators, who are continually watching our Motions. the Bills for establishing post offices, & post roads [*HR-74*], & for excises [*Duties on Distilled Spirits HR-62*] are now in their passage. the latter I fear will prove obnoxious in the extreem, to they southern States. our Delagates have gave it opposition, & will I presume give it their negative. we have succeeded so far, as to excuse from the tax all stills under 35 gallons. those above are to pay 60 cents, per Gallon, including the cap. or qunto, per Gallon, for all the spirits Distili[*d*], given on oath. several Acts of lesser moment have pass'd, the perticulars I forbear to Mention the subject of removal has consum'd much time, & is not Yet finished. the house of representatives, have resolved to hold the next sessions at Baltimore. But the senate have pospond the consideration until Monday weak & I find it is in contemplation to fix the permanent seat at the Potomac, & the temporary residence at Philadelphia. the Dignity of Stations, are not sufficient to exempt mankind from human foibles. party spirits prevail, & private interest are persued, in the grand Council of the nation. the appointments for the Western Teretory are as follows Viz. Coll. [*William*] Blount Governer Genral [*Daniel*] Smith Secretary [*David*] Campbel & [*John*] McNairy Judges the States Attorney not yet appointed for North Carolina Coll. [*William R.*] Davie Judge, John Sitgraves A[*ttorney*] & John Skinner Marshal. Rhod Island have Adopted the Constitution, & their Senators are Dayly expected. Verm[*ont*] only remains to compleat the Union. it was expected that th[*e*] house would rise in June, but I am apprehensive it will not [*be*] the case if we finish the business. the encreased number of Petitions, & remonstrances, consume much time. Congress has resolv'd that the General Government began its opperation on [*the*] 4th March, & the times of the present siting Members will expire next March. by thiss resolution the[*y*] have continue[*d*] the seats of som Members, five months beyond the limits [*of*] the constitution.[1] & others are curtaild twelve months North Carolina must have an Election before next March; or hav[*e*] no Representation I had little expectation of the house dec[*id*]ing on a constitutional question, at thiss early period when seve[*ral*] States were pressing for amendments in that perticular Article their are little expectation of any amendments taking place, [*the*] house refused to appoint a committee to consider the amendm[*ents*] propos'd by North Carolina.[2] Very large Majority were oppos'd [*to*] the measure. we shall bring it before the house once More & endeavour to obtain the Ays, & noes, on the question. Mr. Sevier took his seat the Day before I reciev'd Your favour, I pre[*sume*] You have heard of the Death of Coll. Bland from Virginia. the spring has been sickley but at present the complaints are not frequent.

ALS, Governors' Papers, Nc-Ar. Place to which addressed not indicated.

[1] For the House resolution of 18 May, which the House ordered the Speaker to transmit to all the chief executives of the states on 9 August, see *DHFFC* 3:416. The constitutional provision referred to is Article I, section 4, paragraph 1. This resolution was needed by the states because the second federal election had already begun in some states.

[2] North Carolina's 1789 ratification convention proposed eight amendments to the Constitution, which Williamson presented to the House on 30 March, but his effort to have them committed failed (*DHFFC* 12:871–72).

Thomas Fitzsimons to Benjamin Rush

I deferred answering Your favor of the 12th as Mr. Clymer would inform you of the State of things here—I Reced. yesterday yours of the 18. and will forward Mr. [*Jeremy*] Belknaps letter by tomorrows post.

I have Never made direct Application to any of our Members for their interest in behalf of Mr. Morris[1] except Wynkoop & Scott. the former is a Man of Reflection & of interest in his own Country. And haveing satisfyd. himself as to the propriety of the Measure Considers it to be a duty he owes his Country to use that influence in favor of it—he Assures me it will be Reced. there with great Cordiality—I am not Eno. Acquainted with the others interest to decide upon its extent Nor do I count much upon his Activity but he Expresses his Approbation of our Choice & I hope will take some pains—With the Speaker I can Converse freely—and I shall soon take an oppy. of Explaining to him—all my Views—& asking his Concurrence & Support Which I have No doubt of obtaining—The other Gent. I believe I must leave to their own Choice as I am not Sufficiently Confidential with them I fancy you Can do more With McClay than any person here. I am disposed to think he is favorable to Mr. Morris' Views—Tho perhaps he would not hazard his own to support them. I find he is a Correspondent of Finlays [*William Findley*] and that the former has Warily Evaded Giveing any opinion as to the person he is to Espouse I have been disposed to forget ~~or of~~ or Rather [*lined out*] Overlook some part of his former Conduct in expectation that he has lately Imbibed better principles—but it would seem from your information that he is not to be trusted—& I am well pleased. I did not write to him Upon this Subject—Mr. [*William*] Lewis timidity, nor Finleys duplicity however shall deter me from Continuing my Efforts. I do not Know how they may Suceed but if the Object is Obtained I shall think it Strange [*lined out*] If your Services should be Overlooked—I shall Certainly think it my duty to make them Known—The Massachusetts delegates have Endeavored to Impress their Correspondents with a Very unfavorable opinion of our Conduct as the only Apology for their own but we despise the Calumny & leave them to their own Reflections as a Sufficent punishmt. for their duplicity, & Interested conduct We Know our Strong ground & will not be beaten from it by Whineing or threatning—I shall Rejoice when I am done with the business—being heartily sick of my situation.

ALS, Rush Family Papers, DeU. Place to which addressed not indicated.

[1] In Morris's candidacy for governor of Pennsylvania.

Henry Marchant to John Adams

You will receive this by my Friend Mr. Theodore Foster, of whom I wrote you fully in my last Letter—His Patriotism is very conspicuous in persevering and going forward as a Senator, when it must be his Interest to have accepted the Appointment of Naval Officer for the Port of Providence—I can assure You Sir, you will find Pleasure in the Candour, Modesty and good Sense of Mr. Foster; and his Sentiments very liberal—The Appointment of Our Friend Mr. [*William*] Ellery is very pleasing, and I beleive all the Appointments have given as general Satisfaction as might have taken Place—I presume the [*Rhode Island*] Judiciary Act and the Appointments under it, before this may have taken Place.

ALS, Adams Family Manuscript Trust, MHi. Written from Newport, Rhode Island.

Warner Mifflin to Benjamin Rush

Thy request for me to hand thee a Coppy of my Letter handed William Smith [*S.C.*], induced me therewith to send thee 3 other Little peices I selected from a Number I penned while ~~there~~ in [*New*] York, not with any desire, to spread any thing for ostentation, but as our Society was, there in so illiberal manner asperced, And myself personally held up as a ringleader of Sedition—And some of the debates in the House particularly alluding to some of those performances of mine, and very unjust constructions, thrown out respecting them I thought it would not be amiss to let, at least such as were friendly disposed and were desirous of knowing the truth, of things, have information how things really were—Thou may understand that this letter of mine was deliv'd Smith when in his seat, in Congress, about the middle part of the debates on the slave subject, I wonderd they were not Ashamed at their Conduct, However we must bare with them and am of the Faith it will be Seen that the Earth helpeth the woman.[1]

They Endeavour'd to asperse us very much for being enemies to the revolution, and consequently to the present goverment. *** I told them Generally I was for preserving the Harmony of Goverment though I might conceive there was some rotten pillars, therein. I was not for pulling them out at once in such manner as to endanger the building.

That we were imbarked in the same bottom with them, that our welfare, as to outwards was inseperably connected, and not only our own but our Childrens, that if we injur'd our Country we injurd our selves, and perhaps our posterity—Therefore, if they thought us wrong they ought, to impute it to an error, in judgment, and not to Malicious wickedness, for if we were so, we were so against our selves, as well as them—I also informed them, our principles, bound us to promote the peace of families, the peace of Neighbourhoods, and Surely the Peace of the Goverment that we lived, under, & That we were known to be a peacable people and against War, even against foreign Powers, And that Never any owned by us, were sowers of the seeds of Sedition, or ploters, or conspirators, against any Goverment under which we liv'd, and for our strict adherence to this our principle was the principle cause of so large a part of our Members being branded with the epithet of toryism, however all this I was favourd to bare I trust with becoming Patience, and Christian temperature of mind—The little letter to Abdiel Foster, Chairman of the Committee, and the Queries proposed to them were both deliv'd the Chairman, the piece directed to the Members generally, I had some Young men in New York set one morning after I penn'd it set to coppying and they finish'd for me I believe fourteen coppys, which I sent in by the door keeper and distributed among the Members—One of the days dureing the debates, and which tend to manifest, that those people had no Grounds for flame and foaming except it was that of wanting to shew themselves at home, to keep in with their constituents, which I very much by the by doubt, at least of the long continuance thereof.

Grany Pattin in a letter to my wife speaks that there are some even in Charleston that reprobate their conduct—and Applaud ours, *** I desire to move respecting the Negroe business and there in to do neither less nor more than my duty, Tho the flames from the South should yet raise. I see Nothing Terrible in them, they are but men whose breath as well as mine, is in their Nostrils,[2] and may be presently closed, as poor Blands is I am informed.

P.S. I expect I have a little piece gone out to them now, that thou may perhaps sea at a futer day.

ALS, Rush Papers, PPL at PHi. The enclosures were printed in the [Philadelphia] *American Museum,* probably at Rush's request.

[1] Revelations 12:16.
[2] Isaiah 2:22.

Robert Morris to Mary Morris

I have my Dearest Friend just received your affectionate and welcome letter of the 16th and thank you for the Solicitude which you express, and which I know but too well, that you feel, for my cares & anxieties they seem to increase every day, by one means or other, I have this very Moment come from the Public Office where a pretty difficult jobb, had been cut out for me;[1] to Remove some New Objections to Articles which I thought had been done with. But there seems to be no end to the troubles I am to encounter, I will however persevere untill I surmount all obstacles if possible. I do not Wonder that People are heartily tired of this question of Residence, I am exceedingly so, and often Regret that it was brought on, but our Delegation and some others were bent upon it, and perhaps it may still turn out for the best; We do not despair yet, altho it hangs in a disagreable Situation, No Matter we must now look forward for it will not do to Retreat, I am pleased that You took Notice of Mr. [*van*] Pradelles and doubt not but He will also be pleased therewith.

The Story you have heard respecting Mr. King & me is not true, that I have been Warm in some debates is true, but there was no personalities in the matter I cannot tell yet, when the Session is to end, We are now got to the Important business and it must not be long delayed, I dont like the present position but possibly the Clouds may Clear away and a bright Sky appear in the Political Horizon by & by.

You will be surprized when I tell you (except you should sooner hear it) that [*James*] LaCaze is here, He arrived in the last Packet & left Governeur Morris ~~well~~ in London on the 5th. of May very well, but no good News for me. Mr. [*William Constable*], the two Mrs. Constables & all the children went of[*f*] this Morning for Philipsburg [*New York*] where they are to pass the Summer, So that Mr. Chalmers [*John Chaloner*] & myself are to keep the House but He intends going after them tomorrow Mr. Constable is not well and intends staying a Week so that I shall be lonesome which probably is all for the best as I have much to do—I wish I could have Met [*son*] Robert at the Delaware Works,[2] if [*lined out*] the Packet had not arrived as she did I think it probable that I might have been in Your Company at this hour being now 7 oClock on Saturday Evening June 19th. 1790 perhaps I may add something to this letter tomorrow.

ALS, Morris Papers, CSmH. Place to which addressed not indicated. A postscript dated 21 June is printed under that date, below; for background, see *DHFFC* 8:663–65.

[1] Relating to Morris's cooperation with the treasury department auditor's pending settlement of Morris's secret committee accounts. For background, see *DHFFC* 8:663–65.

[2] The Delaware Works was a nascent complex of mills powered by the Falls of the Delaware and situated across the river from Trenton, New Jersey. Robert Morris bought the complex and the surrounding 450 acres from Samuel Ogden in December 1789, adding to land he began purchasing in 1787 to form Morrisville, Pennsylvania (*Transactions of the American Philosophical Society*, vol. 90, 5[2000]:2n).

Thomas Seymour to Jeremiah Wadsworth

I duly recd. your obliging answer of 14th Instant, to my last—am sensible Mr. [*William*] Imlays circumstances require [*illegible*] that he is personally able to do the Buissiness of a Loan Officer—but is the Union under any Obligations to him? has he rendered two Years personal Service in the most trying period of the Warr—expending his own monies with litle or no Compensation in the prime of Life; you know the fact I thot it was an Equitable & perhaps political principle now & we see it verifyed in most Instances, for the General Government, or the Executive of it, to remember thier Old Servants, & attach them, with their Connections, more ~~friendly~~ closely to their Interest—You will soon recollect with me, that not a Single One, bred in this Capital Town, holds or has held, an Office, under the General Government—this has been remarked—perhaps there are none fit.

I thank you for the good opinion you are pleased to express, of the *Integrity & real merit*, of my Son [*William*]: what can *Hartford* do for him, you know how he has served Connecticut with yourself—This is the more mortifying, when we see Strangers here, who have done nothing, Obtaining the Public favours—since, however, it seems to be a given point though not in all Cases, that new appointments must be continued in the Old line. must beg you not to mention my Son, tho' am Convinced of your good Intentions towards him—You'll allow me to mention another matter for your advice—my Son William you know lost his Limb in Fort Griswould, in Seper. 1781[1] he was allowed by the State £12— ℔ Ann.—that now Ceases—before he or I knew, that he could be further considered by the Superior Court as others who suffered, at same time, & placed on the continental List, the time Expired—will thank you to inform me, if he can petition Congres for Relief, & obtain further allowance, anually—or must his Application be first to Our Legislature, or how? perhaps there may be some precedent in Congress, upon this Subject—Our Comptroller [*Ralph Pomeroy*] has not returned his name among the List of Pensioners, that he may have an Oppoty. to obtain further Allowance, if may be—Your Answer will be very Oblidging.

ALS, Wadsworth Papers, CtHi. Written from Hartford, Connecticut.

[1] At Fort Griswold, located two miles above the mouth of the Thames River in Connecticut, state militia forces failed to halt British General Benedict Arnold's raid against nearby New London on 6 September 1781. William Seymour (d. 1821), who had served in the 5th Regiment of the Connecticut Line in 1775, was apparently lucky to escape with his life; almost half of the fort's 240 defenders were killed or mortally wounded.

Letter from a Member of Congress

Our disputes run high in Congress between 6 and 4 per cent. as the rate of interest at which the debt of the United States must be funded. Many of us hope to carry the latter, if funding must take place, as a just and practicable medium. We have also been extremely agitated about assuming, or not, the State debts, and about the temporary and permanent seats of Congress. The former, though frequently determined in the negative, is not lost sight of; and we have now hopes that we may get the permanent seat of Congress on Patowmack.

[Alexandria] *Virginia Gazette*, 1 July. The editors believe R. B. Lee authored the letter.

Other Documents

Jabez Bowen to George Washington. ALS, Washington Papers, DLC. Written from Providence, Rhode Island. For the full text, see *PGW* 5:533–35.
Office seeking: Benjamin Bourn as federal attorney for the Rhode Island district.

Bartholomew Burges to John Adams. ALS, Adams Family Manuscript Trust, MHi. Written from 3 Little Dock Street, New York.
On Adams's advice, asked Washington for his public support for Burges's proposals (for promoting navigation), which the President declined to do; Burges intends to teach geography in New York, and asks Adams for a three dollar loan; submits his *Indostan Letters* for Adams's perusal.

Solomon Drowne to Louis Guillaume Otto. Copy, Drowne Papers, RPB. Written from Providence, Rhode Island; carried by T. Foster.
Introduces T. Foster who "is a firm Federalist, a friend of the rights of man, and an avowed enemy to Tyranny, whatever form assuming. You will find him a Gentleman poss[*ess*]ed of those amiable qualities of the heart that give the finest zest to social enjoyment. Any Attentions shown to this genuine American" will be appreciated.

Richard Henry Lee to Thomas Lee Shippen. ALS, Shippen Family Papers, DLC. Place to which addressed not indicated. This is a postscript to Lee's letter to Shippen, 17 June, above. Shippen was courting a Miss Allen of Philadelphia in the summer of 1790, perhaps a relation to the Allen household at 155 Chestnut Street, whom Lee may have been referring to as the "Angel Group."

"Since writing as on the other side a dawn of hope presents for our yet going to Philadelphia—But you shall hear more of this so soon as we have tried our new experiment—Remember me to the Angel Group in Chestnut Street."

Samuel Phillips, Jr. to Benjamin Goodhue. ALS, Letters to Goodhue, NNS. Written from Boston.

News of the Massachusetts legislature, in which the House is to report a bill for suspending the state excise as soon as Congress approves an assumption of the state debts; ascribes the only cause of popular discontent with the state's excise to its more stringent enforcement than in the past, and the requirement of payment in specie only; regards to "our worthy Friend Mr. Strong—I am not insensible of his goodness, tho' I have not expressed it to him."

Philip Schuyler to Catherine Schuyler. ALS, Schuyler Papers, NN. Place to which addressed not indicated.

Procures household provisions; Congress has been "in great confusion all last week" about the removal of Congress and the funding system; things "now wear a better face and we have hopes that Congress will remain here four years more, and that Colo. Hamilton funding plan will be in general adopted. I sincerely wish our hopes realized. If so I shall have the happiness to see you in about a fortnight"; reports on probable Anglo-Spanish war; criticizes John Barker Church's gambling habits; notes no letter from Angelica Schuyler Church; reports that all are well.

Theodore Sedgwick to Pamela Sedgwick. ALS, Sedgwick Papers, MHi. Place to which addressed not indicated.

Regrets that his last letter seems to have miscarried; "I have felt myself too severely the pain of neglect ever to inflict it" on her; Pamela's "fortitude and magnanimity, the most distinguishing qualities" of her "delicately sensible" mind, will enable her to withstand the pain of absence and the "loss of friends"; the letter will be delivered by Mr. (Martin?) Hoffman; in the morning visited the home of an "unfortunate gentleman from the southward" who had committed suicide earlier that day and whose Black manservant was barely prevented from committing suicide himself, out of grief.

Theodore Sedgwick to Theodore Sedgwick, Jr. ALS, Sedgwick Papers, MHi. Place to which addressed not indicated.

Letters from his children please Sedgwick more than his to them, "for you have mamma & Brothers & sisters, and I am here alone"; "I depend on you to take care of every thing."

Dummer Sewall to George Thatcher. ALS, Chamberlain Collection, MB. Written from Boston; franked; postmarked 20 June.

After a long debate, the Massachusetts legislature decided the day before to retain its current congressional districting; the state Senate has sent to the House a bill suspending the excise until either its next session or until Congress approves an assumption; recommends a weekly post to Wiscasset and a post office at Bath, Maine, where Sewall would accept an appointment as postmaster if offered him; recommends Davis Sumner as an excise officer if Congress passes an excise.

Benjamin Stelle to George Washington. ALS, Washington Papers, DLC.

Office seeking: naval officer at Providence, Rhode Island; mentions Ellsworth, Maclay, and the Rhode Island Senators as references.

Jeremiah Wadsworth to Harriet Wadsworth. ALS, Wadsworth Papers, CtHi. Addressed to Hartford, Connecticut; franked; postmarked; signed, "Your affectionate friend & Parent." The novel Wadsworth refers to is probably *Zeluco* (New York, 1790), attributed to John Moore (1729–1802).

Is very well; the season is cool and pleasant; does not know when Congress will adjourn, but hopes to visit home on 4 July; Trumbull is well; his brother John is not yet returned (from Philadelphia); describes and promises to send "a new Novel said to be written by Mr. Moore"; thinks it "the best Novel I have read"; attempts to procure household goods.

[Rhode Island] *Providence Gazette*, 19 June.

T. Foster departed for New York this day, carrying the address to George Washington from the Providence Association of Manufacturers and Mechanics; Stanton will leave on 21 June. (There is no known evidence of when Foster may have presented the address, dated 4 June; the Washington Papers dates the reply only as June 1790. Foster took his seat in the Senate on 25 June.)

SUNDAY, 20 JUNE 1790

Hot (Johnson)

Tench Coxe to Benjamin Rush

***

The opinion here seems to be rather in favor [*of*] concession on the part of Spain in their recent Quarrel with England—If she [*Spain*] admits the right to navigate those seas, she will see trouble in her Colonies before the end of this century I think—and if she does not a very severe conflict awaits her this year, & other matters relative to her Southern Dominions will be involved.

Mr. Fitzsimons tells me that Mr. F[*rederick*]. M[*uhlenberg*]. agrees to withdraw in favor of Mr. Morris.[1] Is this so understood amongst friends of the former in Ph[*iladelphi*]a.

I am totally at a loss how to give you an opinion about the Seat of Government—I believe however that the E[*astern*]. Gentlemen are possessed with an Idea, that it will not do for them to return without the Assumption & that [*they*] will try to get that acceded to by means of the other. This entre nous.

I electerized our whole table (among them Messrs. Jefferson, Maddison & a Count [*Paolo*] Andreani of Milan cousin of yr. friend Castiliani[2]) by the relation of the fact relative to Maple Sugar—I wish more particulars of the time—trees tap'd—size & number of Kettles used—hands employed—process &ca. Mr. Jefferson is for [*sending*] Ld. Hawkesbury (C. Jenkinson) a Cask of it[3]—I presume this quantity has converted the unbelievers in Philada.

You have been told that a Comme. of the Senate have reported to give 4 ℔ Ct. & none of the Alternatives—Messrs. McClay, Ellsworth, Lee, King & Paterson were the Come. The first three were in favor of the Report—The Assumption is the great Obstacle to progress in the funding Business, tho the residence & a desire [*lined out*] in some to postpone the public debts till next Session both operate.

***

On the subject of the influence of a friend of mine against Pha. be assured I will convince you of the Error when I see you—I pledge myself to do it— ***

ALS, Rush Papers, PPL at PHi. Place to which addressed not indicated. This undated letter, to which Rush replied on 24 June, was written between 15 June (the date of a Senate committee report that Coxe mentions) and 22 June (the latest possible date of a letter to which Rush would have been able to reply). The probability of a date closer to 20 June is based on two considerations: Coxe indicates that Rush had already been informed of the Senate committee report, and Rush was in the habit of responding immediately to Coxe's letters during this period. The omitted text discusses business matters and recommends one of the "discourses on Davila," attributed to Adams, a sample of which Coxe encloses.

---

[1] In Pennsylvania's upcoming gubernatorial election.

[2] Count Luigi Castiglioni (1757–1832), a noted botanist from Milan, met many prominent members of America's scientific community during his travels through North America, 1785–87, which he wrote about in his famous *Viaggio*, published in 1790 (*PGW: Confederation* 3:453n).

[3] No friend to the United States, Charles Jenkinson (1727–1808) served as Lord North's secretary at war after 1778. In 1786 he became Baron Hawkesbury and chairman of the privy council's committee on trade and plantations. From then until 1794 he virtually dictated British commercial policy toward the United States (Jerald A. Combs, *The Jay Treaty* [Berkeley, Calif., 1970], p. 87).

William Davies to Governor Beverley Randolph

***

Since I had the honor of writing your Excellency last, I have spent two days with Mr. Madison in the examination of the various reports from the public offices here, and am happy to find that under all our disadvantages, should the business of the assumption be brought on again, Virginia will appear at least equal in her exertions to her more immediate antagonists Massachusetts & South Carolina—The two Commissioners [*John Taylor Gilman and John Kean*] for their crude report are disposed to shelter themselves under the excuses of want of time and of misinformation from their principal clerk; and I am inclined to think that the circumstance of some of the unstated papers, bro't on by Mr. [*William*] Winder, being at the time more immediately the object of attention with the principal clerk, induced him, and consequently them, to be more particular with respect to Virginia than any other State, tho' their mode of expression has given so much disgust to most of the southern members, that in the new bill two more Commissioners are provided to be added, and much of that business of the board is proposed to be [*lined out*] transferred to the Comptroller & Auditor of the Treasury, so as to make their continuance less necessary. From the report, Maryland, Virginia North Carolina & Georgia appear to be nearly on the same footing as to the state of preparation in which their accounts are; South Carolina indeed is represented as having her claims regularly stated, & vouched, but at the same time a letter is annexed from her Senators & Representatives dated so late as the 29th April 1790, in which they prefer an additional gross claim of three millions of dollars— ***

ALS, Executive Papers, Vi. Addressed to Richmond, Virginia; postmarked 22 June. For more, see Report of the Commissioners for Settling Accounts between the United States and Individual States, 9 May, above.

Christopher Gore to Rufus King

I do most sincerely hope that your exertions for the Assumption, & establishing the permanent residence of Congress may meet with success—so many unfortunate quarrels among the members of Congress about questions in which few citizens only are interested, to the neglect of those matters in which all are engaged, have afforded grounds of complaint against the government, without raising any friends to advocate the measures of administration—Dalton's Election I think probable—the candidates are numerous—[*Charles*] Jarvis and his party have, in vain, endeavored to obtain a choic by joint ballot, of the two branches, in one room—[*Nathaniel*] Goreham is a candidate, but he declares that he will not frustrate any measures, that may be thought conducive to his D[*alton*].'s success—I wish he woud take an active part in Dalton's favor—this and Strong's influence by letter to his friends, woud insure him an handsome Majority—the time is not yet assign'd for the choice—but a fortnight will probably include the time—You may rest satisfied that no pains will be spared on my part to effect this measure—it is one in ~~which~~ the success of which I shoud greatly & sincerely rejoice—Doctor [*Benjamin J.*] Porter has not come to Boston—I will send the letter to him & shall be happy in his acquaintance, & when he comes this way I will certainly pay him all the attentions in my power—the next week will end my nephew's residence at Harvard[1]—and then I will reply to Your letter on [*seal*] subject.

ALS, King Papers, NHi. Written from Boston; franked; postmarked.

[1] John Callender (1772–1833), son of Gore's sister Elizabeth.

Thomas Hartley to Jasper Yeates

***

We have been on the Ways and Means Bill [*Duties on Distilled Spirits Bill HR-62*]—and you can scarcely conceive what Embarrassments we have—The Eastern People want no Funding without Assumption of the State Debts—and will of course reduce the ways and Means as much as possible—and several Gentlemen of the Senate are agst. the Increase of Duties and Excise—(Indeed I do not like the Excise as proposed, myself but I believe I must take the Dose) so that to Morrow upon the Question—shall the Bill be engrossed I should not be surprized that it will be lost—and then Pennsylvania will be in a good Way—The Eastern men we cannot trust and some of the Southern Gentlemen are whimsical.

The News Papers will tell you what we have been doing here and give you an Idea of the State of Things in Europe—A Spanish war is talked of with England—but the Don I am inclined to think must subscribe to the Terms England shall offer.

The President looks well again.

ALS, Yeates Papers, PHi. Addressed to Lancaster, Pennsylvania; franked; postmarked; answered by post 27 June. In the omitted text, Hartley regrets not receiving a line from Yeates that week and discusses crops.

Thomas Jefferson to James Monroe

***

Congress has been long embarrassed by two of the most irritating questions that ever can be raised among them, 1. the funding the public debt. and 2. the fixing on a more central residence. after exhausting their arguments & patience on these subjects, they have for some time been resting on their oars, unable to get along as to these businesses, and indisposed to attend to any thing else till they are settled. and in fine it has become probable that unless they can be reconciled by some plan of compromise, there will be no funding bill agreed to, our credit, (raised by late prospects to be the first on the exchange at Amsterdam, where our paper is above par) will burst and vanish, and the states separate to take care every one of itself. this prospect appears probable to some well-informed ~~minds~~ and well-disposed minds. endeavours are therefore using to bring about a disposition to some mutual sacrifices. the assumption of the state debts has appeared as revolting to several states as their non-assumption to others. it is proposed to strip the proposition of the injustice it would have done by leaving the states who have redeemed much of their debts on no better footing than those who have redeemed none; on the contrary it is recommended to assume a fixed sum allotting a portion of it to every state in proportion to it's census. consequently every one will receive exactly what they will have to pay, or they will be exonerated so far by the general government's taking their creditors off their hands. there will be no injustice then. but there will be the objection still that Congress must then lay taxes for these debts which could have been much better laid & collected by the state governments. and this is the objection on which the accomodation now hangs with the Non-assumptioners, many of whom committed themselves in their advocation of the new constitution by arguments drawn from the improbability that Congress would ever lay taxes where the states could do it separately. these gentlemen feel the reproaches which will be levelled at them personally. ~~but I think it~~ I have been & still am of their opinion that Congress should always prefer letting the states raise money in their own way where it can be done. but in the present instance I see the necessity of yeilding for this time to the cries of the creditors in certain parts of the union, for the sake of union. and to save us from the greatest of all calamities, the total extinction of our credit in Europe. on the other subject it is proposed to pass an act fixing the temporary residence for 12. or 15 years at Philadelphia, and that at the end of that time it shall stand ipso facto & without further declaration transferred to Georgetown [*Maryland*]. in this way there will be something to displease & something to soothe every part of the Union, but New York, which must be contented with what she has had. if this plan of compromise does not take place I fear one infinitely worse, an unqualified assumption & the perpetual residence on the Delaware. the Pennsylvania & Virginia delegations have conducted themselves honorably & unexceptionably on the question of residence. without descending to talk about bargains they have seen that their true interests lay in not listening to insidious propositions made to divide & defeat them, and we have seen them at times voting against their respective wishes rather than separate.

***

ALS, Monroe Papers, NN. Addressed to Monroe at Charlottesville, Virginia, "to be left in the post office Richmond"; franked; postmarked. For the full text, see *PTJ* 16:536–38. The omitted text expresses hopes of soon seeing Mrs. Elizabeth Kortright Monroe at New York and discusses European affairs.

Thomas Jefferson to Thomas Mann Randolph, Jr.

***

Congress are much embarrassed by the two questions of assumption, and residence. all proceedings seem to be arrested till these can be got over. and for the peace & continuance of the union, a mutual sacrifice of opinion & interest is become the duty of every one: for it is evident that if every one retains inflexibly his present opinion, there will be no bill passed at all for funding the public debts, & if they separate without funding, there is an end of the government. in this situation of things, the only choice is among disagreeable things. the assumption must be admitted, but in so qualified a form as to divest it of it's injustice. this may be done by assuming to the creditors of every state, a sum exactly proportioned to the contributions of the state: so that the state will on the whole neither gain nor lose. there will remain against the measure only the objection that Congress must lay taxes for these debts which might be better laid & collected by the states. on the question of residence, the compromise proposed is to give it to Philadelphia for 15. years, & then permanently to George town by the same act. this is the best arrangement we have now any prospect of, & therefore the one to which all our wishes are at present pointed. if this does not take place, something much worse will; to wit an unqualified assumption & the permanent seat on the Delaware. the delegations of this state ~~have and~~ and Pennsylvania have conducted themselves with great honor and wisdom on these questions. they have by a steady (yet not a stipulated) concurrence avoided insidious baits which have been held out to divide them & defeat their object.

***

ALS, Jefferson Papers, DLC. Place to which addressed not indicated. The omitted text discusses Randolph's settling in Albemarle County, Virginia, and European affairs, and notes enclosure of a letter to "Patsy" (daughter Martha Jefferson Randolph) from a British packet ship.

Benjamin Lincoln to Theodore Sedgwick

I have my dear friend received your favour of the

I wrote to Mr. Ames some time since perhaps three perhaps four weeks[1] giving my ideas of the danger which would arise from making it an unaltrable condition to passing the funding act that of embracing the debts of the United States I wrote my own feelings on the subject perhaps my ideas were wrong—If he has received the letter I presume he thinks them so for he has not even acknowledged the receipt of the letter—If he has not received the letter I am apprehensive that it shall fall into improper hands—I wish you would endeavour to find out whether he has received the letter or not, I shall be made happy on knowing it is in his hands for it was intended for the eye of Mr. Ames only.

If you think the inclosed will avail our friend you will please to seal & deliver it.

ALS, Sedgwick Papers, MHi. Written from Boston. Enclosure not found.

[1] Lincoln's letter to Ames, 20 May, above.

Richard Peters to Thomas Jefferson

*** I wish most sincerely the Affair of your Residence was somehow determined. The Transactions on that Subject cast a Shade on the congressional Character. I had enough of it when I was in the old Congress[1] & I see it is the same Pack of Cards shuffled & used for another Game. An odd Trick is often won I see by those who do not get the Rubber. If the Big Knife[2] would give up Potowmack the Matter would be easily settled. But that you will say, is as unreasonable as it would be to expect a Pennsilvanian to surrender at Discretion to New York. I very much wish you to come here but knowing how uncertain the Thing is, I do not suffer myself to be sanguine. It therefore amuses me to see the Arguments our grave politicians bring forward when I know it will be determined by local Interests which will not suffer Intrigue & Management to grow rusty for Want of Use—Unless indeed the Vote should finally settle down for Germantown or Philada.—In that Case *all the World will see* that Reason & the general Welfare have induced the Measure—You perceive I have not the least Taint of local Attachment—If I had *private* Reasons for desiring you to sojourn here it would be no more reprehensible than it is in one of your great Men who candidly acknowledges he has *private* Reasons against it.[3] As to my Friend Gerry, who moved his Lodging's from a Street here because it was not a sweet one & took up his Quarters opposite our Shambles for the sake of the Air,[4] I never expect his Judgment will be ripe enough to do right in this Residence Bussiness. But I am sorry that Madison, who is a good corrigible Boy a little spoiled by bad Play Mates, should continue to play Truant from us. Let me convey my affectionate Regards to him thro' a Minister of State which he will then receive not for the Value of them but the Channell thro' which they pass; as, if a Man must drink Water, taking it out of a Silver Mug at least gives a luxurious Shew to the homely Tipple—All this [*is*] *Badinage.*

***

ALS, Peters Papers, PHi. Written from "Belmont," Peters's estate outside Philadelphia; postmarked Philadelphia, 21 June; received 23 June. The omitted text relates to a private legal matter and Philadelphia social life. For the full text, see *PTJ* 16:538–40.

[1] Peters was deeply involved in the politics surrounding this issue in the months following the departure of Congress from Philadelphia in June 1783.

[2] A Native American reference to Virginia and Virginians, and, in this case, likely a double entendre for George Washington.

[3] Burke so stated in a House speech on 10 June (*DHFFC* 13:1554).

[4] Gerry served in Congress from 1776 to 1780 and resided in Philadelphia when Congress met there.

William Smith (Md.) to Jeremiah Wadsworth

W. Smith, Requests the favor of Colo. Wadsworth to e[*n*]quire, *on his return to Connecticut*, for a young man of good character, qualified to teach, two or three boys, the languages &ca. He will be accommodated in a genteel family furnished with a Library of Books, either, of Law, Physick, or divinity—the Situation, not exceeding three miles from Baltimore—If Such a person is to be found willing to undertake, a line forwarded to Colo. J[*osias*]. Carvil Hall, or W. S., with the terms, that may be acceptable will oblige.

AN, Wadsworth Papers, CtHi.

John Steele to Governor Alexander Martin

I have written you several letters since my arrival, but whether you have reced. them or not is altogether uncertain. Congress has been and still is much divided respecting the permanent seat of Government, the Assumption of the State debts, the excise bill [*Duties on Distilled Spirits HR-62*], the settlement of Accounts between the United [*States*] and the Individual States [*HR-77*] and the regulation of the Militia [*HR-81*]. These are all important questions and tho' they have been under consideration near six months not one of them is yet decided on.

The Gentlemen from the eastern States differ in sentiments so much from us on the mode of raising revenue and seem to be so unacquainted, or so regardless of the Interest the situation: the feelings and I might add the poverty of the people in the southern States that there is little prospect of doing any thing this Session that will terminate for the good of the whole.

I am well informed that six Million of our continental securities are now in the hands of persons living in Holland, how the people of America will submit to be taxed for the discharge of this debt when they are sensible that these foreigners purchased them at 5/ in the pound, is a question which time must decide. I have been using my utmost exertions to pass the continental post road through Fayetteville [*North Carolina*] it has passed our House, if the Senate concurs I shall be able to be more useful to my constituents by transmitting them timely and regular Information—Yesterday the Brittish packet arrived with advices of a rupture between that nation and Spain a consequence of an insult offered the Brittish flag in the Nootka Sound on the western Coast of the Continent. Perhaps his Catholic Majesty [*Spain*] has been stimulated to this quarrel from the prudential consideration of diverting his subjects from catching the French enthusiasm for liberty, or perhaps his Britannic Majesty may have cast an Eye on the navigation of the Mississippi Be this as it may the Spaniards have captured two brittish Ships and the King of England has called on his faithful Commons for a supply to enable him to resent the injury. America must be benefitted by the struggle. Virginia has given instructions to her Senators to open the doors on the discussion of all legislative business—whether it would be proper for No. Carolina to give similar instructions is not my province to determine However whenever the State thinks proper to interfere I flatter myself she will always speak the language of a SOVEREIGNTY.

FC:lbk, Governors' Papers, Nc-Ar. Place to which addressed not indicated.

James Sullivan to Elbridge Gerry

I thank for yours of the 5th and am very glad to find that the opinion of the Governor and Legislature respecting the assumption is so perfectly agreeable to you and your Colleagues. I hope Congress will lay an Excise and appropriate the proceeds in each State to the particular benefit of the state. unless you assume the debts Congress can never go on with their Government if they tax all the people upon the Score of the debt of the United States exclusive of the demand of the Creditors of the several states, and suffer the Species of Creditors to be ruined. I have lived long enough to see that all world is governed by necessity, and therefore beleive we Shall do right one of these Days. you will have [*Nathaniel*] Gorham for a rival as I am Told in the next Election. our news here is not worth mentioning.

ALS, Gerry Papers, MHi. Written from Boston; franked; postmarked 22 June.

George Thatcher to Sarah Thatcher

Since my last I have received yours of the 6th. continued to the 10th. & of the 12th. inst. In the first you tell me you are "reading Dodd on Death"[1]—this is rather a melancholy treatise & I think you had better lay it aside, for the present—You had better read Fordyce on Education[2]—I do not recommend this Book from my own knowledge—indeed I have read but two or three Dialogues, & do not know enough about it to say whether it is a usefull book or not—and I wish you to read it, that if it is a good one you may ~~profit~~ [*be*] amused by it—and if a trifling thing I may save myself the time & trouble of reading it.

***

I cannot yet fix the time when I shall be at home—but hope it is not a great way off—I did not think you were too impatient at my absence—I ment no more than to assure you I would be at home as soon as I could, without giving occasion for any body to blame my leaving public Business.

***

It gives me great pleasure to hear that [*son*] Phillips continues his school—& loves his school-mistress—I think the more notice you take of her, the more willingly he will go to school—You must be carefull, however, that your attention to her does not make her feel a kind of involuntary obligation to humour & indulge him, even in particular circumstances, where she ought, and otherwise would use due correction—This would be an injury to him.

***

Since the hot weather has come on a scurfy itching humour has broke out on my legs & hands—which is very troublesome—I am tormented also with boils & little sores.

ALS, Thatcher Family Papers, MHi. Place to which addressed not indicated. The omitted text relates to Silas Lee's health and Thatcher's procurement of household goods.

[1] *Reflections on Death* (1763), by the noted British clergyman and author William Dodd (1729–77), whose hanging for forgery was a cause célèbre.

[2] David Fordyce (1711–51), Scottish philosopher, was author of the popular *Dialogues Concerning Education* (2 vols., London, 1745–48).

Unknown to William Smith (Md.)

The paper of the 15th has given us a hope, that Baltimore may be the seat of Congress. That nothing may be wanting on our part a Town meeting was called for tomorrow, at 4 oClock. And I have not the smallest doubt, but a Sum will be raised, in a few hours, fully Sufficient, to prepare a building, to accommodate both houses of Congress, Untill such time, as the funds of the United States will Justify them, in erecting a building, Suitable to the honor & dignity of the Union. Whenever that Shall be the case, they will have, the Square, of 500 feet, on each Side, at the head of Markett Streett. Situate on an eminence, that commands, one of the most delightful prospects in Maryld. or perhaps in the U.S.—*Which Square*, will be given to Congress by Govr. [*John Eager*] Howard. The Area, thereof, will be fully Sufficient to erect thereon, the Federal building. And the Sides, for the Presidents House, the Hotels, of each State, & the officers of government.[1] The water is excellent, the Air pure, & Situation healthy. A number of good dwelling houses to be had for the immediate accomodation, of Public officers. And it is unnecessary to add, that the Boarding houses, are as good as any in America, & Sufficient, *fully*, to Accomodate Congress, to their Satisfaction. It is further to be Observed, That Baltimore is the only commercial Town, of Consequence, in the Union, that has been offered to Congress. And among the few, of deficult access, to an enemy.

We propose a temporary house at the corner of Holiday Street, 100 feet by 40. with committee chambers, runing back, from each corner, which will give a room for the Delegates, 50 feet by 40. an entrey 20 feet wide. And a Senate room, 30 feet by 40. with rooms above for offices.

I have only to add, that the inhabitants are disposed, to pay every attention, in their power, to the Representatives of the Union, & will use every exertion to make their residence comfortable & easey.

Copy, hand of Smith, Butler Papers, PHi. Written from Baltimore. This was an enclosure in Smith to Butler, 25 June, calendared below.

[1] The site is at present-day Broadway and Congress Court, just south of Johns Hopkins Hospital.

Letter from New York

I expected, from the late almost unanimous Vote in Favour of Baltimore, that I should soon have had the Pleasure of congratulating you on its being fixed on for the permanent Seat of Congress; but the Postponement of the Question, by the Senate, has given Time for Intrigues; and it is now confidently asserted, that the Philadelphians have outwitted your Members, by offering to vote for the Patowmac as the permanent Seat, provided they vote for Congress remaining Fifteen Years in Philadelphia, which Bait has been greedily swallowed: It is thought Carrollsburg [*Maryland, in present-day Washington, D.C.*] is the spot fixed on. This will be realizing the Fable of the Two Bitches.[1] When Philadelphia gets Possession of Congress, Carrollsburg will scarcely be able, Fifteen Years hence, to persuade her to part from so good a Friend, and, I suppose, will be too weak to compel a Compliance, against Philadelphia and a Host of Puppies, grown fat and strong in office.

[Baltimore] *Maryland Journal*, 25 June; reprinted at New York City (*NYDA*, *NYDG*, 2 July, *NYP* 3 July) and Poughkeepsie, New York; New Brunswick, New Jersey; Richmond, Virginia; and Edenton, North Carolina.

[1] In Aesop's fable, a house dog was rewarded with the fruits of the hound's labor.

Other Documents

William Channing to Theodore Foster. ALS, Foster Papers, RHi. Written from Newport, Rhode Island. The address sheet includes Channing's directions that an enclosed item be returned in case Walter Channing will have already left New York for Newport.

Offers congratulations on Foster's election; "Your Situation will be pleasing after the great questions now before Congress are decided"; has been informed that day that those questions will soon be resolved in favor of assumption and a removal to Philadelphia; "you will have an opportunity of forming Acquaintance with the most respectable Characters on the Continent," including Senator Henry, Channing's classmate at Princeton, who was "much esteemed" and whom Foster will find "a sensible and a very amiable Character"; sends regards to Henry; office seeking: recommends (Jabez?) Champlin and (brother) Walter Channing, whom he asks Foster to introduce to Henry.

William R. Davie to James Iredell. ALS, Iredell Papers, NcD. Written from Halifax, North Carolina; answered.

Has received letters from Johnston, Steele, and Hawkins since the North Carolina Judiciary Act [HR-68] was passed, but none informs him where the (district and circuit) courts were to be held; supposed that his last letter to Williamson would have prevented his appointment (as federal district judge), which he cannot accept because of its low salary; Johnston wrote him that he and his family were all inoculated against the smallpox and doing very well.

Oliver Ellsworth to Abigail Ellsworth. ALS, Ellsworth Papers, CtHi. Place to which addressed not indicated.

Instructions regarding household finances; is glad that Nabby (daughter Abigail) likes her muslin; Nabby will be able to come either to New York City or Philadelphia; he is not yet certain where Congress will meet next, but believes it not yet improbable it will be in New York; asks for accounts of their children; he was very (happy to receive?) [*torn*] the letter from "Olle" (son Oliver).

Benjamin Goodhue to Stephen Goodhue. ALS, Goodhue Family Papers, MSaE. Addressed to Salem, Massachusetts; franked; postmarked.

"when I wrote you last I thought there was an appearance of accommodation relative to the assumption, but every thing seems yet involved in darkness—the southern members seem consulting. and we are ignorant of their intentions"; advises on joint mercantile affairs; requests news of Lisbon market.

Benjamin Goodhue to an Unknown Recipient. Listing of ALS, *John Heise Catalog* 400(1926):53.

Catharine Greene to Henry Knox. ALS, Knox Papers, Gilder Lehrman Collection, NHi. Written from Bethlehem, Pennsylvania.

Discusses her upcoming claim to Congress; "while it occurs to me, let me te[*ll*] you, that Col., or rather Genl. Jackson is one of the persons who is to be my opponent—this he has declared Publicly."

Henry Jackson to Henry Knox. ALS, Knox Papers, Gilder Lehrman Collection, NHi. Written from Boston.

"From enquiry I find there will be great ~~Interest~~ opposition made to Mr. Daltons Election. they have no particular objection to him, but they say it is best to change, they have the power & will exercise it—he is on the nomination with Doctr. [*Charles*] Jarvis, Mr. [*Nathaniel*] Gorham & Mr.

George Cabbot. it is said if the last mentioned will accept, he will be the man—as they have so in view it will give Mr. D. a better chance, and I hope he will be reelected."

Robert Morris to George Harrison. ALS, Brinton-Coxe Papers, PHi. Place to which addressed not indicated; received and answered 22 June.

Estimates he has had Harrison's last letter for about a week, and blames his silence on his "full occupation"; private business concerns; advises caution on Harrison's agreeing to a proposed partnership, having suffered more because of partners "than from any other cause in the whole course of my Life"; hopes Congress will soon adjourn; "the Important business is now before the Senate and cannot be delayed there."

Robert Parrish to William Bartram. ALS, Miscellaneous Manuscripts, NHi. Addressed to the care of Isaac Gray, Second Street near Race Street, Philadelphia; carried by J(ohn?). Shoemaker. A postscript is calendared under 21 June, below.

The letters to Morris from William Bingham and Bishop William White proved of "considerable advantage" in Parrish's securing subscribers in New York City for Bartram's *Travels* (Philadelphia, 1791); Bartram's illustrations of the crane and the mockingbird are much admired; suggests that the book be dedicated to Adams, Jay, or "Some of the Other first characters here," since Washington has declined.

Philip Schuyler to Catherine Schuyler. ALS, Schuyler Papers, NN. Place to which addressed not indicated. The recipient's identity is based on the salutation, "My Dear and Amiable Child," and the content, which suggests the child was a female. Catherine was the only daughter living at home at this time.

Promises to send pretty things that her sister Cornelia will procure for her.

Philip Schuyler to Catherine Schuyler. ALS, Schuyler Papers, NN. Place to which addressed not indicated.

Is sending sugar, tea, and snuff.

Theodore Sedgwick to Thomas Dwight. No copy known; acknowledged in Dwight to Sedgwick, 24 June.

Theodore Sedgwick to Benjamin Lincoln. No copy known; acknowledged in Lincoln to Sedgwick, 26 June.

John Steele to Joseph Winston. ALS, Steele Papers, NcU. Addressed to Stokes County, North Carolina, in care of Governor Alexander Martin, who forwarded it; franked.

"At present I suppose half of my letters fall by the way a sacrafice to curiosity"; summarizes some provisions of the Duties on Distilled Spirits Bill [HR-62]; "the duty is high, and will operate unequally"; "I have opposed this bill in every stage of its passage and tomorrow will have the yeas, and nays on the last reading; tho' I am apprehensive it will pass by a large majority"; communicate the contents of this letter to "my friend Mr. Houser [*Michael Howser?*], I have not time to write to him."

William Samuel Johnson, Diary. Johnson Papers, CtHi.

"St. Pauls."

MONDAY, 21 JUNE 1790

Cool (Johnson)

William Ellery to Benjamin Huntington

***

I am much obliged to you, to Mr. [*A.*] Foster, and Coll. Partridge and all the gentlemen who have contributed towards my obtaining an appointment which will fill up my time profitably, and, in addition to my income, ~~render~~ give me a comfortable subsistance.

I ~~can~~ may make a shift indeed to mount upon the roost—but an old Cock cannot crow so frequently and so strongly as a young one. By the way of Rhode-Island my wife brought me a fine boy last December, and we named him George Wanton; now if you or either of the gentlemen above named or all of you together can find any connection between George [*an*]d the Collector's Office; and between Wanton, and the Crowing of a cock I will set you down for Conjurors—and by the way of a squint Coll. Partridge's cock never crew in his life. I am glad you are not a senator. if you were I should not dare to trifle with you in this playful manner. Don't for your life say one word to Coll. Partridge about his biddy, or day breaker as our country Quaker Girls call cocks. If you should he would deny it as obstinately as Peter did his master.[1] How to jump ~~to~~ from this to any thing like a sober strain, puzzles me confoundedly. Socrates when he had drank [*the*] poison desired his friend Clito—to remember that he owed a Cock to Æsculapius. If I should be wrong in this peice of history the President of Columbia College [*Johnson*] can set me right. *** I hear that John Bull [*England*] begins to but[*t*] at the Spaniard. The latter may want help, if the former should goad him; and what will the family compact signify if he is not assisted by the French Cock. I find I am getting into European politics, and I had determined not to [*say*] a word in this letter about any sort of politics, otherwise I should have told you long ago that our Antis were very quiet, that the Assembly is to meet in Septemr. when a Representative may or may not be chosen, that one of our Senators Mr. [*T.*] Foster, who is a modest, ingenious man is gone on for N. York, and that his colleague Mr. Stanton, [*lined out*] of whom as I cannot say ~~in~~ any thing in his praise I think it will be most prudent to be silent, soon follow. I should have said something about the Assumption of the State Debts, of the redemption of the Old Conti[*nental*]. or rather the funding of it at one hundred for one, of regulating weights and measures, of coinage, of the Western Posts, and I don't know what; but as I had made that determination, and as I recollect something about servetur ad imum,[2] I think I had better leave of ~~Letter~~ here by saying at least one serious thing in this Letter.

ALS, Benjamin Huntington Correspondence, 1772–1790, R-Ar. Written from Newport, Rhode Island; franked; postmarked; answered 2 July. The omitted text indicates a power of attorney was enclosed, authorizing Huntington to receive money from the treasury department on Ellery's behalf.

---

[1] Matthew 26:34–75.

[2] A paraphrase of the precept coined by the Roman poet Horace, meaning, the tone begun with ought to be retained to the end.

Samuel R. Gerry to Elbridge Gerry

*** We are happy to hear you with Mrs. [*Ann Thompson*] Gerry have recovered [*from*] your Indisposition & pray that your Health may be Con~~firmedtinued~~firmed ~~to you~~ to you—We have a Report circulating here in Salem ~~& beyond~~ that you with Mr. Ames had recd. a Challenge from two of the Southern Members ~~you~~ & that you had accepted & met on the Spot but by the Interposition of your friends on both Sides the duel was happily prevented—& the Cause merely from supporting the Rights of your Constituents, such Matters taking Place ~~alarms the minds~~ in the ~~Grand~~ Great Councils of America alarm the minds of the People greatly & however disposed the Southern Members may be in over bearing come to the touch Stone[1] I believe they will find more than their Match in the Northern States ~~for~~but trust that no Troubles of the Kind may take Place altho the People feels the heavy ~~Tax~~ Burthens Laid on our Navigation & fishery—but may God preserve you from riskg. you Life with such high blooded ~~Chaps~~

Men, who from there great Property Looks on all these Eastern States below them— ***

FC:lbk, Gerry Papers, MHi. Written from Marblehead, Massachusetts. The author was identified by his handwriting and the salutation "Dear Brother." The omitted text laments the poor return on a financial transaction owing to the "impoverished Situation of the Town," regrets "my Entering the Fishery," and relates family news.

[1] The moment of truth.

Robert Morris to Mary Morris

Mr. Fitzsimmons and myself Walked out of Town Yesterday & dined about Two Miles of[*f*], Tom [*Morris*] was engaged and could not be of our party. When We came into the City in the Evening We discovered that the N. Yorkers and Eastern Men had a grand meeting, for the purpose of defeating the plans of the Southern People, and as it happens We Pensylvanians must be the Umpires. Accordingly a Plenipotentiary called on me at near ten oClock last Night, I heard every proposition & Reserved my opinions untill to day meaning to Consult with our Delegation, what We shall make of it I dont know; but the Aspect is rather mended as to Temporary Residence if we abandon the Permanent. dont mention this as I write it for your own Satisfaction only and if you are asked any questions it is enough for the present to say that I have not given the matter up. Tom Francis called on me Yesterday & I asked him to dine with our Delegation to day. This day or tomorrow will probably decide Some important points. Once More adieu.

ALS, Morris Papers, CSmH. Place to which addressed not indicated. This is a postscript to a letter dated 19 June, above.

John Nicholson to Daniel Hiester

I recd. your favor of the 18th. Instant covering the bill for the settlement of the accounts of the several states with the united states [*HR*-77]—The ratio of numbers to ascertain the proportions of the respective states altho it is not the rule which should govern vizt. the amount of property in each state, yet the former may when averaged upon so large a scale operate pretty nearly the same respective amounts to the states with the other and when it is considered how much of the expence to be quotaed on the states will be saved to them all by adopting this rule in preference to any other I am of opinion that at least every Pennsylvanian on a view of the effect should prefer it. The bill leaves into conjecture *what* is to be quotaed by that proportion, I take it for granted it is meant only to apply it to lessen the balences due to all the states equal to the proportion of those states who according to that ratio may have the least balances due to them—If according to the literal terms of the bill it is for apportioning to the states *the expences of the war* instead of the balances or part of the balances of the several states it would be very momentous and important and would supercede the funding and provision making for the payment of those expences. I suppose in the Enumeration Kentuckey will be part of virga. but will not vermont by this rule be exempt from a share in the expences so extingished by the Apportionment on the members of the union however perhaps it is not an object worth attending to on so Great a scale when so little of the expences of the war or national debt will be thus extinguished as she is not yet a member of the union—I like the idea of the balances being non-transferable but I consider discharging the Interest of those balances at any thing less than what is already engaged viz. 6 ℔ Ct. per Ann. a direct infraction of a previous engagement and derogatory to the dignity of the union. The time of payment of the interest should be proportioned to the abilities of the states to make payment and perhaps they ought not now to promise to pay even 4 ℔ Ct. annually for promise what they will, they will not pay if they have not the money and I think there are more engagements entering into than they will find money to discharge but altho they have the time of payment yet in their power. the quantum to be paid is fixed and if they reduce it a farthing below their engagements they fix a principle to reduce it at any time to any thing, under this view I think the senate are more justifiable than the House of Representatives if faith is to be broken let it not be for the paltry Eazement of 7 years Interest of 1/3 of the domestic debt let it be for something worth while if it were not for public faith 4 ℔ cent is too much to speculators but 6 ℔ Cent is little enough for original holders if there were no previous obligation—Impressed deeply for the harmony of the union as well as for the faithful performance of her engagements I wish that the funding bill for the present was confined to the temporary provision now proposed to be made for non subscribers thereby unless it should be changed to payment of 6 ℔ Cent and narrowed for the present to original holders only And that all the rest should be over at least until time would have afforded some experience of the products of the revenues of the united states. I think I would contribute my proportion to the discharge of the equitable and contracted debts of the union as chearfully as any disinterested citizen and yet I would be averse to a promise of immediate payment of the interest permanently in future, and yet if it were funded at all I should desire it to be at the rate promised or at least that the part due not so funded should not be injured but left on the same ground on which it stood before.

I think if good Commissioners be appointed the mode of settlement with the states and the enlarged powers granted them will be for the public good—The idea of allowing the states what they have advanced for the common or particular Defence is calculated to promote the interests of the union—The defence of the different states against the common enemy whether by an individual state or by the united states are in substance the same and the several states were the best judges of the value of services whether of militia or inlisted troops or supplies in their respective states and being actually paid or assumed to be paid by them should be admitted to their credit—The great care should be to guard against false charges which may not have been paid or assumed by the states. A small sum paid by a state and rejected by the united states at settlement would dissatisfy when the admission of it would not only please but perhaps on the whole operate against the interests of that very state.

By an act of this state[1] those who have claims against her are limited till 1st January next—to render them not sooner than a month or six weeks after that date I hope the blanks ~~will be filled up~~ in the bill for limiting the exhibiting to the General Board the claims of the states will be filled—many claims against this state may & will be rendered by the first of January next which cannot and will not be substantiated for long after, wittnesses are scattered vouchers to procure and when they are got perhaps more wanted still—so that if instead of the term "allowed" by near the end of the 3d section it was altered to read unless the same was Exhibited to such state it would be better.

I do not like the power given the Commissioners of reducing the continental money payments made after the 18th. March 1780 because the rule of reducing it in the same manner as the loan office debt after 18th March 1780 would operate more in favor of Pennsylvania than any other state Massachussets excepted and because it is the rule prescribed by the act of Congress first directing the appointment of Commissioners for settling those accounts[2] and under that rule many of the accounts are passed by the Commissioners which as per the bill will not be subject again to examination by this Board so that different principles will govern in ~~different~~ similar cases, to this I might add that the accounts with the states are so Entered on the books of the united states.

I have given you my thoughts on this subject without reserve And with Great freedom for which I ought to apologize but I write to a friend who can bear with me.

The war between England and spain if it commences as a citizen of the world I dislike but as a citizen of America conceive to be advantageous.

FC:dft, Nicholson Papers, PHarH.

---

[1] "An Act to Limit the time for Exchanging and Redeeming Certain Bills of Credit and Certificates," passed by Pennsylvania on 4 December 1789.

[2]On 28 June 1780 Congress established rules for the depreciation of loan office certificates issued between 1 September 1777 and 18 March 1780. These rules were included in the resolutions for settling accounts among the states that Congress adopted on 20 February 1782, and in the ordinances agreed to on 13 October 1786 and 7 May 1787 (*JCC* 17:567–68, 22:85, 31:779–81, 32:262–66).

Aristippus, Anecdote of Kit Congo

KIT CONGO is so whimsical and capricious a mortal, that you would suppose him to be animated by, at least, *sixty four*[1] different souls. He adopts no opinion without debating it a long time, in his own mind; and very frequently, the more insignificant the subject, the more tedious and violent the debate. He delivers his determinations with great solemnity; but you are not hence to conclude that these determinations will be permanent: for, perhaps, he will reject to-day the most solemn resolution of yesterday.

I called in, a few days ago, to see my friend Kit. I knew that his family affairs had been lately very much deranged; that he had contracted heavy debts, for the payment of which his creditors began to be very clamorous; and that it required all his skill and diligence to extricate his affairs from such complicated embarrassments. I also knew, that a very good plan of domestic arrangement had lately been formed, which, if carried into execution, would afford effectual relief. Under these impressions, I very naturally concluded that I should find Kit most seriously engaged in the important business of promoting the welfare of the *whole family*—No such thing. What do you think he was about? Why, he was very gravely and anxiously considering whether he should sit still in the *green room*, where he then was, or remove to the *brown room*, that was separated from it only by a thin partition. Bonds, petitions and accounts were all thrown in confusion under the table; the butcher and the baker were desired to call another day for their money; and all the urgent business of the family was totally suspended, 'till this *very important* matter could be determined. I was really apprehensive that he was growing a madman, or an idiot. "What, in the devil's name! (I exclaimed) Kit, are you about? Is this a moment to sit musing and meditating about the conveniency of a couple of apartments in your house? Is not this a snug room? Have you not a neat table before you? Are you not seated in a very handsome chair? Don't the people bring you your dinner at a very seasonable hour, and in good order? Can't the business of the family be as well conducted here, as in any other place? Depend upon it your household will soon be in a charming uproar; and well they may be so. They expect that you are sedulously engaged in devising means to promote the general good, and have no idea that you are sitting here, wasting your time with these idle fancies. Take up your scattered papers, and proceed at once to business."

This confusion in the mind of my friend, Kit Congo, and the consequent delay and perplexity of his domestic affairs, was principally occasioned by the mischievous suggestions of one of the upper servants of the house, whose name is *Bob* ****** [*Morris*], a fellow of great cunning and indefatigable perseverance. Bob was continually whispering in Kit's ear, many childish reasons for his removal into the *brown room*, such as these:

"My dearest Kit, this creek of salt water running just under the windows of this room, will corrode your tender lungs, and soon make them as spotted as a rusty knife; you are not now exactly in the centre of the house; and every time the servants from the *rice fields* and *tobacco plantations* have any business to transact with you, they are necessitated to go exactly three yards, two feet and five inches farther than they ought to go; a whale or a shark may come up to your very window, spring in and devour you, before you are aware of it; besides, the *money chest* is in the brown room, and, on any emergency, you may more speedily run to it, and take out what you want."

Now, you are not to imagine from all this pretty discourse, that Bob has a superior regard for the prosperity of Kit and his family. The truth of the matter is this—Bob has a snug *closet* in a corner of the *brown room*, which he has pretty well stored with tea and sugar; but, unhappily, his bread and butter begin to run short, so that he is in danger, very shortly, of making but a scanty breakfast. Now Bob imagines, if he can but prevail upon Kit to remove into the brown room, he shall have frequent opportunities after dinner of picking up some of the broken meat, slipping half a loaf of bread or a slice of butter into his closet, and perhaps of finding a sixpence or so that may chance to drop out of Kit's pocket on the floor; for, to say the truth, Kit is rather careless of his cash, and scatters about his sixpences more profusely than his finances can bear.

While I was thus endeavouring to persuade my old friend to quit his childish deliberations, about the superior conveniences of this room or the other, and get his affairs in good order, as soon as possible, we heard an alarming noise at a distance. The people, who had been at work in the fields, and whose accounts Kit had promised to settle long before this time, had formed a resolution of coming to the house, enquiring how matters went on within doors, and ascertaining the true cause of this tedious delay. Kit was confoundedly frightened: "For God's sake, my dear friend (said he) do go out to this clamorous multitude; endeavour to pacify them; assure them upon the word of a man of honour, that I will instantly lay aside every other consideration, and proceed, with all possible dispatch, in the business upon which depends the future wellfare of my whole family."

NYDG, 22 June. The piece was prefaced by: "Mr. [*Archibald*] McLean, Be pleased to insert the following in your useful paper, and thereby gratify your fellow citizens, and much oblige. A SUBSCRIBER." Aristippus was the name of two philosophers, ca. 400 B.C., credited with founding the Cyrenaic School of philosophy, which held pleasure to be the sole purpose of life. "Congo" stands for Congress.

[1] The number of members of the House before the election of Rhode Island's Representative on 31 August.

OTHER DOCUMENTS

Joseph Anderson to George Washington. ALS, Washington Papers, DLC. Written from No. 58 Maiden Lane, New York City. For a partial text, see *PGW* 5:511–12n.

Some days since, waited on Paterson and Read, who informed him that the President had discussed Anderson's character with them; Paterson admitted to informing the President of his limited knowledge of Anderson's legal abilities; Read also was not well acquainted with his legal abilities since Anderson had never practiced in New Jersey or Delaware.

Jonathan Dayton to George Washington. ALS, Washington Papers, DLC. Written from Elizabethtown, New Jersey. For the full text, see *PGW* 5:543–44.

Office seeking: commissioner of loans for New Jersey; is intimately acquainted with many of the members of Congress with whom he served in the last two years of the Confederation Congress.

Robert Parrish to William Bartram. ALS, Miscellaneous Manuscripts, NHi. Addressed to the care of Isaac Gray, Second Street near Race Street, Philadelphia; carried by J(ohn?). Shoemaker. This is a postscript to a letter of 20 June, above. Parrish was still in New York City on 10 July, when he promised to deliver a legal document from Clymer to his son in Philadelphia (George to Henry Clymer, 16 July, ALS, Miscellaneous Manuscripts, DLC).

Spent a very cordial hour with Adams, who added his name to the subscription list for Bartram's *Travels* (Philadelphia, 1791).

John S. Sherburne to John Langdon. ALS, Langdon Papers, NhPoA. Written from Portsmouth, New Hampshire; answered.

Before adjourning, the state Senate failed to vote on ceding the lighthouse at Portsmouth; hopes Langdon will return in time for his brother's (Woodbury) impeachment trial for neglect as a state judge, scheduled for 28 July; election of federal Representatives set for 9 August, "& candidates are not wanting, the six dollars (a day) has too many charms not to excite the wishes of a multitude of *Patriots*"; enquires of the probability of passing a funding act, with or without the assumption of state debts, and of the date of adjournment.

George Washington to Michael Jenifer Stone. AN, hand of William Jackson, Stone Family Papers, DLC. Stone wrote "Commission" on the cover page. At the top of the note, "Old Court Business" was written, probably also by Stone.

"The President of the United States requests the pleasure of Mr. Stone's company to dinner on Thurs-day next at *4 Oclock*.

An answer is requested."

Willing, Morris, & Swanwick to John Langdon. ALS, Langdon Papers, NhPoA. Written from Philadelphia; answered.

Inquiries about purchasing ship masts and spars in New Hampshire, and what rates "your friends" might contract for.

Daniel Hiester, Account Book. PRHi.

Attended "Monday Club" or Mess Day with the Pennsylvania delegation at Fraunces Tavern.

William Samuel Johnson, Diary. Johnson Papers, CtHi.

"Dind. [*Dined at the*] Wadsworths."

NYDA, 22 June; reprinted at Philadelphia.

The Senate has struck out of the Funding Bill every alternative proposed by the House and fixed the interest at four percent.

[*James Madison,*] Letter from New York. [Fredericksburg] *Virginia Herald*, 1 July; reprinted at Winchester, Virginia. The identification of the author is based on the similarity of the language to Madison's letter to Edmund Pendleton, 22 June, below.

"The funding and revenue systems are at present in a critical situation; I think, however, that something effective will yet take place as to both. The case of the state debts has been the great source of delay & embarrassment. The business of the seat of government is a labyrinth which it would be scarcely possible, if there was time, to explain to you. The issue is contingent. The Potowmac has vast difficulties to encounter, and much to fear."

TUESDAY, 22 JUNE 1790

Warm (Johnson)

John Fenno to Joseph Ward

The senate have agreed to fund the Indents and the whole debt at a simple 4 ℔ Cent—so you see the alternatives are rejected—How this will suit the house is hard to say—I rather think it will be agreed to—the Ways & Means [*Duties on Distilled Spirits HR-62*] Bill being rejected by the Eastern people because the State Debts are not assumed, & by some of the Southern on account of the Excise, is lost in the House.

It was a great object with the assumptionists to defeat this bill—supposing it wou'd conduce to their plan—It is now said the assumption is in a fair way—as I still think a fundg. System will be agreed upon the assumption is a consequence—These fluctuations have affected paper—as I wrote you on Sunday last—since when have not heard any price mention'd.

ALS, Ward Papers, ICHi. Addressed to Boston; postmarked.

Benjamin Goodhue to Stephen Goodhue

We are yet in such a situation that I believe no one can see how things may terminate—there is a plan now on foot between the Pensylvanians and the Southern people. that Philadelphia shall have the temporary residence for 10 years and the Patowmac the permanent residence, and we have been given to understand that the assumption may obtain, if We will accede to the measure, but the Patowmack is to our Eastern folks so disagreable, that we think We should never be able to justify our being accessary to so great and lasting an evil, what it may issue in is uncertain—yesterday from a wish to defeat everything which relates to funding unless the debts are assumed, We destroy'd the bill laying impost and excises [*Duties on Distilled Spirits Bill HR-62*]—this cursed residence has put us into the disgracefull situation which has so long and does yet retard all our public measures.

ALS, Goodhue Family Papers, MSaE. Addressed to Salem, Massachusetts; franked; postmarked.

John Henry to George Washington

I have the honor of communicating to the president of the United States the enclosed letter from Doctor [*James*] Manning of Rhode Island. To the favourable Sentiments which it contains, of the character of ~~the~~ Mr. [*Benjamin*] Stelle, I can freely add my own. My acquaintance with him commenced very early in life, and from that period to the present time, I have always understood that he has supported & deserves the character of an honest and upright Man. Having been liberally educated and brought up in the habits of Business, it is probable that his qualifications would enable him to discharge the duties of a more important office than the one he solicits.

ALS, Washington Papers, DLC.

Henry Jackson to Henry Knox

This is since the one I wrote you by Capt. [*Constant?*] Freeman, and I am sorry to inform you that the Senate have also made choice of *Mr. George Cabot* [*for federal Senator*] by a majority of twenty two out of thirty one and is therefore elected, there is no doubt but he will accept, as his mind is firm on the subject.

I feel for Mr. D[*alton*]. as I think it will be a great disappointment to him, and will very much derange his family—Mr. [*Samuel*] Breck, Mr. J[*ohn*]. C[*offin*]. Jones and my friend [*David*] Cobb exerted themselves all in their power, and were not able to obtain more than *six votes* for him at any one time—The House were determind to make a change and used every art to effect it—it was given out last Eveng. & this morning in the House that Mr. Dalton was in favor of high Salaries, and that he voted for seven dolls. to the Senators—this with the influence of the Junto[1] effectually did the business—I wish'd for Mr. D. to be continued [*lined out*] but as that could not be effected, I am glad that Mr. Cabot has succeded in preference to the other candidates—who were Doctr. [*Charles*] Jarvis, Mr. [*Nathaniel*] Gorham & Mr. [*Samuel*] Holten—Mr. G. had the highest number in the first instance—upwards of 40, out of 120—Mr. C. & Doctr. J. had upwards of thirty—& Mr. D. six—the second time—Mr. C— had the highest number Mr. H. upwards 20—the other two fell short, & Mr. D— only one—but no choice—the third time Mr. Cabot had 63 out of 123 and that closed the contention.

***

ALS, The Gilder Lehrman Collection, on Deposit at the New York Historical Society, New York. [GLC 2437.04633] Written from Boston at 7 P.M.; franked; postmarked. The salutation reads, "My dear Harry." The omitted text relates to non-relevant state legislative business.

---

[1] More generally known as the Essex Junto for its power base in Essex County, Massachusetts, this group emerged in the early 1780s to influence what became the state's Federalist

faction, before dispersing by the late 1790s. The typical member was born around 1750, attended Harvard, became a merchant or lawyer, and was likely to be related by marriage to another Junto member's family. Members included George Cabot, Francis Dana, Stephen Higginson, John Lowell, Theophilus Parsons, and, among members of the FFC, Ames and Goodhue (David Hackett Fischer, "The Myth of the Essex Junto," *WMQ* 21[April 1964]:191–235).

James Madison to Edmund Pendleton

The pressure of business as the session approaches its term, the earlier hour at which the House of Representatives has for some time met, and the necessity of devoting a part of the interval to exercise, after so long a confinement, have obliged me to deny myself the pleasure of communicating regularly with my friends. I regret much that this violation of my wishes has unavoidably extended itself to the correspondences on which I set the greatest value, and which, I need not add, include yours. The regret is the greater, as I fear it will not be in my power to atone for past omissions by more punctuality during the residue of the session. In your goodness alone I must consequently look for my title to indulgence.

The funding and Revenue systems are reduced by the discord of opinions into a very critical state. Out of this extremity, however, some effective provision must, I think, still emerge. The affair of the State debts has been the great source of delay and embarrassment, and, from the zeal and perseverance of its patrons, threatens a very unhappy issue to the session, unless some scheme of accommodation should be devised. The business of the seat of Government is become a labyrinth, for which the votes printed furnish no clue, and which it is impossible in a letter to explain to you. We are endeavoring to keep the pretensions of the Potowmac in view, and to give to all the circumstances that occur a turn favorable to it. If any arrangement should be made that will answer our wishes, it will be the effect of a coincidence of causes as fortuitous as it will be propitious. You will see by the papers inclosed that Great Britain is itching for war. I do not see how one can be avoided, unless Spain should be frightened into concessions. The consequences of such an event must have an important relation to the affairs of the United States. I had not the pleasure of seeing Col. [*John*] Hoomes during his momentary stay in New York, but had that of hearing that he gave a very favorable account of your health.

PJM 13:252–53, from Madison, *Letters* 1:520–21.

Samuel Phillips, Jr. to Benjamin Goodhue

Tho' I have but ten minutes before the mail will close, I must thank you for the communication this moment received, of the 17th. instt.—if you persevere with coolness & patience you have great encouragement—pardon me for mentioning *coolness*—you have such trials of fortitude & moderation, that you must be more than than men, or must be indebted to an influence more than human, if you do not sometimes loose the command of yourselves—but let observe, whenever you do, you certainly give the antagonists an advantage: your remarks confirm the opinion before entertained, that *far* more will depend on private interviews, than on public debates.

This day George Cabot Esqr. has been chosen a Senator from this State to succeed Mr. D[*alton*].

A motion has been under considn. of Senate, to instruct our Senators & write to o[*u*]r Reps. on the subject of Compensats. & grants—refered to the next sessn.—A vote of the same natr. afterwards came up from the house (to consider the expediency) not yet acted on.[1]

ALS, Letters to Goodhue, NNS. Written from Boston.

[1] On 23 June, the state Senate concurred with the House resolution for a joint committee to consider instructions on federal salaries. The committee report recommended that Dalton and Strong be instructed to exert "their utmost influence" for a reduction of federal salaries, compensations, and pensions, and that Governor Hancock be requested to transmit a copy of such a resolution to the state's Representatives as well (Miscellaneous Legislative Papers [House], M-Ar). On 24 June, the Senate postponed consideration until February 1791.

Theodore Sedgwick to Pamela Sedgwick

I hope before you receive this you will have received the letter I wrote you by Mr. [*Martin?*] Hoffman. We still continue in a very disagreable and uncertain situation. The pensylvanians seem determined that we shall do nothing unless we gratify them with respect to the residence. Should we do that our friends in this state and Connecticut will be very much disgusted, and it will tend to destroy that union of interests on which good government does at present depend. Besides we think the combining objects of a local and national consideration together will tend to mischivous consequences; From these considerations we have been obliged to act on the defensive. Hence our vote for Baltimore, and hence we have thought ourselves authorised to put a negative on the bill providing the means of funding the debt [*Duties on Distilled Spirits Bill HR-62*]. These Gentlemen have seen these considerations become very serious, and this day explicit propositions have been made to us [?] of assuming the payment of the state debts, provided we will agree to reside 15. years in philadelphia and ultimately to go to the Potomack. Except Mr. Gerry the deligation of Massa. have not the least objection to Philadila. but they cannot, and perhaps ought not to consent to the Potomack scheme. It is far south of the center, but to my mind that is not the greatest objection. The People of Virginia have long been in the habit of extreme jealousy towards the northern and eastern states, and it appears to me that jealousy has produced an inveterate hatred. But enough of musty politics.

I hope yet I shall be able to go home with Mr. Benson, who will undoubtedly leave this on saturday of next week. Should the assumption at that time be determined I shall not wait a moment for any other business, and indeed that being compleated every thing else will follow of course.

Perhaps I may not this week write you by the post. Have you my love heard from [*Ephraim*] Williams since he left stockbridge [*Massachusetts*]? or do you know whether before he went away he recd. my letter, and if he answered it?

ALS, Sedgwick Papers, MHi. Place to which addressed not indicated.

William Smith (Md.) to Thomas Jefferson

I take the liberty to Submit to your perusal the inclosed letter, which was transmitted to me, a few days past, from a merchant in Baltimore.

The prohibition therein complained of Strikes deep, at our East India trade. The article of cotton, from that country, is become a very considerable import, & together with sundry other East India commodities, serve as good remittances to Europe.

If any steps can be devised to afford relief, it will render essential service to this country.

ALS, Miscellaneous Letters, Miscellaneous Correspondence, State Department Records, Record Group 59, DNA. Encloses letter from Stephen Wilson to Smith, dated 10 June and printed above.

A Marylander to Mr. Hayes

THE Town Meeting, held yesterday, may be attended with beneficial consequences to the town of Baltimore, and cannot be injurious—it will evince to Congress and all America, that we are desirous of having their High Mightinesses among us, and rendering their situation comfortable[1]—If they remain among us for several years, it will be advantageous; if only for a session or two, it will be injurious, by introducing a spirit of luxury and dissipation and encroaching upon the domestic habits of such persons among us as have a general acquaintance among the members of Congress, and would wish not to be deemed inhospitable or unsociable—If Congress should remove to this town, it will be entirely owing to the competition and animosity now subsisting between New-York and Philadelphia, as unfortunately more than half of the Maryland delegation are unfriendly to us—The Patowmack interest would sooner have Congress at Portsmouth [*New Hampshire*] or Savannah [*Georgia*] than at Baltimore—It is to be regretted, that we are obliged by our election law, to chuse members residing in six different districts—they ought to be chosen from the state at large without regard to local considerations—If this town and its vicinity have a single spark of spirit, they will make every exertion to turn out Messrs. [*D.*] *Carroll, Contee, Gale*, and *Stone* at the ensuing election in October next, the three first for voting against Congress's coming among us, when it was certainly their duty to agree to any place within the state, proposed for a temporary residence, and although Mr. *Stone* voted for Baltimore, yet he pertinaciously opposed fixing the permanent residence of Congress on the banks of the Susquehannah—had that been done, the present heats would have been avoided, and as the eastern delegates had fixed their eyes on the banks of the Delaware, and the southern ones on those of the Patowmack, the Susquehannah was a medium between the two, and ought to have been agreed to, in order to reconcile parties; besides which it is a central situation, a combined view of the population and extent of the different states—Mr. *Gale* used to be considered a warm friend to Baltimore, as a state Senator, but he has not proved himself so, as our Representative in Congress—We now see the *real* reason, why he was so warmly supported in opposition to our present Senator, Mr. *Henry*, who have ever been our friend, as is Mr. *Seney*—If we do not unanimously support *him* warmly next October, we shall be ungrateful wretches indeed—Our delegate Mr. *Smith*, has been our steady friend.

The accession of Rhode-Island to the union has *now* entirely annihilated all causes of party to respecting our form of government, and we ought to call forth the ablest men into our service without respect to their former political sentiments. If Baltimore-town and county, Hartford and Anne-Arundel move together with the same unanimity as Washington and Frederick, when they supported the federal ticket, they are certainly more numerous, and can effectually shew their resentment to such of their servants as are opposed to their interest—Can the people of Baltimore expect to be served by members from other states, when their own seem disposed to injure them?

[Baltimore] *Maryland Gazette*, 25 June, edited by John Hayes. Written from Baltimore.

[1] For more on the town meeting that was held in response to a House vote on 11 June to move Congress to Baltimore, see *DHFFC* 8:460–61.

OTHER DOCUMENTS

Stephen Goodhue to Benjamin Goodhue. FC:lbk, Goodhue Family Papers, MSaE. Written from Salem, Massachusetts.

"I expect to See you at home in a Short time I hope you will not make your Self uneasy let measures turn as they will"; "I think I Should not write any letters on Politicks at present to any Person."

Samuel Pintard to Elias Boudinot. ALS, Boudinot Papers, PHi. Written from Hempstead, Long Island, New York.

Thanks Boudinot for his letter of 1 June that helped persuade (Pintard's son) Lewis to remain enrolled at Princeton; looks forward to visit from Boudinot and "the Dr. good Old Lady" (Hannah Stockton Boudinot) sometime that summer.

George Thatcher to John Fox. No copy known; acknowledged in Fox to Thatcher, 27 June.

William Samuel Johnson, Diary. Johnson Papers, CtHi.

"Visits."

Letter from Salem, New Jersey. *NYMP*, 29 June.

Pleased to inform the public that the majority of farmers are harvesting without consuming rum, and that the yield is more cleanly cut; three times more farmers will harvest without rum this year than the previous year; in a few years, it will be out of use completely.

WEDNESDAY, 23 JUNE 1790

Rain (Johnson)

Fisher Ames to George R. Minot

I do not suppose you will wish my correspondence, while your duty in the General Court [*legislature*] imposes so hard a task. However, you know that I do not pretend to exact an answer as a right.

I expect all the holders of securities in Boston will be alarmed, when they learn that on Monday the bill for excises, called the supply, or ways and means [*Duties on Distilled Spirits HR-62*] bill, was lost in the House, ayes twenty-three, noes thirty-five. Their anxiety will abate, when they know the circumstances that made it necessary to kill it. The perverseness of the Pennsylvanians has made them risk every thing for Philadelphia. One of them has often defied the friends of the assumption, to hinder the passage of the funding system. The Senate had become a scene of discord upon that subject, and partly from aversion to all funding, and partly from a desire to show that refusing the State debts would make the terms of the other debt worse, they have excluded the alternatives, and offer a simple four per cent. to the creditor. This is playing Rhode Island with one third of the debt,[1] and I cannot think of it without indignation. In short, it was becoming probable that the whole would be postponed to the next session. The negative upon the ways and means, by opening the eyes of the advocates of the funding to a sense of their danger, really contributes to the security of the provision for public credit. It is rather paradoxical, I confess. Besides, a scheme has been ripening, and is agreed upon between the Pennsylvanians and the southern people, to remove to Philadelphia, stay fifteen years, and fix the permanent seat on the Potomac. To do this, and at the same time reject the assumption, is such an outrage upon the feelings of the eastern people, as I persuade myself they dare not commit; and as our claim of justice has been expressed in a loud tone, and our reproaches and resentments have been reiterated since it was denied us, they have become afraid of consequences; and as our zeal and industry have not relaxed, and every instrument of influence has been tried, I think I see strong indications of an assent to the assumption. Those who love peace, and those who fear consequences, will naturally shrink from any side, and however unavailing the debates may have been to procure votes, they have at last silenced opposition. And it is, at the same time, in itself gratifying and a presage of success, that the justice and policy of the assumption, except as it regards the *vox populi*[2] in the south, are no longer denied, or denied so faintly as to indicate merely the repugnance of pride to yielding a contested point. Mr. Morris is a zealous friend of the assumption, (though he has acted crookedly,) and he has strong motives to prevent the convulsions which would ensue, if a bargain for Philadelphia should be supposed the cause of losing the measure. His own wishes, shame, prudence, will concur to exact from all whom he can influence a vote for it, and taking all these things together, I begin to indulge a very confident hope of success. I believe that Congress will sit next at Philadelphia, and if we succeed in the assumption, we shall have nothing of bargain to reproach ourselves with. I confess, my dear friend, with shame, that the world ought to despise our public conduct, when it hears intrigue openly avowed, and sees that great measures are made to depend, not upon reasons, but upon bargains for little ones. This being clear, I should have supposed myself warranted to make a defensive or counter bargain, to prevent the success of the other. But even that would wear an ill aspect, and be disliked by the world. I repeat it, therefore, with pleasure, that we have kept clear of it.

I see by the papers that Mr. Gardiner's reform of the law[3] is not quite extinct; but as our [*Massachusetts*] House is far better than the last, and the Senate absolutely federal, I hope no fresh disturbance will be given to the course of our judicial proceedings. Pray tell your brother Clarke [*Jonas Clark Minot*], that I went to the President on his behalf, and made a strong representation of his losses and merits. The President is well disposed towards him, but I think he will not nominate him to the light-house, because Knox is there *locum tenens*.[4] He will stand well for any vacant place. General Lincoln's vote would go far to serve him. Be so good as to say what I wish to have said to friends, Mr. [*James*] Freeman, &c. My most respectful compliments to Mrs. [*Mary*] Minot. Dear George, if you have leisure, and not else, write to me, for I have long been so vexed by the waves and storms of the political sea, as to wish, as much as the sailors do, for the port, and like them perhaps I shall be willing to quit it again.

Ames 1:81–83.

---

[1] To erase or "spunge" part of the debt.

[2] Voice of the people; the popular will.

[3] John Gardiner's initiative in the Massachusetts legislature to reform legal proceedings; see Ames to William Tudor, 17 January, n. 1, volume 18.

[4] Holding the place, i.e., as deputy. Thomas Knox, a harbor pilot appointed keeper of Boston lighthouse in 1783, was retained in that position by Washington's appointment in March 1790, three months before the lighthouse was even ceded to the federal government; at the same time Benjamin Lincoln was appointed superintendent over all the federal lighthouses in Massachusetts (*PAH* 6:297). The seventy-five foot high Boston lighthouse was reconstructed in 1783 on Little Brewster Island in Boston harbor, where a lighthouse had stood from 1716 until it was destroyed by the British in 1776. Knox served as lighthouse keeper until 1811.

John Langdon to Joshua Brackett

Your Esteemed favor of the 16th. Inst. I Received ℘ post; the Contents shall be particularly Attended to; the funding Bill is not yet passed therefore it is uncertain; what Commissioners will be Appointed—I have long er'e this seen the Conduct of Exeter;[1] and have Constantly endeavour'd, to Check them; but while I have been, Supporting of Portsmouth, I see by the late proceedings of *some of our Gentlemen* ~~of P~~ that they are Supportg. of Exeter. to Answer *their* Private Views.

I have Concluded as it is the desire of many of my Friends, not to Resign untill I return home as it can be done there as well as here; but whether it will be possable, for my patience, to hold out untill Congress Adjourn, I know not—all the *Important* Business of the Session, is now before Congress, and the Houses very Nearly divided on most great Questions, which makes it Impossable for me to leave this place at present, tho' I am very Misserable, while here one Month at most Agreable home, with my dear Family and good Friends, is worth an Age, in this British City of N. york Whether the late Proceeding of Portsmouth. or indeed the General Court [*legislature*] has been Just, Candid, Wise, Generous, or Politick, time will shew—The Salary of the President [*governor*]; one Session of the General Court Seting at Portsmouth; with many other Advantages Naturally Attendant; is lost this Year to Portsmouth; thro' their ill Judged Conduct—your old Acquaintance, has not forgot you, I send the paper Constantly to Mrs. Langdon, for the use of my Friends; which informs you every week of all the News we have here, together with the *unaccountable* proceedgs. of Congress; Heaven knows, where our Politicks will land us; but it is my duty to Attend Watch and pray.

ALS, Sturgis Family Papers, MH. Addressed to Portsmouth, New Hampshire; franked; postmarked (date illegible).

[1] A reference to Portsmouth's rivalry with that town for political and economic influence by means, for example, of the location of New Hampshire's federal district court and, in this case, of the state's commissioner of loans.

Governor Edward Telfair to the Georgia Senators

Having received information that Mr. McGillivray and a number of the warriors of the Creek Nation are on their way to New York, I am induced to furnish you with a certified Copy of the Returns of property taken from the Citizens of this State by the Indians of the said Nation, of which you will make the necessary exhibitions and representations in order That individual restitution may be made as far as the nature of the case will admit from present appearances, I have every reason to hope that a Permanent peace will be established with the aforesaid Indians, and thereby ensure future ease and security to the Citizens of this State—a matter of the highest importance to her political welfare!

The expenditures that have arisen in the defence of the State cannot be fully ascertained at this time, as considerable sums due and owing are not yet liquidated; they shall be forwarded immediately upon a final adjustment.

You have inclosed certified Copies of the several Treaties entered into between this State and the Indians;[1] on this head it is altogether unnecessary for me to comment as they speak for themselves.

FC:lbk, Executive Council Journal, G-Ar. Written from the State House, Augusta, Georgia.

[1]Three treaties were signed by commissioners for Georgia and various representatives of the Creek Indians prior to the FFC: the Treaty of Augusta (1783), which defined territorial boundaries; the Treaty of Galphinton (1785), which confirmed those and additional cessions of Indian land; and the Treaty at Shoulderbone (1786). The last was intended to be a federal treaty, but when the federal commissioners left in the absence of an adequate Creek representation, the remaining state commissioners seized the opportunity to renew the two earlier treaties. The disputed validity of all three treaties was the source of continuing hostilities on the Georgia frontier during the FFC. The treaties are printed in *DHFFC* 2:165–69, 180–83.

Other Documents

Joseph Anderson to George Washington. ALS, Washington Papers, DLC. Addressed from No. 8 Maiden Lane, New York City. For a lengthier summary, see *PGW* 5:512n.

Office seeking: in a conversation the night before, Paterson informed him that the President had expressed his unwillingness to appoint Anderson while his public accounts were still unsettled; considers the accounts settled.

Alexander Hamilton to John Adams. Reply card, hand of Hamilton, Hall Collection, DSI.

Accepts dinner invitation for 30 June.

Thomas Jefferson to Charles G. F. Dumas. FC, Item 121, p. 361, PCC, DNA. Sent to The Hague, Netherlands. For the full text, see *PTJ* 16:551–53.

Believes no one thinks Congress can do anything to alter the terms of funding the foreign debt; the ways and means (Duties on Distilled Spirits HR-62) bill was defeated because an excise was woven into it; its successor will be free of an excise; a majority in Congress seemed to oppose assumption in the belief that the states could more easily raise the taxes to pay their war debts, and spare Congress the odium of the additional taxes; the measure may be modified to a more acceptable form.

Thomas Jefferson to John Coffin Jones. FC, letterpress copy, Jefferson Papers, DLC. For the full text, see *PTJ* 16:554.

A true navigation act for the United States (Trade and Navigation Bill) will probably pass.

James Madison to Governor Beverley Randolph. No copy known; acknowledged in Randolph to Madison, 12 July.

Theodore Sedgwick to Pamela Sedgwick. No copy known; mentioned in Theodore to Pamela Sedgwick, 24 June.

Reuben Shapley to John Langdon. ALS, Langdon Papers, NhPoA. Written from Portsmouth, New Hampshire; marked "Answered."

As Langdon had offered to perform any service for him in New York, encloses a bill for £133 payable to Langdon by the firm of Smith and Wycoff, leaving it up to Langdon to remit it back to Shapley as he thinks best.

John Taylor to George Nicholas. ALS, Henry Clay Papers, DLC. Written from Richmond, Virginia; place to which addressed not indicated. The recipient's identity is based on a reference by Taylor to "your sister," Mrs. Edmund Randolph.

Reports rumors that Congress passed an excise with a heavy tax on country stills while not touching large distilleries in towns, an "obvious instance of New England cunning"; "Madison has several times thought it necessary to make public *protestations* in Congress, that he has *not* changed his principles, and yet ~~that~~ his measures have inlisted all the antis as his warmest advocates, whilst they have lost him the friendship of the mercantile feds."

Letter from Providence, Rhode Island. *GUS*, 23 June; reprinted at Poughkeepsie, New York.

"Gen. JOSEPH STANTON, of Charlestown—and THEODORE FOSTER, Esq. of this town, are chosen Senators of the United States—they are to proceed in a few days. There were *only* 28 candidates."

GUS, 23 June.

"We hear that the Senate of the United States has amended the funding bill, by striking out all the alternatives proposed by the House of Representatives, and fixing the rate of interest on the whole of the public debt at *four per cent.* Also that they have concurred in the bill respecting the indents, so far as to fund them as principal."

THURSDAY, 24 JUNE 1790

Cool (Johnson)

Thomas Dwight to Theodore Sedgwick

***

We almost despair of assumption—and I fear that with the loss of assumption and by your unwearied attention to this and other public business you will lose your health—the conduct of the ~~Pennsylvanians~~,[1] if we are rightly informed is truly contemptible—I rejoice that you invent methods to mar their prospects in regard to residence—if men will sell their principles for such paltry considerations, or sell them at all, it *is honesty* to *defraud* them of the stipulated payment if possible.

***

When will Congress rise? is a question in almost every mans mouth—many load your honorable body with reproaches they are indeed vexed beyond measure at the fate of assumption.

***

ALS, Sedgwick Papers, MHi. Written from Springfield, Massachusetts. The omitted text discusses Sedgwick's financial stake in Nathaniel Kingsley's bankruptcy, reports Jonathan Bliss's upcoming marriage to Mary Worthington, and speculates that the state excise is to be repealed.

[1] This word was probably lined out by someone other than Dwight.

Louis Guillaume Otto to Comte de Montmorin

The Count de Moustier having informed me that there was reason to believe that the Court would not insist immediately on the payment of the arrears owed by the United States and that it would leave them the time to consolidate their financial system, I have taken the opportunity to sound Mr. Hamilton out on his views with regard to the credit of His Majesty. He received this information with gratitude and began to dwell on the natural ties which exist between France and the United States, ties which must necessarily become more firm through the generosity and attachment of which France had not ceased to give them proofs. I endeavored to turn the conversation more particularly to the point in question to satisfy myself whether, conforming to my suspicions, Mr. Hamilton had at this time taken measures to reimburse France by a new loan in Holland. The incoherence and vagueness which he used in his responses have confirmed me in my opinion; and the debates in Congress, at which I have been present since, leave me almost no doubt that the principle of reducing the interest on the foreign debt by means of a new loan will be more powerful than any other consideration. There is talk of bringing this loan to 12,000,000 piastres which will suffice for all the reimbursements either in France or in Spain; and if the public credit is solidly established in this country, it will not be impossible to obtain this loan at the rate of three per cent interest. it will undoubtedly depend on His Majesty to grant this reduction himself; but if political interests induced him to make this sacrifice, it ought to be proposed with much discretion in order not to alarm those Americans who, accustomed to ruse, can ascribe sinister views to the most generous proceedings. It would be useless to observe, My Lord, that in America as in all commercial republics, affections will follow very closely the transactions of money. All the consequences of a transfer of the credit of His Majesty have been expounded by the Count de Moustier with so much clarity and force in the Memoir he drew up on this subject[1] that I could only repeat it here without adding anything very essential to it. I limit myself to observing closely Mr. Hamilton who will transact his operation only because it will give some relief to finances and not for the sake of being of service to France for which he professes an attachment and a veneration which I believe sincere.

This question, My Lord, which is tied essentially to the whole system of stabilizing finances proposed by Mr. Hamilton, would already be decided if the two Houses of Congress could agree on the manner of redeeming the domestic debt. The desire of some members to consolidate the public debts of the particular states and the impatience of some others to attract and establish Congress in Philadelphia continually obstruct the deliberations of this legislature. There is reason to be surprised that Congress has made no progress for the five months that the session has lasted and, in making a recapitulation of the most essential matters which must be decided, one groans to see them all in abeyance. These subjects are reduced to the following articles:

1. Regulation concerning seamen.
2. Ordinance for a new census of Rhode Island.
3. Regulation of commerce with the savages.
4. Bill to charge Congress with the public debts of the particular states.
5. Regulation concerning the treaties to be concluded with the savages.
6. Bill to fund the public debt.
7. Regulation to assure the accounts of the United States with the particular states.
8. Ordinance concerning the invalids [*pensioners*].
9. Regulation of posts.
10. Fixing of the temporary and permanent residence of Congress.
11. Regulation of coasting trade.
12. Increase of the tonnage duty for foreigners.
13. Rate of fees in the Federal Courts.

The House of Representatives having taken more than three months to discuss a bill to fund the public debt, the Senate has rejected it because there was no article concerning the consolidation of the debts of the particular states. The Senate itself proposes, therefore, to draft another bill which can likewise be rejected by the House of Representatives. Dr. Franklin's notion, which at the time of the debates on the Constitution of Pennsylvania compared two legislative chambers to a cart drawn in opposite directions by two equally vigorous horses,[2] has never appeared truer than at the present moment. The two forces have been so well employed since the beginning of this year that the wagon has been able neither to advance nor to retreat. It could be said at first glance that an object which suits the majority of the states ought to be approved by the majority of the two Houses; but it often happens that the simplest questions cause a division of votes between the Senators and the Representatives of the same state, either because they have not received instructions, or because like the members of the English House of Commons they do not consider themselves as bound by these instructions, or they are enrolled individually under the banner of a different party. It is not extraordinary to hear them vote directly against the interests of their constituents because they have made a secret bargain to drop one motion in order to make another succeed. Finally, they are so independent of their constituents that the latter have no other remedy against them than to elect other deputies when their term has expired. The division of the legislature into two Houses no doubt prevents the resolutions from being too hasty, but it prolongs the deliberations amazingly. The theory of counterweights experiences in practice some frictions which it is impossible to evaluate properly in advance, and that is what happens today in the American Government. While wishing to make the Senate resemble England's Upper House, they have forgotten that the Senators were elected by the people and that the same passions, the same prejudices, the same intrigues would agitate the two Houses. Bargains to make certain motions fail or succeed have never been concluded between the two Houses in England; here these bargains are made every day. In England the Upper House is as independent of the people as the King himself; here the Senators are the creatures of the people just like the Representatives, and the counterweight is more ideal than real. The prerogative of the President is another counterweight which will probably always be illusory, as it has been up to now. He would not dare to reject a law proposed to him by the two Houses. In spite of these inconveniences, My Lord, the theory of the American Government is so attractive it is hoped that time will give it more consistency and will realize the advantages which are foreseen till now only through speculation. In the space of one year Pennsylvania, Georgia and South Carolina have remodeled their particular constitutions on the model of that of the United States.[3] All the thirteen governments today have three branches and are united in a general government also divided into three branches. On this point the United States unquestionably has the advantage over other confederated republics. The homogeneous parts which compose the Federal Government will give it an astonishing consistency when time has put the seal of experience on it and local prejudices will be absorbed by the states' long custom of forming themselves into a single national body.

O'Dwyer, pp. 435–38. Otto's letters included in *DHFFC* were usually written over the course of days, and even weeks, following the day they were begun.

---

[1] Moustier's memorandum regarding repayment of the French loan to the United States is dated 7 December 1789 and can be found in Affaires Étrangères, États-unis, 34:326–33, Fr. For background, see *DHFFC* 17:1684–85.

[2] Benjamin Franklin (with Clymer, among others) represented Philadelphia County at the state's constitutional convention in 1776 and was credited at the time with a large role in shaping the final product. His simile to the horse cart was widely retold (*Counter Revolution*, p. 281n; *LDC* 4:422n, 6:430).

[3] The new constitutions of both Georgia (ratified in May 1789, effective the following October) and Pennsylvania (drafted February 1790 but not adopted until September) replaced their unicameral legislatures with bicameral legislatures. South Carolina adopted a new constitution in June 1790, but it perpetuated the bicameral system in place since 1778.

Theodore Sedgwick to Pamela Sedgwick

The letter which I mentioned in mine of yesterday as being carried by mistake to the post office being there observed to have been designed for private conveyance, was sent back by the post master. It is gone by Dudley who sailed this morning.

It will give pleasure to my best beloved to be informed that I am in perfect health, altho I have gone thro a sence of fatigue since I came from home, that was enough to have worn out almost any constitution; the whole business to be transacted out of doors having been in my management.[1] If, as I hope will be the case, success should attend the efforts I have made, I shall feel amply rewarded for all my toils. I have been busy all the morning, and am now going abroad, you will therefore excuse my not adding more.

ALS, Sedgwick Papers, MHi. Place to which addressed not indicated.

---

[1] According to R. B. Lee, Sedgwick was "the chief agent" in striking the deal with certain Maryland and Virginia members that led to the Compromise of 1790.

Michael Jenifer Stone to [*Daniel of St. Thomas Jenifer*]

I have inclosed to my Brother Walter the paper you gave me respecting the property in the Baltimore Iron workes ***

Perhaps while the Question respecting the Seat of Congress is in agitation will be a favorable time for the sale of the Property.[1] ***

To give you any more Specific Idea of the Politicks of the Day than may be found in the papers would fill a very long Letter—I shall only say that *I believe* all the Bustle about the Seat of Govt. will settle in a residence at Phila.

for 10 years & permanently on the Banks of Potowmack; perhaps about George Town perhaps near Connogocheague.

Upon this question the Maryland Delegates have been divided & I believe will not Combine. For my own part I have no Local attachment to any particular Spott in Maryland that are of a Feathers Weight—and my only object is to fix the Seat of Congress Where the Interests of the Union point out—That Spott I think is on the Banks of the Potowmack But if this cannot be attained I shall endeavour to get as near it as I can. I have preserved my temper perfectly cool upon the Subject and have never entered into any Engagement whatever—I allways have found that I am a poor hand at *Bargains* and therefore avoid them in private life—In Publick affairs there are few Cases where they are Justifiable—and yet with respect to residence I am inclined to believe some have been wise and necessary. And The Event has induced me to approve of those Steps in which my feelings prevented me from writing—But—I will at a future time give you a short History of this business.

ALS, Stone Family Papers, DLC. Place to which addressed not indicated. The first sentence corroborates the recipient's identity by its correspondence to the accounts of a "Major Jenifer" mentioned in Stone's letter to Walter Stone, below. Jenifer was known as "Major" by at least 1765, having probably acquired the honorific during the French and Indian War (*CCP* 2:581).

---

[1] The property, which may have included a house that Stone also refers to as part of his deceased brother Thomas's estate, would have been expected to increase in value if Congress had fixed the permanent seat of government nearby. To meet the huge demand for wood to fire the forges, the Baltimore Iron Works (or Baltimore Company) acquired extensive tracts of land in and around Baltimore (*CCP* 2:709–10n).

Michael Jenifer Stone to Walter Stone

*** the question of the Seat of Govt. is in agitation. I do not believe that Congress will ever be at Baltimore but that the permanent seat will be on the Potowmack I hope and Believe—Perhaps the Idea of a removal to Baltimore may prevail in Maryland and if so I conjecture the property in Annapolis will rise. As the Funding Bill is negatived perhaps Finals may fall—I request you therefore to offer the House in Annapolis for Sale £2000.0.0—in [*cash?*] or £3500. in Continental Certificates. The Interest may be calculated on the Certificates to make up this Sum. as I think Principal and Int[*eres*]t. will be funded securely at 4 ℔ Ct. so that in my Idea Cont[*intenta*]ls. are worth 13/4 in the pound.

***

I am in tollerable health—Fred[*erick Stone*]. is well and goes on Handsomely.

***

ALS, Stone Family Papers, DLC. Addressed to Charles County, Maryland; franked; postmarked 28 June; encloses (unlocated) "Statement and account" from Daniel of St. Thomas Jenifer. The omitted text advises on personal business transactions, including settlement of their brother Thomas Stone's estate.

John Wendell to Elbridge Gerry

Yr. Esteemed favours of the 16th Ult. I received with its Inclosure, and observe the Contents, I am happy to find that my Sentiments respecting the Necessity of a Medium, to negotiate the Property of the People at large, meets with yours, and I am equally sure with you, that the fiscal Operations of the Union cannot proceed, without some artificial or real Increase of Money—the latter would be most eligible if possible to effect it, and that I believe Time will effectually do, to so great a degree, that Money will be more plenty in America in ten Years than in any part of the World, but before that comes, Property will change its Owners, and Men, the Production of Chance, will rise superiour to those, whose Ancestors have been the Fathers of America, And the Property of which their Frugality and Industry had saved for their descendants, will soon become the Property of Strangers and Speculators, who have risen upon the Spoils of the Virtuous—The Extravagant Increase of Commissioners Clerks and every Order of Dependants, which lick away the Revenue, creates a Universal Indignation among the People, they would have borne all those Burtherns on Trade, if the Production of the Revenue was applied to the Discharge of the public Debt but the General Surmise is, that whatever the proceeds may be, Ways and Means will be found, to expend it; In short the Expences of civil Governmt. are too high, and the disposal of the public Monies appears to be sported with, instead of payg. the suffering public Creditors, before such Arrangements had taken place, public Credit ought to have been Restored in some Degree—Men might have been found equally honble. able and willing, to serve the Public in every Station, to which any have been appointed for One half the Salaries which have been given. Some say it is to reward them for their Sufferings in the Army—but this is not the Mode, the Public ought to have Quid pro Quo,[1] for any Services; and any appropriations expressly made for certain Purposes should be so considered and applied; Thus if half the Sum applied to the civil List, was given in Compensation for the suffering Soldiery, the People wd. not complain, but to purchase Men into office will not long be suffered, I am able to make my Observations from my general Acquaintance wth. the People of this State They know my Determinations never to accept of any office in Church or State—and therefore am less liable to be deceived—And upon this Ground the Union will not stand long on its present Basis—the People will remove until they can find Men who will not sport with their Monies—I am very glad that Congress are like to agree to pay the Penobscot Expedition, it is reasonable that they should, although as Johnston said of Gt. Brittain[2] that Massachusets undertook it in the *Insolence of official Pride* she was too officious, and too proud to court Assistance And although the Expedition was badly executed, yet it was pro bono publico,[3] and when Her Territories were invaded had she Succeeded the Continent wd. have reaped eventually the Benefit, by weakening the Armaments of our Enemies I cannot see through the Propriety of Assuming all the States Debts, because some of them may arise from local Circumstances, in wch. the Union have been no way interested or benefitted—The Gentlemen of the present Congress would immortalize their Memories, by laying some Plans to enable the People to pay their Debts, for under the Execution of federal Decrees of Court, as soon as they come to be carried into Execution, The People will then show themselves—A Marshal executes his Precept—no Summons attend the Writ, but the original, and unless Bail is given, the Marshal must commit—People not being acquainted with such Process will refuse Bail, and thus Many will stand committed altho' they have sufficient Estates: Our Court [*legislature*] have been abt. *making* making an Exemption Act—to exempt a Debtors Body being taken, who possesses any Estate sufficient to satisfy the Debt.

I am in hopes that Congress will agree that the Notes after Funding, shall be received in Payment of all Excises Duties or Subsidies whatever, and shall issue again out of the Treasury in Payment of all Salaries or Expences of any Name Nature or Kind, I mean only such as are to be bona fide paid by Americans; but that all foreigners shd. pay only Silver and Gold wch. should be sacredly applied to the discharge of the foreign Debt shd. such a Regulation take Place, the public Notes wd. come into Credit, and pass in Currency or Let this Distinction take Place Vizt. That the Interest of the domestic Debt shd. be paid in Certificates receivable at the Treasurers Office in Discharge of Duties due from Americans but not from foreigners.

Or if an American Bank funded on the whole Revenue And Notes issuable & payable in One year, could be erected it will greatly encrease the Quantity of Money in the Next Year, for the Possessors of these Notes knowing that after one year, they can receive the Cash for them, will support their Credit and take them in the Currcy. and before they become payable the Treasurer will have another years Revenue due to the Union.

If a Mint was established at which the People might have their Plate exchanged, many Thousands of Pounds would be sent to be coined, Our Gold smiths got their whole Stock at 5/6 ℔ oz. in great Plenty. In short my Friend, real Property (on which the whole Burthen of the Revolution has been laid) is depreciated in some Instances to 2/3d of their Value, and in General one half, I mean in the Northern States—they must rise again in a few years, but not to the advantage of their present Possessors—Let your fertile Genius at Invention, suggest to you some Mode of Relief, so that it may not be considered as Paper Money—Then *tu eris mihi Magnus Appollo*[4]—Excuse the Length of this Epistle and consider it as the Epistle of Johannes in Eremo.[5]

I was very sorry to see in the Prints an Account of the Death of yr. Brother Thos. Gerry Esquire, it is the only Intelligence I have had—I sincerely sympathize with you in your repeated Losses, but I know yr. philosophic Mind judges rightly of these Dispensations of Providence, and considers them as Decrees of Fate, agst. which there can be no Provision, but by a humble Resignation to sovereign Will.

ALS, Gerry-Townsend Papers, NN. Written from Portsmouth, New Hampshire.

[1] That for which, or a fair exchange.
[2] Probably a reference to Dr. Samuel Johnson's "Introduction to the Political State of Great Britain," which he published in the first issue of the *Literary Magazine* (May 1756).
[3] For the public good.
[4] You will be to me, the great Apollo.
[5] John (the Baptist) in the wilderness; a voice crying out futilely.

A Correspondent

It is but justice, (says a correspondent, who has watched the late electioneering,) to observe, in respect to Doctor [*Charles*] *Jarvis*, that he erased his own name from the list of Senators, which was placed in the House of Representatives; and thus refused even being considered as a candidate, as he, on all occasions, declined the offers of support, which were made him by his friends; and as to the Hon. Mr. *Dalton*, the small number of votes which appeared in his favor, must have arisen from the conflict of parties, and a prevailing disapprobation of the high grants, salaries and compensations, in favor of which this, (in other respects) very worthy character is said to have voted. How far the newly appointed Senator [*George Cabot*] differs from his predecessor in office, in this point, time will evince.

[Boston] *Independent Chronicle*, 24 June.

Other Documents

Shearjashub Bourne to George Thatcher. ALS, Chamberlain Collection, MB. Written from Boston; franked; postmarked 27 June.

Will make no further effort to induce his son (John D.) to return home, but thanks Thatcher for his trouble in the attempt, and for advances which Bourne will repay; reports George Cabot's election to the Senate in place of Dalton, "which Shews Us how uncertain things are in a Repub. Govt."; "We are anxious for Congress to assume the State Debts"; in that case, hopes Dr. Samuel Savage will be remembered for an appointment.

Stephen Choate to Benjamin Goodhue. ALS, Letters to Goodhue, NNS. Written from Boston.

Perceives from Goodhue's letter to Phillips, 17 June, that congressional affairs "have a more favourable aspect"; people are worried about the "late divisions in Congress"; George Cabot is elected to succeed Dalton; the state's excise is to be repealed as soon as Congress assumes the state debts; that morning, the state Senate is to consider a joint committee report in favor of a motion for instructing the Massachusetts delegation to try to obtain a reduction of federal salaries; expects the motion will be referred to next session; "I am not Very fond of being So buisey and Liberal by way of instructions"; hopes Goodhue can bear up "under your trying circumstances."

Benjamin Goodhue to Stephen Goodhue. ALS, Goodhue Family Papers, MSaE. Addressed to Salem, Massachusetts; franked; postmarked.

Personal mercantile affairs; "nothing new."

James Madison to John Dawson. No copy known; acknowledged in Dawson to Madison, 4 July.

Benjamin Rush to Tench Coxe. ALS, Coxe Papers, PHi. Written from Philadelphia.

Identifies Adams as the author of *Davila*; "If he were as busy in disseminating the means of easy education thro' our Country as he is in disseminating his detestable British and European principles, the change in the Conditions of men which he so much pants for, would be rendered for ever unnecessary"; in several letters to friends, F. A. Muhlenberg unequivocably declines Pennsylvania's governorship; Morris's friends, who have been working to remove prejudices against him in York and Lancaster counties will undoubtedly prove successful in his favor; dreads the sight of newspapers because of their nearly exclusive coverage of residence, public debt, and public credit; "The Old Congress at no period of its existence was ever more unpopular than the new. they must leave New York, or the *people* will leave them."

George Thatcher to Sarah Thatcher. ALS, Thatcher Family Papers, MHi. Place to which addressed not indicated.

Has had second thoughts about son Phillips's transferring to a school in Wiscasset, Maine; has envisioned his "too delicious" reunion with Phillips upon his return; objects to Phillips's missing school for a single day; expects to be home within four weeks, or "if you are unwell, & for particular reasons wish me to be home sooner, I will get leave of absence as soon as one or two things shall be accomplished"; has sent some muslin cloth home, for dresses for daughter Sally, since "I admire to see little girls dressed in white"; directions for household purchases with the twenty dollars he sent to (Thomas?) Dakin in Boston the previous Sunday; instructs Sarah to tell the children that when he returns home he will examine them to see which one reads better.

George Washington, Diary. ViHi.

Representatives Gerry, Goodhue, Grout, Leonard, Huntington, Benson, Boudinot, Cadwalader, Sinnickson, Hiester, Scott, Contee, Stone, Brown, and Moore dined at the President's.

Friday, 25 June 1790

Violent Rain (Johnson)

Elbridge Gerry to James Bowdoin

I am favoured with your letter of the 15th, mentioning Mr. John Ewing & Mr. Samuel Waldo as candidates for offices under the federal Government—Whether the assumption will take place or not this session is at present problematical, altho I think the assumptionists have the power of attaining the object: but the misfortune is, that some of them are influenced by the pennsylvanians, all of whom, even those who are firmly attached to the assumption will hazard it & every thing else of the highest importance to the Union, for the paltry object of the temporary residence of Congress. the Rhode Island Senators are arrived & the questions respecting both the permanent & temporary residence are to be agitated on monday next in the senate: upon the issue of these matters we shall be able to form some judgment of what will be the fate of the state debts, & should an oppertunity offer of promoting your wishes respecting your nephews, I shall be very happy in cooperating in the measures. The House consists of two classes the funders & anti-funders; & the former are subdivided into assumptionists & anti-assumptionists. part of the assumptionists have formed a junction with the antifunders & have thrown out the revenue bill [*Duties on Distilled Spirits Bill HR-62*], which has puzzled the residue of the funders, some of whom would be also for the assumption had not the residence of Congress been blended therewth. since the bill was rejected I have seen the secretary of the Treasury & find he is pleased with the measure & think[*s it*] a good stroke of policy. I have only time to assure you that with great esteem & respect I remain.

ALS, Bowdoin-Temple Papers, MHi. Addressed to Boston; franked; postmarked 27 June.

Elbridge Gerry to James Monroe

I am favoured with yours of the 6th of march & should have returned an earlier answer, had not the influenza disqualified me for a considerable time from attending to business, which afterwards pressed in an increased degree & prevented me from being punctual in my correspondence. I have exchanged with Mr. [*Burwell*] Starke several letters on the subject of my demand against Colo. Randolph's estate & have taken a deposition to enable him to make use of Colo. [*Benjamin*] Harrison's evidence[1]—We have been in great expectation of seeing you & your lovely Mrs. [*Elizabeth Kortright*] Munroe here this spring with your little folks, but have been hitherto disappointed & I fear we shall leave the city without that pleasure. we have only one child alive, having lost a lovely boy last fall about twelve months old, but Mrs. G. [*Ann Thompson Gerry*] is hourly expecting an addition to her family & I wish the conflict was well over.[2]

As to politicks, I can say nothing about them that will be very pleasing. I was in some expectation that the new government would for a time have risen superior to local veiws & prejudices, but confess to you that I am greatly disappointed, for I think the evil exists in as great a degree as it did under the confederation. the two houses are much divided about the assumption & their embarassments are increased by blending this with the permanent & temporary residence of Congress. intrigues cabals & combinations are the consequence & what will be the issue, time must determine. Congress are much divided on other points touching the funding system & I see no great prospect of our placing public credit on a solid basis: but you know I am not apt to despond & on this occasion I am determined to anticipate good, untill evil shall exclude every ray of hope.

ALS, Monroe Papers, DLC. Place to which addressed not indicated.

[1] The heavily indebted estate of Richard Randolph of Virginia (ca. 1725–1786) was the subject of much litigation throughout the 1790s. Burwell Starke was one of the many attorneys for Randolph's estate, and Benjamin Harrison, Jr., one of its even more numerous creditors (*John Marshall* 5:117–20, 134).

[2] The Gerrys' son Thomas (b. 1788) died on 1 November 1789. At this time they were expecting the birth of their daughter, Eleanor.

Thomas Hartley to Jasper Yeates

We have been engaged in various Business for some Days past. but the Funding System seems to be suspended and whether we can have ~~another~~ a Resurrection or not is very uncertain.

In the Senate the Bill for fixing a Temporary Residence—as well as permanent Residence of Congress—was brought forward to Day—but the Decision thereon was postponed by the vote of the President of the Senate until Monday.

The two Rhode Island Senators took their Seats this Morning and the Senate is quite full—Our Friends in Senate will strive to fix the Temporary Residence at Philada. for ten Years or more but the permanent Residence would [*go*] to the Banks of the Potomac whether they will succeed in either *is still uncertain*—I am sorry our affairs are in so desparate a Situation.

The Rhode Islanders are I presume made Prisoners by the New Yorkers already—we fight here to great Disadvantage.

ALS, Yeates Papers, PHi. Addressed to Lancaster, Pennsylvania; franked; postmarked. A postscript written on 27 June is printed under that date, below.

Benjamin Huntington to Anne Huntington

By Capt. Parker I Recd. no letter but Mr. Thomas Lothrop & his wife & Mrs. Hannah Huntington cam[*e*] with him and Inform that they have lately seen you riding out by which I conclude you are in no worse health than when I heard from you last—I was mentioning your Case to a Lady of the Name of Bedlow[1] who said she had a Julep which was a most Powerful thing for present Relief in the Chollir [*choler?*] and was kind Enough to furnish me with a Recipe by which I have got the Articles put up and Sent it to you filled to take a Dose is a table Spoon full at once I have sent home the Recipe and wish it may be kept Safe and that you would let Dr. [*Elisha?*] Tracy see it and take his advice before taking any lest there might be some of the Articles it contains improper for you I have a bad opinion of Quackery and would not have the medicine used without advice It was used by a Very famous Physician for Mrs. Be[*d*]low in a very difficult Case and gave her Immediate

Relief and she has used the same for the Chollir more than thirty years and it always has the same Effect.

I am in hopes of Coming home in two or three Weeks or in the Month of July but cannot say when—I [*am*] in comfortable health but a little Troubled with the Billious disorder & but hope to git quite Rid of it when I come home and Relax from Business and hope to find you in better health, and that you will not omit Riding out as often as you can—But after all our Efforts for Self Preservation, our whole Trust must be in that being who alone is Able to help us for vain is the help of Man.

[*P. S.*] Mr. Lothrop tills me Gurdon [*Huntington*] is Coming here which I hope he will not [*in*] fact ~~to~~ do by the next Packett whilst I am here.

ALS, Huntington Papers, CtHi. Addressed to Norwich, Connecticut, "with a bottle of medicine for Mrs. Huntington."

[1] Probably the wife of New York City postmaster William Bedlow, the only Bedlow listed in the city directory at this time.

Woodbury Langdon to John Langdon

I receiv'd. yours of the 17th. Inst., have no particular News to write this is principally to observe to you that [*lined out*] I perceive that Massachusetts are allowed for the Penobscot Expedition, you therefore will take particular care that we are allowed also for our Ship[1] you remember that she was the ~~bes~~ largest and best fitted Ship in the whole Fleet, don't forget Archibald Mercer, your friends are all well here and desire remembrance.

ALS, Langdon Papers, NhPoA. Written from Portsmouth, New Hampshire.

[1] The fleet organized in the summer of 1779 for the Penobscot Expedition against the British base at Castine, Maine, consisted of nineteen vessels, not including transports. In addition to twelve privateers in that state's service, New Hampshire contributed from its state navy the twenty gun brig *Hampden*, commanded by Captain Titus Salter. On 15 August, when most of the rest of the fleet was burned to avoid capture, the *Hampden* was one of the few to fall into British hands (Gordon Allen, *Navy History of the American Revolution* [Boston, 1913], ch. 12; John F. Millar, *American Ships of the Colonial and Revolutionary Periods* [New York, 1978], pp. 233–34.).

James Nicholson to John Barry

You will find By the Enclosed paper the fate of our petition[1] desided on yesterday, The Speakers in our favor where Messrs. Jackson, Burke, Hartley, Stone Seney & Huntington & Page. The whole of which did all that honest sincere Men could do & to whom we ought to look upon ourselves much

Indebted, The Violent opposers where Sedwick, Shearman & Bouedinot & Baldin 23 to 31 was the difference, John Lawrence did not say a syllable in our favour & Mr. Smith of S.C. Voted against us. your Philadelphia friends was likewise silent. only Mr. Gerry & Mr. Huntington Voted for us of the whole ~~of the~~ Eastern Members, J. Laurance only of this State The whole of your State where [*were*] with us, Mr. Vining Kept out of the way, As did Mr. Carroll, Mr. Contee against us, all the other Marylanders with us, Colo. Griffin & Mr. Maddison was also out of the way all the other Virginians where [*were*] for us. The North Carrolianians against us, S. Carrolinians, Burke & Huger with us, Georgians Jackson & Mathews with us. Mr. Stone still presevers & says he will have it, if it is five years hence, but believe there is an end to the business. If Colo. Hartley had been Supported by his Colleagues we should have had a good chance, but suppose they are too much engaged in fixing the Seat of Government in your City to disend to triffels (but this to yourself).

ALS, Barry-Hayes Collection, Independence Seaport Museum, Philadelphia. Addressed to "Strawberry Hill," Philadelphia.

[1] The Petition of the Officers of the Late United States Navy; see *DHFFC* 7:438–43.

Henry Wynkoop to Reading Beatty

I left home on tuesday morning last at 5 & arived here at 7 that evening, the Bill for raising aditional Revenue [*Duties on Distilled Spirits Bill HR-62*] was rejected on monday arising from two Causes the eastern people voted against it on account of the State Debts being unassumed & the Southern from an aversion to an Excise; The Committee appointed to ~~report~~ prepare another Bill have not yet reported.

*** It is not yet impossible but that Congress may hold their next Session at Philadelphia. The funding Bill yet lay's with the Senate undecided that Body being desirous first to see the Ways & Means provided by the Representatives.

ALS, Wynkoop Papers, PDoBHi. Written in the morning; place to which addressed not indicated. The omitted text relates to Wynkoop's debts.

Newspaper Article

A correspondent observes, that Congress have *little leisure*, yet mean to purchase a library—a library to suit the various tastes which must exist in such a mixed assembly, composed of every intermediate degree of character from Mr. G—n [*Gunn?*] to R. S—r—n [*Sherman*], must be numerous, various, and costly. I would recommend the purchase of a *Corderii*[1] and an attentive perusal of the first lesson; beginning with *Quid agis*—What are you doing—And translate it for the benefit of those who had no occasion, which will comprehend the majority.

IG, 3 July, cited a New York newspaper dated 25 June as the source. The original printing was actually in *NYJ*, 29 June.

---

[1] *Corderii Colloquiorum* was designed for the use of beginners in the Latin language and had gone through many editions since its publication in 1700.

[*David Daggett,*] A Republican to Messrs. Printers (No. 6)

IN the house of representatives, on the 10th inst. the yeas and nays were taken twice on the question of adjournment till the succeeding day, and the house was nearly equally divided both times. What could have caused such party-spirit—such opposition about so simple and unimportant a question? What—but the irritation and animosity which has been created by the discussion of questions whose decisions will be governed by local prejudices? We may justly be alarmed when we see such jealousies—we may justly fear that the publick good will be sacrificed to gratify private resentments, and that the most important national questions will be subjected to a determination from minds influenced by the most violent prejudices.

By the last papers it appears, that the committee appointed to select a library, have reported that a 1000 dollars be expended the present year, and 500 dollars every subsequent year, during the pleasure of Congress, for the purchase of books. This report is not yet accepted, and we can but hope that a regard to the dignity of Congress will compel them to reject it. This measure is not only unprecedented, but contemptible. If you employed a divine, and physician or a *lawyer*, (tell Frederick to carp and snarl at that last word;)[1] if you hired a labourer or a mechanic, would you not suppose yourselves insulted, to hear them demand of you, the books or implements of their various occupations? A measure of this kind would prepare the way for many others of a similar nature. If a library is furnished at public expence, why not servants, horses, carriages, and the whole equipage of an American *nobleman*? If 1000 or 500 dollars is now appropriated annually for such purposes, how much will they demand when they see the people tamely submit to such unjust, unrighteous, unprecedented, and iniquitous exactions?

But it may be said, all these evils which I have attempted to point out, are the necessary attendants of a Congress. Is this indeed the case? Is a wasting of the public money—sloth in the dispatch of business—violent contentions about the most trifling points and an almost total neglect of the great objects of legislation—are these necessary to the existence of a public body? No one is stupid enough to believe it, and yet are none of these evils ascribable to the present Congress? If not—more than 2 millions of people judge erroneously—and is it a matter of small moment that the public expectation has been so egregiously disappointed? Should it not have been a primary object with Congress to have rendered their administration so pleasing, that those who considered the constitution objectionable might have been reconciled to it, and thus all the subjects attached to the government? Instead of that, every opponent has been confirmed in his opposition, and the most firm supporters of the new system, shaken in their opinions. But suppose we admit that Congress act under a fatal necessity—and that their proceedings are the unavoidable result of their existence—then I contend, that we had better create no more congresses. I am not fanatic enough in religion, to suppose that Deity ever created any beings and obliged them to sin, on purpose to render them eternally miserable. I do not believe this, because it is repugnant to his justice and goodness; nor do I believe it the duty of the people to create another congress, if the certain consequence of their existence is such measures as have already been adopted, or such neglects as have taken place. But it may also be said, any member of Congress has a right to introduce any question which he pleases, and the house are obliged to deliberate upon it, and therefore the objection which arises from *delay* ceases; shall we then be silent while our property is sported with by the introduction and discussion of the most trifling subjects? Suppose a member should move that all the *quails* and *partridges* in the United States should be enumerated, or that a return should be made from every town and state, of the number of persons who have *red hair*—'tis true Congress must consider of this question, but shall we not charge the man who introduced it with stupidity, and the house, if they should not immediately dismiss it, with a most flagrant and gross mispence of time?

One thing is very obvious, viz. that two of the most important objects before Congress are the establishment of publick credit, and the restoration of a decayed commerce. It was principally for these purposes that the old constitution was despised and rejected and a new system of government established—and yet what measures have been adopted on these subjects? Not a word has been mentioned, in the legislature, tending to benefit commerce, and not an act passed to rescue us from the burthen of an accumulated debt and the consequent contempt and calumny of our publick creditors; but these topics have been sacrificed to admit repeated and warm debates about removing the seat of government—discussions about the pay of an officer in the army—harangues about African slavery, and—but I forbear.

[New Haven] *Connecticut Journal*, 30 June; reprinted at Norwich, Connecticut. For information on this series and its authorship, see A Republican to Messrs. Printers (No. 1), 15 May, above.

[1] See Frederick to Messrs. Printers, 26 May, above.

Other Documents

Pierce Butler to John Coffin. FC:lbk, Butler Papers, PHi.

Has received information from Daniel Hall regarding Butler's runaway "Negro Man," now in Nova Scotia; encloses power of attorney for Coffin to retrieve him and bring him back to New York City or Charleston, South Carolina.

Thomas Fitzsimons to Benjamin Rush. Summary of two page ALS, *Parke-Bernet Catalog* 468(1943):item 96.

Refers to Morris.

Alexander Hamilton to Robert Morris. AN, Montague Collection, NN.

"Mr Hamilton ~~being~~ wishes to converse with Mr. Morris on the subject of the 44 Shares of bank [*of North America*] Stock but being unwell he will be obliged to Mr. Morris to call on him at his house sometime before he goes to Senate."

George Hite to [*James Madison*]. ALS, Madison Papers, DLC. Written from Berkeley County, West Virginia. The recipient's identification is based on the letter's location. For the full text, see *PJM* 13:253–54.

Knowing no one else in New York City, asks Madison to serve White notice of Hite's taking depositions for a lawsuit, in which he is a complainant, against his brother John's children and others, over the estate of his father Jacob Hite; notice must be served by 24 July and acknowledged by either receipt or a sworn affidavit, which Hite asks Madison to return; visiting Isaac Hite the day before, he learned that "my Aunt [*Nelly Conway*] Madison was better than she had been for some time past."

Governor John Eager Howard to an Unknown Recipient. FC, incomplete, Miscellaneous Vertical File, MdHi. Written from Annapolis, Maryland. The recipient was probably a federal official or a member of the Maryland congressional delegation.

Encloses list of invalid pensioners paid by the state; requests to know who, among several Continental Army officers listed, are excluded from commutation.

John Henry Livingston to Egbert Benson. ALS, Dreer Collection, PHi.

Before Benson leaves New York to meet the Vermont commissioners, calls his attention to preserving the title of New York's Dutch Church to royal grants of land "in that Country which were given for pious purposes and the promotion of Literature."

Daniel Denton Rogers to Thomas Jefferson. ALS, Washington Papers, DLC. Written from Broad Street, New York City. For a partial text, see *PTJ* 17:248.

Office seeking: Henry Bromfield as consul at London; mentions Adams as reference.

William Smith (Md.) to Pierce Butler. ANS, Butler Papers, PHi. The enclosure, Unknown to Smith, dated 20 June, is printed above.

"Having been informed, that the question, for adjourning to Philadelphia, & Potomac, is to come before the senate to day—I take the liberty to hand you the enclosed extract of a letter, recd. by me last evening from Baltimore."

John Updike and William Earle to Theodore Foster. No copy known; listed as an enclosure in Thomas Jefferson to Silvanus Bourn, 25 August (*PTJ* 17:421n). The letter concerned seizure of Updike and Earle's sloop *Nancy* by French revenue officers in St. Louis, St. Domingue (Haiti).

George Washington to John Cannon. FC:lbk, Washington Papers, DLC. For the full text, see *PGW* 5:550–52. Washington employed Cannon as agent for his land on Millers Run, Washington County, Pennsylvania, on which Scott's brother James was a tenant.

Per Cannon's request, has applied to Scott for £50, which Scott will arrange to pay, although it far exceeds what he thought was due.

NYDA, 26 June.

Stanton and T. Foster arrived at New York.

GUS, 26 June.

"We hear that a motion made in the Senate of the United States yesterday, to take into consideration the bill for determining the permanent and temporary seat of government, was negatived, 15 to 14. Monday is the time assigned to consider this subject, by a former vote."

SATURDAY, 26 JUNE 1790

Cloudy misty (Johnson)

Theodore Foster to George Washington

I have the Honor to inform your Excellency that on the Twelfth Day of the present Month, I was appointed by the Legislature of the State of Rhode Island and Providence Plantations One of the Senators to represent that State, in the National Government. That on the Evening before last I arrived in this City and yesterday had the Honor of being admitted and sworn as a Member of the Senate of the United States.

Be pleased, Sir, to permit Me on the present Occasion to assure you of my most sincere Disposition to promote your personal Honor and private Happiness and to establish the Credit Glory and Prosperity of the Nation at large over which you preside. Your Excellency will ever find Me anxious to render you all the Aid and Support due to the Cheif Magistrate in the Administration of the National Government.

Accept my most Sincere Thanks for your Goodness in my Appointment to the Naval Office in the District of Providence.[1] At the Time I took the Liberty to write to Your Excellency respecting that office I had no Expectation of the Senatorial Trust I now hold. I undertook the latter not knowing that the former would be confided to Me. As they are incompatible if it would not be deemed presumptuous I would beg leave to request that the Honble. Ebenezer Thompson Esqr. of Providence may be appointed to that office. I will pledge myself for his Abilities, his Integrity and for his Fidelity in the Discharge of the Duties of the Office, and I am well assured that his Appointment will give more general Satisfaction to all Parties in the State then that of any other Person.

The Providence Association of Mechanics and Manufacturers, consisting of about Two Hundred of the Reputable Citizens of that Town have honored Me with the Care of an Address to your Excellency from their Corporation, a Copy of which I herewith inclose. If it be agreeable to your Excellency to receive it I will do myself the Honor to present it—at such Time as you will be pleased to appoint.[2]

The Honorable Joseph Stanton Esq. is my Colleague in the Senatorial Representation of Rhode Island. He has Communications which he wishes to make. If your Excellency will be pleased to admit us to an Interveiw we will wait on you to make our personal Respects, and gratefully acknowledge the Honor done us.

ALS, Miscellaneous Letters, Miscellaneous Correspondence, State Department Records, Record Group 59, DNA. For the text of the enclosed address, signed by Charles Keen and dated 4 June, see *PGW* 5:558n.

[1] Foster's election to the Senate was not yet known when his appointment as naval officer was confirmed in the Senate on 14 June.

[2] Foster may have presented the address during his first known official meeting with the President at the Washingtons' formal dinner on 1 July (*DGW* 6:80).

Rufus King to Caleb Strong

Suffer me my dear Sir, to request your examination of the inclosed—It is difficult to Know ourselves; if I have any Knowledge of my own heart, I can assure you that I am governed in the present case by public, and not by private, considerations—I most certainly believe this to be your situation.

[*Enclosure*]

Mr. Carrrol will propose Philadelphia & Potomack for the temporary & permanent Residence of Congress; it is not very probable that this project will succeed, but to satisfy existing engagements it may be necessary to try it—A motion to adjourn to Philadelphia will follow the loss of Mr. Carrols project—and it may have been suggested, as it formerly was, that the assumption will depend on its success—the Virginians may suppose a removal to Philadelphia will frustrate the Assumption, while on equally fallacious grounds some gentlemen may imagine it will favor the accomplishment of that Event.

The assumption being a just measure will prevail from the force of those considerations which urge its adoption—The opposition is weakened, and the original Objections have dwindled to a mere resistance of the manner proposed for its Establishment.

The question of residence may be decided independent of the assumption, and without exposing that measure to new Difficulties: but if the two Subjects must be connected, it may deserve examination, whether the assumption will not gain more friends by a decision in favor of the temporary residence at New york, and the permanent at Baltimore, than by an abrupt removal to Philadelphia. Pennsylvania might be displeased because this arrangement was preferred to a residence in their Capital, but they would be as little justified in carrying their resentment to any improper length, as New York would be in another Event, in suffering a sacrifice of their interest and wishes, to disturb their Judgment. In the present State of things, the votes in each house would be nearly equal on the question of Newyork and Baltimore, exclusive of the Delegates of Massachusetts. with their votes the measure can be established, and the Government composed on this Subject.

There is no Doubt that this arrangement would meet the approbation of a very large majority of Congress if every gentleman was at liberty to pursue his own convictions on the Subject; and this consideration induces a Belief that the measure will receive a very general approbation from the People of the several States.

The Alternative seems to be New york & Baltimore or Philadelphia. if the former fails, the latter must obtain—In this Situation the Gentlemen of massachusetts may suppose it most prudent to take no part in favor of either. but it is most certain as the business now stands, that not agreeing to New york and Baltimore is embracing Philadelphia—the Idea therefore of not taking a part, is as effectually promoting the views of the opponents of the measure of New york & Baltimore, as the most decisive adoption of their System.

The question of Residence has too long disturbed the public Councils—the conduct of those who have agitated the subject will best explain their views—A removal to Philadelphia leaves the business of residence afloat—It has been the reflected opinion of the friends of the union that this question should be decided—If this should not be the case, but congress should remove to Philadelphia the gratification of the turbulent partizans of that measure would be great, but it would not exceed the Chagrin of those at whose Expence it would be effected.

Newyork will ask nothing that will promote her views, unless the interest of the United States is also promoted, but she must possess uncommon apathy not to feel, and with pretty strong emotions too, that a measure which seems calculated to accomplish both, should be lost by the Silence, of those whose interest she anxiously desires to promote.

ANS and Ms., hand of King, formerly at MSonHi. A draft and a retained copy of this document, in King's hand, are in the King Papers, NHi. Because of the substantial differences between the draft and the final version, the editors are including it here:

Mr.

Mr. Carrol with Mr. Morris & others, propose Philadelphia and Potomack as the temporary & permanent Residence of Congress.

It is not presumable that this arrangement will succeed, but existing engagements may render it necessary to try the question in Senate.

The subsequent Step will be an unqualified proposition to remove the residence of Congress from New-York to Philadelphia. perhaps there may be expectations entertained in respect to the assumption; the Vi[*r*]ginians may suppose the ~~measure~~ asumption will not obtain, while the Eastern Gentlemen may imagine a removal to Philadelphia will brighten the prospects of that Event.

The assumption is a measure which must succeed, from the force of those considerations which urge its adoption—Every day demonstrates the opposition to be weakened, and the inclination of its opponents to adopt the measure to be increased. [*lined out*] The question of Residence may & perhaps ought to be decided independent of ~~that of~~ the assumption—if however they must be connected, it is worthy of consideration whether the assumption would not gain more friends, by a decision fixing the temporary Residence at N. York & the permanent at Baltimore, than by a removal from N. York to Philadelphia.

For N. York & Baltimore the votes will stand nearly divided excluding the votes of Mass. with their votes the measure may be established—if the Southern and eastern States concur in this Decision the question will be finally settled, and the probability is that a much larger portion of the People of the U.S. will be satisfied thereby than by any other Arrangement.

The Scheme of New York and Baltimore is the only one which can defeat the immediate removal to Philadelphia; what national reasons urge the step ~~I know not~~, has not been publickly stated—Philadelphia wd. be gratified New York wd. be disgusted—the Delegates of Mass. may say that they will take no part on this subject. But to take no part in favor of New York & Baltimore, is taking an effectual part in favor of Philadelphia.

The *permanent residence* may disturb the government even in Philadelphia; wd. it not be more for the public interest to decide the question as soon as possible.

Is there any hope of establishing that Residence east of Baltimore? if not, and the residence ought to be fixed, why not decide the question—N. Yk. can expect nothing from any State which will promote her wishes, unless the interest of the U.S. is also promoted—But she may feel with keen sensations that a measure which seems calculated to accomplish both, shd. be lost by the votes of those, whose interest she will always desire to advance.

One point is certain, that not acting with those ~~measure~~ who will propose New York & Baltimore, is embracing ~~that measure wh.~~ Philadelphia.

Richard Bland Lee to Theodorick Lee

I have received your letter from Dumfries [*Virginia*] of the 17th. Instant—and was glad to hear that the crops of wheat were then safe—tho' I am still very very apprehensive that the heavy rains which you have had will very much injure or destroy them.

Your accounts relative to the election are flattering. Tho' I can assure you that I should feel very little solicitude on that occasion, if a repulse would not be a kind of sanction to the malice of some of my adversaries.

We have a plan which is ripe for execution tomorrow—by which we hope to secure the permanent seat of the government to the Potowmack at the expiration of ten years. It's success depends on nice movements—and therefore not so certain as I could wish—but very probable This week will decide the fate of the potowmack forever. If we are successful the place to be elected will be left to the discretion of the President Georgetown [*Maryland*], as is probable should be the fortunate spot—tho the public buildings will be erected in Maryland—the Bill will be so framed as to admit Alexandria, if it should be deemed proper into the ten miles square. If this plan should succeed Philadelphia will be the temporary residence of the government in the meantime. Indeed an harmonious conclusion of our session depends much on the success of this arrangement. This measure is so calculated to conciliate the ~~the~~ most populous & wealthy portion of the United states, that I have no doubt if it should be agreed to, ~~that~~ we shall close the session with honor to ourselves and satisfaction to the Community—and that the past expectations of the friends of the government will begin to be realised—and that an harmonious and permanent arrangement of our finances will be the immediate consequence If it fails I fear we shall break up abruptly in disgust & confusion.

I hope to be with you in the course of a month. I want the sum of money very much which I wrote to you about ***

ALS, Custis-Lee Family Papers, DLC. Addressed to "Sully," Loudoun County, Virginia, by way of Alexandria; franked; postmarked 28 June. The omitted text relates to private business transactions.

William Maclay to Benjamin Rush

Yours of the 23d is now in my hands the mistake of which you make mention is not worth a further thought. were reason Œconomy Justice or any of the avowed principles of sound Policy to govern, on the subject of the Residence. We would not have been here so long. Tomorrow We go at it again in the Senate. The Vote of the Representatives in favour of Baltimore is not Yet decided upon. But the Matter has taken a new face. A Bill is now before Us. to fix the permanent Residence at Potowmack and the Temporary One for 10 Years in Philada. We must do as well as We can. But every Principle of situation improvements Wealth and Population, confirms it to Us, And I must regard it as a political Robbery to deprive Us of it, in any View. Ten Years will however turn up strange things, new and unexpected, Incidents will influence public Measures, and the reins of Government will be held by ~~new~~ other hands to act on anything like the principles of a croked or deceitful policy, is what I detest, nor will I admit such a thought. And Yet after all perhaps the most that we can do is to rule well for the present. leaving future Transactions to be governed by future circumstances. History, all past Experience, is full of the Vanity of endeavouring to perpetuate laws customs or even Religion There is a Lapse in things. a perpetual Shifting of the political Scenery. The Change of Men Works much of this. but You even see the same Men unstable as Water. Up today, and down tomorrow, on the same Question.

You shall hear from me when anything certain is decided.

ALS, Rush Papers, DLC. Addressed to Third Street, Philadelphia; franked; postmarked 28 June.

Pamela Sedgwick to Theodore Sedgwick

I was disopointed my dearest Mr. Sedwick of the pleasure of Sending to you last week as our Post did not go to Kinderhook [*New York*] was however faverd with a Line from you on Satterday Evening You Say not a Word of comeing home—I am Told my dear by Mr. Cornelius Vansc[*h*]aack that It is sopo[*s*]ed Congress will Set until August—I Sicken at the Thought of your being Absent for so long a Time. Tho I have very Long been deprived of the pleasure of your Company Yet I cannot Possiblely reconcile my feal-ings or make my self Happy in this State of Widdowhood. It grows more & more disagreeable To me evry day it is very True—I have many Agreeable acquaintance but what are Theay or the World to me while my Protector my Husband my Bosome friend is gone frome me—my Children want a father I evry day sensiblely feal what Theay suffer from the Loss of ~~an~~ the assidious Care of a Wise and Tender Parent—I must not however Suffer my Self to write or Speake on this Subject—It is Too much for me to Contemplate—and I would not willingly Vex and greive you with my Troubles— ***

[*Nephew*] Theodore is still here and Somewhat disopointed that he could not get a Birth in the Armmy—He has now Turnd his thoughts Toards Jennesee but what can he doe without assistance he is unwilling to ask it of You—I have desired him to write and let you know what his determina-tions and wishes are and Told him that If you could once Se him Act with Spirit and resolution It would I doubted not be an inducement with you to give him the nesecary Assistance Toards makeing a begining in the new world—do my dearest Love write me the first opportunity a longger letter than Your last as your letters are all I have of you I must not be denied a portion of them.

Give me some hope at least that you will return home Soon. The Children are well Roberts Leg remains much as It was. [*Daughter*] Eliza has been gone to the Spring [*at New Lebanon, New York?*] near a fortnight—I expect her home next week.

ALS, Sedgwick Papers, MHi. Written from Stockbridge, Massachusetts. The omitted text discusses Pamela's "Vexsatious fealings,"along with Silas Pepoon and others, over Nathaniel Kingsley's bankruptcy and Sedgwick's resulting liability.

Alexander White to George Washington

It is with great diffidence I offer the enclosed[1] but having taken that lib-erty will not add to your trouble by Apologies. I will only state such Facts as may enable you to judge whether this institution is like to be useful. the nature of the Country in general, its salubrity and fertility you are well acquainted with—The Academy has been supported ~~by~~ several years by private Donations, and the monies arising from Tuition, notwithstanding another Grammar School and a number of English and Dutch Schools have been kept up in the Town by private subscriptions.

The Assembly of Virginia at their last Session [*December 1789*] granted to the Trustees a Lot in Winchester, and two Tracts of Land—One on Cedar Creek containing 200 acres the other on Back Creek containing 900 acres—it is proposed to erect the Buildings on the Lot and to rent the Lands, which in ~~their~~ the present State of their improvements, may not yield much, but will be very valuable in future—If you think this infant Seminary, deserving of any share of your Patronage you will signify it in the manner most agreeable to yourself.

ALS, Washington Papers, DLC.

[1] The enclosure, dated February 1790, was a subscription list of the benefactors of the Winchester Academy, incorporated in Winchester, Virginia, in October 1786 (*PGW* 5:564n).

Newspaper Article

A country gentleman, who came to town on a visit of a few days, in hopes of being entertained in hearing the debates of Congress, begs leave to present his compliments to a number of elegant looking citizens, who come to the gallery every day. The request which the country gentleman has now to make is, that those who are fond of almonds, walnuts and brown hullers, will be so good as to have them cracked at home every morning, so that, when they make their exhibition in the gallery, they may proceed to eating, as the platoon firing of teeth against the corps of nut shells prevents the spectators from hearing some of the best speakers in the house.

N. B. After the gentlemen have secured the kernels, it is requested they would be so obliging as to pocket the shells, as the noise of pedestrial troops, proudly crushing them to atomi, produces the most inharmonious sounds that could possibly be invented to distract the ears of those who may happen to have musical souls, in the vicinity of this crash of matter.

NYDG, 26 June; reprinted at Philadelphia and Alexandria, Virginia.

OTHER DOCUMENTS

William Crocker to George Thatcher. ALS, Thatcher Papers, MeHi. On the address sheet, Crocker wrote "Present" under Thatcher's name, perhaps as a direction for delivery on the floor of the House.

Office seeking: excise officer at Portland, in preference to Machias, Maine; does not mean to recommend himself, "but can afford you, & others in you[*r*] conspicuous Line such recommendation, as will be satisfactory."

Elbridge Gerry to James Sullivan. No copy known; acknowledged in Sullivan to Gerry, 18 [*July*].

John Taylor Gilman to Governor Josiah Bartlett. ALS, Chamberlain Collection, MB. Place to which addressed not indicated.

Thinks Congress will not adjourn until sometime in August, although some think the session will end in a few days; can form no opinion whether anything will be done this session regarding the public debt; parties in the House charge each other with bargaining "for Residence, Assumption &c."; the ways and means (Duties on Distilled Spirits [*HR-62*]) bill was defeated in the House; assumptionists seem determined to provide for no public debts unless the states' war debts are included; fears Congress will rise without a funding bill; "The Galleries of the House being open many of the Speeches are for them, & for the Press; Indeed the House is over done with long Speeches—which very seldom tends to throw light on the Subject."

Benjamin Hawkins to Armand John DeRosset. Summary and excerpt of two page ALS, *The Collector* 62(1949):item 2570. Addressed to Wilmington, North Carolina; franked; postmarked. The ellipses are in the source.

"Thanking him for a copy of his thesis (*Dissertation Medica Inauguralis de Febribus Intermittendibus* [Philadelphia, 1790], on intermittent fevers) and wishing him success in the medical profession. '. . . I do not presume to take on myself to judge of the performance being incompetent; but some of my Medical friends who are really learned say it has considerable Merit,' etc."

Benjamin Lincoln to Theodore Sedgwick. ALS, Sedgwick Papers, MHi. Written from Boston; franked; postmarked 27 June.

"The public creditors have, here, more hopes respecting the State debt than they had some weeks since—The assumption is an event most ardently to be wished for, to the attainment of which no measures should be left untried while there is hope for I have little expectation that we can long exist as a government without it, and never untill it shall be effected live in peace and quietness"; reports that a state bill for ceding lighthouses to the federal government was enacted without Governor John Hancock's assent; has just been informed the Senate has passed the funding bill "as put up."

Henry Marchant to John Adams. ALS, Adams Family Manuscript Trust, MHi. Written from Newport, Rhode Island. The enclosed letter, signed by George Hazard, George Champlin, Peleg Clarke, William Tripp, Geo. Sears, William Ellery, George Gibbs, Chris. Champlin, Saml. Fowler, Caleb Gardner, and James Robinson, is in the same location. An endorsement in Adams's hand reads, "referred to me by the Prest." A copy of the letter in the same collection in Adams's hand was evidently produced for Marchant's comments; Marchant's annotation includes: "Our Senator Mr. Foster will know them all, and they are generally known by the first Characters in New York."

Office seeking: federal district judge for the Rhode Island district; considered any recommendation for that office "from Merchants as indellicate and improper"; "I meant to rest the Matter entirely upon the Knowledge which Members of Congress might Themselves have of me, or procure by Enquiry"; "a few gentlemen have now insisted upon my receiving and forwarding their best Wishes that I should succeed to that office—I have consented to enclose it to you Sir, for your Perusal and better Judgment as to the Propriety or Expediency of delivering it to the President."

William Pike to George Washington. ALS, Washington Papers, DLC. Written from Newburyport, Massachusetts. For the full text, see *PGW* 5:561.

Office seeking: excise collector for the district including Newburyport; Gerry has written that he would nominate Pike; mentions in addition King and Dalton as references.

James Sullivan to John Langdon. ALS, Langdon Papers, NhPoA. Written from York, "Prov[*ince of*] Main"; answered.

Stopped at Langdon's home a few days earlier and found Langdon's wife and daughter well; proposes that those two come to Sullivan's house (in Boston) to meet Langdon on his journey home from Congress.

Sunday, 27 June 1790

Warm (Johnson)

Fisher Ames to Thomas Dwight

Your favour of the 24th. tho ~~not~~ [*lined out*] I expected the connection between our friend [*Mary Worthington*] & Mr. B. [*Jonathan Bliss*] wd. be soon formed, has rather surprised me—I was not prepared for so much haste, and yet, as they are agreed, & have no time to lose why should they delay—You will believe me that my esteem for M[*ary*]. makes me feel a sensible regret for her removal to N. Brunswick [*Canada*]—The loss of the society of so excellent a woman is scarcely to be compensated. ~~except~~ to her, the event is not formidable—for the merit & good sense of Mr. B. as you paint him will make that foggy region more than tolerable to our friend—You reproach your & my tardiness—but Mr. B. by making a business of it, has done more courting in two months than I have done in a year—I leave your own affair to your conscience—If F. [*Frances Worthington*] thought half as well of me as Hh. [*Hannah Worthington*] does of you, there would be some reason for your remark—In the actual state of things, my *conscience* is the most at ease of all my rational faculties—while I am shut up here in this pigsty, smelling the perfumes from wharves, and the raking of gutters, I long for the air & company of Springfield [*Massachusetts*]—while Maria [*Mary Worthington*] is just upon the wing I am impatient to see her—because I expect it will be a long while before we enjoy that pleasure again—The parting will be hard—Some fine eyes will be rub'd till they are red—and the old Gentleman[1] too with all his firmness will suffer greatly at the thought of (possibly) a final adieu—That peaceful house so long the seat of tranquility & good order will be disturbed by unusual emotions—Their very joy will have a sadness in it, because it will quicken the sense of what they are going to lose—At this time, my visit wd. not afford me the usual pleasure—but the sympathy I shd. feel with them wd. upon the whole make it a most interesting visit—and I cannot think with any moderation upon the delay of my journey till M[*ari*]a. shall be gone—If business shd. be in a state to make it barely possible to leave it, I will see you next week.

Your fears are strong that we shall lose the assumption mine have been so, as I have often signified in my letters—Now, I am pretty confident of a better issue to this long contest—conviction seems at last to have its way to men whose prejudices seemed to have bar'd up the passage—we hear no more about the injustice of the assumption at last, it is tacitly allowed that it will promote justice, & it is asked, let it rest till the next session, & then we shall doubtless assume—This looks like coming over—Besides consequences are feared—The N. Engd. states demand it as a debt of justice with a tone so loud & threat'ning, that they fear the convulsions whh. wd. probably ensue—Further they are going to fix the residence permanently on the Potowmac, & by the apostacy of Pensylva. will do it—removing however immediately to Phila. & staying there ten Years—Two such injuries wd. be too much. They dare not, I trust, carry Congress so far south, & leave the debts upon us—R. Morris too is really warm for the assumpn. & as he is the Fac-totum in the business he will not fail to insist upon the original friends of it, & who have ever been a majority, voting for it—with five pensylvns., our former aid from that delegation, we can carry it—or at least obtain four fifths of the debts, to be assumed—Accordingly, they begin to say, these violent feuds must be composed—too much is hazarded to break up in this temper, Maryland is the most alarmed, as well as, next to Virginia, most anxious for the Potowmac. I am beginning to be sanguine in the hope of success—This week may decide If so, the next will carry me to Springfield—But while such immense objects are depending, at the very crisis too, you will see that I cannot desert, without being chargeable with a breach of duty, & taking a risk of consequences & a weight of reproach that I ought not to bear—with my own consent—Please to give me your opinion upon these circumstances—and if you think with me, pray intimate to my friends & particularly to Maria, the force of that necessity which may detain me—for perhaps this week & next may be employed here in the business—we shall adjourn soon, The impatience to get to Phila. will make it tedious to stay in N. York—& others wish to see their families—Poor Dalton suffers the pains of a public man—I cannot think that G. Cabot[2] will serve—Dear friend, I am in haste—going to spend the day abroad—and at the hazard of writing nonsense I have scrabbled what I wished you to know without delay.

ALS, Ames Papers, MDedHi. Place to which addressed not indicated.

[1] Ames's future father-in-law, Col. John Worthington (ca. 1719–1800) of Springfield, Massachusetts.

[2] The Massachusetts legislature elected George Cabot in place of Dalton, who had drawn a two year term when the Senate first formed in 1789.

Thomas Hartley to Jasper Yeates

I last Evening received your Favor of the 20th. inst. and am glad to hear that you and the Family are well—no Change of any Consequence has taken place since the 25th. except that a Committee of both houses of which Committee I was a Member agreed Yesterday Morning to report to the respective Houses that Congress should adjourn on the 15th. of July.

Among the Business which we say ought to be finished this Session—Is making Provision for the Payment of the National Debt—our affairs are so broken ([*lined out*] as I said upon a former occasion) I can draw no Conclusions.

ALS, Yeates Papers, PHi. Addressed to Lancaster, Pennsylvania; postmarked. This is a postscript to a letter written 25 June, above.

Thomas Jefferson to George Gilmer

*** Congressional proceedings go on rather heavily. the question for assuming the state debts, has created greater animosities than I ever yet saw take place on any occasion. there are three ways in which it may yet terminate. 1. a rejection of the measure which will prevent their funding any part of the public debt, and will be something very like a dissolution of the government. 2. a bargain between the Eastern members who have it so much at heart, & the middle members who are indifferent about it, to adopt those debts without any modification on condition of removing the seat of government to Philadelphia or Baltimore. 3. an adoption of them with this modification that the whole sum to be assumed shall be divided among the states in proportion to their census; so that each shall receive as much as they are to pay; & perhaps this might bring about so much good humour as to induce them to give the temporary seat of government to Philadelphia, & then to George town permanently. it is evident that this last is the least bad of all the terms the thing can take. the only objection to it will be that Congress will then will have to lay & collect taxes to pay these debts, which could much better have been laid & collected by the state governments. this, tho' an evil, is a less one than any of the others in which it may issue, and will probably give [*lined out*] us the seat of government at a day not very distant, which will vivify our agriculture & commerce by circulating thro' our state an additional sum every year of half a million of dollars ***

FC, letterpress copy, Jefferson Papers, DLC. Place to which addressed not indicated. The omitted text discusses European news. For the full text, see *PTJ* 16:574–75.

Theodore Sedgwick to Pamela Sedgwick

I have not, my dearest love, received a single line from you this week. I will notwithstanding continue to write. Does my love receive pleasure by my hasty letters, and can you believe me less pleased by reading yours? I will not repeat to you how much I suffer by your neglect. Do not I pray you repeat it. I have thought for these several weeks that the next must bring the question of assumption to a conclusion. It would be idle to bring it forward untill the wicked subject of residence was disposed of. It now seems impossible not to be decided this week. The moment it is I will go home either with or without leave.

Mr. Dalton is not reelected Senator but Mr. George Cabot. the former gentleman must be greatly chagrined, for there certainly is no more reason to leave him out than there was originally to choose him.

Adieu dearest Love, tell the little lazy girls [*Eliza and Frances Sedgwick*] papa can hardly forgive them & if he dared he would make the same declaration to their Mamma.

ALS, Sedgwick Papers, MHi. Place to which addressed not indicated.

George Thatcher to Sarah Thatcher

Thinking as I do, and persuaded as I am of the great influence of education on men, you will not wonder at my so frequently touching on this subject—Almost all the diversities that distinguish one from another are owing to the difference of their education—If all men are not wise, it is not because nature brought any of them forth fools—If all men are not virtuous and honest, we ought not to charge their vices or their dishonesty to nature—All men are born ignorant, but no one was ever brought into the world wicked. Wickedness as well as virtue and Goodness is the result of education and the particular circumstances men are placed in. If then, these positions be true—and I have no doubt of them—how vastly important is the charge every parent has committed to him! Is a child vicious—or ignorant? So far as his father or mother had the charge of him he, or she must be answerable for his vice, and his department, or success in the world—Most people seem sensible of this so far as Education relates to Reading, writing and common Arithmitic—and I might add some of the externals of Religion—such as going to meeting, saying their prayers, & a general complyance with the forms of the Country—And these things, tho not the most essential to the compleat education of the man, are highly usefull, and ought not to be omitted—Yet they are not to be put in competition with the moral part of a compleat education—I mean that, which more immediately relates to the heart and affections—On this depends his character as to virtue, or vice—A man may be virtuous, honest and benevolent tho he does not know his Letters, or able to write his name—and in my estimation is a thousand times more amiable than one who is skillfull in this Learning, and ingenious in wickedness.

Children are all naturally selfish—because they cannot have an idea of any bodys feelings & interest except their own—'tis impossible they should before they are some years old—I am therefore of opinion that it is a good method to begin very early to learn children to be kind and benevolent to others—in order to accomplish this every thing should be avoided that usually irritates children against one another—no child should ever be countenanced in striking another—And if it could well be avoided, one child should not be corrected before another—Yet I see this cannot be avoided in common schools—but let it be attended to where & as often as it can—Children will love those whom their parents appear to esteem and respect—Love is thus far an habit, & may be strengthened by imitation—To illustrate this more clearly I will give you an example in the family of our friends Mr. & Mrs. [*Nathaniel and Sally*] Barrell of York [*Maine*]—As often as I go there I am struck with the affection evidently discovered towards me by the little children—they come round me, & look wishfully upon me, as tho they wanted to do me some act of kindness—This is a moral phenomenon I have frequently noticed, & reflected upon—I could mention the like in several other families—What can this arise from? I never gave them any thing in my life, tho frequently there—For this inattention of mine to so much young benevolence of theirs I have more than once reproached myself.

The children, as well those of very tender ages as such that are of riper discreation, see the particular attention of their father & mother to me, and undoubtedly often hear them speake of me, in my absence, in terms of respect and friendship—Thus the practice of friendship and benevolence, before children, will beget in them the very principle of these virtues—In this manner we may make children love & embrace children—but the sincerity of our professions and actions must not be doubtfull—if it is—a very different Lesson will be taught our children.

I am persuaded, my dear, you will not think I am reading you an admonitory Lecture, when I say—that all scolding, harsh ~~censure~~ censure and severity on the conduct of others, in the presence of children, will certainly make an impression on their tender minds altogether adverse to the kind, humane and amiable feelings that they ought to entertain towards every individual of the human race—What an unhappy creature is an angry, ill-natured child! And how can children be otherwise than such, if they have constantly before them ill-natured & angry objects—perhaps too their parents, whom they are, in other things, taught to imitate—Is it possible for a child to imitate a person in one instance & not in others? I doubt it—especially when he is set before them for that purpose.

Servants, & all domestics should be placed [*placid?*] and in good humor, as well as always cheerful, before children—as children are more familiar with these, they are so much the more likely to copy their actions and imbibe their passions & dispositions.

Yours of the 17th. & 19th. inst. came to hand last evening—I am glad to find Mr. [*Silas*] Lee is well enough to attend Court at York—I am very glad you approve of my Sermon as you call my Letter of the 8th. inst. And I hope the Sermons which gave occasion to that Letter will be as agreeable when they arrive.

I would not have you write me any more after the 7th. or 8th. of July—because I expect Congress will adjourn by the 14th. and I shall be on my way home.

Kiss our dear children.

ALS, Thatcher Family Papers, MHi. Place to which addressed not indicated. Signed "most tenderly yours."

Abishai Thomas to John Gray Blount

*** The Southern Legislators are laboring to remove Congress and I believe will effect it, the Pennsylvania members have offered to join in giving the permanent residence to the Patowmac at the end of ten years if Philadelphia may have the temporary until that time, there will be a nice question in Senate where the bill originated & is to be acted upon tomorrow, if carried there, the general opinion appears to be that it will obtain by a considerable majority in the House of representatives—The bill for funding the domestic debt is considerably alter'd by the Senate, they have Struck out the alternatives of Land &c. as proposed by the House and say the whole shall be funded at 4 ℔ Ct. including Indents, old Continental money is to be funded at 100 for 1 *** The post office bill [*HR-74*] proposes the route through N.C. to be by Halifax Tarboro Smithfield Fayett Haley's Ferry &c. & to have Cross posts from Petersburg on the old line to Edenton, From Tarboro. through Greenville & Washington to New Bern & from Fayette to Wilmington, I take it one of our Senators will oppose it,[1] The assumptionists have not yet relinquish'd their cause but I trust they lose ground— ***

ALS, John Gray Blount Papers, Nc-Ar. Addressed to Washington, North Carolina; carried by Capt. Houston. For the full text, see *Blount* 2:72–73.

[1] Probably Johnston, who came from the tidewater counties that stood to be bypassed by the main post road. He served on the Senate committee to which HR-74 had been referred on 24 June, and which would present its report on 30 June, striking out the proposed postal route in North Carolina (*DHFFC* 6:1707–8).

Letter from New York

The Question now before Congress is, whether they shall adjourn to Philadelphia, for Ten or Fifteen Years, and after that Period, fix their Permanent

Residence on the Patowmack; or remain at New York for Two Years, and their Permanent Residence be at Baltimore.

The Parties in Congress, on those Two Questions, are nearly equal: Nothing but the Opposition of the Majority of the Maryland Members, can prevent Baltimore being the fortunate Spot. I am informed that the Address of Baltimore[1] will be read To-Morrow, in Congress; and although I scarce think it will have Weight with your own Members, yet, I am induced to think, it will have influence with the Members of the other States.

[Baltimore] *Maryland Journal*, 2 July.

[1] On 28 June, Carroll successfully moved the reading of the "representation" of John O'Donnell and other citizens of Baltimore; it was presented in the House by Smith (Md.) and read on 6 July. For background and descriptions of the non-extant address, see *DHFFC* 8:460–61.

Letter from New York

To-morrow, it is expected, the final decision in the *Senate* will be made respecting the Temporary and Permanent Residence of Congress. The last ideas I have heard suggested, are, that Philadelphia should be the temporary seat of government, say, from 5 to 10 years—and the Potomack, by the same act, be fixed on as the permanent residence. The Rhode Island Senators arrived on Friday—One of them, at about 11 o'clock A.M. A motion had been previously made, to take up this business, as reported in a Bill brought in some time since by Mr. Butler. The question was not determined until the Rhode-Island Members were qualified. They voted against taking up the business, which made the numbers 13 and 13. The Vice-President turned the question in favour of the negative.

As to the present state of politicks, it is almost impossible to describe. Assumption and Residence clog the wheels, and make the Funding-Bill lag. When the Residence business is finished, I believe the Assumption will take place, the Funding-Bill pass, and the Adjournment take place immediately. Meantime other less important, though essential business, is picked up, and dispatched.

As to the Residence, it is much expected that the next Congress will meet in Philadelphia. But all that is with compass of human abilities will be done to prevent it. I am persuaded, that if this question was not involved with that of Assumption, New-York and Philadelphia would be left to contest it themselves, *i.e.* Congress would stay where they are for the present. Some are of opinion, however, that merely being here, tends to embarrass publick business—others, that so long as the question remains undetermined, it will poison our publick council, others, again, that it is a ruinous project to think of removing at all in the present state of the Government.

The lots drawn by the Rhode-Island Senators, were, Mr. STANTON 4, and Mr. FOSTER, two years.

[Boston] *Columbian Centinel*, 3 July; reprinted, in whole or in part, at Portland, Maine; Exeter, New Hampshire; and New York City (*NYMP*, 10 July).

Letter from New York

I was extremely surprised to hear as I did last night, that the Hon. Mr. DALTON was superceded—as I have never heard any thing suggested against his conduct, either at home, or since my arrival here. Though his successor is a most excellent and amiable character; I assure you, that if Mr. DALTON has been charged of voting on any question against what is generally supposed to be the true interest of the United States, he has been slandered. I rather fear his being superceded is only preparatory to considerable changes in the representation from Massachusetts. If this should be the case, it will not only discover fickleness, but be subversive of our prospects, arising from abilities, matured by experience—and in some instances, at least, would deprive our State of abilities, independence and industry second to none in the United States.

[Boston] *Columbian Centinel*, 3 July.

Letter from New York

I am very glad to find that Mr. Dalton is superceeded. It is full time that the people should show their disapprobation of the measures of Congress; and I hope this will be preparatory to a general change in the representation of every State in the Union. For let me tell you, the present Congress have got into such parties, that the sooner the members are changed the better; and as it is our misfortune not to have it in our power to recall our Members, we have only this check to *replace them*, 'till we get men that either understand the public business, or have a disposition to study those things that will restore our credit, which has been sacrificed this session to mere party views, and disgraceful combinations.

Boston Gazette, 5 July; reprinted at Portland, Maine; Norwich and Hartford, Connecticut; New York City (*NYMP*, 10 July; *NYJ*, 13 July); Philadelphia; Baltimore; and Fredericksburg and Richmond, Virginia.

OTHER DOCUMENTS

Pierce Butler to Peter Spence. FC, Butler Letterbook, ScU. For the full text, see *Butler Letters*, pp. 52–54.

Defends himself from charge of neglect in their friendship; "Luke warmness where I profess a friendship, unsteadiness or Instability are not to be placed among my deficiencies"; meditates on the rapidity of aging and on having arrived at his forty-fifth year; "I have got to the top of the hill without once looking about me" and "without a knowledge of how I got here"; "I feel I am growing serious—I will quit it, tho' this is a day, Sunday, which I generally give to thought and serious reflection"; Mrs. (Mary Middleton) Butler "is much indisposed, nearly confined to her bed; a shadow of what she was. I am not free from painful apprehensions at her situation"; discusses private business; inquires about hiring a housekeeper for £30 and passage from England; discusses lamentable condition of private credit in South Carolina; does not know when Congress will adjourn; observes that the residence question "somewhat agitates Congress" and predicts it will be determined in favor of the Potomac and Philadelphia; "my mind is at ease" regarding the education of his son (Thomas).

Lambert Cadwalader to James Monroe. FC:dft, Cadwalader Papers, PHi.

Directions for Monroe's conduct in a private legal transaction involving Cadwalader and his family.

Joseph Crocker to George Thatcher. ALS, Thatcher Papers, MeHi. Written from Boston; franked; postmarked.

Office seeking: brother William Crocker for impost or excise appointment in Casco Bay, Machias, or preferably Portland, Maine; "I trust you have some acquaintance with him."

John Fenno to Joseph Ward. ALS, Ward Papers, ICHi. Addressed to the Land Office, State Street, Boston; carried by (Silvanus) Bourn. For the full text, see *AASP* 89(1979):367–80.

Dalton's loss of his bid for reelection "may be right, but it savors of fickleness," since "his conduct has never been impeached to my knowledge"; expects the residence and assumption will be settled that week; seems as if assumption's supporters will prevail.

John Fox to George Thatcher. ALS, Thatcher Papers, MeHi. Written from Boston, in the evening.

Acknowledges Thatcher's letter of 22 June and its expressions of support for (Ebenezer) Mays's appointment (as Portland Head, Maine, lighthouse keeper); completion of the lighthouse could not possibly cost $2500; "if you should mention so large a sum it may defeat the whole plan"; the best estimate is less than $1500, of which Massachusetts' cession act already provided £300; other lighthouses will cost twice as much to complete, which he mentions to show that Portland Head lighthouse "will not be so burthensome on the Continent as others"; (Daniel) Davis also supports Mays's appointment.

Benjamin Goodhue to Stephen Goodhue. ALS, Goodhue Family Papers, MSaE. Addressed to Salem, Massachusetts; franked; postmarked.

Private mercantile business; "We have nothing new, expect we shall adjourn in all next month."

Thomas Jefferson to David Ramsay. FC, Jefferson Papers, DLC. For the full text, see *PTJ* 16:577.

"Congress proceed heavily. their funding plans are embarrassed with a proposition to assume the state debts, which is as disagreeable to a part of the Union as desireable to another part. I hope some compromise will be found. great endeavors are using to get the temporary seat of government to Philadelphia, & the permanent one to George town. the counterproject is New York & Baltimore. no time for their adjournment can be yet calculated on."

Thomas Jefferson to Martha Jefferson Randolph. ALS, Jefferson's Letters to His Daughter, NNP. For the full text, see *PTJ* 16:577.

"I think it probable that Congress will pass a bill for removing to Philadelphia for ten years, and then to Georgetown. the question will be brought on tomorrow, and it's fate be determined probably in the course of the ensuing week."

Jeremiah Wadsworth to Harriet Wadsworth. ALS, Wadsworth Papers, CtHi. Addressed to Hartford, Connecticut; franked; postmarked. Signed "Your affectionate friend & parent."

Is pleased with (son) Daniel's recovery; discusses his own purchase of household goods; Laurance's wife (Elizabeth) "is confined and her health such as gives little reason to expect a recovery I have not seen her this ten days"; America Frances (de Crèvecoeur) Otto sends regards; Trumbull is well; (his brother) John is still in Philadelphia.

William Samuel Johnson, Diary. Johnson Papers, CtHi.

"St. Pauls."

MONDAY, 28 JUNE 1790

Hot (Johnson)

Christopher Gore to Rufus King

***

You will long before this have known the state of our election—Dalton was universally opposed in the house, merely because he was a senator—the advocates for the other candidates warmly encouraged the prejudices against the present members, by inveighing against large salaries compensations, & the want of industry in Congress—this unjustifiable conduct had great effect—and cleard the way for ~~others~~ other candidates, of which there were many—[*George*] Cabot will serve, and sitting aside the mortification to an honourable man—& the fickleness displayed by the Government in abandoning one who has conducted unexceptionably well, the choice is good—I very much question, if any of our delegation attempted, by a correspondence with their friends, to promote Mr. D.'s reelection.

ALS, King Papers, NHi. Written from Boston. The omitted text discusses the relative advantage of King's half-brother Cyrus' (d. 1817) attending Harvard rather than Columbia College. For the full text, see *King* 1:389–90.

William Plumer to Abiel Foster

It is with pleasure I acknowledge your obliging favor of [*10*] May last. You misunderstood me upon the subject of funding the Continental debt; but I have not now leisure to state my opinion upon that important subject.

The Commonwealth of Massachusetts has, it seems instructed their Senators & Representatives in Congress to urge the assumption of the State debts. 'Tis said those instructions will have an influence upon the national Legislature.

The last week of the session of the General Court of this State, a committee was raised to draw up a remonstrance to Congress agt. the Assumption—& to report a resolve to ~~instrct~~ instruct our Senators & request you & your Colleagues to use your influence agt. the adoption of a system so partial & injurious to some of the States, particularly to this. But as ill-luck & the demon of strife & discord would have it, the business was winked out of sight, & the attention of the House was arrested upon the subject of *Tender laws*, & exempting the bodies of debtors from gaol. A few members strenuously advocated these iniquitous measures—a committee was appointed—

a bill offered, not by the committee, but by one of its members without their knowledge. The bill was in direct violation of the constitutions of the United States & this State, of the rights of citizens, & of sound policy. And to the satisfaction of the friends of order & good government it was negatived by a large & respectable majority.

*** You may rest assured that a majority of the Court [*legislature*] are with me against the assumption of the State debts.

***

Copy, Plumer Papers, DLC. Written from Epping, New Hampshire. The omitted text relates to state politics. The concluding paragraph, concerning New Hampshire's second federal election, is printed in that section in Correspondence: Third Session.

William Smith (S.C.) to Edward Rutledge

After much impatience I had the pleasure of gratifying my curiosity in the perusal of your Letter & the new Constitution. Your letter has reconciled me in a considerable degree to some parts which I thought highly objectionable; the Seat of govt., the rotation in offices, the exclusion from the governor's chair, the size of the representation in both houses & some other points struck me as injudicious regulations;[1] I am however satisfied on reflection that local considerations will always supercede strict political maxims & that you were obliged to pay due attention to those considerations. I should have wished the representn. of one house not to have exceeded 60 or 70—& that of the other 20 or 25. I should have wished the Executive re-eligible & vested with a qualifd. negative & elected for a longer period & the Senators to have been chosen thro the medium of Electors. Most of those persons with whom I have conversed concur with me on these heads—Upon the whole the constitn. is much better than the former one & admits of a convenient mode of amendment: I am only apprehensive that Columbia is too well established by the Constitn. to flatter ourselves with the prospect of a change, as it will require the concurrence of two thirds of the *whole representation* & not of the *members present.* you are however the best judge of this, being on the spot & acquainted with all the secret springs of action.

With respect to ourselves, it is so long since I have had an opportunity of writing to you that I should write a volume were I to enter into a detail of our proceedings; many strange & unexpected occurrences have arisen within some weeks past & tho little has apparently been done by Congress yet I can assure you we have not been idle; but where there ~~are~~ is such a complication of interests & views to adjust & bring to a point, it is almost a matter of astonishment that any of the great questions now before us promise a termination this Session. Were each question brought forward seperately, an opinion might be speedily given on their respective merits, but they are so closely entangled one with the other that a member does not know how to vote on one without considering the effect it will have on Several others. Some will not vote for the assumption until the residence is fixed; others withhold their assent to the funding bill & the ways & means until the assumption is carried—a motion was carried in the Reprs. that Congress should hold its next Session at Philada.—the Senate negatived it—it was renewed in the Represens. & there changed by the Eastern Members to Baltimore—the Senate postponed the consideration of it to this day & originated a Bill for fixing the permanent Seat of Governt.—for this fortnight past considerable negotiations have been carrying on—some of the Southn. Senators (including ours) are desirous of New York as the temporary residence for 8 or 10 years & Baltimore as the permanent Seat at the Expiratn. of that period; the Eastn. members who are averse to such a southern position will not concur & it is to be feared the plan will fail: on the other hand Morris with the Virgina. & Maryland Senators have formed another confederacy which is to go to Philada. for ten years & then to the Potowmac as the permant. Seat: thus matters stand at present. The funding Bill past our house & was altered by the Senate, by striking out all the alternatives & funding the Debt at 4 per cent, reserving the Lands as a sinking fund. The Bill has not been sent back to us yet, as some of the Senators detain it with the hopes of reconsidering it, while others retain it as a hostage for the assumption. I don't think our house will agree to the amendmts. The Excise [*Duties on Distilled Spirits HR-62*] Bill was rejected in the Reps.—some voted against it viz., Virga., No. Cara., part of So. Car., and Georgia, from a dislike to the Excise, while the Eastern people voted it out because the assumption had been rejected.

A Committee have reported additional Impost & Tonnage—this will bear hard on the Southern States & will encounter great opposition—We are now in a very embarassing Situation & may possibly adjourn without bringing any of these great questions to a conclusion; some of the Eastn. members think the assumption will stand a better chance if we go to Philada. & begin to waver in their opposition to the removal; they are in general fixed in their determination to oppose any funding, independent of the State debts, & many members who are opposed to any funding at all will heartily join them; this circumstance, with the difficulty of agreeing on the ways & means, places the public debt in great jeopardy this Session. This unfortunate situation is the result of Sumpter's voting against us; had the assumption been carried, the funding system wod. have been passed some time ago, no motion for a removal would have been obtained on the public business & we should have adjourned some time ago to the general satisfaction. As long ago, as 9th. March we carried the question, it was recommitted by the vote of Sumpter, & here we are 28th. June as far back as ever. The Pensya.

Members were tempted to take advantage of their situation & to make this question subservient to their wishes; the three antifederal New-Yorkers[2] were apprized of this & informed that they wod. lose Congress if they voted against the Assumption, but they obstinately stood out; now they begin to repent & will vote for ~~the Assump~~ it; when perhaps it is too late.

We have passed in our house a Bill making provision for the Settlemt. of Accots. between the Several States & the U.S. [*HR*-77]—it is very favorable to our State & I hope the Senate will not alter it. I got the time for delivering our claims extended to July 1791, which circumstance I hope our State will avail herself of & lose no time in collecting & transmitting our further claims; shod. the Assumption be lost, this Bill ~~may~~ will be the best substitute we can expect, for we have claims which if brought forward in time will give us a Ballance of two or three millions of dollars; the Ratio by which our Quota is to be ascertained is highly favorable, as we shall after the next Census be not more than 1/16th. of the Union, whereas we are now 1/13th. We have lost a very worthy Member Col. Bland, I had a great esteem for him & regret his loss exceedingly: he was a truly honest good man—candid, open & fair—quite the gentleman & man of education & by far the best man in the whole [*Virginia*] Delegation—tho not the ablest. The No. Cara. Delegn. is complete—The Rhode Island Senators have taken their Seats.

ALS, Smith Papers, ScHi. Place to which addressed not indicated. A postscript written on 29 June is calendared under that date, below.

---

[1] The new constitution of South Carolina established Columbia as the state capital, excluded the governor from serving a second term until four years had passed, limited judges to one four year term, and provided for a House of 124 members and a Senate of thirty-six.

[2] Floyd, Hathorn, and Van Rensselaer.

John Wilson to James Madison

It is now nearly two Months since I addressed a Petition to the Hon'ble. House Representatives in Congress Assembled, praying that the Hon'ble. House would be pleased to consider my situation as an Invalied and grant me relief in the premises.

I would not wish to trouble you Sir, with a detail of my Losses & Expences that I sustained since the period of my being wounded and during of my Illness of said Wounds: the Vouchers produced I hope will amply testify my situation, and as I am *here* at Expences and in no circumstances to defray those Expences, nor of sufficient ability for to Labour to get my Livelihood, I should hope to meet the favor, countenance, & support of my Country in whose service I have been rendered incapable of earning my Bread.

The distinguished part which you have taken in behalf of the Soldiery of the late Army hath induced me to address you Sir, in particular humbly to sollicit your countenance, and aid, in getting me that support which my services entitle me to, and which is Justified by precedent; and the principals of Justice & Equity. I have no particular reasons for addressing you on this occasion than as a Philanthropist and I humbly trust that my address will not be in vain—relying much on the favor of your countenance & support, at all events I have the satisfaction of feeling a gratitude stimulated by your laudable endeavours for the injured Soldiery.

ALS, Madison Papers, DLC. In a letter to Washington on this date, asking for public employment, Wilson indicated he was residing at Jacob Reed's tavern on Little Water Street, New York (*PGW* 5:565–68). For background on Wilson's petition attempt during the FFC, see *DHFFC* 7:346–47.

Newspaper Article

A correspondent is happy to find, that the General Court have so pointedly shewn their Disapprobation of Congressional Measures, particularly in their Expenditures, by NOT electing Mr. *Dalton* a Federal Senator, when it was thought that Gentleman had been in Favour of such extravagant Compensations. It is not doubted the People will show a similar Disposition in the choice of Representatives.

Boston Gazette, 28 June; reprinted at Albany and New York City (*NYJ*, 7 July), New York.

Connecticut to the Connecticut Delegation in Congress

YOUR constituents, who read the debates of your honorable body, are a little surprised to see the questions of temporary and permanent residence again brought forward to throw Congress into a ferment. We expected that the censures Congress incurred the last session for wasting so much time and debate on the proposition for fixing the permanent residence would have prevented a motion of the kind this session. In opposing the bringing forward of the question, you have undoubtedly contended for the interest of the union. It is said by some gentlemen that their constituents are uneasy and dissatisfied that Congress do not remove to a more central situation. We, on the other hand, believe that their constituents, in general think and care very little about it. We consider the dispute as a mere contest between Philadelphia and New-York cities; we cannot conceive how the union at large is concerned in the question. New-York is indeed nearly in the center of the land communication of the Atlantic states, and if it were not, it is not necessary to have the seat of government in the center of jurisdiction. There is not a metropolis in Europe which is near the local center of dominion; yet we hear nothing about removing the government. Accident has generally fixed the capitals of empires; and often upon the borders of them; but was it ever a national dispute where should be the seat of government? It appears to us that centrality is the most trifling consideration in deciding this question: markets, safety, salubrity of climate, accommodations are of infinitely more consequence.

Philadelphia will undoubtedly be the seat of government, and we have no objection to it at a proper time. Wait only until you have paid a debt of gratitude to New York, which justice and honor demand of you for her uncommon exertions and expences, and until Philadelphia shall have provided you with accommodations that are at least half as convenient as those you now occupy. If you remove before this is done, we shall consider Congress as abandoning themselves to party-views, and deserting the dignified station they hold as Legislators of a great republic. These may be relied on as the sentiments of Connecticut.

[Hartford] *Connecticut Courant*, 28 June; reprinted at Pittsfield, Massachusetts; Providence, Rhode Island; Litchfield, Connecticut; New York City (*NYJ*, 2 July); and Philadelphia.

Yankey to Messrs. Hudson and Goodwin

"THE *Assumption was the Bastard of Eastern Speculators*"—So says Greenleaf's Journal.[1] This I deny, as well as most of the deductions, reasonings, &c. which are so ludicrously detailed from that text. The author of that performance is most undoubtedly a person of letters, wit and refined language; but of very doubtful morals—He has given us the most finished piece of *Blackguardism* which I have ever seen published. Tho I might forgive him the ridicule so liberally dealt out to my countrymen; yet I cannot subscribe to his doctrines. Is it possible this writer can believe his own assertions true? Are the PEOPLE of the *Eastern States* so far turned *Speculators*, as that they could have induced their representatives so generally, to adopt and support the *Secretary's plan of finance*, on the *ground* of *speculation?* or does he suppose the *Eastern Delegation* are so far *personally* concerned in speculations, in their own States paper, as to have influenced their conduct on this great national question? They who know them most intimately *at home*, believe no such thing of them. They know it to be a *false* and *groundless* assertion, brought forward (as they believe) only with a view of rendering this measure odious.

I presume our southern neighbors will like us never the worse for having laid aside *our puritanical manners* with our *ancient dress*; and for having repealed the laws by which they were formerly established.

I shall leave *Mr. Hamilton* to defend his own plans of finance—he is very competent to this business, and does not stand in need of my feeble aid. Mr. *Gerry* will, I hope, prove a discreet and able *nurse*, and if *pumpkin* and *molasses* does not make the child grow, let him substitute *boiled rice and hoe-cake*, and add, as the bantling can bare more substantial food, *great and little homeny and opossum fat.*[2] Messieurs *Sherman, Livermore, Fitzsimons,* &c. will doubtless pursue their plan, invariably, until they effect their purpose; at least if they are honest men they will, let the *seat of government* remain at New-York, or be removed to Philadelphia, Susquehanna or the Potomac. If Mr. Fitzsimons has lost sight of his first object in caballing about the seat of government, it is a reproach to him as a legislator; if he has only given up the assumption, as an *impracticable scheme* at this juncture, this *seeming inconsistence* of conduct is done away; he can best determine this point. Mr. *Sedgwick's zeal* may have carried him too great lengths in urging a favorite plan; it may have been *intemperate*, and in that respect merit reproof. It should have however been more gently administered: I presume he has not merited the severe sarcasms contained in the piece alluded to, and *he* should consider, that when punishment exceeds the crime for which it is inflicted, *every good man* will take part with the *injured person*, and much more, when an *innocent person* is unjustly aspersed. Mr. Sedgwick may console himself with this reflection, at least, that the writer considered him as a man of abilities, or he would not have loaded him with such a torrent of abuse.

Dr. Williamson is not the first of his profession who has, by *quackery*, destroyed very hopeful patients; and tho the *parents of this child of promise*, may justly lament its *untimely* and *unnatural death*; I hope they will have more christian fortitude than to sink under this stroke, this *adverse* stroke of *politicks*. It was not the *only hopes* of their house. They have *many sons and daughters*, (tho but *few servants* and *dependants*) on whom they may rely for aid in trouble, and support in old age. They can even spare a few to their neighbours to repair their losses, and help them forward with the common business of life; or the more arduous ones of defending their property from the inroads of their enemies, or for perfecting their civil police and legislation. Tho we have not *coaches* to carry our *pigs to market*; yet we may bring them to as *good a market* as our neighbors.

[Hartford] *Connecticut Courant*, 28 June, edited by Barzillai Hudson and George Goodwin.

[1] X to Mr. Greenleaf, *NYJ*, 11 June, above.
[2] That is, food associated with the Southern states.

Other Documents

Silvanus Bourn to James Madison. ALS, Madison Papers, DLC. For the full text, see *PJM* 13:257–58.

Has heard that some Representatives are opposed to allowing any "emoluments" to United States consuls; requests Madison's influence in allowing consuls "a small Contribution chargeable on each Vessell according to its size—and a specific regulation of the fees"; a consul's unavoidable expenses "must be intuitively obvious to one of your extensive information"; thinks that the House committee on the Consuls and Vice Consuls Bill [HR-86] will rely on Jefferson's opinion which, "aided by your kind exertions," will help ensure the proposal's success; "the little acquaintance I have had the honour of cultivating with you can hardly justify the Liberty taken."

John Montgomery to John Adams. ALS, Adams Family Manuscript Trust, MHi. Written from Boston.

Office seeking: his brother Robert for consul at Alicante, Spain.

Theodore Sedgwick to Benjamin Lincoln. No copy known; acknowledged in Lincoln to Sedgwick, 6 July.

Roger Sherman to Samuel Hopkins. ALS, Sherman Papers, DLC. Place to which addressed not indicated.

Has recently read Hopkins's *Inquiry into the Nature of True Holiness* (Newport, R.I., 1773) and explains his objections to some points.

Joseph Whipple to John Langdon. ALS, Langdon Papers, NhPoA. Written from Portsmouth, New Hampshire. A draft of this letter added that Whipple had complied on 18 February with Hamilton's 20 January request for an account of the emoluments of office in the first six months, and that "I was in hopes that the result of his enqueries would have produced some addition [*lined out*] by this time" (Sturgis Family Papers, MH).

State gubernatorial election and legislative news; legislature rose without ceding the Portsmouth lighthouse, which it maintains for £170 per year; asks when Congress expects to adjourn; does not trust rumors of an adjournment by 1 July, since it must take several months to complete its business.

Daniel Hiester, Account Book. PRHi. Maclay indicated that the delegation invited Adams, Chief Justice Jay, and the three departmental secretaries, but that only Hamilton, Jefferson, and Knox attended (*DHFFC* 9:306).

Attended "Monday Club" or Mess day with the Pennsylvania delegation at Fraunces Tavern.

Intelligence Extraordinary. *NYDG*, 28 June.

A satire on removal of the seat of government to Philadelphia; reminds readers of the mob attacks on members of public bodies and the "old practice of hissing members from the gallery" of the Pennsylvania State House; "whenever it shall so happen that such obstinate Senators as Governor J[*ohnsto*]n, General S[*chuyle*]r or Mr. K[*in*]g, &c. &c. shall vote against the interests of our [*Schuylkill*] river, we will pardon the first offence; for the second, we will *reward* them with baptism gratis, by a dip in the font which we have prepared; and for the third offence, they may expect an handsome plunge amongst cat-fish as large as sharks."

NYDG, 29 June.

Hears that the Senate agreed to a permanent seat of government on the Potomac; the duration of a temporary residence elsewhere was not yet decided; lists roll calls of the 16-7 vote in favor of Potomac (the informer mistakenly lists Paterson as a "yea" and T. Foster as a "nay" vote), and the 13-12 vote in favor of the temporary residence at New York City, with Gunn being absent. (*NYDG*, 30 June, corrected the transposition of Paterson's and Foster's names in a reprinting of the two roll call votes.)

NYJ, 29 June.

Gunn's "indisposition" prevented his attendance at the Senate; the successful vote for New York as the temporary seat of government will be taken up again "on Mr. Gunn's appearing on the floor."

Letter from New York. *PP*, 30 June, dated "3 o'clock afternoon"; reprinted at Richmond, Virginia.

"The Senate have this day agreed, 16 to 9, to fix the permanent seat of the government at Patowmack. The house of Representatives will most assuredly agree to the proposition, as it will put an end to the very disagreeable altercations which have taken place upon the subject. By this vote we [*Philadelphia*] shall have the honour of the seat of government until the necessary buildings, &c. are prepared."

[Windsor] *Vermont Journal*, 10 August.

T. Foster presented an address to Washington from the Mechanics and Manufacturers of Providence, Rhode Island.

Tuesday, 29 June 1790

Cool (Johnson)

Stephen Hall to John Langdon

Before Congress adjourns I guess some further appointments will be made in this part of the Country. I wish to be a Candidate for an agreeable one. I expected to have been Collector of Impost, & had reason for it. I do not say that my friend, Mr. Thacher, unjustly deprived me of it. A more favourite friend of his [*Nathaniel Fosdick*], whose pretentions compared with mine I should have despised, now enjoys both that, & the Naval Office; tho' the due Collection of the revenue requires a Naval Officer at this Port, & the Emoluments are abundantly sufficient to support one. When I last had the honor & pleasure of seeing You at Portsmouth [*New Hampshire*] I fully stated to You the Case. The Collectorship of Excise would probably be as honorary & agreeable to me, as the Collectorship of Impost. I hope my friend Thacher will not be able to deprive me of an appointment now, if he did before. Will You permit me dear Sir, to sollicit your friendship in mentioning me to the President: I believe that would be effectual to obtain for me an agreeable appointment. Very accidentally I have come at the knowledge of my good friend Thacher's Manoevres. He has written to his brother [*Daniel*] Davis that a Collector of Excise is to be appointed, & wishes to have a person, he has named to him, recommended as suitable for the appointment. This I suppose he means to make use of with the President to obtain it. The letter however fell into the hands of Mr. [*John*] Fox, our other Representative,[1] who tho't. a different person ought to be recommended. Neither Mr. Fox, nor Mr. Davis, nor any other person in town knows of my aplication. I have kept it from them agreeably to your advice. I could easily obtain a long list of subscribers in my favor, if I would propose it. I suppose there is scarcely a Gentleman in Town, but would give me his name, if I was to ask it. But such a step I suppose to be both needless, & improper. I imagine a friend's mentioning me to the President woud be of more avail, than any list of subscribers, who must be unknown to him. I hope You are happy in the enjoyment of health, & in seeing things go on agreeable to You.

ALS, Langdon Papers, NhPoS. Written from Portland, Maine.

[1] Portland's member of the Massachusetts legislature.

Thomas Jefferson to Elias Boudinot

As it is desireable that we should receive from our Consuls an exact report of all our vessels with their cargoes which go to the countries of their residence, such fees appear necessary as may induce them to be watchful that every such vessel is noted. at the same time the fee should not be so large as to induce them to connive at foreign vessels reporting themselves as American, merely to give them the fee. five & ten dollars appear to me well proportioned.

While I was in Europe I found there was a great want of some legal mode of taking and authenticating instruments and evidence in general, to be sent to this country; such as depositions, affidavits, copies of wills, records, deeds, powers of attorney &c. I thought it would be proper, as soon as we should have consuls established, to make their authentications under the seal of their office, good evidence in our courts. I take the liberty of submitting to you whether a clause for these purposes might not be properly placed in this bill. I assure you the occasions for it are extremely frequent.

ALS, Washburn Papers, MHi. Addressed to No. 12 Wall Street. Boudinot served with Gerry and Huntington on the committee for considering consular fees, leading to the Consuls and Vice Consuls Bill [HR-86].

Richard Henry Lee to Thomas Lee Shippen

*** If I were to attempt the detail of all the Votes, Manoeuvres, & detours that have perplexed Congress upon the business of Residence, I should tire both you and myself—Let this therefore remain for conversation hereafter—At present I think that a very fair prospect opens for our being with you next Session—I think it right that it should be so, and therefore you may be sure that my efforts shall not be wanting.

From the first of our meeting in 1774 to the present minute there has never been any altercation between the gentleman you mention[1] and myself, but on the contrary, perfect civility and good humor—But such is the temper of the times, that if a Man believes a twentieth part of what he hears he will believe more than enough— ***

[*P. S.*] Mr. Wyncoob [*Wynkoop*] has not spoke further to me about your fathers [*William, Jr.*] order—perhaps he waits for the close of the Session.

ALS, Shippen Family Papers, DLC. Place to which addressed not indicated. The omitted text relates to business matters. For the full text, see *Lee* 2:529.

[1] None of the letters from Shippen that Lee might have been answering with this comment is known to be extant. Assuming Lee referred to a fellow member of the First Continental Congress of 1774 who was also in the federal government in 1790, the "gentleman" mentioned may have been Floyd, Read, Sherman, Jay, or, most likely, Adams.

Governor Alexander Martin to Hugh Williamson

Your Letter of the 13th. Ulto. I have been duly favored with and is the last I have received: the successful opposition you made to the Assumption of the State Debts was announced to me from the public prints before your Letter reached me. The Council of State who lately met at the Rockingham Springs and our Citizens in General as far as I have received information are pleased with the part you have taken and the unanimity of your Colleagues in opposing so iniquitous a measure taking effect fraught as they conceived with ruin to this State. We are much surprised the Northern Representatives should so unremitingly persevere in a project so obnoxious to a great body of the people of the United States, especially of those States who adopted the Constitution of the General Government with small majorities among which are Virginia and North Carolina. The walk of Congress ought to be with caution, and their conduct conciliatory when so great an opposition has been made to their present form of existence, that in this early Stage of Sovereignty they should establish this new Government on the affections of the People, not exercise powers that appear to be doubtful, that may entail a curse rather then a blessing on themselves and posterity. What have Congress to do with the Contracts made with our own Citizens, where they are satisfied with the mode of payment, why compell them to receive twenty Shillings in the pound when they are contented with four? where will such a Presedent lead will not the General Government quickly bear down the State Governments, not even our civil list, or any pecuniary State transaction will escape their entrusion and interference. However in whatever shape that Demon shall again appear, it is hoped there will be Justice and integrity sufficient in the Congress of the United States to lay him.

***

FC:lbk, Governors' Papers, Nc-Ar. Written from "Danbury," Rockingham County, North Carolina. The omitted text discusses details of Williamson's job as commissioner of state accounts, including the Council of State's authorization for a clerk to assist him, which Martin encloses.

Governor Alexander Martin to Hugh Williamson and Abishai Thomas

I do myself the Honour to enclose you a resolution of the Council of State respecting the disposal of the remainder of the final settlement Certificates, which agreeably to the resolution of the late Assembly, I expect soon will be delivered to the Executive.

You will please to communicate by the earliest opportunity such information the Council, request, & your sentiments relative thereto.

[*Enclosure*]

That it is the opinion of the Council that his Excellency should be acquainted by our representatives in Congress, and agents for settling the Accounts between this State and the United States whether the final settlements remaining in the Treasury will not be received and passed to the Credit of the State and whether any other specialties and what sort are of more Value.

FC:lbk, Governors' Papers, Nc-Ar. Written from "Danbury," Rockingham County, North Carolina; addressed to the "Commisrs. of public Accounts for N. Carolina in New York." The enclosure, dated 25 June, is in the Council of State Journal, Nc-Ar.

Roger Sherman to William Ellery

I received your favr. of the the 21st. instant I am glad that we Succeeded in obtaining Your Appointment to the Office of Collector. It is an important trust, which I doubt not will be executed with fidelity, I have had the pleasure of an interview with the Senators from your State, and am pleased with the Sentiments that they expressed on public affairs.

I hope there will be an agrement to provide for the State debts before Congress closes the present session. The matter of weights & measures, & Coinage, was ea[*r*]ly taken up in Congress, and referred to the Secretary of State. He has not Yet reported upon it, but he lately Shewed me a report which he had prepared,[1] but I believe no law will be passed upon it this session A Committee of both Houses have reported, the business necessary to be finished before Congress adjourn, ~~wh~~ they Suppose it may be accomplished by the 15th of July. I dont think a war will take place between Spain & Britain, neither of them are prepared for it.

Provision is made by Congress for intercourse with foreign nations [*Foreign Intercourse Act HR-52*]. & I Suppose Some kind of Minister will be Sent to London—I hope France will not be involved in a war. before they have Settled a free & effective Government. I think it will be an important event to the European Nations in general, as well as to us. These States, I hope will enjoy peace, until the time when the Nations Shall learn war no more.[2]

ALS, Sherman Collection, CtY. Place to which addressed not indicated.

[1] Jefferson completed a comprehensive draft of his famous report on coins, weights, and measures as early as 20 May, but withheld it to make ongoing corrections, such as those made possible by fresh information he received from Europe between 15 and 18 June. Sherman may have seen the version that Jefferson shared with David Rittenhouse on 12 June. For background and texts relating to the report, submitted to the House in final form on 13 July, see *DHFFC* 8:482–503.

[2] Isaiah 2:4.

Joseph Stanton, Jr. to George Champlin

Agreable to a promise I Now Commence a Negociation with you By Letter, And Shall Undoutedly gain thereby, I wish you not to Suffer, You will find by the Several News Papers I Send you, Which contains Better information than I Can Otherwise Communicate That the Two questions that principally Ingross the Attention of Congress, Is that of Temporary & Permanent Residence; I greatly fear Congress will adjurn to Philadelphia, The Newhampshire Senators are decidedly for philadelphia and if Congress adjurns to that place, I will Venter to provicy [*prophesy*] it will not be in the power of the Southern States to Carry it farther Southward Either to Baltimore or the Patomack.

P. S. my Compliments to the Honle. H[*enry*]. Marchant, tell him Not to dispare, In haste & tide waits for no man.

ALS, Champlin Papers, RHi. Addressed to Newport, Rhode Island; franked.

Joseph Stanton, Jr. and Theodore Foster to George Washington

It being necessary that the Vacancy, in the Naval Office, in the District of Providence, in the State of Rhode Island and Providence Plantations should be filled soon, we beg leave to recommend and request that Ebenezer Thompson Esqr. of Providence may be appointed to that office. He was educated in the Mercantile Business which he followed till the late War. He is a Good Accountant and well acquainted with Book-Keeping. His Moral Character and his Integrity are every way unimpeachable. He has been intrusted with various public Offices which he has discharged to General Satisfaction. He has been a Representative for the Town of Providence and a Member of the upper House, in the Legislature of that State. He is much esteemed and respected, in the Town of Providence being now the President of the Town Council there, who by the Laws of that State transact the Business of the Probate Courts in the other States. He is not now concerned in Navigation or Mercantile Business, or likely to be under the undue Influence of any Gentlemen in that Line, a Recommendation which every Candidate ought to have. His Firmness of Character, his Integrity, and his Abilities entitle him to the Confidence of the Public. Recommendations in his Behalf could be procured from respectable Characters of all Parties in Rhode Island and we believe his Appointment would tend to compose and reconcile the Spirit of Party in that State. And we are satisfied that it is the General Wish and hope of the People in the Town of Providence as well as throughout the District that he may be appointed, his Conduct as late Collector for the State having given very general Satisfaction.

We assure you, Sir, that we have no private Veiws to answer in this Recommendation which is made purely from a conviction that the Appointment of Mr. Thompson as Naval Officer, in that District will Subserve and promote the Public Good more than that of any other Who we heard has made application for the office.

[*P. S*] We also beg leave to mention the Names of the following Persons as Surveyors, Viz.,

Zachariah Rhodes for the Port of Pawtuxet, in the District of Providence.

Job Comstock for the Port of East Greenwich in the District of Newport.

Bowen Card for the Port of North Kingstown, in the same District.

George Stillman for Pawcatuck River in the same District.

Nathaniel Phillips for Warren and Barrington in the same District.

ALS, hand of Foster, Washington Papers, DLC.

George Thatcher to Sarah Thatcher

This Letter is really the production of indolence, if such a thing can be— It is cloudy, dull, & rainy weather this afternoon—I feel indisposed for reading—and cannot walk out—to write is less tedious than to set altogether idle—I have talked politics, & listened to them for an hour or two since dinner—so that no further amusement can spring from that source— indeed I am very weary of the whole subject of politics—'tis an old saying, that too much of one thing is good for nothing—And never was a maxim more litterally verifyed that [*than*] this.

How charming it would pass off this insiped afternoon if I could call, & drink Tea with you & the two dear children—Oh it would be too much!

too much! as our Polly used to say—But perhaps in three weeks it may be realised—And in the mean time let me talk a little about our dear Sally.

In yours of the nineteenth inst. you tell me "that Sam"— (you ought to have wrote Phillips, but I see you will not mind my Commands) "begins to learn—but is not so forward as you could wish him to be" "that Sally is all Life and sprightliness"—Now I must confess I am not at all more anxious on account of Phillips dullness in learning, than of Sally's excessive sprightliness and vivacity—for tho the former is sometimes the forerunner of real stupidity, it is nevertheless as frequently the mark of future good sense & solid abilities—I dont desire any thing more of him, at present, than to see him capable of progress in what is attempted to be taught him—I am very little concerned at the slowness of his progress—provided he can be induced to persevere—which I am persuaded may be done—Attention & application will overcome every thing. Constancy in going to school—regularity and order at home—agreeable play mates—with some small encouragements, from time to time, will produce an habitual attachment to his Book—I beleive I have before observed that *reading & school confinement* can not, of themselves, be otherwise than disagreeable to children—nothing is pleasing to children but motion & what produced quick, & lively sensations—Hence children are continually runing about—and would fly if they could—Every body must have noted the extreme difficulty in regulating children in this respect—If they are told to do a thing—to hand a stick, a knife, & go a cross the room—they will always run—& nothing is so impracticable, for a considerable time, as to make them walk slowly & with regularity—The greatest punishment, except actual pain, a child can be put to is to set or stand still—How often have I observed this in our Phillips & Sally—the latter more especially—And I am inclined to think we shall find it as hard a task to reduce her to regularity in her behaviour as to learn Phillips to read—And yet she appears to me to be a tractable child; but her excessive vivacity keeps her constantly on the wing—To overcome this, & turn it to a good purpose, it will be a prudent step to have her set by you several times a day, for a quarter of an hour at a time, or for a longer or shorter period as it may be convenient—begining with a short space & lengthening them by degrees—in these little trials of discipline you may direct her to set in any position; & with her hands & feet as you would wish to have her carry them at all times—excepting when she sets at Table, she ought to set in a chair, or on a stool that has the same relation to her body & heighth, that Chairs in general have to grown people—a stool, or block is to be prefered, because they have neither arms or back—Children of three or four years old should be taught to set without leaning, or loling—at this age their Bodies as well as their minds may be formed and moulded in any manner you please—And if there be any such thing as grace and elegance in the deportment of children the earlier you begin with them the more natural and easy all their motions will appear—Children take more instruction from example than precept—And this for two reasons—What they see has a more lively effect on them than what they hear, and examples are more constantly before their eyes, than precepts can be delt out to them by those who have the care of their education—Hence, during those periods of Discipline whoever is in the room with children should be careful, that they set, stand, or walk in the same manner the children are taught to—Indeed every motion, gesture & position before children ought to be a patern of elegance and propriety—To contradict your lessons by your actions will very soon make children neglect both—I think we have seen the good effect of Phillips & Sally's seting with us at the Table when we dine—And tho Sally was much under three, & Phillips short of five, their behaviour convinced me that Children, in some things, and particular personal deportment, cannot be too early treated like men and women.

When you are alone afternoons—Let our dear children set with you at the Tea table—It will be company for you—Tell Sally she must learn to make Tea for her papa, & the Ladies—and must therefore take notice how her Mama conducts the things—If she breaks a cup or saucer tis a trifle to the advantage the experiment will be to her—I verily beleive in this mode of treatment, little Girls might might be brought to behave, by the age of six or seven, like women—And were we to consult nothing but our own convenience, this will be the most effectual method to prevent their runing about, making a noise and disturbing a room full of company—How much less troublesome would this be than the various expedients practiced by fond mothers and indulgent fathers—What do they do? as often as a child comes into the room he falls a crying, get a piece of cake—takes a scolding—disturbs the company, puts father and mother to making apologies, and then scuds [?] into the Kitchen & plagues the Domestics—Begin, in season, to educate children by example as well as precept—and much time & Trouble will be saved—Take a child at the age of three, & make her set properly fifteen minutes in a day—and at the age of five or six she will be a perfect woman.

ALS, Thatcher Family Papers, MHi. Place to which addressed not indicated.

Newspaper Article

A correspondent observes, that Congress have *little leisure*, yet mean to purchase a library—a library to suit the various tastes which must exist in such a mixed assembly; composed of every intermediate degree of character from Mr. G—n [*Gunn*] to R. S—r—n [*Sherman*], must be numerous, various, and costly. I would recommend the purchase of a *Corderis*[1] and an attentive perusal of the first lesson; beginning with, *Quis agis*—What are you doing—and translate it for the benefit of those who had no education, which will comprehend the majority.

NYJ, 29 June; reprinted at Bennington, Vermont; New Haven and Litchfield, Connecticut; Poughkeepsie, New York; Philadelphia; and Edenton, North Carolina. For background on the House committee's report recommending titles for a congressional library, presented on 23 June, see *DHFFC* 8:653–62.

---

[1] Corderius (1478–1567) was a Swiss grammarian whose Latin *Colloquies* was a popular educational text available in several English editions in the eighteenth century. *Corderius Americanus* was also a book on the education of children by Cotton Mather (reprint, Boston, 1774).

Of the Residence of Congress

We learn, that the several questions, respecting the *permanent* and *temporary* residence of Congress, were yesterday taken up in Senate, agreeably to postponement, and debated upon with some warmth. The question for a *permanent* residence was first taken, and carried in favor of the POTOMACK by a majority of ONE. Some debate ensued respecting the term of time Congress should continue at their temporary residence; *three, five,* and *ten* years were mentioned, but no decision took place. The question for the *temporary* residence was then put, and carried in favor of NEW-YORK by a majority of ONE.

We could not ascertain the yeas and nays for this day.

We are informed, that the indisposition of the hon. Mr. *Gunn* prevented his attendance on this interesting occasion. It is further said, that the question will be *called up* again on Mr. Gunn's appearing on the floor, which WE flatter ourselves will render OUR majority *doubly* respectable.

Very little business was done yesterday in the House of Representatives, except reading of petitions—the *pervading mind* appearing considerably agitated (suppose on account of the grand question in Senate) the house adjourned at an early hour.

NYJ, 29 June.

Letter from New York

The Senate have been this day upon the bill for the permanent and temporary residence. Yesterday the blank for the temporary residence was filled up with *New York*: this day a motion was made to insert *ten years*, which, together with the *place*, was struck out by the casting vote of the vice-president. Another motion was made for five years at New York and five years at Philadelphia, which was negatived by a large majority. A motion was then made to insert *Philadelphia* and *ten years*, which was negatived by the casting vote of the vice-president. By these several motions, and the votes upon them, you will plainly see that the removal from this city is out of the question, as neither house can agree upon the place to go to.

PP, 1 July; written at 3 P.M.; reprinted at Baltimore.

[*Philip Freneau,*]
Nanny, the Philadelphia House Maid, to Nabby, her friend in New York

SIX WEEKS my dear mistress has been in a fret
And nothing but CONGRESS will do for her yet,
She says they must come, or her senses she'll lose,
From morning till night she is reading the news,
And loves the dear fellows that vote for *our town*
(Since no one can relish New-York but a clown,
Where your beef is so lean, it would make people laugh,
And folks are too haughty to worship—a CALF:[1])
She tells us as how she has read in her books
That God gives them meat but the devil sends cooks;
And *Grumbleton*[2] told us (who often shoots flying)
That fish you have plenty—but spoil them in frying;
That your streets are as crooked as crooked can be
Right forward three perches he never could see
But his view was cut short with a house or a shop
That stood in his way—and compel'd him to stop.
Those speakers that wish for New-York to decide,
'Tis a pity that talents are so misapplied;
My mistress declares she is vext to the heart
That genius should take such a pitiful part;
For *the question*, indeed, she is daily distrest,
And *G*__ [*Gerry*], I think, she will ever detest,
Who did all he could, with his tongue and his pen
To keep the dear Congress shut up in your den.
She insists, the expence of removing is small,
And that *two* or *three thousands* will answer it all,

If that is too much, and we're so very poor—
The passage by water is cheaper, be sure;
If people object the expence of a team,
Here's [*John*] *Fitch*, with his wherry, will bring them *by steam*;
And, Nabby! if once he should take them on board,
The HONOUR will be a sufficient reward.
  But, as to myself, I vow and declare
I wish it would suit them to stay where they are;
I plainly foresee, that if once they remove
From morning to night we shall drive and be drove,
My madam's red rag[3] will ring like a bell
And the hall and the parlour will never look well;
Such scowering will be as has never been seen,
We shall always be cleaning, and never be clean
And threats in abundance will work on my fears
Of blows on the back and of slaps on the ears—
Two trifles, at present, discourage her paw,
The fear of the Lord and the fear of the law—
But if *Congress* arrive, she will have such a sway
That gospel and law will be both done away;
For the sake of a place I must bear all her din,
And if ever so angry, do nothing but grin;
So Congress, I hope in your town will remain
And Nanny will thank them again and again.

NYDA, 1 July; reprinted at Boston; Providence and Newport, Rhode Island; New York City (*NYWM*, 3 July); Philadelphia; Wilmington, Delaware; and Charleston, South Carolina. An 1809 edition of Philip Freneau's poetry identified him as the author of this piece and filled in the blank with "Gerry." A sequel is printed under 14 July, volume 20.

[1] Exodus 32:4.
[2] A derisive term for a member of the political opposition.
[3] Tongue.

Other Documents

Elias Boudinot to William Bradford. No copy known; acknowledged in Bradford to Boudinot, 1 July.

Pierce Butler to James Seagrove. No copy known; acknowledged in Seagrove to Butler, 9 August.

Governor Alexander Martin to Benjamin Hawkins and Samuel Johnston. FC:lbk, Governors' Papers, Nc-Ar. Written from "Danbury," Rockingham County, North Carolina.

Reports action of 24 June by the Council of State for paying the "Martinique Debt"; repeats request for information about which French authorities should receive the payment and where it should be made.

William Smith (S.C.) to Edward Rutledge. ALS, Smith Papers, ScHi. Place to which addressed not indicated. This is a postscript to a letter begun on 28 June, above.

"The Senate have before them the Bill for a temporary & permanent residence but can't agree upon any place.

I take an opporty. of a gentleman's going to Philada. to forward this to you & shall write again by [*John*] Motley in about a week—[*William*] Elliott is not arrived—we expect him."

Henry Wynkoop to Reading Beatty. ALS, Wynkoop Papers, PDoBHi. Written at "6 oClock in the morning"; place to which addressed not indicated. For the full text, see *PMHB* 38(April 1914):200.

Sends half dozen pair of men's stockings; directions for delivery of enclosed letter to Mr. Hutchinson; joint committee reported an adjournment date of 15 July; most of the remaining business is pending before the Senate, "it chiefly depends on that Body wether we shall get away at the time allotted"; the Senate voted for the Potomac seat of government, but he has not heard about the temporary residence; refers Beatty to the newspapers for "general Information of what is doing here."

William Samuel Johnson, Diary. Johnson Papers, CtHi.

"Mrs. J[*ohnson*]. returnd."

NYDA, 30 June; reprinted at New York City (*NYMP*, 1 July).

Reports Senate action on the Residence Act; notes the last clause, which provided that Congress remain at New York until 1800, was defeated by only two or three votes (the vote was actually 16–9).

GUS, 30 June; a summary appeared the same day in *NYDG*.

Heard that the Residence Act had a second reading in the Senate, that New York, Philadelphia, and Baltimore were rejected as the temporary residence, and that "the Potomac stands" as the permanent seat after ten years; "the whole subject is still open to discussion."

WEDNESDAY, 30 JUNE 1790

Cool (Johnson)

Elbridge Gerry to Samuel R. Gerry

I received last evening your letter of the 21st ***

I informed you in my last of the measures which I wished you to pursue for obtaining an appointment under the United States & shall therefore say nothing further at present on the occasion.

***

The report respecting a duel is misrepresented in part: last session debates ran very high in the House & a Gentleman from the southward who was a friend of mine & on the same side as myself of a question respecting the amendments proposed by the States to the Constitution, took offence at Mr. Ames who was on the other side of the question & hinted an intention to call him out: but Mr. Ames made an apology in the House & finished the dispute: immediately on this another gentleman who was also on Mr. Ames's side of the question, said if Gentlemen talked of calling out, he had reason to be offended at something I had said & should use the same freedom with me. I instantly informed him, I had not the least objection & should meet any proposition which he might think proper to make out of the House: but he never tho't it advisable to make any & so the matter ended[1]—I know not whether the report originated from this or from another circumstance: there was a misunderstanding between the Secretary of the Treasury & Judge Burke of South Carolina which must have terminated in a duel, but ~~for~~ by the interference of ~~myself~~ some of their friends of whom I was appointed one by the parties, the matter was accomodated.[2]

ALS, Samuel R. Gerry Papers, MHi. Addressed to Marblehead, Massachusetts; franked; postmarked 1 July; answered 25 July. The salutation reads "Dear Comm[*issione*]r." The omitted text discusses friends and business.

---

[1] The debate to which Gerry refers is probably that of 15 August 1789 in which he declared that the supporters and opponents of the Constitution "ought not to have been distinguished by federalists and antifederalists, but by rats and antirats" (*DHFFC* 11:1254–82; quotation on p. 1262). Smith (S.C.) thought "there has been more ill-humour & rudeness displayed to day than has existed since the meeting of Congress—allowing to Gerry & one or two more" (*DHFFC* 16:1327).

[2] For more on the Burke-Hamilton affair of honor, see *DHFFC* 8:476–80.

Rufus King, Notes on the Residence Issue in Second Session

The house some weeks since passed a Resolve to remove to Philadelphia at the expiration of the present Session, Before the resolve came up to the Senate Majr. Butler brought in a Bill for the establishment of both permanent & temporary Residence—Morris & others urged the Resolution when it came up—his opponents moved to postpone it until Mr. Few & Govr. Johns[*t*]on who were sick could attend—morris objected that the postponement wd. give Time for the arrival of the Senators of R. Island. finally Mr. Few and Govr. Johnson being sent for attended—and the question of concurrence was negatived Thirteen to Eleven—a resolution was the next day past in the House for the adjournment of Congress at the close of the Session to Baltimore—this resolution was by a majority of 13. to 11 of the senate postponed a fortnight—during this Interval a Bargain was made between Pennsylvania, Delaware, Maryland, and Virginia to remove at the end of the Session to Philadelphia there to remain for ten years and afterwards to remove to and permanently remain at the Potomack.

The negative of the Resolution for Phila. and the postponement of that, for ~~an adjournment to~~ Baltimore, were effected by the senators of Georgia So. & No. Carolina. Mr. Paterson & the senators of N. Yk. Cont. & Mass.—after the Postponement of the Baltimore Resolution the Senators of R. Island took their Seats and the Bill brought in by mr. Butler was called up by Mr. Carrol—Mr. King ~~applied~~ proposed to Mr. Henry of Maryland to agree to a temporary Residence at New York and to remove from thence to Baltimore for the permanent Seat. Mr. H. told him the ~~application~~ Proposition was too late & that he cd. not vote for it—Mr. K. and his friends proposed to the Six southern Senators & to those of the States of Cont. & Mass. to concur with those of New York in fixing the temporary residence in New York 5 years and the permanent Resid. at Baltimore—the Six southern senators assured Mr. K. they wd. concur if the measure could be carried Connecticut agreed to the measure. R. Island had no Objection But Massachusetts declined—the conduct of Mass. was explained by the Secy. of the Treasury who called on Mr. K. (and afterwards ~~explained~~ held the same or similar conversation with Mr. K. & Colo. Laurance) and informed him that *He had made up his mind thus.* the funding System including the assumption is the primary national Object—all subordinate points which oppose it must be sacrificed, the project of Philadelphia & Potomack is bad, but it will insure the funding system and the Assumption—~~Disagreeing to remove to Philadelphia after the present session will~~ Agreeing to remain in New Yk. will defeat it—Agreeing to New York & Baltimore will defeat it, so that in the present state of things nothing but Philada. or Phila. & Potomack will insure it—Massachusetts therefore will not agree to NYk. & Baltimore, because her ~~great~~ Object is the assumption—Mr. K. remonst[*r*]ated with Mr. Secy. in this arrangement—and in a subsequent Conversation told him that, great & good ~~measures~~ Schemes ought to succeed on their own merits and not by intrigue or the establishment of bad measures—Mr. K. added that he had been influenced by national views, that he wished national & not state maxims to prevail. but that if instead thereof. the reverse was ~~the case~~ to regulate the Government he must submit ~~to the same~~; and shd. pursue as others found it their interest to do, State or local views—If a bargain existed between the Southern States who wished ~~without Reason~~ for the Seat of Government on the Potomack, Pensylvania who wished Congress in Philada. and the Massachusetts People who were anxious for the Assumption—the measure cod. succeed not because Virga. Mas. or the whole of Pen. desired the assumption, nor because Mass. wished the temporary Residence in Phila. nor because Mass. Pen. or Del. wished the permanent Residence on the Potomack, but because the whole of them could not be gratified any other way.

In a subsequent conversation, Mr. Secy. informed Mr. K. that the measure or combination ~~might~~ had been like to fail, for that from an apprehension (Mr. Morris apprehensive) that the assumption wd. not prevail if Mr. K. shd. be against it, *it had been had* required of the Senators of Del. Maryl. & Virga. to furnish a vote for the assumption in *his* Mr. K.'s Place (from whence Mr. K. clearly inferred what ~~I~~ he had supposed to be the case that the Massachusetts people had authority to expect the assumption if they did not vote for New York & Baltimore, which alone could have defeated the Phila. & Potomack project) and that they had produced a Senator wh. engaged in the last extremity to vote the assumption.

Finally on the question for staying 5 yrs. in New Yk. and 5 in Phila. 2 in New Yk. & 8 In Phila. being negatived by the vote of the vice President—and for a temporary Residence in Philadelphia for 10 yrs. & permanently on the Potomack being also negatived by him. Majr. Butler joined the Philadelphians ~~and~~ inserted the clause, and the Bill was passed to a third reading.

The inference at this moment in Mr. K. mind is satisfactorily clear that the assumption looses NYk. the residence—upon numbering the votes in the H. of R. the Representatives of Penn. found the measure could not succeed without their votes, & although they were in favor of the measure they witheld their votes until they cd. obtain the ~~Assumpt~~ removal to Phila. to accomplish this Plan the combination above alluded to was formed.

Ms., hand of King, King Papers, NHi. King labeled these notes "Residence 2d session."

Richard Henry Lee to Thomas Lee Shippen

Just going to bed I have but a moment to inform you that this day in Senate by a Majority of 16 to 10 we ordered to the third reading a Bill for carrying Congress to Philadelphia after this Session, there to remain for Ten years, and then to go to Potomac. We have little doubt but that we shall pass this Bill in the Senate, and we are assured that a Majority in the H. of R. is there ready to receive & pass it—Of the success of this you will be informed in due season—The Gentleman[1] who will deliver you this, is the Nephew of our late worthy friend Colo. Bland, and he deserves your civilities.

ALS, Shippen Family Papers, DLC. Place to which addressed not indicated.

[1] Probably John Randolph "of Roanoke" or his brother Theodorick Bland Randolph, both of whom left New York at about this time.

Jeremiah Libbey to John Langdon

I last post recd. your kind favour Inclosing the Post Office Bill [*HR*-74]—am pleased that a post is to be established from this to Concord [*New Hampshire*]—and shall not forget Mr. [*Nathaniel*] Bean.

The Bill is so extensive that I do not think my self Competent to make up a Judgement on it, especially as I have had only time to read it once over. hope it will prove beneficial. it appears to me that, the duty of the Post Masters (If done) are greatly Increased, hope the Compensation will be equal—on my reading it I tho't. it carried an Idea. that the former post Masters behaved badly in not rendering their Accounts & paying the Balances they incurred [*?*] but the 27th. Section of it, is very pointed, and [*illegible*] us *very good news*, it appears to me, it will throw more on the Post Master General than is reasonable.

Suppose, (If it may be supposable) that a Post Master, at Portsmouth [*New Hampshire*], or Savannah in Georgia—on the first day of Jany. (the day the Quarter expires,) should be sick, or some accident happen to him or family that he could not possibly send on his Account & the money, at the time; on the first day of February, the Post Master General is to commence an Action against him, shall I ask where is the Action to be commenced? where the General Office is kept, 700 or 1000 miles from the place where the Post Master lives? or is it to be commenc'd where the Man lives? If so the Post Master General must give Orders for the Action perhaps, before it can be known whether the Accounts & moneys were not sent on, tho' not arrived at the General Office for If the Action is not bro't within one month, the Post Master General is to [*be*] charged with it, but it is only a hint whether in requiring so much it may prove not to require very little in the end. as punctuality is design'd, so much may be required as will destroy it—when the Bill is Compleated and the Post Master General has made his Arrangements of forms, Hours, &c. &c. I should be pleased to receive them, that I may comply as far as possible and that he may not by any neglect of mine suffer. was it our old Friend Mr. [*Ebenezer*] Hazard that was now in Office, I should be sure of being Inform'd, but as Mr. [*Samuel*] Osgood and I are Strangers I must not expect what I might in other circumstances.

How does our Good Friend Mr. Hazard do? is he in Business? or like to be provi[*ded for?*] please to present my best regards to him [*torn*] you will oblige me If you have oppertunity (after the Bill is gone thro) to talk with Mr. Osgood on the Subject of the Post Office, to Inform him, that I shall esteem it a favour to be furnished with the particular forms &c. that he wished the Accounts to be kept in.

Hopeing to see you safe returnd to Portsmo. as Soon as the Public Business will permit.

ALS, Langdon Papers, NhPoA. Written from Portsmouth, New Hampshire.

A Correspondent Says

It is true, that a *Committee* of the Legislature of this State reported in favour of *instructing* the Senators from this State, in Congress, "*to use their endeavours to obtain a reduction of the salaries, compensations,* &c. granted *by Congress.*"[1] But it is almost as certain, that the Legislature never can accept a report which will so flagrantly interfere with the proceedings of the General Government—and which is, in its nature, so directly *ex post facto.*

When the subject of compensating the members was before Congress, it was urged by those who were in favour of the sum they have received, that it was the average sum granted by the several States to their Members in Congress—that voting a less sum would be indirectly to charge the Legislatures of the several States with extravagance—and that it was not *in fact* a compensation for the sacrifices of business, waste of interest during their absence, &c. which those members who live at a distance from the seat of government must make and suffer. To arguments, cogent and reasonable as these were, no reply could be made by those who were in favour of a less sum, than the inability of the country to pay it: This, as being a mere matter of opinion, was denied by those in favour of the sum granted. The members from States which had granted the highest sums would not consent to any reduction below the average sum, and being a majority, fixed the compensation. The yeas and nays were taken on this question, and those who complain so much on the subject, are referred thereto, before they continue their murmurs, and wishes for *removals*, &c. Many of the compensations to Officers of the United States are not higher than similar officers under some of the individual states enjoy. And if they are higher than are given in Massachusetts, it must be considered, that she alone cannot dictate to her *Twelve* sisters; and that the files of her Legislature abound in complaints of some of her most respectable and dignified officers, that their compensations have not been adequate to their support—and that some of them have been obliged to resign their offices on that account.

[Boston] *Columbian Centinel*, 30 June; reprinted at Portland, Maine; New York City (*NYDA*, 7 June); Philadelphia; and Winchester, Virginia.

---

[1] The Massachusetts legislature's joint committee report was presented on 24 June, but consideration of it was postponed in both houses.

Newspaper Article

Those who attended to the late election of a Federal Senator, says a correspondent, must be surprized at the affrontery and baseness of those who attempt to injure the reputation of the Legislature, by charging it with an electionering manœuvre therein. The principal Candidates in the House, after Dr. [*Charles*] JARVIS had declined standing, were, Mr. DALTON, Mr. [*George*] CABOT, and Mr. [*Nathaniel*] GORHAM. The friends of each of those gentlemen were not averse to the choice of either—In the first regular return, Mr. GORHAM and Mr. CABOT stood the highest—those who voted for Mr. DALTON, Mr. [*Nathan*] DANE and others, then voted for Mr. CABOT in the second trial—which made Mr. CABOT stand the highest; therefore in the third trial many of those who had before voted for Mr. GORHAM, and Dr. JARVIS, gave Mr. CABOT their votes, which made a majority; and it is asserted by several of the Members of the House, that had not Mr. CABOT been chosen in the third trial, in the fourth he would have had a very great majority. The correspondent of the Gazette therefore who has thus charged the Legislature must either have been blinded by prejudice and party-spirit, or must have willfully misrepresented facts. it might have been said, with more propriety, that Mr. CABOT was chosen by a majority of nearly four-fifths than that he was chosen by a majority of one. The votes for him, in the Senate, being 24 of 31—in the House 62 votes *made a choice*; and Mr. CABOT had 63.

[Boston] *Columbian Centinel*, 30 June.

Letter from New Haven, Connecticut

I remember when I was a boy my schoolfellows had a play called BROTHER I'M BOB'D; the fun of which consisted in artifice and deception, and every boy upon whom the trick was played, without being sensible that he was the dupe, was to say BROTHER I'M BOB'D. I am informed that this amusement in your metropolis is not confined to the boys, but that it is lately growing fashionable even among the great ones. You have a society established something on the plan of the old Robin Hood society, I am told it is creeping into reputation there, and that a considerable number of the members, if they would play the game fairly, wou'd say, BROTHER I'M BOB'D. I was always passionately fond of knowing the etymology of every thing, and shall thank you, if, from amidst your antique researches, you can tell me, whether, as the person *Bob'd* is always *duped*, the play took its name from one of the name of Bob, who was noted for a greater share of *plausibility* and *artifice* than real candor and sincerity.

NYDA, 9 July; reprinted at New Haven, Connecticut. Robert Morris, called by his enemies "Bobby the Cofferer," was the "Bob" referred to in this piece.

Letter from Massachusetts

YOU will doubtless be informed, if you do not see the News Papers from this quarter, that the demon of discord is exceedingly busy at this time; the proceedings of our National Legislature, being faulted by many impatient persons, gives occasion to a few candidates for public notice, to traduce the general government in a way that indicates what sort of materials the scriblers are composed of. My reliance is on the firmness, disinterestedness and patriotism of a majority of Congress. When I was at New-York, similar remarks to those published in the papers, were often made by persons whom I found either unfriendly to the government, or destitute of a proper idea of a free constitution. I remember particularly being one day in the gallery, a member rose at the close of a debate which had been continued through the whole forenoon, and made a speech of about 10 minutes length—I thought very much to the purpose; but a man who sat next me, appeared to be in a perfect agony of impatience—and expressed himself in such a manner as convinced me that if he could have had his will, the member would have been precluded from offering his sentiments of the subject. I just observed, "that in a free assembly every member had a right to give his opinion; and if controuled as to the *time*, or *mode* of speaking, there was an end to all freedom of debate." I tell some of my uneasy friends that "*patience must have its perfect work*"—that however, there is *one way* of shortening the sessions of Congress, and preventing long speeches, which the *people* can adopt, and but one—and that is to change the government from a *free republic* to a *despotism*—but would this be an alteration for the better? The Legislature of the United States is composed of characters, selected from the people with as much coolness, and freedom from party influence, as any that will perhaps ever be chosen. According to all the observations that I have been able to make here, from the printed accounts, or from being an eye-witness, there is an evident solicitude to promote the general interest of the Union—but every man knows, who knows any thing, that it is in the power of one or two individuals in a free assembly, to protract and embarrass their proceedings—it is also to be considered that Congress have as it were but a "choice of difficulties"—and their situation is different perhaps from that of any Legislature that ever existed before. A session in the political history of America, even of a year, is but a point of time, and if the result of Congressional deliberations at this important period, should be a judicious system of finance, whatever may be the present sentiment, posterity will bestow a just tribute of applause on their decisions.

We regret very much that it is thought necessary to bring forward the subject of residence again—and some people talk very strangely; however, it begins to be considered that this and every other question can be introduced at the pleasure of one or two members, and much more so at the instance of a whole State; and therefore to say that such things shall not be, is to say, we will not submit to a free government. I wish the business was once fairly settled, that all contest on the subject may be at an end. I have often reflected on the observation of a gentleman who had had long experience of human nature, in public life—"the new Constitution," said he, "appears to be agreeable in theory—the people are greatly elated at the prospect which presents itself to their imagination—but a Constitution is *one thing*, and the administration of it is *another*; those who will be elected into public office will have a trying time—and it will be well if the Constitution is not made to share the blame with the administration, of all the real or imaginary evils that weakness, credulity or wickedness may conjure up." I observed in reply, that all that could be done was to wait the event—acknowledging at the same time—"*that it was yet to be determined, whether any given number of the human race could be found, who possessed wisdom and self denial adequate to supporting a government of their* OWN INSTITUTING."

GUS, 14 July; reprinted at Concord, New Hampshire, and Bennington, Vermont.

Other Documents

John J. Bleecker to Philip Schuyler. ALS, Schuyler Papers, NN. Written from Albany, New York.

Provides a summary of financial accounts with the commissioners for Indian affairs from 1779 to 1784, as requested for Schuyler by (Volckert) Douw upon the latter's return from New York.

Andrew Craigie to Elnathan Haskell. FC:dft, Craigie Papers, MWA. Sent to Charleston, South Carolina; duplicate sent by schooner with Capt. Wilson.

Never more satisfied of the probability of assumption taking place; the letter is being sent via Philadelphia, and "possibly may reach you before any very encouraging acct. of the Assumption."

Thomas Jefferson to David Rittenhouse. FC, letterpress copy, Jefferson Papers, DLC. For the full text, see *PTJ* 16:587–88.

There is an idea that Congress will adjourn the middle of July; if the Senate's vote on convening the third session of the FFC in Philadelphia is successful, thinks the Residence Bill will pass through all subsequent stages.

Joshua Martin to John Langdon. ALS, Langdon Papers, NhPoA. Written from Portsmouth, New Hampshire.

Reports mixed success commanding Langdon's ship *Eliza* in the West Indies; hopes Langdon has recovered from "your Indisposition this summer"; Mrs. Elizabeth and daughter Eliza Langdon are well.

Theodore Sedgwick to Pamela Sedgwick. No copy known; mentioned in Theodore to Pamela Sedgwick, 1 July.

William Samuel Johnson, Diary. Johnson Papers, CtHi.

"Visits."

Dinner List. Ms., hand of Hamilton, Hull Collection, DSI. This list appears on the reverse of Hamilton's reply card, 23 June, above, for a dinner hosted by the Vice President on this date. The names are probably those who attended.

(Franco and Pieter) Van Berckel, Knox, (José Ignacio) Viar, Jefferson, Hamilton, (Louis Guillaume) Otto, (Paolo) Andreani, (Theophile) Cazenove, Izard, Butler, Smith (S.C.), Morris, Kaine (John Kean?), (Thomas) Barclay, (Antoine-Verrance Gabriel?) Rey, and (Tench) Coxe.

[Boston] *Columbian Centinel*, 30 June; reprinted in Portland, Maine, and Portsmouth and Concord, New Hampshire.

"Letters from New-York, by last night's mail, say, that there is yet a prospect, that the Assumption will take place this session."

NYDA, 1 July.

"We are informed that the Senate had the RESIDENCE Bill again under consideration yesterday—and that they have determined to establish the permanent Residence on the Banks of the *Potowmac*, and that in the mean time the temporary Residence shall be in PHILADELPHIA. This Bill was ordered to be engrossed in order to have a third reading to-day."

NYDG, 1 July. The Latin phrase translates, "The times change."

"The report of yesterday was, that the Senate had determined, by a majority of *two*, to adjourn to Philadelphia. *Tempora mutantur.*"

Letter from New York. *PP*, 2 July; reprinted at Burlington, New Jersey; Germantown, Pennsylvania; Baltimore; Fredericksburg, Virginia; and Savannah, Georgia.

"I have the pleasure to communicate, that the senate this moment passed a bill for the residence of Congress in Philadelphia, for the term of ten years. After the expiration of that time they are to make their permanent seat on the Potowmack—sixteen for, and ten against.

There is no doubt but the house of Representatives will concur—so you may make preparations for the reception of that august body."

[Fredericksburg] *Virginia Herald*, 8 July.

"A letter from the speaker of the house of delegates of the united states, received at Philadelphia in the evening of the 1st current, says, 'The senate, by a majority of *seven*, have agreed for the temporary seat of Congress to be at *Philadelphia* for ten years; and the permanent seat on the *Potowmack*'."

Z to Mr. Russell. [Boston] *Columbian Centinel*, 30 June; edited by Benjamin Russell. This comment stimulated a discussion regarding Ames between the *Centinel* and the *Boston Gazette* in July and August.

Introduces Ames's speech of 25 May on assumption; "it stands a monument of the candour, intelligence and ability of the gentleman who delivered it."

JUNE 1790 UNDATED

Thomas Jefferson,
Memoranda on Candidates and Places for Consular Appointments

Sweden.	Gottenburgh.	
Hamburgh.	this is a considerable deposit of our rice for the consumption of the Northern countries of Europe: being very free in it's commerce, it is a good deal frequented by our vessels; and might be worthy of a consulship were a good native citizen to desire it, or an Englishman, as the English have great privileges there. John Parish named by mr. Morris.	
Holland.	Amsterdam.	Mr. [*James*] Greenleaf is married & settled there. mr. Cassinove [*Theophile Cazenove*] speaks of him as a discreet young man. if we should have a Chargé des affaires there, it would be less important who should be the Consul. but if we have no Chargé there, I imagine it would be important to appoint such a person Consul as might be rendered useful in the very great money transactions we shall have there; & who might keep an eye over our bankers there, which will be found necessary.
Spain.	Cadiz.	Richard [*Hanson*] Harrison already nominated. [*John*] Welsh asks the appointment. I believe he is a native of Britain. With respect to these a general observation must be made. in those countries disposed to be friendly to us, & not so to Great Britain, the governments would be jealous of seeing a Briton employed as American Consul, because they could so easily cover British bottoms under the American flag. in France, where we have considerable privileges denied to the English, the government has been much perplexed and defrauded by British ships under false American colours. and these suspicions have produced embarrasments to vessels really ours. tho' I do not know that we have any privileges in Spain which the English have not, yet that government is not friendly to the British, & therefore the appointment of a native

		of Britain to be American Consul might draw an unfavorable shade over the appointment. in countries where British commerce is favored, it might be advantageous sometimes to appoint an Englishman our Consul, in order to partake of the favor of his nation.
	Bilboa.	Edward Church of Massachusetts already named.
The Canaries.	Teneriffe.	Thomas Thompson of Virginia already named. [*Francisco*] Sarmento asks it.[1] he is said by mr. Fitzsimmons to be a Spaniard, married to a miss Craig of Philadelphia, settled at Teneriffe, to have a good deal of the American business & to be of excellent character. qu. if it be sufficiently important to have any ~~appoint~~ appointment here, unless it were a good native?
Portugal.	Lisbon.	John Marsden Pintard, of New York, will probably prefer this to Madeira. he is not at present in New York.
Madeira Is.	Madeira.	Wm. Hill Wells is proposed, if mr. [*John Marsden*] Pintard does not accept. He is the nephew of Henry Hill of Philadelphia. mr. Morris sais he is a very clever fellow. he is 22. years old.
Azores.	Angra,	in the island of Tercera, is the metropolis of the Azores. It is said to be the only station for ships in all the seven islands, and is the residence of the English, French and Dutch consuls. It is the port at which the Brazil ships refresh, and where intelligence of that country may be had.
	Fayal.	messrs. Morris and Fitzsimmons recommend John Street of Fayal to be Consul. They say he is a native of England, but has resided in Fayal so long that he is considered as a Portuguese: that he is 30. years old & of very good character.
	St. Michaels.	Thomas Hickling of Boston, asks the consulship of the Azores or Western islands. he sets forth that he has resided several years at St. Michael's, is well versed in the Portuguese language & in their laws & customs respecting trade: that on the acknolegement of our independence, he, being

		the only American residing in those islands, was appointed by the Chief judge Consul for the protection of our commerce to the Western islands in which office he has acted since 1783. mr. [*Robert?*] Yates of New York sais that Hickling is a respectable man of property, & that he has long corresponded with him. qu. if this appointment might not as well be left in it's present state till some good native can be found who will settle at Angra? which is central to all the islands? it's connection with Brazil gives it advantage over any other position in these islands.
Gr. Britain.	London.	
	Liverpool.	James Maury of Virginia already named. is not this port sufficient for the Western coast?
	Cowes.	in the Isle of Wight. this is a port at which many of our vessels touch, and where patronage against the Custom house officers will certainly be useful. Thomas Auldjo, a native of Britain, of the house of Strachan, Mackenzie & co. is recommended by mr. Morris. I know him personally, & think him a good man. the Custom house officers seem devoted to him. he is the only merchant of any note there, & has the care of almost all the Carolina rice deposited there. this port would suffice for all the Southern coast of England.
Ireland.	Dublin.	William Knox, of Massachusetts, decidedly prefers this consulship to all others. he will decide within two or three days whether he will accept it. [*Paul*] Randall, who was nominated, declines accepting. mr. Morris recommends a mr. Wilson of Dublin.[2]
	Newry.	Wm. Eugene Imlay of [*New*] Jersey already nominated.
France.	Marseilles.	Stephen Cathalan, a Frenchman.
	Bordeaux.	Joseph Fenwick. of Maryland.
	Nantes.	Burrell Carnes. of Massachusets.
	Havre.	La Motte. a Frenchman. already nominated.
	Rouen.	Nathaniel Barrett of Massachusets.
	Lorient.	

	Isle of Rhé.	very unimportant in my opinion. perhaps it would be as well to let the Consul for Nantes (to which place I believe it is nearer than Bordeaux) appoint T. Baudin[3] his Agent there. Baudin desires it for the sake of the honor, & sais he has done several good offices for our vessels there. He is a Frenchman.
French islands.	Hispaniola.	The ports are the Cape, Port au Prince & aux Cayes. Sylvanus Bourne already named.
Guadaloupé.	Point à petre.	
Martinique.	Port royal.	Fulwar Skipwith of Virginia already named.
St. Lucie.	Carenage.	
Tobago.	Scarboro.	These two islands lying nearer to Martinique than to any other Consulship, & seeming too inconsiderable for separate Consulships, may as well perhaps be agencies under the Consul of Martinique. and indeed, considering how many Consuls are destined for France & it's dependancies, it may be doubted whether it would not be better to make Guadaloupe also an Agency of Martinique (to which it is so near) till a very good native shall offer for it?
Isle of France.		
China.	Canton.	Samuel Shaw of Massachusets. already named. Thomas Randall Vice-Consul. there is a complaint against him for malpractice; received from Jacob Sarly.

Ms, hand of Jefferson, Madison Papers, DLC. The editors believe this document was written after the 22 June consular nominations but before those of 2 August. *PTJ* 17:252 dates it between 27 May and 4 June. The date on which it came into Madison's possession is unknown. In a separate undated document regarding consuls (*PTJ* 17:256), Jefferson indicated that Dalton recommended Richard Codman of Massachusetts for Cadiz, Spain; that Dalton and Adams recommended Henry Bromfield of Massachusetts for London; that Morris recommended Walter Stone of Maryland for London; and that D. Carroll recommended Alexander Sloane of Scotland for Civita Vecchia, the port of Rome.

[1] Jefferson indicates elsewhere (*PTJ* 17:256) that D. Carroll recommended Sarmento for this position and, apparently, also for Oporto, Portugal.

[2] Apparently the Joseph Wilson whom Fitzsimons recommended to William Jackson on 5 May and who served in the position from 1794 to 1809. Morris referred to him as "Philip" Wilson in his note to Jefferson dated 1 May. For both documents, see under their respective dates, above.

[3] Jefferson probably meant François Baudin, a merchant at St. Martin on Ile de Ré who had sought the American consulship there as early as 1788.

William J. Vredenburgh to [*John Laurance?*]

Upon the Report of the Secretary of the Treasury that Warrants had been granted to Joseph Howell, Jr. P[*ay*] M[*aster*] Genl. by the late Board of Treasury for four months Specie Pay due for the year 1783 to non commissioned officers and privates of the Virginia Line. On the 29th Sept. 1789 Congress appropriated a Sum not exceeding $190,000 for discharging warrants remaining unpaid. That in consequence of the above said appropriation, I caused to be purchased from said Soldiers at a generous price amounts due them and received their several assignments duly Executed before two witnesses and attested before one of the Magistrates of the County the Soldier was then in—These assignments were presented to the P. M. Genl. in   and acknowledged by him to be duly executed &c. and noted for payment but the State of the Treasury was not then in a situation to pay them. That by a late Resolve of Congress   it appears that   . That in Consequence of this Resolve the P. M. Genl. has his doubt whether it does not exclude me from receiving Payment for those assignments in the Manner they now are.

PTJ 18:623 from a transcript in E. Ruell Smith, Note Book II, p. 27. Laurance is identified as the recipient because Vredenburgh was his constituent. This letter or memorandum was probably drawn up shortly after the President signed the Resolution on Compensation Lists on 7 June; see *DHFFC* 6:2063–70 and May 1790 Undated, above.

Letter from New York

No doubt you have heard, that the Echo British sloop of war lately arrived here. Her dispatches were for some little time kept a profound secret; but you may depend (as I have good information) that the British court has offered to open a free navigation of the Mississippi, provided we allow them to hold the western posts and enjoy the fur trade—also a commercial treaty is now on the carpet. A Spanish sloop of war has also arrived here a few days past;[1] dispatches of consequence came in her—it has been whispered, that a free navigation of the Mississippi is granted to the Americans, and other important privileges. The court of Spain expects a perfect neutrality on the part of America, if a war should take place between Spain and England—I presume to say that in the present troubles, America will do well to milch the cow. I think in the present approaching storm, Carolina and Georgia would do well to put their militia on a respectable footing, as the Dons are near neighbours, and already jealous of the growing power of America. I do not believe Congress will pass any bankrupt law this session; I think it highly necessary for your state, as from what we hear, that the citizens of

Carolina are in a deplorable situation—indeed the giving up of so many of your great men, has struck us with horror.

[Charleston] *State Gazette of South Carolina*, 26 July; reprinted at Portland, Maine; Exeter, New Hampshire; Windsor, Vermont; Newport, Rhode Island; Philadelphia and York, Pennsylvania; and Savannah and Augusta, Georgia.

---

[1] On 25 June, according to *NYDA*, 29 June.

Other Documents

Fisher Ames to Benjamin Russell. No copy known; mentioned in Russell to Thomas Jefferson, 15 June.

Benjamin Goodhue to Benjamin Russell. No copy known; mentioned in Russell to Thomas Jefferson, 15 June.

John Hurt, Notes on David Ramsay's *History of the American Revolution* (Philadelphia, 1789). Ms., Madison Papers, DLC. Postmarked; franked. The author and date are identified in Madison's endorsement, which also specifies that Hurt corrects errors in Ramsay's account. The twelve page commentary is too long and painstaking to have come to Madison unsolicited; it may have been sought as a matter of general historiographic interest, which motive also lay behind Madison's encouraging George Rogers Clark to write a history of the Revolutionary War in the Northwest Territory (see *DHFFC* 16:946n). For more on this document, see *PJM* 13:233.

Provides details, frequently in a first person narrative, of the battles of Long Island, Trenton, Princeton, and Brandywine.

David Olyphant to George Washington. ALS, Washington Papers, DLC. Place from which written not indicated; received on 9 June. For the full text, see *PGW* 5:499.

Office seeking: collector for Newport, Rhode Island; mentions Izard, Butler, Tucker, and the other South Carolina members of Congress as references.

Daniel Hiester, Account Book. PRHi. The entry's placement in the account book also allows for a date in early July.

Took an excursion to Flatbush on Long Island with Wynkoop.

Letter from Providence, Rhode Island. *GUS*, 23 June.

Stanton of Charlestown and T. Foster of Providence were elected Senators; "they are to proceed in a few days"; "There were *only* 28 candidates."

The Compromise of 1790

By June 1790 the level of frustration, tension, accusation, and even disgust among members of Congress had become acute, and the necessity of a fundamental compromise would not be as desperate again until the crisis of 1819. To some American political leaders the survival of the Union was at stake. Northerners could not persuade even a bare majority to vote in favor of federal assumption of the Revolutionary War debts of the states. Pennsylvanians and their allies were unable to put together a coalition to move the seat of federal government from New York to Philadelphia. And Southerners feared the permanent seat of government would be located to the north and east of the Potomac River before reapportionment of the House provided the votes that they expected would situate it on that river.

The basic terms of a compromise were obvious to all: some sort of bargain linking assumption and the location of the seat of government, temporarily at least and perhaps permanently. Since early April "negotiations, cabals, meetings, plots & counterplots" involving two if not all three of these issues had taken place at boarding houses, taverns, private dinners, and surreptitious rendezvous at the Battery, "without yet ripening to any decision."[1] Finally, by the third week of June, congressional leaders, with the active and essential assistance of the executive branch, particularly Secretary of the Treasury Hamilton, had assembled the votes necessary to assume the state debts, locate the permanent seat of government on the Potomac River, and move to Philadelphia at the end of the session. Often referred to as the "Dinner Table Bargain" because of the success of the negotiations that took place between Hamilton and Representative Madison of Virginia at a dinner hosted by Secretary of State Jefferson, it was the first of three great Union-saving compromises that would occur like clockwork every thirty years, until the final one disintegrated into civil war.[2]

It is likely that the dinner took place on Sunday, 20 June, although the date will never be known for certain unless new evidence becomes available. But one has only to read the letters written from New York in June 1790, printed above, to sense the abrupt change in congressional temperament during the days surrounding the weekend of 19–20 June. New Englanders, like Massachusetts Representatives Ames of Boston and Goodhue of Salem, who had been fighting doggedly for assumption since the strength of the opposition had first become apparent in March, despaired of success as late as 13 June.[3] Virginia Representative Lee, whose Potomac River congressional district stretched from Harpers Ferry south to fifty miles below Alexandria, feared as late as Tuesday, 15 June, that his state's dream of locating the permanent seat of government on its waters was not to happen. As the weekend approached the tone began to change as the result of a new and intense round of bargaining. New Englanders suddenly saw "hopes," even "great hopes," for assumption. By 19 June Lee saw "hopes" for the Potomac while his older cousin, Virginia Senator Lee, saw a "dawn of hope for Philadelphia," as the temporary seat.[4]

On Sunday, 20 June, Jefferson, who had been involved in the bargaining since at least the previous Tuesday,[5] sent two significant letters to Virginia, a personal one to his son-in-law Thomas Mann Randolph, Jr. and a more restrained one to soon-to-be-elected Senator Monroe. To the latter he reported that residence and assumption would be "reconciled by some plan of compromise" and that endeavors were underway "to bring about a disposition to some mutual sacrifices." More open with Randolph, the secretary of state asserted that "the peace and continuance of the union" demanded "mutual sacrifice" from every one; indeed, it was their duty.

Massachusetts Representative Sedgwick, a critical leader in implementing the bargain, reported on 22 June that explicit promises of support for assumption had been made in exchange for northern acquiescence to Philadelphia and the Potomac. Goodhue noted the same day that "we have been given to understand that the assumption may obtain, if We will accede to ten years at Philadelphia and then the Potomac River." Even Ames expressed optimism on 23 June, the day on which Hamilton told Pennsylvania Senator Morris that he no longer opposed the federal government's moving to Philadelphia at the end of the current session. The next day the Pennsylvania delegation caucused and committed itself to support a Philadelphia-Potomac residence bill.[6]

On 26 June Representative Lee predicted that "this week will decide the fate of the potowmack forever." That same day New York Senator King mounted a vigorous counterattack on the Philadelphia-Potomac-assumption bargain by trying to broker a deal retaining the seat of government at New York City for five years and then moving permanently to Baltimore, a pairing he believed would guarantee assumption as well. The proposal made considerable headway until the large and influential Massachusetts delegation surprisingly refused to agree. It became the surely painful duty of Hamilton, one of New York's leading citizens, to explain why, first to King and then to Laurance, the city's Representative: "the project of Philadelphia & Potomack is bad, but it will insure the funding system and the Assumption. . . . Agreeing to N. Y[*or*]k. & Baltimore will defeat it."[7]

By then non-federal officials with access to important people had also begun to express optimism. *GUS* editor John Fenno thought both residence and assumption would be settled during the upcoming week. On 30 June certificate speculator Andrew Craigie, who resided in a boarding house with Ames, Sedgwick, and Massachusetts Senator Strong, declared himself never more satisfied that assumption would pass. A week later he could report "an accommodation has been made (call it a bargain if you please) by which the residence, temporary and permanent, [*and*] the funding and assumption are secured. This is not publicly known although by some people suspected."[8]

As the Residence and Funding bills slowly worked their way through Congress in July, news that a compromise had been reached spread out from New York City, even to the point of naming the congressmen who had participated one way or another in the deal.[9] But the role of Jefferson's dinner did not become public knowledge until 1829 when his grandson published portions of Jefferson's "Anas," which included an introduction, written in 1818, detailing the bargain. By the Civil War the dinner had become ingrained in American political history.[10]

Important new evidence about the Compromise of 1790—minus the dinner—came to light in December 2004 when Christie's auctioned a very detailed four and one half page manuscript entitled, "The Seat of Government: Memorandum or Statement of the Compromise or Arrangement originally made in Congress between the friends of the establishment of the permanent seat of Government in District of Columbia & the funding system." Written to argue against the removal of the seat of government from the Potomac River after the British had burned several of its federal buildings in late August 1814, the document is in the hand of Richard Bland Lee, who penned it between September and November 1814. He explained that an agreement had become necessary to end the stalemate that Congress found itself in by May 1790. It "grew out of necessity and the Spirit of Compromise which had just before produced the establishment of the Constitution itself. The compromise was known & approved by Mr. Jefferson late President of the United States, Mr. Madison, now President of the United States and many other distinguished characters."[11]

---

[1] Smith (S.C.) to Edward Rutledge, 14 June; *DHFFC* 9:292.

[2] Jacob E. Cooke, "The Compromise of 1790," *WMQ* 27(1970):523–45; Kenneth R. Bowling, "Dinner at Jefferson's: A Note on Jacob E. Cooke's 'The Compromise of 1790' with a Rebuttal by Jacob E. Cooke," ibid., 28(1971):629–48.

[3] Ames to Thomas Dwight, 11 June; Benjamin to Stephen Goodhue, 13 June.

[4] R. B. Lee to Theodorick Lee, 15 June; Benjamin to Stephen Goodhue, 17 June; Theodore to Pamela Sedgwick, 17 June; George to Josiah Thatcher, 17 June; Letter from a Member of Congress, 19 June, [Alexandria] *Virginia Gazette*, 1 July; R. H. Lee to Thomas Lee Shippen, 19 June.

[5] *DHFFC* 9:293.

[6] Theodore to Pamela Sedgwick, 22 June; Benjamin to Stephen Goodhue, 22 June; Ames to George Richards Minot, 23 June; *DHFFC* 9:301.

[7] R. B. Lee to Theodorick Lee, 26 June; King to Strong, 26 June; King, Notes on the Residence Issue in Second Session, 30 June.

[8] Fenno to Joseph Ward, 26 June; Craigie to Elnathan Haskell, 30 June; Craigie to Daniel Parker, 8 July.

[9] Smith (S.C.) to Edward Rutledge, 26 July; B. L., 26 July, in *IG*, 7 Aug.
[10] Bowling, ibid., p. 630n.
[11] *Christie's Catalog* 1450(2004):item 377. Lee stressed the importance of the decision and his role in it on other occasions: Lee to Theodorick Lee, [1793], *This Month at Goodspeed's* (Feb.–March 1951), p. 118; Lee Letter, [Philadelphia] *American Daily Advertiser*, 12 February 1795; Lee to Madison, 31 January, 7 February 1815, Madison Papers, DLC.

Thomas Jefferson, The Assumption [*1792–94?*]

The assumption of the state debts in 1790. was a supplementary measure in Hamilton's fiscal system. when attempted in the House of Representatives it failed. this threw Hamilton himself & a number of members into deep dismay. going to the President's one day I met Hamilton as I approached the door. his look was sombre, haggard, & dejected beyond description. even his dress uncouth and neglected. he asked to speak with me. we stood in the street near the door. he opened the subject of the assumption of the state debts, the necessity of it in the general fiscal arrangement & ~~the~~ it's indispensible necessity towards a preservation of the union: and particularly of the New England states, who had made great expenditures during the war, on expeditions which tho' of their own undertaking were for the common cause: that they considered the assumption of these by the Union so just, and it's denial so palpably injurious, that they would make it a sine qua non of a continuance of the Union. that as to his own part, if he had not credit enough to carry such a measure as that, he could be of no use, & was determd. to resign. he observed at the same time, that tho' our particular business laid in separate departments, yet the administration & it's success was a common ~~thing~~ concern, and that we should make common cause in supporting one another. he added his wish that I would interest my friends from the South, who were those most opposed to it. I answered that I had been so long absent from my country that I had lost a familiarity with it's affairs, and being but lately returned had not yet got into the train of them, that the fiscal system being out of my department, I had not yet undertaken to consider & understand it, that the assumption had struck me in an unfavorable light, but still not having considered it sufficiently I had not concerned in it, but that I would revolve what he had urged in my mind. it was a real fact that the Eastern & Southern members (S. Carolina however was with the former) had got into the most extreme ill humor with one another, this broke out on every question with the most alarming heat, the bitterest animosities seemed to be engendered, and tho they met every day, little or nothing could be done from mutual distrust & antipathy. on considering the situation of things I thought the first step towards some conciliation of views would be to bring mr. Madison & Colo. Hamilton to a friendly discussion of the subject. I immediately wrote to each to come and dine with me the next day, mentioning that we should be alone, that the object was to find some temperament for the present ~~difference~~ fever, and that I was persuaded that men of sound heads and honest views needed nothing more than explanation and mutual understanding to enable them to unite in some measures which might enable us to get along. They came. I opened the subject to them, acknoleged that my situation [*lined out*] had not permitted me to understand it sufficiently but encouraged them to consider the thing together. they did so. it ended in mr. Madison's acquiescence in a proposition that the question should be again brought before the house by way of amendment from the Senate, that tho' he would not vote for it, nor entirely withdraw his opposition, yet he should not be strenuous, but leave it to it's fate [*lined out*]. it was observed, I forget by which of them, that as the pill would be a bitter one to the Southern states, something should be done to soothe them; that the removal of the seat of government to the Patowmac was a just measure, & would probably be a popular one with them, and would be a proper one to follow the assumption [*lined out*]. it was agreed to speak to mr. White and mr. Lee, whose districts lay on the Patowmac and to refer to them to consider how far the interests of their particular districts might be a sufficient inducement to them to yield to the assumption. this was done. [*lined out*] Lee came into it without hesitation. mr. White had some qualms, but finally agreed. [*lined out*] the measure came down by way of amendment from the Senate and was finally carried by the change of White's and Lee's votes. but the removal to Patowmac could not be carried unless Pennsylvania could be engaged in it. this Hamilton took on himself, and chiefly, as I understood, through the agency of Robert Morris, obtained the vote of that state, on agreeing to an intermediate residence at Philadelphia. this is the real history of the assumption, about which many erroneous conjectures have been published. it was unjust, ~~impolitic, & itself~~ oppressive to the states, and was acquiesced in merely from a fear of disunion, while our government was still in it's most infant state. it enabled Hamilton so to strengthen himself by corrupt services to many, that he could afterwards carry his bank scheme, and every measure he proposed in defiance of all opposition: in fact it was a principal ground where on was reared up that Speculating phalanx, in & out of Congress which has since been able to give laws & to change the political complexion of the government of the U.S.

Ms., hand of Jefferson, Jefferson Papers, DLC. The date of this document cannot be determined precisely. Julian Boyd argues for a late 1792 date; Paul Leicester Ford, for "Feb.? 1793"; and Dumas Malone, for "late in 1793 or early in 1794" (*PTJ* 17:207–8).

Thomas Jefferson, Explanations of the Three Volumes Bound in Marbled Paper [*Anas*], 4 February 1818

*** this game[1] was over, and another was on the carpet at the moment of my arrival; and to this I was most ignorantly and innocently made to hold the candle. this fiscal maneuvre is well known by the name of the Assumption. independantly of the debts of Congress, the states had during the war, contracted separate and heavy debts; and Massachusets particularly in an absurd attempt, absurdly conducted, on the British post of Penobscot: and the more debt Hamilton could rake up, the more plunder[*lined out*] for his mercenaries. this money, whether wisely or foolishly spent, was pretended to have been spent for general purposes, and ought therefore to be paid from the general purse. but it was objected that nobody knew what these debts were, what their amount, nor what their proofs. no matter; we will guess them to be 20. millions, but of these 20. millions we do not know how much should be reimbursed to one state, nor how much to another. no matter; we will guess. and so another scramble was set on foot among the several states, and some got much, some little, some nothing. but the main object was obtained, the phalanx of the treasury was reinforced by additional recruits. this measure produced the most bitter and ~~bloody~~ angry contests ever known in Congress, before or since the union of the states. I arrived in the midst of it. but a stranger to the ground, a stranger to the actors on it, so long absent as to have lost all familiarity with the subject, and as yet unaware of it's object, I took no concern in it. the great and trying question however was lost in the H. of Representatives. so high were the feuds excited by this subject, that on it's rejection, business was suspended. Congress met and adjourned from day to day without doing any thing, the parties being too much out of temper to do business together. the Eastern members particularly, who, with ~~some~~ *Smith from South Carolina, were the principal gamblers in these scenes, threatened a secession and dissolution. Hamilton was in despair. as I was going to the President's one day, I met him in the street. he walked me backwards & forwards before the ~~door~~ President's door for half an hour. he painted pathetically the temper into which the legislature had been wrought, the disgust of those who were called the Creditor states, the danger of the secession of their members, and the separation of the states. he observed that the members of the administration ought to act in concert, that tho' this question was not of my department, yet a common

*~~I do not know that any member from S. Carolina engaged in this infamous business, except William Smith, whom I think it a duty to name therefore, to relieve the others from imputation.~~

duty should make it a common concern; that the President was the center on which all administrative questions ultimately rested, and that all of us should rally around him, and support with joint efforts measures approved by him; and that the question having been lost by a small majority only, it was probable that an appeal from me to the judgment and discretion of some of my friends might effect a change in the vote, and the machine of government, now suspended, might be again set into motion. I told him that I was really a stranger to the whole subject; not having yet informed myself of the system of finance adopted, I knew not how far this was a necessary sequence; that undoubtedly if it's rejection endangered a dissolution of our union at this incipient stage, I should deem that the most unfortunate of all consequences, to avert which all partial and temporary evils should be yielded. I proposed to him however to dine with me the next day, and I would invite another friend or two, bring them into conference together, and I thought it impossible ~~but~~ that reasonable men, consulting together coolly, could fail, by some mutual sacrifices, of opinion, to form a compromise which was to save the union. the discussion took place. I could take no part in it, but an exhortatory one, because I was a stranger to the circumstances which should govern it. but it was finally agreed that, whatever importance had been attached to the rejection of this proposition, the preservation of the union, & of concord among the states was more important, and that therefore it would be better that the vote of rejection should be rescinded, to effect which some members should change their votes. but it was observed that this pill would be peculiarly bitter to the Southern states, and that some concomitant measure should be adopted to sweeten it a little to them. there had before been propositions to fix the seat of government either at Philadelphia, or at Georgetown on the Patomac; and it was thought that by giving it to Philadelphia for ten years, and to Georgetown permanently afterwards, this might, as an anodyne, calm in some degree the ferment which might be excited by the other measure alone. so two of the Patomac members (White & Lee, but White with a revulsion of stomach almost convulsive) agreed to change their votes, & Hamilton undertook to carry the other point. in doing this the influence he had established over the Eastern members, with the agency of Robert Morris with those of the middle states, effected his side of the engagement, and so the assumption was passed, and 20. millions of stock divided among favored states, and thrown in as pabulum to the stock-jobbing herd. this added to the number of votaries to the treasury and made it's Chief the master of every vote in the legislature, which might give to the government the direction suited to his political views. I know well, and so must be understood, that nothing like a majority in Congress had yielded to this corruption. far from it. but a division, not very unequal, had already taken place in the honest part of that body, between the parties ~~now~~ styled republican and federal. the latter being monarchists in principle, adhered to Hamilton of course, as their leader in that principle, and this mercenary phalanx added to them ensured him always a majority in both houses: so that the whole action of the legislature was now under the direction of the treasury. ***

Ms., hand of Jefferson, Jefferson Papers, DLC.

[1] I.e., the frenzied speculation in public securities.